Praise for Best Places® Guidebooks

"Best Places *are the best regional restaurant and guide books in America.*"
—THE SEATTLE TIMES

"Best Places *covers must-see portions of the West Coast with style and authority. In-the-know locals offer thorough info on restaurants, lodgings, and the sights.*"
—NATIONAL GEOGRAPHIC TRAVELER

"*. . . travelers swear by the recommendations in the* Best Places *guidebooks . . .*"
—SUNSET MAGAZINE

"*For travel collections covering the Northwest, the* Best Places *series takes precedence over all similar guides.*"
—BOOKLIST

"Best Places Northwest *is the bible of discriminating travellers to BC, Washington and Oregon. It promises, and delivers, the best of everything in the region.*"
—THE VANCOUVER SUN

"*Not only the best travel guide in the region, but maybe one of the most definitive guides in the country, which many look forward to with the anticipation usually sparked by a best-selling novel. A browser's delight,* Best Places Northwest *should be chained to dashboards throughout the Northwest.*"
—THE OREGONIAN

"*Still the region's undisputed heavyweight champ of guidebooks.*"
—SEATTLE POST-INTELLIGENCER

"*Trusting the natives is usually good advice, so visitors to Washington, Oregon, and British Columbia would do well to pick up* Best Places Northwest *for an exhaustive review of food and lodging in the region. . . . An indispensable glove-compartment companion.*"
—TRAVEL AND LEISURE

"Best Places Southern California *is just about all the inspiration you need to start planning your next road trip or summer vacation with the kids.*"
—THE FRESNO BEE

"Best Places Alaska *is the one guide to recommend to anyone visiting Alaska for the first or one-hundredth time.*"
—KETCHIKAN DAILY NEWS

"Best Places Northern California *is great fun to read even if you're not going anywhere.*"
—SAN FRANCISCO CHRONICLE

TRUST THE LOCALS

The original insider's guides, written by local experts

COMPLETELY INDEPENDENT
- No advertisers
- No sponsors

EVERY PLACE STAR-RATED & RECOMMENDED

★★★★ The very best in the city

★★★ Distinguished; many outstanding features

★★ Excellent; some wonderful qualities

★ A good place

MONEY-BACK GUARANTEE
We're so sure you'll be satisfied, we guarantee it!

HELPFUL ICONS
Watch for these quick-reference symbols throughout the book:

 FAMILY FUN

 GOOD VALUE

 ROMANTIC

 EDITORS' CHOICE

BEST PLACES®

NORTHWEST

The Locals' Guide to the Best Restaurants, Lodgings, Sights, Shopping, and More!

Edited by
GISELLE SMITH

EDITION **15**

SASQUATCH BOOKS
SEATTLE

Printed in the United States of America
Published by Sasquatch Books
Distributed by Publishers Group West

Fifteenth edition
09 08 07 06 05 04   6 5 4 3 2 1

ISBN: 1-57061-417-2
ISSN: 1041-2484

Cover and interior design: Nancy Gellos
Interior composition: Bill Quinby
Maps: GreenEye Design

SPECIAL SALES

Best Places guidebooks are available at special discounts on bulk purchases for corporate, club, or organization sales promotions, premiums, and gifts. Special editions, including personalized covers, excerpts of existing guides, and corporate imprints, can be created in large quantities for specific needs. For more information, contact your local bookseller or Special Sales, Best Places Guidebooks, 119 South Main Street, Suite 400, Seattle, Washington 98104, 800/775-0817.

SASQUATCH BOOKS
119 South Main Street, Suite 400
Seattle, Washington 98104
206/467-4300
www.sasquatchbooks.com
custserv@sasquatchbooks.com

CONTENTS

Contributors and Acknowledgments **xi**
About Best Places® Guidebooks **xiii**
How to Use This Book **xiv**
    Best Places® Star Ratings **xv**

Oregon

PORTLAND AND ENVIRONS **1**
Access and Information, **3**; Portland, **4**; Forest Grove, **29**; Lake Oswego, West Linn, and Oregon City, **30**
    Map, **2**
    Portland Three-Day Tour, **5**
    An Empire Built on Beer, **16**

COLUMBIA RIVER GORGE AND MOUNT HOOD **31**
Access and Information, **33**; Columbia River Gorge National Scenic Area, **34**; Troutdale, **34**; Cascade Locks, **35**; Hood River, **36**; Mosier, **40**; The Dalles, **41**; Mount Hood, **43**; Welches, **47**; Sandy, **48**
    Map, **32**
    Columbia River Gorge Three-Day Tour, **36**
    Native American Fishing, **45**

WILLAMETTE VALLEY **49**
Access and Information, **51**; Wine Country, **52**; Newberg, **54**; Dundee, **54**; Dayton, **55**; Carlton and Yamhill, **56**; McMinnville, **57**; Bellevue, **59**; Grande Ronde, **60**; Salem and Vicinity, **61**; Aurora, **61**; Mount Angel, **62**; Silverton, **63**; Salem, **64**; Independence, **66**; Albany and Corvallis, **67**; Albany, **67**; Corvallis, **68**; Eugene, **71**; Springfield, **77**
    Map, **50**
    Willamette Valley Three-Day Tour, **53**
    Latino Woodburn, **61**

NORTHERN OREGON COAST **79**
Access and Information, **81**; Astoria, **82**; Gearhart and Seaside, **86**; Cannon Beach, **88**; Arch Cape, **90**; Manzanita, **91**; Garibaldi, Bay City, and Tillamook, **93**; Oceanside, **94**; Pacific City, **95**; Neskowin, **96**; Lincoln City, **96**; Gleneden Beach, **99**; Depoe Bay, **100**; Newport, **102**; Waldport, **105**; Yachats, **106**
    Map, **80**
    Northern Oregon Coast Three-Day Tour, **83**
    See the Whales, **97**
    Coastal Celebrations, **101**

SOUTHERN OREGON COAST 109

Access and Information, 111; Florence, 112; Reedsport and Winchester Bay, 113; North Bend, Coos Bay, and Charleston, 114; Bandon, 117; Port Orford, 120; Gold Beach, 121; Brookings, 124

> Map, 110
> Southern Oregon Coast Three-Day Tour, 114
> Oregon Dunes National Recreation Area, 123

SOUTHERN OREGON AND THE CASCADES 127

Access and Information, 129; Roseburg and the Umpqua Valley, 129; Roseburg, 130; The Rogue River Valley, 133; Grants Pass, 133; Oregon Caves National Monument, 135; Medford, 136; Jacksonville, 137; Talent, 139; Ashland, 140; Klamath Falls, 145; Lakeview and Lake County, 146; Summer Lake, 147; Crater Lake National Park, 147; Diamond Lake and Mount Bailey, 148; Cascade Lakes Area, 148; Odell Lake, 149; Bend and Mount Bachelor, 149; Bend, 150; Mount Bachelor, 154; Elk Lake, 155; Sisters and the Deschutes River Area, 155; Redmond, 155; Sisters, 156; Camp Sherman, 157; Warm Springs, 157

> Map, 128
> Oregon Cascades Three-Day Tour, 132
> Shakespeare Festival Tips, 137
> The Big Glassy, 141

EASTERN OREGON 159

Access and Information, 161; Pendleton, 161; Condon, 164; The Wallowas and Hells Canyon, 164; La Grande, 164; Union, 165; Enterprise, 166; Joseph, 166; Halfway, 168; Baker City and Haines, 169; John Day, 170; Prairie City, 171; Southeast High Desert, 172; Burns, 172; Diamond, 173; Frenchglen, 173

> Map, 160
> Northeastern Oregon Three-Day Tour, 162
> The Wallowas' First Residents, 167
> Birds of the Malheur, 172

Washington

SEATTLE AND ENVIRONS 175

Access and Information, 177; Seattle, 179; The Eastside, 205; Bellevue, 205; Redmond, 206; Kirkland, 207; Woodinville, 208; Issaquah, 210; Seattle-Tacoma International Airport, 210

> Map, 176
> Seattle Three-Day Tour, 178
> Raw and Roll, 188

PUGET SOUND 211

Access and Information, **213**; Edmonds, **213**; Everett Area, **214**; Everett, **215**; Mukilteo, **216**; Snohomish, **217**; Stanwood, **218**; Camano Island, **218**; Whidbey Island, **218**; Langley, **219**; Freeland, **222**; Greenbank, **222**; Coupeville, **223**; Oak Harbor, **225**; Deception Pass State Park, **225**; The Skagit Valley, **225**; Mount Vernon, **226**; La Conner, **226**; Chuckanut Drive, **230**; Bellingham and Area, **232**; Lummi Island, **237**; Lynden, **238**; Blaine, **238**; Anacortes and the San Juan Islands, **239**; Anacortes, **239**; Lopez Island, **241**; Orcas Island, **243**; San Juan Island, **247**; Tacoma, Olympia, and the South Sound, **251**; Vashon Island, **251**; Tacoma, **253**; Puyallup, **258**; Parkland, **258**; Gig Harbor, **259**; Steilacoom and Anderson Island, **261**; Olympia, **262**; Tenino and Yelm, **266**
Map, **212**
North Puget Sound Three-Day Tour, **214**
No Experience Necessary, **227**

OLYMPIC PENINSULA 267

Access and Information, **269**; Kitsap Peninsula, **271**; Port Orchard, **271**; Bremerton, **272**; Seabeck, **273**; Silverdale, **273**; Poulsbo, **274**; Suquamish, **275**; Port Gamble, **275**; Hansville, **275**; Hood Canal and the Northeast Corner, **276**; Shelton, **277**; Union, **277**; Quilcene, **278**; Port Ludlow, **278**; Port Hadlock, **278**; Marrowstone Island, **279**; Port Townsend, **280**; Sequim and the Dungeness Valley, **285**; Port Angeles and the Strait of Juan de Fuca, **288**; Port Angeles, **288**; Lake Crescent, **291**; Sol Duc Hot Springs, **292**; Clallam Bay and Sekiu, **292**; Neah Bay, **293**; Forks and the Hoh River Valley, **293**; Forks, **293**; La Push and Pacific Ocean Beaches, **295**; Lake Quinault, **295**
Map, **268**
Olympic Peninsula Three-Day Tour, **270**
From Timber to Tourism, **276**
How to Eat an Oyster, **288**

NORTH CASCADES 297

Access and Information, **299**; Mount Baker, **299**; Everson, **301**; Deming, **301**; Glacier, **302**; North Cascades Scenic Highway, **302**; Marblemount, **303**; North Cascades National Park, **303**; Diablo and Ross Lake, **304**; The Methow Valley, **304**; Mazama, **304**; Winthrop, **307**; Twisp, **310**; Pateros, **312**; Lake Chelan, **312**; Chelan, **313**; Stehekin, **315**
Map, **298**
North Cascades Three-Day Tour, **300**
Cross-Country Skiing the Methow, **305**
Mountain Loop Highway, **310**

CENTRAL CASCADES 317

Access and Information, **319**; US Highway 2 and Stevens Pass, **319**; Lake Wenatchee, **320**; Plain, **320**; Leavenworth, **322**; Cashmere, **327**; Wenatchee, **327**; Interstate 90 and Snoqualmie Pass, **329**; Carnation, **329**; Snoqualmie, **330**; Snoqualmie Pass, **330**; Roslyn, **331**; Cle Elum, **331**; Mount Rainier National Park, **332**; Black Diamond, **333**; Greenwater, **334**; Crystal Mountain, **334**; Sunrise, **334**; Eatonville, **335**; Ashford, **335**; Longmire and Paradise, **337**; White Pass, **337**

Map, **318**
Central Cascades Three-Day Tour, **321**
Bloomin' Wonderful Fruit, **326**
From a Wagon Road to the Pacific Crest Trail, **333**

SOUTHWEST WASHINGTON 339

Access and Information, **341**; Grays Harbor and Ocean Shores, **342**; Aberdeen and Hoquiam, **342**; Ocean Shores, **344**; Copalis, **346**; Pacific Beach, **347**; Moclips, **347**; Westport, **347**; Long Beach Peninsula and Willapa Bay, **348**; Chinook, **349**; Ilwaco, **350**; Seaview, **351**; Long Beach, **354**; Ocean Park, Nahcotta, and Oysterville, **355**; Longview, **357**; Mount St. Helens National Volcanic Monument, **358**; Castle Rock, **358**; Vancouver, **359**; Mount Adams and the Columbia River Gorge, **361**; Stevenson, **362**; Carson, **362**; White Salmon, **363**; Trout Lake, **364**; Glenwood, **364**; Lyle, **365**; Goldendale, **365**

Map, **340**
Southwest Washington Three-Day Tour, **343**
Mount St. Helens and the Columbia Gorge Three-Day Tour, **352**

SOUTHEAST WASHINGTON 367

Access and Information, **369**; Columbia Basin, **370**; Vantage and George, **370**; Ellensburg and Yakima Valleys, **370**; Ellensburg, **371**; Yakima, **373**; Naches, **376**; Toppenish, **376**; Yakima Valley Wine Country, **377**; Zillah, **377**; Sunnyside, Outlook, and Grandview, **377**; Prosser, **379**; The Tri-Cities, **379**; Richland, **379**; Kennewick, **381**; Pasco, **382**; Walla Walla and the Blue Mountains, **382**; Walla Walla, **383**; Dayton, **387**; Pullman and the Palouse, **389**; Pullman, **390**

Map, **368**
Southeast Washington Three-Day Tour, **374**
Lewis and Clark Trail Bicentennial, **384**
Southeast Washington Three-Day Wine Tour, **388**

SPOKANE AND NORTHEASTERN WASHINGTON 393

Access and Information, **395**; Spokane, **396**; Pend Oreille and Colville River Valleys, **404**; The Pend Oreille, **404**; Colville and Kettle Falls Area, **405**;

Grand Coulee Area, **406**; Grand Coulee Dam, **406**; Soap Lake, **408**; Omak, **409**
Map, **394**
Northeastern Washington Three-Day Tour, **397**
Spokane Valley Wine Touring, **402**
Inland Northwest Golf, **407**

British Columbia

VANCOUVER AND ENVIRONS   411
Access and Information, **413**; Vancouver, **414**; Around Vancouver, **438**;
Richmond, **438**; North Vancouver, **439**
Map, **412**
Vancouver Three-Day Tour, **416**
Greasy Spoons, **422**

LOWER MAINLAND BRITISH COLUMBIA   441
Access and Information, **443**; Sea to Sky Highway (Highway 99), **444**;
Squamish, **444**; Whistler, **446**; Pemberton and Mount Currie, **455**; Lillooet,
456; Fraser Valley, **458**; Fort Langley, **458**; Chilliwack, **458**; Harrison Lake,
459; Hope, **460**; The Sunshine Coast, **460**; Gibsons, **462**; Roberts Creek,
463; Sechelt, **465**; Pender Harbour, **466**; Egmont, **467**; Powell River, **467**;
Lund, **468**
Map, **442**
Sea to Sky Three-Day Tour, **446**
Eagle Eyes, **456**
Reaching the Peaks, **464**

VICTORIA AND VANCOUVER ISLAND   471
Access and Information, **473**; Victoria, **474**; Sooke to Port Renfrew, **484**;
Sidney and the Saanich Peninsula, **488**; Malahat, **490**; The Gulf Islands, **491**;
Salt Spring Island, **492**; North and South Pender Islands, **497**; Saturna
Island, **498**; Mayne Island, **498**; Galiano Island, **499**; Denman and Hornby
Islands, **502**; Discovery Islands, **503**; The Cowichan Valley and Southeast
Shore, **504**; Cowichan Bay, **505**; Duncan, **506**; Chemainus, **507**; Ladysmith,
508; Nanaimo, **509**; Parksville, **510**; Qualicum Beach, **511**; Barkley Sound
and Tofino, **513**; Port Alberni, **513**; Bamfield, **513**; Ucluelet, **514**;
Tofino, **516**; The Comox Valley, **520**; Fanny Bay, **520**; Courtenay and
Comox, **521**; Campbell River and North Vancouver Island, **522**; Gold River,
525; Port McNeill and Telegraph Cove, **525**; Port Hardy, **526**
Map, **472**
Victoria Three-Day Tour, **476**
Vancouver Island Three-Day Tour, **478**
Surf's Up, Eh?, **523**

SOUTHERN INTERIOR AND THE KOOTENAYS 527

Access and Information, **529**; The Thompson Plateau, **529**; Merritt, **530**; Cache Creek, **531**; Kamloops, **532**; Sun Peaks Resort, **534**; The Okanagan Valley, **535**; Vernon and Silver Star Mountain Resort, **536**; Kelowna, **538**; Big White, **541**; Penticton and Apex Mountain Resort, **541**; Naramata, **543**; Oliver and Osoyoos, **544**; The Kootenays, **545**; Rossland and Red Mountain Ski Area, **546**; Nakusp, **548**; Kaslo, **548**; Ainsworth Hot Springs, **549**; Crawford Bay, **550**; Nelson, **550**; Kimberley and Kimberley Alpine Resort, **553**; Fernie, **554**; Fairmont Hot Springs, **555**; Invermere and Panorama Mountain Village, **555**; Radium Hot Springs, **556**; Trans-Canada Highway and the National Parks, Field, **556**; Golden and Kicking Horse Mountain Resort, **557**; Revelstoke, **558**

Map, **528**
Southern Interior Three-Day Tour, **530**
Skiing the Southern Interior, **537**

NORTHERN MAINLAND BRITISH COLUMBIA 561

Access and Information, **563**; The Cariboo Highway (Hwy 97), **564**; Clinton, **564**; Interlakes District, **566**; 100 Mile House, **567**; Williams Lake, **569**; Prince George, **569**; The Northwest Coast, **570**; Prince Rupert, **570**; Haida Gwaii/Queen Charlotte Islands, **571**

Map, **562**
Northern Mainland BC Three-Day Tour, **565**
Tour of the Totems, **568**

Index **573**
Money-Back Guarantee **591**
Best Places® Report Form **592**

Contributors and Acknowledgments

Pulling together a guide as large and wide-ranging as *Best Places Northwest* is necessarily a collaborative effort, but the efforts of the following contributors were critical to its publication.

Seattle native **KAREN BULLARD** currently divides her time between Seattle and Hood River, Oregon, and has traveled extensively throughout the Northwest as a bicycle tour guide and lifetime resident.

Writer-broadcaster **JACK CHRISTIE** is one of the best-known sources for adventure travel information in his region, and won the 2004 Tourism British Columbia Travel Media Award. To learn more, visit *www.jackchristie.com*.

Seattle-based writer **TERI CITTERMAN** does public relations for restaurants and wineries, and is a contributing writer for the *Puget Sound Business Journal* and *Portland Business Journal*.

Longtime coastal resident **RICHARD FENCSAK** writes a weekly restaurant review and is a frequent contributor to the *Oregonian* travel section and other Northwest publications. He's also the owner of an Astoria bike store and an avid hiker, runner, and cyclist.

LAURA GRONEWOLD is a former Sasquatch Books and Best Places editor who recently completed a Master's degree in Literature at the University of Montana. When she's not teaching English classes, she spends time in Seattle and continues to travel the Pacific Northwest.

JUDY JEWELL has lived most of her life in Oregon, and loves to explore the state, with a special eye to its campgrounds and swimming pools (she also swims across the Columbia River once a year). Judy is the author of *Camping! Oregon* (Sasquatch Books) and several other books about Oregon, Montana, and Utah.

Salt Spring Island-based freelance writer **SUE KERNAGHAN** has written about the Pacific Northwest for publications including the *Seattle Post-Intelligencer* and Vancouver's *Georgia Straight*. She has also contributed to several guidebooks about the area.

A founding member of the performance group Typing Explosion Union Local 898, **RACHEL KESSLER** has staged poetry type-ins all over the world. In addition, she has written articles on subjects such as food and travel for *The Stranger*, *Metro News*, and *UrbanView*.

Washington native and Northwest explorer **JENA MCPHERSON** is a former staff editor and regular contributor to *Sunset* magazine. She also writes for *Journey* and has contributed to several guidebooks. She is the author of a travel book on the Northwest.

A California native, writer and editor **DANA PERKINS** teaches high school English in Seattle and explores the Northwest in her spare time.

Raised in the unspoiled wonderlands of New Zealand and Hawaii, **BARBARA VRANA** has been enthralled by the Northwest for the past 27 years, particularly the region's many options for hiking, swimming, and local flavors. Vrana has written for *Adobe Magazine* and is a former managing editor of *TWIST Weekly*.

KASEY WILSON is an award-winning freelance food and travel writer, broadcaster, and author whose career spans both print and electronic media. She co-hosts a weekly radio show, "The Best of Food and Wine," on CFUN, has written several cookbooks, and contributes regularly to national magazines. In addition, she edited the most recent edition of *Best Places Vancouver*.

Three-time *Best Places Northwest* editor **GISELLE SMITH** is a lifelong Seattleite with a passion for the highways, mountains, forests, and beaches of the Northwest. She is a contributor to several regional and travel magazines, is a past editor of *Seattle Magazine* and *Alaska Airlines Magazine*, and has edited *Best Places Seattle* and Insight Guides to Seattle, the Northwest, and Alaska.

Thank you as well to contributors to recent past editions of *Best Places Northwest* and others who lent their expert advice: Les Campbell, Kim Carlson, Providence Cicero, Nick Gallo, Jan Halliday, Susan Hauser, Andrew Hempstead, Bonnie Henderson, Leslie Kelly, Mark Laba, Vanessa McGrady, Shannon O'Leary, Melissa O'Neil, and Alisa Smith.

At Sasquatch Books, the driving forces behind this publication were managing editor Heidi Schuessler, Terence Maikels, Kurt Stephan, and Cassandra Mitchell. Thanks also for the contributions of designer Bill Quinby, copy editor Karen Parkin, proofreader Shari Miranda, and indexer Michael Ferreira.

About Best Places® Guidebooks

People trust us. Best Places guidebooks, which have been published continuously since 1975, represent one of the most respected regional travel series in the country. Our reviewers know their territory, and seek out the very best a city or region has to offer. We provide tough, candid reports about places that have rested too long on their laurels, and delight in new places that deserve recognition. We describe the true strengths, foibles, and unique characteristics of each establishment listed.

Best Places Northwest is written by and for locals, and is therefore coveted by travelers. It's written for people who live here and who enjoy exploring the region's bounty and its out-of-the-way places of high character and individualism. It's these very characteristics that make Best Places Northwest ideal for tourists, too. The best places in and around the region are the ones that denizens favor: independently owned establishments of good value, touched with local history, run by lively individuals, and graced with natural beauty. With this fifteenth edition of Best Places Northwest, travelers will find the information they need: where to go and when, what to order, which rooms to request (and which to avoid), where the best skiing, hiking, wilderness getaways, and local attractions are, and how to find the region's hidden secrets.

We're so sure you'll be satisfied with our guide, we guarantee it.

NOTE: *The reviews in this edition are based on information available at press time and are subject to change. Readers are advised that places listed in previous editions may have closed or changed management or may no longer be recommended by this series. The editors welcome information conveyed by users of this book. A report form is provided at the end of the book, and feedback is also welcome via email: bestplaces@sasquatchbooks.com.*

How to Use This Book

This book is divided into 20 regional chapters covering a wide range of establishments, destinations, and activities. All evaluations are based on numerous reports from local and traveling inspectors. Final judgments are made by Sasquatch editors. **EVERY PLACE FEATURED IN THIS BOOK IS RECOMMENDED.**

STAR RATINGS *(for restaurants and lodgings only)* Restaurants and lodgings are rated on a scale of one to four stars (with half stars in between), based on uniqueness, loyalty of local clientele, performance measured against the establishment's goals, excellence of cooking, cleanliness, value, and professionalism of service. Reviews are listed alphabetically by region, and every place is recommended.

★★★★ The very best in the region
★★★ Distinguished; many outstanding features
★★ Excellent; some wonderful qualities
★ A good place

(For more on how we rate places, see the Best Places Star Ratings box below.)

PRICE RANGE *(for restaurants and lodgings only)* Prices for restaurants are based primarily on dinner for two, including dessert and tip, but not alcohol. Prices for lodgings are based on peak season rates for one night's lodging for two people (i.e., double occupancy). Peak season is typically Memorial Day to Labor Day for summer destinations, or November through March for winter destinations; off-season rates vary but often can be significantly less. Call ahead to verify, as all prices are subject to change.

$$$$ Very expensive (more than $100 for dinner for two; more than $200 for one night's lodging for two)
$$$ Expensive (between $65 and $100 for dinner for two; between $120 and $200 for one night's lodging for two)
$$ Moderate (between $35 and $65 for dinner for two; between $80 and $120 for one night's lodging for two)
$ Inexpensive (less than $35 for dinner for two; less than $80 for one night's lodging for two)

RESERVATIONS *(for restaurants only)* For each dining establishment listed in the book, we used one of the following terms for its reservations policy: reservations required, reservations recommended, or no reservations.

ADDRESSES AND PHONE NUMBERS Every attempt has been made to provide accurate information on an establishment's location and phone number, but it's always a good idea to call ahead and confirm.

EMAIL AND WEB SITE ADDRESSES Web site or email addresses for establishments have been included where available. Please note that the Web is a fluid and evolving medium, and that Web pages are often "under construction" or, as with all time-sensitive information, may no longer be valid.

BEST PLACES® STAR RATINGS

Any travel guide that rates establishments is inherently subjective—and Best Places is no exception. We rely on our professional experience, yes, but also on a gut feeling. And, occasionally, we even give in to soft spot for a favorite neighborhood hangout. Our star-rating system is not simply a checklist; it's judgmental, critical, sometimes fickle, and highly personal.

For each new edition, we send local food and travel experts out to review restaurants and lodgings. and then to rate them on a scale of one to four, based on uniqueness, loyalty of local clientele, performance measured against the establishment's goals, excellence of cooking, cleanliness, value, and professionalism or service. That doesn't mean a one-star establishment isn't worth dining or sleeping at. Far from it! When we say that all the places listed in our books are recommended, we mean it. That one-star pizza joint may be just the ticket for the end of a whirlwind day of shopping with the kids. But if you're planning something more special, the star ratings can help you choose an eatery or hotel that will wow your new clients or be a stunning, romantic place to celebrate an anniversary or impress a first date.

We award four-star ratings sparingly, reserving them for what we consider truly the best. And once an establishment has earned our highest rating, everyone's expectations seem to rise. Readers often write us letters specifically to point out the faults in four-star establishments. With changes in chefs, management, styles, and trends, it's always easier to get knocked off the pedestal than to ascend it. Three-star establishments, on the other hand, seem to generate healthy praise. They exhibit outstanding qualities, and we get lots of love letters about them. The difference between two and three stars can sometimes be a very fine line. Two-star establishments are doing a good, solid job and are gaining attention, while one-star places are often dependable spots that have been around forever.

The restaurants and lodgings described in *Best Places Northwest* have earned their stars from hard work and good service (and good food). They're proud to be included in this book: look for our Best Places sticker in their windows. And we're proud to honor them in this, the fifteenth edition of *Best Places Northwest*.

CHECKS AND CREDIT CARDS Many establishments that accept checks also require a major credit card for identification. Note that some places accept only local checks. Credit cards are abbreviated in this book as follows: American Express (AE), Carte Blanche (CB), Diners Club (DC), Discover (DIS), Enroute (E), Japanese credit card (JCB), MasterCard (MC), Visa (V).

ACCESS AND INFORMATION At the beginning of each chapter, you'll find general guidelines about how to get to a particular region and what types of transportation are available, as well as basic sources for any additional tourist information you might need. Also check individual town listings for specifics about visiting those places.

MAPS AND DIRECTIONS Each chapter in the book begins with a regional map that shows the general area being covered. Throughout the book, basic directions are provided with each entry. Whenever possible, call ahead to confirm hours and location.

THREE-DAY TOURS In every chapter, we've included a quick-reference, three-day itinerary designed for travelers with a short amount of time. Perfect for weekend getaways, these tours outline the highlights of a region or town; each of the establishments or attractions that appear in boldface within the tour are discussed in greater detail elsewhere in the chapter.

HELPFUL ICONS Watch for these quick-reference symbols throughout the book:

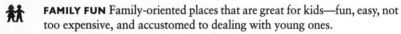 **FAMILY FUN** Family-oriented places that are great for kids—fun, easy, not too expensive, and accustomed to dealing with young ones.

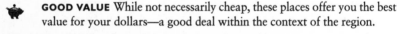 **GOOD VALUE** While not necessarily cheap, these places offer you the best value for your dollars—a good deal within the context of the region.

ROMANTIC These spots offer candlelight, atmosphere, intimacy, or other romantic qualities—kisses and proposals are encouraged!

EDITORS' CHOICE These are places that are unique and special to the Northwest and beyond, such as a restaurant owned by a beloved local chef or a tourist attraction recognized around the globe.

Appears after listings for establishments that have wheelchair-accessible facilities.

INDEXES All restaurants, lodgings, town names, and major tourist attractions are listed alphabetically at the back of the book.

MONEY-BACK GUARANTEE Please see "We Stand by Our Reviews" at the end of this book.

READER REPORTS At the end of the book is a report form. We receive hundreds of reports from readers suggesting new places or agreeing or disagreeing with our assessments. They greatly help in our evaluations, and we encourage you to respond.

PORTLAND AND ENVIRONS

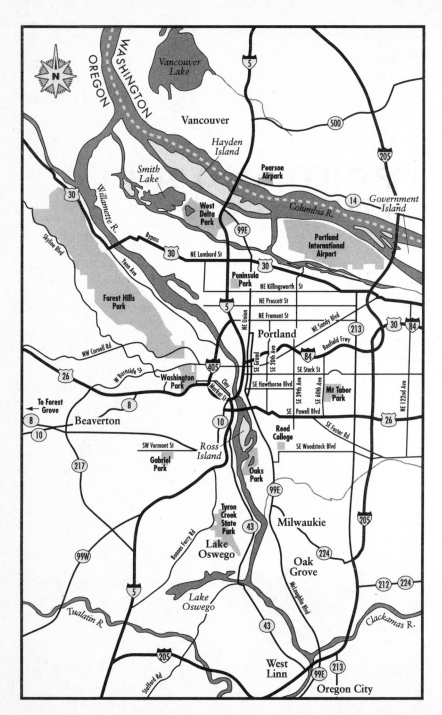

PORTLAND AND ENVIRONS

Although Portland has had a stellar reputation among American cities, it has recently come into its own as a destination, and with good reason. It's got a great location, a nice size, and an up-and-coming restaurant scene.

This city with a river running through it is watched over by a pair of dramatic, volcanic mountains (Hood and Adams), and the beautiful Willamette Valley spreads away from it to the south.

In addition, Portland is not so big that it's an expedition to get downtown from the suburban or residential areas (each of which has its own personality), or so small that there's nothing going on once you get there. Downtown bustles with commerce and culture, and is an easy place to spend a few days—or a few years.

The residents are a mix of lifelong Oregonians (with strong opinions about such issues as salmon recovery, educational reform, and radical-minded newcomers) and newcomers (with their own strong opinions about salmon and schools—and about conservative old-timers). But what's heartening here is the way everyone comes together for classic events such as the Portland Rose Festival and the Mount Hood Festival of Jazz; nobody's a newcomer for long. Portlanders know how to throw a party when the occasion calls for one (there's a killer blues festival every Fourth of July), and they take seriously their civic responsibilities, as evidenced by the urban planning that's become a model for the country, a burgeoning arts scene, and an ever-expanding library and parks system.

Like many Northwest urban areas, the City of Roses shines in late summer and early fall; Indian summer (September and October) is usually glorious, but a few showers are needed to keep the place green all year.

ACCESS AND INFORMATION

PORTLAND INTERNATIONAL AIRPORT, or PDX (7000 NE Airport Wy; 503/460-4234; *www.portlandairportpdx.com*), is served by most major airlines, with excellent connections from points around the Pacific Northwest and beyond. Allow plenty of time, especially during rush hours, to get from airport to town—30 minutes at least—and the same on your return. All major **CAR RENTAL** companies operate from the airport. Taxis and shuttles are readily available; expect to pay at least $25 for the trip downtown. The most economical ride ($1.55) is via the shiny new airport **METROPOLITAN AREA EXPRESS (MAX)** train. Catch a sleek MAX light-rail train just outside baggage claim; the ride to Pioneer Courthouse Square takes 38 minutes. Another mode of transportation is the **GRAYLINE OF PORTLAND AIRPORT EXPRESS** (503/285-9845); buses leave every 45 minutes.

Most drivers reach Portland via either **INTERSTATE 5**, which runs north-south, or **INTERSTATE 84** (east-west). **US HIGHWAY 26** goes to Beaverton; **INTERSTATE 205** loops off Interstate 5 and passes near Lake Oswego, West Linn, Oregon City, and Milwaukie, among other towns. Rush hours in Portland can mean standstill traffic, but if you arrive midday (after 9am, but before 3pm) or after 7pm, you should have clear sailing into town.

AMTRAK (503/273-4866 locally or 800/USA-RAIL; *www.amtrak.com*) operates out of lovely **UNION STATION** (800 NW 6th Ave) just north of downtown. This romantic structure memorializes the bygone era of the great railways. Trains come and go from points north, east, and south daily. The nearby **GREYHOUND** station (550 NW 6th Ave; 503/243-2357 or 800/231-2222; *www.greyhound.com*) has a complete daily schedule of buses. Both stations are within walking distance (about 12 blocks) of downtown.

In Portland, **TRI-MET** (503/238-7433; *www.trimet.org*) operates the city bus system and **MAX**; tickets for the two are interchangeable. Almost all bus lines run through the **PORTLAND TRANSIT MALL** (SW 5th and 6th Aves); MAX lines also pass through downtown. You can ride free downtown in "Fareless Square," which also extends across the river to the Convention Center; from downtown to most outlying neighborhoods, you'll need a two-zone ticket ($1.25), which you can purchase on the bus (exact change only) or at MAX stops. Another popular transportation option that travels from the South Park Blocks to NW 23rd Avenue through the Pearl District is the new **PORTLAND STREETCAR** (*www.portlandstreetcar.org*), which costs the same as Tri-Met.

Portland

Portland has much to offer, and its increasing number of citizens make the most of it. The nationally noted light-rail service goes east to Gresham, west to Beaverton, and now to the airport. A cultural district downtown is home to a jewel of a performing arts center, a first-class art museum, and a historical center, all located along a greenbelt called the **SOUTH PARK BLOCKS**, which run from **PORTLAND STATE UNIVERSITY** north to Salmon Street. In the lively downtown core, lunchtime concerts entertain summer weekday crowds at **PIONEER COURTHOUSE SQUARE**, at SW Broadway and SW Yamhill Streets. Also in town are a major convention center, pleasant strolling neighborhoods, an attractively remodeled minor-league ballpark, and stunning digs for a favorite all-ages hangout: the **OREGON MUSEUM OF SCIENCE AND INDUSTRY** (see Major Attractions section).

MAJOR ATTRACTIONS

Outfit yourself with information at the new visitor center in **PIONEER COURTHOUSE SQUARE** (503/275-8355; *www.travelportland.com*). Here you can make hotel or dinner reservations, buy tickets to events, and talk with someone who's eager to give you the lay of the city.

OMSI, the **OREGON MUSEUM OF SCIENCE AND INDUSTRY** (1945 SE Water Ave; 503/797-4000; *www.omsi.edu*), is an engaging place to take the whole family. There's a submarine moored in the Willamette to board, an IMAX theater, fascinating exhibits, even a toddler room. The **OREGON HISTORY CENTER** (1200 SW Park Ave; 503/222-1741) pays tribute to our ancestors—Native Americans, white settlers, seafarers, and others. Its gift shop is first-rate. Not exactly a museum, but having an impressive (living) collection nonetheless, is the **OREGON ZOO** (4001 SW Canyon Rd; 503/226-1561; *www.zooregon.org*), where myriad exhibits include many species common to the Pacific Northwest; ride MAX for an easy trip from downtown. **CM2**, a.k.a. the **CHILDREN'S MUSEUM 2ND GENERATION**, is located across the parking lot (503/223-6500; *www.portlandcm2.org*).

PORTLAND THREE-DAY TOUR

DAY ONE: Spend your first day exploring downtown Portland. Wake up to breakfast at the **BIJOU CAFÉ**, then stretch your legs along the elm-lined **SOUTH PARK BLOCKS**. Art lovers should head to the **PORTLAND ART MUSEUM**, history buffs to the **OREGON HISTORY CENTER**, and shoppers to **PIONEER PLACE**. For lunch, stop at **MOTHER'S BISTRO & BAR**. In the afternoon, catch an art film at the **KOIN CINEMAS** (SW 3rd Ave and SW Clay St; 503/225-5555, ext 4608 for recorded film schedules) or restrain yourself in the **PEARL DISTRICT**'s art galleries and shops. If you get tired, hop on MAX to get around, but save some time (and energy) for **POWELL'S CITY OF BOOKS**. Make a dinner reservation in advance at **HIGGINS** or **EL GAUCHO**. Then check into the elegant **HEATHMAN HOTEL**, or the **5TH AVENUE SUITES**.

DAY TWO: Excellent breakfasts are the norm at **ZELL'S: AN AMERICAN CAFÉ**, after which, head for the hills, the **WEST HILLS**, that is, to explore some of the city's parks. Views are dramatic from the **WASHINGTON PARK INTERNATIONAL ROSE TEST GARDEN** or the **JAPANESE GARDEN**. For a bit more of a workout, hike through **HOYT ARBORETUM** on the Wildwood Trail (start near the **OREGON ZOO**—itself an intriguing place to visit). When you're getting hungry, point your car toward trendy **NW 23RD AVENUE** and stop in at **THE RAM'S HEAD** (2282 NW Hoyt; 503/221-0098; *mcmenamins.com*), a McMenamin's pub. Then spend the afternoon exploring the boutiques and shops along NW 23rd and 21st Avenues. Stay in the neighborhood and eat dinner at **CAFFE MINGO**.

DAY THREE: Sleep in late on your last morning in Portland and, if you time your visit right, begin the day with a visit to Portland's **SATURDAY MARKET**, where you can grab coffee and a snack. If it's not Saturday, stroll **TOM MCCALL WATERFRONT PARK** instead. Have lunch at **BREAD AND INK CAFÉ**, or head to the **HAWTHORNE STREET ALEHOUSE** (3632 SE Hawthorne Blvd; 503/233-6540). Spend the afternoon in the **HAWTHORNE DISTRICT**, and enjoy a fine dinner at **CASTAGNE** before calling it a night.

During the month of June, the city's roses—and its **ROSE FESTIVAL**—are in full bloom. Highlights of this monthlong extravaganza include three parades, the largest of which is the Grand Floral Parade; an air show; a carnival in Tom McCall Waterfront Park; the Festival of Flowers, for which Pioneer Courthouse Square is transformed with some 25,000 potted plants; and, of course, a world-class rose show.

The Willamette River flows right through the middle of town, and Portlanders flock to one of their city's two major waterways—the other, of course, being the mighty Columbia River just to the north. **TOM MCCALL WATERFRONT PARK**, on the west side of the Willamette, is the perfect place for a run or stroll. The **PORTLAND SPIRIT** riverboat (503/226-2517; *www.portlandspirit.com*) docks here. The new **EASTBANK ESPLANADE**, a floating walkway that extends from the Steel Bridge to the Hawthorne Bridge on the east side of the river, makes it possible to enjoy a 3-mile loop along both banks.

Just north of downtown, on a city block surrounded by parking lots and high-rises, is the **CLASSICAL CHINESE GARDEN**, the **GARDEN OF THE AWAKENING ORCHID** (corner of NW Everett St and NW 3rd Ave; 503/228-8131). Completed in 2000, this garden has quickly become a favorite stop for visitors who appreciate its authenticity (it was designed and built by garden experts from Portland's sister city, Suzhou). Stop for tea in the tea house.

The old warehouse district just west of the Chinese garden known as the **PEARL DISTRICT** (between NW 9th and NW 15th Aves, and NW Burnside and NW Lovejoy Sts) is the gentrified home of art galleries, restaurants, and shops—as well as **POWELL'S CITY OF BOOKS**, the country's largest bookstore (see "A Literary Legend" in this chapter).

GALLERIES AND MUSEUMS

Gallery walks once a month (on "First Thursdays") encourage visitors to expose themselves to art; galleries, clustered in the Pearl District or downtown, showcase both local and national works. The **PORTLAND ART MUSEUM** (1219 SW Park Ave; 503/226-2811; *www.portlandartmuseum.org*) is the big name for exhibits of international acclaim. Past presentations have included priceless objects from the Imperial Tombs of China and Russia's Stroganoff Palace; renowned collections of Pre-Raphaelite and ancient Egyptian art are scheduled for exhibition in 2005 and 2006. Check out the smaller **CONTEMPORARY CRAFTS MUSEUM & GALLERY** (3934 SW Corbett Ave; 503/223-2654; *www.contemporarycrafts.org*), a good place to purchase a unique art gift, perhaps chess sets by various artists, contemporary basketry, quilts, and affordable ceramics, as well as more costly sculpture.

The city is popping with public art, too; pick up the "Public Art: Walking Tour" booklet, free at the **REGIONAL ARTS AND CULTURE COUNCIL** (620 SW Main St, Ste 420; 503/823-5111) to hunt down these treasures. Pioneer Courthouse Square, at SW Broadway and SW Yamhill Streets, is a good place to begin, and the stunningly renovated **CENTRAL LIBRARY** (801 SW 10th Ave; 503/988-5123) is a great place to end.

PARKS AND GARDENS

Besides the sprawling and primitive **FOREST PARK** (see Sports and Recreation section), the city has nearly 150 other parks, and **WASHINGTON PARK** (West Hills; 503/823-3636) is home to several of them: The **HOYT ARBORETUM** (503/228-8733), close to the Oregon Zoo (see Major Attractions section), has an impressive collection of native and exotic flora and well-kept trails. More formal grounds are the **INTERNATIONAL ROSE TEST GARDEN** (503/823-3636), the **JAPANESE GARDEN** (503/223-1321), and, across town, the **CRYSTAL SPRINGS RHODODENDRON GARDEN** (503/823-3640). Also in Washington Park is the largest memorial of its kind in the nation, the **VIETNAM VETERANS' LIVING MEMORIAL**, an inspiring outdoor cathedral commemorating the Oregon victims of that conflict. It's possible for a person to walk from one of these parks to another without really realizing it, so continuous is their reach of trails through Portland's West Hills. Although parts of Washington Park have a wild, overgrown feeling, much of it is well tended. Forest Park, on the other hand, is not a manicured park at all, but is rather a "wilderness" for the city.

SHOPPING

A few uniquely Portland shops not to miss: **POWELL'S CITY OF BOOKS** (1005 W Burnside St; 503/228-4651; *www.powells.com*), which is legendary for its number of volumes, both new and used; **TWIST** (30 NW 23rd Pl; 503/224-0334), where jewelry and folk art rise to new heights of function and form; **MADE IN OREGON** (10 NW 1st Ave; 503/273-8354; and branches), where such names as Jantzen and Pendleton get top billing; and **IN GOOD TASTE** (231 NW 11th Ave; 503/248-2015), one of the city's many stores for cooks, complete with its own class schedule and top-drawer lunch counter.

Crafts—and a carnival atmosphere—can be found weekends at **SATURDAY MARKET** under the Burnside Bridge (closed Jan to Feb). Upscale specialty shops and eateries are found downtown, many in the area around Pioneer Courthouse Square, including the expansive **PIONEER PLACE** (between SW Morrison and Yamhill Sts, and SW 3rd and 5th Aves). Across the river near the Convention Center is **LLOYD CENTER MALL** (between NE Halsey and Multnomah Sts, and NE 9th and 15th Aves), with its beloved ice-skating rink. Posh and happy **NW 23RD AVENUE**, the arty **PEARL DISTRICT** (north of Burnside St between NW 9th and 15th Aves), and countercultural **SE HAWTHORNE BOULEVARD** (between 20th and 45th Aves) are must-visits for shoppers. **SELLWOOD**, southeast of downtown, across the Sellwood Bridge, is an entire neighborhood of antique stores.

PERFORMING ARTS

Portlanders pack the **ARLENE SCHNITZER CONCERT HALL** (1000 SW Broadway) 52 weeks a year for concerts and lectures; contact the box office in the **PORTLAND CENTER FOR THE PERFORMING ARTS** (PCPA; 1111 SW Broadway; 503/796-9293) for tickets. One company that plays regularly at "the Schnitz" is the **OREGON SYMPHONY ORCHESTRA** (503/228-1353; *www.orsymphony.org*), under conductor James DePreist. Classical music fans should also know about **CHAMBER MUSIC NORTHWEST** (522 SW 5th Ave, Ste 725; 503/294-6400; *www.cmnw.org*), which presents a summer festival spanning four centuries of music and events throughout the season in various venues.

The PCPA's resident theater company, **PORTLAND CENTER STAGE** (1111 SW Broadway; 503/274-6588; *www.pcs.org*), offers excellent production values, whatever the play. You can always be assured of work by Shakespeare with productions by **TYGRES HEART** (503/288-8400; *www.tygresheart.org*), housed in the same facility. Plays by **ARTISTS REPERTORY THEATRE**, staged at the **REIERSGAARD THEATRE** (1516 SW Alder St; 503/241-1278; *www.art.org*), often garner lavish critical praise.

The **OREGON BALLET THEATER** (Keller Auditorium, 222 SW Clay St; 503/222-5538; *www.obt.org*) enlists youth and daring to serve the needs of Portland's ballet fans. Also watch for performances presented by **WHITE BIRD**, an organization that exists solely to promote dance (at various venues; 503/245-1600). Finally, contemporary art fans are energetically served by the performances and exhibitions of **PICA** (Portland Institute for Contemporary Art; 503/242-1519; *www.pica.org*).

NIGHTLIFE

For what's happening in the popular music world, check the calendar listings in *Willamette Week,* the *Portland Mercury,* or the *Oregonian*'s A&E section. Some popular music venues in town include the **ALADDIN THEATER** (116 SE 11th Ave; 503/234-9698) for everything from bluegrass to punk; the alcohol-free **B COMPLEX** (320 SE 2nd Ave; 503/235-4424) for hip hop and electronica; and the **CRYSTAL BALLROOM** (1332 W Burnside St; 503/225-0047) where there are musical acts from reggae to ballroom. **HOLOCENE** (1001 SE Morrison St; 503/239-7639) is a hip DJ dance venue; and **THE KNOW** (2022 NE Alberta St; 503/284-6397; all ages) captures Portland's grassroots arts and music scenes.

SPORTS AND RECREATION

The town's big-league action can be found at the **ROSE GARDEN ARENA** (1 Center Ct), a huge dome easily visible from Interstate 5, home of the NBA's **PORTLAND TRAIL BLAZERS** (Ticketmaster: 503/224-4400; *www.nba.com/blazers/*). The Blazers may have a reputation as the NBA's bad boys, but they often make the playoffs (although they haven't won the championship since 1977). The **PORTLAND WINTER HAWKS** (Ticketmaster: 503/224-4400; *www.winterhawks.com*), of the Western Hockey League, play at **MEMORIAL COLISEUM** (1401 N Wheeler Ave) or Rose Garden Arena, and hit the ice 36 times a season at home. Baseball fans are still waiting for the major league, but content themselves with the **PORTLAND BEAVERS**—who play to loyal crowds at refurbished **PGE PARK** (SW 20th Ave and SW Morrison St). The **PORTLAND TIMBERS** soccer team also plays the park. (For PGE Park tickets, call 503/553-5555; *www.pgepark.com.*)

Individual sports thrive in the region: runners, hikers, and mountain bikers have access to more than 50 miles of trails in primitive 5,000-acre **FOREST PARK** (503/823-7529; *www.parks.ci.portland.or.us/Parks/ForestPark.htm*), easily accessed at points throughout the West Hills. A good map of Forest Park is a must; the Audubon Society of Portland's **NATURE STORE** (5151 NW Cornell Rd; 503/292-9453; *www.audubonportland.org/store*) is a great resource for maps and information. Rowers are guaranteed miles of flat water on the Willamette; and cyclists use hundreds of miles of off- and on-street paved bike paths in the greater Portland area, including the new Eastbank Esplanade along the Willamette River.

RESTAURANTS

Andina / ★★★

1314 NW GLISAN ST, PORTLAND; 503/228-9535 This Pearl District newcomer serves *novo* ("new") Peruvian cuisine. You might start with ensalada Macchu Pichu, a quinoa-and-vegetable salad with avocado and duck confit, or with *anticuchos,* marinated beef skewered with grilled yucca and served with salsa criolla. For the main course, consider *pachamanca del Inca,* a traditional hunter's meal of venison and pheasant baked in a clay pot, or *bonito con nopal,* sautéed albacore tuna marinated in a sauce of passion fruit, bell pepper, and lime and served on a cactus leaf. Don't leave without trying Peru's signature drink, *pisco,* a white-grape brandy.

Enjoy it with dinner or sip it in the spacious bar, where you're likely to find Latin Americans cheering a *futbol* (soccer) match on the TV. *$$–$$$; AE, DIS, MC, V; local checks only; lunch Mon–Fri, dinner Mon–Sat, brunch Sun; full bar; reservations recommended; www.andinarestaurant.com; at NW 13th.* &

BeWon Korean Restaurant / ★★★

1203 NW 23RD AVE, PORTLAND; 503/464-9222 There are two routes to take at BeWon: the prix-fixe path of *han jung shik*, an eight-course extravaganza that approximates a traditional Korean meal for an unbelievably affordable $24.95; or a dinner constructed of à la carte orders. Try both. *Han jung shik* is a stimulating meal that takes diners on a memorable tour of the five flavors of Asian cooking (salt, sweet, sour, hot, and bitter). Ordering à la carte allows sampling of not-to-be-missed dishes that aren't in the prix fixe. Main courses, such as broiled mackerel caked in sea salt and sliced pork in a red-pepper barbecue sauce, are satisfying, but they take a backseat to the vivid parade of accompanying side dishes. Teensy saucers hold the likes of dried cod, kimchi, small pancakes chunked with vegetables and crab, delicious flank-steak strips, and dried kelp flakes sprinkled with sugar. The restaurant has gained a legion of new Korean food lovers; try it once, and you may soon BeWon. *$$; AE, DIS, MC, V; no checks; lunch Mon–Sat, dinner every day; beer and wine; reservations recommended; at Northrup St.* &

Bijou Café / ★★⯪

132 SW 3RD AVE, PORTLAND; 503/222-3187 The handsome Bijou Café long ago attained breakfast-landmark status in Portland, and the remodeling of neither the restaurant nor the surrounding neighborhood has changed its position. Lunch, with its one-third pound Painted Hills beef burger, phenomenal milkshakes, soba noodle salad, and seasonal specials ranging from an avocado-grapefruit salad to steamed fish with red curry sauce and basmati rice, can pack quite a full house. But the real crush still happens before noon, especially on weekends, when the lines stretch out the door for grilled cinnamon bread, terrific scrambled eggs, and as many as three kinds of pancakes. The tofu scramble is the best in town, the spicy French toast is made with thick brioche, and salmon hash has a reverent following. *$–$$; MC, V; local checks only; breakfast every day, lunch Mon–Fri; beer and wine; no reservations; at Pine.* &

Bluehour / ★★★

250 NW 13TH AVE, PORTLAND; 503/226-3394 Love it or shun it, everyone's got an opinion about Bluehour, including those who have never stepped inside the cavernous, million-dollar restaurant. Some complain it's too chic for its own good; but Portland's not a lumberjack town anymore. Co-owner Bruce Carey has done oodles to elevate the culinary standard in Stumptown. The cosmopolitan interior is part of the fun, but chef Kenny Giambalvo validates the cash outlay with seriously well-crafted food. His signature gnocchi are velvety, cheesy cushions with a salty kick and a hint of black truffle. Made-to-order risotto takes longer to prepare than most appetizers, but the first bite assuages the wait. Seared sea scallops cosseted by strips of bacon are a heady, reliable treat. Watercress and a sweet-onion salad lend perkiness to grilled hanger steak; grapefruit and leeks accompany excellent seared foie gras. Even desserts, such as chocolate caramel tart spiked with *Fleur de Sel*, take a walk on the wildish side. *$$$; AE, DC, MC, V; checks OK; dinner Tues–Sat; full bar; reservations recommended; www.bluehouronline.com; corner of NW Everett St.* ও

Bread and Ink Café / ★★

3610 NE HAWTHORNE BLVD, PORTLAND; 503/239-4756 There's more to the beloved Bread and Ink than its blintzes. This homey, light-filled bistro in the heart of the funky Hawthorne District serves a marvelous Jamaican jerk-chicken sandwich, grilled black-bean cakes, and panfried oysters with chipotle-lime aioli for lunch. At dinner, you can't go wrong with its chèvre, arugula, and hazelnut salad; its risotto primavera; or its pork tenderloin in fresh rosemary, garlic, and white wine. Regulars rave about its oversized hamburger with homemade condiments, and its impressive baked desserts. With intriguing framed line drawings on the walls and huge windows onto Hawthorne, there are more reasons the place has become a neighborhood landmark. But the biggest is the hallowed blintzes. *$$; AE, DIS, MC, V; checks OK; breakfast, lunch, dinner Mon–Sat, brunch Sun; beer and wine; reservations recommended; at SE 36th Ave.*

Caffe Mingo / ★★★☆

807 NW 21ST AVE, PORTLAND; 503/226-4646 Caffe Mingo is what so many places aspire to: always packed, buzzing with good humor, and absolutely confident in its ability to produce splendid, uncomplicated meals. Diners eagerly wait in line for spiedini with prawns and croutons, gorgonzola and walnut raviolini, and juicy chicken breast with fluffy gnocchi. Seasonal salads—such as beets with green beans and wax beans in nutty garlic-almond dressing—are one-of-a-kind beauties. The menu has grown more ambitious over time, pushing the prices up a bit, but not sky-high. *$$; AE, DC, DIS, MC, V; no checks; dinner every day; beer and wine; reservations recommended; between NW Johnson and Kearny Sts.*

Caprial's Bistro / ★★★

7015 SE MILWAUKIE AVE, PORTLAND; 503/236-6457 Open kitchens permit a close-up peek at the fairly chaotic business of readying meals at breakneck pace: a chance to glimpse chefs tending to four pans with one hand while creating spunky garnishes with the other. At Caprial's, the best spot in the house may be at the end of the kitchen counter, where you get to witness a cook's occasional meltdown and hear waiters cursing when they deliver salmon and duck to the couple who ordered vegetarian tamales. (You won't see that on any of foodie celeb Caprial Pence's public TV shows.) Only four or five entrées are offered nightly, but they explode with flavor and include embellished sides that get as much love as the main dish. Pork loin chop, marinated and glazed in a maple-spiked pork stock reduction to extract robust flavor, is served with fried cheddar-bacon grits and sautéed chard. Appetizers are even more attention-grabbing; prawns sautéed sticky-sweet in a garlic-chile glaze, served with noodles and chopped cashews, are a lip-tingling starter. *$$$; AE, MC, V; checks OK; lunch, dinner Tues–Sat; full bar; reservations recommended; www.caprial.com; in Westmoreland.*

Castagna / ★★★★

1752 SE HAWTHORNE BLVD, PORTLAND; 503/231-7373 As impeccable as Castagna's entrées are, crafting a meal from several starters can be even more seductive. This approach allows you to sample more of Castagna's pristine cooking, such as irresistible duck confit agnolotti (stuffed crescent-shaped pasta), white bean soup, and the Trio: an ever-changing mix that might include fried parsnip curls, magenta beets, and delicately perfumed chick-peas. One of the most striking first courses is also the simplest: butter lettuce leaves stacked to resemble a whole head of the stuff and drizzled with an herby vinaigrette. Everything looks beautiful on the plate, nothing more so than the towering haystack of down-market French fries next to a grilled New York steak reclining in porcini butter. While Castagna is for those *dolce vita* nights, it's more relaxed next-door offspring, Café Castagna ($$; 1758 SE Hawthorne Blvd; 503/231-9959), offers affordable, everyday indulgences like the crisp gem of a Caesar salad or the robust cheeseburger. Each simple dish is executed with enviable prowess. Arancini, fried risotto dumplings with oozing centers, crepe-thin pizzas, and brownie sundaes feed your jones for comfort food. *$$$; AE, MC, V; checks OK; dinner Wed–Sat; full bar; reservations recommended; at SE 17th Ave.* ♿

clarklewis / ★★☆

1001 SE WATER AVE, PORTLAND; 503/235-2294 Michael Hebb and Naomi Pomeroy, whose Ripe catering business has been impressing Portland diners since 1999, opened clarklewis in spring 2004, and it was an immediate hit. The space, in the city's industrial Southeast neighborhood, inspires words like "edgy," "urban," and "chic." It's got cement floors, exposed ceiling ducts, and a wall of glass-paned garage doors. Top-notch ingredients are used with a sure hand by Morgan Brownlow in the kitchen, which is visible from just about every corner of the large room (a former loading dock). The Northern Italian–style food is the most important detail. From a simple plate of radishes with sweet butter and salt, to scaloppini of pork with prosciutto and sage cooked to nearly fork-tender perfection, the food here is simple, straightforward, and superb. Menu categories include starters, pasta and "from the stove" (wood-fired hearth), and sides. You can order anything—including bread and butter—in "small," "large," or "family" portions. The little bistro chairs are not so comfortable, but there's so much going on you may not notice. The candlelit space is too loud to be considered intimate, but if you like your romance with a frisson of excitement, even passion, this is the place. *$$; AE, MC, V; checks OK; lunch, dinner Mon–Sat; full bar; reservations recommended; at SE Yamhill.* ♿

El Gaucho / ★★★

319 SW BROADWAY, PORTLAND; 503/227-8794 Couples seeking shadowy romance come to El Gaucho for moody, elegant sophistication; others come to maybe catch a glimpse of local and visiting celebs and politicos. A menu complete with steakhouse traditions opens with oysters Rockefeller, shrimp Louis, and Caesar salad tossed tableside. Steaks include the signature Roquefort baseball cut—a 16-ounce, 4-inch round of tender, 28-day dry-aged New York Angus—and chateaubriand for two. Non-carnivores order fish broiled with lemon butter and sea scallops on linguine. Bananas Foster and cherries jubilee are flambéed dessert classics. A first-class international wine list is heavy on reds. *$$$$; AE, DC, MC, V; checks OK; lunch Mon–Fri, dinner every day; full bar; reservations recommended; www.elgaucho.com; corner of SW Washington, in the Benson Hotel.* &

Esparza's Tex-Mex Café / ★★

2725 SE ANKENY ST, PORTLAND; 503/234-7909 People may wonder how a Tex-Mex restaurant has become a landmark in Portland—but the surprise doesn't survive the first visit, and certainly not the first smoked beef-brisket taco. Servers will help you choose the right tequila to match the Cowboy Tacos— hearty handfuls filled with thick slabs of smoked sirloin, barbecue sauce, guacamole, and pico de gallo—or the Uvalde, a smoked-lamb enchilada. For an appetizer, go for *nopalitos,* a tasty cactus dish. Augmented by daily specials, the menu has quite a reach, running the gamut from red snapper (smothered with sautéed peppers and tomatoes) to smoked pork loin (stuffed with spiced buffalo). *$$; AE, DC, DIS, MC, V; no checks; lunch, dinner Tues–Sat; full bar; reservations recommended; at SE 28th St.* &

Fernando's Hideaway / ★★★⯪

824 SW 1ST AVE, PORTLAND; 503/248-4709 Fernando's drips with a seedy, lived-in sensuality that confirms it as the most romantic and seductive of Portland's Spanish eateries. Its roaring bar is a first-rate singles' scene, and the upstairs area hosts salsa dancing (free lessons Thurs–Sat) and flamenco exhibitions. Many folks come to sup on the extensive menu of Andalusian-style tapas. Favorites are the *gambas pil pil,* prawns sautéed in a hot chile garlic oil; *tarta de congrejo,* crab cakes with lobster sauce; *tortilla Española,* a potato-and-egg pie; and *pulpo a la gallega,* marinated octopus with picante sauce. Sequester yourselves in a rear booth for an authentic paella, or opt for the marvelous *chuleta de ternera,* a grilled veal chop topped with a dried-cherry and red-wine sauce. Desserts are impressive—Catalan crème brûlée flavored with cinnamon and lemon, for instance—and the long list of Spanish wines is one of the finest in the country. *$$–$$$; AE, MC, V; checks OK; lunch Mon–Fri, dinner every day; full bar; reservations recommended; www.fernandosportland.com; at SW Taylor.* &

Genoa / ★★★★

2832 SE BELMONT ST, PORTLAND; 503/238-1464 One of Portland's truly great restaurants, Genoa seduces with rustic simplicity, not haute cuisine. The seven-course menu changes every two weeks, but some favorite dishes reappear year after year. The *bagna cauda* antipasto, served with homemade breadsticks, crisp raw carrots, fennel, radicchio, and celery, is one such true-blue dish. This might be followed by a bowl of Sicilian-inspired gazpacho, then a fresh egg pasta tossed with chanterelles and black olives. Salmon marinated in fennel, Dijon mustard, and sugar, broiled to coax a caramelized crust, is occasionally offered as one of three entrée choices. Naturally, Genoa's pasta course is unerring. Hand-cut pappardelle with rabbit ragout sings with nutmeg. The ravioli *di zucca* enfolds squash, sweet potato, and biscotti crumbs in its thin sheets. The whole extravagant meal comes to a lovely close with wedges of fresh fruit. *$$$$; AE, DC, MC, V; checks OK; dinner every day; full bar; reservations required; www.genoarestaurant.com; at SE 29th Ave.*

Giorgio's / ★★★

1131 NW HOYT ST, PORTLAND; 503/221-1888 The warm bistro ambiance at Giorgio's is entirely inviting; the service is crisp, the food is sublime, and it's even located in the Pearl District. Chef Michael Clancy's puréed vegetable soups, spiked with star anise, or the mushroom strudel that's dressed up as a spring roll and served with a few wonderfully dry duck slices, are marvelous starters. Next comes a plate of homemade pasta: choose among the rice-paper-thin sweet potato ravioli with sugar snap peas and prosciutto; browned, bullet-sized gnocchi with sprightly spot prawns and fresh artichoke hearts; or foot-long pappardelle noodles tossed with shredded wild boar, fennel, and tomatoes. All are devastatingly delicious. *$$–$$$; AE, MC, V; no checks; lunch Tues–Fri, dinner Tues–Sat; full bar; reservations recommended; between 11th and 12th Aves.* &

The Heathman Restaurant and Bar / ★★★★

1001 SW BROADWAY, PORTLAND; 503/241-4100 Philippe Boulot has produced a consistently impressive kitchen to go with a dining room that continues to be the center of Portland power breakfasts and lunches. In 2001, he brought home the James Beard Award of Excellence, and he keeps pushing the envelope with his precise cooking. After making his own strong statements about Northwest cuisine—such as salmon in a pesto crust—Boulot has returned to his Gallic roots. That means foie gras in a rhubarb sauce and leg of lamb cooked for seven hours. Of course, there are still heartening Northwestern dishes, such as crab cakes in a red-curry butter sauce. Dinners are accompanied by a marvelous wine list dominated by Northwest and French vintages. All possible excuses should be made to dive into dessert creations, such as chocolate pear tart with pear-brandy sauce and *dulce de leche* ice cream. During the holidays, the Heathman offers high tea in the Tea Court. Make reservations early (September) to ensure a taste of cucumber crostini, scones, and delicate opera cakes. *$$$; AE, DC, DIS, MC, V; checks OK; breakfast, lunch, dinner every day; full bar; reservations recommended; www.heathman hotel.com; at SW Salmon St.* &

Higgins / ★★★★

1239 SW BROADWAY, PORTLAND; 503/222-9070 Pioneering chef Greg Higgins cooks with skill and principle. Dedicated to local producers and the idea of sustainability, Higgins crafts deft, creative dishes: medallions of pork loin and foie gras, crab and shrimp cakes with chipotle crème fraîche, and saffron bourride of regional shellfish. Part of Higgins's policy is to always provide a compelling vegetarian entrée; examples include a forest-mushroom tamale with hazelnut mole and tangerine salsa, and a black-and-white-truffle risotto. Spectacular presentation endures, especially in desserts, which might be a roasted pear in phyllo or a chocolate-almond-apricot tart. The adjacent bar at Higgins offers a cozy, less-formal environment; its very reasonable bistro menu features a peerless ground-sirloin burger, a mound of herbed chèvre with olives, and roasted heirloom potatoes with red pepper rouille. The bar's enormous stable of imported beers can, in one cool swig, transport the drinker to Belgium or Germany. *$$–$$$; AE, DC, DIS, MC, V; local checks only; lunch Mon–Fri, dinner every day; full bar; reservations recommended; higgins@europa.com; corner of SE Jefferson St.* &

Jake's Famous Crawfish / ★★

401 SW 12TH AVE, PORTLAND; 503/226-1419 Jake's probably makes more tourist itineraries than any other Portland restaurant. Behind its sociable, trendy scene lies a vigorous 112-year history, still apparent in the clubby wood bar, high-backed booths, and shiny mahogany paneling. If the seafood isn't fresh, it isn't on the menu. What's more, any fish can be ordered simply broiled with lemon butter or prepared "to match its origins": catfish with pecans and jalapeño chutney, for instance. Signature clam chowder, cedar-planked salmon, and whole-leaf Caesar salad take honors. Chocolate truffle cake, however, became so popular it is sold commercially, and three-berry cobbler earns raves. The bar scene is legendary, and a dense wine list showcases some of Oregon's finest vintages. A part of the city for three centuries, Jake's *is* Portland—not the top cuisine but a favorite son. *$$; AE, DC, DIS, MC, V; no checks; lunch Mon–Fri, dinner every day; full bar; reservations recommended; www.mccormickandschmicks.com; at SW Stark St.* &

Khun Pic's Bahn Thai / ★★

3429 SE BELMONT ST, PORTLAND; 503/235-1610 Culinary DNA must account for the success of two Thai sisters, daughters of a mother who owned one of Portland's first popular Thai restaurants. Shelley Siripatrapa has Lemongrass Thai (see review), while Mary Ogard operates Khun Pic's. Ogard's husband, Jon, manages the dining rooms, freeing Mary to run the kitchen solo. Since food is made to order, service can be interminably slow. Despite the pace, diners forgive all when her intensely seasoned food arrives at their table. Most are familiar: phad thai (including a great vegetarian version); *tom yum goong* (hot-and-sour prawn soup); crispy fried tofu with peanut sauce; fragrant curries; freshly grated green-papaya salad; and mango sorbet. *$$; no credit cards; checks OK; dinner Tues–Sat; beer and wine; reservations recommended; at SE 34th.*

La Calaca Comelona / ★★

2304 SE BELMONT ST, PORTLAND; 503/239-9675 La Calaca Comelona's authentic Mexican fare once consisted of inexpensive, bulging tacos, tostadas, and quesadillas, but it has evolved into a full-service restaurant with sophisticated entrées and a full liquor license. The expanded menu offers *especialidades de casa,* including *mole en pipían,* a medium-hot green mole ladled over hunks of chicken, studded with *pepitas* (hulled pumpkin seeds). *Puerco con chile negro* couples a grilled pork loin with smoky-black chile sauce and grilled almonds. The nuts, along with handmade tortillas, serve to balance the startlingly sharp flavor of the chile. *$–$$; AE, DC, DIS, MC, V; no checks; dinner Mon–Sat; full bar; reservations recommended; www.lacalacacomelona.com; at Belmont and SE 23rd Ave.* &

Laslow's Northwest / ★★★

2327 NW KEARNEY ST, PORTLAND; 503/241-8092 From an inexpensive happy-hour hot sheet to the well-rounded bistro list and top-shelf dinner menu, Laslow's Northwest makes its mouth-watering fare accessible to any budget. Happy hour and bar offerings reflect chef Eric Laslow's Cuban ancestry. You'll find tostones (fried green plantains), potato-salt-cod fritters, picadillo-stuffed empanadas, and a terrific sloppy joe. The $10-and-under bistro fare also includes a killer burger with smoked mozzarella and applewood-smoked bacon, and Laslow's signature pumpkin-custard crab cakes. The second story of this Victorian house-turned-restaurant serves as the more formal dining room. Main dishes are at once refined and filling. Expert risotto with kabocha squash, mushrooms, and baby spinach, for example, is an ultimate comfort food composed of premium ingredients. *$$–$$$; AE, MC, V; checks OK; dinner every day; full bar; reservations recommended; at NW 23rd.* &

Le Bouchon / ★★

517 NW 14TH AVE, PORTLAND; 503/248-2193 Here is a Left Bank–style bistro that is perfectly compatible with the Northwest lifestyle. Chef Claude Musquin excels in French-country and traditional bistro fare, and his wonderful sauces are a highlight of dining here. Dishes prepared *à la minuit* include salmon draped in fresh dill sauce with potatoes au gratin. Classic French onion soup requires a spoon to break through a perfect cheese crust to reach rich broth and onions. After your escargot, lamb chops, and *grand-mere*'s noodles, you won't forgive yourself if you haven't left room for a dense white-and-dark-chocolate mousse in a martini glass. *$$; AE, DIS, MC, V; no checks; lunch Fri, dinner Tues–Sat; beer and wine; reservations recommended; at Glisan.* &

Lemongrass Thai / ★★⯪

1705 NE COUCH ST, PORTLAND; 503/231-3053 Shelly Siripatrapa's Lemongrass is nestled in a sweet, subdued Victorian house in leafy Buckman. Siripatrapa prepares and serves much of the food herself. The zesty noodle dishes and be-still-my-heart curries have a spiciness scale that runs from 1 to 20. Lemongrass cuisine is also notable for its emphasis on crisp textures and the heady scents of Thai herbs and spices: grassy basil and cilantro, aromatic kaffir leaves and lemongrass, tart slivers of lime. Service can be slow, but patient diners still pour in for the crispy-chewy salad rolls, the creamy *tom yum* soup, and the palate-scorching Thai Noodle (phad thai). *$$; no credit cards; checks OK; lunch Tues–Fri, dinner Tues–Sat; beer and wine; no reservations; at NE 17th Ave.*

Lucère / ★★

1510 SW HARBOR WY (RIVERPLACE HOTEL), PORTLAND; 503/228-3233 Since Lucère first dropped anchor as resident restaurant of the RiverPlace Hotel (see review), its fortunes have ebbed, flowed, and finally caught a swell; there are many delights on the menu crafted by Matthew Young. Northwest produce provides much of the flavor here, from the wild mushrooms in a perfectly al dente risotto, to the heirloom tomatoes in a chilled salad, to that daub of triple cream on the artisan cheese plate. Execution of the entrées is expert—the grilled fillets of beef and pork

AN EMPIRE BUILT ON BEER

Most cities in the world have McDonald's; for that matter, Portland has McDonald's. But Portland also has McMenamin's, and when it comes to choosing between a Big Mac, fries, and a Coke at the Golden Arches or choosing a Communication Breakdown Burger, fries, and a glass of Terminator Ale at the **HILLSDALE BREWERY AND PUB** (1505 SW Sunset Blvd; 503/246-3938), there's no contest. McMenamin pubs—and there are dozens in the greater Portland area—are old-fashioned, art-filled hangouts, where you meet friends and linger long into the evening to the strains of the Grateful Dead, for instance, or grab a quick dinner with the family.

Brothers Brian and Mike McMenamin have been making handmade ales for a couple of decades now, but you won't find their brews in your grocer's cooler; they are sold only in the McMenamin pubs—and McMenamin hotels, movie theaters, and dance halls. The McMenamins' diverse establishments are tied together by a comfortable, quirky, slightly mystic decorating scheme, including paintings created by artists who are members of the staff.

One of the special things these guys do, besides provide appealing, mostly non-smoking spots for Portlanders to get out of the rain, is refurbish old, dilapidated build-ings. Several sites are on the National Register of Historic Places and have interesting histories. **EDGEFIELD** (2126 SW Halsey St, Troutdale; 503/669-8610), for example, a "destination resort" (20 minutes from downtown Portland), was a former poor farm; the **KENNEDY SCHOOL** (5736 NE 33rd Ave, Portland; 503/249-3983) in northeast Portland was a grade school; and the **GRAND LODGE** (3505 Pacific Ave, Forest Grove; 503/992-9533) was the former Masonic and Eastern Star Home.

You may not appreciate the ambiance of every McMenamin establishment, but chances are great that if you're in Portland long enough, you'll find one you like well enough to visit again. Check out *www.mcmenamins.com* for more information, including menus, current movie offerings, and room rates.

—Kim Carlson

tenderloin are prepared with delicately rendered sauces and careful, artistic plating. An intelligent wine list contains dozens of Northwest entries, many available by the glass. *$$$; AE, DC, DIS, JCB, MC, V; checks OK; breakfast, lunch, dinner every day; full bar; reservations recommended; www.riverplacehotel.com; Downtown.* &

Lucy's Table / ★★★

704 NW 21ST AVE, PORTLAND; 503/226-6126 What you really must know about Lucy's Table is that pound for pound, it's less expensive than many of its peers. Chef Thomas McLaughlin's weekly menu follows the seasons and veers from fragrant braised duck breast to a deep bowl of risotto that teems with some of the meatiest wild mushrooms you've ever met. Roast pork loin is stuffed with a complementary mix of plump Carnaroli rice, nuts, and dried fruits and served with a similarly bulging sweet roasted onion and is surprisingly reasonably priced. *$$; AE, DC, MC, V; checks OK; dinner Mon–Sat; full bar; reservations recommended; www.lucystable.com; at NW Irving.* &

McCormick & Schmick's Seafood Restaurant / ★★

235 SW 1ST AVE, PORTLAND; 503/224-7522 The seafood variety has made a success of this sophisticated homegrown chain-gone-national. The kitchen favors simple preparations of favorites such as crawfish from Lake Billy Chinook, Polly Creek Alaska razor clams, and Suva Fiji yellowfin tuna. The restaurant is solidly styled, with high-backed wood booths ideal for business or urban banter. The international wine list and beers on tap encourage a brisk bar scene. *$$–$$$; AE, DC, MC, V; no checks; lunch Mon–Sat, dinner every day; full bar; reservations recommended; www.mccormickandschmicks.com; at SW Oak St.* &

Mint / ★★☆

816 N RUSSELL ST, PORTLAND; 503/284-5518 Mint owner Lucy Brennan is a master mixologist, turning out intelligent drinks that have the power to become instant classics. One such triumph is the blended avocado daiquiri, a supple surprise that is neither cloying nor heavy. Take a seat in the modern, cool-hued restaurant and your server will bring a bowl of toasted *pepitas* to stave your hunger. The Caribbean-spiced menu features a fair amount of seafood—and intense flavors. The calamari salad, rich with avocado and diced tomatoes, is a pleasing mix of textures. A lamb burger offers a departure from the standard beef, turkey, and vegetable varieties—plus, it's topped with a nice mint *chimichurri*. *$$; AE, MC, V; no checks; dinner Mon–Sat; full bar; reservations recommended; www.mintrestaurant .com; near N Interstate Ave, at N Albina Ave.* &

Morton's of Chicago / ★★★☆

213 SW CLAY ST, PORTLAND; 503/248-2100 Portland has several fine steak houses, but none carries the reputation of Morton's—and none has earned it more. Consistently outstanding food, compelling service, and expense-account prices are earmarks of this establishment, whose 64 restaurants can be found in most major U.S. cities and abroad. Chances are you'll order a tender and juicy steak, but a few nonbeef specialties (lamb, chicken, fish, and lobster) are on the menu as well. Everything is ordered à la carte, which means you'll pay extra for your appetizer, your house salad, your baked Idaho potato, and your fresh asparagus. Wines by the glass disappoint, but the list of bottles is excellent. *$$$$; AE, DC, MC, V; checks OK; dinner every day; full bar; reservations recommended; www.mortons.com; at 2nd Ave.* &

Mother's Bistro & Bar / ★★★☆

409 SW 2ND AVE, PORTLAND; 503/464-1122 This is the way your mother should have cooked but almost certainly didn't, unless you're closely related to proprietor Lisa Schroeder. After cooking in Paris and

New York, Schroeder opened the most comfortable of comfort-food restaurants in Portland, offering the likes of matzo-ball soup, pot roast, and chicken with dumplings. The place flies in H&H bagels from New York but cures its own smoked salmon. The substantial, three-meals-a-day menu is not only reassuring, but also impressively skilled. Not surprisingly, Mother's turns out mean cookies and wicked devil's food cake. *$$; AE, MC, V; no checks; breakfast, lunch Tues–Sun, dinner Tues–Sat; full bar; reservations recommended; at Stark St.* &

Navarre / ★★☆

10 NE 28TH AVE, LAURELHURST; 503/232-3555 The menu at airy new Navarre will wake you from dining doldrums. It's a checklist of about 32 choices, loosely grouped into bar snacks, appetizers, salads, starches, and entrées, though you won't see any headings as such. Bucking the trend of elaborately detailed dishes, you'll find no descriptions telling you where the baby lettuces were grown or from which waters a fish was plucked. "Trout baked in parchment" is about as explicit as it gets. The diner's job is to craft a meal from as few or as many dishes (all are tapas-sized portions) as desired, marking items on the list and handing it to the waiter. Ordering from Navarre's oblique list may be a leap of faith, but your daring will be richly rewarded. Don't miss chef/co-owner John Taboada's gorgeous foie gras, delicate crab crepes, signature braised greens, and frico (crispy-fried cheese). As befits a wine bar, the vintage selection is unique and flawlessly chosen. *$$; AE, MC, V; checks OK; dinner Mon–Sat; beer and wine; reservations for large groups; www.navarrepdx.com; at E Burnside.* &

¡Oba! / ★★☆

555 NW 12TH AVE, PORTLAND; 503/228-6161 ¡Oba! has two identities. There's ¡Oba! the restaurant—a subdued, serious dining room serving one Nuevo Latino concoction after another—and there's ¡Oba! the bar, a cavernous expanse where trendy clothes and high-pitched revelry rule. Chef Scott Neuman rocked the city when the place opened in 1998, and he continues to please palates with herbed ricotta enchiladas with pasilla-tomato sauce, and crispy coconut prawns with jalapeño marmalade. The chopped-vegetable salad with avocado-buttermilk dressing, and ¡Oba!'s Caesar with roasted corn and manchego cheese, are definite highlights. ¡Oba!'s exotic fresh-fruit margarita, shaken and served on the rocks in a tall pint glass, invites customers to veer from the traditional lime variety. *$$; AE, DC, MC, V; no checks; dinner every day; full bar; reservations recommended; www.obarestaurant.com; at NW Hoyt St.* &

Paley's Place / ★★★★

1204 NW 21ST AVE, PORTLAND; 503/243-2403 Though it's been nearly 10 years since Vitaly and Kimberly Paley waltzed into Portland from New York and swept diners off their feet, Paley's continues to dazzle, warm, and thrill Portlanders. Kimberly is known to dance around the intimate, thoughtfully designed dining room the way she once did on national stages, closely watching everything her husband—a Russian-born former concert pianist—sends out from the kitchen. Together, they maintain an atmosphere as artful as the French-influenced Northwest regional cuisine Vitaly prepares. In winter, their seasonal menu might offer crispy veal sweetbreads with a pomegranate demi-glace and a potato-bacon galette, or roasted rabbit with mustard cream and Gruyère mashed potatoes. Other seasons might bring a bisque of spring asparagus, broccoli, or steelhead set off by smoked seafood sausage. From one of the city's best crème brûlées to the warm chocolate soufflé cake to homemade sorbets and ice creams, there's something to satisfy every sweet tooth. In summer, dine on the porch or sidewalk. *$$$; AE, MC, V; no checks; dinner every day; full bar; reservations recommended; www.paleysplace.com; at NW Northrup St.* ⅃

Papa Haydn / ★★

701 NW 23RD AVE, PORTLAND; 503/228-7317 At Papa Haydn, cakes, tortes, and tarts are towering architectural marvels. Chocolate-buttermilk St. Moritz cake with coconut-pecan filling and lemon Bavarian are just a sampling of the confections. As a prelude to the last course, Papa Haydn offers salads and sandwiches (try the chicken club with avocado and sun-dried tomato mayonnaise) at lunch, and daily dinner choices such as pasta with scallops and Gorgonzola cream, succulent grilled chicken breast marinated in apple brandy and mustard, and filet mignon bresaola. The Northwest Portland outpost extends across most of a block, incorporating Jo Bar. *$$; AE, MC, V; no checks; lunch, dinner every day, brunch Sun; full bar; reservations for large groups; jobarhaydn@aol.com; papahaydn.citysearch.com; at NW Irving St.* ⅃

Pho Van / ★★★

1012 NW GLISAN ST, PORTLAND; 503/248-2171 The original SE 82nd café of former Vietnamese army officer Khiet Van earned a sterling reputation for aromatic pho, presented numerous ways. His snazzy new bistro serves two skinnier soups: one with round steak and lean brisket, the other a chicken noodle with *rau ram* (Vietnamese coriander). That leaves room for refreshing salads, grilled pork and chicken dishes, and delicate seafood entrées. Hints of honey punctuate many of Pho Van's offerings, from the lightly battered tilapia filet with garlic sauce and a snowy, steamed Chilean sea bass to the caramelized chicken and pork stews. Don't overlook the unusual hand rolls such as *chao tom*, a pâté of finely minced shrimp and chicken molded around sugarcane stalks and grilled. *$$; AE, DIS, MC, V; no checks; lunch, dinner Mon–Sat; beer and wine; reservations for 5 or more; north of the Eastgate Theater.* ⅃

Plainfield's Mayur / ★★

852 SW 21ST AVE, PORTLAND; 503/223-2995 Richard and Rehka Plainfield pioneered Indian cuisine in Portland back in 1977. Family members still tend the kitchen and oversee service in the restored Victorian home that houses Plainfield's. India's cultural and geographical diversity provides inspiration for familiar pappadams and curries, and exotics such as duck in almond sauce with cheese-stuffed apricots, and vegetables braised in cardamom-nut sauce. Regulars rave about *bhel* salad, an Indian street food of fried lentils, spinach, potatoes, and tomatoes in a tamarind dressing that dances on your tongue. A tandoor oven bakes naan, chicken, and fish. Plainfield's has assembled a credible wine list and Richard Plainfield will happily discuss the merits of a pinot or Gewürztraminer with *saag paneer*. *$$; AE,*

DIS, MC, V; checks OK; dinner every day; full bar; reservations recommended; www.plainfields.com; at SW Taylor. &

Red Star Tavern & Roast House / ★★☆

503 SW ALDER ST (5TH AVENUE SUITES), PORTLAND; 503/222-0005 Rob Pando's regional American cuisine covers the continent impressively, from seared Nantucket scallops to Kansas City baby back ribs to Pacific Northwest halibut, using the huge wood-burning grill and rotisserie at the back of the restaurant. And he exercises the kind of culinary subtlety that produces splendid crab-and-smoked-salmon cakes or ravioli of winter squash and goat cheese. For dessert, try the pear in house-made mascarpone with candied hazelnuts and Oregon pinot-noir sauce. The range is considerable, portions are sizable, the atmosphere is entertaining, service is uniformly excellent, and you couldn't be closer to the middle of downtown. $$; AE, DC, DIS, JCB, MC, V; checks OK; breakfast, lunch, dinner every day; full bar; reservations recommended; www.5thavenuesuites.com; at SW 5th Ave. &

Restaurant Murata / ★★★

200 SW MARKET ST, PORTLAND; 503/227-0080 This tiny, exquisite Japanese restaurant attracts both savvy locals and visiting Tokyo businessmen who seek authentic food, service, and atmosphere. Behind an eight-seat, L-shaped sushi bar, Japanese master chef Murata deftly slices *toro* (tuna belly) and *uni* (sea urchin) and molds them over rice, displaying the confidence of more than 50 years' experience. At lunch, traditional *teishoku* (set meals) include tempura, teriyaki, and tonkatsu, plus hot and cold udon and soba noodle bowls. Murata is one of the few places offering *kaiseki-ryori*, a traditional ceremonial meal of set dishes chosen by the chef to embody the elegance and serenity of each ingredient. $$$; AE, DC, JCB, MC, V; no checks; lunch Mon–Fri, dinner Mon–Sat; beer and wine; reservations recommended; murata@teleport.com; between SW 2nd and 3rd Aves. &

Rivers Restaurant / ★★☆

0470 SW HAMILTON CT, PORTLAND; 503/802-5850 In this fine-dining establishment adjacent to the Avalon Hotel and Spa (see review), the affable Rolland Wesen prepares a synthesis of modern American comfort food and classic French bistro fare. Panfried Dungeness crab cakes are served with a frisée salad and peppercorn aioli. A fresh arugula salad pairs wonderfully with roasted garlic and a balsamic vinaigrette. A simmering iron skillet loaded with clams, prawns, mussels, halibut, and salmon is served in a "fire pot" of tomato and saffron broth. Roasted chicken with garlic-sautéed spinach and mashed potatoes competes for your attention with cassoulet-style halibut on fava-bean risotto and a plate of duck livers and hearts. Desserts feature local fruits and berries, and there's always a mouth-watering triple chocolate cake. $$$; AE, DC, DIS, MC, V; checks OK; breakfast, lunch, dinner every day; full bar; reservations recommended; www.avalonhotelandspa.com; Hamilton Court off of SW Macadam Ave. &

Saucebox / ★★★

214 SW BROADWAY, PORTLAND; 503/241-3393 Proprietor Bruce Carey never lets things get stale at this hole-in-the-wall hot spot—as evidenced by a constantly updated menu and a recent expansion. Salty *edamame* and addictive, fried sweet-potato spring rolls make a promising start to a meal. Move on to the baby back ribs, snowy steamed halibut, or perennial favorite roasted salmon—crisped in soy, garlic, and ginger, topped with frizzled leeks and served with perfumed jasmine rice. The creative entrées are made with fresh, top-quality ingredients—as are the widely touted drinks. *$$; AE, MC, V; local checks only; dinner Tues–Sat; full bar; reservations recommended; www.saucebox.com; across from Benson Hotel.* &

750 ml / ★★

232 NW 12TH AVE, PORTLAND; 503/224-1432 Wine and food receive equal billing at this rehabbed Pearl District wine bistro-bar-retail shop, and a sheaf of menus encourages nonlinear sipping and grazing. Dozens of wines can be ordered by the taste, glass, or bottle, and the dinner menu consists of first plates (starters) and second plates (entrée-type offerings). All plates are bitsy, but the small portions also allow for broader sampling. There is no better starter combo than 750's clams steamed in a broth of white wine, garlic, shallots, and parsley—paired with amazing truffle-scented *pommes frites*. And each grain of rice in the spinach risotto is properly articulated, but the dish is creamy as a whole. Braised lamb with silky, house-made pappardelle, chopped artichoke, and olives vanishes from your plate much too quickly. *$$; AE, DIS, MC, V; checks OK; lunch, dinner Mon–Sat; full bar; reservations recommended; www.750-ml.com; between NW Everett and NW Davis.* &

Sungari Restaurant / ★★☆
Sungari Pearl / ★★☆

735 SW 1ST AVE, PORTLAND; 503/224-0800 / 1105 NW LOVEJOY ST, PORTLAND; 971/222-7327 Sungari uses fresh, quality ingredients, which sets it apart from lazier Chinese joints whose scallops don't taste as sweet and whose broccoli is past its prime. Though not strictly Sichuan, many of its entrées are peppery; yet even with the spiciest dishes, heat does not obscure pure flavor. Diners can taste the individual flavors of plump prawns, peanuts, water chestnuts, and celery, each intensified by chilies, garlic, and ginger. Sungari Duck Slices is a fantastic medley of tender duck, snow peas, carrots, and mushrooms in a subtly spiced sauce. And small culinary touches such as ginger chicken made with young ginger—a type with pale skin possessed of a milder zing than mature ginger—go a long way. *$$; AE, DC, MC, V (Pearl), AE, MC, V (downtown); no checks; lunch Mon–Fri, dinner every day (downtown), lunch, dinner every day (Pearl); full bar; reservations recommended; www.sungarirestaurant.com; one block west of waterfront park (downtown), between 11th and 12th (Pearl).* &

Syun Izakaya / ★★

209 NE LINCOLN ST, HILLSBORO; 503/640-3131 This downtown Hillsboro sushi-and-sake bar draws locals and expatriate Japanese techies. It offers a lively, informal mood, but the sushi and traditional dishes are first rate—as fresh and carefully prepared as you'd find in any more formal setting. And the 35-bottle sake collection is impressive. An extensive menu offers snacks such as *edamame,* yakitori, soba, and chilled tofu with ginger and bonito. You'll also get meals of domburi, grilled mackerel, tempura, and tonkatsu, plus eclectic desserts such as banana tempura with red-bean paste and black-tea pudding. *$$; AE, DC, DIS, MC, V; local checks only; lunch Mon–Fri, dinner every day; full bar; reservations recommended; in Hillsboro.* &

Taqueria Nueve / ★★★

28 NE 28TH AVE, PORTLAND; 503/236-6195 Eastside favorite Taqueria Nueve has expanded into an adjacent storefront and shed its former rustic cantina ambiance. The menu also is refurbished, though quite a few original dishes fortunately remain: piquant seviche, *coctel de pulpo* (spicy lime-cured octopus), and several taco varieties—including the wonderful achiote-seasoned pork, wild boar, and roasted beef tongue. The intricate mole tops a plate of tortillas, shredded chicken, cheese, and crema. Delicious grilled top sirloin is paired with sweet-and-sour onions and chipotle salsa. In addition to its wonderful, orange-tinged flan, Taqueria Nueve has introduced a three-milk layer cake with chocolate mocha icing and pecans. *$$; AE, MC, V; no checks; dinner every day; full bar; reservations for 6 or more; at Burnside.* &

Typhoon! / ★★★

2310 NW EVERETT ST, PORTLAND; 503/243-7557 / 400 SW BROADWAY (HOTEL LUCIA), PORTLAND; 503/224-8385 Typhoon! is expanding into a small empire. The original Northwest Portland space has been joined by a stylish downtown location in the Hotel Lucia, two new cafés in suburban Portland, and two more in the Seattle area. From openers of *miang kum* (spinach leaves to be filled with a half-dozen ingredients) and mouth-filling soups, the menu moves into a kaleidoscope of flavors. You can't go wrong with curries, inspired seafood dishes, and multiple pungent Thai noodle dishes. *$$; AE, DC, MC, V; no checks; lunch Mon–Sat, dinner every day (NW Portland), breakfast, lunch, dinner every day (downtown); full bar; reservations recommended; www.typhoonrestaurants.com; at NW 23rd Ave (NW Portland), between SW Stark and Washington Sts (downtown).* &

Veritable Quandary / ★★★

1220 SW 1ST AVE, PORTLAND; 503/227-7342 Peppered with local ingredients ranging from Fraga Farm goat cheese to Cotton Creek lamb, Veritable Quandary's market-driven menu is a swell representation of what the rain-soaked Northwest brings to the table. When available, the must-have appetizer is Gruyère-and-Granny Smith beignets, weightless fritters oozing cheese and sweet-tart apple pieces. For the main course, if not chef Anne Barnette's signature osso bucco, try one of the fresh fish specials, such as red snapper and sweet crab paired with piquant kumquat slices. Veritable Quandary boasts an extensive by-the-glass program of about 50 wines and a smart cellar with plenty of bottles in the $20 to $30 range. *$$–$$$; AE, DC, DIS, MC, V; no checks; lunch Mon–Fri, brunch Sat–Sun, dinner every day; full bar; reservations recommended; www.veritablequandary.com; near Jefferson St, west of the Hawthorne Bridge.* &

Wildwood / ★★★½

1221 NW 21ST AVE, PORTLAND; 503/248-9663 Wildwood's reputation as one of Portland's top tables is completely deserved. Recipient of a James Beard award in 1998, native son Cory Schreiber is diligent in his quest to create explosively flavorful food. Wildwood's menu changes weekly but is always solidly Northwest, taking full advantage of local bounty. Schreiber and his loyal team let quality ingredients do most of the work, building dishes around beautiful shell beans, Chioggia beets, abalone, crayfish, and leg of lamb, for example. Robust heirloom tomatoes make a wedge of snowy halibut sing, while a zingy gremolata massages the lamb's deep flavor. Pork loin is stuffed with lobster mushrooms and sausage and paired with white-corn grits and peaches bathing in a maple-syrup glaze. A pleasing wine list and intense fruit desserts further the delicious dining experience. Watching your dining budget? Check out the bar's Chalkboard Menu, a smart selection of uncomplicated pizzas, shellfish, salads, and a $10 burger. *$$–$$$; AE, MC, V; checks OK; lunch Sun, dinner every day; full bar; reservations recommended; www.wildwoodrestaurant.com; at NW Overton St.* &

Winterborne / ★★★

3520 NE 42ND AVE, PORTLAND; 503/249-8486 This tiny seafood restaurant is always highly ranked by Portlanders as well as outsiders. The limited menu, which reflects the style of Alsatian chef Gilbert Henri, includes sautéed oysters with a tangy aioli, escargots in a garlicky herb butter, and the wonderful Bouillabaisse Royale: a flavorful stew rife with lobster, salmon, and various shellfish. To another dish, Henri adds a touch of Southeast Asia: prawns à la Thailandaise are laced with garlic, basil, ginger, and coconut milk. Bringing new continental inspiration to Northwest seafood, this chef can stretch a halibut from Astoria to Alsace. Winterborne is an intimate, seven-table restaurant; guests feel the warmth and care that such a size allows. *$$; AE, DIS, MC, V; local checks only; dinner Wed–Sat; beer and wine; reservations recommended; at NE Fremont.* &

Zell's: An American Cafe / ★★

1300 SE MORRISON ST, PORTLAND; 503/239-0196 Simply put, Zellçs serves one of the best breakfasts in this time zone. The brilliance of the hot-from-the-griddle specialties (try the ginger pancakes, when available) is matched by a medley of inspired egg dishes. The trademark chorizo-and-peppers omelet is joined by a worthy Brie-and-tomato effort. If you prefer scrambles, you won't be disappointed by the gently mixed eggs with smoked salmon, Gruyère, and green onions. The catch, especially on weekend mornings, is a long wait for a table. *$; AE, DIS, MC, V; checks OK; breakfast, lunch every day; beer and wine; no reservations; at SE 13th Ave.* &

LODGINGS

Avalon Hotel & Spa / ★★

0455 SW HAMILTON CT, PORTLAND; 503/802-5800 OR 888/556-4402 An oasis of calm a short hop from downtown, the Avalon overlooks the Willamette River from the John's Landing district off Macadam Avenue (Route 43). The contemporary, red-brick boutique hotel includes a popular day spa. Seventy-eight of the Avalon's 99 rooms, including all 18 fireplace suites, have river-view balconies; all feature marble baths with double vanities, CD players, and high-speed Internet access. If you're headed downtown, leave your car parked here and take the complimentary Town Car service. The beautiful, 13,000-square-foot Avalon Spa & Fitness Club (503/802-5900) offers traditional European and Asian treatments. Adjacent Rivers Restaurant (see review) thrives with the culinary touch of Rolland Wesen. *$$$; AE, DC, DIS, MC, V; checks OK; www.avalonhotelandspa.com; take exit 299A off I-5.* &

The Benson Hotel / ★★★

309 SW BROADWAY, PORTLAND; 503/228-2000 OR 800/426-0670 Although the 21st century has brought a slew of new luxury hotels to downtown Portland, the Benson, open since 1913, remains the grand dame of them all. The palatial lobby features a stamped-tin ceiling, mammoth chandeliers, stately columns, and a generous fireplace. Guest rooms may lack the grandeur of the public areas, but they are dignified and sophisticated, with modern furnishings in conservative blacks and beiges. Characterized by service that's impeccably competent, if sometimes impersonal, the Benson is literally and figuratively corporate (owned by Coast Hotels & Resorts) but the place is well loved nonetheless. The London Grill caters to an old-fashioned dining crowd; El Gaucho (see review) features fresh seafood and steak and is also quite formal. *$$$–$$$$; AE, CB, DC, DIS, JCB, MC, V; checks OK; www.bensonhotel.com; south of downtown, exit 299A off I-5.* &

Embassy Suites Portland Downtown / ★★★☆

319 SW PINE ST, PORTLAND; 503/279-9000 This newish hotel has a pedigree: It's the former Multnomah Hotel, a lavish hostelry that hosted U.S. presidents, royalty, and Hollywood stars who passed through town, from 1912 until its closure in 1965. The Embassy Suites chain bought it in 1997 and remodeled it to restore some of its original grandeur. The spacious lobby is easily the finest room, with its gilt-touched columns and grand piano. The 275 guest rooms, all two-room suites, boast nice touches—marble baths, queen-sized sofa sleepers, and wet bars with microwave ovens and mini-refrigerators. In underground Arcadian Gardens, complimentary hot breakfasts and happy hours are offered. *$$$; AE, DC, DIS, MC, V; no checks; www.embassysuites.com; between 2nd and 3rd Aves.* &

5th Avenue Suites Hotel / ★★★

506 SW WASHINGTON ST, PORTLAND; 503/222-0001 OR 800/711-2971 Built in 1912, this elegant but aging structure was transformed into a fine 10-story hotel by the Kimpton Boutique Hotels group in 1996. Nearly two-thirds of the 221 rooms are spacious suites, but even those that are not have a sense of grandeur. Each suite has three phones (with data ports), a television, plus an ironing board, hair dryer, and plush cotton robes. The work-out room is open 24 hours. The staff is gracious and the bellhops are extremely attentive; and, like its sister inn, the Hotel Vintage Plaza, 5th Avenue Suites welcomes the occasional dog or lizard. The Kimpton group has covered its bases: from indoor parking to the welcoming lobby with its large corner fireplace, where you'll find complimentary coffee and newspapers in the morning, and wine tastings come evening. *$$$; AE, DC, DIS, JCB, MC, V; checks OK; www.5thavenuesuites.com; at 5th Ave.* &

The Governor Hotel / ★★☆

611 SW 10TH AVE, PORTLAND; 503/224-3400 OR 800/554-3456 Opened in 1909, in the heady days following Portland's 1905 Lewis and Clark Exposition, the hotel lives and breathes the Northwest. Arts and Crafts–style furnishings, leather club chairs, mahogany, and a wood-burning fireplace give the lobby a clubby feel. The 100 spacious guest rooms are decorated in earth tones and hung with early photos of Northwest Indian tribes; all have standard furnishings and upscale amenities. Suites feature gas-burning fireplaces, wet bars, and balconies. Guests have 24-hour maid service and business-center access, as well as use of the adults-only athletic club. *$$$; AE, DC, DIS, JCB, MC, V; checks OK; www.govhotel.com; at SW Alder St.* &

The Heathman Hotel / ★★★★

1001 SW BROADWAY, PORTLAND; 503/241-4100 OR 800/551-0011 A revolutionary personal-service concept has helped the intimate, elegant Heathman rise to the top of Portland's downtown lodgings. In 2001, the traditional front desk was replaced by "floating consoles"—manned by young men and women who serve not only as desk clerks but also as personal concierges, room-service attendants, and even tour guides. The Heathman's location in the heart of the Cultural District (a breezeway links it to Arlene Schnitzer Concert Hall and the Center for Performing Arts) is underscored by its commitment to the arts; 20 signed Andy Warhol original lithographs are just part of a collection that includes a fanciful Henk Pander mural and two large 18th-century oils by Claude Galle. The common rooms are handsomely appointed with teak or eucalyptus paneling, and the elegant Tea Room is a great place to enjoy an afternoon cup or evening jazz performance. Depending on your interests, you might be impressed by the video collection, the library (with author-signed volumes from those who have stayed here), or the fitness suite (personal trainer available). And you're just steps away from the Heathman Restaurant, one of the city's finest restaurants, where chef Philippe Boulot designs culinary masterpieces. *$$$–$$$$; AE, DC, DIS, JCB, MC, V; checks OK; www.heathmanhotel.com; at SW Salmon St.* &

Heron Haus Bed and Breakfast / ★★

2545 NW WESTOVER RD, PORTLAND; 503/274-1846 Hostess Julie Keppeler loves "stuff that moves." Her spacious 1904 English Tudor home, at the foot of the West Hills just four blocks from Northwest "Trendy-Third" Street, is a tasteful museum of mobiles and motion toys. Each of the six guest rooms has a king- or queen-sized bed, private bath, fireplace, air-conditioning, cable TV, and data port: a midweek corporate rate attracts single business people. The Kulia Room features an elevated spa tub with a city view and deluxe bathing accoutrements. Breakfast, served in the dining room, is an artistic affair. *$$$; MC, V; checks OK; www.heronhaus.com; near NW 25th Ave and Johnson St.*

Hotel Lucia / ★★½

400 SW BROADWAY, PORTLAND; 503/225-1717 OR 877/225-1717 Black-and-white photographs by Pulitzer Prize–winning journalist David Hume Kennerly, a former Oregonian and one-time official White House cameraman, give this innovative hotel a touch of contemporary elegance. Opened in April 2002 after a $5 million redesign, the Lucia boasts an ambiance of sophisticated minimalism that extends from the lobby to the 128 guest rooms. The white-limestone lobby is accented by walls of dark *sapele,* an African rainforest tree. Chrome and stainless steel are evident in the decor of the spacious rooms, which feature plush bedding, high-speed wireless Internet access, and top-of-the-line amenities. Room service is from the fine Thai restaurant Typhoon! (see review), which adjoins the Lucia's lobby. *$$$; AE, DC, DIS, MC, V; checks OK; www.hotellucia.com; downtown, on the corner of Broadway and Stark.* &

Hotel Vintage Plaza / ★★★

422 SW BROADWAY, PORTLAND; 503/228-1212 OR 800/243-0555 This intimate (107-room) boutique hotel of the Kimpton group is as playful yet satisfying as a glass of good pinot noir. Lodged in a restored 1894 National Register building with an upscale European-inn appeal, the 10-story hotel has a gracious staff and a charming lobby with antique furnishings and a marble fireplace. An Oregon wine theme extends to the guest rooms, although the layered-tapestry look is more reminiscent of Italy. Particularly delightful are the top-floor Starlight rooms, with angled, greenhouse-style windows for romantic bedtime planet viewing. Below are nine two-story townhouse units. If you have a pet, you'll find it so welcome that the desk staff serves "treats"; the hotel also has a small fitness center. This hotel is a good value, especially on weekends, when rates drop. *$$–$$$; AE, DC, DIS, JCB, MC, V; checks OK; www.vintageplaza.com; at SW Washington.* &

Inn @ Northrup Station / ★★

2025 NW NORTHRUP ST, PORTLAND; 503/224-0543 OR 800/224-1180 The sole hotel in the heart of trendy Northwest Portland, the Inn @ Northrup Station is also the city's most eclectic in decor. Industrial chic with nods to art deco and '70s retro, this all-suite boutique hotel startles the newcomer with colors the hotel defines as "energetic." Parking is free, or there's a streetcar stop (the "station") outside the front door. Opposite the small registration desk is a sleek lobby, where a continental breakfast is served daily beside a fireplace. Long hallways lead to the suites, all with marble bathrooms and executive desks (with two-line phones and data ports). The fully furnished kitchens may inspire you to stay in and cook, but several of Portland's finest restaurants are just around the corner. *$$–$$$; AE, DC, DIS, MC, V; checks OK; www.northrupstation.com; between NW 20th and 21st Aves.* &

The Kennedy School / ★★☆

5736 NE 33RD AVE, PORTLAND; 503/249-3983 If you're not familiar with the McMenamin brothers' enterprises, you may find this place perplexing, but if you're in the loop, you're bound to like the Kennedy School. Located in a former 1915 public-school building, built in Italian Renaissance style, the Kennedy School features 35 bed-and-breakfast guest rooms—two to a classroom—each featuring a private bath, Indonesian antiques, and (in some) chalkboards still in place. There are the requisite bars, a brewery, and the Courtyard Restaurant. There are also some not-so-common public areas: an excellent movie theater, a gymnasium, and a hot-water soaking pool. *$$; AE, DIS, MC, V; checks OK; www.mcmenamins.com; between NE Ainsworth and NE Killingsworth.* ♿

The Lion and the Rose / ★★★☆

1810 NE 15TH AVE, PORTLAND; 503/287-9245 OR 800/955-1647 Occupying the 1906 Freiwald House, a Queen Anne mansion in the historic Irvington District, the Lion and the Rose maintains its status as one of Portland's finest B&Bs. Our favorites of the six rooms are Joseph's (rich colors contrast with ample natural light), the Starina (strong, dark colors with a map theme), and the Lavonna (done in lavender and white, with a spacious reading nook in the turret). Breakfast, served in the formal dining room, is lavish, and tea is offered to guests, 4–6pm. Business travelers find plenty of phone lines (with data ports) and other amenities. *$$$; AE, DC, DIS, MC, V; checks OK; www.lionrose.com; north of NE Broadway.*

MacMaster House / ★★

1041 SW VISTA AVE, PORTLAND; 503/223-7362 OR 800/774-9523 Contrasts set the tone at this centrally located bed-and-breakfast inn. A massive portico flanked by Doric columns makes for an imposing exterior, but the interior is dreamy and Victorian. Though the decor is florid and eclectic, rooms are quiet and gracious. The half-dozen rooms range from small and bookish to large and fanciful. All have antiques and modern compact-disc players. Four boast fireplaces and two have private baths. Located in the King's Hill Historic District, the manor is two blocks from the east entrance to Washington Park and a straight shot down to NW 23rd Avenue. *$$; AE, DIS, MC, V; checks OK; www.macmaster.com; at SW Main St.* ♿

Mallory Hotel / ★

729 SW 15TH AVE, PORTLAND; 503/223-6311 OR 800/228-8657 Rufus Mallory was 81 years old when the hotel that bears his name opened for business in 1912. It was a "strictly modern, high-class, eight-story, fireproof structure." Now the homey Mallory is one of the best bargains in town: $90 for a spotless double, $165 for a suite. The Mallory—on a quiet hillside just a 10- to 15-minute stroll from Pioneer Courthouse Square—offers free parking in its garage. Crystal chandeliers hang above sturdy, leather-upholstered furniture in the broad lobby. Guest rooms aren't fancy, but they have refrigerators and wireless Internet access, and your pet is welcome ($10 fee). A continental breakfast is included, or opt for German pancakes in the charming café. Before retiring, enjoy a drink in the quirky Driftwood Lounge. *$$; AE, DC, DIS, JCB, MC, V; checks OK; www.malloryhotel.com; at SW Yamhill St.* ♿

The Mark Spencer Hotel / ★★☆

 409 SW 11TH AVE, PORTLAND; 503/224-3293 OR 800/548-3934 Perhaps no Portland hotel is more dedicated to the local arts community than the Mark Spencer. Powell's Books and the galleries of the Pearl District have dubbed it their "official" hotel; arts packages include admission to major shows or Portland Art Museum exhibits. Every room is nicely but not ostentatiously decorated, with a fully equipped kitchen and wireless Internet access; suites also have sofa sleepers. The pet-friendly property rises around an entry courtyard; amenities include a guest laundry, library, and rooftop garden, complimentary continental breakfast and afternoon tea, and a copy of the day's *New York Times*. Three floors are dedicated to nonsmokers. *$$; AE, DC, DIS, MC, V; checks OK; www.markspencer.com; at SW Stark.* &

The Paramount Hotel / ★★★☆

808 SW TAYLOR ST, PORTLAND; 503/223-9900 OR 800/663-1144 This 15-story luxury hotel, which opened in 2000, has built a reputation for sophistication and innovation. A compact yet elegant seating area sits front and center in the marble-floored lobby, from which doors on either side open to the Dragonfish Asian Cafe and Bar (breakfast, lunch, and dinner; 503/243-5991). Elevators rise to 154 guest rooms, each one simply yet impressively decorated with Biedermeier furnishings, and provided with a granite-finished bathroom and high-speed wireless Internet access. The hotel also has a modern fitness center, a business center, and a staff that will take the time to help you with any directions or arrangements. *$$$–$$$$; AE, CB, DC, DIS, JCB, MC, V; checks OK; www.paramounthotel.net; at Park Ave.* &

Portland Guest House / ★★☆

1720 NE 15TH AVE, PORTLAND; 503/282-1402 Since 1987, owner Susan Gisvold has maintained this simple urban retreat just off busy NE Broadway in the historic Irvington District. Gisvold doesn't live here, but she's usually around to advise you on Portland doings. In the morning, she'll drop in to serve a home-cooked breakfast of low-fat cottage-cheese pancakes, scones, fresh strawberries, and coffee or tea. Each of the seven rooms (five have private baths) has its own phone and clock, making this a good place for business travelers. *$–$$; MC, V; checks OK; www.teleport.com/~pgh/; at NE Broadway.*

Portland's White House / ★★★

1914 NE 22ND AVE, PORTLAND; 503/287-7131 On the outside, Portland's White House looks a bit like its Washington, D.C., namesake, complete with fountains, a circular driveway, and a carriage house that contains three guest rooms with baths. Inside are five more guest rooms, all with private baths. The Canopy Suite features a large canopied bed and bright bath; the Baron's Suite boasts a Victorian claw-footed tub. A full gourmet breakfast is served in the main dining room every morning; the signature dish is salmon eggs Benedict with an orange hollandaise. White House catering specialists host numerous weddings and social gatherings in its garden. *$$–$$$; AE, DIS, MC, V; checks OK; www.portlandswhitehouse.com; 2 blocks north of NE Broadway.*

RiverPlace Hotel / ★★★

1510 SW HARBOR WY, PORTLAND; 503/228-3233 OR 800/227-1333
Facing directly upon the busy Willamette River (and the boat show that comes with it), this casually elegant hotel is lovely to look in at and glorious to look out from. The best rooms among 74 kings, doubles, and suites face the water or look north across park lawns to the downtown cityscape. Decor has a Cape Cod appeal, with beiges and powder blues, picking up the river's nuances. Live plants and botanical prints bring the outside in. Plush furnishings include teak and oak paneling, overstuffed sofas, and CD players. Ten adjacent private condominiums—with dining and living rooms and wood-burning fireplaces—are popular with visiting entertainers and athletes. Concierge service is among the best in the city; 24-hour room service is available from the stunning Lucère restaurant (see review); and a complimentary continental breakfast can be brought to your room along with the day's newspaper. Massage and spa treatments are available by appointment. There's no charge to use the adjacent RiverPlace Athletic Club (including an indoor pool and running track), but on nice days there's plenty of opportunity for outdoor exercise: wide, paved paths lead through the fountains and monuments of adjacent Gov. Tom McCall Waterfront Park. *$$$–$$$$; AE, DC, DIS, JCB, MC, V; checks OK; www.riverplacehotel.com; south end of waterfront park.* &

Forest Grove

Pacific University is why most people come here, and the towering firs on the small campus do justice to the town's name. But there's also quite a collection of local wineries, making the area worth exploring, perhaps on your way to the ocean. South of town on Highway 47 is the huge **MONTINORE VINEYARDS** (3663 SW Dilley Rd, Forest Grove; 503/359-5012; *www.montinore.com*), with a fancy tasting room and wines that improve with each vintage. In nearby Gaston, **ELK COVE VINEYARDS** (27751 NW Olson Rd, Gaston; 503/985-7760; *www.elkcove.com*) has a spectacular site for a tasting room perched on a forested ridge, and **KRAMER VINEYARDS** (26830 NW Olson Rd, Gaston; 503/662-4545; *www.kramerwine.com*) is a tiny place in the woods with tasty pinot noir and excellent raspberry wine. West of Forest Grove on Highway 8, on the site of a historic Oregon winery, **LAUREL RIDGE WINERY** (46350 NW David Hill Rd, Forest Grove; 503/852-7050) specializes in sparkling wines and makes good sauvignon blanc. **SHAFER VINEYARDS** (6200 NW Gales Creek Rd, Forest Grove; 503/357-6604; *www.shafervineyardcellars.com*) has produced some fine, ageable chardonnays, and **TUALATIN ESTATE VINEYARDS** (10850 NW Seavey Rd, Forest Grove; 503/357-5005; *www.oregonvineyardland .com*) produces exquisite chardonnay, as well as an excellent Müller Thurgau. Finally, just outside of town you can sample sake from **MOMOKAWA SAKE** (820 Elm St, Forest Grove; 503/357-7056; *www.sakeone.com*), where quality rice wines are brewed on-site.

Lake Oswego, West Linn, and Oregon City

South of Portland, these three towns have differing characters and qualities but taken together make a nice excursion. You might start with a walk in Lake Oswego's 645-acre **TRYON CREEK STATE PARK** (11321 SW Terwilliger Blvd, Lake Oswego; 503/636-9886), where—in early spring—you'll see the trillium light up the hiking trails. The scenic campus of **LEWIS AND CLARK COLLEGE** (0615 SW Palatine Hill Rd; 503/768-7000; *www.lclark.edu*) is nearby, as is the lake itself, though swimming and boating access is private.

Next, drive south on Highway 43 to Interstate 205 and go east to historic Oregon City. Visit the **END OF THE OREGON TRAIL INTERPRETIVE CENTER** (1726 Washington St, Oregon City; 503/657-9336; *www.endoftheoregontrail.org*), with its easy-to-spot covered-wagon architecture. See what it was like coming to Oregon 150 years ago—but call ahead for show times. You won't be allowed into the multimedia presentation unless you're on the tour, except to see a few exhibits and the well-stocked museum store.

COLUMBIA RIVER GORGE AND MOUNT HOOD

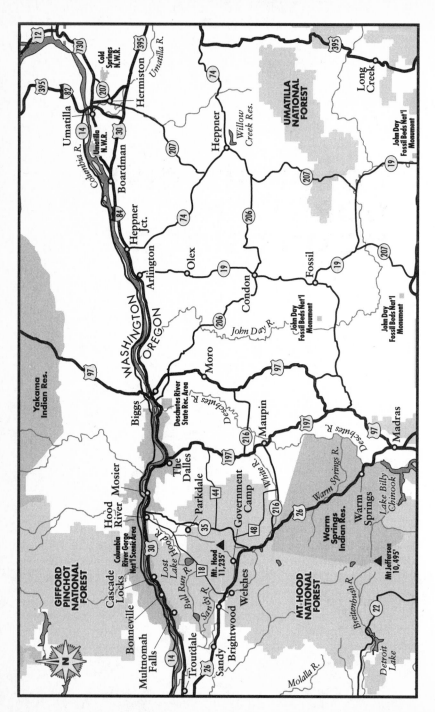

COLUMBIA RIVER GORGE AND MOUNT HOOD

Cataclysmic ice-age floods carved the Columbia Gorge about 15,000 years ago, leaving cliffs as high as 4,000 feet. Streams plunged into the newly created canyon, becoming the waterfalls that still grace the gorge's steep, craggy walls. Until the Columbia River Highway opened in 1915, views of the gorge were enjoyed mainly by Native Americans, who for centuries netted salmon from the Columbia River, and by Oregon Trail pioneers, who reached the Willamette Valley via the river or across the flanks of Mount Hood. The highway, built to display the gorge rather than to blemish it, was an engineering marvel of its day, featuring intricate stonework, arched bridges, viaducts, tunnels, and lookout points. For a memorable excursion, drive a stretch of the old highway from Troutdale to Multnomah Falls.

On the western edge of The Dalles, the beautifully designed Columbia Gorge Discovery Center offers a look at the gorge from prehistory to the present. Hood River, the gorge's only other real city, is the sailboard capital of the Pacific Northwest and has been long renowned for its fruit trees. A drive on Highway 35 takes you past acres of apple and pear orchards, and eventually to the snowy slopes of Mount Hood.

The mountain's crown jewel, Timberline Lodge, is worth a visit in any season. President Franklin D. Roosevelt dedicated it in 1937, praising the masons, craftsmen, and artists who made this mountain lodge an enduring classic. High above the lodge, chair lifts transport skiers and snowboarders to Palmer Snowfield nearly year-round. In 1845 Joel Palmer stood here to scout what would become the last leg of the Oregon Trail, Barlow Road. At several places westward along US Highway 26, you can still see wagon ruts cut into the ground, indelible traces of the first white settlers.

ACCESS AND INFORMATION

The Columbia River Gorge and Mount Hood are most commonly approached from Portland, via **INTERSTATE 84** east; follow the freeway through the gorge to Hood River and The Dalles. Another option is exiting at Troutdale to follow the **HISTORIC COLUMBIA RIVER HIGHWAY**, or cutting over to **HIGHWAY 26** and heading southeast to Mount Hood.

In winter, usually after mid-November, traction devices are required on Mount Hood. Call the **OREGON DEPARTMENT OF TRANSPORTATION** (503/588-2941 outside of Oregon or 800/977-6368; *www.tripcheck.com*) to see if roads are snowy or icy on Mount Hood. Also, an Oregon Department of Transportation **WINTER SNO-PARK PERMIT** is required if you plan to ski, board, sled, or snowshoe. Permits are sold at Timberline Lodge (see review), as well as service stations, Department of Motor Vehicle offices, and sporting goods stores in the gorge and on the mountain: $3 for one day; $7 for three days; $15 for the season.

GREYHOUND (503/243-2357 or 800/231-2222; *www.greyhound.com*) has daily bus service up the Columbia River Gorge from Portland, stopping at Hood

River and The Dalles, as well as service from Portland to Government Camp on Mount Hood.

The **COLUMBIA RIVER GORGE VISITORS ASSOCIATION** (2149 W Cascade Ave #106A, Hood River; 800/984-6743; *www.crgva.org*) and **MOUNT HOOD INFORMATION CENTER** (65000 E Hwy 26, Welches; 503/622-3017; *www.mthood.org*) provide tourist information.

Columbia River Gorge National Scenic Area

The Columbia River Gorge National Scenic Area was created by an act of Congress in 1986 to shield the river corridor from rapacious development, while also fostering and guiding industry in designated urban areas. It begins near the mouth of the Sandy River, near Troutdale, and ends at the Deschutes River, east of The Dalles. It encompasses 292,500 acres in Oregon and Washington.

Troutdale

Named for the town founder's trout ponds, Troutdale was a welcome sight to Oregon Trail pioneers who rafted their covered wagons here from about 40 miles up the Columbia River. From the freeway, Troutdale now looks like a jarring assortment of truck stops, factory outlets, and fast-food joints. But behind all the neon you'll find the town's heart, a quaint street of antique shops, galleries, and cafés that marks the beginning of the **HISTORIC COLUMBIA RIVER HIGHWAY**, built in 1913–15. Until it merges with Interstate 84, 5 miles east of Multnomah Falls, the highway winds along 22 miles of breathtaking views and awesome waterfalls. **THE VISTA HOUSE** (40700 E Historic Columbia River Hwy; 503/695-2230) at Crown Point, constructed in 1916–18 as a rest stop, sits atop a 733-foot-high cliff. Built of stone, its interior features a marble floor and stairs, elegant wainscoting, ornate carvings, stained glass, and other decorative elements. It's open May through October and has historic displays, a gift shop, and rest rooms. For more information contact the **TROUTDALE CHAMBER OF COMMERCE** (338 E Historic Columbia River Hwy; 503/669-7473; *www.troutdalechamber.org*).

RESTAURANTS

Multnomah Falls Lodge

53000 HISTORIC COLUMBIA RIVER HWY 30 E, BRIDAL VEIL; 503/695-2376
Designed by Portland architect A. E. Doyle, this rustic lodge was built in 1925 with every type of stone found in the gorge. For a great view of the falls, sit in the restaurant's back room. The food is basic but satisfying (sandwiches at lunch; prime rib and salmon at dinner), especially when it follows a vigorous hike. A big-leaf maple forms the backdrop to the cozy bar; try to nab a seat on the Mission-style couch by the fireplace. *$$; AE, DIS, MC, V; no checks; breakfast, lunch,*

*dinner every day, brunch Sun; full bar; no reservations; www.multnomahfallslodge
.com; exit 31 from I-84.* &

Tad's Chicken 'n' Dumplins

1325 E HISTORIC COLUMBIA RIVER HWY, TROUTDALE; 503/666-5337 Tired of
trendy Northwest cuisine? Then plan a dinner at Tad's, where comfort food is
served up without a hint of fake sophisticated irony. Though stewed chicken with
giant dumplings is the signature dish, Tad's also serves seafood, steaks, and liver and
onions. Come prepared to wait, especially on weekends. But even the wait can be
pleasant—Tad's is right on the Sandy River. *$; AE, MC, V; checks OK; dinner every
day; full bar; no reservations; just southeast of the Sandy River bridge.* &

LODGINGS

McMenamin's Edgefield / ★

2126 SW HALSEY ST, TROUTDALE; 503/669-8610 OR 800/669-8610 Built in
1911 as the county poor farm, Edgefield was transformed by local microbrew
barons Mike and Brian McMenamin into a sprawling complex of lodging,
libations, eateries, golf, and a cinema. About 100 rooms, most with shared baths, all
free of telephones and TVs, are furnished with 1930s-era furniture and brightened
by whimsical paintings. Murals and paintings on doors and walls are a virtual gallery of ex-hippie artistry, and there's plenty to do, from golfing on the 18-hole par-3
course to catching a recent release at the Power Station Movie Theater to strolling
the gardens on the 38-acre estate. Choose from several bars—with much of the beer,
wine, and spirits produced on-site—for lunch or dinner. Guests are served com-
plimentary breakfast in the Black Rabbit Restaurant. *$$; AE, MC, V; checks OK;
edge@mcmenaminspubs.com; www.mcmenamins.com; Wood Village exit off I-84,
south to Halsey St, turn left, drive ¼ mile to Edgefield sign on right.* &

Cascade Locks

The cascades (rapids) here were once so treacherous that boats had to be portaged.
Navigational locks built in 1896 solved the problem, but when Bonneville Dam
was built in 1937 and the river behind it rose 60 feet, the locks, for which this
town was named, were submerged. Now the former home of the lock tender is a
museum, next door to the ticket office for the **STERNWHEELER COLUMBIA GORGE**
(Cascade Locks Marina Park, 355 Wa-Na-Pa St; 541/374-8427 or 800-643-1354;
www.sternwheeler.com). This 600-passenger replica of turn-of-the-20th-century
paddle-wheel riverboats that used to churn their way east from Portland makes two
two-hour narrated excursions daily during summer, as well as brunch and dinner
cruises on weekends year-round. During December, the stern-wheeler sails out of
Portland; call for scheduling details.

Just west of town is the **BONNEVILLE DAM** (exit 40 from I-84 or Hwy 14;
541/374-8820; *www.nwp.usace.army.mil/op/b/*), built in 1937, and the 1909
BONNEVILLE FISH HATCHERY (541/374-8393). No matter what you may think of
hatchery programs, it's worth stopping to visit the giant green sturgeon at the nicely

COLUMBIA RIVER GORGE THREE-DAY TOUR

DAY ONE: Begin in Troutdale after spending the night at **MCMENAMIN'S EDGE-FIELD**; enjoy your complimentary breakfast, then head east on a 22-mile stretch of the **HISTORIC COLUMBIA RIVER HIGHWAY**, across the Sandy River and into the hills above the Columbia River Gorge. Follow the highway to Multnomah Falls and stop for a hike and lunch at **MULTNOMAH FALLS LODGE**. (It's a steep 1-mile hike on a mostly paved trail to the head of the falls.) Get on Interstate 84 and drive to the **BONNE-VILLE DAM VISITOR CENTER**. Watch fish swim up the fish ladder, then check out the giant sturgeon at the **BONNEVILLE FISH HATCHERY**. For the rest of the afternoon, either stop in Cascade Locks and ride the **STERN-WHEELER COLUMBIA GORGE** or continue east to Hood River and ride the rails on the **MOUNT HOOD RAILROAD** past apple, pear, apricot, and cherry orchards. No matter how you spend the afternoon, enjoy dinner at **BRIAN'S POURHOUSE** in Hood River and bed down at the elegant **COLUMBIA GORGE HOTEL** or, for budget travelers, next door at the **VAGABOND LODGE**.

    DAY TWO: Eat the bountiful farmhouse breakfast at the Columbia Gorge Hotel or pick up some pear panini at **PANZANELLA** and head east. At Mosier, exit the freeway and take a walk along the hiker/biker stretch of the **HISTORIC COLUMBIA RIVER**

landscaped hatchery. One dam visitor center is on Bradford Island and another is on the Washington shore, at the second powerhouse, built in 1981. At the navigational locks, built in 1993, watch barges and boats moving up- or downriver.

    A perfect spot for watching river traffic is **CHARBURGER** (714 SW Wa-Na-Pa St; 541/374-8477), a cafeteria-style restaurant with great burgers and homemade pie. From a booth next to the large windows, you can admire the river and the graceful **BRIDGE OF THE GODS**, a cantilever toll bridge built in 1926 to link Oregon and Washington. The bridge is also part of the 2,000-mile Pacific Crest National Scenic Trail, which runs from Mexico to Canada.

    For more information contact the **CASCADE LOCKS VISITOR CENTER** (Cascade Locks Marina Park; 541/374-8619; *www.cascade-locks.or.us*).

Hood River

Once known simply for the glorious fruit orchards in the neighboring hills, Hood River has broadened its appeal. The vibrant town owes its renaissance to the adventurers who come from all points of the globe to launch sailboards and kiteboards on the Columbia River. The closest of Mount Hood's five ski areas is just 27 miles away; a multitude of hiking and biking trails are similarly close. Rent gear or sign up for lessons at **BRIAN'S WINDSURFING** (Hood River Marina Park; 541/386-1423; *www.brianswindsurfing.com*).

HIGHWAY STATE TRAIL. Back in your car, head east along another 9-mile stretch of the historic highway to Rowena Crest viewpoint and the **TOM MCCALL PRESERVE**. Stop at the crest to take in a spectacular view and acres of wildflowers and native plants. Continue east along the historic highway to The Dalles, and lunch at the **BALDWIN SALOON**. Spend a couple of hours going through the **COLUMBIA GORGE DIS-COVERY CENTER** and adjoining **WASCO COUNTY HISTORICAL MUSEUM**. Return west to Hood River for dinner at **ABRUZZO**, then head 15 miles south on Highway 35 to the **MOUNT HOOD HAMLET BED & BREAKFAST** for the night.

DAY THREE: When you open your eyes and look out your bedroom window, you'll think Mount Hood is close enough to touch. Take your time; you're almost there. After a leisurely breakfast, have a soak in the outdoor spa with its heated deck. Drive south and then west over Bennett and Barlow Passes to Government Camp. Have a late lunch here, perhaps a gourmet personal pizza, at **THE BREW PUB AT MOUNT HOOD BREWING CO**. Spend the afternoon hiking and exploring the mountain. You'll work up an appetite for dinner at the **CASCADE DINING ROOM** at **TIMBERLINE LODGE** and be ready to sink into bed while the snowy peak of Mount Hood shimmers in moonlight.

The Hood River Valley's rich volcanic soil continues to support thousands of fruit trees, particularly pears, which are widely available in the fall from roadside stands along Highway 35 south of town. For more information, contact the **HOOD RIVER COUNTY CHAMBER OF COMMERCE** (405 Portway Ave; 541/386-2000 or 800/366-3530; *www.hoodriver.org*). Trees are beautiful in spring, when they blossom, kicking off a months-long series of festivals, highlighted by the **HOOD RIVER VALLEY BLOSSOM FESTIVAL** in April and **HOOD RIVER VALLEY HARVEST FESTIVAL** in October.

The **FRUIT BLOSSOM SPECIAL**, a spring rail excursion through the orchards, is one of many special-occasion trips on the **MOUNT HOOD RAILROAD** (110 Railroad Ave; 541/386-3556 or 800/872-4661; *www.mthoodrr.com*). The restored trains depart from the historic 1911 depot and follow their original route through the valley, past packing plants, lumber mills, and orchards. Excursion trains and brunch or dinner trains run regularly from March through mid-December.

Even though downtown Hood River has become a place to see (and shop for) the Northwest recreational-chic look, it still has room for businesses such as **FRANZ HARDWARE** (116 Oak St; 541/386-1141). Owned and operated by the same family since 1909, it still sells nails and bolts individually. Just up the street, at **ANNZPANZ** (315 Oak St; 541/387-2654), you'll find stylish cookware alongside a gourmet lunch counter. Across the street at **WAUCOMA BOOKS** (212 Oak St; 541/386-5353) are books for every taste and age, and local pottery. Visit elaborately carved carousel animals at the **INTERNATIONAL MUSEUM OF CAROUSEL ART** (304 Oak St; 541/387-4622), then stop by **FULL SAIL BREWERY AND PUB** (506 Columbia St; 541/386-2247) for a tour and a taste of some of Oregon's best microbrews.

RESTAURANTS

Abruzzo / ★★

1810 W CASCADE ST, HOOD RIVER; 541/386-7779 It's easy to miss this small olive-green building on the busy commercial strip just west of downtown. But to pass it by would mean missing one of Hood River's most inviting restaurants. The cement floors and wood tabletops lend an informal note, and the friendly staff and hearty food give it true warmth and character. Locals gather here to eat huge plates of pasta topped with rich sauces, many featuring pancetta or tasty Italian sausage. *$; MC, V; local checks only; dinner Tues–Sat; full bar; no reservations; west of downtown on north side of Cascade St.* &

Brian's Pourhouse / ★★

606 OAK ST, HOOD RIVER; 541/387-4344 Over the past few years, Brian's has become a Hood River classic. Just like the town itself, Brian's is laid-back but upscale. Though the lively front-room bar can be a little daunting to first-time visitors, the dining areas of this old house are much quieter and very family-friendly. The menu runs the gamut from small pizzas, large hamburgers, and fish tacos to more grown-up dinners, such as a wild mushroom sauté with pumpkin ravioli, or grilled marlin with couscous. During summer, there's seating on an outside deck. *$$; MC, V; local checks only; dinner Tues–Sat, open for lunch in summer; full bar; no reservations; between 6th and 7th.* &

North Oak Brasserie / ★★☆

113 3RD ST, HOOD RIVER; 541/387-2310 The adventure begins when you descend a stairway from the sidewalk to the basement level. Inside, you enter a place apart from the sporty, sunny bluster of Hood River—at once a cozy locals' lunch spot and a sophisticated wine lovers' bistro. Owners Mike and Shawna Caldwell (who also own the restaurant Stonehedge Gardens) make a great team; Mike, the former cellar master at Flerchinger Vineyards, selected about 150 wines for a list that complements the food. Shawna, a former art teacher, gave the basement a warm Mediterranean glow and adds her touch to the menu. Prosciutto-wrapped shrimp skewers whet your appetite for one of the several pasta offerings, such as seafood cannelloni, or a main course like pork loin in a peppercorn sauce. Kids are welcome. *$$; AE, DIS, MC, V; checks OK; lunch, dinner every day; full bar; reservations recommended; northoak@gorge.net; www.hoodriverrestaurants .com; downtown, at Oak St.*

Panzanella Artisan Bakery and Italian Deli / ★

102 5TH ST, HOOD RIVER; 541/386-2048 Carbohydrate lovers rejoice! Finally, there's a good bakery in Hood River. Dense, chewy pear and walnut *panini,* dark-crusted loaves of whole wheat *levain,* and a deli case full of sandwiches (even the tuna salad is irresistible). Don't look for a sit-down atmosphere here; high counters are lined with stools, but most folks take their sandwiches and bread on the run. Breakfasts are light, such as toast with mascarpone cheese or preserves. Lunch items are, according to the crew, "whatever we felt like making," but usually include a couple of crusty pizzas, such as a wonderful potato, onion, and Gorgonzola, sold by the slice. Panzanella comes with a pretty good Hood River pedigree; it's owned by baker Matt Botti and Abruzzo co-owners Glen Pearce and Mark DeResta. *$; MC, V; checks OK; breakfast, lunch Mon–Sat; no alcohol; no reservations; 5th St at Cascade Ave.* &

Stonehedge Gardens / ★★☆

3405 CASCADE DR, HOOD RIVER; 541/386-3940 Much of the charm of Stonehedge Gardens is in its setting; the historic house was built in 1898 as a summer residence for a prominent Portland family. A huge five-level, landscaped garden houses dozens of tables, making this the best outdoor dining in the gorge. Inside, the old house is charming, but a little shabby. Either inside or out, the food is good, in an almost retro gourmet way. "Bistro classics," such as seafood crepes, are best for smaller appetites; main courses, such as seared ahi tuna or steak Diane, are large meals served with salad, bread, and vegetables. Owners Mike and Shawna Caldwell (who also own the North Oak Brasserie in town) and their engaging staff work hard to make Stonehedge simultaneously comfortable and nice enough for special celebrations. *$$; AE, DIS, MC, V; checks OK; dinner every day; full bar; reservations recommended; stonehedge@gorge.net; www.hood riverrestaurants.com; exit 62 off I-84, look for sign on south side of Cascade Dr, follow gravel road for ⅓ mile.* &

LODGINGS

Columbia Gorge Hotel / ★★

4000 WESTCLIFF DR, HOOD RIVER; 541/386-5566 OR 800/345-1921 Timber baron Simon Benson built his luxury hotel in 1921 to accommodate motorists on the new Columbia River Highway; it's now on the National Register of Historic Places. This Spanish-style, golden stucco beauty with green shutters and a red-tile roof has elegant, spacious common areas, but many rooms are a tad cozy. Some larger suites have fireplaces; a few rooms have polished brass or canopy beds. Enjoy acres of beautiful gardens, stone bridges, and a 208-foot waterfall cascading to the Columbia. The hotel features nightly entertainment, and evening turndown service includes a rose and chocolate. Included in the room rate is the five-course "World Famous Farm Breakfast," with eggs, pancakes, fresh fruit, and oatmeal. *$$$; AE, DIS, MC, V; checks OK; cghotel@gorge.net; www.columbiagorgehotel.com; 1 mile west of Hood River, exit 62 off I-84.* &

Hood River Hotel / ★

102 OAK AVE, HOOD RIVER; 541/386-1900 OR 800/386-1859 This sweet, old downtown hotel was built in 1912 as the annex to the long-gone Mount Hood Hotel. The lobby, with inviting chairs and a fireplace, is a pleasant place to relax; the rooms themselves are small and, though tastefully decorated with antique reproductions, not overly fancy. As with all gorge hotels, there's a bit of noise from night trains and highway traffic. The river-view rooms aren't really worth the extra fee (the parking lot and the Mount Hood Railroad depot are much more prominent than the river) and the "rooftop garden" also houses the hotel's HVAC equipment. All that said, it's still a charming hotel in a prime downtown location. *$$; AE, DIS, MC, V; checks OK; hrhotel@gorge.net; www.hoodriverhotel.com; at 1st Ave.* &

Pheasant Valley Orchards Bed and Breakfast / ★★

3890 ACREE DR, HOOD RIVER; 541/386-2803 Nestled in the foothills of Mount Hood, this delightful farmhouse overlooks 40 acres of organic pear and apple orchards. Working farmers Scott and Gail Hagee opened their home as a B&B in spring 2001, but also continue to grow, pack, and ship eight varieties of pears and apples. Comfortably off the beaten path, the cheerfully decorated house welcomes travelers with two large living rooms and a wide view porch. Upstairs rooms feature private baths and lovely views of the orchards, mountains, and surrounding Hood River Valley. The main-floor suite has a shared bath and looks out into the orchard. The slightly more expensive Comice Suite, considerably larger than the other guest rooms, includes a king-sized bed, Jacuzzi tub, and private deck. Each morning guests sit down to breakfast (which always features fresh fruits from the orchard), sip hot coffee, and look out the large windows at towering Mount Hood. The Hagees are also full of ideas for activities in Hood River or day trips. *$$; MC, V; checks OK; innkeeper@pheasantvalleyorchards.com; www.pheasantvalleyorchards.com; about 5 miles south of downtown Hood River, ½ mile east of Tucker Rd on Acree Dr.*

Vagabond Lodge

4070 WESTCLIFF DR, HOOD RIVER; 541/386-2992 OR 877/386-2992 Turn in just past the cement buffalo to find one of Hood River's best lodging values. The motel itself wins no beauty prizes, but if you ask for a riverfront room you'll get an outstanding view at a good price. Several suites are available, including some with kitchens. The Vagabond, on 4 acres in a park-like setting with a playground, is right next door to the Columbia Gorge Hotel (see review), where folks pay about $100 more for the same views. For an evening stroll, cut across the parking lot to the fancier hotel's gardens. *$; AE, DC, DIS, MC, V; no checks; info@vagabondlodge.com; www.vagabondlodge.com; go west on Westcliff Dr past Columbia Gorge Hotel.*

Mosier

Of all the Columbia Gorge towns, Mosier has the most serenely beautiful location, surrounded by cherry orchards and set between two stunning sections of the Historic Columbia River Highway—one stretch open to cars, and the other section kept for non-motorized traffic. Follow the 9-mile stretch of the old highway east to The Dalles, ascending to **ROWENA CREST**, a high bluff overlooking the gorge, and the **TOM MCCALL PRESERVE**, a 230-acre Nature Conservancy refuge for native plants, including rare and endangered wildflowers. Trailhead parking is just beyond mile 6 on historic Highway 30. A 1-mile trail leads along the plateau, and a 3-mile trail gains 1,000 feet in elevation and is open only May through November.

About a half mile west of town, along Rock Creek Road, is the **HISTORIC COLUMBIA RIVER HIGHWAY STATE TRAIL**, a 4½-mile hiking, biking, and wheelchair-accessible trail along the old highway to Hood River, passing through the **MOSIER TWIN TUNNELS**. The tunnels, which took highway engineers two years to complete in 1921, proved too narrow for modern cars but are perfect for cyclists.

RESTAURANTS

Wildflower Café / ★

904 2ND AVE, MOSIER; 541/478-0111 For years, visitors to Mosier who wanted to eat something beyond coffee and ice cream had to head to Hood River or The Dalles. Since the Wildflower Café opened in 2001, all that has changed; now people travel from Hood River to eat at this friendly Mosier hot spot. The Wildflower was constructed largely from salvaged wood, including boards from a 100-year-old Willamette Valley grain mill, and has a screened-in porch with a good view of the Columbia. It's a comfortable place to relax after a morning of hiking or bicycling, or to fuel up (say with a salmon-and-pear omelet) for a hike in the Tom McCall Preserve. The food is on the simple side, and all the better for it. Nothing really messes with the freshness of salmon in a grilled sandwich, or with the richness of the deliciously smooth steamed date bread pudding. *$$; AE, DIS, MC, V; checks OK; breakfast, lunch, dinner Tues–Sat in summer (shorter and varied winter hours); beer and wine; no reservations; on the eastern edge of "downtown" Mosier.* ఉ

LODGINGS

Mosier House Bed & Breakfast / ★

704 3RD AVE, MOSIER; 541/478-3640 This beautiful 1904 Queen Anne home was built by Jefferson Newton Mosier, son of the town's founder and a civic leader in his own right. The current owner, Matt Koerner, spent many years lovingly restoring the house, which had become rather dilapidated, and has followed in Mosier's footsteps as a civic leader. Sitting on a knoll with a great view of the river (and some rumble from Interstate 84), the home is on the National Register of Historic Places. Up the wooden staircase are four rooms with shared baths; the master guest room has a private bath (with a claw-footed tub and shower) and a private entrance and porch. An abundant breakfast is served in the dining room, which overlooks manicured gardens. *$$; MC, V; checks OK; innkeeper@mosierhouse. com; www.mosierhouse.com; turn up Washington St and go left on 3rd St.*

The Dalles

French traders and voyageurs dubbed this point on the river Le Dalle, meaning "the trough," referring to fierce rapids that flowed through a narrow channel, now covered by the reservoir behind The Dalles Dam. Lewis and Clark shot those rapids in large canoes, then camped at Rock Fort, just west of what is now downtown The Dalles. About 40 years later, The Dalles became the decision point for Oregon Trail pioneers. From here they either hired rafts to float their wagons downriver, or continued on a land route southwest across Mount Hood's foothills. Samuel Barlow blazed the trail in 1845 then charged a toll for wagons and livestock. Although travelers on the Barlow Road avoided an arduous river journey, their trip was just as difficult and dangerous.

Be sure to spend several hours at the **COLUMBIA GORGE DISCOVERY CENTER** and the adjoining **WASCO COUNTY HISTORICAL MUSEUM** (5000

Discovery Dr; 541/296-8600; *www.gorgediscovery.org*), which overlooks the river 3 miles west of town. You'll learn about the origins of the Columbia River Gorge and the history of the area, including Native Americans, Lewis and Clark, and the Oregon Trail. Interactive exhibits bring you up to date, even offering a simulated ride on a sailboard. **FORT DALLES MUSEUM** (15th and Garrison Sts; 541/296-4547), housed in the fort's 1857 surgeon's quarters, has its own collection of memorabilia from pioneer days. **ST. PETER'S LANDMARK** (3rd and Lincoln Sts; 541/296-5686), an 1898 Gothic Revival church, was built of local red brick and adorned with stained-glass windows made by Portland's famed Povey Brothers. The spire is adorned with a 6-foot rooster.

At **THE DALLES DAM** (2 miles east of The Dalles, off I-84; 541/296-9778; *www.nwp.usace.army.mil/op/D*), a free train tour departs from the visitor center and makes stops at the dam, powerhouse, fish ladders, and a picnic area.

Seventeen miles east of The Dalles is **DESCHUTES STATE PARK** (on the frontage road off I-84) on the Deschutes River, renowned for steelhead and trout fishing, white-water rafting, and a rails-to-trails bike path along the eastern bank of the river. The park has a campground with RV hookups, hiking and biking trails, fishing, and swimming.

RESTAURANTS

Baldwin Saloon / ★

205 COURT ST, THE DALLES; 541/296-5666 After stints as a steamboat office, a warehouse, a coffin storage site, an employment office, and a saddlery, the 1876 Baldwin Saloon has returned to its roots, right down to the original brick walls and fir floor. Gracing those walls and flanking the antique mahogany bar is an impressive collection of turn-of-the-20th-century Northwest landscape oil paintings. Seafood's a specialty here—try Salmon Rockefeller with parmesan sauce, one of the chef's favorites (he also serves the Rockefeller sauce, made with spinach and licorice liqueur, on oysters). The long list of homemade desserts includes a Snickers-like mousse. *$; MC, V; checks OK; lunch, dinner Mon–Sat; full bar; reservations recommended for 6 or more; at 1st St.* &

Romul's / ★★

312 COURT ST, THE DALLES; 541/296-9771 The Dalles, long a meat-and-potatoes town, has embraced Mediterranean food with the opening of Romul's. Romul Grivov, formerly the owner of the Baldwin Saloon, is Bulgarian with Greek roots; he takes classic Mediterranean cuisines and gives them his own twist. A variety of pasta dishes are offered, as well as eggplant primigana, an Italianized pork schnitzel, and the lovely seafood romesco, with pan-seared prawns and scallops tossed with a hazelnut-almond pesto. Lighter meals (including mixed grill skewers of seafood, meat, and vegetables) are available in the bar. Warm colors, wall murals, and statues scattered among the sturdy wood tables give this downtown restaurant a homey touch. *$$; MC, V; checks OK; dinner Mon–Sat; full bar; reservations for large groups; just off 3rd St (Hwy 30).* &

Mount Hood

Topping out at 11,245 feet, Mount Hood is Oregon's highest point. Dotted with lakes, campgrounds, and hiking and biking trails, the mountain has abundant recreation year-round. Its five ski areas attract skiers and snowboarders of all levels.

From the east via Hood River, drive 27 miles south on Highway 35 and you'll first encounter **COOPER SPUR** (11000 Cloud Cap Rd; 541/352-7803; *www.cooper_spur.com*), elevation 4,500 feet, on the north side of the mountain. It's an inexpensive day- and night-skiing area popular with beginners, with one chair lift, a T-bar, and three rope tows. Next you'll come to **MOUNT HOOD MEADOWS** (2 miles north of Hwy 35 on Forest Rd 3555; 503/337-2222; *www.skihood.com*). At 7,300 feet elevation, it's the largest area on the mountain, with 87 runs, four high-speed quads, six double chair lifts, and a Nordic center with groomed tracks, instructors, and rentals. Many of the lodgings in the Hood River–Mount Hood area offer their guests bargain-priced Meadows lift tickets.

From Portland, drive 53 miles east on Highway 26 to the town of **GOVERNMENT CAMP**, so named because a contingent of U.S. Army Rifles (mounted riflemen) wintered here in 1849. Here you'll find **MOUNT HOOD SKIBOWL** (87000 E Hwy 26; 503/272-3206 or 503/222-2695, recorded information; *www.skibowl.com*), at 5,026 feet, America's largest night-ski area with 34 lighted runs, four double chair lifts, and a tubing hill. Right next to the rest area at the east end of Government Camp, at 4,306 feet, **SUMMIT** (54 miles east of Portland on Hwy 26; 503/272-0256; *www.summitskiarea.com*) is good for beginners or families who want to slide on inner tubes; ski and tube rentals are available. At 6,000 feet, **TIMBERLINE** (4 miles north of Hwy 26, just east of Government Camp; 503/622-7979; *www.timberlinelodge.com*) has six lifts; four—including Palmer Lift, which takes skiers up to Palmer Snowfield for year-round skiing—are high-speed quads.

Timberline is popular with people who never want to put their skis away, including the U.S. Ski Team, which trains here in summer. Summer also offers plenty of hiking, biking, horseback riding, golf, and other sports. The **MOUNT HOOD SKIBOWL SUMMER ACTION PARK** (87000 E Hwy 26; 503/272-3206 or 503/222-2695, recorded information; *www.skibowl.com*; open 11am–6pm weekdays, 10am–7pm weekends) boasts more than 25 summertime activities, including a half-mile dual alpine slide, Indy Karts, miniature golf, croquet, bungee jumping, a mountain-bike park with 40 miles of trails, horseback and pony rides, batting cages, volleyball, horseshoes, and other attractions. Get an all-day pass or pay for individual activities.

Climbers who want to scale the mountain's 11,235 feet must register and obtain a free mandatory wilderness permit in the 24-hour climbing room of Timberline's Wy'east Day Lodge. Guided climbs are available through **TIMBERLINE MOUNTAIN GUIDES** (541/312-9242). Recreation on the south side of Mount Hood (the easiest climbing route) is managed by the **ZIGZAG RANGER DISTRICT** (503/622-3191).

TIMBERLINE LODGE (see review) is another popular stop for summer visitors. From here, the Palmer Snowfield is accessible even to nonskiers. It takes just 6 minutes to travel the **MAGIC MILE SUPER EXPRESS** chair lift 1,000 vertical feet to Palmer Junction. The Magic Mile Interpretive Trail leads back to Timberline Lodge.

RESTAURANTS

The Brew Pub at Mount Hood Brewing Co.

87304 E GOVERNMENT CAMP LOOP HWY, GOVERNMENT CAMP; 503/622-0724 Tuck into an armchair and look out onto the snow from this warm, inviting pub. If you're not driving back down the mountain, sample such bold brews as a strong Scottish ale, a porter, a barley wine, and an oatmeal stout. Spring visitors should try Illumination Ale, an herbal ale flavored with tea, elderberries and elder flowers, ginger, and a host of other flowers and herbs. Fill up on Tuscan-style white pizza, topped with garlic dressing, spinach, red onion, zucchini, asparagus, red pepper, oregano, and a three-cheese blend. The extensive kids' menu includes quesadillas, burgers, and grilled cheese sandwiches. *$; AE, DIS, MC, V; checks OK; lunch, dinner every day; beer and wine; no reservations; pubinfo@mthoodbrewing .com; www.mthoodbrewing.com; west end of Government Camp, next to Mount Hood Inn.* &

Cascade Dining Room / ★★★

TIMBERLINE LODGE, TIMBERLINE; 503/622-0700 Beyond the hand-forged iron gate on the lodge's second level is the Cascade Dining Room, renowned for 20 years for the award-winning cuisine of executive chef Leif Eric Benson. Don't let the rustic setting fool you: the food here is very sophisticated, with a wine list to match. Although Benson is Swiss, he loves to showcase foods of the Northwest, such as grilled wild salmon served with a sea clam and fennel chowder, a wild mushroom timbale, or apple wood–smoked pork loin. The fine food and service are two reasons many Portlanders make the drive here for special occasions. *$$$; AE, MC, V; checks OK; breakfast, lunch, dinner every day; full bar; dinner reservations recommended; food@timberlinelodge.com; www.timberlinelodge.com; 60 miles east of Portland off Hwy 26.* &

LODGINGS

Falcon's Crest Inn / ★☆

87287 GOVERNMENT CAMP LOOP HWY, GOVERNMENT CAMP; 541/272-3403 OR 800/624-7384 This Government Camp B&B is a good base for groups of friends or extended families. On both the second and third floors, a central lounge area is dominated by floor-to-ceiling windows and flanked by bedrooms, including the exuberantly decorated Safari Room and the more subdued Mexicalli Suite, complete with a Jacuzzi for two. With advance notice, hosts Bob and Melody Johnson will prepare an elaborate six-course dinner (you don't need to stay at the inn to eat dinner here, but reservations are a must). *$$$; AE, DIS, MC, V; checks OK; info@falconscrest .com; www.falconscrest.com; just off Loop Rd, on north side.*

Mount Hood Hamlet Bed & Breakfast / ★★

6741 HWY 35, MOUNT HOOD; 541/352-3574 OR 800/407-0570 The newly built 18th-century-style New England colonial sits on a hill overlooking the farm where owner Paul Romans was raised. After careers as schoolteachers, he and his wife, Diane, returned and built this gorgeous house, inspired by the family's ancestral home in Rhode Island. Three second-floor guest rooms

NATIVE AMERICAN FISHING

For centuries the shores of the Columbia River were a meeting ground for Native Americans who came from hundreds—even thousands—of miles away to trade. The commodity that local tribes traded was like gold—red gold. It was the flavorful and nourishing meat, either fresh or dried, of the wild salmon. You can still see Native Americans from the Umatilla, Nez Perce, Warm Springs, or Yakama tribes fishing with dip nets from the river's shore, often from wooden platforms.

CELILO FALLS, flooded and filled when The Dalles Dam was built in 1957, was a vital fishing area for about 10,000 years. Petroglyphs and pictographs preserved near The Dalles attest to the native peoples' ancient presence. The touring train at the dam (see The Dalles section) takes you to **PETROGLYPH WALL**, where pictures of faces, animals, figures, spirals, spirits, and symbols are displayed. The famous petroglyph, Tsagaglalal—"She Who Watches"—is on the Washington shore at Horsethief State Park. This and other petroglyphs may be seen only on ranger-guided tours (509/767-1159; 10am Fri–Sat Apr–Oct); reservations are required.

To get an idea of how powerful and magnificent Celilo Falls were, visit the **COLUMBIA GORGE DISCOVERY CENTER** (5000 Discovery Dr; 541/296-8600) in The Dalles and watch documentary film clips dating from 1910 to 1950, when the roar of the falls was deafening. Also at the museum is a 33-foot-long model of the Columbia River that shows its before- and after-dam appearance. As the water recedes, the rock formations and falls appear, as well as Memaloose Island, which was the largest Native American burial island on the river and now is only partially above water.

Local Native Americans still mourn the loss of the falls but continue to celebrate the arrival of the first spring chinook salmon at Celilo Village. The village longhouses are open to the public for the **CELILO SALMON FEED** on the second weekend of April; contact **THE DALLES CONVENTION & VISITORS BUREAU** (404 2nd St; 541/296-6616 or 800/255-3385).

—*Susan Hauser*

have private baths and TVs, one with a fireplace and Jacuzzi; all have views. Ample common areas include a warm, inviting library, which shares a fireplace with the great room, where guests can read or enjoy the view of Mount Hood. Full breakfasts, served family-style in the dining room or on the 44-foot-long patio, feature fruits of the valley or berries from the Romanses' own garden, and homemade jams and jellies. Breakfast offerings may be a Belgian waffle with fruit topping or an omelet soufflé. The outdoor spa can be used year-round and has a heated deck and an extraordinary view of Mounts Hood and Adams. *$$$; AE, DIS, MC, V; checks OK; innkeeper@mthoodhamlet.com; www.mthoodhamlet.com; 20 miles north of Mount Hood Meadows on Hwy 35.* &

Old Parkdale Inn / ★

4932 BASELINE RD, PARKDALE; 541/352-5551 Parkdale, with its friendly brew pub, its great views of Mount Hood, and its surrounding pear orchards, is a fine base for exploring either the mountain or Hood River. Colorful gardens surround this 1911 Craftsman house, and the decor in each of the three guest rooms is inspired by a different artist. Pick Monet for a quiet floral theme, O'Keefe for southwestern vibrancy, or Gauguin for wild color and a view right into the treetops. Two of the rooms are actually suites with complete kitchens and can sleep up to four. Innkeeper Mary Pelligrini will deliver breakfast to your room or serve it in the dining room. *$$$; MC, V; checks OK; parkdale@hoodriverlodging.com; www.hoodriverlodging.com; Hwy 35 north from Mount Hood, turn off to Parkdale and look for sign on right.*

Summit Meadow Cabins

JUST OFF FOREST RD 2560, GOVERNMENT CAMP; 503/272-3494 A visit to one of these Trillium Basin cabins is plenty of fun in summer, when hiking and mountain biking outings may lead to swims in nearby Trillium Lake. But staying here is truly special in winter, when it takes a 1½-mile cross-country ski or snowshoe journey to reach the cabins. The trek is long enough to gain you bragging rights, but—and only you need to know this—it's not particularly arduous. Groomed cross-country ski trails abound; in fact, the Summit Meadows crew manicures trails all over the Trillium Basin. All the cabins—from the cozy Mineral Creek Cabin to the large chalets that sleep up to 12—are more functional than elegant; each comes equipped with cookware, bedding, and towels. Good dogs are welcome. *$$$; no credit cards; checks OK; 2-night min; info@summitmeadow.com; www.summitmeadow.com; north of Still Creek Campground off Hwy 26 (about 1 mile south of Government Camp).*

Timberline Lodge / ★★★☆

TIMBERLINE SKI AREA, TIMBERLINE; 503/622-7979 OR 800/547-1406 Built at the 6,000-foot level on Mount Hood as a Civilian Conservation Corps project during the Depression, this rustic stone-and-timber lodge was dedicated by President Franklin D. Roosevelt in 1937 and is now a National Historic Landmark. A huge central stone fireplace, the focal point of both levels, is surrounded by handmade furnishings and artwork, including wonderful examples of wood- and ironworking, rug weaving, mosaics, and painting. The 70 rooms range from dorm rooms with bunk beds and shared baths to the Timberline Fireplace Room. Many of the upholsteries, draperies, rugs, and bedspreads in the public and guest rooms have been re-created in their original patterns—in some cases with the help of the original craftspeople. A wintertime dip in the outdoor heated pool is a bracing experience, best followed by a sauna. In summer, Timberline is a great base for hikers, can't-quit skiers, and poolside loungers. The lodge's Cascade Dining Room (see review), the Blue Ox Bar, and the Ram's Head Bar are all fun places to eat. *$$$; AE, MC, V; checks OK; reservations@timberlinelodge.com; www.timberlinelodge.com; 60 miles east of Portland off Hwy 26.* &

Welches

Coming west off Mount Hood, you reach Welches, which takes its name from Samuel Welch, who welcomed travelers at the hotel he built in 1890 (now the Old Welches Inn). Stop by the **FLYING FROG** (67211 E Hwy 26, in the Arrah Wanna Rendezvous Center; 503/622-7638) for the best cup of tea on the mountain and a delicious pastry. (Full breakfasts and lunches are also served in the cheery café.)

RESTAURANTS

The Rendezvous Grill and Tap Room / ★★

67149 E HWY 26, WELCHES; 503/622-6837 Tucked into a nicer-than-average strip mall is one of Mount Hood's best restaurants. Although her emphasis is on seasonal, local products, including chanterelle mushrooms and huckleberries, chef/co-owner Kathryn Bliss is quick to try something new, such as hosting a harvest moon tribal belly-dance festival with a fine spread of vegetarian noshes. On a more normal night, expect to choose from rigatoni with alder-smoked chicken in a champagne cream sauce with toasted hazelnuts, dried cranberries, and fresh spinach; sake-glazed salmon; or fried Willapa Bay oysters with rémoulade sauce. Choosing a bottle of wine is easy with succinct but conversational reviews written by co-owner Tom Anderson—they're like little wine newsletters, with information about featured wines. *$$; AE, DIS, MC, V; checks OK; lunch, dinner every day; full bar; reservations recommended; rndzvgrill@aol.com; www.rendezvousgrill.net; north side of Hwy 26, just west of traffic light.* &

LODGINGS

Old Welches Inn / ★

26401 E WELCHES RD, WELCHES; 503/622-3754 You'd never guess this rambling blue-roofed white house behind a picket fence is more than a century old. Built in 1890, it was the first hotel and summer resort on Mount Hood; the Welch family converted it into their private home in the 1930s. The four cozy guest rooms in the main house are named after wildflowers. Three of the rooms are on the second floor, while the Forget-Me-Not Room is tucked away atop two flights of stairs. Whole families, and their pets, are welcome at the cottage next door. It's a bit more modern—built in 1901—with two bedrooms, a bath, a kitchen, and a living room with fireplace. The lush lawn extends all the way to the shore of the Salmon River. *$$; AE, MC, V; checks OK; info@mthoodlodging.com; www.mthoodlodging.com; 1 mile south of Hwy 26.*

The Resort at the Mountain / ★★

68010 E FAIRWAY AVE, WELCHES; 503/622-3101 OR 800/669-7666 Clan crests decorate the lobby walls, the Scottish Shoppe sells all manner of Scottish collectibles, and the Highlands Dining Room and Tartans Inn are your sources for food and drink. And, just as in Scotland, golf is a big deal here. Though many come for the 27-hole golf course, you'll also find tennis, croquet, lawn bowling, volleyball, badminton, swimming, hiking, biking, fishing, and, of course, skiing just up the road. Many of the 160 spacious, modern guest rooms have fireplaces, and the grounds, much like the surrounding forests, seem to go on forever. Condos and suites face the fairway; other rooms face the wooded courtyard and pool area. *$$$; AE, DC, DIS, MC, V; checks OK; www.theresort.com; 1 mile south of Hwy 26.*

Sandy

Sandy fairly hops in the winter, when carloads of skiers and snowboarders clog the highway on their way to and from Mount Hood. En route, folks may stop here for cross-country ski rentals, advice, and gear at **OTTO'S** (38716 Hwy 26; 503/668-5947) or for the area's cheapest gas at the local filling station.

On a clear day, turn off Highway 26 at Bluff Road and go 1 mile north to **JONSRUD VIEWPOINT**, where interpretive signs help you find where the last leg of the Oregon Trail came down the mountainside. It's a spectacular lookout over the Sandy River and the forested foothills of Mount Hood.

About 5 miles east of Sandy, stop at the **OREGON CANDY FARM** (48620 SE Hwy 26; 503/668-5066) and watch caramels, marshmallows, and chocolates—including Bavarian truffles—being made the old-fashioned way. Plenty to taste and buy here.

RESTAURANTS

The Elusive Trout Pub

39333 PROCTOR BLVD, SANDY; 503/668-7884 The trout is indeed elusive—it's only found in the names of the burgers and sandwiches on the menu here. The Eastern brookie is a steak sandwich, the German brown a reuben, and the Hatchery a ham and cheese. Nineteen Northwest microbrews are on tap here, and a row of German beer steins hangs from the rafters. Owners Jim and Kim Simonek keep things in a casual Northwest perspective, noting on the menu, "Hours change according to economic conditions, weather, family needs, current political administration, etc." *$; AE, MC, V; local checks only; lunch, dinner Tues–Sun; beer and wine; no reservations; on westbound Hwy 26 at Hoffman Ave.* &

WILLAMETTE VALLEY

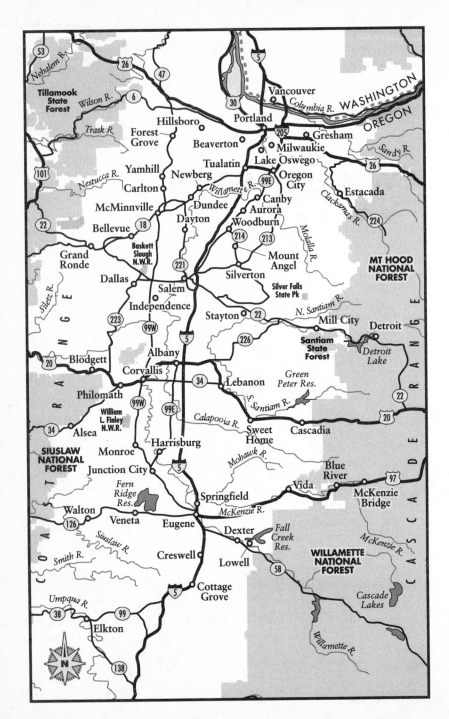

WILLAMETTE VALLEY

A lush, temperate river valley edged by mountains and dotted with farms and small towns, often rainy in winter but rarely snowy. Sound quintessentially like Oregon? In fact, most of the state is in mountains or high desert. But it's the Willamette Valley that most people picture when they think of this state. And it's here that nine out of ten Oregonians live, Salem being the second-largest city in Oregon and Eugene the third. In that sense, the Willamette Valley *is* Oregon.

The Willamette River defines the valley. Its forks wind their way out of the Central Cascade mountains to merge southeast of Eugene; from there, the river heads north to meet the Columbia at Portland. The valley, barely 10 miles wide near Eugene but broadening to more than 30 miles wide near Salem, is also defined by mountains: the Coast Range to the west, the Cascades to the east, and—south of Eugene—the Siskiyous. That broad, flat valley and the uncrowded rural roads that traverse it are inviting to cyclists, as are extensive networks of paved bicycle paths, especially in Eugene and Corvallis. Venture into the foothills of those ranges for some memorable hiking—past waterfalls, through wild bird refuges, to the summits of modest peaks.

When the pioneers pushed west with covered wagons in the mid-1800s, they were lured by promises of an agricultural paradise. What they found, and what you'll find today, isn't too far off the mark. Wherever you live in the United States, there's a good chance your Christmas tree, dahlias, and irises, the berries in your pie, the hazelnuts in your biscotti—even your front lawn—were grown in the Willamette Valley. Driving from Portland to Eugene along Highway 99W west of the Willamette River, and along lesser routes, you'll still find roadside stands with fresh produce, flowers, honey, and jams, spring through fall; some are open year-round. On weekends, farmers markets bloom in many town centers.

The wine at your table may also have come from here, especially if you favor fine reds; pinot noir has emerged as the Willamette Valley's star varietal. First came the vines, some 35 years ago, and then came the wineries. Happily for travelers, fine dining was the next step.

So what about that rain? There's plenty, but not more than in a lot of places: around 45 inches a year. Locals don't necessarily wait for the sun to shine to get out hiking, nursery browsing, or touring wine country. Less well-known is the valley's summer surprise: sunny and hot, with low humidity, from about July 5 into September and sometimes through October.

ACCESS AND INFORMATION

Commuter airlines America West, Horizon Air, United, and United Express serve the **EUGENE AIRPORT** (north of town, off Hwy 99; 541/682-5430; *www.eugeneairport.com*). The greatest choice of flights is to and from Portland, Seattle, San Francisco, and Denver. **CAR RENTALS** are available at the airport and in town.

Most travelers arrive by car via **INTERSTATE 5**, its four lanes (at Eugene) widening to six around Salem. This is the express route; figure less than two hours from Eugene to Portland. More leisurely north-south travelers prefer scenic old

US HIGHWAY 99W, parallel to Interstate 5 west of the Willamette. At the north end it's known as the "wine road," where it passes through the wine-country hubs of Newberg, Dundee, and McMinnville; unobtrusive blue signs point the way to wineries. For road conditions, contact the **OREGON DEPARTMENT OF TRANSPORTATION** (503/588-2941 or 800/977-6368 outside of Oregon). The online **TRAVEL ADVISOR** (*www.tripcheck.com*) also has helpful, up-to-date information on road conditions.

AMTRAK (800/USA-RAIL; *www.amtrak.com*) from Seattle and Portland stops at Salem, Albany, and Eugene; the Coast Starlight continues south to Los Angeles. Service and schedule improvements have made the train more attractive for getting into and out of the Willamette Valley; Spanish-made Talgo trains have a little less legroom and no white-linen dinner service, but they're faster, with contemporary amenities such as plug-ins for laptops (and a snack bar). If you want to go by train, make sure that's what you're getting when you make reservations; Amtrak uses motor coaches on some links.

The **WILLAMETTE VALLEY VISITOR'S ASSOCIATION** (866/548-5018; *www .willamettevalley.org*) is a good source for information on the area as are the individual city Web sites listed there.

Wine Country

Wine is a growth industry in Oregon: acres of grapes and numbers of wineries have more than doubled in the past decade. The greatest concentration of the now 175-plus wineries is in Yamhill County, mostly between Newberg and McMinnville. Here among rolling oak-covered hills are increasing numbers of vineyards and enough wineries (more than 50 in the North Willamette Valley appellation) to keep touring wine lovers tipsy for a week. The wine country stretches south past Salem and Eugene, west of the Willamette; wineries down this way are more widely scattered but well worth visiting. For more information, contact the **YAMHILL COUNTY WINERIES ASSOCIATION** (503/646-2985; *www.yamhillwine.com*).

So many of Oregon's pinot noirs have achieved international renown that many of the better-known bottlings are quite pricey. But ardent wine explorers can still find up-and-coming producers cheerfully selling fabulous wine at reasonable prices out of winery front doors. Summer weekends, as well as Memorial Day and Thanksgiving weekends, can be busy but are good times to visit because some wineries are only open then. Most are open year-round, at least on weekends (though a few are not open to visitors at all). Many are small family operations well off the beaten track, and visitors are rare enough that you'll receive a hearty welcome. Tasting is free most places; some charge a small fee to try a sampling of wines, or just for "premium pours"—worth paying, since visitors are fewer at these spots and you tend to get more time to converse with your host. (The fee may be applied toward any wine you purchase.) Or stop at an independent tasting room where, for a small fee, you can sample the best of the lesser-known labels.

The best advice is to arm yourself with a map (it's easy to get lost on the backroads) and the winery guide from the **OREGON WINE ADVISORY BOARD** (1200

WILLAMETTE VALLEY THREE-DAY TOUR

DAY ONE: Start out in the heart of **YAMHILL COUNTY** and Oregon wine country and drive between **NEWBERG** and **MCMINNVILLE**, touring the plentiful local wineries along the way. Lunch in McMinnville at **BISTRO MAISON**, sitting in the outside courtyard if weather permits, and sample fine French cuisine in a relaxed setting. Walk off lunch along **THIRD STREET**, where you can browse speciality shops and boutiques or stop for a local brew at **GOLDEN VALLEY BREWERY & PUB**. If you're historically inclined, drive to the **EVERGREEN AVIATION MUSEUM** to check out Howard Hughes' *Spruce Goose* and other aviation wonders. Afterward, head to **YOUNGBERG HILL VINEYARDS & INN**, where your room awaits. Relax and enjoy the view before heading back down the road to nearby Dayton and a quintessential dining experience at the **JOEL PALMER HOUSE**.

DAY TWO: Savor your three-course breakfast at the inn before heading out for the day. Hire a bike for a morning ride around the scenic countryside or stroll the grounds of the inn; there's plenty of room to wander. Consider leaving early to drive to Salem to explore the **BUSH HOUSE**, a beautiful historic home in a large park that includes a conservatory, rose gardens, and hiking trails. Have an elegant lunch at **ALESSANDRO'S 120** or **J. JAMES RESTAURANT**. Then you might want to stop by the **WILLAMETTE VALLEY VINEYARDS**, just south of town, to sample some excellent pinot noir and chardonnay. Leave an hour to drive to the hip college town of Corvallis, where you'll spend the night at **HANSON COUNTRY INN**. Arrive with enough time to view the grounds and visit with the innkeeper. Dine at **IOVINO'S** on First Street, across from **RIVERFRONT PARK**, where you can take a leisurely stroll after dinner.

DAY THREE: It's only another hour farther south to Eugene, where even more adventures await. For those athletically inclined, hike to the top of **SPENCER'S BUTTE** for an amazing view of the entire city, valley, and rivers below. Hire a canoe or raft to enjoy the waters of the **WILLAMETTE** or **MCKENZIE RIVERS**, or wander down to **FIFTH STREET PUBLIC MARKET** for local color and fun shopping, or over to Eighth and Oak Streets if the **SATURDAY MARKET** is in swing; food booths at either spot can provide lunch. For dinner, check out the newly opened **RED AGAVE** restaurant, across from the train station. Or sample the fresh seafood at **ADAM'S PLACE** on Broadway.

NW Naito Pkwy, Ste 400, Portland, OR 97209; 503/228-8336 or 800/242-2363; *www.oregonwine.org*) or from any member winery. Use it to seek out your favorites: a particular varietal, sparkling wines, or boutique wineries. When you come across a wine you especially like, ask the vintner (or whoever's pouring) to suggest other wineries in that vein to visit. In fine weather, take along a picnic; many wineries have tables outside, and some sell chilled wine and lunch supplies.

Newberg

LODGINGS

Springbrook Hazelnut Farm / ★★

30295 N HWY 99W, NEWBERG; 503/538-4606 OR 800/793-8528 Informal Oregonians are surprised by the colorful elegance of this landmark farmhouse. Owner Ellen McClure, an artist by training, has created an exquisitely decorated B&B filled with original art. The large paneled dining room makes you feel as if you're in an Italian palazzo. Two upstairs wicker-furnished guest rooms share a sitting room and a bathroom; downstairs, two more guest rooms are furnished with antiques and have half-baths, sharing a full bath down the hall. The Rose Cottage and Carriage House are behind the main house; each is a perfect little private suite with a kitchen well stocked with breakfast fixings. They're near the old barn, which now houses a one-man winery. Guests may explore the 60-acre filbert orchard, take a swim in the pool, or play tennis on the newly refinished private court. *$$–$$$; DIS, MC, V; checks OK; ellen@nutfarm.com; www.nutfarm.com; just off Hwy 99W, north of Newberg.*

Dundee

Not much more than a wide spot in the road a generation ago, Dundee has become the culinary capital of Northern Oregon's wine country. Highway 99W—the wine road—runs right through town, and crossing it on foot is a challenge on weekends. But it's one worth taking, to hop from **DUNDEE BISTRO** (see review) to the sparkling wines awaiting your palate at **ARGYLE WINERY** (691 Hwy 99W; 503/538-8520 or 888/427-4953; *www.argylewinery.com*). A handful of stellar restaurants now lines the highway's west side; any one is worth a visit. Some say Dundee is a bit like Napa 25 years ago—a farming town still rough around the edges, with touches of refinement. Visit now so you can say you knew it when.

RESTAURANTS

Dundee Bistro / ★★★

🌲 **100-A SW 7TH ST, DUNDEE; 503/554-1650** This smart, bustling bistro-pizzeria-bar on Dundee's restaurant row was built by the Ponzi family, respected local wine makers. The courtyard arrangement and large windows, walls, and floor in tones of sage and pumpkin lend it a Tuscan air, but the food is inventively, seasonally Northwestern. Daily menu changes focus on ingredients available at nearby farms and ranches, and a local farmers market can be found in front of the restaurant on Sundays. A fall dinner might start with garnet yam flan with smoked salmon, or roasted butternut squash soup with comice pear. The half-dozen entrée choices could include mesquite-roasted chicken with apples and fig vinaigrette, or locally grown pork loin with hedgehog mushrooms and applesauce. Pizza appears as an appetizer at dinner or an entrée at lunch, topped with unusual combinations, such as air-dried sausage, crimini mushrooms, roasted onion, and Gorgonzola. The same care is evidenced in the handful of desserts and eclectic wine list: not long, but well chosen, with a dozen available by the glass. Next door is the Ponzi Wine Bar, where you can taste Ponzi and other premium Oregon wines. *$$; AE, MC, V; local checks only; lunch, dinner every day; full bar; reservations recommended; www .dundeebistro.com; on Hwy 99W at 7th St.* &

Red Hills Provincial Dining / ★★★

276 HWY 99W, DUNDEE; 503/538-8224 You'll be warmly received in this 1912 Craftsman-style house-turned-restaurant. The simple European-country dinner menu changes often, and the choices are all intriguing: veal osso buco with creamy polenta, perhaps, or fricassee of game hen with chanterelles and black trumpet mushrooms, or a classic coquilles St.-Jacques. All the details are just right, whether it's bread dusted with fresh rosemary or a crisp mesclun salad, or poached pears with caramel sauce and chocolate ganache. Add to this an award-winning wine list with a huge selection from all over the world. A private dining room seats up to 12. *$$; AE, MC, V; checks OK; dinner every day; full bar; reservations recommended; redhills@teleport.com; www.redhillsdining.com; north edge of town.*

Tina's / ★★★

760 HWY 99W, DUNDEE; 503/538-8880 This jewel box of a restaurant— something of a gathering place for the local wine crowd—resides in a small, unassuming house on the side of the highway. Inside, it's stylish and pretty, bright with white walls and warmed by a fireplace. Chef-proprietors Tina and David Bergen seem to be taking their culinary cues from contemporary French cuisine, with a bias toward fresh, local ingredients cooked perfectly: the sea scallops and thyme-infused sauce, for example, or purée of corn soup, creamy without cream. Surprises include salmon spring rolls served with a hazelnut sauce. The green salad is perfectly fresh; the herbs flavoring your entrée are likely homegrown. The list of house-made desserts is short and the wine list long: the right proportion in these parts. *$$; AE, DIS, MC, V; checks OK; lunch Tues–Fri, dinner every day; full bar; reservations recommended; center of town, across from fire station.* &

Dayton

RESTAURANTS

Joel Palmer House / ★★★★

600 FERRY ST, DAYTON; 503/864-2995 A trip to Oregon's wine country is no longer complete without a pilgrimage to the Joel Palmer House. Chef Jack Czarnecki is a renowned authority on cooking with mushrooms, and rare is the dish that emerges from his kitchen without some variety of fungus in either a starring or supporting role. Appetizers might include a three-mushroom tart, escargot with black chanterelles, or a silky corn chowder with dried cèpes. The rack of lamb comes with a rich pinot noir–hazelnut sauce, while wild mushroom duxelles and a Creole–pinot gris sauce accompany tender sautéed scallops. Or, consider Jack's Mushroom Madness, a prix-fixe multicourse dinner emphasizing—what else?—wild mushrooms. Service is attentive if somewhat haphazard, but the chef's presence and the setting—a white Southern Revival home built in the 1850s by town co-founder Gen. Joel Palmer—give a sense of romance and formality. The extensive wine list is a gushing ode to Oregon pinot noir. *$$–$$$; AE, DIS, MC, V; local checks only; dinner Tues–Sat; full bar; reservations required; joelpalmerhouse @onlinemac.com; www.joelpalmerhouse.com; downtown.* ᕼ

LODGINGS

Wine Country Farm / ★

6855 BREYMAN ORCHARDS RD, DAYTON; 503/864-3446 OR 800/261-3446 In the "red hills of Dundee" (the soil really is red), surrounded by vineyards, you'll find the Wine Country Farm. From the hilltop, watch clouds drift across the valley; the setting and view are the draws here. All six guest rooms in the white stucco 1910 house have private baths and down comforters, and two have fireplaces. Guests can enjoy a hot tub and sauna, and massage is available on-site. The farm also has a commercial winery next door to the inn, Wine Country Farm Cellars, with a public tasting room that was recently expanded to seat 150 guests and has hosted numerous weddings. Three spacious suites, one with a sitting room, occupy the second floor and are also available to guests. In warm weather, enjoy the hearty farm breakfast on the sun-washed deck. Owners of the 13-acre farm also raise Arabian horses; guided trail rides to nearby wineries and horse-drawn buggy rides are available. *$$–$$$; MC, V; checks OK; innkeeper@winecountryfarm.com; www .winecountryfarm.com; right onto McDougal just past Sokol Blosser Winery, then right to Breyman Orchards Rd.*

Carlton and Yamhill

At the western edge of Yamhill wine country and just a few miles apart, these two towns are worthwhile destinations in a driving tour of the valley's north end. Carlton's 19th-century brick and stone storefronts, old-fashioned feed store, and gentle pace are a tonic. Enjoy the shops (quilting, garden, arts) arrayed along Main Street, check out **CUNEO CELLARS** (750 W Lincoln St; 503/852-0002; *www .cuneocellars.com*) at the north end of town, and stop to taste (small fee) and chat with the knowledgeable owner at **THE TASTING ROOM** (105 W Main St; 503/852-6733), which offers wines from nearby wineries that are generally closed to the public. Yamhill is worth a stop if only to browse the antiques at **RD STEEVES IMPORTS** (140 W Main St; 503/662-3999). The **FLYING M RANCH** (23029 NW Flying M Rd; 503/662-3222; *www.flying-m-ranch.com*), 10 miles west of town, is great for families and offers horseback riding, spartan overnighting, an airstrip for private pilots, and meat-and-potatoes fare in a big log lodge.

RESTAURANTS

Caffe Bisbo / ★

214 MAIN ST, CARLTON; 503/852-7248 When Claudio and Joanne Bisbocci opened their trattoria in little Carlton, fourth-generation restaurateur Claudio could barely speak English. But communication has never been a problem; this Italian speaks volumes with his food and his infectious enthusiasm. The food is straight-ahead, traditional Northern Italian, the likes of rice torta redolent with extra-virgin olive oil and basil, Genoa shrimp with garlic and marsala, and fresh cannelloni. Minestrone is thick and basily; salad dressed simply in the Italian manner—much as you would expect somewhere along the Cinque Terre, Claudio's home turf. The tiramisù is the real thing, and wines (by the glass or bottle) are mostly modestly priced Italian and Northwest. Come to enjoy the food and a small-town Italian welcome. *$$; MC, V; local checks only; lunch and dinner Thurs–Sat; beer and wine; dinner reservations required; downtown.* &

McMinnville

McMinnville is growing up; the feed stores are still here, now cheek by jowl with stores supplying the burgeoning wine industry. Driving through town, turn off the highway onto historic Third Street to reach the gracious old tree-shaded city center sporting a growing collection of wine shops, cafés, and boutiques housed in buildings built between 1885 and 1912. Its central location makes this town a good headquarters for wine touring; pick up information at the **MCMINNVILLE CHAMBER OF COMMERCE** (417 N Adams St; 503/472-6196; *www.mcminnville.org*). Serious wine lovers can OD on great wine and food while hobnobbing with wine celebrities (including some of France's hot young wine makers) at the three-day **INTERNATIONAL PINOT NOIR CELEBRATION** (503/472-8964 or 800/775-4762; *www.inpc.org*), held in late July or early August on the campus of Linfield College; tickets tend to sell out well in advance. Check out the **FARMERS MARKET** on Thursday afternoons, 3–6pm, at S Cowls St between Second and Third, June–September. Don't miss the **EVERGREEN AVIATION MUSEUM** (3685 NE Cumulus Ave, off of Highway 18; 503/434-4180; *www.sprucegoose.org*), featuring Howard Hughes' Flying Boat, the *Spruce Goose*.

RESTAURANTS

Bistro Maison / ★★

729 E 3RD ST, MCMINNVILLE; 503/474-1888 Opened in 2003, this French café run by chef Jean-Jacques and his wife, Deborah, is a welcome addition to downtown McMinnville. Based on the ground floor of a historic bungalow on NE Third—the owners live upstairs—it is decorated with cheery French country wallpaper and red leather-backed booths. There is a wine-tasting bar up front as well as a comfortable waiting area at the top of the stairs. Start with an apertif and sample the moules—cooked in three different styles—served with frites and saffron aioli. Classics such as escargots en croûte de Bourgogne, coq au vin, steak tartar, as well as daily specials, such as poached leeks, are mouth-watering fare. In sunny weather, choose the charming outdoor seating in the private courtyard. Local hazelnuts are offered at the end of the meal. *$$; DIS, MC, V; local checks only; lunch Wed–Fri, dinner Wed–Sun, brunch Sun; full bar; reservations recommended; deborah@bistromaison .com; www.bistromaison.com; on 3rd next to the train station.*

Golden Valley Brewery & Pub / ★

980 E 4TH ST, MCMINNVILLE; 503/472-2739 For a nice break from wine touring, try this local pub for its refreshing ales and bustling atmosphere. Housed in a recycled bottling plant, local brews such as Erratic Rock Amber and Red Thistle Ale, as well as a selection of seasonal beers, are offered with an extensive menu that includes something for everyone: homemade soups, specialty salads, sandwiches, burgers, pastas, and pub favorites. A prime rib special is available Friday and Saturday nights. The 15-foot ceilings and abundant woodwork are tastefully installed and add to the ambiance. You can also shop online for brew pub paraphernalia. *$; AE, DIS, MC, V; local checks only; lunch, dinner every day, brunch Sun; full bar; no reservations; www.goldenvalleybrewery.com; 1 mile off Highway 18.* &

Nick's Italian Café / ★★

521 E 3RD ST, MCMINNVILLE; 503/434-4471 Long before Dundee's restaurant row emerged, Nick's in McMinnville was the culinary headquarters of Oregon's wine country, with owner Nick Peirano turning out the Northern Italian cooking he learned at his mother's knee. Today you'll find new chef Christopher Gayer, and although it's still a winner, it's been eclipsed by more dazzling restaurants in nearby Dundee, and its funky charm—mismatched plates, the location a former luncheonette—is wearing thin. Still, there's plenty to enjoy in the prix-fixe, five-course meal, including the second-course tureen of heavenly, garlicky minestrone and the simply dressed green salad. The seasonal antipasto might include shellfish in winter or melon with prosciutto in summer. The fourth course is always delicious pasta. Entrées could include perfectly grilled swordfish steak, or top sirloin marinated in garlic and rosemary. Dessert choices include crème brûlée, truffles, and tiramisù. Guests are welcome to order à la carte. *$$$; AE, MC, V; checks OK; dinner Tues–Sun; beer and wine; reservations recommended; www.nicks italiancafe.com; next door to Hotel Oregon.* &

LODGINGS

Hotel Oregon / ★★

310 NE EVANS ST, MCMINNVILLE; 503/472-8427 OR 888/472-8427 Oregon's ubiquitous microbrew *meisters,* the McMenamin brothers, have revitalized a 1905 hotel in the center of McMinnville, contributing to its downtown renaissance and giving adventurous wine-country tourers a rather spartan but lively new lodging option. Ceilings are high, beds firm, furnishings predominately antique, and decor a bit brooding (including original artwork). Only a handful of the 42 rooms have private baths; the rest either share a bath with an adjoining room or utilize one down the hall (terry-cloth robes provided). All have phones, but no TVs. Late-night street noise can be a bit much, due in part to the hotel's own pub downstairs. As at other McMenamin accommodations, a featured activity is drinking, with a large main-floor pub as well as diminutive basement and rooftop bars starring the brothers' formidable brews and wines from their Edgefield winery. Breakfast, lunch, and dinner—tasty tavern fare—are served in the pub. Breakfast vouchers provided to overnighters cover most options, from steel-cut oats with all the trimmings to creative variations on eggs Benedict. *$$; AE, DIS, MC, V; checks OK; reserve@hoteloregon.mcmenamins.com; www.hoteloregon.com; at 3rd St.* &

Steiger Haus Inn / ★

360 SE WILSON ST, MCMINNVILLE; 503/472-0821 Tucked in a neighborhood of older homes on the edge of the Linfield College campus, Steiger Haus is a peaceful oasis. The contemporary cedar-shingled house has a comfortable Northwest feel, with lots of light. Predecessors of current hosts Susan and Dale DuRette designed the inn as a B&B, so downstairs rooms have private decks, offering guests the opportunity to sip coffee outside and enjoy the large, woodsy backyard. All five rooms and suites (three downstairs, two up) have private baths; one downstairs has a fireplace, another, a jetted tub; the upstairs suite has a soaking tub and bay window. Full breakfast might include fresh poached pears, raisin muffins, and German pancakes; the DuRettes provide a specially roasted coffee. *$$; DIS, MC, V; checks OK; steigerhaus@onlinemac.com; www.steigerhaus.com; ¼ mile east of Linfield College entrance.*

Youngberg Hill Vineyards & Inn / ★★★

10660 YOUNGBERG HILL RD, MCMINNVILLE; 503/472-2727 OR 888/657-8668 The setting of this gracious inn can't be beat: from the crest of a 700-foot hill you have views that stretch 180 degrees across the Willamette Valley, including the inn's own 12-acre vineyard. Even in winter, guests may want to take their coffee on the wraparound porch. The inn's vineyard skirts the house, and new owners Wayne and Nicolette Bailey have exciting plans to renovate and expand the current offerings (extending the vineyard, adding spa facilities, and scheduling more weddings, for example). Built in 1989, the rambling contemporary house has seven spacious rooms and suites (three with fireplaces), private baths, fabulous views, and comfortable furnishings. Common areas include a cozy music room and gracious living room, as well as a small gift shop where local wines are sold. A sample breakfast might include guava juice and banana chocolate-chip muffins, followed by a baked apple stuffed with nuts and currants, and then a third course of eggs florentine served with salmon on the grill and spiced yams. The quiet is deeply refreshing, and guests can walk for miles on old logging roads. *$$$; MC, V; checks OK; youngberg@netscape.net; www.youngberghill.com; 12 miles southwest of McMinnville off Youngberg Hill Rd, call for directions.* &

Bellevue

A crossroads 8 miles southwest of McMinnville on Highway 18, this wide spot in the road from Portland to the beach at Lincoln City is a destination in itself, mainly for the **LAWRENCE GALLERY** (19700 SW Hwy 18; 503/843-3633), Oregon's largest—and some say finest—art gallery; don't miss the water-and-sculpture garden outside. The attached **OREGON WINE TASTING ROOM** (19690 SW Hwy 18; 503/843-3787; *www.winesnw.com/oregonwinetastingroom.htm*) lets you sample offerings from some two dozen Oregon wineries. Across the street, **FIRE'S EYE** (19915 SW Muddy Valley Rd; 503/843-9797; *www.fireseye gallery.com*) features clay artists.

RESTAURANTS

Fresh Palate Café / ★

19706 SW HWY 18, BELLEVUE; 503/843-4400 Break up a drive to the beach with breakfast or lunch at this pleasant atelier café. The informal, airy space feels like an extension of the Lawrence Gallery it overlooks, with original art on the walls. To the west, windows look toward forest and farmland, and the door opens onto a broad deck (for summer supping). Everything is freshly made, from salad dressings to bread and desserts. The lunch menu includes sandwiches and entrées, such as pasta dishes and acclaimed crab cakes. At dinner choose from a half-dozen entrées, from grilled honey-mustard filet mignon to a Northwest cioppino. On the 60-bottle list of local wines, at least 15 are always available by the glass. *$$; AE, MC, V; checks OK; lunch every day, full bar; reservations recommended; freshpalatecafe@aol.com; www.freshpalatecafe.com; 7 miles southwest of McMinnville.*

Grande Ronde

This small valley community serves as hub for the Confederated Tribes of Grande Ronde, flourishing largely thanks to the success of **SPIRIT MOUNTAIN CASINO** (27100 SW Salmon River Hwy, Willamina; 800/760-7977; *www.spirit-mountain .com*). The public is also welcome at the tribes' annual powwow in August, and at the **SPIRIT MOUNTAIN STAMPEDE** rodeo in June.

LODGINGS

Spirit Mountain Lodge / ★

27100 SW SALMON RIVER HWY, GRANDE RONDE; 888/668-7366 Oregon's number-one tourist attraction? Spirit Mountain Casino, the state's largest gaming facility. Surprisingly, the attached 5-story, 100-room lodge completed in 1998 is under-stated, stylish, and comfy—a refreshing contrast to the casino's glare and glitz. Pendleton blankets drape every bed; quiet touches of Native American art adorn the walls. Colors are muted and earthy, and solid soundproofing keeps the slots out of earshot. It's everything you'd expect of a modern resort hotel in a remote location—except there's not much to do but gamble: no pool, no spa, no stationary bicycles, not even a walking trail. There is a play area for kids and a video arcade for teens. Food is served in the Legends Restaurant and Coyote Buffet, as well as in two 24-hour cafes, Rock Creek (light meals and snack foods) and Spirit Mountain Café (espresso and pastries). *$$; AE, DIS, MC, V; checks OK; www.spirit-mountain .com; ¼ mile west of Valley Junction.* &

LATINO WOODBURN

When the highway bypassed historic Woodburn's city center, the town's fate seemed sealed, finished off by construction of a huge outlet mall along Interstate 5 in 1999. But a transformation has since taken place here, as local Latinos have reclaimed the 100-year-old brick-and-stone buildings for cafés, shops, and tortillerias reminiscent of their roots in Mexico and Central America.

Take the Woodburn exit (exit 271) from Interstate 5, head east 1½ miles, then follow signs right (Settlemeier Ave) and left (Garfield St) to the city center, minutes from the freeway. Most Latino-owned businesses are clustered within a block or two of First and Hayes Streets.

Your first stop should be **SALVADOR'S BAKERY** (405 N 1st St; 503/982-4513) for fresh-baked sugar cookies or *bolillos*, or traditional Mexican deli items such as *carnitas* or *queso cotija*. Stop in at **LA MORENITA TORTILLERIA** (270 Grant St; 503/982-8221) for tortillas fresh off the griddle or for masa to make your own.

You'll find several fast and inexpensive taquerias, with flavors more familiar in Michoacán than middle America. These aren't the fish tacos they serve at the upscale restaurants back home; **TAQUERIA EL REY** (966 N Pacific Hwy; 503/982-1303), for instance, lists *cabeza* (head), *tripa* (tripe), and *lengua* (tongue) on its taco menu, but no *pescado* (fish).

LUPITA'S RESTAURANT (311 N Front St; 503/982-0483) is a good choice for a sit-down meal; the English-Spanish menu includes offerings from several regional cuisines. **MEXICO LINDO** (430 N 1st St; 503/982-1832) is one of the oldest Latino restaurants in Woodburn and has an attached import shop. There and at **SU CASA IMPORTS** (297 S Front St; 503/981-7361), you can find piñatas, religious statuary, and other staples of Latin American culture.

—*Bonnie Henderson*

Salem and Vicinity

What was once a staid state capitol surrounded by sleepy farmland is now growing like crazy, as Portlanders' notion of an acceptable commute broadens. Look beyond the interstate and its malls, though; you'll still find the upper valley's rural heart in small towns and fields of tulips and irises, brilliant in spring.

Aurora

Antique hunters find a fertile field in this well-preserved historic village. In 1856 Dr. William Keil brought a group of Pennsylvania Germans called the Harmonites to establish a communal settlement. After the death of its founder, the commune faded away; today most visitors are drawn to the town, on the National Register of Historic Places, to comb through antique stores occupying the many clapboard and Victorian houses along US Highway 99E. A former ox barn is now the **OLD AURORA COLONY MUSEUM** (corner of 2nd and Liberty; 503/678-5754; *www.auroracolonymuseum.com*), with unusual and well-displayed artifacts.

History-minded visitors also enjoy nearby **CHAMPOEG STATE PARK** (off Hwy 99W, 7 miles east of Newberg; 503/678-1251; *www.oregonstateparks.org/park_113.php*), site of a historic meeting in 1843 to create the first provisional government by Americans on the Pacific; it's now a fine place to picnic, hike, browse the heirloom garden, or camp in cabins, yurts, or one's own tent or RV. Rose lovers journey a few miles farther up the river (west on Champoeg Rd and across Hwy 219) to **HEIRLOOM OLD GARDEN ROSES** (503/538-1576), one of the country's premier commercial growers of old garden roses.

LODGINGS

Willamette Gables Riverside Estate / ★★

10323 SCHULER RD NE, AURORA; 503/678-2195 It could be an old mansion, well restored, but in fact it's a new mansion, built as a B&B in Southern Plantation style and perched on a bluff overlooking the Willamette. Open since spring 1999, it's a favorite for weddings, with beautifully landscaped grounds and an elegantly appointed interior. Follow the spiral staircase upstairs to five guest rooms, each with a private bath and individually decorated with antiques and convincing reproductions. The Captain's Room features a king-sized sleigh bed, fireplace, and claw-footed tub; the Music Room has a four-poster double bed with wedding ring quilt. The Monet Room also has its own wood-burning fireplace. Downstairs, settle into the lower parlor with its fireplace and baby grand piano, or enjoy a full breakfast with a river view. *$$$; MC, V; checks OK; w.gables@juno .com; www.willamettegables.com; 5 miles west of I-5 at exit 282B, call for directions.* &

Mount Angel

Visit **MOUNT ANGEL ABBEY** (1 Abbey Dr, St. Benedict; 503/845-3030; *www .mtangel.edu*), a century-old Benedictine seminary, on a foggy morning when its celestial setting atop a butte sacred to local Native Americans makes it seem as if it's floating in the clouds. The seminary's library (503/845-3303) is a gem by the internationally celebrated Finnish architect Alvar Aalto. The town is best known for its pull-out-the-stops **OKTOBERFEST** (503/845-9440) in mid-September; the rest of the year, try the home brew and hearty fare at cavernous **MOUNT ANGEL BREWING COMPANY** (210 Monroe St; 503/845-9624; *www.mtangelbrewing.com*).

Silverton

The historic downtown is pretty in summer, with hanging baskets overflowing with flowers and interesting shops to browse; take tea or enjoy lunch at the **OREGON TEA GARDEN** (305 Oak St; 503/873-1230; *www.oregonteagarden.com*). It's named after the **OREGON GARDEN** (503/874-8100; *www.oregongarden.org*), about 2 miles southwest of town off Highway 213, which opened in May 2000; its 240 landscaped acres should make this a world-class attraction as plantings mature. Southeast of town is lush, dramatic **SILVER FALLS STATE PARK** (off Hwy 214, 26 miles east of Salem; 503/873-8681; *www.oregonstateparks.org/park_211.php*), with its concentration of waterfalls, plus camping and hiking, biking, and horse trails. Iris farmers cultivate acres of fields around the town, creating a brilliant palette in late May; that's also the time to wander **COOLEY'S IRIS DISPLAY GARDENS** (11553 Silverton Rd NE; 503/873-5463; *www.cooleysgardens.com*).

RESTAURANTS

Silver Grille Café & Wines / ★★★

206 E MAIN ST, SILVERTON; 503/873-4035 Chef Jeff Nizlek runs this well-known contemporary bistro and wine shop in Silverton's historic downtown. Inside, it's as elegant as a lacquered Chinese box, dimly lit with dark wood wainscoting below dark red grass-paper walls. The menu changes seasonally, with specials chalked on a blackboard, and it is the seasons, and the bounty of Willamette Valley farms and fields, that set direction. Fall finds three locally foraged wild mushrooms merged with white Oregon truffles in a faultless risotto, and a perfectly seared ahi fillet on a bed of black rice, wrapped in a truffle wine sauce. Start with a salad of local organic greens or a terrine of smoked salmon and bay shrimp, and wind up with, say, a dense chocolate cake graced with essence of marionberries; desserts are as seasonal and sensational as entrées. The wine selection is displayed just inside the front door, convenient for retail customers; diners choose here, too, then add a modest corkage fee. *$$; AE, MC, V; checks OK; dinner Wed–Sun; full bar; reservations recommended; silvergrillecafe@aol.com; www.silvergrille.com; at 1st St.* &

LODGINGS

Water Street Inn Bed and Breakfast / ★★

421 WATER ST, SILVERTON; 503/873-3344 OR 866/873-3344 This beautifully appointed B&B reflects the efforts of mother- and daughter-in-law team Sheila and Laurie Rosborough. Closed for a year and renovated throughout, this spacious historic home, originally built in 1890 as the Wolfard Hotel, boasts five immensely comfortable guest rooms, all with private baths—several with double whirlpool tubs and one with a double shower, as well as all the amenities you'd expect of a modern hotel: Internet access, cable TV, and air conditioning. The attention to detail is evident, from the added period crown molding and wall sconces to the exquisite décor and linens in the bedrooms. At breakfast you might be served Grand Marnier french toast, eggs Benedict, or lemon soufflette. The shared formal rooms are gracious and spacious, and the innkeeper's English accent adds to the elegant feel of a time gone by. *$$–$$$; AE, MC, V; checks OK; www.thewaterstreetinn.com; downtown, 1 block off Silver Creek.*

Salem

Handsome parks flank Oregon's 1938 **CAPITOL BUILDING** (900 Court St NE; 503/986-1388; *www.leg.state.or.us/capinfo*), topped by a pioneer sheathed in gold; take in the Depression-era murals in the rotunda on your own or on a free tour, offered daily in summer. Just behind is **WILLAMETTE UNIVERSITY** (900 State St; 503/370-6300; *www.willamette.edu*), the oldest university in the West, founded in 1842. The campus is a happy blend of old and new brick buildings, with Mill Creek nicely incorporated into the landscape. It's a pleasant place to stroll, and plant lovers should visit the small but well-tended botanical gardens. The university's **HALLIE FORD MUSEUM OF ART** (700 State St; 503/370-6855; *www.willamette.edu/museum_of_art*) is the second largest in the state, with some 3,000 pieces of art from around the globe.

Across the road from Willamette University is **HISTORIC MISSION MILL VILLAGE** (1313 Mill St SE; 503/585-7012; *www.missionmill.org*). The impressive 42-acre cluster of restored buildings from the 1800s includes a woolen mill, a parsonage, a Presbyterian church, and several homes. The mill, which drew its power from Mill Creek, now houses a museum that literally makes the sounds of the factory come alive. **JASON LEE HOUSE**, dating from 1841, is the Northwest's oldest remaining frame house; picnic along the stream and feed the ducks. The **SALEM VISITOR INFORMATION CENTER** (503/581-4325 or 800/874-7012; *www.scva.org*) is part of the complex. Also try the **SALEM CHAMBER OF COMMERCE** (1110 Commercial St NE; 503/581-1466; *www.salemchamber.org*) for more information on the surrounding area.

BUSH HOUSE (600 Mission St SE; 503/363-4714; *www.oregonlink.com/bush_house*) is a Victorian home built in 1877 by pioneer newspaper publisher Aashal Bush. It sits in a large park complete with conservatory, rose gardens, hiking paths, and barn turned art gallery. Tours are available Tues to Sun, noon to 5pm May to Sept, and 2–5pm Oct to Apr (last tour begins at 4:30pm).

GILBERT HOUSE CHILDREN'S MUSEUM (116 Marion St NE; 503/371-3631; *www.acgilbert.org*) on the downtown riverfront between the bridges is a delightful hands-on learning and play center for young children. Kids also appreciate **ENCHANTED FOREST** (8462 Enchanted Wy SE, Turner; 503/363-3060 or 503/371-4242; *www.enchantedforest.com*), a nicely wooded storybook park with picnic space.

WILLAMETTE VALLEY VINEYARDS (8800 Enchanted Wy SE, Turner; 503/588-9463; *www.oregonpinot.com*), a big investor-owned winery offering a broad range of wines, commands a spectacular view just south of town. Follow Highway 221 northwest of town to visit several smaller noteworthy wineries, including Stangeland, Witness Tree, Cristom, and Bethel Heights.

For family entertainment featuring music, dance, food, crafts, games, and activities from all over the world, check out late June's **WORLD BEAT FESTIVAL** (503/581-2004; *www.worldbeatfestival.org*) held in Riverfront Park. If you visit during the 10 days of the **OREGON STATE FAIR** (503/947-3247; *www.oregonstatefair.org*), held around Labor Day, don't miss it—it's one of the Northwest's biggest.

RESTAURANTS

Alessandro's 120 / ★★

120 COMMERCIAL ST NE, SALEM; 503/370-9951 Simple, elegant pasta and sea-food dishes are the strong suit at this longtime downtown favorite. The menu isn't particularly original, but the classics are mostly done well, starting with fresh ingredients: perfectly cooked veal piccata, rich meat-stuffed tortellini in light cream sauce. In addition to the regular menu, a multicourse dinner is offered; the staff asks if there's a particular dish you *don't* like, and they surprise you with the rest. The wine menu is strong on Italy. Service is quiet and professional, and jazz is live Friday and Saturday nights. *$$; AE, DIS, MC, V; no checks; lunch Mon–Fri, dinner every day; full bar; reservations recommended; info@alessandros120.com; www.alessandros120.com; near Court St.* ♿

The Arbor Café / ★★

380 HIGH ST NE, SALEM; 503/588-2353 The Arbor Café feels a bit out of place—an informal, airy garden café camped in a steel-and-concrete "plaza" at the foot of a downtown office tower. It's not the most elegant spot, but it's the locals' eatery of choice. Stop for continental breakfast—house-made pastries and espresso. Midday, try a muffuletta *panini*, some homemade soup, maybe honey-mustard chicken salad. At dinner, you can go simple with soup and a sandwich, but entrées are compelling: Sichuan stir-fry is lightly spicy and comes with beef or prawns, and cashew chicken is sauced with ginger, lime, and chile. Provençal meatloaf dresses up this old chestnut with a savory roasted-shallot brown gravy. A number of microbrews are joined by a small selection of Oregon and Italian wines. Desserts perform solidly, particularly dense, flavorful cakes. *$$; MC, V; local checks only; breakfast, lunch Mon–Sat, dinner Wed–Sat; beer and wine; reservations for 6 or more; between Center and Chemeketa Sts.* ♿

j. james restaurant / ★★

325 HIGH ST SE, SALEM; 503/362-0888 Chef-owner Jeff James's eponymous restaurant is a bright light in the Salem dining scene. An Oregon native, James uses the region's ingredients in simple but creative dishes, including starters such as Oregon shrimp, whole kernel corn, and fresh dill risotto or Bandon white cheddar and goat cheese tart with spicy onion jam and citrus reduction. There are entrées to please all tastes, like grilled pork loin marinated in molasses or salmon poached in a lightly spiced broth. The kitchen occasionally missteps—overdone fish in one daily special and a mustard vinaigrette that overwhelmed a salad—but the chef's experience more than often prevails. The large, awkward space by a parking garage is softened by white linens, floor-to-ceiling windows, and bold paint. The service is crisp and professional, the wine list moderately priced. *$$; AE, MC, V; checks OK; lunch Mon–Fri, dinner Mon–Sat; full bar; reservations recommended; www.jjamesrestaurant.com; downtown, in Pringle Park Plaza.* ♿

Morton's Bistro Northwest / ★★★

1128 EDGEWATER NW, SALEM; 503/585-1113 A clever design puts the diner below roadway level, looking out on an attractive courtyard backed by an ivy-covered wall that screens a busy highway. The interior is intimate, with dark wood beams, soft lighting, and a convivial feel from the ricocheting conversations. The menu is solidly Northwestern with hints of international influences, and everything on the plate works together brilliantly. A salmon fillet might be accompanied by a potato-pumpkin mash with basil and balsamic braised tomatoes; vegetarian lasagne combines roasted red peppers, mushrooms, goat cheese, and spinach. Give serious consideration to the mixed grill or the cioppino. Service is expert and pleasant, and the selection of reasonably priced Northwest wines is good. *$$; MC, V; checks OK; dinner Tues–Sat; full bar; reservations recommended; steve@mortonsbistronw.com; www.mortonsbistronw.com; between Gerth and McNary Aves in West Salem.* &

LODGINGS

Mill Creek Inn

3125 RYAN DR SE, SALEM; 503/585-3332 OR 800/346-9659 In a town dominated by chain lodgings, this well-kept motel run by Best Western is the nicest of the lot. The 109 spacious guest rooms all have microwaves, minifridges, data ports, even irons and ironing boards. Amenities include an indoor pool, Jacuzzi, and fitness room. It's just off Interstate 5, but close enough to the city center to be convenient for business or pleasure travelers. *$; AE, DC, DIS, MC, V; no checks; www.bestwestern.com/millcreekinn; exit 253 off I-5.* &

Independence

This riverside town looks pretty untouched by modern times. If you want to remind yourself (or learn) what an old-fashioned fountain was like, visit **TAYLOR'S FOUNTAIN AND GIFT** (296 S Main St; 503/838-1124), at Monmouth St. The **RIVER GALLERY** (184 S Main St; 503/838-6171; *www.oregonlink.com/rivergallery*) exhibits the work of local artists, who also take turns staffing the place; in September the gallery organizes an annual "Fish Run," in which foam-core salmon embellished by area artists are displayed outdoors and auctioned off to fund an art scholarship. Just northeast of the town center is Independence State Airport, where you can grab a basic breakfast at **ANNIE'S AT THE AIRPORT** (4705 Airport Rd; 503/838-5632) and hobnob with pilots of the small and often homebuilt planes that frequent the place. Southeast of town the four-car **BUENA VISTA FERRY** (503/588-7979) still shuttles cars across the Willamette the old-fashioned way (Wed to Sun, Apr to Oct).

RESTAURANTS

Buena Vista House Café and Lodging / ★★

11265 RIVERVIEW ST, INDEPENDENCE; 503/838-6364 "Sort of a wayward house for people who like good food, good music, and quiet places" is how innkeeper Claudia Prevost describes the welcoming hostelry she's created out of a 110-year-old house two blocks from the Buena Vista Ferry. Stop for a stellar scone and an excellent cup of coffee or espresso, or stay for lunch, choosing from a small menu that might include salmon croquettes one day or wild mushroom quiche another. In sunny weather, sit under the ancient apple trees in the garden out back. Three guest rooms upstairs are appointed with antiques in a refreshingly spare country style; all share one large bath. *$; no credit cards; checks OK; breakfast, lunch Wed–Sat, brunch Sun; no alcohol; reservations required for Sunday brunch; south of Independence on the ferry access road.*

Albany and Corvallis

Time and the interstate have bypassed Albany, which is probably a blessing. Once you get off the freeway (ignore the smell of the nearby pulp mill), you'll discover a fine representative of the small-town Oregon of an earlier era, with broad, quiet streets, neat houses, and a slow pace. Corvallis is a pleasant mix of old river town and funky university burg. In 1998 Corvallis was the first city in Oregon to ban all smoking in restaurants, bars, and taverns, and it's ideal for biking and running; most streets include wide bike lanes, and routes follow both the Willamette and Marys Rivers.

Albany

Once an important transportation hub in the Willamette Valley, Albany has an unequaled selection of historic homes and buildings in a wide variety of styles; many of them have been lovingly restored. You can see 13 distinct architectural styles in the 50-block, 368-building Monteith Historic District. Then there are the Hackleman (28 blocks, 210 buildings) and Downtown (9½ blocks, 80 buildings) Historic Districts. Many buildings are open for inspection on annual tours—the last Saturday in July and the Sunday evening before Christmas Eve. A handy, free guide, "Seems Like Old Times," is available from the **ALBANY CONVENTION AND VISITORS CENTER** (300 SW 2nd; 800/526-2256; *www.albanyvisitors.com*).

Wander First Avenue, where it all began: have a cup at **BOCCHERINI'S COFFEE AND TEA HOUSE** (208 1st Ave SW; 541/926-6703) or a pint at **WYATT'S EATERY & BREWHOUSE** (211 1st Ave NW; 541/917-3727). In summer, enjoy an outdoor concert as part of the River Rhythms series at **MONTEITH RIVERPARK** (Water Ave and Washington St; 541/917-7772; *www.riverrhythms.org*).

The covered bridges that were so characteristic of this area in the mid-1900s are disappearing; from 300 throughout Oregon, their number has dwindled to fewer than 50. But that's still more than in any state west of the Mississippi. Most remaining bridges are in the Willamette Valley counties of Lane and Linn and, to the west, Lincoln. Best starting points for easy-to-follow circuits of the bridges are Albany, Eugene, and Cottage Grove. Six bridges lie within an 8-mile radius of Scio, northeast of Albany; for a map, contact the Albany Convention and Visitors Center. For other tours, send an SASE with two first-class stamps to the **COVERED BRIDGE**

SOCIETY OF OREGON (PO Box 1804, Newport, OR 97365; 541/265-2934; *coveredbridges.stateoforegon.com*).

RESTAURANTS

Sybaris / ★★★

442 SW 1ST AVE, ALBANY; 541/928-8157 This elegant restaurant opened in 2001 in the former Capriccio Ristorante space on Albany's historic First Ave. The former owners kept the exposed brick and large windows when they renovated, adding an English-style wood-burning fireplace and scattering tables around the high-ceilinged room. Enter current chef-owner Matt Bennett, whose menus reflect a fearless and playful approach to food. On any given day, "spaghetti and meatballs" might mean balls of ahi tuna in a ginger-tomato sauce with black squid ink pasta; "roast" could be venison loin with mashed root vegetables and a huckleberry-port sauce. Bennett relies on a couple of local farms for many of his ingredients and plans his monthly menus according to what's in season. The generous entrées may lead you to pass on dessert, which would be a shame, for you'd miss the Sybaris chocolate hazelnut cake, a dense, flourless, decadent work of art filled with a cache of crème brûlée. The wine list is short but well matched to the menu. *$$; AE, MC, V; checks OK; dinner Tues–Sat; full bar; reservations recommended; www.sybarisbistro.com.* &

Corvallis

The Willamette River lines small, lively downtown Corvallis, with the 19th-century **BENTON COUNTY COURTHOUSE** (120 NW 4th St) lending a nostalgic charm. Get touring information downtown at **CORVALLIS TOURISM** (553 NW Harrison Blvd; 541/757-1544 or 800/334-8118; *www.visitcorvallis.com*). Poke around interesting shops, and stop for pastry and coffee at **NEW MORNING BAKERY** (219 SW 2nd St; 541/754-0181) or **THE BEANERY** (500 SW 2nd St; 541/753-7442). Don't miss the newly renovated **RIVERFRONT PARK** at First and Madison, a beautifully paved pedestrian esplanade that runs for several blocks along the Willamette River. You'll find a lovely fountain, stone benches, picnic tables, and interesting sculpture by Northwest artists. This is also the home of the local **SATURDAY FARMERS MARKET**, May through October.

The **OREGON STATE UNIVERSITY** (15th and Jefferson Sts; 541/737-0123; *www.orst.edu*) campus is typical of big Northwest universities, with a gracious core of old buildings, magnificent trees, and open space. Corvallis has a thriving arts scene; visit the **CORVALLIS ART CENTER** (700 SW Madison Ave; 541/754-1551; *www.caclbca.org*) in a renovated 1889 Episcopal church off Central Park.

Tree lovers will enjoy **MCDONALD STATE FOREST** (off Hwy 99W, 6 miles north of Corvallis), with its 10 miles of biking, horseback riding, and hiking trails, including one among the native and exotic plants of **PEAVY ARBORETUM**. For a bigger outing, head west on Highway 34 to **MARY'S PEAK**, the tallest point in the Coast Range at 4,097 feet; stroll the last mile to the summit, or try any of several interconnecting forest paths. **WALDPORT RANGER DISTRICT** (541/563-3211) has details. Look for dusky Canada geese from trails in **FINLEY NATIONAL WILDLIFE REFUGE** (541/757-7236), 10 miles south of town on Highway 99W.

RESTAURANTS

Big River / ★★★

101 NW JACKSON ST, CORVALLIS; 541/757-0694 Arty, jazzy, noisy—Big River brought big flavors to Corvallis and became a big hit. Against an industrial-strength background (high ceilings with exposed beams and ductwork), Big River has added lots of bold original art, color, and whimsy. Food is bold as well, and solidly, eclecticly Northwest, with a taste of Sichuan here, a bit of curry there, and lots of fresh (often organic) local produce. Appetizers range from grilled homemade bread with kalamata olive tapenade to garlicky steamed Manila clams. You'll find at least a dozen entrées, half of them vegetarian, on the menu, which changes daily; consider the rolled polenta with spinach, provolone, and portobellos, or the duck with orange and dried black cherry sauce. Interesting pizzas are baked in a wood-fired oven, and desserts are equally original and good. Or order off the menu in the Bow Truss Bar; perch at a high table or burrow into an upholstered chair to enjoy live jazz and a glass of wine or a shot from a long menu of Kentucky bourbons and single-malt Scotches. The glass dessert case is unbearably tantalizing; a private dining room seats up to 100. *$$; AE, DC, MC, V; checks OK; lunch Mon–Fri, dinner Mon–Sat; full bar; reservations for 8 or more; www.bigriverrest.com; at 1st St.* &

Bombs Away Cafe / ★

2527 NW MONROE AVE, CORVALLIS; 541/757-7221 This is a taqueria with an attitude. You'll find several Tex-Mex favorites—with a wholesome twist: heaps of herb-flavored brown rice and black beans and hardly any fat. Among the favorites are flautas stuffed with duck confit, top sirloin steak with tasty tomatillo chipotle sauce, and a smoked tofu, shiitake, peppers, and zucchini chimichanga. The menu is loaded with vegetarian options, and has a short list of simple, inexpensive kids' meals. Order at the counter in the front room. The ambiance is basic college campus casual, the help is friendly, and the service speedy. The bar in back offers an impressive variety of tequilas. Saturday night is Mom's night; mothers eat half price when accompanied by their children. *$; MC, V; checks OK; lunch Mon–Fri, dinner every day; full bar; reservations for 6 or more; www.bombs awaycafe.com; at NW 25th St.* &

Iovino's / ★★★

126 SW 1ST ST, CORVALLIS; 541/738-9015 From concrete floors to high ceilings in this former garage, Iovino's has the industrial feel of a converted New York loft—and a stylish sophistication you don't expect in Corvallis. Nothing on the nouvelle Italian menu is quite what you'd anticipate, and the surprises are all pleasant. Consider starting with bruschetta swathed in piquant caramelized onions, tomatoes, capers, and Gorgonzola (you'll need a fork for this finger food), or *insalata di noce*—chopped greens and a cache of minced hazelnuts. The sweet marsala sauce on the turkey scallops melds brilliantly with mashed ricotta potatoes, and a basil dressing happily marries the plate of tiger prawns to the herb-breaded eggplant underneath. Many entrées come in either small or full-sized portions. The tiramisù is terrific, as is chocolate mousse served in a lemonade glass. The short wine list is matched by an inventive martini menu. *$$; AE, MC, V; checks OK; lunch Mon–Fri, dinner every day; full bar; reservations for 6 or more; at Monroe Ave.* &

Le Bistro / ★★

150 SW MADISON AVE, CORVALLIS; 541/754-6680 The name is misleading: this is a fine French restaurant, a modest *chef d'oeuvre* of French chef Robert Merlet, who arrived in Corvallis via Paris, Bordeaux, and the San Francisco Bay Area. The atmosphere is quiet and intimate, the food lovingly prepared in the classic French manner: no fireworks, but ingredients are fresh and everything is cooked just right. Roast duckling might come with fresh rhubarb and a French sweet-and-sour demi-glace; grilled fish choices are lightly sauced; cheese tortellini comes with diced vegetables and roasted-garlic pesto. Not all restaurants get risotto right, but Le Bistro does. You know it's French when the menu includes not only escargots and sweetbreads but the simplicity of sliced tomatoes with a bit of anchovy and feta, and dessert choices include profiteroles, a fresh fruit tartlet, and melt-in-your-mouth mousse. *$$; MC, V; local checks only; dinner Tues–Sat; full bar; reservations recommended; www.lebistro.com; downtown near NW 1st St.*

Magenta / ★★

1425 NW MONROE AVE, STE A, CORVALLIS; 541/758-3494 "European style with Asian flair" is how chef-owner Kim Hoang, former Nike executive, describes her elegant little bistro just off campus. Inside she's created the feel of a genteel establishment in French colonial Vietnam—antiques and tropical plants—and her eclectic menu of well-prepared dishes follows suit. You'll find seafood and fowl on the menu, but Hoang specializes in unusual meats, from buffalo steak to cabernet-glazed emu. Appetizers might include green papaya salad or fresh spring rolls. A menu of small dishes is available in the bar all evening and in the dining room after 8:30pm. *$$; AE, DIS, MC, V; lunch Mon–Fri, dinner every day; full bar; reservations recommended; next to Oregon State University.* &

LODGINGS

Hanson Country Inn / ★★

795 SW HANSON ST, CORVALLIS; 541/752-2919 The inn is just a few minutes from town, but you'll feel you're in the country when you reach this wood-and-brick 1928 farmhouse. Formerly a prosperous poultry ranch, it's now a registered historic home, thanks to extensive renovation by former San Franciscan Patricia Covey. The gleaming living room (with piano and fireplace), sun-room, and library are often used for weddings. Step outside to a formal lawn and garden. Two large guest suites upstairs are luxuriously wallpapered and linened, each with its own sitting room, deck, and private bath. After breakfasting on crepes with blackberries, or a fresh frittata, explore the grounds and the original egg house. If you're traveling with kids, take the two-bedroom cottage behind the main house with fully equipped kitchen, private bath, and living area. *$$–$$$; AE, DIS, MC, V; checks OK; hcibb@aol.com; www.hcinn.com; 5 minutes west of town.*

Harrison House Bed and Breakfast / ★

2310 NW HARRISON BLVD, CORVALLIS; 541/752-6248 OR 800/233-6248 Three blocks from the Oregon State University campus, Harrison House makes a homey base camp for a Corvallis stay—nothing innovative in the way of decor, but nicely appointed and immaculate. The restored 1939 Dutch Colonial is in a neighborhood of older homes, and owners Maria and Charlie Tomlinson are gracious and accommodating. Four large rooms are furnished with a mix of antiques and reproductions and all have private baths. The English Garden Cottage comes with kitchenette and sitting area; it's available when the hosts' sons are out of town. Enjoy a microbrew or a glass of wine when you arrive, and let Maria know your breakfast preferences for the next morning: just fruit with scones or muffins, or a full meal with the likes of eggs Benedict or stuffed crepes. *$$; AE, DC, DIS, JCB, MC, V; checks OK; stay@corvallis-lodging.com; www.corvallis-lodging.com; at 23rd St.*

Eugene

Portland's laid-back sister to the south may be the state's second-largest urban area, but it's still something of an overgrown small town, with enough local color—from tree-hugging hippies to pro-growth developers—to keep life interesting. There's no skyline here—unless you count the grain elevator and 12-story Hilton—and a Eugenean's idea of a traffic jam is when it takes more than five minutes to traverse downtown.

Still there's a sophisticated cultural scene, with respected symphony, ballet, opera, and theater companies. The **UNIVERSITY OF OREGON** (13th Ave and University St; 541/346-3111; *www.uoregon.edu*)—the state's flagship institution—provides more speakers and events than one could possibly attend. The university also features natural history and art museums, several historic landmark buildings, and a good bookstore (541/346-4331). There are other good bookstores in town—don't miss **SMITH FAMILY BOOKSTORE** (768 E 13th Ave; 541/345-1651 or 541/343-4714)—as well as the requisite number of coffeehouses, fabulous bakeries, and trendy brew pubs. Try **STEELHEAD** (199 E 5th Ave; 541/686-2739), in the Fifth Avenue historic district, or the **WILD DUCK** (169 W 6th Ave; 541/485-3825; *www.wildduckbrewery.com*). Two serious chocolatiers set up shop here: **EUPHORIA** (6 W 17th Ave; 541/345-1990; *www.euphoriachocolate.com*) and **FENTON & LEE** (35 E 8th Ave; 541/343-7629; *www.fentonandlee.com*), and there's an elegant French tea shop—**SAVOURE** (201 W Broadway; 541/242-1010) in the new Broadway Place development. Breathe deep; every restaurant and bar in town is smoke-free by law.

The **WILLAMETTE AND MCKENZIE RIVERS** run through or near town and provide opportunities for canoeists and rafters. Hikers find miles of forest trails just outside the city limits. Runners love the city's several groomed, packed running trails. Run along the banks of the Willamette through **ALTON BAKER PARK** (off Centennial

Blvd) on the groomed **PREFONTAINE TRAIL**. Solo runners may feel safer on the sloughside circuit that borders **AMAZON PARK** (off Amazon Pkwy). **HENDRICKS PARK** (follow signs from Fairmont Blvd), the city's oldest, features an outstanding 10-acre rhododendron garden; best blooms are in May and early June.

Whatever else you do in Eugene, hike the 1½-mile trail up **SPENCER'S BUTTE** (off S Willamette St), the landmark just south of town, for a spectacular view of the city, valley, and its two rivers. Spend a morning at **SATURDAY MARKET** (Oak St at Broadway; 541/686-8885; April through fall), the state's oldest outdoor crafts fair; shop and eat your way through the **FIFTH AVENUE PUBLIC MARKET** (5th Ave and High St) one afternoon; and attend the **HULT CENTER FOR THE PERFORMING ARTS** (7th Ave and Willamette St; 541/342-5746; *www.hultcenter.org*), the city's world-class concert facility, with two architecturally striking halls. In early July, don't miss the area's oldest and wildest countercultural celebration, the **OREGON COUNTRY FAIR** (541/343-4298; *www.oregoncountryfair.org*).

RESTAURANTS

Adam's Place / ★★★

30 E BROADWAY, EUGENE; 541/344-6948 Adam Bernstein, a third-generation restaurateur who trained at the Culinary Institute of America, has tastefully decorated this intimate downtown spot by adding mahogany wainscoting, arches, pillars, sconces, and a lovely fireplace. The result is quietly sophisticated, unpretentious yet classy—think San Francisco. Service is attentive, presentation exquisite, and the cuisine inventive, with a menu that changes seasonally. Catch the salmon and dill potato pancake with dill crème frâiche and salsa appetizer; or the grilled eggplant, tomato, and warm duck salad. For an entrée, consider salmon—perfectly undercooked—topped with a sweet, tangy, chutneylike orange glaze; or seared Hawaiian ahi over marinated cucumber in soy-ginger sauce. Vegetarian options are always interesting, and desserts are stunning. An award-winning wine list, with many by the glass, adds to the experience. Attached to the restaurant, Luna is the spot to hear live jazz; it has lighter pub fare featuring Spanish tapas. *$$–$$$; AE, MC, V; checks OK; dinner Tues–Sat; full bar; reservations recommended; www.adamsplacerestaurant.com; on the downtown mall.* &

Ambrosia / ★

174 E BROADWAY, EUGENE; 541/342-4141 Pizzas are wonderful here: small, crisp pies topped with rich plum tomato sauce and trendy ingredients (sun-dried tomatoes, artichoke hearts, roasted eggplant), baked in a huge wood-burning oven. But Ambrosia is much more than a designer pizzeria: take the ravioli San Remo, homemade and stuffed with veal, chicken, and ricotta; or the dill-sauced crepes filled with smoked salmon, spinach, and ricotta. Low lighting creates a warm, intimate atmosphere in this cavernous restaurant, where tables are tucked into "rooms" on the ground floor or scattered on an airy mezzanine; sit at the gorgeous wooden bar to take in the chefs' oven action. End the evening with a cool bowl of homemade gelato. *$$; MC, V; local checks only; lunch Mon–Fri, dinner every day; full bar; reservations recommended for 6 or more; www.ambrosiarestaurant.com; at Pearl St.* &

Beppe and Gianni's Trattoria / ★★★

1646 E 19TH AVE, EUGENE; 541/683-6661 John Barofsky and Italian native Beppe Macchi have created a neighborhood trattoria with the spirit and flavor of Beppe's homeland. The old house it occupies retained most of its interior walls, creating nice nooks for intimate dining, though there's a family feel to the place, with Beppe shouting greetings to friends and customers, and tables jammed with a town-and-gown crowd. Antipasto choices include bruschetta and melon with prosciutto di Parma. Salads include a lovely fresh orange-and-grapefruit arrangement with a light Sicilian vinaigrette. Primi dishes—mostly imported or homemade pasta with lovely, light sauces and accompaniments—are generous enough to serve as the main course, including melt-in-your-mouth ravioli of the day and excellent risottos. Secondi entrées are classical presentations of, for example, grilled fish, sautéed chicken breast (with wild mushrooms in a marsala sauce), or rosemary-perfumed lamb chops. Choose a glass or bottle from a short, modestly priced wine list. *Bambini* have several inexpensive menu choices. Desserts don't disappoint. *$$; MC, V; checks OK; dinner every day; beer and wine; reservations for 8 or more Sun–Thurs; east of Agate St.* &

Café Soriah / ★★

384 W 13TH AVE, EUGENE; 541/342-4410 In this jewel box of a neighborhood restaurant, chef-owner Ibrahim Hamide has wrapped an adventurous Mediterranean and Middle Eastern menu in an elegant little package, comfortable enough for everyday dining but deserving of special occasions. Squeeze past the tiny bar—a work of art in wood—to reach the pretty, well-appointed dining room, airy and smart with original art and fine woodworking; the atmosphere is intimate but not claustrophobic. In good weather, dine outdoors in the leafy, stylish walled terrace. Hamide's roots are revealed in the menu, starting with a stellar appetizer plate of hummus, *baba gannoujh,* and stuffed grape leaves sized for two or more. The menu changes monthly and might include roasted salmon with a coconut-curry sauce, or marlin Gaza-style (spicy); count on favorites such as lamb tagine and moussaka. Memorable desserts range from wonderful amalgams of sponge cake and buttercream to a subtly exotic cardamom-scented flan. *$$; AE, MC, V; checks OK; lunch Mon–Fri, dinner every day; full bar; reservations recommended; www.soriah.com; at Lawrence St.* &

Chanterelle / ★★

207 E 5TH ST, EUGENE; 541/484-4065 Chef Ralf Schmidt's intimate restaurant is sophisticated and understated, with a small menu that reflects Schmidt's classical French culinary sensibilities and hints at his Austrian roots. You'll find escargots bourguignonne and oysters Rockefeller among a handful of appetizers; the traditional baked French onion soup is deeply satisfying. A dozen entrée choices—from delicate coquilles St. Jacques to richly sauced tournedos of beef and a classic zwiebelsteak—are supplemented by a wide selection of specials, from spring lamb to chinook salmon. All come with salad and choice of potatoes or spaetzle. You'll find a respectable wine list and extraordinary desserts made by the chef's wife, Gisela. *$$$;*

AE, DC, MC, V; checks OK; dinner Tues–Sat; full bar; reservations recommended; across from public market. &

Excelsior Inn Ristorante Italiano / ★★★

754 E 13TH AVE, EUGENE; 541/342-6963 OR 800/321-6963 When it opened some 30 years ago, the Excelsior was the first restaurant to bring European sophistication to Eugene; it's since met with serious competition, but the Ex remains one of Eugene's better restaurants. Current owner–executive chef Maurizio Paparo has brought his Italian background to bear in the menu and the interior. Look for medallions of elk sauced with a fig-molasses demi-glace, or fresh fettucini with chicken in a garlic-rosemary-sherry sauce. The filet mignon, topped with a brandy-mushroom demi-glace, may be the best in town. Desserts by pastry chef Milka Babich are themselves worth a visit, ranging from the simplicity of crème caramel to the Grand Marnier–infused Maurizio's cake topped with white and dark chocolate curls. The wine list is well chosen and extensive. Sit by the fireplace in the formal dining room, in the airy European-style bar on the skylit terrace, or in the walled courtyard out front. *$$–$$$; AE, DC, DIS, MC, V; checks OK; breakfast, dinner every day, lunch Mon–Fri, brunch Sun; full bar; reservations recommended; info@excelsiorinn.com; www.excelsiorinn.com; across from Sacred Heart Medical Center.* &

The LocoMotive Restaurant / ★★

291 E 5TH AVE, EUGENE; 541/465-4754 Owners Lee and Eitan Zucker came to Eugene via Israel, the Caribbean, and Manhattan, and they bring sophistication and subtlety to vegetarian cooking in their friendly restaurant backed against the railroad tracks in the lively Fifth Street Public Market district. The menu is 100 percent vegetarian (vegan on request), ingredients nearly 100 percent organic, and results 100 percent delicious. The Zuckers know the world's variety of legumes and grains and enjoy playing with them. With your bread, you're served an "appetizer mix" of nicely seasoned beans. The menu changes weekly but always includes wonderful soups; try the South Indian *rasam*. Musts include portobello mushrooms in reduced red wine sauce with garlic mashed potatoes, and curried eggs with house-made chutney. Don't miss the Oregon Snow—creamy white sorbet with flavors of lime and coconut. *$$; MC, V; checks OK; dinner Wed–Sat (closed 2–3 weeks in Jan and July); beer and wine; reservations recommended; www.thelocomotive.com; across from public market.* &

Marché / ★★★

296 E 5TH AVE, EUGENE; 541/342-3612 The name of this elegant restaurant, on the ground floor of the Fifth Street Public Market, says it all: Marché's menu is an ode to the seasonal Northwest bounty, prepared with French sensibility. Each day's menu lists well-crafted combinations of fresh and often organically grown local foodstuffs. In fall, locally raised pork chops may come with an autumn fruit-and-onion confit, and the sage-infused roasted leg of venison is accompanied by sweet potato purée, baked apple, and huckleberry sauce. Lunch is lighter, with the addition of a few *pizzettas* (picture pancetta, *delicata* squash, sage, and Romano cheese) and sandwiches (consider portobello mushroom with sun-dried tomato relish and smoked mozzarella on homemade flatbread). The wine list and dessert menu reflect the same regional leanings and attention to detail. The interior is elegantly hip with dark gleaming wood and wry artwork. In a hurry? Try Café Marché upstairs. *$$–$$$; AE, DC, DIS, MC, V; checks OK; lunch, dinner every day, brunch Sun; full bar; reservations recommended; www.marcherestaurant .com; in public market.* &

Red Agave / ★★

454 WILLAMETTE ST, EUGENE; 541/683-2206 Voted best new restaurant by the *Eugene Weekly* in 2003, Red Agave is a distinctive blend of Nuevo-Latino cuisine. It was opened by locals (and former roommates) Sara Willis and Katie Marcus-Brown, and Jeff Dessler. The high ceilings and warm yellow walls make the open floor plan feel lively and vibrant. Start with a whole-leaf Tijuana Caesar salad for two and move on to local pattypan squash vegetarian tamales or rum-marinated pork loin, pan seared and served with a jalapeño-Jamaica drizzle. Mixmaster Jeff Morgenthaler adds his own special twist to the full bar, and desserts range from spiced Mexican chocolate cheesecake with warm caramel-arbol chile sauce to an aged manchego cheese plate served with quince paste, cayenne, toasted almonds, and Palace Bakery baguette. Quite a mouthful, whatever you choose. *$$–$$$; AE, MC, V; local checks only; dinner Tues–Sun, brunch Sat–Sun; full bar; reservations recommended; across from train station.* &

Ring of Fire / ★★

1099 CHAMBERS ST, EUGENE; 541/344-6475 Pull open the heavy entry door, inhale the exotic fragrances from the kitchen, and allow Ring of Fire's elegant, tranquil ambiance to transport you far from busy, strip-malled W 11th Street. The menu claims inspiration from many Pacific Rim cuisines, mainly Thai and Indonesian. Start with a Korean-style vegetable tempura served with homemade plum sauce, or a taste of beef satay with black bean–ginger sauce. Curries are coconut-based, Thai style, and noodle dishes include the reliable phad thai as well as phad se yu, with sweet wheat noodles and broccoli. Crispy ginger red snapper comes with roasted garlic and vegetables. Many dishes offer meat, tofu, or tempeh options. Portions are generous. Takeout is available until midnight. Try a "My Thai" or other original tropical drink from the stylish little Lava Lounge. *$$; MC, V; no checks; lunch, dinner every day; full bar; reservations recommended; rof@ringoffirerestaurant.com; www.ringoffirerestaurant.com; off W 11th Ave.* &

Zenon Cafe / ★★★

898 PEARL ST, EUGENE; 541/343-3005 A compelling combination of culinary imagination and consistency has made Zenon one of Eugene's best restaurants. Urbane, noisy, crowded, and invariably interesting, Zenon offers an ever-changing international menu featuring, on any given night, Italian, Greek, Middle Eastern, Cajun, Caribbean, Thai, and Northwest cuisines. Nothing disappoints, from Chinese "Hot as Hell" skewered pork tenderloin with cucumber relish and daikon-carrot salad, to sautéed duck breast with raspberry demi-glace, sautéed shiitake mushrooms, and wild rice. Vegetarian dishes range from a lovely eggplant-based dish named "The Priest Fainted" to Southwest-inspired black bean–posole chili. For a light meal, have a bowl of the day's soup and a basket of fresh breads. A good selection of regional wines by the glass (and bottle) is available, as is Zenon's complex summer sangria, juicy with fresh seasonal fruits. Zenon's dessert list is the city's largest and one of the best. In the spirit of lively European restaurants, this is a good place for kids; it's already loud, and the chef is happy to provide plates of plain fettucine with cheese. *$$; MC, V; checks OK; breakfast, lunch, dinner every day; beer and wine; no reservations; corner of E Broadway.* &

LODGINGS

Campbell House / ★★★

252 PEARL ST, EUGENE; 541/343-1119 OR 800/264-2519 Built in 1892 and restored as a grand bed-and-breakfast inn, Campbell House has everything: a location that's quiet (an acre of beautifully landscaped grounds) yet convenient (two blocks from Fifth Street Public Market); elegant, light-filled rooms with Old World charm (four-poster beds, high ceilings, dormer windows) and modern amenities (TVs and VCRs tastefully hidden, wireless Internet access, stocked minifridges); and smart, attentive service. Each of the 18 rooms has a private bath, several have gas fireplaces, and one—the Dr. Eva Johnson Room—has a luxurious bathroom alcove with jetted tub. The inn is designated nonsmoking, but the Cogswell Room offers a private entrance that opens onto a pretty patio for those who must. Or check out the Celeste Cottage, a separate guest house located next door and available as a one- or two-bedroom, complete with gas fireplace and wet bar. If you like the personalized service of a B&B but don't like to feel hovered over, if you love country-cottage decor but lament Laura Ashley frills, this is your kind of place. Full breakfast features waffles, homemade granola, and a special egg dish. *$$–$$$$; AE, DC, DIS, MC, V; no checks; campbellhouse@campbellhouse.com; www.campbellhouse.com; 2 blocks north of public market.* &

Excelsior Inn / ★★

754 E 13TH AVE, EUGENE; 541/342-6963 OR 800/321-6963 This European-style inn sits atop the Excelsior restaurant, 2 blocks from the University of Oregon. Each of the 14 rooms is named for a composer and is charmingly decorated, featuring hardwood floors, arched windows, vaulted ceilings, and marble-and-tile baths with fluffy towels. There are a variety of rooms for every budget but all rooms have TVs, VCRs, and computer hookups; two have Jacuzzi tubs. The Bach Room, with its king-sized sleigh bed, pretty sitting area, and Jacuzzi, is a favorite. The downside: most rooms are small, some with a view of a blank wall, and the reception at the inn's alley entrance can be uncertain; you may have to chase down an innkeeper at the attached restaurant. The upside: Old World ambiance, good soundproofing, and amenities that cover the bases. An excellent complimentary breakfast is served in the restaurant, where guests order from the regular menu. *$–$$$$; AE, DC, DIS, MC, V; no checks; info@excelsiorinn.com; www.excelsiorinn.com; across from Sacred Heart Medical Center.* &

Hilton Eugene and Conference Center / ★

66 E 6TH AVE, EUGENE; 541/342-2000 OR 800/937-6660 For convenience to downtown, the Hilton fits the bill. Many of the guest rooms were remodeled in 2002 and have nice city views from south-facing rooms and quiet views of Skinner Butte from north-facing rooms. It's attached to the Eugene Conference Center, across a brick courtyard from the Hult Center for the Performing Arts, a block from the downtown mall, and within easy strolling distance of most of Eugene's best restaurants. Amenities include a (very small) indoor pool along with sauna, Jacuzzi, fitness room, bike rentals, and on-site Hertz rental car office. *$$–$$$; AE, DC, DIS, MC, V; checks OK; www.eugene.hilton.com; exit 194B off I-5.* &

Secret Garden / ★★

1910 UNIVERSITY ST, EUGENE; 541/484-6755 OR 888/484-6755 Originally a 1910 farmhouse, this is now an airy, enchanting 10-room inn on a hilltop just south of the University of Oregon campus. Thoughtfully chosen art and antiques give the inn a refined feeling reminiscent of the Edwardian era from which the novel of the same name sprung. Each room is individually decorated, taking cues from the garden, from the rusticity of the Barn Owl to the refinement of the Scented Garden. All rooms have private baths as well as TV/VCRs, minifridges, and phones. Fix yourself a cup of tea in the second-story sitting room, or lounge in the Great Room downstairs, where you may meet Angus (the house dog) or a guest playing the baby grand piano. Breakfasts are inventive and generous. Depending upon the season, the street noise in this university neighborhood can be a bit much. *$$–$$$$; AE, DIS, MC, V; checks OK; gardenbb@att.net; www.secretgardenbbinn.com; 1 block south of campus.* &

Valley River Inn / ★★

1000 VALLEY RIVER WY, EUGENE; 541/687-0123 OR 800/543-8266 This elegant, low-profile hotel is neighbor to a regional shopping mall with acres of parking, but the hotel itself looks toward the Willamette River for its ambiance. With pretty inner courtyards, lovely plantings, and an inviting pool, this sprawling complex effectively creates a world of its own. All 257 rooms were recently renovated and are oversized and well decorated, with the best ones facing the river. Guests can use a workout room, sauna, Jacuzzi, and outdoor pool, or rent bicycles for a spin on the paved riverside path just out the door. The inn's Sweetwaters restaurant has an outdoor dining area overlooking the river that is wonderful for drinks and hors d'oeuvres. *$$$–$$$$; AE, DC, DIS, MC, V; checks OK; reserve@valleyriverinn.com; www.valleyriverinn.com; exit 194B off I-5.* &

Springfield

"Gateway" is the catchword for Springfield, Eugene's smaller neighbor to the east. The town promotes itself as the gateway to the **MCKENZIE RIVER**, wild with white-water upstream but placid where it flows by town. And the Gateway district along Interstate 5 is fast becoming the de facto town center. Here you'll find chain motels, fast food, and the large **GATEWAY MALL** (300 Gateway St; 541/747-3123).

The old downtown isn't much to look at these days, but secondhand and collectibles shops sometimes yield a gem. **LIVELY PARK SWIM CENTER** (6100 Thurston Rd; 541/736-4244), the state's first wave pool, is a kid magnet at the east end of town. Down by the river, wander the old orchards and riverside paths of **DORRIS RANCH LIVING HISTORY FARM** (2nd St S and Dorris St; 541/747-5552), birthplace of the state's hazelnut industry (they're still called filberts here).

RESTAURANTS

Kuraya's

1410 MOHAWK BLVD, SPRINGFIELD; 541/746-2951 Its location is off the beaten path, but Kuraya's remains a popular spot with local Thai-food fanciers. The casual atmosphere, friendly service, and large, inventive menu keep people coming back. So do the seafood baskets—shrimp and scallops in a hot, coconutty sauce—and the Bangkok prawns, charcoal broiled and served with a crabmeat-and-peanut dipping sauce. *$; MC, V; no checks; lunch Mon–Sat, dinner every day; beer and wine; reservations for 7 or more; at Market St.* &

Mookie's Place / ★

1507 CENTENNIAL BLVD, SPRINGFIELD; 541/744-4148 OR 541-746-8298 Housed in a former drive-in, Mookie's is a local favorite for come-as-you-are, sit-down dinners or ready-to-eat takeout. It's not nouvelle cuisine, but chef Randy Hollister's menu is playful and surprising, like spicy Cajun chicken Alfredo, honey-marinated grilled salmon, and hot artichoke dip with garbanzo beans. Slow-roasted prime rib is offered Friday and Saturday nights and the desserts are all homemade. Eat in, in the newly remodeled dining area, or order to go, from an entire meal to just your favorite sauce or salad dressing. Expect to take something home in either case: portions are generous. There's a decent selection of microbrews, several West Coast wines, and an extensive children's menu. *$–$$; AE, MC, V; checks OK; lunch Tues–Fri, dinner Tues–Sat; beer and wine; no reservations; www.mookiesplace.com; at Mohawk Blvd.* &

LODGINGS

McKenzie View Bed & Breakfast / ★★★

34922 MCKENZIE VIEW DR, SPRINGFIELD; 541/726-3887 OR 888/625-8439 Roberta and Scott Bolling's large, contemporary country home is 15 minutes—and a world away—from downtown Eugene. There's nothing between your room and the wide, placid lower McKenzie River but a broad back porch, immaculate gardens, lawns dotted with hammocks, and a maple-shaded deck hanging over the river's edge. The four rooms have private baths and range from good-sized to spacious (the pricing reflects amenities offered); three overlook the river through large picture windows, and two have gas fireplaces. Rooms have no TVs, VCRs, or phones, but guests can get their fix in the common areas. Roberta's full breakfasts are inventive and satisfying, and you are welcome to raid a well-stocked minifridge and cookie jar. The transplanted Midwesterners have furnished the house with antiques and quality reproductions, giving it a conservative feel by Oregon standards, but one freshened by the Bollings' enthusiasm for innkeeping and for their adopted home. *$–$$$$; AE, DC, MC, V; checks OK; mckenzieview@worldnet.att.net; www.mckenzie-view .com; exit 199 off I-5.* &

NORTHERN
OREGON COAST

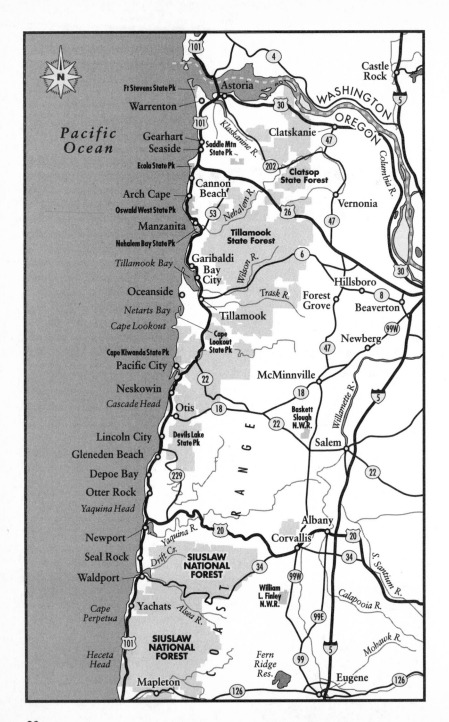

NORTHERN OREGON COAST

Native Americans considered the Northern Oregon Coast paradise, with unlimited trees to build their longhouses and canoes, plentiful game, edible wild flora, and a benevolent year-round climate. Contemporary residents—an eclectic mix of loggers, fisherfolk, entrepreneurs, artists, and retirees—continue to appreciate the region's easy living. But the place is changing. Even though everyone comes to escape the big city, aspects of urban life, such as fast-food franchises, big-box retailers, and outlet malls, are already part of the landscape. Summer traffic through Seaside, or between Lincoln City and Newport, can be stifling.

Fortunately, commercial progress hasn't undermined the area's breathtaking geography. From Astoria to Yachats—the mouth of the Columbia River to Cape Perpetua—this rugged coastline is embossed with a series of spectacular headlands holding out against Neptune's fury, separated by broad expanses of sand. Stark sandstone cliffs sculpted by weather and waves distinguish other points of land, such as Pacific City's Cape Kiwanda. Many stretches of coastline remain pristine, preserved as state parks, and Oregon's "beach bill" (unique in the United States) guarantees public access to the state's shoreline.

The Oregon Coast Trail begins at the South Jetty of the Columbia River (within Warrenton's Fort Stevens State Park), then traverses capes and beaches to the California border. "Boardheads" will tell you The Point in Seaside boasts the best surfing waves north of Santa Cruz, and that the north coast's windsurfing conditions are second only to the Columbia River Gorge's. Thousands of cyclists pedal US Highway 101 every summer, and kayakers paddle the region's numerous rivers, lakes, and backwaters.

Tourism now fuels the north coast's economic engine. Tiny hamlets of a few hundred people—Manzanita, in Tillamook County, for example—showcase upscale lodgings and galleries. Once a culinary wasteland, this area is now loaded with top-tier restaurants, and outside investment is increasing. Even those quintessential Northwest urban establishments, brew pubs, are thriving in Astoria, Cannon Beach, Pacific City, Lincoln City, and Newport.

Certainly it rains—55 to 80 inches a year; that's why the landscape is forever green. Winter storms that carry much of the moisture—sou'westers, locals call them—afford one of nature's greatest spectacles: rain falls in horizontal sheets, beach sands swirl, and the Pacific becomes a frothing cauldron. What residents keep to themselves is that come summer, days are mostly sunny, temperatures rarely dip below 55°F or crest 80°F, and a refreshing breeze blows daily.

ACCESS AND INFORMATION

Driving is your best bet to and from the Northern Oregon Coast. From Seattle, take Interstate 5 to Longview, Washington, cross the interstate bridge, and follow US Highway 30 west to Astoria. From downtown Portland, take US Highway 26 west (the road traverses the Coast Range mountains and can be dangerous in winter) to its intersection with US Highway 101 at the Cannon Beach Junction. **HIGHWAY 101** (also known as the Coast Highway) is the only route along Oregon's coast. The **STATE WELCOME CENTER** (111 W Marine Dr, Astoria; 503/325-6311 or 800/875-6807; *www.oldoregon.com*) or the **SEASIDE VISITORS BUREAU** (7 N Roosevelt Dr, Seaside; 503/738-3097 or 888/306-2326; *www.seasideor.com*) are good starting points.

Transportation options via bus and air change frequently. Check with either of the above agencies, or the **GREATER NEWPORT CHAMBER OF COMMERCE** (555 SW Coast Hwy, Newport; 541/265-8801 or 800/262-7844; *www.newportchamber .org*) for current information.

Weather on the north coast is rainy in winter and dry—but almost never hot—in summer (generally July 4 through September). The tourist season now runs from spring break in late March to the onset of the wet season, usually mid- to late October.

Astoria

The oldest American city west of the Rockies is undergoing a renaissance. Restaurants, lodgings, and galleries are popping up as fast as the annual fall crop of mushrooms in the surrounding fields and forests. Victorian homes dot the hillside, a river walkway and a year-round trolley grace the bustling Columbia River waterfront, and the seasonal downtown **SUNDAY MARKET** (mid-May to early October) draws thousands. Sundry historical attractions await visitors. The **COLUMBIA RIVER MAR-ITIME MUSEUM** (1792 Marine Dr; 503/325-2323; *www.crmm.org*) features interactive exhibits and visitor-friendly galleries depicting different aspects of the region's maritime history (the lightship *Columbia* is moored outside and open to visitors). Named for a prominent 19th-century businessman and one of the first Columbia River bar pilots, **CAPTAIN GEORGE FLAVEL HOUSE** (8th and Duane Sts; 503/325-2563; *www.clatsophistoricalsociety.org*) is the city's best example of ornate Queen Anne architecture. Local history is showcased inside and at the restored **HERITAGE MUSEUM** (1618 Exchange St; 503/325-2203), eight blocks away. Six miles southwest of Astoria, off Highway 101, the Lewis and Clark Expedition's 1805–06 winter encampment is re-created at **FORT CLATSOP NATIONAL MEMORIAL** (92343 Fort Clatsop Rd; 503/861-2471; *www.nps.gov/focl*). You can watch videos and view period artifacts in the visitor center and, during summer, enjoy living-history demonstrations, such as musket firing, and canoe and candle making (expect crowds during the 2005–06 bicentennial).

For a breathtaking panorama of the Columbia River estuary and more, climb the 166 steps of the **ASTORIA COLUMN** (drive to the top of 16th St and follow the signs), which sits atop Coxcomb Hill, Astoria's highest point.

FORT STEVENS STATE PARK (off Ridge Rd, Hammond; 503/861-1671; *www .oregonstateparks.org/park_179.php*), 20 minutes northwest of Astoria off Highway 101, is a 3,500-acre outdoor wonderland of forest trails, paved bike paths, a freshwater lake, and uncrowded beaches—including the permanent resting place of the *Peter Iredale*, a sailing vessel wrecked in 1906. The **SOUTH JETTY** lookout tower, perched at Oregon's northwesternmost point, is a supreme storm-watching spot and a good place to spy whales in calmer weather. It also marks the start of the **OREGON COAST TRAIL**, which traverses sandy beaches and forested headlands all the way to the California border.

NORTHERN OREGON COAST THREE-DAY TOUR

DAY ONE: Drive up to the **ASTORIA COLUMN** and soak in the pleasing prospects of the Columbia River estuary and the ocean beyond; you may spy a bald eagle soaring overhead. Meander back down the hill along Franklin and Grand Avenues (between 16th and 17th Sts) for a look at some of the restored **VICTORIAN HOMES**. At the foot of 17th, tour the **COLUMBIA RIVER MARITIME MUSEUM** (and the lightship *Columbia*), then stroll west along the riverfront walkway. Retire to the **CANNERY CAFE** for lunch. Check in at the **HOTEL ELLIOTT** (if it's a summer Sunday, Astoria's outdoor market will be in full swing). Next, drive south to **FORT STEVENS STATE PARK**, where you can frolic on the beach, inspect the remains of the *Peter Iredale*, and climb the South Jetty viewing tower. Detour back to Astoria via **FORT CLATSOP NATIONAL MEMORIAL**. Have dinner at the funky but fun **COLUMBIAN CAFE** then take a riverfront walk to the Sixth Street viewing tower, where you can watch seals, sea lions, and river traffic.

 DAY TWO: Following a sumptuous breakfast at the **CANNERY CAFE**, head south to Cannon Beach and browse the **SHOPS AND GALLERIES** along Hemlock Street (public parking lots are in downtown and midtown, with free bus service between the two). Walk to the beach and majestic **HAYSTACK ROCK**, or drive north into **ECOLA STATE PARK**, where a cliff-side trail affords wondrous vistas. Enjoy a slice at **PIZZA 'A FETTA** or a more ambitious lunch (and a craft brew) at **BILL'S TAVERN & BREWHOUSE**, then drive south and check in at **THE INN AT MANZANITA**. Drop off your bags and drive north again to the **NEAHKAHNIE MOUNTAIN TRAILHEAD** (look for a green sign on the highway's east side). The trail to the summit is steep, but you'll be rewarded with the north coast's finest panorama. Return to Manzanita, take a quick spa, and dine at the fusion-food-oriented **BLUE SKY CAFE**. The beach is a couple of blocks away and ideal for an evening stroll, especially at low tide.

 DAY THREE: Nothing like a bracing morning walk or jog on the beach to get the blood going. Afterwards, head 2 miles south for breakfast at **WANDA'S CAFE** (Hwy 101; 503/368-8100) in Nehalem, then continue on Highway 101 to the **TILLAMOOK CHEESE PLANT**. Take the tour, buy an ice cream cone, and detour to **THREE CAPES SCENIC DRIVE**, a route that rejoins Highway 101 just south of Pacific City (where craft beers await at the beachfront **PELICAN PUB & BREWERY**). Continue on to Lincoln City and savor lunch at the **BLACKFISH CAFE**. On the north end of Newport, drive into the **YAQUINA HEAD OUTSTANDING NATURAL AREA** and tour **YAQUINA HEAD LIGHTHOUSE**. Late afternoon entertainment comes courtesy of the finny, feathery, and furry critters at Newport's **OREGON COAST AQUARIUM**. Check in to the literary-inclined **SYLVIA BEACH HOTEL** for a restful night of reading and stimulating dinner conversation at the hotel's **TABLES OF CONTENT** restaurant. Or venture across the street to **APRIL'S**, for some Mediterranean-inspired cuisine.

RESTAURANTS

Cannery Cafe / ★

I 6TH ST, ASTORIA; 503/325-8642 Locals flock to this aptly named eatery, housed in a century-old former cannery building perched on pilings over the Columbia River. Every table offers a superb view of sea lions, seals, and ship traffic. Clam chowder is credible, panini are built around thick focaccia slices, and desserts are terrific (try the vanilla cheesecake). More substantial fare includes tangy sautéed lime prawns, crab and shrimp cakes, baked or grilled halibut, and pan-Asian salmon finished with an orange-sake sauce. Carnivores can savor a bacon-wrapped rib-eye or free-range fowl infused with honey and bourbon. After your meal, stroll to the end of the Sixth Street pier (or to the top of an adjacent viewing tower) for even finer Columbia River vistas. *$$; DIS, MC, V; checks OK; lunch, dinner every day; full bar; reservations recommended; on 6th St pier.* &

Columbian Cafe / ★★

1114 MARINE DR, ASTORIA; 503/325-2233 It hasn't changed much in the last decade, but this smallish (a few booths, counter seating, and tables next door), veggie-oriented café continues to woo customers. Crepes fashioned with savory fixings, sumptuous soups ranging from borscht to vegetable bisque, a wilted spinach salad redolent of walnuts and blue cheese, and fabulous seafood-pasta preparations are drawing cards. Usually manning a small grill in the open kitchen, chef Uriah Hulsey presides over the place like a prince in his palace. If you're feeling frisky, order his Chef's Mercy, a surprise potpourri of the day's best fixings. The adjacent (nonsmoking) Voodoo Lounge offers pizza and other light fare, plus regular live music. *$$; no credit cards; checks OK; breakfast, lunch, dinner Mon–Sat; beer and wine; no reservations; at 11th St.* &

Fulio's Pastaria / ★★

1149 COMMERCIAL ST, ASTORIA; 503/325-9001 Humble pastas come alive under chef Peter Roscoe's care, their flavors and textures extending well beyond spaghetti and meat sauce or fettuccine Alfredo. Creamy rigatoni mustard showcases flavor bursts of excellent sausage, while penne puttanesca and rigatoni salsa rosa represent the simple and hearty richness of Italian cooking. Grilled Columbia River sturgeon topped with a refreshing avocado–sun-dried tomato salsa, then sided with sautéed spinach spiked with sliced garlic, is a preparation reminiscent of the red-white-and-green Italian flag. Panini paired with penne and rosemary potatoes make a lusty lunch. The restaurant's space is understated but appealing, somewhere between a laid-back trattoria and a more formal ristorante. *$$; AE, DIS, MC, V; checks OK; lunch, dinner every day; beer and wine; reservations recommended (dinner); between 11th and 12th Sts.* &

LODGINGS

Benjamin Young Inn / ★

3652 DUANE ST, ASTORIA; 503/325-6172 OR 800/201-1286 Painted in antique gold and bedecked with scalloped shingles, this 20-room mansion was built in 1888 on Astoria's east side for Benjamin Young, a Swedish immigrant and pioneer salmon packer. The B&B now sits on a three-quarter-acre estate planted with lush greenery. Wrought-iron gates lead to an expansive front porch outfitted with wicker furniture. Elegant drapes, red-velvet settees, and a huge white-brick fireplace adorn the living quarters. Five guest rooms (one downstairs, four upstairs) are lavishly decorated; all have river views. The Honeymoon Suite has antique Eastlake furnishings and a turret with a sitting room overlooking the garden and the river. *$$–$$$; AE, DIS, MC, V; checks OK; benjamin@benjaminyounginn .com; www.benjaminyounginn.com; 1 block above Marine Dr.*

Clementine's Bed and Breakfast / ★★

847 EXCHANGE ST, ASTORIA; 503/325-2005 OR 800/521-6801 This stylish Italianate built in 1888 sits across the street from the Flavel House (Astoria's most recognized Victorian) and on the edge of downtown. Innkeepers Judith and Cliff Taylor possess a wealth of local knowledge, and their B&B has a lived-in look, with a baby grand piano and a crystal chandelier in the living room and a bevy of antiques throughout, including a collection of vintage glassware and bowls. Upstairs rooms feature private balconies and captivating river vistas. Next door are two suites equipped with kitchens, fireplaces, and two bedrooms apiece (ideal for families and pets). Judith also serves one of Astoria's finest breakfasts: pumpkin pancakes, Dutch babies with raspberries from her garden, and wild mushroom and cream crepes, to name three, plus a stunning array of sweet treats. *$$; AE, DIS, MC, V; checks OK; closed Jan 1–mid-Feb; jtaylor@clementines-bb.com; www.clementines-bb.com; across 8th St from Flavel House.* &

Hotel Elliott / ★★★

357 12TH ST, ASTORIA; 503/325-2222 OR 877/378-1924 Built in 1924 and the oldest hotel in downtown Astoria, the Elliott has undergone a $4 million transformation and reclaimed its former glory, including its reputation for uncommon comfort (a huge original sign painted on the hotel's north side proclaims "wonderful beds"). Dark brown mahogany wainscoting wraps the lobby walls, and the original reception desk welcomes guests. A gold-leaf frieze along the perimeter of the ceiling has been meticulously restored, and historical photos and artwork of Astoria and environs hang throughout. In the basement is a wine cellar, bar, and cigar lounge. Upstairs, the Elliott offers 21 standard rooms and 11 suites on 4 floors (the old hotel had 68 rooms), all appointed with lovely furniture, heated stone bathroom floors, and beds to die for, draped with 460-count Egyptian cotton sheets and topped with four goose-down pillows. Premium suites are appointed with wet bars, fireplaces, and bathrooms finished with floor-to-ceiling stone, and showcase scintillating views of downtown and the Columbia River. An opulent Presidential Suite penthouse features a circular staircase winding to a crow's nest room adjacent to a rooftop garden and outfitted with another signature Elliott bed. *$$–$$$$; AE, DIS,*

MC, V; checks OK; info@hotelelliott.com; www.hotelelliott.com; on 12th between Commercial and Duane Sts.

Rosebriar Hotel / ★★

636 14TH ST, ASTORIA; 503/325-7427 OR 800/487-0224 Ensconced in a residential area three blocks above the waterfront, the Rosebriar is an example of the small, intimate hotels popular on the Oregon Coast. Inside, a homey lobby is furnished with comfy chairs and a fireplace. Guest quarters (all with private baths) range from cozy rooms trimmed with richly stained fir to more spacious view units featuring fireplaces and spas. Best vistas are from the top-floor Captain's Suite, with vaulted ceilings, private staircase, and a kitchenette. Down below, a separate carriage house—built in 1885, it predates the main building by 17 years—has a full kitchen. The included full breakfast might feature cherry quiche, deep-dish French toast, and sundry fresh-baked goodies. Outside, a man-made "brook" flows through the lush side yard, while a shrine made of stones and seashells is a reminder that the Rosebriar was formerly a convent. *$$–$$$; AE, DIS, MC, V; checks OK; info@rosebriar.net; www.rosebriar.net; corner of Franklin Ave.* &

Gearhart and Seaside

Isolated from Highway 101, Gearhart is a bedroom community backed by grassy dunes and a wide, uncrowded beach reminiscent of an earlier Cape Cod. Seaside, conversely, is the Oregon Coast's oldest resort town and sprawls north and south along Highway 101. Visitors stroll Broadway, eyeing the entertainment parlors, bumper cars, and sweet-treat concessions, and then emerge at **THE PROM**, the 2-mile cement walkway that parallels the beach. Throughout town are the coast's most delightful street-side gardens, planted with a collage of flowers, shrubs, and plants. Duck into **PACIFIC BENTO** (2111 Broadway, Ste 12; 503/738-2079) for nutritious fast food—try charbroiled chicken over yakisoba noodles. Out on the highway, **MORNING STAR CAFE** (280 S Roosevelt Dr; 503/717-8188) serves espresso and light fare in a retro coffeehouse atmosphere. Surf fishing is popular in the Cove area (along Sunset Boulevard). Steelhead and salmon can be taken (in season) from the **NECANICUM RIVER**, which flows through town. **QUATAT MARINE PARK** (downtown Seaside, along Necanicum River) is a relaxing picnic spot and the setting for summer concerts.

RESTAURANTS

Corpeny's / ★

2281 BEACH DR, SEASIDE; 503/738-7353 Morning regulars at this delightful corner café with a rock fireplace and porcelain tile floors swear by the Torres omelet bursting with jalapeños, roasted garlic, mushrooms, zucchini, and pork sausage. Noontime fare revolves around extraordinary sandwiches, such as chicken salad spiked with toasted almonds, dried cranberries, and pineapple on Tuscan peasant bread. Adventurous eaters can opt for a tamale pie built with sausage and veggies tucked inside a moist polenta-style crust swathed in melted cheeses.

French apple tarts, lemon poppy-seed scones, raspberry-streusel muffins, and Seaside's yummiest coffee cake are irresistible snacks. *$; no credit cards; checks OK; breakfast, lunch Thurs–Sun; no alcohol; no reservations; corpenys@pacifier.com; at Ave U, 1 block from beach.* &

Kalypso / ★★

619 BROADWAY, SEASIDE; 503/738-6302 John Nelson took a half-year respite from restaurant cooking, then opened this roomier, more bistro-like version of Kalypso (the older one was in Cannon Beach) and immediately began serving imaginative renditions of old standbys using the freshest local fixings. There's crispy-skinned rotisserie chicken infused with apple-citrus juice and paired with comforting cornbread stuffing. Lovely linguine is well stocked with shrimp and mildly spicy andouille sausage, then tossed in a tomato-clam broth sweetened by bits of carrot. Salmon and halibut skewers washed with tomato-fennel sauce score high on any seafood-lover's scale. Pastry chef Jennifer Nelson's moist and crunchy coconut cake crowned with caramel sauce and her Swedish cream topped with strawberry purée will delight even the most persnickety diner. *$$; DC, DIS, MC, V; checks OK; dinner Tues–Sun; full bar; reservations recommended; corner of Broadway and Holladay.* &

Lil' Bayou / ★

20 N HOLLADAY DR, SEASIDE; 503/717-0624 Fried catfish is as common on the Oregon Coast as a 70°F December day—except at this storefront bastion of Cajun-Creole cuisine, where a moist fillet is dredged in sassy seasonings, pan-blackened, then coated with crawfish aioli. You also might find fried alligator, pork- or crawfish-filled boudin (sausage), a delectable creamed corn called *mague choux,* and muffuletta sandwiches filled with salami, ham, cheeses, and a chopped-olive dressing. Sweet potato–pecan pie is an appealing dessert. *$$; DIS, MC, V; checks OK; lunch, dinner every day (closed Tues–Wed in winter); reservations recommended (dinner); on Holladay, just north of Broadway.* &

Pacific Way Bakery & Cafe / ★★

601 PACIFIC WY, GEARHART; 503/738-0245 The concept of a casual coastal café goes back two decades in Oregon, and this welcoming chic and airy establishment was one of the first. Lisa Allen's baked goods—artisan breads, croissants, cinnamon rolls, and cheesecakes, among others—are stellar. So is a broiled Island Ham sandwich garnished with dilled cream cheese and a zippy, cilantro-pineapple-jalapeño relish, or a grilled portobello burger with melted provolone and a smear of roasted red pepper mayo. Panfried cashew razor clams, grilled halibut freshened with mango-ginger chutney, and a bowl of snappy seafood stew are superior catches. Pizzas (especially the tomato-basil pie) are super, and homemade ice creams and sorbets hit the mark every time. *$$; MC, V; checks OK; lunch, dinner Thurs–Mon; beer and wine; reservations recommended (dinner); corner of Cottage Ave.*

LODGINGS

Gilbert Inn / ★★

🌲 **341 BEACH DR, SEASIDE; 503/738-9770 OR 800/410-9770** Seaside is becoming ever more crowded (especially with the massive beachfront time-share condos at the west end of Broadway, completed in 2003). But this Queen Anne–style house, built in 1892 by a former French consul and mayor of Seaside, is the city's finest lodging and an oasis of comfort on the edge of downtown. All 10 guest rooms within the light-yellow structure are appointed with period furnishings and include down quilts and private baths. Richly finished tongue-and-groove fir covers walls and ceilings throughout, and a brick fireplace dominates the downstairs parlor, decorated with family heirlooms and cushy couches. What remains of the original Gilbert cottage has been incorporated into the house and serves as a main-floor suite with a sitting room. Upstairs, the Turret Room has a four-poster bed and an ocean view. The Garret, a third-floor suite with three hand-hewn fir beds, is right for families. Breakfasts, served in summer on the side porch, are superior. *$$; AE, DIS, MC, V; checks OK; closed Jan; info@gilbertinn.com; www.gilbertinn.com; at Ave G.*

Cannon Beach

Chic and trendy, Cannon Beach is an oft-crowded coastal destination showcasing aesthetically pleasing structures constructed with cedar and weathered wood (no neon signs are allowed). Still, the main draw is the wide-open white-sand beach, dominated by **HAYSTACK ROCK**, one of the world's largest coastal monoliths and approachable at low tide. In summer, interpreters with the **HAYSTACK ROCK AWARENESS PROGRAM** (503/436-1581; *www.hrap.org*; on the beach) explain the geology and marine life.

Cannon Beach counts some of the coast's best galleries, most clustered along Hemlock Street. Not to be missed are the **WHITE BIRD** (251 N Hemlock St; 503/436-2681; *www.whitebirdgallery.com*), with an eclectic collection on two levels; **DRAGON FIRE GALLERY** (123 S Hemlock St; 503/436-1533) exhibits paintings, stained glass, jewelry, and metal sculpture; while soft-hued watercolors are displayed at **JEFFREY HULL GALLERY** (172 N Hemlock St; 503/436-2600; *www.hullgallery.com*); watch two glass blowers working in tandem at **ICEFIRE GLASSWORKS** (116 Gower St; 503/436-2359). Quick eats can be found at **ECOLA SEAFOOD MARKET** (208 N Spruce St; 503/436-9130) and **PIZZA 'A FETTA** (231 N Hemlock St; 503/436-0333). Quaff a handcrafted beer at **BILL'S TAVERN & BREWHOUSE** (188 N Hemlock St; 503/436-2202). A natural gas–powered free shuttle travels the length of town (along Hemlock St) year-round.

ECOLA STATE PARK (on the town's north end; *www.oregonstateparks.org/park_188.php*) offers fabulous vistas, picnic areas, and fantastic hiking trails (primitive camping only). A mile offshore is the former **TILLAMOOK ROCK LIGHTHOUSE**, built more than a century ago and decommissioned in 1957. **TOLOVANA PARK**, as the locals call the south side of Cannon Beach, has a laid-back, residential feel. Leave your vehicle at the **TOLOVANA BEACH WAYSIDE** (at Hemlock St and Warren Wy), with parking and rest rooms, and stroll the quiet beach, especially in the off-season.

RESTAURANTS

The Bistro / ★★

263 N HEMLOCK ST, CANNON BEACH; 503/436-2661 Unpretentious seafood entrees (grilled salmon festooned with roasted corn–red pepper relish or grilled halibut garnished with avocado salsa), premier pasta plates (*pansotti*—ravioli-like triangles stuffed with spinach, cheeses, and chard), and understated beef dishes (broiled rib-eye with caramelized onions or port-flavored tenderloin piled with portobellos) all share the limelight at this charming eatery tucked into a row of shops at downtown's north end. Dreamy-eyed couples sip wine by the glass in the pint-sized bar while sharing grilled Dungeness cakes (sided with a lemon-sake sauce) and Swedish crème capped with raspberry compote. Live acoustic guitar music most weekends, too. *$$; MC, V; local checks only; dinner every day (Thurs–Mon in winter); full bar; reservations recommended; opposite Spruce St downtown.* &

Cafe Mango / ★

1235 S HEMLOCK ST, CANNON BEACH; 503/436-2393 The egg-and-pesto scrambles, oat-buttermilk pancakes, and buffalo burgers are always appetizing, but what sets this midtown café apart is a lineup of savory crepes crafted from organic buckwheat flour and filled with everything from smoked salmon to spinach and mushrooms. Dessert crepes fashioned with organic white flour, then folded with fruits, nuts, chocolate, and dollops of yogurt, are fine anytime. *$–$$; no credit cards; checks OK; breakfast, lunch Thurs–Mon; no alcohol; no reservations; 8 blocks south of downtown.*

Warren House Pub / ★

3301 S HEMLOCK ST, CANNON BEACH; 503/436-1130 A British-style pub in Cannon Beach? Believe it, thanks to owners Jim Oyala and Ken Campbell, who transformed a former historic home (from the floor plan on up) into a haven for adventuresome diners. Smoked lamb pita pockets, ahi coated in yogurt and wasabi, pork ribs glazed with a citrus barbecue sauce, and a carnivore's dream burger blended with top sirloin and bacon are some of the options. On tap are craft beers from Bill's Tavern & Brewhouse (see Cannon Beach Introduction). *$–$$; DIS, MC, V; checks OK; full bar; no reservations; breakfast Sat–Sun, lunch, dinner Thurs–Mon; on Hemlock, south of town.* &

LODGINGS

Cannon Beach Hotel / ★

1116 S HEMLOCK ST, CANNON BEACH; 503/436-1392 OR 800/238-4107 In view of sprawling resort motels, this century-old former boardinghouse a block from the beach feels like a tidy European inn. A fireplace, flowers, and a huge bowl of fresh fruit grace the lobby, and complimentary hot beverages are served in the evening. Nine guest rooms (eight upstairs, one at ground level) are decorated with original art and vary from a nicely appointed one-bedroom to a suite with gas fireplace, spa, and ocean peeks. A continental breakfast and a newspaper are brought to your door in a French market basket. (If the hotel is full, ask about the Courtyard or the Hearthstone, both nearby and under the same management.) Adjacent to the hotel, bistro-casual JP's serves superb salads and seafood chowder, fettuccine tossed with chicken and mushrooms in a rousing pesto, and broiled mint-infused prawns wrapped in bacon. *$$; AE, DC, DIS, MC, V; checks OK; info@cannonbeachhotel .com; www.cannonbeachhotel.com; corner of Gower St.*

The Ocean Lodge / ★★

2864 S PACIFIC ST, CANNON BEACH; 503/436-2241 OR 888/777-4047 Like the Stephanie Inn next door, this newer wooden lodge is smack-dab above the beach. Inside, an eye-catching array of blonde and brown timbers rise from a richly finished hardwood floor. The 37 guest units, all with gas fireplaces, decks, and in-room amenities (including irons, ironing boards, and hair dryers), have fabulous ocean views. Some rooms enjoy king beds and spas. Eight additional units (all with spas, some with ocean vistas) are apportioned among a quartet of bungalows situated farther back from the ocean. Largest is the Cottage, which sleeps four. All guests are served continental breakfast in the Mountain View dining nook adjacent to the library. *$$$$; AE, DC, DIS, MC, V; checks OK; oceanlodge@charter .net; www.theoceanlodge.com; oceanfront, between Nelchena and Chisana.* &

Stephanie Inn / ★★★

2740 S PACIFIC ST, TOLOVANA PARK; 503/436-2221 OR 800/633-3466 Perhaps the most attractive lodging on the north coast, this gorgeous ocean-front getaway radiates the elegance of a large New England country inn: 50 spacious rooms are luxuriously appointed with gas fireplaces, spas, wet bars, and exquisite furnishings. Most rooms (some are two-bedroom suites, and a separate Carriage House has four suites) have outdoor balconies or patio decks with ocean or mountain scenes. Every afternoon, Northwest wines are served in the chart room, with a wall of windows overlooking the ocean. A masseuse is on call, a shuttle transports guests downtown, and a complimentary breakfast buffet is served in the second-floor dining room overlooking the Coast Range mountains. Dinners are the finest in town: elegant, four-course, prix-fixe affairs prepared by coastal food luminary John Newman (reservations required). Look for porcini risotto, gingered seafood cakes, shrimp and cabbage rolled in rice paper, marinated flank steak grilled with sweet peppers and red onions, and maybe even passion fruit cheesecake for two. *$$$$; AE, DC, DIS, MC, V; checks OK; 2-night min weekends and Aug; info@stephanie-inn.com; www.stephanie-inn.com; oceanfront at Matanuska.* &

Arch Cape

A quiet community of shoreside residences, Arch Cape has one of the two highway tunnels along Oregon's shoreline (the other is the Cape Creek tunnel south of

Yachats). The **OREGON COAST TRAIL** winds up and over Arch Cape (beginning at east end of Hwy 101, just north of tunnel; ask for directions at the post office, 79330 Hwy 101) and into **OSWALD WEST STATE PARK** (along Hwy 101; 800/551-6949), where you walk a half mile from a parking lot to tent sites (wheelbarrows are available to carry your gear) among old-growth trees. The ocean, with a protected cove and tide pools, is just beyond. Surfing and kayaking are favorite year-round activities. No reservations are taken, and the place gets packed in summer.

LODGINGS

St. Bernards / ★★

3 E OCEAN RD, ARCH CAPE; 503/436-2800 OR 800/436-2848 World travelers Don and Deanna Bernard built their palatial-looking wooden lodging in 1995, then sold it eight years later. Wisely, new innkeeper Barbara Dau has maintained the charm and finery that has made St. Bernards a desired destination. An impressive interior boasts tiled floors, elegant tapestries, French Provincial furnishings, and winding castlelike stairways. All seven rooms have spacious private baths, gas fireplaces, TV/VCRs, and refrigerators. The Provence suite features a spa and French doors leading to a private patio. Best views are from the top-floor Tower, a multilevel abode equipped with a soaking tub. Breakfasts are best described as extraordinary: goat cheese–cornmeal muffins, mixed-berry yogurt parfaits, sautéed bananas, curried eggs, and German apple pancakes, among other delectables. Guests can enjoy a sauna and work-out room, and the beach is a short stroll across the highway. No children under 12 permitted. *$$$; AE, MC, V; checks OK; bernards@pacifier.com; www.st-bernards.com; across from post office.* &

Manzanita

Growing but still uncrowded, this cozy, uncluttered community is a popular destination for urban overnighters, some of them windsurfers who flock to the usually breezy oceanfront and nearby Nehalem Bay. Overlooking the town is **NEAHKAHNIE MOUNTAIN** (1 mile north of Manzanita, along Hwy 101), with a steep, switch-backed trail leading to its 1,600-foot summit, the best panorama on the Northern Oregon Coast.

Three miles south of Manzanita, **NEHALEM BAY STATE PARK** (off Hwy 101; 503/368-5154) offers hiking and paved biking trails as well as miles of little-used beaches.

For sweet treats and espresso, visit **MANZANITA NEWS AND ESPRESSO** (500 Laneda Ave; 503/368-7450). Take-out burritos are the specialty at **LEFT COAST SIESTA** (288 Laneda Ave; 503/368-7997), while **MARZANO'S** (60 Laneda Ave; 503/368-3663) purveys calzones and pizza. Boats and tackle to explore or fish Nehalem Bay can be rented at **WHEELER MARINA** (278 Marine Dr, Wheeler; 503/368-5780); rent kayaks at **WHEELER ON THE BAY LODGE** (580 Marine Dr, Wheeler; 503/368-5858).

RESTAURANTS

Blue Sky Cafe / ★★★

154 LANEDA AVE, MANZANITA; 503/368-5712 Forget your cell phones (they're taboo) but bring a sense of culinary adventure to this postfusion dinner house, where the seasonal menu runs the gamut from oven-roasted pork chops paired with pumpkin-sage bread pudding to the Big Sky Thai stir-fried with veggies, rice noodles, chicken, or tofu. Warm pecan-crusted goat cheese (in a port reduction) and masa dough stuffed with smoked fowl, cheese, and spices make standard starters look obsolete. And peppercorn-coated black cod over house-crafted linguine, or crab and pan-seared-scallop risotto enriched with a chive-truffle emulsion are unorthodox house takes on typical seafood entrées. Even desserts, such as a pumpkin–white chocolate cheesecake Napoleon in a sage foam, enter unfamiliar—but tasty—territory. The stylishly lit, low-slung interior hung with avant-garde art resembles a gallery more than a restaurant, but closely spaced tables and beautifully finished woodwork lend a warm and welcoming feel. *$$–$$$; no credit cards; checks OK; dinner every day (Fri–Sat in winter); full bar; reservations recommended; at 2nd.* ও

Bread and Ocean / ★

387 LANEDA AVE, MANZANITA; 503/368-5823 Something about a quality bakery makes a town more livable. This artisan bread-box of a storefront (owned and operated by local food goddess Julie Barker) certainly ups Manzanita's quality of life a notch or two. Loaves du jour include polenta, fig-walnut, and brioche, plus eight sandwiches and nine panini can be had. Some put an unusual spin on old favorites: pastrami on rye with Gruyère, tomatoes, greens, and a smear of horseradish, for example. Other selections, such as prosciutto stuffed into a couple slices of seed-specked focaccia spread with pesto, tapenade, and fresh mozzarella, enter novel sandwich territory. A picnic box lunch comes with soup or salad and a smile-sustaining cookie. No inside tables; takeout only. *$; no credit cards; checks OK; Tues–Sun; no alcohol; no reservations; at 4th.*

Nehalem River Inn / ★★★

34910 OREGON HWY 53, MOHLER; 503/368-7708 OR 800/368-6499 Nestled against the verdant green Nehalem River shoreline, this reconverted tavern is a culinary oasis in the heart of cow country. First-time patrons are surprised at the scope of chef Stephen Tinkham's menu: selections range from a Cognac-flamed filet mignon (finished with a juniper berry demi-glace) to crayfish paired with chipotle aioli. Salmon might arrive brushed with a dill and lemon tapenade, while roast duckling enhanced with herbs, gooseberries, and kumquats is sweet protein at its finest. Vegetarians can rejoice in a Fantasia Platter replete with sautéed wild fixings, many from the garden out back. Wild huckleberry cheesecake crowned with citrus crème fraîche, a seven-chocolate torte, and other desserts sound like prized entries from a fantasy cookbook, and taste accordingly. Meals are presented in a lodgelike dining area. A covered outdoor porch overlooking some massive old-growth spruce trees affords additional seating. Dinner is a happening that lasts 90 minutes or more. *$$$; AE, DIS, MC, V; checks OK; dinner Thurs–Mon; full bar;*

reservations recommended; info@river-inn.com; www.river-inn.com; on Hwy 53 in Mohler. &

LODGINGS

Coast Cabins / ★★

635 LANEDA AVE, MANZANITA; 503/368-7113 Though the location (not far from the highway and unprotected from road noise) leaves a bit to be desired, you won't find more stylishly appointed accommodations in Manzanita. These five shake-sided cabins are decorated with quality cotton linens, goose-down pillows and comforters, and Scandinavian-style furniture. Three cabins have two-story towers, with sleeping quarters in the lofts; two have full kitchens (the other three, kitchenettes). A one-story cabin has a fireplace and laundry facilities. Extras include CD players and VCRs in the rooms. The pet-friendly owners have also done a remarkable job with the grounds. *$$$–$$$$; AE, MC, V; checks OK; info@coastcabins.com; www.coastcabins.com; 6 blocks from the beach.* &

The Inn at Manzanita / ★★

67 LANEDA AVE, MANZANITA; 503/368-6754 A few hundred feet from soul-soothing sand and surf, this tranquil retreat divided into four earth-colored structures occupies a multilevel, woodsy setting similar to a Japanese garden. Each of the 13 spacious, nonsmoking units is finished in pine or cedar and decorated with stained glass. Each room has a gas fireplace, a good-sized spa, TV/VCR, and some enjoy balconies and treetop ocean views. The larger Cottage unit is equipped with a full kitchen and a separate bedroom. Extra touches for all guests include terry-cloth robes, fresh flowers daily, and morning paper delivery. *$$$; MC, V; checks OK; 2-night min weekends and summer; info@innatmanzanita .com; www.inn@manzanita.com; 1 block from beach.*

Ocean Inn / ★★

32 LANEDA AVE, MANZANITA; 503/368-7701 OR 866/368-7701 You're so close to the beach here, the tide practically laps at your bedpost. Four remodeled cottage-like units (three have wood stoves, two enjoy ocean-side decks, and one has a spa) are nestled on a grassy bluff a seagull's flight from the surf. All have knotty-pine interiors and good-sized kitchens (with microwaves and dishwashers). Six newer units (9 is our favorite) boast vaulted ceilings with stained-glass chandeliers and gorgeous fir woodwork. Most enjoy full kitchens and wood heaters set in brick alcoves. Number 10 is equipped for persons with disabilities, and 2, 3, and 4 allow pets. Covered parking is provided. *$$$; MC, V; checks OK; 1-week min July–Aug (except units 5 and 10); oceaninn@nehalemtel.net; www.oceaninn@manzanita .com; at the beach.* &

Garibaldi, Bay City, and Tillamook

TILLAMOOK BAY is a mecca for salmon fishermen, and these burgs along Highway 101 are good places for fresh seafood. Drive out on the pier at Bay City's **PACIFIC OYSTER COMPANY** (5150 Oyster Dr, Bay City; 503/377-2323) for 'sters and a view.

Numerous charter boats operate from Garibaldi and are good for whale-watching as well as fishing (see "See the Whales" in this chapter for more information). Anglers routinely haul in 30-pound chinook from the Ghost's Hole section of Tillamook Bay, and area rivers are well-regarded salmon and steelhead streams.

Best known as dairy country, the town of Tillamook is in a broad, flat expanse of bottomland formed by the confluence of three rivers: the Tillamook, Trask, and Wilson. On the north end of town sits the home of world-renowned Tillamook Cheese, the **TILLAMOOK COUNTY CREAMERY ASSOCIATION** plant and visitor center (4175 Hwy 101N, Tillamook; 503/842-4481 or 800/542-7290). The tour is self-guided but interesting, and 31 flavors of Tillamook ice cream are sold. Three dozen meticulously restored aircraft are on display in a former blimp hangar at the **TILLAMOOK AIR MUSEUM** (6030 Hangar Rd, Tillamook; 503/842-1130). **MUNSON CREEK FALLS** is 7 miles south of Tillamook (turn off Hwy 101 to Munson Creek Rd) and features a 319-foot waterfall—Oregon's second tallest.

Oceanside

A quaint seaside hamlet, Oceanside lies 8 miles west of Tillamook along the 34-mile **THREE CAPES SCENIC DRIVE**. Tracing one of Oregon's most magnificent stretches of coastline, the narrow, winding road skirts the outline of Tillamook Bay and climbs over Cape Meares. At **CAPE MEARES STATE PARK** (just north of Oceanside), you can walk up to and inside **CAPE MEARES LIGHTHOUSE** (503/842-2244) and inspect an oddly shaped Sitka spruce known as the Octopus Tree. The Three Capes route winds along Netarts Bay before reaching **CAPE LOOKOUT STATE PARK** (1300 Whiskey Creek Rd; 503/842-4981; *www.oregonstateparks.org/park_186 .php*), with 212 campsites (and 13 yurts), as well as headland-hugging trails and a huge expanse of beach. After scaling Cape Lookout, the westernmost headland on the Northern Oregon Coast, the scenic drive traverses a desertlike landscape of sandy dunes. The road to Pacific City and the route's third cape, Kiwanda, runs through lush, green dairy country.

RESTAURANTS

Roseanna's Oceanside Café / ★★

1490 PACIFIC ST, OCEANSIDE; 503/842-7351 The town's lone fine-dining experience, this converted grocery store is fronted by wooden walkways and a weathered facade. Views of the ocean and offshore Three Arch Rocks make meals memorable, and the seafood is sublime. A simple shellfish sauté arrives bathed in apricot curry or cream blended with ginger and marsala wine; up the heat quotient with a garlic-chili sauce. Willapa oysters come coated with bread crumbs and parsley or poached in wine, then sprinkled with Parmesan and finished in the oven. Rarely seen preparations (in these parts, anyway) include Angels on Horseback (oysters wrapped in bacon) and Saints on a Wire (skewered scallops and bacon). Lighter eaters can order penne tossed with a variety of sauces (spicy ginger or Gorgonzola-pear, for instance) or a bowl of excellent clam chowder. Chocolate-caramel crunch cake and Toll House pie topped with Tillamook ice cream headline the dessert board. *$$; MC, V; checks OK; breakfast Sun, lunch, dinner Thurs–Tues; full bar; no reservations; on main drag.* &

Pacific City

A tidy river and ocean community, Pacific City is home to the **DORY FLEET**, composed of Oregon's classic salmon-fishing boats. The vessels are launched from the beach in the lee of **CAPE KIWANDA** (a brilliantly colored sandstone headland), sometimes competing with sea lions, surfers, and kayakers for water space. If the wind is right, hang gliders swoop off the sandy slopes of the cape and land on the beach below. Just south of the cape, **PELICAN PUB & BREWERY** (33180 Cape Kiwanda Dr; 503/965-7007) has garnered awards for its Kiwanda Cream Ale and Tsunami Stout. The region's second **HAYSTACK ROCK** sits a half mile offshore (Cannon Beach has the other). **ROBERT STRAUB STATE PARK** (at the south end of town; 800/551-6949) occupies most of the Nestucca beach sand spit. The Nestucca and Little Nestucca Rivers are top-notch salmon and steelhead streams.

RESTAURANTS

Grateful Bread Bakery / ★

34805 BROOTEN RD, PACIFIC CITY; 503/965-7337 The owners have changed, but the appealing, low-priced food and the cheery ambiance remain intact at this bakery with a catchy name. Gingerbread pancakes, a smoked-salmon scramble, and challah French toast remain morning standouts. Black-bean chili, Tillamook cheese and corn chowder, and a host of sandwiches built with house bread highlight the lunch menu (for something different, try a cheese and nut loaf sandwich on multigrain). New is a dinner lineup that includes local dory-caught grilled cod, pizza, and seafood pasta plates, along with a number of vegetarian options. A spacious deck allows alfresco dining. *$; MC, V; checks OK; breakfast, lunch, dinner Thurs–Mon (no Mon dinners fall and winter); no alcohol; no reservations; on Pacific City loop road.* &

LODGINGS

Eagle's View Bed & Breakfast / ★

37975 BROOTEN RD, PACIFIC CITY; 503/965-7600 OR 888/846-3292 Real-world stress melts away at this enchanting B&B perched on a steep hill backdropped by forest and boasting bird's-eye views of Nestucca Bay and adjacent dairy lands. Built in 1995, the structure is an attractive two-story country cottage set on 4 acres (with walking trails and a fish pond). Amenities include a covered porch, a wraparound deck with hot tub (for a daytime or evening soak), rocking chairs, and comfy country decor throughout. Five guest rooms, all with private baths, have TV/VCRs and CD players (there's a video and CD library); three feature spa tubs. Enjoy a full breakfast in the privacy of your room, or dine with other guests in the downstairs great room or out on the deck. *$$; AE, DIS, MC, V; checks OK; eagle@wcn.net; www.eaglesviewbb.com; ½ mile east of Hwy 101.* &

Neskowin

A mostly residential hamlet lying in the lee of Cascade Head—a steeply sloped and forested promontory—Neskowin is the final port of refuge before the touristy "20 miracle miles" (as the stretch from Lincoln City south to Newport used to be called). The beach here is narrower but less crowded than other locales. Just south, **CASCADE HEAD** has miles of little-used hiking trails that traverse rain forests and meadows; begin your hike at a marked trailhead about 2 miles south of Neskowin (visible from Hwy 101). The **OLD NESKOWIN ROAD** (turn east off Hwy 101, 1 mile south of Neskowin), a narrow route that winds through horse farms and past old-growth groves, provides an enchanting side trip.

RESTAURANTS

Hawk Creek Cafe / ★

4505 SALEM AVE, NESKOWIN; 503/392-3838 Before or after a foray to Neskowin's delightful beach, this pint-sized eatery showcasing lots of windows and gorgeous woodwork is a must-stop. Be prepared to wait for a table: locals swarm the joint for breakfast omelets and scrumptious pancakes, then return for prodigious burgers, bowls of stalwart black bean–turkey chili, and hand-crafted pizzas baked in a wood-fired oven. A warming gas stove, soft music, and an extensive beer selection (5 on tap, 25 by the bottle) keep patrons lingering. Summer crowds overflow onto a creek-side wraparound deck exposed to sea breezes. *$; MC, V; checks OK; breakfast, lunch, dinner every day; beer and wine; no reservations; off Hwy 101, adjacent to Neskowin Beach Wayside.*

LODGINGS

The Chelan / ★

48750 BREAKERS BLVD, NESKOWIN; 503/392-3270 Nestled among the trees in narrow-laned Neskowin, this hidden gem lies near private homes, yet feels like a getaway retreat. A manicured front lawn and lush gardens add to the seclusion. Eight condominium units each have two bedrooms (a ninth unit has three), well-equipped kitchens, and large living rooms with picture windows and fireplaces. Ground-floor units each have a private entrance to a tiny backyard, with the ocean just beyond. Upstairs accommodations (off-limits to children) enjoy private balconies. *$$; MC, V; checks OK; just off Salem Blvd.*

Lincoln City

Just when you think there's no room for more development, another motel pops up in this coastal congestion zone. Still, Lincoln City's restaurant scene is vibrant, the shopping choices are legion, and 7 miles of broad, sandy beaches stretch from

SEE THE WHALES

Gray whales are soooo inconsiderate. The leviathans migrate past Oregon's coastline (they winter in Baja, California, and Mexico, and spend the summer in Arctic waters) during some of the worst weather of the year, typically the end of the year and late March. Not to worry; the north coast affords a few sheltered spots to spy these magnificent creatures. Spotting them usually isn't difficult: adults measure 45 feet and weigh 35 tons, and more than 22,000 whales of all sizes take part in the two annual migrations. During **WHALE WATCH WEEK** (last weeks of Dec and Mar; call 541/563-2002 for information), volunteers are on hand at the following sites (and numerous others) to answer questions.

ECOLA STATE PARK (2 miles north of Cannon Beach, off Hwy 101): A short walk from the parking area is a spacious, covered picnic shelter with cliff-side vistas of—one hopes—spouting whales.

Lincoln City's **INN AT SPANISH HEAD** (4009 SW Hwy 101; 541/996-2161 or 800/452-8127): The inn's 10th-floor viewing lounge is open for whale-watchers.

The **CAPE PERPETUA INTERPRETIVE CENTER** (south of Yachats on Hwy 101): Good looks can be had from inside the center or outside on a covered deck.

Want a closer look? Get eye to eye with gray whales from the safety of a chartered boat. These giant mammals travel less than 5 mph during their migrations and sometimes will surface almost alongside your craft. Weather permitting, many charter operators on Oregon's north coast offer tours. Check with the chamber of commerce or visitor center serving the port from which you hope to depart. Newport's **MARINE DISCOVERY TOURS** (345 SW Bay Blvd; 541/265-6200 or 800/903-2628) is the most family-friendly operator on the Oregon Coast.

—*Richard Fencsak*

Road's End (north end of town) to the peaceful shores of Siletz Bay. Kite festivals (see "Coastal Celebrations" in this chapter) are held at **D RIVER BEACH WAYSIDE** (milepost 115, halfway through town).

Amid the chaos on Lincoln City's north end, retire to **LIGHTHOUSE BREWPUB** (4157 N Hwy 101; 541/994-7238) for handcrafted ales and good grub. **BARNACLE BILL'S SEAFOOD MARKET** (2174 NE Hwy 101; 541/994-3022) has fresh and smoked seafood galore. Walk among rhododendrons, azaleas, irises, and other flowers and plants that thrive in a coastal climate at the **CONNIE HANSEN GARDEN** (1931 NW 33rd St; 541/994-6338).

The arts flourish here ("keeper" glass floats created by local artists are distributed along Lincoln City beaches every winter; 800/452-2151). North of town, the quarter-century-old **RYAN GALLERY** (4270 N Hwy 101; 541/994-5391) has 3,000 square feet filled with the work of Northwest artists. On the south side of Lincoln

City, the **FREED GALLERY** (6119 SW Hwy 101; 541/994-5600) exhibits functional and decorative glass, furniture, and sculptures, as well as paintings.

Stop by the **LINCOLN CITY VISITORS & CONVENTION BUREAU** (801 SW Hwy 101, Suite 1, Lincoln City; 541/994-8378 or 800/452-2151; *www.oregoncoast.org*) for an overview.

RESTAURANTS

Bay House / ★★★★

5911 SW HWY 101, LINCOLN CITY; 541/996-3222 Chefs come and go, but the spectacularly situated Bay House—with Siletz Bay out the back window and the ocean just beyond—continues as the Oregon Coast's finest upscale eatery. Richly finished wood and brass, crisp tablecloths, and seasoned service personnel garbed in black and white lend a traditional ambiance, and the wine list is exemplary. With chef Jesse Otero at the helm, the always difficult-to-define Bay House menu leans as much toward Europe as the Pacific Rim. Stellar starters include salad niçoise (Dungeness crab stands in for tuna), cornmeal-crusted oysters sided with apple-cabbage slaw, and a superb trio of artisan cheeses—say, a Taleggio from Italy, French fourme d'Ambert, and a Camembert crafted in New York's Hudson Valley. Entrées range from the forever-popular Oregon rack of lamb (cumin-seasoned and finished with an unusual cinnamon-cabernet sauce) to wild chinook salmon crusted with mustard seeds, then christened with a spiced coconut broth. Although he has imprinted the kitchen, Otero knows patrons might take umbrage if he modified the traditional house soup, a creamy caramelized-onion concoction garnished with bay shrimp. Ethereal ginger crème brûlée (topped with fresh raspberries) remains a dessert standby. But look out calorie counters: Otero has added lemon curd cheesecake, coffee-Kahlua ice cream, and an over-the-top strawberry-almond tart garnished with both chantilly cream and crème anglaise. A new Sunday brunch menu offers everything from huckleberry pancakes to pan-fried trout piccata. *$$$–$$$$; AE, DIS, MC, V; checks OK; dinner every day (Wed–Sun in winter), brunch Sun; full bar; reservations recommended; bayhouse@wcn.net; www.bayhouserestaurant.com; south end of town.* &

Blackfish Cafe / ★★★

2733 NW HWY 101, LINCOLN CITY; 541/996-1007 Rob Pounding (past head honcho in Salishan's kitchen) and his wife, Mary, ventured into the challenging world of restaurant ownership in 1999 and immediately struck gold with a three-pronged concept that has revolutionized Oregon coastal dining: Concentrate on sourcing the finest Northwest ingredients; scale down the prices, but not the portions or the culinary creativity; and serve the food in a casual, bistro-like atmosphere. The Poundings' frequently changing menu reads like a regional geography book—Tillamook cheeses, Yaquina Bay oysters, veggies from Yachats, Willamette Valley pork loin chops, Oregon pink shrimp, Pacific City dory-caught salmon and black bass. A sirloin steak comes bathed in an Oregon pinot noir sauce, Coast Range huckleberries garnish a grilled duck breast, and the top round for burgers is from Carlton, Oregon, cows. Side dishes such as blue cheese potato gratin, walnut-sage risotto, and roasted sweet-corn broth are equally enticing. Lighter fare includes fried buttermilk-dipped and cornmeal-breaded oysters, beer-battered rockfish-and-chips, and exemplary clam chowder. Chocolate fanciers save room for the Blackfish "ding dong," an ultrarich fudge cake oozing creamy innards. *$$; AE, DIS, MC, V; checks OK; lunch, dinner Wed–Mon (Thurs–Mon in winter); beer and wine; reservations recommended; www.blackfishcafe.com; west side of Hwy 101.* &

LODGINGS

O'dysius Hotel / ★

120 NW INLET CT, LINCOLN CITY; 541/994-4121 OR 800/869-8069 Boxy, nondescript motels rule Lincoln City's shoreline, backed by still more uninspiring lodgings along Highway 101. The upscale oceanfront O'dysius (with 7 miles of beach just outside) offers an alternative. Attractive furnishings, fireplaces, whirlpool baths, down comforters, and TV/VCRs (and a selection of videos) grace the 30 units. All enjoy private decks or balconies looking seaward; suites have full kitchens. Slippers and terry-cloth robes are provided for lounging. Wine is served afternoons in the lobby sitting room, which also houses a well-stocked library. Continental breakfast and the newspaper arrive at your doorstep in the morning. *$$$; AE, DIS, MC, V; checks OK; odysius@harborside.com; www.odysius.com; just north of D River Beach Wayside.* &

Gleneden Beach

Across the highway from the famous Salishan Lodge, a cluster of shops includes the **GALLERY AT SALISHAN** (7760 N Hwy 101; 541/764-2318), which sells wood carvings, wool tapestry, pottery, paintings, even furniture. **EDEN HALL** (6675 Gleneden Beach Loop Rd; 541/764-3825) stages local and regional music and theater.

RESTAURANTS

Side Door Cafe / ★★

6675 GLENEDEN BEACH LOOP RD, GLENEDEN BEACH; 541/764-3825 Unique on the Oregon Coast, this establishment combines an open, airy eatery exuding a bistro feel with a cozy entertainment venue named Eden Hall. The café occupies a large, stylized room with an exquisite wood-and-marble fireplace and colorful backdrops from theatrical presentations. Creatively cooked and plated food draws as many raves as the shows next door. Try the macadamia- and hazelnut-encrusted pork tenderloin graced with a cherry-mango chutney, for example, or Northwest bouillabaisse partnered with Parmesan risotto, curried mussels, and a seared-salmon Caesar salad. Vegetarian meals—such as ravioli plump with wild mushrooms and ricotta, and Asian spring rolls matched with a hot mustard-soy dipping sauce—are spot-on. Cheesecakes headline the dessert tray. *$$; MC, V; local checks only; lunch, dinner Wed–Mon; full bar; reservations recommended; info@sidedoorcafe.com; www.sidedoorcafe.com; on old highway.* &

LODGINGS

Salishan Lodge & Golf Resort / ★★★

**7760 N HWY 101, GLENEDEN BEACH; 541/764-2371 OR 888/
SALISHAN** Back in 1965 when it was built, Salishan was a one-of-a-kind retreat. Dispersed over an idyllic, 750-acre forested landscape, the resort still boasts more amenities than any other coastal lodging, and service personnel are well informed and eager to please. Native American themes permeate the decor within the 205 guest accommodations, which are arranged in eight-plexes on a hillside rising from the main entrance. All units have gas fireplaces and balconies that overlook the forest, golf course, or Siletz Bay. The best deals are traditional rooms—about the size of a typical motel room, only considerably nicer. Premier accommodations enjoy spa tubs, exquisitely appointed parlors, and Siletz Bay vistas; suites can easily accommodate four. Golfers like the remodeled 18-hole course (par 72), driving range, 18-hole putting course, pro shop, and resident PGA professional. Guests can swim in a covered pool, play indoor or outdoor tennis, exercise in the sizable fitness center, sweat in a sauna, soak in a hot tub, or jog and hike the forested trails. Kids have their own game room and can join regularly scheduled guided activities. The massive wooden lodge houses two restaurants, an attic lounge, a library, conference rooms, and the splendid Out of the Woods gift shop. The main dining room—a stunning venue with lovely views and a Northwest-oriented menu—has garnered multiple awards, but is no longer a top-tier coastal eatery. The wine cellar, however, remains one of the Northwest's finest (it has an entire wall of Oregon pinot noirs) and hosts occasional wine dinners. *$$$–$$$$; AE, DC, DIS, MC, V; checks OK; reservations@salishan.com; www.salishan.com; east side of Hwy 101.* &

Depoe Bay

Amid the coastal sprawl, parts of this still-charming community remain intact, including its picturesque and tiny harbor (billed as the smallest anywhere). **WHALE-WATCHING** is big here, and during the gray whale migratory season (Dec–Apr), the leviathans may cruise within hailing distance of headlands, sometimes rubbing against offshore rock formations to rid themselves of troublesome barnacles (see "See the Whales" in this chapter). Metal art, ceramics, and unusual indoor fountains can be seen at **DANCING COYOTE GALLERY** (34 NE Hwy 101; 541/765-3366). Three miles south at Otter Rock, **FLYING DUTCHMAN WINERY** (915 W 1st St; 541/765-2060; *www.dutchmanwinery.com*) offers free tastes, tours, and beach access.

RESTAURANTS

Tidal Raves / ★★

279 NW HWY 101, DEPOE BAY; 541/765-2995 The parking lot always seems full at this classy, cliff-side eatery. True, the vistas of swirling surf crashing on shoreside rocks and partially submerged reefs (plus peeks at spouting whales

COASTAL CELEBRATIONS

Oregon's coastal festivals highlight everything from Scandinavian dancers and sandcastles to clams and kites. Some of the best festivals center on food.

Eat, drink, and be merry with thousands of revelers at February's **SEAFOOD & WINE FESTIVAL** (800/262-7844) in Newport, the coast's original (and, many say, still the best) seafood bash. Add an ethnic bent to your revelry at June's **SCANDINAVIAN MIDSUMMER FESTIVAL** in Astoria (800/875-6807), featuring costumed dancers and a good-luck troll. Seaside (Visitors Bureau: 888/306-2326) holds a **COFFEE & CHOCOLATE LOVERS FESTIVAL** in February, and the coast's biggest **VOLLEYBALL BASH** (more than 2,500 players) in August.

Experienced and novice kite flyers gravitate to Lincoln City—situated on the 45th parallel, halfway between the equator and the North Pole, and considered one of America's premier kite-flying venues—for a spring gathering (usually in May) and the grandiose **FALL KITE FESTIVAL** (800/452-2151). Probably the coast's best-known festival is Cannon Beach's annual **SANDCASTLE DAY** (503/436-2623), a contest that attracts national attention, until the tide comes in and washes away the magnificent sculptures.

Other possibilities include Newport's classically oriented July **ERNEST BLOCH MUSIC FESTIVAL** (800/262-7844) and August's **TILLAMOOK COUNTY FAIR** (503/842-2272)—don't miss the pig 'n' Ford races, where drivers share vintage Model Ts with squealing porkers. Depoe Bay's **INDIAN SALMON BAKE** (877/485-8348) is a sumptuous September feast. Astoria's **GREAT COLUMBIA CROSSING AND SILVER SALMON FESTIVAL** (800/875-6807) affords runners and walkers their only opportunity to traverse the interstate bridge on foot. Cannon Beach's appropriately named November **STORMY WEATHER ARTS FESTIVAL** (503/436-2623) features music, theater, gallery hopping, and wave watching.

—*Richard Fencsak*

during migrating season) are stupendous from every table. But what customers consistently rave about is the seafood, even though choosing from the extensive menu can be irksome. Smoked-salmon chowder, garlic shrimp, and spinach-oyster bisque are splendid starters. So is Seahawk bread, a baguette spread with smoked salmon, shrimp, cream cheese, onions, and havarti. Thai-grilled tiger shrimp marinated in curry, a signature dish, is a can't-miss entrée. Ditto for cioppino, an unbelievably rich Dungeness crab casserole, and oysters coated with spicy cornmeal crust, sided with chipotle sauce. See what we mean about too many choices? *$$; DIS, MC, V; Oregon checks only; lunch, dinner every day; beer and wine; reservations recommended; west side of Hwy 101.*

LODGINGS

Channel House / ★★

35 ELLINGSON ST, DEPOE BAY; 541/765-2140 OR 800/447-2140 You can't sleep any closer to the ocean than this without spending the night aboard a boat. A rocky shoreline—not beach—lies below Channel House, so surf crashes right outside your room. And the contemporary-styled lodging is spectacularly situated on a cliff above the Depoe Bay channel and the Pacific. All 12 units include pine furnishings, private baths, and ocean views. Ten units are truly special, outfitted with private decks, gas fireplaces, and spas (the seven roomier, and spendier, suites feature oceanfront spas on private decks). Two additional (and similarly appointed) units are located in the owner's house a few doors away. Every unit is equipped with binoculars, a bonus during whale-watching season. Come morning, you enjoy a continental buffet breakfast (fruits, cereals, fresh-baked breads and pastries) in an ocean-side dining area. No children. *$$$–$$$$; AE, DIS, MC, V; checks OK; cfinseth@channelhouse.com; www.channelhouse.com; end of Ellingson St.*

Newport

The coast's busiest destination, Newport offers a potpourri of activities and attractions. The historic **NYE BEACH AREA**, on the ocean side of the highway, has a funky arts-community feel and an easily accessible beach. Here the **NEWPORT PERFORMING ARTS CENTER** (777 S Olive St; 541/265-ARTS; *www.coastarts.org/pac*) hosts music, theater, and other events, some national caliber. **PANINI BAKERY** (232 NW Coast St; 541/265-5033) purveys artisan breads, sandwiches, pastries, and Newport's best pizza, while **TEA & TOMES LTD** (716 NW Beach Dr; 541/265-2867; *www.virtualtea.com/tnt*) re-creates the ritual and elegance of English afternoon tea.

To the east is the **YAQUINA BAY** front, a working harbor going full tilt, where all types of fishing boats berth year-round. Many charter boat companies offer fishing trips, whale-watching excursions, and eco-trips. Quaff a native beer (Shakespeare Stout or Mocha Porter, for instance) at **ROGUE ALES PUBLIC HOUSE** (748 SW Bay Blvd; 541/265-3188; *www.rogue.com*), with upstairs "bed & beer" rooms; or head for the brew pub **BREWERS ON THE BAY** (2320 OSU Dr; 541/867-3664; *www.rogue.com/brewery.html*), located directly under the Yaquina Bay Bridge. **SHARK'S SEAFOOD BAR & STEAMER CO.** (852 SW Bay Blvd; 541/574-0590) serves fresh fish and fine chowder. Just up the hill, the supposedly haunted **YAQUINA BAY LIGHTHOUSE** (536 Bay Front St; 541/265-5679) is open for tours.

Art reigns at numerous Newport galleries. **OCEANIC ARTS CENTER** (444 SW Bay Blvd; 541/265-5963) displays jewelry, paintings, pottery, and sculpture. The **WOOD GALLERY** (818 SW Bay Blvd; 541/265-6843) exhibits woodwork, pottery, and weaving. Watch glass blowing at **PYROMANIA GLASS STUDIO** (3101 Ferry Slip Rd; 541/867-4650 or 888/743-4116). For a bird's-eye perspective of boats, bay, and ocean, take a drive through **YAQUINA BAY STATE PARK** (under Yaquina Bay Bridge), which wraps around the south end of town.

On the southeast side of the Yaquina Bay Bridge, Oregon State University's **HATFIELD MARINE SCIENCE CENTER** (2030 S Marine Science Dr; 541/867-0100; *hmsc.oregonstate.edu*) has an octopus tank (and a touch tank with other marine animals), interactive video displays and computer games, ecology classes, and nature walks. Nearby is the **OREGON COAST AQUARIUM** (2820 SE Ferry Slip Rd; 541/867-3474; *www.aquarium.org*), home to 15,000 furry, finny, and feathery critters cavorting in re-created tide pools, cliffs, and caves. The blockbuster "Passages of the Deep" exhibit lets visitors stroll through an underwater acrylic tunnel surrounded by marine life. A couple of miles farther south is the area's best and most extensive camping site (including yurts), **SOUTH BEACH STATE PARK** (off Hwy 101; 541/867-4715; *www.oregonstateparks.org/park_209.php*).

North of town, above Agate Beach, **YAQUINA HEAD OUTSTANDING NATURAL AREA** (off Hwy 101; 541/574-3100) includes the restored Yaquina Head Lighthouse (circa 1873; open to the public), an interpretive center, hiking trails, and an intertidal area (for viewing marine organisms from seaweeds to shore crabs) that's accessible for people with disabilities and safe for kids.

RESTAURANTS

April's / ★★

749 NW 3RD ST, NEWPORT; 541/265-6855 Mediterranean flavors with an Italian accent shine as brightly as a dazzling summer sunset at this diminutive café (just a dozen tables) pressed up against the Nye Beach sidewalk. Simple, skillfully crafted preparations dominate the regular menu and the specials sheet. Delicate pasta pomodoro tossed with fresh tomatoes and flecked with Parmesan, chili flakes, and bread crumbs might remind seasoned travelers of their last trip to Naples. Polenta comes crowned with apple-turkey sausage, while Tuscan grilled chicken is infused with lemon and thyme. Pan-seared salmon might receive a zinfandel and rosemary treatment; halibut, a romesco sauce. But regulars swoon over the myriad fish and shellfish rolled into cannelloni tubes redolent of dill and tarragon. The wine list includes 70 bottles, with upwards of 15 wines sold by the glass at reasonable prices. *$$; AE, DIS, MC, V; checks OK; dinner Wed–Sun (closed Jan); beer and wine; reservations recommended; aprils@newportnet.com; across from Sylvia Beach Hotel.* &

Canyon Way Restaurant and Bookstore / ★

1216 SW CANYON WY, NEWPORT; 541/265-8319 Central-coast cognoscenti book a table at this hillside eatery tucked into the back of a century-old building, then arrive early to peruse the on-site bookstore and gift shop, Newport's choicest browse with 20,000 titles. The restaurant, likewise, affords a pleasingly diverse lineup: pan-fried cod "fingers" paired with "angel hair" onion rings, French onion soup showcasing three cheeses, and ginger-garlic chicken sautéed with peppers and mushrooms for lunch. In the evening, there's grilled local salmon with saffron risotto, honey-roasted duck breast, Oregon bouillabaisse, and filet mignon graced with a green peppercorn sauce. Summer dining can be delightful on the deck overlooking Yaquina Bay. For daytime takeout, consider a humongous Sidewalk sub sandwich from the deli. *$$; AE, DIS, MC, V; checks OK; lunch, dinner Tues–Sat (deli Tues–Sat, bookstore Mon–Sat); full bar; reservations recommended; between Hurbert and Bay Sts.* &

Saffron Salmon / ★★

859 SW BAY BLVD, NEWPORT; 541/265-8921 Bet you can't eat just one of the fabulous crispy frites at Newport's newest "rave" restaurant. It's worth a visit to this bay-front eatery painted in soft earth tones and adorned with eye-catching art simply to sample these squiggly, twice-cooked, candylike shoestring potatoes. Pair an order with a grilled Black Angus burger topped with Tillamook cheddar and apple-smoked bacon, or a messy-good slab of salmon sandwiched into toasted focaccia slices (from Newport's Panini Bakery). Come dinner, a larger fillet of that same local salmon arrives oven-roasted and coated with a signature orange-saffron concoction. Save some sauce for the accompanying hazelnut risotto cake. White bean soup simmered with herbs and veggies or an avocado-tomato salad graced with Dungeness crab and grilled prawns are ideal starters or light-appetite entrees. Four-berry (strawberry, blueberry, raspberry, marionberry) cobbler à la mode and lemon curd–filled layer cake frosted with white chocolate are favored desserts. Grab a window table and watch sea lions frolic in the bay below or ogle seagulls as they zoom to and fro from a pier-side wooden railing. *$$; DIS, MC, V; checks OK; lunch, dinner Thurs–Tues; beer and wine; reservations recommended; south end of the bay front.* &

Whale's Tale / ★

452 SW BAY BLVD, NEWPORT; 541/265-8660 It's been around for more than a quarter century, but this whale ain't stale. Open the wooden door and step into a cavelike interior decorated with marine-mammal paraphernalia and frequented by a diverse clientele. The person at the next table might be a commercial fisherperson, a suit from "uptown" Newport, or an adventurous tourist. Poppy-seed pancakes and jalapeño omelets are morning favorites. At noon, a Yaquina oyster sandwich and a lusty fisherman's stew draw raves. Troll-caught salmon prepared several ways, pan-fried tiger prawns, and sausage or veggie lasagne are top evening choices. *$$; AE, DC, DIS, MC, V; checks OK; breakfast, lunch, dinner every day; beer and wine; no reservations; bay front at Hurbert St.*

LODGINGS

Nye Beach Hotel & Café / ★

219 NW CLIFF ST, NEWPORT; 541/265-3334 This funky, '50s-looking oceanfront lodging built in 1992 fits right in with Historic Nye Beach, a section of town that has been welcoming vacationers for more than a century. Green metal railings lead to second and third floors with narrow carpeted hallways sporting wildly shaped mirrors and myriad greenery. All 18 tidy guest rooms have private baths, fireplaces, willow love seats, balconies, and ocean views (a half-dozen units have spas). A piano, a tiny bar, and a chirpy cockatiel are attention-getters in the lobby. Steps lead down to a bistro-like area that's a must-stop for a morning beverage or an evening libation. An available-anytime menu lists Scotch eggs, Mexican quiche, shrimp étouffée, even biscuits and gravy. Outside is an expansive heated deck for above-the-beach lounging or dining. *$$; AE, DIS, MC, V; checks OK; hotel@nyebeach.com; www.nyebeach.com; just south of Sylvia Beach Hotel.* ♿

Sylvia Beach Hotel / ★★★

 267 NW CLIFF ST, NEWPORT; 541/265-5428 OR 888/795-8422 In lieu of overnighting in a library, this rambling and sometimes creaky four-story structure seemingly plunked on a bluff above Nye Beach is the preferred sleepover for voracious readers. Owners Goody Cable and Sally Ford have dedicated each of their 20 guest rooms to a renowned author. The spendiest rooms are the ocean-facing "classics," with fireplaces and decks. The Agatha Christie Suite is bedecked in lush green chintz, and "clues" abound (shoes poking out from beneath a curtain, bottles labeled "poison" in the medicine cabinet). "Best sellers" (views) and "novels" (no views) are smaller and less impressive, but equally imaginative (a mechanized pendulum swings over the third-floor Edgar Allan Poe bed, for example). Tomes and periodicals are everywhere, especially in the ocean-front upstairs reading room that ascends into the attic. A warming fireplace and complimentary hot wine (served at 10pm) enhance the bookish ambiance. Guests gather family-style for meals (breakfast is included) in the downstairs Tables of Content restaurant, where interaction is encouraged. Simply prepared seafood gets top billing at the prix-fixe, reservation-only dinners. As at breakfast, the food is noteworthy, but meals take a backseat to the company. No phones, TVs, or radios. *$$–$$$; AE, MC, V; checks OK; www.sylviabeachhotel.com; oceanfront.* ♿

Waldport

Bookended by better-known neighbors (Newport and Yachats), Waldport is a sleepy town with a city center unspoiled by tourism. The **ALSEA BAY BRIDGE**, built in 1937 and rebuilt in 1991 (on Hwy 101), is the coast's most picturesque span, and protected walkways extend on either side of its half-mile-plus length. At the south end of the bridge, an interpretive center exhibits photos and historical transportation displays. In the middle of town, **GRAND CENTRAL PIZZA** (235 Hwy 101; 541/563-3232) offers massive "grinder" sandwiches, pizza, and second-deck dining overlooking Alsea Bay.

East in the Old Town section, **DOCK OF THE BAY MARINA** (1245 Mill St; 541/563-2003) sells angling equipment and rents boats, crab rings, and kayaks. Buy some bait and try your luck from the Port of Alsea pier (Port St and the bay front).

LODGINGS

Cliff House Bed and Breakfast / ★★

1450 ADAHI RD, WALDPORT; 541/563-2506 Waldport's finest views can be enjoyed from Cliff House, a romantic retreat perched above the Alsea River's mouth and geared to cuddling couples. Innkeepers Sharon and Keith Robinson continue to add personal touches to their historic home—handcrafted copper cut-out art, quilts sewn by their parents, and such. Four rooms, all with ocean views, are appointed with antiques, TV/VCRs, and refrigerators (and satiny robes for guests); three have balconies (the cozy Redwood Room has an adjacent, but private, bath). A king four-poster bed, a century-old parlor stove, chandeliers, and a fully mirrored bath with spa grace the opulent Suite, a honeymooners' dream. In the ocean-facing Great Room, guests can munch Sharon's cookies and sip beverages, warm to a woodstove fire, and savor memorable sunsets. Out back, a 65-foot-long ocean-view deck is surrounded by glass and outfitted with a hot tub. A trail leads to the beach below. Massages ($50 per hour by appointment) are administered in the front-yard gazebo, ensconced in a garden complete with a putting green. Full breakfasts might include Dungeness crab quiche, cheese blintzes, sugar-plum scones, and raspberry-hazelnut muffins. *$$$–$$$$; MC, V; checks OK; innkeeper@cliff houseoregon.com; www.cliffhouseoregon.com; 1 block west of Hwy 101.*

Edgewater Cottages / ★

3978 SW PACIFIC COAST HWY, WALDPORT; 541/563-2240 The owners live on the premises, contributing to the homey atmosphere at these shaked, shingled, and very popular (full all summer) lodgings situated on a knoll above the beach. All eight units have ocean views, fireplaces (wood provided), well-equipped kitchens, and sun decks, but no phones (guests can use the office phone). The pint-sized Wheel House (with a queen bed and three skylights) is strictly a couple's affair, while the commodious three-bedroom, three-bath Beachcomber can accommodate as many as 15. Children are welcome; even pets can stay with prior approval (and a $10 surcharge). Out back, a short trail leads to 8 miles of uncrowded sand. *$$–$$$; no credit cards; checks OK; min stay requirements; 2¼ miles south of Waldport.*

Yachats

Called the "gem of the Oregon Coast," Yachats (pronounced "YA-hots") recently has graduated from village to small-town status, which the resident mix of aging countercultural types, ex-loggers, and transplanted urban boomers may or may not consider a positive step. Either way, the place continues to exude a hip, artsy ambiance and counts numerous galleries. **EARTHWORKS GALLERY** (2222 N Hwy 101; 541/547-4300) is a remodeled myrtlewood factory specializing in ceramics, hand-blown glass, and metal-and-wood sculptures. **TOUCHSTONE GALLERY** (2118 Hwy 101; 541/547-4121) sells exquisite jewelry, glass, paintings, and ceramics. North of town, the **TOLE TREE** (2334 Hwy 101; 541/547-3608) is a decorative and folk arts center offering supplies and classes.

Beachcombers flock to the Yachats River, which intersects downtown and emp-ties into the Pacific, providing a playground for seabirds, seals, and sea lions. **SMELT SANDS STATE RECREATION AREA** (off Hwy 101), a small day-use area on the north side of town, is the beginning of Yachats 804 Oceanfront Trail, a wheelchair-accessible, paved path that meanders north almost a mile above driftwood-strewn coves.

A 2,700-acre rain forest boasting twice the botanical mass, per square acre, of the Amazon jungle, the **CAPE PERPETUA SCENIC AREA** is just south of town. To get oriented, head for the **CAPE PERPETUA INTERPRETIVE CENTER** (2400 Hwy 101, 3 miles south of Yachats; 541/547-3289; *www.newportnet.com/capeperpetua/*), which features please-touch exhibits and family environmental programs, such as tide-pool explorations, on spring and summer weekends. On a clear day, the West Shelter (above the Interpretive Center; accessible by road or trail) affords the coast's finest view, a 150-mile, north-to-south panorama from Cape Foulweather to Cape Blanco and 40 miles out to sea.

RESTAURANTS

The Drift Inn / ★

124 HIGHWAY 101N, YACHATS; 541/547-4477 From the outside, you might expect a traditional Oregon Coast watering hole selling suds, pepperoni sticks, and hardboiled eggs from a jar. But the atmosphere and menu are hardly tavernlike at this welcoming local hangout fronting the highway. Inside are polished hardwood floors, wooden booths, an attractive bar running the full length of the inn, spunky servers, and stout tables capable of supporting multiple platters of food. Mixing and matching is the preferred ordering strategy. You might begin with a crab cocktail or a plate of sweet-potato empanadas, then move on to but-ternut squash ravioli, a creamy chanterelle casserole (in season), or a teriyaki burger. Cappuccino cheesecake and pumpkin bread pudding are delish. The beverage list is legion: Italian sodas and cremosas; 15 beers in the bottle, 10 on tap; 15 wines (by the bottle or glass); even a trio of sparkling wines and a port. Regular live music, too. *$–$$; MC, V; checks OK; lunch, dinner every day; full bar; no reservations; east side of Hwy 101, midway through town.*

La Serre / ★

160 W 2ND ST, YACHATS; 541/547-3420 French influences are evident inside this distinctive (a high-beamed ceiling, overhead skylights) and expansive fine-dining establishment. The restaurant's name, after all, is French and translates to "the greenhouse." But Gallic fare is limited to the selection of crepes, a warm wedge of Brie accompanied by garlic toast, and the house-specialty clam puffs—clams, herbs, and cream cheese baked in puff pastry. Simply prepared dishes, such as Dungeness crab cakes paired with pork ribs, breaded Umpqua oysters, fish-erman's stew, oven-roasted free-range fowl, and a half-pound filet mignon wrapped in bacon and crowned with mushrooms, highlight the menu. La Serre also is one of the few coastal restaurants to purvey both New England- and Manhattan-style clam chowder. A cozy lounge with cushy couches and a fireplace is a fine locale to enjoy a post-meal libation. *$$; AE, MC, V; local checks only; dinner Wed–Mon (closed Jan); full bar; reservations recommended; at Beach Rd, downtown.*

LODGINGS

Sea Quest Bed & Breakfast / ★★★

 95354 HWY 101, YACHATS; 541/547-3782 OR 800/341-4878 An exquisitely appointed palatial structure situated on a 2½-acre bench of land right above the Pacific, Sea Quest is rightly ranked among the coast's best B&Bs. All five guest rooms enjoy bathtub spas, private entrances, and ocean views, and are close enough to the Pacific to feel the pull of the tides. In the inviting living room, guests can scan the horizon with a mounted spyglass or plunk down with a good book in one of the gaily upholstered plush chairs. Outside is a wraparound deck; go ahead, grab the house binoculars and gaze seaward toward far-off freighters or spot a migrating gray whale. Elaine Ireland, who runs the place with her husband, George Rozsa, is renowned for her breakfast buffet of fresh pastries, fruits, homemade granola, and a special du jour—perhaps blintzes topped with seasonal berries, Dutch babies, or egg casseroles plump with scrumptious innards. *$$$; DIS, MC, V; checks OK; seaquest@newportnet.com; www.seaq.com; 6½ miles south of Yachats.*

Ziggurat Bed & Breakfast / ★★

 95330 HWY 101, YACHATS; 541/547-3925 A four-story, glass-and-wood structure that takes its name from the ancient Sumerian word for "terraced pyramid," this is surely the coast's most visually stunning B&B. The location is equally dramatic, on a sandy knoll just back from the ocean and beside the gurgling waters of Tenmile Creek. The entire ground floor is devoted to guests, and two spacious suites are available: the Southeast Suite faces the Coast Range mountains and boasts a sauna and an additional bed; the West Suite enjoys a round, glass-block shower and stellar seascapes enhanced by a 27-foot wall of glass. A woodstove and a baby grand piano highlight the expansive living quarters. No children younger than 14. *$$$; no credit cards; checks OK; www.newportnet.com/ziggurat; 6½ miles south of Yachats.*

SOUTHERN
OREGON COAST

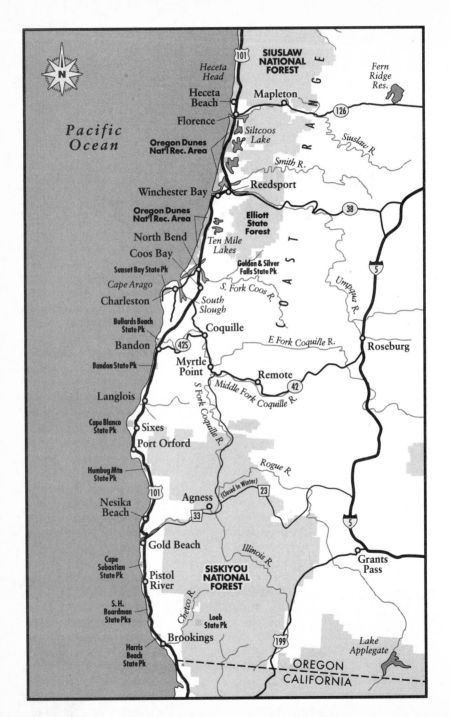

Pacific
Ocean

Heceta
Head

SIUSLAW
NATIONAL
FOREST

Fern
Ridge
Res.

Heceta
Beach

Mapleton

Florence

Siltcoos
Lake

Oregon Dunes
Nat'l Rec. Area

Smith R.

Winchester Bay

Reedsport

Oregon Dunes
Nat'l Rec. Area

Elliott
State
Forest

North Bend

Ten Mile
Lakes

Coos Bay

Golden & Silver
Falls State Pk

Sunset Bay State Pk

S. Fork Coos R.

Cape Arago

South
Slough

Charleston

Bullards Beach
State Pk

Coquille

E Fork Coquille R.

Roseburg

Bandon

Bandon State Pk

Myrtle
Point

Remote

Middle Fork Coquille R.

Langlois

S Fork Coquille R.

Cape Blanco
State Pk

Sixes

Port Orford

Humbug Mtn
State Pk

Rogue R.

(Closed In Winter)

Nesika
Beach

Agness

Gold Beach

Cape
Sebastian
State Pk

Illinois R.

SISKIYOU
NATIONAL
FOREST

Grants
Pass

Pistol
River

S. H.
Boardman
State Pks

Chetco R.

Loeb
State Pk

Brookings

Harris
Beach
State Pk

Lake
Applegate

OREGON

CALIFORNIA

Siuslaw R.

Umpqua R.

SOUTHERN OREGON COAST

Out of reach of any urban center, much of Oregon's south coast is isolated and undeveloped. Only a few cities of any size break up this 150-mile stretch of mostly wild seashore. The eight major towns are ports situated near the mouths of rivers: Florence, on the Siuslaw; Reedsport and Winchester Bay, on the Umpqua; Coos Bay and North Bend, on the Coos; Bandon, on the Coquille; Gold Beach, on the Rogue; and Brookings, on the Chetco, with a location almost equidistant from Portland and San Francisco and an eight-hour drive from either.

The south coast geography is world-class. Sahara-sized dunes within the Oregon Dunes National Recreation Area extend south from Florence almost 50 miles to North Bend. Farther along, a series of state parks encompasses rocky headlands forested with myrtlewood trees, wild azaleas, rhododendrons, and various conifers, including aromatic Port Orford cedars and, near Brookings, magnificent towering redwoods.

Coos Bay is the largest natural bay north of San Francisco, and for years was the Southern Oregon Coast's center for resource extraction—everything from gold and coal to oysters and forest products. There's far less maritime traffic these days, but the city (and neighboring North Bend) retains its unscrubbed, rough 'n' tumble look. The pristine Coos estuary is habitat for thousands of migrating waterfowl. From lookouts on the rugged cliffs of Cape Arago, you can view offshore rocks populated with seabirds, seals, and barking sea lions and, during early and late winter, watch gray whales migrating south to Mexico or north toward Arctic feeding grounds.

Reedsport, Gold Beach, and tiny Port Orford are seeing surges of tourism. Florence and Brookings are bustling retirement communities. And Bandon has become a renowned golfing destination: the seashore topography has been reconfigured into two golf courses, Bandon Dunes and Pacific Dunes; both are reminiscent of Scotland's St. Andrews and California's Pebble Beach (a third course, Bandon Trails, is under construction and is expected to be completed by summer 2005). Throughout the region, recreational opportunities such as hiking, fishing, kayaking, surfing, mountain biking, windsurfing, and beachcombing are virtually unlimited. Ask the locals where to go or what to do; they're fiercely independent and almost universally friendly.

ACCESS AND INFORMATION

US HIGHWAY 101 follows the Pacific coastline from Washington to Southern California and links most of the towns along the Southern Oregon Coast. From Interstate 5, four two-lane paved roads follow rivers west to the south coast: from Eugene, **HIGHWAY 126** follows the Siuslaw River to Florence; from Drain, **HIGHWAY 38** follows the Umpqua River to Reedsport; from Roseburg, **HIGHWAY 42** follows the Coquille River to Bandon and Coos Bay; and from Grants Pass, **US HIGHWAY 199** follows the Smith River, then cuts through the redwoods and dips into Northern California near the Oregon border and Brookings. All are scenic routes. Air service between Portland and North Bend is offered on **HORIZON AIR** (800/547-9308; *www.horizonair.com*); **GREYHOUND** (800/231-2222; *www.greyhound.com*) has regular bus service.

Florence

Intersected by the deep, green Siuslaw River, Florence is surrounded by the beauty of the **OREGON DUNES NATIONAL RECREATION AREA**. The geography here—and for 50 miles south—is devoid of the trademark rugged Oregon coastal headlands. Instead, expansive, wind-sculpted sand dunes dominate the landscape. Orient yourself to this intriguing ecosystem by exploring **SOUTH JETTY ROAD**, just south of the bridge across the Siuslaw River, or the **OREGON DUNES OVERLOOK**, 11 miles south on Highway 101. The dunes (some tower 600 feet high) hide excellent swimming lakes; just east, several larger lakes are circled by pines and, in spring and summer, bright pink and red rhododendrons.

Florence is a growing tourist mecca with strip development up and down Hwy 101, but **OLD TOWN**, a continually upgraded few blocks of shops, restaurants, and lodgings, has become visitor-oriented without selling out to schlock. The best java is blended at **SIUSLAW RIVER COFFEE ROASTERS** (1240 Bay St; 541/997-3443), with a river view from the deck and a paperback book library. A small sternwheeler, **WESTWARD HO!** (Maple and Bay Sts; 541/997-9691), offers half-hour and dinner river cruises from Old Town. If you want a closer view, launch a kayak from **CENTRAL COAST WATERSPORTS** (1560 2nd St; 541/997-1812).

DARLINGTONIA BOTANICAL WAYSIDE (5 miles north of Florence on the east side of Hwy 101) is a bog featuring *Darlingtonia californica,* pitcher plants with unusual burgundy flowers that bloom in May and devour insects. Farther north, 14 miles of trails await equestrians on Cape Mountain. Stop at **C & M STABLES** (90241 Hwy 101; 541/997-7540) to rent a steed. **SEA LION CAVES** (91560 Hwy 101; 541/547-3111; *www.sealioncaves.com*)—far less kitschy than the advance hype might suggest—are situated on the breathtaking cliffs of **HECETA HEAD**. You descend 21 stories to a peephole in a natural, surf-swept cavern, where hundreds of golden brown Steller's sea lions frolic or doze on the rocks. **HECETA HEAD LIGHTHOUSE** is the Oregon Coast's most powerful beacon. Perched atop a rock outcropping just off Highway 101, the 56-foot-high lighthouse isn't open to the public, but the grounds, with a trail to Heceta Head Lighthouse State Viewpoint, are yours for a $3 day-use fee. The former lightkeeper's quarters now house a bed and breakfast (541/547-3696).

RESTAURANTS

Cafe Francais / ★★☆

3056 HWY 101, FLORENCE; 541/997-6767 From the outside, it looks like just another nondescript residence-turned-restaurant, but this relocated (from Winchester Bay, 25 miles south) Gallic café is Florence's finest dinner house. An engaging interior, arrayed with a few handsome wood tables draped with flowered linens, is presided over by chef Francois Pere, a finicky-about-freshness Frenchman. His unpretentious country cooking is memorable from the first bite of crusty house bread—French, of course. Starters such as Cajun prawns and stuffed mushrooms are superb, and the café's escargot is unsurpassed on the coast. Entrées (served with soup and salad, vegetables and potato) include salmon finished with lemon-butter sauce; quail paired with seasonal mushrooms; garlic, rosemary, and thyme-infused rack of lamb; and duck l'orange. The well-chosen wine list features French, Oregon, and California selections; desserts (crepe flambé, creme brûlée, chocolate mousse) are not to be overlooked. *$$$; MC, V; checks OK; dinner Wed–Sun; beer and wine; reservations recommended; on Hwy 101, north end of town.*

Firehouse Restaurant / ★

1263 BAY ST, FLORENCE; 541/902-8675 Real firemen *do* eat quiche. That is, when they're not enticed by this Old Town eatery's prime rib hash topped with a couple of eggs or a smoked-salmon omelet sized for a firefighter's appetite. The quiche of the day is plenty tempting and comes stocked with, say, bacon, tomatoes, spinach, and cheeses. Sides such as fried grits and sweet-potato home fries delight with every bite. Lunch and dinner options range from a tri-tip steak sandwiched into a husky hoagie (all sandwiches can be ordered first-, second-, or third-alarm hot) to salmon Oscar splashed with a béarnaise sauce. Even "unmanly" eggplant Parmesan and a veggie stir-fry are offered, and there's a "future firefighters" menu for the small-fry, who will revel in the firefighter memorabilia decorating the restaurant's walls. Everybody (even quiche eaters) has a hard time resisting the cinnamon ice cream. *$–$$; MC, V; checks OK; breakfast, lunch, dinner Tues–Sat; full bar; no reservations; west end of Old Town.*

LODGINGS

Edwin K Bed & Breakfast / ★★

1155 BAY ST, FLORENCE; 541/997-8360 OR 800/8ED-WINK Ensconced in a quiet residential neighborhood just beyond the bustle of Old Town, this roomy, Craftsman-style home was built in 1914 by one of Florence's founders and remains a tribute to the woodcrafters' art. Inside, the place looks formal but feels warm and homey. Ivory wall-to-wall carpeting contrasts nicely with aged and swarthy Douglas fir built-in bookcases and rectangular ceiling panels. Six spacious guest rooms (four upstairs, two down) and one apartment are fitted with ultraplush baths and adorned with antiques. The Spring room features a double shower and spa, while a queen sleigh bed highlights the Autumn room, where French doors open to a backyard garden and waterfall. Innkeepers Inez and Victor West serve top-flight multicourse breakfasts in the exquisitely appointed dining room at a table that seats 12. *$$$; DIS, MC, V; checks OK; edwink@presys.com; www.edwink.com; west edge of Old Town.*

Reedsport and Winchester Bay

Reedsport is a port town on the Umpqua River a few miles inland, and Winchester Bay sits at the river's mouth. Headquarters for the **OREGON DUNES NATIONAL RECREATION AREA** is in Reedsport; orient yourself at the visitor center (855 Hwy 101; 541/271-3611; *www.fs.fed.us/r6/siuslaw/*; see "Oregon Dunes National Recreation Area" in this chapter). On a wharf in Old Town Reedsport is the **UMPQUA DISCOVERY CENTER MUSEUM** (409 Riverfront Wy; 541/271-4816), which features a weather station and exhibits on Native American tribal history and culture, marine life, ocean beaches, and logging. Observe wild elk grazing on the protected

SOUTHERN OREGON COAST THREE-DAY TOUR

DAY ONE: Breakfast in Florence's Old Town at **THE FIREHOUSE**, then head north to **HECETA HEAD** and the **SEA LION CAVES**; take in the scintillating vistas and ride the elevator from the top of the cliff into a natural ocean cave. Back in Florence, stop for coffee and check out the waterfront shops in **OLD TOWN**. Then take the one-hour lunch cruise aboard the **WESTWARD HO!** stern-wheeler on the Siuslaw River, or pack a picnic and hike through the sand dunes at **JESSIE M. HONEYMAN STATE PARK** south of town. Following a country-French dinner at Florence's **CAFE FRANCAIS**, spend the night at the **EDWIN K BED & BREAKFAST**.

    DAY TWO: After breakfast at the Edwin K, drive Hwy 101 south to Coos Bay and west to Charleston. Snag some fish-and-chips and sweet treats at **CHARLESTON STATION**, and explore the trails, gardens, and overlooks at **SUNSET BAY** and **SHORE ACRES STATE PARKS**. Stop by the interpretive center at **SOUTH SLOUGH NATIONAL ESTUARINE RESEARCH CENTER RESERVE**, then continue south on Seven Devils Road, the side alternate route that reconnects with Highway 101 north of Bandon. If you've arranged a tee time for **BANDON DUNES** or **PACIFIC DUNES**

salt marsh and meadow, and watch for new calves in June at the **DEAN CREEK ELK RESERVE**, 4 miles east on Highway 38.

    Tours of the **UMPQUA LIGHTHOUSE** (1020 Lighthouse Wy, Winchester Bay; 541/271-4631; *www.oregonstateparks.org/park_121.php*) are available Wednesday through Sunday in summer; an adjacent museum in the former Coast Guard administration building displays photographs and pioneer history.

North Bend, Coos Bay, and Charleston

It seems ironic that these cities that share so many geographical advantages, including the finest natural harbor between San Francisco and Seattle, presently suffer from lack of investment, high unemployment, and a pervasive rough 'n' tumble appearance. Formerly the world's foremost wood-products exporters, the bay area of North Bend and Coos Bay has been undercut by a sagging timber industry, resulting in far less calls from foreign ships. The cities are making a slow transition from a natural resources–extraction economy to a service-oriented one.

    In the plus column, the Coquille Indian Tribe transformed a former Weyerhaeuser plywood mill into the **MILL RESORT & CASINO** (3201 Tremont Ave, North Bend; 541/756-8800; *www.themillcasino.com*), with a restaurant overlooking the waterfront. The three-story hotel is furnished like a rustic lodge, and most rooms have sunrise views of the bay, river, and Coast Range mountains.

    THE HOUSE OF MYRTLEWOOD (1125 S 1st St, Coos Bay; 541/267-7804; *www.oregonconnection.com* or *www.houseofmyrtlewood.com*) combines wood

GOLF COURSE, play 18 holes; if you haven't, check out the lodge (a sunny lounge with a full-service bar—and espresso—overlooks the first course). Golfers will want to spend the night at this four-star-rated resort. Those who don't golf can go directly to **OLD TOWN** Bandon to browse and enjoy cranberry fudge, then follow the Coquille River to the jetty at its mouth and hike the spectacular beach past enormous haystack rocks. Grab dinner at **HARP'S**, overlooking the river and the historic lighthouse. Reserve the Gray Whale room at Bandon's **LIGHTHOUSE BED AND BREAKFAST** and, from your whirlpool tub for two, watch the sun set and moon rise.

DAY THREE: Rise at the crack of dawn, thermos of something hot in hand, and drive 40 scenic miles to **GOLD BEACH**; try to resist the charms of Cape Blanco and Humbug Mountain State Parks (near Port Orford) so you can go on a daylong **JET-BOAT TRIP** up the Rogue River (make arrangements in advance)—a stop is made for lunch on the way upriver. Check in at **TU TU'TUN LODGE** overlooking the Rogue, and request a room with a hot tub on your deck. After dinner in the lodge's majestic dining room, have a soak and, perhaps, spy an eagle or osprey soaring overhead in the fading light. Spend the evening wrapped in a robe in front of your private fireplace.

products and tourism, annually drawing thousands of visitors who stop to buy the bowls, plates, salt shakers, and clocks (among other items) the factor has been making since 1929. Oregon's myrtlewood tree, related to the California bay tree, grows only within a 90-square-mile area on the south Oregon coast, between Coos Bay and the California border.

Fishing boats, tugs, and historical photographs can be seen on the **COOS BAY WATERFRONT**. The local arts scene includes the **COOS ART MUSEUM** (235 Anderson Ave, Coos Bay; 541/267-3901; *www.coosart.org*), with many big city–quality exhibits; **SOUTHWESTERN OREGON COMMUNITY COLLEGE** (1988 Newmark Ave, Coos Bay; 541/888-2525; *www.socc.edu*), which schedules art shows and musical performances; and July's two-week **OREGON COAST MUSIC FESTIVAL** (541/267-0938; *www.coosnet.com/music/*), which features classical, jazz, and world music. West of town, **CHARLESTON'S DOCKS** moor Coos Bay's commercial fishing fleet. Fresh seafood is readily available at **CHUCK'S SEAFOOD** (5055 Boat Basin Dr; 541/888-5525) and **QUALMAN OYSTER FARMS** (4898 Crown Point Rd; 541/888-3145). Buy bagels, donuts, fruit fritters, cinnamon rolls, cobblers, and other baked goodies at **CHARLESTON STATION** (91120 Cape Arago Hwy; 541/888-3306). Hikers, canoeists, and kayakers (no motor boats) explore the **SOUTH SLOUGH NATIONAL ESTUARINE RESEARCH CENTER RESERVE** (61907 Seven Devils Rd; 541/888-5558), 4 miles south of Charleston.

Southwest of Charleston on the Cape Arago Highway, **SUNSET BAY STATE PARK** (12 miles southwest of Coos Bay; 541/888-3778), with year-round camping (including yurts), has a bowl-shaped cove with 50-foot cliffs on either side—good for a swim because the water is perpetually calm, though cold. Farther down the road at **SHORE ACRES STATE PARK** (541/888-3732), a cliff-side botanical garden contains a restored caretaker's house (impressively lit at Christmas) and an impeccably maintained display of native and exotic plants. Watch winter storms—or whales—from an enclosed shelter here. Still farther south, **CAPE ARAGO STATE PARK** (541/888-3778) overlooks the **OREGON ISLANDS NATIONAL WILDLIFE REFUGE** (541/867-4550; *oregoncoast.fws.gov/oregonislands/*), home to seabirds, seals, and sea lions. The Oregon Coast Trail winds through all three parks. For more information, contact the Oregon Parks and Recreation Department (503/378-6305; *www.prd.state.or.us/*); for camping reservations, call 800/452-5687.

RESTAURANTS

Blue Heron Bistro / ★

100 W COMMERCIAL AVE, COOS BAY; 541/267-3933 It looks a bit tired inside and out (as do many structures in town), but this bistro still packs culinary pop. The reasonably priced menu lists a plethora of options: choose from omelets; breakfast parfaits (yogurt, fruit, and muesli); salads; and myriad sandwiches, such as a Reuben fashioned with pastrami, smoked Gouda, and apple-infused sauerkraut. Continent-hopping evening fare runs the gamut from blackened snapper Southern style (with rice, black beans, and corn relish), to a fine veggie lasagne with spinach and three cheeses, to Tex-Mex entrées and a German sausage plate. The dessert lineup showcases a fine apple pie and variations on a chocolate theme. Order from a list of more than 40 kinds of bottled beer. *$$; MC, V; local checks only; breakfast, lunch, dinner every day; beer and wine; reservations for 6 or more; at Hwy 101.* &

Cedar Grill / ★

201 CENTRAL AVE, COOS BAY; 541/267-7100 This popular Bay Area hangout occupies a former brew pub (formerly a bank). The stately building lends a chummy atmosphere, but food is the main attraction. Lunch brings downtown business types and tourists, who feast on open-faced steak sandwiches with enormous onion rings on the side, tuna burgers paired with Asian pasta salads, and pork ribs slathered with mango barbecue sauce. Everyone from the cool and hip to Coos Bay's hard-core blue-collar crowd drops in for dinner. Lightly breaded local oysters, signature cedar-planked salmon or halibut, grandiose cuts of prime rib, and sambuca prawn linguine are evening favorites. *$$; AE, MC, V; local checks only; lunch, dinner Tues–Sat; full bar; reservations recommended; corner of 2nd.* &

LODGINGS

Coos Bay Manor Bed & Breakfast / ★

955 S 5TH ST, COOS BAY; 541/269-1224 OR 800/269-1224 A grand 1912 Colonial-style structure (built by two Finnish brothers) with large rooms and high ceilings, this B&B sits on a beautifully landscaped residential street overlooking the waterfront, but up the hill from Highway 101's commercial glitz. Five guest rooms (three with private baths) are distinctively decorated—the Baron's Room has a four-poster canopy bed in brocade and tapestry; the Victorian features lots of lace and ruffles. On mellow summer mornings, innkeepers Pam and Bill

Bate serve breakfast on the upstairs open-air balcony patio. Quiz Bill about where to go and what to do in the Coos Bay area. Families are welcome. *$–$$; DIS, MC, V; checks OK; cbmanor@charter.net; www.coosbaymanor.com; 4 blocks above waterfront.*

The Old Tower House / ★★

476 NEWMARK AVE, COOS BAY; 541/888-6058 One of the few historic houses remaining in the former bustling Empire district of Coos Bay (on the road to Charleston), this lovely Victorian built by Dr. C. W. Tower in 1872 overlooks in- and outbound ships. Owners Don and Julia Spangler have restored the historic home and filled it with a bevy of antiques. The main structure contains three guest rooms, which share two spacious baths. Our choice, the Rose Room, has a 150-year-old four-poster bed with a handmade fishnet canopy. Outside, a private garden includes the original apple orchard, dozens of whimsical birdhouses, and two separate quarters (both with private baths): the Ivy Cottage, done in green and white; and the Carriage House, a ship-themed suite with its own kitchen. Full breakfast is served on white linen, china, and vintage crystal in the cozy sun-room. *$$; DIS, MC, V; checks OK; oldtowerhouse@yahoo.com; www.oldtowerhouse .com; take Charleston exit from downtown.*

Bandon

Some locals believe Bandon, the south coast's trendiest town, sits on a "ley line," an underground crystalline structure reputed to be the focus of powerful cosmic energies. Whatever; there's no doubt about the grandeur of the scenery—river views, huge haystack and monolithic offshore rocks, and sweeping Pacific vistas.

Begin in **OLD TOWN**, where the Coquille River waterfront is best seen from the public pier (1st St and Chicago Ave). Other must-stops include the **SECOND STREET GALLERY** (210 2nd St; 541/347-4133) and **BANDON GOURMET** (92 2nd St; 541/347-3237) for artisan breads, breakfasts, takeout sandwiches, and desserts. For another treat, try the candies (and generous free samples) at **CRANBERRY SWEETS** (1st St and Chicago Ave; 541/347-9475). Buy the local catch at **BANDON FISHERIES** (250 1st St SW; 541/347-4282). Watch glassblowers ply their craft at the **BANDON GLASS ART STUDIO** (240 Hwy 101; 541/347-4723; *bandonbythesea .com/bglass.htm*).

The best beach access is from the south jetty in town or from Face Rock Viewpoint on **BEACH LOOP ROAD**. This route parallels the ocean in view of weather-sculpted rock formations and is a good alternative (especially by bicycle) to Highway 101. Two miles north of Bandon, **BULLARDS BEACH STATE PARK** (541/347-2209) occupies an expansive area crisscrossed with hiking and biking trails leading to uncrowded driftwood- and kelp-cluttered beaches. The campground, with yurts near the entrance, is nestled in the pines. Built in 1896, the **COQUILLE RIVER LIGHTHOUSE** (open to the public) is at the end of the park's main road. Good windsurfing is on the river side of the park's spit. Tour the gently flowing Coquille River before the afternoon winds kick up, and poke around the edges of **BANDON MARSH NATIONAL WILDLIFE REFUGE** (look for osprey, harriers, and egrets) in a kayak from **ADVENTURE KAYAK** (315 1st St; 541/347-3480; *www.adventurekayak.com*).

Bandon's cranberry bogs make it one of the nation's premier producers and are the reason for the **BANDON CRANBERRY FESTIVAL** (541/347-9619) in September. Call **FABER FARMS** (541/347-1166) for directions to its tasting room (harvest tours begin in October). Seven miles south of Bandon on Highway 101, you can view lions, tigers, elk, and more at the **WEST COAST GAME PARK SAFARI** (541/347-3106; *www.gameparksafari.com*).

HARP'S ON THE BAY RESTAURANT, arguably Bandon's best-regarded and best-situated eatery (on the Coquille River, in view of the lighthouse and the Pacific), was sold in spring 2004. Like Harps, the new **BANDON CHANNEL HOUSE** (480 First St SW, Bandon; 541/347-9057) specializes in local seafood.

RESTAURANTS

Lord Bennett's / ★★

1695 BEACH LOOP DR, BANDON; 541/347-3663 Named for Bandon's founder, doubly damned for bringing invasive Scotch broom and prickly gorse with him from Scotland, this upscale eatery is directly across Beach Loop Drive from ocean-side cliffs and towering offshore rock formations, so views are scintillating. The cuisine is fancy, fussy, and filling. Veal bolognese is layered with prosciutto and Gruyère; Coos Bay oysters are lavished with spinach, bacon, and Pernod; and grilled hazelnut-encrusted lamb chops arrive on a mound of caramelized onions. Fowl is fantastic: chicken receives an herb marinade and port-cranberry-pomegranate treatment, or is stuffed with spinach and pancetta, baked, and finished with ginger-lime butter. Homemade ice cream is a reliable dessert, and the wine list is extensive, with many Oregon pours available by the glass. Weekend brunches showcase crab enchiladas, shrimp-topped eggs Benedict, lemon soufflé pancakes, and sundry three-egg omelets. *$$–$$$; AE, DIS, MC, V; checks OK; lunch daily (Mon–Fri in winter), dinner daily, brunch Sat–Sun; full bar; reservations recommended; www.bandonbythesea.com/lord_ben.htm; next to Sunset Motel.*

Wild Rose Bistro / ★

130 CHICAGO ST, BANDON; 541/347-4428 Ensconced inside a diminutive Old Town storefront that has seen restaurants come and go is this up-and-coming eatery (with new owners) painted brick red and green. The surprisingly broad menu offers lamb osso buco braised in a wild mushroom sauce; a bounty of seafood stewed with potatoes; and one of the south coast's only renditions of paella, this version packed with chicken, *linguica*, and shellfish. Already, the Wild Rose purveys Bandon's premier vegetarian plates—grilled portobellos layered with seasonal sautéed vegetables, for example, or a tart fat with cheese and onions baked in puff pastry. Specials might include herb-rubbed then seared King salmon, and pork loin stuffed with roasted garlic and rosemary. *$$; AE, DIS, MC, V; checks OK; dinner Thurs–Sun; full bar; reservations recommended; midblock on Chicago Ave in Old Town.*

LODGINGS

Bandon Dunes Golf Resort / ★★★★

ROUND LAKE DR, BANDON; 541/347-4380 OR 888/345-6008 This is golfers' heaven—the soul of the game resides in Bandon Dunes and Pacific Dunes, two walking, 18-hole Scottish links courses designed by Scot architect David McLay Kidd and Tom Doak, respectively. Both courses have garnered worldwide kudos from the golf press and have been named among the top 10 venues in the United States (virtually every golf publication has named the latter the best new course in America; a third course is under construction). Both courses are beloved by scratch players and duffers alike, in part because the prevailing attitude is fun and relaxed, instead of country-club formal. Rather than motor around in golf carts, players walk (and children, especially young golfers, are welcome, too). After navigating the links, many end up in the timber-and-shake clubhouse Lodge, with four monolithic spires of columnar basalt in the lobby and subtle Celtic symbols throughout. The Lodge is also a favored place to stay, offering 19 single rooms and a quartet of suites on the second floor. Four secluded "cottages" surrounding a lily pad–covered pond have 48 additional rooms with queen beds; 84 Chrome Lake rooms and suites all have oversized king beds. Every unit is tastefully appointed, and some have ocean views. Hiking trails meander through dunes and forest (one reaches the beach), and salmon and steelhead fishing trips to the nearby Sixes and Elk Rivers can be arranged. Excellent repasts—everything from meatloaf and a prawn martini to cranberry barbecued chicken and a South Coast bourride (cioppino)—are served in the Gallery Restaurant (with full bar) every day. The adjacent Tufted Puffin lounge offers a full menu and libations until the wee hours; the Bunker Bar has lighter fare and a pool table; while Mulligan's Pub boasts traditional Scottish grub, craft beers, and single-malt Scotches. *$$$–$$$$; AE, DC, DIS, MC, V; no checks; reservations@bandondunesgolf.com; www.bandondunesgolf.com; north end of Coquille River bridge.* &

Beach Street Bed and Breakfast / ★★

200 BEACH ST, BANDON; 541/347-5124 OR 888/335-1076 A homey, romantic place, Beach Street is perfect for small wedding parties and honeymooners. The inn features floral bedspreads on king-sized beds, dried flowers, and a huge vaulted-ceilinged Great Room with comfy chairs, skylights, and an eight-foot-wide fireplace. Some of the six guest accommodations have gas fireplaces and private balconies; all enjoy unobstructed westerly ocean views. Five rooms have two-person spa tubs (our favorites are the Windsor and Oak Rooms). Breakfasts—perhaps blueberry and cran-orange muffins, fruit salad, and Mediterranean quiche—are served in the living/dining room; guests can request a favorite Benedict or crepe, and hosts Sidney and Edel Zeller will add it to the morning repast. No children (unless you rent all the rooms) or pets allowed. *$$$; AE, DIS, MC, V; checks OK; innkeeper@beach-street.com; www.beach-street.com; across from riding stable.*

Lighthouse Bed and Breakfast / ★★

650 JETTY RD, BANDON; 541/347-9316 Spacious and appealing, this contemporary home has windows opening toward the mouth of the Coquille River, its lighthouse, and the ocean, a short walk away. Guests can watch fishing boats, windsurfers, seals, and seabirds, and maybe spy the spout of a migrating gray whale. Five guest rooms (all with ocean or river vistas) are roomy and wonderfully appointed. The top-of-the-inn Gray Whale Room is a stunner, with a king-sized bed, wood-burning stove, TV, and whirlpool tub for two in a view alcove. Breakfasts are top notch. No children or pets. *$$–$$$; MC, V; checks OK; lighthouse@lighthouselodging.com; www.lighthouselodging.com; at 1st St.*

Port Orford

Port Orford is the south coast's oldest town, dating to the mid-19th century, when settlers and Native Americans fought at **BATTLE ROCK** (in town, along Hwy 101); interpretive signs now tell the story. These days, locals are sheep ranchers, cranberry farmers, sea urchin divers, retirees, and fishermen (who use a five-story hoist to launch their boats into the ocean). Check out the **PORT ORFORD HEADS LIFE-SAVING STATION** (edge of town, on 9th St; 541/332-2352; *www.oregonstateparks .org/park_61.php*; open seasonally), built in 1934 and one of the best remaining examples of period architecture. A gem of a grocery store, **PORT ORFORD BREAD-WORKS** (190 6th St; 541/332-4022) purveys artisan loaves (country French, herb and cheese, kalamata olive), imported cheeses and meats (real French Roquefort, mascarpone, finocchiona salami, slabs of prosciutto), and black truffle oil, among other goodies; plus oceanfront dining.

About 10 miles north of town is **BOICE-COPE COUNTY PARK** (south of Langlois off Hwy 101; 541/247-7011), site of fresh-water **FLORAS LAKE**, popular with boaters and windsurfers. A trail system that skirts oceanfront cliffs and wanders through dense forests is suitable for hiking, running, horseback riding, and mountain biking (careful: some of the trails are in disrepair). Fisherfolk visit the Elk and Sixes Rivers for salmon and steelhead.

CAPE BLANCO LIGHTHOUSE (541/332-2207) in **CAPE BLANCO STATE PARK** (5 miles north of Port Orford and 6 miles west of Hwy 101; 541/332-6774; *www.oregonstateparks.org/park_62.php*) is the oldest (since 1870) and most westerly lighthouse in the Lower 48 states—and the windiest station on the coast. The lighthouse, 245 feet above the ocean, and small interpretive center are open seasonally to the public. West of the light station, a path leads to the end of the cape. On the way to Cape Blanco, check out the restored **HUGHES HOUSE** (open Thurs–Mon Apr–Oct), built by the English-born Hughes family, the area's first non-native settlers.

HUMBUG MOUNTAIN STATE PARK (5 miles south of Port Orford off Hwy 101; 541/332-6774) features a steep switchbacked trail to a top-of-the-world panorama at the summit.

LODGINGS

Home by the Sea Bed and Breakfast / ★

444 JACKSON ST, PORT ORFORD; 541/332-2855 OR 877/332-2855 Beach access is easy from this modest, homey B&B atop a bluff near Battle Rock, and guests have the run of a large, pleasantly cluttered dining/living room with a view (plus laundry privileges). Quiche, waffles, omelets, and fresh fruit are morning mainstays. Surf the Internet with chatty Alan Mitchell, a friendly whirlwind of information and a Mac enthusiast who'll gladly give you the local scoop (and daily weather forecasts off the Web). Go online to check out the B&B's south-facing Pacific panorama from the two guest rooms (both on the second floor). *$$; MC, V; checks OK; reservations@home bythesea.com; www.homebythesea.com; 1 block west of Hwy 101.*

Gold Beach

Named for the gold found here in the 19th century, Gold Beach is renowned as the town at the ocean end of the **ROGUE RIVER**, a favorite with whitewater enthusiasts. It's also a supply town for hikers heading up the Rogue into the remote **KALMIOPSIS WILDERNESS AREA**, or for anglers hoping to hook a salmon or steelhead. Catch angling tips or rent clam shovels and fishing gear at the **ROGUE OUTDOOR STORE** (29865 Ellensburg Ave; 541/247-7142). Pick up maps and hiking or rafting information from the **U.S. FOREST SERVICE** (1225 S Ellensburg Ave; 541/247-3600), then determine your course while sipping espresso at **GOLD BEACH BOOKS AND BISCUIT COFFEEHOUSE & ART GALLERY** (29707 Ellensburg Ave; 541/247-2495); with two floors of tomes and a sophisticated urban feel, it's the town's hippest hangout.

    JET-BOAT TRIPS are a popular way to explore the backcountry. Guides discuss the area's natural history and stop to observe wildlife (otter, beaver, blue herons, bald eagles, and deer) on these thrilling forays (64–104 miles) up the Rogue. Boats dock at lodges along the way for lunch and sometimes dinner. (Prepare for sun exposure; most boats are open.) Outfits include **JERRY'S ROGUE RIVER JET BOAT TRIPS** (541/247-4571 or 800/451-3645; *www.roguejets.com*) and **MAIL BOAT HYDRO-JETS** (541/247-7033 or 800/458-3511; *www.mailboat.com*). Call **ROGUE RIVER RESERVATIONS** (541/247-6504 or 800/525-2161) for information on Rogue River outings, jet-boat trips, or overnight stays in the wilderness (including backcountry lodges).

    The little-used **OREGON COAST TRAIL** (800/525-2334) traverses headlands and skirts untraveled beaches between Gold Beach and Brookings. A portion of the trail winds up and over **CAPE SEBASTIAN**, 3 miles south of town off Highway 101. Take the steep drive to the top of the cape for breathtaking vistas. Gold Beach also is part of Oregon's coastal "banana belt," which stretches to the California border and boasts warmer winter temperatures, an earlier spring, and more sunshine.

RESTAURANTS

Chives / ★★★⯪

29212 US HWY 101, GOLD BEACH; 541/247-4121 OR 800/4CHIVES You may have heard the buzz about Chives ranking among the three or four finest restaurants anywhere along Oregon's shoreline. Folks are chatting up the inviting ocean-facing dining room with a dozen tables lit with candles and warmed by a towering river-rock fireplace, the superior wine list, and the conviviality of owners Rick and Carla Jackson. But mostly, people are raving about the food. Rick Jackson adds flair to an assortment of traditional dishes and gives an occasional nod to fusion—say, ethereal gnocchi awash in a garlic-cream sauce, a homegrown beet-and-asparagus salad enhanced with bits of bacon, or perfectly prepared risotto infused with wasabi. Carnivores are well served by myriad entrées: grilled rib-eye encrusted with pecan, garlic, and blue cheese; chicken breast stuffed with Brie and hazelnuts; a rack of lamb accompanied by minted couscous and comforting ratatouille; and Jackson's signature veal osso buco paired with a mound of garlic mashed spuds. Sautéed shrimp served with lemon-pepper pasta, classic cioppino, crispy salmon cakes, and a trio of fishes (cobia, fluke, and grouper) poached in a Thai ginger concoction are also excellent catches. Desserts such as a fruit cup freshened with frothy sabayon; bread pudding spiked with currants, nuts, and Jack Daniels sauce; and a killer version of bananas Foster put an emphatic cap on any meal. *$$–$$$; AE, DIS, MC, V; checks OK; dinner Wed–Sun (closed Jan); full bar; reservations recommended; chives@harborside.com; www.chives.net; west side of Hwy 101.* &

Spinner's Seafood, Steak & Chop House / ★★

29430 ELLENSBURG AVE, GOLD BEACH; 541/247-5160 As the name suggests, the menu at Gold Beach's most popular eatery is extensive. You might begin with a wild mushroom (raised in the nearby Pistol River valley) napoleon bathed in a Cognac-herb sauce, then move on to, say, a charbroiled strip-steak marinated in Scotch and crusted with peppercorns, or cedar-planked salmon garnished with a pinot noir reduction. Pork chops come with warm apples and orange marmalade, an impressive Caesar salad can be had with fried oysters, and Key West chicken arrives bathed in a honey-lime sauce. Pasta Maricella mates fettuccine with prawns, sea scallops, and pea pods, all tossed in a creamy Asiago mixture; while pasta Campagnola is blended with sun-dried tomatoes, shiitakes, and spinach. Seafood purists opt for unadorned Dungeness crab cakes or jumbo prawns and scallops served "naked" over jasmine-scented rice. Burgers—humongous half-pounders paired with shoe-string fries—are outstanding (try a Gold Beach burger slathered with blue cheese and 'shrooms). Every table enjoys an ocean view, and the sunset panoramas are only slightly more impressive than the cuisine. *$$–$$$; AE, MC, V; checks OK; lunch, dinner every day (lunch Mon–Fri in winter); full bar; reservations recommended; on Hwy 101, north end of town.*

OREGON DUNES NATIONAL RECREATION AREA

Between Florence and North Bend is an area of coast like no other. This 50-mile swath encompasses the Oregon Dunes National Recreation Area, a paradoxical land of desertlike panoramas. But water is, literally, everywhere. These 32,000 acres of desolate sand are dotted with multisized lakes, intersected by streams and backed by the Pacific. Islands of greenery—trees trapped by shifting sand—are remnants of an earlier, more expansive forest, and reminders that the sand here will bury anything in its way.

Even though the dunes are federally managed, a good access point is within **JESSIE M. HONEYMAN STATE PARK** south of Florence. Hundred-foot-high dunes and a surrealistic terrain loom just beyond the **CLEAWOX LAKE** day-use area. Eleven miles south is the **OREGON DUNES OVERLOOK**, another day-use area and a good orientation site with interpretive displays. Farther south, the **SILTCOOS RIVER** area features an estuary, a lagoon, beaches, wetland ponds, numerous trails, and a variety of wildlife. There are dune buggy concessions along Highway 101, and overnighters can stay in any of 13 campgrounds. Bring your hiking shoes, binoculars, even your pail and shovel. Most of all, bring your curiosity and sense of wonder to this varied ecosystem of stark, bare dunes interspersed by blue water and green foliage. The **OREGON DUNES VISITOR CENTER** (855 Hwy 101, Reedsport; 541/271-3611) has more information.

—*Richard Fencsak*

LODGINGS

Inn at Nesika Beach / ★

33026 NESIKA RD, GOLD BEACH; 541/247-6434 The setting is unbeatable at this three-story neo-Victorian (built in 1992) occupying a bluff in quiet Nesika Beach. The inn boasts lovely landscaping, a relaxing wraparound covered porch (including an enclosed sun-room, with spotting scope, in the southeast corner), and a backyard within view of waves, fishing boats, and migrating gray whales. The expansive interior, with hardwood floors and attractive area rugs, is sparsely but elegantly decorated. Four large upstairs guest rooms all enjoy fabulous ocean views, uncommonly comfortable feather beds (ideal for cuddling couples), and private baths with deep whirlpool tubs. So what could be wrong? Well, at press time, the owner was selling and the inn feels in limbo, without a warm presence (we had the place to ourselves). Paint is peeling from the window sills and rafters, and during our visit, there were no wine and nibbles served in the evening (no one was around to serve them). Breakfast was adequate, but not worthy of the inn's former three-star rating. Hopefully, new owners can breathe life into this gem of a structure. *$$$; no credit cards; checks OK; 5 miles north of Gold Beach.*

Tu Tu'Tun Lodge / ★★★★

 96550 NORTH BANK ROGUE, GOLD BEACH; 541/247-6664 OR 800/864-6357 This lodgelike resort, named after a local Native American tribe and located 7 miles inland, is among the loveliest in the country. Tall, mist-clouded trees line the north shore of the Rogue River, and hosts Dirk and Laurie Van Zante will help you get a line in for salmon, steelhead, or trout. The main building is handsomely designed, with lots of windows, fireplaces, private porches overlooking the river, racks for fishing gear, and stylish decor. The two-story main building holds 16 units, and the adjacent lodge has two larger kitchen suites, all with river views. In the apple orchard is the lovely Garden House, which sleeps six and features a large stone fireplace. The nearby two-bedroom/two-bath River House, open in summer, is the spendiest and most luxurious, with a cedar-vaulted living room, outdoor spa, satellite TV, and washer/dryer. Guests can swim in the heated lap pool, use the four-hole pitch-and-putt course, play horseshoes, relax around the mammoth rock fireplace in the main lodge, kayak, hike, or fish. A fire is lit every evening on the terrace, and you might spot resident bald eagles. Breakfast and hors d'oeuvres are served, and a four-course prix-fixe dinner (available for an additional fee, May 1–Oct 26) might include your own fish. *$$$–$$$$; MC, V; checks OK; tututun@harborside.com; www.tututun.com; 7 miles up from Rogue River bridge (north road).*

Brookings

Situated 6 miles north of the California line, Brookings is bookended by breathtaking beauty and enjoys the state's mildest winter temperatures. To the north are **SAMUEL H. BOARDMAN** and **HARRIS BEACH STATE PARKS** (541/469-0224 or 800/452-5687). The verdant Siskiyou Mountains, deeply cut by the Chetco and Winchuck Rivers, are to the east, and ancient redwood groves lie to the south. Most of the **EASTER LILIES** sold in North America are grown in this favorable clime. Retirees have inundated the area, and the hills hum with new housing.

BRIAN SCOTT GALLERY & THE SNUG OCEAN VIEW COFFEE HOUSE (515 Chetco Ave; 541/412-8687; *brianscottgallery.com*) is a fine stop to view art and sip espresso or British teas, especially on the ocean-view patio. Hundreds of multicolored and shaped teapots line the windows at **THE TEA ROOM CAFÉ** (434 Redwood St; 541/469-7240), a pleasant venue for sandwiches and dessert. **WILD RIVER BREWING & PIZZA COMPANY** (16279 Hwy 101S; 541/469-7454; *www.wildriver brewing.com*) is the place for local craft beers. At **AZALEA PARK** (just east of Hwy 101 at the south end of town; 541/469-3181) fragrant western azaleas bloom in May, amid wild strawberries, fruit trees, and rhodies (and a marvelous kids' play area); picnic amid the splendor.

MYRTLEWOOD (which grows only on the Southern Oregon Coast and in Palestine) can be seen in groves in **LOEB PARK** (8 miles east of town on North Bank River Rd; 541/469-2021). Drive 4 miles up curvy Carpenterville Road from N Highway 101 to visit the tasting room at **BRANDY PEAK DISTILLERY** (18526 Tetley Rd;

541/469-0194; *www.brandypeak.com*), a family-owned microdistillery producing fruit brandies, grappa, and eau-de-vie.

The **REDWOOD NATURE TRAIL** in Siskiyou National Forest winds through one of the few remaining groves of old-growth coastal redwoods in Oregon. See where a Japanese pilot dropped a bomb during World War II—the only place in the contiguous United States bombed by a foreign power—on **BOMBSITE TRAIL**, a pretty walk through the redwoods. Contact the **U.S. FOREST SERVICE** (555 5th St; 541/469-2196) for directions to trails.

Fishing is renowned here, and Brookings boasts the Oregon Coast's safest harbor. The fleet operates from the south end of town. Stop in at **SPORTHAVEN MARINA** (16374 Lower Harbor Rd; 541/469-3301 or 800/421-4249) for supplies and info, or at nearby **TIDEWIND CHARTERS** (16368 Lower Harbor Rd; 541/469-0337) for oceangoing fishing adventures. Soak up the harbor ambiance, purchase the freshest catch, and order grilled-fish lunch and dinners at the fishermen-owned **CHETCO SEAFOOD CO** (16182 Lower Harbor Rd; 541/469-9251). **SURFING** can be splendid at nearby Sporthaven Beach.

RESTAURANTS

The Great American Smokehouse & Seafood Company / ★★☆

15657 HWY 101S, BROOKINGS; 541/469-6903 OR 800/828-3474 An incredible assortment of fresh and smoked salmon, sturgeon, tuna, calamari, cod, shark, and more, plus sundry gift packs and nautical gifts, awaits visitors inside this blue and white retail-restaurant combo south of town (look for the large "smoked salmon jerky" sign). The eatery is a double-decker affair, finished with wood floors and paneling, oversized cushioned captain's chairs, hanging glass floats, and a fish tank. Upstairs is even cozier, with windows and portholes looking out across the highway at farmers' fields and the ocean just beyond. Fresh seafood, simply prepared, is the way to order (otherwise the menu is mostly unimaginative). Try a broiled halibut steak brushed with garlic-lemon butter, blackened snapper, or an albacore fillet wrapped in bacon. Always a good bet is the smoked salmon and albacore platter, with sweet-hot mustard and Bandon cheddar for backup. Fish-and-chips fans can select their fave from among a dozen choices, including salmon, swordfish, and sole. Deep-fried calamari rings, mozzarella sticks, and an irresistible dessert lineup (turtle cheesecake, chocolate mousse pie) are sure to please the youngsters. *$$; DIS, MC, V; checks OK; lunch, dinner every day; beer and wine; no reservations; nancy@smokehouse-salmon.com; www.smokehouse-salmon.com; south of town along Hwy 101.*

LODGINGS

Chetco River Inn Bed and Breakfast Retreat / ★★

21202 HIGH PRAIRIE RD, BROOKINGS; 541/670-1645 OR 800/327-2688 Expect a culture shock: this secluded, alternative-energy retreat/farm planted with lavender sits on 35 forested acres of a peninsula formed by a sharp bend in the turquoise Chetco River, 18 mostly paved miles east of Brookings. Solitude is blissful; the five nicely furnished bedrooms and a family-oriented cottage have no phones, and cell service is iffy at best. But you can read by safety propane lights and, in the cottage, watch TV via satellite (there's also a VCR). An expansive common room features a vaulted cedar ceiling, a fireplace crafted from local rock, and a deep-green marble floor draped here and there with Oriental carpets; windows offer vistas of the river, myrtlewood groves, and wild-life. Full breakfast is included; make special arrangements for a deluxe sack lunch or exemplary five-course dinner ($30 a person). Anglers and crack-of-dawn hikers (the Kalmiopsis Wilderness is nearby) are served early-riser breakfasts. *$$$; MC, V; checks OK; chetcoriverinn@chetcoriverinn.com; www.chetcoriverinn.com; off North Bank Rd, call for directions.*

South Coast Inn / ★★

516 REDWOOD ST, BROOKINGS; 541/469-5557 OR 800/525-9273 Twin gargoyles guard this handsome, 4,000-square-foot Craftsman-style home designed in 1917 by renowned San Francisco architect Bernard Maybeck. Though it's two blocks above downtown, trees and shrubs—some of them flower all year in the mild climate—muffle the traffic noise. A spacious, partially covered deck, lighted in evening, extends around most of the lodging. Four luxurious bed-rooms (two with ocean views) are appointed with antiques, and guests can access an extensive collection of classic and contemporary films to view in their quarters. The spacious, first-floor Maybeck Room has cherry wood decor, a gas fireplace, and a private patio. Downstairs, a stone fireplace and grand piano grace the parlor. An unattached garden cottage (with kitchen; continental breakfast is provided) is outfitted with rustic log furniture. Innkeepers Gro and Shell Lent will arrange for guests to be picked up at the Brookings or nearby Crescent City (California) airport. No children younger than 12 permitted. *$$–$$$; AE, DIS, MC, V; checks OK; innkeeper@southcoastinn.com; www.southcoastinn.com; 2 blocks above Hwy 101.*

SOUTHERN OREGON
AND THE CASCADES

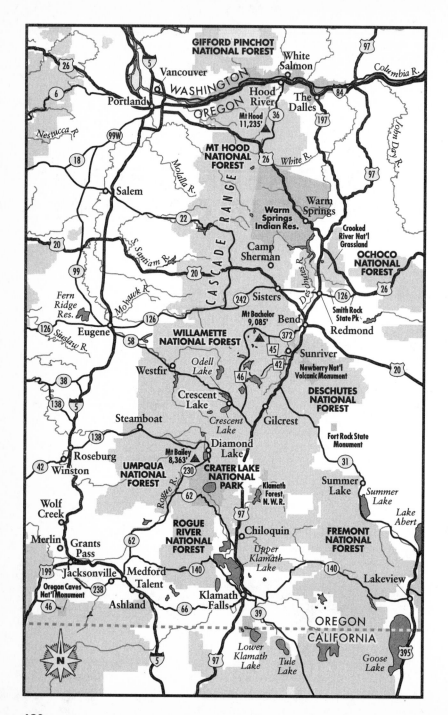

SOUTHERN OREGON AND THE CASCADES

The Cascade Mountain range forms a massive ridge through Oregon, like an army of sentinels marching north to south. Predominantly old and deeply eroded, these broad mountains are dominated to the east by a second, younger chain of magnificent—if somewhat scabrous—volcanic peaks that tower over the old guard.

The Cascades—including Mounts Jefferson, Washington, Bachelor, Sisters, and Broken Top—split Oregon into two distinct regions: one wet and one dry. Heavy rainfall and creek runoff keep the western, more populous region surrounding the Willamette Valley lush and verdant, while Eastern Oregon's high plains and ancient lake basin, 4,000 feet above sea level, remain an arid outback of Ponderosa pine, juniper, and sage, pocked with alkali lakes and riddled with lava. Unlike other North American deserts, Oregon's high desert receives about 30 inches of snow annually, providing it with enough sun and snow to attract outdoor enthusiasts year-round.

Just north of the California border, the Cascades intersect with the Siskiyou Mountains. Within the folds of these converging mountains, a series of warm, dry pockets extends from the Oregon Caves to the Cascade-Siskiyou National Monument, spawning rare and unusual flora and fauna, such as carnivorous cobra lilies, rough-skinned newts, copper butterflies, and kangaroo rats.

ACCESS AND INFORMATION

A major north-south highway runs along each side of the Cascades: **INTERSTATE 5** on the west, and **US HIGHWAY 97** on the east. **US HIGHWAY 26**, the main route between Portland and the desert, crosses Mount Hood southeast and connects with US Highway 97. Routes to Bend, the largest town on the east side of the Cascades, depart from Salem on **HIGHWAY 22**, from Albany on **US HIGHWAY 20**, and from Eugene on **HIGHWAY 126** (McKenzie Pass). From Eugene, follow **HIGHWAY 58** (Willamette Pass) to US Highway 97 at the halfway point between Bend and Klamath Falls. The most scenic route to the east side of the mountains, open only in summer, is the narrow **OLD MCKENZIE HIGHWAY** (Hwy 242) from Eugene. Farther south, Crater Lake is accessible from Roseburg on **HIGHWAY 138** (Diamond Lake) and from Medford on **HIGHWAY 62**. The most southerly routes are from Medford on **HIGHWAY 140** and from Ashland on the **GREEN SPRINGS HIGHWAY** (Hwy 66).

Flights between Portland and Bend/Redmond, Klamath Falls, and Medford are offered daily on **HORIZON AIR** (800/547-9308; *www.horizonair.com*) and other carriers. **AMTRAK** (800/USA-RAIL; *www.amtrak.com*), bound for California from Portland, crosses Willamette Pass into Klamath Falls, bypassing Southern Oregon with the exception of a stop in tiny Chemult.

Roseburg and the Umpqua Valley

The Willamette Valley and Interstate 5 corridor south of Eugene lead to Roseburg and the Umpqua River Valley. The "Wild and Scenic" North Umpqua River (so named under the Wild and Scenic River Act) is famed worldwide among serious fly-fishers, and the valley is gaining recognition for its wine-growing endeavors.

Roseburg

Timber still plays a significant, yet lesser, role in the town of Roseburg, where you can find artifacts of the industry at the **DOUGLAS COUNTY MUSEUM OF HISTORY AND NATURAL HISTORY** (off I-5 at fairgrounds, exit 123; 541/957-7007; *www.co.douglas.or.us/museum*). Here you'll also find a good history of the area, including its mining and pioneer past.

Find fresh pies and produce at family-run **KRUSE FARMS** (532 Melrose Rd; 541/672-5697 or 888/575-4268; *www.krusefarms.com*; open April–January, except holidays), dating to 1923. It wouldn't be a Southern Oregon road trip without an ice cream shake from the **K-R DRIVE-IN** (off I-5, Rice Hill exit, 30 miles north of Roseburg); a neon arrow marks this favorite spot.

The Roseburg area now has more than a half-dozen wineries, including **ABACELA VINEYARDS & WINERY** (12500 Lookingglass Rd; 541/679-6642; *www.abacela.com*), **CHAMPAGNE CREEK** (340 Busenbark Ln; 541/673-7901; *www.champagnecreek.com*), **DENINO UMPQUA RIVER VINEYARDS** (451 Hess Ln; 541/673-1975), **GIRARDET** (895 Reston Rd; 541/679-7252; *www.girardetwine.com*), **HENRY ESTATE WINERY** (687 Hubbard Creek Rd, Umpqua; 541/459-5120 or 800/782-2686; *www.henryestate.com*), **HILLCREST** (240 Vineyard Ln; 541/673-3709 or 800/736-3709), **MELROSE VINEYARDS** (885 Melqua Rd; 541/672-6080), **LA GARZA CELLARS & GOURMET KITCHEN** (491 Winery Ln; 541/679-9654; *www.lagarza.com*), and **PALOTAI VINEYARDS** (272 Capital Ln; 541/464-8127). Most are open for tastings during spring and summer; some are closed or require an appointment in fall and winter. La Garza's tasting room has an indoor dining area and an outdoor patio, where you can enjoy a reasonably priced, gourmet summer lunch, such as perfectly cooked salmon with a creamy dill sauce, or freshly made ravioli.

The humans are the only caged animals at the **WILDLIFE SAFARI** (Hwy 99, 4 miles west of I-5, exit 119; 541/679-6761 or 800/355-4848; *www.wildlifesafari.org*) as they drive through 600 acres of grasslands and woods packed with cheetahs, giraffes, and other exotic species.

RESTAURANTS

Roseburg Station Pub & Brewery / ★

700 SHERIDAN ST, ROSEBURG; 541/672-1934 The brothers McMenamin have brought their robust ales, tasty pub grub, and peculiar art to yet another historic site: Roseburg's 90-year-old train depot. This brick fortress, adorned with an eclectic collection of brass chandeliers, is a charming oasis in the summer heat with its polished wood booths, tall ceilings, and covered patio overlooking the tracks for the Southern Pacific Railroad's now-defunct Shasta Route. McMenamins' beer (Hammerhead, Terminator Stout, and Ruby) is brewed onsite. Enjoy it with a Captain Neon burger, ale-battered halibut and chips, or a chicken Caesar salad. *$; AE, DIS,*

*MC, V; local checks only; lunch, dinner every day; full bar; no reservations; www
.mcmenamins.com; across from Village Bistro.* &

LODGINGS

Seven Feathers Hotel and Casino Resort / ★★

146 CHIEF MILWALETA LN, CANYONVILLE; 800/548-8461 Owned by the Cow
Creek Band of the Umpqua Tribe, this resort is located about 25 miles south of
Roseburg, and includes the most luxurious hotel on Oregon's Interstate-5 corridor.
Funded by a thousand-plus slots and gaming tables, the four-story, 146-room hotel
(with indoor swimming pool and spa) is one of the better bargains on weekdays.
Choose a package for two that includes a room, breakfast, and a round (including
cart) at the 18-hole Myrtle Creek championship course (541/863-GOLF), or chance
your luck in the casino (check out the new nonsmoking addition). The dramatic
crystal-chandeliered Camas Room offers fine Northwest cuisine dinners and a truly
exceptional Sunday brunch. *$$; AE, DIS, MC, V; local checks only; lunch, dinner
every day, brunch Sun; full bar; www.sevenfeathers.com.* &

Steamboat Inn / ★★

42705 N HWY 138, STEAMBOAT; 541/498-2230 OR 800/840-8825
On the banks of the North Umpqua sits this homey lodge, run for
many years by Jim and Sharon Van Loan. Eight small cabins share a
common veranda that parallels the river; each unit has knotty pine walls and a bath-
room with a Japanese-style soaking tub. A mile upstream you'll find five secluded
cottages with living rooms and kitchens, suitable for small groups or families. Across
the river, four three-bedroom houses are offered through an arrangement with the
State of Oregon and the U.S. Forest Service. Remarkably good family-style dinners
are served in the main building each night at about 8pm, by reservation ($45 per
person). In spring, guest winemakers and chefs whip up special meals ($80 per
person). The inn also serves breakfast and lunch every day, and is entirely non-
smoking. No pets. *$$$; MC, V; checks OK; weekends only Mar–Apr and Nov–Dec,
closed Jan–Feb; www.thesteamboatinn.com; 38 miles east of Roseburg.*

Wolf Creek Inn / ★

100 FRONT ST, WOLF CREEK; 541/866-2474 This hand-hewn, two-
story inn has been in operation most of the 120 years since it was built.
Purchased by the state in 1975, the inn was restored in 1979 to its
former, glamorous self when frequented by famous writers and movie stars in the
1920s. Nine nicely furnished guest rooms, including one suite, have comfortable
antique beds. All have private, basic baths. Downstairs, a cozy dining room features
the best of both coasts with fresh Northwest fare and New York–style pizza and
calzone. Children OK; no pets; no smoking. *$$; MC, V; local checks only; closed
Mon–Tues Oct–May; www.thewolfcreekinn.com; 25 miles north of Grants Pass,
exit 76 off I-5.* &

OREGON CASCADES THREE-DAY TOUR

DAY ONE: From Portland, head out early on Highway 26 to see the unique architecture and displays at the **MUSEUM AT WARM SPRINGS**. Continue south to Bend and have a late lunch at the **ALPENGLOW CAFE**. Take a quick detour to **PILOT BUTTE STATE PARK** to orient yourself amidst the majestic Cascade peaks before checking in at the **INN OF THE SEVENTH MOUNTAIN**. Pick up the **DESCHUTES RIVER TRAIL** from the inn's nature trail for a 10-minute hike to **BENHAM FALLS** in summer, or ski **MOUNT BACHELOR**'s downhill or groomed Nordic trails in winter. After a soak, head downtown to the breezeway off Wall Street to bar hop and then dine at **MERENDA RESTAURANT AND WINE BAR**. If you're still energized after 10pm, head to **THE GROVE CANTINA** (1033 NW Bond, Bend; 541/318-8578) for dancing and dessert.

    DAY TWO: After checking out, savor coffee and a pastry at **A CUP OF MAGIC** (1304 Galveston Ave, Bend; 541/330-5539), then grab a bag lunch across the street at **MOTHER'S** (1255 NW Galveston Ave, Bend; 541/318-0989). In summer, drive the one-lane road off County Road 21 to **PAULINA PEAK** for a jaw-dropping view of the Newberry caldera, Paulina and East Lakes, and the Obsidian flow; visit the **HIGH DESERT MUSEUM** year-round. Continue south on US Highway 97 to either Highway 138 in summer for the north entrance to **CRATER LAKE NATIONAL PARK**, or to Highway 62 just north of Klamath Falls in winter to the south entrance. Drink in the heady blue of Crater Lake as you eat lunch on the rim. Drive westward on Highway 62 and then Interstate 5 to Ashland and check in at cozy **COWSLIP'S BELLE**. Walk to the **OREGON SHAKESPEARE FESTIVAL** for the Green Show, taking the long way home through Lithia Park before dining at **NEW SAMMY'S COWBOY BISTRO** (reserve in advance). Follow dinner with a long soak and bed.

    DAY THREE: Get some laps in at the **ASHLAND RACQUET CLUB**'s pool before a leisurely breakfast. Then, head north on Highway 99 for a self-guided wine and farm tour, starting with **RISING SUN FARM** (5126 S Pacific Hwy, Phoenix; 541/535-8350; *www.risingsunfarms.com*) and **HARRY AND DAVID'S COUNTRY VILLAGE**. Detour north on Interstate 5 to the **ROGUE VALLEY CREAMERY** (311 N Front St, Central Point; 541/665-1155)—be sure to mind the speed limits—then shoot south on Hanley Rd (Exit 31) to **VALLEY VIEW WINERY'S TASTING ROOM** in Jacksonville. Take a stroll on historic California Street and visit the **JACKSONVILLE MUSEUM**. If you're feeling peckish, have a bite at **BELLA UNION** before heading west on Highway 238 and south on Highway 199 to **FORIS VINEYARDS**. Catch the last tour of the day at **OREGON CAVES NATIONAL MONUMENT** before heading north for your final night at **FLERY MANOR** in Grants Pass.

The Rogue River Valley

The Rogue River is one of most beautiful and wild rivers in Southern Oregon. Percolating out of crystal clear springs in Crater Lake National Park, the river drives a rough and erratic route from the Cascades to the coastal range through miles of protected wilderness. It forms sheer canyons, rabid white water, and placid pools before spilling into the Pacific Ocean, carrying loads of steelhead and King salmon. Many rustic lodges along the river cater specifically to fly-fishers and rafters, and are often accessible only by boat. Flanked by the Upper Rogue to the south and west, Grants Pass offers the best access for fishing and rafting.

Grants Pass

Two companies offer guided tours of the Rogue River. **HELLGATE JETBOAT EXCURSIONS** (966 SW 6th St; 541/479-7204 or 800/648-4874; *www.hellgate.com*) departs from the **RIVERSIDE INN** (971 SE 6th St; 541/476-6873 or 800/334-4567; *www.riverside-inn.com*) in Grants Pass. **ORANGE TORPEDO TRIPS** (209 Merlin Rd, Merlin; 541/479-5061; *www.orangetorpedo.com*) conducts popular whitewater trips on inflatable kayaks and rafts.

RESTAURANTS

Hamilton River House / ★

1936 ROGUE RIVER HWY/HWY 99, GRANTS PASS; 541/479-3938 Long a local favorite, Doug Hamilton's restaurant—with an an awe-inspiring view of the Rogue—serves dependable fare at excellent prices. Count on tender barbecued ribs, succulent seafood fettucini, and mouth-watering filet mignon. Tex-Mex fare is a house favorite, so the daily sheet might feature fish tacos with mahimahi or a moist pan-blackened salmon. *$; AE, DIS, MC, V; checks OK; dinner every day; full bar; reservations recommended; Grants Pass exit off I-5.* &

Matsukaze

1675 NE 7TH ST, GRANTS PASS; 541/479-2961 This conveniently located restaurant serves authentic Japanese fare where you'd least expect it. The vegetable and meat teriyakis are flavorful, fresh, and satisfying. Grace Tamashiro's sauces are delicious and available for sale. Other offerings include tempura, sukiyaki, California and Philadelphia sushi rolls, and plate lunches served with salad, rice, vegetables, and hot tea. Or try crispy mahimahi coated with *panko* breadcrumbs and fried in soy oil. Finish up with refreshing green tea ice cream. *$; DIS, MC, V; no checks; lunch Mon–Fri, dinner Mon–Sat; beer and wine; no reservations; corner of Hillcrest Dr.* &

Summer Jo's / ★★

2315 UPPER RIVER RD LOOP, GRANTS PASS; 541/476-6882 Sitting on 6½ acres of flower, vegetable, and herb gardens and fruit trees, this cheery country restaurant belongs in a Merchant Ivory film. The certified organic gardens are both ornamental and functional, providing color and flavor for salads and entrées. Philip Accetta, who trained at the Hyde Park Culinary Institute, creates fresh versions of the classics, such as smoked chicken fettucine Alfredo with fresh roma tomatoes, spinach, and pine nuts, or New York strip-steak with sun-dried tomato butter and herby mashed potatoes. Carefully selected wines from around the world provide the perfect accompaniment. *$–$$; AE, MC, V; local checks only; lunch, dinner Wed–Sat (closed mid-Dec–mid-Feb); full bar; no reservations; www .summerjo.com; exit 58 off I-5.* &

LODGINGS

Flery Manor / ★★

2000 JUMPOFF JOE CREEK RD, GRANTS PASS; 541/476-3591 OR 541/ 471-2303 This classy two-story, 5,000-square-foot 1990s rural home on 7 acres of wooded mountainside became a B&B in 1996. Owners John and Marla Vidrinskas have added waterfalls, ponds (with black swans), hammocks, and a gazebo to create an idyllic setting for romance. Inside, the showpiece is the Moonlight Suite, favored by honeymooners and second-honeymooners. Its king-sized canopied bed sits in front of a fireplace. French doors open to a private balcony. The bath has a double vanity, double Jacuzzi, and glassed-in shower. A second suite offers the same luxury with a private first-floor patio. Three additional guest rooms are elegantly furnished with period decor. Marla serves a three-course breakfast in a formal dining room, with baked goods, quiches, and frittatas (featured in several gourmet magazines). No pets; no smoking; no children under 10. *$$–$$$; MC, V; checks OK; flery@flerymanor.com; www.flerymanor.com; 10 miles north of Grants Pass, Hugo exit 66 off I-5.* &

Morrison's Rogue River Lodge / ★★

8500 GALICE RD, MERLIN; 541/476-3825 OR 800/826-1963 Start your Rogue River rafting adventures here and you'll follow in the footsteps of former presidents George H. W. Bush and Jimmy Carter. Within yodeling range of Hellgate Canyon, Morrison's is one of the best Rogue River lodges, favored by anglers and river runners alike, and one of the easiest to reach. While others are accessible only by boat or plane, Morrison's is accessed via a paved road. Built in the 1940s, the lodge has four guest rooms and nine river-view cottages, all recently updated with new beds and fresh paint. One- or two-bedroom cottages and lodge rooms have private baths; cottages also feature fireplaces, refrigerators, covered parking, and private decks. The lodge operates a rafting outfit that provides three- and four-day camping or lodge-stay excursions on the Upper Rogue; fly-fishing packages are also available. Rates include breakfast and a four-course dinner, which might feature grilled pork with blackberry beurre rouge, spinach salad with chutney dressing, Morrison's famous orange rolls, and homemade chocolate torte; the dining room is open to (and often frequented by) nonguests, by reservation. *$$–$$$; DIS, MC, V; checks OK; closed Nov–Apr; info@morrisonslodge.com; www.morrisonslodge.com; 12 miles west of I-5.*

Weasku Inn / ★★

🌲 **5560 ROGUE RIVER HWY/HWY 99, GRANTS PASS; 541/471-8000 OR 800/ 493-2758** On the banks of the Rogue River, the Weasku Inn (pronounced "we-ask-you") is an idyllic place to stay, with its river-rock fireplace, giant trees, and friendly staff. Once the private residence of fly-fisher "Rainbow" Gibson, host to Hollywood luminaries such as Clark Gable and Bing Crosby, the homey lodge was completely restored in the 1990s; the nine fishing cabins were rebuilt from the river bank up. All accommodations are expansive, with vaulted ceilings and lodgepole furnishings; river cabins also have gas fireplaces, gleaming baths with slate floors, and decks to catch the morning sun. Any potential traffic noise is drowned out by the rush of water over Savage Rapids Dam. A short trail from the cabins to the rocky shore below the dam brings you to a bird-watching spot; look for mergansers, mallards, osprey, and herons. Complimentary continental breakfast is served in the lodge dining room, and evening wine and cheese next to the fireplace. *$$$; AE, DIS, MC, V; no checks; www.weasku.com; exit 48 off I-5.*

Oregon Caves National Monument

Cave Junction is 28 miles southwest of Grants Pass on US Highway 199 and the area is home to two of Oregon's better wineries: **FORIS VINEYARDS WINERY** (654 Kendall Rd; 541/592-3752 or 800/84FORIS; *www.foriswine.com*) and **BRIDGEVIEW VINEYARDS & WINERY** (4210 Holland Loop Rd; 541/592-4688 or 877/273-4843; *www.bridgeviewwine.com*). Both have tasting rooms open daily.

About 20 miles east of Cave Junction, on Highway 46, is **OREGON CAVES NATIONAL MONUMENT** (19000 Caves Hwy; 541/592-2100; *www.nps.gov/orca*), an active marble cave filled with glistening mineral formations, wet with moon milk, set among redwoods at 4,000 feet elevation. Tours leave hourly every day, mid-March through November, and every 15 minutes, late June through August. Come prepared for 75 minutes of cool (41°F) temperatures, strenuous climbing (500 steps), and less oxygen than usual. It's well worth the effort. Part of the caves' walkway is wheelchair-accessible. Children must meet a height requirement. In summer, arrive before 11am or plan on a late-afternoon, or candlelight, tour.

OREGON CAVES LODGE (541/592-2100; open May–Oct) is completely hand-built and somewhat unusual: This shaggy 22-room lodge is built across a ravine and has a stream running through the dining room.

LODGINGS

Out 'n' About Treesort / ★

🌲 👫 **300 PAGE CREEK RD, CAVE JUNCTION; 541/592-2208 OR 800/200- 5484** After a nationally publicized "tree-ring circus" with courts and planning officials, owner-builder Michael Garnier's treehouse B&B was officially approved in 1998 as a commercial enterprise. This out-on-a-limb B&B is continually growing and now counts 18 different structures swinging from the trees: tree houses, platforms, forts, ladders, a ropes course, and a floating ship "piratree." Accommodations include 11 units and range from the Tree Room Schoolhouse

Suite for six with a kitchenette, sitting area, and bathroom with clawfooted tub, to the Peacock Perch for two, with refrigerator and sink. Treemusketeers (kids of all ages) and their families can engage in rappeling, horseback riding, rafting—even craft making. Full breakfast is included. Book early; summer reservations go fast. The resort also offers tours and treehouse-building workshops. *$$; AE, DIS, MC, V; checks OK; treesort@treehouses.com; www.treehouses.com; 10 miles southeast of Cave Junction near Takilma.*

Medford

While Southern Oregon's largest city may not win any beauty contests, Medford has achieved national recognition for its shapely pears, due to the marketing efforts of Harry and David's, a local mail-order giant. **HARRY AND DAVID'S COUNTRY VILLAGE** (1314 Center Dr; 541/776-2277; *www.harrydavid.com*) offers "seconds" from gift packs and numerous other items; it's the departure point for tours (877/322-8000) of the corporate complex, also home to **JACKSON & PERKINS** (*www.jacksonandperkins.com*), the world's largest rose growers.

The **CRATERIAN GINGER ROGERS THEATER** (23 S Central Ave; 541/779-3000; *www.craterian.org*) is Medford's showpiece, a downtown performing arts center with a 742-seat theater that opened in 1997. (The 1924 building was originally The Craterian, a vaudeville and silent-movie house.) Why Ginger Rogers? The actress owned a ranch on the nearby Rogue River for many years, once danced on The Craterian stage, and in the last couple of years before her death helped raise money for the theater's $5.3 million renovation.

Locals like lunch and dinner at **SAMOVAR** (101 E Main St; 541/779-4967), a Russian café with fabulous pastries; for Thai food they flock to **ALI'S THAI KITCHEN** (2392 N Pacific Hwy; 541/770-3104), a humble spot north of town with good, inexpensive fare.

LODGINGS

Under the Greenwood Tree / ★★★☆

3045 BELLINGER LN, MEDFORD; 541/776-0000 OR 800/766-8099 When you stay at this stately inn, owner Renate Ellam will encourage you to loaf amid the 300-year-old trees, beautiful rose gardens, gazebo, and antique farm buildings from the Civil War era. She'll spoil you, too. Trained at Cordon Bleu, she'll serve you elaborate three-course gourmet breakfasts and tea and treats on the redwood deck. You'll also get ironed pillowcases, fresh flowers, the daily post, and a terry-cloth robe. The inn was built in 1862 and includes five graciously appointed rooms, each with a private bath. Massages can be booked in-room or out in the rose garden. Popular for weddings, the B&B has a dance floor under the stars. Smoking permitted outside. Children under 10 by advance arrangement only. *$$; V; checks OK; grwdtree@internetcds.com; www.greenwoodtree.com; exit 27 off I-5.* &

SHAKESPEARE FESTIVAL TIPS

The Oregon Shakespeare Festival mounts plays in three theaters. In the outdoor **ELIZABETHAN THEATER**, which seats 1,200, famous and authentic nighttime productions of Shakespeare are staged (three each summer). The festival opened a new indoor theater in 2002; it's the first time a venue has been added in 25 years. The season for the two indoor theaters, the **NEW THEATRE** and the **ANGUS BOWMER THEATRE**, runs February through November and includes comedies, contemporary fare, and some experimental works. (The Festival is dark on Mondays.)

Visit the **EXHIBIT CENTER**, where you can clown around in costumes from plays past. Directors, actors, and scholars discuss the plays at noon lectures, and actors provide excellent backstage tours each morning. Each summer evening in the courtyard, resident musicians present nearly an hour of new and old compositions for the general public, accompanied by modern dance. The "Green Show" rotates three different shows nightly; some have themes to match that night's outdoor play. Music and dance concerts are also held across the street in Carpenter Hall, Wednesdays and Saturdays at noon through August.

The best way to get current information and tickets (last-minute tickets in summer are rare) is through a comprehensive agency: **SOUTHERN OREGON RESERVATION CENTER** (541/488-1011 or 800/547-8052; www.sorc.com; Mon–Fri), or the festival box office (15 S Pioneer St, Ashland; 541/482-4331; www.osfashland.org).

Ashland is also home to a growing number of smaller theater groups that are worth watching, such as the award-winning **ARTATTACK THEATER ENSEMBLE** (310 Oak St; 541/482-6505; www.artattacktheatre.com). Festival actors often join in these small companies to have a bit of fun. **OREGON CABARET THEATER** (1st and Hargadine Sts; 541/488-2902; www.oregoncabaret.com) presents musicals and comedies through much of the year, serving dinners, hors d'oeuvres, and desserts.

Jacksonville

Resembling a set from your favorite Western, this chestnut of a town has relied heavily on its good looks and historic merit for survival ever since the Pacific Railroad bypassed the town and laid rails through Medford, a few miles east. Because the lush landscape and mild winters of the Applegate valley were well suited for orchards and other crops, miners dropped their pans and picked up their ploughs when the Gold Rush ended. Much of the original 19th-century city, declared a National Historic Landmark in 1966, has been restored; Jacksonville now boasts more than 100 historic homes and buildings, several along California Street.

The **JACKSONVILLE MUSEUM** (206 N 5th St; 541/773-6536; *www.sohs.org*), housed in the stately 1883 Italianate-style courthouse, follows the history of the Rogue River Valley with photos and artifacts and displays works by Peter Britt (see Britt Festival below). In the adjacent **CHILDREN'S MUSEUM**, kids walk through various miniature pioneer settings (jail, tepee, schoolhouse). Walking trails thread around old gold diggings in the hills; the longest (3 miles) is **RICH GULCH HISTORIC TRAIL** (trailhead off 1st and Fir Sts), an easy climb to a panoramic view. Also stroll through the 1875 "country gothic" **BEEKMAN HOUSE AND GARDENS** (on east end of California St; 541/773-6536).

VALLEY VIEW WINERY (1000 Upper Applegate Rd; 541/899-8468 or 800/781-WINE; *www.valleyviewwinery.com*) is at Ruch, 6 miles southwest of Jacksonville on Highway 238, and offers free tastings at the winery and in Jacksonville, at their **VALLEY VIEW WINERY TASTING ROOM** (125 W California St; 541/899-1001 or 800/781-9463).

The **BRITT FESTIVAL** (541/773-6077 or 800/882-7488; *www.brittfest.org*; June–Sept), an outdoor music-and-arts series, is held on the hillside field where Peter Britt, a famous local photographer and horticulturist, lived. Listeners often picnic while enjoying music ranging from jazz and bluegrass to folk, country, and classical, as well as musical theater and dance. The series has improved in recent years and sometimes includes artists such as James Brown, Allison Krauss and Union Station, George Benson, and Tracy Chapman. Begun in 1963, the festival now draws some 70,000 visitors each summer.

RESTAURANTS

Bella Union / ★★

170 W CALIFORNIA ST, JACKSONVILLE; 541/899-1770 This restaurant, in the original century-old Bella Union Saloon (half of which was reconstructed when *The Great Northfield, Minnesota Raid* was filmed in Jacksonville in 1969), has everything from pizza and pasta to elegant dinners and summer picnic baskets. Outdoor dining under a magnificent old wisteria is popular with guests. Proprietor Jerry Hayes, a wine fancier, pours a wide variety of labels by the glass as well as by the bottle. *$$; AE, DIS, MC, V; checks OK; lunch, dinner every day, brunch Sun; full bar; reservations for 6 or more; greatfood@bellau.com; www.bellau.com; downtown.*

Caterina's Trattoria / ★★

505 N 5TH ST, JACKSONVILLE; 541/899-6975 New-kid-on-the-block Catherine Moore serves flavorful, rustic dishes inspired by the Piemonte region of Northern Italy at this small trattoria, which is cozy and intimate enough for a romantic interlude, while retaining the crispness of a classy, well-run dinner house. The menu features a healthy list of antipasto dishes, first and second courses, pizzas, and regional wines. All dishes use imported meats, cheeses, extra-virgin olive oils, and balsamic vinegar. Bread and pasta are baked fresh each day and the desserts change too frequently to print. Try the "leap in your mouth" chicken breast layered with fresh sage, prosciutto, and fontina cheese, served with buttery Yukon Gold potatoes; or order the slow-cooked beef infused with espresso and red wine, then tossed with roasted garlic, tomatoes, and pasta. Finish up with an espresso and dolci. Picnic boxes (for the Britt Fest) available on request. *$$$; AE, MC, V; checks OK; dinner Tues–Sun; beer and wine; reservations recommended; 4 blocks north of California St.*

Jacksonville Inn / ★★

175 E CALIFORNIA ST, JACKSONVILLE; 541/899-1900 OR 800/321-9344
Ask a native to name the area's best restaurant, and the answer is often the Jacksonville Inn. The staff is considerate, and the antique-furnished dining room, housed in the original 1863 building, is elegant and intimate. The inn's restaurant features seasonal specials such as elk, venison, and buffalo, and year-round Northwest favorites, such as steak, salmon, pasta, and vegetarian entrées, including a handful of heart-friendly, low-cholesterol meals. Jerry Evans maintains one of the best-stocked wine cellars in Oregon, with more than 2,000 domestic and imported labels. Upstairs, eight rooms named for local, historic figures are decorated with 19th-century details: antique beds, patchwork quilts, and original brickwork on the walls. Modern amenities include private baths and air conditioning (a boon on 100-degree summer days). The inn has four honeymoon cottages nearby, all with king-sized canopied beds, two-person Jacuzzis, fireplaces, and stereo systems; the newest one has a dining room where the inn's chef can serve a meal. Guests enjoy a full breakfast. Reserve in advance, especially during the Britt Festival. *$$$; AE, DC, DIS, MC, V; checks OK; breakfast, dinner every day, lunch Tues–Sat, brunch Sun; full bar; reservations recommended; jvinn@mind.net; www.jacksonvilleinn .com; on main thoroughfare.*

McCully House Inn / ★★

240 E CALIFORNIA ST, JACKSONVILLE; 541/899-1942 OR 800/367-1942 McCully House, an elegant Gothic Revival mansion, was built in 1860 for Jacksonville's first doctor. Inside, four intimate dining rooms draw raves for ambiance and a menu crafted by Grants Pass native Derenda Hurst. The daily blue-plate special features comfort foods, such as meatloaf and spinach-mushroom crepes with Swiss cheese sauce, complementing the more cosmopolitan choices—tequila-lime prawns with orzo and seasonal vegetables, for example. The best of the three guest rooms flaunts a fireplace, huge claw-footed pedestal tub, and the original black-walnut furnishings that traveled 'round the Horn with J.W. McCully. Children welcome (with well-behaved parents); no pets. *$$$; AE, DC, DIS, JCB, MC, V; checks OK; dinner every day, brunch Sun; full bar; reservations recommended; mccully@wave.net; www.mccullyhouseinn.com; downtown.* &

Talent

RESTAURANTS

New Sammy's Cowboy Bistro / ★★★

2210 S PACIFIC HWY/HWY 99, TALENT; 541/535-2779 Proprietors Vernon and Charlene Rollins played their part in the culinary movement sweeping Sonoma

County in the 1970s (they ran the New Boonville Hotel in Medocino County) and have a huge foodie following despite their complete lack of advertising or evidence of a real sign (look instead for a flashing light and the consortium of expensive cars parked off the highway). Since 1985, they've been dazzling diners with such creations as clam chowder with a dollop of fresh corn ice cream, and ricotta gnocchi in sorrel sauce with Alaska spot prawns. With just six tables, reservations are a must, and you may have to wait a couple of weeks. The menu usually features a four- or five-course dinner special that might include wild, striped bass with tarragon sauce, mashed potatoes in phyllo crust, and beet purée with *gribiche,* plus a handful of entrées, such as seared scallops, roasted rack of lamb, and grilled sturgeon. The Rollins grow many of their own ingredients in their organic garden. A veritable wine encyclopedia with legs, Vernon stocks the cellar with thousands of wines from Oregon, California, and France. Once the kitchen has your food order, ask for the long wine list. *$$$; MC, V; checks OK; dinner Thurs–Sun (Fri–Sat in midwinter); beer and wine; reservations required; 3 miles N of Ashland on Hwy 99.*

Ashland

The remarkable success of the **OREGON SHAKESPEARE FESTIVAL** (see "Shakespeare Festival Tips" in this chapter), since its first performance of *Twelfth Night* in 1935, has transformed this sleepy town into one with, per capita, the region's best tourist amenities. The festival draws more than 380,000 people through the eight-month season, filling its theaters to an extraordinary 95 percent capacity. Visitors pour into this town of 20,000, and fine shops, restaurants, and bed-and-breakfasts spring up in anticipation. Amazingly, the town still has its soul: for the most part, it seems a happy little college town, set amid lovely ranch country, that just happens to house the largest repertory company in the nation.

Designed by the creator of San Francisco's Golden Gate Park, **LITHIA PARK**, Ashland's central park, runs for 100 acres behind the outdoor theater, with duck ponds, Japanese gardens, grassy lawns, playgrounds, and groomed or dirt trails for hiking and jogging; locals find it a pleasant place to play guitar or practice Qigong. There's even an ice-skating rink in winter. **SCHNEIDER MUSEUM OF ART** (1250 Siskiyou Blvd; 541/552-6245) at the south end of the Southern Oregon University campus is the best art gallery in town. **WEISINGER'S OF ASHLAND WINERY** (3150 Siskiyou Blvd; 541/488-5989; *www.weisingers.com*) and **ASHLAND VINEYARDS** (I-5 exit 14; 541/488-0088; *www.winenet.com*) offer opportunities to sample Ashland vintages.

Nearby daytime attractions include river rafting, picnicking, and historical touring. Get picnic supplies at the **ASHLAND COMMUNITY FOOD STORE** (237 N 1st St; 541/482-2237; *www.ashlandfood.coop*). Shoppers drive from neighboring counties to buy organically grown produce, fresh breads, gourmet cheeses, deli fare, and dry goods at this spacious, member-owned co-op. The **ROGUE RIVER RECREATION AREA** has fine swimming on sizzling summer days, as does the lovely Applegate River. Less than an hour's drive up scenic Dead Indian Memorial Road are two lake resorts: **HOWARD PRAIRIE LAKE RESORT** (3249 Hyatt Prairie Rd; 541/

THE BIG GLASSY

One of the premier attractions of **NEWBERRY NATIONAL VOLCANIC MONU-MENT** is an enormous mound of volcanic glass that sits in the middle of Newberry caldera, east of La Pine. The eruption of the Big Obsidian flow, just 1,300 years ago, is the most recent dated volcanic event in Central Oregon. The flow covers just over 1 square mile to an average depth of 300 feet.

The razor-sharp glassy shards of obsidian were put to good use by the area's early residents. Broken bits of glass were shaped into arrowheads, knives, and extraordinary cutting tools, as well as being used for barter. Obsidian from Newberry has been found in archaeology sites as far east as Missouri and as far north as Alaska. Older obsidian flows in Newberry caldera may be one of the reasons the earliest North Americans chose to live here at least 9,500 years ago.

Today a 1-mile **INTERPRETIVE TRAIL** leads up and into the obsidian flow; there you can see magnificent views of 7,985-foot-high Paulina Peak and topaz-blue Paulina Lake, one of two large "crater" lakes that fill the 100,000-year-old caldera floor. Follow US Highway 97 about 15 miles south of Sunriver, and watch for Newberry Crater signs to the east.

For more information, contact the **DESCHUTES NATIONAL FOREST LAVA LANDS VISITOR CENTER** (541/593-2421).

—*Jan Halliday*

482-1979) is open seasonally; newly renovated **LAKE OF THE WOODS** (950 Harriman Rd, Klamath Falls; 541/949-8300; *www.lakeofthewoodsresort.com*) rents cabins year-round. **SKI ASHLAND** (1745 Hwy 66; 541/482-2897; *www.mtashland.com*), on nearby Mount Ashland, 18 miles south of town, offers 22 runs for all classes of skiers (usually Thanksgiving to mid-April).

RESTAURANTS

Amuse Restaurant / ★★★

15 N FIRST ST, ASHLAND; 541/488-9000 The French expression *amuse-bouche,* or "fun for the mouth," provides the name for this elegant restaurant bent on providing deep fun for food lovers. Husband-and-wife team Erik Brown and Jamie North opened the restaurant in 2000, bringing several years of chef experience at notable Napa Valley restaurants. Their French-style dishes make extensive use of fresh local organic produce and meats, and are served in eye-appealing compositions. Tease your palette with sweet corn purée with basil oil, or creamy Normandy Camembert with currants and thyme-flavored honey, then sate your appetite with pan-roasted Oregon rabbit and potato risotto, or Niman Ranch rib-eye with shallot-thyme butter and French fries. The wine list includes several excellent Oregon and California labels and a few from France. For dessert, try North's deep-fried pastry lavished in whipped cream and berry jam. *$$$; AE, DC, DIS, MC, V; local checks OK; dinner Tues–Sun (April–Oct), Wed–Sun (Nov–March), closed Dec; beer and wine; www.amuserestaurant.com; one block from the Plaza.* &

Breadboard Restaurant & Bakery / ★

744 N MAIN ST, ASHLAND; 541/488-0295 Diners return again and again to this unassuming eatery on the edge of town for dependable and hearty home cooking. Owners Pete, Sarah, and Nikki Foster opened the Breadboard in 1983 and have since added covered patios with gorgeous views of the rolling hills. The sizable menu appeals to vegetarians and carnivores alike, and offers a wide selection of inexpensive breakfast and lunch choices. In the morning, try a tofu scramble with fresh salsa, chicken-fried steak, or sourdough pancakes with a side of crispy bacon. Midday specialties include burgers, meatloaf on a French roll, garden burgers smothered in grilled portobello mushrooms, hot roast beef au jus, and grilled ginger chicken salad. Breads, muffins, and pastries are baked fresh each day and are served with homemade jam. *$; MC, V; local checks only; breakfast, lunch every day (closed holidays); no alcohol; no reservations; 1 mile north of town.* &

Chateaulin / ★★★

50 E MAIN ST, ASHLAND; 541/482-2264 Less than a block from the theaters is a romantic café reminiscent of New York's Upper West Side. During Shakespeare season, the place bustles with before- and after-theater crowds gathered for fine French cuisine or drinks at the bar. House specialties are pâtés and veal dishes, but seafood and poultry are also impressive. Each season, chef David Taub and co-owner Jason Doss change the à la carte menu. The bar menu is a favorite of the after-show crowd: baked goat cheese in puff pastry with carmelized onions served on mesclun green salad with olive and lemon vinaigrette gets raves, as does a delicious onion soup; coffee and champagne drinks round out the menu. The three-course prix-fixe specials, including wine, are a great deal at $32.50; these might incorporate other Mediterranean flavors, such as lamb osso buco with Greek salad and raspberry sorbet. Service is polished and smooth even during the rush. The restaurant has an inside door to its sister business, a wine and gourmet-food shop. *$$; AE, DIS, MC, V; checks OK; dinner every day (closed Mon–Tues in winter); full bar; reservations recommended; www.chateaulin.com; down walkway from Angus Bowmer Theater.* &

Cucina Biazzi / ★★

568 E MAIN ST, ASHLAND; 541/488-3739 Restaurant king Beasy McMillan has owned several successful restaurants in Ashland over the years, but this traditional Tuscan-style trattoria is her best-loved to date. Four-course dinners are served on white linen in what was once the living room in this former residence. Don't fill up on the delicious antipasto course alone (though it's tempting): Asiago cheese, imported olives, marinated mushrooms and seasonal vegetables, and bean salad, with plenty of warm bread. Pasta portions, made with fresh pasta and creamy cheeses, are filling, followed by a full plate of fish or a meat entrée, such as rack of lamb, chicken, or veal. Dinner finishes with a perfectly dressed green salad. Desserts might be warm chocolate cake, tiramisù, or homemade ice cream. *$$$;*

MC, V; checks OK; dinner every day; full bar; reservations recommended; near fire station on E Main St.

Monet / ★★★

36 S 2ND ST, ASHLAND; 541/482-1339 Pierre and Dale Verger have created a gentrified French restaurant that is the talk of Ashland (and even gets mentioned in Portland). Favorite dishes in this gracious house include shrimp sautéed in white wine and Pernod, and filet mignon flambeed in Cognac then served in a four-pepper-corn cream sauce. Pierre Verger goes out of his way to make interesting vegetarian choices, such as eggplant on a bed of creamy German pasta topped with tomatoes, herbs, and Swiss cheese, as well as a simple French-country dish called *la crique Ardechoise,* a kind of gourmet potato pancake with garlic and parsley. The wine list is extensive. Dine outdoors in summer. *$$$; MC, V; local checks only; dinner Tue–Sun (Tues–Sat off-season, closed Jan–mid-Feb); full bar; reservations recommended; www.mind.net/monet; ½ block from Main St.*

LODGINGS

Chanticleer Inn / ★★★

120 GRESHAM ST, ASHLAND; 541/482-1919 OR 800/898-1950 Ellen and Howie Wilcox have spared no expense updating the six guest rooms in this beautiful 1920 Craftsman with antiques, designer fabrics, and classic bathroom fixtures to create a pleasing French provincial effect. Each room has a view of the Cascade foothills or a private patio entrance with a garden view. The largest room has a gas fireplace; all have private baths and cotton robes for the trek to the Jacuzzi out back. Modern amenities include DVD players and air conditioning for sweltering summer days. A gourmet breakfast (orange eggs Benedict with smoked salmon is a favorite) is served in the dining room, and complimentary afternoon wine, sherry, port, and homemade cookies are available. Children over 12 OK; no pets. *$$$; AE, MC, V; checks OK; innkeeper@ashland-bed-breakfast.com; www.ashland-bed-breakfast.com; 2 blocks from library, off Main St.*

Country Willows Inn / ★★★

1313 CLAY ST, ASHLAND; 541/488-1590 OR 800/945-5697 Set on 5 acres of farm-land seven minutes from downtown, this rebuilt 1896 country home offers peace and quiet and a lovely view of the hills. Dan Durant and David Newton offer five rooms, three suites, and a separate cottage, all with air-conditioning and private baths. A newly rebuilt swimming pool and hot tub await on the large back deck. The best room is in the barn: the Pine Ridge Suite has a bed/living room with a lodgepole-pine king-sized bed, and a bathroom bigger than most bedrooms. Beds feature plump down pillows and new mattresses. Breakfast, presented on a pretty sun porch, is organic juices and unique egg dishes, such as poached eggs on grilled polenta with pesto and garden-fresh tomatoes, sausages, or bacon. Cherry, pear, apple, and grape yields are used in preserves, available for sale on-site. The grounds offer running and hiking trails into the adjacent foothills; the owners keep a small flock of ducks, a gaggle of geese, and even a couple of goats. Children over 12

OK; no pets. *$$–$$$; AE, DIS, MC, V; checks OK; www.countrywillowsinn.com; 4 blocks south of Siskiyou Blvd.* &

Cowslip's Belle / ★★

159 N MAIN ST, ASHLAND; 541/488-2901 OR 800/888-6819 Named after a flower mentioned in *A Midsummer Night's Dream* and *The Tempest,* this home has a cheery charm, with its swing chair on the front porch, vintage furniture, and fresh flowers inside. A huge deck with a redwood arbor overlooks a koi pond and lagoon. Two lovely bedrooms (one a suite) are in the main house—a 1913 Craftsman bungalow—and three more in a romantic carriage house in back; the newest one has a spa tub and a private balcony overlooking the mountains. Each room has cable Internet access; wireless access is available throughout. Jon and Carmen Reinhardt, owners for 20 years, provide turndown service (with chocolate truffles and teddy bears) and full breakfasts, such as fritatta or cheese blintz soufflé with a side of maple bacon or chicken apple sausage and Jon's brioche, scones, and other baked goods (his wholesale bakery, City Dunkers Gourmet Cookie Company, is on the premises, so the inn always smells heavenly). Work up an appetite at the Ashland Racquet Club, compliments of your hosts. No children under 10; no pets; no smoking. *$$$; no credit cards; checks OK; stay@cowslip.com; www.cowslip .com; 3 blocks north of theaters.* &

Mount Ashland Inn / ★★★

550 MOUNT ASHLAND RD, ASHLAND; 541/482-8707 OR 800/830-8707 Wind your way up Mount Ashland Ski Road and you discover a huge, two-story log cabin, crafted from incense cedars from the 40-acre property in 1987. Chuck and Laurel Biegert bought the inn in 1995 and created five suites for absolute comfort; each includes a gas fireplace, a Jacuzzi, thick Turkish robes, as well as a microwave and a refrigerator. A scant 30 minutes from culture, the inn is within reach of alpine trails and skiing; at a 5,500-foot elevation, it's above the clouds in the winter and 10 degrees cooler than town in summer. Enjoy spectacular views of Mounts Shasta and McLoughlin from the dining room. An outdoor spa and sauna, cross-country skis, snowshoes, and mountain bikes are available for guests' use. Sumptuous, multicourse breakfasts are available for an additional charge. Expect snow November through April. No children under 10; no pets. *$$$; DIS, MC, V; checks OK for deposits; www.mtashlandinn.com; follow signs to Mount Ashland Ski Area.*

Peerless Hotel / ★★

243 4TH ST, ASHLAND; 541/488-1082 OR 800/460-8758 Originally a hotel in Ashland's now-historic railroad district in 1900, the building fell into disrepair but was saved by Chrissy Barnett. She merged hotel rooms into six B&B units (two of them suites), decorated them with antiques collected from places as disparate as New Orleans and Hawaii, and painted murals on the walls and ceilings. High ceilings and oversized bathrooms are trademarks. Suite 3 features a bath with two claw-footed tubs and a glassed-in shower. Several rooms include Jacuzzis; all rooms feature turndown service, evening port or sherry, and access to the Ashland Racquet Club. Breakfast is served in the restaurant (open to the public for dinner) across the garden; you can walk to the theaters. Children over 14 OK. *$$$–$$$$; AE, DIS, MC, V; checks OK; crissy@peerlesshotel.com; www.peerlesshotel.com; between "A" and "B" Sts.* &

Romeo Inn / ★★★

295 IDAHO ST, ASHLAND; 541/488-0884 OR 800/915-8899 This imposing 1932 Cape Cod home has four plush guest rooms and two suites, some decorated in English country with antiques, some neoclassical. Spacious rooms have king-sized beds, phones, and private baths. The Stratford Suite is a separate structure with its own bedroom, bath, and kitchen; it features a vaulted ceiling with skylight, marble-tiled wood fireplace, and raised whirlpool tub for two. The Cambridge Suite has a fireplace, patio, and private entrance. The heated pool on the large back deck is open seasonally, and the hot tub is inviting year-round. For breakfast, innkeepers Don and Deana Politis serve freshly squeezed orange juice and three courses that might include coffee cake, poached pears in walnut-mint sauce, baked eggs Lorraine, and rosemary roasted potatoes. Complimentary cookies and tea are available all day, home-baked treats in the afternoon, and chocolate before bed. No pets or children under 12. *$$$; DIS, MC, V; checks OK; innkeeper@romeoinn.com; www.romeoinn.com; south of Siskiyou Blvd.*

Klamath Falls

For decades, the wide open spaces around this city of 19,000 (called "K Falls" by locals) attracted few but cattle ranchers and crop farmers, lured by the 1902 Reclamation Act that offered homesteads to veterans. Recent drought conditions brought water issues to a boil when the Endangered Species Act—drafted in part to protect suckers and coho salmon in Upper Klamath Lake—restricted irrigation, leaving farmers high and dry. While the Feds work on creative solutions to quench everyone's thirst, Klamath Falls is hardly going down the drain. Oregon's "City of Sunshine" redeveloped the downtown area and is diversifying its economic base by promoting the natural beauty of the area; tourism and real estate are on the rise and the town now sports several hotel chains.

The $250 million **RUNNING Y RANCH RESORT** (5500 Running Y Rd; 888/850-0275; *www.runningy.com*) provides recreation and real estate services with its 85-room lodge, Arnold Palmer 18-hole golf course, restaurant, and condo development on 9,000 acres on Klamath Lake, 10 miles out of town. The Klamath Indian Tribe, a confederation of the Klamath, Modoc, and Yahooskin Natives who have occupied the region for thousands of years, opened their **KLA-MO-YA CASINO** (541/783-7529 or 888/552-6692; *www.klamoya.com*) on US Highway 97 at Chiloquin, just a few miles north of the Klamath Falls Airport.

The **FAVELL MUSEUM OF WESTERN ART AND INDIAN ARTIFACTS** (125 W Main St; 541/882-9996; *www.favellmuseum.com*) is a true Western museum, with arrowheads, Native artifacts, and the works of more than 300 Western artists. **KLAMATH COUNTY MUSEUM** (1451 Main St; 541/883-4208) exhibits the volcanic geology of the region, regional Native artifacts, and relics from pioneer days. The **BALDWIN HOTEL MUSEUM** (31 Main St; 541/883-4207; open June–Sept), in a spooky 1906 hotel, retains many fixtures of the era. The geothermally heated **ROSS RAGLAND THEATER** (218 N 7th St; 541/884-0651 or 888/627-5484; *www.rrtheater.org*), a onetime art deco movie theater, now presents more than 60 plays, concerts, and Broadway shows each year.

UPPER KLAMATH LAKE lies on the remains of a larger ancient lake system and, at 143 square miles, is the largest lake in Oregon; it's fine for fishing and serves as the nesting grounds for many birds, including white pelicans, eagles, and herons. The Williamson River, which flows into the lake, yields plenty of trout. **THE VOLCANIC LEGACY SCENIC BYWAY** (Highway 140) runs alongside the lake and through the beautiful Wood River Valley.

RESTAURANTS

Fiorella's / ★★

6139 SIMMERS AVE, KLAMATH FALLS; 541/882-1878 In 1986, Fiorella and Renato Durighellois came here from a town near Venice, Italy, and re-created the ambiance of their homeland in a former residence, with white tablecloths, fresh flowers, plastered walls, wood-beamed ceilings, and a copper polenta pot nestled in the fireplace. Specials may include osso buco with risotto, or chicken cacciatore with penne. Fresh fruit pie or tiramisù top it off nicely. *$$; AE, MC, V; local checks only; dinner Tues–Sat (closed Jan); full bar; no reservations; S 6th St to Simmers Ave.*

Lakeview and Lake County

At nearly 4,800 feet elevation, Lakeview calls itself "The Tallest Town in Oregon." While most of Lake County exceeds 4,300 feet elevation, this prehistoric and alkaline lake basin is more noteworthy for its hot springs and fabulous hang gliding or paragliding. **HUNTER'S HOT SPRINGS** (US Hwy 395; 800/858-8266; 2 miles north of town) has two pools (the outdoor pool is perfect for stargazing) with direct hookups to geyser springs that blow every 40 seconds at Old Perpetual. Further north into the Oregon Outback is **SUMMER LAKE HOT SPRINGS** (41777 Highway 31, Paisley; 877/492-8554; milepost 92), a rustic bathhouse in a desolate setting.

Paragliding championships are held above Lakeview at **BLACK CAP LAUNCH** (follow signs in Lakeview for Hang Glider Port), which offers tremendous views for those without wings. A popular gliding site is Tague's Butte on **ABERT RIM**, a massive fault scarp that stretches 30 miles and towers 2,000 feet over Lake Abert.

WARNER CANYON SKI AREA (10 miles north of Lakeview; 541/947-5001) offers 17 weeks of skiing each year, beginning in mid-December, with no lines for the 700-foot vertical chair lift. A modest ski lodge has a fireplace and a small restaurant.

For authentic campfire cuisine and Western-style cabins, visit the **WILLOW SPRINGS GUEST RANCH** (Clover Flat Rd, Lakeview; 541/947-5499; *www.willowspringsguestranch.com*), a working cattle ranch that generates its own power. The wood-fired hot tub overlooks acres of meadows.

Summer Lake

From Summer Lake, continue north on Highway 31 and you'll pass **FORT ROCK STATE MONUMENT** (541/388-6055), remnants of an ancient volcanic blast, where Klamath Indians found refuge when Mount Mazama exploded 6,800 years ago. In one of Fort Rock's caves, archeologists found what they believe to be the oldest shoes on record: a pair of woven sandals that date back 10,000 years. **SUMMER LAKE STORE** (37580 Highway 31; 541/943-3164), a mom-and-pop grocery store, and a small pioneer museum nearby are usually open.

LODGINGS

Summer Lake Inn / ★★

47531 HWY 31, SUMMER LAKE; 541/943-3983 OR 800/261-2778 If you are looking for luxury in a remote setting, this is it—about 110 miles southeast of Bend on the edge of one of Oregon's largest bird refuges, Summer Lake Wildlife Refuge. From the inn's hot tub on the wide deck you can see across miles of unmarred desert and, at night, more stars than you can count. Stay in one of Darrell Seven and Jean Sage's six new cabins, which have kitchens, Jacuzzis, and fireplaces. Cabins in the converted stable are attractive and cheaper but get traffic noise; two cabins include Jacuzzis but share a kitchen. Breakfast is served American-style every morning except Monday, when large continental breakfast baskets are available. The cedar-and-glass dining room serves dinner six days a week by reservation February through December. The area has considerable natural charms, which you'll have mostly to yourself—hiking in the Gearhart Mountain Wilderness Area to the south, fly-fishing, birdwatching, and viewing petroglyphs. If you're looking for the lake, you might be disappointed; Summer Lake often recedes to little more than a swamp in summer. Enjoy a canoe ride in the pond instead. Dogs and horses are welcome (for a fee). $$; AE, DIS, MC, V; checks OK; www.summerlakeinn.com; between mileposts 81 and 82. ▲

Crater Lake National Park

Heading north from Klamath Falls on US Highway 97, then west on Highway 62, you'll reach the south entrance to **CRATER LAKE NATIONAL PARK**. Some 7,700 years ago, 10,000- to 12,000-foot Mount Mazama was the Mount St. Helens of its day. It blew up and left behind a 4,000-foot-deep crater—now a lake filled by rainwater and snowmelt. With the water plunging to 1,932 feet, it's the deepest lake in the United States and probably the bluest. A prospector searching for gold found this treasure in 1853; it was designated a national park in 1902, the only one in Oregon.

Crater Lake National Park is extraordinary: the impossibly blue lake, eerie volcanic formations, a vast geological wonderland. The **STEEL INFORMATION CENTER** (near the south entrance at park headquarters; 541/594-3000; www .nps.gov/crla) offers an information desk, books, and an interpretive video year-round; in summer, a second visitors center operates in Rim Village. Visitors can camp at **MAZAMA VILLAGE CAMPGROUND** or book a room at the 40-unit **MAZAMA**

VILLAGE MOTOR INN (541/830-8700); be sure to plan early, as space fills fast. The 33-mile **RIM DRIVE** along the top of the caldera offers many vistas; the two-hour boat ride from Cleetwood Cove out to Wizard Island requires a short but strenuous hike (back to the parking lot). There are dozens of trails and climbs to magnificent lookouts. In winter, when the crowds thin, only the south and west entrance roads are open. Then, cross-country skiing and snowshoe walks are popular.

LODGINGS

Crater Lake Lodge / ★★

RIM DR, CRATER LAKE NATIONAL PARK; 541/830-8700 Originally built in 1909, the historic wood-and-stone building, perched at 7,000 feet on the rim of the caldera, was weakened considerably by decades of heavy snowfall. The four-story summer lodge, with 71 rooms, was restored in the mid-1990s with a $15 million taxpayer-funded makeover. Although only 26 rooms face the lake, all have great views. Best are the eight with claw-footed bathtubs in window alcoves. You won't find TVs or in-room phones here. The dining-room motif is 1930s lodge decor, but the menu (breakfast, lunch, dinner) is contemporary. Guests should reserve space in the tiny dining room up to 30 days before arrival. If the dining room is full, choose between two less-than-grand restaurants at Rim Village, 500 feet from the lodge. $$$; DIS, MC, V; checks OK; open mid-May–mid-Oct; www.craterlakelodge.com; via Hwy 138 (north) or Hwy 62.

Diamond Lake and Mount Bailey

MOUNT BAILEY ALPINE SKI TOURS (off Hwy 138, just north of Crater Lake; 541/793-3348 or 800/446-4555; www.mountbailey.com) offers true backcountry skiing, with experienced, safety-conscious guides and snow cats instead of helicopters to take you to the top of this 8,363-foot ancient volcano. **DIAMOND LAKE RESORT** (800/733-7593; www.diamondlake.net) is headquarters for the guide service. Also popular in winter: snowmobiling, cross-country skiing, inner-tubing, snowboarding, and ice-skating. When the snow melts, the operation turns to mountain-bike touring, boating, swimming, and hiking.

Cascade Lakes Area

The 100-mile scenic **CASCADE LAKES HIGHWAY** (Hwy 58) tour needs several hours and a picnic lunch for full appreciation; stunning mountain views and a number of lakes and rustic fishing resorts are tucked along the way. Odell and Davis Lakes, near Willamette Pass on Highway 58, mark the southern end of the tour that winds its way north, eventually following the Deschutes River on Century Drive to Bend.

Odell Lake

LODGINGS

Odell Lake Lodge and Resort

E ODELL LAKE ACCESS OFF HWY 58, CRESCENT LAKE; 541/433-2540 OR 800/434-2540 This resort on the shore of Odell Lake is ideal for the fisher, hiker, and skier in all of us. The lake's a bit alpine for swimming; instead, cast for Mackinaw, rainbow, or kokanee trout. (Most sports equipment—fishing rods to snowshoes—is rentable here.) The small library is perfect for sinking into an overstuffed chair in front of the fireplace. Request a lakeside room, one of seven in the hotel. (Room 3, specifically, is a corner suite warmed with knotty-pine paneling and lake and stream views.) If you'd prefer one of the 12 cabins, spend the few additional dollars to get one lakeside. Pets OK in cabins. The restaurant is open year-round for three squares a day. *$$; DIS, MC, V; checks OK; 2-night min holidays and weekends; www.odell lakeresort.com; from Oakridge on Hwy 58, head east for 30 miles, take E Odell Lake exit.* &

Bend and Mount Bachelor

Bend was just another quiet desert town founded on timber until word got out about the powdery snow and bountiful sunshine on nearby **MOUNT BACHELOR** (formerly named Bachelor Butte). Bachelor was converted into an alpine playground, followed by golf courses in Bend, an airstrip, bike trails, river-rafting companies, hikers, tennis players, and rockhounds. The city's popularity—and population (now more than 55,000)—has steadily increased ever since.

Heading north from Summer Lake on Highway 31 or Klamath Falls on US Highway 97, the road to Bend passes through **NEWBERRY NATIONAL VOLCANIC MONUMENT** (between La Pine and Bend on both sides of US Hwy 97; 541/593-2421 or 541/383-4771; *www.fs.fed.us*), a 56,000-acre monument in the Deschutes National Forest that showcases geologic attractions tens of thousands of years old. Within the **NEWBERRY CRATER**, 13 miles east of US Highway 97 on Forest Road 21, lies the Big Obsidian Flow, Paulina Falls, and East and Paulina Lakes; each lake includes a small resort. The 7,985-foot Paulina Peak is accessible by road in summer and provides an excellent vantage point over the features within the collapsed caldera, which spans 500 square miles. Tour **LAVA RIVER CAVE**, a mile-long lava tube on US Highway 97 (13 miles south of Bend). As you descend into the dark and surprisingly eerie depths, you'll need a warm sweater. **LAVA LANDS VISITOR CENTER** at the base of Lava Butte (12 miles south of Bend; 541/593-2421; closed in winter) is the interpretive center for the miles of lava beds. Drive or—when cars are barred—take the shuttle up Lava Butte, formed by a volcanic fissure, for a sweeping, dramatic view of the moonlike landscape. Seasons for Newberry attractions vary depending on snow, but generally run mid-May through September.

Bend

The main thoroughfare through Bend—US Highway 97's 10 miles of uninspired strip development—bypasses the historical town center, which thrives just to the west. To the south, all but the powerhouse buildings and smokestacks from the former timber mill were torn down and replaced with a sleek glass-and-split-rail complex of restaurants, shops, and galleries on the Deschutes riverbank now called the **OLD MILL DISTRICT** (*www.theoldmill.com*). Across the river, the **LES SCHWAB AMPHITHEATER** (541/322-9383; *www.lsabend.com*) seats 7,500 for summer concerts. Toward the center of town, the **DESCHUTES HISTORICAL CENTER** (NW Idaho and Wall Sts; 541/389-1813) features regional history and interesting pioneer paraphernalia. Look west of the downtown area for the new location of much-lauded **CAFE ROSEMARY** (1110 NW Newport Ave), scheduled to reopen in late 2004.

The **HIGH DESERT MUSEUM** (59800 S Hwy 97, 4 miles south of Bend; 541/382-4754; *www.highdesert.org*) is an outstanding educational resource and nonprofit center for natural and cultural history. This modern structure, built from pine and lava rocks, is set on 20 acres of natural trails. Outdoor exhibits offer replicas of covered wagons, a sheepherder's camp, a settlers' cabin, and an old sawmill; three river otters, three porcupines, and about a half-dozen raptors are in residence (presentations daily). The museum also has an extensive collection of Columbia Plateau Indian artifacts on display.

Part of Bend's charm comes from the blindingly blue sky and pine-scented air, the other part from its proximity to outdoor attractions. Mountain bike or hike for 9 miles along the **DESCHUTES RIVER TRAIL**, from downtown Bend past the Inn of the Seventh Mountain (see review) and a series of waterfalls. **PILOT BUTTE STATE PARK** (541/388-6055), just east of town on US Highway 20, is a red-cinder-cone park with a mile-long road to a knockout vista on top.

RESTAURANTS

Alpenglow Cafe / ★

1040 NW BOND ST, BEND; 541/383-7676 The glow they're referring to is probably the warm feeling you'll have after eating their mountain of breakfast (served all day). Orange juice is fresh squeezed and full of pulp, bacon and ham are locally smoked (salmon is brined and smoked in-house), and all breads are homemade. Chunky potato pancakes, made with cheddar and bacon, are served with homemade applesauce or sour cream. The salmon eggs Benedict is huge—two eggs on two English muffin halves, topped with smoked king salmon, fresh basil, tomatoes, and a rich, lemony hollandaise. Even the huevos rancheros have the Alpenglow touch—a generous dollop of cilantro pesto and fresh salsa on top. Entrées come with a pile of home fries and coffee cake or fresh fruit. $; AE, DIS, MC, V; *local checks only; breakfast, lunch every day; no alcohol; no reservations; next to Deschutes Brewery.* &

Broken Top Restaurant / ★★

62000 BROKEN TOP DR, BEND; 541/383-8210 Hidden in the clubhouse of the Broken Top Golf Course is one of Oregon's most elegant dining establishments with exceptional views of the Cascades beyond the course and lake. Make your reservation for a half hour before sundown, and if Mother Nature is accommodating, you'll see a spectacular sunset over the jagged Broken Top and Three Sisters. The food is equally sensational; try the grilled beef tournedos with potato gnocchi, tossed in applewood-smoked bacon and cheddar cream. New York steak is always on the menu, as are Northwest game and a vegetarian entrée. Note: The restaurant is often closed for members-only events Saturday evenings. *$$; AE, MC, V; local checks only; lunch Tues–Fri, dinner Tues–Sat; full bar; reservations recommended; www.brokentop.com; just off Mount Washington Dr from Century Dr.* &

Hans / ★★☆

915 NW WALL ST, BEND; 541/389-9700 A casual, bright café with hardwood floors and big windows, Hans offers a fine selection of salads and interesting daily specials. Service is sometimes brisk, but the bustle is hospitable. Lunch menus have mix-and-match sandwiches with all kinds of breads, cheeses, and other ingredients. Dinner brings finer dining, ranging from grilled portobello appetizers, unique pizzas, and seafood pasta, to salmon in a lemon–herb beurre blanc, and tenderloin, all with creative yet simple sauces and flavors. A case full of pastries and sweets tempts for dessert. *$; MC, V; checks OK; lunch Tues–Sat, dinner Wed–Sat; beer and wine; reservations recommended; downtown.* &

Marz Planetary Bistro / ★★

163 NW MINNESOTA AVE, BEND; 541/389-2025 Perfect for social occasions (or people watching), this artful, bustling bistro delivers ethnic flavors in interesting combinations, without the attitude. The mainstays are Thai crab cakes; rice paper–wrapped fish and veggies; jambalaya; and grilled chicken breast marinated in rum, mint and citrus, served with mango salsa and smoked rice. Specials might include bacon-wrapped filet mignon with Southwest-style black beans and rice, or pan-seared mahimahi in dill rémoulade. Desserts take no prisoners and are made daily: flour-free chocolate cake, crème brûlée, and pear-cherry torte, for example. A wide selection of wines and a handful of microbrews provide the perfect accompaniment. *$$; DIS, MC, V; checks OK; dinner every day; beer and wine; reservations for 6 or more; between NW Bond and NW Wall Sts.* &

Merenda Restaurant and Wine Bar / ★★★

900 NW WALL ST, BEND; 541/330-2304 This spacious new restaurant and wine bar with balcony seating is beautifully crafted with brick and wood details, and fills up nightly with satisfied diners. Owner and chef Jody Denton and his wife, Michelle, offer rustic comfort food from Southern France and Northern Italy with simple, high-quality ingredients—at competitive prices. The menu includes pasta and pizza dishes, fish, pork, steak, and a nightly wood-fired special. Or you can customize your dinner from the extensive list of tapas-style plates, vegetable side dishes, imported cheeses, hors d'oeuvres, and antipasti. Try goat cheese–stuffed figs in prosciutto, and Spanish white anchovies marinated in sherry and olive oil, or rib-eye for two with porcini butter, and baked potato with pancetta and crème fraîche. Wine flights are popular; eight choices include four hearty tastes of reds or whites from around the world. More than 65 wines are available by the glass. The bartenders are friendly and informative. *$$–$$$; AE, DC, DIS, MC, V; local checks only; lunch, dinner daily (except holidays); full bar; reservations recommended; at the corner of NW Wall and Minnesota, downtown.* &

Pine Tavern Restaurant / ★★

967 NW BROOKS ST, BEND; 541/382-5581 The Pine Tavern is all you want in a dinner house: good food, service, atmosphere, and a decent value for your dollar. This establishment has 68 years of history and a reputation for quality. Request a table by the window (overlooking placid Mirror Pond) in the main dining room and marvel at the 200-year-old tree growing through the floor; outdoor dining is now available, weather permitting. Naturally grown Oregon prime rib is the restaurant's forte. Hearty scones and honey butter are served first, but are worth saving for dessert. *$$; AE, DIS, MC, V; checks OK; lunch Mon–Sat, dinner every day; full bar; no reservations; www.pinetavern.com; foot of Oregon Ave.*

LODGINGS

The Bend Phoenix Inn / ★

300 NW FRANKLIN AVE, BEND; 541/317-9292 OR 888/291-4764 Huge, spotless minisuites with leather couches, microwaves, refrigerators, coffeemakers, and other amenities make you feel at home in this establishment, which recently added 32 rooms for a grand total of 117. Request a room with a mountain view. The staff is informative and friendly. There's a pool, Jacuzzi, and fitness center. But the best thing about this inn is its downtown location (and local calls are free). The continental breakfast buffet in a comfortable dining room includes fresh pastries, fruit, and newspapers. *$$–$$$; AE, DC, DIS, MC, V; checks OK; www.phoenixinn7 .citysearch.com; downtown.*

Inn of the Seventh Mountain / ★★

18575 SW CENTURY DR, BEND; 541/382-8711 OR 800/452-6810 The Inn offers the closest accommodations to Mount Bachelor and is popular with families, no doubt due to the vast menu of activities built into the multi-condominium facility and the reasonable prices. Much of the central facility has been renovated and condominiums are in the process; the estimated completion date is late 2004. An ice rink (which converts to a roller rink in April), huge co-ed sauna, three bubbling hot tubs, a water slide, and heated swimming pool vie for guests' attention, along with tennis, horseback riding, biking, skating, rafting—you name it. The Gray Hawk Grill offers fine Northwest dining, as well as breakfast and lunch, in the spacious lounge downstairs. Individually owned units are available for two-night stays through Central Oregon Accomodations (866/617-0179; *www.centraloregonaccomm.com*). *$$–$$$; AE, DIS, MC, V; checks OK; www.innofthe7thmountain.com; 7 miles west of downtown.* &

Mount Bachelor Village / ★★

19717 MOUNT BACHELOR DR, BEND; 541/389-5900 OR 800/452-9846 What this development has over some of its more famous neighbors is spacious rooms. Every unit (130 in all) has a furnished kitchen, wood-burning fireplace, and private deck. We prefer the newer units, where the color scheme is modern and light, and sound-proofing helps mute the thud of ski boots. Some units look out to the busy mountain road, but the River Ridge addition looks out over the Deschutes River. Amenities include two outdoor Jacuzzis, seasonal outdoor heated pool, six tennis courts, a 2.2-mile nature trail, and complimentary access to the exclusive Athletic Club of Bend, on the property. Children OK; no pets. *$$$; AE, DIS, MC, V; checks OK; www.mtbachelorvillage.com; toward Mount Bachelor on Century Dr.* &

Pine Ridge Inn / ★★★

1200 SW CENTURY DR, BEND; 541/389-6137 OR 800/600-4095 Perched on the edge of the river canyon on Century Drive, this privately owned 20-suite inn is smaller than neighboring resorts but big on privacy, luxury, and south-facing bird's-eye views of the Deschutes River. Suites have step-down living rooms with antique and reproduction furniture, and gas-log fireplaces, private porches, and roomy, well-stocked baths; several include Jacuzzis. Innkeepers Judy and Don Moilanen are attentive and personable, pampering guests with wine or beer tastings each afternoon, turndown services (fresh towels, bottled water, and pillow treats) each evening, and homemade complimentary breakfasts each morning. Well-behaved children are welcome; they can choose from a well-stocked library of videos, munch popcorn in their room, and get a special turndown treat of hot chocolate and cookies before bed. The Moilanens have extended the lawn to better serve small, intimate family gatherings and weddings (for parties of 25 or fewer). Budget tip: six rooms facing the parking lot are less expensive. *$$$–$$$$; AE, DC, DIS, MC, V; checks OK; pineridge@empnet.com; www.pineridgeinn.com; just before Mount Bachelor Village.* &

Rock Springs Guest Ranch / ★★

64201 TYLER RD, BEND; 541/382-1957 OR 800/225-3833 From late June through late August and at Thanksgiving, the emphasis here is on family vacations. (The rest of the year, it's a top-notch conference center.) Counselors take care of kids in daylong special programs while adults hit the trail, laze in the pool, play tennis, or meet for evening hors d'oeuvres on the deck. Digs are comfy knotty-pine two- and three-room cottages with fireplaces. Only 50 guests stay at the ranch at one time, so it's easy to get to know everyone, particularly since you eat family-style in the lodge. The setting, amid ponderosa pines and junipers alongside a small lake, is secluded and lovely. The main activity here is riding, with 9 wranglers and a stable of 70 horses. Summer season is booked by the week ($2,050 per person—kids for less, children under 2 free), which includes virtually everything. Look for lighted tennis courts, a free-form whirlpool, a sand volleyball court under the tall pines, guided canoe trips, golf courses, mountain biking, and fishing in the ranch pond. It's ideal for weddings or reunions. *$$$; AE, MC, V; checks OK; info@rocksprings .com; www.rocksprings.com; 8 miles north of Bend off Hwy 20.* &

Sunriver Lodge / ★★★

SUNRIVER; 541/593-1000 OR 800/547-3922 More than a resort, Sunriver is an organized community with its own post office, chamber of commerce, realty offices, outdoor mall, grocery store, and more than 1,500 residents. The unincorporated town sprawls over 3,300 acres, and its own paved runway for private air commuting does brisk business. Sunriver's specialty is big-time escapist vacationing, and the resort has all the facilities to keep families, couples, or groups busy all week long, year-round. The guest list in summer 2003 included President George W. Bush. A two-level indoor club and spa provides tennis courts, a lap pool, and a full slate of services, from massages to aromatherapy. Summer offers golf (three 18-hole courses), tennis (28 courts), rafting, canoeing, fishing, swimming (three pools, two complexes of hot tubs), biking (30 miles of paved trails), and horseback riding. In winter the resort is home base for skiing (Nordic and alpine), ice-skating, and snowmobiling. For the best bargain, deal through the lodge reservation service, request one of the large contemporary homes (often with hot tubs, barbecues, and decks), and split expenses with another family; the lodge extends club and pool access to all properties it manages (that makes up for the whopping 17 percent lodge tax). Even the bedroom units in the lodge village have small decks and fireplaces and come with privileges like discounted recreation, depending on the season. Four complexes hold 38 luxury River Lodges, each with a deck or balcony overlooking the Meadows golf course, slate-floored bathrooms with soaker tubs and separate showers, and gas fireplaces. Lodge dining includes the Meadows restaurant, a much-acclaimed showplace for lunch, dinner, and Sunday brunch. Elsewhere in the town of Sunriver, choose anything from Chinese to pizza. We like breakfast at the Trout House at the Sunriver Marina, too. *$$$–$$$$; AE, DIS, MC, V; checks OK; www.sunriverresort .com; 15 miles south of Bend.*

Mount Bachelor

MOUNT BACHELOR SKI AREA (22 miles southwest of Bend, on Century Dr; 541/382-7888 for ski report, or 800/829-2442; *www.mtbachelor.com*) is now under the ownership Powdr Corp., based in Park City, Utah. It's one of the largest ski areas in the Pacific Northwest, with 7 high-speed lifts (10 lifts in all) feeding skiers onto 3,100 vertical feet of groomed and dry-powder slopes. Snowboarders and skiers can enjoy a full park with rails and jumps, a minipark for beginners, and the **SUPERPIPE**—a 400-foot-long halfpipe with 17-foot walls. The tubing park has a surface lift and five groomed runs. The **SKIER'S PALATE** (at midmountain Pine Marten Lodge) serves excellent lunches; **SCAPOLO'S** (on the lodge's lower level) features Italian cuisine. Skiing closes Memorial Day and the slopes reopen July 1 for summer sightseeing. High-season amenities include ski school, racing, day care, rentals, and an entire Nordic program and trails.

Elk Lake

LODGINGS

Elk Lake Resort

CENTURY DR, BEND; 541/480-7228 This remote fishing lodge 11 miles past Mt. Bachelor—reached by snow cat or 10 miles of cross-country skiing in the winter (or by car in the summer)—consists of 10 self-contained cabins, with kitchens, bathrooms, and sleeping quarters for 4 to 12, and a small store. It's nothing grand, but the place is favored by Bend dwellers and the scenery is wonderful. Summer visitors can choose among 3 primitive cabins and 13 tent sites. The dining room has changing daily specials and serves three squares a day. Reserve in advance for cabins or dining, and bring bug juice in summer—mosquitoes can be ravenous. *$$–$$$; MC, V; no checks; www.elklakeresort.com; look for signs to Elk Lake.*

Sisters and the Deschutes River Area

From Bend, US Highway 20 heads northwest to Sisters, and from Sisters, Highway 126 goes east to Redmond; together with US Highway 97 these roads form a triangle in an area rich with rivers and parks. North from Madras on US Highway 26 is the Warm Springs Indian Reservation. And through it all runs the **DESCHUTES RIVER**, designated a scenic waterway north of Warm Springs.

Redmond

Often overlooked in favor of its big sister to the south (Bend), Redmond offers a nice alternative base for exploring the Sisters region. About 6 miles north of Redmond, east of Terrebonne, some of the finest rock climbers gather to test their skills on the red-rock cliffs of **SMITH ROCK STATE PARK** (off US Hwy 97; 541/548-7501). Year-round camping is available.

Experience a train robbery over Sunday brunch on the **CROOKED RIVER DINNER TRAIN** (4075 NE O'Neil Rd; 541/548-8630; *www.crookedriverrailroad.com*) as it ambles up the 38-mile Crooked River valley between Redmond and Prineville. Three-hour scenic excursions include white tablecloth dinner service and sometimes have special themes, such as Western murder-mystery theater and cowboy cookouts. Reservations required.

LODGINGS

Inn at Eagle Crest / ★★

1522 CLINE FALLS HWY, REDMOND; 541/923-2453 OR 800/MUCH-SUN Sisters has Black Butte, Bend has Sunriver, and Redmond has Eagle Crest. The private homes at this full resort rim the 18-hole golf course, and visitors choose one of the 100 rooms in the hotel (best ones have decks facing the course) or a condominium. The resort has two recreation centers: Ridge Sports has an indoor basketball court, a swimming pool, and a full day spa; and Resort Sports includes indoor tennis, squash, and racquetball courts; a workout room; a masseuse; a tanning salon; a heated outdoor pool; and tennis courts. The resort also has miles of biking and jogging trails, an equestrian center, and playfields. The food at the resort's formal Niblick & Greene (dinner only) is predictable for such a clubby atmosphere, with rancher-sized portions. The three-tiered deck outside provides a good view. *$$; AE, MC, V; checks OK; www.eagle-crest.com; 5 miles west of Redmond.*

Sisters

Named after the three mountain peaks (Faith, Hope, and Charity) that dominate the horizon, this little community is becoming a mecca for tired urbanites looking for a taste of cowboy escapism. On a clear day (about 250 a year here), Sisters is exquisitely beautiful. Surrounded by mountains, trout streams, and pine and cedar forests, this small town capitalizes on the influx of winter skiers and summer camping and fishing enthusiasts.

There's mixed sentiment about the pseudo-Western storefronts that thematically organize the town's commerce, but then again, Sisters hosts 56,000 visitors for each of four shows during June's annual **SISTERS RODEO**. In July, the town also has the world's largest outdoor quilt show, the longtime **SISTERS OUTDOOR QUILT SHOW**, with 800 quilts hanging from balconies and storefronts. Call the **VISITOR CENTER** (541/549-0251) for information on either event.

In the early 1970s, Sisters developed the Western theme, but it's grown much more sophisticated. The town, built on about 30 feet of pumice dust spewed over centuries from the nearby volcanoes, has added mini-mall shopping clusters with courtyards and sidewalks to eliminate blowing dust. There are several large art galleries, good bakeries, an excellent fly-fishing shop, **THE FLY FISHER'S PLACE** (151 W Main Ave; 541/549-3474; *www.theflyfishersplace.com*), and even freshly roasted coffee at **SISTERS COFFEE COMPANY** (273 W Hood Ave; 541/549-0527). Although the town population is about 1,000, more than 7,500 live in the surrounding area on miniranches.

RESTAURANTS

Bronco Billy's Ranch Grill and Saloon / ★

190 E CASCADE ST, SISTERS; 541/549-RIBS Formerly known as the Hotel Sisters Restaurant, this bar and eatery serves ranch cooking—good burgers and some Mexican fare. Seafood is fresh, filet mignon grilled perfectly, chicken and ribs succulent. The wait staff is friendly and diligent. The decor is mostly authentic 1900s, with a touch of "Hee Haw!" and "Haunted House" thrown in for entertainment value; full-sized straw-stuffed dolls in period dress occupy the corners. Owners John Keenan, Bill Reed, and John Tehan have succeeded in turning old friendships into a growing business consortium, re-creating the look of a first-class 1900 hotel. The upstairs hotel rooms are now private dining rooms, perfect for banquets. The covered patio is a good place for drinks. *$$; MC,*

V; checks OK; lunch, dinner every day (lunch Sat–Sun only in winter); full bar; reservations recommended; at Fir St. &

LODGINGS

Black Butte Ranch / ★★★

HWY 20, BLACK BUTTE RANCH; 541/595-6211 OR 800/452-7455 With 1,800 acres, this vacation and recreation wonderland remains the darling of Northwest resorts. Rimmed by the Three Sisters mountains and scented by a plain of ponderosa pines, these rental condos and private homes draw families year-round to swim, ski, fish, golf, bike, boat, ride horses (summer only), and play tennis. The best way to make a reservation is to state the size of your party and whether you want a home (most are large and contemporary) or simply a good-sized bed and bath (lodge condominiums suffice, though some are dark and dated, with too much orange Formica and brown furniture). The main lodge is handsome, but not overwhelming, and serves as dining headquarters (breakfast, lunch, dinner). Tables at the Lodge Restaurant (closed Mon–Wed Jan–mid-March) are tiered so everyone can appreciate the meadow panorama beyond. You can also dine next door at the Big Meadow Clubhouse restaurant. *$$$; AE, DIS, MC, V; checks OK; 2-night min July–August; info@blackbutteranch.com; www.blackbutteranch.com; 8 miles west of Sisters.* &

Camp Sherman

This tiny settlement midway between Sisters and Santiam Pass is lush and green despite raging fires in summer 2003. Reservations are recommended at the popular **KOKANEE CAFE** (25545 SW Forest Service Rd 1419; 541/595-6420; April–Oct).

LODGINGS

Metolius River Resort / ★★

25551 SW FOREST SERVICE RD 1419, CAMP SHERMAN; 541/595-6281 OR 800/81-TROUT Not to be confused with the lower-priced, circa-1923 Metolius River Lodges across the bridge, these 11 upscale cabins on the west bank are wood-shake with large decks and river-rock fireplaces. Most have bedroom lofts, furnished kitchens, river-facing decks, cable television, and barbecues. Because the pricey cabins are privately owned, interiors differ, but most include luxurious lodge-style furnishings and all are meticulously maintained. Management prohibits group rentals, children, and pets to maintain a tranquil atmosphere. Two-night minimum stay. *$$$; AE, DIS, MC, V; checks OK; reservations@metolius-river-resort.com; www.metolius-river-resort.com; 5 miles north of US Hwy 20.*

Warm Springs

Many travelers pass through the Warm Springs Indian Reservation on their way south to Bend or north to Mount Hood. If you're not spending a night at the

Kah-Nee-Ta High Desert Resort (see review), be sure to stop and visit the incredible **MUSEUM AT WARM SPRINGS** (541/553-3331; *www.warmsprings.biz/museum*). The award-winning facility includes a stunning exhibit of a Wasco wedding ceremony, a contemporary art gallery, and a gift shop.

LODGINGS

Kah-Nee-Ta High Desert Resort / ★★

100 MAIN ST, WARM SPRINGS; 541/553-1112 OR 800/554-4786 The sulfur-free hot springs near the Warm Springs River are the center of this resort on the Warm Springs Indian Reservation, nestled below the barren Mutton Mountains. The resort includes two houses with full kitchens and hot tubs, five RV spaces, a 20-teepee encampment, a 30-room motel, a gift shop, tennis courts, and an 18-hole golf course. Farther up the road, the lodge and casino are perched on the canyon wall. Angular and lovely, the lodge has swimming pools and sweeping southerly views, but the 139 rooms are otherwise unremarkable and belie the nonsmoking policy. Popular Indian-style salmon bakes, sometimes with dance performances, are held Saturdays during summer. From mid-March through late September, the main lodge's Juniper Room offers fine dining while the Chinook Room offers buffet service and food to go (breakfast, lunch, and dinner). From October through March, the Chinook Room offers a more elaborate dining menu in addition to sit-down breakfasts and lunches. The resort is a peaceful getaway 11 miles from US Highway 26. *$$–$$$; AE, DC, DIS, MC, V; checks OK; www.kah-nee-taresort.com; 11 miles north of Warm Springs on Hwy 3.* &

EASTERN OREGON

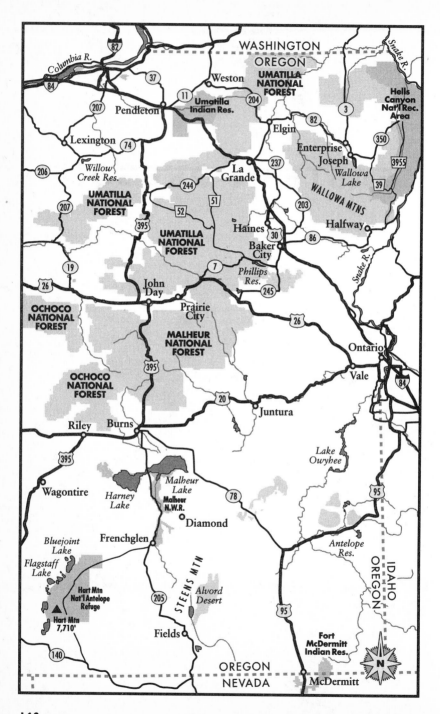

EASTERN OREGON

Eastern Oregon is as different from Western Oregon as it is from, say, Kansas, and it's commonly misrepresented by Western Oregonians, who refer to it as a "desert." Sure, some areas here are pretty dry, with about a million pickup loads' worth of sagebrush, but Eastern Oregon also has mountains galore, where winter snows pile up and springtime snowmelt feeds streams and wetlands. Lava flows and glaciers formed much of the landscape, including Steens Mountain, the world's largest fault block. The Wallowa Mountains, in the northeast corner of the state, are classic examples of glacial action—their crags and cirques and gemlike lakes were all formed by ice-age glaciers.

Oregon Trail pioneers got across this land as quickly as they could, but some returned after a short stay in Western Oregon. Back here, they became gold miners and cattle ranchers. Today, though the bulk of the gold has been grabbed, this is still cattle country, where a rugged Western spirit prevails.

ACCESS AND INFORMATION
INTERSTATE 84 is the main route across Eastern Oregon, connecting Pendleton, La Grande, and Baker City with Portland to the west and Boise, Idaho, to the east. The other east-west routes are **US HIGHWAY 26** through Prineville, John Day, and Prairie City, and **US HIGHWAY 20**, the route from Bend to Burns and Ontario. **US HIGHWAY 395** is the main north-south route, with Pendleton, John Day, and Burns along its way. Between Pendleton and La Grande, Interstate 84 crosses the Blue Mountains at 4,193 feet; this pass often closes down for a day or so after a heavy snow. For road conditions throughout the state, check in with the **OREGON DEPARTMENT OF TRANSPORTATION** (503/588-2941 outside of Oregon or 800/977-6368 in state); their excellent online **TRAVEL ADVISOR** (*www.tripcheck.com*) is the best place to check on road conditions.

HORIZON AIR (800/547-9308; *www.horizonair.com*) flies to Pendleton and Redmond from Portland. Buses are another option out here. **GREYHOUND** (800/231-2222; *www.greyhound.com*) runs along Interstate 84 and stops in towns such as La Grande and Pendleton; the **PEOPLE MOVER** bus (541/575-2370 or 800/527-2370) travels between Prairie City and Bend; **WALLOWA VALLEY STAGE LINES** (541/569-2284) makes the trip between Wallowa Lake and La Grande.

Pendleton

Looking for the Wild West? Stop by Pendleton in mid-September, when the whole town devotes itself to staging the **PENDLETON ROUND-UP** (1205 SW Court St; 800/457-6336 tickets and information). The event features a dandy rodeo and a crazy street scene.

PENDLETON WOOLEN MILLS (1307 SE Court Pl; 541/276-6911; *www.pendleton-usa.com*; tours Mon–Fri) sells woolen clothing and fabric and imperfect versions of its famous blankets at reduced prices. **PENDLETON UNDERGROUND TOURS** (37 SW Emigrant Ave; 541/276-0730 or 800/226-6398) offers a 90-minute

---

NORTHEASTERN OREGON THREE-DAY TOUR

DAY ONE: Start the day in La Grande with breakfast at **FOLEY STATION**. Wander around downtown and stop in at **SUNFLOWER BOOKS** (1114 Washington Ave; 541/963-8057), which has a cozy café and a wide selection of books. Then hop in the car and head east along Highway 82. Several antique stores make up the whole of small-town Elgin, and it's a nice place to get out of the car. By the time you reach Enterprise, the Wallowa Mountains dominate the scenery. Stop by the huge **WALLOWA MOUNTAIN VISITORS CENTER**, on the bluff as you enter Enterprise, for information on hiking, mountain biking, or cross-country skiing. From Enterprise, it's just 6 miles to Joseph, where the **WILDFLOUR BAKERY** is a good lunch spot. Spend the afternoon browsing the galleries and shops along Main Street, then check into the **BRONZE ANTLER B&B**. For a casual dinner, drive the 6 miles to Enterprise and relax at the **TERMINAL GRAVITY BREWPUB**.

  DAY TWO: Eat a hearty breakfast at Joseph's **OLD TOWN CAFE** to prepare for a hike or horseback ride; **EAGLE CAP WILDERNESS PACK STATION** can set you up with a horse and guide. For an easy ride (sans horse) to mountaintop views, hitch a ride

---

walk through Pendleton's subterranean history to view the remains of businesses that date back to the turn of the century: bordellos, opium dens, and Chinese jails. Reservations are necessary; make them at least 24 hours in advance; $10 per person, no children under 6. If you don't have the necessary reservations or time for the underground tour, tour Pendleton's history at the newly renovated **HERITAGE STATION MUSEUM** (108 SW Frazer Ave; 541/276-0012).

The Confederated Tribes of the Umatilla's **TÁMASTSLIKT** ("ta-MUST-ah-luck") **CULTURAL INSTITUTE** (72789 Hwy 331; 541/966-9748), on 640 acres behind the Wildhorse Gaming Resort, tells the story of Oregon from the Native point of view and mounts some very exciting art exhibits.

RESTAURANTS

Raphael's / ★★

233 SE 4TH ST, PENDLETON; 541/276-8500 OR 888/944-2433 You know you're well east of the Cascades when you walk in the front door and see the row of cowboy hats hanging from coat hooks. This also tells you that you're at a classy joint, where men actually remove their hats before sitting down at the table. The decor is simple, with Craftsman-style chairs and impressive art on the sage-colored walls. The menu ranges from light dinners, such as a salmon sauté, to an autumn selection of "Hunters' Specials," including rattlesnake and rabbit sausage tossed with sautéed vegetables and pasta, or marionberry-barbequed elk rack. You'll likely find Raphael Hoffman, the owner and Nez Perce tribal member, behind the bar while her husband, Rob, does the cooking. *$$; AE, DIS, MC, V; checks OK; dinner Tues–Sat; full bar; reservations recommended; between Court Pl and Dorion Ave.* &

on the **WALLOWA LAKE TRAMWAY**. For lunch, take another swing by the Wildflour Bakery. Head east out of town, then turn south onto Forest Road 39, a paved road that takes you high above **HELLS CANYON** (be sure to take the 3-mile detour to the scenic overlook) to link up to Highway 86. Head west on 86 into Halfway. Even though it's only 65 miles between Joseph and Halfway, allow at least two hours for the drive, and remember: This is remote country, with no restaurants, stores, or gas stations. (Forest Rd 39 is closed in winter.) In Halfway, stay and eat at **PINE VALLEY LODGE**.

DAY THREE: After breakfast at the lodge, backtrack east along Highway 86 to the **SNAKE RIVER**. Choose a noisy jet-boat ride or a quiet hike. If you opt for the latter, drive north from Oxbow Dam until the long, dusty dirt road ends. Park and walk. For lunch, grab a bite at the **COWBOY CAFE** (241 S Main St; 541/742-7777) in downtown Halfway. Then take Highway 86 west to the **NATIONAL HISTORIC OREGON TRAIL INTERPRETIVE CENTER** in Baker City for both the indoor exhibits and the trail to the wagon ruts. By late afternoon, leave the dusty trail behind and check into the **GEISER GRAND HOTEL** for a little rest before dinner at **BARLEY BROWN'S BREWPUB**.

LODGINGS

Parker House Bed and Breakfast / ★★

311 N MAIN ST, PENDLETON; 541/276-8581 OR 800/700-8581 Don't underestimate Pendleton's capacity for grandeur. What seems to be a fairly roughand-tumble town, especially at Round-Up time, has some spectacular old houses, not the least of which is the pink stucco Parker House, just up the hill and across the Umatilla River from downtown. Built in 1917, the Italian Renaissance–style house is in great condition and retains many of its original fittings, including beautiful Chinese silk wall fabrics and, in the shared bathroom, what may be the world's most unusual shower. (It only *looks* like a torture chamber.) Of the five rooms, Gwendolyn is the grandest, with a fireplace and French doors. *$$; MC, V; checks OK; www.parkerhousebnb.com; north on Hwy 11, follow City Center signs to downtown, head north on Main St, cross Umatilla River to N Main St.*

The Working Girl's Hotel

17 SW EMIGRANT AVE, PENDLETON; 541/276-0730 OR 800/226-6398 Just upstairs from the Pendleton Underground Tours, this nonprofit hotel, designed to bring tourism to Pendleton, gets its name from its former incarnation as a bordello. The girls are gone, but the five spacious rooms (one long flight up) in this classic downtown brick building are still welcoming. Each has 18-foot ceilings and antique furnishings. The plumbing's pretty close to the original stuff, so you'll need to cross a hall to the bath—but that's a small price to pay for such a fun night's stay. A full kitchen and dining area are available. In the grand bordello tradition, this is an adults-only hotel. *$; MC, V; checks OK; between Main and SW 1st Sts.*

Condon

LODGINGS

Hotel Condon / ★★☆

202 S MAIN ST, CONDON; 541/384-4624 OR 800/201-6706 Condon makes a good base for exploring the John Day country, and the Hotel Condon makes such a weekend trip all the more appealing. The renovated hotel is—much like the people who live in Condon—an attractive mix of country and sophistication. Rooms are spare and elegant, decorated with steel gray carpeting, white down comforters, and classy black-and-white photos of the striking local landscape. Downstairs at the Sage Lounge, conversations tend either to art or to cattle, with a good dose of the local gossip. A light continental breakfast is laid out in the upstairs reading area, and the hotel restaurant serves just about the best restaurant food in all of Gilliam County. *$$; AE, DIS, MC, V; checks OK; info@hotelcondon.com; www .hotelcondon.com; downtown at corner of 2nd and Main Sts.* &

The Wallowas and Hells Canyon

This is the ancestral home of Chief Joseph; he fled from here with a band of Nez Perce to his last stand near the Canadian border. Although Chief Joseph's remains are interred far from his beloved land of the winding water, he saw to it that his father, Old Chief Joseph, would be buried here, on the north shore of Wallowa Lake (see "The Wallowas' First Residents" in this chapter). **HELLS CANYON NATIONAL RECREATION AREA** (35 miles east of Joseph) encompasses the continent's deepest gorge, an awesome trench cut by the Snake River through sheer lava walls.

La Grande

RESTAURANTS

Foley Station / ★★

🌲 **1114 ADAMS AVE, LA GRANDE; 541/963-7473** If you want to hang with the happening folks in La Grande, show up at Foley Station at 7am. That's when the doors open to Eastern Oregon's most sophisticated breakfast joint. Settle into a booth or perch at the bar and get down to the formidable task of deciding what to eat. It seems like every local has a breakfast favorite here, from such classics as huevos rancheros or biscuits and gravy to the Valley Gardener, a nutritious pile of sautéed vegetables, potatoes, and herbs topped with a satisfying layer of cheese. Wash it all down with coffee poured from a giant French-press carafe, or tea. Foley's does dinner, too; the menu changes monthly to feature seasonal specials, but a wide selection of steaks and pasta dishes, including a delicious smoked salmon pasta with a dill-caper cream sauce, is available year-round. Chef-owner Merlyn Baker emphasizes locally grown produce and local meats (providing an outlet for Eastern Oregon emu ranchers). In 2003, Foley's was forced to move across the street from its original location; Baker has poured his seemingly limitless energy into making the new venue as inviting and as popular as the old place. *$$; MC, V; checks OK; breakfast, lunch Wed–Sun, dinner Thurs–Sat; full bar; reservations recommended; foleystation@restaurant.com; www.restaurant.com/ foleystation; between 4th and Depot Sts.* &

Ten Depot Street

10 DEPOT ST, LA GRANDE; 541/963-8766 Ten Depot, a longtime local favorite, is a good place to get a feeling for this friendly town. The dining room, in an old brick building with antique furnishings, is nice, but it's more fun to eat dinner in the bar, with its beautiful carved-wood back bar. Bargain hunters order the blue-plate special; other dinners range from a two-fisted (half-pound) burger to chicken-and-pesto pasta to prime rib (the house specialty). Prepare for a hearty meal: dinners include appetizers, bread, and salad. *$$; AE, MC, V; checks OK; lunch, dinner Mon–Sat; full bar; reservations recommended; 2 blocks west of Adams Ave.* &

LODGINGS

Stange Manor Inn / ★

1612 WALNUT ST, LA GRANDE; 541/963-2400 OR 888/286-9463 This restored timber baron's house on the hill behind town lends a touch of elegance to La Grande. It's a huge place, with four bedrooms at the top of a sweeping staircase. The master suite is best, but even if you opt for the former maid's quarters with its seven doors and angled walls, you'll feel pampered. The B&B's innkeeper, Carolyn Jensen, is a culinary-school grad and takes special care with breakfast. The Stange Manor is, popular with business travelers. Kids over 10 are welcome. *$$; MC, V; checks OK; innkeeper@stangmanor.com; www.stangmanor.com; at Spring St.*

Union

LODGINGS

Union Hotel

326 N MAIN ST, UNION; 541/562-6135 It's hard to miss the Union Hotel; the huge brick building dominates Main Street. Inside, room by room, it's turning into a darn nice place to stay in this small town on the back road between La Grande and Baker City. Built in 1921, it was neglected long enough for it to become something of an Eastern Oregon squat (a sheep was among the residents). The parlor's dark woodwork and wicker furniture evoke the 1920s; the 15 renovated rooms are all different and range from the modest, old-fashioned Original Room to the more modern Northwest Room, with a separate kitchenette and huge soaking tub. (Most of the rooms have clawfooted tubs.) Many of the rooms are actually two-bedroom suites, making this a great place for families with kids. The attached restaurant is a handy spot for dinner and breakfast, though it's an easy drive into La Grande for a fancier meal. *$; DIS, MC, V; checks OK; info@theunionhotel.com; www.the unionhotel.com; 14 miles southeast of La Grande, at corner of Presbiterin.*

Enterprise

RESTAURANTS

Terminal Gravity Brewery

803 SCHOOL ST, ENTERPRISE; 541/426-0158 Find a place on the front porch of this old country house turned brew pub, settle in with a glass of the rich, smooth IPA, and admire the fancifully carved and painted screen door. (It features batlike monsters holding glasses of beer.) Before long you'll either be playing volleyball out on the lawn with the regulars, or venturing inside for a game of darts. Don't fight the temptation to stay on into the dinner hour: the food at this down-home spot is as good as you'll find anywhere in town. Weekend specials are a cut above pub grub and may include such dishes as jambalaya, blackened catfish, or meatloaf. *$; no credit cards; checks OK; dinner Thurs–Sat; beer and wine; no reservations; south end of town on School St.*

Joseph

Artists, especially bronze artists, thrive in Joseph. The many galleries include **MANUEL MUSEUM AND STUDIO** (400 N Main St; 541/432-7235), featuring the work of David Manuel, and **VALLEY BRONZE OF OREGON** (307 W Alder St; 541/432-7551), with a foundry, a showroom, and weekday tours. Even if you don't set foot in a gallery, a walk down Main Street is an art walk in itself; large bronzes by local artists adorn nearly every block.

    WALLOWA LAKE STATE PARK (just south of Joseph on the edge of the lake) is full of campers and camper-friendly deer all summer; it's near trailheads that lead into the **EAGLE CAP WILDERNESS AREA**, a rugged mountain wilderness that looks more Alpine than Oregonian. (This resemblance isn't lost on the Joseph tourist board; an **ALPENFEST** with music, dancing, and Bavarian feasts occurs in September.)

    Scoot to the top of 8,200-foot Mount Howard on the **WALLOWA LAKE TRAMWAY** (59919 Wallowa Lake Hwy; 541/432-5331), a four-person summer gondola that shimmies you up to spectacular overlooks and 2 miles of hiking trails. Maps of the region's roads and trails, and information on conditions, are available at the **WALLOWA MOUNTAINS VISITOR CENTER** (88401 Hwy 82, Enterprise; 541/426-5546).

    As you hike down into Hells Canyon or up to the lake-laden Eagle Cap Wilderness, let a llama lug your gear with **HURRICANE CREEK LLAMA TREKS** (541/432-4455 or 800/528-9609; *www.hcltrek.com*; June–Aug). A day's hike takes you 4 to 8 miles, and hearty meals are included; reserve well in advance. Sign up for a morning horseback ride or an extended wilderness pack trip at the **EAGLE CAP WILDERNESS PACK STATION** (59761 Wallowa Lake Hwy; 541/432-4145 or 800/681-6222; *www.eaglecapwildernesspackstation.com*).

    Don't let winter stop you from exploring the Wallowas. Head into the back-country for a few days of guided telemark skiing with **WING RIDGE SKI TOURS** (541/426-4322 or 800/646-9050; *www.wingski.com*). Experienced backcountry ski

THE WALLOWAS' FIRST RESIDENTS

The beautiful Wallowa Valley is the homeland of the **NEZ PERCE TRIBE**. Outside town and off the main roads, little has changed since the tribe wintered in the canyon bottoms, dug camas lilies on the prairies, and hunted at the base of the Wallowa Mountains.

LEWIS AND CLARK'S CORPS OF DISCOVERY brought the first whites encountered by the Nez Perce. They had an exceptionally good relationship, and relations with whites remained good even as pioneers began to settle the valley. In 1877, the government ordered the Nez Perce to a reservation in north-central Idaho. The Wallowa Valley bands were reluctantly ready to comply, when a few young men lashed out by killing white settlers. Their band feared retribution and thus began one of history's great and tragic treks, as more than 800 American Indians sought safety in Canada, east of the Continental Divide. The U.S. Army pursued the Nez Perce, suffered some defeats, but ultimately wore them down, killing not only warriors but also women and children. The Nez Perce finally surrendered in northern Montana, where Chief Joseph gained his fame as an orator.

Surviving Nez Perce were sent to Oklahoma, and eventually back to the Northwest, where they were split between reservations in Idaho and Colville, Washington. Chief Joseph is buried on the Colville reservation; his father, Old Chief Joseph, is buried at the northern end of Wallowa Lake.

—Judy Jewell

guides lead you to accommodations in a rustic cabin or wood-floored tent shelters (conveniently located next to a wood-fired sauna tent).

RESTAURANTS

Old Town Cafe

8 S MAIN ST, JOSEPH; 541/432-9898 Locals and tourists pack this place, which has a modern-day, Western chat 'n' chew atmosphere. Breakfast burritos (eat 'em any time of day, smothered in homemade salsa) and artery-plugging desserts are among the favorites here. *$; MC, V; checks OK; breakfast, lunch Fri–Wed, dinner Fri–Sat; beer and wine; no reservations; downtown.*

Wildflour Bakery / ★

600 N MAIN ST, JOSEPH; 541/432-7225 It's easy to cruise right by this glorified double-wide on the north side of downtown Joseph, but if you keep your eyes open, you'll see a bunch of happy noshers out on the front deck. Inside, the Wildflour Bakery is light and airy, staffed by friendly folks who are proud of their organic, slowly risen breads. If a loaf of bread isn't proper hiking fuel for you, grab a marionberry turnover from the pastry case, or hang around and eat a full breakfast (the tasty and filling Santa Fe corn cake is stuffed with black beans and grilled veggies and topped with homemade salsa). Good sandwiches appear at lunch, and it's as easy to go vegetarian here as it is to order the delicious grilled sausage sandwich. *$; no credit cards; checks OK; breakfast, lunch Wed–Mon; no alcohol; no reservations; north end of town.* &

LODGINGS

Bronze Antler B&B

309 S MAIN ST, JOSEPH; 541/432-0230 OR 866/520-9769 This quiet inn is just a couple of blocks from the summertime bustle of downtown Joseph's art, shopping, and restaurant scene. The detailed Craftsman bungalow was built in 1925 and has been carefully restored with the help of local craftspeople. The innkeepers, Bill Finney and Heather Tyreman, are retired from military careers, during which they traveled widely and ended up with a fine selection of European antiques, now incorporated in the B&B's decor. (The European sensibility extends to bidets in the bathrooms.) Each of the three rooms has a fine view, but go for the Chief Joseph room if you want to wake up to an eyeful of the Wallowas. *$$; AE, DIS, MC, V; checks OK; info@bronzeantler.com; www.bronzeantler.com; 4th and Main.*

Wallowa Lake Lodge / ★

60060 WALLOWA LAKE HWY, JOSEPH; 541/432-9821 This rustic lodge is like a scaled-down version of a great national park lodge. Many of the guest rooms are quite small, but that shouldn't matter; you're here to hike the trails, knock around downtown Joseph, and try for the perfect photo of Wallowa Lake. That said, the lake-view rooms with balconies have a little more space, and evenings are best spent sprawled in front of the big stone fireplace in the lobby. If you plan to stay longer than a night, the lakeside cabins, each with a living room, fireplace, and kitchen, allow for a bit more flexibility. Neither lodge rooms nor cabins have TVs or phones, which contributes to the quiet appeal. The lodge and its restaurant are open only on weekends and holidays from mid-October through Memorial Day, but cabins are available year-round. *$$; DIS, MC, V; checks OK; info@wallowalake.com; www .wallowalake.com; near Wallowa Lake State Park.*

Halfway

Once just a midway stop between two bustling mining towns, Halfway is now the quiet but quirky centerpiece of Pine Valley—stashed between the fruitful southern slopes of the Wallowa Mountains and the steep cliffs of Hells Canyon.

The continent's deepest gorge, **HELLS CANYON**, begins at **OXBOW DAM**, 16 miles east of Halfway. For spectacular views of the **SNAKE RIVER**, drive from Oxbow to Joseph (take Hwy 86 to Forest Rd 39; summers only). Maps of the region's roads and trails are available from the U.S. Forest Service ranger station in Pine (541/742-7511), 1½ miles outside Halfway. The folks at **WALLOWA LLAMAS** (36678 Allstead Ln; 541/742-2961; *wallama@Pinetel.com*; *www.wallowallamas .com*) lead three- to seven-day trips into the pristine Eagle Cap Wilderness high in the Wallowas, while their surefooted beasts lug your gear and plenty of food. For those who would rather experience the raging river up close, **HELLS CANYON ADVENTURES** (4200 Hells Canyon Dam Rd; 541/785-3352; *www.hellscanyon adventures.com*) in Oxbow arranges jet-boat or white-water raft tours leaving from Hells Canyon Dam.

LODGINGS

Pine Valley Lodge / ★★

MAIN ST, HALFWAY; 541/742-2027 A wacky good spirit came to Halfway with Babette and Dale Beatty. They've put together an eccentric complex of lodgings on one side of Main Street and a restaurant and gallery on the other. Rent a room in the main lodge, the Love Shack, or the Blue Dog House—they're all comfortable and loaded with whimsy. And take the time to chat with Babette and Dale. Upstairs from the breakfast area, look for the inaugural *Sports Illustrated* swimsuit issue from 1963, where you'll recognize young Babette on the cover. Next to '60s fashion magazine covers, you'll see her extensive cookbook collection, and nearby is the art studio where she paints (mostly on silk) and Dale builds giant fanciful fishing rods and lures. If you happen by on a night when the lodge's Halfway Supper Club is serving dinner, be sure to jump at the chance to eat some wonderful food. *$$; no credit cards; checks OK; www.pvlodge.com; downtown.*

Baker City and Haines

Baker City is still a cow town, albeit a sophisticated one. For proof that it's still cowboy, just stay over on a Saturday night when the streets (and bars) fill with hats, boots, and big belt buckles. A sign of its sophistication is **BELLA** (2023 Main St, 541/523-7490), a popular downtown market with good coffee, a variety of classy housewares, and Eastern Oregon's best wine selection.

Located in the valley between the Wallowas and the Elkhorns, Baker City makes a good base for forays into the nearby mountain Gold Rush towns. The **NATIONAL HISTORIC OREGON TRAIL INTERPRETIVE CENTER** at Flagstaff Hill (Hwy 86, Baker City; 541/523-1843), 4 miles east of Interstate 84, is worth a detour. The multimedia walk-through brings the Oregon Trail experience to life. Open every day; admission is $5 per adult or $10 per carload.

Tour the Elkhorn Mountains, west of Baker City, flush with **MINING GHOST TOWNS**, on a 100-mile loop from Baker City (some on unpaved roads). The loop begins on Highway 7 then leads through the deserted towns of Bourne, Granite, Bonanza, and Whitney. A restored narrow-gauge steam train, the **SUMPTER VALLEY RAILWAY** (541/894-2268; *www.svry.com*), makes the short run between McEwen, just west of Phillips Lake, and Sumpter, from Memorial Day through September. **ANTHONY LAKES SKI AREA** (20 miles west of North Powder on Forest Rd 73; 541/856-3277) has good powder snow, one chair lift, cross-country trails, and snow-cat skiing.

RESTAURANTS

Barley Brown's Brewpub

2190 MAIN ST, BAKER CITY; 541/523-4266 Downtown Baker City's best (and biggest) dinners come from this family-friendly brew pub, housed in a former bakery on Main Street. Though half the space is a bar, the other half is a casual restaurant, nicely decked out with wooden booths and a pressed-tin ceiling. The menu features a wide range of pasta dishes, including "mad" pasta—bacon, mushrooms, peppers, and onions in a spicy tomato sauce. (The truly mad can opt to add alligator meat to the dish.) Seafood is also good here; someone in the kitchen knows how to cook it just about perfectly. The brewery makes a full line of tasty beers, including Tumble Off Pale Ale and seasonal brews such as Sled Wreck Winter Ale. Weekend nights often feature live music in the bar. *$; AE, DC, DIS, MC, V; checks OK; dinner Mon–Sat; full bar; no reservations; at Main and Church.* &

Haines Steak House / ★

910 FRONT ST, HAINES; 541/856-3639 There's no mistaking that you're in cattle country, so get ready to chow down on a giant steak. Some say this is the state's best steak house; it certainly is popular with Eastern Oregonians. Teenage boys in cowboy hats try to act suave at the salad bar to impress their dates, but the minute the meat is served, it's all eyes on the plate. Don't stray from beef here—it's well selected, well cut, and well cooked (rare, natch). *$$; AE, DC, MC, V; checks OK; lunch Sun, dinner Wed–Mon; full bar; reservations recommended; on old Hwy 30.* &

LODGINGS

Geiser Grand Hotel / ★★

1996 MAIN ST, BAKER CITY; 541/523-1889 OR 888/434-7374 A $7-million restoration to this landmark downtown hotel made all of Oregon look up and pay attention to Baker City. A highlight of the restoration is the Palm Court, a dining area that rises three stories to a huge stained-glass skylight. If the biggest stained glass in the Pacific Northwest doesn't shed enough light, check out the bejeweled chandeliers—they're probably not what you would choose for your own house, but they fit right into this 1889 Italianate Renaissance Revival–style hotel. The 30 rooms are large and comfortable—the cupola suites are a bit of a splurge but have great views of the mountains and downtown Baker City through the original 10-foot-high windows. All in all, a night at the Geiser Grand makes a trip to Baker City something special. Well-behaved dogs are welcome. *$$; AE, DIS, MC, V; checks OK; www.geisergrand.com; downtown at Washington Ave.* &

John Day

John Day looks like just another cow town, but its surroundings are loaded with history. It's just off the Oregon Trail, and before the 1860s, the whole region was packed tight with gold (in 1862, $26 million in gold was mined down the road in Canyon City). **KAM WAH CHUNG MUSEUM** (250 NW Canton St; 541/575-0028;

open May–Oct, closed Fri) was the stone-walled home of a Chinese herbalist early in the 20th century. A tour makes for an interesting glimpse of the Chinese settlement in the West: opium-stained walls, shrines, and herbal medicines are on display, as well as a small general store.

JOHN DAY FOSSIL BEDS NATIONAL MONUMENT lies 40 to 120 miles west, in three distinct groupings: the colorfully banded hillsides of the Painted Hills Unit, an ancient fossilized forest at the Clarno Unit, and fascinating geological layers at the Sheep Rock Unit. Stop by the visitor center and museum near the Sheep Rock Unit (on Hwy 19, 10 miles northwest of Dayville; 541/987-2333; open daily 9am–5pm) for a look at the choicest fossils.

LODGINGS

The Ponderosa Guest Ranch / ★★★

PO BOX 190, SENECA; 541/542-2403 Been fantasizing about trading in your tennis shoes for pointy-toed boots? Checking out the cowboy Web sites? Well, pardner, must be time for the Ponderosa. This isn't some big-shot developer's fluffed-up idea of a ranch—it's a real working cattle ranch, with all the buckaroos to prove it. Guests help staff cowboys manage 2,500 to 4,000 head of cattle—this can mean assisting with a bovine cesarean section, branding, or driving cattle to mountain pastures—all the little things that go into that nice steak dinner you're gonna get at the end of a long day's work. But nobody here is going to make you get on a horse. You can grab a field guide and rustle up some wildflowers, or look for antelope, bear, groundhogs, eagles, sandhill cranes, cinnamon ducks, and sage hens. Hearty ranch fare (included in the price) is served family style. Guest operations are scaled back in winter. Ages 18 and up only. *$$$; MC, V; checks OK; 3-night min; ride@ponderosaranch.com; www.ponderosaguestranch.com; on Hwy 395, halfway between Burns and John Day.*

Prairie City

LODGINGS

Strawberry Mountain Inn

E HWY 26, PRAIRIE CITY; 541/820-4522 OR 800/545-6913 Anyone in Prairie City will tell you what a classy five-room B&B Linda Harrington runs, with prime views of the Strawberry Mountains, rising from the horse pasture across the road. Ask for one of the two rooms with mountain views. The backyard is nice, with a little orchard and a garden, but it's the mountains that give Prairie City its life. In addition to the requisite B&B reading room, there's a hot tub, a pool table, and plenty of videos and CDs. Unlike many B&B hosts, the Harringtons welcome kids and have a play area in the yard. Breakfasts fuel you for a hike into the Strawberry Mountain Wilderness Area. *$$; AE, MC, V; checks OK; linda@ortelco.net; www.strawberrymountaininn.com; just east of downtown.*

BIRDS OF THE MALHEUR

MALHEUR NATIONAL WILDLIFE REFUGE is ground zero for Eastern Oregon birding—its 187,000 acres of wetlands make it a hospitable stop for migrating birds. Spring is the best time to see birds; more than 130 species nest on the refuge, and many more make rest stops. Sandhill cranes (with 8-foot wingspans) and tundra swans may show up as early as February, followed by waterfowl in March, shorebirds in April, and songbirds late in May, when other birds are beginning to fly off. During the hot summer months, trumpeter swans swim the refuge ponds. Sandhill cranes, ducks, and geese return in the fall, and then fly on to California, leaving the winter to eagles and hawks.

Start your trip to Malheur with a visit to the **REFUGE HEADQUARTERS** (32 miles southeast of Burns on south side of Malheur Lake; 541/493-2612), where you can pick up maps and brochures. Visit the **GEORGE BENSON MEMORIAL MUSEUM** (chock-full of mounted birds) and spy on birds in the pond and in the trees around headquarters. From there, drive south on **CENTRAL PATROL ROAD**, a good gravel road that passes a number of ponds before ending at **P RANCH**, right near the **FRENCHGLEN HOTEL**. In order to protect the wildlife, most areas are closed to hiking, but if you need to burn off some energy, it's okay to mountain bike along Central Patrol Road.

—Judy Jewell

Southeast High Desert

MALHEUR NATIONAL WILDLIFE REFUGE (37 miles south of Burns on Hwy 205; 541/493-2612) is one of the country's major bird refuges—187,000 acres of wetlands and lakes (see "Birds of the Malheur" in this chapter).

Burns

The town of Burns, once the center of impressive cattle kingdoms, is still a market town, but a pretty quiet one. Walking downtown, you can hear a luff as a flock of quail takes flight from a parking lot.

CRYSTAL CRANE HOT SPRINGS (25 miles southeast of Burns on Hwy 78, Crane; 541/493-2312) is a good place to take a break from driving and swim in the hot-springs pond or soak in a water trough turned hot tub.

RESTAURANTS

Pine Room Cafe

543 W MONROE ST, BURNS; 541/573-6631 This may be Burns's fanciest restaurant, but that doesn't mean you have to take your cowboy hat off at the dinner table. It's a good-natured, chummy spot where locals call out to each other and comment, sotto voce, on who's dining with whom. But it's not cliquish, and the staff is eager to make out-of-towners feel like hanging around the bar after dinner. Besides the expected array of steaks, popular entrées include the Chicken Artichoke and fish dishes (though don't count on your halibut being flown in fresh). The bread is homemade, and the steaks hand-cut in the kitchen. *$$; MC, V; local checks only; dinner Tues–Sat; full bar; reservations recommended; at Egan Ave.* &

LODGINGS

Sage Country Inn / ★

351½ W MONROE ST, BURNS; 541/573-7243 Set well back from the main drag through Burns, the Sage Country Inn is a comfortable base for a southeastern Oregon adventure. The rooms in this 1907 Georgian Colonial house are comfortable but not cloying—the Cattle Baron's Room is as manly a room as you'll ever find in a B&B. All three rooms are filled with antiques and stacks of books on local history and ranchers' witticisms. Read up and save your questions for breakfast—the Husebys can tell you all about life present and past in southeastern Oregon. *$$; MC, V; checks OK; mchuseby@centurytel.net; www.sagecountryinn .com; at S Court Ave.*

Diamond

LODGINGS

Hotel Diamond

12 MILES EAST OF HWY 205, DIAMOND; 541/493-1898 When you drive into Diamond, the first things you see are dilapidated stone buildings tucked under giant old poplar trees. Buzz by and you might mistake Diamond for a ghost town; however, its few residents keep the looming ghosts at bay. Shirley Thompson, David Thompson, and Gretchen Nichols, longtime Diamond Valley residents and owners of the nearby McCoy Creek Inn, have brought a surge of energy to this little hotel. The Diamond, which doubles as a general store (watch the pickups pull in at 5pm for the evening six-pack) has five small bedrooms upstairs sharing two baths and a sitting area; three larger rooms off the front porch have private baths. Dinners are available for hotel guests (a big family-style meal if the house is full; cheeseburgers when the crowds go away). An old icehouse attached to the hotel has been turned into Frazier's, a tiny pub named after the owners' great-grandparents, who managed the hotel more than 100 years ago. *$; MC, V; checks OK; www.central-oregon.com/hoteldiamond; closed Nov 15–Mar 15 (call for exact dates); 12 miles east of Hwy 205.*

Frenchglen

This beautiful little town (population about 15) 60 miles south of Burns is a favorite stopover for those visiting the **MALHEUR NATIONAL WILDLIFE REFUGE** (see "Birds of the Malheur" in this chapter) or **STEENS MOUNTAIN**. Steens rises gently from the west to an elevation of 9,670 feet and then drops sharply to the Alvord Desert in the east. A road goes all the way to the ridgetop (summers only), and another makes a long loop around Steens—passing the vast borax hardpan of the former Alvord Lake, numerous hot springs, and, near the northeastern end of the route, good fishing in Mann Lake. Contact the **BUREAU OF LAND MANAGEMENT** (Hwy 20W, Hines; 541/573-4400) just southwest of Burns for information about Steens Mountain.

It's a rough but scenic ride from Frenchglen to the 275,000-acre **HART MOUNTAIN NATIONAL ANTELOPE REFUGE** (509/947-3315). Turn west off Highway 205 and follow Rock Creek Road to the visitor center, where you can learn about recent wildlife sightings. Pronghorn, of course, are frequently noted, and bighorn sheep live east of the headquarters on the steep cliffs that form the western boundary of fault-block Hart Mountain. No visit here is really complete without a prolonged dip in the local hot spring. It's south of the visitor center in the campground—very rustic and absolutely free.

LODGINGS

Frenchglen Hotel / ★

🌲 **HWY 205, FRENCHGLEN; 541/493-2825** One of the handful of historical hotels owned by the Oregon State Parks system, the Frenchglen is a small, white frame American Foursquare–style building that dates back to the mid-1920s. Nothing's very square or level here, and that's part of the charm. Upstairs, eight small, plain bedrooms are free from the shackles of TVs and telephones; all the rooms share baths. Room 2 is the largest and nicest, and the only one with a view of Steens Mountain. Downstairs are a large screened-in front porch and the dining room, where guests mingle and compare travel notes. Many of the guests are birders, and the lobby is well stocked with field guides. John Ross, the hotel manager, and his local crew cook up good, simple meals for guests and drop-by visitors. Ranch-style dinner is one seating only (6:30pm sharp) and reservations are a must. $; MC, V; checks OK; closed mid-Nov–mid-Mar; fghotel@ptinet.net; on Hwy 205, 60 miles south of Burns.

SEATTLE AND ENVIRONS

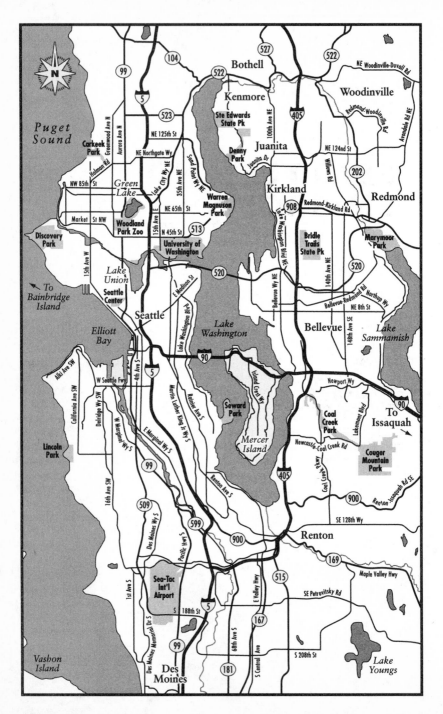

SEATTLE AND ENVIRONS

Seattle has been changing. While the company that once seemed like the city's benevolent father, Boeing, has diminished its role, a few former upstarts have stepped up like older siblings: Microsoft, Amazon.com, and Starbucks. Seattle's got a larger population now—and it's more diverse, including people from all over the United States and the world. In the last decade, this city that used to be considered a little *boring* by big-city standards has seen riots (related to the World Trade Organization meeting and Mardi Gras) and scandals.

Meanwhile, other things haven't changed at all. The area's geography, which draws many immigrants yet keeps the natives, is as striking as ever: the Olympic Mountains on the west, the Cascades on the east, and around-the-compass waterways (Elliott Bay, Lake Union, Lake Washington, and Lake Sammamish). Despite the city's reputation for rain (not entirely undeserved), the sun does shake its cover on a regular basis, and the resulting Technicolor perfection makes it hard not to hum "the bluest skies you've ever seen are in Seattle" as you run, bike, kayak, sail, windsurf, or skate on your way.

The lush landscape also creates a sense of expectation with something compelling—mountains, skyscrapers, water, floatplanes, boats, bridges—always visible in the near distance. This yin-yang pattern is repeated in the urban grid: historic Pike Place Market gives way to swanky retail on Fifth and Sixth Avenues; Fremont, Capitol Hill, and Belltown each claim a distinctive corner of the city's hip neighborhood triangle. Seattle's sibling suburbs are a study in divergent personalities: the mini-metropolis glam of Bellevue, corporate sprawl of Redmond, charming waterfront styles of Kirkland and Bainbridge Island, and the wanna-be-village quaintness of Issaquah.

Even Seattle's longtime architectural conservatism has begun to bend. The Frank Gehry–designed, Paul Allen–owned Experience Music Project museum threatens to eclipse the adjacent Space Needle in attitude if not altitude (especially with the 2004 addition of the Science Fiction Museum and Hall of Fame). Its lumpy psychedelic exterior at first drew mews of dislike, but then Pritzker Prize–winning Dutch architect Rem Koolhaas was called to design the new downtown public library, which opened in 2004. And when a city's library is cutting new architectural ground, a corner undeniably has been turned.

ACCESS AND INFORMATION

The nightmare traffic story has become something of a competitive sport in Seattle. It doesn't require dramatic license: a recent national study pegged Seattle as having the second-worst traffic jams in the nation (behind Los Angeles). And though a long-awaited light-rail system should alleviate some of the carbon-monoxide crush, it's not set to go online until 2009.

In the meantime, the best defense is a sense of humor and street smarts. The road basics: **INTERSTATE 5** is the main north-south arterial; two east-west arterials connect it to Eastside communities (such as Bellevue) via two floating bridges—**INTERSTATE 90** (south of downtown) and **HIGHWAY 520** (north of downtown); the major Eastside north-south highway is **INTERSTATE 405**. Downtown Seattle is divided

SEATTLE THREE-DAY TOUR

DAY ONE: You'll find it's easy being car-less in Seattle. Don't bother with a sit-down breakfast on your first morning; just grab a coffee from the original **STARBUCKS** (1912 Pike Pl; 206/448-8762), then get an apple fritter from the **THREE GIRLS BAKERY** (1514 Pike Pl; 206/622-1045) and meander through the bustling **PIKE PLACE MARKET**. Swing by **TICKET/TICKET** in the Market to pick up half-price day-of-show tickets for that evening's entertainment, then hit **ELLIOTT'S OYSTER HOUSE** on the waterfront for lunch. Spend the afternoon strolling through the **SEATTLE ART MUSEUM**. Back in your room at the **INN AT THE MARKET** (more moderately priced rooms can be had at the nearby **ACE HOTEL**), you'll have time for a shower and change before dinner at downstairs **CAMPAGNE**. Then it's a leisurely walk to **BENAROYA HALL** and an evening of **SEATTLE SYMPHONY** music. Cab back for a nightcap in Campagne's bar before tucking in for the night.

DAY TWO: Rise early, but indulge in a room-service breakfast from **BACCO** before descending the Pike Place Hillclimb to hop the vintage waterfront trolley for historic **PIONEER SQUARE**. After taking the **UNDERGROUND TOUR** of old Seattle, resurface to peruse the Square's collection of **GALLERIES** and the **ELLIOTT BAY BOOK CO.**, then head east to the city's Chinatown/International District, where you can lunch on dim sum at the spacious **HOUSE OF HONG** (409 8th Ave S; 206/622-7997). The **WING LUKE ASIAN MUSEUM** was named for the city's first Chinese American city

into "avenues" (starting with First near the waterfront) running north-south, and "streets" running west-east (many are one-way).

Getting to downtown from **SEATTLE-TACOMA INTERNATIONAL AIRPORT** (17801 Pacific Hwy S, SeaTac; 206/431-4444; *www.portseattle.org/seatac*) is a 35-minute straight shot north on Interstate 5 (avoid peak rush hours 7–9:30am and 4:30–7pm). **GRAY LINE AIRPORT EXPRESS** (206/626-6088; *www.graylineofseattle .com*) runs airport passengers to and from major downtown hotels for about $8.50 one-way ($14 round trip). Taxis from the airport cost $30–$35. By law, however, taxis to the airport from downtown Seattle charge a flat fee of $25 (though some cabbies might need reminding). Large car rental agencies have locations near the airport, in downtown Seattle, and in the outlying suburbs.

AMTRAK (3rd Ave S and S Jackson St; 800/USA-RAIL; *www.amtrak.com*) trains arrive at and depart from King Street Station, and **GREYHOUND** (811 Stewart St; 800/231-2222; *greyhound.com*) also serves the city.

METRO TRANSIT (206/553-3000; *transit.metrokc.gov*) serves the city and the Eastside with more than 300 routes and connects with buses from greater Puget Sound to the north and south. Metro buses are free until 7pm in the downtown core (between the waterfront and I-5, and Jackson and Battery Sts). The **WATER-FRONT STREETCAR** (part of Metro) serves the waterfront, Pioneer Square, and the council member and has a collection that integrates the experiences of 10 Asian-Pacific American groups. Marvel at the range of Asian specialties at **UWAJIMAYA VILLAGE** (600 5th Ave S; 206/624-6248) and stay for dinner at **CHINOISE CAFÉ**. In keeping with the afternoon's theme, find out what's playing at **NORTHWEST ASIAN AMERICAN THEATRE** (409 7th Ave S; 206/340-1445; *nwaat.org*), which offers a variety of cross-cultural programs.

DAY THREE: Wake up like a local with a latte and pastry (or bowl of fresh fruit) at Belltown's **MACRINA BAKERY AND CAFE**. Then it's off for some serious shopping and people-watching at the splashy **PACIFIC PLACE** mall and flagship **NORDSTROM**. Take kids to the high-end **GAMEWORKS** (1511 7th Ave; 206/521-0952; *www.gameworks.com*) video arcade. If it's Sunday and the **MARINERS** are in town, baseball fans can catch a bus to **SAFECO FIELD**—pregame activities should include partaking of a mess of ribs at **PECOS'S PIT BBQ** (2260 1st Ave S; 206/623-0629). If not, walk to Westlake Center, from where the **MONORAIL** will whisk you to **SEATTLE CENTER**. Grab lunch at one of the myriad options in the **CENTER HOUSE**, then settle in for an afternoon of high-tech musical exploration at the **EXPERIENCE MUSIC PROJECT**. Before winding up your day and your stay with dinner at Belltown's **FLYING FISH**, say goodbye to the city from atop the landmark **SPACE NEEDLE**.

city's Chinatown/International District. For off-road transport, ride the space-age **MONORAIL** (also part of Metro), which glides between downtown's **WESTLAKE CENTER** (Pine St and 4th Ave, 3rd floor) and the Seattle Center in 2 minutes, or catch a **WASHINGTON STATE FERRY** (206/464-6400 or 888/808-7977; *www.wsdot.wa.gov/ferries/*) at Pier 52 to nearby islands and across the Sound.

The **SEATTLE–KING COUNTY CONVENTION AND VISITORS BUREAU** (800 Convention Pl, Galleria level; 206/461-5840; *www.seeseattle.org*) is a good source for information and maps. In summer, visit the **OUTDOOR KIOSKS** at Seattle Center and Pioneer Square.

Seattle

Traditionalists yearn for Seattle's small-town Pleasantville past: those carefree—and, by comparison, car-free—days before our clothes, musicians, and hot beverages were hijacked as fashion statements, and the only jet set we knew built planes at Boeing. Seattle's sheltered location in the far corner of the national map afforded a blissfully long childhood, but the city has gained some of the more intriguing complications and entertaining perks of adulthood.

MAJOR ATTRACTIONS
Even first-timers can probably rattle off the big must-sees in Seattle: **PIKE PLACE MARKET** (Pike St and 1st Ave), **PIONEER SQUARE** (along 1st and 2nd Aves, between

James and S Jackson Sts; *www.pioneersquare.org*), and the **SPACE NEEDLE**. The Needle actually anchors a corner of another major attraction, the **SEATTLE CENTER** (between Denny Wy and Mercer St, between 1st Ave N and 5th Ave N; 206/684-8582; *www.seattlecenter.com*). Born out of the 1962 World's Fair, the 74-acre park is home to arts and athletics venues—such as **MARION OLIVER MCCAW HALL** and **KEY ARENA**—as well as the **PACIFIC SCIENCE CENTER** (200 2nd Ave N; 206/443-2880; *www.pacsci.org*), with cool hands-on science exhibits and an IMAX theater.

Water-based exhibits are the focus of **ODYSSEY, THE MARITIME DISCOVERY CENTER** (2205 Alaskan Wy, Pier 66; 206/374-4000; *www.ody.org*) and the **SEATTLE AQUARIUM** (1483 Alaskan Wy, Pier 59; 206/386-4320; *www.seattleaquarium .org*), which boasts a 400,000-gallon Underwater Dome. Visitors and animals come breathtakingly close in the **WOODLAND PARK ZOO**'s (5500 Phinney Ave N; 206/684-4800; *www.zoo.org*) animal-friendly natural habitats.

In Pioneer Square, the hokey-but-fun **UNDERGROUND TOUR** (610 1st Ave; 206/682-4646; *www.undergroundtour.com*) lets visitors take in the sights—and some of the smells—of old Seattle, preserved from the 1889 great fire that leveled much of the city. Downtown art galleries open new shows for the popular monthly **FIRST THURSDAY** art walks.

MUSEUMS

The striking street-corner Hammering Man sculpture directs patrons into the **SEATTLE ART MUSEUM** (100 University St; 206/654-3100; *www.seattleartmuseum .org*), home to impressive Asian, African, and Northwest Native art collections, as well as national traveling exhibits. The **HENRY ART GALLERY** (15th Ave NE and NE 41st St; 206/543-2280; *www.henryart.org*), on the University of Washington campus, is known for its photography collection and more experimental shows, particularly video installations. First Hill's once-stodgy **FRYE ART MUSEUM** (704 Terry Ave; 206/622-9250; *www.fryeart.org*) has been redesigned inside and out, adding imaginative exhibits and music and film events.

The **CHILDREN'S MUSEUM** (Seattle Center; 206/441-1768; *www.thechildrens museum.org*) encourages exploration of other cultures with hands-on activities and inventive exhibits, such as a global village featuring child-sized dwellings from Japan, Ghana, and the Philippines. The **WING LUKE ASIAN MUSEUM** (407 7th Ave S; 206/623-5124; *www.wingluke.org*) examines the Asian-American experience in the Northwest, including an exhibit concerning the internment of Japanese Americans during World War II. Bankrolled by Microsoft co-founder Paul Allen, the eye-and-ear-popping **EXPERIENCE MUSIC PROJECT** (Seattle Center; 206/770-2700; *www.emplive.com*) celebrates rock 'n' roll and its roots with high-tech installations, hands-on exhibits, and more. The new **SCIENCE FICTION MUSEUM AND HALL OF FAME** (206-SCI-FICT; *www.sciencefictionexperience.com*) opened in the same building in June 2004. The **BURKE MUSEUM OF NATURAL HISTORY AND CULTURE** (17th Ave NE and NE 45th St; 206/543-5590; *www.burkemuseum.org*) on the UW campus harbors the Pacific Northwest's only dinosaurs (snap a shot of Junior sitting on the 5-foot-tall sauropod thigh bone). Twenty-six full-sized airplanes are suspended in midair at the **MUSEUM OF FLIGHT** (9404 E Marginal Wy S; 206/764-5720; *www.museumofflight.org*).

PARKS AND GARDENS

Throw a rock, hit a park. Local favorites include **DISCOVERY PARK** (3801 W Government Wy; 206/386-4236), with 534 wild and woodsy acres, miles of trails, beach, and Sound views. **WASHINGTON PARK ARBORETUM** (2300 Arboretum Dr E; 206/543-8800) has 200 wooded acres, walking and running trails, and a Japanese garden. **VOLUNTEER PARK** (1247 15th Ave E; 206/684-4075) features a 1912 conservatory full of hothouse plants and a view from the top of the water tower; it's also home to the **SEATTLE ASIAN ART MUSEUM** (206/654-3100). **GAS WORKS PARK** (N Northlake Wy; 206/684-4075) is where Seattleites go to fly a kite. Joggers, dog walkers, and strollers flock to **GREEN LAKE** (*www.cityofseattle.net/parks/*).

SHOPPING

NORDSTROM's downtown flagship store (500 Pine St; 206/628-2111) includes a spa and five floors of clothes and accessories. Connected to Nordie's via a glass sky bridge is **PACIFIC PLACE** (600 Pine St; 206/405-2655), a splashy four-level commercial cathedral stocked with name retailers, restaurants, and a cinema. Downtown now has most major chain stores, from the youth-oriented **URBAN OUTFITTERS** and **OLD NAVY**, to middle-of-the-road **POTTERY BARN** and **J. CREW**, to upscale **TIFFANY & CO.** and **BARNEYS NEW YORK**.

Neighborhoods are where to find unusual or handmade goods, from harps and hammered dulcimers at Fremont's **DUSTY STRINGS** (3406 Fremont Ave N; 206/634-1662) to shabby chic relics at Capitol Hill's **PRIVATE SCREENING** (1530 Melrose Ave; 206/839-0759). **PIONEER SQUARE** has cutting-edge galleries and old-fashioned shops, while the **PIKE PLACE MARKET** is justly famous for its fresh fruit, flower, and fish stalls, and authentic crafts, including **MILAGROS MEXICAN FOLK ART** (1530 Post Alley; 206/464-0490).

PERFORMING ARTS

Theater/Dance

The big three playhouses are **A CONTEMPORARY THEATRE (ACT)** (700 Union St; 206/292-7676; *www.acttheatre.org*), **INTIMAN THEATRE** (Seattle Center; 206/269-1900; *www.intiman.org*), and **SEATTLE REPERTORY THEATRE** (Seattle Center; 206/443-2222; *www.seattlerep.org*). The toasts of Broadway land at the **5TH AVENUE THEATRE** (1308 5th Ave; 206/625-1900; *www.5thavenuetheatre.org*) and **PARAMOUNT THEATRE** (911 Pine St; 206/443-1744; *www.theparamount.com*), while wonderfully imaginative, and surprisingly sophisticated, productions play out at **SEATTLE CHILDREN'S THEATRE** (Seattle Center; 206/441-3322; *www.sct.org*). Classics are at the core of the city's premiere dance company, the **PACIFIC NORTHWEST BALLET** (Seattle Center; 206/441-2424; *www.pnb.org*); an annual holiday favorite, *The Nutcracker*, features spectacular Maurice Sendak sets.

Music

Music of all genres—from alternative rock and reggae to chamber and classical—is amply represented in Seattle these days. The **SEATTLE SYMPHONY** (200 University St; 206/215-4747; *www.seattlesymphony.org*), under the baton of Gerard Schwarz, has an elegant downtown home in Benaroya Hall. In summer 2003, the **SEATTLE OPERA** (Seattle Center; 206/389-7676; *www.seattleopera.org*), guided by Speight

Jenkins, moved into its refurbished permanent home, Marion Oliver McCaw Hall. First-rate jazz clubs include classy **DIMITRIOU'S JAZZ ALLEY** (2033 6th Ave; 206/441-9729; *www.jazzalley.com*) and cozy **TULA'S** (2214 2nd Ave; 206/443-4221; *www.tulas.com*).

Some of the city's most anticipated festivals revolve around music. The **NORTH-WEST FOLKLIFE FESTIVAL** (Seattle Center; 206/684-7300; *www.nwfolklife.org*) showcases a melting pot of talent—from African marimba players to American fiddlers—over Memorial Day weekend. **BUMBERSHOOT** (Seattle Center; 206/281-8111; *www.bumbershoot.org*), over Labor Day weekend, hosts headliner acts ranging from Beck to Tony Bennett. And jazz artists, representing bebop to swing, make the rounds of local clubs for the **EARSHOT JAZZ FESTIVAL** (206/547-9787; *www.earshot.org*) in October.

Literature/Film

Seattle's reputation for being well-read is reinforced by almost-daily author readings at the **ELLIOTT BAY BOOK CO.** (101 S Main St; 206/624-6600; *www.elliottbaybook.com*) in Pioneer Square and the annual **SEATTLE ARTS AND LECTURES** series (206/621-2230; *www.lectures.org*), which brings prominent authors to town.

The **SEATTLE INTERNATIONAL FILM FESTIVAL** (various theaters; 206/324-9996; *www.seattlefilm.org*) brings together world premieres, stars, filmmakers, and film buffs for a staggering three-plus weeks starting in late May.

Check the free weeklies, *Seattle Weekly* or *The Stranger,* for event listings. Most theater and event tickets are sold through **TICKETMASTER** (206-292-ARTS; *www.ticketmaster.com*); **TICKET/TICKET** (401 Broadway Ave E and Pike Place Information Booth, 1st Ave and Pike St; 206/324-2744) sells half-price, day-of-show tickets.

NIGHTLIFE

Although Seattle isn't really a party-all-night kind of city, some of its urban neighborhoods give it an honest effort. Some of the best see-and-be-seen nightspots are on Capitol Hill, a favorite with Seattle's gay and lesbian population, and in Belltown. Hot spots on the Hill range from the high-energy dance beats at **NEIGHBORS** (1509 Broadway Ave; 206/324-5358) to the retro-chic of the **BALTIC ROOM** (1207 Pine St; 206/625-4444) and the **CENTURY BALLROOM** (915 E Pine St, 2nd Floor; 324-7263), a former theater offering swing and salsa dancing. Belltown offers funky hybrids such as the live-music club/café **CROCODILE CAFE** (2200 2nd Ave; 206/441-5611) and the high-tech dance floor/high-class pool hall atmo of **BELLTOWN BILLIARDS** (90 Blanchard St; 206/448-6779).

Downtown, all-ages rock shows are held at the largely volunteer-run **VERA PROJECT** (1916 4th Ave; 206/956-VERA). In Fremont, hipsters listen to live music at **TOST** (513 N 36th St; 206/547-0240), and in Ballard, the **TRACTOR TAVERN** (5213 Ballard Ave NW; 206/789-3599; *www.tractortavern.citysearch.com*) books folk, alt-country, and bluegrass acts—among others.

SPORTS AND RECREATION

Even when they don't win pennants, the **SEATTLE MARINERS** (206/346-4000; *www.mariners.mlb.com*) have a hit on their hands with open-air **SAFECO FIELD** (between Royal Brougham Wy and S Atlantic St; 206/346-4003), popular even with nonbaseball fans (public tours available). **QWEST FIELD** (formerly Seahawks Stadium) next door, opened in fall 2002, is home for the Paul Allen–owned **SEATTLE SEAHAWKS** (206/682-2800; *www.seahawks.com*) and also hosts the **SEATTLE SOUNDERS** (206/622-3415 or 800/796-KICK; *www.seattlesounders.net*). The **UNIVERSITY OF WASHINGTON HUSKIES** (Husky Stadium, 3800 Montlake Blvd NE; 206/543-2200; *www.gohuskies.com*) thrill rabid fans from their Lake Washington–backed gridiron. Seattle's pro women's basketball team, the WNBA's **SEATTLE STORM** (206/283-DUNK; *www.wnba.com/storm/*), tips off in the **KEY ARENA** (305 N Harrison St) in summer; the **SEATTLE SUPERSONICS** (206/283-DUNK; *www.nba.com/sonics/*) dominate the Key, November through April.

Plenty of outlets appeal to amateur athletes. In-line skaters and bikers work up a sweat along the 14-mile **BURKE-GILMAN TRAIL**, a stretch of blacktop running from north Lake Union to the Eastside. Along the trail, the **BICYCLE CENTER** (4529 Sand Point Wy NE; 206/523-8300) rents bikes and skates. For a map of Seattle bike routes, contact the city **BICYCLE AND PEDESTRIAN PROGRAM** (206/684-7583; *www.seattle.gov/transportation/bikeprogram.htm*). Kayakers, rowers, and canoeists ply the waters of Lake Union and Lake Washington. Rent a kayak from **NORTHWEST OUTDOOR CENTER** (2100 Westlake Ave N, Ste 1, Westlake; 206/281-9694 or 800/683-0637; *www.nwoc.com*) or a canoe at the **UNIVERSITY OF WASHINGTON WATERFRONT ACTIVITIES CENTER** (206/543-9433; *depts.washington.edu/ima/IMA.wac.html*). Outdoor enthusiasts of all stripes flock to the two-level flagship **REI** (222 Yale Ave N; 206/223-1944 or 888/873-1938; *www.rei.com*), which, along with an abundance of equipment, houses an indoor climbing wall, an outdoor mountain bike/hiking test trail, and the U.S. Forest Service's **OUTDOOR RECREATION INFORMATION CENTER** (206/470-4060; *www.nps.gov/ccso/oric.htm*) for trip planning.

RESTAURANTS

Afrikando / ★★

2904 1ST AVE, SEATTLE; 206/374-9714 If you dream of French West Africa, head for lively Afrikando, where the menu recalls chef Jacques Sarr's native Senegal. Start with *akra,* light fritters of black-eyed peas in a spicy tomato sauce with bay shrimp. The star entrée is the *poisson frite* (French for "fried fish"), a whole fried tilapia served with rice and tomato sauce. Other favorites include *debe,* grilled lamb chops with spicy onion-mustard sauce and couscous, and *thiebu djen,* the national Senegalese dish of fish in rich tomato sauce with vegetables and *jollof* rice. The beer and wine list features selections from South Africa and Kenya. For nonalcoholic alternatives, try one of the homemade Senegalese juices—hibiscus, ginger, or tamarind. Sarr's mango tart is perfect with a cup of hot ginger tea. *$; MC, V; checks OK; lunch Mon–Fri, dinner every day; beer and wine; reservations recommended; Belltown.* &

Agua Verde Cafe & Paddle Club / ★★☆

1303 NE BOAT ST, SEATTLE; 206/545-8570 Even on the grayest Seattle days, this bay-side café exudes the essence of sun-drenched Baja. Brightly colored walls fill the cottage with a tropical glow, while stripped floorboards resemble an oceanfront boardwalk. Around lunch, count on a crowd, and on sunny afternoons, expect to stand in line with paddlers who've rented kayaks from the club downstairs. The menu features Baja classics—fish tacos, salads, seviche—and plenty of vegetarian plates. The taco de *mero,* grilled halibut and shredded cabbage enlivened with a squirt of fresh lime, is love at first bite. We also favor the *de carne,* a sliced flank steak taco with onions, peppers, and crumbles of cotija cheese, as well as *de carnitas,* shredded pork with cabbage and salsa. The vegetarian *de boniato* is a surprising combination of sweet potatoes sautéed with mild chiles, served with onions, cotija, and a cooling, creamy avocado sauce. Don't miss the salsa cart, which offers a smoky chipotle and a three-alarm tomato salsa. The cafeteria-style lunch, frequented by local University of Washington students and staff, gives way to full service at dinnertime, where table service can be hit-or-miss. Partner any meal with Mexican beer, a margarita, or fresh-squeezed juice. *$; DIS, MC, V; checks OK; lunch, dinner Mon–Sat; full bar; reservations recommended; www.aguaverde.com; University District.* &

Anthony's Pier 66 / ★★★

2201 ALASKAN WY, PIER 66, SEATTLE; 206/448-6688 This handsome top-floor restaurant at the Bell Street Pier is the flagship of the Anthony's seafood restaurant chain. Pier 66 has the most jaw-dropping view of Seattle's working waterfront, and the Asian-inflected menu of local and regional seafood is priced accordingly. Ginger Penn Cove mussels steamed with sake will get you off to a good start, as will the Potlatch, an impressive collection of Northwest steamer clams, mussels, split snow-crab legs, and half-shell oysters. Planked wild chinook salmon or Alaskan halibut are always reliable entrées. Two sister restaurants, in the same building, offer lower-priced alternatives. For lunch or casual dinners by Elliott Bay, the boisterous Bell Street Diner downstairs is a good choice, offering a wide selection of less formal fare: seafood, chowders, burgers, generous salads, rice bowls, and fish tacos; for a quick, no-frills bite, take the kids and join the sea gulls waterside at Anthony's Fish Bar. *$$; AE, MC, V; checks OK; dinner every day; full bar; reservations recommended; www.anthonys.com; waterfront.* &

Brasa / ★★★☆

2107 3RD AVE, SEATTLE; 206/728-4220 Recently, Brasa owners Tamara Murphy and Bryan Hill improved on what was already one of the most striking restaurants in the city. Awash in warm orange tones and amber light, the dual-tiered dining room is still sumptuous, while the copper-topped bar, cinched in tuck-and-roll glitter vinyl, remains one of the hippest spots in town, but the white tablecloths are gone. Hill is at the door waiting to welcome everyone into his dining room, while in the kitchen Murphy cooks honest food (often over live coals) for her guests. From the dinner menu, the perfume of *cataplana* mussels marooned in curry, coriander, and coconut milk turns heads, as does the sensual beef carpaccio with minced shallots and heady white truffle oil. Savory favorites include the Oregon hare with figs, pine nuts, and potato dumplings, as well as the grilled squab with wilted spinach, house-cured bacon, and goat cheese. Tarry over a glass of red wine from Hill's glass-pour list or shake up the routine with a frozen lemon mousse with raspberries. *$$; AE, DC, MC, V; checks OK; dinner every day; full bar; reservations recommended; www.brasa.com; Belltown.* &

Campagne / ★★★⯪

86 PINE ST (INN AT THE MARKET), SEATTLE; 206/728-2800 Tucked away in a courtyard in Pike Place Market and adjacent to the Inn at the Market, rain or shine, Campagne is a ray of light from sun-drenched Southern France. To help keep your focus on what owner Peter Lewis calls "the adventure at the table," the candlelit room and bar are warmly finished with cherry-wood floors, farmhouse-yellow walls, and sumptuous draperies. Chef Daisley Gordon's menu is a passionate union of Northwest and French influences. Don't pass up the earthy leeks in truffle vinaigrette, served with crostini and perfect with a glass of chenin blanc from the Loire Valley. Worthy hors d'oeuvres include pan-roasted sea scallops over carrot purée, or the *tartare de boeuf aux herbes,* raw beef with herbs, capers, and parsley. For the main event, dishes range from grilled king salmon, served over chard-potato gnocchi and pancetta in a sorrel cream sauce with oyster mushrooms, to grilled lamb loin and house-made lamb *crépinette* accompanied by potato *galette,* olives, and a red wine–fennel glaze. Pastry chef Asia Johnson prepares tarts, ice creams, and granités. The crème brûlée tasting (a selection of three) is our idea of heaven. Wine director and frequent host Shawn Mead has composed a wine list that calls to mind vineyards of France. Smoking is permitted in the bar after 10pm. Just below is the slightly lower priced, but no less popular, Café Campagne (206/728-2233). *$$$; AE, DC, MC, V; no checks; dinner every day, lunch Mon–Fri; full bar; reservations recommended; campagnerestaurant .com; in Pike Place Market.* &

Canlis / ★★★★

2576 AURORA AVE N, SEATTLE; 206/283-3313 Those now celebrating their umpteenth whatever will still find old favorites at Seattle's most popular special-occasion view restaurant, now under co-chefs Jeff Taton and Aaron Wright. Canlis also still has the verve and zing that helped it land a Top 50 rating from *Gourmet* magazine in 2001. The Northwest Seafood Extravaganza starts a meal with three tiers of fresh delights. Kobe-style Washington beef comes as impeccable steak tartare, or cooked to order from the famous copper broiler. Other broiler items—salmon, ahi, more steaks—enjoy the company of reliable sides, such as a mighty baked potato. Dungeness crab legs come encased in a chick-pea crust with ponzu and Asian vegetables. Give a half-hour notice for the knockout Grand Marnier soufflé. Sommelier Shyn Bjornholm presides over the massive and much-lauded wine list that ranges from many options in the $30 range to a $1,000 bottle. Expect to be treated like royalty and to pay accordingly in this beautifully delicious anachronism. *$$$$; AE, DC, DIS, MC, V; checks OK; dinner*

Mon–Sat; full bar; reservations required; www.canlis.com; on Aurora Ave, just south of the bridge. &

Carmelita / ★★★

7314 GREENWOOD AVE N, SEATTLE; 206/706-7703 Here is a vegetarian restaurant that even a carnivore can love, thanks to chef Dan Braun's innovative and tasty menu. And it's gorgeous. Owners Kathryn Newmann and Michael Hughes, visual artists in their spare time, transformed a dilapidated retail space into a theatrically lit, art-filled haven of color and texture. Neighbors from Greenwood and Phinney Ridge warmly embraced Carmelita from the beginning, and the sophisticated, seasonal vegetarian menu remains enticing. Expect to find such entrées as English pea agnolotti stuffed with asparagus, foraged mushrooms, and truffle butter sauce, or portobello mushroom roulade with green beans, roasted-shallot mashed potatoes, and mushroom demi-glace. *$$; MC, V; local checks only; dinner Tues–Sun; beer and wine; reservations recommended; reserve@carmelita.net; carmelita.net; Greenwood.* &

Cascadia Restaurant / ★★★★

2328 1ST AVE, SEATTLE; 206/448-8884 Cascadia benefits from its spare but luxurious space and its chef-owner Kerry Sear, who uses indigenous foods and flavors of Cascadia (the region he defines as between the Pacific Ocean and Montana) and beyond. A sculpted-glass wall between the dining room and kitchen has water sluicing through it like rain against a window. The bar now offers pocketbook- and palate-friendly noshes, ranging from skillet-roasted prawns to mini-cheeseburgers. The dining room features such à la carte exotica as an appetizer of foie gras *torchon* with brandied cherries and black truffle jam, or entrées such as pork tenderloin served with grilled peaches, fingerling potatoes, and grilled eggplant. Or choose one of three seven-course tasting menus, including an ambitious all-vegetarian selection; a new three-course tasting menu is a deal at $25. The wine list features handcrafted wines of character and quality, chosen to flatter the cuisine. *$$$$; AE, DC, DIS, MC, V; no checks; dinner Mon–Sat; full bar; reservations recommended; www.cascadiarestaurant.com; Belltown.* &

Chinoise Café / ★★☆

610 5TH AVE S, UWAJIMAYA VILLAGE, SEATTLE (AND BRANCHES); 206/254-0413 Opened two years ago in the International District's theme park–worthy Uwajimaya Village, this was the third Chinoise Café in Seattle. Eclectically but assuredly Asian, Chinoise is a reliable place for Vietnamese salad rolls, Japanese sukiyaki, Thai curries, Chinese stir-fry, and noodles. The vibrant Vietnamese lemongrass chicken salad is worth a visit, but for a multicourse meal, start with delicate summer salad rolls or an order of pot stickers, and move on to General Tsao's Chicken or a yakisoba. At the Uwajimaya location, Chinoise offers some Korean dishes and a full bar in its neon-lit lounge. Branches on Queen Anne (12 Boston St; 206/284-6671), in the Madison Valley (2801 E Madison St; 206/323-0171), and in Wallingford (1618 N 45th St; 206/633-1160) all have slightly different characters. *$; AE, DC, DIS, MC, V; no checks; lunch Mon–Fri, dinner every day; full bar; no reservations; www.chinoisecafe.com; International District.* &

Chinook's at Salmon Bay / ★★

1900 W NICKERSON ST, SEATTLE; 206/283-4665 The Anthony's folks (see review of Anthony's Pier 66) are using the right bait here at Fisherman's Terminal. The light-industrial decor—steel countertops, visible ventilation ducts—is secondary to the bustle of the working marina outside the big windows. The Anthony's group owns a wholesale fish business, so fish is immaculately fresh. The regular menu is large and can be overwhelming. Fail-safe choices are creamy oyster stew, with wonderful chunks of yearling Quilcene oysters throughout; tender halibut-and-chips; and mahimahi tacos. The daily special sheet is the place to look, with offerings such as wild king salmon charred with sun-dried tomato-basil butter, or garlic-baked prawns with lemon and gremolata. There's a great all-you-can-eat tempura bar—don't miss the fat, tender *panko*-coated onion rings. For dessert, try warm wild-blackberry cobbler. *$$; AE, MC, V; checks OK; breakfast Sat–Sun, lunch, dinner every day; full bar; no reservations; www.anthonys restaurants.com; at Fisherman's Terminal in Interbay.* &

Dahlia Lounge / ★★★☆

2001 4TH AVE, SEATTLE; 206/682-4142 Under the direction of Tom Douglas, head chef Mark Fuller gracefully guides this legendary restaurant. Matching a spirited decor of crimson, gold brocade, and papier-mâché fish lanterns is an exuberant, global approach from the kitchen. We confess to rarely ordering from the regularly updated main dishes on the right side of the menu—too many delights on the left side. That's where you'll find appetizers—from crispy veal sweetbreads masterfully presented with crayfish, fava beans, and roasted cauliflower to curried vegetable *samosas* with tamarind and coriander dipping sauces—and the always tempting "Little Tastes from the Sea Bar" list, starring a seasonally changing Sea Bar Sampler that never fails to serve up tender chunks of smoked salmon with spicy mustard and some incarnation of fatty tuna. Select entrées based on their accompaniments, because better sautéed bitter greens and toasted *farro* you will not find. Dessert can be such down-to-earth yet cosmic delectables as a bag of doughnuts fried to order with mascarpone and raspberry, plum, and apricot jams. *$$$; AE, DC, DIS, MC, V; local checks only; lunch Mon–Fri, dinner every day; full bar; reservations recommended; www.tomdouglas.com; downtown at Virginia.* &

Daniel's Broiler Prime Steak & Chops / ★★☆

809 FAIRVIEW PL N, SEATTLE (AND BRANCHES); 206/621-8262 It's all about meat at this luxurious classic steak house on the southernmost shore of Lake Union. Masculine and well-appointed in copper, wood, and windows, this swanky Schwartz Brothers flagship offers splendiferous lake views of yachts gliding by. And prime seafood, too, such as giant Australian lobster tails, salmon, halibut, and Dungeness crab, but the deal's definitely the meat. The beef is Midwestern, corn-fed, aged, cut huge, and cooked to order in the space-age 1,800°F broilers. We suggest one of the mighty porterhouses, T-bones, or the herb-encrusted, cut-it-with-a-fork prime rib, but Daniel's does a great job on the veal chop and the French-cut lamb chops, as well. Expect slavish service, a mighty wine list, and all the usual steak-house choices—Caesar salads, garlic mashers, or a baked potato the size of your

RAW AND ROLL

Seattle is a sushi town not only when it comes to tony Belltown restaurants, but also in a growing number of neighborhood sushi bars, such as **CHISO** (3520 Fremont Ave, Fremont; 206/632-3430), **KISAKU** (2101 N 55th; 206/545-9050; www.kisaku.com), **NISHINO** (3130 E Madison St, Madison Park; 206/322-5800), **MASHIKO** (4725 California Ave SW, West Seattle; 206/935-4339), and **SANMI SUSHI** (2601 West Marina Pl, Interbay; 206/283-9978). For sushi that's easier on the wallet, try **BENTO SUSHI** (8501 15th Ave NW, Crown Hill; 206/782-3000), Wallingford's crowd-drawing **MUSASHI'S** (1400 N 45th St; 206/633-0212), or **RICENROLL** (Westlake Center, Bellevue Square, or 214 Madison St downtown; 206/262-0381). The kaiten craze—reasonably priced sushi grabbable from a moving conveyor belt—has hit town with the sleek **BLUE C SUSHI** (3411 Fremont Ave N, Fremont; 206/633-3411) and the busy Queen Anne **MARINEPOLIS SUSHI LAND** (803 5th Ave N; 206/267-7621).

—Michael Hood

shoe. All three Daniel's Broilers—the others are in Leschi (200 Lake Washington Blvd; 206/329-4191) and Bellevue (Bank of America Building, 10500 NE 8th St; 425/462-4662)—have great water views, luxurious service, and large, well-priced, and praiseworthy wine lists. *$$$; AE, DC, DIS, MC, V; checks OK; lunch Mon–Fri, dinner every day; full bar; reservations recommended; info@schwartzbros.com; www.schwartzbros.com; South Lake Union.* &

El Gaucho / ★★★

2505 1ST AVE, SEATTLE; 206/728-1337 El Gaucho is a retro-swank, Paul Mackay remake of the '70s-era uptown hangout with mink-lined booths and nearly extinct tableside service. Located in Belltown (as well as in Tacoma and Portland), the current version has dark, wide-open spaces where cooks scurry at a wood-fired broiler and servers make classic Caesar salads to order, beside your table. Patrons seated at comfy banquettes in the senate-style dining room feast on any number of (trademarked) Custom 28-day, Dry Aged Certified Angus Beef Prime cuts, which include New York, the Baseball cut of top sirloin, filet mignon, and fillet of New York—none fewer than 8 ounces. Seafood lovers can dredge garlic bread in buttery Wicked Shrimp or slurp saffron-scented broth from an artful bouillabaisse (although they may be even better served at Mackay's seafood palace, Waterfront Seafood Grill: 2801 Alaskan Wy; 206/956-9171; *www.elgaucho.com/waterfrontpier70*). Bananas Foster is a decadent and sublime capper to the evening. In the bar, a well-heeled crowd sips martinis as a piano player noodles jazz riffs on a baby grand. The wine card is formidable, supplemented by a premium reserve list. Serious imbibers will be heartened by the lengthy single-malt Scotch list. The Pampas Room downstairs, open for dancing and drinking on Friday and Saturday, offers the full El Gaucho menu. *$$$$; AE, DIS, MC, V; checks OK; dinner every day; full bar; reservations recommended; elgaucho.com; Belltown.* &

Elliott's Oyster House / ★★★

1201 ALASKAN WY, PIER 56, SEATTLE; 206/623-4340 They call it Oyster House for a reason: it's the best in town, with an extensive selection. Elliott's annual Oyster New Year is a world-class all-you-can-slurp pig out. But the restaurant is more than that: it's a classic fish house with plenty of innovative seafood alternatives served up in a sparkling redo of an old Seattle waterfront favorite. Designers envisioned a classic yacht when they spent $2 million on the remodeled setting, best described as nautical but nice. Tourist boat docks next door provide appropriate visual action. Or focus on a pink-tinged Dungeness crab chowder with a touch of cayenne. The iced shellfish extravaganzas serve two, four, or six people. Whole Dungeness is offered hot and spicy, simply steamed, or chilled with dipping sauces. Alaska weathervane scallops are grilled over mesquite then drowned in crab beurre blanc. Wild, troll-caught king salmon gets aromatically alder planked and served with smoked tomato beurre blanc, or mesquite grilled, or lightly alder smoked and char-grilled. At lunch, the mesquite-grilled mahimahi tacos are salsa mayo-ed and wrapped in thick tortillas. It wouldn't be Seattle without Dungeness crab cakes, and these are exceptional, with rock shrimp and a crab beurre blanc blended with the juice of blood oranges. The wine list is safe but seafood-friendly. *$$$; AE, DC, DIS, MC, V; checks OK; lunch, dinner every day; full bar; reservations recommended; www.elliottsoysterhouse.com; waterfront.* &

Eva Restaurant and Wine Bar / ★★★

2227 N 56TH ST, SEATTLE; 206/633-3538 A few blocks east of Seattle's popular Green Lake, James Hondros and spouse/chef Amy McCray transformed a well-windowed, warm-wooded room into a first-rate bistro. McCray spent years honing her skills at the Dahlia Lounge and Chez Shea, where she was lead chef. She also lured pastry chef JoAnna Cruz, and the resulting kitchen chemistry is captivating palates across the city with an absolute imperative: yes, enjoy dinner, but save room for dessert. Panfried oysters rolled in the crumbs of pappadams (Indian flatbread) and served with a raita sauce and cilantro pesto typifies the simplicity and originality of the menu. The light, smooth, Cabrales flan is a blue-cheese blast offset with a tangy-sweet pear relish and anchored to the earth with a buttery walnut cracker. Basic bistro entrées include grilled and roasted fish, steaks, and poultry. Cruz's desserts are flawless, and Hondros's well-chosen wine list has plenty of bottles in the $30s—and nearly a dozen good half bottles. One drawback is that only the wood is absorbing the sound. And while an open kitchen is one thing, an open dishwashing station is a nerve-jangling something else. *$$; AE, MC, V; checks OK; dinner Tues–Sun; full bar; reservations recommended; between Keystone and Kirkwood.* &

Flying Fish / ★★★★

2234 1ST AVE, SEATTLE; 206/728-8595 Even on nights when neighboring Belltown joints are quiet, Flying Fish jumps; it leaps, it soars. And it's a foodie's dream come true. Chef-owner Christine Keff not only knows and loves seafood, but also has created a place where everybody wants to be, and where ultrafriendly staffers haul platters and plates to exuberant wine-imbibing diners.

Order the small starter plates, two or three of which can make a meal. Entrée choices range from lobster ravioli with yellow-foot mushrooms in a puddle of lobster velouté, to a pile of crispy fried calamari with a hot-sweet honey jalapeño mayonnaise, to grilled scallops in a creamy herb polenta served with sautéed mixed greens. Everything is achingly fresh and artistically presented. Keff encourages large parties to opt for the sharing platters that are sold by the pound, such as the whole fried rockfish or her famous Sister-in-Law Mussels with chile-lime dipping sauce. The wine list is expansive and accessible, with many Northwest and California offerings as well as tons of midrange bottlings from around the world. *$$; AE, DC, MC, V; local checks only; dinner every day; full bar; reservations recommended; info@flyingfishseattle.com; www.flyingfishseattle.com; Belltown.* &

Harvest Vine / ★★★☆

2701 E MADISON ST, SEATTLE; 206/320-9771 As in Spain, conviviality is the point of this tiny tapas emporium, and Joseph Jimenez de Jimenez's infinitely shareable menu will frustrate a solo diner. Once seated, ask for a glass of fino sherry and start ordering *platitos* from the more than two dozen seasonally inspired tapas. Simply superb are the grilled sardines with lemon, the meltingly tender braised octopus with grilled potatoes, and warm salad of partridge with morels and corn. The sweet *piquillo* peppers stuffed with potato mousse and salt cod prove that good food doesn't have to be precious. A seat at the copper-top bar provides front-row-center viewing of Jimenez and his wee crew as they turn out dish after dish with precision and humor. Tables offer an intimate, although not ideal for lingering, option. The chef's wife and award-winning pastry patrona Carolin Messier de Jimenez breathes new life into classic Spanish and Basque desserts. Be advised: Harvest Vine does not take reservations, except for the "harvest table," located in the *txoko* (the small subterranean addition that doubled their seating capacity), which can be reserved in advance for parties of eight or more. Waits can be long and there is no lounge or reception area, but we think the experience is well worth any inconvenience. *$$; MC, V; checks OK; dinner Tues–Sat; beer and wine; no reservations; Madison Valley.* &

Il Terrazzo Carmine / ★★★

411 1ST AVE S, SEATTLE; 206/467-7797 More than a few consider this Seattle's top Italian restaurant. Those who disagree often do so without conviction. Carmine Smeraldo's handsome and romantic restaurant is nestled in an urban-renewed alley, with entrances through the lobby of an office building on First Avenue or through the back courtyard. The airy room and small terrace outside are a perfect environment for the kind of romantic but decisive tête-à-tête it requires to navigate the formidable and tempting menu. For a lusty starter, choose calamari in *padella* (Italian frying pan), tender squid in a heady tomato-garlic sauté, or fresh spinach sautéed with lemon and garlic. The creamy soup of prawns and roast peppers is rich and unusual. Cannelloni is creamy and bubbly with ricotta and filled with veal and spinach; the fettuccine is tossed with house-smoked salmon, mushrooms, and peas. The outstanding osso buco is braised in red wine and served with buttered fettuccine. The prime-cut tenderloin is roasted and served with a wine and pancetta sauce. Tiramisù and crème brûlée are appropriately decadent and well crafted, as are ever-changing choices such as cheesecakes, cannolis, or house-made gelati that showcase local fruits in season. A guitarist plays classical music most nights, adding to the dreamy escapism of this exceptional restaurant. *$$$; AE, DC, DIS, MC, V; no checks; lunch Mon–Fri, dinner Mon–Sat; full bar; reservations recommended; www.ilterrazzocarmine.com; Pioneer Square.* &

India Bistro / ★★☆

2301 NW MARKET ST, SEATTLE; 206/783-5080 Run by three partners—manager Mike Panjabi and chef Gian Jaswal and his assistant Gurmohan Singh—India Bistro is one of the most enduring Indian restaurants in the city. The exotic smells of the Malabar Coast or Kashmiri Province come from an unlikely corner of Seattle's old Norwegian neighborhood, Ballard, and it is the destination of frequent pilgrimages by Indian nationals. The long menu has curries, vegetarian dishes, Indian breads, and meats from the tandoor—the super hot, vertical clay oven. Try the *pakoras*, little bundles of vegetables, chicken, or fish fried in a lentil-flour batter, served with mint chutney, and the mulligatawny soup. Infinitely shareable entrées include *kabli masala*, delicate garbanzo beans cooked with onions and spices, and lamb *vindaloo*, a spicy stew with potatoes and a splash of vinegar. Accompanying rice is buttery, flaky, and fragrant. Order the cooling raita on the side if these specialties are too spicy (heat is determined by the star system). From the tandoor, don't miss the delectable and inexpensive lamb rack or the fish cooked amazingly moist at 800°F. The tender naan is the best way to soak up rich gravies and sauces. *$; AE, DC, DIS, MC, V; no checks; lunch Mon–Sat, dinner every day; beer and wine; reservations recommended; in Ballard.* &

Kingfish Café / ★★★☆

602 19TH AVE E, SEATTLE; 206/320-8757 The Coaston sisters have their restaurant just the way they want it—busy. The cuisine is sassy Southern classics served in a stylish, casual, contemporary space with enlarged sepia-tinted photos from the family album on the walls—including one of distant cousin Langston Hughes. They take no reservations, so expect lines of chatty people, wine glasses in hand. It's worth it for the likes of Jazz It Slow Gumbo, loaded with tasso and prawns; velvety pumpkin soup; catfish cakes with green-tomato tartar sauce; and the famous buttermilk fried chicken. Lunch is a bargain—try the pulled pork sandwich with peach and watermelon barbecue sauce. Save room for three-layer red velvet cake or strawberry shortcake. At Sunday brunch, crab and catfish cakes are topped with a poached egg and hollandaise. *$$; MC V; checks OK; lunch, dinner every day (except Tues), brunch Sun; beer and wine; no reservations; East Capitol Hill.* &

Lampreia / ★★★★

2400 1ST AVE, SEATTLE; 206/443-3301 From most seats in his urbane, spare dining room, chef-owner Scott Carsberg can be seen in the kitchen five nights a week, performing magic. How can something this simple be this spectacular? Maybe it's a single slice of seared tuna topped with citrus slices. Possibly it's a veal chop, drizzled with a fonduta sauce. Carsberg is often described as a minimalist, letting a few flavors speak volumes. Many in his near-cultish following consider him a genius. What keeps the sheep's milk cheese gnocchi from floating right off the plate? Others wonder why all the fuss—smallish portions, high prices, big-city attitude. He's a local boy—raised in West Seattle when it was still a blue-collar neighborhood—who made his way to the East Coast and was mentored by a master Tyrolean chef who took him to Italy. Carsberg returned to open his own show in 1992, bringing a New York sensibility and a master chef's sensitivity. Menu descriptors—appetizer, intermezzo, and main course—are also simple, such as "lentils from Verona served as a salad with guinea hen terrine," or "thin sheets of pasta filled with foie gras in beef consommé." He features prize mushrooms—matsutakes and morels, truffles and chanterelles—and artisan cheeses, served perfectly after a meal, an end unto themselves, or as prelude to a delicate lemon tart. Service, as directed by Carsberg's wife, Hyun Joo Paek, is seamless and reverential. *$$$; AE, MC, V; no checks; dinner Tues–Sat; full bar; reservations recommended; www .lampreiarestaurant.com; Belltown.* &

Lark / ★★★

926 12TH AVE, SEATTLE; 206/323-5275 Bring a group of friends to this new Capitol Hill hot spot and plan to stay a while. The multipage menu of small plates is unusual, but servers will happily help you compose a meal from categories such as "cheese," "vegetable/grains," and "charcuterie." Plates—expertly prepared from perfectly fresh ingredients—are intended for sharing, but you may want to hoard every bite of dishes such as baby beets with sherry vinegar and tangerine oil; *Pommes de terre Robuchon* (baked mashed potatoes); flatiron steak with parsley salad and blue cheese; smoked prosciutto with a 12th-century chutney; and halibut cheeks with stone-ground grits. Flowing white curtains can be cleverly arranged to create an aura of privacy in the softly lit, wood-floored open space. Chef Johnathan Sundstrom earned a following at Seattle's Earth & Ocean and Dahlia Lounge, and the crowd here is food-savvy and sophisticated. The no-reservations policy (except for large groups) can cause a crush at the tiny bar in the back. Have patience—and a glass of wine from the small, quirky list—the meal will be worth the wait. *$$$; MC, V; checks OK; dinner Tues–Sun; reservations for large groups; full bar; between Prospect and Aloha.* &

Le Gourmand / ★★★

425 NW MARKET ST, SEATTLE; 206/784-3463 Bruce Naftaly is one of the seminal purveyors of Northwest regional cooking. He combs the region for ingredients, and in his French kitchen uses vegetables and flowers from his own garden and from producers he's cultivated for many years. With the advent of the Italian-joint-on-every-corner era, his unlikely French storefront on the edge of Ballard has endured and matured into fine-honed perfection. Service is personal and capable in this quiet, romantic room, with its ceiling painted like a clear spring day and a trompe l'oeil wall of trees, hollyhocks, and lupines. Naftaly's prix-fixe menu includes appetizer choices, entrées, and salade après. His fortes are sauces, such as a creamy one with local caviars gracing the sole, or a huskier one with shiitakes, Cognac, and fresh sage accompanying the loin of rabbit. Naftaly married Sara Lavenstein, a pastry chef, a fortunate coupling for us all. The wine list features bottles from France, California, and the Northwest, with plenty of good midrange price options. *$$$; AE, MC, V; local checks only; dinner Wed–Sat; beer and wine; reservations recommended; Ballard.* &

Le Pichet / ★★☆

1933 1ST AVE, SEATTLE; 206/256-1499 Stepping into this narrow *café à vin* near Pike Place Market feels like walking into a vintage black-and-white postcard of la Rive Gauche. Owned by chef Jim Drohman (a Campagne expat) and business partner Joanne Herron (formerly of the Ruins), this café features a collection of house-made charcuterie—pâtés, sausages, and confits—that lesser places would buy from France. Parisian ambiance with warm overhead lighting and wood-framed mirrors puts tables together so couples are seated with strangers—before long expect to be offering bites of the *tartare de boeuf* in exchange for potted pork. The petit zinc bar, manned most nights by David Butler, is just long enough to sit a handful of patrons for espresso and brioche in the morning and Alsatian beer or a glass of Bordeaux *la nuit*. It is hard to imagine a more transporting start to a Parisian meal than curly endive salad with lardons, fingerling potatoes, and poached egg. Next should be the chicken liver terrine, followed by the grilled pork and garlic sausage over red pepper and white bean stew or the sautéed hangar steak with potatoes, fava beans, and Madeira pan sauce. The how-do-they-charge-that-and-stay-in-business wine list has about 50 labels, mostly French, and most under $25 and available by the glass, *pichet* (two-thirds of a 750ml bottle), or *demi-pichet* (two glasses). *$$; MC, V; no checks; breakfast every day, lunch, dinner Thurs–Mon; full bar; reservations recommended; downtown.* &

Macrina Bakery & Cafe / ★★

2408 1ST AVE, SEATTLE; 206/448-4032 Artisanal baker Leslie Mackie cast a spell on Seattle when she opened Macrina Bakery & Café 10 years ago in the (then upstart) Belltown neighborhood. The enchantment renews each morning as fresh bread, pastry, and the aroma of espresso greet still-sleepy downtown residents and on-the-go commuters. Folks fortunate enough to linger over breakfast secure a table or counter stool and start their day with homemade bread pudding with fresh fruit and cream or house-made granola and yogurt. Lunch charms with simple salads, sandwiches, and a meze—your choice of three Mediterranean-inspired noshes. Afternoon lulls are banished with a pick-me-up cookie and a strong cup of organic coffee. Arguably producing the best loaves in town, Marcrina's wholesale division supplies many of Seattle's best restaurants with a variety of Mackie's loaves (which are also available for purchase). Recently, Mackie came out with a new cookbook (*Macrina Bakery and Café Cookbook*) and a second café location on the west side of Queen Anne Hill (615 W McGraw St; 206/283-5900)—the magic continues. *$; MC, V; local checks only; breakfast, lunch Mon–Fri, brunch Sat–Sun; beer and wine; no reservations; www.macrinabakery.com; Belltown.* &

Malay Satay Hut / ★★☆

212 12TH AVE S, SEATTLE; 206/324-4091 After a fire in 2001, fans of this tasty strip-mall storefront in Seattle's Little Saigon fretted that this flavor hub where Malaysia meets China, India, and Thailand might be gone forever. But all's well. Sam and Jessy Yoo first opened a long-planned new location in Redmond, then reopened the noisy, ambiance-free Seattle location. It's easy to get addicted to the high intensity flavors of the Hut's seafood, curries, wontons, stir-fries, and satays. Order the *roti canai*, Indian flatbread served with a potato-chicken curry sauce; the Penang-style hot and sour noodle soup; or Buddha's Yam Pot, a chicken, shrimp, and vegetable stir-fry in a deep-fried basket of grated yams. The service is fast; to-go orders are recommended if you want to avoid waiting for seats. The Eastside place (15230 NE 24th St, Redmond; 425/564-0888), kitsched up with lava lamps and retro junk, has the same incredible food and prices and is every bit as busy, but a little less chaotic. *$; MC, V; no checks; lunch, dinner every day; beer and wine; reservations for 6 or more; Chinatown/International District.* &

Marjorie / ★★★

2331 2ND AVE, SEATTLE; 206/441-9842 When Donna Moodie and then-husband Marco Rulff split the linen, their two dinner restaurants stayed in the family. He got his namesake Marco's Supperclub (2510 1st Ave; 206/441-7801) and she the lovely Lush Life, which she transformed from dreamy Italian to romantic eclectic and renamed after her mother. In bold jewel tones, colorful raw silk, and dynamic metal work, this vaguely Moroccan room is stunning but comfortable. Chef Tyler Boring is well traveled and his menu shows it. Onion pakoras, thick rings fried in chick-pea batter, resemble a huge cinnamon roll with layers to be pulled off and dipped in curried ketchup and green coriander chutney. Pan-globals such as Sri Lankan curried eggplant, baked ricotta ravioli, and fleur de sel–roasted chicken with sour-cherry sauce are all served up with handmade chapatis. Moodie is the architect of simple-sounding desserts, such as the huge pieces of chocolate layer or lemon chiffon cake, which are, like her restaurant, studies in richness and triumphs of presentation. *$$; AE, MC, DIS, V; checks OK; dinner Tues–Sun; full bar; reservations recommended; marjorie@trenchtownrocks.com; www.trenchtownrocks.com; Belltown.*

Matt's in the Market / ★★★

94 PIKE ST, 3RD FLOOR, SEATTLE; 206/467-7909 Matt's is Seattle's worst-kept secret. It's tucked away in a tiny space on the third floor of the Corner Market Building, with a handful of tables that look out large-paned windows over the Market to Elliott Bay and the Olympic Mountains. From the tiny kitchen space, the durable chef, Erik Canella, turns out food that's not only well crafted, but also some of the freshest and most innovative downtown. It's no wonder it's fresh—cooks shop the Market twice a day. Seafood is the best bet here: try the rare-seared albacore, the smoked catfish salad, the whopping oyster po' boys, heady filé gumbo, or clams and mussels in an ouzo-infused broth. Owner Matt Janke does everything except cook—waiting, greeting, busing, prepping, and washing dishes. Sometimes he manages to squeeze musicians in to play live jazz. *$$; MC, V; no checks; lunch, dinner Mon–Sat; beer and wine; reservations recommended; Pike Place Market.*

Monsoon / ★★★

615 19TH AVE E, SEATTLE; 206/325-2111 Restaurant-savvy siblings Sophie, Eric, and Yen Banh took Seattle by storm when they opened Monsoon in 1999. Like the wind after which this sleek restaurant was named, the menus at Monsoon change direction with the seasons. An innovative approach to local, seasonal product is Monsoon's calling. Dishes are prepared in a gleaming open kitchen that fills the spare dining room with exotic fragrances. Don't miss signature appetizers, such as the crispy spring roll stuffed with Dungeness crab, shrimp or duck salad with green cabbage and vermicelli, or the traditional tamarind soup with chicken and gulf shrimp. The entrée portions are agreeably ample. Share the five-spice flank steak with Chinese celery and hothouse tomatoes or the seared scallops with bok choy and black-bean sauce. Vegetable dishes, such as the oven-baked Asian eggplant with grilled lobster mushroom and spicy green beans with butternut squash, make the menu welcoming to vegetarians. Waits can be long and the dining room is noisy when full. *$$; MC, V; no checks; lunch Tues–Fri, dinner Tues–Sun; beer and wine; reservations recommended; www.monsoonseattle.com; east Capitol Hill.* &

The Oceanaire Seafood Room / ★★★☆

1700 7TH AVE, SEATTLE; 206/267-2277 Seattleites were skeptical about this chain restaurant's nostalgic take on the classic fish house. But then they got a load of chef Kevin Davis's massive menu with 30 daily-changing seafoods, high standards for freshness, and huge portions. The service is seamless in this room that's a 1940s supper club in steamship moderne. It's got art deco styling, comfy booths, and walls decked with stuffed groupers and swordfish. Look for all the fish house classics—oysters Rockefeller, fish-and-chips—but don't miss Davis's herb-crusted sturgeon or Aunt Joy's Stuffed Petrale with Dungeness crab, bay shrimp, and Brie. Everything's à la carte, which can make this an expensive outing. The good news is that half orders of the immense side dishes, such as au gratin potatoes, green beans almandine, matchstick fries, or coleslaw, will feed four. Desserts are big, too—from the towering inferno of the baked Alaskas to the crème brûlée in vats. *$$$; AE, B, DC, DIS, JCB, MC, V; checks OK; lunch Mon–Fri, dinner every day; full bar; reservations recommended; www.oceanaireseafoodroom.com; downtown.* &

Palace Kitchen / ★★

2030 5TH AVE, SEATTLE; 206/448-2001 The enormous mural on the restaurant's south wall is a tip-off to owner Tom Douglas's goal here. The 17th-century period piece is a lusty scene of scullery maids and castle servants feasting on roast meats while guzzling red wine in the "palace kitchen." The palatial open kitchen staffed by talented cooks and the lively center-stage bar scene circulate a constant energy buzz. Although primarily a bar, the Palace delivers stick-to-your-ribs fare. To get in the convivial spirit, order shareable selections, such as the fat and spicy grilled chicken wings; bowls of clams; or crispy-fried, semolina-coated anchovies. The goat-cheese fondue with chunks of bread and apple slices is also a crowd pleaser. For a more formal supper, order the *plin*, tender raviolis plumped with chard and sausage, or one of the night's specials from the applewood grill, including the pit-roasted lamb, chicken, or whole fish. The wine list, written by the folks at Pike & Western Wine Shop, offers well-priced dinner accompaniments, while knowing bartenders make some of the best cocktails in town. If you are lucky enough to sit at one of LaDawn King's tables, you will know the joys of Seattle-style service at its best. *$$$; AE, DC, DIS, MC, V; checks OK; lunch Mon–Fri, dinner every day; full bar; reservations recommended; www.tomdouglas.com; Belltown.* &

Palisade / ★★☆

2601 W MARINA PL, SEATTLE; 206/285-1000 This tourist-pleaser has one of the most incredible waterfront settings in the area, with a splendid 180-degree view of Elliott Bay, Alki Point, and the Seattle skyline. The view is pretty distracting, especially during long Northwest summer sunsets, but the interior, with its huge radiating beams, Japanese garden with bonsais, and bubbling brook, is stunning, too. Go for an after-work drink and pupu platters of steamed butter clams and Whidbey Island mussels with sun-dried tomatoes and fresh thyme. Chefs use an applewood grill, wood oven, and wood-fired rotisserie for the extensive menu of fish and meat. Check the daily fresh sheet for local fish, such as steelhead, Columbia River sturgeon, or signature wild salmon steak roasted on a red-cedar plank. Don't miss the Granny Smith apple tart with cinnamon ice cream and warm caramel sauce. *$$; AE, DC, DIS, MC, V; checks OK; dinner every day, brunch Sun; full bar; reservations recommended; palisaderestaurant.com; Magnolia/Interbay.* &

Ray's Boathouse / ★★★

6049 SEAVIEW AVE NW, SEATTLE; 206/789-3770 Warm wood and a greeting to match welcome locals and tourists alike to Ray's Boathouse. Regional seafood dominates the menu at this Seattle landmark restaurant. Satisfying starters include the Penn Cove mussels luxuriating in a rosy, silken stew of coconut and red curry, heady with the perfume of Thai basil, chiles, garlic, lemongrass, and ginger, or the Manila clams in butter and dill broth from the Skookum Inlet. Salmon is always great (Ray's was the first restaurant to acquire its own fish buyer's license) and all fish are usually wild and always fresh. The rich Chatham Straits black cod is a signature selection, which can be applewood smoked or marinated *kasu*-style in sake lees, encrusted in sesame seeds, and served with a sesame-scented rice cake and wasabi-ginger emulsion. Under general manager Maureen "Mo" Shaw, the well-trained staff is gracious and capable. Expect an extensive selection of Northwest wines on the list.

Upstairs, Ray's Café serves up lower-priced, lighter fare, though guests are welcome to order from the downstairs menu. Choices include fish-and-chips, burgers, salads, or classic clam linguine. Diehard Northwesterners sit on the outside deck, toddy in hand, any time of the night or year (there are blankets for the asking). Make reservations for weekday lunches in the café. *$$$; AE, DC, DIS, MC, V; checks OK; dinner every day (Boathouse), lunch, dinner every day (Café); full bar; reservations recommended; www.rays.com; Ballard, near Shilshole.* &

Rover's / ★★★★

2808 E MADISON ST, SEATTLE; 206/325-7442 Though Rover's puckish "Chef in the Hat" Thierry Rautureau has won the hearts of Seattleites, half his customers are out-of-towners making pilgrimages to get a taste of the kitchen that has won Rautureau national renown. Guests approach through a courtyard that blossoms behind an unassuming arcade. Rover's welcoming reception area proffers a gentle transition from the street to the dining room, full of sunny hues and ambient light. Choose from three prix-fixe menus (one vegetarian) that progress from delicate flavors to bolder expressions with elegant sufficiency. Rautureau is a master of sauces, using stocks, reductions, herb-infused oils, and purées to enhance slices of sturgeon, steamed Maine lobster, wild mushrooms, breasts of quail, and the requisite foie gras. Expect professional service from the loyal staff. Rautureau, a Frenchman, is serious about wine. Cellar master and sommelier Cyril Frechier manages the 5,500-bottle collection and is on hand to bring guests the perfect partner for any meal. Dining in the courtyard, weather permitting, is enchanting. *$$$$; AE, DC, MC, V; checks OK; dinner Tues–Sat; beer and wine; reservations required; rovers-seattle.com; Madison Valley.* &

Saito's Japanese Cafe & Bar / ★★★⯪

2120 2ND AVE, SEATTLE; 206/728-1333 On any given night in this smart Belltown place you might see the Japanese ambassador or—more impressively—Mariners superstar Ichiro Suzuki, who is a regular. They come for Saito-san's sushi, arguably the best in town. The fish is immaculately fresh and cut thicker than you'll usually find in Seattle—one of the reasons he's so popular with Japanese visitors. The modern mirrored dining room is served well by Saito-san's vivacious wife, Anita, and a staff of knowledgeable servers. Items from the hot kitchen are innovative; stray from the teriyaki and try the butter *itame,* a geoduck sauté with sugar snaps and shiitakes. Saito's kitchen goes further than the traditional Japanese with vegetable tempura, picking what's fresh from the Market: sugar snaps; squash blossoms; and matsutake, oyster, and morel mushrooms all cut thin and fried delicately in batter. Be sure to try the house-made ice-cream sampler, with flavors such as green tea, mango, or sweet plum. *$$$; AE, DIS, E, MC, V; no checks; lunch Tues–Fri, dinner Tues–Sat; full bar; reservations recommended; info@saitos.net; www.saitos .net; Belltown.* &

Salumi / ★★

309 3RD AVE S, SEATTLE; 206/621-8772 If you're thinking of going vegetarian, eat here first. In this little wedge of Italy near the King Street train station, arias soar and angels sing. Armandino Batali (the father of famed New York chef Mario Batali) is a retired aeronautics engineer who after 31 years at Boeing dusted off his family recipes, went to culinary school in New York, worked in a salami factory in Queens, and apprenticed with butchers in Tuscany. He cures his own *coppa,* three kinds of salami, lamb or pork prosciutto, spicy *finocchiona,* and citrusy *soppressata,* a lamb and orange sausage. They're cut to order and all sold cheaply by the pound for takeout, or let Batali slice you some to lay on a crusty baguette slathered with an anchovy-rich pesto or garlic sauce. Try the braised oxtail or the amazing meatball sandwich on a rosetta roll, piled high with sautéed peppers and onions. If you're still considering vegetarianism, there's Swiss chard, dandelion greens, or Roman beans. Batali's weekly private dinners are booked up months in advance (reservations required for parties of 10 or more), but lunch at communal tables is for everyone. *$; AE, MC, V; checks OK; lunch Tues–Fri, dinner Sat; beer and wine; reservations required (dinner); Pioneer Square.* &

Thaiku / ★★⯪

5410 BALLARD AVE NW, SEATTLE; 206/706-7807 When the beloved Fremont Noodle House was moved to Old Ballard, owner Jon Alberts renamed it Thaiku, and he calls what he does here "culinary Zen." Dark red walls are graced by bright Thai fabric, Indonesian antiques, and the head of a Javanese carnivorous wooden deer. A rubber-tired Djakarta pony cart hangs from the ceiling alongside balloon-tired bicycles. Votives flicker on every surface. The authentic food from an expanded menu is as good as ever, with soupy slurp-'em-up noodles such as Guay Tiow Talay, prawns, scallops, squid, and vegetables; or stir-fries such as classic phad thai or a list of rice dishes. Nang Kwak, the ubiquitous goddess of Thai businesses, beckons you, and prosperity, in the door. Her juju seems to be working, though she can't take all the credit—the food and service match the incredible decor. *$; AE, DIS, MC, V; no checks; lunch, dinner every day; full bar, reservations for 6 or more; Ballard.* ♿

Union / ★★★

1400 UNION ST, SEATTLE; 206/838-8000 As the son of Pacific Northwest Ballet co-directors Francia Russell and Kent Stowell, chef Ethan Stowell is akin to a Seattle prince. Though his talents fall some distance from the family tree, they are no less artistic. The menu, which is divided into firsts, seconds, and entrées, encourages diners to create a meal of small plates. The menu changes daily, but you might begin with seared foie gras or a subtle celery soup served over a salty cod fish cake, then choose an entrée of sturgeon perfectly matched with Brussels sprouts or roasted squab. The small portions make the large white plates look spacious; complex flavors more than fill them. Such modest portions leave ample room for dessert: perhaps chocolate cake with mint ice cream. Though the ambiance suffers from a many-windowed view onto a gritty urban street corner, and acoustics amplify the kitchen clatter to diner decibels, nothing in the less-than-cozy contemporary space is likely to distract from what's on the plate: Stowell creates some of the city's best food, which is reason enough to go. *$$$; AE, DIS, MC, V; no checks; lunch, Mon–Fri, dinner every day; full bar; reservations recommended; www.unionseattle.com; on the corner of 1st and Union.* ♿

Wild Ginger Asian Restaurant and Satay Bar / ★★★

1401 THIRD AVENUE, SEATTLE; 206/623-4450 After a move to massively larger digs (some say too large) in 2000 that made locals whine about the prospect of Wild Ginger losing its soul, this landmark is still remarkable and wildly popular with Seattleites and visitors—especially those attending Seattle Symphony performances at Benaroya Hall down the street. The huge, bilevel dining room has street-side views and an elegant spiral stairway leading up to private banquet rooms. Owners Rick and Ann Yoder's culinary vision, inspired by time spent in Southeast Asia, changed the Seattle restaurant scene and pan-Asian cuisine everywhere. Wild Ginger offers a wide range of multiethnic dishes from Bangkok, Singapore, Saigon, and Djakarta. At the mahogany satay bar, order from a wide array of sizzling skewered selections, like the mountain lamb and Saigon scallop satay. Indulge in the succulent Singapore-style stir-fried crab, fresh from live tanks and redolent of ginger and garlic; the celebrated fragrant duck served with steamed buns and plum sauce; or *laksa*, a spicy Malaysian seafood soup, with soft, crunchy, and slippery textures and hot and salty flavors that encompass everything good about Southeast Asian food. *$$$; AE, DC, DIS, MC, V; no checks; lunch Mon–Sat, dinner every day; full bar; reservations recommended; downtown.* &

LODGINGS

Ace Hotel / ★★

🌲 **2423 1ST AVE, SEATTLE; 206/448-4721** The 30-room Ace is *A Clockwork Orange* without the bright colors. This futuristic, hostel-like hotel is so hip it hurts. White wood floors, white walls (some rooms have black-and-white Andy Warhol–like murals), mostly white bedding, and white robes give the Ace a stylishly clean, spare look. Fourteen standard rooms each have a stainless sink and counter and baths down the hall. Sixteen deluxe rooms have their own baths and king- or queen-sized beds. No down comforters here; low beds have simple wool French Army blankets. With its ultracool location above the Cyclops Café and within walking distance of Pike Place Market and Belltown galleries and shops, this is the place to experience the urban hipness of Seattle. Amenities include small wall TVs, phones with data ports, minibars, and CD players. There's no room service, but with all of Belltown's eateries at your command, you can eat around the world during your stay. Rooms on First Avenue can be noisy. Pets OK. *$$–$$$; AE, DC, DIS, JCB, MC, V; checks OK; www.acehotel.com; Belltown.*

Alexis Hotel / ★★★

1007 1ST AVE, SEATTLE; 206/624-4844 OR 888/850-1155 The luxurious Alexis takes its motto "A Work of Art" seriously, placing original artwork throughout the guest rooms and common areas. This whimsical yet elegant boutique-style hotel inside a turn-of-the-19th-century building has 109 rooms, including spacious executive suites, fireplace suites, spa suites, and one- and two-bedroom suites with kitchens. Theme suites include the John Lennon Suite, with reproductions of his artwork and CDs of his music; the Author's Suite, with autographed copies of books by authors who have stayed there, such as Chuck Palahniuk (*Fight Club*) and Donna Tartt (*The Little Friend*); and the Honeymoon Suite, with in-the-mood music by Marvin Gaye and Barry White. In each of the romantic spa suites on the top floor, step up to a giant, two-person tub surrounded by mirrors. North-facing rooms have a view of Elliott Bay; First Avenue rooms might be a little noisy. Amenities range from voice mail, data ports, and complimentary morning tea and coffee and newspaper of your choice, to shoeshines, a fitness room, an on-call masseuse, and the Aveda Day Spa. Live jazz every Wednesday provides nice background for evening wine tasting. The Library Bistro, which replaced the Painted Table in 2003, serves breakfast and lunch only, but it will provide guests with picnics to go and tours of Pike Place Market. Pets OK. *$$$–$$$$; AE, DC, DIS, JCB, MC, V; checks OK; seattleres@kimptongroup.com; alexishotel.com; downtown.* &

The Edgewater / ★★☆

2411 ALASKAN WY, PIER 67, SEATTLE; 206/728-7000 OR 800/624-0670 A longtime waterfront landmark, the Edgewater is home to some of the Emerald City's most unusual claims to fame. It's the only Seattle hotel literally over the water (you've probably seen the famous 1964 photo of the Beatles fishing out their hotel window—which isn't allowed anymore, unfortunately). Just throw open your window to breathe the fresh, salty air, listen to the ferry horns, and watch para-sailers float by. The 234-room hotel has a metal log-cabin exterior, with aluminum shingles meant to evoke silvery fish scales, and a Northwest-lodge theme inside. All rooms have fireplaces and log bed frames. The sleek Six Seven Restaurant & Lounge (named for the pier) serves Northwest cuisine with pan-Asian influences. The eatery's uninterrupted views of Elliott Bay, Puget Sound, and the Olympics extend to a balcony over the water. It's a short walk to Bell Street Pier (Pier 66), with restaurants and an overpass to nearby Pike Place Market. Pets OK. *$$$; AE, DC, DIS, MC, V; checks OK; www.edgewaterhotel.com; waterfront.* ♿

Fairmont Olympic Hotel / ★★★★

411 UNIVERSITY ST, SEATTLE; 206/621-1700 OR 800/441-1414 It may be a cliché, but "Old World luxury" is the perfect description for the 80-year-old Fairmont Olympic. On the site of the original University of Washington, and formerly named the Four Seasons Olympic, the only four-star hotel in Seattle was bought by Fairmont Hotels in August 2003. The changeover didn't significantly alter this historic landmark: impeccable service and exceptional pampering are hallmarks of this 1924 Italian Renaissance icon. Creamy white walls, warm wood accents, huge chandeliers, and rich fabrics make you feel as if you've stepped back in time to an era when travelers expected opulent accommodations. That luxury extends from the 450 guest rooms (219 of them suites), including baths with showers, soaking tubs, and terry-cloth robes, to the venerable restaurant, The Georgian (206/621-7889). Executive suites feature king-sized beds separated from elegant sitting rooms by French doors. Amenities include 24-hour room service, 24-hour concierge staff, twice-daily housekeeping service, complimentary shoeshine, three-line telephones (so you can e-mail, fax, and talk at the same time), bathroom phone, CD player, town-car service, high-speed Internet access, Shuckers oyster bar (206/621-1984), and two lounges. Several swank meeting rooms and a dozen chichi shops flank the lobby. Enjoy afternoon tea in The Georgian, work out in the health club, or relax in the hot tub and pool (a massage therapist is on call). The Fairmont's prices are steep, but this is Seattle's one world-class contender. And it's not just for grown-ups. The hotel goes out of its way for children and infants, providing them with their own welcome bag, loaner Sony PlayStation, video tapes, cribs, kid-sized bathrobes, and even bottle warmers and babysitting service. Pets OK. *$$$$; AE, DC, DIS, JCB, MC, V; checks OK; www.fairmont.com/seattle; downtown.* ♿

Hotel Monaco / ★★★

1101 4TH AVE, SEATTLE; 206/621-1770 OR 800/945-2240 The Monaco's bold style is a welcome respite on gray Seattle days. All 189 rooms are sumptuously appointed in a blend of eye-popping stripes and florals in reds and yellows, which strike some as insanely busy, others as utterly charming. All rooms have queen- or king-sized beds; 10 Mediterranean Suites feature deluxe bathrooms with two-person Fuji jet tubs. As with many downtown hotels, views take a backseat to service and design (business travelers appreciate 6,000 square feet of meeting space). Amenities include complimentary high-speed Internet access, 24-hour room service, two-line phones, leopard-print bathrobes, 24-hour business services, evening wine tasting, fitness center, and privileges at a local health club. Monaco's campy principality extends to the Southern-inspired Sazerac restaurant (206/624-7755), named for the bar's signature drink. Pets OK; or ask for a loaner goldfish in its own bowl. *$$$–$$$$; AE, DC, DIS, JCB, MC, V; checks OK; www.monaco-seattle.com; downtown.* ♿

Hotel Vintage Park / ★★★

1100 5TH AVE, SEATTLE; 206/624-8000 OR 800/624-4433 From the lobby's plush velvet settees and leather armchairs to the Grand Suite's double-sided fireplace, the Vintage Park looks like the ideal spot to break out a smoking jacket and a nice Chianti. The 126 rooms are named after Washington wineries and vineyards, with Tuscany-inspired decor and cherry furniture, and a complimentary fireside Northwest wine tasting every evening. Part of the San Francisco–based Kimpton Group, the personable Vintage Park offers rooms facing inward or outward (exterior rooms have a bit more space but not much of a view, but corner rooms on the west side have views of the courthouse's row of maple trees). Rooms come with fax machines, double phone lines with data ports, and phones in the bathrooms. Nice touches include "left arm" chairs (the left arm is high, the right arm is low, providing a very comfortable sort of slouch), in-room fitness equipment, privileges at a local health club, and 24-hour room service (including lunch or dinner from the hotel's excellent Italian restaurant Tulio: 206/624-5500; *www.tulio.com*). A nearby Interstate 5 on-ramp makes lower floors a bit noisy; upper floors are more removed from traffic noise. Pets OK. *$$$; AE, DC, DIS, JCB, MC, V; checks OK; www.hotelvintagepark.com; downtown.* ♿

Inn at Harbor Steps / ★★

1221 1ST AVE, SEATTLE; 206/748-0973 OR 888/728-8910 Tucked inside a swanky high-rise retail-and-residential complex across from the Seattle Art Museum, rooms at the Inn are shielded from the surrounding urban hubbub. It's hard to remember you're in the middle of downtown with views of the Inn's quiet interior courtyard with its lush greenery and arch from the old Victoria Hotel, which occupied this site decades ago. Part of the California-based Four Sisters Inns (another Northwest property is Whidbey Island's Saratoga Inn), Harbor Steps offers 28 rooms with sleek furnishings, garden views, fireplaces (in most rooms), air-conditioning, king- or queen-sized beds, sitting areas, wet bars, fridges, data ports, and voice mail. Deluxe rooms include spa tubs. Each double-queen room has an angled wall that extends partway into the room, separating the beds for a bit of privacy. Among the amenities are 24-hour concierge/innkeeper services, evening room service from Wolfgang Puck Café (4–10pm), complimentary evening hors d'oeuvres and wine, and a full gourmet breakfast. Guests have access to an indoor pool, resistance pool, sauna, Jacuzzi, exercise room, and meeting rooms. Complimentary fresh cookies and computers with Web access in the lobby. *$$$; AE, DC, MC, V; no checks; www.foursisters.com; downtown.* &

Inn at the Market / ★★★⯪

86 PINE ST, SEATTLE; 206/443-3600 OR 800/446-4484 Everything about the Inn at the Market oozes quintessential Seattle atmosphere: views of Elliott Bay and the Olympics from most rooms, close proximity to bustling Pike Place Market, and room service from country-French Campagne (see review). An ivy-draped courtyard wraps around its entrance amid high-end retailers and restaurants. The 70 rooms are handsomely dressed in soft taupe, copper, and green, and have oversized bathrooms, robes, two-line phones with data ports, Nintendo, and floor-to-ceiling bay windows that open. West-facing windows have incredible views of the Sound. (Don't fret if the weather turns gloomy; some of the most memorable views come through rain-streaked windows.) Rise early to sample the Market's fresh foods; or sleep late and indulge in room service from Bacco in the courtyard. In-room dinners come courtesy of Campagne. Campagne's bar is a snug, if smoky, spot for a nightcap. *$$$–$$$$; AE, DC, DIS, JCB, MC, V; checks OK; info@innatthemarket.com; www.innatthemarket.com; Pike Place Market.* &

Mayflower Park Hotel / ★★

405 OLIVE WY, SEATTLE; 206/623-8700 OR 800/426-5100 Past and present come together at this handsome 1927 hotel set in the heart of the city's retail district (it's connected to Westlake Center mall). A member of the National Trust Historic Hotels of America, the Mayflower has a lobby decorated with lovely antique Chinese artwork and furniture. The 171 rooms are fairly small, but preserve reminders of the hotel's past: Oriental brass and antique appointments, elegant dark-wood furniture, deep tubs, thick walls, and double-glazed windows that keep out noise. Twenty suites offer comfortable sitting areas and most have wet bars. Slightly bigger corner suites have better views; ask for one on a higher floor. Amenities include free high-speed wireless Internet, robes, Nintendo, telephones with data ports, 24-hour room service, and same-day laundry service. For refreshments, you can't beat Andaluca (206/382-6999), an upscale restaurant combining Northwest and Mediterranean themes, or you can sip one of Seattle's best martinis at the popular bar, Oliver's. Kids 10 and under get a free full breakfast. *$$–$$$; AE, DC, DIS, MC, V; checks OK; valet parking; mayflowerpark@mayflowerpark.com; www.mayflowerpark.com; downtown.* &

Panama Hotel / ★★⯪

605½ S MAIN ST, SEATTLE; 206/223-9242 This historic European-style hotel with shared bathrooms down the hall was built in 1910 in old Japantown as a workingman's hotel for Japanese immigrants, Alaskan fishermen, and international travelers. Remodeled in the late 1980s (although a few old-timers still have apartments here), the hotel has 100 rooms with hardwood floors, antique furnishings, unique bedding collected from around the world, down comforters, lace curtains, and single sinks. Men's and women's baths are small but clean. Street-side rooms can be a little noisy. Ask for a tour of the basement to see the only remaining Japanese bathhouse left intact in the United States. There's no room service, but the adjacent Panama Hotel Tea & Coffee House has yummy snacks and teas and also displays artifacts left behind by Japanese families going to WWII internment camps. Pets OK, but notify staff beforehand. Weekly rates available. *$–$$; AE, MC, V; no checks; reservations@panamahotelseattle.com; www.panamahotelseattle.com; Chinatown/International District.*

Pensione Nichols / ★★⯪

1923 1ST AVE, SEATTLE; 206/441-7125 OR 800/440-7125 If you're turned off by megahotels but want the ambiance of downtown, Pensione Nichols (the only bed-and-breakfast in Seattle's downtown core) is the place for you. Perched above Pike Place Market and furnished with antiques from the 1920s and '30s, 10 guest rooms share 4 bathrooms. Some rooms face noisy First Avenue; others have bright skylights instead of windows and are quieter. Two spacious suites have private baths, full kitchens, and living rooms with jaw-dropping water views. A large, appealing common room on the third floor has a similarly spectacular view of Elliott Bay; it's here the bountiful continental breakfast—including fresh treats from the Market—is served. Couch potatoes be warned: the stair climb from street level is steep. Summer weekends bring a two-night minimum stay; discounts for long-term stays. Kids OK, as well as pets. *$$; AE, DC, DIS, MC, V; checks OK; www.seattle-bed-breakfast.com; downtown.*

Sorrento Hotel / ★★★⯪

900 MADISON ST, SEATTLE; 206/622-6400 OR 800/426-1265 When it opened in the first decade of the 1900s, the Sorrento was a grand Italianate masterpiece holding court on a corner of the First Hill neighborhood, just east of downtown. And it's every bit as grand today. Evoking a classic European hostelry, the beauty of the Sorrento is in details: elegant furnishings, Italian marble bathrooms, an assortment of pillows in four different firmness levels, and the plush Fireside Room just off the lobby, perfect for taking afternoon tea or for a cocktail while listening to evening jazz. Splurge for a special package, such as the Sorrento Romance or Breakfast-in-Bed, and you'll get rose petals on your pillow or a hot water bottle in winter. The 76 rooms and suites are comfortably luxurious in an old-fashioned way, but offer DIRECTV, CD players, free high-speed Internet access, and fax/printer/scanners. There's also a small exercise room. Top-floor suites make posh quarters for meetings or parties. The Hunt Club (206/343-6156) serves Northwest and Mediterranean cuisine. Complimentary town-car service takes guests downtown. The Sorrento is a short, though hilly, five-minute walk to the heart of the city—perfect for getting away from it all, without being too far away. Small pets OK. *$$$$; AE, DC, DIS, JCB, MC, V; checks OK; reservations@hotelsorrento.com; www.hotelsorrento.com; First Hill.* &

W Seattle Hotel / ★★★⯪

1112 4TH AVE, SEATTLE; 206/264-6000 OR 877/W-HOTELS The W is in a class all its own: dressed in postmodern art, velvet drapes, plush modern furniture, and oversized chess sets—and that's just the lobby. The two-story lobby is one of those see-and-be-seen kind of places—especially once a month when a DJ gives the place a nightclub feel. Though the black-clad staff is hard to see in the much-too-dark hallways (it's supposed to set a mood, but instead makes it hard to find your room key), they're friendly and helpful. Rooms are stylishly simple: taupe and black, with stainless steel- and glass-accented bathrooms, coffeemakers, desks, and Zen-inspired water sculptures. Goose-down duvets and pillows, and honor bars with wax lips and "intimacy kits" make for a sexy stay. Many rooms (particularly higher corner rooms) have impressive downtown views. Room service is available 24 hours, as is the fitness room; meeting space totals 10,000 square feet. The W is also totally wired: each room has a 27-inch TV with Internet access, CD and video player, two-line desk phone with high-speed Internet connection, conference calling, and cordless handset. A Pet Amenity Program provides pet beds and treats. You don't have to go far for great food—just cross the lobby to Earth & Ocean (206/264-6060). If you want a little privacy, unequivocal do not disturb signs tell visitors to "Go Away." *$$$$; AE, DC, DIS, JCB, MC, V; checks OK; www.whotels .com; downtown.* &

Watertown / ★★

4242 ROOSEVELT WY NE, SEATTLE; 206/826-4242 OR 866/944-4242 The upscale sister hotel of the University Inn just two blocks south, the more luxurious Watertown was built in 2002. It has postmodern furniture and bamboo floors in the lobby. The 100 studios and suites in this totally nonsmoking hotel have free high-speed Internet access, microwaves, refrigerators, coffeemakers, and TVs that swivel to face the bathroom if you need your news fix while shaving. Closets open from both the bedroom and bathroom sides. Suites have pull-out sofa beds and wet bars. Jacuzzi suites have two-person tubs. The hotel has a fitness center, general store, free underground parking, free local shuttle, and three meeting rooms, and offers free newspapers and continental breakfast, and access to the seasonal pool and spa at University Inn. Thoughtful touches include loaner bicycles and "Ala Carts" (push carts filled with board games or spa amenities delivered to your room). The hotel is secure—guests must use room cards to access guest floors. *$$; AE, DC, DIS, MC, V; checks OK; reservations@watertownseattle.com; www.watertownseattle.com; University District.* &

The Westin Seattle / ★★★

1900 5TH AVE, SEATTLE; 206/728-1000 OR 800/WESTIN-1 The Westin's twin cylindrical towers evoke all sorts of comparisons by local wits: corncobs, trash cans, mountain-bike handlebars. It's a '60s-era kind of look, but the spacious rooms provide some of the best views in the city, especially above the 20th floor. The gargantuan size of the hotel (891 rooms and 34 suites) contributes to some lapses in service: the check-in counter can resemble a busy day at the airport, and the concierge staff gets harried. But rooms are comfortable, and beds have cozy pillow-top mattresses. Hotel amenities are corporate minded: business center, convention facilities, and a multilingual staff. You'll also find a large pool and whirlpool tub with city view, an exercise room, and a large lobby suitable for cocktails or business meetings. On the top floors are some ritzy suites. The Westin's location, near Westlake Center and the Monorail station, is excellent, as are meals at Roy's (206/256-7697)—save room for gooey-in-the-center chocolate soufflés. *$$$$; AE, DC, DIS, JCB, MC, V; checks OK; westin.com; downtown.* &

The Eastside

The suburbs—and suburban cities—on the east side of Lake Washington across from Seattle are collectively known as "the Eastside." They include Bellevue, Redmond, Kirkland, Woodinville, and Issaquah. The **EAST KING COUNTY CONVENTION & VISITORS BUREAU** (425/455-1926; *www.eastkingcounty.org*) has the lowdown on Eastside goings-on.

Bellevue

Washington's fourth-largest city has been making noises for years about shaking its shopping-mall image. It now has an impressive downtown skyline populated by glass high-rises. The fairly new **MEYDENBAUER CENTER** (11100 NE 6th St; 425/637-1020; *www.meydenbauer.com*) hosts myriad arts performances.

But shopping is still the main attraction. Consider the conglomeration of retail might: **BELLEVUE SQUARE** (NE 8th St; 425/454-8096; *www.bellevuesquare.com*), packed with a triple-decker Nordstrom store and Crate & Barrel, plus 200 shops and restaurants; kitty-corner is glitzy **BELLEVUE PLACE** (10500 NE 8th; 425/453-5634); and, farther east, family-oriented **CROSSROADS SHOPPING CENTER** (15600 NE 8th; 425/644-1111; *www.crossroadsbellevue.com*). The barn-sized **BARNES & NOBLE** bookstore (626 106th NE; 425/644-1650; *www.barnesandnoble.com*) is worth a look. And, the 19-acre **DOWNTOWN PARK**, possessed of a fine waterfall and promenade in the southern shadow of Bellevue Square, offers shoppers a nature break.

RESTAURANTS

Sans Souci / ★★★

10520 NE 8TH ST, BELLEVUE; 425/467-9490 Carefully hidden from the world in the second floor of Bellevue Place's Wintergarden, Sans Souci seems to carry on, as its name means, "without worry." No matter that few know it's there and even fewer ever penetrate this multipurpose fortress of a development, northeast of Bellevue Square. After so many years in the restaurant business—including introducing Seattle to fine northern Italian fare at legendary Settebello (in the '80s)—Luciano Bardinelli can cope. More than cope; his handsome, mostly Italian–partly French restaurant usually delivers. Skilled servers present the Harry's Bar carpaccio appetizer, a gorgeous plate of shaved raw tenderloin as served in the famous American expat hangout in Paris. The crab cakes are just that—nothing more. The onion soup, built on a sturdy base of veal broth, can make a meal. *Paniscia di Novara* is a simple, meat-laden Northern Italian risotto, and the osso buco is a sure bet. The well-chosen wine list ranges from the upper $20s to multiple hundreds. The handsome dining room sports pumpkin-colored walls, wood accents, and white linen. Save room for super sweet tiramisù. *$$; AE, DC, DIS, MC, V; checks OK; lunch Mon–Fri, dinner every day; full bar; reservations recommended; www.sanssoucibistrot.com; at Bellevue Wy.* &

Seastar Restaurant and Raw Bar / ★★★☆

205 108TH AVE NE, BELLEVUE; 425/456-0010 It seemed a bold move when John Howie, who had served as executive chef at Palisade for nearly a decade, left to open an upscale seafood restaurant smack dab in the middle of a recession. How bold you discover when you step into his sparkling seafood emporium. The horseshoe-shaped restaurant wraps sensually around Howie's state-of-the-art kitchen: nary a corner can be found in the shimmering, curvy ocean-inspired rooms. Don't let a glossy clique of hostesses at the door throw you. The wait staff has fun with playful guests and converses easily about the food. The Best of Show cold appetizer is a multilevel raw bar sampler: Hawaiian ahi poke, California roll, and scallop seviche. On the hot side, we like flash-seared divers sea scallops with tropical fruit chutney and ginger-soy reduction, and the Kauai shrimp, wrapped in saifun noodles, deep fried and drizzled with *Sriracha* (an Asian chili-garlic concoction) butter and scallions. At dinner or lunch, request the sesame-peppercorn crusted ahi with creamy wasabi and ginger-soy reduction. And while it's clear the lure of Seastar is seafood, carnivores will never go hungry, not with a 9-ounce Snake River Farms American Kobe beef rib-eye on the grill. Seastar's nationally celebrated wine list is written by the ever-affable Erik Liedholm, who's on the floor most nights to offer knowing recommendations and tailored service. *$$$; AE, DC, DIS, MC, V; local checks OK; lunch, dinner every day; full bar; reservations recommended; www.seastarrestaurant.com; at NE 2nd.* &

LODGINGS

Bellevue Club Hotel / ★★★

11200 SE 6TH ST, BELLEVUE; 425/454-4424 OR 800/579-1110 One of the most elegant hotels in the area, the Bellevue Club is part hotel, part upscale athletic club, hidden inside lush plantings in an office park just blocks from Interstate 405. The 67 rooms feature sunken tubs and original pieces by Northwest artists, as well as cherry-wood furniture custom-made on Whidbey Island. Many of the Asian-inspired rooms overlook the tennis courts; French doors in some guest rooms open onto private terra-cotta patios. A great benefit is the attached athletic facilities, including an Olympic-sized swimming pool, indoor tennis, racquetball, and squash courts, and aerobics classes. Oversized limestone-and-marble bathrooms—with spalike tubs—are perfect for post-workout soaks. The club offers fine dining at Polaris Restaurant (425/637-4608) and casual fare at Splash. *$$$–$$$$; AE, DC, DIS, MC V; checks OK; bellevueclub.com; at 112th Ave SE.* &

Redmond

Once a bucolic valley farming community, Redmond today is a sprawling McTown of freeway overpasses, offices (Microsoft and Nintendo are headquartered here), subdivisions, and retailers, including the open-air, 100-plus-shop **REDMOND TOWN CENTER AND CINEMAS** (16495 NE 74th; 425/867-0808; *www.redmondtown center.com*). Some of Redmond's pastoral past remains. It's not dubbed the bicycle capital of the Northwest for nothing: bikers can pedal the 10-mile **SAMMAMISH RIVER TRAIL** or check out races on the 400-meter **MARYMOOR VELODROME** (2400 Lake Sammamish Pkwy; 206/675-1424; *marymoor.velodrome.org*). In summer, 522-acre **MARYMOOR PARK** (6046 W Lake Sammamish Pkwy NE; 206/296-2966; *www.metrokc.gov/parks/rentals/pomjun99.htm*) draws crowds for picnics. The **CONCERTS AT MARYMOOR** series (6046 W Lake Sammamish Pkwy NE; 206/628-0888; *concertsatmarymoor.com*) hosts a popular summer program that has featured artists from Norah Jones to Ringo Starr.

Kirkland

Sure, there's a crunch of expensive condos and traffic, but this fetching town tucked into the eastern shore of Lake Washington has avoided the Eastside's typical strip-mall syndrome. People *stroll* here among congenially arranged eateries, galleries, and boutique retailers. In summer, sidewalks fill with locals and tourists, as do **PETER KIRK PARK** and the **KIRKLAND MARINA**, where you can catch an **ARGOSY** (206/623-1445; *www.argosycruises.com*) boat for a lake cruise, April through September. Welcome downtown additions include the 402-seat **KIRKLAND PERFORMANCE CENTER** (350 Kirkland Ave; 425/893-9900; *www.kpcenter.org*). Even the obligatory mall, **KIRKLAND PARKPLACE** (6th St and Central Wy; 425/828-4468), doesn't spoil the townscape—it's several blocks east of the waterfront.

RESTAURANTS

Cafe Juanita / ★★★⯪

9702 NE 12TH PL, KIRKLAND; 425/823-1505 It's still a humble little converted white-brick house, but its reputation—on both sides of the lake—is like a brick house. The theme is Northern Italy. The execution by Holly Smith is precise; the presentation flawless. A professional wait staff brings elegant cuisine that changes with the seasons, created lovingly from first-rate ingredients, including herbs grown in the kitchen garden viewed through dining-room windows. Grilled octopus with fennel might start a meal, as could a pear salad with pine nuts, Parmigiano-Reggiano, and white truffle oil. Tagliatelle with sea-urchin white truffle crema could be a destination, or a stopping point before a whole-roasted fish, rib-eye chop, or Muscovy duck breast, each prepared with flair. The dessert list is formidable and irresistible, with select cheeses or Valrhona-chocolate-truffle cake with vanilla gelato, espresso sauce, and crisp almond wafer. After training at Dahlia Lounge and Brasa, Smith is now the one to emulate. The carefully considered wine list has plenty of Italian bottles, with a fair Northwest representation and a range for varied pocketbooks and tastes. *$$$; AE, MC, V; no checks; dinner Tues–Sun; full bar; reservations recommended; www.cafejuanita.com; Juanita area.* &

Yarrow Bay Grill / ★★☆

1270 CARILLON PT, KIRKLAND; 425/889-9052 Yes, you can go home again. Chef Vicky McCaffree did, back to the Yarrow Bay Grill in summer 2002 after a two-year term opening the Waterfront Seafood Grill in Seattle. Her purview here, the upstairs Grill, still has the great views and the understated, elegant decor. The service has slipped at times, beyond what one would expect at a fine venue. Now McCaffree, who made a name for herself with pan-Asian cuisine, has downplayed that part of her repertoire, though you still can get the Seven-Spice Seared Ahi and Thai Seafood Stew, with its coconut milk–lemongrass broth. A grilled nectarine chutney graces the seared pork tenderloin, and Gorgonzola-Madeira demi-glace accompanies the beef tenderloin. New Mexico corn ravioli further stretches the geographical perspective. *$$$; AE, DC, DIS, JCB, MC, V; no checks; dinner every day; full bar; reservations recommended; www.ybgrill.com; at Carillon Point.* ঠ

LODGINGS

The Woodmark Hotel on Lake Washington / ★★★

1200 CARILLON POINT, KIRKLAND; 425/822-3700 OR 800/822-3700 The only hotel nestled right on the shoreline of Lake Washington, the Woodmark is tucked inside the elite enclave of Carillon Point on the Eastside. The four-story brick hotel blends seamlessly with surrounding shops and restaurants and is just steps from the marina and shoreline path. Away from busy streets, you're more likely to hear the rustling of boat sails than a car. One hundred guest rooms, about half with stunning lake views, offer a relaxing retreat of cream-colored furnishings and extras, such as minibars and refrigerators, the comfiest robes (terry on the inside, silky on the outside), and prompt, friendly service. Some rooms have balconies. Suites include the palatial Woodmark, with a lake and mountain view, dining space for six, and 950 square feet of parlor space. Smaller suites feature varying parlor sizes. All guests get a complimentary newspaper, free Internet access, and a chance to "raid the pantry" when the restaurant lays out a complimentary late-night buffet. Down the grand staircase is the comfortable Library Bar, with grand piano and overstuffed chairs in front of the fireplace. The hotel's restaurant, Waters (425/803-5595; *www.watersbistro.com*), features Northwest cuisine focusing on local and organic foods; other restaurants and specialty shops (including The Spa at Woodmark) are nearby. *$$$–$$$$; AE, DC, JCB, MC, V; checks OK; mail@thewoodmark.com; www.thewoodmark.com; at Carillon Point.* ঠ

Woodinville

Oenophiles and hopheads (the microbrew kind) love this little Eastside town. **CHATEAU STE. MICHELLE** (14111 NE 145th St; 425/488-1133; *chateaustemichelle .com*), the state's largest winery, offers daily tastings and tours and popular summer concerts on its lovely 87-acre estate. Across the street, **COLUMBIA WINERY** (14030 NE 145th St; 425/488-2776; *columbiawinery.com*) has daily tastings and weekend tours. Or wet your whistle at one of the state's first microbreweries, **REDHOOK ALE BREWERY** (14300 NE 145th St; 425/483-3232; *redhook.com*), which, along with daily $1 tours (including a souvenir glass and plenty of samples), has a pub with tasty grub and live music Fridays and Saturdays.

RESTAURANTS

The Herbfarm / ★★★★

14590 NE 145TH ST, WOODINVILLE; 425/485-5300 It is often placed in the upper echelon of American restaurants—a must-experience place for anyone who loves serious food and formal service, and can pay the freight. The nine-course prix-fixe dinner with accompanying wines costs around $175 per person. After a devastating fire followed by a short time in a temporary location, Ron Zimmerman and Carrie Van Dyke moved their foodie shrine to brand-new gorgeous digs in the Woodinville "wine country," near the Ste. Michelle and Columbia Wineries, on the property of the posh Willows Lodge. Nationally renowned chef Jerry Traunfeld presides over seasonal menus of local produce and herbs—much of which are grown in the Herbfarm's own substantial gardens. The food is immaculately presented and carefully explained. A night's repast could typically encompass tempura squash blossoms stuffed with goat cheese; crab salad with fennel and chives; pea flan with caviar; sweet corn soup with smoked mussels and chanterelles; salmon smoked in basilwood; herb-crusted lamb; cheeses; desserts such as a roasted Italian plum tart and a caramelized pear soufflé with rose-geranium sauce; and a selection of small treats—miniature s'mores with cinnamon and basil, chocolates, or lemon-thyme espresso truffles—to go with your coffee. The army of staff attends to every service detail, wiping your brow, pouring your wines, and clearing away the Christofle flatware and crystal as you use it. The rooms are filled with a tasteful mass of framed art and memorabilia. Arrive a half hour before dinner for Van Dyke's tour around the gardens. This is a coveted, one-of-a-kind destination—reservations usually need to be booked months in advance, especially for holidays. *$$$$; AE, MC, V; checks OK; dinner Thurs–Sun; beer and wine; reservations required; reservations@theherbfarm .com; theherbfarm.com; next to Willows Lodge.* &

LODGINGS

Willows Lodge / ★★★⯪

14580 NE 145TH ST, WOODINVILLE; 425/424-3900 OR 877/424-3930 Willows Lodge is the quintessential Northwest hotel, combining casual grace with a recycling aesthetic unique to the region. It's only two stories tall, so it blends in with its wooded surroundings. While the burned-out shell of a 1,500-year-old cedar—trucked over from the Olympic Peninsula—stands sentinel near the entry, 100-year-old reclaimed Douglas fir forms the beams and stairs in the two-level lobby. World-class wineries and lush gardens surround this 88-room luxe lodge. Rooms are classified as "nice," "nicer," and "nicest." Even "nice" rooms are fabulous: slate bath tile, recycled slate desks, balconies or patios, reclaimed timber shelves, rock-lined fireplaces, stereo/DVD/CD systems (borrow CDs and DVDs at the front desk), free high-speed Internet connections, lush bathrooms ("nicest" rooms have jetted tubs and heated towel racks), safes large enough for your laptop, and complimentary breakfast. Add enticing views of the gardens, Chateau Ste. Michelle and Columbia wineries next door and across the street (a dozen more are a short drive away), the Sammamish River (and its popular bike trail), or Mount Rainier (on a clear day). Service is Northwest casual, but quick and professional. The "nicest" of six suites ($750 per night) boasts a whirlpool bath and flat-screen TV. Other lodge amenities include a spa, a 24-hour fitness room, a Japanese garden, and evening wine tastings. The Barking Frog (425/424-2999) restaurant serves Mediterranean-influenced dinners and weekend brunches. Guests also have access to nine-course meals at the renowned Herbfarm Restaurant (see review), which, along with its famed herb gardens, occupies its own site on the grounds. *$$$$; AE, DC, DIS, JCB, MC, V; checks OK; mail@willowslodge.com; willowslodge.com; next to Redhook Brewery.* &

Issaquah

Though every so often a cougar shows up in this wealthy Cascade-foothills suburb 15 miles east of Seattle, Issaquah is pleasantly mild mannered. Historic **GILMAN VILLAGE** (317 NW Gilman Blvd; 425/392-6802; *www.gilmanvillage.com*), composed of refurbished old farmhouses, offers an agreeable day of poking about in its 40 or so shops, and the **VILLAGE THEATRE** (120 Front St N and 303 Front St N; 425/392-2202; *www.villagetheatre.org*) entertains with mostly original, mainly musical productions at two downtown theaters. Seattleites cross the Interstate 90 bridge in packs during summer weekends to "scale" the Issaquah Alps, which have miles of trails from easy to challenging; the **ISSAQUAH ALPS TRAILS CLUB** (425/328-0480; *issaquahalps.org*) offers organized day hikes. Drop in the first weekend of October for **ISSAQUAH SALMON DAYS** (425/392-7024; *www.salmon days.org*), a celebration—including food, crafts, music, and a parade—marking the return of the salmon that surge up Issaquah Creek.

Seattle-Tacoma International Airport

LODGINGS

Hilton Seattle Airport Hotel / ★★☆

17620 INTERNATIONAL BLVD, SEATAC; 206/244-4800 OR 800/HILTONS A huge renovation a few years back doubled the size of this well-run hotel to a total of 396 rooms, including 7 suites. Rooms are set around two landscaped courtyards with a pool and an indoor/outdoor Jacuzzi. The hotel also has a fitness room and 40,000-square-foot, state-of-the-art conference center. Rooms include comfortable desks, computer hookups, high-speed Internet access, coffeemakers, and WebTV. A 24-hour business center caters to worker bees. The hotel's restaurant, Spencer's for Steaks and Chops (206/248-7153), serves all meals. Room service is 5am to midnight, but the complimentary airport shuttle is 24 hours. *$$–$$$; AE, DC, DIS, JCB, MC, V; checks OK; www.hilton.com; corner of S 176th St and Pacific Hwy S.* &

PUGET SOUND

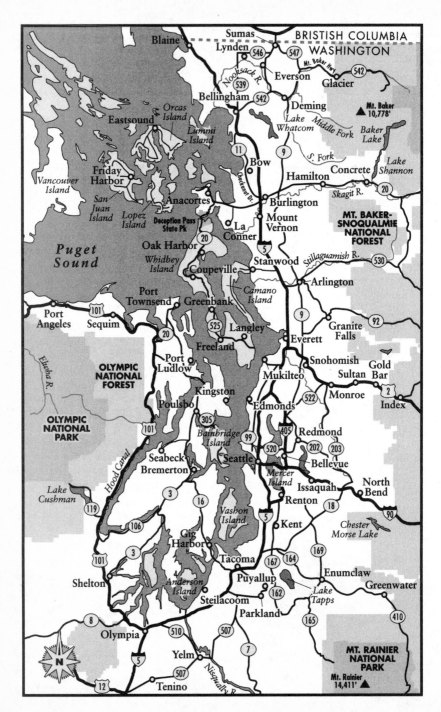

PUGET SOUND

The Puget Sound region—from Olympia at the southern end of Puget Sound to Blaine at the border with Canada—is not only the cradle of the state's port, shipping, fishing, and naval industry, it also offers some of the area's most idyllic getaways. Its transportation corridor, Interstate 5, is flanked by a richly populated, verdant stretch of Washington State. Waterways, islands, farmlands and forest, and stunning mountain views dominate the landscape.

Driving north from Seattle, I-5 carries you to the artsy suburb of Edmonds, the port city of Everett, the tulip town of Mount Vernon, and the university community of Bellingham. The area is best explored by leaving the freeway and traveling the back roads, routes that lead to the state's most visited islands—including Whidbey and the San Juans—as well as to waterfront towns and villages—Langley, Coupeville, Anacortes, and La Conner—that invite travelers to linger and explore.

ACCESS AND INFORMATION

Fly into **SEATTLE-TACOMA INTERNATIONAL AIRPORT** (17801 Pacific Hwy S, SeaTac; 206/431-4444; *www.portseattle.org*)—13 miles south of Seattle and 16 miles north of Tacoma—and you have easy access to Interstate 5. You'll need a car to best explore the region; most **CAR RENTAL** agencies have outlets at Sea-Tac.

Train travel offers a different view. **AMTRAK** (303 S Jackson St, Seattle; 206/382-4125 or 800/USA-RAIL; *www.amtrak.com*) has daily runs between Portland and Seattle's King Street Station, and Seattle and Vancouver, with stops including Everett and Bellingham.

WASHINGTON STATE FERRIES (Pier 52, Seattle; 206/464-6400 or 800/843-3779; *www.wsdot.wa.gov/ferries/*) access the San Juan Islands, Whidbey, Vashon, and other islands in Puget Sound.

Edmonds

This former mill town, and popular suburb 15 miles north of downtown Seattle, has managed to hang onto its small-town feel despite growth and the daily stream of ferry commuters who take the Edmonds–Kingston ferry. This active arts community hosts the **EDMONDS ARTS FESTIVAL** (*www.edmondsartsfestival.com*) each June, a good month to appreciate the creative hanging baskets and pots of flowers that are a city tradition. Explore small galleries, antique stores, and specialty shops downtown. Take in a show at the classic **EDMONDS THEATER** (415½ Main St, Edmonds; 425/778-4554), or enjoy saltwater views, tidal pools, and outdoor sculptures as you stroll waterfront **BRACKETT'S LANDING PARK**. A train station and nearby **EDMONDS HARBOR INN** (130 W Dayton; 800/441-8033; *www.nwcountryinns .com/edmonds/html*) make it an overnight destination as well. Numerous eateries include the **SHELL CREEK GRILL & WINE BAR** (526 Main St; 425/775-4566) for fine dining in a casual atmosphere and **CHANTERELLE'S** (316 Main St; 425/774-0650), a popular gathering spot.

NORTH PUGET SOUND THREE-DAY TOUR

DAY ONE: From Interstate 5, go west to the **MUKILTEO FERRY**. A 20-minute ferry ride puts you at Clinton, on the southeast end of Whidbey Island. Exit off the main highway to Langley, a cliff-side village overlooking Saratoga Passage. Grab coffee and a pastry at **THE BRAEBURN** on Second Street, then explore **FIRST STREET** galleries, antiques shops, and boutiques. Head to the **STAR BISTRO CAFÉ AND BAR** for lunch, then complete your tour. Check into the **INN AT LANGLEY**, then seek out an order of the island's own Penn Cove mussels at **CAFE LANGLEY**. Enjoy a soak while watching boats in Saratoga Passage before bed.

DAY TWO: Breakfast at the inn gets you ready to head up-island to Coupeville. Drop by the **ISLAND COUNTY HISTORICAL MUSEUM**, tour the exhibits, and watch the informative video about island history. Pick up a map there for exploring **EBEY'S LANDING**, then have lunch at **TOBY'S 1890 TAVERN**. Go for a hike on the beach at **FORT EBEY STATE PARK**, particularly inspiring with views west to the water and setting sun. For a rustic, historical experience, overnight at the **CAPTAIN WHIDBEY INN**, where you also have dinner.

DAY THREE: Breakfast at the inn or at **KNEAD & FEED**. Continue north on the island, stop at **DECEPTION PASS STATE PARK** for a ground-level view of the furious waters in the pass, then cross the **DECEPTION PASS BRIDGE** and get a glimpse from above. Swing through Anacortes and browse at **MARINE SUPPLY AND HARDWARE** or the **ANACORTES MUSEUM**. Grab a bite at the **CALICO CUPBOARD**, then head south to La Conner, where you can stroll through town and have an early dinner at **KERSTIN'S** or **NELL THORN'S**. Take the back route out of La Conner and stop at **SNOW GOOSE PRODUCE** and **ROOZENGARDE** demonstration garden if it's spring, then rejoin Interstate 5 at Conway, or stay on back roads to Stanwood and Camano Island. Check in at the **CAMANO ISLAND INN**, relaxing by the fireplace while watching the sun set behind Whidbey Island, where you began your journey.

Everett Area

The Everett area extends from Edmonds on the south to Stanwood on the north. US Highway 2 heads east from Everett, and ferries head west from Mukilteo just south of Everett. Timber and fishing once supported this Snohomish County seat. Now, Boeing's Paine Field facility and the state-of-the-art U.S. naval base here add more to the area's growing economy and its ever-increasing population.

Everett

The grand, new $70-plus million **EVERETT EVENTS CENTER** (2000 Hewitt Ave, 425/322-2600; *www.everetteventscenter.com*) has added a sizzle long missing in downtown Everett. Home to the **SILVERTIPS** (425/252-5100; *www.everett silvertips.com*), Everett's new Western Hockey League franchise team, the center also hosts big-name entertainment in its 10,000-seat facility. The **EVERETT AQUASOX** (3802 Broadway; 425/258-3673; *www.aquasox.com*), the single-A, short-season farm team for the Seattle Mariners, draws folks away from Seattle to enjoy baseball at the small, old-fashioned field. Don't miss the chili dogs.

The beautifully redeveloped and historic Monte Cristo Hotel, now the **EVERETT CENTER FOR THE ARTS** (1507 Wall St; 425/257-8380; *www.everettwa.org/ community/*), is home to the Everett Symphony, the Arts Council, and a stunning display of Pilchuck glass. The **EVERETT PERFORMING ARTS CENTER** (2710 Wetmore Ave; 425/257-8600 box office or 888/257-3722; *www.everettwa.org/ community/*) hosts a variety of plays, concerts, dance, and other events.

BOEING'S SOUTH EVERETT PLANT (exit 189 west from I-5 to Hwy 526, follow signs; 206/544-1264; *www.boeing.com*) offers 90-minute tours of the world's largest building (in volume), where you can watch the assembly of the aviation giant's 747s, 767s, and 777s. Tours (admission charge) run Monday through Friday, fill early, and have strict height requirements for children; a gift shop is on-site.

Downtown Everett has an excellent bakery, **PAVÉ** (2613 Colby Ave; 425/252-0250; *www.pavebakery.com*), with sandwiches made fresh; however, the hazelnut tarts or the sour cherry and chocolate bread (when available) are reason enough to stop.

RESTAURANTS

Alligator Soul / ★

2013½ HEWITT AVE, EVERETT; 425/259-6311 Exposed brick, Mardi Gras beads, hot-pepper lights, and heaping portions of Southern smoked ribs with a hot barbecue sauce give this place its soul. The sides alone could make a meal: jalapeño cornbread, corn salad, and cool coleslaw. Other dishes—the Creole hot pot, crawfish étouffée, catfish gumbo (special order), fried catfish with hush puppies—have even diehard Northwesterners longing to go south. Bread pudding, packed with pecans and peaches, is delicious served with a sweet bourbon sauce. You can purchase Alligator Soul hot sauce to take home. Live music some evenings. *$$; MC, V; no checks; lunch, dinner every day; beer and wine; reservations recommended; near Broadway, across from the new arena.*

Emory's Lake House / ★

11830 19TH AVE SE; EVERETT; 425/337-7772 A former roadhouse on a country lake, Emory's sits in the midst of southeast suburban Everett, offering aged steaks and seafood—such as salmon, halibut, and a cannelloni with Dungeness crab—pasta, salads, and burgers. The Key lime cheesecake is worth the calorie splurge. Emory's has an easygoing pub-style charm, lake views, and deck dining in warmer weather. After your meal, explore the nearby dock. *$$; AE, DIS, MC, V; no checks; lunch, dinner every day; full bar; reservations recommended; at Silver Lake.* &

The Sisters

2804 GRAND ST, EVERETT; 425/252-0480 This place is as popular as it is funky. Soups such as corn and cheese chowder or beef and mushroom barley can be outstanding. Sandwiches range from average deli stuff to a vegetarian burger made with chopped cashews and sunflower seeds. Morning favorites are pecan hotcakes or scrambled eggs wrapped in flour tortillas. Fresh-squeezed lemonade quenches your thirst; a big slice of marionberry pie cures what ails you. *$; MC, V; checks OK; breakfast, lunch Mon–Fri; no alcohol; no reservations; in Everett Public Market.* &

LODGINGS

The Inn at Port Gardner / ★★

1700 W MARINE VIEW DR, EVERETT; 425/252-6779 OR 888/252-6779 Industrial chic mixes with warm touches—an inviting lobby fireplace and colorful art accents—to create a stylish getaway, or a comfortable stay for corporate travelers. The inn views the marina and is next to Lombardi's Italian restaurant. Thirty-three sophisticated rooms are done up in neutral tones. Suites have separate bedrooms and fireplaces. Continental breakfast is included. *$$–$$$; AE, DC, DIS, MC, V; local checks only; reservations@innatportgardner.com; www.innat portgardner.com; exit 193 off I-5.* &

Marina Village Inn / ★

1728 W MARINE VIEW DR, EVERETT; 425/259-4040 OR 800/281-7037 The Puget Sound waterfront location of this 26-room inn on Port Gardner Bay can't be beat, even if lobby areas look dated. Rooms are contemporary with oak furnishings, satellite TVs, handcrafted ceramic sinks, trouser presses, and refrigerators. Many have jetted tubs; most have telescopes. Book a room on the harbor side; sea lions might be lollygagging on the nearby jetty. Anthony's Home Port restaurant is next door. *$$; AE, DC, DIS, MC, V; checks OK; mvi1728@aol.com; www.gtesupersite .com/marinavilinn; exit 193 off I-5.* &

Mukilteo

On the southwest edge of Everett, Mukilteo is known for the congestion caused by ferry traffic to Whidbey Island (see Access and Information in this chapter). A mini-mall collection of old-fashioned shops located just south of the ferry has a coffee shop and bookstore to explore. A block or two south of the ferry terminal (follow signs from freeway), a small waterfront park has a historical lighthouse worth seeing. Get fish and chips or chowder at **IVAR'S** (720 Front St; 425/742-6180; *www.ivars.net*) next to the terminal.

RESTAURANTS

Amici's Bistro / ★

8004 MUKILTEO SPEEDWAY, MUKILTEO; 425/438-9544 The strip-mall location doesn't look promising, yet once you're inside this Italian bistro, the food, wait staff, and atmosphere—especially in the cozy back room with a fireplace—make you forget the busy ferry traffic. Butternut squash soup is a favorite, as is the tender Pollo Marsala entrée. An avid fisherman, chef Peter Orel (formerly with New York's Tavern on the Green) specializes in a catch of the day, so that's always a good bet. The dinner menu is offered to go. *$$; AE, MC, V; no checks; lunch Mon–Fri, dinner daily; beer and wine; reservations recommended; off 80th.* &

Charles at Smugglers Cove / ★★

8340 53RD AVE W, MUKILTEO; 425/347-2700 Chef Claude Faure and his wife, Janet, turned this landmark building (a 1929 speakeasy set on a bluff above Possession Sound) into an elegant restaurant. The atmosphere is country French, and a terrace views the Sound. Dishes such as veal chop with tarragon and *poulet aux crevettes* (breast of chicken with prawns) grace the classically French menu. Save room for crêpes suzette or Grand Marnier soufflé. For lunch try a tasty salad niçoise. A bistro menu offers lighter and less expensive choices. *$$$; AE, MC, V; local checks only; lunch Tues–Fri, dinner Mon–Sat; full bar; reservations recommended; www.charlesatsmugglerscove.com; at Hwys 525 and 526.* &

LODGINGS

Silver Cloud Inn / ★★

718 FRONT ST, MUKILTEO; 425/423-8600 OR 800/311-1461 It's hard to beat the location of this waterfront inn adjacent to the Mukilteo ferry. It's built over the water, and half of the 70 guest rooms have spectacular Puget Sound views. The floral-decorated rooms have traditional furniture, microwaves, and small refrigerators; some view rooms have jetted tubs and gas fireplaces. A generous continental breakfast is included and can be enjoyed in the surprisingly homey fireplace sitting room off the lobby. Ask about special packages. *$$–$$$; AE, DIS, MC, V; checks OK; www.silvercloud.com; exit 189 from I-5.*

Snohomish

Once an active lumber town, this small community southeast of Everett now bills itself as the "Antique Capital of the Northwest." Antique shops fill the downtown historical district; the **STAR CENTER MALL** (829 2nd St; 360/568-2131) is the largest, with 200 dealers from all over the area, and a restaurant, **COLLECTOR'S CHOICE** (360/568-1277), on the lower level. Take tea at **PICCADILLY CIRCUS** (1104 1st St; 360/568-8212) or buy imported English teapots and foods. Visit the **SNOHOMISH PIE COMPANY** (915 1st St; 360/568-3589) and try the lunch special—a half sandwich, bowl of soup, and slice of pie.

When you're through taking in the old, get a new perspective on Snohomish from the air: charter a scenic flight at **HARVEY FIELD** (9900 Airport Wy; 360/ 568-1541; www.snohomishflying.com), take a trip with **AIRIAL HOT AIR BALLOON COMPANY** (10123 Airport Wy; 360/568-3025; www.airialballoon.com), or enjoy a parachute adventure with **SKYDIVE SNOHOMISH** (9912 Airport Wy; 360/568-7703; www.skydivesnohomish.com).

Stanwood

A once sleepy farm village of Scandinavian heritage, Stanwood, like many idyllic country locales, has been caught up in suburban sprawl. Still, its old town along Main Street is worth exploring, and the **STANWOOD GRILL** (8628 271st NW; 360/629-5253) is a worthy stop for a prime rib meal. Near town is the 54-acre campus of internationally renowned glass-art **PILCHUCK SCHOOL** (206/621-8422; *www.pilchuck.com*), founded in 1971 by local glass artist Dale Chihuly and Seattle art patrons John Hauberg and Anne Gould Hauberg. Students live and study on campus. Spring tours and a summer open house (admission $20 to $30) give folks a chance to see artists at work; call for times and directions.

Camano Island

The 'burbs have spread to parts of this island west of Stanwood, an hour's drive from Seattle. Once primarily a summer enclave, Camano still has plenty of that "away from it all" feel—besides, there's no ferry to catch to get there. **CAMANO ISLAND STATE PARK** (360/387-3031; *www.parks.wa.gov/alpha.asp*) on the south-west side is a day-use park with a beach and picnic shelters. On your way to the park, stop at the **UTSALADY GROCERY** (50 E North Camano Dr; 360/387-3915) for delicious clam chowder to go. Visit the island over Mother's Day weekend and take in the **CAMANO ARTS ASSOCIATION STUDIO TOUR** (360/387-7146; *www.camanoarts.org*).

LODGINGS

Camano Island Inn / ★★

1054 W CAMANO DR, CAMANO ISLAND; 360/387-0783 OR 888/718-0783
This luxurious waterfront inn has spectacular water views. Cozy up in the sitting room with its rustic river-rock fireplace; sink into king-sized feather beds. Six guest rooms (all with water views) have private waterfront decks and large bathrooms; some have jetted tubs. The breakfast room showcases island artists. Kayaks are available for guests ($20 per use); massages can be arranged. *$$; AE, DIS, MC, V; checks OK (in advance); rsvp@camanoislandinn.com; www.camano islandinn.com; exit 212 from I-5, follow Hwy 532 onto the island.*

Whidbey Island

Whidbey Island is one of only eight islands that make up Island County (with Camano, Ben Ure, Strawberry, Minor, Baby, Smith, and Deception). Named for Capt. Joseph Whidbey, a sailing master for Capt. George Vancouver, Whidbey Island was first surveyed and mapped by the two explorers in 1792. More than 200 years later, its largest employer is the government (thanks to the Oak Harbor navy base). The island boasts pretty towns, historical parks, sandy beaches, and pastoral farmland.

Depart from the mainland at Mukilteo (see the Everett Area section), about 25 miles north of Seattle, for a 25-minute ferry ride (see Access and Information in this chapter) to Clinton on the south end of the island. Expect long car waits on sunny weekends. You can also drive onto Whidbey at its north end, on Highway 20 south of Anacortes. Here the island is described from south to north.

Langley

The nicest town on Whidbey carries its small-town virtues well. With the addition of **LANGLEY VILLAGE**, a charming collection of old-style shops on Second Street, it has grown into a two-street town with plenty of antiques, arts, and specialty shops to explore.

Look for original Northwest paintings, pottery, sculpture, and glass at **GASKILL-OLSON GALLERY** (302 1st St; 360/221-2978; *www.gaskillolson.com*); and stop to enjoy the Georgia Gerber sculpture of Reggie, a well-known town terrier, in front of the gallery. Next door at **HELLEBORE GLASS GALLERY** (308 1st St; 360/221-2067; *www.helleboreglass.com*), you can watch glassblower George Springer at work. **MUSEO** (215 1st St; 360/221-7737; *www.museogallery.com*) features regional and national glass art and handcrafts.

The **BRAEBURN** (197 2nd St; 360/221-3211) is a good spot for espresso, breakfast, and light meals; head to the **DOG HOUSE** (230 1st St; 360/221-9825) for a microbrew (18 on tap) after a movie at **THE CLYDE** (213 1st St; 360/221-5525). The pesto pizza by the slice at **LANGLEY VILLAGE BAKERY** (221 2nd St; 360/221-3525) is a local favorite. Try the rhubarb wine at the **WHIDBEY ISLAND WINERY** (5237 S Langley Rd; 360/221-2040) tasting room a few minutes south of town.

RESTAURANTS

Cafe Langley / ★★

113 1ST ST, LANGLEY; 360/221-3090 Owners Shant and Arshavir Garibyan maintain the sparkling consistency that established this café as the town's best bet from the moment it opened. Make a reservation (especially on weekends) and prepare for fine Mediterranean dining. Appetizers include hummus and warm pita bread, and Penn Cove mussels in saffron broth. Try moussaka for lunch; the Greek salad is perfect before a feast of seafood stew, a lamb shish kebab, or a creative preparation of Northwest salmon or halibut, in season. Split the Russian cream for dessert. *$$; AE, MC, V; checks OK; lunch Wed–Mon, dinner every day (closed Tues in winter); beer and wine; reservations recommended; www.langley-wa.com/cl; on the main street.* &

The Fish Bowl / ★★

317 2ND ST; LANGLEY; 360/221-6511 The Fish Bowl is a recent, welcome addition to the Langley food scene. Owners Ray and Maureen Cooke and executive chef Micah Noack focus on fresh fish and shellfish and serve them up in a comfortably elegant old building overlooking town. The menu changes frequently, however you'll usually find a half-dozen appetizers featuring ingredients from the sea—crab cakes, clam chowder, oysters, prawns, mussels, and calamari. One islander calls the halibut entrée served with caramelized apples and a mushroom-and-walnut sauce a "swoonable dish." It's a signature item, as is the wild salmon served on a bed of baby bok choy with a ginger-carrot sauce. Vegetarian items are always available. *$$–$$$; AE, DIS, MC, V; local checks only; dinner Tues–Sun; full bar; reservations recommended; www.fishbowlrestaurant.com; in Langley.* &

Star Bistro Café & Bar / ★

201½ 1ST ST, LANGLEY; 360/221-2627 An island favorite, the Star Bistro Café & Bar (above the Star Store) is a fun, color-splashed place that hops on weekends and after local events. Chef Paul Davina's menu includes pastry-enclosed French onion soup, salads, pasta, and burgers, along with seasonal specials such as creamy oyster stew. There's a breezy, sun-drenched deck. Pull up a stool at the red-topped bar for excellent martinis or margaritas. *$$; AE, MC, V; no checks; lunch, dinner every day (dinner Tues–Sun in winter); full bar; reservations recommended; bistro@whidbey .com; www.star-bistro.com; on the main street.*

Trattoria Giuseppe / ★

4141 E HWY 525, LANGLEY; 360/341-3454 Inside this trattoria—an unexpected discovery in a little strip mall on Highway 525—the scent of garlic and taverna decor are reminiscent of little places in the Tuscan countryside. Penn Cove mussels are prepared marinara. We like the fusilli primavera with prawns and scallops and the *salmone con spinaci*—salmon on a bed of spinach with lemon butter sauce. Finish with a traditional Italian dessert such as cannoli. Enjoy live music on Friday (during high season) or Saturday nights. *$$; AE, DIS, MC, V; checks OK; lunch Mon–Fri, dinner every day; full bar; reservations recommended; dine@trattoriagiuseppe.com; www.trattoriagiuseppe.com; at Langley Rd.*

LODGINGS

Boatyard Inn / ★★

200 WHARF ST, LANGLEY; 360/221-5120 The industrial siding and metal roofs of this inn mesh well with Langley's working waterfront. Big windows, pine accents, and back-to-basics Eddie Bauer–esque furnishings characterize 10 breezy suites (the smallest is 600 square feet), each with a gas fireplace, galley kitchen, queen-sized bed, sofa bed, cable TV, private deck, and water view. Loft units are suitable for small groups. *$$$; AE, DC, DIS, MC, V; local checks only; boatyard@whidbey.com; www.boatyardinn.com; take Wharf St downhill.* &

Chauntecleer House, Dove House, and Potting Shed Cottages / ★★★

5081 SARATOGA RD, LANGLEY; 360/221-5494 OR 800/637-4436 Our only quibble with these gorgeous cottages on a quiet bluff north of downtown Langley is that it's too hard to choose one. Decorating these hideaways was a labor of love for transplanted Southerner Bunny Meals. We prefer Chauntecleer House, but only by a nose—or a beak (Chauntecleer is the name Chaucer used for a rooster in one of his Canterbury Tales)—for its sun-yellow walls, view of Saratoga Passage, wood-burning fireplace, and outdoor hot tub. Dove House doesn't share the view but is charmingly decorated with a mix of furniture and art (the bronze otter was sculpted by Georgia Gerber, Seattle's Pike Place Market Rachel-the-pig artist). A wood stove adds coziness, a second bedroom has bunks for the kids. The Potting Shed has a whimsical garden theme, "twig" bed, two-person jetted tub, and glass-front wood stove. A full breakfast is left in each kitchen. *$$$; AE, MC, V; checks OK; bunny@dovehouse.com; www.dovehouse .com; take 2nd St west from town.*

The Garden Path Suites / ★★☆

111 1ST ST, LANGLEY; 360/221-5121 There are only two suites here, but the charm and comfort of these stylish hideaways, right in the center of the action, is worth seeking out. The large front suite has water and main street views, a full kitchen, and a separate dining room. The back suite is smaller, but just as beautifully decorated. It comes as no surprise that host Linda Lundgren also owns the interiors shop downstairs. No children or pets. *$$$; AE, MC, V; www.islandsgetaways.com; off 1st St.*

Inn at Langley / ★★★★

400 1ST ST, LANGLEY; 360/221-3033 It's difficult to imagine a more idyllic getaway, or one more evocative of the Pacific Northwest, than the first private venture of former Seattle mayor Paul Schell and his wife, Pam. Architect Alan Grainger combined three themes: Frank Lloyd Wright style, Northwest ruggedness, and Pacific Rim tranquility. Inside this rough-hewn, shingled building, built elegantly into the bluff over Saratoga Passage, are 24 rooms with simple Asian-influenced furnishings, trimmings of three different woods, and quarry-tiled bathrooms with hooks made from alder twigs. Every room of the four-story inn views the water (you can watch boat traffic from the Jacuzzi); we prefer the upper-level rooms. Two townhouse cottages—with living room, bedroom, and master bath—just east of the inn offer more expansive and expensive options. Spa services are available on-site. Continental breakfast included. New chef Matt Costello, formerly of Seattle's Dahlia Lounge, creates the six-course prix-fixe dinners (served weekends only by reservation, and open to the public) celebrating Northwest foods. *$$$–$$$$; AE, MC, V; local checks only; www.innatlangley.com; edge of town.* &

Island Tyme / ★

4940 S BAYVIEW, LANGLEY; 360/221-5078 OR 800/898-8963 At Island Tyme, on a quiet 10 acres, 2 miles from downtown Langley, innkeepers Cliff and Carol Wisman raise pheasants and pygmy goats. Rooms in the Victorian-style inn are unfussy, romantic retreats, especially the Heirloom Suite, with its fireplace, two-person jetted tub, and deck. All five rooms have private baths, TVs, and VCRs. One room allows pets. Don't miss the apple tree mural around the front door. *$$; AE, MC, V; checks OK; info@islandtymebb.com; www.islandtymebb .com; call for directions.* &

Saratoga Inn / ★★★

201 CASCADE AVE, LANGLEY; 360/221-5801 OR 800/698-2910 It's a two-minute walk from downtown Langley to the Saratoga Inn, which has architectural touches reminiscent of New England. Each of the 15 view rooms is festooned in warm plaids or prints and furnished with a gas fireplace, an armoire, and an entertainment center. Breakfast can be delivered to your chamber. Solitude seekers like the separate Carriage House, with a full kitchen, stone fireplace, and king-sized sleigh bed. Small conferences are held in the Library Boardroom; guests socialize in the tea room. The Four Sisters Inn group manages the property. *$$$; AE, DC, MC, V; no checks; www.foursisters.com; corner of 2nd St.*

Freeland

Freeland is home to **NICHOLS BROTHERS BOAT BUILDERS** (5400 S Cameron Rd; 360/331-5500; *www.nicholsboats.com*), manufacturers of cruise boats and stern-wheelers, and the town's largest employer. Like other small island communities, Freeland has grown in recent years and now boasts a small shopping center. The **FREELAND CAFÉ AND LOUNGE** (1642 Main St; 360/331-9945; *www.whidbey .com/freelandcafe*), an old-fashioned non-fancy spot where locals hang out, is open 6am to 9pm and serves breakfast all day. **FREELAND PARK** on Holmes Harbor has picnic tables, a play area, and a sandy beach.

LODGINGS

Cliff House / ★★★

727 WINDMILL RD, FREELAND; 360/331-1566 At the end of a winding road through the forest and perched on a cliff above Admiralty Inlet, this extraordinary getaway, designed by Seattle architect Arne Bystrom, is full of light from lofty windows. The focus of the home is a 30-foot-high native plant–filled atrium and a sunken living room with a wood-burning fireplace. For a staggering $450 a night, two can have use of the entire luxuriously furnished house and its 14 acres of woods. There are hammocks, benches, and a deck with a hot tub high on the cliff. The elfish Sea Cliff Cottage is more modestly priced ($195) and includes a queen-sized feather bed, kitchenette, and deck overlooking the water. *$$$$; no credit cards; checks OK; 2-night min; wink@whidbey.com; www.cliffhouse.net; Bush Point Rd to Windmill Rd.*

Greenbank

Here on the narrowest part of the island, stop by **WHIDBEY'S GREENBANK FARM** (765 E Wonn Rd; 360/678-7700, *www.greenbankfarm.com*), at one time the largest loganberry farm in the country. You can taste wines, browse the wine shop, which specializes in small wineries of the Northwest, or rest a while in **WHIDBEY PIES CAFE** over coffee and a slice of loganberry pie. The grounds have picnicking spots and trails for walking.

LODGINGS

Guest House Log Cottages / ★★

24371 HWY 525, GREENBANK; 360/678-3115 We love this place, partly because playing house here fulfills long-lost storybook dreams. Six dwellings set in a woodland-fringed clearing include the pine-log

Tennessee Cottage with a king-sized feather bed and river-rock fireplace. Comparatively modest and less expensive, but just as cozy, is the Farm Guest Cottage. Everybody's favorite is the Lodge, a $325-a-night log home for two at the edge of a spring-fed pond; a tall stone fireplace plays center stage in a space that combines the old (a wood stove) with the new (a dishwasher). Breakfast makings are left in the fully equipped kitchens. All accommodations have TVs and VCRs (the video library boasts 500 flicks), and whirlpool spas for two. An outdoor pool is seasonally heated. No smoking, pets, or children over 4 months old. *$$$; DIS, MC, V; checks OK; guesthse@whidbey.net; www.guesthouselogcottages.com; 1 mile south of Greenbank.*

Coupeville

The second-oldest incorporated town in the state dates back to the mid-1850s; no wonder the town has a strict agenda of historical preservation. Coupeville's downtown consists of a handful of gift and antique shops and several restaurants. **ISLAND COUNTY HISTORICAL MUSEUM** (NW Alexander St and Front St; 360/678-3310; *www.islandhistory.org*) tells the story of Whidbey Island's early days. Community events include the **COUPEVILLE ARTS & CRAFTS FESTIVAL** the second weekend in August, and March's **PENN COVE MUSSEL FESTIVAL**; for information, contact the **CENTRAL WHIDBEY CHAMBER OF COMMERCE** (302 N Main St; 360/678-5434; *www.centralwhidbeychamber.com*).

   TOBY'S 1890 TAVERN (8 NW Front St; 360/678-4222) is a good spot for burgers, beer, mussels, and a game of pool. Homemade breads, pies, soups, and salads make **KNEAD & FEED** (4 NW Front St; 360/678-5431) a worthy stop; and real coffee lives at **GREAT TIMES** (12 NW Front St; 360/678-5358), a waterfront coffee house and café with light meals. Gourmets can't miss **BAYLEAF** (901 Grace St; 360/678-6603; *www.bayleaf.us*), a tiny wine and cheese specialty shop and deli.

   An extra bike lane follows Engle Road 3 miles south of Coupeville to **FORT CASEY STATE PARK** (360/678-4519; *www.parks.wa.gov/parks/*), a decommissioned fort with splendid gun mounts, a lighthouse, beaches, and commanding bluffs. Explore the magnificent bluff and beach at the nearby 17,000-acre **EBEY'S LANDING NATIONAL HISTORIC RESERVE** and **FORT EBEY STATE PARK** (360/678-4636). The **KEYSTONE FERRY** (888/808-7977 in WA; 206/464-6400 outside WA; *www.wsdot.wa.gov/ferries/*) connecting Whidbey to Port Townsend on the Olympic Peninsula leaves from Admiralty Head, just south of Fort Casey.

RESTAURANTS

The Oystercatcher / ★★★

   901 GRACE ST, COUPEVILLE; 360/678-0683 The menu here is as small as the size of this delightful pocket bistro overlooking Coupeville and Penn Cove might suggest. Yet chef-owner Susan Vanderbeek (who honed her skills at Seattle's Campagne restaurant) serves up simply delicious offerings that could include an appetizer of tender, sautéed Blau oysters with basil-lemon mayonnaise or an entrée of pan-roasted chicken with chanterelle mushrooms, onions, and bacon, and a porcini glaze. Always, there is a fresh catch on the menu. Desserts, as Vanderbeek says, are "at the whim of the chef." *$$; AE, MC, V; checks OK; dinner Wed–Sat; reservations recommended; beer and wine; downtown.* &

LODGINGS

Anchorage Inn / ★

807 N MAIN ST, COUPEVILLE; 360/376-8282 OR 877/230-1313 A modern Victorian, the Anchorage offers moderately priced lodgings on Coupeville's Main St. Six rooms have private baths; we especially like the water-view room with the four-poster king-sized bed, the room in the turret, and the top-floor Crow's Nest suite with fireplace. All rooms have TVs, VCRs, and cable. Full breakfast (included) is served in the antique-filled dining room. *$$; DIS, MC, V; checks OK; crowsnest@anchorage-inn.com; www.anchorage-inn.com; on Main St.*

Captain Whidbey Inn / ★★

2072 W CAPTAIN WHIDBEY INN RD, COUPEVILLE; 360/678-4097 OR 800/366-4097 This handsome 1907 inn on Penn Cove, built of sturdy madrona logs, is a Northwest institution. In such a beloved place, history sometimes outranks comfort; the thin walls seem to talk, sniffle, and sneeze. Upstairs, 12 small, original rooms (two are suites) have sinks and share two bathrooms, one for each gender. Avoid rooms above the bar unless you're planning to be up until closing time. Four furnished cabins include fireplaces and baths, and three newer cottages have full kitchens, fireplaces, two bedrooms, and hot tubs. Best bets are 13 lagoon rooms with private baths and inlet views. Feather beds and down comforters grace all beds and rooms are decorated in light and airy tones. Public rooms include a lantern-lit dining room, warm-weather deck, woodsy bar, well-stocked library, and folksy fireplace lobby. The restaurant features Penn Cove mussels (you're looking out at the mussel beds), fresh seafood, and other Northwest seasonal ingredients. New restaurant owners (the Stone family still owns the inn itself) are scheduling more private functions; you may find it difficult to simply drop by on a Saturday afternoon for an appetizer and wine on the deck, so call in advance. *$$; AE, DIS, MC, V; local checks OK; info@captainwhidbey.com; www.captainwhidbey.com; off Madrona Wy.*

Fort Casey Inn / ★

1124 S ENGLE RD, COUPEVILLE; 360/678-8792 OR 866/661-6604 Built in 1909 as officers' quarters for nearby Fort Casey, this row of nine houses offers tidy, no-frills accommodations with a historical bent and touches of patriotic memorabilia. Houses are divided into two-bedroom duplexes with fully equipped kitchens (coffee is provided, but bring your own breakfast fixings). Garrison Hall, with a small reception area and its own private bedroom and bath, can be rented for weddings or private parties. The inn welcomes kids. It's a 10-minute walk to the beach and there's plenty to explore in Fort Casey State Park, the bird sanctuary at Crockett Lake, or nearby Ebey's Landing National Historic Reserve. *$$–$$$; MC, V; checks OK; stay@fortcaseyinn.com; www.fortcaseyinn.com; 2 miles south of Coupeville.*

Oak Harbor

Named for the thriving Garry oak trees, Oak Harbor is Whidbey's largest city and home to **NAVAL AIR STATION WHIDBEY ISLAND,** a large air base for electronic attack, patrol, and reconnaissance squadrons as well as Navy Search and Rescue; group tours are currently limited on a case-by-case basis by reservation (360/257-2286). For the most part, Oak Harbor is engulfed in new and retired military folk. Kids at heart should visit **BLUE FOX DRIVE-IN THEATER AND BRATTLAND GO-KARTS** (1403 Monroe Landing Rd; 360/675-5667; *www.bluefoxdrivein.com*), 2 miles south of Oak Harbor.

RESTAURANTS

Kasteel Franssen / ★

33575 HWY 20 (AULD HOLLAND INN), OAK HARBOR; 360/675-0724 Classically trained chef Scott Fraser has maintained Kasteel Franssen's solid reputation for fine dining featuring seafood and game. Expect the unexpected—ostrich, for example. Or try a Northwest version of Hawaiian *laulau* with red snapper, prawns, scallops, and julienne vegetables all steamed in ti leaves. Fraser also serves delicious, lean buffalo short ribs, a favorite of "Galloping Gourmet" television chef Graham Kerr, who sometimes visits. Catch live music Thursdays and most Saturdays. The restaurant is a delightful surprise within the Auld Holland Inn, owned and operated by Joe and Elisa Franssen. A shade close to the highway, the motel with its trademark windmill has a regal European feel; some upper-story rooms have antiques; six have private hot tubs. There's a tennis court, hot tub, outdoor pool, and children's play area. Continental breakfast included. *$$; AE, DIS, DC, MC, V; local checks only; dinner every day (Mon–Sat in winter); full bar; reservations recommended; www.auld hollandinn.com; ¼ mile north of Oak Harbor, 8 miles south of Deception Pass.*

Deception Pass State Park

Beautiful, treacherous **DECEPTION PASS**, at the north end of the island, has a lovely, if crowded, park (41229 Hwy 20; 360/675-2417; *www.parks.wa.gov/alpha*)—the state's most popular—offering 3,600 acres of prime camping land, forests, and beach. The park's centerpiece—a stunning steel bridge connecting Whidbey and Fidalgo Islands—is not to be missed. Park in the highway pullouts at either end and walk across.

The Skagit Valley

To travelers on Interstate 5, the Skagit Valley is little more than a blur—except in spring, when the lush farmlands are brilliantly swathed in daffodils (mid-Mar–mid-Apr), tulips (Apr–early May), and irises (mid-May–mid-June). The countryside is ideal for bicyclists, except during the annual **TULIP FESTIVAL** (360/428-5959; *www.tulipfestival.org*; usually late Mar–early Apr). Mount Vernon is the county seat of this food- and flower-growing valley. For information on **HARVEST**

FESTIVALS—June is strawberries; September, apples—contact the **MOUNT VERNON CHAMBER OF COMMERCE** (117 N 1st St, Ste 4; 360/428-8547; *www.mount vernonchamber.com*).

Mount Vernon

Mount Vernon is the "big city" of surrounding Skagit and Island Counties. Browse **SCOTT'S BOOKSTORE** (121 Freeway Dr; 360/336-6181) in the historical Granary Building at the north end of town, then have a pastry at the **CALICO CUPBOARD** (121-B Freeway Dr; 360/336-3107) next door. Or drop into the **SKAGIT RIVER BREWING CO.** (404 S 3rd St; 360/336-2884) to sample house-brewed suds and pub grub, including pizza from a wood-fired oven. The **CHUCK WAGON DRIVE INN** (800 N 4th St; 360/336-2732) offers 50 different burgers and the world's largest collection of whiskey-bottle cowboys. **PACIONI'S PIZZERIA** (606 S 1st St; 360/336-3314) is a good family stop that serves up award-winning vegetarian pies.

La Conner

La Conner was founded in 1867 by John Conner, a trading-post operator, who named the town after his wife, Louisa A. Conner. Much of what you see today was built before railroads arrived in the late 1880s, when fishing and farming communities on Puget Sound traded largely by water. In an age of conformity, the town became a literal backwater and a haven for nonconformists (Wobblies, WWII COs, McCarthy-era escapees, beatniks, hippies, and bikers), always with a smattering of artists and writers, including Mark Tobey, Morris Graves, Guy Anderson, and Tom Robbins.

This long-standing live-and-let-live attitude has allowed the neighboring Native American Swinomish community to contribute to the exceptional cultural richness of La Conner. Merchants here have created a unique American bazaar with shops like **COTTONS** (608 S 1st St; 360/466-5825) with comfortable clothing; **NASTY JACK'S ANTIQUES** (1st and Morris Sts; 360/466-3209; *www.nastyjacksantiques .com*); the **OLIVE SHOPPE** (205 E Morris; 360/466-4101; *oliveshoppe.com*), and **GO OUTSIDE** (111 Morris St; 360/466-4836), a small but choice garden store. If all this shopping leaves you in need of respite, stop by the stylish **LA CONNER BREWING CO** (117 S 1st St; 360/466-1415) for fine ales and tasty wood-fired pizzas. Kids like **WHISKERS CAFE** (128 S 1st St; 360/466-1008), a casual burger stop on the dock.

GACHES MANSION (703 S 2nd St; 360/466-4288; *www.laconnerquilts.com*), home to the not-to-be-missed **QUILT MUSEUM**, is a wonderful example of American Victorian architecture, with period furnishings and a widow's walk that looks out on the entire Skagit Valley. The **MUSEUM OF NORTHWEST ART** (121 S 1st St; 360/466-4446; *www.museumofnwart.org*; open Tues–Sun) focusing on major Northwest artists, is a regional gem with changing exhibits and a small permanent collection. Each November, the community hosts **ARTS ALIVE** (360/466-4778 or 888/642-9284; *www.laconnerchamber.com*), a weekend festival with galleries and specialty stores that showcase the work of modern Northwest artists and artisans.

NO EXPERIENCE NECESSARY

Sea kayaking is an elegant, delightful way to exercise as you explore the waterways, bays, and islands of Puget Sound. Miles of secluded coastline and engaging wildlife—including eagles and other birds, harbor seals, river otters, minke whales, even orcas—guarantee you're never bored. A real plus is that sea kayaking is surprisingly easy, even for novices. All you need is good health, an adventurous spirit, and a good teacher/guide. Half-day or shorter outings help you "get your feet wet." Ambitious overnight trips with provisions are like specialized backpacking/camping trips—by water—and become more of an adventure and an investment.

Several outfitters from Gig Harbor and Vashon Island to Anacortes, Bellingham, and the San Juan Islands offer short or long trips: at **GIG HARBOR KAYAK CENTER** (888/429-2548; *www.clearlight.com/kayak*) you can explore the bay in a few hours or sign up for a guided tour that takes you farther afloat. **VASHON ISLAND KAYAK COMPANY** (206/463-9257; *www.pugetsoundkayak.com*) offers instruction and day trips, as well.

SAN JUAN SAFARIS (San Juan Island; 360/378-6545; *www.sanjuansafaris.com*) trips leave from Roche Harbor and Friday Harbor; ask about whale-watching trips. **SHEARWATER KAYAK TOURS** (Eastsound, Orcas Island; 360/376-4699; *shearwaterkayaks.com*) does half-day and longer trips from Eastsound and Rosario Resort. **MOONDANCE** (Bellingham; 360/738-7664; *moondancekayak.com*) offers half-day and longer outings, including exploring the petroglyphs of Bellingham Bay. With **NORTHERN LIGHTS EXPEDITIONS** (Fairhaven; 800/754-7402, *www.seakayaking.com*), take an extensive trip (with gourmet meals) up the Inside Passage and into western Canada.

—Jena MacPherson

If you come into La Conner via Conway off I-5, stop at **SNOW GOOSE PRODUCE** (on Fir Island Rd; 360/445-6908) for ice cream in a homemade waffle cone. You can buy local produce, specialty food items, fresh seafood, and tulips in spring. You can also buy bulbs and see the spring bloom at 3-acre **ROOZENGARDE**, the demonstration garden for the **WASHINGTON BULB COMPANY** (on Beaver Marsh Rd; 866/488-5477 toll free; *www.tulips.com*). Beware: It is jam-packed in spring.

RESTAURANTS

Calico Cupboard / ★

720 S 1ST ST, LA CONNER (AND BRANCHES); 360/466-4451 The Calico Cupboard tradition of hearty breakfasts and soup-and-sandwich lunches continues—but most folks come for the pastries, such as delicious cinnamon rolls, hot apple dumplings, and cranberry scones. Our advice for avoiding the weekend crowds: buy your goodies from the take-out counter and find a sunny bench by the water. Two other Calicos are in Anacortes (901 Commercial Ave; 360/293-7315) and Mount Vernon (121-B Freeway Dr; 360/336-3107). *$; MC, V; checks OK; breakfast, lunch every day (early dinner Fri–Sat in Mount Vernon); beer and wine; no reservations; on main drag.*

Kerstin's / ★★

505 S 1ST ST, LA CONNER; 360/466-9111 The former Black Swan, with its postage-stamp lower level and upstairs dining room viewing Swinomish Channel, continues to draw raves. Chef and co-owner David Poor (formerly of La Petite in Anacortes) and his wife, Kerstin, a former New York ballet dancer, have lightened up these charming old main street digs. While the menu changes seasonally, count on moist, fall-off-the-bone-tender lamb shank served with cabernet sauce over roasted-garlic risotto, and Samish Island oysters, baked in the shell with garlic cilantro butter and a small kick of Tabasco. The vegetarian special is a savory, layered dish of roasted vegetables including portobello mushrooms, caramelized red onions, and eggplant. A small outdoor deck offers good-weather dining with a channel view. *$$; AE, DC, MC, V; local checks only; lunch, dinner Wed–Mon; full bar; reservations recommended; dpoor@fidalgo.net; east side of 1st St.*

Nell Thorn Restaurant & Pub / ★★

205 WASHINGTON, LA CONNER; 360/466-4261 Newcomer Nell Thorn's, with its focus on local and organic foods and stone-oven artisan breads, is already a local hit. The rustic-elegant charm of the "old favorite" location (the former home of Palmers) in the La Conner Country Inn (see review) is hard to beat. The stylish blackberry walls and French-style floral carpet add comfortable sizzle. Two levels offer dining options to fit your mood: the warm and cozy pub downstairs, or the quieter "loft" upstairs. Start with bread and a warm olive appetizer, or the very popular endive salad with Jonagold apple vinaigrette, and goat cheese rolled in candied walnuts. Chef Casey Schanen's pork tenderloin with dried apricots and rosemary is a delicious entrée, or choose troll-caught salmon or a rack of lamb. For a more casual meal, order the half-pound hamburger on a homemade bun with rainbow relish. Any meal is perfect when you finish off with the signature Skagit Mud Brownie. *$$–$$$; AE, MC, V; breakfast Wed–Sun, dinner Tues–Sat (lunch on a seasonal schedule); full bar; reservations recommended; www.nellthorn.com; one block off 1st St.* &

Palmers at the Lighthouse / ★★

512 S 1ST ST, LA CONNER; 360/466-3147 Thomas and Danielle Palmer's popular eatery (formerly in the La Conner Country Inn) is La Conner's only waterfront fine-dining restaurant. With sage green walls and high-gloss ivory woodwork, the spacious digs have a Nantucket flair enhanced by expansive channel views; there's also a channel-front deck for warm-weather outdoor dining. Regulars love the seasoned, slow-cooked prime rib. Breast of duckling with fresh ginger and raspberry demi-glace shows the kitchen can work just as successfully with more exotic offerings. The restaurant is nonsmoking, but a wine and port bar, with separate entrance and ventilation, allows smoking. *$$; AE, MC, V; local checks OK; lunch, dinner every day; full bar; reservations recommended; left off Morris at 1st St.* &

LODGINGS

The Heron Inn & Watergrass Day Spa / ★★

117 MAPLE AVE, LA CONNER; 360/466-4626 OR 877/883-8899 The Heron is one of the prettiest hostelries in town, with 12 jewel-box rooms. Splurge on Room 31, the Bridal Suite, with a jetted tub and gas fireplace, or Room 32, with gas fireplace, spacious sitting area, and a wonderful view of the Skagit Valley and Cascades. Downstairs is an elegant living room with wing chairs and a formal dining room, where full breakfast is served. Out back, barbecue in the stone fire pit or slip into the hot tub. The day spa (open to inn guests and the public) has two treatment rooms and offers a variety of massages, facials, and skin treatments. *$$; AE, MC, V; checks OK; heroninn@ncia.com; www.theheron.com; edge of town.*

Hotel Planter / ★

715 S 1ST ST, LA CONNER; 360/466-4710 OR 800/488-5409 A hotel since 1907, this Victorian-style brick establishment has known the most famous (and infamous) characters of La Conner's colorful past. Current owner Don Hoskins used his connoisseur's eye and artisan's care to create a tasteful blend of past (original woodwork staircase and entrance) and present (private baths and armoire-hidden TVs in every room). Four of the 12 rooms face the waterfront (and the often noisy main street); four others overlook a garden courtyard (guests reserve time in the hot tub); four have limited views. The staff, well versed on the Skagit Valley, is exemplary. *$$; AE, MC, V; checks OK; hotelplanter@aol.com; www .hotelplanter.com; south end of main street.*

La Conner Country Inn / ★

107 S 2ND ST, LA CONNER; 360/466-3101 OR 888/466-4113 Despite its name, the La Conner Country Inn is more of a classy motel than a true country inn. All 28 rooms have gas fireplaces and country pine furnishings. The inn is especially accommodating to families; rooms with two double beds are generously sized. Complimentary breakfasts are served in the library, where an enormous fieldstone fireplace and comfy couches beckon. *$$; AE, DC, MC, V; checks OK; www .laconnerlodging.com; downtown off Morris St.* &

Skagit Bay Hideaway / ★★

17430 GOLDENVIEW AVE, LA CONNER; 360/466-2262 OR 888/466-2262 A sybaritic and romantic spot, this Northwest shingle-style cottage, designed by architect Earlene Beckes and operated by her and partner Kevin Haberly, is a luxury waterfront hideaway with two 600-square-foot suites sporting minikitchens and double-headed showers. You can watch the sun set over the water from your rooftop spa or enjoy a fire in your own cozy living room. Full breakfast served in your suite. *$$$; AE, DIS, MC, V; checks OK; hideaway@skagitbay.com; www.skagitbay.com; 1¼ miles west of La Conner across Rainbow Bridge.*

White Swan Guest House / ★★

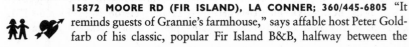

15872 MOORE RD (FIR ISLAND), LA CONNER; 360/445-6805 "It reminds guests of Grannie's farmhouse," says affable host Peter Goldfarb of his classic, popular Fir Island B&B, halfway between the

La Conner exit (at Conway) off Interstate 5 and the town itself. Poplars line the driveway, Adirondack chairs dot the garden, and the grounds are full of perennials. Tranquil farm fields stretch beyond. The house is splashed with warm yellow, salmon, evergreen, and peach wall tones and fabric accents and seems to soak up the sunlight—even in the rain. Pamper yourself with a soak in the large claw-footed tub (three guest rooms share two baths), or curl up on the sofa in front of the woodstove. Dog lovers enjoy meeting Goldfarb's three friendly canines. Goldfarb serves a country continental breakfast of fresh scones or muffins, fruit, and coffee; his wonderful chocolate chip cookies are waiting in the afternoons. Bring binoculars for bird-watching and bikes for touring the island's flat farmlands. A charming guest cottage out back provides an especially private accommodation, great for families or romantics; it has an open first floor with living/dining room and kitchen area, and a queen-bedded room upstairs. *$$; MC, V; checks OK; www.thewhiteswan.com; 6 miles southeast of La Conner, call for directions.*

The Wild Iris Inn / ★★

121 MAPLE AVE, LA CONNER; 360/466-1400 OR 800/477-1400 This romantic 16-room inn with spacious suites is located at the edge of town, giving you the "country" feel of the setting. Nine rooms are deluxe suites featuring gas fireplaces, oversized jetted tubs, and panoramic Cascade and farmland views from decks or balconies. Each room is individually decorated. Most standard rooms face the parking lot and seem a bit cramped. Breakfast is served in the dining room, to your order. *$$$; AE, MC, V; checks OK; www.wildiris.com; edge of town.* &

Chuckanut Drive

This famous stretch of road (Hwy 11) between Burlington or Bow and Bellingham was once part of the Pacific Highway; now it is one of the prettiest drives in the state, curving along the Chuckanut Mountains and overlooking Samish Bay and its many islands. If you're in the driver's seat, however, you'll have to keep your eyes on the narrow and winding road. Take the Chuckanut Drive exit (exit 231) off Interstate 5 northbound (or follow 12th St south out of Bellingham, exit 250 from I-5).

As you wend north to Bellingham through bucolic communities, it's hard to believe Interstate 5 is only minutes away. Removed from traffic and shopping malls, you'll discover orchards, oyster beds, slow-moving tractors, and fields of mustard. For an interesting detour, visit the **PADILLA BAY NATIONAL ESTUARINE RESEARCH RESERVE AND BREAZEALE INTERPRETIVE CENTER** (1043 Bayview-Edison Rd; 360/428-1558; *www.inlet.geol.sc.edu/PDB*; open Wed–Sun 10am–5pm). Learn about the Padilla Bay estuary through displays, saltwater tanks, and a library. A 2-mile shoreline trail begins a short drive south of the center. Nearby **BAYVIEW STATE PARK** (360/757-0227; *www.parks.wa.gov/parkpage*) has overnight camping and beach-front picnic sites, perfect for winter bird-watching.

Permanent and part-time residents inhabit **SAMISH ISLAND**, as do numerous oyster beds. **BLAU OYSTER COMPANY** (11321 Blue Heron Rd; 360/766-6171; *www.blauoyster.com*; open Mon–Sat 8am–5pm; 7 miles west of Edison via

Bayview-Edison Rd and Samish Island Rd) has been selling Samish Bay oysters, clams, and other seafood since 1935; follow signs to the shucking plant. You'll also find oysters, etc., at **TAYLOR SHELLFISH FARMS** (2182 Chuckanut Dr, 360/766-6002; *www.taylorshellfish.com*), open daily in summer. If you're hungry or thirsty as you make your way through Edison, stop at the (smoky) **LONGHORN SALOON & GRILL** (5754 Cains Ct; 360/766-6330; 21 and over) for burgers, steaks, local oysters, crab dinners, and a full-service bar; owner Steve Mains has fancied up the place and the menu (you can now get a hand-cut New York steak with oysters), but you can still get a delicious burger.

    LARRABEE STATE PARK (off Chuckanut Dr; 360/902-8844; *www.parks.wa.gov*; 7 miles south of Bellingham) was Washington's first state park. Beautiful sandstone-sculpted beaches and cliffs provide a backdrop for exploring abundant sea life. Picnic areas and camping are good. The **INTERURBAN TRAIL**, once the electric rail route from Bellingham to Mount Vernon, is now a 5-mile trail connecting three parks on Chuckanut Drive: Larrabee State Park to Arroyo Park to Fairhaven Park (in Bellingham). Formerly a nude beach, **TEDDY BEAR COVE** (*www.co.whatcom .wa.us/parks/*) is a lovely secluded beach along **CHUCKANUT DRIVE** (*www.chuckanut drive.com*) just south of the Bellingham city limits. Watch for a parking lot on the east side of the road.

RESTAURANTS

The Oyster Bar on Chuckanut Drive / ★★★

🌲 **2578 CHUCKANUT DR, BOW; 360/766-6185** This famed Chuckanut Drive restaurant has been spiffed up over the years, but little can improve upon the spectacular view of Samish Bay, gourmet fare, and award-winning wines—they're still tops. The frequently changing menu focuses on seafood and local bounty. You'll find panfried yearling oysters on the lunch menu; for dinner start with a half-dozen raw oysters fresh from the bay. Entrées might be a generous cedar-planked fillet of wild salmon or a perfectly cooked filet mignon. A creamy cheesecake is often on the menu—try the chef's sorbet trio for a light finish. No children under 10, please. *$$$; AE, MC, V; local checks only; lunch and dinner every day; beer and wine; reservations recommended; www.theoysterbaronchuckanutdrive .com; north of Bow.*

The Rhododendron Cafe / ★★

5521 CHUCKANUT DR, BOW; 360/766-6667 The Rhododendron Cafe is the perfect starting or ending point for a scenic trek on Chuckanut Drive. It may not have the view of other eateries, but the commitment to making everything from scratch—including basil and shallot buns for sandwiches—makes this a delicious stop. Once the site of the Red Crown Service Station in the early 1900s, the Rhody serves homemade soup (chowder is excellent) and a tasty portobello burger. Lightly breaded and panfried Samish Bay oysters are delicious for lunch or dinner. The latter also brings grilled pork loin and chicken Parmesan. A nightly seafood stew has an ethnic theme—check the blackboard or the Web site for the theme of the month. *$$; AE, MC, V; checks OK; breakfast Sat–Sun, lunch, dinner Wed–Sun (closed late Nov–Jan); beer and wine; www.rhodycafe.com; reservations recommended; at Bow–Edison junction.*

LODGINGS

Benson Farmstead Bed & Breakfast / ★

10113 AVON-ALLEN RD, BOW; 360/757-0578 OR 800/441-9814 Once part of a working dairy farm, this 17-room house, surrounded by English-style gardens, is packed with antiques and Scandinavian memorabilia. Four upstairs guest rooms (all with private baths) are outfitted with iron beds and custom quilts. Best are the Wildflowers and the English Garden Rooms. A cottage-style family suite is in the granary out back; there's also a self-contained (stove, fridge, sitting area) suite by the new waterfall gardens in a restored well house. Kids especially like the playroom and the three cats. In the evening, relax in the parlor, sharing Sharon Benson's desserts and coffee. Jerry and Sharon Benson cook a country breakfast. Don't be surprised to hear music in the air; the Bensons are talented pianists and violinists. Ask about their separate La Conner beach-front rental. *$$; MC, V; checks OK; bensonfarmstead@hotmail.com; www.bbhosts.com/bensonbnb; exit 232 west off I-5.*

Samish Point by the Bay / ★★

4465 SAMISH POINT RD, BOW; 360/766-6610 OR 800/916-6161 Theresa and Herb Goldston's tranquil getaway on their estatelike property at Samish Island's west end offers miles of wooded trails, a beach, mountain views, and solitude. Their three-bedroom cottage has a gas fireplace in the cozy living room and a hot tub on the back deck. It accommodates two to six (rates based on party size). The kitchen is stocked with continental breakfast fixings. *$$$; AE, MC, V; checks OK; tg@samishpoint.com; www.samishpoint.com; on Samish Island.*

Bellingham and Area

Bellingham, the hub of northwestern Washington, is situated where the Nooksack River flows into Bellingham Bay. This community—full of fine old houses, award-winning university architecture, stately streets, and lovely parks—has been rediscovered in recent years. A development on Squalicum Harbor, called **BELLWETHER**, with a park, outside amphitheater, shops, galleries, restaurants, and a mini-grand hotel (see Hotel Bellwether review in Lodgings section) finally takes advantage of the town's waterfront location.

WESTERN WASHINGTON UNIVERSITY (on Sehome Hill south of downtown; 360/650-3000; *www.wwu.edu*) is a fine expression of the spirit of Northwest architecture: warm materials, formal echoes of European styles, and respect for context and the natural backdrop. The visitor-parking kiosk on the south side of campus has maps of the university's outdoor sculpture collection (*outdoorsculpture.wwu.edu*).

The Old Town around Commercial and W Holly Streets hosts antique and junk shops and some decent eateries. The **BELLINGHAM FARMERS MARKET** (downtown at Railroad Ave and Chestnut St, Sat, Apr–Oct; in Historic Fairhaven at 11th and Mill Sts, afternoons June–Sept; 360/647-2060; *www.bellinghamfarmers.org*) features produce—including the county's famed berry harvests—fresh seafood, herbs, flowers, and crafts.

The **WHATCOM MUSEUM OF HISTORY AND ART** (121 Prospect St; 360/676-6981; *www.whatcommuseum.org*) is a four-building campus. The main building is a massive 1892 Romanesque structure used as a city hall until 1940. It has permanent exhibits on historic Bellingham as well as an adventurous exhibition schedule. Check out the **SYRE EDUCATION CENTER** (201 Prospect St) down the block, focusing on Native American culture, and the **WHATCOM CHILDREN'S MUSEUM** (227 Prospect St) a few doors farther north. Across the street, the **ARCO BUILDING** has changing art and history displays. One block from the main museum is **HENDERSON BOOKS** (116 Grand Ave; 360/734-6855), a 7,000-square-foot store with 250,000 volumes of used books in excellent shape (the staff is fanatical about the condition of the books) and a good collection of art books. A short walk away is the **AMERICAN MUSEUM OF RADIO** (1312 Bay St; 360/738-3886; *www.american radiomuseum.org*), a delight for young and old. Also downtown is **GREENHOUSE** (1235 Cornwall Ave; 360/676-1161), an eclectic home-furnishings shop.

The summer **BELLINGHAM MUSIC FESTIVAL** (360/676-5997 or 800/335-5550; *www.bellinghamfestival.org*; late July–mid-Aug) has quickly become an institution, featuring more than two weeks of orchestral, chamber, and jazz performances. The **MOUNT BAKER THEATRE** (104 N Commercial St; 360/734-6080; *www.mount bakertheatre.com*), built in 1927 and renovated in 1995, is home to the **WHATCOM SYMPHONY ORCHESTRA** (*www.whatcomsymphony.com*) and hosts other concerts, plays, films, and special events.

SEHOME HILL ARBORETUM (Bellingham Parks and Recreation; 360/676-6985; *www.ac.wwu.edu/~sha/*), adjacent to WWU campus, sports more than 3 miles of trails, with prime views of the city, Bellingham Bay, and the San Juans. **WHATCOM FALLS PARK** (1401 Electric Ave; 360/676-6985) has more than 5 miles of trails overlooking several scenic falls, a fish hatchery, picnic sites, and more. **BIG ROCK GARDEN PARK** (2900 Sylvan St, near Lake Whatcom; 360/676-6985; Apr–Oct) is a wonderful woodland site with a vast array of azaleas, rhododendrons, and Japanese maples that focuses on outdoor garden art and sculpture. **LAKE WHATCOM RAILWAY** (on Hwy 9 at Wickersham; 360/595-2218; *www.lakewhatcomrailway.com*) makes scenic runs on July and August Saturdays using an old Northern Pacific engine. **MOUNT BAKER VINEYARDS** (11 miles east of Bellingham on Mount Baker Hwy/Hwy 542; 360/592-2300; open every day), in a cedar-sided, sky-lit facility, specializes in lesser-known varietals such as Müller Thurgau and Madeleine Angevine, as well as more familiar chardonnays, cabs, merlots, and syrahs. The **SKI-TO-SEA RACE** (360/734-1330; *www.bellingham.com/skitosea/*) attracts teams from all over the world to an annual seven-event relay on Memorial Day weekend.

Bellingham has a variety of eateries to try. **BOUNDARY BAY BREWERY** (1107 Railroad St; 360/647-5593) downtown is a popular hangout and serves a delicious lamb burger and other tasty pub grub. French bistro–style **CAFÉ TOULOUSE** (114 W Magnolia St, 360/733-8996) is well known for their huge, well-orchestrated breakfasts including dishes such as Greek and provençal frittatas or huevos rancheros. Ethnic favorites are **INDIA GRILL** (1215½ Cornwall Ave; 360/714-0314), with Northern Indian cuisine, a long list of vegetarian choices, and a generous, inexpensive lunch buffet; and **LEMON GRASS CAFÉ** (111 N Samish Wy; 360/676-4102), serving Thai food.

South of the university, **FAIRHAVEN**, a once-separate town that was the result of a short-lived railroad boom in 1889–93, retains its old-time charm and offers plenty of exploring. The **MARKETPLACE** (Harris and 12th Sts), the grand dame of the attractive old buildings, was restored in 1988 and houses shops and dining options. The district is rich with diversions: crafts galleries, coffeehouses, bookstores, a charming garden/nursery emporium, and a lively evening scene. **VILLAGE BOOKS** (1200 11th St; 360/671-2626; *www.villagebooks.com*) carries an eclectic mix of new and used best-selling, children's, and regional titles and hosts many author readings and special events. Downstairs is **THE COLOPHON CAFÉ** (360/647-0092; *www.colophoncafe.com*; also downtown at 308 W Champion St, 360/676-6257), known for its African peanut soup and real cream pies. **TONY'S COFFEES** (1101 Harris Ave, 360/738-4710) is the local beanmeister; an adjacent café serves breakfast and lunch. Stop at the **ARCHER ALE HOUSE** (1212 10th St; 360/647-7002) for a selection of brews, including hard-to-find Belgian beers, and tasty pizza and focaccia.

The cruise terminal, a handsome port facility in Fairhaven, houses the southern terminus of the **ALASKA MARINE HIGHWAY SYSTEM** (355 Harris Ave; 360/676-8445 or 800/642-0066; *www.dot.state.ak.us/amhs/*); here travelers begin the long coastal journey through Alaska's famed Inside Passage. Also from here (in summer), the **SAN JUAN ISLAND COMMUTER** (888/734-8180; *islandcommuter.com*) offers daily sightseeing and whale-watching cruises to San Juan Island, and associate **VICTORIA SAN JUAN CRUISES** (360/738-8099 or 800/443-4552, *www.whales .com*) offers overnight cruise and whale-watching packages to Victoria. The **AMTRAK** (*www.amtrak.com*) station is nearby.

RESTAURANTS

The Calumet Restaurant / ★★

113 E MAGNOLIA ST, BELLINGHAM; 360/733-3331 Art on exposed brick walls, a freestanding fireplace, and soft sculpture fish on the ceiling soften the old rectangular space of this casual downtown bistro that claims fans of all ages. Delicious meal choices are white fish tacos, a lamb burger with marinated tomatoes, a house made gnocchi, and panfried oysters. An impressively stocked bar (more than 30 types of vodka) and an extensive fancy drinks menu make this a great after-theater destination. If the menu seems a bit pricey, take heart—the weekday happy-hour menu (4–6pm) is a real deal. *$$–$$$; AE, MC, V; checks OK; lunch Mon–Fri, dinner daily; full bar; reservations recommended; at Railroad Ave.*

Coppa Mediterranean Bistro / ★★

1224 HARRIS AVE, FAIRHAVEN; 360/312-5050 This new Fairhaven bistro has already become a neighborhood hangout. The delicious mix of Mediterranean foods—dishes from Spain, Italy, Turkey, Portugal, and Morocco—is generous and well priced. Come here with friends and order the tapas sampler (four selections, including hummus and tabbouleh, that you scoop up with boats of romaine or spread onto tender pita bread) and a very thin pizza-like flatbread (the tomato sauce, pine nuts, and fresh mozzarella is excellent). No bottle on the list of 30 wines is more than $20. With tile floors and crisp blue-and-white-tile-topped tables (owner Fahri Ugurlu brought the tiles from Turkey) you'd expect noise, and there is: laughter and lively conversation. The low ceiling and lounge music favorites like "Mr. Saturday Night" on the stereo system soften the sounds; you're simply aware of a happy buzz that resonates from contentment. *$$; DIS, MC, V; local checks only; dinner daily; full bar; reservations for 6 or more; www.coppabistro .com; at 13th St.* &

Pacific Cafe / ★★★

100 N COMMERCIAL ST, BELLINGHAM; 360/647-0800 The Pacific Café continues its reputation as a sparkling gem for gastronomes. Tucked into the Mount Baker Theatre building, its ambiance is civilized and modern—with abstract watercolors and quiet jazz—and service is superb. Co-owner Robert Fong's Hawaiian background and years of travel in Europe, India, China, and Malaysia influence the sophisticated menu. Fong has fish flown in directly from the Honolulu fish auction and seared ahi poke (mildly spiced seared tuna on greens) is a specialty. New on the menu is organic Oregon beef filet mignon, grilled with a Shiraz sauce. Expect wonderful desserts from pastry chef Wayne Kent, such as *lilikoi* (passion fruit) sorbet, butter-pecan ice cream, and hand-dipped Valrhona chocolate truffles. Quality vintages reflect a fine-tuned palate. Check on special wine dinners and food events. *$$; AE, MC, V; local checks only; lunch Mon–Fri, dinner Mon–Sat; beer and wine; reservations recommended; www.thepacificcafe.com; near Champion St.* &

Pepper Sisters / ★★

1055 N STATE ST, BELLINGHAM; 360/671-3414 "We really try to rock the house," says owner Susan Albert about the innovative, Southwestern fare served at Pepper Sisters. That attitude combined with cheerful, knowledgeable service, a great location in a vintage brick building, and a wide-awake kitchen have made the restaurant an institution. Seafood specials mix local provender with a "high desert" approach; the marinated, grilled king-salmon taco on a soft blue-corn tortilla with accents of kalamata olives, garlic, chipotle aioli, and fresh arugula is wildly popular; it's a blackboard special, so try it when you see it. The kitchen shows the same verve with traditional favorites: delicious chiles rellenos are prepared with herbed chèvre, jack cheese, cilantro, and blue cornmeal crust. A daily vegetarian special is also offered. For dessert, count on delicious traditional flan. *$; MC, V; checks OK; dinner Tues–Sun; beer and wine; reservations for 5 or more; south of downtown.* &

LODGINGS

Best Western Heritage Inn / ★★

151 E MCLEOD RD, BELLINGHAM; 360/647-1912 OR 888/333-2080 Three tasteful, shuttered, and dormered structures nestle amid a small grove of trees adjacent to Interstate 5 and a conglomeration of malls. This Best Western is one of the most professionally run hotels in the area. Rooms have a classic elegance with wing chairs in rich fabrics and cherry wood furnishings. Thoughtful touches include free newspapers, a guest laundry facility, an outdoor pool (in season), and indoor hot tub. Request a room away from the freeway.

European-style continental breakfast is included. *$$; AE, DC, DIS, MC, V; checks OK; heritageinnbham@aol.com; www.bestwestern.com/heritageinnbellingham; exit 256 off I-5.*

The Chrysalis Inn & Spa / ★★★

804 10TH ST, BELLINGHAM; 360/756-1005 OR 888/808-0005 Perched on the water just north of Fairhaven, this Northwest Craftsman-style hotel is a stylish, romantic retreat. All 43 guest rooms (9 are luxury suites) have oversized soaking or jetted tubs, window seats, fireplaces, and water views. We like the corner suites—pricey, but you could move in and be happy ever after. Spend an afternoon in the spa. Dine in the onsite restaurant, Fino's, a sophisticated wine bar/restaurant with terrific water views (binoculars are a nice amenity), and creative food beautifully presented—though with a lot of wood, metal, and glass, it can be noisy. A breakfast buffet is included and served in Fino's. Secure underground parking is available for guests. *$$$–$$$$; AE, DC, DIS, MC, V; checks OK; info@thechrysalisinn.com; www.thechrysalisinn.com; Old Fairhaven Pkwy exit off I-5.* &

Fairhaven Village Inn / ★★

1200 10TH ST, BELLINGHAM; 360/733-1311 OR 877/733-1100 This Victorian-style boutique hotel offers a great location in the heart of historic Fairhaven. Twenty-two large guest rooms have bay or park views. Though not individually decorated, rooms are light filled and appointed with traditional-style cherry wood furnishings, feather beds, and muted natural toned comforters. The second-story terrace overlooks the bay and cruise terminal. Small conference rooms are also available. A hearty continental breakfast is included. *$$–$$$; AE, DC, DIS, MC, V; checks OK; guestservices@fairhavenvillageinn.com; www.fairhavenvillageinn.com; exit 250 from I-5 and follow Old Fairhaven Pkwy.* &

Hotel Bellwether / ★★★★

1 BELLWETHER WY, BELLINGHAM; 360/392-3100 OR 877/411-1200 Bellingham now has a perfect small "grand" hotel located in a perfect spot. Many of the 68 rooms are on the waterfront overlooking Bellingham Bay and have terrific sunset views from private balconies or patios. Rooms have gas fireplaces, soaking tubs that can take in the view or be closed off (they also have separate glassed-in showers), and are richly decorated with furniture imported from Italy. A turndown service provides fine chocolates on your Hungarian down pillow (the dreamy beds are made up with Austrian bed linens). The dramatic Lighthouse Suite, a few steps from the hotel, offers three levels of seclusion and comes with its own private butler, champagne, and caviar. The hotel's friendly Harborside Bistro (877/411-1200 or 360/392-3200; lunch, dinner daily) offers views and casual fine dining, focusing on Northwest seafood and French-style steaks; breakfast is served in the smaller, more intimate Compass Room. Enjoy a libation and watch the sun sink in the west from the Sunset Lounge. If you arrive by boat, you can "park" at the hotel's private dock. Security car parking is included. *$$–$$$$; AE, DC, DIS, MC, V; local checks only; reservations@hotelbellwether.com; www.hotelbellwether.com; exit 256 off I-5, turn right on Squalicum Wy.* &

Schnauzer Crossing / ★★★

4421 LAKEWAY DR, BELLINGHAM; 360/734-2808 OR 800/562-2808 Donna and Monty McAllister's lovely contemporary home in a garden setting overlooking Lake Whatcom is a stalwart on the Bellingham bed-and-breakfast scene—what's better, the experience here is consistently top notch. Maybe that's because it's a labor of love. You'll see it in the extra touches—such as the miniature teahouse that Monty handcrafted and set in an idyllic glade in their Japanese-style garden. The grounds also include a meditation garden, wisteria arbor, hammock, koi pond, and hot tub. (Ask to hear the story of the artful new doghouse in the garden.) Three accommodations are available. The spacious and elegant Garden Suite, with fireplace, Jacuzzi, TV/VCR, and the separate cottage overlooking the lake are most luxurious. Guests staying in the simpler Queen Room enjoy the surroundings without the pricey amenities. All guests enjoy extra-thick towels, bathrobes and slippers, and gorgeous flowers year-round. Donna is known for her breakfasts—such as baked oatmeal served with ice cream "snowballs," hazelnut waffles, or a parfait of summer fruits from the garden. Children are welcome (breakfast is staggered for guests seeking quiet). The three resident Schnauzers are the top dogs here, so please leave yours at home. *$$$–$$$$; DIS, MC, V; checks OK; schnauzerx@aol.com; www.schnauzercrossing.com; exit 253 off I-5.*

Lummi Island

Located just off Gooseberry Point northwest of Bellingham, Lummi is one of the most overlooked islands of the ferry-accessible San Juans. It echoes the days when the San Juan Islands were a hidden treasure, visited only by folks seeking bucolic surroundings. Private ownership has locked up most of this pastoral isle, so you won't find state parks or resorts. To stretch your limbs, bring bikes and enjoy the quiet country roads. Plan ahead; dining options are sparse. Not far from the ferry landing, the **BEACH STORE CAFÉ** (2200 N Nugent Rd; 360/758-2233) is an island gathering place for pizza or seafood chowder and special reef-caught pink salmon and chips, but don't overlook daily specials. The **WILLOWS INN** (see review) has a small café with espresso drinks, soups, and sandwiches.

Lummi is serviced by the tiny **WHATCOM CHIEF FERRY** (360/676-6759 or 360/676-6730; *www.co.whatcom.wa.us/publicworks/ferry*), which leaves Gooseberry Point at 10 minutes past the hour from 7am until midnight (more frequently on weekdays). It's easy to find (follow signs to Lummi Island from I-5, north of Bellingham), cheap ($5 round-trip for a car and two passengers), and quick (six-minute crossing). The ferry returns from Lummi on the hour.

LODGINGS

The Willows Inn / ★★☆

2579 W SHORE DR, LUMMI ISLAND; 360/758-2620 OR 888/294-2620 Owners Judy Olsen and Riley Starks, who also own nearby Nettles Farm, preside over this old favorite inn, now a country-casual food resort. Weekend dinners and

Sunday brunch are served, and the Willows has a small espresso café and pub, The Taproot, with three Northwest beers on tap; it's a local hot spot in the afternoons. Cooking classes are offered (check Web site). In the main house, four guest rooms with private baths include two on the main floor with private entrances. A small cottage for two has a tiny kitchen and a terrific view; a two-bedroom guesthouse looks out to the water from a deck. For couples traveling together, the last is our favorite for its gas fireplace, whirlpool tub, and natural woodsy feel. Kitchens are stocked with basics. The decor is farm-style chic, sometimes spare but always restful. Ask about picnic boat excursions from the inn to tiny nearby islands. *$$$; AE, MC, V; checks OK; innkeeper@willows-inn.com; www. willows-inn.com; north on Nugent Rd for 3½ miles.* &

Lynden

This tidy community, with many immaculate yards and colorful gardens, adopted a Dutch theme in tribute to its early settlers. To explore this heritage, visit the **DUTCH BAKERY** (421 Front St; 360/354-3911), a great place to find traditional pastries. **HOLLANDIA** restaurant (655 Front St; 360/354-4133), in Lynden's unusual shopping mall (there's a stream running through it), offers a taste of the Netherlands with dishes such as schnitzel and *groentesoep* (firm, tasty meatballs in a luscious vegetable broth). The **DUTCH VILLAGE INN** (655 Front St; 360/354-4440) is a bed-and-breakfast with lodging in a windmill; the six rooms are named after Dutch provinces.

Visit the charming **PIONEER MUSEUM** (217 Front St; 360/354-3675; *www .lyndenpioneermuseum.com*), full of local memorabilia, antique buggies, and motorcars. Come in December for the community's elaborate show of holiday lights (*www.lynden.org*).

Golfers take note—east of town is **HOMESTEAD FARMS GOLF RESORT** (115 E Homestead Blvd; 360/354-1196 or 800/354-1196; *www.homesteadfarmsgolf .com*), an upscale 18-hole golf course with clubhouse and restaurant, and condominium (including some deluxe) accommodations; golf packages are available. The resort's 30-unit hotel is slated for completion in late 2004.

Blaine

The northernmost city along the Interstate 5 corridor, Blaine is the state's most popular—and most beautiful—border crossing into British Columbia. Home to the grand white **INTERNATIONAL PEACE ARCH MONUMENT**, which spans the U.S.–Canadian border, the surrounding park borders on Boundary Bay and is filled with lovely gardens and sculptures. Each June there's a Peace Arch celebration.

LODGINGS

Resort Semiahmoo / ★★★

 9565 SEMIAHMOO PKWY, BLAINE; 360/318-2000 OR 800/770-7992 Nestled on a 1,100-acre wildlife preserve on Semi-ah-moo Spit, Resort Semiahmoo offers golf, acres of wooded trails, waterfront, and views west to the sea and the San Juans and east to Drayton Harbor. Amenities include a salon, fitness center, spa, heated indoor/outdoor pool, kayaking and paddle boating, racquetball, tennis, and more. Comfortably spacious rooms have classy earth-tone furnishings. Most of the 198 rooms (12 are suites) have water views and fireplaces; some overlook the parking lot. Two restaurants (Stars is a fine dining eatery offering breakfast and dinner daily) and a café provide views and a range of culinary alternatives. The Arnold Palmer–designed golf course has long, unencumbered fairways surrounded by dense woods and lovely sculptural sand traps. Adjacent is a convention center in revamped cannery buildings. **DRAYTON HARBOR MARITIME MUSEUM** (1218 4th St, Blaine; 360/332-5742; *www.draytonharbormaritime.org*) is nearby. *$$$–$$$$; AE, DC, DIS, MC, V; checks OK; info@semiahmoo.com; www.semiahmoo.com; exit 270 off I-5.*

Anacortes and the San Juan Islands

There are 743 islands at low tide and 428 at high tide; 172 have names, 60 are populated, and only 4 have major ferry service. The San Juans are varied, remote, and breathtakingly beautiful. They lie in the rain shadow of the Olympic Mountains; most receive half the rainfall of Seattle. Of the main islands, three—Lopez, Orcas, and San Juan—have lodgings, eateries, and some beautiful parks.

ACCESS AND INFORMATION

The most obvious and cost-effective way to reach the San Juans is via the **WASHINGTON STATE FERRIES** (206/464-6400 or 800/843-3779; *www.wsdot.wa.gov/ferries/*), which run year-round from Anacortes (see Anacortes section below). The sparsely populated islands are overrun in summer, and getting your car on a ferry out of Anacortes can mean a three-hour-plus wait. Bring a good book—or park the car and board with a bike. Money-saving tip: Cars pay only westbound. If you plan to visit more than one island, arrange to go to the farthest first (San Juan) and work your way east.

Other summer options for those who don't bring a car include the high-speed **VICTORIA CLIPPER** (2701 Alaskan Wy, Seattle; 206/448-5000; *www.victoriaclipper.com*), which travels daily in season from downtown Seattle to Friday Harbor; whale-watching trips and accommodation packages are also offered. **KENMORE AIR** (425/486-1257 or 866/435-9524; *www.kenmoreair.com*) schedules five floatplane flights a day during peak season; fewer in off-season. Round-trip flights start at about $165 per person and leave from downtown Seattle at Lake Union and from north Lake Washington; luggage is weight-limited. **WEST ISLE AIR** (800/874-4434; *www.westisleair.com*) offers scheduled daily flights from Boeing Field to the San Juan Islands, Anacortes, and Bellingham.

Anacortes

Anacortes, the gateway to the San Juans, is itself on an island: Fidalgo. Though most travelers rush through on their way to the ferry, this town adorned with colorful, life-sized cutouts of early pioneers is quietly becoming a place that warrants slowing down.

Seafaring folks should poke around **MARINE SUPPLY AND HARDWARE** (202 Commercial Ave; 360/293-3014); established in 1913, it's packed to the rafters with basic and hard-to-find specialty marine items. For the history of Fidalgo Island, visit the **ANACORTES MUSEUM** (1305 8th St; 360/293-1915; *www.anacorteshistory museum.org*). Those who plan to kayak stop by **ISLAND OUTFITTERS** (2403 Commercial Ave; 360/299-2300 or 866/445-7506; *www.seakayakshop.com*), which offers tours out of **CAP SANTE MARINA** (360/293-0694; *portofanacortes.com*). Test a kayak in the harbor, take a lesson, or rent one for a San Juan weekend; reservations necessary.

Casual eateries abound. In fact, a town favorite spot for burgers is **STORK'S** (2821 Commercial Ave; 360/293-7500) in the local bowling alley. Try **GEPPETTO'S** (3320 Commercial Ave; 360/293-5033) for Italian takeout; those with more time head to **GERE-A-DELI** (502 Commercial Ave; 360/293-7383), a friendly hangout with good homemade food in an airy former bank. **CALICO CUPBOARD** (901 Commercial Ave; 360/293-7315) is an offshoot of the popular café/bakery in La Conner known for its cinnamon rolls. In fact, baked goods in this town are plentiful. You'll find artisan breads, fancy cakes, sandwiches, and more at **LA VIE EN ROSE FRENCH BAKERY AND PASTRY SHOP** (418 Commercial Ave; 360/299-9546; *www.laviebakery.com*); and more decadent indulgences at **THE DONUT HOUSE** (2719 Commercial Ave; 360/293-4053), open 24 hours most days. **THE BAKERY AT THE STORE** (919 37th St, near south end of Commercial Ave; 360/293-2851) specializes in huge, diet-killer muffins in irresistible flavors, such as coconut cream pie or peaches 'n' cream; a deli is also on the premises.

WASHINGTON PARK is less than a mile west of the ferry terminal. Here you'll find scenic picnic areas and a paved 2½-mile trail looping through an old-growth forest with great San Juan views. Near the ferry terminal is **SHIP HARBOR INN** (5316 Ferry Terminal Rd; 360/293-5177 or 800/852-8568; *www.shipharborinn .com*), a comfortable mix of older motel-style rooms and cabins with views that makes a good overnight choice if you're aiming for an early ferry.

RESTAURANTS

Bella Isola at Nantucket Inn / ★★

3402 COMMERCIAL AVE, ANACORTES; 360/299-8398 Early in 2004, chef-owner Andy Ferguson and wife Julianne moved their popular Italian eatery from the heart of downtown Anacortes into the main floor of the eye-catching Nantucket Inn and into surroundings more fitting the specials that keep regulars coming back. The setting is new, yet the food is the same delicious Italian that has garnered a loyal following: try *penne con vodka* (penne pasta tossed in a creamy rose sauce with proscuitto and chile-pepper vodka), or the delicious grilled sirloin steak with balsamic glaze and Gorgonzola sauce. Five delightful (some antique-filled) rooms are upstairs. *$$; AE, DC, DIS, MC, V; checks OK; dinner every day; full bar; reservations recommended; as you enter town.*

Billy Ray's / ★

5320 FERRY TERMINAL RD, ANACORTES; 360/588-0491 Locals give Bill Ray, owner of this bistro-style hangout in an old building near the ferry terminal, high marks as a chef. Understandable—his restaurant hits just the right chord of fun, ease, expertise, and good food. The decor is energetic—walls of rich colors and inverted patio umbrellas decorate the ceiling—and the wait staff is cheerful. Soups, salads, pizzas, and fish-and-chips make good lunch choices; curries and more elaborate dishes, including seafood and nightly specials—such as chili-crusted deep sea scallops—show up on the dinner menu. Desserts include slices of chocolate or carrot cake. A good place to head if you have a long ferry wait, it's got a deck for warm-weather dining. *$$; MC, V; checks OK; lunch, dinner every day; beer and wine; reservations recommended; on your right as you approach the ferry terminal.* &

Flounder Bay Cafe / ★

2201 SKYLINE WY, ANACORTES; 360/293-3680 Light-filled and contemporary, this waterside café in Skyline Marina captures the casual and carefree boaters' spirit seductive to us all. Colorful sails overhead contribute to the decor and sense of fun. On your plate, the emphasis is fresh, seasonal, and seafood—choices such as Dungeness crab cakes, Blau oysters, wild salmon, tiger prawns, and almond-coated cod. Many locals believe the café serves the town's best Sunday brunch. Early evening special-price meals and warm-season dinner cruises are offered, too. *$$; AE, DIS, MC, V; local checks only; full bar; reservations recommended on weekends; www.flounderbaycafe.com; at Skyline Marina, west of town.* &

Lopez Island

Lopez Island, flat and shaped like a jigsaw-puzzle piece, is a sleepy, bucolic place, famous for friendly locals (drivers almost always wave) and gentle inclines. The latter makes it the easiest bicycling in the islands: a mostly level 30-mile circuit suitable for the whole family. If you don't bring one, rent a bike from **LOPEZ BICYCLE WORKS** (2847 Fisherman Bay Rd; 360/468-2847; *www.lopezbicycleworks.com*); you can also rent kayaks there (*www.lopezkayaks.com*) mid-April through October.

Two day parks with beach access—**OTIS PERKINS** and **AGATE COUNTY**—are great for exploring. You can camp at 80-acre **ODLIN COUNTY PARK** (on right, about 1 mile south of ferry dock; 360/468-2496) or 130-acre **SPENCER SPIT STATE PARK** (on left, about 5 miles south of ferry dock; 888/226-7688; *www.parks.wa.gov*), both on the island's north side. Odlin has many nooks and crannies, and grassy sites among Douglas firs, shrubs, and clover. Spencer Spit has 37 tent sites and 7 walk-in beach sites. Seals and bald eagles can often be seen from the rocky promontory off Shark Reef Park (off Shark Reef Rd), on the island's southwestern shore.

LOPEZ VILLAGE, 4 miles south of the ferry dock on the west shore near Fisherman Bay, is basic but has a few spots worth knowing about, such as **HOLLY B'S BAKERY** (Lopez Plaza; 360/468-2133; Apr–Nov), with fresh bread and pastries—try the cinnamon rolls—and coffee to wash them down, and the **LOVE DOG CAFÉ** (1 Village Ctr; 360/468-2150) for Italian food.

The village also boasts a 60-slip marina at **LOPEZ ISLANDER RESORT** (Fisherman Bay Rd, 360/468-2233 or 800/736-3434; *www.lopezislander.com*).

RESTAURANTS

The Bay Cafe / ★★★

9 OLD POST RD, LOPEZ ISLAND; 360/468-3700 The Bay Café has long been reason enough to come to this serene isle. Its modern digs close to the beach (old fans remember its smaller, funkier location in the village) are spacious and retain some of its eclectic flair. A great sunset view of Fisherman Bay's entrance is a bonus. It's a come-as-you-are kind of place—and people do. The oft-changing menu might include steamed mussels, Oregon bay shrimp cakes, or grilled tofu with chickpea potato cakes (vegetarians never suffer). The daily seasonal fish special could be salmon, halibut, or fresh mahimahi. Dinners include soup and a salad of local greens. *$$; AE, DIS, MC, V; checks OK; dinner every day (Thurs–Sun in winter); full bar; reservations recommended; baycafe@hotmail.com; www.bay-cafe.com; junction of Lopez Rd S and Lopez Rd N, Lopez Village.*

LODGINGS

Edenwild Inn / ★★

132 LOPEZ RD, LOPEZ ISLAND; 360/468-3238 OR 800/606-0662 This modern Victorian manse with a garden features eight individually decorated rooms, some with fireplaces, some with king-sized Victorian sleigh beds, all with private baths and beautiful hardwood floors. The inn is not on the water, yet front rooms upstairs have fine views: Room 6 features Fisherman Bay vistas. Breakfast is served at individual tables in the dining room. Village restaurants and shops are within walking distance. *$$$; AE, MC, V; checks OK; edenwild@rockisland.com; www.edenwildinn.com; Lopez Village.* &

Inn at Swifts Bay / ★★★

856 PORT STANLEY RD, LOPEZ ISLAND; 360/468-3636 OR 800/903-9536 Nature and luxury blend charmingly in this Tudor retreat. You may be greeted by friendly deer or see rabbits cavorting in the yard. While the setting is "back to nature," accommodations are well above it. Five beautifully appointed rooms (three are suites with gas fireplaces and outside entrances) have queen-sized beds with down comforters—or lambswool, if you prefer—and are meticulously clean. On cool evenings, retreat to the living room, choose a book or magazine, and sink into a winged chair to enjoy a crackling fire. You can watch movies in the den (the video collection is impressive), make popcorn, and help yourself to tea. Reserve private time in the secluded hot tub, down a stone path at the edge of the forest. Guests are treated to fresh morning muffins, homemade jams, and the inn's secret fresh juice blend. You can drive, bike, hike, or get a ride (the innkeepers will arrange this) from the ferry. *$$–$$$; MC, V; checks OK; inn@swiftsbay.com; www.swiftsbay.com; 2 miles south of ferry landing.*

MacKaye Harbor Inn / ★

949 MACKAYE HARBOR RD, LOPEZ ISLAND; 360/468-2253 OR 888/314-6140 Bicyclists call this paradise after a sweaty trek from the ferry on the north end of the island to the little harbor on the south end. The tall white Victorian house, built in 1927, sits above a sandy, shell-strewn beach, perfect for sunset strolls or pushing off in a kayak. The Harbor Suite is our choice, with fireplace, private bath, and enclosed sitting area facing the beach. Rent kayaks or borrow mountain bikes; ask friendly innkeepers Mike and Robin Bergstrom to share their island secrets, and you're off to explore. Return later for fresh-baked cookies. If you do come by bike, be warned: the closest restaurant is 6 miles back in town. *$$$; MC, V; checks OK; innkeeper@mackayeharborinn.com; www.mackayeharborinn.com; 12 miles south of ferry landing.*

Orcas Island

Named not for the whales (the large cetaceans tend to congregate on the west side of San Juan Island and are rarely spotted here) but for a Spanish explorer, Revilla Gigedo de Orcasitas, Orcas Island has a reputation as the most beautiful of the four main San Juan Islands. It's also the biggest (geographically) and the hilliest, boasting 2,407-foot **MOUNT CONSTITUTION** as the centerpiece of **MORAN STATE PARK** (800/233-0321; *www.parks.wa.gov/alpha.asp*). Drive, hike, or—if you're up to it—bike to the top; from the old stone tower you can see Vancouver, Mount Rainier, and everything between. The 5,252-acre state park, 13 miles northeast of the ferry landing, also has lakes and nice campsites, obtained through a central reservation service (888/226-7688; *www.parks.wa.gov*) at least two weeks in advance.

The man responsible for the park was shipbuilding tycoon Robert Moran. His old mansion is now the focal point of **ROSARIO RESORT & SPA** (see review), just west of the park. Even if you don't stay there, the mansion, decked out in period memorabilia, is worth a stop. Its enormous pipe organ is still used for performances.

Shaped like a pair of inflated lungs, with the village of Eastsound running up its breastbone, Orcas has a ferry landing that is a good 8 miles from town, so most people bring their cars to the island; but you can walk on the ferry and rent a bicycle for the fairly level ride to town. Rent bicycles by the hour, day, or week from **DOLPHIN BAY BICYCLES** (at ferry landing; 360/376-4157; *www.rockisland .com/~dolphin*) or **WILD LIFE CYCLES** (in Eastsound; 360/376-4708). Walk-ons can also stay at the historic **ORCAS HOTEL** (360/376-4300 or 888/672-2792; *www .orcashotel.com*) at the landing.

RESTAURANTS

Bilbo's Festivo / ★

NORTH BEACH RD, EASTSOUND; 360/376-4728 Patrons speak of this cozy place with reverence. Its eclectic decor and setting—mud walls, Mexican tiles, fireplace, Navajo and Chimayo weavings in a small house with generous garden courtyards—are charming. Note the highly varnished tables and wraparound bench fashioned from old-growth cedar. For more than 28 years, owner Cy Fraser has served up fare with Mexican and New Mexican flair; choose from enchiladas, burritos, chiles rellenos, and mesquite-grilled specials that include seafood and vegetarian options. Fraser broils the tomatoes, peppers, and other vegetables for his sauces to intensify flavors. Summer lunch is served taqueria-style, grilled-to-order outdoors. *$; MC, V; local checks only; lunch every day June–Sept and weekends Apr–May, dinner every day; full bar; reservations recommended; at A St.*

Cafe Olga / ★

OLGA JUNCTION (11 POINT LAWRENCE RD), OLGA; 360/376-5098 While you wait for your table at Cafe Olga, browse the adjoining Orcas Island Artworks, a sprawling crafts gallery in a renovated strawberry-packing barn. Home-style choices at this popular island stop include fish of the day and local oysters, sandwiches on homemade bread, and huge salads. For dessert, try the terrific blackberry pie or the tiramisù. *$; MC, V; local checks only; open daily (closed Tues off-season and Jan–early Feb); beer and wine; no reservations; at Olga Junction.* &

Christina's / ★★★

310 MAIN ST, EASTSOUND; 360/376-4904 Perched over Eastsound and built above a 1930s gas station, Christina's offers a bewitching blend of provincial locale and urban sophistication. And the water view from the dining room and deck doesn't hurt. Christina Orchid's classic continental food keeps patrons returning. Local oysters are routinely on the menu. King salmon might come with scallops, sorrel, and Jack Daniels cream sauce; and the fillet of beef could arrive with a horseradish potato gratin and an apple shiitake demi-glace. These kinds of dishes have made Christina's reputation. Servings tend toward generous; appetizers are sized to share or to enjoy as a light meal. *$$$; AE, DC, MC, V; checks OK; dinner every day (Thurs–Mon in winter); full bar; reservations recommended; www.christinas.net; at N Beach Rd.*

Inn at Ship Bay / ★★★

326 OLGA RD, EASTSOUND; 360/376-5886 OR 877/276-7296 Geddes Martin, the new chef-owner here, was formerly the executive chef at Rosario Resort. That's a fortunate transition for this classic old farmhouse restaurant (formerly the Ship Bay Oyster House) with a view of Ship Bay. Martin emphasizes fresh, local organic produce and seafood. You'll find Judd Cove oysters, Kamilche Seafarms mussels, and troll-caught wild salmon (served with wild mushrooms). Specialties include handcrafted foods, such as ricotta ravioli with caramelized onions, kale, olives, and herb broth. Martin also makes his own ice creams—try the honey version served with his delicious flourless chocolate cake. He continues the inn's tradition of serving enticing "good deal" appetizers in the lounge or on the outdoor view patio. Eleven deluxe rooms (one an executive suite with whirlpool bath) have extremely comfortable pillow-top king beds, fireplaces, and bay views. Innkeeper Luke Ryan was also formerly with Rosario Resort. *$$$; AE, DC, DIS, MC, V; checks OK; dinner every day (Tues–Sun Mar–Apr and Oct–Nov, closed Dec–Jan); full bar; reservations recommended; shipbay@rockisland.com; www.innatshipbay .com; east of Eastsound on Olga Rd.* &

LODGINGS

Cascade Harbor Inn / ★★

1800 ROSARIO RD, EASTSOUND; 360/376-6360 OR 800/201-2120 The inn shares its vistas of pristine Cascade Bay and beach access with sprawling Rosario Resort next door. Forty-five modern units—some studios with Murphy beds, some two-queen rooms, some in-between—have decks and water views, and many configure into multi-unit suites with full kitchens. Continental breakfast is included in summer. This is a smoke-free facility; no pets are allowed. *$$$; AE, DIS, MC, V; checks OK; cascade@rockisland.com; www.cascadeharborinn.com; just east of Rosario.*

Deer Harbor Inn and Restaurant / ★★

33 INN LN, DEER HARBOR; 360/376-4110 OR 877/377-4110 Over the years, owners Pam and Craig Carpenter have shored up this rustic old lodge, built in 1915 in an apple orchard overlooking Deer Harbor. Lodge rooms are small, with peeled-log furniture. Newer cabins have a beachy feel—knotty pine walls, log furniture, woodstoves or fireplaces, and private hot tubs; the two-bedroom, two-bath Pond Cottage is roomy with a full kitchen, fireplace, and deck. Beds are heaped with quilts. Off-season, breakfast is included; fresh baked goods and hot coffee are delivered to your door. In summer, breakfast (for a charge) is available at the restaurant. Dinners are served nightly in the lodge's rustic dining room. *$$–$$$; AE, MC, V; checks OK; stay@deerharborinn.com; www.deerharborinn.com; from ferry landing, follow signs past West Sound to Deer Harbor.* &

The Inn on Orcas Island / ★★★

114 CHANNEL ROAD, DEER HARBOR; 360/376-5227 OR 888/886-1661 Part Nantucket cottage, part English manor house, this stunning inn at the tip of Deer Harbor, built in 2002, was a labor of love for owners Jeremy Trumble and John Gibbs. The two former Southern California gallery owners, both Anglo-philes, showcase collections of English paintings, needlepoint, engravings, and china throughout their property (ask to see the stunning display of majolica in the kitchen)—the art alone is worth a visit. Six manor rooms are individually decorated; your king suite (suites have gas fireplaces, double sinks, and a jetted tub) may sport a four-poster bed hung with rich fabric panels and adorned with an antique tapestry pillow. The topaz-colored entry and sitting rooms are cheery on the rainiest day. Enjoy a three-course breakfast in the ruby-colored dining room, or, weather permit-ting, on the veranda overlooking the water; then you can birdwatch or beach comb on the grounds. All rooms have water views. The six-acre property also has a car-riage house with a fully equipped kitchen and a waterside cottage. *$$$–$$$$; AE, MC, V; checks OK; jeremy@theinnonorcasisland.com; www.theinnonorcasisland .com; from ferry landing, follow signs past West Sound to Deer Harbor.* &

Outlook Inn / ★

171 MAIN ST, EASTSOUND; 360/376-2200 OR 888/688-5665 If you stay in East-sound—Orcas's "big city"—stay at the legendary 1888 Outlook Inn. Like the proverbial hippies who once flocked here, the 45-room inn has traded its counter-cultural spirit for luxuries money can buy. Though the old portion (with shared baths) is still available and affordable, newer swank suites have bang-up views, fireplaces, decks, whirlpool baths, and heated towel racks—and command prices a hippie would surely protest. We remember its humble past, so the renovated Outlook Inn feels a little soulless to us. But the bar and restaurant (under new direction by the folks from the popular nearby Sunflower Café) have a loyal local clientele. *$$$; AE, DIS, MC, V; local checks only; info@outlook-inn.com; www.outlook-inn .com; downtown.* ♿

Rosario Resort & Spa / ★★★

1400 ROSARIO RD, ROSARIO; 360/376-2222 OR 800/562-8820 This waterfront estate, built by 1900s Seattle industrialist Robert Moran and listed in the National Register of Historic Places, was converted to a resort in the 1960s. Now owned by Rock Resorts, Rosario has seen expensive renovation in recent years to update the facilities and to return the mansion to its former elegance. Teak floors, mahogany paneling, original furnishings, and Tiffany accents give a feel for the home's past. Now the ugly duckling is a dazzling swan. One thing can't be overcome: most of the 116 guest rooms are perched on a hillside behind the mansion—a steep climb unless you take the resort's van service. Rooms have a cheery upscale country style; most offer bay views (22 are junior suites, 2 have kitchens, and 2 are guest houses). The mansion itself is home to a museum and music room (don't miss the organ recital by historian Christopher Peacock), gift shops, lounge, veranda, and restaurants. Spa services and a pool are on the lower level. Also on the grounds are a kayaking concession, dive shop, and conference facilities. *$$$–$$$$; AE, DC, DIS, MC, V; checks OK; info@rosarioresort .com; www.rosario.rockresorts.com; from Eastsound, drive east on Olga Rd for 3 miles.* ♿

Spring Bay Inn / ★★★

464 SPRING BAY TRAIL, OLGA; 360/376-5531 It's a long dirt road getting here, but rarely is a drive so amply rewarded. On 57 wooded seafront acres, the inn's interior reflects the naturalist sensibilities of innkeepers Sandy Playa and Carl Burger, a youthful pair of retired state park rangers. The angular great room, with fieldstone fireplace, showcases a stunning view. Upstairs, four thoughtfully decorated guest rooms have private baths and fireplaces; two have balconies. The light-filled Treetop room is one of the most uplifting spaces we've seen. Coffee, muffins, and fruit are delivered to each door—sustenance for a complimentary two-hour guided kayak tour. Return for a healthy brunch. The property, laced with hiking trails and teeming with wildlife, is adjacent to Obstruction Pass State Park. Ease tired muscles with a soak under the stars in the bay-side hot tub. *$$$; DIS, MC, V; checks OK; info@springbayinn.com; www.springbayinn.com; Obstruction Pass Rd to Trailhead Rd, left onto Spring Bay Trail.*

Turtleback Farm Inn / ★★★

1981 CROW VALLEY RD, EASTSOUND; 360/376-4914 OR 800/376-4914 At Turtleback Farm—located in the Crow Valley amidst rolling pastures, trees, and ponds, in the shadow of Turtleback Mountain— you get the contented feeling that not much has changed here in a long, long time. In some ways you are right. The crisp green and white farmhouse does date back to the late 1800s. Yet it has been restored and renovated comfortably by owners Bill and Susan Fletcher into one of the top B&Bs around, a perennial favorite and Northwest icon for more than 20 years. Glowing wood floors and accents and tastefully simple decor—rocking and winged chairs, area rugs—keep the old-time feeling alive. Of the 11 rooms, our favorites are in the farmhouse and have private decks overlooking the garden, meadow, or valley. However, for luxury and privacy, it's hard to beat the Orchard House, a barn-style building a short stroll from the farmhouse. Four spacious suites have expansive valley views; fir flooring, trim, and doors; a Vermont Casting stove; king-sized bed; bar-sized refrigerator; and spacious bath with large claw-footed tub and shower, and all have private decks. Delicious breakfasts (check out the inn's cookbook) are served in the dining room or outside on the view deck in warmer weather, or delivered discreetly to the suites. Children are welcome in suites by prior arrangement. *$$$–$$$$; AE, DIS, MC, V; checks OK; www.turtlebackinn .com; 6 miles from ferry on Crow Valley Rd.* &

San Juan Island

San Juan Island, the most populated in the archipelago, supports the biggest town, Friday Harbor. The **SAN JUAN HISTORICAL MUSEUM** (405 Price St; 360/378-3949; *www.sjmuseum.org*) is filled with memorabilia from the island's early days. Another bit of history is hidden away at **ROCHE HARBOR RESORT** (see review). Here you'll find a mausoleum, a bizarre monument that may tell more about timber tycoon John McMillin than does all the rest of Roche Harbor. The ashes of family members are contained in a set of stone chairs that surround a concrete dining-room table. They're ringed by a set of 30-foot-high columns, symbolic of McMillin's adherence to Masonic beliefs. At the entrance to Roche Harbor Resort Village, a 19-acre preserve on Westcott Bay contains more than 80 sculptural works by renowned artists.

Other island attractions include the mid-19th-century sites of the **AMERICAN** and **ENGLISH CAMPS** (360/378-2240; *www.nps.gov/sajh*), established when ownership of the island was under dispute. The conflict led to the infamous Pig War of 1859–60, so called because the sole casualty was a pig. Americans and British shared joint occupation until 1872, when the dispute was settled in favor of the United States. The English camp, toward the island's northwest end, is wooded and secluded; the American camp at the south end is open, windy prairie and beach. Either makes a fine picnic spot. So does beautiful **SAN JUAN COUNTY PARK** (50 San Juan Park Rd; 360/378-2992; *www.co.san-juan.wa.us/parks/sanjuan.html*) on the island's west side, where it's possible to camp on 22 sites on a pretty cove (reservations recommended). Another camping option is **LAKEDALE RESORT** (2627 Roche Harbor Rd; 360/378-2350 or 800/617-2267; *www.lakedale.com*; reservations recommended), a private campground on 84 acres with three lakes for swimming and fishing, a 10-room lodge, 6 2-bedroom log cabins, and a seasonal 3-bedroom guest house. Bed-and-breakfast establishments are plentiful on the island; check the **SAN JUAN ISLAND BED AND BREAKFAST ASSOCIATION** (360/378-3030 or 866/645-3030; *www.san-juan-island.net*).

The best diving in the archipelago is here (some claim it's the best cold-water diving in the world); **ISLAND DIVE & WATER SPORTS** (in Friday Harbor; 360/378-2772 or 800/303-8386; *www.divesanjuan.com*) has rentals, charters, and instruction. Several charter boats are available for whale-watching (primarily Orcas); try the **WESTERN PRINCE** (1 block from ferry landing; 360/378-5315 or 800/757-ORCA; *www.orcawhalewatch.com*). Those distrustful of their sea legs can visit the marvelous **WHALE MUSEUM** (62 1st St N; 360/378-4710 or 800/946-7227; *www.whalemuseum.com*), with exhibits devoted to the resident cetaceans; or go to the nation's first official whale-watching park at **LIME KILN POINT STATE PARK** on the island's west side. Bring binoculars and patience. Orcas are resident whales in the Northwest—primarily traveling the waters of Southwestern BC, the San Juans, and Puget Sound—not migrating whales like the grays you see off the Oregon/California coast at a particular time of year. Check the Whale Museum Web site hotline for whale-sighting information.

Oyster fans happily visit **WESTCOTT BAY SEA FARMS** (904 Westcott Dr; 360/378-2489; *www.westcottbay.com*) off Roche Harbor Road, 2 miles south of Roche Harbor Resort, where you can help yourself to oysters at bargain prices.

RESTAURANTS

Duck Soup Inn / ★★

50 DUCK SOUP LN, FRIDAY HARBOR; 360/378-4878 For more than 26 years, Richard and Gretchen Allison have served up special food in this shingled cottage, with its arbor, stone fireplace, and pond views. Their menu is ambitious. The focus is on local seafoods and seasonal ingredients, and they've succeeded admirably with house specialties such as applewood-smoked Westcott Bay oysters and grilled fresh fish. House-baked bread, a small bowl of perfectly seasoned soup, and a large green salad accompany ample portions. *$$; DIS, MC, V; checks OK; dinner Wed–Sun (closed in winter); beer and wine; reservations recommended; www.ducksoupinn .com; 5 miles northwest of Friday Harbor.* &

The Place Bar & Grill / ★

I SPRING ST, FRIDAY HARBOR; 360/378-8707 Behind the unassuming name and waterside location is this striving concern, garnering much local praise. Chef-owner Steven Anderson features a rotating world of cuisines, focusing on fish and shellfish, from BC king salmon to Westcott Bay oysters. Salmon might come with gingery citrus sauce; or try black-bean ravioli topped with tiger prawns in a buttery glaze. In summer, crab cakes flavored with ginger and lemongrass are a sure bet. Servers know exactly how much time you have if your boat's in sight: with luck, enough to savor the sumptuous crème brûlée. *$$; MC, V; local checks only; dinner every day (Tues–Sat in winter); full bar; reservations recommended; at foot of Spring St.* &

Vinny's / ★★

165 WEST ST, FRIDAY HARBOR; 360/378-1934 Don't be fooled by a name that conjures up visions of pizza and red-checked tablecloths. Vinny's is a sophisticated, Tuscan-style eatery offering Italian specialties and daily fresh seafood specials—such as pan-seared Alaskan halibut with tangy lemon thyme butter or Wescott Bay clams steamed in a sherry garlic broth. The breast of duck with lavender, honey, garlic, and fresh cranberries is delicious. Pasta dishes are generous; for a "hot" meal, split a salad and an order of "Pasta from Hell"—a combo of garlic, pine nuts, raisins, and bell peppers in a very spicy curry cream sauce. To cool the heat, try an offering from the extensive wine list or fancy drinks menu. Cheerful service and the restaurant's eye-pleasing golden interior and panoramic harbor view add to the experience. *$$-$$$; MC, V; local checks only; dinner daily; full bar; reservations recommended; downtown off 1st St.* ⅄

LODGINGS

The Argyle House / ★★★

685 ARGYLE RD, FRIDAY HARBOR; 360/378-4084 OR 800/624-3459 Two blocks from downtown Friday Harbor, Argyle House is a vintage 1910 Craftsman-style home set on a gardened acre with fish pond, brick patio, and outdoor spa tub. Accommodations include three upstairs rooms with private baths, a downstairs two-bedroom suite with claw-footed tub, and a honeymoon cottage with private deck. The main house has lovely hardwood floors, high ceilings, and a cozy living area, where owners Bill and Chris Carli have been known to join guests in impromptu musical reveries (Bill plays guitar and harmonica). Immaculate bedrooms are nicely appointed; the honeymoon cottage has a beamed sky-lit ceiling, lace curtains, a hope chest with extra towels, and a kitchenette with microwave, minifridge, coffeemaker, and beverages—plus a private hot tub and shatter-proof champagne glasses. At breakfast you might feast on exceptional French toast with berries, homemade granola, coffee cake, and fresh fruit (if you leave before breakfast, they'll pack you something to go). *$$$-$$$$; MC, V; checks OK; info@argylehouse.net; argyle house.net; 4 blocks from ferry.*

Friday Harbor House / ★★★

130 WEST ST, FRIDAY HARBOR; 360/378-8455 OR 866/722-7356 To many, the contemporary architecture of San Juan Island's poshest inn, a sister property of Whidbey Island's Inn at Langley, is a welcome relief from Victorian B&Bs. The interior is a bastion of spare serenity, a mood abetted by professional management. Twenty rooms are decorated in muted modern tones and have gas fireplaces and (noisy) jetted tubs positioned to absorb both the fire's warmth and the harbor view. Some rooms have tiny balconies; not all offer full waterfront views. Breakfast is continental, with delicious hot scones. The view dining room (open to the public for dinner) maintains the inn's spartan cool, warming considerably when you're presented with dishes such as panfried Westcott Bay oysters, grilled salmon with sautéed chanterelles, or Oregon tenderloin with buttermilk mashed potatoes and a chutney of onions and figs. *$$$$; AE, DIS, MC, V; checks OK; fhhouse@rockisland.com; www.fridayharborhouse.com; from ferry, left on Spring St, right on 1st St, right on West St.* ⅄

Friday's Historic Inn / ★

35 1ST ST, FRIDAY HARBOR; 360/378-5848 OR 800/352-2632 This extensively renovated 1891 historic building in downtown Friday Harbor is a great place to stay to be in the center of the action. Of the 15 rooms, the best is the Eagle Cove, a third-floor, water-view perch with a deck, kitchen, double shower, and Jacuzzi. Some (economy) rooms share baths. Heated bathroom floors and fresh-baked cookies in the afternoon are just two thoughtful touches. The continental breakfast often includes freshly baked scones with fresh fruit. There are no grounds here, yet in warm weather you can retreat to the very pleasant outdoor deck. *$$; MC, V; checks OK; stay@friday-harbor.com; www.friday-harbor.com; 2 blocks from ferry.* &

Harrison House Suites / ★★★

235 C ST, FRIDAY HARBOR; 360/378-3587 OR 800/407-7933 This crisply renovated Craftsman inn, run by the effusive Farhad Ghatan, features five impressive suites, all with kitchens and private baths, four with decks, four with whirlpool tubs. Rooms with views overlook the scenic sweep of Friday Harbor. A pretty water garden, plus flower, fruit, and vegetable gardens for guest use make this the only place we've seen in the islands where you can pick your own salad and toss it in your own kitchen. Fresh-baked breads are served each evening; mornings, it's fresh scones. Kayaks and mountain bikes are available for guests. Ghatan also runs a little café—guests only—for private dinners and catered events. The inn is great for families or groups. *$$$–$$$$; AE, DIS, MC, V; checks OK; hhsuites@rockisland.com; www.san-juan-lodging.com; 2 blocks from downtown.* &

Highland Inn / ★★★

WEST SIDE OF SAN JUAN ISLAND; 360/378-9450 OR 888/400-9850 Helen King, the former owner of the famous Babbling Brook Inn in Santa Cruz, California, moved north and built the inn of her dreams on the west side of San Juan Island. Now she has just two lovely suites, one at each end of her house. Licensed for only two couples a night (no children), the Highland Inn is everything you could ask for in privacy and hospitality. Suites are huge, with sitting rooms, wood-burning fireplaces, marble bathrooms—each with a jetted tub for two and steam-cabinet shower—and views of the Olympic Mountains, Victoria, and Haro Strait from the 88-foot-long covered veranda. In the afternoons, King serves tea and "Mrs. King's Cookies"—white-and-dark-chocolate-chip cookies. *$$$–$$$$; AE, MC, V; checks OK; helen@highlandinn.com; www.highlandinn.com; call for directions.*

Lonesome Cove Resort / ★

416 LONESOME COVE RD, FRIDAY HARBOR; 360/378-4477 A fixture on the island since the 1940s, this 10-acre resort offers classic log-cottage-in-the-woods charm. Six immaculate little cabins at the water's edge, manicured lawns, and deer that wander the woods make the place a favorite for lighthearted honeymooners. Sunsets are spectacular. No pets—too many baby ducks. *$$–$$$; MC, V; checks OK; 2-night min, 5-night min in summer; cabins@lonesomecove.com; www.lonesome cove.com; take Roche Harbor Rd 9 miles north to Lonesome Cove Rd.* &

Roche Harbor Resort / ★★

ROCHE HARBOR; 360/378-2155 OR 800/451-8910 There are few places in the region that take you back in time as surely as a visit to Roche Harbor Resort. The trellis-fronted, ivy-clad Hotel de Haro, centerpiece of the resort, was built by Tacoma lawyer-industrialist John McMillin in 1886 (around the foot-thick walls of a Hudson's Bay post). History buffs relish the piecework wallpaper and period furnishings, the creaky, uneven floorboards, and the thought that Teddy Roosevelt was once an honored guest. The view from the hotel entry takes in the flower garden, cobblestoned waterfront, and yacht-crammed bay. Nearby are remnants of McMillin's lime quarry, once the largest west of the Mississippi. The hotel offers 20 rooms; only 4 have private bathrooms. Separate accommodations include 4 luxury view suites (in McMillin's old house) with claw-footed soaking tubs. A few nicely renovated cottages (ask for one viewing the water) and condos (a good walk away from the main inn) are available. A fine-dining restaurant, café, and casual eatery are on the grounds. Stroll the gardens, swim, kayak, play tennis, and visit the mausoleum (really). *$$$–$$$$; AE, MC, V; checks OK; roche@rocheharbor.com; www.rocheharbor.com; on waterfront at northwest end of island.* &

Wharfside Bed & Breakfast on the Slowseason / ★

🌲 **K DOCK, #13, FRIDAY HARBOR; 360/378-5661 OR 800/899-3030** If nothing lulls you to sleep like the gentle lap of the waves, the Wharfside's for you. Two guest rooms on the 60-foot ketch-rigged motor sailer are nicely finished, with full amenities and the compact precision that only boat living can inspire. Staterooms, fore and aft, have queen-sized beds. Aft has its own bathroom; fore (with bow-area space suitable for children, at an extra charge) uses the bath in the main cabin. When the weather's good, enjoy the huge breakfast on deck and watch boaters head to sea. *$$$–$$$$; AE, MC, V; checks OK; slowseason@rockisland .com; www.slowseason.com; marina is north of ferry terminal.*

Tacoma, Olympia, and the South Sound

Going south from Seattle, Interstate 5 takes you to the state's second-largest city, Tacoma—which is experiencing a renaissance, especially in the arts—and to the state's picturesque bayside capital of Olympia.

Vashon Island

Vashon Island is a close-in, wonderful place to sample Northwest island life, especially by bicycle (although the first long hill from the north-end ferry dock is a killer). An active arts community and plentiful organic and vegetarian restaurant offerings remind you this was once a countercultural refuge. Vashon village is the island's commercial hub. Few beaches are open to the public, but some public spots invite a stroll and offer a view. It's a short ferry ride from downtown Seattle (foot passengers only), West Seattle (the Fauntleroy ferry), or Tacoma (Point Defiance ferry), all via **WASHINGTON STATE FERRIES** (206/464-6400 or 800/843-3779; www.wsdot.wa.gov/ferries/).

Island arts are displayed at **BLUE HERON ART CENTER** (19704 Vashon Hwy SW; 206/463-5131; www.vashonalliedarts.com); **HERON'S NEST** (17600 Vashon Hwy SW; 206/463-5252), an arts and crafts gallery; and at **SILVERWOOD GALLERY**

(23927 Vashon Hwy SW; 206/463-1722; *www.silverwoodgallery.com*) in Burton. **SEATTLE'S BEST COFFEE** (19529 Vashon Hwy SW; 206/463-5050) roasting headquarters are here, yet you'll only find brewed coffee for sale. Cozy **CAFÉ LUNA** (9924 SW Bank Rd; 206/463-0777), in the village, is the place islanders get their lattes. If you have even the faintest green thumb, don't miss **DIG, WEEKEND GARDENER** (19028 Vashon Hwy SW; 206/463-5096), a delightful nursery showcasing plants and garden art. The **COUNTRY STORE AND GARDENS** (20211 Vashon Hwy SW; 206/463-3655) is an old-fashioned general store stocking many island-made products, including Wax Orchards fruit preserves (*www.waxorchards.com*) and Maury Island Farms jams (*www.goodjam.com*), housewares, and gardening supplies. **VASHON ISLAND KAYAK COMPANY** (Jensen Acres boathouse at Quartermaster Harbor; 206/463-9257; *www.pugetsoundkayak.com*) offers instruction and day trips.

Islanders host several annual events; best known is the July **STRAWBERRY FESTIVAL** (contact the chamber; 206/463-6217; *www.vashonchamber.com*). The Vashon Community Calendar has a detailed events listing, including a garden show and first Friday gallery walks.

RESTAURANTS

Back Bay Inn / ★★

2407 VASHON HIGHWAY SW, VASHON; 206/463-5355 Though it was built in the early 1990s, this Victorian-style inn fits the 100-year-old feel of the tiny harbor village of Burton, near Vashon's south end. This is the place islanders come for white-tablecloth dining. Chef Curtis Gray offers welcome classics—from Dungeness crab cakes and other seafood and pasta, to delicious filet mignon and a mouth-watering bourbon-glazed pork chop; of course there are vegetarian entrées. An outdoor terrace with fireplace is a cozy retreat. Upstairs lodging includes four queen-bedded rooms, two with great views. *$$–$$$; AE, MC, V; checks OK; dinner Wed–Sat; full bar; reservations recommended; stay@thebackbayinn.com; www.thebackbayinn .com; follow Vashon Highway south to Burton.*

Express Cuisine / ★★

17629 VASHON HWY SW, VASHON; 206/463-6626 This storefront restaurant and catering company may not look like the island's most popular eatery, but locals line up to take out gourmet dinners or to fill communal tables and enjoy tender prime rib, mouth-watering sirloin stroganoff, and smoked salmon over linguine with a mushroom Alfredo sauce. Dinners include soup or salad (if seafood chowder is on the list, choose it). Service is counter-style. Come early or call ahead for takeout; otherwise, you might have to wait. *$–$$; no credit cards; local checks only; dinner Wed–Sat; beer and wine; no reservations; near Bank Rd.* ♿

The Homegrown Cafe / ★

17614 VASHON HWY SW, VASHON; 206/463-6302 Reminiscent of a country kitchen, this small café with its yellow and white "sunny-side up" decor may be the island's favorite breakfast spot (check the blackboard specials) with a generous menu of omelets, biscuits and gravy, and other offerings. The focus is on fresh organic eggs, meat, and island produce, whenever possible. A good destination for family meals (it has a children's menu), the café offers dinners such as roasted chicken, seafood, vegetarian, and vegan choices. *$–$$; MC, V; local checks only; breakfast, lunch, dinner daily; beer and wine; no reservations; in Vashon village.* &

Stray Dog Cafe / ★

17530 VASHON HWY SW, VASHON; 206/463-7833 This small village bistro has an eclectic menu that could include meatloaf and mashed potatoes or French Vietnamese chicken crepes; the hearty and generous black bean soup with salsa and sour cream makes a delicious meal any time it is offered. Named after a St. Petersburg, Russia, eatery that was famous in the 1930s as a refuge for artists, the café displays art on red-toned walls. A decor of slightly shabby chic adds to the artistic flair. The wine bar is a cozy gathering spot. The weekend champagne brunch is popular. *$–$$; MC, V; checks OK; breakfast, lunch, dinner every day (closed Tues); beer and wine; no reservations; in Vashon village.* &

Tacoma

Flanked by Commencement Bay and the Tacoma Narrows and backed by Mount Rainier, Tacoma is no longer just a blue-collar mill town, but a growing urban center with a thriving cultural core and a plethora of wonderful new and old, small and large, modest and grand museums.

Perhaps the brightest star is the $63 million **MUSEUM OF GLASS INTERNATIONAL CENTER FOR CONTEMPORARY ART** (on Thea Foss Waterway; 253/396-1768; *www.museumofglass.org*), designed by famed architect Arthur Erickson. New and sleekly modern, the nearby **TACOMA ART MUSEUM** (12th St and Pacific Ave; 253/272-4258; *www.tacomaartmuseum.org*) is home to paintings by Degas, Renoir, and Sargent, and to the country's largest permanent public collection of glass art by Tacoma native Dale Chihuly. The **WASHINGTON STATE HISTORY MUSEUM** (1911 Pacific Ave; 888/238-4373; *www.wshs.org*) occupies a handsome building just south of Union Station. A state-of-the-art museum experience, it provides history and innovation under the same roof; from the outside, the museum has been designed to complement the old train stop, Union Station, next door.

JOB CARR'S CABIN (2350 N 30th St; 253/627-5405; *www.jobcarrmuseum.org*) is a tiny Old Town museum that marks the city's birthplace. The **WORKING WATERFRONT MUSEUM** (705 Dock St; 253/272-2750; *www.wwfrontmuseum.org*) is a work in progress with plenty of boats on display. The free **KARPELES MANUSCRIPT MUSEUM** (407 S "G" St; 253/383-2575; *www.rain.org/~karpeles*), with changing exhibits displaying papers and signatures of famous figures, is located across from **WRIGHT PARK** (Division and I Sts), a serene in-city park with trees, a duck-filled pond, and a beautifully maintained 1908 glass-and-steel conservatory. The **RUSTON WAY WATERFRONT** (between N 49th and N 54th Sts) is a popular 2-mile mix of parks and restaurants.

Three theaters comprise the **BROADWAY CENTER FOR THE PERFORMING ARTS** (901 Broadway Plaza; 253/591-5894; *www.broadwaycenter.org*): the restored

1,100-seat **PANTAGES THEATER** (901 Broadway Plaza), originally designed in 1918 by nationally known movie-theater architect B. Marcus Priteca, is the focal point of the reviving downtown cultural life—with dance, music, and stage presentations; the **RIALTO THEATER**, a former old movie house, and the contemporary and colorful **THEATER IN THE SQUARE** are nearby.

Historic buildings in the downtown warehouse district have been converted from industrial use to hip residential and commercial functions; the **UNIVERSITY OF WASHINGTON** (1900 Commerce St; 253/692-4000 or 800/736-7750; *www .washington.edu*) has a branch campus here. Stately homes and cobblestone streets in the north end are often used as sets by Hollywood moviemakers.

History and architecture buffs delight in **OLD CITY HALL** (625 Commerce St), with its coppered roof and Renaissance clock; the Romanesque **FIRST PRESBYTERIAN CHURCH** (20 Tacoma Ave S); the rococo **PYTHIAN LODGE** (925½ Broadway Plaza); the one-of-a-kind **UNION STATION** (17th St and Pacific Ave), built in 1911; and the much-praised **FEDERAL COURTHOUSE** (with some spectacular Chihuly glass on public display). Also of note is the turreted chateau of **STADIUM HIGH SCHOOL** (N 1st St and Stadium Wy), site of several big-screen movie sets.

POINT DEFIANCE PARK (northwest side of Tacoma, call for directions; 253/305-1000) has 500 acres of untouched forest jutting out into Puget Sound and is one of the country's most dramatically sited and creatively planned city parks. The wooded 5-mile drive and parallel hiking trails open up now and then for sweeping views of the water, Vashon Island, Gig Harbor, and the Olympic Mountains. There are rose, rhododendron, Japanese, and Northwest native gardens; a railroad village with a working steam engine; a reconstruction of Fort Nisqually (originally built in 1833); a museum; a swimming beach; and the much acclaimed **POINT DEFIANCE ZOO & AQUARIUM** (5400 N Pearl St; 253/591-5335; *www.pdza.org*). Watching the play of sea otters, polar bears, walruses, and white beluga whales from underwater vantage points is a rare treat.

The 20-year-old **TACOMA DOME** (2727 E "D" St; 253/572-3663; *www.tacoma dome.org*), one of the world's largest wooden domes, is the site of trade, entertainment, and sports shows. Fans of baseball in a first-class ballpark head to **CHENEY STADIUM** to watch the **TACOMA RAINIERS** (2502 S Tyler St; 253/752-7707; *www .tacomarainiers.com*), the triple-A affiliate of the Seattle Mariners.

Thirsty? **ENGINE HOUSE NO 9** (611 N Pine St; 253/272-3435) near the University of Puget Sound is a friendly, pizza-and-beer-lover's dream tavern (minus the smoke). Other fun watering holes include **THE SPAR** (2121 N 30th St; 253/627-8215) in Old Town. The **HARMON** brew pub (1938 Pacific Ave; 253/383-2739), across from the history museum, and the nearby **SWISS PUB** (1904 S Jefferson Ave; 253/572-2821) are local favorites. **LAKEWOLD GARDENS** (12317 Gravelly Lake Dr SW, Lakewood; exit 124 off I-5 to Gravelly Lake Dr; 253/584-3360 or 888/858-4106; *www.lakewold.org*; open Wed–Sun Apr–Sept, Fri–Sun in winter), one of the area's largest estates, lies 10 minutes south of Tacoma on a beautiful 10-acre site overlooking Gravelly Lake in Lakewood. Recognized as one of America's outstanding gardens, Lakewold Gardens offers guided and nonguided tours.

RESTAURANTS

Altezzo / ★★

1320 BROADWAY PLAZA (SHERATON TACOMA HOTEL), TACOMA; 253/572-3200
Atop the Sheraton (see review), this restaurant is "lofty" in space and attitude.
Request a window table for great downtown and area views—and some of the best
Italian cuisine in Tacoma. Chef James VandeBerg offers a delicious cioppino, or
ravioli with spinach and chard in tomato cream sauce. Tiramisù is the real McCoy,
and there's a wonderful fresh pear and berry tart with ice cream and cinnamon
sauce. The newly renovated bar is a great place to kick back with a glass of wine
and a plate of antipasto to enjoy the view. *$$; AE, DC, MC, V; dinner every day;
full bar; reservations recommended; www.sheratontacoma.com/html/Dining.htm;
between 13th and 15th Sts.* &

The Cliff House / ★★

6300 MARINE VIEW DR, TACOMA; 253/927-0400 Commanding views of Com-
mencement Bay, Mount Rainier, and the Tacoma skyline, and its formal decor and
"memory lane" desserts—cherries jubilee and crepes suzette flambéed tableside—
make this a special occasion eatery for some. A more casual restaurant downstairs
offers the same great views and less expensive offerings. *$$$; AE, DC, DIS, MC,
V; no checks; lunch, dinner every day; full bar; reservations recommended; www
.cliffhouserestaurant.com; top of Marine View Dr (Highway 509).*

East & West Cafe / ★

5319 TACOMA MALL BLVD, TACOMA; 253/475-7755 What this restaurant
lacks in location, it makes up for tenfold in great food and charm. It's a haven
of Asian delights on the busy thoroughfare south of Tacoma Mall. Owner
Vien Floyd, a Saigon native, has gained a loyal local following and has remodeled
and doubled her space twice in recent years. Her incomparable personality helps
make meals here a treat. The emphasis is on Vietnamese and Thai cuisine; the Saigon
Crepe is filled with chicken, prawns, and vegetables. Vegetables are crisp, bright,
and full of flavor; sauces have character; meats are tender. For the price, it's hard to
have a better meal in Tacoma. *$; AE, DIS, MC, V; local checks only; lunch, dinner
Mon–Sat; beer and wine; no reservations; www.eastwestcafe.com; 56th St exit off
I-5.* &

El Gaucho / ★★★

2119 PACIFIC AVE, TACOMA; 253/272-1510 Tacoma's new El Gaucho, like its
older sibling in Seattle, is a ritzy steak house with dark, sophisticated interiors
and an atmosphere reminiscent of '60s Doris Day flicks of stylish New York City
life. You come here for classic (pricey) meals—a martini starter; tableside-tossed
Caesar salad; amazing, thick Angus steak; such as chateaubriand for two; or a
showy flaming shish kebab. A cigar lounge and four private dining rooms enhance
the clubby atmosphere, as does the live piano music. *$$$; AE, DIS, MC, V; checks
OK; dinner every day; full bar; reservations recommended; www.elgaucho.com; on
Pacific in the museum district.* &

Fujiya / ★★

1125 COURT C, TACOMA; 253/627-5319 Absolute consistency and authentic hospitality are what attract a loyal clientele from near and far to Masahiro Endo's stylish downtown Japanese restaurant for sushi and sashimi. Begin with *gyoza* (savory pork-stuffed dumplings). The real test of a Japanese restaurant is tempura, and Endo's is feathery crisp. Those who prefer seafood cooked can try the *yosenabe* (seafood stew) served in a small cast-iron pot. The owner is a generous and friendly man; seldom a meal goes by that he doesn't offer a complimentary *omaki*—a gift tidbit. *$$; AE, MC, V; checks OK; lunch Mon–Fri, dinner Mon–Sat; beer and wine; reservations recommended; between Broadway and Market St.*

Harbor Lights / ★

2761 RUSTON WY, TACOMA; 253/752-8600 Anthony's now owns Harbor Lights, but blessedly the only changes at Tacoma's pioneer Ruston Way waterfront restaurant have been new, generous containers of summer flowers and a general spruce-up. Decor is circa 1950, with glass floats, stuffed prize fish, and a giant lobster. Up-to-the-minute it may not be, but that doesn't bother seafood fans who regularly crowd the noisy dining room for buckets of steamed clams and mounds of perfectly cooked panfried oysters. Fillet of sole is grilled to perfection; halibut-and-chips are the best around, as are crisp hash browns. Portions are gargantuan. Expect a broth-style chowder (not creamy New England). *$$–$$$; AE, DC, DIS, MC, V; checks OK; lunch Mon–Sat, dinner every day; full bar; reservations recommended; www.Anthony.com/restaurants/info/harborlights.html; City Center exit off I-5.*

Over the Moon Café / ★

709 OPERA ALLEY/COURT C, TACOMA; 253/284-3722 Exposed brick walls, comfortably mismatched furniture, floral curtains, and books of poetry on the tables all add to the artsy style perfect in this intimate Opera Alley café. Ambitious dinner entrées include bourbon-glazed Atlantic salmon, breast of duck, and beef Wellington. For lunch, try the grilled cheese sandwich—thick slices of sourdough bread with sweet wine-soaked Gruyère cheese. This is a fun destination after exploring the nearby shops, or for a meal before or after a performance at nearby Broadway Center. *$$; AE, MC, V; local checks only; lunch, dinner daily; beer and wine; reservations recommended; www.overthemooncafe.com; off St Helens.*

The Primo Grill / ★★★

601 S PINE ST, TACOMA; 253/383-7000 Come here for great food and a hit of high energy. Belfast-born chef Charlie McManus (formerly at Altezzo, in the Sheraton) has created a contemporary, bistro-style restaurant in a developing district at Sixth and Pine. He's not afraid to use spices, and anything on the menu in this energetic art-filled spot is delicious. Try a "small bite" of crispy polenta with melted goat cheese and roasted pepper coulis; an entrée of grilled pork chop with cinnamon caramelized onions or fire-roasted prawns; or a special favorite of the house—warm bread salad with sausage, tomatoes, and onions. Finish with a warm hazelnut brownie and vanilla ice cream. Even when the restaurant isn't crowded, the vibrant colors, art, and design seem to radiate a kind of buzz you might associate with San

Francisco. Check the Web site for recipes, cooking classes, and special events. *$$; AE, MC, V; local checks only; lunch Mon–Fri, dinner every day; full bar; reservations recommended; www.primogrilltacoma.com; off 6th St at Pine St.* &

Stanley and Seaforts Steak, Chop, and Fish House / ★★

115 E 34TH ST, TACOMA; 253/473-7300 Every seat in this restaurant has a panoramic view of Tacoma, its busy harbor, and, on a clear day, the Olympics. But the emphasis here is on quality meats and seafood simply grilled over applewood with flavorings of herbs and fruits. That and dependable preparation have made Stanley and Seaforts a favorite for two decades. The spacious bar features distinctive Scotch whiskeys—and a great sunset. *$$; AE, DC, DIS, MC, V; local checks only; lunch Mon–Fri, dinner every day; full bar; reservations recommended; City Center exit off I-5.* &

LODGINGS

Chinaberry Hill / ★★★

302 TACOMA AVE N, TACOMA; 253/272-1282 This 1889 grand Victorian (on the National Register of Historic Places) in Tacoma's historic Stadium District has been beautifully restored by Cecil and Yarrow Wayman. Now an eclectic B&B, it is richly inviting. Lovers of old homes delight in the detailed woodwork, stained glass, and period lighting. Three rooms are in the main house: we prefer the Pantages Suite, with its view of Commencement Bay and a Jacuzzi, or the Wild Rose Suite, which has a fireplace, a Jacuzzi, and bay windows overlooking the garden. Families enjoy the Catchpenny Cottage behind the main house; once the estate's carriage house, it has been converted into a lovely two-story retreat that sleeps up to seven. A new suite on the third floor (be prepared to climb some steep stairs) has a kitchen, two bedrooms, a sitting room, and bay views. The Waymans serve full breakfast in the dining room or on the veranda. *$$$; MC, V; checks OK; chinaberry@wa.net; www.chinaberryhill.com; City Center exit off I-5.*

Silver Cloud Inn / ★★

2317 N RUSTON WY, TACOMA; 253/272-1300 OR 866/820-8448 This Pacific Northwest chain has claimed one of the region's best locations with this new hostelry jutting into Commencement Bay from Tacoma's waterfront promenade, Ruston Way. Contemporary with a sunny country decor—furnishings combine neutral tones and bold prints—that fits nicely with the blues and grays of surrounding water and sky. Ninety rooms offer water views, almost all have fireplaces. The most romantic rooms are the king-sized suites with jetted tubs. Rooms are stocked with microwaves, coffee makers, and refrigerators. Continental breakfast is included. Ask about special packages. *$$–$$$; AE, DIS, MC, V; checks OK; www.silvercloud.com; from I-5 take exit 133 (I-705) north and follow to Schuster Pkwy exit, follow to Ruston Way exit.*

Thornewood Castle B&B Inn / ★★★

8601 N THORNE LN, LAKEWOOD; 253/584-4393 "B&B" and "castle" may be contradictory terms, yet the two come together beautifully in this 28,000-square-foot Gothic–Tudor Revival hybrid built by Chester A. Thorne in

1908. It once hosted presidents Howard Taft and Theodore Roosevelt. Now owned by innkeepers Wayne and Deanna Robinson, it has more recently served as the set for an ABC miniseries *Rose Red*, by Stephen King. On four acres overlooking American Lake, the architecturally grand home has impressive reception rooms—a ballroom, music room, great hall, gentlemen's parlor, and more—with extensive wood paneling and medieval stained-glass window accents. Ten guest rooms are decorated with antiques; the impressive bridal suite is done in ivory tones. Some rooms have fireplaces and jetted or antique soaking tubs; all have terry-cloth robes, TV/VCRs, and CD players. Roam the grounds, exploring the sunken Olmsted-designed English garden; fish, swim, or boat on the lake. Mystery tours are sometimes conducted (check the Web site). *$$$–$$$$; AE, DIS, MC, V; checks OK in advance; www .thornewoodcastle.com; take I-5 exit 123 south of Tacoma to Thorne Ln.*

Puyallup

At the head of the fertile Puyallup Valley southeast of Tacoma, this frontier farm town serves as one gateway to Mount Rainier, with Highway 410 leading to Chinook Pass, and Highways 162 and 165 leading to the Carbon River and Mowich Lake. The bulb, rhubarb, and berry farmland continues to be cultivated, but much of it has been strip-malled and auto-row-ravaged around the edges. Avoid the fast-food strip on Highway 161 to the south and head east up the valley to Sumner and the White River (Hwy 410), or Orting, Wilkeson, and Carbonado (Hwys 162 and 165).

The **EZRA MEEKER MANSION** (312 Spring St; 253/848-1770; *www.meeker mansion.org*; open Wed–Sun 1–4pm, mid-Mar–mid-Dec) is the finest original pioneer mansion left in Washington. Its builder and first occupant, Ezra Meeker, introduced hops to the Puyallup Valley. The lavish 17-room Italianate house (circa 1890) now stands beautifully restored in the rear parking lot of a Main Street furniture store.

Puyallup is big on old-time seasonal celebrations and hosts two of the Northwest's largest: April's **DAFFODIL FESTIVAL AND PARADE** (253/627-6176) and September's Western Washington Fair—better known as the **PUYALLUP FAIR** (110 9th Ave SW; 253/841-5045; *www.thefair.com*)—one of the nation's biggest fairs, with food, games, rides, and premier touring bands. The **PUYALLUP DOWNTOWN FARMERS MARKET** is held Saturday mornings at Pioneer Park (corner of Pioneer and Meridian Sts) and runs through the growing season (usually late May–Sept).

Parkland

RESTAURANTS

From the Bayou / ★★

508 GARFIELD ST, PARKLAND; 253/539-4269 Four former school friends from Louisiana launched this Parkland restaurant that has claimed a loyal following.

The smoked-salmon cheesecake appetizer is unexpectedly addictive. Then there's a tantalizing array of Cajun food such as étouffée, gumbo, alligator, and po' boys to satisfy you. Even the stuffed halibut entrée—or praline cream pie—is worth the trip. The setting is a bonus, too, with Zydeco music playing and black-and-white photos of Acadian villages gracing the walls. Live jazz on weekends. *$–$$; AE, DIS, V; checks OK; lunch, dinner Mon–Sat; beer and wine; reservations recommended; cajun@fromthebayou.com; www.fromthebayou.com; take Hwy 512E exit from I-5, then the Pacific Ave exit to Parkland.* &

Marzano's / ★

516 GARFIELD ST, PARKLAND; 253/537-4191 The reputation of Lisa Marzano's voluptuous cooking has people arriving from miles away. In fair weather, outside seating on two deck areas is an added plus to this large space. Meals begin with fresh-baked crusty bread, ready to be topped with shredded Parmesan and herbed olive oil. For entrées, try the stubby rigatoni, perfect for capturing the extraordinary *boscaiola* sauce made with mushrooms and ham; lasagne is sumptuous, as is elegant chicken piccata pungent with capers and lemons. Finish with the many-layered chocolate poppy-seed cake floating in whipped cream. *$$; DIS, MC, V; checks OK; lunch Tues–Fri, dinner Tues–Sat; beer and wine; reservations required (call near meal time; there's no answering machine); adjacent to Pacific Lutheran University, Hwy 512 exit from I-5.* &

Gig Harbor

Once an undisturbed fishing village (and still homeport to an active commercial fleet) northwest of Tacoma across the Narrows Bridge on Highway 16, Gig Harbor is now part suburbia, part retirement destination, and quietly getting better and better as a weekend getaway. Boating is still important, with good anchorage and various moorage docks attracting gunwale-to-gunwale pleasure craft. When the clouds break, Mount Rainier holds court for all. An especially good view can been had at **ANTHONY'S HOMEPORT** (8827 N Harborview Dr; 253/853-6353). A variety of interesting shops and galleries lines **HARBORVIEW DRIVE**, which almost encircles the harbor. It's a picturesque spot for browsing and window-shopping. Sea-kayaking classes from **GIG HARBOR KAYAK CENTER** (8809 N Harborview Dr; 253/851-7987 or 888/429-2548) are fun and thorough; rental boats are available and you can explore the bay in a few hours, or sign up for a guided tour that takes you farther afloat.

Gig Harbor was planned for boat traffic, not automobiles (with resulting traffic congestion and limited parking), yet it's a good place for celebrations. An arts festival in mid-July, a maritime festival in June, and a **SCANDINAVIAN FEST** (*www.ghscanfest.org*) in October are main events. The Saturday **GIG HARBOR FARMERS MARKET** (*www.gigharborfarmersmarket.com*; mid-Apr–Oct) features locally grown produce, plants, and Northwest gifts. Check the events calendar on the **GIG HARBOR CHAMBER OF COMMERCE** (3302 Harborview Dr; 253/851-6865; *www.gigharborchamber.com*) Web site.

In recent years, two large inns have dramatically increased lodging options; both are a drive from downtown. The New England lodge–style **BEST WESTERN WESLEY INN** (6575 Kimball Dr; 253/858-9690 or 888/462-0002; *www.wesleyinn .com*) has an outdoor swimming pool. The Northwestern-style **INN AT GIG HARBOR** (3211 56th St NW; 253/858-1111 or 800/795-9980; *www.innatgigharbor.com*) has an on-site restaurant featuring seafood specialties.

PARADISE CABARET THEATRE (6615 38th Ave NW; 253/851-7529; *www .paradisetheatre.org*) and **ENCORE! THEATER** (253/858-2282; *www.encoretheater .org*), Gig Harbor's resident groups, mount enjoyable productions year-round. In winter, there's dinner theater at Paradise and family theater at Encore. Summer shows are staged outside; theatergoers bring picnics and blankets and watch beneath the stars. It's turned into a wonderful small-town custom.

PENINSULA GARDENS NURSERY (5503 Wollochet Dr NW; 253/851-8115) southwest of town is fun to explore and sells espresso. Nearby **KOPACHUCK STATE PARK** (follow signs from Hwy 16; 253/265-3606) is popular, as are **PENROSE POINT** and **JOEMMA STATE PARKS** on the Key Peninsula (south of Hwy 302, west of Hwy 16 at Purdy), all with beaches for clam digging. Purdy Spit, right on Highway 302, is most accessible.

RESTAURANTS

The Green Turtle / ★★

2905 HARBORVIEW DR, GIG HARBOR; 253/851-3167 At this fun and funky waterfront restaurant, with its undersea decor, owners Nolan and Sue Glenn, and chef Roman Aguillon, present a seafood-focused menu popular with community regulars and fun for visitors. A piquant pear-and-spiced-walnut salad is a nice starter. King salmon comes crusted with sesame seeds; spicy seafood sauté is dressed-up phad thai with shrimp, scallops, and clams. The Turtle Surf and Turf (jumbo scampi in creamy lemon sauce with filet mignon in cabernet demi-glace) is a little pricey but garners raves. Desserts, such as banana toffee or Key lime pie, are worth the extra calories. In fine weather, dine on the deck overlooking the harbor. *$$–$$$; AE, DIS, MC, V; checks OK; lunch Tues–Fri, dinner Tues–Sun; beer and wine; reservations recommended; www.thegreenturtle.com; past Tides Tavern.* &

Marco's Ristorante Italiano / ★

7707 PIONEER WY, GIG HARBOR; 253/858-2899 Everyone in the area loves Marco's. It shows in the busy, crowded bustle of the place. The menu ranges from traditional (spaghetti and meatballs, handmade tortellini in fresh pesto) to more original specials (a dense, tender piece of tuna sautéed in red wine). Deep-fried olives are an unusual starter. *$$; AE, MC, V; checks OK; lunch, dinner Tues–Sat; beer and wine; reservations recommended; 2 blocks from harbor.*

Tides Tavern

2925 HARBORVIEW DR, GIG HARBOR; 253/858-3982 "Meet you at the Tides" has become such a universal invitation that this tavern perched over the harbor often has standing room only, especially on sunny days when the deck is open. People come by boat, seaplane, and car. Originally a general store next to the ferry landing, the Tides is a full-service tavern (no minors) with pool table, Gig Harbor memorabilia, and live music on weekends. Indulge in clam chowder, man-sized sandwiches, huge charbroiled burgers, a gargantuan shrimp salad, and highly touted fish-and-chips (pizzas are only passable). *$–$$; AE, MC, V; checks OK; lunch, dinner every day; beer and wine; reservations recommended Mon–Thurs Sept–May; www.tidestavern.com; downtown Gig Harbor.*

LODGINGS

Aloha Beachside Bed and Breakfast / ★★★

8318 STATE RTE 302, GIG HARBOR; 888/256-4222 It may take a while to get your bearings: seductive Hawaiian music, an expansive beach, a waterfall tumbling over rocks, and a fishing pond (trout) make this feel like Maui. Creature comforts include the sparkling smile of innkeeper Lalaine Wong, the dynamo who runs this two-room B&B with husband Greg. Lalaine loves desserts for breakfast—perhaps cheesecake or fruit crepes. The comfortable guest rooms, named Orchid and Pikake, claim the top (entry) floor and have queen-sized feather beds, water views, and private baths. A spacious balcony between the two overlooks the Sound. The kitchen and a sitting area, also with views, are one floor down. In good weather there's nothing better than breakfast on the deck, with the soothing waterfall and water view. *$$–$$$; MC, V; checks OK; lalaine@alohabeachsidebb .com; www.alohabeachsidebb.com; 7 miles west of Narrows Bridge, take exit 302 and turn left over Purdy Bridge.*

The Maritime Inn

3212 HARBORVIEW DR, GIG HARBOR; 253/858-1818 The Maritime Inn is well located in downtown Gig Harbor, walking distance to shops and restaurants and across from the waterfront. Fifteen individually decorated rooms are comfortably appointed with queen-sized beds, gas fireplaces, and TVs; some offer a bit more space, including sun decks, at a slightly higher cost. Space or no, the price is a bit high considering the lack of conversational privacy in the rooms. Avoid rooms at the front of the inn closest to the street. *$$; AE, DIS, MC, V; checks OK; info@maritimeinn.com; www.maritimeinn.com; downtown.* &

Steilacoom and Anderson Island

Once a Native American village and later the Washington Territory's first incorporated town (1854), Steilacoom today is a quiet community of old trees and houses, with no vestige of its heyday, when a trolley line ran from Bair's drugstore northeast to Tacoma. October's **APPLE SQUEEZE FESTIVAL** (*www.steilacoom.org/museum/*) and midsummer's **SALMON BAKE**, with canoe and kayak races, are popular. The **STEILACOOM TRIBAL MUSEUM** (1515 Lafayette St; 253/584-6308) is in a turn-of-the-century church overlooking the South Sound islands and the Olympic range. **CITY HALL** (253/581-1900; *www.steilacoom.org*) has tourist information.

PIERCE COUNTY FERRIES (253/798-2766 recording; *www.co.pierce.wa.us/text/ services/transpo/ferrysch.htm*) run from here to bucolic off-the-beaten-path Anderson Island.

RESTAURANTS

The Bair Restaurant at the Bair Drug and Hardware Store

🌲 **1617 LAFAYETTE ST, STEILACOOM; 253/588-9668** Side orders of nostalgia are gratis when you step into Bair Drug. Except for the customers, little has changed since it was built in 1895. Products your grandparents might have used—cigars, washtubs, perfume, and apple peelers—are on display. Old post office boxes mask the bakery, which turns out berry and apple pies and other pastries. Best of all is a 1906 soda fountain, where you can still get a sarsaparilla, a Green River, or a genuine ice-cream soda. Traditional high tea, complete with tiny tea sandwiches and tartlets, is served every afternoon except Sunday, by 24-hour advance reservation. In summer, old-fashioned meals such as skillet fried chicken or meatloaf are served on Friday and Saturday nights. The crab and artichoke dip appetizer is delicious. *$; MC, V; no checks; breakfast, lunch every day, dinner Fri–Sat in summer; beer and wine; reservations recommended; www.thebairrestaurant.com; at Wilkes St.* ♿

ER Rogers Mansion / ★

1702 COMMERCIAL ST, STEILACOOM; 253/582-0280 View restaurants on Puget Sound are not novelties, but views like this are still exceptional, particularly from a restored 100-year-old Queen Anne–style home. The Steilacoom special prime rib, first roasted and then sliced and quickly seared, is tops. The huge Sunday buffet brunch offers a selection of seafood: oysters on the half shell, cold poached or kippered salmon, flavorful smoked salmon, cracked crab, pickled herring, steamed clams, and fettuccine with shrimp. An upstairs bar has a widow's walk just wide enough for one row of tables. *$$$; MC, V; checks OK; dinner every day, brunch Sun; full bar; reservations recommended; www.ERRogers.com; corner of Wilkes St.* ♿

LODGINGS

Anderson House on Oro Bay / ★★

12024 ECKENSTAM-JOHNSON RD, ANDERSON ISLAND; 253/884-4088 OR 800/750-4088 A short ferry ride from Steilacoom and a few miles from the dock is a large house surrounded by 200 acres of farmland and woods. The Anderson family operates this landmark home, with original artwork, antique furnishings, and four large guest rooms. Although the hosts live on-site, use of the whole house can be arranged. Breakfasts feature breads hot from the oven, fruit pizzas, and other treats. A short bike ride takes you to a mile-long secluded beach. Arrangements can be made to pick up guests from the ferry. Art and writing workshops are offered; check the Web site or call for more information. A nine-hole golf course is nearby. Boaters and those with seaplanes have their own dock. *$$–$$$; MC, V; checks OK; ahouse@centurytel.net; www.non.com/anderson; call for directions.*

Olympia

The state capital's centerpiece—visible from the freeway—is the classic dome of the **WASHINGTON STATE LEGISLATIVE BUILDING** (416 14th Ave; 360/586-8687). Lavishly fitted with bronze and marble, this striking Romanesque structure houses the offices of the governor and other state executives. Damaged during an earthquake in February 2001, the building is undergoing repair and renovation, and is expected to open sometime in January 2005 for tours. Meanwhile, take a virtual tour on the Web (*www.ga.wa.gov*).

Opposite the Legislative Building rises the pillared **TEMPLE OF JUSTICE**, seat of the State Supreme Court. To the west is the red brick **GOVERNOR'S MANSION**, which also sustained exterior damage during the 2001 earthquake; it is expected to re-open in December 2004 for free Wednesday afternoon tours (360/586-8687; reservations required).

The **STATE CAPITOL MUSEUM** (211 W 21st Ave; 360/753-2580; *www .wshs.org*) houses a permanent exhibit documenting the state's political past. The **WASHINGTON STATE LIBRARY** (6880 Capitol Blvd S, Tumwater; 360/753-5592; *www.statelib.wa.gov*) is open to the public during business hours.

Downtown, on Seventh Avenue between Washington and Franklin Streets, is the restored **OLD CAPITOL**, whose pointed towers and high-arched windows suggest a late-medieval chateau. The **WASHINGTON CENTER FOR THE PERFORMING ARTS** (on Washington St between 5th Ave and Legion Wy; 360/753-8586; *www.washington center.org*) presents a wide variety of national and international performances as well as being home to more than a dozen local performance groups. Across Fifth Avenue, the **CAPITOL THEATER** (206 E 5th Ave; 360/754-5378) provides a showcase for the active **OLYMPIA FILM SOCIETY** (360/754-6670; *www.olyfilm.org*) and locally produced plays and musicals. A few blocks from the heart of downtown, **CAPITOL LAKE** offers views and grassy areas for an informal picnic.

Toward the harbor, the lively **OLYMPIA FARMERS MARKET** (near Percival Landing; 360/352-9096; *www.farmers-market.org*; open Thurs–Sun Apr–Oct (during growing season), weekends Nov–Dec up to Christmas) displays produce, flowers, and crafts from all over the South Sound. The waterfront park of **PERCIVAL LANDING** (700 N Capitol Wy) is a community focal point, the site of several harbor festivals. In another part of downtown, just off the Plum Street exit from Interstate 5 and adjacent to City Hall, is the serene **YASHIRO JAPANESE GARDEN**, honoring one of Olympia's sister cities.

The historic heart of the area (Olympia, Lacey, and Tumwater) is **TUMWATER FALLS** (exit 103 off I-5), where the Deschutes River flows into Capitol Lake. A nice walk along the river takes you past several waterfalls. For something sweet after strolling the falls, stop at **DESSERTS BY TASHA NICOLE** (2822 Capitol Blvd; 360/352-3717; *www.tashanicole.com*) in Tumwater: chocolate-dipped cheesecake on a stick is to die for.

THE EVERGREEN STATE COLLEGE (2700 Evergreen Pkwy NW; 360/866-6000; *www.evergreen.edu*) west of Olympia on Cooper Point, offers a regular schedule of plays, films, experimental theater, and special events. Its library and pool are public.

The area's finest nature preserve lies well outside the city limits. This is the relatively unspoiled Nisqually Delta—outlet of the Nisqually River that forms at the foot of a Mount Rainier glacier and enters the Sound just north of Olympia. Take exit 114 off Interstate 5 and follow signs to the **NISQUALLY NATIONAL WILDLIFE REFUGE** and visitor's center (360/753-9467; *www.nisqually.fws.gov*). Five trails include a 5-mile hiking trail following an old dike around the delta through a wetland alive with birds, and a handicapped-accessible mile-plus boardwalk through freshwater wetlands. Just south, a rookery of great blue herons occupies the treetops. Between the delta and Tacoma to the north is **FORT LEWIS MILITARY RESERVATION**.

Several restaurants downtown are worth knowing about. **SWEET OASIS** (507 Capitol Wy; 360/956-0470) serves delicious Mediterranean-style lunches and dinners at value prices; it has a bakery and active take-out business—get a pita or gyro sandwich and enjoy it by Capitol Lake. At **SANTOSH** (116 4th Ave W, Olympia; 360/943-3442), you'll find delicious handcrafted Northern Indian tandoori-style dishes. Next door is **BEN MOORE'S** (112 4th Ave W; 360/357-7527), a shabby but longtime favorite old American-style café that serves razor clams or geoduck in season.

RESTAURANTS

Budd Bay Cafe / ★★☆

525 N COLUMBIA ST, OLYMPIA; 360/357-6963 It's a slice of the 1970s—a waterfront seafood restaurant with wood floors and armchairs, maritime murals, and a fishing net on the ceiling. But it's a nice slice. Large windows overlook the marina, there's outdoor deck seating for warm weather dining, and a small publike bar at the entry. Service is friendly and upbeat. The food is better than you'd expect. The clam chowder (with a splash of cream sherry offered as a seasoning) is delicious; blackened grilled salmon is a specialty. This is a longtime after-hours haunt of many state government movers and shakers. *$$; AE, DC, DIS, MC, V; checks OK; lunch Mon–Sat, dinner every day, brunch Sun; full bar; reservations recommended; bbaybcafe@olywa.net; www.buddbaycafe.com; between A and B Sts.* &

Gardner's Seafood and Pasta / ★★

111 W THURSTON ST, OLYMPIA; 360/786-8466 For more than 21 years, Leon and Jane Longan have packed loyal fans into their cozy eatery—it has only 11 tables and counter seating for six—near the marina. Yet, the size lends intimacy and many claim you feel as though you're in the home (with fresh flower touches) of a friend who cooks like a dream—serving up good, simple food that always hits the spot. During the right season, you might find a dozen Olympia oysters, each the size of a quarter, served on the half shell. Pastas are homemade and can be bland; appetizers, such as sautéed rock shrimp with garlic and lemon, never are. *$$; AE, MC, V; checks OK; dinner Tues–Sat; beer and wine; reservations recommended; north on Capitol Wy to Thurston St.* &

The Mark / ★★★

407 COLUMBIA ST SW, OLYMPIA; 360/754-4414 The white rectangular building lit with a yellow-and-white Michelin Man sign looks like a garage—and it once was. Yet inside this newcomer to Olympia's food scene there's a nightclub atmosphere. Art on gleaming wood walls, a simple, low-lit, chic lounge of booths and tables, and truly special food—emphasizing French and Spanish cheeses, olives, fresh and organic foods, handcrafted pastas, and rustic breads—turn this into a food sophisticate's destination. Try the cheese ravioli—fat pillows of tender pasta with walnuts—or a free-range Oregon steak. The fancy drinks menu is extensive. Two rooms off the main lounge can be reserved—and hopping—for parties. *$$–$$$; AE, DIS, MC, V; checks OK; reservations recommended; www.themarkolympia.com; full bar; downtown between 4th and 5th Aves.* &

Portofino / ★★

101 DIVISION NW, OLYMPIA; 360/352-2803 For more than 20 years, this tiny, converted 1890s farmhouse—overshadowed by a beetling office building—has been a quiet, elegant refuge for Olympians seeking imaginative, skillfully prepared Northwest cuisine influenced by Italian and French cooking styles. Garlic lovers must try their garlic and spinach purée soup; a house-made fresh ravioli changes daily, as does much of the menu. Crab cakes are made fresh from shrimp and crab shucked on the spot. There is an extensive wine list. In spring or summer, sit on the restaurant's glassed-in porch—though the view of over-trafficked Division Street may make you long for the days when this place was a farm. *$$; AE, MC, V; checks OK; dinner Tues–Sun; full bar; reservations required; 1 block south of Harrison Ave.* &

The Spar Cafe and Bar / ★

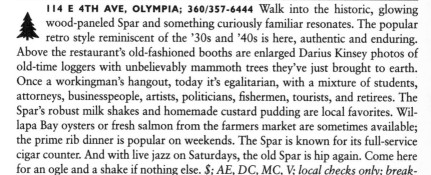

114 E 4TH AVE, OLYMPIA; 360/357-6444 Walk into the historic, glowing wood-paneled Spar and something curiously familiar resonates. The popular retro style reminiscent of the '30s and '40s is here, authentic and enduring. Above the restaurant's old-fashioned booths are enlarged Darius Kinsey photos of old-time loggers with unbelievably mammoth trees they've just brought to earth. Once a workingman's hangout, today it's egalitarian, with a mixture of students, attorneys, businesspeople, artists, politicians, fishermen, tourists, and retirees. The Spar's robust milk shakes and homemade custard pudding are local favorites. Willapa Bay oysters or fresh salmon from the farmers market are sometimes available; the prime rib dinner is popular on weekends. The Spar is known for its full-service cigar counter. And with live jazz on Saturdays, the old Spar is hip again. Come here for an ogle and a shake if nothing else. *$; AE, DC, MC, V; local checks only; breakfast, lunch, dinner every day; full bar; no reservations; 1 block east of Capitol Wy.*

LODGINGS

Harbinger Inn / ★★

1136 E BAY DR, OLYMPIA; 360/754-0389 Occupying a restored 1910 mansion, this B&B offers Mission-style furnishings, a fine outlook over Budd Inlet and the distant Olympic Mountains, and five choice guest rooms. Nicest is the top-floor Innkeeper's Suite, with its king-sized bed, sitting room, gas fireplace, and large bathroom with soaking tub. Rooms at the front of the house have views, but rooms on the back side are farther from the street, with only the sound of a small artesian-fed waterfall to disturb the tranquility. All have private baths (although the bath for the Cloisonné Room is on the main floor, directly below the room). The inn is situated near excellent routes for bicycle riding, and Priest Point Park is close by. Full breakfast is served. *$$; AE, MC, V; checks OK; www.harbingerinn.com; ¼ mile north of State St.*

Tenino and Yelm

This once quiet, now growing area south of Olympia on Highway 99 is known for **WOLF HAVEN** (3111 Offut Lake Rd; 360/264-4695; *www.wolfhaven.org*), an educational, nonprofit research facility that teaches wolf appreciation and studies the question of whether to reintroduce wolves into the wild. The public is invited to see the wolves or join them in a howl-in. Tenino is also known for the country dining destination **ALICE'S RESTAURANT** (19248 Johnson Creek Rd SE; 360/264-2887; *www.alicesdinners.com*). Another nearby and growing rural community, Yelm also has a bucolic dining destination: **ARNOLD'S COUNTRY INN** (717 Yelm Ave E; 360/458-3977), a great place to stop for seafood, steaks, chicken, and freshly baked rolls and pies on the way to Mount Rainier.

OLYMPIC PENINSULA

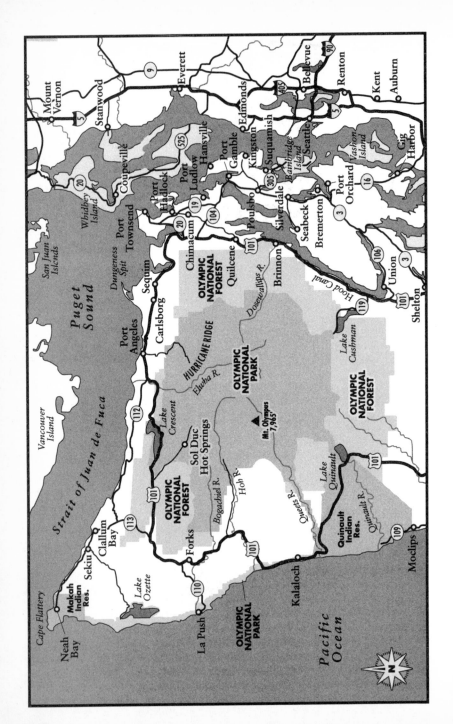

OLYMPIC PENINSULA

The wonders of the Olympic Peninsula draw visitors from all over the world. Olympic National Park, with its mountainous terrain blended with a diverse ocean landscape, combined with the lush temperate rain forest, gives the impression of three parks rolled into one.

As it is inside the park, the scenery throughout the entire 5,000 square miles of the Kitsap and Olympic Peninsulas is diverse and distinct. In Kitsap County, you'll see Silverdale's mall country, with neon lights and fast-food joints, get caught up in Poulsbo's Scandinavian atmosphere, or ponder history through the dollhouse homes in the historic mill town of Port Gamble. Then cross the Hood Canal Bridge to the Olympic Peninsula's land of emerald farmland carpets, hulking forests of cedar and fir, crashing swells that pound the Pacific coast, and the charming Victoriana of Port Townsend. Native peoples have inhabited the lands for thousands of years, and traditions rooted in logging and fishing are evident in every community.

Each change in topography brings a change in climate. You could bask in the sun in Sequim (popular with retirees, in the rain shadow of the Olympics), and two hours later find yourself pelted by hammering raindrops in Forks. The variations make planning a trip easy: bring everything. Good sturdy shoes and a water-repellent jacket are musts year-round. The only thing you probably won't need is formal wear.

Countless opportunities exist here for picnicking, hiking, camping, photography, boating, fishing, shopping, and more. Other Olympic Peninsula perks include restaurants serving plenty of fresh seafood, unique lodgings and hot springs, and a "winery loop."

And, of course, there are the forests. US Highway 101 wraps snugly around an empire built and ruled by Mother Nature. In the center, Olympic National Park is home to some 1,200 plant species, 300 bird species, and 70 different kinds of mammals. More than 5 million people every year come to soak in the hot springs, wander the forest, hug the 250- to 500-year-old fir and cedar trees, and sneak a peek at wildlife adept at the art of camouflage. Visitor centers at Hurricane Ridge and the Hoh Rain Forest feature interpretive, hands-on learning exhibits and helpful rangers.

Perhaps the Olympic Peninsula's rainy winter weather (rainfall ranges from 24 inches annually in Port Angeles to more than 130 inches in the Hoh Rain Forest) is nature's way of attracting the serious type of visitor. If you don't mind getting wet, though, you'll learn why 200,000 people call it home.

ACCESS AND INFORMATION

The best route to the Olympic Peninsula is by way of the scenic **WASHINGTON STATE FERRIES** (206/464-6400 or 800/843-3779; *www.wsdot.wa.gov/ferries/*), which run regularly between downtown Seattle and Bremerton on the Kitsap Peninsula, or Bainbridge Island. Boats also dock in Port Townsend (from Keystone on Whidbey Island), on the Kitsap Peninsula in Kingston (from Edmonds), and in Southworth, near Port Orchard (from Fauntleroy in West Seattle). You can also drive around Puget Sound to reach the peninsula.

OLYMPIC PENINSULA THREE-DAY TOUR

DAY ONE: Catch an early ferry to Kingston from Mukilteo, then follow the signs toward Port Townsend. On your way, take a detour through charming little Port Gamble for ice cream or a coffee at the **PORT GAMBLE GENERAL STORE**. Cross the Hood Canal Bridge to the Olympic Peninsula and follow signs to Port Townsend. Slow down on your way through the Chimacum Valley to drink in the bucolic splendor—this is dairy-farm country. Once in Port Townsend, check in at the **QUIMPER INN**, then wander through the Uptown district and stop at **SENTOSA** for lunch. Go downtown via the Taylor Street steps, built to accommodate ladies who took tiny steps in their tight Victorian skirts, to **HALLER FOUNTAIN**. Window-shop downtown, finishing up with wine tasting at the **WINE SELLER**. Then take dinner at the **SILVERWATER CAFÉ** and perhaps a movie at the **ROSE THEATER**.

DAY TWO: After breakfast at the inn, head out of town and take Highway 20 to Highway 101 west toward Sequim. Take the Sequim exit for a roving **MURAL TOUR**—the main street is peppered with trompe l'oeil works. Continue down 101—it joins up with the main street as you head west—toward Port Angeles. Pick up a sandwich and a cranberry muffin at **SUNNY FARMS COUNTRY STORE** (261461 Hwy 101; 360/683-8003), between Sequim and Port Angeles. Follow signs to **HURRICANE RIDGE** in **OLYMPIC NATIONAL PARK**, where summer meadows are filled with wildflowers, and winter activities include free guided snowshoe tours and cross-country skiing. After playing all day, return to Port Angeles and check into the **TUDOR INN** and soak in a nice hot bath; then head to dinner at **C'EST SI BON**.

DAY THREE: After breakfast at the inn, continue west on Highway 101 to Forks, stopping at **RIVERRUN COFFEE** for coffee or the **RAINDROP CAFÉ** (111 S Forks Ave; 360/374-6612) for lunch. Then visit the **TIMBER MUSEUM** to learn about the forest and the logging industry. Head east into the **HOH RAIN FOREST** to tromp trails flanked by ancient trees dripping with lacy moss, and perhaps spy a herd of Roosevelt elk. On the way back to Forks, pick up some groceries and find your way to the **SHADY NOOK COTTAGE**, where you can cook your own dinner and relax before tomorrow's drive home.

Arriving in Port Angeles by boat is a snap (crossing time is one hour) from Victoria, British Columbia, with the **MV COHO**, operated by Black Ball Transportation (360/457-4491; twice daily year-round, except during January dry docking), and via the much quicker **VICTORIA EXPRESS** (360/452-8088 or 800/633-1589; *www.victoriaexpress.com*), a foot-passenger ferry that runs two or three times daily, summer and fall (cash only). In summer, **ROYAL VICTORIA TOURS** (888/381-1800; *www.royaltours.ca*) offers guided bus trips to Victoria and Butchart Gardens.

PUBLIC BUS TRANSPORTATION between communities is available through Kitsap Transit (360/373-BUSS or 800/501-RIDE), Jefferson County Transit and West Jefferson Transit (360/385-4777 or 800/371-0497), Clallam Transit System (360/452-4511 or 800/858-3747), and Mason County Transit Authority (360/426-9434 or 800/281-9434).

SMALL PLANES land at airports in Bremerton, Jefferson County, Shelton, Sequim, and Port Angeles. The largest airline to serve the peninsula is HORIZON AIR (800/547-9308; *www.horizonair.com*), which lands at Fairchild International Airport in Port Angeles.

Olympic Peninsula temperatures range from 45°F in January to 72°F in August. Rainfall averages 2–3 inches per month, less in Sequim and more—up to 121 inches annually—in Forks. For information on visiting the area, contact the PORT TOWNSEND CHAMBER OF COMMERCE VISITOR INFORMATION CENTER (2437 E Sims Wy, Port Townsend; 360/385-2722 or 888/ENJOYPT; *www.ptchamber .org*) or the NORTH OLYMPIC PENINSULA VISITOR & CONVENTION BUREAU (360/452-8552 or 800/942-4042; *travel@olypen.com*; *www.northwestsecretplaces .com/vcb/*) in Port Angeles.

Kitsap Peninsula

The Kitsap Peninsula, between the larger Olympic Peninsula and the mainland, is roughly defined by Puget Sound (and Bainbridge and Vashon Islands) on the east and Hood Canal on the west. Connected to the Olympic Peninsula by a small stretch of land at the southern end of Hood Canal, the Kitsap Peninsula links to the body of Western Washington via the Tacoma Narrows Bridge. The Hood Canal Bridge connects Kitsap's northern end to the Olympic Peninsula.

Port Orchard

Known as the antique capital of the Kitsap Peninsula, the center of this small town hugs the southern shoreline of one of Puget Sound's many fingers of water: Sinclair Inlet. With its boardwalk and beach access, the waterfront area is a true gathering place. The PORT ORCHARD FARMERS MARKET (Marina Park, 1 block from Bay St.; Sat late Apr–Oct) and WEDNESDAY MARKET (South Kitsap Community Park, use Lund Ave entrance; May–Oct) offer a selection of cut flowers, fresh vegetables, baked goods, and crafts. Take home Hood Canal oysters or ask the Oyster Lady to grill a few. Antique shops abound, and the SIDNEY ART GALLERY AND MUSEUM (202 Sidney Ave; 360/876-3693) displays Northwest art.

KITSAP TRANSIT (360/478-6230) operates a daily foot ferry between downtown Port Orchard and the main ferry terminal at Bremerton. Otherwise, drive north on Highway 3.

LODGINGS

Reflections Bed and Breakfast Inn / ★★

3878 REFLECTION LN E, PORT ORCHARD; 360/871-5582 This sprawling inn, set on a hillside overlooking Sinclair Inlet with a backdrop of the Olympic Mountains, is an impressive manor with a New England flair. Former New Englander Cathy Hall extends warm hospitality and serves a hearty breakfast. Guests are asked the night before to agree by consensus on the next morning's menu and serving time. The inn has four guest rooms (two with private baths) adorned with family antiques, including heirloom quilts. The largest room has a private porch and a soaking tub. All have water views. The well-tended grounds include a hot tub, a gazebo, and birds eating and preening at various feeders. *$$; MC, V; no checks; jimreflect@seanet.com; www.portorchard.com/reflections; east of Port Orchard off Beach Dr.* &

Bremerton

In the 1890s, a young German, William Bremer, sold close to 200 acres of bay front to the U.S. Navy for $9,587. The naval shipyards are still located in downtown Bremerton, and rows of moth-gray ghost ships—silent reminders of past naval battles—loom offshore. Only the destroyer **USS TURNER JOY** (300 Washington Beach Ave; 360/792-2457), which saw action off Vietnam, is open for self-guided tours (daily May–Sept, weekends only Oct–Apr). Adjacent to the ferry terminal and the *Turner Joy*, the **BREMERTON NAVAL MUSEUM** (360/479-7447) depicts the region's shipbuilding history back to bowsprit-and-sail days; open every day in summer, closed Mondays, Labor Day through Memorial Day.

Farther north on the Kitsap Peninsula is the **TRIDENT NUCLEAR SUBMARINE BASE** at Bangor. Occasionally a pod of orcas can be sighted escorting one of the mammoth submarines through the local waters to deep-sea duty. Since 1915, Keyport has been the major U.S. site for undersea torpedo testing. Now it also is home to the extraordinary **NAVAL UNDERSEA MUSEUM** (360/396-4148; open every day, closed Tues Oct–May; *www.lcss.net/num*), housing the first Revolutionary War submarine.

RESTAURANTS

Boat Shed / ★

101 SHORE DR, BREMERTON; 360/377-2600 This casual seafood restaurant overhanging the Port Washington Narrows offers waterfront dining and is suitably named. Dock access makes it a convenient drop-in for nearby boaters. Walls inside and out are paneled in rough wood, and a solitary fish tank serves as decor. Local seafood is the main attraction here: salmon, herb-crusted halibut, pan-fried oysters, rich clam chowder, and popular Dungeness crab cakes. Pastas, salads, and steaks round out the menu. *$; AE, DC, MC, V; local checks only; lunch, dinner every day, brunch Sun; full bar; reservations recommended; east side of Manette Bridge.* &

Seabeck

LODGINGS

Willcox House / ★★★

▲ **2390 TEKIU RD, SEABECK; 360/830-4492 OR 800/725-9477** Col. Julian Willcox and his wife, Constance, once played host to Clark Gable at this copper-roofed, 10,000-square-foot, art deco manse on the east side of Hood Canal. Now owners Phillip and Cecilia Hughes serve a hearty breakfast, offer lunch to multinight guests, and provide prix-fixe dinners (open to nonguests by reservation). Diners love the roasted pork tenderloin served Saturdays, and if you're lucky, you'll come on a night when Cecilia has made one of her famous chocolate truffle cakes. Oak parquet floors, walnut-paneled walls, and a copper-framed marble fireplace—one of five fireplaces in the house—grace the front rooms. All five guest rooms have private baths and views of Hood Canal and the Olympics. One room has a fireplace; another, a double soaking tub. Comb the beach for oysters, fish from the dock, or hike the hillside trails. The house is about a half-hour drive from the Bremerton ferry, though some guests arrive by boat or floatplane. *$$$; MC, V; checks OK; www.willcoxhouse.com; 9 miles south of Seabeck, call for directions.*

Silverdale

RESTAURANTS

Bahn Thai / ★★

9811 MICKELBERRY RD, SILVERDALE; 360/698-3663 Come with a group to share a variety of the brightly flavored dishes of Thailand: *tod mun*—spicy, crisp patties of minced fish, green beans, and lime leaves; *tom yum goong*, a favorite soup of prawns and lemongrass; and six exotic curries, including *mussamun*—beef and potatoes sauced with a medium curry infused with coconut milk and cloves, nutmeg, and cinnamon. Fifteen years of cooking at Seattle's Bahn Thai put Rattana Vilaiporn in perfect position to take over operations at the Silverdale location. She's kept the menu and the same clean, exotic look of the place, with sunken tables and lots of Thai art. *$; AE, MC, V; local checks only; lunch, dinner weekdays, dinner on weekends; beer and wine; reservations not necessary; kbahnthai@excite.com; ½ block north of Bucklin Hill Rd.* &

Yacht Club Broiler / ★

9226 BAYSHORE DR, SILVERDALE; 360/698-1601 This simple restaurant boasts one of the best happy hours in town. As you might expect from its name and location (on Dyes Inlet), seafood is big here. More unexpected is the high quality of that seafood (as the commercial fishermen who eat here will attest), be it sweet, moist Dungeness crab cakes, Cajun-seared ahi tuna with Asian slaw, or prawn and shrimp skewers. At happy hour, appetizers and drinks are half price (every day 3–6pm, Saturday 11am–6pm, and all day Sunday). *$$; AE, DC, MC, V; checks OK; lunch,* *dinner every day, brunch Sun; full bar; reservations recommended; Silverdale exit off Hwy 3.* &

LODGINGS

Red Lion Silverdale Hotel

3073 NW BUCKLIN HILL RD, SILVERDALE; 360/698-1000 OR 800/544-9799 This resort hotel was scheduled for a remodel as we went to press, but is expected to serve the same clientele as before: conference attendees and getaway travelers. Encroaching shopping malls are a distraction, but many of the 150 rooms and suites have balconies with sweeping views over Dyes Inlet. In addition, some rooms have fireplaces and all have high-speed Internet access. Extras include an indoor lap pool, a large brick sun deck, a sauna, a weight room, and a video-game room. The Mariner Grill offers tables with white linens, professional service, and nicely prepared meals that aren't too pricey. The crab chimichanga took first place in a local restaurant competition. Enjoy a breakfast of boardinghouse-style biscuits and gravy, or Belgian waffles piled with strawberries and cream. *$$; AE, DC, DIS, MC, V; no checks; silverdalesales@redlion.com; www.redlion.com; at Silverdale Wy.*

Poulsbo

Poulsbo, once a community of primarily Scandinavian fishermen and loggers, is referred to as "little Norway." Today, it's a popular stop, full of gift shops and yachts. Its Scandinavian heritage is apparent—Front Street sports its "Velkommen til Poulsbo" signs, and the architecture is a dolled-up version of the fjord villages of Norway. Stroll the boardwalk along Liberty Bay, or rent a kayak from **OLYMPIC OUTDOOR CENTER** (360/697-6095).

The **HULA GRILL CAFE** (18927 E Front St; 360/779-2763) serves Hawaiian-style food—hot and cold sandwiches, soups, salads, and smoothies; or select something from the overwhelming choices at the famed **SLUY'S BAKERY** (18924 Front St NE; 360/779-2798). Too crowded? Walk south a block to **LIBERTY BAY BAKERY AND CAFE** (18996 Front St NE; 360/779-2828; closed Mon). **BOEHM'S CHOCOLATES** (18864 Front St NE; 360/697-3318) also has an outpost here.

RESTAURANTS

Benson's Restaurant / ★★★

18820 FRONT ST, POULSBO; 360/697-3449 White linens add to the elegant ambiance of one of Poulsbo's nicest downtown neighbors. Signature selections include pan-seared and oven-roasted duck sliced thin with a cranberry port sauce, and crab-and-spinach-stuffed Alaskan halibut served with a lemon beurre blanc sauce. Owners Kelly and Jeffrey Benson go out of their way to make friendly suggestions for appropriate wines and specials. For dessert try chocolate mousse torte, or appetizingly presented apple tart under caramel glaze, with vanilla ice cream. Wednesdays are good for wine lovers: bottles and glasses are half price. *$$; AE, MC, V; checks OK; lunch, dinner Tues–Sat, brunch Sun; full bar; reservations recommended; jef_ben@msn.com; from Lincoln St NE, head toward water.* &

LODGINGS

Manor Farm Inn / ★★

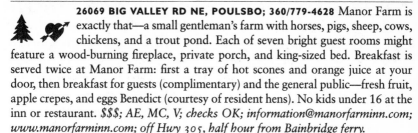 **26069 BIG VALLEY RD NE, POULSBO; 360/779-4628** Manor Farm is exactly that—a small gentleman's farm with horses, pigs, sheep, cows, chickens, and a trout pond. Each of seven bright guest rooms might feature a wood-burning fireplace, private porch, and king-sized bed. Breakfast is served twice at Manor Farm: first a tray of hot scones and orange juice at your door, then breakfast for guests (complimentary) and the general public—fresh fruit, apple crepes, and eggs Benedict (courtesy of resident hens). No kids under 16 at the inn or restaurant. *$$$; AE, MC, V; checks OK; information@manorfarminn.com; www.manorfarminn.com; off Hwy 305, half hour from Bainbridge ferry.*

Suquamish

In Suquamish, on the Port Madison Indian Reservation (follow signs past Agate Pass), the **SUQUAMISH MUSEUM** in the Tribal Center (15838 Sandy Hook Rd NE; 360/598-3311) is devoted to Puget Sound Salish Indian culture. Chief Sealth's grave is nearby, on the grounds of St. Peter's Catholic Mission Church. Twin dugout canoes rest on a log frame over the stone, which reads, "The firm friend of the whites, and for him the city of Seattle was named."

Port Gamble

Located on Hwy 104 between Kingston and Hood Canal, this picture-postcard town was built in the mid-19th century by the Pope & Talbot timber company. Andrew Jackson Pope and Frederic Talbot traveled here by clipper ship from Maine, and created the quintessential company town. Everything is still company-owned and maintained—though the company is now Olympic Resource Management, not Pope & Talbot—and the dozen or so Victorian houses are beauties. The town, modeled on a New England village, also boasts a lovely church and a vital and well-stocked company store. The historic **PORT GAMBLE MUSEUM** (on Rainier Ave; 360/297-8074) offers an ideal presentation of a community's society and industrial heritage, designed by Alec James, creator of the displays for the Royal Provincial Museum in Victoria. The lumber mill no longer operates.

Hansville

A couple of the prettiest, most accessible, and least explored beaches on the peninsula lie to the east of Hansville. **POINT NO POINT**, marked by a lighthouse, is great for a family outing. Follow the road from Hansville to the west and you'll reach **CAPE FOULWEATHER**. The short trail through the woods can be tough to find, so look for the Nature Conservancy sign on the south side of the road.

FROM TIMBER TO TOURISM

Dennis Chastain passes his chain saw across a cubic yard of cedar, with sawdust flying like sparks. He switches to a smaller saw and gingerly shaves down rough edges with the care of a barber giving a young boy his first crew cut. After about 20 minutes, a cuddly looking grizzly bear emerges from the block.

Chastain is a master chain-saw carver: he's won and placed in competitions all over the Northwest. People from around the world stop to admire and buy the works he creates from an outdoor shop, **DEN'S WOOD DEN**, behind his home a few miles south of Forks on Highway 101.

"When we moved here it was known as the last frontier," he says, recalling the virgin timber and big-money jobs.

That was three decades ago, when Chastain and his wife, Margaret, came from Salem, Oregon. He took a production job in a mill that eventually went belly-up. Others in the timber industry faced the same problem in the 1980s, when overlogging and new environmental rules sent shock waves through the corridor of Highway 101: timber could no longer sustain the community.

"They wanted me to sit around on my butt and answer the telephone, and I just couldn't do that," Chastain says.

So, in 1988, he turned his carving hobby into full-time work where he could gulp in the aroma of fresh cedar sawdust; Margaret takes care of sales. The Chastains' company is part of the Olympic Peninsula's evolution to a tourism-based economy. The towns of Port Angeles, Sequim, and Forks have stepped up efforts to bring in people to play at Olympic National Park, roam the rocky coast, and shop for antiques and local art.

The Chastains have seen some of their best friends leave town to pursue logging careers in other places, such as Alaska, Dennis says. But the Olympic Peninsula is his home: "I have a funny feeling we may be planted here."

—*Vanessa McGrady*

Hood Canal and the Northeast Corner

Highway 101 hugs the west side of Hood Canal through tiny towns with names like Lilliwaup, Hamma Hamma, Duckabush, and Union, and vacation homes line the miles of scenic shoreline. In bays and inlets along the way, oyster and clam populations are making a comeback; stop at any roadside stand or store for fresh crab and oysters. Sample the wines at the little **HOODSPORT WINERY** tasting room (N 23501 Hwy 101; 360/877-9894; Mon–Fri 10am–6pm).

Once serious timber country—the logging community of Shelton still sells thousands upon thousands of Christmas trees nationwide each year—this stretch of highway also serves as the jumping-off spot for many recreational areas in the Olympic National Forest, including **LAKE CUSHMAN** and its state park (7211 N Lake Cushman Rd; 360/877-5491). Numerous hiking trails lead to remote, cloud-draped alpine lakes and meadows.

The **ALDERBROOK RESORT AND SPA** (10 E Alderbrook Dr, Union; 360/898-2200 or 800/622-9370; *www.alderbrookresort.com*) recently reopened after a two-year renovation and now has an 18-hole golf course, fitness center, meeting space for as many as 200 people, 77 guest rooms, and 16 beachfront cottages.

Shelton

RESTAURANTS

Xinh's Clam & Oyster House / ★★

221 W RAILROAD AVE, STE D, SHELTON; 360/427-8709 A five-time West Coast oyster-shucking champion, chef Xinh Dwelley knows her shellfish. For 20 years, she worked as the quality control manager (and did her fair share of shucking) at Taylor United Inc., a Shelton shellfish company. Today, Xinh runs not only Shelton's finest seafood restaurant, but also one of the best and freshest little clam and oyster houses on the Olympic Peninsula. Xinh herself picks out the best of each day's haul. Slide down a few fresh Olympias or Steamboat Island Pacifics on the half shell and then see what she can do with a sauce. For guests who order raw oysters, Xinh will shuck them herself. The menu features fusion cooking with a weekly featured curry dish, and a few Italian dishes. You won't find a better heaping plate of mussels in a Vietnamese curry sauce. *$$; MC, V; checks OK; dinner Tues–Sat; beer and wine; reservations recommended; www.taylorshellfish.com; at 3rd St.* &

Union

RESTAURANTS

Robin Hood / ★★

6790 HWY 106, UNION; 360/898-4400 The stone-and-log structure on the east bank of Hood Canal has been a stopover since the early 1930s. It has functioned as a lively dance hall and tavern, a drugstore, and a B&B, but in the past decade it has evolved into one of the area's better eateries. High-beamed ceilings, a fireplace, and large windows set the scene for equally appealing food. Seafood can be exceptional, and portions of prime rib are ample. Robin Hood's signatures include Mediterranean mussels with crème fraîche and lavender garlic broth, and pan-seared Alaskan scallops with Israeli couscous. Desserts are imaginative and rich. Live jazz Sundays, 6–9pm. Live music or a DJ on Saturdays after 10pm. *$$;*

MC, V; checks OK; lunch Wed–Sun in Pub & Oyster Bar, dinner Thurs–Sun; full bar; reservations recommended; ¼ mile west of Alderbrook Resort and Spa. ♿

Quilcene

Every summer weekend, this popular access point to the Olympic Mountains holds renowned concerts by the internationally acclaimed, Seattle-based Philadelphia String Quartet and world-class guest artists at the **OLYMPIC MUSIC FESTIVAL** (11 miles west of Hood Canal Bridge on Hwy 104, then ¼ mile south from Quilcene exit; 360/732-4000; *www.olympicmusicfestival.org*). Music lovers sit on hay bales in a century-old Dutch Colonial barn or stretch out with a picnic on the gentle hillside while listening to chamber music. Nearby, **MOUNT WALKER**, a 6-mile hike or drive, promises spectacular views of Puget Sound including Seattle, Quilcene, and Dabob Bay.

Port Ludlow

LODGINGS

The Resort at Port Ludlow / ★★

1 HERON RD, PORT LUDLOW; 360/437-0411 OR 877/805-0868 A popular resort facility inspired by New England's classic coastal summer homes, the Resort at Port Ludlow offers breathtaking views of the Olympic Mountains and beyond. This spectacular setting is ideal for family vacations, executive retreats, and conferences, with 27 holes of golf, meeting space, spa services, and a wide variety of hiking and cycling trails. Guests choose an individual guest room at the Inn at Port Ludlow, the two-bedroom Pintail House, or a two- or four-bedroom condominium. The inn has 37 spacious rooms decorated in classic mission-style furnishings; each has a fireplace, sitting area, and oversized jetted tub. Unfortunately a few of the town homes in the neighboring community have direct views into some guest rooms. Two restaurants at the resort offer casual and fine dining. *$$$; AE, MC, V; checks OK; info@ludlowbayresort.com; www.ludlowbayresort.com; 6 miles north of Hood Canal Bridge on west side.*

Port Hadlock

Hugging the shorelines of Oak Bay and Port Townsend Bay, the false-front, Old West–style buildings in Port Hadlock sport the same hot pinks, blues, and purples that some supermarkets use to ice cakes—a new take on "local color." South of Hadlock on Highway 19, the **CHIMACUM CAFE** (9253 Rhody Dr; 360/732-4631) serves great homemade pie. A transplanted Frenchman and his American wife bake heart-achingly delicious bread and pastries at the **VILLAGE BAKER** (10644 Rhody Dr; 360/379-5310). Heading north, at the Shold Business Park off Highway 19, buy a bag of superb fresh bagels (baked daily) and toppings to go at **BAGEL**

HAVEN BAKERY & CAFE (227 W Patison St; 360/385-6788). Local events include a Fourth of July Celebration, Hadlock Days in July, and musical performances at Fort Flagler.

RESTAURANTS

Ajax Cafe / ★

271 WATER ST, PORT HADLOCK; 360/385-3450 Colorful chapeaus from sombreros to safari hats decorate the whimsical walls of the Ajax, and owners Tom and Linda Weiner have been known to encourage guests to try them on for size. An eclectic mix of mismatched dishes and glasses garnish the tables, but the flavors and aromas floating from the kitchen harmonize perfectly. The signature dish is a flavorful Mediterranean-style fishermen's stew: clams, mussels, and whitefish simmer in a leek and saffron broth served with garlic aioli. A local favorite is macadamia nut–encrusted halibut served with an orange basil beurre blanc sauce. The Weiners use only the finest Oregon country beef for steaks and ribs. Local live music (jazz, blues, folk) plays Thursday through Saturday. *$$; MC, V; local checks only; dinner Tues–Sun; beer and wine; reservations recommended; www.ajaxcafe.com; on waterfront, off Oak Bay Rd.* &

Marrowstone Island

Long ago, Marrowstone's enterprise was turkey farming. Today, locals farm oysters and harvest clams. To get to Marrowstone from Ports Ludlow or Hadlock, watch for signs directing you to Indian Island, Fort Flagler State Park, and Marrowstone from Oak Bay Road. **FORT FLAGLER STATE PARK** (10541 Flagler Rd; 360/385-1259), an old coastal fortification, offers acres of trails, grassy fields, and miles of beaches to walk, as well as RV and tent camping. Seals hang out at the end of a sand spit, as do nesting gulls. At the historic **NORDLAND GENERAL STORE** (5180 Flagler Rd; 360/385-0777), with its oiled floors and covered porch, you can pick up a bag of oysters or, in summer, rent a small boat to paddle on Mystery Bay. In winter, locals gather with espresso around the woodstove in the back of the store.

LODGINGS

Beach Cottages on Marrowstone / ★

10 BEACH DR, NORDLAND; 360/385-3077 OR 800/871-3077 Formerly known as The Ecologic Place, this gathering of eight quaint cabins offers "nothing," as the innkeepers like to say. When was the last time you did nothing? The rustic resort, complete with a meeting hall that sometimes hosts live local music, is peaceful and picturesque. The resort borders on a tidal estuary that flows into Oak Bay and then Puget Sound and offers a view of the Olympics and Mount Rainier. Cabins provide equipped kitchens, Tempur-Pedic beds, and fine-for-the-children bunks and twin beds. Bring a good book, a pair of binoculars, and a bathing suit. *$$; MC, V; checks OK; www.beachcottagegetaway.com; right at "Welcome to Marrowstone" sign.*

Port Townsend

Wealthy folk settled here in the mid-1800s and built more than 200 Victorian homes; foreign consuls off ships from around the globe added a cosmopolitan flavor to the port town's social life. When the mineral deposits petered out, the railroad never came, and the elite investors left, Port Townsend became a land of vanished dreams and vacant mansions. The restored buildings with wraparound views, in what is now a National Historic Landmark District, lie at the heart of the town's charm. A **VICTORIAN HOMES FESTIVAL** (360/379-0668; *www.victorian festival.org*) in March includes tours of newly renovated Victorian homes. The **HISTORIC-HOMES TOUR** (888/ENJOYPT) happens in September, and the **JEFFERSON COUNTY HISTORICAL SOCIETY** (210 Madison St; 360/385-1003) has a fascinating museum in the original city hall. The **ROTHSCHILD HOUSE** (*www.olympus.net/ftworden/rh.html*) on Taylor (between Jefferson and Franklin) is one of Washington's smallest state parks, measuring 50 by 200 feet. The pre-Victorian house with a heritage rose and herb garden is open for self-guided tours daily May through September, weekends in November.

Colorful shops line Water Street. **ANCESTRAL SPIRITS GALLERY** (701 Water St; 360/385-0078) has an abundant and elegant collection of sculpture, prints, paintings, jewelry, and music by Native craftspeople across the country. **PACIFIC TRADITIONS GALLERY** (in lobby of Water Street Hotel, 637 Water St; 360/385-4770; *www .pacifictraditions.com*), owned by Mary Hewitt, represents indigenous artwork, jewelry, and books from many tribes and nationally renowned artists. There's **WILLIAM JAMES BOOKSELLER** (829 Water St; 360/385-7313) and **EARTHEN WORKS** (702 Water St; 360/385-0328), specializing in high-quality Washington crafts. You'll find the best antique selection at the **PORT TOWNSEND ANTIQUE MALL** (802 Washington St; 360/379-8069).

The best ice cream cones can be had at **ELEVATED ICE CREAM** (627 Water St; 360/385-1156); the best pastries at **BREAD AND ROSES BAKERY** (230 Quincy St; 360/385-1044); and for picnic fare, coffee, homemade chocolates, and people watching, try **MCKENZIE'S** (221 Taylor St; 360/385-3961). At the **WINE SELLER** (940 Water St; 360/385-7673), proprietor and jazz guitarist Joe Euro stocks gourmet snacks, a selection of high-end beer, and wines from around the globe.

SIRENS (823 Water St; 360/379-1100), hidden up a flight of stairs in the historic Bartlett Building, is a delightful place to enjoy a glass of wine, shoot some pool, and listen to music on the deck overlooking the bay. The **ROSE THEATER** (235 Taylor St; 360/385-1039), a beautifully restored art house, has red velvet curtains, ancient frescoed walls, and the world's best popcorn. It's also home to the annual **PORT TOWNSEND FILM FESTIVAL** (360/379-1333; *www.ptfilmfest.com*)

CHETZEMOKA PARK (Jackson and Blaine Sts), a memorial in the northeast corner of town to the S'Klallam Indian chief who became a friend of the first white settlers, has a charming gazebo, picnic tables, tall Douglas firs, and a grassy slope down to the beach. You can see the chief's likeness carved in the huge pillars in front of the post office or in a bronze sculpture at the golf course. **HALLER FOUNTAIN** (Washington and Tyler Sts) is where Port Townsend's brazen goddess lives. Galatea, her voluptuous body draped beneath a diaphanous robe, has graced this intersection since 1906.

The **RHODODENDRON FESTIVAL** (888/ENJOYPT) in May, with a parade and crowning of the queen, is the oldest festival in town. The Wooden Boat Foundation (380 Jefferson St; 360/385-3628; *info@woodenboat.org*; *www.woodenboat.org*) presents the **WOODEN BOAT FESTIVAL**, at Point Hudson Marina on the weekend after Labor Day: a celebration of traditional crafts and a showcase for everything from kayaks to tugboats. The first weekend of October finds lunatic geniuses racing human-powered contraptions across town, on the water, and through a mud bog in the **KINETIC SCULPTURE RACE** (360/385-3741).

FORT WORDEN STATE PARK (200 Battery Wy; 360/385-4730; *www.olympus .net/ftworden/*), along with sister forts on Marrowstone and Whidbey Islands, was part of the defense system established to protect Puget Sound a century ago. The 433-acre complex overlooking Admiralty Inlet now incorporates turn-of-the-century officers' quarters (now available for lodging), campgrounds, gardens, a theater, and a concert hall. A huge central field, formerly the parade ground, is perfect for games or kite flying. The setting may look familiar to those who saw the movie *An Officer and a Gentleman,* most of which was filmed here. At the water's edge, an enormous pier juts into the bay—it's the summer home to the **MARINE SCIENCE CENTER** (360/385-5582 or 800/566-3932; *www.ptmsc.org*) and its expanded natural history exhibit, with touch tanks, displays of sea creatures, and cruises to nearby Protection Island, the region's largest seabird rookery. Here, too, is a safe, protected swimming beach and access to miles of other beaches. On the hillside above, you can spend hours exploring deserted concrete bunkers.

Fort Worden is also home to Centrum, which sponsors concerts, workshops, and festivals throughout the year. Many of these take place in the old balloon hangar, reborn as McCurdy Pavilion. The **CENTRUM SUMMER SEASON** (360/385-3102; *www.centrum.org*; June–Sept) is one of the most successful cultural programs in the state, with dance, fiddle tunes, chamber music, a writers' conference, jazz, blues, and theater performances.

The **PUGET SOUND EXPRESS** (360/385-5288) and **CAPTAIN JACKS** (877/278-5225) run whale-watching tours.

RESTAURANTS

Fountain Cafe / ★★

920 WASHINGTON ST, PORT TOWNSEND; 360/385-1364 Kris Nelson, owner and local treasure, shows her passion for great flavors. Her breakfast menu features seafood crepes with béchamel sauce and a cowboy omelet. Dinner favorites include an award-winning warm salad with sautéed potatoes, proscuitto, and fresh vegetables. The café is known for its signature dessert: fresh homemade gingerbread served with warm custard. Nelson uses organic, local produce whenever she can. There are only 10 tables, and it's well worth the wait. *$$; MC, V; checks OK; lunch, dinner every day, breakfast Wed–Sat; beer and wine; no reservations; 1 block north of Water St.*

Lonny's / ★★★

2330 WASHINGTON ST, PORT TOWNSEND; 360/385-0700 Known as one of the most hospitable hosts in town, Lonny Ritter creates a cuisine destination that people travel for miles to experience. Lonny's has been known to connect with the local Rose Theater and replicate outrageous dinners to complement featured films such as *Big Night* and *Mostly Martha*. Lonny's regularly features distinctive Italian pasta entrées, locally harvested seafood, fresh meats, poultry, and game. Try the oyster stew, made with sweet cream, fennel, and diced pancetta, or the char-grilled lamb sirloin. Lonny's trademark dessert, Coco Halva, is a frozen extravaganza made with layers of chocolate, marble-nut halvah, toasted coconut, and Häagen-Dazs vanilla ice cream. *$$; AE, DC, DIS, MC, V; checks OK; dinner Wed–Mon; beer and wine; reservations recommended; lonnys@olypen.com; www.lonnys.com; adjacent to harbor.* ⓓ

Manresa Castle / ★★★

7TH AND SHERIDAN STS, PORT TOWNSEND; 360/385-5750 OR 800/732-1281 The Castle was built in 1892 for Charles and Kate Eisenbeis, prominent members of the early Port Townsend business community. It offers a design similar to some of the castles in the Eisenbeis's native Prussia. With 30 rooms, it was the largest private residence ever built in Port Townsend. Today, the Castle is a Victorian inn and elegant dining room, under the established and creative leadership of Swiss-German chef Walter Santchi. He's cultivated an international menu of inventively prepared and artfully presented seasonal dishes. Favorites include king salmon rosette or exotic curry chicken Casimir. Sunday brunch is exquisite and a great value. It's impossible to leave hungry after Santchi's signature Swiss *roesti*, a heap of shredded potatoes browned with bacon and ham, then topped with Swiss cheese and two fried eggs. The Castle can accommodate banquets and weddings, with reception space for 80. *$$; DIS, MC, V; checks OK; dinner every day May–Oct (Wed–Sat Oct–May), brunch Sun; full bar; reservations recommended; www.manresacastle.com; heading into town on Sims Wy, take a left onto Sheridan St.*

The Public House / ★

1038 WATER ST, PORT TOWNSEND; 360/385-9708 An inverted eight-oared rowing shell, 60 feet long and built in the 1950s, hangs suspended from soaring ceilings in this large space. In summer, the boat is used by the Wooden Boat Foundation. The comfortable and casual Public House offers a signature dish of a creamy fennel-laced seafood stew among an extensive variety of gourmet burgers and salads. Owner Joann Saul also owns Sentosa Sushi and Fins Coastal Cuisine, which provides fine dining on the waterfront. Down a beer from the impressive list of drafts and watch the world go by through the big front windows. Or catch live music on weekends in a nonsmoking bar. *$; AE, DIS, MC, V; checks OK; lunch, dinner every day; full bar; no reservations; www.thepublichouse.com; north side of street.* ⓓ

Sentosa Sushi / ★★

218 POLK ST, PORT TOWNSEND; 360/385-2378 Operated by the same owners as the Public House, Fins Coastal Cuisine, and Dream City Catering, Sentosa features a variety of stir-fried noodle and rice bowl dishes, local seafood, and sushi. Its popular dishes include Seven Elements Albacore with toasted peanuts, and honey garlic chicken udon in a black bean sauce. Chef Tomoko Tolson uses seasonal ingredients, shape, placement, color orientation, and flavor alchemy to create a large assortment of sushi. Try the Port Townsend and the Sentosa rolls. *$$; MC, V; checks OK; lunch, dinner served every day in summer; lunch and dinner Tues–Sat Nov–Apr; no reservations; www.dreamcitycatering.com/sentosa; across from Heliotrope Bakery.*

Silverwater Café / ★

237 TAYLOR ST, PORT TOWNSEND; 360/385-6448 Owners David and Alison Hero have created a unique combination of simple but elegant flavors at this local favorite. The menu includes a variety of Northwest cuisine and a selection of vegetarian dishes. Sandwich favorites include one with artichoke hearts, roasted red bell peppers, chicken, and havarti. Another unique dish is pan-seared sesame-encrusted tofu placed around a rice island surrounded by red curry coconut sauce and topped with crystallized ginger. Local raves for dinner are green-peppercorn steaks, amaretto chicken in a tart and spicy lemon and curry sauce, and seafood pasta loaded with prawns and wild mushrooms and doused with brandy. Chef Alison uses mostly organic products and makes everything from scratch. She has created her own line of blended spices sold at the restaurant and at Sur La Table stores nationwide. *$$; MC, V; checks OK; lunch, dinner every day; full bar; reservations recommended; next to Rose Theater.* ੬

LODGINGS

Ann Starrett Mansion / ★★

744 CLAY ST, PORT TOWNSEND; 360/385-3205 OR 800/321-0644 The most opulent Victorian in Port Townsend, this multigabled Queen Anne hybrid was built in 1889 by George Starrett for his wife, Ann, as a wedding present. A three-tiered, free-hung spiral staircase rises to a 70-foot octagonal tower. At the top, a ceiling fresco depicts angelic (though scantily clad) maidens representing the four seasons. Rooms are furnished with rich tapestries of vibrant color and finely crafted antiques. The Drawing Room (with a tin claw-footed bathtub) opens to views of the Sound and Mount Baker, while the romantic Gable Suite occupies the whole third floor with a skylight, a breathtaking view, and a spacious seating area. For a romantic indulgence, book the Master Suite with its canopy bed and antique fainting couch. The house is open for public tours, noon to 3pm, when any unoccupied bedrooms are cordoned off for viewing. *$$; AE, DIS, MC, V; checks OK; edel@starrettmansion .com; www.starrettmansion.com; at Adams St.* ੬

Bay Cottage / ★★

4346 S DISCOVERY RD, PORT TOWNSEND; 360/385-2035 This quiet, private backdrop is perfect for a writer's refuge or an artist's retreat. One might expect to see the smoke of Hemingway's pipe wafting in the air. Susan Atkins, a gracious host and owner, has two rustic cottages on the shore of Discovery Bay. The cottages have fully equipped kitchens, cozy feather beds, and access to a private sandy beach—marvelous for swimming, bonfires, and beachcombing. Atkins stocks each kitchen with basic breakfast necessities, and each cottage has its own picnic basket, binoculars, and library. The rose garden is a perfect place to sit quietly enjoying the view and the waves lapping at the beach. If you catch her in the mood, Atkins has been known to bake homemade cookies for guests to enjoy. It's an ideal retreat for romantics or small families. No pets. *$$$; no credit cards; checks OK; www.baycottagegetaway .com; ¼ mile west of Four Corners Grocery.*

Fort Worden / ★

200 BATTERY WY, PORT TOWNSEND; 360/344-4400 Fort Casey, Fort Flagler, and Fort Worden were built between 1897 and 1911 and formed the first line of defense guarding Puget Sound cities and the Bremerton naval shipyard. Today, Fort Worden is a beautiful park situated on the edge of Puget Sound, offering a variety of accommodations, a conference center, a youth hostel (great for teenagers biking the peninsula), and Centrum, the splendid Center for Arts and Creative Education, which presents the Centrum Summer Season. Twenty-four former officers' quarters—nobly proportioned structures dating back to 1904—front the old parade ground. These two-story houses are spacious lodgings, each with a complete kitchen, at bargain rates (great for family reunions; a few smaller homes suit couples). The most coveted of the one-bedroom lodgings is Bliss Vista, perched on the bluff, with a fireplace and plenty of romantic appeal. Alexander's Castle, a mini-monument with a three-story turret, is charming in its antiquity, sequestered away from the officers' houses on the opposite side of the fort's grand lawn. RV and tent sites are near the beach and tucked into the woods. Make summer reservations well in advance. *$$; DIS, MC, V; checks OK; www.olympus.net/ftworden; 1 mile north of downtown, in Fort Worden State Park.*

Hastings House/Old Consulate Inn / ★★

313 WALKER ST, PORT TOWNSEND; 360/385-6753 OR 800/300-6753 This ornately turreted red Victorian on the hill is one of the most frequently photographed of Port Townsend's "painted ladies." It is also one of its most comfortable. The exquisite Master Suite (our favorite) is perfect for a luxurious, romantic getaway. The suite encompasses the entire water-view side of the second floor. Soak in a claw-footed bathtub, sip coffee in the turret alcove overlooking the water, lounge in the canopied four-poster bed, and warm up in front of the antique fireplace. The third-floor Tower Suite, with a sweeping bay view and swathed in lace, is the essence of a Victorian-style romantic valentine. The hot tub in the backyard sits in a glass gazebo and lends a perfect perspective on a stormy evening. Owners Michael and Sue DeLong provide king-sized beds and private baths in each room and serve a great breakfast featuring wild-rice pancakes with double buttermilk syrup (their secret recipe) or Eggs Port Townsend. *$$$; AE, DC, MC, V; checks OK; www.oldconsulateinn.com; on bluff at Washington St.*

The James House / ★★★

1238 WASHINGTON ST, PORT TOWNSEND; 360/385-1238 OR 800/385-1238 With sweeping views over sparkling waters and snow-capped mountains, this exquisite Victorian mansion was built in 1889 and reigns as the first B&B in the Northwest. Owner Carol McGough freshens the 12 rooms by varying the antiques and linens, and adds new wonders to the delightful garden. Front rooms have the best water views; all rooms have private baths. The main floor offers two comfortable parlors, each with a fireplace and plenty of reading material. Breakfast is served either at the big dining-room table or in the kitchen with its antique cook stove. Ask about the private bungalow on the bluff, perfect for a romantic getaway. *$$$; AE, DIS, MC, V; checks OK; innkeeper@jameshouse.com; www.jameshouse .com; corner of Harrison St.*

Quimper Inn Bed and Breakfast / ★★☆

1306 FRANKLIN ST, PORT TOWNSEND; 360/385-1060 OR 800/557-1060 The turn-of-the-20th-century Richardsonian-style Quimper Inn sits nestled among the grand Victorians with great distinction. The décor is simple with rich earthy colors and wild cherry wood. Hosts Sue and Ron Ramage welcome guests to a crackling fire in the cozy bay-windowed parlor. Rooms are named for family members and each has its own distinctive mood. The Michelle Room, for example, has a soft rose tint and a large bathroom with a deep claw-footed tub. Most have views of the gardens, mountains, or water. The second-floor balcony is perfect for morning tea, and favorite breakfast dishes include baked pear soufflé and fresh cranberry and white chocolate scones. The inn is within walking distance of town and the Ramages thoughtfully provide menus for most local restaurants. Trust their suggestions. *$$; MC, V; checks OK; rooms@quimperinn.com; www.quimperinn.com; corner of Harrison St.*

Sequim and the Dungeness Valley

Sequim (pronounced "skwim") was once a carefully kept secret. The town sits smack in the middle of the rain shadow cast by the Olympic Mountains, so the sun shines 306 days a year here, and annual rainfall is only 16 inches. Now Sequim has been discovered, especially by retirees, and is growing fast; golf courses sprout in what used to be pastures.

On Sequim Bay, near Blyn, the S'Klallam Indians operate the unique **NORTH-WEST NATIVE EXPRESSIONS** art gallery (1033 Old Blyn Hwy; 360/681-4640; www .jamestowntribe.org/gallery.htm). Across the highway stands the **7 CEDARS** (270756 Hwy 101; 800/4LUCKY7; www.7cedarscasino.com), a mammoth gambling casino with valet parking and good food. **CEDARBROOK HERB FARM** (1345 S Sequim Ave; 360/683-7733; daily Mar–Dec 23), Washington's oldest herb farm, has a vast range of plants—including scented geraniums—fresh-cut herbs, and a pleasant gift shop. The July **LAVENDER FESTIVAL** (877-681-3035; info@lavenderfestival.com) is truly an experience for all the senses.

OLYMPIC GAME FARM (1423 Ward Rd, 5 miles north of Sequim; 360/683-4295; www.olygamefarm.com) is the retirement center for Hollywood animal stars and endangered species. Take the hour-long guided walking tour mid-May through Labor Day, or the driving tour year-round.

DUNGENESS SPIT (360/457-8451), one of the world's longest natural sand spits, extends 6 miles northwest of Sequim and is a national wildlife refuge for birds (more than 275 species have been sighted). A long walk down the narrow 5½-mile beach takes you to a remote lighthouse (check a tide table before you start).

For more information, contact the **NORTH OLYMPIC PENINSULA VISITOR & CONVENTION BUREAU** (*www.northwestsecretplaces.com/vcb/*) or **DESTINATION SEQUIM** (800/942-4042; *www.visitsun.com*).

RESTAURANTS

Khu Larb Thai II / ★

120 W BELL ST, SEQUIM; 360/681-8550 A new menu features fresh Northwest flavors with Thai spice. Guests will find all the usual Thai dishes, including *tum kah gai* (a chicken soup with coconut milk and lime broth), phad thai (sweet, spicy noodles stir-fried with egg, tofu, and vegetables), and garlic pork. Aromatic curries appeal to more adventurous diners. New items include seasonal, fresh coho or Copper River salmon baked on a cedar plank with kaffir lime leaves, lemongrass, and a red curry paste; and New York steak with asparagus and shiitake mushrooms served with a mango salsa. The owners are the Itti family, who also own Thai Peppers in Port Angeles and Khu Larb Thai in Port Townsend. *$; MC, V; local checks only; lunch, dinner Tues–Sun; beer and wine; no reservations; at Sequim Ave.* &

Oak Table Cafe / ★

292 W BELL ST, SEQUIM; 360/683-2179 The Oak Table Cafe is known for its ample breakfasts (served until 3pm); prepare for a feast. The apple pancake is a custard-baked batter with apples and a cinnamon-sugar glaze. The signature dish, Eggs Nicole—named for owner Billy Nagler's daughter—combines eggs, Swiss cheese, spinach, mushrooms, and onions topped with hollandaise and served on a toasted croissant with a side of potato pancakes. Other house specialties include Swedish pancakes, fruit blintzes, and crepes. Service is friendly and familial. Good old-fashioned lunch options include turkey sandwiches, soothing—but unexciting—soups, and a few interesting salads such as sesame chicken. The Nagler family also owns the Chestnut Cottage (see review) and First Street Haven in Port Angeles. *$$; AE, DC, MC, V; checks OK; breakfast daily, lunch Mon–Sat; no alcohol; no reservations; www.oaktablecafe.com; at 3rd Ave.* &

Petals Garden Cafe / ★★

1345 S SEQUIM AVE, SEQUIM; 360/683-4541 Adjacent to the Cedarbrook Herb Farm, Petals opened four years ago with its main dining room in a converted greenhouse. Owner Brandy Salmon serves earthy, simple flavors with an Australian flair. Lamb cutlets with roasted root vegetables and mint ginger syrup, corn fritters with fruit chutney, and the ploughman's lunch—rustic bread, sausage, sweet hot lavender mustard, cheese, and tomato—are among the favorites. Petals features a good selection of salads and two daily soup specials. Afternoon tea, by reservation only, is served after 3pm. Complete your meal with a decadent piece of creamy lavender cheesecake. *$$; AE, DIS, MC, V; checks OK; lunch, dinner every day; reservations recommended; www.petalscafe.com; on Sequim Ave.* &

LODGINGS

Groveland Cottage / ★

4861 SEQUIM-DUNGENESS WY, SEQUIM; 360/683-3565 OR 800/879-8859 At the turn of the 20th century, this was a family home in Dungeness—just a short drive from the beach. Now the place has the comfortable salty-air feel of an old summer house with a great room where guests convene around the fireplace. Four cheerful guest rooms are accented with Native American fabrics and tapestries. Each room has a private bath, two have whirlpool tubs, and one has a large private deck. A one-room cottage out back is simply furnished with its own cooking space and allows pets. Owner and avid gardener Simone Nichols serves fresh raspberries and cuts flowers from the yard. No children under 6 permitted. *$$; AE, DIS, MC, V; checks OK; simone@olypen.com; www.sequimvalley.com; follow signs toward Three Crabs.*

Juan de Fuca Cottages / ★

182 MARINE DR, SEQUIM; 360/683-4433 Any of these five comfortable cottages—overlooking Dungeness Spit, offering views of the Olympics—is special, whether for a winter weekend or a longer summer getaway. A two-bedroom suite has a welcoming fireplace. Each cottage is equipped with a jetted tub, robes and slippers, a full kitchen, games, and reading material, as well as a CD player, cable TV, and a VCR; choose an old movie from the vast video library. Outside across the road is the spit, with a private beach begging for long walks and clam digging. Perfect for couples and families, or reserve all five for reunions or family gatherings. *$$$; DIS, MC, V; checks OK; 2-night min on weekends year-round and Jul–Aug; www.juandefuca.com; 7 miles north of Sequim.*

Lost Mountain Lodge / ★★★

303 SUNNY VIEW DR, SEQUIM; 360/683-2431 Romantic and elegant, this lodge is tucked away on 6 acres of sunny meadows. Owners Lisa and Dwight Hostvedt attend to the smallest details and add a personal touch to create a perfectly romantic affair. The great room is lined with windows for wildlife watching or cozying up to the two-story fieldstone fireplace. The three private suites are spacious and airy with king beds, fireplaces, and large private bathrooms, one with a steam room. Breakfast is prepared in individual baskets, so guests can take it back to their rooms for dining privately or outside on the deck overlooking ponds and waterfalls. The Guest House and Farm House, in nearby buildings, are ideal for families with small children. Both have upscale amenities and the convenience of new kitchens. Children of all ages are welcome in the houses; infant- and toddler-friendly amenities are provided upon request. *$$$; AE, DIS, MC, V; checks OK; 2-night min; getaway@lostmountainlodge.com; www.lostmountainlodge.com; 3 miles west of Sequim.* &

HOW TO EAT AN OYSTER

Despite their reputed powers as an aphrodisiac, oysters are not for everyone. But don't assume you won't like them just because they're ugly—especially if you've never tried one of the Northwest's famous shellfish.

Restaurants all over the region offer a multitude of preparations, from sautéeing to frying, but purists insist the slippery mollusks are best raw; many chefs concoct special sauces to go with uncooked oysters as well. Xinh Dwelley of Xinh's Clam & Oyster House, in Shelton on Hood Canal, offers the following tips:

1. Place the oyster on a towel draped over your open palm, using caution to avoid the sharp edges (wear work gloves). Hold the oyster firmly with one hand, and in your dominant hand, hold an oyster knife.

2. Slip the blade between the top and bottom shell near the hinge.

3. Run the knife around the oyster until you get to the other side. This sounds easy, but be careful; people are most likely to cut themselves at this step.

4. Using a twisting motion, pry the top and bottom shells apart. Be gentle but firm so you do not spill the oyster "liquor" inside.

5. Cut the oyster free from the shell by slicing through tough connection membrane.

6. Eat your oyster. Slurp it plain, or add Tabasco, cocktail sauce, or a squeeze of lemon to dress up the ugly but lovable bivalve.

—Vanessa McGrady

Port Angeles and the Strait of Juan de Fuca

The north shore of the Olympic Peninsula was home to several thriving Native American tribes long before outside explorers laid claim to the area. Today this region is anchored by the blue-collar mill town Port Angeles—"where the Olympics greet the sea." Port Angeles Harbor, protected against wind and waves by Ediz Hook sand spit, is the largest natural deep-water harbor north of San Francisco. It is also a jumping-off point to Victoria, British Columbia, 17 miles across the Strait of Juan de Fuca.

Port Angeles

Port Angeles is the northern gateway to **OLYMPIC NATIONAL PARK** (360/565-3130; *www.nps.gov/olym*) The park, as big as Rhode Island, with a buffer zone of national forest surrounding it, contains the largest remaining herd of the huge Roosevelt elk, which occasionally create "elk jams" along Highway 101. The park offers plenty of hiking trails in summer, and good cross-country skiing and a weekend poma-lift downhill-skiing-and-tubing area in winter. Seasonal snowshoe rental and guided snowshoe nature walks are offered through March. Check road conditions before you go (360/565-3131; 24-hour recorded message). **OLYMPIC RAFT AND KAYAK SERVICE** (360/452-1443 or 888/452-1443) offers easy floats and kayaking ventures on the Elwha and Hoh Rivers.

In downtown Port Angeles, **PORT BOOK AND NEWS** (104 E 1st St; 360/452-6367) sells a wide selection of magazines and daily newspapers such as the *New York Times* and the *Wall Street Journal*. **MOMBASA COFFEE COMPANY** (113 W 1st St; 360/452-3238) serves excellent fresh-roasted coffee. **GINA'S BAKERY** (710 S Lincoln St; 360/457-3279), near the library, is a good place to buy picnic food, especially pastries, cinnamon rolls, and freshly made sandwiches. Browse **SWAIN'S GENERAL STORE** (602 E 1st St; 360/452-2357) for everything else.

The October **DUNGENESS CRAB & SEAFOOD FESTIVAL** (*www.crabfestival.org*) showcases and celebrates the foods and traditions of the Olympic Peninsula. In and around Port Angeles, several small and notable wineries dot the map. Most offer tastings, including **CAMARADERIE CELLARS** (334 Benson Rd; 360/417-3564; *www .camaraderiecellars.com*; open weekends May–Sept), **LOST MOUNTAIN WINERY** (3174 Lost Mountain Rd; 360/683-5229; *www.lostmountain.com*; tastings by arrangement or chance), **BLACK DIAMOND WINERY** (2976 Black Diamond Rd; 360/ 457-0748; *pages.prodigy.net/sharonlance*; open Thurs–Sun Feb–Dec, or by appointment), and **OLYMPIC CELLARS WINERY** (255410 Hwy 101E; 360/452-0160; *www.olympiccellars.com*; daily in summer, Wed–Sun in winter).

RESTAURANTS

Bella Italia / ★★★

118 E 1ST ST, PORT ANGELES; 360/457-5442 A local favorite, Bella Italia specializes in Olympic coast cuisine and features fresh seafood, locally grown organic vegetables, a wine bar, and retail wine sales. Its signature dish is an espresso-smoked duck breast with a port demi-glace sauce. Regulars also love the smoked salmon fettucine, locally smoked in a garlic-tomato cream sauce. Owner Neil Conklin has a passion for wine and good company. He grew up in an East Coast Italian neighborhood, where he learned the art of hospitality and generosity that goes along with sitting at an Italian dinner table. Bella Italia received *Wine Spectator*'s Award of Excellence for its listing of more than 500 wine selections. *$$; AE, DIS, MC, V; checks OK; dinner every day; full bar; reservations recommended; bella@olypen.com; www.bellaitaliapa.com; on 1st, between Laurel and Lincoln.* &

C'est Si Bon / ★★

23 CEDAR PARK DR, PORT ANGELES; 360/452-8888 Married for 40 years, the spirited team of Michéle and Norbert Juhasz has transplanted a local treasure straight out of Leon, France. Dine leisurely in a French home setting: the best tables are in window bays that overlook the rose garden; a glass conservatory is a favorite for large parties and weddings. Host Norbert Juhasz regales waiting guests with tales of his musical experiences in France and Hollywood and has been known to bring out his violin on occasion, while Chef Michéle sends wafting flavors from the kitchen. A big bowl of onion soup, bubbling under a brown crust of cheese, can serve as a meal in itself, particularly when followed by a refreshing salad. The most popular dish here is *Pave du Roi*—filet mignon topped with sautéed Dungeness crab. Other features include braised lamb, classic steak au poivre, or fresh halibut and salmon in season. The chocolate mousse is wickedly rich, and the wine list has good choices. *$$$; AE, DIS, MC, V; local checks only; dinner Tues–Sun; full bar; reservations recommended; 4 miles east of Port Angeles.* &

Chestnut Cottage / ★

929 E FRONT ST, PORT ANGELES; 360/452-8344 The Chestnut Cottage is the place to go for an exceptional breakfast in delightful Victorian-style country surroundings smack in the middle of downtown. Owners Diane Nagler and Ken Nemirow are particular when it comes to quality food and service. It shows. A custardy apple and walnut French toast is only one of several morning treats; others include Belgian waffles, pancakes, quiches, frittatas, or lemon blintzes drizzled with raspberry purée. Children are delighted by the breakfast pizza (ham and eggs on pita). Simple porridge with berries is another kid-friendly option. Nagler and Nemirow also own First Street Haven (107 E 1st St; 360/457-0352), an equally good place for more casual breakfasts and fresh lunches with reasonable prices. *$$; AE, DIS, MC, V; checks OK; breakfast, lunch every day; beer and wine; no reservations; east of town center.* &

Hacienda del Mar / ★

408 S LINCOLN ST, PORT ANGELES; 360/452-5296 Hacienda del Mar is a local choice with a charming staff, but be warned: your waiter will have you saying *si* to another margarita and dessert before you know it. Salsa gets points for being thick and zesty with a comfortable balance of cilantro and heat. The standards—fajitas, burritos, tacos—are all fine, but specialties are where the house shines. Try spinach-filled tamales with a cream cheese sauce, or seafood enchiladas. *$; AE, DIS, MC, V; checks OK; lunch, dinner every day; beer and wine; no reservations; between 4th and 5th Sts.* &

LODGINGS

Domaine Madeleine / ★★★

146 WILDFLOWER LN, PORT ANGELES; 360/457-4174 OR 888/811-8376 Jeri Weinhold upholds many of the traditions started by the original French owner who gave Domaine Madeleine her name. The inn sits nestled in the forest, with sweeping views of the Strait of Juan de Fuca. Each of the five rooms has a fireplace and most have whirlpool tubs. Three of the rooms have separate entrances. A secluded, cozy cottage is a perfect newlywed getaway. Thai chefs Victor Posten and Ann Chaummalung prepare a unique dining experience with a five-course breakfast that features apple crepes and salmon with mango salsa. Guests can stroll through the acres of landscaped gardens, including the rose- and clematis-covered arches of a garden replica of Monet's *Petites Allees*, bamboo forests, and Japanese gardens. Ideal for weddings. *$$$; AE, DIS, MC, V; checks OK; 2-night min Apr–Oct and all weekends Oct–Apr; 7 miles between Sequim and Port*

Angeles; romance@domainemadeleine.com; www.domainemadeleine.com; ½ mile from Sequim.

Five SeaSuns / ★

1006 S LINCOLN ST, PORT ANGELES; 360/452-8248 OR 800/708-0777 This 1926 Dutch Colonial house was home to only three families before owners Bob and Jan Harbick took over and turned it into a B&B in 1996. It has a well-kept interior with sunny rooms, elegantly crafted architectural details, and polished hardwood floors. A parlor outfitted with comfy couches gives guests a homey sitting space, and rooms are decorated to evoke the feeling of the four seasons. Pick of the lot is the Winter room, with a private white-tiled bath, queen-sized brass bed, wicker furniture, well-placed antiques, and hats and hatboxes of a bygone era. The Carriage House is for rent, too, with rustic, wood-paneled decor and full kitchen. Breakfast—your choice of two sittings—is filling and artfully presented. *$$–$$$; AE, MC, V; checks OK; www.seasuns.com; corner of E 10th St.*

Tudor Inn / ★★

1108 S OAK ST, PORT ANGELES; 360/452-3138 OR 866/286-2224 New owner Betsy Reed Schultz creates a home away from home in one of the oldest and most charming B&Bs in town. Crisp linens and turn-of-the-20th-century antiques decorate the five rooms; the best has a balcony with a mountain view, fireplace, claw-footed tub, and shower. Schultz prepares a three-course breakfast with homemade granola and baked goods and has nine rotating menus so guests on extended stay will never eat the same meal twice. From October 15 through May 15, the Tudor Inn Teahouse serves a traditional English tea for parties of 4 to 32 guests, with traditional fare such as crumpets, fresh fruit, and finger sandwiches. It's a unique event for bridal or baby showers, or wedding anniversaries. Schultz can also put together an ideal tea party for children 12 and under, perfect for birthdays. *$$; AE, DIS, MC, V; checks OK; info@tudorinn.com; www.tudorinn.com; at 11th St.*

Lake Crescent

Highway 101 skirts the south shore of 600-foot-deep Lake Crescent with numerous scenic pullouts. The Fairholm store and boat launch are on the far west end of the lake, with East Beach 10 miles away. Lake Crescent is home to rainbow trout and steelhead, to Beardslee and the famous Crescenti trout, which lurk in its depths. Rental boats are available. Ask about the easy 1-mile hike to 90-foot Marymere Falls.

LODGINGS

Lake Crescent Lodge / ★

416 LAKE CRESCENT RD, PORT ANGELES; 360/928-3211 Well-maintained Lake Crescent Lodge has been well worn since the days when it was known as Singer's Tavern. Built 85 years ago, the historic main building has a grand veranda that overlooks the deep, crystal blue waters of Lake Crescent, an average restaurant, and a relaxed bar. Upstairs rooms are noisy and rustic—a euphemism that means the bathroom is down the hall. Motel rooms are the best buy, but the clutter of tiny basic cabins, with porches and fireplaces, can be fun and charming—though bear in mind that they were built in 1937, when President Franklin Roosevelt came to visit. Service consists of enthusiastic college kids having a nice summer. It's true this side of the lake sees less sun than the north side, but you don't come to the rain forest to see sun, do you? *$$; AE, CB, DC, DIS, MC, V; checks OK; closed Nov–Apr; www .lakecrescentlodge.com; 20 miles west of Port Angeles.* &

Sol Duc Hot Springs

Whether you arrive by car after an impressive 12-mile drive through old-growth forests, or on foot after days of hiking mountain ridges, these hot springs are the ideal trail's end. The Quileute Indians called the area Sol Duc—"sparkling water." In the early 1900s, **SOL DUC HOT SPRINGS** (28 miles west of Port Angeles; 360/327-3583; open daily mid-May–Sept; Thurs–Sun Apr–mid-May and Oct, closed Nov–Mar) became a mecca for travelers seeking relief from aches and pains. Melt away tension and relax into the serene setting of forested peaks and the babbling Sol Duc River. For $10, you can have a hot soak followed by a swim in a cold pool. You can also opt for a lengthy massage ($60 for an hour). The hike to nearby **SOL DUC FALLS** passes through one of the loveliest stands of old-growth forest anywhere.

LODGINGS

Sol Duc Hot Springs Resort / ★★

SOL DUC RD AND HWY 101, PORT ANGELES; 360/327-3583 Tucked away deep in the forest, 32 small cedar-roofed sleeping cabins are clustered in a grassy meadow. The favorites are those with river-facing porches. Up to four guests can share a cabin, which is carpeted and has a private bath and double bed. Duplex units have kitchens, and in keeping with the natural serenity, there are no TVs anywhere (and a no-smoking policy everywhere). Camping and RV sites are available. The Springs Restaurant serves breakfast and dinner in summer, and a deli is open midday through the season. Use of the hot springs and the pool is included in the cabin rental fee. *$$; AE, DIS, MC, V; checks OK; open daily seasonally, limited hours spring and fall; pamsdr@aol.com; www.northolympic.com/solduc/; turn off a few miles west of Lake Crescent, then drive 12 miles south of Hwy 101.*

Clallam Bay and Sekiu

Twenty-one miles south on Hoko-Ozette Road from Sekiu is Lake Ozette, the largest natural body of freshwater in the state. Nearby are the Ozette Trail, the Sand Point Trail, Cape Alava, the Ozette Indian Reservation, the Indian Village Trail, ancient Indian petroglyphs, and Flattery Rocks National Wildlife Refuge. At the north end of the lake is a campground and trails leading to several beaches where you can see the eerie, eroded coastal cliffs. It was near here in the 1960s that tidal erosion exposed a 500-year-old Native American village—once covered by a mud slide—with homes perfectly preserved. The archaeological dig was closed in 1981 after 11 years of excavation; artifacts are on display at the Makah Cultural and Research Center in Neah Bay (see Neah Bay section).

Neah Bay

This is the end of the road, literally: Highway 112 ends at this small waterside town on the northern edge of the **MAKAH INDIAN RESERVATION**. Two 8-mile-long rutted roads lead to **CAPE FLATTERY**—take the west one coming and going. The Makah allow public access across their ancestral lands—a half-mile walk on a new boardwalk to **LAND'S END**, the far northwestern corner of Washington's coast. From these high-cliffed headlands, cow-calf pairs of gray whales can often be seen migrating north in April and May. Outlooks offer views of Tatoosh Island and the entrance to the Strait of Juan de Fuca. Sandy **HOBUCK BEACH** is open for picnics (no fires) and surfing, and farther on, the **TSOO-YAS BEACH** (pronounced "sooes") is accessible (pay the landowners a parking fee). Call the **PORT ANGELES VISITORS CENTER** (877/456-8372; *www.portangeles .org*) for coastal access information. The **MAKAH CULTURAL AND RESEARCH CENTER** (Front St; 360/645-2711) has a stunning exhibit of artifacts from the village discovered under Lake Ozette; it also serves as an ad hoc tourist information center.

Forks and the Hoh River Valley

With an average yearly rainfall of 133.58 inches, the **HOH RAIN FOREST** in Olympic National Park is the wettest location in the contiguous United States. This steady moisture nurtures more than 3,000 species of plant life—including the Rain Forest Monarch, a giant Sitka spruce more than 500 years old towering close to 300 feet over the moss- and fern-carpeted forest floor. Take the spur road off Highway 101, 13 miles south of Forks, to the visitors center and campground (30 miles southeast of Forks; 360/374-6925). For those with more time, one- to three-day round-trip hikes up **MOUNT OLYMPUS** provide some of the best hiking in the world. The longer trip to **GLACIER MEADOWS** is best mid-July through October. Stop in at **PEAK 6 ADVENTURE STORE** (about 5 miles up the road to the Hoh; 360/374-5254), a veritable miniature REI right where you need it most.

Forks

From this little town on the west end of the Olympic Peninsula, you can explore the wild coastal beaches, hook a steelhead, or go mountain biking, camping, or hiking. The pristine waters of the Hoh, Bogachiel, Calawah, and Sol Duc Rivers all flow near Forks, making it a key fishing destination. Ask your innkeeper, the informative **FORKS VISITORS CENTER** (1411 S Forks Ave; 360/374-2531 or 800/44-FORKS; *www.forks-web.com/fg/visitorscenter.htm*), or **OLYMPIC SPORTING GOODS** (190 N Forks Ave; 360/374-6330) for information on recommended guides, licenses, or where to land the Big One.

On the outskirts of town, the **TIMBER MUSEUM** (1421 S Forks Ave; 360/374-9663) tells the story of the West End's logging heritage. Next door at the visitors center, pick up a map for **ARTTREK**, a self-guided tour of nearly two dozen local studios and galleries; most are in artists' homes, but if the Arttrek sign is out, you're welcome. A delightful mingling of espresso, art, and unique gifts can be found where **THE ERRANT ELK, RIVERRUN COFFEE**, and **HOME & ABROAD DECOR** combine into one space (71 N Forks Ave; 360/374-4037).

LODGINGS

Eagle Point Inn / ★★

384 STORMIN' NORMAN LN, FORKS; 360/327-3236 One of the most impressive places to stay near the rain forest, the Eagle Point Inn rests on five acres in a bend of the Sol Duc River. Chris and Dan Christensen designed this spacious log lodge and combine comfort with style. Heavy down comforters cover queen-sized beds in the two downstairs bedrooms, each with a large, private bathroom. The open two-story common living quarters house Chris's collection of kerosene lamps and other interesting antiques but leave plenty of room for guests to relax in front of the stone fireplace, made of rocks from the Sol Duc River. The Christensens live nearby in what was the original lodge, leaving you just the right amount of privacy. Even if you need to get up before dawn to fish, a hearty breakfast will be ready. You can barbecue your own dinner in a covered outdoor kitchen near the river. *$$; no credit cards; checks OK; info@eaglepointinn.com; www.eaglepoint.com; 10 miles north of Forks.*

Huckleberry Lodge / ★

1171 BIG PINE WY, FORKS; 360/374-6008 OR 888/822-6008 Avid outdoors enthusiasts Kitty and Bill Speery go the extra mile to accommodate guests, whether it's waking them with breakfast at 4:30am before their fishing excursion or making arrangements for a full day of fly-fishing or ATV adventures. On request, the owners provide niceties (toiletries, hot tub under the evergreens, sauna) and naughties (poker chips, a heated outdoor smoking canopy). The hosts' philosophy is the more the merrier. This is a great place if you come with friends for a fun weekend. There's a pool table in the family room, a buffalo head (among numerous other items) in the living room, and Native American artifacts on display throughout. The cabins, complete with kitchens, are a good choice for the more independently minded or for those wanting longer stays. A couple of RV hookups accommodate those who want to get away from the hubbub of busy RV parks. *$$; MC, V; checks OK; hucklodg@olypen.com; www.huckleberrylodge.com; north end of Forks.*

Shady Nook Cottage / ★

81 ASH AVE, FORKS; 360/374-5497 Innkeeper Deannie Hoien operates three guest cottages surrounded by a beautiful English garden, tucked away only a few blocks from downtown Forks. Hoien, an accomplished stained-glass artist, continually updates the decor with her creations. Down comforters and handmade quilts create a welcoming charm. Cottages come equipped with full kitchens, microwaves, and TVs. The gardens surrounding the cottages are full of bright flowers and graceful foliage. *$$; no credit cards; checks OK; open Apr–Nov, other times by arrangement;*

shadynook@northolympic.com; www.shadynookcottage.com; turn west at N Forks Ave, go 2 blocks, and turn right onto Ash Ave.

La Push and Pacific Ocean Beaches

The Dickey, Quillayute, Calawah, and Sol Duc Rivers merge and enter the ocean near La Push. To the north and south extend miles of wilderness coastline—the last such stretch remaining in the United States outside of Alaska—much of which is protected as part of Olympic National Park. It is home to the Quileute Indians, and today the small community still revolves around its fishing heritage. The lure of wild ocean beaches, with jagged offshore rocks and teeming tide pools, attracts those seeking adventurous solitude. The only nearby lodging is **OCEAN PARK RESORT AT LA PUSH** (360/374-5267 or 800/487-1267; *www.ocean-park.org*), which offers motel rooms, cabins, duplexes, and camping.

A mixture of pristine beaches makes up the largest section of wilderness coast in the lower 48 states. Hike 0.8 mile to reach remote **SECOND BEACH** (low tide is the best time to visit), where a natural arch and the Quillayute Needles cover the landscape. **THIRD BEACH**, a 1.4-mile hike, is more crowded with surfers and whale watchers. **RIALTO BEACH**, just north of La Push, is a 0.1-mile walk to the beach on a paved trail. **RUBY BEACH**, located just 400 yards off U.S. Highway 101 and named for the tiny garnet crystals that fleck its sand, offers excellent views of Destruction Island. Nearby, a trail leads to the world's largest western red cedar. Warning: All ocean beaches can be extremely dangerous due to fluctuating tides and unfordable creeks during periods of heavy rain.

Several more beaches make good explorations as you continue south—particularly at Kalaloch, which has a campground and a fine clamming beach. **KALALOCH LODGE** (157151 Hwy 101, Forks; 360/962-2271; *www.visitkalaloch.com*) is one of the most isolated beachside resorts in Washington. Unfortunately, accommodations are rudimentary and the food in the restaurant is standard at best. If you're looking for a view you can't beat it, but those in the know, camp.

Lake Quinault

Lake Quinault, at the inland apex of the **QUINAULT INDIAN RESERVATION**, is usually the first or the last stop on Highway 101's scenic 31-mile loop around the peninsula's Olympic National Park and Forest. The glacier-carved lake is surrounded by cathedral-like firs, and the fishing is memorable. The **GRAVES CREEK RANGER STATION** (360/288-2444) provides hiking and trail information for all levels.

LODGINGS

Lake Quinault Lodge / ★★

S SHORE RD, QUINAULT; 360/288-2900 OR 800/562-6672 (WA AND OR ONLY) Built in 1926 and located in the middle of the rain forest, Lake Quinault Lodge is a resort hotel in the tradition of the Old Faithful Inn at

Yellowstone and the Sun Valley Lodge in Idaho. An immense cedar-shingled structure, this grand old lodge arcs around the sweeping lawns that descend to the lake. The rustic public rooms resemble grandma's sun porch in wicker and antiques, with a massive stone fireplace in the lobby; the dining room overlooks the lawns. Rooms in the main building are small but nice; half have lake views. The 36 newer lakeside rooms are a short walk from the lodge. Amenities consist of a sauna, an indoor heated pool, a game room, canoes and rowboats, and well-maintained trails for hiking or running. It's a good idea to make summer reservations four to five months in advance, but winter is wide open—and a great time to experience the rain forest. Lunches are classic national park (Monte Cristos and logger burgers), and dinners are a bit more creative, with entrées such as ginger-seared halibut or blackened salmon. On occasion, conventioneers abound, drawn by the spalike features of the resort, but somehow the old place still exudes the quiet elegance of its past. *$$–$$$; AE, MC, V; checks OK; www.visitlakequinalt.com; from Hwy 101, turn east at milepost 125 onto S Shore Rd.*

NORTH CASCADES

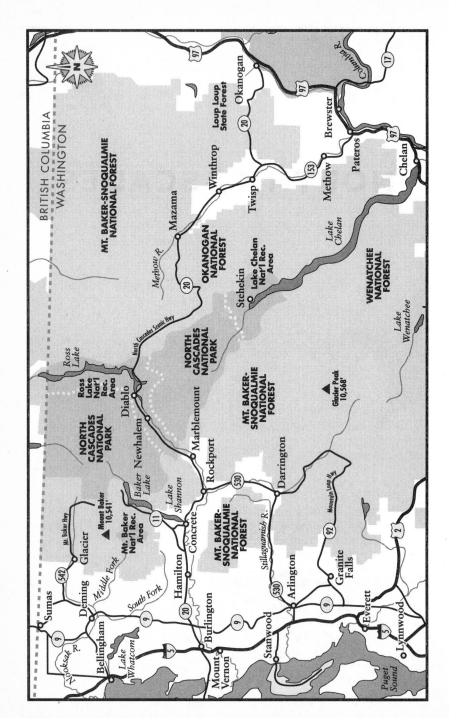

NORTH CASCADES

Few regions in Washington have the allure of the North Cascades. This mountainous area in the northwest part of the state is world renowned for ice-draped peaks, alpine meadows, and vast stands of old-growth forest. North Cascades National Park is a cluster of magnificent peaks (part of the Cascade Range) surrounded by a jigsaw puzzle of federally protected wilderness areas. It's nirvana for hikers and campers.

Broadly speaking, the North Cascades includes more than just the park; the region encompasses Mount Baker to the north, the breathtaking North Cascades Scenic Highway that cuts across the park's center, the wide-open Methow Valley east of the Cascades, and, farther south, the popular playground of Lake Chelan.

Relatively unscathed by development, the North Cascades contains no cities, few resorts, and little tourist-town sprawl—though that means food and lodging aren't plentiful, either. The towns scattered throughout the region still feel like small-town America; they may have espresso stands at almost every corner, but the owners keep local hours rather than cater to tourists. These are friendly, hospitable spots. And locals know the region's best feature is their backyards: each is a gateway to the Great Outdoors, an invitation to hiking, camping, mountain biking, fishing, boating, and downhill and cross-country skiing.

ACCESS AND INFORMATION

Travelers tour the North Cascades via car (there are no airports or train stations within this region) on the **NORTH CASCADES SCENIC HIGHWAY** (Hwy 20), an east-west corridor that links Sedro-Woolley near Interstate 5 (exit 230, 65 miles north of Seattle) to the town of Twisp. East of the Cascades, the Twisp–Chelan leg is connected by **HIGHWAY 153** and **US HIGHWAY 97**.

Snow closes the North Cascades Highway—typically the stretch between Mazama on the east side and Diablo on the west—from approximately mid-November to mid-April, depending on the weather. In winter, Puget Sound visitors travel to the Methow Valley by crossing the Cascades via the longer, more southerly routes of US Highway 2 or Interstate 90.

For information, contact the **NORTH CASCADES VISITOR CENTER** (502 Newhalem St, Newhalem, WA 98283; 206/386-4495; *www.nps.gov/noca/*) or the **LAKE CHELAN VISITOR BUREAU** (PO Box 216, Chelan, WA 98816; 800/4-CHELAN; *www.lakechelan.com*).

Mount Baker

The **MOUNT BAKER HIGHWAY** (Hwy 542) rises from Bellingham, paralleling the sparkling Nooksack River and passing several Christmas tree farms and little towns such as Deming and Glacier, to reach two of the state's loveliest sights: 10,778-foot Mount Baker and 9,131-foot Mount Shuksan. Extreme skiers and snowboarders from all over the world journey to **MOUNT BAKER SKI AREA** (360/734-6771; 360/671-0211 snow conditions; *www.mtbakerskiarea.com*), 56 miles east of

NORTH CASCADES THREE-DAY TOUR

DAY ONE: Start your day in the Puget Sound area and head eastbound on the **NORTH CASCADES SCENIC HIGHWAY** for a daylong drive. Pack a lunch or grab a burger at the café with the **GOOD FOOD** (59924 Hwy 20; 360/873-9309) sign in Marblemount before making your first must-stop: the **NORTH CASCADES VISITOR CENTER** in Newhalem. Enjoy the center's exhibits, then take a short, easy hike to view the **PICKET RANGE**. Back in the car, begin your drive across the mountains, allowing at least two hours for stops. The overlooks at **DIABLO LAKE** and **WASHINGTON PASS** have sweeping, panoramic vistas. Continue your drive into the Methow Valley and collapse in the arms of luxurious comfort at the **FREESTONE INN AND EARLY WINTERS CABINS** in Mazama, where you'll have dinner.

DAY TWO: After your complimentary breakfast at the inn, drive into Winthrop and take the morning to explore its frontier atmosphere. Mosey around the pioneer buildings of **SHAFER MUSEUM**. Poke through the main street's Old West storefronts, antique stores, and blacksmith shop. Stop for lunch nearby at the **TOPO CAFÉ**, where you can enjoy healthy, Asian-inspired cuisine. Use the afternoon to unwind at **PEARRYGIN LAKE STATE PARK**. Go for a swim, rent a boat, or simply relax with a book under one of the shade trees. Wrap things up with an intimate dinner at the **FIDDLEHEAD BISTRO** in Twisp, or the impressive dining room above Winthrop at **SUN MOUNTAIN LODGE**, then return to your hotel.

DAY THREE: Head for Winthrop's **DUCK BRAND HOTEL & CANTINA** for a hearty breakfast of huevos rancheros, fluffy omelet, or scramble, before starting your drive to **CHELAN**. The 56-mile trip takes about 1½ hours, but allow time to stop in Twisp to pick up snacks at **CINNAMON TWISP** or to visit the **CONFLUENCE GALLERY**. Once you reach Chelan, check into **CAMPBELL'S RESORT ON LAKE CHELAN** and settle into a lakeside lawn chair on the lodge's sandy beach to soak up the sun. If you get restless, saunter out to explore town; everything is within walking distance. Enjoy dinner at **CAMPBELL HOUSE CAFE** and wind up the day with an evening stroll through **RIVERWALK PARK**.

Bellingham. The mountain has the highest average annual snowfall (595 inches) in North America, and during the 1998–99 season set a world record for snowfall with 1,140 inches. It has the kind of steep terrain that satisfies avid boarders, who are welcome on all runs. The area typically is open mid-November to mid-May (the longest season in the state). In summer, enjoy beautiful vistas and exhilarating day hikes.

The region has a range of lodging options, including cabin rentals through **MOUNT BAKER LODGING** (360/599-2453 or 800/709-SNOW; *www.mtbaker*

lodging.com). Many of the privately owned cabins have hot tubs, fireplaces, and barbecues.

Just north of Maple Falls, the **BLACK MOUNTAIN FORESTRY CENTER** (360/599-2623; *www.blackmountainforestry.com*) is a nonprofit organization dedicated to forestry education. The museum, located in a historic log home hewn from a single cedar tree, features photographs, antique tools, and an adjacent working sawmill.

Everson

RESTAURANTS

Black Forest Steak & Schnitzel House / ★

203 W MAIN ST, EVERSON; 360/966-2855 Dinner at Jack Niemann's Black Forest feels like a special night out in a small town—casual and a little kitschy. The front of the menu quotes the founder and chef: "My culinary art is wasted on those who salt before they've tasted." The low-ceilinged interior has a hunting-lodge look with log supports and a brick wall—and a window into the kitchen that lets you watch your steak being cooked on the mesquite broiler. The menu features seven kinds of schnitzel, and even more options for steaks, from filet mignon to sirloin Cajun style, which are very good. Entrées come with lentil soup, goulash soup, or Caesar salad. Desserts are classic steak house: apple strudel, black forest cake, burned cream caramel. *$$; MC, V; no checks; dinner every day; full bar; no reservations; take Sunset exit off I-5 onto Hwy 542, turn left to Everson-Goshen Rd, left on E Pole Rd, right on Kale, which becomes Main.* &

Deming

RESTAURANTS

The North Fork / ★

6186 MT BAKER HWY, DEMING; 360/599-BEER Touting itself as a "brewery, pizzeria, beer shrine, and wedding chapel," the North Fork draws a diverse clientele that includes locals as well as everyone who plays (winter or summer) at Mount Baker. Families settle in at wood tables next to 20-somethings, while the locals and old-timers tend to congregate in the bar. The thin-crust pizza (served on an elevated platter) is good (choose from a few prearranged pies or build your own), the spicy steamer clams have a loyal following, and the brews (also available to go by the jug) are tasty and inventively named. Service is friendly and familiar. An ordained minister is on-site for those who want to tie the knot; the "shrine" consists of empty bottles and cans collected over the past 90 years. Your (reasonable) bill comes with fortune cookies, if you're less ready to commit. *$; MC, V; local checks only; lunch Sat–Sun, dinner every day; beer and wine; no reservations; www.northfork brewery.com; milepost 21 on the Mt Baker Hwy.* &

Glacier

RESTAURANTS

Milano's Restaurant and Deli / ★★

9990 MT BAKER HWY, GLACIER; 360/599-2863 You might overlook this unassuming little restaurant-market-deli on your way to (or from) Mount Baker, but that'd be a mistake. It's the best bet for several miles. Check out the blackboard for specials, then sit at an (unclothed) table for some good Italian food: fresh pasta comes with creative fillings and sauces. Linguine vongole is clam-packed; chicken Gorgonzola is smothered in a rich, savory sauce; and mushroom risotto is rich enough to save half for later. Tasty raviolis are stuffed with spinach, porcini mushrooms, or smoked salmon. Enjoy a beer or a glass of wine from the well-priced selection, then consider the contents of the dessert case: chocolate truffles, Mt. Baker apple pie, tiramisù, or perhaps a dense and delicious cappuccino chocolate torte. The deli does a brisk business in take-out sandwiches, too. *$$; MC, V; local checks only; breakfast Sat–Sun, lunch, dinner every day; beer and wine; reservations recommended; milanodeli@aol.com; on Hwy 542 in Glacier.* &

LODGINGS

Inn at Mount Baker / ★★★½

8174 MT BAKER HWY, GLACIER; 360/599-1776 Carole MacDonald and Bill Snyder spent more than three years looking for just the right site for their B&B, then built it from the ground up, carefully positioning it so that all five guest rooms (three downstairs, two up) have views of both Mount Baker and the Nooksack River. Guests enjoy the same view from the large outdoor hot tub (with an umbrella for rainy nights). MacDonald stocks her B&B with all the comforts of a fine hotel: feather beds; down duvets; deep 6-foot tubs; rocking chairs; silky, terry-lined robes; flowers; and plenty of space for guests to spread out their belongings. Privacy is respected: your room is made up daily only if you request it. The lower-level guest lounge has an impressive video collection (rooms have TVs and VCRs, but no TV reception) and a kitchenette with chilled beverages and snack fixings. Gourmet breakfasts served in the view dining room might be apples in puff pastry with roasted garlic–turkey sausage, French toast, or three kinds of eggs Benedict (regular, vegetarian, or smoked salmon). *$$$; AE, DIS, JVC, MC, V; no checks; tiamb@earthlink.net; www.theinnatmtbaker.com; just before milepost 28 on the Mt Baker Hwy.*

North Cascades Scenic Highway

The heart of this region is the **NORTH CASCADES SCENIC HIGHWAY** (Hwy 20), frequently heralded as one of the nation's top scenic highways. Winter snow closes the park highway from approximately mid-November to mid-April, depending on the weather, but when it's open, the two-lane road, completed in 1972, slices through the mountains to provide stunning roadside mountain vistas. Almost as impressive are the brilliantly hued, jade-green and turquoise **DIABLO** and **ROSS LAKES** created by a hydroelectric dam project.

The highway, the most northerly cross-state route, connects the wet, west, forested side of the Cascades to the semiarid, sunlit world east of the mountains. More than 130 miles and a few hours' driving time, it climbs from peaceful farmland and lush, thick evergreens to rugged mountains and immense glaciers via **RAINY** and **WASHINGTON PASSES**, then glides down into a wide-open pastoral valley and grassy meadowlands.

Marblemount

Hundreds of **BALD EAGLES** perch along the Skagit River from December through February, scavenging on spawned-out salmon. You can spy a number from the road, along Highway 20 between Rockport and Marblemount (bring binoculars). However, the best view is from the river, via a two- to three-hour **FLOAT TOUR**. Call **CHINOOK EXPEDITIONS** (800/241-3451; *www.chinookexpeditions.com*), **WILDWATER RIVER TOURS** (800/522-WILD; *www.wildwater-river.com*), or the **MOUNT BAKER RANGER DISTRICT** (2105 Hwy 20, Sedro-Woolley; 360/856-5700; *www.fs.fed.us/r6/mbs/about/mbrd.shtml*) for other float-trip operators.

North Cascades National Park

The North Cascades are sometimes called America's Alps—or Washington's, at any rate. Like their European counterparts, the mountains possess extraordinary grandeur and majesty, along with a wild quality that makes them a worldwide draw.

In 1968, a 505,000-acre section immediately south of the U.S.-Canadian border won national park status. The huge park contains jagged peaks draped in ice, 318 glaciers, and unspoiled wilderness hidden from everyone but the most intrepid of hikers. Part of the Cascade Range, the peaks are not especially tall—the highest hover around 9,000 feet—but their vertical rise takes them from almost sea level into the clouds, making them steep-walled, enchanting to view, and, in many places, inaccessible.

Although the North Cascades Highway bisects the wilderness area and provides dramatic views, the inner sanctum contains no network of roads, no lodges or visitor centers. The park will not reveal its treasures easily; you have to discover them on foot. Fortunately, the adventurous have been given 386 miles of maintained trails in the territory to explore—and the rest can take solace in a stunning scenic drive.

Access to the park, about a three-hour drive from Seattle, is via the North Cascades Scenic Highway (Hwy 20). Food, lodging, and gas are minimal within the park. The main highway provides access to dozens of trails, including the **PACIFIC CREST NATIONAL SCENIC TRAIL**. Backpackers also hike into the park from Stehekin, located at the north end of Lake Chelan (see Stehekin section). Hiking usually starts in June; snow commonly melts off from all but the highest trails by July. But summer storms are frequent; be prepared with rain gear. Expect four-legged company in the backcountry: this is home to black bears, elk, mountain goats, mountain lions, and a few grizzlies.

Backcountry camping requires a free permit, available at the **NORTH CASCADES NATIONAL PARK HEADQUARTERS** (2105 Hwy 20, Sedro-Woolley; 360/856-5700; *www.nps.gov/noca/*) or the **WILDERNESS INFORMATION CENTER** (7280 Ranger Station Rd, Marblemount; 360/873-4500). Both offices have park information.

Diablo and Ross Lake

Since the only road access to Ross Lake is south from Hope, BC, the best way to get to the lake and its main attractions—campgrounds and the cabins built on log floats at **ROSS LAKE RESORT** (Rockport; 206/386-4437)—is on the **SEATTLE CITY LIGHT FERRY** (500 Newhalem St, Rockport; 206/386-4393) from Diablo. Here Seattle City Light built an outpost for crews constructing and servicing the dams on the Skagit River. The ferry leaves twice daily (8:30am and 3pm), running from mid-June through the end of October. Cost is $5 one-way; no reservations needed. Tours of Diablo Lake are available through **SEATTLE CITY LIGHT** (206/684-3030; *www.seattle.gov/light/tours/skagit*); tours were suspended for a time after September 11, 2001, and are still restricted from visiting certain parts of the Skagit River Hydroelectric Project. Visit the Newhalem **SKAGIT TOURS OFFICE** (500 Newhalem St; 206/233-2709; June–Sept) for more information.

The Methow Valley

Just east of the Cascades, Highway 20 descends into the Methow (pronounced "MET-how") Valley. Popular in winter with skiers and in summer with hikers and mountain bikers, the Methow recalls the Old West, from the faux-Western storefronts of Winthrop to the valley's working ranches and farms, to the Big Sky–and–sagebrush landscape.

Mazama

The best things to do in tiny Mazama (pronounced "ma-ZAH-ma") are fly-fish, hike, or cross-country ski, depending on the season. If it's civilization you're after, head for the **MAZAMA STORE** (50 Lost River Rd; 509/996-2855), where a sociable soup-and-espresso counter sits beside products that range from Tim's Potato Chips to fine wines to Patagonia shirts. The store also has a picnic area (complete with grillmeister in summer), and the last (or first) gas pumps for more than 70 miles if you're traveling across the mountains. In summer, the town is home to the **METHOW MUSIC FESTIVAL** (800/340-1458), a classical-music series held in local barns and meadows.

If you've got the rig for it (four-wheel drive is best; trailers are allowed), jump off from Mazama on the Methow Valley Road (County Rd 9140) for a 19-mile, knee-buckling sojourn up a steep, rough, one-lane road, complete with hairpin curves, no

CROSS-COUNTRY SKIING THE METHOW

Bright winter sunshine, dry powder snow, jaw-dropping views of mountain peaks—add almost 200 kilometers of well-groomed trails, and you have one of the nation's premier cross-country ski destinations. The **METHOW VALLEY SPORT TRAILS ASSOCIATION (MVSTA)** maintains this vast network of trails, the second largest in the United States. The system consists of four linked sections, many of which go directly past the valley's popular accommodations, so you can literally ski from your door. (In summer, the trails are used by mountain bikers.) Ski season usually begins in early December and continues through March. For updates on snow and trail conditions, contact the MVSTA (509/996-3287 or 800/682-5787; *www.mvsta.com*).

The largest section surrounds **SUN MOUNTAIN LODGE** in Winthrop, where 70 kilometers of trail cut through rolling hills. Below it, the **COMMUNITY TRAIL** snakes past farms and bottomland as it meanders from Winthrop to Mazama. Mazama's flat terrain and open meadows are ideal for novices.

The remaining section, called **RENDEZVOUS**, is recommended for intermediate to expert skiers only. Set above the valley at 3,500 to 4,000 feet, the trail passes through rugged forestland, where five huts are located at strategic points for overnight stays. Each hut bunks up to eight people and has a woodstove and a propane cookstove. Huts rent for $35 per person per night (or $150–175 for an entire hut). **CENTRAL RESERVATIONS** (800/422-3048; *www.mvcentralres.com*) has maps and information and makes reservations (required) for the **HUT-TO-HUT SYSTEM**. (For $85, Rendezvous Outfitters will lighten your load by hauling your group's gear and food to the huts.) Special trails are also set aside for **SNOWSHOERS**. Skiing on MVSTA trails requires trail passes, available at ski shops in the valley.

—*Nick Gallo*

guardrails, and 1,000-foot dropoffs. Your reward: **HARTS PASS** and **SLATE PEAK**, the state's highest drivable point at 7,440 feet. Open only in summer, Harts Pass delivers spectacular views of the Cascades, hiking trails, campgrounds, and fragrant meadows of wildflowers.

RESTAURANTS

Freestone Inn / ★★★

17798 HWY 20, MAZAMA; 509/996-3906 OR 800/639-3809 A floor-to-ceiling river-rock fireplace stands in the center of the Freestone Inn (see review) and separates the lobby on one side from the dining room on the other. In this intimate room, diners sit at white-clothed, candlelit tables for dinners of Northwest specialties. Chef Todd Brown's simple, elegant menu changes seasonally as it features ingredients grown by local purveyors (complemented by a wine selection heavy on Washington vintners). Start with skillet-roasted black tiger shrimp or grilled smoked garlic sausage. A baby spinach salad might come with roasted beets, Gorgonzola, apple, and sweet Walla Walla onion vinaigrette. Brown's hearty entrées range from a noble panfried trout to spice-roasted duck breast. Finish with profiteroles, a fruit crisp with cinammon ice cream, or a glass of Courvoisier. Breakfast might be banana spice bread French toast or Eggs provençal, baked with tomatoes, goat cheese, and herbs. *$$$; AE, DC, DIS, MC, V; local checks only; breakfast every day, dinner Tues–Sun; beer and wine; reservations recommended; info@freestoneinn .com; www.freestoneinn.com; 1½ miles west of Mazama.* &

LODGINGS

Freestone Inn and Early Winters Cabins / ★★★

17798 HWY 20, MAZAMA; 509/996-3906 OR 800/639-3809 Drive up to the 21-room log lodge that is the Freestone Inn, and you'll feel you've reached *Bonanza*'s Ponderosa. The inn sets an elegant, rustic tone for the 1,200-acre Wilson Ranch. The two-story lodge blends into the landscape, and gentle touches lend environmental appeal. A massive river-rock fireplace is the lobby centerpiece, and there's a little library nook nearby. The earth-toned rooms are subdued and classy, trimmed in pine with big stone fireplaces, large bathrooms with soaking tubs, wrought-iron fixtures, and old black-and-white photographs of the ranch. The original ground-floor rooms are our favorites, with king-sized beds and access to the lakefront lawn or snowy banks. An outdoor hot tub is just between Freestone Lake—a pond enlarged into a lake and stocked with trout—and the lodge. Although views from the inn are more territorial than grand, activities here are as vast as the Methow Valley itself; Jack's Hut serves as a base camp for outdoor activities from skiing to white-water rafting, fly-fishing to mountain biking. Additional lodging options include a luxurious Lakeside Lodge (complete with a kitchen and lots of room for families or friends) and 15 smaller Early Winters Cabins. Continental breakfast in the dining room is complimentary for guests at the inn (but not in the cabins). *$$$; AE, DC, DIS, MC, V; local checks only; info@freestoneinn.com; www.freestoneinn.com; 1½ miles west of Mazama.* &

Mazama Country Inn / ★★

42 LOST RIVER RD, MAZAMA; 509/996-2681 OR 800/843-7951 (IN WA) Quilts on the beds and comfortable sitting areas on two floors, stocked with books and games, give you the feeling of being in your own very large mountain cabin. A view of the North Cascades from nearly every window makes this spacious 8,000-square-foot lodge a good year-round destination (especially for horseback riders and cross-country skiers). The lodge has 18 good-sized rooms, all with private baths, of wooden construction with cedar beams; 10 are in the main lodge and 4 each in two additions. Some of the guest rooms (all fairly standard) have air-conditioning, nice on hot summer Eastern Washington nights. Amenities include an outdoor pool, sauna, and hot tub, as well as tennis and squash. In summer, breakfast, lunch, and dinner are offered in the lodge restaurant (best are meat selections, such as beef tenderloin or spicy ribs); winter brings family-style breakfasts and dinners. Thirteen cabins (each with kitchen and bath) are available for families

or groups of up to ten. No children under 13 in winter; no smoking; no pets. *$–$$;
MC, V; checks OK; info@mazamacountryinn.com; www.mazamacountryinn.com;
14 miles west of Winthrop.*

Mazama Ranch House / ★

42 LOST RIVER RD, MAZAMA; 509/996-2040 Horses and kids stay free at these economical accommodations just behind the Mazama Store. Owners Steve and Kristin Devin run the ranch house (which sleeps up to 13 guests) and the eight-room motel-style addition. The main house has five beds and a full kitchen and is perfect for family retreats. Each room in the addition has entrances on both sides—one to the parking lot and one to a sunny deck that fronts the valley's trail system (and the hot tub). An additional cabin, the rustic Longhorn, has its own kitchen, sleeping loft, and woodstove. The rural ranch atmosphere is the real deal: the barn, corral, and arena are available to overnighters who arrive with horses—and in summer, many do. For the horseless, two excellent outfitters are located within a few miles: Rocking Horse Ranch (509/996-2768) and Early Winters Outfitting (509/996-2659 or 800/737-8750; *www.earlywintersoutfitting .com). $$; MC, V; checks OK; www.mazamaranchhouse.com; just off Lost River Rd, across from Mazama Country Inn.* &

Winthrop

The Western motif of this mountain town fits the sun-baked (or snow-drifted) hills and wide-open sky. The old-fashioned storefronts and boardwalks feel a bit like something out of a John Wayne movie, and this is where most "tourism" takes place in the Methow Valley. Stop in the **SHAFER MUSEUM** (285 Castle Ave; 509/996-2712; *www.winthropwashington.com/winthrop/shafer/*), housed in pioneer Guy Waring's 1897 log cabin on the hill behind the main street, to learn about the area's early history; exhibits include old cars, a stagecoach, and horse-drawn vehicles.

The valley offers fine white-water rafting, spectacular hiking in the North Cascades, horseback riding, mountain biking, fishing, and cross-country or helicopter skiing. After you've had a big day outside, quaff a beer at the **WINTHROP BREWING COMPANY** (155 Riverside Ave; 509/996-3183), in a diminutive old schoolhouse on the main street (the interior belies its appearance; a deck and patio expand the seating in summer). **WINTHROP MOUNTAIN SPORTS** (257 Riverside Ave; 509/996-2886; *www.winthropmountainsports.com*) sells outdoor-activity equipment and supplies, and rents bikes, skis, snowshoes, and ice skates. The **TENDERFOOT GENERAL STORE** (corner of Riverside Ave and Hwy 20; 509/996-2288) has anything else you might have forgotten. **PEARRYGIN LAKE STATE PARK** (509/996-2370), 5 miles north of town, offers good swimming and campsites.

METHOW VALLEY CENTRAL RESERVATIONS (303 Riverside Ave; 800/422-3048; *www.mvcentralres.com*) books lodging for the entire valley and sells tickets for major events, such as mid-July's **RHYTHM AND BLUES FESTIVAL**. For more info, contact the **METHOW VALLEY INFORMATION CENTER** (241 Riverside Ave; 888/463-8469; *www.methow.com*).

RESTAURANTS

Duck Brand Hotel & Cantina / ★

246 RIVERSIDE AVE, WINTHROP; 509/996-2192 OR 800/996-2192 For more than a decade, this funky, eclectic restaurant built to replicate a frontier-style hotel has been a popular gathering spot and provisioner of good, filling meals at modest prices. Start the day with huevos rancheros or a big breakfast burrito; lunch on teriyaki chicken salad or a turkey avocado sandwich; then conclude your day with barbecued duck breast, cilantro quesadilla, fajitas, New York steak, halibut with pesto sauce, hoisin chicken breast, or myriad other options. The in-house bakery produces delicious baked goods, including biscotti, cinnamon rolls, and fruit pies. Beware: lines form in summer. Upstairs, the Duck Brand Hotel has six sparsely furnished rooms, priced right. *$$; AE, DC, DIS, MC, V; local checks only; breakfast, lunch, dinner every day; full bar; no reservations; duckbrand@methow.com; www.methownet.com/duck; on main street in Winthrop.*

Sun Mountain Lodge / ★★★☆

PATTERSON LAKE RD, WINTHROP; 509/996-2211 OR 800/572-0493 All tables here have beautiful views of the Methow Valley, giving diners the impression they are eating in a fantastical tree fort. Chef Patrick Miller changes the menu frequently, offers a different three-course taste meal every night, and strives to use organic and local high-quality ingredients whenever possible. The crab cakes come artfully arranged, two pillowy, rich, perfectly cooked dreams. Many delights accompany the beef tenderloin—mashed Yukon Golds and a morel demi-glace, seared squash, and two elaborate horns of crispy turnip. The wild salmon cooked with lavender and citrus butter can feature asparagus, a risotto cake, and grilled tomatoes. The obsequious staff gives good advice and provides seamless service. Overall, the food is delicious, though you'll pay for the experience. Lunch and breakfast are more simple, as is the menu in the adjoining Eagle's Nest Lounge. The wine cellar holds more than 5,000 bottles, and the list features 400 different labels, 150 of them from Washington State. *$$$; AE, DC, MC, V; local checks only; breakfast, lunch, dinner every day; full bar; reservations recommended; smtnsale@methow.com; www.sunmountainlodge.com; 9.6 miles southwest of Winthrop.* &

Topo Café / ★

253 RIVERSIDE AVE, WINTHROP; 509/996-4596 An Asian restaurant in Western-themed Winthrop? Surprisingly, it works. The old house on Riverside Ave (Hwy 20) fits the look of the street, but inside the place takes on a simple, serene elegance. Light colors stain the interior beams, complementing dark wood chairs and tables; live green plants and sheer white curtains on the many windows complete the fresh feel. The menu is Methow-Valley healthy: begin with *edamame*, spring rolls, or satay, then enjoy pho (Vietnamese soup), phad thai, spicy Singapore noodles, or Japanese *katsu* cutlet. Choose from a small but tasteful wine list, several bottled beers, and an assortment of teas. *$$; MC, V; local checks only; lunch and dinner Thurs–Tues (winter), every day (summer); beer and wine; reservations for 6 or more; topocafe@ mymethow.com; www.methownet.com/topo; on the main road through town.*

LODGINGS

Hotel Rio Vista / ★

285 RIVERSIDE AVE, WINTHROP; 509/996-3535 OR 800/398-0911 Rebuilt and reopened in 2003 as one hotel (after a fire destroyed the two motels formerly on this spot), the Hotel Rio Vista is much nicer than you'd expect of a hotel just south of downtown Winthrop. The Western-looking street-side appearance hides the confluence of the Methow and Chewuch Rivers, onto which all 29 rooms (and the glass-enclosed hot tub) have a view. Each room has a king- or two queen-sized beds, air-conditioning, and data port phone. King rooms have kitchenettes and DVD players. The management also rents out a cozy, lofted cabin, 10 minutes west of Winthrop, that sleeps six. *$$; MC, V; checks OK; info@hotelriovista .com; www.hotelriovista.com; on main street, at south end of town.*

Sun Mountain Lodge / ★★★☆

PATTERSON LAKE RD, WINTHROP; 509/996-2211 OR 800/572-0493 The showpiece of the Methow Valley is Sun Mountain Lodge, a resort offering luxury accommodations (as well as some that cater more to families), recreational activities for every season, fine dining, and stunning scenery. High on a hill above the valley and facing the North Cascades, the massive timber-and-stone lodge offers expansive views from most guest rooms and the on-site dining room (see review). The lobby features two huge wood-burning fireplaces, and a large concierge desk. Guest rooms offer casual ranch-style comfort, with log furniture, wrought-iron sconces, glass coffee tables, and thick, soft blankets. The Mount Robinson rooms are the newest and are stunning, with towering views even from the whirlpool bath; more reasonably priced Gardner rooms aren't quite as large, but still have gas fireplaces and private decks or patios; older main lodge rooms offer many of the same amenities (robes, coffeemakers, fine toiletries). Sixteen appealing one- or two-bedroom cabins are available just down the hill at Patterson Lake. (Children's play areas and child care/activity programs are available.) Much of the Sun Mountain experience stems from the outdoors. In summer, try tennis, horseback riding, swimming (two heated, seasonal pools), fly-fishing or rafting trips, golf (nearby), mountain biking, and more; in winter, resort trails are part of the valley's 175-kilometer cross-country trail system, or you can arrange ice skating, snowshoeing, or a sleigh ride. Soak in one of two outdoor hot tubs, or splurge on a spa treatment. Reserve early for summer or winter ski-season dates. *$$$–$$$$; AE, DC, MC, V; checks OK; 2-night min on weekends; sunmtn@methow.com; www.sunmountainlodge.com; 9.6 miles southwest of Winthrop.* &

WolfRidge Resort / ★★

412-B WOLF CREEK RD, WINTHROP; 509/996-2828 OR 800/237-2388 About 5 miles from the main highway, this collection of log buildings is everything a mountain retreat should be: rustic yet comfortable, serene, and private. Seven buildings contain 19 units divided into two-bedroom town houses, one-bedroom suites, hotel-style rooms, and three cabins. Lodgings are tastefully, if simply, furnished with handcrafted log furniture. Larger units have full kitchens (studios have kitchenettes), so you can grocery shop in town and then stay here for

MOUNTAIN LOOP HIGHWAY

The Mountain Loop Highway is one of Washington's less-recognized gems, overshadowed by the spectacular North Cascades Scenic Highway to the northeast. Located east of Everett, the Mountain Loop Highway is a 78-mile scenic drive that follows three swift rivers as it swings through the foothills of the western Cascades. The prime section is a 50-mile stretch past the town of Granite Falls that makes for an ideal weekend drive (especially in fall, when the colors are out). The highway also offers access to more than 300 miles of hiking trails, ranging from baby-stroller romps to rugged climbs into remote mountains. Note: Snow closes upper elevations of the highway during winter.

The highway consists of three roads: Highway 92, Forest Road 20, and Highway 530. It starts in **GRANITE FALLS**, 14 miles east of Everett (exit 194 off I-5), which isn't much to look at, but is the best spot to grab lunch or last-minute supplies. Choose from pizza places, diner fare, or ethnic-food restaurants.

Eastbound from Granite Falls, the highway retraces an old railway bed, passing through the town of Verlot; the **VERLOT RANGER STATION** (33515 Mountain Loop Hwy, Granite Falls; 360/691-7791) has information on hikes and sights. During the late 1880s, prospectors discovered gold, silver, and other metals in nearby mountains. Eastern investors built a railroad to haul ore to a smelter in Everett. But after a brief flurry of activity, the endeavor was undone by high costs, constant floods, and an economic depression. The mines closed in 1907.

days, only venturing out on skis or bikes on the Methow Valley trail system that runs right outside your door. Even without the trails, the 60-acre riverside setting impresses: lovely ponderosas blow in the wind, mountain peaks dance behind a curtain of green forest, a glorious meadow lets in the sun. For sybarites, there's an outdoor pool and a hot tub in a river-rock setting. *$$–$$$; AE, MC, V; checks OK; www.wolfridgeresort.com; south of Winthrop head up Twin Lakes Rd for 1½ miles, turn right on Wolf Creek Rd, and travel 4 miles to entrance on right.*

Twisp

Eight miles away from Winthrop, ordinary-looking Twisp (the name is said to come from a Native American word for the noise made by a yellow jacket) doesn't possess any of its sister city's gussied-up Western ornamentation, but it's worth a stop. On Saturday mornings, the thriving **METHOW VALLEY FARMERS MARKET** operates next to the community center April 15 through October 15. Poke around Glover Street and you'll find local arts and crafts at the **CONFLUENCE GALLERY** (104 Glover St; 509/997-ARTS; www.confluencegallery.com), theater performances during summer at the **MERC PLAYHOUSE** (101 Glover St; 509/997-PLAY; www.merc playhouse.com), and wonderful pastries and fresh bread—served hot 9am–11am—at

Outside Granite Falls, the highway turns into a gravel road that plunges into thick forest as it follows the "Stilly"—the darting, fast-flowing South Fork of the Stillaguamish River. Campgrounds appear at regular intervals, offering convenient places to picnic. The following hikes make nice outings: **OLD ROBE TRAIL** (mile 9 from Granite Falls; easy; 3 miles round-trip) leads to two former railroad tunnels; **MOUNT PILCHUCK LOOKOUT** (mile 11; difficult; 6 miles round-trip) climbs 2,100 feet and scrambles over boulders to reach a 5,300-foot lookout tower; **BIG FOUR ICE CAVES** (mile 25; easy; 2 miles round-trip), popular with families, leads to year-round ice caves (don't go inside the caves; ice crashing down from the ceiling makes it dangerous); and **MONTE CRISTO** (mile 31; easy; 8.6 miles round-trip) goes to a former gold-mining town, but there's little there now except for a few shacks.

At **BARLOW PASS**, the highway pavement ends and a 14-mile stretch of winding gravel on Forest Road 20 drops down from the mountains before it emerges in farmland near the timber town of **DARRINGTON**. The **COUNTRY COFFEE & DELI** (1015 E Sauk Rd, Darrington; 360/436-0213) will replenish you with sandwiches, ice cream, and espresso. At Darrington, the Mountain Loop Highway swings west on Highway 530 and loops back to Arlington near Interstate 5; or head 19 miles on Forest Road 20 to connect to the North Cascades Scenic Highway in Rockport.

—Nick Gallo

CINNAMON TWISP (116 Glover St; 509/997-5030; *www.cinnamontwisp.com*). For more info, contact the **TWISP VISITOR INFORMATION CENTER** (509/997-2926) or the **TWISP CHAMBER OF COMMERCE** (*www.twispinfo.com*).

RESTAURANTS

Fiddlehead Bistro / ★★

201 GLOVER ST, TWISP; 509/997-0343 Live music, eclectic cuisine, an intimate space, and friendly locals all make this one of the best dining experiences in the Methow Valley. The warm bistro features locally produced, organic vegetables and fruit in a perfectly balanced seasonal menu. Dishes might include curried chicken soup, rich cioppino, butternut-squash risotto with spicy greens and spicy pecans, a braised lamb shank with apricot-balsamic glaze, or grilled swordfish niçoise. The owners are on-site, and the staff is personable and knowledgeable. The wine list is relatively short but offers exquisite choices, many from France and Italy, and great prices. Desserts are rich—don't pass up the chocolate ecstasy cake. Music (usually performed by local musicians) can be hit or miss, but even when it misses it doesn't detract from the experience. *$–$$; MC, V; checks OK; breakfast Sun, lunch Sun–Tues and Thurs–Fri, dinner Thurs–Sun; beer and wine; reservations recommended; downtown.* &

Twisp River Pub / ★

HWY 20, TWISP; 888/220-3360 Spacious and clean, the new Twisp River Pub, home of the Methow Brewing Company, has room for a crowd, and often draws one. For lunch, order salads, sandwiches, or burgers. Dinner entrées (which come with bread and soup or salad) change regularly but might include bratwurst, curry, seafood, steak, and pastas. A children's menu attests to the popularity of this place with families. Desserts are worth considering. The full bar features 12 rotating taps that pour a variety of Northwest beers, especially the handcrafted brews of the Methow Valley Brewing Co. Live music is regularly scheduled, including an open mic night every Saturday at 9pm; work by local artists decorates the expansive walls. *$$; AE, DC, DIS, MC, V; checks OK; lunch and dinner Wed–Sun; full bar; no reservations; www.twispriverpub.com; at the west end of Twisp, on the main highway.*

Pateros

LODGINGS

Amy's Manor Inn / ★★

435 HWY 153, PATEROS; 509/923-2334 Built in 1928, this enchanting manor is dramatically situated at the foot of the Cascades overlooking the Methow River, in an impressive stand of maples, oaks, and large pines. Stone fences line the property; 5 acres of flower gardens produce bursts of color. Three guest rooms, country French in character, have a quiet elegance and share two baths. Not surprisingly, the location is often booked for weddings. But the hidden treasures here are the culinary creations of owner Pamela Ahl. Combine the seasonal harvest from her organic garden with her skills in the kitchen, and the table's breakfast bounty never disappoints. Ahl teaches cooking classes in spring and fall. *$$; MC, V; checks OK; www.amysmanor.com; 5 miles north of Pateros.*

Lake Chelan

South of the Methow Valley, Lake Chelan sits with half a mind in the mountains and the other half in vacation playland.

Some think Chelan is the best of the Northwest, just three and a half hours from Seattle. Others turn up their noses at the proliferation of shoulder-to-shoulder summer homes. Time-share condo developments (some more than 30 years old) and a few well-established resorts claim the primo waterfront sites with lots of beach access, docks, tennis, swimming pools, and activities. Many families have been coming here for generations; it's a Lake Tahoe kind of place, where Gen-Xers bring their young families, and college kids congregate on Memorial Day and Labor Day weekends, which makes the town and lake feel a bit like Florida on spring break.

The 55-mile-long, fjordlike lake is never more than 2 miles wide and is one of the nation's deepest lakes. Those who eschew summer's busy family fun/party atmosphere at the lake's south end (it's one of the state's most popular summer swimming, boating, and fishing destinations) often love the remote community of Stehekin at its northern tip, where you have a sense of slicing right into the Cascades. Or, they visit in the off-season, when even in Chelan, the pace slows to a crawl.

Chelan

The small town that anchors this resort area is blessed with a springtime profusion of apple blossoms, beautiful Lake Chelan thrusting into tall mountains, 300 days of sunshine a year, and good skiing, hunting, fishing, hiking, and sailing nearby.

One of the top attractions is the cruise up Lake Chelan to Stehekin on *Lady of the Lake II*, an old-fashioned tour boat, or one of its faster, more modern siblings. In summer, three boats are in operation. The *Lady II*, the largest of the vessels, holds 350 passengers and provides a leisurely four-hour trip uplake, with a 90-minute layover in Stehekin. It departs Chelan daily at 8:30am and returns around 6pm ($22 per person round-trip; kids 6–11 years old travel half price). The faster, smaller *Lady Express* shortens the trip to just over two hours one-way, with a one-hour stop in Stehekin before heading back (round-trip tickets $41). The *Lady Cat*, a catamaran that whips across the lake at 50 mph, makes the trip in 75 minutes; cost is $79 round-trip. Many travelers opt for the "combination trip," traveling uplake on the *Lady Express* and returning on the *Lady II*, which allows for a three-hour, 15-minute layover in Stehekin and a return by 6pm. Reservations are not needed for the *Lady II*, but the two faster boats almost always book up; advance purchase is necessary. During the off-season—November 1 through May 1—the boat schedule cuts back drastically. For full details, contact the **LAKE CHELAN BOAT COMPANY** (1418 W Woodin Ave; 509/682-2224 or 509/682-4584; *www.ladyofthelake.com*).

Alternatively, **CHELAN AIRWAYS** (1328 W Woodin Ave; 509/682-5065 or 509/682-5555; *www.chelanairways.com*) offers daily seaplane service to Stehekin ($120 round-trip), as well as scenic tours of the mountains. Chelan Butte Lookout, 9 miles west of Chelan, also provides a view of the lake, the Columbia River, and the orchard-blanketed countryside.

The best reason for going to Chelan is Lake Chelan itself, where some of the best accommodations are shoreside condos. **CHELAN QUALITY VACATION PROPERTIES** (888/977-1748; www.lakechelanvacationrentals.com), a rental clearing-house, has listings for condos and private vacation homes in the area. Each condo or house is privately owned, so furnishings and taste vary greatly. **CONDOS AT WAPATO POINT** (1 Wapato Point Wy, Manson; 509/687-9511 or 888/768-9511; *www.wapatopoint.com*), a full-fledged resort in neighboring Manson, are rented directly through its office.

Chelan's hot summer weather and the lake's clear, cool water beg you to get waterborne. Waterskiing, windsurfing, pleasure boating (personal watercraft, kayak, motorboat), and swimming—stick close to the lake's lower end for the warmest water—are popular activities. Rent boats and water-ski gear at Chelan Boat Rentals (1210 W Woodin Ave; 509/682-4444). Popular public boat docks in the area are Don Morse Park (the city park), Riverwalk Park, Lake Chelan State

Park, 25 Mile Creek State Park, and Old Mill Park. Slidewaters (102 Waterslide Dr; 509/682-5751; *www.slidewaters.com*), one of the Northwest's largest waterslide parks, keeps the kids happy.

Fishing for steelhead, rainbow, cutthroat, and chinook is very good in Lake Chelan. Stocked in the lake since the mid-1970s, chinook are the lake's prized catch. **GRAYBILL'S GUIDE SERVICE** (509/682-4292) is a reputable outfit; check with the **LAKE CHELAN CHAMBER OF COMMERCE** (800/4-CHELAN; *www.lakechelan .com*) for more guides. The chamber also has maps for the growing number of tiny boutique wineries in the area.

Good dining options in the area are limited, but locals rave about **LOCAL MYTH PIZZA** (122 S Emerson; 509/682-2914) and **HUNGRY BELLY** (246 W Manson Hwy; 509/682-8630).

RESTAURANTS

Campbell House Cafe / ★★

104 W WOODIN AVE, CHELAN; 509/682-4250 The decor is somewhat dowdy and the menu sticks to safe, predictable choices, but this is where you'll find Chelan's freshest seafood, dependable steaks, and acceptable pastas. An award-winning Washington State wine list is a plus. Breakfast is popular, with apple pancakes, biscuits and gravy, and other standards leading the way. Upstairs, you can find casual fare—burgers, fish-and-chips, salads—and a good selection of single-malt scotches at the Second Floor Pub & Veranda. The outdoor deck is a choice spot to catch a bite on a warm evening and people-watch. *$$$; AE, MC, V; checks OK; breakfast (Café), lunch, dinner every day; full bar; reservations recommended (Café), no reservations (Pub); www.campbellsresort.com; downtown, facing main street near lake.* ⅋

LODGINGS

Best Western Lakeside Lodge / ★

2312 W WOODIN AVE, CHELAN; 509/682-4396 OR 800/468-2781 This 65-unit complex, sharp-looking in a green sage and cedar trim exterior, offers spacious rooms (vaulted ceilings on the top floor), a cheerful indoor pool (and one outside too), and complimentary breakfast in an airy, gazebo-shaped conference room with full-length windows facing the lake. The biggest reason to stay might be the back-yard: nicely landscaped grounds slope down to a small, adjoining park fronting the water, where uplake views of the North Cascades' snowy peaks are delightful. *$$$; AE, DC, DIS, MC, V; checks OK; info@lakesidelodge.net; www.lakesidelodge.net; 2 miles south of Chelan on Hwy 97A.* ⅋

Campbell's Resort on Lake Chelan / ★★

104 W WOODIN AVE, CHELAN; 509/682-2561 OR 800/553-8225 Chelan's landmark resort—the hotel was built by C.C. Campbell in 1901—continues to be the most popular place for visitors. Its major draw is prime lakeside property and a sandy 1,200-foot beach in the heart of this classic small town. The 170 rooms, many with kitchenettes and all with patios or decks, are spread out in five buildings of varying vintage. The majority are more comfortable than plush, with the most attractive in Lodge 1 or 4. Amenities include two heated outdoor pools, two outdoor hot tubs, boat moorage, and a day spa. With a conference center that holds 300 people, Campbell's is undeniably a large-scale operation, but it still has an amiable, personable quality, thanks to the fact that the same family who built the resort still owns and operates it four generations later. Reservations are scarce in high season. *$$–$$$; AE, MC, V; checks OK; res@campbellsresort.com; www.campbellsresort.com; on lake at end of main street near downtown.*

Kelly's Resort / ★★

12801 S LAKESHORE RD, CHELAN; 509/687-3220 OR 800/561-8978 Kelly-owned for half a century, this longtime getaway qualifies as a "find" for urban escapees. It's a peaceful retreat, though it's also like summer camp for families who return year after year to claim the same cabin. You can walk on woodland trails or take a boat out on the water, but most people seem happy to sunbathe on the sunny deck. The 11 cabins set back in the woods are a bit dark, shaded by the forest, but they're fully equipped with kitchens, fireplaces, and TVs. A great feature is an outdoor heated pool in the woods. Kelly's also offers five modern condo units on the lake (from the lower units, you can walk right off the deck into the water), a three-bedroom house for rent, a convenience store, and a Ping-Pong table. The only off note: the budget prices have gone up. *$$$–$$$$; AE, MC, V; checks OK; www.kellysresort.com; 14 miles uplake on south shore.*

Stehekin

A passage to Stehekin, the little community at the head of Lake Chelan, is like traveling back in time. This jumping-off point for exploring rugged and remote North Cascades National Park is reached only by a four-hour boat trip from Chelan on *Lady of the Lake II* or one of its faster counterparts, by **CHELAN AIRWAYS FLOAT-PLANE**, by hiking, or by private boat. For a shorter boat ride, catch one of the boats uplake at Field's Point. At Stehekin, you can take a bus tour, eat lunch, enjoy close-up views of the North Cascades' rugged peaks, and be back onboard the boat in time for the return voyage. The **STEHEKIN PASTRY COMPANY** (summer only), a pleasant stroll from the boat landing, fills the mountain air with fresh-from-the-oven, sugary smells of cinnamon rolls.

Exploration is the prime reason for coming here. Good day hikes include a lovely one along the lakeshore and another along a stream through the **BUCKNER ORCHARD**; numerous splendid backcountry trails attract serious backpackers. In winter, fine touring opportunities for cross-country skiers or snowshoe enthusiasts abound, though the town pretty much shuts down for the season. The **RANGER STATION** at Chelan (428 W Woodin Ave, Chelan; 509/682-2576), open year-round, is an excellent information source. A **NATIONAL PARK SERVICE SHUTTLE BUS** (509/682-2549) provides transportation from Stehekin to trailheads, campgrounds, fishing holes, and scenic areas mid-May through mid-October.

Part of the national park complex near the Stehekin landing, **NORTH CASCADES STEHEKIN LODGE** (at head of Lake Chelan; 509/682-4494; *www.stehekin.com*) is a year-round lodge featuring 28 rooms, a full-service restaurant, a general store, and a rental shop for bikes, boats, skis, and snowshoes.

The Courtney family will pick you up at Stehekin in an old bus and take you to their **STEHEKIN VALLEY RANCH** (800/536-0745; *www.courtneycountry.com*) at the farthest end of the valley, where you can enjoy river rafting and hiking or opt for seclusion. Open in summer, the ranch rents 12 units, 7 of which are rustic tent-cabins offering the basics (screened windows, a kerosene lamp, showers in the main building). The price is decent ($75–$85 per night per person), considering it includes three hearty, family-style meals and valley transportation. **CASCADE CORRALS** (509/682-7742), also run by the family, arranges horseback rides and mountain pack trips.

LODGINGS

Silver Bay Inn / ★★

10 SILVER BAY RD, STEHEKIN; 509/682-2212 OR 800/555-7781 (WA AND OR ONLY) The Silver Bay Inn, at the nexus of the Stehekin River and Lake Chelan, is a gracious, memorable retreat. Friendly Kathy and Randall Dinwiddie welcome guests to this passive-solar home and spectacular setting: 700 feet of waterfront with a broad green lawn rolling down to the lake. Formerly a B&B, the inn has changed its configuration slightly. The main house now rents out as a single unit. The two-bedroom, two-bath house, decorated with antiques, has a 30-foot-long sun-room, two view decks, a soaking tub, and a faraway view. The house includes an apartment-sized unit with a private entrance, rented separately. Two lakeside cabins are remarkably convenient (dishwasher, microwave, all linens) and sleep four and six. Bicycles, canoes, croquet, and hammocks are available. The hot tub has a 360-degree view of the lake and surrounding mountains. During summer, units have a two- to five-night minimum stay and kids under 9 are not allowed (though they're welcome other months). *$$–$$$; MC, V; checks OK; stehekin@silverbayinn.com; www.silverbayinn.com; 1¼ miles up Stehekin Valley Rd from landing.*

CENTRAL CASCADES

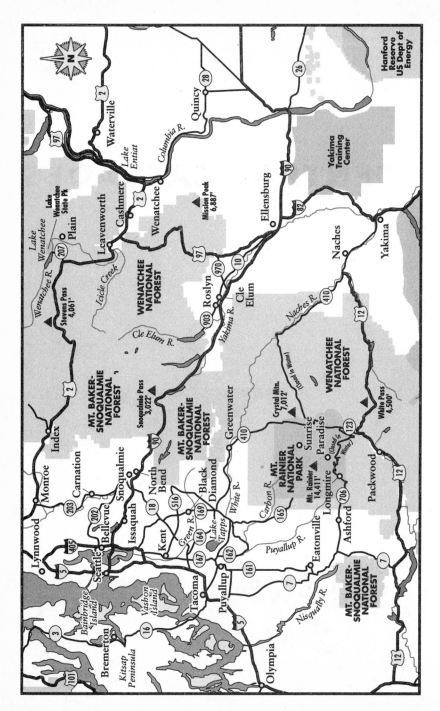

CENTRAL CASCADES

Anyone seeking a quintessential mountain experience will find it in the Central Cascades. The state's best recreation destinations are here, along with the main arteries between Western and Eastern Washington—Interstate 90 and US Highways 2 and 12. In summer, these thoroughfares are jammed with those seeking fir- and pine-perfumed air, pristine lakes, mountain trails, rock walls to climb, and campsites in forested glades. In winter, the routes can be choked with snow, and skiers and snowboarders flock to the summits of Snoqualmie, Stevens, and White Passes to schuss the slopes.

The mountains around the Bavarian-style village of Leavenworth, and north to the tiny village of Plain, contain countless all-season mountain getaways. Leavenworth's many festivals draw visitors year-round. The Central Cascades are also home to quite probably the world's most beautiful mountain—Mount Rainier. In summer, many Northwesterners make a tradition of picnicking amid wildflower meadows, an experience that on a sunny day feels like a fat slice of heaven. No wonder it's called Paradise. The mountain is an easy day trip—or overnight in one of the B&Bs or lodges nearby.

ACCESS AND INFORMATION

One of the Northwest's most beautiful drives, the 400-mile **CASCADE LOOP** follows US Highway 2 from Everett, takes in Leavenworth and Wenatchee, and heads north (see North Cascades chapter) to Lake Chelan, Winthrop, and the North Cascades Scenic Highway. The route can be accessed from Interstate 90 at Cle Elum by taking Highway 970 to US Highway 97 north. It joins US Highway 2 just east of Leavenworth. A brochure is available from the **CASCADE LOOP ASSOCIATION** (PO Box 3245, Wenatchee, WA 98807; 509/662-3888; *www.cascadeloop.com*).

The most popular east-west route across Washington, **INTERSTATE 90** connects Interstate 5 at Seattle with Ellensburg, Moses Lake, and Spokane (and beyond). Highway highlights include Snoqualmie Falls, the ski areas at Snoqualmie Pass, and towns such as Cle Elum and Roslyn. It is an elegant multilane freeway, designated a National Scenic Byway in 1998, which roughly traces the South Fork of the Snoqualmie River east into the Cascade foothills, cutting through the verdant Snoqualmie Valley and fir-thick hillsides like a wide boulevard. A map of outings and activities along the route and a heritage tour map are available from the **MOUNTAINS TO SOUND GREENWAY TRUST** (1011 Western Ave, Ste 606, Seattle; 206/382-5565; *MTSGreenway@tpl.org*; *www.mtsgreenway.org*).

US Highway 2 and Stevens Pass

Highway 2 heads east-west across the state, from Interstate 5 at Everett to Spokane, winding up to Stevens Pass along the Skykomish River. **STEVENS PASS** itself (exit 194 off Hwy 2; 206/812-4510; *www.stevenspass.com*), operating late November to early April, is a favorite destination of Seattle-area skiers, offering downhill and cross-country skiing as well as snowshoeing (the **NORDIC CENTER** is located

5 miles east of the summit). Day lodges at the summit also include a half-dozen casual eateries. From the pass, Highway 2 drops down to the Wenatchee River. Along the way, the towns of Leavenworth, Cashmere, and Wenatchee give travelers reason to stop.

Lake Wenatchee

Lake Wenatchee, about 5 miles north of Highway 2 on Highway 207 at Coles Corner (and the same distance northwest of Plain), has a state park at one end, with a large, sandy public swimming beach and campsites (888/226-7688; *www.parks.wa.gov*; overnight fee) in the woods closer to the Wenatchee River and lake. The Forest Service's **GLACIER VIEW CAMPGROUND**, 5 miles west on Cedar Brae Road, also has lakeside campsites. About a quarter of a mile before you reach the campground you'll see the trailhead to **HIDDEN LAKE** (a half-mile family hike to a small alpine lake). Ask about camping, hiking, or other day hikes at the **RANGER STATION** (22976 Hwy 207, at Lake Wenatchee; 509/763-3103) on the north side of the lake. Play golf or tennis at **KAHLER GLEN GOLF AND SKI RESORT** (20890 Kahler Dr, Leavenworth; 509/763-2121 or 800/440-2994; *www.kahlerglen.com*).

Plain

LODGINGS

Mountain Springs Lodge / ★★

19115 CHIWAWA LOOP RD, PLAIN; 509/763-2713 OR 800/858-2276 Arriving at this high mountain lodge evokes images of coming home to the Ponderosa. Check in at Beaver Creek Lodge, which houses two spacious Ralph Lauren–style suites upstairs, and a restaurant (meals available by reservation) and espresso bar. Two 20-person-plus lodges and two smaller A-frame chalets face a sprawling lawn, good for volleyball, croquet, or cartwheels. The brook leads to the barn, where events as special as weddings or as down-home as a family reunion chuck-wagon barbecue take place. This is a good place for anyone anytime but is best when you've got an energetic group and rent one of the lodges. Hot tubs and massive rock fireplaces are magnets after a day of snowmobiling (available here), in the saddle (you can take guided horseback and wagon rides here in summer), or on sleigh rides (on-site in winter). Several private, offsite homes are also available to rent; ask for details. $$$; DIS, MC, V; checks OK; info@mtsprings.com; www.mtsprings.com; *14 miles northwest of Leavenworth, then 1 mile north of Plain.*

Natapoc Lodging / ★★★

12348 BRETZ RD, LEAVENWORTH; 509/763-3313 OR 888/NATAPOC Natapoc offers an idyllic "cabin in the woods" experience that delights first-time visitors and is addictive to regulars who come here for romantic interludes or large family reunions. Choose from cozy-for-2 or spacious-for-20 secluded log houses on acreage along the Wenatchee River. All have gas grills, TV/VCRs, and

CENTRAL CASCADES THREE-DAY TOUR

DAY ONE: Head east on Interstate 90 from Seattle. Take exit 22, past Preston, a turn-of-the-20th-century Scandinavian mill town, and Fall City, the final upstream landing for early steamboats. Highway 202 takes you to dramatic 268-foot **SNOQUALMIE FALLS**, where you can lunch at **SALISH LODGE & SPA** in fancy surroundings with views of the falls. Then tour the little town of Snoqualmie. At North Bend, where the rocky face of Mount Si rises to the north, return to Interstate 90 and continue east to Snoqualmie Pass. The terrain begs you to stop for a view—or a hike. East of the summit, take a swing through historic Roslyn, then on to Cle Elum to spend the night in a caboose at the **IRON HORSE INN B&B**.

DAY TWO: After breakfast at your B&B, stock up on road snacks in town: choose goodies at the **CLE ELUM BAKERY** or pick up beef jerky at **OWEN'S MEATS**. Follow signs north to Blewett/Swauk Pass (US Hwy 97), a scenic drive that drops along Peshastin Creek to Highway 2; head east. Swing through Cashmere and visit the **PIO-NEER VILLAGE** and **LIBERTY ORCHARDS** for fruit candy samples, then continue to Wenatchee. Watch for the **ANJOU BAKERY** sign and stop for a macaroon or fudgy chocolate cookie, or lunch on a sandwich or slice of torta. Your destination on a clear spring or summer day is **OHME GARDENS**, just north of town. Head west on Highway 2 to Leavenworth. Check into **HOTEL PENSION ANNA** and relax before dinner. Dine **AT CAFE MOZART** or **VISCONTI'S**.

DAY THREE: Have a leisurely breakfast, then explore Leavenworth's **FRONT STREET SHOPS**. Enjoy a lunch crepe at **PAVZ**, or buy a bratwurst from a street vendor. If you want to burn calories, check in at the ranger station for suggested hikes. Stay in Leavenworth a second night at **SLEEPING LADY**, if space is available, and take in a concert at the **ICICLE CREEK MUSIC CENTER** (9286 Icicle Rd, Leavenworth; 509/548-6347; www.icicle.org; call ahead for performance schedules). The following day take Highway 2 west, enjoying the views at Stevens Pass, as you return to the Seattle area.

fully equipped kitchens with dishwashers and microwaves. Book early for holidays or special weekends (a year in advance if you're aiming for Christmas). Ambitious types can fish nearby, cross-country ski in winter, or shop in Leavenworth. But if vegging out is your idea of heaven, sit on the deck and listen to the river or gaze at the stars as you slip into the soothing waters of your hot tub. *$$$; AE, MC, V; checks OK; info@natapoc.com; www.natapoc.com; 4 miles south of Lake Wenatchee.*

Leavenworth

A former struggling mill town, self-styled in the 1960s as a Bavarian village, Leavenworth has more than found its niche: it is proudly, unabashedly, a theme town. Bavarian food, architecture, music, and festivals have become part of the fabric of life here. If you think that's not your cup of tea, try it anyway. Behind the shutters and flower-box architecture, the yodeling and accordion fests, there's a lot to explore in this stunning alpine setting. Excellent lodging is plentiful—some of it is top quality, and Bavarian in style. Popular festivals are held year-round. Call the Leavenworth Chamber of Commerce (see below) for information.

If you possess even one shopping gene, you'll enjoy exploring the dozens of shops along Front Street, the town's festival showcase and main promenade. Specialty stops include **DIE MUSIK BOX** (933 Front St; 509/548-6152 or 800/288-5883; *www.musicbox.com*), with a dazzling—sometimes noisy—array of music boxes; **THE BAVARIAN CLOTHING COMPANY** (933 Front St; 509/548-2442), where you can custom order genuine Lederhosen or buy dirndls and beautiful capes; or **KRIS KRINGL** (907 Front St; 509/548-6867 or 888/KKRINGL), to shop for Christmas year-round.

Cultural offerings are varied and growing. The **HI STRUNG MUSIC & PICKIN' PARLOR** (923 Commercial St; 509/548-8663; *www.histrungmusic.com*) focuses on acoustic music with guitars ranging from a few hundred to many thousands of dollars and an excellent CD collection. The **COMMUNITY COFFEE HOUSE** offers live music every Friday night at the Chumstick Grange Hall (621 Front St; 509/548-7374; *www.leavenworthcoffeehouse.com*). Off the beaten path, seek out the new **MILLER FINE ARTS GALLERY** (210 Division St; 509/548-8010) featuring work by Eastern Washington artists, or check out the natural history and cultural exhibits at **LEAVENWORTH AUDUBON CENTER** and **UPPER VALLEY MUSEUM**, which share space in a historic building, formerly Haus Lorelei B&B (347 Division St; 509/548-0181; *wa.audubon.org* or *www.wenatcheevalleymuseum.com*; open weekends). For a lighter browse, visit **THE LEAVENWORTH NUTCRACKER MUSEUM** (735 Front St; 509/548-4573; *www.nutcrackermuseum.com*; open afternoons May–Oct, call for other times) to view 5,000 nutcrackers, from thumb-sized to life-sized.

Boutique wineries are cropping up in the valley and include **EAGLE CREEK WINERY** (509/548-7668; *www.eaglecreekwinery.com*) near town, **ICICLE RIDGE WINERY** (509/548-7851; *www.icicleridgewinery.com*) in Peshastin, **LA TOSCANA WINERY** (509/548-5448; *http://groups.msn.com/LaToscana*) in Cashmere, and **WEDGE MOUNTAIN WINERY** (509/548-7068; *www.wedgemountainwinery.com*) on the Wenatchee River. Tasting rooms are open on weekends or by appointment. Contact the winery association (509/782-0708; *www.columbiacascadewines.com*) for information about two summer wine festivals. There's even a new **SILVER LAKE WINERY** tasting room (714 Front St, #A1, Leavenworth; 509/548-5788; *www.silverlakewinery.com*). For a picnic, pair wine with goodies from **THE CHEESEMONGER'S SHOP** (633 Front St, Ste F; 509/548-9011; *www.cheesemongersshop.com*). Stop by the Front Street crepery, **PAVZ** (833 Front St; 509/548-2103; *www.pavz.com*), for a savory or dessert crepe and espresso in a stylish, casual setting, or enjoy a glass of wine with your meal at **EDEL HAUS** (320 9th St; 509/548-4412 or 800/487-3335), one of the best places in town to dine alfresco.

Outdoor activities abound here; check with the **LEAVENWORTH RANGER STATION** just off Highway 2 (600 Sherbourne St, eastern edge of town; 509/548-6977) or the **LEAVENWORTH CHAMBER OF COMMERCE** (in the Obertal Mall at 9th and Commercial Sts; 509/548-5807; *www.leavenworth.org*) for maps and information on hiking, fishing, skiing, mountain biking, rafting, kayaking, river running, golf, and horseback riding.

RESTAURANTS

Cafe Mozart / ★★★

829 FRONT ST, LEAVENWORTH; 509/548-0600 Nibble on schnitzel, pork medallions, or lighter fare, such as fish of the day, in this family-run dining retreat overlooking Front Street. A new "wine attic" can be viewed from the dining area, and wines include a selection of local offerings. The downstairs restaurant, Andreas Keller, is run by the same family, has a beer-hall atmosphere, and serves heartier food, such as sausage, sauerkraut, and German-style potato salad. *$$; DIS, MC, V; checks OK; lunch and dinner every day; beer and wine; reservations recommended; www.cafemozartrestaurant.com; on Front St across from the park.*

Visconti's / ★★★

636 FRONT ST, LEAVENWORTH; 509/548-1213 / 1737 N WENATCHEE AVE, WENATCHEE; 509/662-5013 Italian food is served up in a lively fine-dining atmosphere in the upper levels of Leavenworth's former brewery. Pizza and lots of other delicious items—including savory mussels—come out of the wood-fired ovens. The Leavenworth branch has a shorter menu than the original Visconti's (a fancy roadhouse on the main drag in Wenatchee). Both are popular and frequently packed. *$$; DIS, MC, V; checks OK; dinner every day; beer and wine; reservations recommended; www.viscontis.com; on Front St across from the park.*

LODGINGS

Abendblume Pension / ★★★

12570 RANGER RD, LEAVENWORTH; 509/548-4059 OR 800/669-7634 Come here to leave everything behind (especially the kids). Austrian chalet–style Abendblume continues to grow in popularity. And no wonder: it's one of the most elegant, sophisticated inns in town, run by a gracious host. A beautiful sweeping staircase leads upstairs. The two best upper-level rooms have wood-burning fireplaces, Italian marble bathrooms with whirlpool tubs discreetly opening to the rooms, and sun-drenched window seats with views. A recent remodel on the main floor turned a double-bedded room into a king-bedded room with two twin Murphy beds. Every room is an escape, regardless of size. Outside is a patio hot tub. Breakfast at your own pace in the pine-trimmed morning room; *abelskivers* (a pancake) are a specialty. *$$$; AE, DIS, MC, V; checks OK; abendblm@rightathome.com; www.abendblume.com; north on Ski Hill Dr at west end of town.*

All Seasons River Inn / ★★★

8751 ICICLE RD, LEAVENWORTH; 509/548-1425 This modern two-story cedar house with rustic touches and a relaxing riverside location has six rooms with antique furnishings, river views, and jetted tubs. Some rooms have sitting areas; several have fireplaces. One room has its own pocket garden and swing overlooking the river. Happy amenities include chocolates and evening treats. Owners Kathy and Jeff Falconer are happy to arrange massages or desserts for special events. Kathy's breakfasts are so popular she's compiled her recipes into a booklet for guests. An adult retreat; no TVs in rooms. *$$$; MC, V; checks OK; allriver@rightathome.com; www.allseasonsriverinn.com; 1 mile south of Hwy 2.*

Bosch Garten / ★

9846 DYE RD, LEAVENWORTH; 509/548-6900 OR 800/535-0069 Friendly hosts and stylish, homey comfort make this modern two-story home, in a residential area at the eastern outskirts of town, a good choice. Three rooms with private baths are perfect for those traveling in small groups—then the house is yours. A garden gazebo hot tub and a tiny orchard make this particularly relaxing on warm summer evenings. Children over 14 OK. *$$$; MC, V; checks OK; innkeeper@nwi.net; www.boschgarten.com; east of town.*

Haus Rohrbach Pension / ★★☆

12881 RANGER RD, LEAVENWORTH; 509/548-7024 OR 800/548-4477 Since it opened in 1975, Leavenworth's first B&B has collected a loyal following, especially among hikers and skiers. So, a few years ago, fans fretted when the original owners, Bob and Kathryn Harrild, sold their Bavarian-style inn overlooking the Leavenworth Valley. Would the beloved routines of this nonfussy, family-oriented establishment disappear? The Dutch Babies (puffed pancakes) and orange rye French toast? The chocolate-coated peanut butter pie and milkshakes and sundaes (offered at nominal cost) and the evening dessert hour? Not to worry. New owners (and former loyal guests) Carol and Mike Wentink wouldn't dream of letting go of these treasured traditions. While they have added hammocks to the grounds, remodeled the kitchen, and plan modest cosmetic improvements (sorely needed, we think), they are not interested in changing the basic nature of this retreat. Of course the swimming pool, spring-fed pond, and great hiking hill behind the inn remain, as do the two quieter suites up the hill preferred by couples. *$$–$$$; AE, DIS, MC, V; checks OK; info@hausrohrbach.com; www.hausrohrbach.com; north of Hwy 2, north onto Ski Hill Rd, and left onto Ranger Rd.*

Hotel Pension Anna / ★★☆

926 COMMERCIAL ST, LEAVENWORTH; 509/548-6273 OR 800/509-ANNA Pension Anna could be on a side street in an Austrian village. Owners Robert and Anne Smith travel frequently to Germany and Austria, and return with more than ideas. The pine beds, eiderdown comforters, and duvets have been directly imported. Bob's handcrafted armoire, adorning a hall, is hard to distinguish from the old-country one nearby. The breakfast room, rich with pine paneling, coffered ceiling, and Austrian-style fireplace, is a cozy retreat to enjoy the sliced meats, cheeses, and egg-in-an-egg-cup breakfast. All 16 guest rooms are spacious; most have balconies. Suites have jetted tubs and fireplaces. The stunner is the adjacent former church that's been converted into two suites. On the whole, we could wish for more expansive views or larger grounds, but why? The beauty here is that you're wrapped in quality half a block from the center of town. *$$$; DIS, MC, V; checks OK; www.pensionanna .com; two blocks south of Hwy 2.* &

Mountain Home Lodge / ★★★☆

8201 MOUNTAIN HOME RD, LEAVENWORTH; 509/548-7077 OR 800/414-2378 This contemporary lodge claims a commanding site a mile above Leavenworth in a breathtaking mountaintop setting. Reach it in summer by driving 3 miles of dirt road; in winter, a heated snow-cat picks you up from the parking lot at the bottom of Mountain Home Road. Cross-country skiers enjoy miles of tracked trails outside the back door; you can snowshoe and sled, or try the 1,700-foot toboggan run. Summer activities include hiking, horseshoes, badminton, and tennis; the hot tub and swimming pool overlook a broad meadow and mountains. Ten charming rooms are decorated with quilts and outdoor-themed accessories. Nearby, two newer private pine cabins offer solitude and views. Gourmet meals in the dining area might include squash soup, pheasant, or wild mushroom–glazed tenderloin, and possibly a decadent chocolate tart; top Northwest offerings grace the wine list. No kids. Meals included in winter. *$$$; DIS, MC, V; checks OK; info@mthome .com; www.mthome.com; off E Leavenworth Rd and Hwy 2.*

Run of the River / ★★★★

9308 E LEAVENWORTH RD, LEAVENWORTH; 509/548-7171 OR 800/288-6491 Attention to detail keeps guests returning to this elegant log inn on the Icicle River. Innkeepers Monty and Karen Turner are consummate hosts. It's a pleasure to find the day's paper waiting on your ottoman, or the vintage typewriter and stationery for romantic missives or notes for the guest book. Each of the six rooms is a luxurious suite with river-rock fireplace; hand-hewn, four-poster burl-wood log bed; jetted tub for two surrounded by river rock; and work by local artists. We like the cozy log-cabin ambiance, warm colors, and privacy of the Kingfisher (it has a separate entrance). Some rooms have reading lofts. All suites boast solitude and comfort. Spend the day on large, private decks, reading or watching wildlife in the refuge across the river (binoculars provided). You'll also find cable TV and a bubble kit, in case stargazing from the hot tub isn't enough entertainment. Hearty breakfasts emphasize seasonal produce. Bikes are available. The Turners have printed an excellent array of area-specific activity guides. This is a must-stay place. Our only regret is that all rooms are pricey; check for Internet value packages. *$$$$; DIS, MC, V; checks OK; info@runoftheriver.com; www.runoftheriver.com; 1 mile east of Hwy 2.*

Sleeping Lady / ★★★

7375 ICICLE RD, LEAVENWORTH; 509/548-6344 OR 800/574-2123 This is a one-of-a-kind place—a quintessential Northwest retreat with an acute awareness of the environment and a devotion to music and performing arts. A former Civilian Conservation Corps camp, the place is well set up for conferences; buildings—from a dance studio to a spacious 60-person meeting house—are

BLOOMIN' WONDERFUL FRUIT

The Wenatchee Valley is one of Washington State's most famous and picturesque fruit regions, with climate-perfect hot summers and cold winters to produce crisp, juicy apples. Spring and fall are the best times to visit.

Bloom time is usually around the end of April or first week of May. Side roads between Leavenworth and Wenatchee offer grand blossom-touring opportunities. Head east from Leavenworth along Highway 2, exit at the tiny villages of Peshastin or Dryden, and meander through orchard country. Since the valley is cozy and intimate in scale—roads usually loop back to the main highway—it's hard to get lost, and fun to try. Wenatchee's **WASHINGTON STATE APPLE BLOSSOM FESTIVAL**—the state's oldest major fest—coincides with peak bloom, weather cooperating.

Apples ripen in September and early October, which is a great time to visit, stopping by fruit stands to buy boxes of apples, pears, or other tree fruits. Try **SMALLWOOD HARVEST** (1 mile east of Leavenworth on Hwy 2; 509/548-4196; Apr–Oct) for fruits, wines, and specialty foods. **PREY'S FRUIT** (just east of Leavenworth on Hwy 2; 509/548-5771) is another good stop. Top apple varieties include Jonagold, Gala, and Criterion.

The **WASHINGTON APPLE COMMISSION VISITORS CENTER** (2900 Euclid Ave, Wenatchee; 509/663-9600; *www.bestapples.com*; weekdays year-round, weekends May–Dec) offers bloom-time information, as well as displays, apple gift items for sale, and free juice or fruit samples.

—*Jena MacPherson*

comfortably elegant, with touches such as Oriental rugs and woodstoves, but all are high-tech ready. The old fieldstone chapel is now a 200-seat performing arts theater (the Icicle Creek Music Center's resident string ensemble performs here; 509/548-6347; *www.icicle.org*). The guest rooms—with log beds and sometimes additional beds in alcoves or lofts—are set in six different clusters. Two separate cabins include the romantic, secluded Eyrie, with a woodstove and whirlpool bath. Two woodland-style rock pools include a large heated pool, used May through September, and a small heated soaking pool (year-round). Conferences have first dibs on reservations, but there's flexibility for other guests, as space allows. Chef Damian Browne serves an excellent meal in a (slightly disconcerting) buffet-style dining room; prices include meals. The Grotto is a separate, casual retreat for before- or after-dinner drinks; O'Grady's is a coffee and deli stop with tables and a fireplace and is open to the public. Look for the outdoor glass "icicle" sculpture by Dale Chihuly. *$$–$$$;*

AE, DIS, MC, V; checks OK; info@sleepinglady.com; www.sleepinglady.com; 2 miles southwest of Leavenworth.

Cashmere

This little orchard town gives cross-mountain travelers who aren't in a Bavarian mood an alternative to Leavenworth. Western storefronts line the low-key main street; a river and railroad border the town.

The **CASHMERE MUSEUM** (600 Cottage Ave; 509/782-3230; *www.cashmere museum.com*) has an extensive collection of Native artifacts and archaeological material; the adjoining **PIONEER VILLAGE** puts 21 old buildings, carefully restored and equipped, into a nostalgic grouping. The waterwheel is on the National Register of Historic Places. The museum and village alone are worth a stop.

Aplets and Cotlets, confections made with local fruit and walnuts from an old Armenian recipe, have been produced in Cashmere for decades. You can tour the plant at **LIBERTY ORCHARDS** (117 Mission St; 509/782-2191 or 800/231-3242; *www.aplets.com*) and sample a few.

In an orchard off Highway 2, 1 mile east of Cashmere, is **ANJOU BAKERY** (3898 Old Monitor Hwy; 509/782-4360), a great stop for rustic breads, streusel-topped apple pies, macaroons, chocolate cookies, and other baked goods. Premade sandwiches and soups are ready for takeout; a handful of tables are available.

Wenatchee

A visit to Wenatchee in the center of Washington puts you in the heart of apple country, with an **APPLE BLOSSOM FESTIVAL** at the end of April; call the Wenatchee Valley Convention & Visitors Bureau (116 N Wenatchee Ave; 800/572-7753; *www.wenatcheevalley.org*). **OHME GARDENS** (just north of town on US Hwy 97A; 509/662-5785; *www.ohmegardens.com*) is a 9-acre alpine retreat with cool glades and water features. It sits on a promontory 600 feet above the Columbia River, offering splendid views of the valley, river, city, and mountains. The **RIVERFRONT LOOP TRAIL** on the banks of the Columbia makes for a pleasant evening stroll or an easy bike ride; the 11-mile loop traverses both sides of the river (and crosses two bridges) from Wenatchee to East Wenatchee. The best place to join the trail is via a pedestrian overpass at the east end of First Street. The **WENATCHEE VALLEY MUSEUM AND CULTURAL CENTER** (127 S Mission, Wenatchee; 509/664-3340; *www.wenatcheevalleymuseum.com*; Tues–Sat 10am–4pm) has permanent exhibits on the pioneers, Native Americans, and petroglyphs from the Columbia River.

MISSION RIDGE (13 miles southwest on Squilchuck Rd; 509/663-6543; *www.missionridge.com*) offers some of the region's best powder, served by four chairlifts; ask for ski-and-lodging package info. On the second or third Sunday in April, hordes of spectators watch athletes compete in six grueling events—including skiing, running, biking, and paddling—in the **RIDGE-TO-RIVER RELAY** (509/662-8799; *www.r2r.org*).

RESTAURANTS

John Horan House / ★★

2 HORAN RD, WENATCHEE; 509/663-0018 Many of the orchards once surrounding this 1899 Victorian farmhouse, built by Wenatchee pioneer John Horan, are gone. Yet the roundabout drive to the house, near the confluence of the Wenatchee and Columbia Rivers, sets the tone for an evening that harkens back to more gracious times. Proprietor Inga Peters offers country hospitality; chef Amilee Cappell orchestrates seasonally fresh seafood, and you'll be equally impressed with her Angus beef preparations. The Carriage House Café next door—a friendly stop for a glass of wine, a Northwest microbrew, or a game of cribbage—offers casual fare. *$$–$$$; AE, DIS, MC, V; checks OK; dinner Mon–Sat in summer (off-season, call for hours); full bar; reservations recommended; johninga@johnhoranhouse.com; www.john horanhouse.com; just south of K-Mart plaza.*

Shakti's / ★★★

218 N MISSION, WENATCHEE; 509/662-3321 Shakti Lanphere (formerly a chef in Seattle and Methow Valley restaurants) and her mother, Renee, partnered to create this welcome oasis. A luscious gold dining room with maple touches is a stylistic mix of Asia and Tuscany. With linen tablecloths and romantic lighting, it feels like a slice of design-chic Seattle. The food—such as braised rabbit, nightly risotto, or pasta specials—has more in common with rustic northern Italian cuisine. You can get a great steak, too, pan-seared with pancetta, shallots, and rosemary, alongside fresh spinach lightly sautéed in garlic, lemon juice, and olive oil. Bread from Anjou Bakery arrives with herbs and spiced oil for dipping; the bread also goes into pudding that may be the best we've had. Reasonably priced wine selections are well matched to the menu, and the pours are generous. Friendly, informed servers pamper you. Refreshing for Wenatchee is a full-service, nonsmoking lounge—stop for calamari and a martini or glass of wine. In warm weather, try the back patio. *$$–$$$; AE, MC, V; checks OK; lunch Tues–Fri, dinner Tues–Sat; reservations recommended; in Mission Square, downtown.* &

The Windmill / ★★

1501 N WENATCHEE AVE, WENATCHEE; 509/665-9529 This former roadside diner looks offbeat, but it retains much of its simple charm. Before your first dinner is over, you'll probably be planning a return visit. Although the owners have changed once, the waitresses stay and stay. Meals are western American classics. Plenty of steaks and prime rib come out of the kitchen. Yes, there's seafood, but don't be a fool—stick with the meat. If the barbecued pork ribs are on the menu, indulge—they're worth it. Finish with a piece of pie made daily on the premises—the fat apple double crust or coconut cream are our picks. *$$; DIS, MC, V; checks OK; dinner Mon–Sat; beer and wine; no reservations Fri–Sat; 1¼ miles south of Hwy 2 exit.*

LODGINGS

Coast Wenatchee Center Hotel / ★

201 N WENATCHEE AVE, WENATCHEE; 509/662-1234 This is the nicest hotel on the strip (a very plain strip, mind you, with numerous motels), with a city and river view. The nine-story hotel has five nonsmoking levels. Rooms are classic in style with floral accents. For the best rates, reserve in advance and ask about packages. The Wenatchee Roaster and Ale House, on the top floor, has live DJ entertainment Tuesday through Saturday and serves breakfast, lunch, and dinner daily. The city's convention center next door is connected by a sky bridge. Swimmers enjoy outdoor and indoor pools. *$$; AE, DC, DIS, MC, V; checks OK; www.coasthotels.com or www.wenatcheecenter.com; center of town.*

The Warm Springs Inn / ★★★

1611 LOVE LN, WENATCHEE; 509/662-8365 OR 800/543-3645 You approach the estatelike grounds of this three-story 1917 manor house via a winding drive bordered by orchards. A pillared, ivy-covered entrance and dark-green-and-rustic-brick exterior lend majesty to Jim and Kathy Welsh's B&B. Six guest rooms are decorated with a comfortable mix of antiques. All have private baths, sophisticated color schemes, and river views; a favorite is the blue and yellow room, an airy and uplifting retreat. Guests can relax in the living room, watch movies on the plasma TV in the sun-room, or take in the sun on the veranda. Better yet, follow the path behind the inn through landscaped gardens to the river and claim a spot on the swing overlooking the Wenatchee River. *$$; AE, DIS, MC, V; checks OK; warmsi@warmspringsinn.com; www.warmspringsinn.com; turn south off Hwy 2 onto Lower Sunnyslope Rd, then right onto Love Ln.*

Interstate 90 and Snoqualmie Pass

Carnation

Carnation is a verdant stretch of cow country nestled in the Snoqualmie Valley along bucolic Highway 203 (which connects I-90 to Hwy 2 at Monroe). At **TOLT MACDONALD MEMORIAL PARK** (Fall City Rd and NE 40th St; *www.metrokc .gov/parks/parks/toltmac.htm*), meandering trails and an old-fashioned suspension bridge across the Snoqualmie River provide a great family picnic setting; campsites are also available year-round (to reserve a picnic shelter or group campsite, call 206/205-7532).

Go to the source for your favorite fruits and vegetables at **REMLINGER FARMS** U-pick farm (on NE 32nd St, off Hwy 203; 425/333-4135; *www.remlingerfarms .com*), south of Carnation. The **RHUBARB FESTIVAL** starts the season in May. The **STRAWBERRY FESTIVAL** in June draws crowds. Throughout summer, choose the best in raspberries, apples, corn, and grapes. In October, kids love tromping through the fields in search of the perfect jack-o'-lantern-to-be.

Snoqualmie

The lovely **SNOQUALMIE VALLEY**, where the mountains unfold into meadowland, is best known for its falls and its scenery, once the setting for the TV series *Twin Peaks*. The 268-foot **SNOQUALMIE FALLS**, just up Highway 202 from Interstate 90 (parking lot adjacent to Salish Lodge & Spa; see review), has always been a thundering spectacle. Use the observation deck or, better yet, take a lightweight picnic down the 1-mile trail to the base of the falls.

The **NORTHWEST RAILWAY MUSEUM** (38625 SE King St; 425/888-3030; *www .trainmuseum.org*) runs a scenic tour to Snoqualmie Falls gorge from the towns of Snoqualmie and North Bend most Saturdays and Sundays, May through October; the depot museum is open all year Thursday through Monday.

LODGINGS

The Salish Lodge & Spa / ★★★☆

 6501 RAILROAD AVE SE, SNOQUALMIE; 425/888-2556 Native American tribes believed the spectacular 268-foot Snoqualmie Falls were sacred and long ago frequently gathered at the foot of the falls. You won't get that view (unless you hike down the hill), but stay in Salish Lodge and you will have a luxurious spot to watch mist rising and water frothing as it tumbles to the valley floor. Rooms are spacious, with bed covers and chairs in calm taupe fabrics, light, clean-lined wood furnishings, balconies, flagstone fireplaces (with full wood boxes), and armoires. Guests appreciate the rooms' discreet, small details: a cleverly concealed TV, plush bathrobes, a phone in each room, even a swinging window that separates the bedroom from the Jacuzzi tub. Tea is served to lodging guests daily, 4pm to 6pm, in the main-floor library. On the fourth level is an extensive spa, with beautifully appointed Asian-style massage and treatment rooms and hydrotherapy soaking spas. The Attic offers casual meals for lunch and dinner on the top floor. The excessive multicourse brunch that made the lodge famous is a thing of the past—although the signature oatmeal is still available. The dinner menu emphasizes fish, game, and Northwest produce. With more than 1,000 labels, the wine list is almost legendary. *$$$; AE, DC, DIS, MC, V; checks OK; www.salishlodge.com; take exit 25 off I-90.*

Snoqualmie Pass

Four associated ski areas—**ALPENTAL**, **SUMMIT WEST**, **SUMMIT CENTRAL**, and **SUMMIT EAST**, collectively called **THE SUMMIT AT SNOQUALMIE** (52 miles east of Seattle on I-90; 425/434-7669; *www.summitatsnoqualmie.com*)—offer the closest downhill and cross-country skiing for Seattleites (with a free shuttle that runs between areas on weekends), as well as the largest night-skiing program in the Northwest. Alpental is most challenging; Summit West, with one of the largest ski schools in the country, has excellent instruction for beginners through racers; Summit Central has some challenging bump runs and a great tubing hill; and the smallest, Summit East, is a favored spot for cross-country skiers, with lighted, groomed cross-country tracks and miles of trails.

In summer, the relatively low-lying transmountain route is a good starting point for many hikes. Contact the **NORTH BEND RANGER STATION** (425/888-1421; *www.fs.fed.us/r6/mbs/*) for more information. The **BEST WESTERN SUMMIT INN AT SNOQUALMIE PASS** (603 Hwy 906; 425/434-6300 or 800/557-STAY; *www.bwsummitinn.com*) is your only choice for year-round lodging.

Roslyn

Modest turn-of-the-century homes in this onetime coal-mining town have become weekend places for city folk. But the main intersection still offers a cross section of the town's character. In Roslyn, once the stage set for the hit TV series *Northern Exposure,* fans will recognize the old stone tavern, inexplicably called **THE BRICK** (100 W Pennsylvania Ave; 509/649-2643), with a water-fed spittoon running the length of the bar. Also familiar is the **ROSLYN CAFE** (201 W Pennsylvania Ave; 509/649-2763), remodeled inside and under new ownership. The small **ROSLYN BREWING COMPANY** (208 W Pennsylvania Ave; 509/649-2232) is open weekends. Down the road, behind the town's junkyard, you'll find **CAREK'S MARKET** (510 S "A" St; 509/649-2930), one of the state's better purveyors of fine specialty meats and sausages; try the beef jerky.

Cle Elum

This small mining town of about 2,000 parallels Interstate 90. Freeway access, at either end of town, leads to First Street, Cle Elum's main thoroughfare, making it a handy stop when you need to grab a burger and fill your gas tank. **CLE ELUM BAKERY** (1st St and Peoh Ave; 509/674-2233) is a longtime local institution, also popular with travelers. From one of the last brick ovens in the Northwest come delicious baked goods such as *torchetti* (an Italian butter pastry rolled in sugar) and cinnamon rolls. **OWEN'S MEATS** (502 E 1st St; 509/674-2530), across the street, is an excellent stop for fresh meats, and beef and turkey jerky. **MAMA VALLONE'S STEAK HOUSE** (302 W First St, Cle Elum; 509/674-5174) offers cozy Italian dishes such as lasagne and spaghetti, as well as beef, in a pleasant country-style home on the main street.

LODGINGS

Hidden Valley Guest Ranch / ★★

3942 HIDDEN VALLEY RD, CLE ELUM; 509/857-2322 OR 800/5-COWBOY
A short hour from Seattle is the state's oldest dude ranch on 300 beautiful, private acres. Bruce and Kim Coe have spruced up some of the cabins: the uneven wood floors, homemade quilts, and potbelly stoves add to the charm. Of the 13 cabins, our favorites are the older ones, particularly Apple Tree and Spruce Number 5. Newer ones, though fine, trade some charm for separate bedrooms and

kitchenettes. Miles of trails, horseback riding (packages can include daily rides), nearby trout fishing, a pool, hot tub, and basketball hoop make up for the basic accommodations. Look for indoor fun in the ranch house (table tennis, pool table); meals (included) are taken in the cookhouse dining room. *$$; MC, V; checks OK; open May–Oct; info@hvranch.com; www.hvranch.com; off Hwy 970 at milepost 8.*

Iron Horse Inn B&B / ★

526 MARIE AVE, SOUTH CLE ELUM; 509/674-5939 OR 800/2-2-TWAIN This B&B was built in 1909 to house employees of the Chicago, Milwaukee, St. Paul & Pacific Railroads. Now listed on the National Register of Historic Places, the bunkhouse, with seven guest rooms including a honeymoon suite, is pleasantly furnished with reproduction antiques. Railroad memorabilia—vintage photographs, model trains, schedules, and more—is on display. Three cabooses in the side yard are equipped with baths, refrigerators, queen-sized beds, and private decks; the garden boasts a hot tub. Owners Mary and Doug Pittis are railroad buffs (Mary's father was a Milwaukee railroad man); check the Web site for information on the new train museum nearby. Kids OK; no pets. *$$; MC, V; checks OK; maryp@ironhorseinnbb.com; www.ironhorseinnbb.com; adjacent to Iron Horse State Park Trail.*

Mount Rainier National Park

The majestic mountain is the abiding symbol of natural grandeur in the Northwest, and one of the most awesome mountains in the world. Its cone rises 14,411 feet above sea level, several thousand feet higher than other peaks in the Cascade Range. The best way to appreciate Rainier is to explore its flanks: 300 miles of backcountry and self-guiding nature trails lead to ancient forests, massive glaciers, waterfalls, and alpine meadows lush with wildflowers during the mountain's short summer.

Chinook and Cayuse Passes are closed in winter; you can take the loop trip or the road to Sunrise late May through October. The road from Longmire to Paradise remains open during daylight hours in winter; carry tire chains and a shovel, and check current road and weather conditions by calling a 24-hour information service (360/569-2211). Obligatory backcountry-use permits for overnight stays can be obtained from any of the ranger stations. Of the five entrance stations (entrance fee is $10 per automobile or $5 per person on foot, bicycle, or motorcycle), the three most popular are described here; the northwest entrances (Carbon River and Mowich Lake) have few visitor facilities and unpaved roads.

Highway 410 heads east from Sumner to Enumclaw, the **WHITE RIVER ENTRANCE** to the park, and Sunrise Visitors Center, continuing on to connect with Highway 12 near Naches. Note that the road beyond the Crystal Mountain spur is closed in winter, limiting access to Sunrise, and Cayuse and Chinook Passes. Highways 7 and 706 connect the main **NISQUALLY ENTRANCE** with Tacoma and Interstate 5; Nisqually is open year-round to Paradise. The **STEVENS CANYON ENTRANCE** (southeast corner) on Highway 123, which connects Highways 410 and 12, is closed in winter; in summer, **OHANAPECOSH** is a favorite stop.

FROM A WAGON ROAD TO THE PACIFIC CREST TRAIL

Hikers can access a portion of one of the nation's most famous trails, the **PACIFIC CREST NATIONAL SCENIC TRAIL**—a 2,600-plus-mile route through high country from Mexico to Canada—at Snoqualmie Pass. North from the pass, the trail leads through the **ALPINE LAKES WILDERNESS AREA**, a "hikers' dream" destination. This area can be experienced on an overnight, or it can take at least five days to **HIKE THE PACIFIC CREST TRAIL** segment from Interstate 90 north to Highway 2.

Shorter hikes, such as the **WAGON ROAD TRAIL**, take much less planning. Beginning near the Denny Creek Campground 3 miles off Interstate 90 (exit 47), it follows the original Snoqualmie Pass Wagon Road on an easy 2-mile loop winding through mostly old-growth forest.

For more information, contact the **NORTH BEND RANGER STATION** (425/888-1421) or check out Web sites for the **WASHINGTON TRAILS ASSOCIATION** (www .wta.org) or the **PACIFIC CREST TRAIL ASSOCIATION** (www.pcta.org).

—Jena MacPherson

You can climb the mountain with **RAINIER MOUNTAINEERING INC.** (PO Box Q, Ashford, WA 98304; 360/569-2227; *www.rmiguides.com*)—the concessionaire guide service—or in your own party. Unless you are qualified to do it on your own—and this is a big, difficult, and dangerous mountain on which many people have been killed—you must climb with the guide service. If you plan to climb with your own party, you must register and pay a fee ($30 per person) at one of the **RANGER STATIONS** in Mount Rainier National Park (Paradise Old Station, and White River or Wilkeson Wilderness Information Centers; 360/569-2211). Reservations are required for summer climbing; solo climbs must be approved in advance. Generally, best climbing is in late June through early September.

Black Diamond

This quiet, former coal-mining town is located on Highway 169, in Maple Valley, about 10 miles north of Enumclaw. Hundred-year-old **BLACK DIAMOND BAKERY** (32805 Railroad Ave; 360/886-2741) boasts the last wood-fired brick oven in the area; the bread that comes out is excellent—26 different kinds, including cinnamon, sour rye, potato, and garlic French—and perfect for a Rainier excursion. A soup and sandwich restaurant is on the premises.

Greenwater

A tiny blink-and-you-miss-it community as you head east to Crystal resort, Green-water offers several reasons to stop: a friendly tavern, fun ski clothing store, and a couple of espresso vendors. The **NACHES TAVERN** (58411 Hwy 410E; 360/633-2267) is a comfy spot where loggers, locals, and the après-ski crowd mix easily to play pool or cribbage, or to snooze by the fire; the staff fires up the grill and serves hamburgers on the weekends.

Crystal Mountain

CRYSTAL MOUNTAIN SKI RESORT (off Hwy 410 just west of Chinook Pass, on northeast edge of Mount Rainier National Park; 360/663-2265; *www.skicrystal .com*), southeast of Enumclaw, is the state's best ski area and offers incredible panoramic views when you reach the top. There are runs for beginners and experts, plus fine backcountry skiing. Less well-known are summer facilities, which include hiking and horseback riding. Rent on-mountain condominiums from **CRYSTAL MOUNTAIN LODGING** (360/663-2558; *www.crystalmtlodging-wa.com*), hotel rooms from **CRYSTAL MOUNTAIN HOTELS** (360/663-2262; *www.crystalhotels .com*; often closed in summer), or cabins from **ALTA CRYSTAL RESORT** (360/663-2500; *www.altacrystalresort.com*).

LODGINGS

Silver Skis Chalet / ★★

CRYSTAL MOUNTAIN BLVD, CRYSTAL MOUNTAIN; 360/663-2558 OR 888/668-4368 These individually decorated condos are your best bet if you want to stay right on the mountain. Pick and choose among 60 units for details such as a fireplace (all have kitchens). Great for families, with the perk of an outdoor pool heated to 95°F, they're nonsmoking and have one or two bedrooms. Nonholiday midweek packages offer extra value. *$$$–$$$$; AE, MC, V; checks OK; crystalmtlodging@tx3.com; www.crystalmtlodging-wa.com; off Hwy 410, at end of Crystal Mountain Rd.*

Sunrise

Open only during summer, **SUNRISE** (6,400 feet) is the closest you can drive to Rainier's peak. The old lodge has no overnight accommodations but does offer a **VISITOR CENTER** (northeast corner of park, 31 miles north of Ohanapecosh; 360/569-2177, ext 2357; *www.nps.gov/mora/*), snack bar, and mountain exhibits. Dozens of trails begin here, such as the short one to a magnificent view of **EMMONS GLACIER CANYON**.

Eatonville

At Eatonville, just east of Highway 7, 17 miles south of Puyallup, the big draw is **NORTHWEST TREK** (on Meridian/Hwy 161; 360/832-6117; *www.nwtrek.org*). Here visitors board small open-air trams for hour-long tours of the 435-acre grounds to see elk, moose, deer, bighorn sheep, and bison—the herd steals the show. New in 2003 are the red fox and coyote exhibits. Open daily mid-February through October, weekends and holidays the rest of the year; group rates available.

RESTAURANTS

Noodles on the Move

311 CENTER ST E, EATONVILLE; 360/832-3777 This small lace-curtained restaurant—formerly Between the Bread—is cozy (eight tables), the staff extremely friendly, and the service makes you feel at home. You'll find typical breakfast fare, daily specials such as meat loaf, wonderful desserts, and a children's menu. Lunch includes sandwiches, soups, and salads; dinner ranges from pasta to seafood to steaks. Noodle casseroles are a specialty and can be enjoyed on-site or ordered as takeout. There's outside seating in summer. *$–$$; DIS, MC, V; checks OK; breakfast, lunch every day, dinner Wed–Sun; beer and wine, no reservations; downtown Eatonville.*

Ashford

If Ashford is the gateway to Paradise, then **WHITTAKER'S BUNKHOUSE** (30205 Hwy 706E; 360/569-2439; *www.welcometoashford.com*) is the place to stop on the way to the very top—of Mount Rainier, that is. It's a good place to meet the guides, climbers, hikers, and skiers of the mountain. Rooms are basic and cheap (bunks available in summer) but plush compared to camping. **MOUNT TAHOMA SKI HUTS**, run by the Mount Tahoma Trails Association (360/569-2451; *www.skimtta.com*), is Western Washington's first hut-to-hut ski trail system. It offers about 50 miles of trails (20 groomed), three huts, and one yurt in a spectacular area south and west of Mount Rainier National Park.

LODGINGS

Alexander's Country Inn & Restaurant / ★★☆

37515 HWY 706E, ASHFORD; 360/569-2300 OR 800/654-7615 This historic Victorian inn, one of the state's oldest, opened in 1912 when travelers came to visit the mountain by horse and buggy. It retains the flavor of that time even though it's been remodeled in recent years. Stop for lunch or dinner, or spend a night in one of 14 rooms (including a tower suite); 9 have private baths. Your stay includes breakfast, evening wine, and access to the hot tub. The restaurant specializes in Northwest cuisine; trout comes from the pond on the premises and is delicious. Its Web site includes not just the inn's history, rooms, rates, and menus, but also recipes (especially for cookies) from chef Martin Larson. *$$$; MC, V; checks OK; open year-round; 1 mile from Mount Rainier National Park, Nisqually entrance.*

Mountain Meadows Inn and B&B / ★★

28912 HWY 706E, ASHFORD; 360/569-2788 This gracious 1910 home offers seclusion and relaxation near the base of one of Washington's busiest tourist destinations. Just off the main road, the inn is privately situated on 11 landscaped acres, with a trout pond, nature trails, an outdoor fire pit, and a 23-jet cedar grove hot tub. Three large guest rooms in the main house are filled with an eclectic mix of antiques. There's nothing kitschy here; just a tasteful home filled with John Muir memorabilia, a nature library, and some Native American baskets. Seats on the spacious porch look out to the forest. A guest house has three studio apartments; the main house has more appeal. *$$$; MC, V; checks OK; stay@mountainmeadowsinn .com; www.mountainmeadowsinn.com; 6 miles west of Nisqually park entrance.*

Nisqually Lodge / ★

31609 HWY 706E, ASHFORD; 360/569-8804 Reasonably priced and clean, this 24-room, two-story lodge just west of the Nisqually entrance to Mount Rainier National Park offers welcome respite to those willing to trade some charm for a phone, satellite TV, and air-conditioning. Though walls are somewhat thin, returnees like the lobby's stone fireplace and the outdoor hot tub. Coffee and pastries are served for breakfast; conference and laundry facilities are available. *$$; AE, MC, V; no checks; www.escapetothemountains.com; 5 miles from Nisqually park entrance.*

Stormking Spa and Cabins / ★★

37311 SR 706E, ASHFORD; 360/569-2964 In 2003, hosts Steve Brown and Deborah Sample turned their former B&B, a historic 1890 homestead located just a mile from the Nisqually entrance to Mount Rainier National Park, into a spa offering massage therapy, seaweed wraps, aromatherapy, and facial massage. Three cabins provide lodging: the Eagle, with a two-person greenhouse shower, gas fireplace, and private outdoor hot tub; the Raven, a yurt-style cedar retreat with a skylight and a river-rock rain shower; and the Bear, with three bedrooms and a fully equipped kitchen that is great for small groups (it is located more than a mile from the main house). Enjoy nature trails and an outdoor hot tub. Children over age 12 OK at spa; pets allowed in Bear cabin with prior permission. Continental breakfast is provided in the Eagle and Raven cabins. *$$-$$$; MC, V; checks OK; stormking@stormkingspa.com; www.stormkingspa.com; 4½ miles east of Ashford.*

Wellspring / ★★

54922 KERNAHAN RD, ASHFORD; 360/569-2514 For more than 20 years, Wellspring has quietly greeted outdoor enthusiasts with two spas nestled in a sylvan glade surrounded by evergreens. In that time, it has grown from a handful of cabins to 14 units, including permanent tent sites with themes (you'll find sand on the floor of the Tropics tent), older rustic cabins, and new deluxe ones. Four-poster feather beds, jetted tubs, and stone fireplaces grace some units. While this is primarily a couples' retreat, the Three Bears cottage—with four rooms, a full kitchen, and washer and dryer—accommodates children. Make an advance appointment with owner Sunny Thompson-Ward for an hour's massage and you'll tuck in perfectly. *$$-$$$; MC, V; checks OK; 3 miles east of Ashford.*

Longmire and Paradise

A few miles inside the southwestern park border, the village of **LONGMIRE** has the 25-room (19 with private baths) **NATIONAL PARK INN** (360/569-2275; *www .guestservices.com/rainier*), with tasteful, hickory-style furnishings. A small museum with wildlife exhibits, a **HIKING INFORMATION CENTER** (360/569-4453; Apr—Sept), and snowshoe and cross-country **SKI RENTAL** (360/569-2411) are nearby.

At 5,400 feet, **PARADISE** is the most popular destination on Rainier. You'll catch wonderful views of Narada Falls and Nisqually Glacier on the way to the paved parking lot and the **HENRY M. JACKSON MEMORIAL VISITOR CENTER** (just before Paradise; 360/569-2211, ext 2328). The center, housed in a flying saucer–like building, has a standard cafeteria and gift shop, extensive nature exhibits and films, and a superb view of the mountain from its observation deck. Depending on the season, you can picnic (best to bring your own) among the wildflowers, explore the trails (rangers offer guided walks), let the kids slide on inner tubes in the snow-play area, try a little cross-country skiing, or even take a guided snowshoe tromp. Reserve one of the 118 rooms (30 without private baths) at **PARADISE INN** (at the end of the road, 20 miles from the southwest—Nisqually—entrance; 360/569-2275; *www.guestservices.com/rainier*), a massive 1917 lodge with a wonderfully nostalgic feel, and comfortably spend the night in one of the most unique locations in the state.

White Pass

WHITE PASS (509/672-3101; *www.skiwhitepass.com*) is an off-the-beaten-path ski destination offering downhill (with a high-speed quad lift) and cross-country skiing, located 12 miles southeast of Mount Rainier National Park at the summit of Highway 12. Its base is the highest on the Cascade crest, at 4,500 feet. A Nordic center near the day lodge serves cross-country skiers with about 18 miles of trails. Summer hiking can be found in adjacent William O. Douglas and Goat Rocks Wilderness Areas.

LODGINGS

Hotel Packwood / ★

104 MAIN ST, PACKWOOD; 360/494-5431 A couple of motels in Packwood may have more modern amenities—air-conditioning, for instance—but this spartan lodge, open since 1912, remains a favorite. The aroma from the lobby woodstove makes you feel as if you're in the middle of the forest, even though you're in downtown Packwood. Climb a flight of stairs to seven simple guest rooms that share baths. Two with private bathrooms are the best bets. *$; DIS, MC, V; checks OK; just off Hwy 12 at Main St.*

SOUTHWEST WASHINGTON

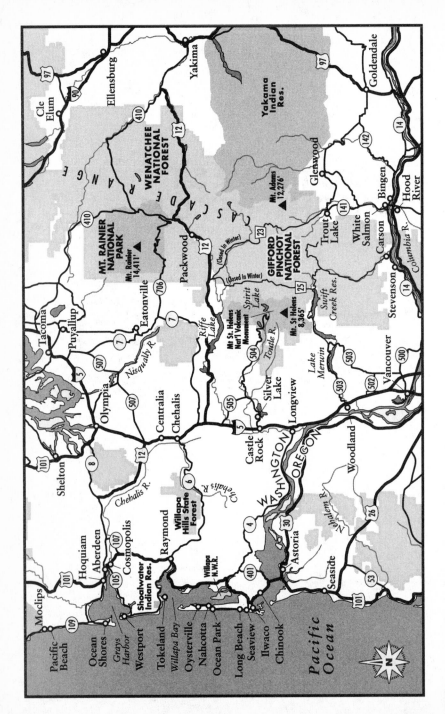

SOUTHWEST WASHINGTON

Nearly all of the varied terrain, scenery, and weather that make up the Pacific Northwest are on display in Southwest Washington. You can play on flat, sandy beaches that spread for miles along the Pacific Coast, basking in an often wet but always mild marine climate. Or trek up the slopes of geologically young mountains—including one (Mount St. Helens) devastated by the same volcanic forces that built its neighbors. Across the mountains, following the gorge cut by one of the country's mightiest rivers, you can experience long, hot, arid summers.

History looms large here. Native Americans first settled what is now Southwest Washington during the last ice age, when a land bridge stretched across much of the Bering Sea between North America and Asia. Initial contact between these Native American groups and European (English, French, Spanish, Russian) and American explorers and fur traders began in the late 1700s. American Captain Robert Gray of Boston was the first to sail into the Columbia River on May 11, 1792, and named it after his vessel, *Columbia Rediviva*. From then onward, the broad mouth where the river spills into the Pacific became the graveyard of more than 2,000 vessels large and small, and can still be treacherous sailing today, particularly during winter storms, when waves can swell 30 feet high or more and break on the Columbia River bar.

Overland fur traders and, eventually, settlers, followed in the footsteps of American explorers Meriwether Lewis and William Clark, who blazed a trail overland to the region 200 years ago, ending their epic journey in 1805 near what is now the town of Chinook. The Corps of Discovery—as the Lewis and Clark Expedition came to be called—traveled the last leg of their trek both by canoe on the Columbia and on foot along its shoreline. Today's traveler finds signs and numerous updated interpretive monuments that mark their trail. The Lewis and Clark Bicentennial celebration is ongoing through 2006, with many local and regional activities (see "Lewis and Clark Trail Bicentennial" in Southeast Washington chapter).

ACCESS AND INFORMATION

Most travelers exploring Southwest Washington via car approach from **INTERSTATE 5**, the multilane freeway between Seattle and Portland. Between the two metropolises, you'll find Vancouver just north of the Columbia and Longview a 45-minute drive farther north.

Other major highways that provide access in the region include **US HIGHWAY 12** (traveling through sleepy, tree-filled coastal mountains to Aberdeen/Hoquiam); **US HIGHWAY 101** (running south from Aberdeen to the Columbia at Astoria); and **HIGHWAY 14** (from Vancouver into the Columbia River Gorge), which frequently crosses the trail of Lewis and Clark and enters rugged cliffs and sloping grasslands to connect with **US HIGHWAY 97** north to Goldendale.

AMTRAK's (800/USA-RAIL; *www.amtrak.com*) Coast Starlight route runs between Seattle and Portland, with stops at Kelso-Longview (501 S 1st Ave; 360/578-1870) and Vancouver (1301 W 11th St; 360/694-7307). **GREYHOUND** bus service (800/231-2222; *www.greyhound.com*) is available to Castle Rock, Kelso-Longview, Woodland, Vancouver, and Goldendale.

Grays Harbor and Ocean Shores

Grays Harbor has attracted folks since Captain Robert Gray first sailed in on his 1792 expedition. Generations of loggers have begun to give over their land to retirees drawn by bargain-priced real estate—and the natural beauty of the region. A half-million Arctic-bound shorebirds migrate to the area from as far south as Argentina, and congregate on the tidal mudflats at the wildlife refuge of **BOWERMAN BASIN** (just beyond the Hoquiam airport, Airport Wy off Hwy 109) each spring from about mid-April through the first week of May. At high tide, the birds rise in unison in flocks that shimmer through the air, twisting and turning, and then drop again to feed. The **GRAYS HARBOR NATIONAL WILDLIFE REFUGE** (Hwy 109, 1½ miles west of Hoquiam; 360/753-9467) has further information.

Aberdeen and Hoquiam

The timber industry brought riches to these twin towns. Evidence can be seen in numerous mansions and the splendid **7TH STREET THEATRE** (313 7th St; 360/532-0302), a restored turn-of-the-20th-century edifice that hosts a variety of productions. Logging and sawmilling are just shadows of their early-1900s heyday, but tourism is slowly rising to take their place. One attraction is the **GRAYS HARBOR HISTORICAL SEAPORT** (east side of Aberdeen; 360/532-8611), home to a full-scale replica of Captain Robert Gray's *Lady Washington,* a 105-foot 18th-century square rigger. The ship, available for onboard tours and cruises, is often at other ports of call, so phone ahead. In 2002–03, it journeyed to St. Vincent via Panama to star as the *HMS Interceptor* in the Disney blockbuster *Pirates of the Caribbean.*

On the Harbor—From Black Friday to Nirvana is a fascinating history of the area by local newspaper editor and publisher John Hughes. (The late grunge superstar Kurt Cobain grew up in Aberdeen.)

RESTAURANTS

Billy's Bar and Grill / ★

322 E HERON ST, ABERDEEN; 360/533-7144 Billy's aims to recall Aberdeen's bawdy past and is named for the infamous Billy Gohl, who terrorized the waterfront in 1907. Gohl shanghaied sailors and robbed loggers, consigning their bodies to the murky Wishkah River through a trapdoor in a saloon just one block away from the present-day Billy's—where you get a square-deal meal (thick burgers and seasoned fries) and an honest drink, without much damage to your pocketbook. *$; AE, DC, MC, V; local checks only; breakfast, lunch, dinner every day; full bar; no reservations; corner of G St.* &

Bridges

112 N "G" ST, ABERDEEN; 360/532-6563 Nicely decorated with a country-club atmosphere and a library room in the center of the dining area, Bridges is probably the most popular place in Aberdeen and has been for decades. The food is good, but not gourmet; reliable, but not exciting. Salads are fresh, but it's the prime rib

SOUTHWEST WASHINGTON THREE-DAY TOUR

DAY ONE: Start the day from the Puget Sound area with a drive to Ocean Shores. Take lunch at the **GALWAY BAY RESTAURANT & PUB**, and then spend the afternoon beachcombing, or perhaps horseback riding on the beach. When you tire of dodging rented mopeds on the main beach, head a little south down to **DAMON POINT**, also called Protection Island, the fourth-largest estuary on the Pacific Coast. Look for harbor seals and bring binoculars for bird-watching. Check into the **CAROLINE INN** for a comfortable night in a Southern-inspired two-story suite, then head back into Ocean Shores proper for dinner at **ALEC'S BY THE SEA**. After dinner, relax in your Jacuzzi with a view.

DAY TWO: Enjoy a breakfast you make yourself in your full kitchen; before checking out, make dinner reservations at the **SHOALWATER** in Seaview. Head south down Highway 101 about 90 miles to the Long Beach Peninsula. In Long Beach, make a visit to **MARSH'S FREE MUSEUM** to ogle the oddities, stop in to the **WORLD KITE MUSEUM**, and then shop for a kite to fly on the beach. After lunch at **PAULY'S BISTRO** in Ilwaco, fly your kite for a while and then check in at **CHINA BEACH RETREAT** and get ready for dinner at the Shoalwater in Seaview.

DAY THREE: After a healthy breakfast at the **SHELBURNE INN** (where China Beach guests are served), pack a picnic lunch and drive down to Ilwaco and **CAPE DISAPPOINTMENT STATE PARK**, where you can visit the **LEWIS AND CLARK INTERPRETIVE CENTER** and the park's two **LIGHTHOUSES**, located at North Head and Cape Disappointment. Then have dinner at **THE DEPOT** in Seaview, followed by a half-mile stroll to the beach. Head home along Highway 4, which follows the Columbia River (and what used to be called the "forgotten shore") east to Longview.

that keeps the regulars coming back for more. *$$; AE, DC, DIS, MC, V; checks OK; lunch, dinner every day; full bar; reservations recommended; between 1st and F.* &

Mallard's Bistro & Grill / ★

118 E WISHKAH ST, ABERDEEN; 360/532-0731 A favorite among local professionals, Mallard's has a cozy atmosphere to complement its outsized menu, which (sometimes crazily) runs the gamut from French to Italian to Asian to American cuisine, with a natural emphasis on seafood. Tiger prawns in Pernod make a tasty opener before moving onto entrées such as rosemary and garlic pork tenderloin or coquilles St. Jacques. Note: Mallard's offers sensational meat dishes, but no vegetarian options. *$$; MC, V; local checks only; lunch Tues–Fri, dinner Tues–Sat; beer and wine; reservations recommended; between S I St and S Broadway.*

Ocean Palace

112 E WISHKAH, ABERDEEN; 360/533-6966 Nestled amid a minefield of frightening Chinese restaurants, the humongous Ocean Palace is just a good, reasonably priced Chinese restaurant. The restaurant's main selling point, besides being inexpensive, is the perpetually warm and smiling owners, who also serve. A great place for families, the expansive dining room (it can accommodate 200) is just right for restless children, who may be entertained by playing hide-n-seek with the owners' extremely well-behaved kids. *$; AE, MC, V; local checks only; lunch, dinner Mon–Sat; beer and wine; no reservations; on main thoroughfare.* &

LODGINGS

Hoquiam's Castle Bed & Breakfast / ★★☆

515 CHENAULT AVE, HOQUIAM; 360/533-2005 If you've ever wished you could slip under the ropes at a museum and lounge on the antiques in Victorian splendor, Hoquiam's Castle Bed & Breakfast gives you your chance. Previously open only to tours, the mansion was purchased by David and Linda Carpenter in 1999, extensively renovated, and debuted in 2000 as an inn. Guests can relax by the rosewood grand piano in the parlor beneath a cut-crystal chandelier, watch the sun set on Grays Harbor from the panoramic Princess' Room, or twirl across the Ballroom floor on their way to the Den, a snug saloon with an ornate bar and custom stained-glass windows installed by timber potentate Robert Lytle (who built the mansion). All five guest rooms have private baths. Kids under 12 are discouraged. *$$–$$$; AE, DC, MC, V; no checks; info@hoquiamcastle.com; www.hoquiamcastle.com; west on Emerson, right on Garfield St, up hill to Chenault Ave.*

Ocean Shores

Despite the best efforts of real estate speculators and celebrity investors in the 1960s, Ocean Shores did not develop into a Las Vegas of the north. Instead, residents managed to wrest control from the land barons, build schools, and create a real town, albeit one with strangely broad urban streets (a legacy of its pie-in-the-sky city planning).

That isn't to say building isn't booming. In addition to numerous hotels, Ocean Shores boasts a big convention center, busy year-round. An ambitious $20 million, 23-acre Aquarium Project complex is slated for construction over 2004–2006. Nearby is the Quinault Indian Reservation's luxurious and popular **QUINAULT BEACH RESORT AND CASINO** (78 SR 115; 360/289-7789; *www.quinaultbchresort.com*), with indoor pool, hot tub, sauna, steam room and spa, tables and slots, and a hopping lounge dance floor almost any night of the week—though you're better off dining in town. July's **SUN & SURF RUN** welcomes Harley-Davidson owners, the Cossacks Motorcycle Stunt Team, and others for a parade with fireworks on the beach; November brings the **DIXIELAND JAZZ FESTIVAL**. Contact the **OCEAN SHORES CHAMBER OF COMMERCE AND VISITORS CENTER** (800/762-3224; *www.oceanshores.com*) for more information on these and other events.

Outside the downtown hubbub, consider reserving one of the **PRIVATE BEACH COTTAGES** (888/702-3224; *www.oceanshores.com*) that owners make available.

The long, flat beach is great for clamming—for seasons and license requirements, check with the **DEPARTMENT OF FISH AND WILDLIFE** (48 Devonshire Rd, Montesano; 360/249-4628; *wdfw.wa.gov*). Beachcombing is popular; hunt for Japanese glass floats, Russian bottles holding messages, and other treasures during incoming tides, fall through early spring. Fly kites in the near-constant wind, build a bonfire, and even drive—if you dare. For those who want to ride on the beach, **NAN-SEA STABLES** (360/289-0194) brings a string of horses to the beach in front of the Shilo Inn; and **CHENOIS CREEK HORSE RENTALS** (just show up on the beach) has mounts available at the end of Damon Road, across from the Best Western Lighthouse Suites Inn.

RESTAURANTS

Alec's by the Sea / ★

131 E CHANCE A LA MER BLVD NE, OCEAN SHORES; 360/289-4026 Alec's by the Sea heads a list of otherwise uninspiring dining options in Ocean Shores. Reminiscent of a coffee shop, Alec's doesn't offer ocean views, but boasts the best waitresses in town and a vast menu. Choices include fresh seafood (such as an oven-broiled seafood platter of salmon, scallops, prawns, crab, oysters, and more), steaks, pasta (smoked-salmon fettuccine is a winner), poultry, burgers, and sandwiches (try the Philadelphia prime sandwich with grilled onions, bell peppers, and Swiss cheese), as well as a house-made thick, rich, buttery clam chowder, made fresh daily. Alec's has three hallmarks of the family restaurant: large portions, early-bird specials (4–6pm), and crayons for kids. *$$; AE, DC, DIS, MC, V; local checks only; lunch, dinner every day; full bar; no reservations; off Point Brown Rd.* &

Galway Bay Restaurant & Pub / ★

880 POINT BROWN RD, OCEAN SHORES; 360/289-2300 Take off the chill in the best Irish fashion in this pub with a small but tasty traditional menu. One of Hoquiam's raved-about restaurants, Parma, closed in 2001, but that city's loss was Ocean Shores' gain: The Galway hired chef Rob Paylor and moved to a new location, which features a fireplace and an authentic Irish phone booth. Order a pint of Guinness (on tap), then dine on Irish stew (browned lamb, potatoes, carrots, and sautéed onions in a rich, creamy sauce), chicken and mushroom pasty, Limerick sausage roll, or Forfar bridies (chopped steak with sautéed onions, carrots, and potatoes baked in puff pastry). Note the shamrock lovingly cut from a potato atop the satisfying shepherd's pie. Finish with a tot of 16-year-old single-malt whiskey. Or start the day right—if a bit late—with the Galway's acclaimed breakfast (served 11am–2pm) featuring hearty Irish favorites, such as corned beef hash and soda bread. If you're ready to cut a reel, there's live Irish music most weekends and some weeknights, too. *$$; AE, DIS, MC, V; checks OK; breakfast, lunch, dinner every day; full bar; no reservations; www.galway-bay.com; by the entrance to Ocean Shores.* &

Mike's Seafood

830 POINT BROWN RD, OCEAN SHORES; 360/289-0532 If you have a kitchenette, the best dining option in Ocean Shores is to pick up some fresh fish, oysters, clams or other local seasonal seafood from Mike's and cook it up yourself. The restaurant around back fries up straight-ahead fresh fish-and-chips that are so popular they can only be offered on a first-come, first-served basis—so get there early. *$; MC, V; checks OK; lunch, dinner every day; no alcohol; no reservations; on main road off hwy into town.*

LODGINGS

The Caroline Inn / ★★

1341 OCEAN SHORES BLVD SW, OCEAN SHORES; 360/289-0450 Down a long road, at the end of the peninsula, is the Caroline Inn—a gleaming white Southern Gothic mini-mansion rising above the sea grass. Each of four two-story suites has a first-floor living room with a fireplace and a balcony facing the ocean, a dining room, and a fully outfitted kitchen (you're well removed from the restaurants and entertainment in town, but that's much of the appeal). In the upstairs bedroom, you can relax in the Jacuzzi while gazing out at the beach, or step onto another balcony for a better view. These tastefully furnished suites are popular year-round; reserve at least a month in advance for weekends. *$$$; MC, V; checks OK; www.oceanshores.com/lodging/caroline; toward end of peninsula, near Cutlass Ct.*

The Shilo Inn / ★

707 OCEAN SHORES BLVD NW, OCEAN SHORES; 360/289-4600 OR 800/222-2244 Something of a crown jewel in the nation's largest privately owned hotel chain, the Shilo Inn at Ocean Shores delivers a lot for your money. Every one of its 113 rooms is a junior suite: sitting room, bedroom, and oceanview balcony, plus microwave, refrigerator, wet bar, four phones, three TVs with free cable—even one in the bathroom—fireplace, and free newspaper. Downstairs is a guest laundry, 24-hour indoor pool, spa, sauna and fitness center, a surprisingly good restaurant, and a beautiful 3,000-gallon aquarium in the otherwise sterile lobby. No pets permitted. *$$$; AE, DC, MC, V; checks OK; www.shiloinns.com; at Chance a la Mer Blvd.*

Copalis

LODGINGS

Iron Springs Ocean Beach Resort / ★

3707 HWY 109, COPALIS BEACH; 360/276-4230 Beloved by generations (and run by the same family for 50 years), Iron Springs' rustic-yet-charming homelike cottages spread over wooded grounds offer a real getaway for everyone from privacy-seeking couples to large groups to people traveling with dogs ($10 per night) and kids. Each cottage has a unique, custom-made fireplace or woodstove and boasts ocean views. Hike the nearby nature trails, take a dip in the steamy (if well worn) indoor heated pool, and then fall asleep (on a sometimes lumpy bed) to the sound of the surf crashing. Wake up to complimentary fresh coffee and homemade cinnamon rolls, available in the office every morning, along with newspapers and hospitality from two generations of innkeepers. All cottages have kitchenettes, satellite TV, VCRs, but no phones. Many units are reserved months in advance. *$$; AE, DIS, MC, V; checks OK; www.ironspringsresort.com; 3 miles north of Copalis Beach.* &

Pacific Beach

LODGINGS

Sandpiper / ★★

4159 HWY 109, PACIFIC BEACH; 360/276-4580 The large, clean Sandpiper is perfect for a family reunion, or just some peaceful quality time with the nuclear family at the ocean. Two four-story complexes have suites with amenities including sitting rooms, kitchens, baths with heated towel bars, small porches, and real log-burning fireplaces. No phones or TV (or restaurant—you'll whip up the haute cuisine in the kitchen or on the outdoor barbecue), but there's a nice kids' play area, plus a gift shop that sells board games, kites, and sand pails. Pets are welcome with advance notice and deposit. Many units are reserved months in advance. *$$–$$$; MC, V; checks OK; min stays weekends and summer; www.oceanshores .com/lodging/sandpiper; 1¼ miles south of town.*

Moclips

LODGINGS

Ocean Crest Resort / ★

HWY 109N, MOCLIPS; 360/276-4465 The tremendous view the Ocean Crest Resort commands from its cliffside perch among the spruce—as well as amenities such as an indoor pool and spa, exercise room, tanning bed, and a massage therapist—has made this inn a perennial hit, with minimum stays required during peak periods. Rooms run from bargain studio units with no view to kitchen and fireplace units to two-bedroom suites (logs provided free). Rates are reasonable even in summer. Best views are from the large studios in Building 5. The resort's somewhat pricey view restaurant, serving fresh seafood, pasta, steaks, and more, is the best dining within a half-hour's drive. *$$–$$$; AE, DIS, MC, V; checks OK; www.oceanshores.com/lodging/oceancrest; 18 miles north of Ocean Shores.*

Westport

A spate of oceanfront condos proves that retirees and urban escapees have begun to flock to Westport, just as fishers have for years. Charter fishing is still the town's lifeblood, as the cluster of motels near the docks (and the fact that you can eat breakfast at just about any restaurant before 5am) attests. Changes in the salmon fishery have resulted in more charter bottom-fishing trips (for halibut and snapper, among others), and popular whale-watching cruises. Gray whales migrate off the coast, March through May, on their way toward Arctic feeding waters, where they'll fatten up for the trip back down to their breeding lagoons in Baja come fall. Some of the best charters include **CACHALOT** (2511 Westhaven Dr; 360/268-0323), **NEPTUNE** (2601 Westhaven Dr; 360/268-0124), **OCEAN** (2315 W Westhaven Dr; 360/268-9144), and **WESTPORT** (2411 W Westhaven Dr; 360/268-9120 or 800/562-0157).

If you're not enthused about catching your own, Westport has plenty of places to buy seafood. Try **BRADY'S OYSTERS** (3714 Oyster Pl, Aberdeen; 360/268-0077), just east of town on Highway 105; **MERINO SEAFOODS** (301 E Harbor St; 360/268-2510), near the docks; or **WESTPORT SEAFOOD** (609 Neddie Rose Dr; 360/268-0133).

The **WESTPORT LIGHTHOUSE** (turn left at the town's only stoplight) towers 100 feet over the dunes; call the **COAST GUARD** (360/268-0121) for a guided tour. A scenic 2½-mile (round-trip) trail leads through the dunes from Westport Lighthouse State Park to Westhaven State Park; it's paved and wheelchair-accessible. In town, exhibits at the **WESTPORT MARITIME MUSEUM** (2201 Westhaven Dr; 360/268-0078; open daily in summer, weekends and holidays, Jan–Feb, and Thurs–Mon the rest of the year) trace seafarers back to the 1700s; the museum also shows collections of local Coast Guard, industry, and whaling artifacts.

LODGINGS

Chateau Westport / ★

710 W HANCOCK, WESTPORT; 360/268-9101 OR 800/255-9101 The Chateau Westport is '60s-boxy on the outside but pretty comfy and vaguely continental on the inside. More than 100 rooms and suites are available, some with fireplaces, kitchens, and balconies. Ocean-facing views (especially from the third and fourth floors) are quite lovely. An indoor heated pool and hot tub are available, as is free continental breakfast. Bargain winter rates apply during prime whale-watching months. No pets allowed. *$$; AE, DC, MC, V; no checks; chateau@tss.net; www.chateauwestport.com; at S Forest St.* &

Long Beach Peninsula and Willapa Bay

The ocean conjures up restful visions of soothing waves lapping the shore, but some "destination" beach areas offer a shrill edge instead. Sure, the Long Beach Peninsula has its share of campy bumper boats and seashell tchotchkes—and the population triples in July and August—but it delivers the real deal: beautiful, serene beaches blessed by a gentle marine climate. Beyond scenery and souvenirs, the peninsula offers renowned kite flying, cranberry bogs, famous Willapa Bay oysters, rhododendrons, historic lodgings, and a concentration of fine restaurants unmatched on the Northwest coast.

With its 37-mile-long stretch of flat beach (the "world's longest," local boosters say), the peninsula's topography and attractions make it perfect for a lengthy exploration by bicycle, though cars are allowed on the beach. Also, be aware that the **LEWIS AND CLARK BICENTENNIAL** (*www.lewisandclark200.org*) is ongoing, with a substantial increase in visitors predicted.

If you really want to get away from it all, visit Willapa Bay's Long Island (accessible only by boat) and its 274-acre old-growth cedar grove, part of the **WILLAPA NATIONAL WILDLIFE REFUGE** (10 miles north of Seaview on Hwy 101; 360/484-3482; *willapa.fws.gov/Willapa/WR_Index.htm*). Campsites are available; check at the refuge's headquarters.

Chinook

From primeval times to the present, fishing has loomed large in Chinook, located southeast of the peninsula on US Highway 101. Salmon was a dominant figure in the Native American cosmology and a staple of the local diet. Late in the 1800s, when most members of the native Chinook Nation had been decimated by disease, thousands of super-efficient salmon traps owned by Chinook's white residents made the town one of the richest per capita in the United States. The traps were outlawed (you can see their remnants at low tide), but the town is still a sport-fishing mecca.

On Scarborough Hill, **FORT COLUMBIA STATE PARK** (1 mile southeast of Chinook on Hwy 101; 360/777-8221; open daily) hosts a collection of restored turn-of-the-20th-century wooden buildings that once housed soldiers guarding the river mouth. The former commander's house is now a **MILITARY MUSEUM** (open mid-May–Sept). For a fun getaway, rent the fully furnished Steward's House (two bedrooms) or Scarborough House (five bedrooms); advance reservation required (800/360-4240).

RESTAURANTS

The Sanctuary Restaurant / ★★

794 SR 101, CHINOOK; 360/777-8380 Dining among religious statues and saintly images inside this former Methodist church is a heavenly experience. Lightly sautéed Willapa oysters swimming in a pool of sherry are downright blissful. Linguine tossed with steamers and andouille sausage, salmon drizzled with a pomegranate vinaigrette, Svenska Kottbullar (Swedish meatballs) sided with pickled beets, even Swedish pancakes served with pea soup (owner-chef Joanne Leech is Swedish), are sinfully satisfying. And Leech's chocolate-caramel fondue and lemon sherbet will make you believe you've gone to a culinary version of the sweet by-and-by. Adjacent Little Ocean Annie's serves mighty fine chowder, fish-and-chips, and such (lunch, dinner on weekends). *$$–$$$; AE, DIS, MC, V; checks OK; dinner Wed–Sun (Thu–Sun in winter); full bar; reservations recommended; Highway 101 and Hazel St.*

Ilwaco

Known as a salmon-fishing and processing port and not much else a decade ago, Ilwaco's harbor is pulsating with new energy, particularly at **ILWACO HARBOR VILLAGE**, an array of galleries, restaurants, and shops fronting the boat basin. **SHOALWATER COVE GALLERY** (177 Howerton Wy SE; 360/642-4020 or 877/665-4382) features local artist Marie Powell's soft pastels and watercolors. Sip wine and savor chicken-basil sausage hoagies at **THE CANOE ROOM CAFE** (161 Howerton Wy SE; 360/642-4899). A seasonal **SATURDAY MARKET** (May–Sept) also happens here.

Despite the vagaries of the salmon fishery, Ilwaco is still a charter fishing hot spot. Two popular operators, located at the port docks, are **COHO CHARTERS** (237 Howerton Wy SE; 360/642-3333; *www.cohocharters.com*) and **SEA BREEZE CHARTERS** (185 Howerton Wy SE; 360/642-2300; *www.seabreezecharters.net*). Many charter operators also offer eco-tours. The **ILWACO HERITAGE MUSEUM** (115 SE Lake St; 360/642-3446; *www.ilwacoheritagemuseum.org*) does a fine job illuminating the area's history, with exhibits of Native American artifacts, cranberry agriculture, logging, fishing, and more. Nearby **CAPE DISAPPOINTMENT STATE PARK** (3 miles southwest of Ilwaco off Hwy 101; 360/642-3078) is one of Washington's most popular attractions, with almost 2,000 acres stretching from picturesque **NORTH HEAD LIGHTHOUSE** to Cape Disappointment, where another stately sentinel illuminates the Columbia River's mouth (both lighthouses approachable by trail; North Head is open for summer tours). Open all year, the park has yurts available for comfortable winter stays and is home to the expanded **LEWIS AND CLARK INTERPRETIVE CENTER** (360/642-3029; *www.parks.wa.gov/lcinterpctr.asp*), which affords visitors a fresh and vivid retelling of the explorers' monumental journey that began in St. Louis and ended on the Pacific shore. Other displays interpret lighthouses (there's a handsome first-order Fresnel lens on display), lifesaving, and shipwreck lore. But the biggest draw here is the view, the region's finest.

RESTAURANTS

Pauly's Bistro / ★★☆

235 HOWERTON ST, ILWACO; 360/642-8447 Opened in 2003, this cute-yet-kitschy establishment at Ilwaco's rejuvenated harbor offers fare that's equal parts eclectic and enthusiastic; in fact, it's all over the culinary map, a post-fusion celebration that busts down gastronomic boundaries: Tuscan grilled bread salad, troll-caught salmon piccata, meat loaf drizzled with cranberry–sundried tomato ketchup, pork posole, beef short ribs braised in Rhone wine, and an "Assortment of All Things Yummy" (a platter of grilled veggies, hummus, roasted garlic cloves, and a Gorgonzola-pear terrine, among other delights). Portions are prodigious and prices are low. In bistro tradition, wine by the glass or half glass is served in tumblers, and summer sangria plus some exotic soft drinks (strawberry-lavender lemonade, pomegranate ice tea) are offered. The place is like an indoor picnic, with more tempting fare. *$–$$; MC, V; checks OK; lunch, dinner Tues–Sun; beer and wine; no reservations; east end of Ilwaco Harbor Village.* &

LODGINGS

China Beach Retreat / ★★★

222 CAPTAIN ROBERT GRAY DR, ILWACO; 360/642-5660 OR 800/466-1896 You might spot a soaring bald eagle or a great blue heron gliding gracefully above the water during your visit to this charming secluded lodging named after the Chinese who worked the local canneries. Constructed in 1907, the retreat has been lovingly remodeled and is dedicated entirely to guests (owners David Campiche and Laurie Anderson live elsewhere). A wall of west-facing windows affords stunning vistas of the Ilwaco boat channel, Cape Disappointment, and the Pacific; a large spyglass and binoculars facilitate gazing. One ground-floor and two upstairs guest rooms are furnished with an assortment of 18th- and 19th-century Asian and European period antiques, spa tubs, and eclectic art (including watercolors by Campiche's father, John, a renowned local painter). History buffs will appreciate that Captain Robert Gray (who named the Columbia River) anchored just downstream more than two centuries ago, and Lewis and Clark bushwhacked around the bay and probably crossed what's now the retreat's front yard. Guests savor the Peninsula's best breakfast (included) at the Shelburne Inn (Campiche and Anderson own and operate both lodgings), 2 miles away in Seaview. *$$$; AE, MC, V; checks OK; innkeeper@theshelburneinn.com; www.chinabeachretreat.com; ½ mile west of downtown Ilwaco.*

Seaview

Touted as an ocean retreat for Portlanders early in the 20th century (visitors arrived via river steamer, then transferred to a local railroad), Seaview now enjoys a legacy of older, stately beach homes, a pretty beach front, and some of the best dining and lodging on the peninsula. Nearly every road headed west reaches the ocean, and you can park your car and stroll the dunes. The Lewis and Clark trail stretching from Long Beach to Ilwaco is a work in progress.

RESTAURANTS

The Depot Restaurant / ★★★

1208 38TH PL, SEAVIEW; 360/642-7880 This refreshingly modest eatery occupies the former train station for the Long Beach Peninsula's "clamshell railroad," so called because it ran by the tides. Look for substantial portions of inspired bistro fare—herbes de Provence–infused fowl, steak in a port-shallot reduction, and penne enhanced with andouille sausage and smoked mozzarella, then tossed in a heady Creole sauce. The third-of-a-pound Depot burger topped with garnishes galore and sided with house-cut fries is a bona fide three-napkin delight (served Thursdays only). Chef Michael Lalewicz can get creative, too: Witness his duck-prosciutto salad, venison wrapped in wild-boar bacon, or mammoth morel stuffed with salmon mousse and bathed in a pool of sherry. Desserts, such as hazelnut tart sprinkled with raisins and spiked with rum, or a raspberry-walnut cobbler, are consistently luscious. Seasonal repasts might include a summer Hawaiian Luau or a fall Lewis and

MOUNT ST. HELENS AND THE
COLUMBIA GORGE THREE-DAY TOUR

DAY ONE: Spend the day touring **MOUNT ST. HELENS**. Though all of the five visitor centers are interesting, if it's a sunny day plan to spend most of your time at the **JOHNSTON RIDGE OBSERVATORY**, with its spectacular views of the volcano's crater. Once you've had your fill of volcanic activity, seismographs, and steam vents, head south on Interstate 5 to Vancouver to check in at the **HEATHMAN LODGE**. Enjoy dinner at **BACCHUS** (make reservations in advance), then return to your hotel to sip a glass of wine by the stone fireplace in the lobby before bed.

DAY TWO: Have a tasty breakfast at **HUDSON'S BAR & GRILL**, then explore historic Vancouver—visit the re-created **FORT VANCOUVER** and **OFFICERS ROW**, then walk along the riverfront and stop for lunch at **MCMENAMIN'S ON THE COLUMBIA**. Afterward head east on Highway 14 and take in the magnificent scenery along the **COLUMBIA RIVER GORGE**. Stop for dinner at **FIDEL'S** in Bingen, then turn north onto Highway 141 for the short drive to the **INN OF THE WHITE SALMON** for the night.

DAY THREE: After a sumptuous breakfast at the inn, rouse your sense of adventure for a raft trip down the **WHITE SALMON RIVER**. If river-running doesn't strike your fancy, head down to the Columbia River and check out the petroglyphs at **HORSETHIEF LAKE STATE PARK** or tour the **LOCAL WINERIES**. Head east on Highway 14 to the **MARYHILL MUSEUM OF ART**, have a simple lunch in the museum café, and steep yourself in Rodin sculptures, elaborate chess sets, and fashion dolls. A little farther down the road you'll find the **STONEHENGE REPLICA**. Drive back down the gorge to Lyle and settle into the **LYLE HOTEL** for dinner and a good night's sleep.

Clark Wild Game Dinner. *$$; DIS, MC, V; checks OK; dinner Tues–Sun (closed Sun in winter); beer and wine; no reservations; on the Seaview beach approach.*

The 42nd Street Café / ★★★

4201 PACIFIC HWY, SEAVIEW; 360/642-2323 Skillet-fried chicken with mashed potatoes and gravy, pork chops dripping cranberry barbecue sauce, halibut stew, and even a crunchy peanut-butter-and-marionberry-jam sandwich can be had at this homey eatery that once housed a Coast Guard barracks. But chef Cheri Walker (an accomplished harpist who often plays for patrons) purveys more than comfort food. Charbroiled ahi freshened with watercress mayonnaise, fettuccine and smoked salmon tossed in a bourbon-dill cream sauce, and sweet-pepper ravioli plump with walnuts and feta are always possibilities. Anything concocted with local wild mushrooms—say, portobello–chicken liver pate or puff pastry graced with chanterelles—is a winner, and desserts are top-drawer. Under the tutelage of Walker's husband, Blaine, the evolving wine list is following suit. Come morning, don't miss the bacon waffles dripping maple syrup, the jambalaya omelet, or the beignets served with French press café au lait. *$$–$$$; MC, V; checks OK; breakfast, lunch, dinner every day; beer and wine; reservations recommended (dinner); blaine@42ndstreetcafe.com; www.42ndstreetcafe.com; at 42nd St.* ₺

The Heron and Beaver Pub / ★

4415 PACIFIC HWY, SEAVIEW; 360/642-4142 True, it's part of the Shoalwater Restaurant (see review) and the food comes from the same kitchen, but this exceedingly handsome, pint-sized pub is an eatery unto itself. Graze on a country Caesar sprinkled with shrimp or nosh on baked ham and Gruyère sandwiched into slices of rye smeared with basil-pesto mayonnaise. Crab and shrimp cakes, a grilled bratwurst hoagie, ravioli du jour, and occasional sushi are other appetizing options. The wine and single-malt Scotch selections are extensive, and a deck out of the wind overlooks the Victorian gardens of the Shelburne Inn (the historic hotel whose space the pub shares; see review). *$$; AE, DC, MC, V; checks OK; lunch Mon–Sat, dinner every day, brunch Sun; full bar; no reservations; reservations@shoalwater.com; www.shoalwater.com/pub; at N 45th St.* ₺

The Shoalwater Restaurant / ★★★½

4415 PACIFIC HWY, SEAVIEW; 360/642-4142 More than two decades ago, this bastion of Northwest cuisine ensconced in a lovely dining area decorated with dark wood and bronze demonstrated that stellar dining wasn't limited to urban enclaves. These days, Lynne "Red" Pelletier's seasonal menu ranges from the simple to the sublime, from an unmatchable bowl of mussel-and-clam chowder to an herb-encrusted duck breast sweetened by a wine-berry-and-butter sauce graced with shaved truffles. Seafood is showcased in numerous imaginative preparations: baked scallops coated with caviar beurre blanc, *tako* salad topped with steamed octopus, and a Willapa Bay Oyster Picker puff pastry pie overflowing with wild mushrooms and tarragon cream. Desserts, such as cappuccino-fudge ice cream or an impossibly rich French silk pie, consistently draw raves, and the wine list is the coast's finest (*Wine Spectator* has bestowed an Award of Excellence on it every year since 1988). The Shoalwater's Winemakers' Dinner Series (from late fall through spring) features stunning seven-course meals designed around wines from visiting Northwest winemakers; reserve well in advance. *$$$; AE, DC, MC, V; checks OK; lunch, dinner every day, brunch Sun; full bar; reservations recommended; reservations@shoalwater.com; www.shoalwater.com; at N 45th St.* ₺

LODGINGS

The Shelburne Country Inn / ★★★½

4415 PACIFIC HWY S, SEAVIEW; 360/642-2442 OR 800/466-1896 Well-worn, warm, and filled with antiques and friendly appeal, the Shelburne is listed in the National Register of Historic Places and is cherished in the hearts of many a romantic traveler. The 1896 inn—said to be

Washington's oldest continuously operating lodging—has 15 rooms filled with lovely quilt-covered four-poster beds, stained-glass windows, hand-braided rugs, and other Victorian furnishings. All have private baths, and many have decks. Owners David Campiche and Laurie Anderson prepare memorable breakfasts with fresh, seasonal ingredients. Entrée choices always number at least five; possibilities might include a warming bowl of huckleberry-apple oatmeal, smoked-salmon or smoked-chicken frittatas, house-made Italian sausage omelets, or a shrimp soufflé roll oozing ricotta. Petite Willapa Bay oysters and wild mushrooms often make appearances. If you're interested in foraging for the latter, ask Campiche, a Peninsula native who knows where the chanterelles and porcinis grow. Anderson's fresh-baked goodies—treats as varied as zucchini muffins and banana-nut bread—grace every morning repast (included for guests), served at a massive oak table backed by couches and a fireplace. Lunch and dinner are available at the Shoalwater Restaurant or Heron and Beaver Pub (under separate ownership; see reviews). Busy Highway 103 is right out front—request a west-facing room for maximum quiet. Best-value rooms are on the third floor, if you're up for the stairs. *$$$; AE, MC, V; checks OK; innkeeper@ theshelburneinn.com; www.theshelburneinn.com; at N 45th St.* &

Long Beach

The epicenter of Peninsula tourist activity, Long Beach hosts throngs of summer visitors who browse the assortment of gift shops and amusement arcades and wander the beach boardwalk—a pedestrian-only half-mile stroll with night lighting (wheelchairs and baby strollers welcome). The paved **LEWIS AND CLARK TRAIL** begins here, too.

A big draw is August's week-long **INTERNATIONAL KITE FESTIVAL**, when the town swells to more than 50,000. Visit the **WORLD KITE MUSEUM AND HALL OF FAME** (112 3rd St NW; 360/642-4020; *www.worldkitemuseum.com*), or get in on the fun yourself by shopping at **LONG BEACH KITES** (115 Pacific Ave N; 360/642-2202 or 800/234-1033) or **OCEAN KITES** (511 Pacific Ave S; 360/642-2229). For a tastier museum visit, check out the **CRANBERRY MUSEUM AND GIFT SHOP** (2907 Pioneer Rd; 360/642-5553; *www.cranberrymuseum.com*; open daily Apr–Dec) and take a self-guided tour of the bogs. **ANNA LENA'S PANTRY** (111 Bolstad Ave E; 360/642-8585) has 20 or so varieties of fudge, including a quartet of cranberry fudges; it's also a quilters' destination, with 2,500 bolts of fabric and a huge assortment of books and patterns. **CAMPICHE STUDIOS** (101 Pacific Ave S; 360/642-2264) exhibits watercolors, pottery, and scenic photos. Grab a hefty sandwich or a pizza to go at **SURFER SANDS** (1113 Pacific Hwy S; 360/642-7873).

Kitschy and fun, **MARSH'S FREE MUSEUM** (409 S Pacific Ave; 360/642-2188; *www.marshsfreemuseum.com*) displays an enormous selection of knickknacks for sale, and you can play the antique coin-operated arcade machines and music boxes. The museum's star attraction, nationally famous Jake the Alligator Man, is a mummified half-man, half-alligator who has inspired a line of "Believe It Or Not"–style sportswear.

LODGINGS

Boreas Bed & Breakfast / ★★

607 N OCEAN BEACH BLVD, LONG BEACH; 360/642-8069 OR 800/642-8069 Owners Susie Goldsmith and Bill Verner have polished their inn into a romantic gem. Each of five guest rooms in this 1920s beach house situated amid the dunes (and just steps, via trail, from the beach) has a private bath, including the Dunes Suite with its Impressionist wall mural and spa tub. The living room, with large windows facing the ocean, is graced with a marble fireplace and a baby grand piano. Breakfast possibilities include omelets plump with wild mushrooms and smoked salmon, yogurt pancakes topped with berries, a soufflé-like French toast freshened with Grand Marnier and sprinkled with almonds, and herb-kissed home fries. Braised bananas, stuffed pears, brownies, and cranberry sorbet are other specialties. The paved Lewis and Clark dunes trail, a nice way to stroll into downtown, courses between Boreas and the beach. The owners also offer a separate, more private two-bedroom beach cottage, built in the 1890s and filled with antiques and charm. *$$$; AE, DC, MC, V; checks OK; boreas@boreasinn.com; www.boreasinn .com; 1 block west of Hwy 103.*

Ocean Park, Nahcotta, and Oysterville

Ocean Park was once a Methodist retreat, which offered summers free of vice. But the senses are in for a bigger shock nowadays—at least during the **JUNE GARLIC FESTIVAL**, which features a Northwest Wine Tasting and Brew Garden. Contact the **OCEAN PARK CHAMBER OF COMMERCE** (888/751-9354; *www.opwa.com*) for current dates.

The **WIEGARDT STUDIO GALLERY** (2607 Bay Ave; 360/665-5976; *www .ericwiegardt.com*) displays Eric Wiegardt's seascapes and other delicate watercolors in a restored Victorian house. **JACK'S COUNTRY STORE** (Hwy 103 and Bay Ave; 360/665-4989) dates from 1885 and can supply almost every need, or perhaps a seashore knickknack that will grace your living room mantle. **SWEET WILLIAMS** (1311 Bay Ave; 360/665-3266) affords an eclectic browse, everything from books and candles to Polish pottery.

A healthy population of seagulls attests to Nahcotta's tenure as a center for oysters. Several storefronts purvey the tasty bivalves, including **JOLLY ROGER SEAFOODS** (273rd and Sandridge Rd, on old Nahcotta dock; 360/665-4111), where you can watch the oyster business in action. On the same pier you can visit the **WILLAPA BAY INTERPRETIVE CENTER** (273rd and Sandridge Rd, next to the Ark restaurant; 360/665-4547; summer weekends) to learn the history of the century-and-a-half-old oyster industry.

Founded as a 19th-century sea town, Oysterville is the Northwest's prettiest village, and its double row of wooden houses with picket fences is listed as a Historic District with the National Register. The photogenic 1892 Baptist church no longer holds services but is open for visitors.

OYSTERVILLE SEA FARMS (1st and Clark; 360/665-6585 or 800/CRANBERRY; *www.oysterville.net*) is the sole industry here, with a retail store that sells a variety of fresh and vacuum-packed oysters in flavors ranging from smoked to habañero, as well as Anna Lena preserves, dried fruits, baking mixes, and more.

LEADBETTER POINT STATE PARK (3 miles north of Oysterville, on Stackpole Rd) is a large wildlife refuge that attracts thousands of birds. Miles of hiking trails lead to mostly untouched beaches along Willapa Bay; no camping.

RESTAURANTS

The Ark Restaurant / ★★★

273RD AND SANDRIDGE RD, NAHCOTTA; 360/665-4133 Thanks to owners Jimella Lucas and Nanci Main, the Ark is more than a restaurant; this eatery with the picture-postcard setting is a culinary legend renowned throughout the Northwest and beyond (and was a favorite of the late James Beard, America's preeminent food writer). Lucas masterminds the Ark's kitchen, where she crafts meals ranging from grilled Thai oysters or oysters Italiano to veal medallions mated with cumin potato cakes. Main commandeers the bakery (a treasure trove of treats), creates desserts such as brioche bread pudding and a raspberry torte topped with Devonshire sauce, and lends her flamboyant presence to the dining area. During Sunday brunch, don't miss Main's muffins spread with cranberry butter, or the poached eggs paired with Dungeness crab hash. *$$$; AE, MC, V; checks OK; dinner Tues–Sun (Thurs–Sun in winter), brunch Sun; full bar; reservations recommended; info@arkrestaurant.com; www.arkrestaurant.com; on old Nahcotta dock, next to the oyster fleet.*

Moby Dick Hotel and Oyster Farm / ★★★☆

25814 SANDRIDGE RD, NAHCOTTA; 360/665-4543 Don't tell Jeff McMahon that life on the Long Beach Peninsula is unexciting. Well, maybe by New York or Portland standards, where the 30-something chef worked in well-regarded restaurants, most recently at Saucebox, Portland's über outpost of pan-Asian cuisine. Now he oversees an essentially one-man operation at this pleasantly funky hotel-restaurant combo beached in a virtual culinary Garden of Eden on the Willapa Bay shoreline. McMahon's Mediterranean-inspired offerings are more comforting and down home than cutting-edge, yet the variety of his menus (which change twice monthly) seems limited only by what land and sea can provide. An organic garden out front furnishes produce that he picks just prior to preparation; oysters are harvested from Willapa Bay out back. Curried potato soup; wild mushroom risotto cakes; spaghetti with smoked oysters and pancetta; roasted free-range fowl basted with a lemon-garlic sauce; monkfish stuffed with ham, spinach, and pine nuts; pistachio cakes bedecked with honey tangerines; black currant and cherry-bourbon ice creams—the list goes on, and the fruits of McMahon's labors are nothing short of scintillating. *$$–$$$; AE, DIS, MC, V; checks OK; dinner Thurs–Mon; full bar; reservations recommended; mobydickhotel@willapabay.org; www.nwplace.com/mobydick .html; south of Bay Ave on Sandridge Rd.*

LODGINGS

Caswell's on the Bay Bed & Breakfast / ★★★

25204 SANDRIDGE RD, OCEAN PARK; 360/665-6535 OR 888-553-2319 Take the long driveway off quiet Sandridge Road and prepare to be stunned by this gleaming yellow neo-Victorian mansion tucked away on 5 sheltered acres along Willapa Bay's shoreline. Inside you'll find a large parlor offering an amazing waterfront panorama backdropped by mountains. A sun-room outfitted with a spyglass is an ideal spot to gaze and enjoy afternoon tea and cookies. Five commodious guest rooms are furnished with antiques and feature second-floor vistas of the gardens (the house is surrounded by rhododendrons and other magnificent flora) or bay. Innkeepers Bob and Marilyn Caswell purvey fabulous morning feasts; Bob's hangtown fry stuffed with local oysters has garnered national awards. Many honeymooners land here, and the B&B frequently hosts weddings. *$$$; MC, V; checks OK; bcaswell@willapabay.org; www.caswellsinn .com; 1 mile south of Bay Ave/Sandridge Rd intersection.*

Shakti Cove Cottages / ★

ON 253RD PL, OCEAN PARK; 360/665-4000 Though the Shakti Cove Cottages are just off Highway 103, they feel miles from the outside world. Ten small cedar-shingled cabins stand in a semicircle around a gentle green, each funky-cozy, with its own carport, bath, and kitchen facilities. Amble a quarter mile down a private gravel road to the beach, likely passing black-tailed deer grabbing a meal along the way. Shakti Cove is popular with gays and lesbians, as well as travelers with dogs (even large ones), but "covekeepers" Celia and Liz Cavalli make all visitors feel at home. *$$; MC, V; checks OK; info@shakticove.com; www .shakticove.com; 1 block west of Pacific Hwy 103.*

Longview

Perched at the edge of Washington State, on the lip of the Columbia River, Longview is a convenient crossroads for travelers headed north to Seattle, south to Portland, or west to the Long Beach Peninsula. For a relaxing walk, stroll through the park surrounding Lake Sacajawea.

RESTAURANTS

Country Village Nutrition Shoppe and Cafe

711 VANDERCOOK WY, LONGVIEW; 360/425-8100 A good place to pick up organic foods before heading off to ocean beaches or Mount St. Helens, this is also a great stop for a tasty, filling, and inexpensive lunch. Though it sounds unlikely, the chopped nut sandwich is a winner, as is the cauliflower slaw. Scared of "healthy" food? Opt for a pastrami sandwich. *$; DIS, MC, V; checks OK; lunch Mon–Fri; no alcohol; no reservations; I-5 exit 39, just off Washington Wy.* &

Mount St. Helens National Volcanic Monument

The May 18, 1980, explosion of Mount St. Helens's volcanic fury created a drastically changed landscape, as well as an attraction for the attention of hundreds of scientists and thousands of visitors from around the world. While the region can be explored via Randle in the north (on US Hwy 12) or Cougar in the south (off Hwy 503), most visitors opt to travel Highway 504, also known as **SPIRIT LAKE MEMORIAL HIGHWAY**, which heads east from Interstate 5 at Castle Rock. Five excellent visitor centers dot its length, and the route ends with a bird's-eye view of the volcano's still-steaming crater at **JOHNSTON RIDGE OBSERVATORY** (mile 52; 360/274-2140). A fee ($6 per adult, $2 for ages 5–15) lets you visit Johnston Ridge as well as the **SILVER LAKE** and **COLDWATER RIDGE** visitor centers (all along Hwy 504). The **HOFFSTADT BLUFF REST AREA AND VIEWPOINT** (run by Cowlitz County) and the **WEYERHAEUSER FOREST LEARNING CENTER** (run by Weyerhaeuser) are free to visit.

Castle Rock

This small town at the intersection of Highway 504 and Interstate 5 is a gateway to Mount St. Helens. **THE CINEDOME THEATER** (1239 Mount St. Helens Wy NE/Hwy 504; 360/274-9844) boasts "Mount St. Helens erupts here every 45 minutes!" and shows the Omnimax film *The Eruption of Mount St. Helens* every day (a great introduction to your mountain tour). The theater also shows first-run theatrical movies in the evening, employing the three-story, 55-foot screen and its seat-rumbling sound system. Plenty of souvenirs—from kitschy ash creations to valuable interpretive guides—can be found in town.

LODGINGS

Blue Heron Inn / ★

2846 SPIRIT LAKE HWY, CASTLE ROCK; 360/274-9595 OR 800/959-4049 John and Jeanne Robards built the lodge-style, log-and-stone Blue Heron Inn in 1996. The inn—located next to Seaquest State Park, just across from the Silver Lake Mount St. Helens Visitors Center—makes a comfy base of operations from which to explore Mount St. Helens. Each of the seven rooms (including the Jacuzzi Suite) has a private bath, as well as a balcony with marvelous views of the volcano and Silver Lake. A substantial family-style breakfast is included. *$$$; MC, V; checks OK; info@blueheroninn.com; www.blueheroninn.com; Hwy 504 about 6 miles east of I-5 and just west of U.S. Forest Service Mount St. Helens Visitors Center.* &

Vancouver

One of the oldest white settlements in the Pacific Northwest, Vancouver had a big growth spurt during the late 1990s, when the high-tech industry drew people to the area. And even when the jobs went south, most of the people stayed.

In the early 19th century, the British Hudson's Bay Company ensconced itself in **FORT VANCOUVER** (1501 E Evergreen Blvd; 360/696-7655), and the fort became an American military base when the territory passed to the United States. The stockade wall and some of the fort buildings have been reconstructed, and the visitor center features a museum and heirloom garden. Just across the Parade Grounds from the fort is **OFFICERS ROW** (E Evergreen Blvd, between I-5 and E Reserve St), a leafy street of restored homes where officers billeted in bygone days; the Heritage Trust of Clark County (360/737-6066) gives tours.

Just north of downtown, the **CLARK COUNTY HISTORICAL MUSEUM** (1511 Main St; 360/695-4681) reproduces pioneer stores and businesses. **COVINGTON HOUSE** (4201 Main St; 360/695-6750) is the oldest log house (1846) in the state; call to make tour arrangements.

Downtown comes alive weekend mornings when the **VANCOUVER FARMERS MARKET** (Apr–Oct) takes up several blocks around Esther Short Park (6th and Columbia) with local produce, flowers, food vendors, and craftspeople. A lovely 4-mile waterfront walk along Columbia Way begins just under the Interstate 5 bridge (next to the Red Lion Inn at the Quay), passes the Northwest's oldest apple tree, and heads to the **WATER RESOURCES CENTER** (4600 SE Columbia Wy; 360/696-8478), with interactive exhibits, a giant fish tank filled with denizens of the Columbia, and a superb view of the Columbia River, at the east end of Columbia Way on the edge of Marine Park.

RIDGEFIELD NATIONAL WILDLIFE REFUGE (3 miles west of I-5, exit 14; 360/887-3883) has nature trails leading to the bird refuge on the lowlands of the Columbia River. For a duck's-eye view of the refuge, rent a kayak from Lake River Kayak (214 Pioneer, Ridgefield; 360/887-2389). **MOULTON FALLS** (NW Lucia Falls Rd near County Rd 16; 360/696-8171) has a three-story-high arched bridge spanning the East Fork of the Lewis River, a 387-acre park, and two waterfalls. It's 2 miles south of Yacolt and 9 miles east of Battle Ground.

RESTAURANTS

Bacchus / ★★☆

3200 SE 164TH AVE, VANCOUVER; 360/882-9672 First-time visitors to Bacchus may worry when they see the restaurant's strip-mall setting. But once safely through the front doors, doubts drop away. Grilled meats scent the air and form a substantial part of the dinner menu (excellent salmon and halibut dishes are also offered). The wine cellar is stocked with a huge variety of bottles, mostly from the Pacific Northwest and California, and there's a bar with live entertainment Thursday through Sunday nights. *$$–$$$; AE, DIS, MC, V; lunch Mon–Fri, dinner every day; full bar; reservations recommended; www.bacchusrestaurant.biz; near Thurston Way exit off Hwy 500 (at South View Center).* &

Hudson's Bar & Grill / ★★☆

7805 GREENWOOD DR (HEATHMAN LODGE), VANCOUVER; 360/816-6100
 Inside the grand, incongruously sited Heathman Lodge (see review), a massive slate fireplace, a real dugout canoe, and plush rugged comfort set the scene for indigenous Northwest cuisine from an open, red-tiled kitchen. Without pretension, chef Mark Hosack prepares meals designed for taste and pleasure, not to dazzle. In the morning, Hudson's serves a custardy bread-pudding French toast and a halibut Benedict. Midday, a crab-cake sandwich with chipotle aioli, grilled halibut with smoked mozzarella and bacon, and beer-battered onion rings are superb. In the evening, oven-roasted venison with sweet-potato hash, and Northwest seafood stew in a charred tomato broth, illustrate respect for local seasonal ingredients. Breads and pastries, baked in-house, appear as flatbread appetizers, pear and apple tarts, and summertime lemonade cake. *$$–$$$; AE, DC, DIS, MC, V; checks OK; breakfast, lunch, dinner every day; full bar; no reservations; www.heathmanlodge .com/hudsons; near Thurston Wy exit off Hwy 500.* ఉ

McMenamin's on the Columbia

1801 SE COLUMBIA RIVER DR, VANCOUVER; 360/699-1521 Of the several riverfront restaurants in Vancouver, this is the least frenetic and most inviting. The food is standard pub fare, familiar to any Northwesterner who has ever dined at one of the McMenamin brothers' restaurants (and by now, that must be nearly everyone). The sandwiches, such as ahi with wasabi mayonnaise, are good but not great. What makes this particular McMenamin's such a pleasant spot is its location on the banks of the Columbia, just a few steps off the riverside footpath. *$; AE, DC, DIS, MC, V; lunch, dinner every day; full bar; no reservations; exit 1A off Hwy 14.* ఉ

Roots Restaurant / ★★

19215 SE 34TH AVE, CAMAS; 360/260-3001 When Brad Root, formerly chef at such noted Portland restaurants as Higgins and Wildwood, looked for a place of his own, he noticed how East Vancouver and Camas were booming. He also noticed that the area had few places to eat except chain restaurants and decided to fix that. The result is an airy restaurant decorated in a classy modern Scandinavian-meets-Northwest style, with ceiling-high wooden doors and equally large windows that look out onto an expansive parking lot and the neighboring Subway and video store. (Well, that's the downside of the Vancouver-to-Camas location.) Chef Root has established strong relationships with local farmers, and the staff can tell you where just about every ingredient on your dinner plate was grown. The vegetables that accompany main dishes such as short ribs or pan-seared salmon are particularly tasty, as are the salad greens (grown right down the road in Ridgefield). The small bar is a good place for a light dinner. *$$; AE, MC, V; no checks; lunch, dinner every day; full bar; reservations recommended; Riverstone Marketplace Shopping Center.* ఉ

Thai Orchid / ★

1004 WASHINGTON ST, VANCOUVER; 360/695-7786 Downtown Vancouver does not have a lively restaurant scene; among the handful of places, Thai Orchid stands out for its fresh, healthy ingredients (and no hydrogenated oils); its huge selection of curried, stir-fried, seafood, rice, and noodle dishes; and its pleasant atmosphere. For both its name and its flavor, you can't go wrong with the Evil Jungle Prince curry (your choice of vegetables, beef, chicken, or pork on a bed of steamed cabbage and broccoli, all topped with curry sauce). Spicy dishes are marked on the menu and can be ordered to suit your courage, and the staff can help you make the leap from phad thai to more exotic dishes. *$; AE, DIS, MC, V; checks OK; lunch, dinner every day; full bar; no reservations; www .thaiorchidrestaurant.com; at Evergreen Blvd.* &

LODGINGS

Heathman Lodge / ★★☆

7801 GREENWOOD DR, VANCOUVER; 360/254-3100 OR 888/475-3100 Vancouver's first luxury hotel—run by the pros who until recently owned Portland's venerable Heathman—gives a distinct first impression: it is stunning but somewhat out of place. The hotel looms like a national-park lodge as you approach it from busy Route 500, but it's set squarely in a Clark County suburb, near a mini-mall and high-tech office space. Huge timbers support the *porte cochère;* nearby is a carved cedar totem pole. Inside the striking lobby, you'll find peeled-log balconies draped with Pendleton blankets, a massive basalt gas fireplace, and dugout canoes hanging from the massive rafters. Lodge rooms (and suites) combine rustic Northwest-style furnishings with modern amenities—two-line phones, data ports, refrigerators, microwaves, coffeemakers, and ironing boards; some have balconies, and some have Tempur-Pedic mattresses. The hotel also offers an indoor pool and fitness center. With a good restaurant just off the lodge's lobby (Hudson's Bar & Grill; see review), you can stay inside over a rainy weekend and never break the illusion that you're tucked away in an alpine haven. *$$–$$$$; AE, DC, DIS, MC, V; checks OK; www.heathmanlodge.com; near Thurston Wy exit off Route 500.* &

Mount Adams and the Columbia River Gorge

The **COLUMBIA GORGE INTERPRETIVE CENTER** (990 SW Rock Creek Dr, Stevenson; 509/427-8211 or 800/991-2338), just west of Stevenson, spins an evocative tale of the region's natural and cultural history, with a nine-projector slide show that re-creates the gorge's cataclysmic formation. In addition to the relatively slick interpretive displays are quirkier exhibits, such as the world's largest collection of rosaries (and their accompanying touch-screen database), that hint at the center's origins as a small-town historical museum.

Mount Adams and its surrounding area, 30 miles north of the Columbia, offer natural splendor largely overlooked by visitors, who seldom venture in from the gorge. Besides climbing to the summit of the 12,276-foot mountain—greater in mass than any of the five other major volcanic peaks in the Northwest—hikers and skiers can explore miles of wilderness trails in the **MOUNT ADAMS WILDERNESS AREA** and **GIFFORD PINCHOT NATIONAL FOREST**. Contact the **MOUNT ADAMS**

RANGER STATION (2455 Hwy 141; 509/395-3400) in Trout Lake to purchase a pass for mountain climbing, or for information on trails and campgrounds.

LODGINGS

Bonneville Hot Springs Resort / ★★

1252 EAST CASCADE DR, NORTH BONNEVILLE; 509/427-7767 OR 866/459-1628
Native Americans, early settlers, and entrepreneurs of all stripe have all been attracted to the seeps and gushes of hot water springing from the ground around these parts. The Bonneville Hot Springs Resort, which opened in 2002 with a hotel, spa, restaurant, and splendid indoor lap pool and outdoor hot tub, makes good use of both the hot water and the beautiful natural setting. Hotel rooms are heated geothermally, and some have balcony hot tubs. Day-use guests are welcome, and whether you're here for a full weekend of spa treatments, or just for a swim and a soak, this a fine place to relax and take the waters. *$$$; AE, DC, DIS, MC, V; checks OK; info@bonnevilleresort .com; www.bonnevilleresort.com; turn north onto Hot Springs Dr. 3 miles west of Bridge of the Gods, then right (east) onto Cascade Dr.* &

Stevenson

A small town blessed by scenery, Stevenson lies within the beginnings of the **GORGE SCENIC HIGHWAY** (Hwy 14) and marks the unofficial boundary of windsurfing country.

LODGINGS

Dolce Skamania Lodge / ★★

🌲 **1131 SW SKAMANIA LODGE WY, STEVENSON; 509/427-7700 OR 800/221-7117** Skamania Lodge was designed to resemble a national park lodge, and it does, with a lot of wood and stone, Mission-style furniture, Native American–style rugs, and beautiful views from its perch above the Columbia River Gorge. The differences are an award-winning 18-hole golf course, an indoor fitness center, a pool, saunas, and a spa. If you don't golf, you can use one of two tennis courts, or rent a bike and follow the map of trails. A formal dining room offers fine cuisine, and the River Rock Lounge serves lunch, appetizers, and light dinners. The lodge is huge—195 rooms, including 34 deluxe rooms with fireplaces, and 5 suites—and, though it caters largely to the meetings and conventions business, it's a great place to use as a base for exploring the Columbia Gorge. *$$$; AE, DC, MC, V; checks OK; www.skamanialodge.dolce.com; turn north onto Rock Creek Dr just west of Stevenson.*

Carson

"Funky" is the word most often used to describe **CARSON MINERAL HOT SPRINGS** (Hot Springs and St. Martin Ave; 509/427-8292). This historic resort has been around since 1897, and while the sheets have been changed since then, not much else has. Reserve ahead for its renowned old-style "treatment"—a (non–co-ed) hot mineral bath—followed by a rest while wrapped snugly in towels and blankets, which you can follow with a professional massage. If you decide you want to stay at this quite rustic, well-worn resort, TV- and phone-free rooms and cabins are available, as well as a restaurant and an 18-hole golf course.

White Salmon

Perched above the Columbia River with lovely views of Mount Hood and Mount Adams, White Salmon is a great base from which to enjoy the gorge. The **WHITE SALMON RIVER**, with its Class II–IV rapids, serene pools, and verdant canyon, is one of the state's most popular rafting and kayaking destinations, April through October. Two of the best outfitters are **ZOLLER'S OUTDOOR ODYSSEYS** (1248 Hwy 141; 509/493-2641 or 800/366-2004; *www.zooraft.com*) and **WET PLANET** (860 Hwy 141; 509/493-8989 or 800/306-1673; *www.wetplanetrafting.com*). At **RAY KLEBBA'S WHITE SALMON BOAT WORKS** (230 E Jewett Blvd; 509/493-4766) the staff can teach you how to make your own woodstrip-construction sea kayak or canoe; buy a kit to take home, or have the skilled crafters build one for you. **NORTHWESTERN LAKE STABLES** (126 Little Buck Creek Rd; 509/493-4965) offers backcountry horseback-riding packages ranging from one hour to overnight.

If a less strenuous outing is in order, visit **WIND RIVER CELLARS** (196 Spring Creek Rd; 509/493-2324). Enjoy complimentary sips in a tasting room with a stunning view of Mount Hood, and bring lunch to enjoy in the pretty grape-arbor picnic area.

RESTAURANTS

Fidel's

120 E STUBEN ST, BINGEN; 509/493-1017 A fancy restaurant would seem out of place in unpretentious Bingen, but Fidel's, a friendly family-owned Mexican place, fits right in. With large portions of home-cooked food, it's a good place to head after a day of rafting the White Salmon or windsurfing the Columbia. The menu offers fish, chicken, or carne asada, chile verde or colorado, and omelets *machaca* (with shredded beef, chicken, or pork). A favorite here is the chicken asada super quesadilla, a soft tortilla with melted cheese topped by marinated chicken breast grilled with onions, tomatoes, and green peppers. *$; MC, V; checks OK; lunch, dinner every day (call ahead in winter); full bar; no reservations; 1 mile east of Hood River toll bridge.*

LODGINGS

Inn of the White Salmon / ★★

172 W JEWETT BLVD, WHITE SALMON; 509/493-2335 OR 800/972-5226 At first glance, the Inn of the White Salmon looks like a 1930s-era brick apartment building, and when it was built in 1937 it did combine hotel rooms and apartments. While it may look rather run-of-the-mill from the street, inside it's a standout: each room has a large, comfy antique bed, as well as private bath, phone, cable TV, and air-conditioning; several are two-room suites. A relaxing parlor and a hot tub provide a chance to socialize, but owners Roger and Janet Holen emphasize that their inn offers the privacy of a hotel with the comfort of a B&B. Breakfast (included) serves up a real groaning board: 20 kinds of pastries and breads; juice, tea, and coffee; and your choice among entrées, such as Italian or artichoke frittatas, chiles rellenos, quiche, and more. Fido can stay for a small extra fee. *$$; MC, V; checks OK; innkeeper@gorge.net; www.innofthewhitesalmon.com; Hwy 141, 1½ miles north of Hwy 14.*

Trout Lake

Trout Lake, about 25 miles north of the gorge on Highway 141, follows the White Salmon River toward its mountain source. Long ago, volcanic activity left the Mount Adams area honeycombed with caves and lava tubes, including the **ICE CAVES** (509/395-3400) near Trout Lake, with stalactites and stalagmites formed by dripping ice. Southwest of Trout Lake is **BIG LAVA BED** (509/395-3400), a 12,500-acre lava field filled with cracks, crevasses, rock piles, and unusual lava formations. Late summer ripens the wild huckleberries growing in abundance in the nearby **INDIAN HEAVEN WILDERNESS AREA**.

LODGINGS

Serenity's Village / ★

2291 HWY 141, TROUT LAKE; 509/395-2500 OR 800/276-7993 These four chalet-style cabins set among the firs and pines are a good base for exploring the Trout Lake valley below Mount Adams. All are tastefully finished, warmed by gas fireplaces (or cooled by air-conditioning), and equipped with basic kitchen facilities, plus TVs, VCRs, stereos, and outdoor barbecues. Two larger units have lofts and jetted tubs, but smaller units are set farther back from the highway. Kids OK; no pets. *$$; MC, V; checks OK; www.serenitys.com; 23 miles north of White Salmon.* &

Glenwood

LODGINGS

Flying L Ranch / ★

25 FLYING L LN, GLENWOOD; 509/364-3488 OR 888/MT-ADAMS If you never went to camp as a kid, the 100-acre Flying L Ranch gives you the chance. Poised at the foot of Mount Adams, the ranch has trails for exploring on foot in summer or on skis in winter. Accommodations are rustic but comfortable. You have three options: six rooms in the main lodge house (some with fireplaces); five rooms in the Guest House (with a small shared kitchen); and cabins about 200 feet from the main buildings (each with its own kitchen, woodstove, and electric heat). Everyone has access to the spacious living room in the main house with its stone fireplace, piano, stereo, and wonderful view, as well as to the kitchen and pantry, and the hot tub in the gazebo. Full ranch breakfasts are served in the separate Cookhouse dining room; lunch and dinner you'll make yourself, or see what you can find in tiny "downtown" Glenwood. *$$; AE, MC, V; checks OK; flyingl@mt-adams.com; www.mt-adams.com; east through Glenwood about ½ mile toward Goldendale, turn north and proceed ¼ mile to driveway on right.*

Lyle

LODGINGS

Lyle Hotel / ★☆

100 7TH ST, LYLE; 509-365-5953 The 10-room Lyle Hotel has the feeling of a roadhouse, where weary travelers lay down their mountain bikes and windsurfing boards, share the local wines, eat hearty meals, and fall into soft feather beds. Indeed, the Lyle was built in 1905 as a railroad hotel, offering bunks to railroad workers and passengers. The hotel retains a simple, old-fashioned style—the 10 rooms share 5 baths, there's no TV, and owners Jim and Penny Rutledge make sure guests are well-informed about local sites, including the Klickitat Trail (a converted railbed) and the wonderful petroglyphs at nearby Horsethief Lake State Park. The library bar is a friendly spot, and in the warmer months, conversations spill out onto the patio. It's best to make a dinner reservation when you call for your room (dinner is served Wed–Sat; on Sundays there's brunch); the food is good, and it's complemented by wines from some of the area's smaller wineries. *$; MC, V; checks OK; info@lylehotel.com; www.lylehotel.com; two blocks south of Hwy. 14. Restaurant &; rooms not &.*

Goldendale

Though Goldendale is the seat of Klickitat County, it's not a case of bright lights, big city. This makes it the perfect location for **GOLDENDALE OBSERVATORY STATE PARK** (602 Observatory Dr; 509/773-3141; *parks.wa.gov*; Wed–Sun in summer, weekends by appointment in winter), 1 mile north of Goldendale just off Columbus Avenue. Visitors can look through the 24½-inch telescope (one of the largest in the nation available to the public) or borrow a portable telescope to gaze at skies largely clear of air and light pollution. Lectures, slide shows, and films are also offered. On the way to visit the nearby **MARYHILL MUSEUM OF ART** (35 Maryhill Museum Dr, Goldendale; 509/773-3733; *www.maryhill museum.org*; Mar–Nov), stop at the **MARYHILL WINERY** (877/627-9445; *www .maryhillwinery.com*) next door. In addition to a tasting room, the winery stages concerts in its 2,500-seat amphitheater. About two miles east of the Maryhill Museum is a life-sized replica of England's neolithic **STONEHENGE**, built to honor fallen World War I soldiers from Klickitat county, and as an antiwar memorial. Goldendale is 10½ miles north of Highway 14 on US Highway 97.

SOUTHEAST WASHINGTON

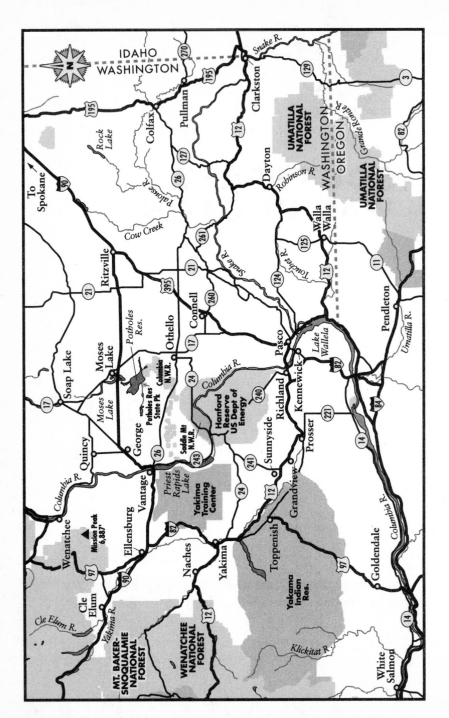

SOUTHEAST WASHINGTON

The southeast quadrant of Washington State encompasses the college towns of Pullman and Ellensburg, the wine country of the Yakima and Walla Walla Valleys, and some high technology thrown in, too. It isn't as evergreen as the rest of the state, but it's rich in sagebrush and agriculture.

Southeast Washington is its own melting pot, with strong influences from Mexican and Native American cultures. Residents are farmers, nuclear scientists, cowboys, college students, entrepreneurs, and good ol' boys. They enjoy a slower, more casual pace than in urban areas.

Of course, each city has bragging points. Ellensburg is famous for its lamb and Labor Day rodeo. Yakima is known for fruit trees, wineries, and outdoor activities. The Tri-Cities claim 300 days of sunshine annually, a Lewis and Clark campsite, and discovery of the 9,300-year-old Kennewick Man bones. (He's not available for public viewing due to government legal wranglings, and the discovery spot is unmarked to prevent vandalism. The best way to see the bones is at a "virtual interpretive center"; *www.kennewick-man.com*.) Washington State University in Pullman is famous for its Cougar Gold cheese. Walla Walla's résumé includes sweet onions, world-class wine, and pioneers.

Appreciating the landscape might take a conscious effort if you're accustomed to snowcapped mountains, green hills, and humidity. But the earth-toned palette reveals its own majestic geological formations, like the 198-foot Palouse Falls and Wallula Gap basalt pillars. Out here, spaces are wide open, the clouds—if there are any—are high above your head, and you feel like you can see a million miles in the clear, dry air.

ACCESS AND INFORMATION

Most people visiting central and Southeast Washington drive. Even if you fly, you'll want to have a car. Numerous highways lead through often sparsely populated country to this dry, sunny corner. Take advantage of rest areas and be sure your gas tank is full. In summer, bring sunblock and a light sweater (for overactive air-conditioners and cool evenings); in winter, a turtleneck and warm, wind-proof jacket.

INTERSTATE 90 is the most practical route from Puget Sound, connecting at Ellensburg with **INTERSTATE 82**, which leads through the Yakima Valley to the Tri-Cities at the confluence of the Yakima, Snake, and Columbia Rivers. From there, Walla Walla is an easy trip via Interstate 82 and **US HIGHWAY 12**.

From Portland, **INTERSTATE 84**—or the two-lane **HIGHWAY 14** on the Washington side—leads to Eastern Washington. If you're heading to Ellensburg or Yakima, turn north on **US HIGHWAY 97**. If your destination is the Tri-Cities, take Interstate 82/**US HIGHWAY 395**. Note: The Tri-Cities include Kennewick, Richland, and Pasco, and freeway signs usually name one of those instead of the region's nickname.

The **TRI-CITIES AIRPORT** (3601 N 20th Ave, Pasco; 509/547-6352; *www .portofpasco.org/aphome.htm*) is served by Horizon Air, Delta, United Express, and SkyWest. **HORIZON AIR** (800/547-9308; *www.horizonair.com*) also serves the region's smaller airports, in Walla Walla, Yakima, and Moses Lake.

Most major **CAR RENTAL** companies operate out of the Tri-Cities Airport. The **PASCO TRAIN STATION** (535 N 1st Ave) serves **AMTRAK** (509/545-1554 or 800/ USA-RAIL; *www.amtrak.com*) and **GREYHOUND** (800/231-2222; *www.greyhound .com*). The local public transit company is **BEN FRANKLIN TRANSIT** (509/735-5100; *www.bft.org*). The **TRI-CITIES VISITOR AND CONVENTION BUREAU** (6951 W Grandridge Blvd, Kennewick; 800/254-5824; *www.visittri-cities.com*) is a good source of information.

Columbia Basin

The Columbia Plateau is a vast tableland that stretches across the center of the state, much of it rich agricultural lands irrigated by the Columbia River Basin. More than 2,000 miles of canals and secondary canals water more than a million acres of fields.

Vantage and George

Situated on a splendid stretch of the Columbia just north of Interstate 90, Vantage doesn't have much food and lodging—but it has incredible scenery. **GINKGO PETRI-FIED FOREST STATE PARK** (exit 136 off I-90; 509/856-2700; *www.parks.wa.gov*) takes you back to the age of dinosaurs. The interpretive center is open daily in summer, by appointment otherwise. It's a great picnic spot.

The small town of George, Washington, also just off Interstate 90, boasts the naturally terraced **GORGE AMPHITHEATER** (*www.hob.com/venues/concerts/gorge/*) with a westward view over the Columbia Gorge. Big names of all musical genres play here—from Joni Mitchell and Radiohead to Bob Dylan and the Dave Matthews Band. Arrive early to avoid country-road traffic jams. You can bring food, but packs are searched and alcohol is not allowed. Rest rooms are scarce, and locals have become less tolerant of rowdy concert-goers. **TICKETMASTER** (206/628-0888; *www.ticketmaster.com*) handles most ticket sales. George is a three-hour drive from Seattle and two hours from Spokane. Nearest accommodations are in Vantage, Ellensburg, Quincy, Ephrata, or Moses Lake. The **GORGE CAMPGROUND** (509/785-2267) charges $35 per vehicle per night.

Ellensburg and Yakima Valleys

The Ellensburg and Kittitas Valleys stretch from the eastern foothills of the Cascades toward the Columbia at Vantage. The region is a key producer of cattle and hay, and it provides a natural gateway along the Yakima River to Yakima and its upper and lower valleys, separated by Union Gap.

The Yakima Valley has more fruit trees than any other county in the United States and is first in production of apples, mint, winter pears, and hops. Tourism in the area reflects the region's agricultural industry base with attractions such as the **AMERICAN HOP MUSEUM** (22 S "B" St; 509/865-4677) in Toppenish, and the

CENTRAL WASHINGTON AGRICULTURAL MUSEUM (4508 Main St, Fullbright Park; 509/457-8735) in Union Gap. The **YAKIMA VALLEY VISITORS AND CONVENTION BUREAU** (10 N 8th St; 800/221-0751; *www.visityakima.com*) has information on enjoying the region's natural beauty.

The Yakima Valley's agricultural industry has drawn migrant workers from Mexico, Texas, and California, resulting in a large Hispanic population and a culturally rich community. Over the years, many migrant families have settled in the area, bringing their native culture—and cuisine—with them.

Ellensburg

Once a contender to be Washington's state capital, Ellensburg now is a combination college-cowboy town. One of the city's biggest draws is the **ELLENSBURG RODEO** (800/637-2444; *www.ellensburgrodeo.com*), held at the county fairgrounds on Labor Day weekend. Started in 1923, it's three days of competition, food, games, country-western music, and the Budweiser Clydesdales.

At **CENTRAL WASHINGTON UNIVERSITY** (400 E 8th Ave; 509/963-2244; *www.cwu.edu*), visit the serene Japanese Garden, designed by Masa Mizuno, and the **CHIMPANZEE AND HUMAN COMMUNICATION INSTITUTE** (14th and "D" Sts; 509/963-2244; *www.cwu.edu/~cwuchci/*), where humans and chimps communicate through American Sign Language. Workshops are offered for a fee, March–November.

A surprising amount of art can be found in this small town. The **SARAH SPURGEON GALLERY** in CWU's fine-arts complex (Randall Fine Arts Bldg; 509/963-2665) holds regional and national art exhibits year-round. The **CLYMER MUSEUM AND GALLERY** (416 N Pearl St; 509/962-6416) honors John Clymer, Ellensburg's chronicler of the western frontier whose work appeared in the *Saturday Evening Post*. **GALLERY ONE** (408½ N Pearl St; 509/925-2670) sells regional crafts and displays contemporary art.

Because the city is at the foot of the Cascades, it's also a popular base for skiing, rafting, and hiking along the Yakima River. Outdoors aficionados enjoy canoe or raft trips through the Yakima River's deep gorges, or fly-fishing for trout. Contact the **ELLENSBURG CHAMBER OF COMMERCE** (801 S Ruby St, Ste 2; 509/925-3137; *www.ellensburg-chamber.com*).

Locals like **CAFÉ NICHOLAS** (601 University Wy; 509/925-3544) for breakfast; but if you're running late, just go to the drive-through at **D&M COFFEE** on Main Street (408 S Main; 509/925-5313).

RESTAURANTS

Pearl's on Pearl Wine Bar & Bistro / ★★

311 N PEARL ST, ELLENSBURG; 509/962-8899 The locals love this place, but the owner (who greets and seats you) is just as friendly to visitors (who are often sent here by the locals). The chef and co-owner changes the menu regularly, but starters might include a sun-dried tomato tart and spicy lemon shrimp. Pearl's signature pasta is farfalle with smoked salmon and sautéed veggies in a champagne cream sauce, and entrées featuring catfish, venison, or crab legs regularly appear on the menu. The wine list is reverentially regional. The brick-walled space is surprisingly large and is broken in the middle by a stage (where a sign reminds that musicians are playing for tips); the bar's in the back. Save room for cheesecake. $$; MC, V; local checks only; lunch Sat–Sun, dinner every day; beer and wine; no reservations; www.pearlsonpearl.com; between 3rd and 4th. &

The Valley Cafe / ★★

105 W 3RD AVE, ELLENSBURG; 509/925-3050 The Valley Cafe has been a regional favorite for years. The decor is authentic art deco, with mahogany booths and a circa 1930s back bar, and the cuisine is fine dining—an unexpected surprise here in Ellensburg. Lunch favorites are sandwiches and salads—the lemon tahini dressing is marvelous—and quiche is a specialty. Dinners are more gourmet, with fresh seafood and Ellensburg lamb. Owner Greg Beach also owns the wine shop next door, so it's no surprise that the café's wine list is award winning; also not surprising is that it's got a strong selection of Washington wines. Desserts include crème brûlée and fresh fruit pies. $$; AE, DC, DIS, MC, V; checks OK; lunch, dinner every day; beer and wine; no reservations; near Main St.

LODGINGS

The Inn at Goose Creek / ★

1720 CANYON RD, ELLENSBURG; 800/533-0822 There's something a bit incongruous about this inn just off Interstate 90. On the one hand, it's one of the most convenient lodging options for cross-state travelers; on the other hand, why put so much effort into the decor of a place just off the highway? Block out the location, however, and you won't find much more comfortable accommodations in Ellensburg: 10 theme rooms, all with private baths, allow you to pick your mood, from romantic to rodeo to year-round Christmas. Best of the bunch is possibly the Sports room—not for the decor but for its view out over spacious fields (other rooms look out onto a gas station or drab building next door). Each features a goose-down comforter, king- or queen-sized bed or two queens, spa tub, TV, and VCR. Our favorite is the Rodeo room, but if you like ruffles and lace, look into the first-floor honeymoon suite with its canopy bed. A continental breakfast is served just off the lobby. No smoking; no pets. $$; AE, MC, V; checks OK; www.innatgoosecreek .com; exit 109 off I-90. &

Meadowlark Guest House / ★★

606 N MAIN ST, ELLENSBURG; 509/962-3706 OR 888/699-0123 The enthusiasm of owner Sarah Ames infects this entire two-room B&B, as well as her little antique/specialty shop on the first floor. In the last 10 years, Ames has worked to make her sunny yellow Queen Anne Victorian house (listed on the National Register of Historic Places) adhere to the strictest standards for B&Bs, with down comforters (which can be switched out for people with allergies), CD players, antiques, multiple down pillows, luxury cotton linens, reading lights on both sides of the four-poster queen-sized beds, and more. Each suite also has a queen sleeper-sofa and a private bath, though the latter is accessed via the hallway.

A gourmet breakfast basket is delivered to your room. *$$; DIS, MC, V; checks OK; www.kittitasvalleyinns.com/Meadowlark/; three blocks from downtown.*

Yakima

This is the preeminent city of central Washington and the seat of county government. Hit the **NORTH FRONT STREET HISTORICAL DISTRICT**, including Yakima Avenue and E "B" Street, where a 22-car train houses restaurants and shops selling everything from women's clothing to stationery and children's toys. The **YAKIMA VALLEY MUSEUM** (2105 Tieton Dr; 509/248-0747; *www.yakimavalleymuseum.org*) appeals to all ages with recently renovated space and exhibits of pioneer equipment, a children's "underground" museum, a display on Yakima native Supreme Court Justice William O. Douglas, and an old-fashioned soda fountain.

The **GREENWAY** (509/453-8280; *www.yakimagreenway.org*) is a 10-mile-long path along the Yakima and Naches Rivers for bicyclists, walkers, runners, and in-line skaters. The paved path has nature trail offshoots—sometimes allowing a view of bald eagles or blue herons—plus playgrounds. The Greenway hosts an annual summer blues and jazz festival. Entrance points are at Sarg Hubbard Park (111 S 18th St), Sherman Park (E Nob Hill Blvd), Rotary Lake ("R" St), Harlan Landing (west side of I-82 between Selah and Yakima), and the east end of Valley Mall Boulevard.

Yakima, naturally, has a wide range of motels; one the nicest is the **OXFORD INN** (1603 E Yakima Ave; 800/521-3050; *www.oxfordsuites.com*).

RESTAURANTS

Barrel House

22 N FIRST ST, YAKIMA; 509/453-3769 This new (April 2002), clubby Yakima restaurant feels a bit like a hangout for lawyers—though more likely the clientele is discussing the wine business. The historic location was built in 1906, but was sleekly updated for its new incarnation. The food is simple but good: salads, sandwiches, and burgers for lunch; all that plus entrées such as London broil, rosemary chicken, king salmon, and a grilled and marinated portobello for dinner. The wine list is appropriately regionally based and good; as is the selection of microbrews. *$$; MC, V; no checks; lunch Mon–Fri, dinner every day; beer and wine; no reservations; mgr@barrelhouse.net; barrelhouse.net; near Yakima Ave.* &

Birchfield Manor / ★★

2018 BIRCHFIELD RD, YAKIMA; 509/452-1960 Birchfield Manor offers country-French dining in an antique-filled room. Trained in Europe, chef and co-owner Wil Masset (with his wife, Sandy) offers six entrées—perhaps double breast of chicken Florentine or an authentic bouillabaisse—and a good list of Washington wines for one seating each on Thursday and Friday, and two seatings on Saturdays. The restaurant has a homey atmosphere in a relaxed, pastoral setting, and a separate cigar room. Private dinners can be held in the Carriage House for up to 16. Five B&B rooms are located above the restaurant, and six more "cottage rooms" are in a

SOUTHEAST WASHINGTON THREE-DAY TOUR

DAY ONE: Grab a hearty breakfast at Ellensburg's **CAFÉ NICHOLAS**, then stroll around downtown and get a feeling for the town. Head south on Interstate 82 to Yakima, then stretch your legs with a nature walk on the **GREENWAY** or window-shop in the **NORTH FRONT STREET HISTORICAL DISTRICT**. Drive to Toppenish to see the western art murals, then visit the **YAKAMA NATION CULTURAL HERITAGE CENTER**, one of the few museums in the state designed and operated by Native Americans. Get back in the car and head to Sunnyside to sample the region's Mexican heritage with lunch at **TAQUERIA LA FOGATA**, then visit **DARIGOLD'S DAIRY FAIR** for a self-guided tour of the cheese factory. Drive over to Grandview and check into the charming **COZY ROSE PRIVATE COUNTRY SUITES**. End the day with a lovely **DINNER AT DYKSTRA HOUSE RESTAURANT**, a quaint 1914 mansion with scrumptious desserts.

DAY TWO: After breakfast at your B&B, dress for the outdoors and head for the Tri-Cities and the roaring Columbia River. Bring sunblock, a hat, sneakers, and a bottle of water, and spend the morning on a **COLUMBIA RIVER JOURNEYS JET-BOAT TOUR** through Hanford Reach. Eat lunch and quaff a Half-life Hefeweizen back in Richland at the **ATOMIC ALE BREWPUB & EATERY**; then hit the **COLUMBIA RIVER EXHIBITION OF HISTORY, SCIENCE & TECHNOLOGY**. Head over to Kennewick to the **PLAYGROUND OF DREAMS** and **FAMILY FISHING POND**, where kids can learn how to catch-and-release. Have dinner next to the Richland Yacht Club at the **SUNDANCE GRILL**, then head down the river and end the day at the **HAMPTON INN**.

DAY THREE: Wake up early and go for a run (or a walk) on the **WATERFRONT TRAIL** right outside your hotel, have breakfast back at the Hampton, then hit the road for Walla Walla. Your first stop is the **WHITMAN MISSION**, where 19th-century missionaries and Native Americans clashed. Next, visit the historic buildings of the **FORT WALLA WALLA MUSEUM**. Lunch in downtown Walla Walla at chic but casual **GRAPE-FIELDS**; then check into the restored 1928 **MARCUS WHITMAN** hotel, in downtown Walla Walla. Take the short drive to the **CREEK TOWN CAFÉ**, and save room for one of a dozen tempting desserts.

separate building. Some have fireplaces or two-person whirlpool tubs, and guests have access to an outdoor pool. Personalized wine tours are available. *$$$; AE, DC, DIS, MC, V; checks OK; dinner Thurs–Sat; beer and wine; reservations recommended; www.birchfieldmanor.com; 2 miles from Yakima, exit 34 off I-82 onto Hwy 24.* &

Gasperetti's Restaurant / ★☆

1013 N FIRST ST, YAKIMA; 509/248-0628 Linen tablecloths and fresh flowers accent the two dining rooms in this 35-year-old restaurant. Walls are painted in an aged stucco style, reminiscent of old Tuscany. Brad Patterson, who helped owner John Gasperetti open the place, has returned as chef after working in Seattle's four-star Lampreia restaurant. Appetizers such as smoked-salmon cheesecake complement a range of entrées, from pastas to Washington filet mignon in a sauce of marsala wine and Gorgonzola. The award-winning wine list offers a solid selection from Washington, California, and Italy. *$$; AE, DIS, MC, V; checks OK; lunch Tues–Fri, dinner Tues–Sat; full bar; reservations recommended; N 1st St exit off I-82.* &

Grant's Brewery Pub / ★

32 N FRONT ST, YAKIMA; 509/575-2922 In 1982, Bert Grant opened the first brew pub in the United States since Prohibition was repealed. Located in Yakima's old train station, the pub is rich with atmosphere and thick with memories, especially now that Grant has passed on. There's seating at the bar, booths, and a few tables. Live music, including folk, can be enjoyed most weekends. Beer ranges from hefeweizen to stouts to cask-conditioned Scottish ales. Food is typical pub fare, with fish-and-chips a favorite. *$; AE, MC, V; checks OK; lunch, dinner every day (Mon–Sat in winter); beer and wine; no reservations; www.grants.com; in the old depot building, from N 1st St head west on Yakima Ave.*

Melange / ★

7 N FRONT ST, YAKIMA; 509/453-0571 Formerly Deli De Pasta, this intimate Mediterranean-influenced café is owned by the daughter and son-in-law, Melissa and Ron Richter, of the original owners. The North Front Street Historical District restaurant features steaks, pastas, and seafood. You might start with a kalamata olive tapenade with chèvre, or fresh mozzarella with tomatoes and basil. Entrées might be dijon tenderloin, veal marsala, or duck with marionberry sauce. The wine list is strong on Washington State vintages. *$; AE, MC, V; checks OK; dinner Mon–Sat; beer and wine; reservations recommended; ½ block off Yakima Ave.*

LODGINGS

Orchard Inn B&B / ★

1207 PECKS CANYON RD, YAKIMA; 509/966-1283 OR 888/858-8284 This pleasant inn, in the middle of a working cherry orchard, has one of the best features of a B&B: an innkeeper, Shari Dover, who loves her work. Dover and her husband purchased the orchard in 1974, and opened the B&B in 1996. Four rooms are decorated in a cherry theme and feature down comforters, phones, and color TVs. All have private baths with jetted tubs. Breakfast is served in the (cherry-themed) dining room off the spacious kitchen. The sitting room has a TV, VCR, video library, CD player, computer, and fax machine for guest use. A selection of Northwest products—many of them cherry-related—is for sale. *$$; MC, V; checks OK; orchardinn@hotmail .com; www.orchardinnbb.com; ¼ mile off Powerhouse Rd.*

A Touch of Europe B&B / ★★

220 N 16TH AVE, YAKIMA; 888/438-7073 This Queen Anne Victorian house was built in 1889 and opened as a B&B by owners Jim and Erika Cenci in 1995. Three antique-filled rooms have private baths and air-conditioning; the Prince Victorian Mahogany Room has a gas fireplace. Erika, the chef, was raised in Germany and has written several cookbooks. Her European-style breakfast is served in the dining room, or privately in the turret by candlelight and classical music. Gourmet lunches, afternoon high tea, and dinners for up to 20 are available by arrangement. No smoking, pets, or children. *$$; AE, MC, V; checks OK; www.winesnw.com/toucheuropeb&b.htm; exit 31 off I-82, west on US Hwy 12.*

Naches

LODGINGS

Whistlin' Jack Lodge / ★★

20800 SR 410, NACHES; 800/827-2299 This 1957 mountain hideaway is ideal for hiking, alpine and cross-country skiing, fishing, or just escaping civilization. Weekend rates vary by type of room: cottage, bungalow, or motel unit. Cottages have full kitchens and hot tubs, and are close to the river (some as little as 10–20 feet away)—and make great private retreats. Guests who come with bigger plans—and want to dine out—opt for motel rooms or bungalows. Some catch their own dinner—but Whistlin' Jack also serves panfried trout in its restaurant, with live music on weekends. The lodge has a convenience store and a 24-hour gas pump. *$$; AE, DIS, MC, V; local checks only; www.whistlinjacklodge.com; 40 miles west of Yakima.*

Toppenish

The town's best-known son, Western artist Fred Oldfield, has turned Toppenish's streets into an art gallery with more than 50 historical murals—and a new one is painted each June. Such efforts by the **TOPPENISH MURAL SOCIETY** (5A Toppenish Ave; 509/865-6516) complement stores selling Western gear, antiques, and art, making this a nice place for a walking tour—and giving an authentic feel to summer rodeos.

The **YAKAMA NATION CULTURAL HERITAGE CENTER** (off US Hwy 97 and Buster Rd; 509/865-2800; *www.yakamamuseum.com*) includes a Native American museum and restaurant, reference library, gift shop, theater, and the 76-foot-tall Winter Lodge for banquets. Nearby is the tribal-run **LEGENDS CASINO** (580 Fort Rd; 509/865-8800; *www.yakamalegendscasino.com*). **FORT SIMCOE STATE PARK** (open May–Sept), a frontier military post built in 1865, stands in desolate grandeur 30 miles west of Toppenish on Highway 220, on the Yakama Indian Reservation.

Yakima Valley Wine Country

The Yakima Valley wine country stretches from Yakima almost as far as the Tri-Cities, encompassing Zillah, Sunnyside, Grandview, Prosser, and Benton City (see "Southeast Washington Three-Day Wine Tour" in this chapter).

Zillah

RESTAURANTS

Squeeze Inn

611 FIRST AVE, ZILLAH; 509/829-6226 Established in 1932, this Yakima Valley fixture was once a single, 8-foot-wide storefront (and customers had to squeeze in). Now it's more spacious, with plenty of room for locals to enjoy well-priced steak dinners that come with shrimp or fruit cocktail, *and* bread, *and* soup or salad, *and* your choice of baked potato, rice pilaf, pasta Alfredo, or garlic mashed potatoes. The music in the background is the best of the oldies, the decor is country farmhouse floral, and service is, well, serviceable. Unusual for the atmosphere, but not for the region, is the two-page wine list. *$; MC, V; local checks only; full bar; breakfast Sat, lunch, dinner Mon–Sat; no reservations; on main street.* &

Sunnyside, Outlook, and Grandview

This is true farm country, and it's famous for its wine grapes, Concords, hops, corn, apples, cherries, cucumbers, onions, peaches, pears, peppers, garlic, and dairy products—with all the accompanying aromas. If you need a snack or want to stretch your legs, stop at **DARIGOLD'S DAIRY FAIR** (400 Alexander Rd, Sunnyside; 509/837-4321). It's open daily for sandwiches, old-fashioned ice cream, free cheese tasting, and self-guided tours of the factory.

Locals recommend the **SUNNY SPOT** (1850 Yakima Valley Hwy, Sunnyside; 509/839-7768) for breakfast.

RESTAURANTS

Dykstra House Restaurant

114 BIRCH AVE, GRANDVIEW; 509/882-2082 Dykstra House—a 1914 mansion—makes bread and rolls from hand-ground whole wheat grown in the surrounding Horse Heaven Hills. Owner Linda Hartshorn also takes advantage of local in-season produce—like asparagus—in her entrées, but her specialty is dessert. Favorites are apple caramel pecan torte and Dykstra House chocolate pie, served since Hartshorn opened the place in 1984. *$$; AE, DC, DIS, MC, V; checks OK; lunch Tues–Sat, dinner Fri–Sat; beer and wine; reservations recommended; exit 75 off I-82.*

Snipes Mountain Microbrewery & Restaurant / ★

905 YAKIMA VALLEY HWY, SUNNYSIDE; 509/837-2739 Snipes is expansive from every angle, and its huge stone fireplace and exposed rafters make the brew pub feel like a mountain lodge. The beers are brewed on-site and the food is good steakhouse fare. Meals can be as fancy as you like, ranging from wood-fired pizza (try the Mountaineer—"beer-b-q" chicken, ale-caramelized onions, smoked Gouda, and pine nuts) to hazelnut-crusted rack of lamb with mustard demi-glace. *$; AE, DIS, MC, V; checks OK; lunch, dinner every day; beer and wine; no reservations; www.snipesmountain.com; exit 63 or 69 off I-82.* &

Taqueria la Fogata

1204 YAKIMA VALLEY HWY, SUNNYSIDE; 509/839-9019 The small, simple Mexican taqueria was remodeled in 1999, although its menu still reflects local tastes. Walls inside are a rich coral, and Michoacán specialties include posole—a stew of pork back, feet, and hominy—and menudo, a tripe-and-cow's-feet stew in a spicy sauce. Less adventurous diners, however, can't go wrong with excellent tacos and burritos. *$; MC, V; checks OK; breakfast, lunch, dinner every day; full bar; no reservations; middle of town.*

LODGINGS

Cozy Rose Private Country Suites / ★

1220 FORSELL RD, GRANDVIEW; 800/575-8381 Owners Mark and Jennie Jackson are dedicated to perfecting the B&B experience; they offer four rooms, each with a private entrance, bathroom, fireplace, cable TV, and stereo. Splurge and get the Secret Garden Suite with a two-person Jacuzzi and "king-sized wonder bed." Breakfast is delivered to your room; typical fare includes French toast, omelets, and pecan pancakes. The Jacksons grow their own strawberries, herbs, and apples. They keep llamas on the property and are near a vineyard for a romantic walk. No smoking; well-behaved children over 12 OK. *$$–$$$; no credit cards; checks OK; stay@cozyroseinn.com; www.cozyroseinn.com; exit 69 off I-82.*

Outlook Guest House / ★

1320 INDEPENDENCE RD, OUTLOOK; 509-549-7244 OR 888-837-7651 This is the house where winemaker Joel Tefft raised his family, back before the landscape around it was planted with wine grapes almost as far as you can see (though some of the original orchards still stand). The former family home has been remodeled to serve as a comfortable guest house for wine country visitors. Each of the three rooms has a queen-sized bed and private bath; or you can rent the entire house, including the full kitchen and comfortable living and dining room. The Teffts supply you with coffee and continental breakfast basics, and you're just across the driveway from the Tefft Cellars winery. When tasting room hours are over, calm prevails. Children only by prior arrangement; no pets. *$$; MC, V; checks OK; tcwinery@aol.com; www.tefftcellars.com; take exit 63 off I-82 and follow signs.*

Prosser

Who can resist a quick stop in Prosser, the self-purported "pleasant place with pleasant people"? Every day, the tasting room at **CHUKAR CHERRIES** (321 Wine Country Rd; 509/786-2055; *www.chukar.com*) gives out samples of the local Bing and Rainier cherries—especially good once they're dried and covered in chocolate.

LODGINGS

The Vintner's Inn at Hinzerling Winery / ★

1524 SHERIDAN AVE, PROSSER; 509/786-2163 OR 800/727-6702 If you'd like an insider's view of life in wine country, the Vintner's Inn is the place. The winery is one of the region's oldest, and the historic home that houses the bed-and-breakfast has built-in, decades-old charm. Hinzerling Winery owners Mike and Frankie Wallace purchased the 1907 Victorian-style house, loaded it onto a truck, and relocated it next to their winery in little Prosser. Accommodations are quaint and comfy; three bedrooms upstairs have private bathrooms. Downstairs, dinner is served, by reservation only, Fridays and Saturdays. The five-course meal is a gourmet treat and might begin with crostini, Brie with carmelized onions, and herbed focaccia. Next might be gazpacho, followed by chicken in a tarragon-sherry-caper cream sauce. A wine bar with patio seating is available on weekends (wines of the region are featured, not just Hinzerling's own). In his organic garden, Mike grows most of the herbs and vegetables used in the kitchen. A continental breakfast prepares guests for a strenuous day of wine touring. No smoking; call ahead to clear pets or children. *$$; DIS, MC, V; checks OK; www.hinzerling.com; just off Wine Country Rd.*

The Tri-Cities

The Tri-Cities' main attractions are the rivers (the Yakima, Snake, and Columbia converge here), wineries (more than a dozen between Prosser and Walla Walla), and golf courses (nine public or private). But the area also has an intriguing history, from Lewis and Clark's stop at what is now **SACAJAWEA STATE PARK** in Pasco to Kennewick's annual summer hydroplane races to Richland's role in ending World War II with top-secret atomic research at Hanford. The region is made up of three cities (although Richland now sports "suburbs" of North and West Richland) and two counties (Benton and Walla Walla), but the **TRI-CITIES VISITOR AND CONVENTION BUREAU** (6951 W Grandridge Blvd, Kennewick; 800/254-5824; *www.visittri-cities.com*) pulls them together to provide a seamless visit.

Richland

Richland was once a secret city, hidden away while the atomic-bomb workers did research in the 1940s. "Atomic City," with a highly educated population, is proud of its nuclear past. The **COLUMBIA RIVER EXHIBITION OF HISTORY, SCIENCE & TECHNOLOGY** (95 Lee Blvd; 509/943-9000; *www.crehst.org*) displays the region's history from ice age through nuclear age. Hands-on exhibits explain how the Tri-Cities area sprang up during World War II, when the federal government created Hanford.

COLUMBIA RIVER JOURNEYS (1229 Columbia Park Trail; 509/734-9941; *www.columbiariverjourneys.com*; May–Oct 15) offers jet-boat tours through **HANFORD REACH**, an ecologically preserved section of the Columbia River. Beautiful **HOWARD AMON PARK** (509/942-7529) lies along the Columbia, with a paved path for bicycling, walking, or in-line skating.

ALLIED ARTS GALLERY (89 Lee Blvd; 509/943-9815) displays the work of local artists and sponsors an annual July art festival.

Local dining opportunities include not just the expected Mexican cuisine, but also Russian (**SAMOVAR**, 1340 Jadwin Ave; 509/946-6655) and Thai (**THE EMERALD OF SIAM**, 1314 Jadwin Ave; 509/946-9328).

RESTAURANTS

Atomic Ale Brewpub & Eatery / ★

1015 LEE BLVD, RICHLAND; 509/946-5465 The microbrews are too good for Homer Simpson's taste in beer, but he'd appreciate their names: Half-life Hefeweizen and Plutonium Porter, for example. The standard pub food—pizza, salads, and soups—is good, and the house specialty is wood-fired gourmet pizza made with garlic, basil, shrimp, and other flavorful morsels. Finish with a B Reactor brownie. *$; AE, DIS, MC, V; checks OK; lunch, dinner Mon–Sat; beer and wine; no reservations; George Washington Wy exit off I-82.*

Sundance Grill / ★

450 COLUMBIA POINT DR, RICHLAND; 509/942-7120 A move to Richland heightened the appeal of this local favorite. A casual, business-lunch atmosphere still segues into dinner with tablecloths and nightly live music, but the new location next to the Richland Yacht Club adds a view and more atmosphere. The regularly changing menu features seasonal fish, meat, and produce, such as seafood creole; prime rib; a mixed grill with sea bass, prawns, and scallops; eggplant Parmesan; or seared and baked duck breast with a black-currant rhubarb sauce. The wine list has more than 100 choices, most from Washington. The restaurant features the only cigar lounge in the Tri-Cities area. *$$; AE, DIS, MC, V; checks OK; lunch, dinner Mon–Sat; full bar; reservations recommended; about 1 mile from Richland, exit from Hwy 240 or 182.* ♿

LODGINGS

Hampton Inn / ★

486 BRADLEY BLVD, RICHLAND; 509/943-4400 Right on the Columbia River, adjacent to the waterfront path, the Hampton Inn is one of the Tri-Cities' newest and most comfortable hotels. Rooms are nicely, if uniformly, decorated, and amenities include a pool, fitness room, and restaurant on-site. A Hampton Inn is a Hampton Inn, but view rooms here take this a step above most Tri-Cities accommodations. *$$; AE, DC, DIS, MC, V; checks OK; take George Washington Wy exit and turn right onto Bradley Blvd at third light.* ♿

Kennewick

Kennewick is the largest of the Tri-Cities, sharing a border with Richland and an architecturally magnificent **CABLE BRIDGE** (lighted at night) with Pasco. The city is known as Southeast Washington's retail center and has several malls, including Columbia Center, but the place to visit is **COLUMBIA PARK** (between Hwy 240 and Columbia River; 509/585-4293). At the park's east end, near the US Highway 395 blue bridge, volunteers in 1999 built the wooden castlelike **PLAYGROUND OF DREAMS** with climbing structures and twisty slides. It's next to the **FAMILY FISHING POND**, where adults can teach children to catch and release. Both are handicapped accessible. The park has a Frisbee golf course and is the site of late July's Columbia Cup unlimited **HYDROPLANE RACES** (509/547-2203; *www.hydroracing.com*). Winter sports fans focus on the **TRI-CITY AMERICANS** hockey team (509/736-0606), which plays at the **COLISEUM** (7100 W Quinault Ave; 509/783-9999).

RESTAURANTS

Casa Chapala / ★

107 E COLUMBIA DR, KENNEWICK; 509/586-4224 / 2100 N BELFAIR PL, KENNEWICK; 509/783-8080 Owners Lupe and Lucina Barragan are known throughout the community for their friendly smiles, and for organizing Tri-Citians in 1999 to make the world's largest burrito. Mexican food here is reasonably authentic and quite filling. The menu has kid-sized choices and several low-fat options. Beware: "Large" margaritas are huge. *$; AE, DIS, MC, V; checks OK; lunch, dinner every day; full bar; no reservations; www.casachapala.com; east end of Kennewick, just east of N Washington St (Columbia Dr), near railroad tracks, just off Columbia Center Blvd (Belfair Pl).*

Cedars Pier I / ★

355 CLOVER ISLAND DR, KENNEWICK; 509/582-2143 Not just "Tri-Cities casual," Cedars is frequented by boaters who dock here after a jaunt on the Columbia River. The cuisine is high-quality surf-and-turf, with various delicious cuts of meat including sirloin and T-bone. The seafood menu might include grilled ahi with a variety of sauces, salmon, and crab—both Dungeness and Alaskan king. The wine list is good, with many excellent regional choices, including the Hogue Genesis series and Glen Fiona syrahs. *$$; AE, DC, DIS, MC, V; checks OK; dinner every day; full bar; reservations recommended; www.cedarsrest.com; follow signs to Clover Island.*

Chez Chaz Bistro / ★

5011 W CLEARWATER AVE, KENNEWICK; 509/735-2138 Don't let the building's outward appearance make you hesitate; inside the decor is tasteful, if whimsical, and the food is good. Chez Chaz offers an enormous tapas menu in addition to ever-changing dinner selections. The tapas, perfect snacks to pair with wine, include traditional Mediterranean choices, like dolmas (rice-stuffed grape leaves) and smoked garlic sausage with polenta and romesco sauce, and fusion choices like spicy sweet chili chicken wings or masa-crusted fried oysters. Entrées include oven-roasted duckling with cherry brandy and grilled rack of Colorado lamb. The Washington wine list is solid. Chez Chaz's sister restaurant and wine bar, Aioli's (94 Lee Blvd, Richland; 509/942-1914; lunch Mon–Sat, dinner Tues–Sat), serves the same tapas menu, plus tasty soups and salads, panini sandwiches, and specialties such as paella and lasagne. *$$; DIS, MC, V; checks OK; lunch Mon–Sat, dinner Tues–Sat; beer and wine; reservations recommended; between Union and Edison Sts.*

Pasco

Pasco has the most diverse population of the Tri-Cities—about half the residents are Hispanic—and an economy based on light manufacturing and food processing. Historically a railroad town, Pasco is home to the **WASHINGTON STATE RAILROADS HISTORICAL SOCIETY MUSEUM** (122 N Tacoma St; 509/543-4159; *www.wsrhs .org*; open Saturdays Apr–Sept), which features old motorcars, railcars, and steam locomotives, including the state's oldest—the Blue Mountain, circa 1877.

Downtown is the **PASCO FARMERS MARKET** (4th Ave and Columbia St; 509/545-0738; open Wednesdays and Saturdays May–Nov), one of the state's largest open-air produce markets. **SACAJAWEA STATE PARK** (off Hwy 12) honors the remarkable Native American woman (see "Lewis and Clark Trail Bicentennial" in this chapter).

LODGINGS

Red Lion Hotel Pasco / ★★

2525 N 20TH AVE, PASCO; 509/547-0701 OR 800/RED-LION Four blocks from the Tri-Cities Airport, the Red Lion Hotel Pasco (for those paying attention, it was last a Doubletree, but prior to that another incarnation of Red Lion) is also right next to Sun Willows Golf Course and Columbia Basin College. The region's largest hotel, with 279 rooms and a huge ballroom, is a popular place for conventions and festivals. The hotel has two outdoor pools and an exercise facility. The hotel's Vineyards Steak House restaurant features vintages from Tri-Cities wineries; the Grizzly Bar is a hot night spot. *$$; AE, DC, DIS, MC, V; checks OK; www.westcoasthotels.com; exit 12 off I-82/US Hwy 395.* ᵬ

Walla Walla and the Blue Mountains

The Walla Walla Valley is an important historical area: the Lewis and Clark Expedition passed through in 1805, fur trappers began traveling up the Columbia River from Fort Astoria in 1811 and set up a fort in 1818, and in 1836 Dr. Marcus Whitman built a mission west of the present town. But when a virulent attack of measles hit area tribes in November 1847, a group of enraged Cayuse men killed the missionaries. The incident came to be called the Whitman Massacre. The excellent interpretive center at the **WHITMAN MISSION NATIONAL HISTORIC SITE** (7 miles west of Walla Walla along US Hwy 12; 509/529-2761; *www.nps.gov/whmi/*) sketches out the story of the mission and the massacre; there aren't any historic buildings, but the simple outline of the mission in the ground is strangely affecting. A hike up an adjacent hill to an overlook offers the best impression of what the area looked like to the Whitmans and their fellow settlers. The mission became an important station on the Oregon Trail, and the Whitman party included the first white women to cross the continent overland.

Agriculture is important to the namesake county, known worldwide for its sweet onions and, more recently, its fine wines (see "Southeast Washington Three-Day Wine Tour" in this chapter). The **WALLA WALLA VALLEY CHAMBER OF COMMERCE** (29 E Sumac St; 877/998-4748; *www.wwchamber.com*) has additional information.

Walla Walla

Infused with tourism centered upon some of the best wines in the country, restored downtown Walla Walla bustles with restaurants, wine-tasting rooms, and galleries. The community is strong on the arts, and the **WALLA WALLA SYMPHONY** (509/529-8020; *www.wwsymphony.com*) is the oldest symphony orchestra west of the Mississippi. Performances are held in **CORDINER HALL** (345 Boyer Ave) on the grounds of private **WHITMAN COLLEGE** (509/527-5176; *www.whitman.edu*), which anchors the town and has a lovely campus. **FORT WALLA WALLA** (The Dalles Military Rd; 509/525-7703; *www.fortwallawallamuseum.org*) has a museum featuring 14 historic buildings and a collection of pioneer artifacts. The adjacent city park features a skateboard park and BMX riding area.

RESTAURANTS

Creek Town Café / ★★

1129 S 2ND AVE, WALLA WALLA; 509/522-4777 Though it's only been open for a couple of years, the Creek Town Café is quickly becoming a Walla Walla favorite. A wait is not uncommon on weekends, when several of the restaurant's four-tops get pushed together to accommodate large parties. A rock half-wall divides the room in two, and dark wood wainscoting complements framed historic photos. Dinner selections include well-prepared seafood, meat, and pasta dishes (with the local providers named on the menu) that might range from a turkey confit ravioli in butternut squash sauce to a flatiron whiskey steak with a kabob of roasted vegetables. Lunches are similar, but a little cheaper. A dozen desserts are listed on the white board behind the attractive deli case, which draws your gaze as soon as you enter the room; save your appetite for treats such as bread pudding, Key lime pie, cheesecake, or maybe coconut cream pie. *$$; AE, DIS, MC, V; checks OK; lunch, dinner daily; beer and wine; reservations recommended; at E Morton St.* &

Grapefields / ★★

4 E MAIN ST, WALLA WALLA; 509/522-3993 Grapefields has a sophisticated bistro attitude, from the art deco bar to tasty tapas. The latter include toast manchego—bread grilled with manchego and served with a tomato-onion herb salsa—and Spanish sardines (not fishy at all) marinated in citrus, vinegar,

LEWIS AND CLARK TRAIL BICENTENNIAL

Exploring the Pacific Northwest is nothing new: the concept was made famous about 200 years ago by Meriwether Lewis and William Clark.

The bicentennial celebration of Lewis and Clark's Corps of Discovery runs through 2006. Washington, Oregon, and the nine other states along the trail are expecting "historical tourists" following all or part of the 3,700-mile route that led to the non-Native settlement of the Northwest. The trail is clearly outlined with signs (featuring the forward-looking silhouettes of Lewis and Clark), historical markers, parks, and interpretive centers. Many sites also delve into the other side of the story: the Corps's long-term effect on the region's Native tribes. What started as friendly relations built on trading and exploring led to great tragedy for many tribal people.

Lewis and Clark started along the Missouri River from Illinois in May 1804, sent out by President Thomas Jefferson to find an overland link to the Pacific Ocean. Five months later, they entered what is now the southeast corner of Washington State on the Snake River. The Alpowai Interpretive Center in **CHIEF TIMOTHY STATE PARK** (on Silcott Rd, 8 miles west of Clarkston; 509/758-9580) focuses on the white explorers' meeting with the Nez Perce Indians. **LEWIS AND CLARK TRAIL STATE PARK** (on Hwy 12, 4½ miles west of Dayton; 509/337-6457; www.parks.wa.gov) offers campsites, picnic areas, and a 1-mile interpretive trail.

The Tri-Cities is the farthest point upriver on the Columbia explored by Lewis and Clark. **SACAJAWEA STATE PARK** (off Hwy 12 near Pasco; 509/545-2361; www.parks.wa.gov), at the confluence of the Snake and Columbia Rivers, is the only park along the trail honoring the Indian woman guide. The 284-acre park includes the

garlic, and olive oil. The café menu offers a traditional charcuterie plate featuring a selection of cured and preserved meats; a perfectly dressed salad verte topped with toasted walnuts, Gorgonzola, and Anjou pear; and hand-tossed pizzas. The dazzling selection of premium wines is both local and international. *$; AE, MC, V; checks OK; lunch Tues–Sat, dinner Tues–Sun; beer and wine; no reservations; just off 2nd Ave.* &

Merchants Ltd. / ★★☆

21 E MAIN ST, WALLA WALLA; 509/525-0900 Merchants has been a mainstay— especially for liberal-arts college students who come for the Wednesday-only spaghetti dinners—since 1976. The huge space (it seats 300) across three storefronts downtown serves healthy morning and midday meals. A full, in-house bakery makes treats like chocolate croissants and pizzas, while a well-stocked deli case serves picnic needs. Look for international groceries, gourmet foodstuffs, organic coffee beans, and wines. *$; AE, DIS, MC, V; checks OK; breakfast, lunch Mon–Sat, dinner Wed; beer and wine; no reservations; 2nd St exit off US Hwy 12.* &

SACAJAWEA INTERPRETIVE CENTER (509/545-2361), housing a collection of Native artifacts; it is run by volunteers and open by appointment for group tours.

Paddling down the Columbia, the explorers talked with Natives near what is now **MARYHILL STATE PARK** (off Hwy 14, Goldendale; 509/773-5007; www.parks .wa.gov; open year-round). **MARYHILL MUSEUM** (35 Maryhill Museum Dr, Goldendale; 509/773-3733; open Mar 15–Nov 15), on the hill across from Biggs, Oregon, has an outstanding display of Indian baskets and stone tools. **BEACON ROCK STATE PARK** (35 miles east of Vancouver on Hwy 14; 509/427-8265 or 800/233-0321) was where the explorers first noticed the effects of the Pacific Ocean's tide.

From the site of what is now **LEWIS AND CLARK CAMPSITE STATE PARK** (2 miles southeast of Chinook on Hwy 101), the 33 weary travelers first saw the Pacific Ocean. Washington State's **LEWIS AND CLARK INTERPRETIVE CENTER** (2½ miles southeast of Ilwaco, off Hwy 101; 360/642-3029; www.parks.wa.gov/lcinterpctr.asp) is on Cape Disappointment, where the explorers officially reached the Pacific.

After being pounded by cold and wet winds, they turned south to establish a winter campsite, at what is now **FORT CLATSOP NATIONAL MEMORIAL** (92343 Fort Clatsop Rd; 503/861-2471; www.nps.gov/focl; open daily), 5 miles southwest of Astoria, Oregon. The visitor center includes a replica of Lewis and Clark's winter quarters.

Those wanting to know more should consult the national park's **LEWIS AND CLARK NATIONAL HISTORIC TRAIL** Web site (www.nps.gov/lecl), the nonprofit **NATIONAL LEWIS AND CLARK BICENTENNIAL COUNCIL** (888/999-1803; www.lewisandclark200.org), or www.lewisandclark.com.

—Melissa O'Neil

Whitehouse-Crawford / ★★★

55 W CHERRY ST, WALLA WALLA; 509/525-2222 A former planing mill from 1905 was rescued and restored to house this airy, chic restaurant that plays host to wine tourists and Carhart-wearing winery owners. Tasty appetizers—try spicy calamari with ginger—pair well with many local wines on the extensive wine list. Entrées are the usual suspects—salmon, steak, and pork tenderloin—but with unexpected twists such as southwest-style salmon with black beans, corn, and squash in a piquant tomato sauce, or pork smoked and served with grilled fresh figs, shallots, and spaetzle. Desserts are divine, including lemon verbena crème brûlée and award-winning twice-baked chocolate cake—a marriage of dense cake and chocolate soufflé. *$$–$$$; AE, MC, V; checks OK; dinner Wed–Sun; full bar; reservations recommended; www.whitehousecrawford.com; downtown, at 3rd Ave.* ❧

LODGINGS

Green Gables Inn / ★★

 922 BONSELLA ST, WALLA WALLA; 888/525-5501 The title character from L.M. Montgomery's *Anne of Green Gables* series loved staying in guest rooms. Margaret and Jim Buchan incorporate that spirit in five rooms named for topics in the popular books, such as Idlewild, with a fireplace and Jacuzzi, and Dryad's Bubble, with a small balcony. The Carriage House is good for families; it is separate from the main house and gives kids more room to run around. Full breakfast is served on fine china by candlelight. A wraparound porch and air-conditioning make for pleasant summer evenings. *$$–$$$; AE, DIS, MC, V; checks OK; innkeeper@greengablesinn.com; www.greengablesinn.com; Clinton St exit off US Hwy 12.*

Inn at Abeja / ★★★

2014 MILL CREEK RD, WALLA WALLA; 509/522-1234 More than 100 years old, this 22-acre farmstead doubles as a working winery and luxurious retreat. Located outside town, surrounded by the rolling Palouse and the Blue Mountains, visitors can experience the tranquility of the country, along with some modern conveniences. Some rooms have satellite TVs; some have dial-up Internet access. The former chicken house and bunkhouse have been transformed with playful good taste into cottages and suites. The Chicken House Cottage has vaulted ceilings, a slate-tiled walk-in shower for two, and an airy full kitchen. Best is the two-story Summer Kitchen Cottage, with a deck overlooking the vineyards, sky-lit bathroom, king-sized bed, claw-footed tub, and full kitchen and living room. A hearty gourmet breakfast is served to all guests in the morning. No smoking or children under 12; pets allowed in Chicken House Cottage only. *$$$–$$$$; MC, V; checks OK; www.millcreekbb.com/inn.htm; 1.6 miles outside downtown.*

Inn at Blackberry Creek / ★★

1126 PLEASANT ST, WALLA WALLA; 509/522-5233 OR 877/522-5233 Just around the corner from Pioneer Park and Whitman College is the charming Inn at Blackberry Creek. The 1912 farmhouse has been lovingly restored by innkeeper Barbara Knudson, whose attention to detail—fresh cookies in the evening, flawlessly decorated rooms—makes for a pleasant stay. The three rooms available, Cezanne's Sanctuary, Monet's Retreat, and Renoir's Studio, all feature king-sized beds, private baths with showers, and peaceful views of the tree-lined property. The light-filled common area overlooks the lawns and invites you to play chess, thumb through magazines, or read in comfortable chairs. Breakfast might include freshly baked pastries, eggs, yogurt, and fresh fruit. No smoking or children under 12. *$$; MC, V; checks OK; bknud@hscis.net; www.innatblackberrycreek.com; 4 blocks southeast of Pioneer Park.*

Marcus Whitman / ★★

6 W ROSE ST, WALLA WALLA; 866/826-9422 One of the largest structures in downtown Walla Walla, the classically elegant, historic (1928), and recently restored (1999) Marcus Whitman offers 91 clean, comfortable rooms. Owner

Kyle Mussman took pains to restore the hotel as accurately as possible, and works hard to make the Whitman part of the community, with events and special dinners (sushi night, for example). The best rooms are suites in the original tower of the hotel (the West Wing was added in the 1960s). Decorated in handsome, almost masculine colors with cherry molding, new carpets, and furnishings, the suites are a good place to stay if you're on business or want to hold a large meeting in one of the hotel conference centers or ballroom; standard rooms share the same look and feel, but are less spacious (and don't have the same city views). Right downtown, the hotel is within walking distance of several good restaurants (and wineries), but if you don't feel like going out, grab dinner at the first-floor Marc restaurant for steaks, salmon, or chicken. The Vineyard Lounge features—of course—a good wine list, with some strong European choices as well as Washington labels. *$–$$$; AE, MC, V; www.marcuswhitmanhotel.com; at 2nd Ave.* ♿

Dayton

Dayton is a small farming town northeast of Walla Walla and one of the first communities established in Washington State. Small wonder it's full of historical buildings—almost 90 Victorian-era structures. The **DAYTON CHAMBER OF COMMERCE** (166 E Main St; 800/882-6299; *www.historicdayton.com*) offers information for self-guided walking tours. The **DAYTON HISTORICAL DEPOT** (222 E Commercial St; 509/382-2026; tours Tues–Sat), built in 1881, is the state's oldest remaining railroad station, now a museum.

Dayton is also known for easy access to **BLUEWOOD SKI RESORT** (22 miles south of Dayton via US Hwy 12; 509/382-4725; *www.bluewood.com*), in Umatilla National Forest in the Blue Mountains. It has clear skies, dry powder, and the second-highest base elevation (4,545 feet) in the state.

RESTAURANTS

Patit Creek Restaurant / ★★★

725 E DAYTON AVE, DAYTON; 509/382-2625 This small-town restaurant is known regionwide for its consistent continental cuisine and is one of the most highly rated restaurants this side of the mountains. Bruce and Heather Hiebert turned a 1920s service station into a 10-table restaurant famous for filets in green peppercorn sauce, chèvre-stuffed dates wrapped in bacon, fresh vegetables, and huckleberry pie. The wine list is strong on Walla Walla selections. Patit Creek is a classic off-the-beaten-path discovery and a classy place to end a day of valley wine touring or skiing at Bluewood. Just don't drop in and expect a table; reservations are recommended at least two weeks in advance. *$$; MC, V; local checks only; lunch Wed–Fri, dinner Wed–Sat; beer and wine; reservations recommended; north end of town.* ♿

SOUTHEAST WASHINGTON THREE-DAY WINE TOUR

Washington is the second-largest wine-producing state in the nation (behind California), and more than half of its wineries are in Eastern Washington, where 99 percent of the 29,000 acres of grapes are grown. The state's $2.4 billion wine industry saw incredible growth in the late 1990s, and the number of wineries now totals about 240. Most, though not all, of these have tasting rooms open for visits year-round.

DAY ONE: Start in Yakima and drive to Zillah and the **WINEGLASS CELLARS** (260 N Bonair Rd; 509/829-3011; *www.wineglasscellars.com*) tasting room. Next sample a few wines at **PORTTEUS** (5201 Highland Dr, Zillah; 509/829-6970; *www.portteus .com*) before heading south on Interstate 82 to the Outlook exit, where you follow the signs to **TEFFT CELLARS** (1320 Independence Rd, Outlook; 509/837-7651; *www.tefft cellars.com*). Take a lunch break at **TAQUERIA LA FOGATA** in Sunnyside and then stop again in Prosser for tasting at **HOGUE CELLARS** (Wine Country Rd; 509/786-4557; *www.hoguecellars.com*). Take an afternoon drive to the Red Mountain growing area near Benton City. Taste at **HEDGES CELLARS** (53511 N Sunset Rd, Benton City; 509/588-3155; *www.hedgescellars.com*); then see the underground barrel-storage tunnels at **TERRA BLANCA** (34715 N DeMoss Rd, Benton City; 509/588-6082; *www .terrablanca.com*). In Prosser, check in at the **VINTNER'S INN**, and enjoy the prix-fixe dinner.

DAY TWO: After breakfast at the inn, shop in Prosser for picnic fixings and take Highway 221 south to the Northwest's largest winery, **COLUMBIA CREST** (Columbia

LODGINGS

The Purple House B&B Inn / ★

415 E CLAY ST, DAYTON; 800/486-2574 This 1882 house really *is* purple, and has been a B&B since the late 1980s. Four rooms have modern amenities, including air-conditioning. Two have private baths, while the others share one large bathroom. A separate carriage house is also available. Innkeeper Christine D. Williscroft is a native of southern Germany, which shows in the inn's decor, as does her passion for Chinese antiques and Oriental rugs. Williscroft has two small dogs and welcomes other small pets with advance warning. Full breakfast might include strudel or crepes, served in a walled-in courtyard next to the private swimming pool. Lunch and dinner can be arranged for in-house guests and groups of six or more. *$$; MC, V; checks OK; purplehousebnb.com; 1 block off US Hwy 12.* &

The Weinhard Hotel / ★

235 E MAIN ST, DAYTON; 509/382-4032 This is one of our favorite places in the Walla Walla Valley. Fresh flowers and fruit greet guests in each room. Owners Dan and Ginny Butler restored the old Weinhard building (built as a saloon and lodge hall in the late 1800s) in tiny, historic Dayton and filled it with

Crest Dr, Patterson; 509/875-2061; *www.columbia-crest.com*), on the Columbia. Taste the wine, take the tour, and then eat lunch on the grounds by the fountain. Return to the Tri-Cities and visit Richland's **BARNARD GRIFFIN WINERY** (878 Tulip Ln; 509/627-0266; *www.barnardgriffin.com*). Then drive toward Walla Walla on US Highway 12, stopping en route to taste award-winning wines at **WOODWARD CANYON WINERY** (11920 W Hwy 12, Lowden; 509/525-4129; *www.woodward canyon.com*) and **L'ECOLE NO. 41** (41 Lowden School Rd, Lowden; 509/525-0940; *www.lecole.com*). Check in at the **INN AT ABEJA** and dine at **WHITEHOUSE-CRAW-FORD** in Walla Walla.

DAY THREE: Fortified by breakfast in the inn's charming barn and a walk in the grape fields, head to historic downtown Walla Walla and be sure to stop at the bright-yellow storefront of **CAYUSE VINEYARDS** (17 E Main St; 509/526-0686; *www .cayusevineyards.com*). Eat a simple lunch across the street at **MERCHANTS LTD.** Stroll down Main Street and stop at another tasting room—**WATERBROOK WINERY** (31 E Main St; 509/522-1262; *www.waterbrook.com*)—then visit **CANOE RIDGE VINEYARD** (1102 W Cherry St; 509/527-0885; *www.canoeridgevineyard.com*) and **SEVEN HILLS WINERY** (212 N 3rd Ave; 877/777-7870; *www.sevenhillswinery.com*). Then head to **WALLA WALLA VINTNERS** (Mill Creek Rd; 509/525-4724; *www.wallawallavintners .com*) if it's a Saturday. Finish the tour in Dayton and check in at your night's lodging, **THE WEINHARD HOTEL**, followed by a gourmet dinner at the highly rated **PATIT CREEK RESTAURANT** (where you made reservations well in advance).

elegant Victorian antiques that they collected from across the country. The 15 rooms are furnished with antique dressers, desks, and canopied beds. (Tall people, however, should ask for one of the longer beds.) All rooms have private baths, and the Signature Room has a jetted tub. Inside the hotel is the recently updated Weinhard Café (*www.weinhard-cafe.com*; lunch, dinner Tues–Sat), serving tasty, inventive fare. Entrées range from halibut cakes with avocado pumpkin-seed salsa to New York steak with Gorgonzola herb butter. No smoking. *$$–$$$; AE, MC, V; checks OK; www.weinhard.com; downtown.* &

Pullman and the Palouse

Washington's golden Palouse region, next to Idaho and north of the Blue Mountains, is made up of seemingly endless, rolling hills covered with wheat, lentils, and other crops. The area also boasts rivers, including the Snake, and several geological wonders.

KAMIAK BUTTE COUNTY PARK (13 miles north of Pullman on Hwy 27) is a good place for a picnic with a view of the undulating hills. **STEPTOE BUTTE STATE**

PARK (about 30 miles north of Pullman on US Hwy 195) is great for a panoramic view or stargazing, but windy.

At **PALOUSE FALLS STATE PARK** (2 miles off Hwy 261 between Washtucna and Tucannon; 509/646-3252 or 800/233-0321), the Palouse River roars over a basalt cliff higher than Niagara Falls, dropping 198 feet into a steep-walled basin on its way to the Snake. A hiking trail leads to an overlook above the falls, most spectacular during spring runoff. Camping and canoeing are allowed in **LYONS FERRY STATE PARK** (on Hwy 261, 7 miles north of Starbuck; 509/646-3252 or 800/233-0321), at the confluence of the Palouse and Snake Rivers; the park also has a public boat launch.

Pullman

The heart of the Palouse beats in Pullman, at the junction of US Highway 195 and Highway 27 near the Idaho border, and the heart of Pullman is **WASHINGTON STATE UNIVERSITY** (Visitor Center: 225 N Grand Ave; 509/335-8633; *www.wsu .edu*). WSU started in 1892 and is where 17,000 die-hard Cougars live during the academic year. Campus tours are available weekdays. A trip through town wouldn't be complete without sampling the ice cream or Cougar Gold cheese made at the WSU creamery, **FERDINAND'S** (inside Agriculture Science Bldg; 509/335-2141; weekdays).

Pullman is also known for its historical buildings, with brick masonry and early 1900s classical and Georgian architecture. Find more info at the **PULLMAN CHAMBER OF COMMERCE** (415 N Grand Ave; 800/365-6948; *www.pullman .com*).

RESTAURANTS

Hilltop Restaurant

920 NW OLSON ST, PULLMAN; 509/334-2555 This steak house has an incredible view of the university and surrounding hills, a romantic vista complemented by linens and attentive service. Red meat is the specialty, from prime rib and steaks to Sunday's midday roast-beef family dinner. Homemade desserts include cheesecakes, mud pie, and chocolate truffles. Hilltop is connected to the three-story, 59-room Hawthorne Inn & Suites (928 NW Olsen St; 509/332-0928; *www.pullman-wa.com/housing/motels/bestwest.htm*), where it offers room service. *$$; AE, DIS, MC, V; checks OK; lunch Mon–Fri, dinner every day; full bar; no reservations; hilltop@pullman.com; www.hilltoprestaurant.com; on Davis Wy.*

Swilly's Cafe & Catering / ★★

200 NE KAMIAKEN ST, PULLMAN; 509/334-3395 The renovated historic Hutchison Photography studio maintains its dedication to art, with local artwork displayed on the dining room's exposed-brick walls. Opened in 1986 by Jill Aesoph, Swilly's overlooks Paradise Creek in downtown Pullman. Casual warmth translates into homemade soups, salads, sandwiches, and burgers, plus more sophisticated dinner entrées such as Moroccan lamb, Thai shrimp, grilled tenderloin, and various pastas.

Microbrews are on tap, and a moderately priced wine list is strong on Washington choices. *$; AE, MC, V; checks OK; lunch, dinner Mon–Sat; beer and wine; no reservations; www.pullman-wa.com/food/swilly.htm; at NW Olson St.* &

LODGINGS

The Churchyard Inn B&B / ★

206 ST. BONIFACE ST, UNIONTOWN; 509/229-3200 The Churchyard Inn is next door to the historic St. Boniface Catholic Church in tiny Uniontown, 16 miles south of Pullman on US Highway 195. The three-story house was built as a parish in 1905, converted to a convent in 1913, then turned into a B&B by Linda and Marvin Entel in 1995. Each of seven uniquely decorated rooms has a private bath. The top-floor 1,200-square-foot Palouse Suite has a great room big enough for seminars or small wedding receptions, a kitchen, dining area, gas fireplace, views from every window, two queen-sized hide-a-beds, and a separate room with a king-sized bed. Breakfast and beverages are served in the dining room with a view of the Palouse farmlands. No smoking, pets, or children under 14. *$$–$$$; MC, V; checks OK; www.church yardinn.com; 2 blocks west of US Hwy 195.* &

SPOKANE AND NORTHEASTERN WASHINGTON

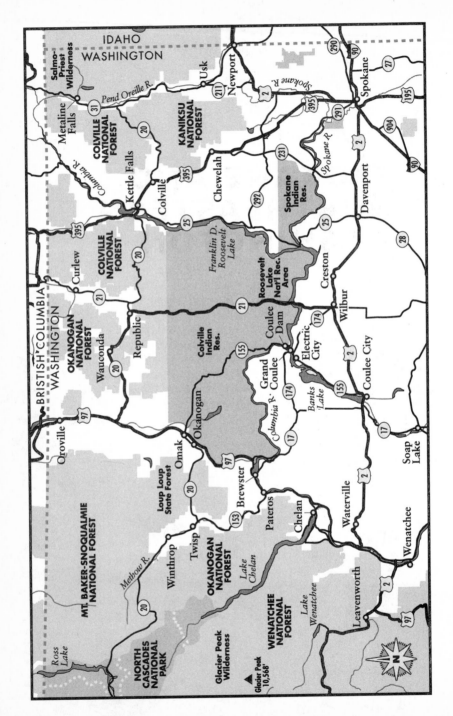

SPOKANE AND NORTHEASTERN WASHINGTON

The northeastern quadrant of Washington State is a study in contrasts compared to the lush, green west side of the Cascades. The upper-right corner of Washington starts in the sleepy spa town of Soap Lake and runs north to the Canadian border near Oroville; along this imaginary north-south line lie the towns of Grand Coulee, Okanogan, and Omak. To the east are the vast Channeled Scablands—the most visible reminder of the great floods that poured from glacial Lake Missoula thousands of years ago. That flat, featureless terrain bumps up against the gorgeous and little-explored Kettle River Range to the north, and near Colville you'll find the spectacular Selkirks, an outlying range of the Canadian Rockies.

The image of everything east of the Cascades being dry couldn't be farther from reality when you consider that the Columbia River, one of the nation's most powerful waterways, runs through this region, though it is much dammed and sedated. Its tributaries include the Pend Oreille, Colville, Spokane, and Okanogan, all of which create riparian areas in an otherwise sere shrub-steppe environment.

Spokane, in the far-eastern reaches of the state near Idaho, is famous for its tree-lined neighborhoods. The city is forested as well, with the spiky ponderosa pines of drier climes rather than the fir-dominated forests of Western Washington. Northeastern Washington years ago was dubbed the Inland Empire, and Spokane is its largest city, some 300 miles from the burgeoning Puget Sound region.

Only a half-hour east of Spokane, Coeur d'Alene, Idaho, makes for a lovely day trip from Spokane. This popular tourist destination offers year-round outdoor activities, as well as a cute downtown area with shopping and restaurants. The **COEUR D'ALENE RESORT** (800/688-5253; *www.cdaresort.com*) is a top-notch facility complete with golf, a boardwalk for strolling, and marvelous views of the lake. The city hosts numerous festivals throughout the year; contact the **COEUR D'ALENE CHAMBER OF COMMERCE** (877/782-9232; *www.coeurdalene.org*) for more information.

ACCESS AND INFORMATION

The fastest, most direct route to Spokane from Seattle is **INTERSTATE 90**; **US HIGHWAY 2** is another east-west route through Northeastern Washington. North-south routes include **US HIGHWAY 97** on the eastern slope of the Cascades and **US HIGHWAY 395**, which runs from Spokane through Colville. The **SPOKANE REGIONAL VISITOR CENTER** (201 W Main Ave; 509/747-3230 or 888/776-5263; *www.visitspokane.com*) can provide details about special events, as well as a list of accommodations and restaurants in the city.

Nine airlines—Alaska, America West, Big Sky, Canadian, Delta, Horizon, Northwest, Southwest, and United—serve **SPOKANE INTERNATIONAL AIRPORT** (W 9000 Airport Dr; 509/455-6455; *www.spokaneairports.net*), a 10-minute drive west of downtown.

AMTRAK's (800/USA-RAIL; *www.amtrak.com*) Empire Builder between Seattle and Chicago rumbles through the city, stopping in the middle of the night at Spokane's **INTERMODAL CENTER** (221 W 1st Ave). The **TRAILWAYS** bus system (509/838-5262; *www.trailways.com*) and **GREYHOUND** (509/624-5251; *www .greyhound.com*) also operate from that depot; buses also serve nearby Cheney.

Spokane

Water is the reason for Spokane's existence. Native American tribes gathered at the massive, thundering falls of the Spokane River every August to harvest salmon. The city was founded in 1879 because of the mill-power provided by the falls, which today is the centerpiece of a spacious downtown oasis, Riverfront Park, built on the site of Expo '74. The river is home to rainbow trout and osprey, including birds that nest within the city limits. It also provides a scenic backdrop for horseback riding, hiking, and golf.

Spokane's urban core continues with its revitalization efforts, spearheaded by a stylish mall that houses upscale retailers. **RIVER PARK SQUARE** (808 W Main Ave; 509/363-0304) tenants include a state-of-the-art multiplex, Nordstrom, Williams-Sonoma, Restoration Hardware, and the Gap, among others. While downtown, stop to admire the fascinating architecture and have a beer at the **STEAM PLANT GRILL** (159 S Lincoln; 509/777-3900), the site of a former plant that provided steam and electrical power to downtown Spokane from 1915 to 1986.

Civic leaders still point to the development of **RIVERFRONT PARK** (downtown; 800/336-PARK; *www.spokaneriverfrontpark.com*) as one of the turning points in the city's history. Formerly railroad yards, this expansive space is full of meandering paved paths and attractions such as an IMAX theater and a mint-condition 1909 carousel built by Charles Looff. From here you can also access the wonderful **CENTENNIAL TRAIL** (*www.spokanecentennialtrail.org*), which runs from downtown through the park to Coeur d'Alene, Idaho. A 2-mile loop passes near the pretty campus of Spokane's **GONZAGA UNIVERSITY** (502 E Boone; 509/328-4220 or 800/986-9585; *www.gonzaga.edu*), itself worth a stop to view the lovely architecture and museums (see below).

One of the best ways to get a feel for Spokane is the **CITY DRIVE**. The 32-mile drive passes gorgeous older Spokane mansions that were built at the beginning of the 20th century, financed with logging and mining money. You can print out a map of the route by visiting *www.spokaneoutdoors.com*. On the drive, a great urban adventure awaits at **MANITO PARK** (at Grand Blvd and 18th Ave) on the city's South Hill, which features a busy duck pond, a stunning rose garden filled with heirloom varieties, a peaceful Japanese garden, and the ever-changing **GAISER CONSERVATORY**—with displays that include coffee plants, exotic orchids, and prickly flowering cactus.

Feeling peckish? The stylish **ROCKWOOD BAKERY** (315 E 18th Ave; 509/747-8691) on South Hill is a favorite sweet spot. In summer months, breakfast and lunch (sandwiches, soups, pastries, and espresso) are offered under towering trees at **THE PARK BENCH** (1928 S Tekoa St; 509/456-8066).

NORTHEASTERN WASHINGTON THREE-DAY TOUR

DAY ONE: Wake up in Spokane with a fine eye-opener at the **CANNON STREET GRILL**—we recommend the veggie frittata. Afterward, explore South Hill's **MANITO PARK**, admiring the park's greens. Then lunch in neighborhood-bistro style at **THE ELK PUBLIC HOUSE** (sit outside in warm weather) or enjoy the mostly vegetarian fare downtown at **MIZUNA**. Check out the shopping at spiffy **RIVER PARK SQUARE**, which includes a 20-screen cinema. Later, rent in-line skates or a bike at **RIVERFRONT PARK** and head out on the **CENTENNIAL TRAIL**, which runs along the scenic Spokane River. After a dinner of creative cuisine at **LUNA**, attend a **SPOKANE SYMPHONY ORCHESTRA** or local theater performance. Retire in European splendor in your room at **HOTEL LUSSO**.

DAY TWO: Enjoy complimentary breakfast at the hotel's **FUGAZZI** restaurant, then head north on US Highway 395 toward Colville for a day's adventure. Golfers can stop in Chewelah to play a round at the **GOLF AND COUNTRY CLUB**; skiers can hit the ski slopes at **49 DEGREES NORTH**. In **COLVILLE**, explore Main Street shops and stop for a velvety cappuccino and a snack at **TALK AND COFFEE**. Head back to Spokane in the early evening and check into your luxurious room at the newly renovated **DAV-ENPORT HOTEL**, then venture about downtown on foot to your dinner at **NIKO'S II GREEK AND MIDDLE EASTERN RESTAURANT**. After dinner, enjoy a drink back in the hotel's **PEACOCK ROOM**.

DAY THREE: Start your day early with a latte and a decadent pastry at **LINDA-MAN'S GOURMET TO GO** and grab lunch to go on your way out of town. Head west on Highway 2 to Wilbur, then northwest on Highway 174 to the famous **GRAND COULEE DAM**. Gape at the mammoth structure FDR built, walk in the historic town of Coulee Dam, or try your luck at the **CASINO**. Have an early dinner of Mexican fare at **LA PRESA** and then continue west to **SOAP LAKE** and your room at **NOTARAS LODGE**. (You can also drive directly to Notaras and have dinner there at **DON'S RESTAURANT**.)

Museum-goers can duck inside to view Bing Crosby memorabilia at the **CROSBY LIBRARY** (Gonzaga University campus, 502 E Boone; 509/328-4220; *www.gonzaga.edu*), the singer's gift to his alma mater. While on the campus, don't miss the **JUNDT ART MUSEUM** (202 E Cataldo Ave; 509/323-6611; *www.gonzaga.edu*) and its eclectic lineup of exhibits. The MAC's $28 million expansion makes the city's dramatically renovated **NORTHWEST MUSEUM OF ARTS & CULTURE** (2316 W 1st Ave; 509/456-3931; *www.northwestmuseum.org*) a worthwhile visit.

Brazilian-born **SPOKANE SYMPHONY** (509/624-1233; *www.spokanesymphony.org*) conductor Fabio Mechetti directs diverse programs such as a pops series—guest artists include native son and internationally known baritone Thomas Hampson—

and the free Labor Day concert at Comstock Park. The **SPOKANE CIVIC THEATRE** (1020 N Howard St; 509/325-2507; *www.spokanecivictheatre.com*) offers a mixed bag of amateur performances, including kid-friendly productions; **INTERPLAYERS** (S 174 Howard St; 509/455-PLAY) is a professional company with a full season featuring well-known works. The 12,000-seat **SPOKANE VETERANS ARENA** (720 W Mallon Ave; 509/324-7000) occasionally attracts major entertainers and bands; most tickets are sold through a local agency, **TICKETSWEST** (509/325-7328 or 800/325-7328; *www.ticketswest.com*).

For a nature escape and wildlife viewing near Spokane, the suburban **RIVERSIDE STATE PARK** (509/456-5064; *www.riversidestatepark.org*), in nearby Nine Mile Falls, extends from residential northwest Spokane to the Little Spokane River, and offers hiking and picnicking as well as the interesting Bowl and Pitcher basalt formations. The **LITTLE SPOKANE NATURAL AREA** at Riverside State Park is a calm, meandering 6-mile stretch of the Little Spokane River—one of the area's premiere paddling spots. It can be accessed off Waikiki Road near St. George's School in north Spokane; a well-marked parking lot is at the canoe launch, a half mile past the school. The area offers prime bird-watching and has one of the nation's highest diversities of nesting songbirds, as well as great blue heron, wood ducks, and widgeons.

City festivals bring visitors from surrounding areas to celebrate in Spokane. More than 60,000 runners and walkers turn out on the first Sunday in May for the 7.46-mile **LILAC BLOOMSDAY RUN** (509/838-1579; *www.bloomsdayrun.org*), while Labor Day weekend's **PIG OUT IN THE PARK** (Riverfront Park; 509/625-6685) attracts food enthusiasts to its many booths.

The Spokane Arena is home to the Western Hockey League's **SPOKANE CHIEFS** (509/535-7825; *www.spokanechiefs.com*). Skiing can be sublime with powdery Inland Northwest snow at **MOUNT SPOKANE** (509/443-1397; *www.mtspokane .com*), 31 miles north of the city on Highway 206, which recently upgraded its terrain under new ownership. Or try 17 kilometers of groomed cross-country trails with two warming huts (a Sno-Park pass is required), 3 miles up the road.

RESTAURANTS

Cannon Street Grill / ★

144 S CANNON ST, SPOKANE; 509/456-8660 There are plenty of good greasy spoons in Spokane, but this cozy little spot in the Browne's Addition neighborhood is a cut above the average breakfast place. The coffee is from Craven's, a local roaster. Morning meals include a stellar frittata made with sautéed mushrooms, red peppers, and sweet onions; plate-filling pancakes; and thick French toast. On Sundays, not-to-be-missed brunch fare includes huevos rancheros with black beans. Lunch consists of simple sandwiches and salads. *$; MC, V; local checks only; breakfast, lunch Tues–Sat, brunch Sun; beer and wine; no reservations; from Maple St exit, north to 2nd Ave, west on Cannon St.* &

Catacombs Pub / ★★☆

110 S MONROE ST, SPOKANE; 509/838-4610 If you're looking for ambiance downtown, check out Catacombs Pub, located in the former boiler room of the Montvale

Hotel. Inspired by European castles, complete with tapestries on the stone walls, Catacombs ups the atmosphere ante with its exposed stone, solid oak beams, and warm brick hearth (do bring a sweater though, as it can get chilly). The menu is mostly Southern Italian fare, with thin-crust pizza and pastas; desserts include the kitschy and fun s'mores that you toast yourself at the table. You're not only coming here for the cuisine, but also for the surroundings. Catacombs' late-night menu is served until midnight and includes tapas, as well as specialty cocktails and a nice wine list, with Northwest wines. *$$; AE, DIS, MC, V; checks OK; lunch Mon–Fri, dinner every day; full bar; reservations for 8 or more (no reservations Fri–Sat); www.catacombspub.com; at 1st and Monroe Ave.*

Chicken-n-More / ★

502 W SPRAGUE AVE, SPOKANE; 509/838-5071 Spokane's sole soul-food joint is located in a small corner storefront downtown. Owner Bob Hemphill is a Texas native who slow-cooks brisket and ribs in a smoker and tops them with his signature sauce. The deep-fried catfish sandwich—slathered with red pepper sauce and ketchup—takes 15 minutes but is worth the wait. Southern-style fried chicken is digit-licking good, especially alongside an order of jo-jo potatoes. Try a side of red beans and rice, or some braised greens; the coleslaw and baked beans are nothing special. The tiny dining room has a half-dozen tables and some counter space. *$; AE, DC, DIS, MC, V; checks OK; lunch, dinner Mon–Fri; no alcohol; reservations for large groups; across from Ridpath Hotel.*

The Elk Public House / ★★

1931 W PACIFIC AVE, SPOKANE; 509/363-1973 Don't underestimate the cuisine at the Elk—on a recent visit we had one of the best meals Spokane has to offer. This lively neighborhood watering hole has an ever-changing selection of microbrews on tap and a menu designed to complement them. The Wisconsin bratwurst is slow-simmered in beer, and the 74th Street gumbo (inspired by a Seattle alehouse of the same name) is wickedly hot. The pork tacos, marinated in chipotle and spices, served with mango-and-pineapple salsa, are to die for. The weekly fresh sheet offers global fare such as Spanish-style cod, Asian-inspired pork chops topped with gingery apricot chutney, or Southern-fried catfish with spicy grits. Vegetarians appreciate the option of subbing grilled tofu in any of the entrées or salads. *$; MC, V; checks OK; lunch, dinner every day; beer and wine; no reservations; at Cannon St.* &

Hill's Someplace Else / ★★

518 W SPRAGUE AVE, SPOKANE; 509/747-3946 Walk in the front door of this dark, smoky spot and it feels more like a bar than a restaurant, but chef-owner Dave Hill cranks out top-notch food in this casual atmosphere. Everything on the menu is made in-house, from the too-good-to-eat-just-one potato chips and spicy beef jerky to the sinful New York–style cheesecake. The lengthy menu includes sandwiches (house-smoked-salmon panini and the Reuben are standouts), meal-sized salads, and an eclectic lineup of house favorites: duck breast with green peppercorn sauce, chicken satay, beer-batter fish-and-chips, fiery shrimp creole, pork tenderloin with sun-dried-cherry chutney. Specials change twice daily (lunch and dinner), and the

Culinary Institute of America–trained Hill has a way with seafood. *$$; AE, MC, V; checks OK; lunch, dinner Tues–Sat; full bar; reservations recommended; across from Ridpath Hotel.* &

The Italian Kitchen / ★

113 N BERNARD ST, SPOKANE; 509/363-1210 Italian is the cuisine du jour for many restaurants, but this trattoria turns out the most authentic fare in Spokane. Chef Bob Staples fills his handmade, tender ravioli with spinach and ricotta or Italian sausage—try it with rich Gorgonzola cream sauce. Lasagne is also built on a foundation of hand-rolled pasta—layered with beef and veal, béchamel, and marinara—and the veal piccata is nicely done. The stylish dining room, done up in warm wood accents and big windows on the street side, dates back to the 1900s. In the lounge, a late-night appetizer menu is served every night. *$$; AE, DIS, MC, V; local checks only; lunch Mon–Fri, dinner every day; full bar; reservations recommended on weekends; 2 blocks south of Opera House.* &

Lindaman's Gourmet-to-Go / ★

1235 GRAND BLVD, SPOKANE; 509/838-3000 This quiet, neighborhood bistro in Spokane's South Hill remains one of the city's most popular places. Lunch and dinner menus are written on a board that hangs above the bustling open kitchen, but the food is also on view in a display case where you order. The menu varies daily, and the casual fare runs the gamut from pine nut–crusted chicken with boursin polenta and roasted-vegetable napoleon to comforting, cheesy casseroles. The house salad with a creamy garlic dressing is not to be missed; same goes for the decadent pastries. Temptations include cheesecake, chocolate sin, and—in summer months—fine fruit pies. The wine selection is exceptional and affordable. *$; AE, MC, V; checks OK; lunch, dinner Mon–Sat; beer and wine; no reservations; www.lindamans.com; near Sacred Heart Medical Center.* &

Luna / ★★★☆

5620 S PERRY ST, SPOKANE; 509/448-2383 If this classy neighborhood spot reminds you of a sun-drenched dining room in California, it's no happy accident. Owners Marcia and William Bond solicited advice from Alice Waters, the queen of nouvelle California cuisine, before they launched their restaurant in 1994. It shows—from the warm welcome to the ever-evolving menu that focuses on fresh ingredients, including herbs and vegetables harvested from a garden just outside the kitchen. First plates might include ahi tuna tartare over mustard greens with wasabi vinaigrette or local mushroom timbale with crispy leeks; main plates offer contemporary takes on classics: coconut curry prawns are a customer favorite. Light eaters can split a plate-sized pizza from the wood-fired oven. Luna has one of the region's best wine lists, with extensive and affordable international selections. For brunch, treat yourself to the delicate hollandaise of Luna's Eggs Benedict or the French toast with carmelized bananas and pecans. *$$$; AE, DIS, MC, V; local checks only; lunch Mon–Fri, dinner every day, brunch Sat–Sun; full bar; reservations recommended; www.lunaspokane.com; corner of 56th St.* &

Mizuna / ★★

214 N HOWARD ST, SPOKANE; 509/747-2004 Spokane's upscale vegetarian restaurant has added seafood to its innovative lineup, in which all dishes feature fresh, seasonal ingredients. At lunch, try the Asian lettuce-wrap—crunchy iceberg leaves enveloping a savory sauté of shiitakes, *seitan*, ginger, and garlic—or the cajun Caesar. For dinner, begin with an appetizer of roasted fall mushrooms with rosemary over warm Brie, then move on to the entrées: popular choices include butternut pecan cannelloni and orange-maple glazed salmon. A cozy wine bar adds to this inviting venue's appeal and offers tastings nightly. *$$$; AE, DIS, MC, V; checks OK; lunch Mon–Fri, dinner Tues–Sat; beer, wine, and specialty cocktails; reservations recommended; www.mizuna.com; just south of Riverfront Park.* &

Niko's II Greek and Middle East Restaurant / ★★

725 W RIVERSIDE AVE, SPOKANE; 509/624-7444 The heart of this downtown restaurant is its sophisticated yet cozy wine bar. Take a tasting tour—several samples of one varietal or a famous wine region—and order the appetizer combo (hummus, *tzatziki, baba gannoujh*) while studying the extensive Mediterranean menu. Solid bets are lamb *souvlakia*, beef kebabs, tomato chutney–topped calamari steak, and chicken curry. Steer clear of dishes with pasta, which can be overcooked. House-made desserts include traditional baklava and elegant crème brûlée. The kitchen stays open until 11pm, with a late-night menu on weekends. *$$; AE, DC, MC, V; checks OK; lunch Mon–Fri, dinner every day; beer and wine; reservations recommended; downtown, at Post St.* &

Paprika / ★★★

1228 S GRAND BLVD, SPOKANE; 509/455-7545 Across the street from the gothic spires of St. John's Cathedral on Spokane's South Hill, this little dining room has the most imaginative food in town. Offerings change seasonally: fall brings warming fare such as elk piccata, sautéed escolar with braised heirloom tomatoes, and rack of pork swimming in a puddle of hard cider sauce. Spring and summer focus on tender greens from local growers and whimsical presentations such as Bloody Mary gazpacho served in a martini glass with a plump prawn. For variety, try chef-owner Karla Graves's weekday bite nights: mini portions at mini prices. The walls at this cozy spot are bathed in the warm tones of the spice for which the restaurant is named. Striking art is painted by the sous-chef, who also prepares some of the desserts. Seasonal creations include updated classics such as a baked Alaska with a creamy Italian meringue. *$$$; AE, MC, V; checks OK; dinner Tues–Sat; beer and wine; reservations recommended; across from St. John's Cathedral.* &

LODGINGS

The Davenport Hotel / ★★★☆

10 S POST ST, SPOKANE; 509/455-8888 OR 800/899-1482 In summer 2002, Spokane's hotel darling revealed its newly renovated property after a facelift that would make any Hollywood surgeon proud, and now it's back to shine its light over Northeast Washington in a grand way. The renovation is truly astounding;

SPOKANE VALLEY WINE TOURING

While few grapes grow in Spokane itself, the area has a healthy wine industry. Seven wineries welcome visitors, especially during the annual spring barrel tasting (usually the first weekend in May) and holiday open house (the weekend before Thanksgiving).

MOUNTAIN DOME WINERY (16315 Temple Rd; 509/928-2788; *www.mountain dome.com*), largely recognized as Washington's finest producer of sparkling wine, is a family-run operation in the foothills of Mount Spokane; tastings and tours are available by appointment.

There's no nicer spot for a picnic than the **CLIFF HOUSE AT ARBOR CREST WINE CELLARS** (4705 Fruithill Rd; 509/927-9463; *www.arborcrest.com*), a historic home that sits high above the Spokane Valley. In summer, enjoy Sunday evening concerts and art exhibits. The family winery has a reputation for fine merlot and sauvignon blanc. The Cliff House tasting room is open noon–5pm daily.

At **LATAH CREEK WINE CELLARS** (13030 E Indiana Ave; 509/926-0164; *www.latahcreek.com*; 9am–5pm), winemaker Mike Conway is almost always on the premises to answer questions about his merlots, cabernets, chardonnay, or their May wine, white wine with strawberry concentrate.

bask in the opulence of the Spanish Renaissance lobby, or take time to walk through and peek into the four ballrooms, all restored to their original condition and wonderful locations for a private party or corporate affair (with 30,000 square feet of meeting space). The 284 guest rooms (each with one king- or two queen-sized beds), including 24 suites, all offer hand-carved, custom-made mahogany furniture, which complements the Travertine marble bathrooms and showers. The many amenities—flat-screen TVs with Lodgenet and Nintendo, high-speed Internet access, and in-room safes—will make you feel spoiled. Separate sleeping and living areas distinguish the deluxe suites, which also feature fireplaces; some offer jetted tubs or wet bars. The Palm Court restaurant features classical Euro-Asian cuisine for breakfast, lunch, and dinner; while the Peacock Room, with its stunning stained-glass ceiling, is an elegant and cozy place to have a brandy. The hotel also features a 24-hour business center, room service, fitness center, indoor lap pool and Jacuzzi, and Spa Paradiso, with a variety of services available to guests. *$$$–$$$$; AE, DC, DIS, MC, V; checks OK; www.thedavenporthotel.com; corner Post and Sprague.* &

Fotheringham House / ★★

2128 W 2ND AVE, SPOKANE; 509/838-1891 Irene and Poul Jensen took over ownership of Fotheringham in spring 2001, bringing with them an aesthetic of pampering guests in high style. The beautifully restored Queen Anne–style mansion in the Browne's Addition neighborhood is entirely and tastefully appointed with period antiques. You don't have to be a politician to enjoy the Mayor's Room, adorned with a four-poster bed draped in delicate lace, a piano desk, and a love seat; it also

KNIPPRATH CELLARS (5634 E Commerce Ave; 509/534-5121; *www.knipprath cellars.com*), located in the old Parkwater Schoolhouse, specializes in varietals crafted in a European style, such as merlot, chardonnay, and a variety of ports, including both tawny and ruby ports. Tasting-room hours are noon–5pm Thurs–Sun, and by appointment.

In an odd juxtaposition, **CATERINA WINERY** (905 N Washington St; 509/328-5069; *www.caterina.com*) sits on the ground floor of the historic Broadview Building, which formerly housed a dairy. Gregarious vintner Michael Scott jokes that's what makes his chardonnays so rich and creamy. The tasting room is open daily, noon–5pm; Friday and Saturday nights the wine bar stays open until 10pm.

At **WYVERN CELLARS** (7217 W 45th Ave; 509/455-7835; tastings 9am–5pm Mon–Fri and noon–5pm Sat–Sun), west of downtown, the friendly tasting-room staff is glad to pour from an extensive lineup that ranges from Riesling to merlot.

The latest addition is **TOWNSHEND CELLAR** (16112 N Greenbluff Rd, Colbert; 509/238-4346; *www.townshendcellar.com*; tastings noon–6pm Fri–Sun), which produces chardonnay, merlot, cabernet, and a huckleberry port.

has a private bath. The Garden Room overlooks an urban bird sanctuary. It shares a bath with the Museum Room and the Mansion Room, named for the historic Patsy Clark mansion across the street. Stroll through the garden in summer and enjoy the lovely lavender display that lines the front walkway. Or enjoy Thursday high tea any time of year—the public is welcome, but make reservations (especially for groups larger than 10). Breakfasts are delicious and may include poached pears, fresh fruit smoothies, and German pancakes with sausage. *$$; MC, V; checks OK; innkeeper@fotheringham.net; www.fotheringham.net; across from Cowley Park.*

Hotel Lusso / ★★★

N 1 POST ST, SPOKANE; 509/747-9750 Step into intimate, romantic Hotel Lusso for our favorite luxury hotel experience in Spokane. Within walking distance of shopping, restaurants, and Riverfront Park, Hotel Lusso was remodeled in 1998, and its new lobby fountain and plush sitting area welcome visitors in splendid style. Guest rooms have oversized windows that offer a view of downtown, although you'll likely turn your gaze inward to the 48 beautifully appointed rooms (all nonsmoking), which include cable TV and Lodgenet, high-speed Internet access, and showers and baths surrounded by Italian marble. Suites feature sitting areas and overstuffed chairs; some have gas fireplaces. Down comforters crown the queen- or king-sized beds; cookies and turn-down service beckon visitors to retire early. Guests are pampered under Lusso's excellent service, which extends to the complimentary breakfast at Fugazzi and complimentary afternoon wine and hors d'oeuvres from 4–6pm every day. Fugazzi restaurant serves European breakfast (every day), lunch (Tues–Fri), and dinner (Tues–Sat); nonsmoking Cavallino Lounge serves dinner (Tues–Sat) and a late-night menu (Fri–Sat 10pm–midnight). *$$$–$$$$; AE, DC, DIS, MC, V; checks OK; www.hotellusso.com; at Post and Sprague.* &

Marianna Stoltz House / ★

427 E INDIANA AVE, SPOKANE; 509/483-4316 OR 800/978-6587 This 1908 four-square home on a tree-lined street near Gonzaga University offers an inviting parlor and living room filled with elegant velvet couches and brocade armchairs. The Blue Room is lit with an ornate chandelier that dates back to when the house was built, and the Green Room has an antique settee. Or try the Ivy Suite, one of our favorites. All have cable TV and air-conditioning. Hostess Phyllis Maguire's attention to detail includes robes, free local calls on the guest phone, a refrigerator to stash beverages, and a ready supply of coffee, tea, and cookies. Breakfast is served in courses, and featured items might include peach-melba parfait, homemade granola, Dutch Baby pancakes, or scrambled eggs tucked into a croissant. *$$; AE, DIS, MC, V; checks OK; info@mariannastolzhouse.com; www.mariannastolzhouse.com; Hamilton St exit off I-90.*

Waverly Place Bed & Breakfast / ★★

709 W WAVERLY PL, SPOKANE; 509/328-1856 OR 866/328-1856 Marge Arndt and her daughter Tammy Arndt are the gracious hosts at this pretty 1902 Victorian located in the Corbin Park historic district just north of downtown. In summer, guests are invited to take a dip in the pool or to linger over afternoon lemonade on the expansive veranda with a view of nearby Corbin Park. The four rooms are on three levels, the grandest quarters being the two-story master suite, with its own sitting room and claw-footed tub in the luxurious bath. Of the two rooms that share a bath, Anna's Room has a window seat that overlooks the park. Breakfast specialties include Swedish pancakes with Idaho huckleberries. *$$; MC, V; checks OK; waverly@waverlyplace.com; www.waverlyplace.com; Division St exit off I-90.*

Pend Oreille and Colville River Valleys

The Pend Oreille Valley remains a hidden secret to many Northeast Washington visitors, and that's just fine with those who come to enjoy the wild terrain, the wildlife, and the region's wide river, the Pend Oreille (pronounced "pon-der-RAY"). The river flows north to Canada, where it dumps into the Columbia just north of the border. The sparsely populated Colville River valley is home to tiny farming and logging communities and is a haven for outdoor recreation, from fishing and boating to cross-country skiing and hunting.

The Pend Oreille

This northernmost corner of the state is generally considered a place to drive through on the way to Canada. In fact, it's nicknamed "the forgotten corner." But don't overlook this delightful region of the state—curve along Highway 20 as it heads north from US Highway 2 at Newport along the **PEND OREILLE RIVER**. The surrounding **SALMO-PRIEST WILDERNESS AREA** is home to grizzly, caribou, and bald eagles, among other elusive wildlife. Its 38 miles of hiking trails traverse 7,300-foot Gypsy Peak. To the west of Metaline Falls, north of Highway 20 on Highway 31, hikers can trek to the Kettle Crest, one of the best hikes in the region. If you're lucky you'll catch a glimpse of black bear, deer, coyotes, and a variety of birds on this 42-mile trip. The Colville branch of the U.S. Forest Service (765 S Main St, Colville; 509/684-7000) has also developed some shorter loop trails that access the crest; the forest service's summer guided wildflower tours here have become so popular that reservations are essential.

Colville and Kettle Falls Area

The working-class feel of a lumber town still personifies Colville and Kettle Falls, tight-knit blue-collar communities where you're likely to spot "Cream of Spotted Owl" bumper stickers on the logging trucks chugging down the road. Kettle Falls is a jumping-off spot for exploring Lake Roosevelt to the south and the Okanogan to the west.

CHEWELAH, 52 miles north of Spokane on US Highway 395, is home to the 18-hole challenging (and inexpensive) **GOLF AND COUNTRY CLUB** (2537 E Sand Canyon; 509/935-6807; *www.chewelahgolf.com*). To the east is the tiny but friendly **49 DEGREES NORTH** ski area (3311 Flowery Trail Rd; 509/935-6649 or 866/376-4949; *www.ski49n.com*), 58 miles northeast of Spokane, which offers free beginner lessons.

Continuing north on US Highway 395, reach Colville, with a quaint Main Street of antique shops and the friendly **TALK AND COFFEE** (119 E Astor Ave; 509/684-2373). When the weather's warm, head for the retro-cool **AUTOVUE DRIVE-IN** (444 AutoVue Rd; 509/684-2863) for first-run movies and special Sunday prices for carloads.

CHINA BEND WINERY (3751 Vineyard Wy; 509/732-6123 or 800/700-6123; *www.chinabend.com*), north of Kettle Falls on Lake Roosevelt, grows organic grapes and has the northernmost vineyards in the state. Owners Bart Loyalty and Victory Israel Alexander are now running a bed-and-breakfast from the winery, as well; their breakfasts and dinners feature gourmet organic meals and organic wines made without sulfites.

Drive west from Kettle Falls on Highway 20, a little-traveled two-lane road, for the multihued splendor of birch and maple trees during fall. Near **SHERMAN PASS** you'll see dramatic remnants of a 1988 forest fire, while the mountain town of **REPUBLIC** offers views of small-town America.

From Republic, Highway 21 heads south to Lake Roosevelt in the Grand Coulee area. If you're hankering to get out and explore the pretty landscape on horseback, head to **K-DIAMOND-K GUEST RANCH** (15661 Hwy 21S; 509/775-3536 or 888/345-5355; *www.kdiamondk.com*). A working dude ranch, it specializes in guided mountain trail rides and down-home hospitality (everyone eats at the family table).

RESTAURANTS

Cafe Italiano

153 W 2ND AVE, COLVILLE; 509/684-5957 This inviting restaurant, with several dining rooms and an outdoor courtyard for summer seating, is run by the Karatzas family. Their Greek heritage shows up on the expansive menu with dishes such as sautéed scampi à la Greca (finished with feta) and filet mignon sautéed with Greek peppers. But the fare is mostly traditional Northern Italian: pastas, pizzas, antipasto, and spumoni, or try the signature veal marsala—always a solid bet. The three to five specials offered daily span the culinary globe, from French to African to Cajun. The house cheesecake is made fresh daily, featuring different toppings. *$$; MC, V; local checks only; lunch Mon–Fri, dinner every day; beer and wine; reservations recommended; 2 blocks west of US Hwy 395.*

Grand Coulee Area

This wonderful area is grand, indeed—from the outsized dimensions of the landscape to the man-made Grand Coulee Dam erected to tame it. The **COLUMBIA RIVER** slices through Northeastern Washington with a quiet power, as the water rushes by in silky strength through enormous chasms. In prehistoric times, glacier-fed water created a river with the largest flow of water ever known. Today it's the second-largest river in the nation, traversing a plateau of equally staggering scale.

Some 15 miles upstream of Grand Coulee Dam, the tiny **KELLER FERRY** (on Hwy 21; 800/695-7623, ext 511) shuttles across the Columbia dozens of times a day at no charge; the *Martha S.* holds just a dozen cars. The crossing takes 15 minutes to traverse the waterborne section of Highway 21, the link between the Colville Indian Reservation to the north of the river and the Columbia Plateau on the south. On the Grand Coulee side is a small store run by the Colville Tribe that sells fishing licenses and some groceries, and rents boats.

For many years **LAKE ROOSEVELT**, the massive 150-mile-long reservoir created by Grand Coulee Dam, was untapped by the RV-on-pontoon fleets. Now several companies offer weekly (or weekend, for a hefty price) **HOUSEBOAT RENTALS**. Some of these vessels have deluxe features such as on-deck hot tubs, stereo systems, gourmet kitchens, and outdoor rinse-off showers. For rates and reservations, contact **ROOSEVELT RECREATIONAL ENTERPRISES** (800/648-LAKE; *www.rrehousboats.com*) or **LAKE ROOSEVELT RESORT & MARINA** (800/635-7585; *www.lakeroosevelt.com*).

Grand Coulee Dam

Clustered around Grand Coulee Dam are the towns of Grand Coulee, Coulee Dam, and Electric City. The **GRAND COULEE DAM** (509/633-9265 or 800/268-5332) is a marvel of engineering and harkens back to a time when man-made dams were the cutting edge of design. Sometimes referred to as the seventh wonder of the world, the dam was conceived as an irrigation project and now supplies water to more than

INLAND NORTHWEST GOLF

When *Golf Digest* named Spokane one of the best places in the country to play on public links, some of the city's duffers were perturbed. It wasn't that they disagreed; they simply didn't want to share their secret.

The good news is, with so many courses in the area—40 within a half-day drive of Spokane—no one should have trouble getting a tee time. And most of those courses are still reasonably priced, averaging less than $30 for 18 holes. Visit *www.spokane parks.org/golf* for general information on city golf courses.

The venerable **INDIAN CANYON** (4304 W West Dr; 509/747-5353) is considered the most beautiful links around—its sweeping fairways are lined with majestic ever-greens. The 19th hole is especially appealing (sit on the deck and enjoy the view) after uphill jaunts on the 17th and 18th holes.

The newest city course, the **CREEK AT QUALCHAN** (301 E Meadowland Rd; 509/448-9317), is rife with water hazards, while one of the oldest courses, **ESMER-ALDA GOLF COURSE** (3933 E Courtland Ave; 509/487-6291), remains a challenge to duffers mostly due to the more than 2,000 trees that edge the fairways.

County and municipal courses include a couple of beauties that sit side by side east of Spokane (visit *www.spokanecounty.org/parks/golfcourses.htm* for more information). **LIBERTY LAKE** (24403 E Sprague Ave; 509/255-6233) nestles up against a wooded hillside, which comes into play on several holes. Golfers are rewarded for their efforts with a fine view of the lake on the 18th green. The neighboring **MEADOWWOOD** (24501 E Valleyview Ave, Liberty Lake; 509/455-9539), which was given *Golf Digest's* four-star seal of approval, is long and rambling with open fairways lined with tricky roughs. Another county course, **HANGMAN VALLEY** (2210 E Hangman Valley Rd; 509/448-1212), has an almost desertlike landscape, with some fine valley views from elevated par fives. You can find information for all three courses at *www.spokanecounty .org/parks/golfcourses.htm*.

—Leslie Kelly

500,000 acres of farmland. World War II gave it a new purpose, generating power for the production of plutonium at Hanford and aluminum for aircraft. As tall as a 46-story building and the length of a dozen city blocks, the dam was completed in 1942. The **VISITOR ARRIVAL CENTER** is open seven days a week and features movies and exhibits; during summer months (end of May through August), the laser light show is a spectacular treat. Visit the **GRAND COULEE DAM AREA CHAMBER OF COMMERCE** (319 Midway Ave; 800/268-5332; *www.grandcouleedam.org*) for more information. If you're feeling lucky, stop in at the **COULEE DAM CASINO** (515 Birch St; 509/633-0766).

RESTAURANTS

La Presa / ★

515 E GRAND COULEE AVE, GRAND COULEE; 509/633-3173 The Hernandez family doesn't make a big deal about calling its food "authentic Mexican," but it is. Most authentic of the 126 dishes featured by the Hernandez clan are the carne asada (cooked over a charcoal fire), the chorizo with eggs, and the dark, cinnamon-scented chicken mole. The menu is huge, with all sorts of steaks and seafood dishes. There's even (oddly enough) chicken teriyaki. You won't go wrong with traditional favorites such as the enchilada verde, made with fresh tomatillos. The decor is strictly velvet paintings and wool blankets, but the welcome is warm and the margaritas are icy cold. *$; DIS, MC, V; checks OK; lunch, dinner every day; full bar; reservations recommended; on Hwy 21, just up from dam.* &

Soap Lake

Soap Lake earned its name on a windy day, when frothy whitecaps dotted the surface of this lake. Many believe the lake, known for its high content of soft minerals (which also gives it a soapy feel), has healing properties. Contact the **SOAP LAKE CHAMBER OF COMMERCE** (300 N Daisy St; 509/246-1821; *www.soaplakecoc.org*) for information on renting canoes and sailboats.

DRY FALLS, off Highway 17 north of town, is an example of the power of ice. When glacial Lake Missoula overflowed its ice-age dam some 12,000 years ago, torrential floods headed west to the Pacific. The force of the water carved out what is now this ancient waterfall, 3½ miles wide and 400 feet high (by comparison, Niagara Falls is 1 mile wide and 165 feet high). The **DRY FALLS INTERPRETIVE CENTER** (inside Sun Lakes State Park, 4 miles southwest of Coulee City on Hwy 17; 509/632-5583), at the top of the canyon a half mile from the scenic overlook, is open every day 10am–6pm, May through September.

SUN LAKES STATE PARK (888/226-7688; *www.parks.wa.gov*), downstream from the falls, offers all kinds of outdoor activities: hiking, canoeing, camping, swimming, boating, fishing, golf, horseback riding, and simple picnicking.

LODGINGS

Notaras Lodge

13 CANNA ST, SOAP LAKE; 509/246-0462 Soap Lake's renowned mineral waters are on tap in the bathrooms, several of which have in-room whirlpools. The lodge was rebuilt after a 1998 fire, and the 15 rooms retain their charm, inspired by Western history—or, for some rooms, a Western character. The Mrs. No room, named after owner Marina Romary's mother, is highlighted by Tennessee cedar woodwork; Luck of the Draw, which you enter by pulling a slot machine handle, tempts guests to visit area casinos. All four lodge buildings are log-cabin style and are right on the lake; six rooms have lake views, and five offer in-room whirlpools. Romary also runs Don's Restaurant (14 Canna St; 509/246-1217; lunch Sun–Fri, dinner every day), which specializes in steak, seafood, and Greek entrées. *$–$$; MC, V; checks OK; notaras@televar.com; www.notaraslodge.com; Soap Lake exit off Hwy 28, at Canna St.* &

Omak

Omak is a town of 4,000, located 50 miles north of Grand Coulee on Highway 155. The climax of the **OMAK STAMPEDE** (509/826-1002 or 800/933-6625; *www.omak stampede.org*) is the famous—and controversial—Suicide Race, when riders drive horses 210 feet downhill at a 62-degree angle, plow through the Okanagon River, and cross 500 feet of Colville Indian land. It routinely injures (or even kills) horses and remains a divisive attraction. The popular rodeo is held the second weekend of August; during the Stampede, Omak's population swells to 30,000.

LODGINGS

The Rodeway Inn

122 N MAIN, OMAK; 509/826-0400 OR 888/700-6625 This basic hotel has the distinction of being the closest lodging to the Stampede grounds. Its 61 rooms include remote-control satellite TV, several Jacuzzi suites, and a few units with kitchens. There are smoking and nonsmoking rooms and an outdoor swimming pool; pets OK. *$; AE, DIS, MC, V; checks OK; next to movie theater.*

VANCOUVER AND ENVIRONS

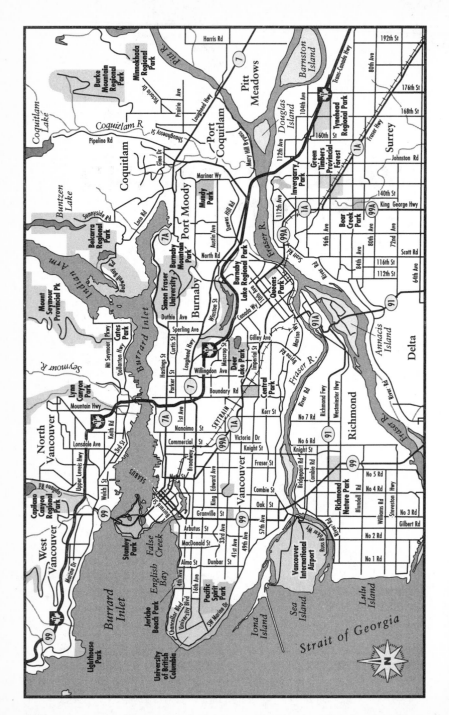

VANCOUVER AND ENVIRONS

The Vancouver area is Canada's fastest-growing metropolis, and the next several years are an opportune time to visit. Preparations are underway for the 2010 Olympic Winter Games, including renovations to existing venues, construction of new facilities, and improvements on the scenic Sea to Sky Highway (which links the lower mainland to Whistler). Vancouverites are excited and proud to show off their home to the rest of the world, and Whistler, already known as a top ski-and-snowboard resort, can now boast an urban sophistication on par with Vancouver.

This city, nestled between mountains and ocean, has long touted itself as Canada's gateway to the Pacific Rim, and British Columbia is fortunate to be plugged into what is still the world's fastest-growing economy. In fact, Vancouver has always accepted the waves of legal immigrants that have landed on its shore. The city seems living proof that a benign environment will produce an easygoing disposition.

ACCESS AND INFORMATION

VANCOUVER INTERNATIONAL AIRPORT (9 miles/15 km south of downtown on Sea Island; 604/207-7077; *www.yvr.ca*) is a major international airport with daily flights to every continent. It has been consistently ranked first among North American airports of its size according to statistics compiled by the International Air Transport Association of Geneva. For advice and basic directions, newcomers can turn to an army of about 200 Green Coats, volunteer goodwill ambassadors for the airport authority who are on hand to greet every flight. Several **CAR RENTAL** agencies, including Avis (604/606-2847), Budget (604/668-7000), and National (604/273-3121), are located on the ground floor of the three-level parkade.

Weathered but still graceful, **PACIFIC CENTRAL STATION** (1150 Station St) is the local terminus of several regional, national, and international bus and rail services. **GREYHOUND CANADA** (604/482-8747 or 800/231-2222; *www.greyhound .ca*) operates five buses daily between Vancouver and Seattle, with connections in Seattle to other U.S. points. **PACIFIC COACH LINES** (604/662-8074 or 800/661-1725; *www.pacificcoach.com*) operates a modern bus service between Vancouver and Victoria via **BC FERRIES** (250/386-3431 or 888/223-3779; *www.bcferries .bc.ca*). **VIA RAIL** (800/561-8630 or 888/VIA-RAIL; *www.viarail.ca*) is Canada's national passenger rail service. **AMTRAK** (800/872-7245; *www.amtrak.com*) trains make daily runs between Seattle and Vancouver.

Travelers by car choose between two major highways. **HIGHWAY 99**, the main north-south highway connecting Vancouver to Seattle, leads south from the city across the fertile delta at the mouth of the Fraser River and connects with Washington State's Interstate 5. Highway 99 also connects Vancouver to the ski resort town of Whistler, about two hours north, and is known as the **SEA TO SKY HIGHWAY**. Transcontinental **HIGHWAY 1**, the main east-west highway, arrives from the east through lower BC mainland and terminates in Vancouver; it runs along the south shore of the Fraser River. Another alternate route is **HIGHWAY 7**, which runs east-west along the north shore.

Western British Columbia is blessed by a temperate maritime climate, and Vancouver's **WEATHER** is the mildest in Canada, thanks to ocean currents and major weather patterns that bring warm, moist air in waves from the Pacific year-round. Spring comes early (by mid-March, usually); July and August are warmest; late summer and autumn days (through October) tend to be warm and sunny, with the occasional shower. Winter is rainy season—roughly November through March—but rain usually falls as showers or drizzle. Heavy continuous downpours are rare, as are thunderstorms and strong winds.

Vancouver

Vancouver, its residents are fond of saying, is one of the few cities in the world where you can go snowboarding and sailing on the same day. How remarkable, then, that it should also be one of the few where, sitting outside a Neapolitan café, you can eavesdrop on an impassioned argument in Hungarian and see graffiti in Khmer. It's also a festive city, with art everywhere, and a fashionable shopping strip—Robson Street—often compared to posh Rodeo Drive in Beverly Hills. Yet glance away from the opulence of the shops as you saunter along Robson and, at the end of a side street, the peaceful waters of Burrard Inlet lap at the shore. Beyond, the mountains on the North Shore glitter with snow for half the year.

No city is homogenous, particularly Vancouver. It's really an amalgam of 23 neighborhoods, each with its own unique character and stories. **YALETOWN**, a whirling high-tech zone that's a case of gentrification gone right, looks across to the glittering condos on the south shore of False Creek. Home to one of the largest urban redevelopment projects ever attempted in North America, the **FALSE CREEK BASIN** has its natural center in the bustling market area and arts community on **GRANVILLE ISLAND**. Equally dynamic alternative cultures of different sorts flourish in **KITSILANO** (known as "Kits," a funky, former low-rent haven for hippies that has been yuppified by baby boomers and young families) and the **WEST END** (home to Canada's most densely populated neighborhood and western Canada's largest gay and lesbian community). The West End is just south of Stanley Park; Kits is west across False Creek. The cultural mix along **COMMERCIAL DRIVE** is the contemporary home of bohemian subculture, where members of Vancouver's lesbian community can be seen alongside the graying curmudgeons of an older generation sipping espresso outside one of the many cafés. If the High Street style of British society is more to your liking, amble over to **AMBLESIDE** and rub shoulders with the sensible-shoe set browsing the private art galleries and lunching on pork pies.

The city's public transit system is an efficient way to get around town; **COAST MOUNTAIN TRANSLINK** (604/521-0400; *www.translink.bc.ca*) covers more than 695 square miles (1,800 square km) with three forms of transit: bus, SeaBus, and SkyTrain. More information is available from the **VANCOUVER TOURIST INFO CENTRE** (200 Burrard St; 604/683-2000; *www.tourismvancouver.com*).

MUSEUMS AND GALLERIES
Downtown's **VANCOUVER ART GALLERY** (750 Hornby St; 604/662-4719; *www.vanartgallery.bc.ca*) was once Francis Rattenbury's elegant old courthouse. It now holds more than 20 major exhibitions a year, and a permanent collection that includes works by Goya, Emily Carr, Gainsborough, and Picasso. Many of the city's

commercial galleries are located on the dozen blocks just south of the Granville Bridge; art galleries here represent internationally renowned painters and photographers. Granville Island, site of the **EMILY CARR INSTITUTE OF ART AND DESIGN** (1399 Johnston St; 604/844-3800; *www.eciad.bc.ca*), has a number of pottery and craft studios. Look for avant-garde art at spaces such as the **MONTE CLARK GALLERY** (2339 Granville St; 604/730-5000; *www.monteclarkgallery.com*).

THE **MUSEUM OF ANTHROPOLOGY** at the University of British Columbia (6393 NW Marine Dr; 604/822-3825; *www.moa.ubc.ca*) has an extensive collection of artifacts from coastal British Columbia Native American cultures (including an impressive display of totem poles and two Haida houses), as well as artifacts from Africa and the Orient.

While away a rainy afternoon in the **GRANVILLE ISLAND MUSEUMS** (1502 Duranleau St; 604/683-1939; *www.granvilleislandmuseums.com*), actually three museums in one building: the **SPORT FISHING MUSEUM** holds the world's biggest public display of recreational fishing artifacts; the **MODEL SHIP MUSEUM** features miniature watercraft—from tugs to battleships to working model subs; and the **MODEL TRAIN MUSEUM** has an impressive collection of toy and model trains, along with a diorama of the Fraser Valley Canyon done in stunning detail—right down to each of the 5,000 handmade trees. Admission to any one of the museums covers all three.

PARKS AND GARDENS

Vancouver's climate is similar to Britain's and is well suited for flowers and greenery. Take a walk through the quiet rain forest in the heart of **STANLEY PARK** (west end of Beach and W Georgia Sts to Lions Gate Bridge; 604/257-8400). This 1,000-acre in-city park is within walking distance of the trendy shops of Robson Street, but feels worlds away; its appeal includes the seawall, formal rose gardens, Vancouver Rowing Club, Vancouver Aquarium, restaurants, painters, totem poles, horse-drawn tours, and numerous wilderness trails. At **QUEEN ELIZABETH PARK**, dramatic winding paths, sunken gardens, and waterfalls skirt the **BLOEDEL CONSERVATORY** (Cambie St and 33rd Ave; 604/257-8570). Near Queen Elizabeth Park, **VANDUSEN BOTANICAL GARDEN** (5251 Oak St; 604/878-9274; *www.vandusen garden.org*) stretches over 55 acres.

THE **UNIVERSITY OF BRITISH COLUMBIA** (UBC campus, 6804 SW Marine Dr; 604/822-9666; *www.ubcbotanicalgarden.org*) boasts superb gardens—the Botanical Garden, Nitobe Memorial Gardens, and Totem Park—along with the Physick Garden, which re-creates a 16th-century monastic herb garden. The **CHINESE CLASSICAL GARDEN** (578 Carrall St; 604/662-3207; *www.vancouver chinesegarden.com*) within Dr. Sun Yat-Sen Park is a spectacular reconstruction of a Chinese scholar's garden, complete with pavilions and water walkways. **KITSILANO BEACH** (Cornwall Ave and Arbutus St, bordering English Bay) is a year-round haven for joggers, dog-walkers, and evening strollers.

SHOPPING

Vancouver has always been bursting with storefronts. In **YALETOWN** (bordered by Pacific Blvd and Nelson, Cambie, and Seymour Sts), brick warehouses have been transformed into loft apartments, offices, chic shops housing ultrahip clothing

VANCOUVER THREE-DAY TOUR

DAY ONE: Start your day at the **GRANVILLE ISLAND PUBLIC MARKET** (1661 Duranleau St; 604/666-6655). It opens at 9am and it's a good place to turn breakfast into a progressive meal: a chai at the **GRANVILLE ISLAND TEA CO.** (#117 1689 Johnston St; 604/683-7491), apple focaccia from **TERRA BREADS** (#107 1689 Johnston St; 604/685-3102), candied salmon from **SEAFOOD CITY** (#143 1689 Johnston St; 604/688-1818). After exploring the shops, studios, and galleries, hop on an aquabus to Yaletown and check into the hip **OPUS HOTEL** or the **YWCA HOTEL/ RESIDENCE**. Next stop: **CHINATOWN**, for dim sum at **HON'S WUN TUN HOUSE** and a guided tour through the **DR. SUN YAT-SEN CLASSICAL CHINESE GARDEN**, before walking the frenzied streets looking for jade treasures or tasting steamed buns from one of Chinatown's many bakeries. Return to your room and change for a run along the **STANLEY PARK SEAWALL** before heading to dinner (with a sunset) at the **RAINCITY GRILL** or the **PARKSIDE**.

DAY TWO: After your first cup of strong coffee at the hotel, head west to the **KITSI- LANO** neighborhood for breakfast—big portions of eggs, pancakes, and waffles are on deck at **SOPHIE'S COSMIC CAFE**. Next, head to the University of British Columbia and the **MUSEUM OF ANTHROPOLOGY** to see jaw-droppingly impressive First

stores (Global Atomic Designs, Atomic Model, Vasanji), high-end home furnishings (Chintz and Company, Liberty, Bernstein & Gold), and the city's most vibrant restaurants. **ROBSON STREET** (between Beatty St and Stanley Park) is the meeting place of cultures and couture, as *tout le monde* strolls among its many boutiques and restaurants. Weekends are crowded, but there's lots to see, from art books, jewelry, and gifts by local artists at the **GALLERY SHOP** in the Vancouver Art Gallery to a string of international fashion stores (Zara, Banana Republic, Nike, French Connection, Gap, Club Monaco), and local fashion chains (Lululemon, Aritzia, Zioni, Boys' Co.). At Robson and Homer, you'll find the main branch of the Vancouver Public Library, designed by world-renowned architect Moshe Safdie and inspired by the Roman Coliseum. Its store **BOOKMARK** (604/331-4040) has literary gifts.

Downtown is full of outstanding shops. In poor weather, head underground to **PACIFIC CENTRE** (700 W Georgia St to 777 Dunsmuir St; 604/688-7236; *www .pacificcentre.ca*), downtown's biggest and busiest mall, with more than 140 outlets, including name retailers **HOLT RENFREW** and **SEARS**, which connects to **VAN- COUVER CENTRE** (604/688-5658). Also downtown is **SINCLAIR CENTRE** (757 W Hastings St; 604/659-1009; *www.sinclaircentre.com*), a striking example of the reclaimed-heritage school of architecture. It contains the high-end designer department store **LEONE**, as well as **PLAZA ESCADA**.

South Granville, from Granville Bridge toward 16th Avenue, borders on the prestigious **SHAUGHNESSY NEIGHBORHOOD** and caters to the carriage trade

Nations artifacts, and the **UBC BOTANICAL GARDEN**, the oldest and one of the finest gardens in Canada. Leave time to freshen up at your hotel before you walk over to the **SUTTON PLACE HOTEL** for high tea or Japanese tea in **FLEURI**. Then stroll **ROBSON STREET**, a trendy boulevard of pret-a-porter boutiques and swank eateries. If you'd like to see a live show—pop, jazz, or an evening at the symphony—walk over to **GRANVILLE STREET**, where the Commodore Ballroom, Orpheum Theatre, and Vogue Theatre sometimes have last-minute tickets available before 8pm. Afterward, treat yourself to a late-night snack of "tapatizers" at **BIN 941 TAPAS PARLOUR**.

DAY THREE: Start the morning in West Vancouver with raspberry scones and hot chocolate at the **SAVARY ISLAND PIE COMPANY**. After breakfast, leisurely browse the shops in Ambleside and Dundarave. Then it's off to **LIGHTHOUSE PARK**'s 1914 lighthouse (Marine Dr at Beaton Ln, West Vancouver) and the rocky outcrop of **POINT ATKINSON**—and its stunning city view. Back in Yaletown, have chowder and a beer at **RODNEY'S OYSTER HOUSE** or sushi and sake at **BLUE WATER CAFE** before browsing upscale boutiques. For dinner, go all out with a four-star meal at **LUMIÈRE** or **WEST**.

with art galleries, British and Occidental antique stores, and a crop of upper-end lifestyle designer clothing and housewares shops. Under the Granville Street Bridge on **GRANVILLE ISLAND** (604/666-5784), warehouses and factories have been transformed into a public market and craft shops. Some of the best local designers are located in the Net Loft building, and the island also has more than 50 shops catering to the marine industry. At the **GRANVILLE ISLAND PUBLIC MARKET** (1689 Johnston St; 604/666-5784; *www.granvilleisland.bc.ca*), you can get everything from ocean-caught and candied salmon to artisan cheese to the best doughnuts in the city.

South Main used to be one of Vancouver's fringe neighborhoods. Today, **SOUTH MAIN**, or **SOMA**—as locals call the area around Main Street and Broadway—has become Vancouver's hottest new shopping district. **EUGENE CHOO** (3683 Main St; 604/874-9773) is the *it* boutique and **BAKER'S DOZEN** (3520 Main St; 604/879-3348) is known around the globe for its rare collection of antique toys and collectibles.

The oldest and biggest of Vancouver's ethnic communities is **CHINATOWN** (off Main St, on Pender and Keefer Sts). The Chinese groceries and apothecaries have been there for generations, and many display remnants of Vancouver's recent-past status as a neon mecca. For jade treasures, don't miss **CHICOCHAI ANTIQUES** (539 Columbia; 604/685-8116). During the summer, there's a weekend open-air night market (6pm–midnight) at Main and Keefer Streets. Vancouver's 60,000 East Indian immigrants have established their own shopping area, called the **PUNJABI MARKET** (in south Vancouver at 49th and Main Sts), where you can bargain for a custom-fit *salwar kameez,* Rajastani jewelry, or the latest Bollywood blockbuster on DVD or videotape.

In West Vancouver, **PARK ROYAL** has the distinction of being Canada's first shopping mall as well as the North Shore's largest and most prestigious shopping center. It straddles Marine Drive in West Vancouver, just across Lions Gate Bridge from the city. (Out-of-towners note: It's too far to walk from downtown, so take the bus or drive.)

PERFORMING ARTS

Theater

THE CENTRE IN VANCOUVER FOR PERFORMING ARTS (777 Homer St; 604/602-0616; *www.centreinvancouver.com*) showcases touring mega-musicals. The multi-million-dollar theater was designed by Moshe Safdie (who also designed Library Square). The two most striking features are the intimacy of the auditorium and the visual power of the seven-story, mirrored-wall grand staircase that unites all levels. The elegant **QUEEN ELIZABETH THEATRE** (Hamilton and W Georgia; 604/665-3050; *www.city.vancouver.bc.ca/theatres*) is still one of Vancouver's main venues for the **VANCOUVER OPERA** (*www.vanopera.bc.ca*) and **BALLET BRITISH COLUMBIA** (*www.balletbc.com*). Next door, the 670-seat (every seat a good one) **VANCOUVER PLAYHOUSE THEATRE COMPANY** (604/873-3311; *www.vancouverplayhouse .com*) presents contemporary and classical productions with spectacular sets, luscious costumes, and terrific soundscapes. In the heart of lively Granville Island, the **GRANVILLE ISLAND STAGE** (1585 Johnston St; 604/687-1644) and neighboring **REVUE STAGE** (604/687-1644) have become local institutions. The latter is home to the award-winning improvisational **VANCOUVER THEATRESPORTS LEAGUE**. A raunchy late-show, *Scared Scriptless,* is not to be missed on weekends at 11:45pm. Contemporary theater in Vancouver is largely centered in the **VANCOUVER EAST CULTURAL CENTRE** (1895 E Venables St; 604/251-1363; *www.vecc.bc.ca*), known to locals as the Cultch.

Music

Over the past decade, the city has witnessed a renaissance in the proliferation of classical, jazz, and world music. Under the leadership of music director Bramwell Tovey, the 74-member **VANCOUVER SYMPHONY ORCHESTRA** (884 Granville St; 604/876-3434; *www.vancouversymphony.ca*) should continue to pursue artistic heights. The **VANCOUVER OPERA** (Hamilton at W Georgia; 604/683-0222; *www.vanopera.bc.ca*) presents four to five productions a year at the Queen Elizabeth Theatre. The **VANCOUVER INTERNATIONAL JAZZ FESTIVAL** (604/872-5200; *www.jazzvancouver.com*) attracts crowds of more than 250,000 jazz lovers each June, and the annual **VANCOUVER FOLK MUSIC FESTIVAL** (604/602-9798; *www.thefestival.bc.ca*) is extremely popular, too. **TICKETMASTER** (604/280-4444; *www.ticketmaster.com*) has more information about musical events and venues.

FOOD AND WINE

Vancouver has become internationally renowned as a gastronomic destination as chefs bring a wealth of multicultural influences to their craft and are totally committed to unparalleled regional ingredients. You'll also find wide-ranging international wine lists, the breadth and depth of which you seldom encounter elsewhere. Two of the city's most popular events are **DINE OUT VANCOUVER** and the **VANCOUVER PLAYHOUSE INTERNATIONAL WINE FESTIVAL**. For two weeks in January and February, Tourism Vancouver showcases Vancouver's best restaurants during Dine Out with exceptional three-course dinner menus offered at $15 and $25. In the spring, the Wine Festival, now in its third decade, attracts more than 150 new and Old World wineries and is considered one of North America's premier consumer and trade wine events. For up-to-the-minute food and wine news, tune in to "The Best of Food & Wine" on CFUN 1410 AM (noon–1pm Saturdays).

NIGHTLIFE

On an evening out in Vancouver, you can enjoy just about every clubbing experience imaginable, from an old-time rock 'n' roll bender to a no-holds-barred striptease show, to a till-dawn rave in a factory warehouse. A piano player rules the roost weekends at the tony **BACCHUS RISTORANTE** (845 Hornby St; 604/608-5319) to serenade imbibers with everything from soft rock to old standards. Live pop, world music, and electronica are the lures that attract schools of new-music aficionados to the **COMMODORE BALLROOM** (868 Granville St; 604/739-SHOW). For live jazz, head to the **CELLAR JAZZ CLUB** (3611 W Broadway; 604/738-1959; *www.cellarjazz.com*). To find out who's playing where, the best sources for up-to-date listings are the *Georgia Straight* (*www.straight.com*) and the Thursday entertainment section of the *Vancouver Sun* (*www.vancouversun.com*). For daily concert updates, contact **TICKETMASTER** (604/280-4444; *www.ticketmaster.ca*).

SPORTS AND RECREATION

Cycling, running, hiking, and water sports are all popular here. A good in-city route for runners or in-line skaters is along the 6½-mile (10.5 km) **STANLEY PARK SEAWALL**. A good one-stop source for bicycling information, including maps and guidebooks, is **CYCLING BRITISH COLUMBIA** (332-1367 W Broadway; 604/737-3034; *www.cycling.bc.ca*). Contact the **OUTDOOR RECREATION COUNCIL OF BRITISH COLUMBIA** (334-1367 W Broadway; 604/737-3058; *www.orcbc.ca*) to reach the Canoeing Association, Whitewater Kayaking Association, or Sea Kayaking Association of British Columbia, or for more information on other sports.

The best bet for spectator sports fans is the NHL's **VANCOUVER CANUCKS**, playing at **GENERAL MOTORS PLACE** (800 Griffiths Wy; 604/899-7400; *www.canucks.com*). The faithful stick with the team through good times and bad, and that makes getting tickets a challenge. Closer to downtown, the Canadian Football League's **BC LIONS** play at **BC PLACE STADIUM** (777 Pacific Blvd; 604/589-7627; *www.bclions.com*). Vancouver's diverse ethnicity has created a ready-made audience for soccer, especially among homesick Brits, Portuguese, and Italians. **SWANGARD STADIUM** (intersection of Boundary Rd and Kingsway; 604/899-9823) hosts the **VANCOUVER WHITECAPS** (once known as the 86ers). Tickets for most sporting events are available at the gates or through **TICKETMASTER** (604/280-4444; *www.ticketmaster.com*). Thoroughbreds race at **HASTINGS PARK** (Hastings St and Renfrew St; 604/254-1631; *www.hastingspark.com*; mid-Apr–Nov), on the grounds of the Pacific National Exhibition.

RESTAURANTS

Aqua Riva / ★★

30-200 GRANVILLE ST, VANCOUVER; 604/683-5599 Located near the working part of Vancouver's inner harbor and adjacent to Canada Place, Aqua River boasts a splendid view outside that melds with the spectacular marine mural and wavy ceiling inside. The servers are so friendly you almost want to share a glass or two with them. Mario Fortin, sous chef from the time Aqua Riva's doors opened seven years ago, has moved up a notch and the executive chef toque fits him well. The proof is in the prawn spring rolls (torpedoes of flavor explosions); the *panko*-fried baby beach oysters, fresh and delicate; and the house smoked-salmon-and-shellfish spaghettini in a roast garlic and basil-infused olive oil, each bite of mussel, clam, and prawn retaining its delicate identity against the robust smoky salmon. The oven-baked thinnest crust pizzas and slow barbecued ribs are also good choices. Considering the opulent room, the prices are surprisingly reasonable. The wine list is good, and many BC wines are featured, most by the glass. *$$; AE, DC, E, MC, V; no checks; lunch, dinner every day, brunch Sun May–Oct; full bar; no reservations; dinner@aquariva.com; www.aquariva.com; at Howe St.* &

Bacchus Ristorante / ★★★

845 HORNBY ST (THE WEDGEWOOD HOTEL), VANCOUVER; 604/608-5319 Wonderfully romantic, this elegant retreat in one of the city's best hotels and is consistently rated "most romantic restaurant in Vancouver." Dark wood paneling and deep burgundy velvet couches are accented by huge bouquets of flowers, creating private niches. At lunch, Bacchus attracts the legal beagles from the courthouse for roast of the day, pizza Bacchus, or the gnocchi with spinach and Parmesan. The changing dinner menu might include pastrami of crab rolls with mango and mint, roasted loin of peppered venison, or a classic coq au vin. Hope that the mango tarte Tatin happens to be on the menu, or surrender to the opera cake. Best of all, Bacchus offers fine French cheese, fine wines, and servers who cater to your every whim. Nightly except Sunday, a pianist tickles the ivories. Stogie aficionados have free rein in the cigar room. *$$$; AE, DC, MC, V; no checks; breakfast, lunch, dinner every day, brunch Sat–Sun; full bar; reservations required; info@wedgewoodhotel .com; www.wedgewoodhotel.com; between Robson and Smithe Sts.* &

Bin 941 Tapas Parlour / ★★★
Bin 942 Tapas Parlour / ★★★

941 DAVIE ST, VANCOUVER; 604/683-1246 / 1521 W BROADWAY, VANCOUVER; 604/734-9421 Get to these stylish tapas bars early: the shoebox-sized restaurants are funky and madcap and with only 40 seats, lineups spill into the street, often before opening. Here, it's all about sharing. Order three or four dishes for two and they come up one at a time. The "tapatizers" change as often as the decor, but some are here to stay: flank steak with maple-chipotle glaze surrounding a nest of the skinniest shoestring fries; the wild sockeye salmon atop Waldorf salad with miso aioli; the mussels TKO with fresh habañeros; and the Navajo fried bread is good with anything. Nothing's over $10. Chef-owner Gord Martin has Mexican infusions throughout the menu. Sit at the bar and watch the frenetic action from the closet-sized kitchen, guaranteed as entertaining and educational as any show on the Food Network. They don't have time or space for complicated cocktails or nonfat vanilla lattes, but instead supply wines by the glass, craft beers, and a selection of single-malt scotch. *$$; MC, V; no checks; dinner every day; beer, wine, liqueurs; reservations recommended; www.bin941.com; between Burrard and Howe Sts (Bin 941), between Fir and Granville Sts (Bin 942).* &

Bishop's / ★★★★

2183 W 4TH AVE, VANCOUVER; 604/738-2025 Where better to eat than in this simple two-level restaurant, long a fixture on busy W Fourth Avenue? "Nowhere" is the answer; John Bishop is the reason. One of the city's first restaurant owners to support local, seasonal ingredients, Bishop proudly states that his restaurant is almost 100 percent organic. Bishop warmly greets his guests (celebrity and otherwise) and demonstrates that he understands personal service, hovering over each table serving, pouring, discussing. Chef Dennis Green's entrées are uncomplicated. Dungeness crab is perfectly matched with pear-cranberry chutney, and wild sockeye or spring salmon is grilled to perfection—while in season, of course. The rack of lamb with goat cheese–mashed potatoes, and sablefish (smoked then steamed, with truffle brandade cake and herb horseradish sabayon) are standouts. Expect light, subtly complex flavors and bright, graphic color. Desserts, such as the moist ginger cake pooled in toffee sauce and the Death by Chocolate, are legendary. Manager Abel Jacinto oversees an eclectic list of fine wines, including more than 50 half bottles. *$$$–$$$$; AE, DC, MC, V; no checks; dinner every day (closed 2 weeks in Jan); full bar; reservations required; inquire@bishopsonline.com; www.bishopsonline.com; between Yew and Arbutus Sts.*

Bistro Pastis / ★★★

2153 W 4TH AVE, VANCOUVER; 604-731-5020 Formerly Pastis, this high-end establishment has morphed into an affordable yet still elegant bistro. With hardwood floors, bold and bright paintings, and mirrors from every wall reflecting well-dressed diners, the room bustles with top-notch staff dishing out authentic bistro choices such as bouillabaisse or New York steak with *pommes frites* and your choice of béarnaise or peppercorn sauce. Set your gastronomic mood with escargot fritters, parsley coulis, and garlic confit—a new take on an old theme, much like the rest of the menu. Try the clever and sublime combination of grilled sablefish with truffle smoked black cod, or the unctuous roasted duck breast with organic beets and cider jus. Ask about the three- or five-course dinners, $45–$60. The smart wine list has many half bottles. *$$–$$$; AE, MC, V; no checks; lunch Tues–Fri, dinner every day, brunch Sat–Sun; full bar; reservations recommended; pastis@telus.net; www.pastis .ca; just west of Arbutus.*

Blue Water Cafe / ★★★☆

1095 HAMILTON ST, VANCOUVER; 604/688-8078 We can't think of a better way to spend an evening than bar-hopping in this posh seafood restaurant in Yaletown. First stop in this 100-year-old converted warehouse: the main bar, to slurp Fanny Bay oysters and sip B.C.'s Blue Mountain Brut. Next stop: the raw bar, for Yoshi's elaborate sushi rolls with chilled sake. Finally, settle into a plush banquette for the

GREASY SPOONS

Greasy-spoon restaurants are fast becoming an endangered species. But like an aging boxer, they refuse to go down, standing up to take one more punch from the cilantro-infested culinary contenders. With home-fried hospitality, they welcome you in from the technological wasteland of modern living, where you can sit back with a good cup of coffee minus the foam, the infusions, and the sprinkles. Here are five of Vancouver's finest.

BERT'S RESTAURANT (2904 Main St; 604/876-1236) is a homey diner on Main Street that proudly displays the Gold Cup Coffee Award it won in 1969. You can't go wrong with the Denver omelet. And the waitresses will capture your heart when they call you "honey."

BON'S OFF BROADWAY (2451 Nanaimo St; 604/253-7242) has a Californian-Tuscan stucco interior with signed *X-Files* cast members' pictures on the walls and one of the cheapest breakfasts in town. All-night ravers mix with truckers and families, and the bottomless cups of coffee will keep you going for days.

formidable signature seafood tower (priced by the tier) followed by exec chef Frank Pabst's miso-crusted sablefish (known south of the border as black cod), Queen Charlotte Island halibut, or bouillabaisse. Or catch the fresh sheet, including six to eight varieties of oysters. For dessert, you might want to go light with the layered homemade sorbet trio. At some point in the evening, try a concoction of chilled vodka and freshly squeezed juices from the menu of hand-shaken cocktails. The wine list is extensive, with a good selection of British Columbia's best. The terrace is heated for alfresco dining. *$$$–$$$$; AE, DC, E, MC, V; no checks; lunch Mon–Fri, dinner every day, brunch Sat–Sun; full bar; info@bluewatercafe.net; www.bluewatercafe.net; at the corner of Helmcken St.*

Bridges / ★★

1696 DURANLEAU ST, VANCOUVER; 604/687-4400 One of the city's most popular hangouts has a superb setting on Granville Island. Seats on the outdoor deck, with sweeping views of downtown and the mountains, are at a premium on warm days. Bridges is actually three separate entities: a casual bistro, a pub, and a more formal second-story dining room. The bistro's seafood Caesar is the best bet; upstairs, the chefs take seafood seriously, but expect to pay top dollar for it. *$$–$$$$; MC, V; no checks; lunch, dinner every day, brunch Sun; full bar; no reservations for bistro, recommended for dining room; info@bridgesrestaurant.com; www.bridgesrestaurant.com; Granville Island.* ♿

C / ★★★☆

1600 HOWE ST, VANCOUVER; 604/681-1164 For the cutting edge on seafood, both in taste and presentation, look no further. Sourcing the best seafoods available, from local waters to the East Coast (each

The homemade ketchup at **THE COTTAGE COFFEE SHOP** (1441 Commercial Dr; 604/254-0306) is all the reason you need to come here. At this coffee shop run by the same family for more than 30 years, French fries are still hand-cut for each order. The location on hip Commercial Drive makes for an interesting crowd, and the price of a burger and fries makes you wonder how the place has stayed in business so long.

Decorated in cowboy paraphernalia that has attracted more than a few movie shoots, **MOLLY'S CAFE** (1832 Columbia St; 604/874-5122) boasts one of the best chicken club sandwiches in town. Both Chinese food and standard greasy-spoon fare make this the ultimate in deep-fryer fusion. The bacon, lettuce, and tomato fajita is truly a strange combo, especially with the addition of hoisin sauce. Plus you can hear all the day's news from the TV crowd that chows down here.

One of the true forerunners of Chinese-Canadian cuisine, the **VARSITY GRILL** (4381 W 10th Ave; 604/224-1822) is a landmark to timeless perseverance. Where else can you get old-fashioned milk shakes and wavy fries—and a fortune cookie on the way out?

—Mark Laba

product sustainable), rates this Zen-like room with a spacious patio and stellar view of False Creek and Granville Island arguably the best seafood restaurant in the country. Chef Rob Clark creates dishes that are as dramatic on the palate as they are on the plate. A must-have is the signature grilled octopus bacon–wrapped scallop, and the Skeena River wild salmon; C has a direct line to the local catch. The halibut fillet in saffron broth or the seared New Zealand John Dory with smoked Pemberton pumpkin gnocchi and pumpkin seed sauce could render you speechless. C is a contemporary artist's idea of restaurant, made with "found objects" and totally innovative design (much like the food). Check out the one-of-a-kind floor lamps and the stand-up bar stools. Plus, the service is impeccable. C gets an A. *$$$–$$$$; AE, DC, E, MC, V; no checks; lunch, dinner every day; full bar; reservations recommended; info@crestaurant.com; www.crestaurant.com; at Beach Ave.*

The Cannery Seafood House / ★★★

2205 COMMISSIONER ST, VANCOUVER; 604/254-9606 Frederic Couton's culinary artistry (he's the garnish maestro) makes your trek out to this relatively remote east-end dockside location unquestionably worthwhile. Due to port security, access is only from the Commissioner Street overpass, off McGill Street. However, boaters can tie up at the 40-foot dock and grab a picnic to go, or stay awhile. First up is Couton's amazing lobster oil—soak it up with bread, drizzle it over just about everything else, and take a bottle home. On any given day, you'll find a baker's dozen of honestly prepared, high-quality seafood options on the fresh sheet; perhaps a delicate arctic char, a juicy grilled swordfish, or a meaty tuna. Salmon Wellington has been a house specialty here since 1971; it's still a winner, yet our favorite is the buttery steamed Alaskan black cod with BC wild mushrooms in a chive-butter sauce. Those who don't go for fish are catered to with smoked rack of lamb or simple grilled beef tenderloin. The award-winning wine list is one of the city's best. Service is enthusiastic and friendly. *$$$; AE, DC, MC, V; no checks; lunch Mon–Fri, dinner every day; full bar; reservations recommended; info@canneryseafood.com; www.canneryseafood.com; off McGill St, east of Renfrew.*

Chartwell / ★★★

791 W GEORGIA ST (THE FOUR SEASONS), VANCOUVER; 604/689-9333 Somewhat unusual for a hotel restaurant, Chartwell attracts a bevy of loyal customers; some for the clubby atmosphere, some for the exceptional service, but most for a gastronomic adventure. Start with an appetizer of three local salmons, and the incredibly aromatic lobster bisque served "cappuccino" style: light and foamy yet with full-bodied flavor. The menu's main focus is the grill, with a mix-and-match menu of steak and chops, a selection of sides, and four sauces sure to please every taste. Try the thick and juicy lamb chop with a stack of fries, or the sautéed sea scallops with herbed gnocchi and wild mushrooms, paired with a wine from the knowledgeable sommelier. Some of Vancouver's finest servers give Chartwell its distinctive stamp of personal service—warm, discreet, and attentive. A pre-theater dinner menu with valet parking is an outstanding value. The wine list is an award winner, and the winemakers' dinners are the most popular in the city. *$$$$; AE, DC, DIS, JCB, MC, V; no checks; dinner Tues–Sat; full bar; reservations recommended; www.fourseasons.com; at Howe St.* &

CinCin Restaurant & Bar / ★★★

1154 ROBSON ST, VANCOUVER; 604/688-7338 Warmth exudes from every corner of the room, from the Mediterranean-inspired decor, the aromas of the wood-fired open kitchen, and the friendly, professional staff. Talented chef Romy Prasad combines European influences and techniques with West Coast flavors and comes up with winners throughout his eclectic menu. Be sure to order the appetizer tasting plate; included is the Parma prosciutto with grilled figs—worthy of ordering by itself. Fettucine with charred cipollini onions and sage butter sprinkled with sunchoke chips is superb; for something meaty, try the local ostrich bathed in a dense and fruity au jus, or the braised leg of rabbit, robustly flavored with blue cheese, black olives, and a four-nut pesto. CinCin boasts a 10,000-bottle cellar, with many good values. Enjoy a cocktail at the bar, sip wine in the lounge (food is served until midnight), or dine on the outdoor heated terrace overlooking Robson Street. *$$$; AE, DC, MC, V; no checks; lunch Mon–Fri, dinner every day; full bar; reservations recommended; cincin@direct.ca; www.cincin.net; between Bute and Thurlow Sts.*

Cioppino's Mediterranean Grill / ★★★★
Cioppino's Enoteca / ★★★★

1133 HAMILTON ST, VANCOUVER; 604/688-7466 The name is a pun on San Francisco's delicious seafood stew, cioppino, and that of the very talented Pino Posteraro. Pino's French-inspired Mediterranean dishes—foie gras and sea bass casserole, sautéed wild chanterelles and morels, spaghettini with truffles—have earned him a loyal following. Stick to a tasting menu and you'll have one of the most brilliant meals in town for the price. Celestino Posteraro and Massimo Piscopo preside over a friendly bar and a serious wine list. And there's a wonderful private dining room for up to 24. Next door, Posteraro has opened Enoteca, a comfortable low-key wine bar with a rotisserie. *$$$–$$$$; AE, DC, MC, V; no checks; lunch Mon–Fri, dinner Mon–Sat; full bar; reservations recommended; pino@cioppinosyaletown .com; www.cioppinosyaletown.com; between Helmcken and Davie Sts.*

Circolo / ★★★

1116 MAINLAND ST, VANCOUVER; 604/687-1116 Settle into a curvy banquette at Umberto Menghi's chic Tuscan eatery for the *bella gente* ("beautiful people"). He set out to capture the moods of his favorite cities, and with one look at the decor in his Yaletown restaurant you'll imagine yourself at a bustling oyster bar in Manhattan, a romantic bistro in Paris, or a classic restaurant in Florence. One of Canada's best-known restaurateurs, Menghi has a syndicated TV show, five cookbooks, and owns Villa Delia, one of Italy's best cooking schools. We suggest starting with fresh oysters and sharing the escargot de Bourgogne. Then on to the Bistecca alla Fiorentina for two: 32 ounces of grilled porterhouse sliced off the bone, chased with a bottle of Bambolo, the owner's upscale Bolgheri red. Everything makes us feel rich and a long way from home. *$$$–$$$$; AE, DC, E, MC, V; no checks; dinner Mon–Sat; full bar; reservations recommended; www.umberto.com/circolo.htm; in Yaletown.* &

Cru / ★★★

1459 W BROADWAY, VANCOUVER; 604/677-4111 Coffee and butterscotch hues from the tall-backed banquette running along one wall set the tone for this warm and inviting room. The focus here is "fun and easy" and the menu definitely gets this point across: each item is color coded with eight components of the wine list (with descriptions such as crisp, luscious, juicy, smooth, and big), and all the wines are sold by the glass. A three-course prix fixe is offered with "mix and match" choices—or go for casual "small plates" that are the size of large appetizers else-where. Chef/co-owner Dana Reinhardt has elevated Caesar salad to an art form. And other dishes rise to the occasion, such as scallops with wild mushrooms, but-ternut squash risotto and brown butter, or the Moroccan lamb chops, good to the bone. Cru may just have the best duck confit in town—crackling skin outside and a hint of vinegar perfectly balances the rich meaty flavor. Save room for the hot plum and ginger Johnnycake: plums poached with cardamom, star anise, and red wine with a cornmeal biscuit topping individually baked and served with a big dollop of whipped cream. *$$; AE, MC, V; no checks; dinner every day; full bar; reservations recommended; www.cru.ca; between Granville and Hemlock Sts.* &

Diva at the Met / ★★★☆

645 HOWE ST (METROPOLITAN HOTEL), VANCOUVER; 604/602-7788 If it's winter, the hearty venison shank with smoked parsnip purée is the perfect choice; for summer, the line-caught halibut is cooked to perfection; and for anytime, try the pan-seared sweetbreads with duck-leg confit and wild mushrooms with a heavenly hazelnut-garlic foam sauce, soon to become another signature dish. Executive chef Scott Baechler, with his light touch and finesse, could very well be Canada's Jamie

Oliver: watch him and his expert crew work the exhibition kitchen from this multi-tiered, spacious room. Using regionally based ingredients emphasizing simplicity, he makes each dish a taste treat. Chocoholics go for Thomas Haas's signature chocolate bar. Diva's well-stocked cellar has more than 500 selections, including many local producers. Don't pass on the opportunity to attend a winemakers' dinner. *$$$–$$$$; AE, DC, JCB, MC, V; no checks; breakfast, lunch, dinner every day, brunch Sat–Sun; full bar; reservations recommended; reservations@divamet.com; www.metropolitan.com; between Dunsmuir and W Georgia St.* &

Elixir / ★★

350 DAVIE ST (OPUS HOTEL), VANCOUVER; 604/642/6786 Slide into an antiqued leather banquette at this brasserie-style bar and restaurant and it's a quick ticket to the Left Bank, where executive chef Don Letendre and his talented crew serve authentic French cuisine inspired by Pacific Coast produce. For dinner, braised dishes are the focus, such as the cured pork belly, rolled, braised and broiled—an unforgettable dish, as is the ethereal foie gras and scallops grounded by *puy* lentils. Also try the skate wing in a brown butter and caper sauce. The grand finale is the apple tarte Tatin with crème fraîche. Prices are surprisingly reasonable given the opulent surroundings, both here and at the Opus lobby bar with its own menu of small plates (all under $20; try the deconstructed bento box and a cocktail while taking in the eclectic interior design—New York cool). Elixir also has a well-rounded wine menu with many glasses and half bottles. *$$–$$$; AE, DC, JCB, MC, V; no checks; breakfast, lunch, dinner every day, brunch Sat–Sun; full bar; reservations recommended; www.elixir-opusbar.com; corner of Hamilton.*

Ezogiku Noodle Cafe / ★

1329 ROBSON ST, VANCOUVER; 604/685-8606 Steely clean, this small gem of a place has a steady following of ramen lovers, of which there are several varieties—ramen, that is. The café caters to Asian food lovers who don't want to spend a lot of money. A modest awning says "noodle cafe," but regulars would say that doesn't begin to describe its value. Several varieties of ramen noodle dishes, many representing a clever combination of Japanese and Chinese culinary tastes, come in huge servings. There's also fried rice, fried noodles, and wonderfully tasty *gyoza*. Be prepared to wait for a seat. Other branches are in Honolulu and Tokyo. *$; cash only; lunch, dinner every day; no alcohol; no reservations; between Jervis and Bute Sts.*

Feenie's / ★★★★

2563 W BROADWAY, VANCOUVER; 604/739-7115 Rob Feenie's casual dining spot, the city's best gourmet bargain, became a neighborhood hangout virtually the day it opened in July 2003. The patio side is laid back, but inside there's a transformation to slick high design. The interior is divided with a second, all-red room with bar and tables, modular and curvy like a spaceship. Look up—there's a wild light fixture—a huge, glowing, peachy fake-fur-covered orb that looks like it could vacuum up your meal. The menu is fun—everything from the eight-buck Feenie's Weenie to a suberb Peking duck clubhouse sandwich. Dine à la carte or try the $35 prix-fixe menu. "Rob's Favs" include the Feenie Burger, all

Angus with mushrooms, cheese, and bacon (add foie gras on top for a bit more); Alsatian pizza; *poutine;* and his famed Calamari sandwich. Save room for thrombotic desserts, like the white chocolate crème brûlée with a pecan honey wafer or the apple galette with vanilla ice cream and warm caramel sauce. The cocktail and beer lists are also serious. *$$–$$$; AE, DC, MC, V; no checks; lunch, dinner every day; full bar; reservations recommended; lumiere@relaischateaux.com; www .relaischateaux.com; between Trafalgar and Larch Sts.* &

The Fish House at Stanley Park / ★★

2099 BEACH AVE, VANCOUVER; 604/681-7275 Pull up a stool at the Oyster Bar, slide into a booth in the Garden Room, intimately dine by the fireplace, or enjoy the gorgeous surroundings of Stanley Park from the patio or heated atrium. Chef Karen Barnaby constantly re-invents her fresh sheet and leaves some dishes just the way regulars like them, such as the tender ahi tuna Diane with green peppercorn cream sauce and buttermilk mashed potatoes. Be sure to try the seafood sampler, with in-house smoked salmon pastrami, calamari wondrously marinated in smoked tomatoes, grilled prawns, and plump mussels. Or, try the tableside flamed prawns with ouzo. And, for anyone on the Atkins diet (or any diet), Barnaby is the low-carb guru, and the servers give expert recommendations. Yes, you can have the German chocolate cheesecake. And you'll want the recipe—pick up a copy of Barnaby's cookbook. Afternoon tea is delightful and so is Sunday brunch, rain or shine. The Fish House boasts one of the largest selections of half bottles in town. *$$; AE, DIS, DC, JCB, MC, V; no checks; lunch Mon–Sat, afternoon tea, dinner every day, brunch Sun; full bar; info@fishhousestanleypark.com; www.fishhousestanleypark.com; at the entrance to Stanley Park.* &

Gotham Steakhouse & Cocktail Bar / ★★★

615 SEYMOUR ST, VANCOUVER; 604/605-8282 Meat is the main course here; USDA prime, to be precise. The stand-alone steaks (vegetables are à la carte) are even more beautiful than the people. From the New York strip ($39.95) to the splendid 24-ounce porterhouse ($48.95), it's a cattle drive for the taste buds. At $5.50–$7.50 per order, you can share mashed potatoes, creamed spinach, or crispy French fries. For sheer entertainment value, take a seat at the bar and engage in some of the best people-watching that Vancouver has to offer. Beware: this place prices under the assumption that everyone has a Swiss bank account. *$$$$; AE, DC, MC, V; no checks; dinner every day; full bar; reservations recommended; www.gothamsteak house.com; at Dunsmuir St.* &

Habibi's / ★★

7-1128 W BROADWAY, VANCOUVER; 604/732-7487 Richard Zeinoun cooks from the heart at this casual Middle Eastern spot. All sorts of surprises start with a complementary meze that whets the appetite for *shinkleesh,* an aged goat cheese; *balila,* warmed chick-peas in garlic-infused oil; or *warak anab,* stuffed grape leaves. There are falafels and both Lebanese- and Israeli-style hummus. Wines chosen to go with the food make Habibi's an unbeatable dining experience. Food is downright cheap; dishes start at $7 and the baklava is $2. Service is friendly and enthusiastic, and underground parking is free. *$; V; lunch, dinner Mon–Sat; beer and wine; no reservations; www.habibis.com; between Spruce and Oak Sts.*

Hon's Wun Tun House / ★

1339 ROBSON ST, VANCOUVER (AND BRANCHES); 604/688-0871 By serving the just-plain-good, basic Chinese specialties you'd find in Hong Kong street-corner restaurants, and by keeping prices to a minimum, what was once a steamy Chinatown noodle house has become a restaurant empire with six branches. Wonton is just one of the more than 90 varieties of soup available, and there's a seemingly endless list of noodle specialties. The trademark pot-sticker dumplings, fried or steamed, are justly famous. Hon's also offers delivery, takeout, and a full line of frozen dim sum. One more thing: those addictive candied walnuts are available on your way out. *$; MC, V; no checks; lunch, dinner every day; beer and wine; no reservations; hons@shinnova.com; www.shinnova.com; between Jervis and Broughton Sts.*

Imperial Chinese Seafood Restaurant / ★★★☆

355 BURRARD ST, VANCOUVER; 604/688-8191 The Imperial may lay claim to being the most opulent Chinese dining room around. There's a feeling of being in a grand ballroom of eras past: a central staircase leads to the balustrade-lined mezzanine, diplomatic dignitaries and rock stars dine in luxurious private rooms, and windows two stories high look out onto the panorama of Burrard Inlet and the North Shore mountains. The food can be equally polished—lobster in black bean sauce with fresh egg noodles; panfried scallops garnished with coconut-laced, deep-fried tapioca-thickened milk; sautéed spinach with minced pork and Chinese anchovies; a superb pan-smoked black cod; and the addictive beef sauté in chiles with honey walnuts. Dim sum is consistently good. Service is ever courteous, informative, and helpful, and the wine list is exceptional. *$$$–$$$$; DC, MC, V; no checks; lunch, dinner every day; full bar; reservations recommended; www.imperialrest .com; between Cordova and Hastings Sts.*

La Régalade / ★★☆

2232 MARINE DR, WEST VANCOUVER; 604/921-2228 This bistro is as near to France as you can get—at least this side of the Atlantic—from the rustic French cuisine to the decor to the background music. And slow-food movement aficionados, look no further; simmering stews and braised meats are de rigeur and comprise several of the daily specials. Not to be missed: *les pots d'escargots* (and no fussing with shells) with plenty of garlic butter, and the *terrine maison*—thick slices of country-style pâte with cornichons. Follow with robust *la côte de porc mijotée en cocotte,* or the exceptional cheese selection. The food here is true to its roots. *Mais oui,* there is an ample French wine list. *$$–$$$; MC, V; no checks; lunch Mon–Fri, dinner Mon–Sat; full bar; reservations recommended; laregalade@hotmail.com; www.laregalade.com; at 22nd between Ambleside and Dundarave Sts.*

Le Crocodile / ★★★★

100-909 BURRARD ST, VANCOUVER; 604/669-4298 France without a passport—that's Le Crocodile. It was named after chef-owner Michel Jacob's favorite restaurant in his hometown of Strasbourg. Everyone wants to order Jacob's savory onion tart served with chilled Alsace Edelzwicker. Entrées of marvelously sauced classics such as sea bass with lobster beurre blanc, double-cut veal chop with porcini mushrooms and veal reduction cream sauce, and panfried sweetbreads with tarragon and Calvados sauce all pay their respects to tradition. He panfries Dover sole to remember. Jacob's treasury of French cheeses makes a fine end to a meal or an even better prelude to a tangy lemon tart paired with house-made raspberry sorbet. The wines of Alsace are proudly poured, but so are many others. France's Loire Valley, Bordeaux, and Burgundy are well represented, as is California. The ever-professional service and chic European atmosphere make dinner at Le Crocodile an event. *$$$; AE, DC, MC, V; no checks; lunch Mon–Fri, dinner Mon–Sat; full bar; reservations recommended; lecrocodile@telus.net; www.lecrocodilerestaurant.com; at Smithe St.* &

Lumière / ★★★★

2551 W BROADWAY, VANCOUVER; 604/739-8185 Rob Feenie's restless energy fuels the passion for perfection that is Lumière, creating arguably the city's best food. Once a tad austere, the main room's third upgrade/ expansion is complete with banquettes running down the center of the room. Food luxuriates in the skill of Feenie's contemporary French kitchen—he always seems to achieve a perfect balance of flavors and textures. Diners can choose a large three-course prix-fixe selection, or one of four seasonally driven tasting menus Three of the tasting menus comprise 8 small dishes, the "Signature" menu has 12, and all are designed to make diners swoon: cornets of salmon tartar in a beach of breadcrumbs, three ravioli—raw milk ricotta, braised short rib, and butternut squash—and an olive-oil poached duck confit on a lily pad of roasted root vegetables. The sublime vegetarian menu can win converts to the no-meat cause. For a relaxed, quicker-meal alternative, the Lumière tasting bar offers a dozen scaled-down versions of classics, all at $12. The desserts are masterful, especially sticky toffee pudding with caramel sauce. The now-substantial wine list is always being improved, and service is informed and attentive. *$$$$; AE, DC, MC, V; no checks; dinner Tues–Sun; full bar; reservations recommended; lumiere@relaischateaux.com; www.relaischateaux .com; between Trafalgar and Larch Sts.* &

Memphis Blues Barbeque House / ★★★

1465 W BROADWAY, VANCOUVER; 604/738-6806 / 1342 COMMERCIAL DR, VANCOUVER; 604/ 215-2565 Get here early. Memphis Blues was an instant success when restaurateur George Sui and wine nut Park Heffelfinger opened their authentic Southern "baah-be-cue" in the fall of 2001. All Memphis favorites—ribs, beef brisket, pulled pork, rib ends, and smoked sausage—are perfectly prepared with sides of coleslaw, cornbread, potato salad, or fries, and barbecue pit beans. The brisket is unsurpassed, spread out in thick, melting tender slices. Cornish hen is tender and juicy, deserving of its signature dish status. Heffelfinger posts a wine list, selected to whistle Dixie with smoked pork treats and available by glass or bottle. The second location on Commercial Drive in the heart of veggieville is an oasis for carnivores. Eating with your hands is the norm. Service is minimal—order at the counter and listen carefully. *$; AE, MC, V; no checks; lunch, dinner every day; beer and wine; reservations not accepted; between Granville and Hemlock Sts.* &

Montri's Thai Restaurant / ★★★

3629 W BROADWAY, VANCOUVER; 604-738-9888 Why go anywhere else for Thai food when Montri's is simply the best in town? What to order? Everything is good. *Tom yum goong* is Thailand's national soup, a lemony prawn broth. The *tod mun* fish cakes blended with prawns and chile curry are excellent, as is the beef or prawn spicy stir-fry served on panfried spinach. Rattanaraj's *Thai gai-yang*, chicken marinated in coconut milk and broiled, is a close cousin to the chicken sold on the beach at Phuket. Have it with *som tum*, a green papaya salad served with sticky rice and wedges of raw cabbage; the cabbage and the rice are coolants, and you'll need them (Thailand's Singha beer also helps). *$$; MC, V; no checks; dinner every day; full bar; no reservations; near Alma St.* &

Nat's New York Pizzeria / ★★

2684 W BROADWAY, VANCOUVER; 604/737-0707 / 1080 DENMAN ST, VANCOUVER; 604/642-0777 The skinniest crust pizza and the thickest, tastiest toppings make these pizzas the best in town. Nat and Franco Bastone learned how to create Naples-style pizza at their uncle's pizza parlor in Yonkers and now serve up some of the best thin-crust pizza around. Take out, or pull up a chair under the Big Apple memorabilia and sink your teeth into a pie loaded with chorizo and mushrooms, or artichokes and pesto, or cappocolo and hot peppers. If you can get past the lunch crowd of high school kids drizzling liquid honey all over their leftover crusts (really), order Nat's new creation—bruscetta with artichokes and red pepper. Regular customers bring in all things New York to hang on the walls. The place is kid-friendly, too. *$; no credit cards; no checks; lunch, dinner Mon–Sat; no alcohol; no reservations; between Stephens and Trafalgar Sts (Broadway), at Helmcken St (Denman).*

Ouzeri / ★★

3189 W BROADWAY, VANCOUVER; 604/739-9378 Traditionally, the Greek *ouzeri* is a place to go to drink and graze tapas-style before going to dinner. In Vancouver, this lively, modern Greek restaurant, located in the heart of Greektown, is where you can go any time of the day and compose a meal of mezethes. Expect all the usual Greek specialties and then some. Signature lamb chops are char-grilled to perfection; moussaka Kitsilano-style is vegetarian; panfried chicken livers are wonderful—crisp on the outside and tender on the inside. Prawns dressed with ouzo and mushrooms are simply amazing. Friendly, casual, happy (with surely the most reasonably priced menu this side of Athens), Ouzeri proves that being Greek doesn't mean you can't be trendy. The tile floor can make it a bit loud. In summer, the restaurant opens onto the sidewalk and small patio. *$$; AE, DC, MC, V; no checks; lunch Tues–Sat, dinner every day; full bar; no reservations; www.ouzeri.ca; at Trutch St.* &

Parkside / ★★★

1906 HARO ST, VANCOUVER; 604/683-6912 After a few incarnations (Delilahs, Zev's), it seems that owners Andre Durbach and Chris Stewart have the right formula to stay put. Their idea: 20 small plates all priced under $20 and a clever wine list comprising 60 bottles under $60 (although they do have a reserve list and a tasting menu for $48). The only problem is making a decision: all of chef Durbach's dishes are as delicious as they are tempting. Begin with the warm salad of red mullet, *puy* lentils, and sauce *vierge:* the mullet's crispy, crackling exterior and delicate, flaky interior will linger as a delightful memory, as will the silkiest foie gras parfait with pear chutney. If it's a wintry night, go for ever-so-slowly braised veal cheeks with polenta and the thickest, richest sauce. To go with a summer breeze on the patio, try heirloom tomato salad with Dungeness crab bisque. *$$–$$$; MC, V; no checks; dinner every day; full bar; reservations recommended; parkside@telus.net; a few blocks north of Denman.*

Quattro on Fourth / ★★★

2611 W 4TH AVE, VANCOUVER; 604/734-4444 Patrick Corsi and the accommodating staff at this comfortable Italian restaurant make sure dining here is a treat in any season. In winter, the restaurant emanates mystery and romance with candlelit, crimson-washed walls and the glow from rustic, wrought-iron chandeliers. An impressive and generous antipasto platter includes no less than a dozen items (grilled tiger prawns, crab and salmon cakes, and salmon gravlax are among its offerings). The beef carpaccio is superb; so, too, the grilled radicchio bocconcini and portobello mushrooms. Kudos for the grilled beef tenderloin cloaked in aged balsamic syrup, the pistachio-crusted sea bass, and the spicy de-boned Cornish game hen. Spaghetti Quattro ("for Italians only") rewards with a well-spiced sauce of chicken, chiles, black beans, and plenty of garlic. Of course, the mostly Italian wine list is stellar, and the Corsi family has the largest selection of grappa in Vancouver. The heated patio seats 35. *$$$; AE, DC, MC, V; no checks; dinner every day; full bar; reservations recommended; www.quattro/ristorante.com; at Trafalgar St.* ♿

Raincity Grill / ★★★

1193 DENMAN ST, VANCOUVER; 604/685-7337 This contemporary restaurant situated at the hip Davie-Denman intersection in the West End dazzles diners with excellent year-round views of English Bay (in summer, loll on the patio). Chef Sean Cousins takes "all things local" seriously, so much so that 98 percent of the menu now comes from the Pacific Northwest; Cousins even uses flax and grape-seed oil rather than olive oil. (The other 2 percent must be coffee, salt, and pepper.) General manager Brent Hayman's award-winning wine list showcases more than 400 West Coast vintages. Start with any combination of delightful "spoons"—*amuse bouche*—and the velvet smooth grilled scallops with rosemary cream. The Dungeness crab cakes set your taste buds in motion for blackberry-marinated bison tenderloin: it's clean and simplistic in design, with the thickest muscat jus that begs for another taste. And for the ultimate in savory dessert, try the chèvre cheesecake with frozen grapes and hazelnut brittle. Each menu item carries a wine suggestion. A glass of dessert wine and the day's tart or pastry make a perfect finish. Expect ever-professional service from Hayman and his staff. *$$$; AE, DC, MC, V; no checks; dinner every day, brunch Sat–Sun; full bar; reservations recommended; info@raincitygrill.com; www.raincitygrill.com; at Davie St.* ♿

Rodney's Oyster House / ★★

1228 HAMILTON ST, VANCOUVER; 604/609-0080 It's hard to find a spot at the bar, as everyone squeezes in to eye the forearms of the young shuckers at Rodney's. A team of experts makes careful checks of temperature, freshness, and quality of more than a dozen types of briny bivalves (many from the East Coast). While the slogan here is "the lemon, the oyster, and your lips are all that's required," you can choose one of Rodney's four sauces instead of taking your oysters straight. (The Seawich is a good choice if you grew up with cocktail sauce on shrimp.) Also offered are a choice of creamy chowders, steamed mussels and clams, local Dungeness crab, and East Coast lobsters. The staff is more than willing to indulge your whims. There are a few tables upstairs, but the bar is where the action is. *$$–$$$; AE, E, MC, V; no checks; lunch, dinner Mon–Sat; beer, wine, cider, and Scotch and Caesars; no reservations; between Davie and Drake Sts.*

Sophie's Cosmic Cafe / ★★

2095 W 4TH AVE, VANCOUVER; 604/732-6810 The walls of this funky Kitsilano diner are the flea market of a kitsch collector's dreams. So don't worry about the wait—there's plenty to look at, including Sophie's collection of colorful lunch boxes and hats that were once stashed in her attic. Evenings, people are drawn by burger platters, pastas, boffo spicy mussels, and chocolate shakes. On weekends, fans queue in the rain for stick-to-the-ribs breakfasts, especially Mexican eggs (with sausage, peppers, and onions, spiced with hot-pepper sauce: it's potent). Vegetarian choices are offered all day. A covered deck accommodates all-weather puffers. *$–$$; MC, V; no checks; breakfast, lunch, dinner every day, brunch Sat–Sun; full bar; no reservations; at Arbutus St.* &

Sun Sui Wah Seafood Restaurant / ★★★

3888 MAIN ST, VANCOUVER; 604/872-8822 Simon Chan brought the proven track record and signature dishes of this successful Hong Kong group to Vancouver, and his team has been playing to packed houses ever since. Reasons are legion: crispy, tender roasted squabs and sculpted Cantonese masterpieces, such as luscious broccoli-skirted steamed chicken interwoven with black mushrooms and Chinese ham; deftly steamed scallops on silky bean curd topped with creamy-crunchy *tobikko* (flying-fish roe) sauce; Alaskan king crab in wine and garlic; lobster hot pot with egg noodles; giant beach oysters steamed in black bean sauce; and lightly sautéed geoduck paired with deep-fried "milk"—fragrant with sweet coconut in a fluffy crust. Reserve early; these are wedding hot spots. Sun Sui Wah has another branch in Richmond (4940 No. 3 Rd, Richmond; 604/273-8208). *$$; AE, MC, V; no checks; lunch, dinner every day; full bar; reservations recommended; www.sunsuiwah.com; at E 23rd Ave.* &

Tojo's / ★★★★

202-777 W BROADWAY, VANCOUVER; 604/872-8050 Hidekazu Tojo is Tojo's. One of the best-known sushi maestros in Vancouver, this beaming mustachioed Japanese chef has a loyal clientele that regularly fills his spacious upstairs restaurant, though most people want to sit at the 10-seat sushi bar. He's endlessly innovative, surgically precise, and committed to fresh ingredients. Check out his Tojo tuna or "special beef" (very thin beef wrapped around asparagus and shrimp) or suntan tuna with plum sauce. Tojo-san created the BC roll (barbecued salmon skin, green onions, cucumber, and daikon), now found in almost every Japanese restaurant in Vancouver. Tempura and teriyaki are always reliable, and everyday specials are usually superb: pine mushroom soup in the fall, steamed monkfish liver from October to May, and cherry blossoms with scallops and sautéed halibut cheeks with shiitake in the spring. Cold Masukagami sake is hot at Tojo's. *$$$$; AE, DC, JCB, MC, V; no checks; dinner Mon–Sat; full bar; reservations recommended; www.tojos.com; between Heather and Willow Sts.* &

Vij's / ★★★⯪

1480 W 11TH AVE, VANCOUVER; 604/736-6664 This is where food writers impress informed eaters from out of town. Bombay native Vikram Vij dishes up imaginative home-cooked Indian fare that evolves at whim. His seasonal menu changes every three months but usually includes a mean curry or a killer *saag*. Decor is minimalist, casual, and modern. Start with a glass of Vij's refreshing fresh-ginger-and-lemon libation, and don't pass on the standout appetizer—small samosas filled with ricotta and served with a Bengali sauce containing a mixture of five spices called *panchpooran*. Try the lamb "popsicles"—dainty racks of lamb charbroiled to perfection without being masked by the accompanying sauce. They're guaranteed to transport you to Nirvana. Not only is it naan-lickin' good, the combination of ingredients is just as mysterious as its country. Courtesy and simplicity rule, as Vij waits carefully on all who arrive early enough to get in—greeting them with a glass of chai before discussing the menu. There is a small but excellent wine list; prices are civilized, too. Next door is Rangoli, Vij's latest venture for lunch, tea, and upscale takeaway. *$$–$$$; AE, DC, MC, V; no checks; dinner every day; beer and wine; no reservations; between Granville and Hemlock Sts.* &

Villa del Lupo / ★★★⯪

869 HAMILTON ST, VANCOUVER; 604/688-7436 Chef-owner Julio Gonzalez Perini's dazzling experiments with flavor bring off-duty local chefs to this elegant Victorian townhouse. Order the veal tenderloin with foie gras–stuffed morels and marvel at the delicate blending of tastes and textures. Prices tend to be high, but so is the quality, and portions are generous. Almost everything else on the Northern Italian menu is wonderful, too. Roasted halibut with bay scallops is remarkable. Osso buco is a hearty house specialty and a consistent favorite. The wine list goes far beyond the Italian border. Grappa and eau-de-vie are available, as well. Service is always amiable and correct. *$$$; AE, DC, MC, V; no checks; dinner every day; full bar; reservations recommended; between Robson and Smithe Sts.*

West / ★★★★

2881 GRANVILLE ST, VANCOUVER; 604/738-8938 Formerly Ouest, West has won countless awards for chef David Hawksworth, including Restaurant of the Year 2003—no small task in a town teeming with exceptional eateries. Recently remodeled (glimpse a reflection of diners' plates in the wavy new ceiling sculpture), the beautifully designed room with a cherry-wood-and-marble bar seats 10 against a backdrop of a ceiling-high "wall of wine." The "wall" includes a custom-built refrigeration system that keeps wines within 2°F of their optimum temperature. Though the room and name have changed, some of Hackworth's dishes have blissfully remained the same. Notably the parfait of foie gras and chicken liver with brioche and apple gelee, the pumpkin ravioli with Parmesan-sage butter, and roast sea bream with black truffle sauce. Service is seamless. *$$$$; AE, DC, E, MC, V; no checks; dinner every day; full bar; reservations recommended; www.westrestaurant .com; between W 12th and W 13th Ave.* &

LODGINGS

The Fairmont Hotel Vancouver / ★★★

900 W GEORGIA ST, VANCOUVER; 604/684-3131 OR 800/441-1414 To revel in the luxury of an earlier era, stay at the Hotel Van. One of the grand French chateau-style hotels built by the Canadian Pacific Railway, this hotel dates back to 1887. The steeply pitched, green-patina copper roof of its current incarnation has dominated the city's skyline since 1939. Stone arches, friezes, and other design elements hidden by earlier remodeling have been restored or re-created in the past few years. The Lobby Bar with oversized club chairs and the elegantly casual 900 West Sea & Steakfood Restaurant and Wine Bar replaced the original main-floor lobby. There's a shopping arcade that includes a Canadian Pacific Store, featuring private-label goods reminiscent of the early days of Canadian travel. Spacious guest rooms retain their elegance with dark-wood furnishings and comfortable seating areas. There's a health club with a lap pool beneath skylights. Try to get a room high above the street noise. *$$$-$$$$; AE, DC, DIS, E, JCB, MC, V; checks OK; concierge@fairmont.com; www.fairmont .com; at Burrard St.* &

The Four Seasons / ★★★★

791 W GEORGIA ST, VANCOUVER; 604/689-9333 OR 800/332-3442 (U.S.) OR 800/268-6285 (CANADA) Guests wallow in luxury at this upscale hotel, which offers meticulous attention to detail. It's a modern tower that's connected to more than 140 shops in the Pacific Centre mall below it. Although the hotel is located in the middle of the high-rise downtown core, many of the guest rooms offer surprising views of the city as well as peeks at the harbor. Amenities include bathrobes, hair dryers, VCRs, shoe shines, 24-hour valet and room service, and complimentary morning coffee and tea in the lobby. Housekeeping takes place twice daily. Facilities include a year-round indoor/outdoor pool, a complimentary health club (with iced towels), and a rooftop garden. Kids are welcomed not only with milk and cookies on arrival, but also with teddy bears in their cribs, a step stool in the bathroom, and their own plush bathrobes. There's also a Dog Recognition Program. Business travelers appreciate phones with voice mail in English, French, or Japanese; modular phone jacks for computer hookup; and full business services. Order a couple of two-olive martinis and sit in the soothing Garden Terrace amid what seems like a jungle, but is actually an award-winning garden of rare flora from Africa. *$$$$; AE, DC, DIS, JCB, MC, V; no checks; vcr.sales@fourseasons.com; www.fourseasons.com; at Howe St.* &

Hotel Le Soleil / ★★★

567 HORNBY ST, VANCOUVER; 604/632-3000 Outside, it's easy to walk right by the bland facade of Le Soleil ("the sun"). But inside, the decor demands attention. The high-ceilinged lobby is a study in gilded opulence. It features original oil paintings, a grand fireplace, and a cozy sitting area. Like the lobby, the 112 guest suites are a little on the small side, but their layout is efficient. Besides, the suites are beautifully decorated in tones of regal red and gold, focusing on Le Soleil's solar theme. Guests have access to the state-of-the-art YWCA Fitness Centre next door for $11 per day. *$$$$; AE, DC, MC, V; no checks; info@lesoleilhotel.com; www.lesoleilhotel.com; between Dunsmuir and Pender.*

Johnson Heritage House / ★★★

2278 W 34TH AVE, VANCOUVER; 604/266-4175 To say that owners Ron and Sandy Johnson are fond of antiques is an understatement. They have restored a 1920s Craftsman-style home on a quiet street in the city's Kerrisdale neighborhood and turned it into one of Vancouver's most intriguing bed-and-breakfasts. Everywhere in the three-story house are relics of the past: coffee grinders, gramophones—even carousel horses. Above the front door, the porch light is a genuine old Vancouver street lamp. Top-floor and basement rooms are cozy; the Carousel Suite, with its mermaid-theme bath and antique slate fireplace, is grandest. Breakfast is served in a bright, airy, cottage-style room. Children 12 and over OK; no pets. *$$; no credit cards; checks OK; fun@johnsons-inn-vancouver.com; www.johnsons-inn-vancouver.com; at Vine St, in Kerrisdale.*

"O Canada" House / ★★★

1114 BARCLAY ST, VANCOUVER; 604/688-0555 OR 877/688-1114 This beautifully restored 1897 Victorian home in the West End is where the national anthem, "O Canada," was written in 1909. Filled with comfort and grace, the front parlor and dining room hearken back to gentler times. Potted palms nestled in Oriental urns; a welcoming fireplace; large, comfy chairs; and soft lights greet you at every turn, along with sherry in the evenings. A wraparound porch looks out onto the English-style garden. The late-Victorian decor continues into the six guest rooms, which have private baths and modern conveniences. The South Suite has an additional adjoining sitting room. The Penthouse Suite offers two gabled sitting areas, skylights, and a view of the downtown area. The separate, diminutive guest cottage, a new addition, has a gas fireplace and private patio. *$$$; MC, V; no checks; info@ocanadahouse.com; www.ocanadahouse.com; at Thurlow St, 1½ blocks south of Robson St.*

Opus Hotel / ★★★★

322 DAVIE ST, VANCOUVER; 604/642-6787 OR 866/642-6787 Fun-loving romantics won't want to leave Vancouver's sexy new multi-million-dollar brick, granite, and glass cocoon in Yaletown. The bold design of each room in this boutique hotel is themed around five fictitious personalities—such as "Bob and Carol" from the hip couple-swapping farce of the '60s, and "Dede," an actress who loves animal prints and fake fur. All rooms and suites feature spa bathrooms with oversized vanities, stainless-steel stand-alone basins, luxurious European

435

toiletries, and ultraplush Frette robes. Courtyard rooms overlook a rooftop garden, and penthouse suites boast double-sided fireplaces, plasma-screen TVs, and deep soaker tubs. If you're into a voyeuristic experience, request a room that overlooks the street; the bathroom has floor-to-ceiling windows and two sets of blinds—one allows you to see out but blocks the view in, the other gives you complete privacy. Have an Ultra-Vox martini in the Opus Bar, the chic lobby lounge, and reserve a corner table in Elixir (see review) for a French-bistro dinner. *$$$; AE, DC, JCB, MC, V; no checks; info@opushotel.com; opushotel.com; at the corner of Davie and Hamilton Sts.* &

Pan Pacific Hotel / ★★★½

300-999 CANADA PLACE WY, VANCOUVER; 604/662-8111 OR 800/663-1515 OR 800/937-1515 (U.S.) No hotel in Vancouver boasts a more stunning location, a better health club, or a more remarkable architectural presence. As part of the Canada Place conference facility, the Pan Pacific juts out into Vancouver's inner harbor with its five famous giant white sails—which are actually the roof of the convention center. It's a little confusing when you first enter the hotel: check-in is on the third floor, guest rooms start on the eighth. Many of the 506 rooms showcase spectacular views of water, mountains, and sky. Soft color schemes, down duvets atop king-sized beds, and marble bathrooms distinguish the rooms. The best views face west, but you can't beat a corner room (with views from your tub). Have a libation in the Cascades Lounge, just off the lobby, and watch ships sail into the sunset. For an incredible dining experience, visit the Five Sails restaurant (dinner only; 604/891-2892) and claim a window table overlooking the harbor and North Shore mountains. Try the luxurious lobster bisque, open ravioli filled with pan-seared prawns, or seared duck. *$$$$; AE, DC, E, JCB, MC, V; no checks; concierge@panpacific-hotel.com; vancouver.panpacific .com; at foot of Burrard St.* &

The Sutton Place Hotel / ★★★★

845 BURRARD ST, VANCOUVER; 604/682-5511 OR 800/961-7555 When Hollywood stars show up in Vancouver, this is often where they stay. With its elegant interior and spectacular original antiques in the public spaces, Sutton Place would rank as a top hotel in any European capital. Each of the 397 soundproofed rooms and suites in this sumptuous residential-style hotel has all the amenities one could want. Housekeeping tidies rooms twice daily. The beds are king-sized; the furnishings are quality reproductions of European antiques. It has 11 nonsmoking floors, the fastest elevators in town, a concierge, and bellhops who snap to attention when you arrive, whether you're in blue jeans and a beat-up truck or in black tie and a limo. The hotel's Fleuri (breakfast, lunch, dinner; 604/642-2900) restaurant and lounges are popular with locals for elegant meals, a civilized tea, and a decadent chocolate buffet. The richly paneled Gerard Lounge is ranked as one of the Northwest's best watering holes by *Vancouver Magazine*. Le Spa is replete with a swimming pool, a fitness room, and beauty salons. Sutton Place also provides the best wheelchair-accessible rooms in the city. High-end rental condominiums at La Grande Residence are located in a separate building connected to the hotel. *$$$$;*

AE, DC, DIS, E, JCB, MC, V; no checks; info@vcr.suttonplace.com; www.sutton place.com; between Robson and Smithe Sts. &

Sylvia Hotel / ★

1154 GILFORD ST, VANCOUVER; 604/681-9321 A favorite for price and location more than for attentive service, this English ivy–covered, eight-story historic brick hotel is a landmark adjacent to English Bay Beach, Vancouver's most popular sand-and-strutting grounds. Try for a south-facing room. A low-rise addition was built to accommodate guests in the busy summer season, when you might just need to settle for any room. Doubles begin at $65 (off-season), and reservations are required well in advance. All 119 rooms, some quite small, have private baths. Families or small groups should request a one-bedroom suite, which can sleep four and includes a kitchen and living room. Covered parking—with no security (and that can be a problem)—is available for an extra charge. The hotel also offers room service, a restaurant, and a lounge. Legend has it that the first cocktail bar in Vancouver opened here in 1954. (On some winter afternoons, it looks as though the original clientele is still in situ.) The variety of cuisines available on Denman Street is more alluring. But the view of the bay at sunset makes a pre-dinner cocktail in the lounge a rewarding experience. *$; AE, DC, MC, V; checks OK; www.sylviahotel.com; corner of Gilford and Beach Aves.*

The Wedgewood Hotel / ★★★

845 HORNBY ST, VANCOUVER; 604/689-7777 OR 800/663-0666 Eleni Skalbania's Wedgewood Hotel is a place you will want to return to time and again. The Wedgewood offers Old World charm and scrupulous attention to every detail. From its ideal downtown location just off Robson Street to its renowned Bacchus Ristorante (see review), this 80-room hotel is all a small urban luxury hotel should be—and then some. The finely appointed rooms—surprisingly large and decorated with vibrant colors and genuine English antiques—have the feel of a grand home. Nightly turndown service, a spa and fitness room, and 24-hour room service are offered. Though views are lost to taller buildings in the neighborhood, this is the place to spend your honeymoon—and many do. For that matter, any weekend at the Wedgewood is a weekend to savor. *$$$; AE, DC, DIS, E, JCB, MC, V; no checks; info@wedgewoodhotel.com; www.wedgewoodhotel.com; between Robson and Smithe Sts.* &

West End Guest House / ★★

1362 HARO ST, VANCOUVER; 604/681-2889 Don't be put off by the blazing-pink exterior of this early-1900s Victorian home. Owner Evan Penner runs a fine eight-room inn (each with private bath), and vacancies are rare during summer. Rooms are generally small but nicely furnished, and there are antiques throughout the house. The staff have all worked in major hotels and know good hospitality. Sherry or iced tea is served in the afternoons on the covered back deck overlooking the verdant English-style garden. Nightly turndown service, feather beds and lambskin mattress covers, robes, telephones—even teddy bears—are provided in every room. Breakfast is a bountiful meal served family-style or delivered to your room. There is guest parking, which is a rarity in the West End. Families with children are accepted, but be careful with the antiques. If you stay, be sure to take a stroll along the garden paths in Barclay Square, one block west, for a quick impression of how the neighborhood looked in the early 1900s. *$$–$$$; AE, DIS, MC, V; checks OK; info@westendguesthouse.com; www.westendguesthouse.com; at Broughton St, 1 block off Robson St.*

YWCA Hotel/Residence / ★★

733 BEATTY ST, VANCOUVER; 604/895-5830 OR 800/663-1424 Built in 1995, the YWCA is close to theaters, sporting venues, and the library. The rooms are functional, immaculately clean, and reasonably priced for a downtown location. All rooms have sinks; baths are private, shared with another room, or "down the hall." Rooms with private baths have TVs. The residence is also remarkably quiet, and although it might not be quite the thing for those accustomed to amenities (no tissues, clocks, or coffee makers here), it does provide meeting rooms, kitchen and laundry facilities, and communal lounges. There isn't a gym, but you can work out for free at the YWCA Fitness Centre, 535 Hornby Street. *$; MC, V; checks OK for deposit only; hotel@ywcavan.org; www.ywcahotel.com; between Georgia and Robson Sts.* &

Around Vancouver

Richmond

This Vancouver suburb, where the airport is located, is south of the city, between the North Arm and the main Fraser River. Many Asians have moved into Richmond, as evidenced by the increasing number of outstanding Chinese restaurants and the new postmodern "Asia West," where Asian pop culture meets the Western strip mall. Here, you'll find convincing iterations of suburban life in Tokyo (Yaohan Centre, 3700 No. 3 Rd, Richmond; 604/231-0601), Taipei (President Plaza, 3320-8181 Cambie Rd, Richmond; 604/270-8677), or Hong Kong (Aberdeen Centre, 4151 Hazelbridge Wy, Richmond; 604/273-1234; Parker Place, 4380 No. 3 Rd, Richmond; 604/273-0276; and Fairchild Square, 4400 Hazelbridge Wy, Richmond; 604/273-1234). From the *rambutans* of Johor to the calligraphies of Shanghai, the wares of Asia are on sale.

LODGINGS

Fairmont Vancouver Airport Place / ★★★

3111 GRANT MCCONACHIE WAY, VANCOUVER INTERNATIONAL AIRPORT, RICHMOND; 604/207-5200 OR 800/676-8922 While most airport hotels simply cater to harried business travelers, here is an oasis of tranquility. Rising above the international terminal, it is the closest hotel to the airport. A waterfall in the lobby and floor-to-ceiling soundproof glass on all floors eliminate outside noise. The Globe at YVR is a reasonably priced restaurant with a full menu. Even if you're not a guest, it's the perfect spot to while away spare boarding time in front of large fireplaces or at the bar. Nonguests can use work-out facilities, plus work-out clothes and robes—for $15. This might be Canada's most technologically advanced and environmentally sound hotel. The room heat turns on when you check in; lights turn on when you insert your key in the door—and turn off when you leave; the "do not disturb" sign illuminates from a central control panel on the nightstand (which also shuts off the doorbell and routes calls to voice mail). *$$; AE, DC, E, MC, V; checks OK; fvares@fairmont.com; www.fairmont.com; on departure level of Vancouver International Airport.*

North Vancouver

A trip to Vancouver isn't complete without a closer look at the natural setting that makes it such a beautiful city. The trip across Lions Gate Bridge makes for picture-postcard views of the North Shore, Stanley Park, and Burrard Inlet. On the way up Capilano Road is Capilano Regional Park, home to a fish hatchery, the huge Cleveland Dam, and the 450-meter (137 meter) **CAPILANO SUSPENSION BRIDGE** (3735 Capilano Rd; 604/985-7474; *www.capbridge.com*), which spans the most picturesque canyon inside any major city. Stopping to take in these sights might help prepare you for the 3,600-foot (1,100 meter) ascent of **GROUSE MOUNTAIN** aboard the Skyride gondola (604/984-0661; *www.grousemtn.com*). A less direct route to the top is the 2,880-foot (880 vertical-meter) **GROUSE GRIND** hiking trail. Either way, on a clear day at the top of Grouse you'll enjoy a superb vista of Vancouver and the Lower Mainland. The casual **BAR 98** restaurant (604/984-0661) is open for lunch. The public market at **LONSDALE QUAY** (123 Carrie Cates Ct; 604/985-6261; *www.lonsdalequay.com*), lesser known than the one at Granville Island, boasts two levels of shops and produce stands, selling everything from toys and crafts to smoked salmon. A large Iranian population has settled in North Vancouver, as the many **IRANIAN MARKETS** and saffron-scented restaurants attest.

RESTAURANTS

Gusto di Quattro / ★★☆

I LONSDALE AVE, NORTH VANCOUVER; 604/924-4444 Gusto makes a great excuse for a minicruise via the SeaBus. There's an air of festivity at all Quattro restaurants, and the intimate Gusto is no exception. Like Quattro at Whistler, *la cucina leggera*, or "the healthy kitchen," is the motto here. Start with the impressive and generous anti-pasto platter. Pastas are beautifully balanced; an outstanding choice is the pappardelle Fagiano—thin ribbons tossed with pheasant and chanterelles in a pheasant reduction. We loved the pistachio-crusted sea bass in a roasted sweet pepper sauce, but if you're really hungry, order the *l'abbuffata* menu for four or more big appetites. Distinctive Italian bottlings and some well-chosen international favorites join a handful of top domestic favorites on the wine list. *$$–$$$; AE, DC, MC, V; no checks; dinner every day; full bar; reservations recommended; quattrogusto@telus.net; www.quattro/ristorante.com; across from Lonsdale Quay Market.* &

The Tomahawk / ★

I550 PHILIP AVE, NORTH VANCOUVER; 604/988-2612 Garden gnomes in a fountain greet you when you step inside this 70-year-old Vancouver institution. Menu names are a match for the kitschy decor: try the legendary, massive all-day Yukon

Breakfast, or if you can say it with a straight face, a Big Chief Skookum Burger—a double beef-patty burger topped with a hot dog plus all the fixings, and a mountainous side order of fries, pickle, and slaw. Cap your feast with baked-on-the-premises pie (perhaps lemon meringue, Dutch apple, or banana cream). *$; AE, DC, MC, V; no checks; breakfast, lunch, dinner every day; no alcohol; no reservations; info@tomahawkrestaurant.com; www.tomahawkrestaurant.com; at Marine Dr.* &

LODGINGS

Thistledown House / ★★★

3910 CAPILANO RD, NORTH VANCOUVER; 604/986-7173 OR 888/633-7173 Set amid a half-acre of lush lawns and gardens, this sparkling white Craftsman-style home was built in 1920 from timber cut on the nearby mountain, and was completely restored in 1996 and luxuriously furnished. Antiques and period pieces intermingle with eclectic international art. All guest rooms offer private baths, thick terry robes, and down or silk duvets. Two rooms have gas fireplaces and separate sitting areas. Our favorite, Under the Apple Tree, has a two-person jetted tub and a private patio. Ideal innkeepers, owners Rex Davidson and Ruth Crameri are a genial former restaurateur and Scottish history expert, and a professional interior designer from five generations of Swiss hoteliers, respectively. A delightful afternoon tea, including European pastries, fruit flans, and sherry, is served on the porch overlooking the flower garden or in the living room by the fireplace, depending on the weather. Breakfast is a sumptuous four-course affair that might include homemade granola with mulled milk or stirred yogurt, a selection of breads and jams, sherried grapefruit, alder-smoked Pacific salmon in puff pastry, and fresh fruits. *$$$; AE, DC, E, MC, V; no checks; davidson@helix.net; www.thistle-down.com; across from Capilano Suspension Bridge.*

LOWER MAINLAND
BRITISH COLUMBIA

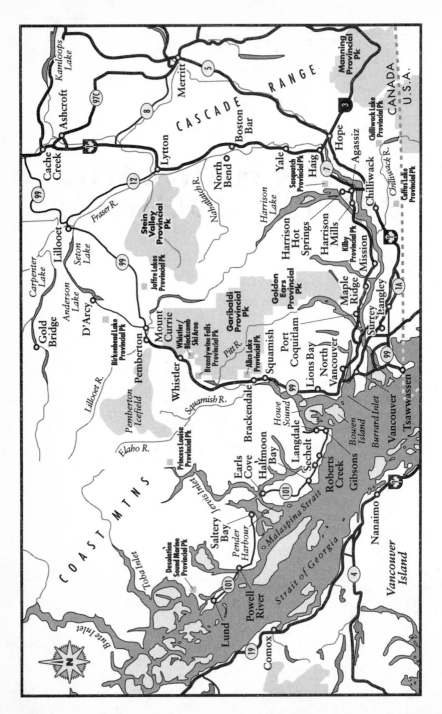

LOWER MAINLAND BRITISH COLUMBIA

More than half of British Columbia's 4 million residents reside in the southwest corner of the province, primarily in the Greater Vancouver Regional District of the Lower Mainland. Early immigration into what was first called the Crown Colony of British Columbia, centered in Victoria, soon spilled over from Vancouver Island into the lush Fraser River estuary and adjacent Fraser Valley. Vancouver Islanders use the term "mainlanders" to emphasize the separation between the two. The Strait of Georgia that divides the island from the Lower Mainland represents as much a psychological schism as it does a physical split. It didn't help when, by the end of the 1800s, Vancouver and the Lower Mainland had stolen the limelight from the government seat in Victoria.

During the past century, the Lower Mainland has grown well beyond the Fraser River basin to encompass not only Greater Vancouver but also the Sunshine Coast, the Sea to Sky corridor, as well as the Fraser Valley regions, all of which are defined by the towering presence of the Coast Mountains that begin here and stretch north to Alaska. The success of Vancouver's bid to host the 2010 Olympic winter games, coupled with Whistler's ascendancy as one of the world's hippest resorts, has thrown a halo around the entire region.

ACCESS AND INFORMATION

Border crossings (and customs) link Washington State and the Lower Mainland at four locations. The busiest are the crossings at Blaine, Washington, where Interstate 5 links with Highway 99 at the Peace Arch, and at Douglas, linking with BC's Highway 15. The others are located just south of Aldergrove, and at Sumas just south of Abbotsford. The nearest major airport is **VANCOUVER INTERNATIONAL AIRPORT** (3211 Grant McConachie Wy, Richmond; 604/207-7077; *www.yvr.ca*).

HIGHWAY 1 (Trans-Canada Hwy) runs east-west and links the south Fraser Valley with Vancouver. **HIGHWAY 17** links BC Ferries' Tsawwassen terminal with **HIGHWAY 99**. The North Shore is reached by traveling west on Highway 1 across the Ironworkers Memorial Second Narrows Bridge, or via the Lions Gate Bridge from downtown Vancouver on Hwy 99A. Highway 1/99A (or the Upper Levels Hwy, as it is called on the North Shore) crosses North and West Vancouver to Horseshoe Bay, site of the BC Ferries terminal connecting the North Shore with Nanaimo on southern Vancouver Island, Langdale (and Highway 101) on the Sunshine Coast, and nearby Bowen Island. From Horseshoe Bay, Highway 99 (the Sea to Sky Hwy) links the North Shore with the upcountry communities of Squamish, Whistler, Pemberton, and Lillooet.

The **VANCOUVER, COAST & MOUNTAINS TOURISM REGION** (250-1508 W 2nd Ave, Vancouver, V6J 1H2; 604/739-9011 or 888/430-3339; *info@vcmbc.com*; *www.vcmbc.com*) is a font of information on the Lower Mainland.

Sea to Sky Highway (Highway 99)

The scenic Sea to Sky Highway crosses paths with two historic routes—the Pemberton Trail and the Gold Rush Heritage Trail—that linked the coast with the interior in the days before automobiles. Along these ancient pathways, generations of Coast Salish people traded with their relations in the Fraser Canyon, and in the 1850s, prospectors stampeded north toward the Cariboo gold fields. By the mid-1960s, the prospect of skiers heading from Vancouver to the fledgling trails on Whistler Mountain prompted the opening of a road north from Horseshoe Bay. Space being at a premium along steep-sided Howe Sound (North America's southernmost fjord), road and BC Rail lines parallel each other for much of the 28 miles (45 km) between Horseshoe Bay and Squamish, at the head of the sound. By 1975, the highway linked Whistler with Pemberton, and by 1995 the last stretch was paved between Pemberton and Lillooet. Today, vehicles cover the entire 142-mile (236 km) Sea to Sky route between Horseshoe Bay and Lillooet in about five hours. Certainly, Whistler's success has propelled development, both commercial and recreational, in other parts of the region, particularly Squamish and Pemberton. So, too, has the popularity of mountain biking, snowmobiling, and sport utility vehicles—all of which make the local backcountry more accessible.

ACCESS AND INFORMATION

GREYHOUND CANADA (604/482-8747 in Vancouver, 604/898-3914 in Squamish, 604/932-6236 in Whistler; *www.greyhound.ca*) offers frequent daily service between Vancouver, Squamish, Whistler, Pemberton, and Mount Currie. **WHISTLER AIR** (604/932-6615; *www.whistlerair.ca*) offers twice-daily floatplane service between Vancouver and Whistler, June–September.

Squamish

Squamish (population 14,250), or "Squish," as it is affectionately known, is a relief. Far smaller than Vancouver, larger than Whistler, and equidistant from both, Squamish is the envy of the south coast. It has so many things going for it—location, geography, wildlife, weather—that as forestry declines as the town's major employer, tourism and outdoor recreation have taken on greater importance.

A gateway to outdoor pursuits, Squamish is strategically situated amidst water and mountains. Depending on the time of year, you can canoe, sea or white-water kayak, sail, horseback ride, backpack, rock climb, mountaineer, cross-country ski, mountain bike, windsurf, kite board, or bird-watch. Not surprisingly, the town crowned itself the outdoor recreation capital of Canada in 2002.

For information on all aspects of life here, contact the **SQUAMISH CHAMBER OF COMMERCE AND VISITOR INFO CENTRE** (37950 Cleveland Ave, Squamish; 604/892-9244; *info@squamishchamber.bc.ca*; *www.squamishchamber.bc.ca*).

RESTAURANTS

Red Heather Grill & Brew Pub / ★★

37801 CLEVELAND AVE (HOWE SOUND INN), SQUAMISH; 604/892-2603 OR 800/919-2537 The Howe Sound Inn's restaurant and brew pub offer the best of both worlds. Whether you put your feet up in the pub or spiffy up for a meal in the Red Heather Grill (Squamish's most upscale dining room), the food for both originates from the same creative kitchen. The Red Heather Grill features tastefully understated decor that matches the indoor-outdoor feel of the inn, minus the sports fare featured on the pub's omnipresent televisions. Pull up a Craftsman chair to a sturdy wooden table, or settle in on an oversize couch beside the fireplace next to the bar. You can't go wrong with seafood specials such as skewers of sweet Thai ahi tuna or the West Coast Salmon Sampler—smoked, candied, and barbecued tips, with mango salsa, red pepper mayonnaise, and assorted relishes. House breads, such as whole wheat focaccia or herb and cheese are baked on premises. (Buy a loaf to go.) The grill has its own wood-fired pizza oven from which inventive creations (with toppings such as lime-cured chicken) emerge. *$$; AE, MC, V; no checks; breakfast, lunch, dinner every day, brunch Sat–Sun; full bar; reservations recommended; hsibrew@howesound.com; www.howesound.com; downtown Squamish.* &

LODGINGS

Howe Sound Inn & Brewing Company / ★

37801 CLEVELAND AVE, SQUAMISH; 604/892-2603 OR 800/919-2537 This 20-room inn, with its massive fieldstone chimney (the exterior of which doubles as a climbing wall), is part pub, part restaurant, and part hotel. Owner Dave Fenn fashioned his gathering place with outdoor enthusiasts in mind. Guests can pick up information on local recreation and get the latest road reports, all while taking in inspiring views of Stawamus Chief Mountain (with its legendary rock-climbing routes), which towers above the inn's front entrance. The modestly sized rooms are decorated in warm tartans and feature comfy beds. Best bets are rooms 13–20 on the quiet side of the inn opposite the pub entrance. *$$; AE, MC, V; no checks; hsibrew@howesound.com; www.howesound.com; downtown Squamish.* &

SunWolf Outdoor Centre / ★

70002 SQUAMISH VALLEY RD, BRACKENDALE; 604/898-1537 OR 877/806-8046 SunWolf's 10 cabins sit at the shaded confluence of the Cheakamus and Cheekye Rivers, whose soothing voices drown out all else. The 5½-acre center makes an ideal base when exploring the outdoors around Squamish. Each of the high-ceilinged cabins (some with kitchenettes) comes equipped with a gas fireplace, fir floors, pine furnishings, and both a double and a single bed. Light meals are available from the café in the center's main lodge, a good place to relax while perusing maps and guidebooks. Staff members offer expert advice on where to go and what to do. White-water rafting and eagle-viewing float trips are two specialties. Rent mountain bikes, canoes, or kayaks. Skiing, fishing, rock climbing, hiking, and horseback riding are other options. *$$; MC, V; checks OK; sunwolf@sunwolf .net; www.sunwolf.net; 2½ miles (4 km) west of Hwy 99 on Squamish Valley Rd.*

SEA TO SKY THREE-DAY TOUR

DAY ONE: Breakfast until Vancouver's morning rush hour is over (North Shore bridges are typically busy until 9am), then begin your journey north to Squamish on the aptly named **SEA TO SKY HIGHWAY** (Hwy 99). Take time for a stroll along **PORTEAU COVE PARK**'s black gravel beach at the road's halfway point along Howe Sound. Lunch at the **BRACKENDALE ART GALLERY AND THEATRE RESTAURANT** (604/898-3333) in north Squamish, then explore **SHANNON FALLS PARK** to view BC's third-highest waterfall. Check in at the nearby **HOWE SOUND INN & BREWING COMPANY** in downtown Squamish. Admire the views of Stawamus Chief Mountain from the pub after choosing from an arm's-long list of microbrews, then freshen up before dining at the inn's **RED HEATHER GRILL**. Get an early night.

    DAY TWO: Breakfast at the inn, and make sure there's film in your camera. The breathtaking drive to Whistler is only 45 minutes nonstop, but take your time. Pause at the **TANTALUS RANGE VIEWPOINT** to see a dozen or more peaks, and at **BRANDYWINE FALLS PARK**, where a short walk leads to the rim of the falls. Lunch in Whistler at **HOZ'S PUB**, where insiders have been heading for decades. Just outside is the beginning of the 12-mile (20 km) **VALLEY TRAIL** that leads past nearby Nita Lake.

Whistler

The Resort Municipality of Whistler (population 8,900) nestles in a narrow valley. High above, hundreds of trails crisscross Blackcomb and Whistler Mountains. No other valley in the Sea to Sky region enjoys such a wealth of small and medium-sized lakes. And no other lakes have quite the scenery to mirror. Remnants of the most recent ice age persist in glaciers on the highest peaks in **GARIBALDI PARK** (*wlapwww.gov.bc.ca/bcparks/*).

Whistler comprises a collection of neighborhoods linked to the hotels and restaurants in the village core by roads and the pedestrian-friendly Valley Trail. Hop on one of the Whistler WAVE (Whistler and Valley Express) public buses, a car-free way to see the valley, which connect with all Whistler neighborhoods, from Function Junction to Emerald Estates, as well as the villages of Pemberton and Mount Currie. **WAVE** (604/932-4020; *www.busonline.ca*) operates a free village shuttle with stops at Whistler Village, Village North, Upper Village, and the Benchlands. All buses are equipped with racks for skis and snowboards in winter, and bikes in summer.

    WHISTLER MOUNTAIN (elevation 7,160 feet/2,182 m) and **BLACKCOMB MOUNTAIN** (elevation 7,494 feet/2,284 m) were rivals for two decades before merging under the Intrawest corporate umbrella in 1997. Together they make what many skiers, snowboarders, and (more recently) mountain bikers consider the premier North American resort. You can just as easily explore one as the other; each offers a complimentary perspective on its companion and has a loyal following of devotees. They have been around long enough (Whistler since 1965, Blackcomb since 1980)

Head north to the **EDGEWATER LODGE** on Green Lake. After checking in, double back into Whistler Village, where, depending on the season, you can catch happy hour with skiers and snowboarders or mountain bikers at the **GARIBALDI LIFT COMPANY (604/905-2220)** beside Whistler Mountain's Village Gondola. Treat yourself to dinner at **ARAXI'S**, or head back to Green Lake for the sunset on Blackcomb and Whistler Mountains and dinner at the **EDGEWATER**.

DAY THREE: Get up early for breakfast at the Edgewater before continuing north. Stop at **NAIRN FALLS PARK** for a quick jaunt to the falls, then into Pemberton and to **GRIMM'S GOURMET & DELI** to pick up picnic supplies. Poke your head in at **NORTH ARM FARM** on Highway 99 between Pemberton and Mount Currie for fresh-baked goodies and produce before you begin the two-hour drive to **LILLOOET**. Pause at one of several roadside sites beside Cayoosh Creek to enjoy your lunch. Just before Lillooet, stop at the **BC HYDRO RECREATION AREA** on turquoise Seton Lake to walk the beach, then walk to the nearby viewpoint. In Lillooet, check into your room at the **4 PINES MOTEL**, then stroll over to **DINA'S PLACE** for dinner. Catch the sunset from the patio as the smell of sagebrush rises in the air.

---

to have developed trails covering more than 7,071 acres that have been shaped, groomed, and gladed to hold snow in winter and provide exciting downhill cycling in summer in the **WHISTLER MOUNTAIN BIKE PARK**. For information on lessons and rentals, as well as ticket prices, contact **WHISTLER-BLACKCOMB GUEST RELATIONS** (604/932-3434 or 800/766-0449; *www.whistler-blackcomb.com*).

Whistler Village's **LOST LAKE PARK** (604/905-0071; *www.crosscountry connection.bc.ca*) features a 20-mile (32 km) network of packed and tracked trails for cross-country skiers, snowshoers, and, in summer, mountain bikers. Skiing around the lake takes 60–90 minutes. Trails are marked for beginners to experts; the 2-mile (4 km) **LOST LAKE LOOP TRAIL** is lit for night skiing.

A designated cross-country ski trail in winter and a hiking/cycling/in-line skating loop in summer, the 12-mile (20 km) **VALLEY TRAIL**'s access points include the Whistler Golf Course (on Hwy 99 in Whistler Village), the Meadow Park Sports Centre (on Hwy 99 in Alpine Meadows), and Rainbow Park (on Alta Lake Rd).

Snowmobiling is big at Whistler: **CANADIAN SNOWMOBILE ADVENTURES** (604/938-1616; *www.canadiansnowmobile.com*) and **COUGAR MOUNTAIN WILDERNESS ADVENTURES** (36-4314 Main St; 604/932-4086; *www.cougar mountainatwhistler.com*), which also offers dogsledding, horseback riding, snowshoeing, fishing, and mountain bike tours.

Heli-skiing/boarding in Whistler can be arranged with **WHISTLER HELI-SKIING** (3-4241 Village Stroll; 604/932-4105; *www.whistlerheliskiing.com*), **COAST RANGE HELISKIING** (604/894-1144 or 800/701-8744; *www.coastrangeheliskiing.com*), and **BLACKCOMB HELICOPTERS** (9990 Heliport; 604/938-1700; *www.blackcomb helicopters.com*).

Some of the most inviting **SNOWSHOE TRAILS** in Whistler are those in the forest surrounding Olympic Station on Whistler Mountain. **OUTDOOR ADVENTURES AT WHISTLER** (4205 Village Square; 604/932-0647; *www.adventureswhistler.com*) offers rentals and guided tours, including evening outings on Blackcomb.

For summer visitors, golf choices include the scenic Arnold Palmer–designed **WHISTLER GOLF CLUB** (4001 Whistler Wy; 604/932-3280), or the equally esteemed Robert Trent Jones Jr. link course at Chateau Whistler (4599 Chateau Blvd; 604/938-2092). There is also **NICKLAUS NORTH** (8080 Nicklaus N Blvd; 604/938-9898), a Jack Nicklaus–designed course in the Green Lake area.

Tourism Whistler's **ACTIVITY AND INFORMATION CENTRE** (4010 Whistler Wy; 604/932-2394) offers advice and arrangements for any winter or summer recreation. Whistler has achieved such a high level of international popularity that on some weekends, rooms cannot be had for love or money. With more than 2 million ski visits alone each winter, advance reservations are recommended for all lodging and restaurants. Many rooms in the area, as well as condos, are owned by different management companies. All may be reached through Tourism Whistler's **CENTRAL RESERVATIONS** (604/932-4222 in Whistler, 604/664-5625 in Vancouver, or 800/944-7853 from the United States and Canada, except BC; *whistler.rezrez .net/vps*). For a complete listing of activities, consult **TOURISM WHISTLER** (4010 Whistler Wy, Whistler; 604/932-3928 in Whistler, 604/664-5625 in Vancouver, or 800/944-7853; *www.mywhistler.com*). The newly renovated **WHISTLER VISITOR INFO CENTRE** (2097 Lake Placid Rd, Whistler Conference Centre; 604/932-5528) provides information about accommodations, restaurants, outfitters, and special events year-round. Three information kiosks are open in the summer: **VILLAGE BOOTH**, at the Greyhound Bus Loop, the **VILLAGE KIOSK** in Village Square, and the **NORTH KIOSK BY THE GAZEBO** in Village North. This resort, where the average house price now tops $1 million, is expensive—sometimes *scary* expensive—but you can generally count on good-to-outstanding value in return.

RESTAURANTS

Araxi Restaurant & Bar / ★★★★

4222 WHISTLER VILLAGE SQUARE, WHISTLER; 604/932-4540 If you only dine out once in Whistler, choose Araxi. Whistler's culinary cornerstone anchors the Village Square's patio scene. The restaurant's cozy ambiance is best experienced from a seat at the mahogany-topped bar, possibly the longest—and least crowded—in town. Dubbed "heaven" by staff veterans, this is where to size up Araxi's expansive wine cellar. With its emphasis on fresh, locally sourced fare prepared with French and Italian influences, Araxi's menu—just like its artwork—undergoes a complete makeover every six months. Perennial favorites run the gamut from Salt Spring Island smoked albacore tuna brochettes with organic peach salsa, minted cucumber, tobiko, and cilantro syrup, to Lillooet honey crème brûlée. Check the Araxi Web site for the latest mouth-watering selections. *$$$; AE, DC, MC, V; no checks; lunch May–Dec, dinner every day; full bar; reservations recommended; info@araxi.com; www.araxi.com; heart of Whistler Village.* &

Caramba! / ★★

4314 MAIN ST (EAGLE LODGE), WHISTLER; 604/938-1879 Caramba! (a.k.a. Wow!) proves dining out in Whistler doesn't have to break the bank. This fun, boisterous, Mediterranean-influenced restaurant holds down a corner of the Town Plaza on one of Village North's busiest walkways. High-energy service twins with big, soul-satisfying portions of pasta, pizza, and roasts. The open kitchen, zinc countertops, alder-fired pizza ovens, and sizzling rotisseries lend a warm, casual tone to the room. The real stars of this menu are appetizers, such as the phenomenal Calamari a la Plancha, a garlic-laden treat that really shines when teamed with sautéed wild mushrooms or Insalada Caprese (ripe tomatoes, young bocconcini). Toss in a bottle of Caramba!'s house wine from Francis Ford Coppola's vineyard and you've got the makings of "Wow! Now." *$; AE, MC, V; no checks; lunch seasonal, dinner every day; full bar; reservations recommended; www.caramba-restaurante .com; Village North, at Town Plaza Square.* &

Chef Bernard's Café / ★

4573 CHATEAU BLVD, WHISTLER; 604/932-7051 Don't be put off if the lineup at Chef Bernard's stretches out the door toward the Chateau Whistler, former home of executive chef Bernard Casavant, now one of Whistler's foremost caterers. As if to belie the café's cramped interior, crack service helps move things along at a brisk pace. After you squeeze inside and place your order, the outdoor patio is *the* place to wake up on a sunny summer morning. Indoors, where Casavant's kitchen jockeys for room with a few wooden tables and a takeout counter, it's catch-as-catch-can. All this makes for instant informality as customers share this little space. Close proximity leads to impromptu conversations with visitors drawn to Whistler from the four corners of the world. Casavant's sure touch at fusing classic French and Pacific Northwest cuisines impresses with dishes such as shrimp meat and caramelized scallops with asparagus, and Brie-and-carrot soup. Fresh sheet dinner specials, such as pan-seared wild salmon fillet in a lemongrass and star anise marinade served with basmati rice and a spicy orange-ginger sauce, are offered both in the café and the adjacent 24-seat BBK Pub run by Casavant's wife, Bonnie. *$; AE, MC, V; no checks; breakfast, lunch every day, dinner seasonal; beer and wine; no reservations; bbks@whooshnet.com; Upper Village, at Blackcomb Wy.* &

Hoz's Pub & El Tipo's Mexican Grill / ★★

2129 LAKE PLACID RD, WHISTLER; 604/932-4424 Good basic fare in a down-to-earth atmosphere might seem elusive in Whistler, but the locals have long known a spot that pleases every palate and wets every whistle. From deluxe burgers, pasta, barbecued chicken, ribs, and big beef bones (served with beans, hand-cut fries, and slaw) to cod or salmon fish-and-chips, Hoz's menu pushes all the right buttons. Owner Ron "Hoz" Hosner, a fixture in the Creekside neighborhood, pursues his culinary passion in an adjacent room, the new 45-seat El Tipo's ("The Dude's") Mexican Grill. Hoz, sporting his trademark desperado mustache, surveys the crowd as he and an assistant prep the Southern California–influenced Mexican dishes of his youth: salmon quesadillas, chimichangas, roll-your-own fajitas, and steak Mazatlan. *$; AE, DC, MC, V; no checks; breakfast, lunch, dinner every day; full bar; reservations not accepted; thebar@hozspub.com; www.hozspub .com; 1 block west of Hwy 99, Creekside area.*

Jayde / ★

1200 ALTA LAKE ROAD, WHISTLER; 604/932-4611 Just off the beaten track, Jayde is worth the 10-minute drive from Whistler Village. Chef/owner Eric Vernice concentrates on modern European cuisine with interesting results. For sheer decadence, go for the foie gras trio: pan-seared with pear; crème brûlée and brioche; and marinated in roasted almond oil. Then move on to a second appetizer of braised rabbit risotto with porcini mushrooms. Vernice serves a wonderful oven-roasted monkfish with root vegetable emulsion and zucchini gratin. Lastly, ask for the dessert symphony. *$$$–$$$$; AE, DC, MC, V; no checks; dinner every day; full bar; reservations recommended; jayde@telus.net; at Twin Lakes Village, 10 minutes south of Whistler Village.*

La Rúa Restaurante / ★★★★

4557 BLACKCOMB WY (LE CHAMOIS), WHISTLER; 604/932-5011 Longtime Whistler restaurateur Mario Enero's stylish, comfortable restaurant is tucked away in Le Chamois hotel at Blackcomb's Upper Village base. Superb dishes created by R.D. Stewart, one of Whistler's top-ranked chefs, are served in portions that will satisfy the most ravenous skier or mountain biker. Start with a pyramid of bocconcini cheese or a seafood tower constructed with layers of Dungeness crab, salmon tartar, avocado salsa, and smoked salmon, and finished with caviar. No one makes better lamb, serving a rack with caramelized garlic sauce and mint dumplings or a shank set atop a mound of root vegetables and lentils. Exotic pastas, such as lumache shells stuffed with spinach, Dungeness crab, and ricotta cheese in a baked shrimp mornay sauce, will win your heart. Save room for a mango-raspberry Napoleon made with layers of fresh berries, mango mousse, and crisp vanilla phyllo. *$$$; AE, DC, MC, V; no checks; dinner every day; full bar; reservations recommended; www.laruarestaurante.com; Upper Village, Lorimer Rd and Blackcomb Wy.* &

Quattro at Whistler / ★★★

🌲 **4319 MAIN ST (PINNACLE INTERNATIONAL HOTEL), WHISTLER; 604/905-4844** Quattro is upbeat, vibrant, and innovative. *La cucina leggera,* or "the healthy kitchen," is the motto here, a concept that fits the West Coast sensibility like a good set of ski boots. Fungi fanciers love the carpaccio featuring sliced portobello mushrooms topped with flavorful white truffle oil and shaved Asiago. Kudos also for the grilled scallops and prawns, served with a painstakingly prepared Dungeness crab risotto inside a phyllo roll. Pasta dishes, such as the gnocchi al Gorgonzola, an idyllic marriage of tender potato-and-semolina dumplings and sharp Gorgonzola topped with roasted pecans, are equally inspired. Entrées of crisp deboned Cornish game hen or roasted lean duck breast, accompanied by sun-dried blueberry and port wine sauce, are irresistible. The portions are generous, and the mainly Italian wine list is stellar. The staff is knowledgeable, friendly, and attentive. Desserts (which change daily) are stunning. *$$$; MC, V; no checks; dinner every day* *(closed mid-Oct–mid-Nov); full bar; reservations recommended; quattro@telus.net; www.quattrorestaurants.com; Village North, at Library Square.*&

Rim Rock Cafe and Oyster Bar / ★★★

2117 WHISTLER RD (HIGHLAND LODGE), WHISTLER; 604/932-5565 OR 877/932-5589 Manager Bob Dawson and chef Rolf Gunther dish out great food in their cozy, woody café with its centerpiece stone fireplace, and the place is filled to the open rafters with locals (who consistently rate this Creekside cornerstone as their favorite place to dine). A daily fresh sheet features fish- and game-themed selections, such as seared foie gras with rare ahi in a red wine reduction accompanied by crisp leeks and apple-raspberry salad, and grilled northern caribou in a porcini mushroom cream sauce with wild mushroom gnocchi and cranberry relish. The wine list emphasizes Pacific Rim selections. Along with its reputation for superb seafood, the service here is ranked the best in town. In winter, book at least a week in advance. In summer, request a table on the cozy back patio and dine amid fresh herbs in the chef's garden. *$$$; AE, MC, V; no checks; dinner every day (closed mid-Oct–mid-Nov); full bar; reservations recommended; rimrock@direct.ca; www.rimrockwhistler.com; 2 miles (3.5 km) south of Whistler Village, at Creekside.*

Splitz Grill / ★

4369 MAIN ST (ALPENGLOW), WHISTLER; 604/938-9300 It's been a long time since a hamburger has been this thick, juicy, and tantalizing. Small wonder Splitz routinely tops the polls as the town's best burger joint. The not-so-humble grilled sandwich on a crusty bun is elevated to new heights with your choice of umpteen toppings, such as Salt Spring Island lamb with *tzatziki* (worthy of china and linen napkins), teriyaki salmon fillet, Italian sausage, or spicy lentil. A satisfying meal is less than $10, half that for kids, whose selections come with thick, house-cut fries and a soft drink. Sweet temptations include ice cream sundaes, floats, shakes, cones, and a caramelized banana split. *$; V; no checks; lunch, dinner every day; beer and wine; no reservations; Village North, across from 7-Eleven.*

Sushi Village / ★★

4272 MOUNTAIN SQUARE (WESTBROOK HOTEL), WHISTLER; 604/932-3330 To satisfy an appetite for healthy portions of Japanese cuisine, locals invariably choose Sushi Village. You can't miss it, even though it's perched on the second floor of the Westbrook Hotel; ravenous young skiers and snowboarders patiently wait in line with upscale sophisticates. It's worth it. Delicious and extremely fresh sushi, sashimi, and maki platters, as well as abundant combinations served in wooden sushi boats, are prepared by animated experts at the counter. Tempura, gyoza, yakitori, teriyaki, and satisfying meal-sized noodle soups are just a few hot dishes. Food is straightforward, dependable, and a good deal. The staff is knowledgeable, gracious, and consistent. Simple Japanese-style decor allows for privacy even with large parties. Semiprivate tatami rooms and takeout are available. *$$; AE, DC, MC, V; no checks; lunch Wed–Sun, dinner every day* *(weekends only off-season); full bar; reservations for 4 or more; info@sushivillage.com; www.sushivillage.com; Whistler Village, at Sundial Cres.* &

Trattoria di Umberto / ★★★☆

4417 SUNDIAL PL (MOUNTAINSIDE LODGE), WHISTLER; 604/932-5858 You can depend on any of Umberto's establishments, and this is no exception. Two large, romantically lit dining rooms separated by a massive open kitchen welcome you to this busy, lively, Northern Italian establishment. Animated conversation is as much a part of the atmosphere as the potted plants and sculptures, the poolside view, and the rustic Italian decor. Service is fast and friendly. Classic Tuscan starters include beef carpaccio topped with shaved Parmesan, accompanied by a mélange of aromatic vegetables, and hearty bean soup. But it's entrées like the grilled quail with sage, or the cioppino (a saffron- and fennel-laced stew combining crab, prawns, mussels, and a variety of fish in a rich tomato broth) that will leave you singing the kitchen's praises. No trattoria can exist without pasta and risotto dishes: smoked-duck-and-portobello risotto, and penne with pesto and smoked salmon, are just two examples at Umberto's. A respectable wine list, desserts large enough to share, cappuccino, and espresso complete the experience. *$$$–$$$$; AE, DC, MC, V; no checks; lunch, dinner every day; full bar; reservations recommended; inquire@umberto.com; www.umberto.com; Whistler Village, at Blackcomb Wy.* &

Val d'Isère / ★★★★

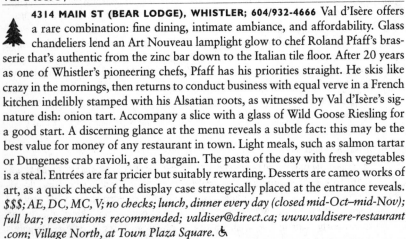

4314 MAIN ST (BEAR LODGE), WHISTLER; 604/932-4666 Val d'Isère offers a rare combination: fine dining, intimate ambiance, and affordability. Glass chandeliers lend an Art Nouveau lamplight glow to chef Roland Pfaff's brasserie that's authentic from the zinc bar down to the Italian tile floor. After 20 years as one of Whistler's pioneering chefs, Pfaff has his priorities straight. He skis like crazy in the mornings, then returns to conduct business with equal verve in a French kitchen indelibly stamped with his Alsatian roots, as witnessed by Val d'Isère's signature dish: onion tart. Accompany a slice with a glass of Wild Goose Riesling for a good start. A discerning glance at the menu reveals a subtle fact: this may be the best value for money of any restaurant in town. Light meals, such as salmon tartar or Dungeness crab ravioli, are a bargain. The pasta of the day with fresh vegetables is a steal. Entrées are far pricier but suitably rewarding. Desserts are cameo works of art, as a quick check of the display case strategically placed at the entrance reveals. *$$$; AE, DC, MC, V; no checks; lunch, dinner every day (closed mid-Oct–mid-Nov); full bar; reservations recommended; valdiser@direct.ca; www.valdisere-restaurant .com; Village North, at Town Plaza Square.* &

LODGINGS

Brew Creek Lodge / ★★

1 BREW CREEK RD, WHISTLER; 604/932-7210 This sparkling hideaway sits at the foot of Brandywine Mountain south of Whistler. A sheltering forest buffers all sounds from the steady stream of nearby traffic on Highway 99. Brew Creek, the lodge's crowning touch, flows through the 12-acre property past a massive post-and-beam main lodge with six spacious bed-and-breakfast rooms with private bathrooms. Nearby are two suites that share the Guest House (sleeps eight), plus the Trappers Cabin (four), and the romantic Treehouse (two), all self-contained. No TVs or phones intrude on Brew Creek's atmosphere of calm, best appreciated from the creek-side hot tub or the main lodge's secluded back deck. Architectural flourishes abound, though it would be hard to improve on the natural beauty. Cross-country and hiking trails encircle the lodge. *$$–$$$; AE, MC, V; no checks; www.brewcreek.com; 12 miles (16 km) south of Whistler.* &

Delta Whistler Resort / ★★

4050 WHISTLER WY, WHISTLER; 604/932-1982 OR 800/515-4050 As the first major hotel to open in Whistler Village at the base of the dual mountain operations in the 1980s, the Delta Whistler Resort nabbed a prime location. Further development has added a year-round tennis facility, a heated outdoor lap pool, as well as a spa and fitness center. The resort's standard rooms are surprisingly ordinary. Executive studios are worth the extra expense, equipped with balconies and fireplaces, full kitchens, Jacuzzis or soaking tubs, and clothes dryers. Also convenient are bike and ski rental shops in the 300-room, pet-friendly hotel. *$$$$; AE, DC, DIS, JCB, MC, V; checks OK; reservations@deltawhistler.com; www.deltawhistler.com; Whistler Village.* &

Durlacher Hof Alpine Country Inn / ★★★

7055 NESTERS RD, WHISTLER; 604/932-1924 OR 877/932-1924 As authentic as edelweiss, this Tyrolean-style farmhouse, owned by Erika and Peter Durlacher, is a traditional country inn right down to hut slippers that await guests' feet. Hand-carved furniture and fixtures adorn all eight rooms, plus the piano bar and cozy kitchen with its *kachenelofen*—an old-fashioned fireplace oven. For simple overnight stays, book one of the second-floor Sunshine rooms with views of Blackcomb and Whistler Mountains just minutes away. If you're lucky enough to be here for an extended stay, try the roomier Premier suite. Romance flourishes on the inn's third floor, which houses two suites with vaulted wooden ceilings and private Jacuzzi tubs. Attention to detail is evident everywhere, such as in the cozy après-ski area where complimentary afternoon tea is served. A groaning sideboard holds lavish breakfasts. From the moment you get up to the last cup of *glüwein* (hot red wine) late at night (the guest lounge is also a licensed bar), sharing the Hof with the Durlachers is a joy. *$$$$; MC, V; checks OK; info@durlacherhof.com; www.durlacherhof.com; Nesters neighborhood.* &

Edgewater Lodge / ★★

8841 HWY 99, WHISTLER; 604/932-0688 OR 888/870-9065 Hands down, this inn commands the best view on Blackcomb and Whistler of any lodging in the valley. Still, owner Jay Simmons purposefully keeps his Green Lake estate low-key. For starters, the entrance to the lodge's intimate restaurant (where guests are treated to a bountiful complimentary breakfast) doubles as the Edgewater's lobby. Twelve modest guest rooms, half of which are furnished with dens and pullout beds, look out through picture windows onto Green Lake. The Edgewater's lakeside location offers quick access to outdoor recreation, such as canoeing, kayaking, and horseback riding. The multi-use recreational Valley Trail links the 45-acre property with the rest of Whistler. Meadow Park Sports Arena—complete with indoor skating rink, fitness center, and swimming pool—lies nearby, as does the Nicklaus North golf course. Pets are welcome. *$$–$$$; AE, DC, MC, V; local checks only; jays@direct .ca; www.edgewater-lodge.com; across from Meadow Park Arena.* &

Fairmont Chateau Whistler Resort / ★★★★

4599 CHATEAU BLVD, WHISTLER; 604/938-8000 OR 800/606-8244 In keeping with the cachet its sister chateaus enjoy in Banff and Lake Louise, the 12-story, 563-room Chateau Whistler is arguably *the* place to experience Whistler. Anchoring the Upper Village neighborhood, the chateau's sun-drenched east face offers sweeping views of the Coast Mountains from its slope-side suites, the Wildflower dining room and Mallard Lounge, the indoor/outdoor pool, and the award-winning spa complex. Not surprisingly, all of the pampering one would expect (guest robes, chocolates on the pillow, daily newspaper delivery, ski valet service) is provided. Given the grand impression of the chateau's foyer, however, standard rooms—particularly junior suites—are only adequately sized. While most rooms are still over-the-top expensive, west-facing accommodations are priced slightly lower. The chateau's public areas are some of the most inviting in Whistler and deserve a look even if you're staying elsewhere. Hooked rugs soften the lobby's slate slab floor, while folk art and twig furniture accent two mammoth limestone fireplaces. Blackcomb's Wizard chairlift lies just steps away, while the heart of the village is a pleasant 5-minute walk. *$$$$; AE, DC, DIS, MC, V; checks OK; reservations@chateauwhister.com; www.fairmont.com; at foot of Blackcomb.* &

Pan Pacific Lodge / ★★★☆

4320 SUNDIAL CRES, WHISTLER; 604/905-2999 OR 888/905-9995 "Lodge" is not the word that first springs to mind when you arrive at Pan Pacific Hotels' Whistler property. Its modest lobby shares an entrance with an Irish pub. Only a deer-antler chandelier and Morris chairs arranged beside a river-rock fireplace evoke the spirit of classic mountain lodges. On the eight floors above, 121 studios, 1-bedroom suites, and 2-bedroom suites with floor-to-ceiling windows give the impression you're floating among the peaks. All have fireplaces, soaker tubs, plush robes, Internet hookups, full kitchens (occasionally more irritating than convenient, as refrigerators in studio suites can be noisy), and private balconies. A heated outdoor pool and hot tubs grace the lodge's second-floor terrace, with a spa, fitness center, and steam room tucked inside. In spring, après-ski action on the adjacent Skier's Plaza heats up. During April's 10-day World Ski and Snowboard Festival, those seeking tranquility should book elsewhere. The Pan Pacific Whistler Village Centre is slated to open in December 2004. *$$$$; AE, DC, MC, V; no checks; whistler_res@panpacific.com; www.whistler.panpacific.com; off Blackcomb Wy.* &

Whistler Village Inn & Suites / ★★

429 SUNDIAL PL, WHISTLER; 604/932-4004 OR 800/663-6418 With the debut of Blackcomb Mountain in 1980, the heart of Whistler Village began to take shape. It was as exciting to stay at this inn then as it is today. Completely renovated in 2000, with more touches added in 2001, this

89-room boutique hotel sits just around the corner from the base of the lifts for both mountains in the pedestrian-friendly heart of the village. Shops, bars, restaurants, and equipment rentals are just steps away. The inn's view suites, with full kitchens, wood-burning fireplaces, patios, and cozy sleeping lofts, provide a comfortable family ambiance. There's also a heated outdoor pool, a steaming hot tub, and a sauna. Complimentary continental breakfast is served in the lobby under the baleful gaze of a regal moose head. *$$–$$$$; AE, DC, DIS, MC, V; no checks; wvi@direct .ca; www.whistlervillageinn.bc.ca; heart of Whistler Village.* &

Pemberton and Mount Currie

In the decades before Highway 99 linked with Pemberton, this farming community that's quickly evolving into a Whistler suburb existed in splendid isolation from the rest of the Lower Mainland. Travelers moved in and out of its broad valley by rail (a tradition that sadly came to an uncertain end when BC Rail cancelled its passenger service in 2003). Public transit now connects Pemberton and nearby Mount Currie (3.7 miles/6 km east) with Whistler (22 miles/35 km south). For schedule and fare information, contact WAVE (604/938-0388; *www.busonline.ca*).

Today, this agriculturally and recreationally rich valley is experiencing phenomenal growth in both visitors and new residents, many of whom work in Whistler. Quick access to golfing, hiking, climbing, mountain biking, and backcountry snow touring is one reason for the surge. Another is affordability.

To get the feel—and taste—of this small town, attend the annual **CANADA DAY** celebration during the last week in June. At that time of year there won't be a potato in sight (Pemberton—or Spud Valley—is renowned for the quality of its seed potatoes, which growers ship to farms throughout North America), however you can try other local specialties, including calorie-packed desserts such as rhubarb coffee cake that tastes as if it came fresh from a wood-burning oven. By then there will also be locally grown produce to sample at **NORTH ARM FARMS** (1888 Sea to Sky Hwy; 604/894-6650), midway between Pemberton and Mount Currie on Hwy 99).

Mount Currie's brawny profile dominates the local skyline. Not incidentally, this region is also the traditional territory of the Lil'wat people, who today are headquartered in the towns of Mount Currie and D'Arcy (23½ miles/38 km north of Mount Currie). Everyone is welcome at First Nation events, such as the **LILLOOET LAKE RODEO**, held each May in Mount Currie, and August's **D'ARCY SALMON FESTIVAL**.

The quaint **PEMBERTON PIONEER MUSEUM** (Camus and Prospect, Pemberton; 604/894-6135) offers a glimpse of pioneer life. **PEMBERTON CHAMBER OF COMMERCE TOURISM INFORMATION** (7400 Prospect St; 604/894-6175; *www .pemberton.net*) provides details on all activities. The Pemberton Visitor Info Centre is open May 15–Sept 1 on Highway 99 and Portage Road.

In Pemberton, seek out small cafés such as **PONY ESPRESSO** (1426 Portage Rd; 604/894-5700) and **GRIMM'S GOURMET & DELI** (7433 Frontier Ave; 604/894-5303). **WICKED WHEEL PIZZA** (2021 Portage Rd; 604/894-6622), in nearby Mount Currie, is packed on all-you-can-eat nights.

EAGLE EYES

The largest gathering of bald eagles in southwestern British Columbia occurs along the banks of the Squamish River as it flows past Brackendale. Each year, from November until mid-February, thousands of these majestic birds come from points north and east to feast on a late-fall salmon run. Vast numbers roost along the river during the winter.

In 1996, the BC government created the **BRACKENDALE BALD EAGLE SANC-TUARY** (an hour's drive north of Vancouver, along Hwy 99), an act that recognized the importance of this area. It's a bit surprising to find the names of so many birds recently taken off the endangered species list. Indeed, if you walk the trails or riverbanks here in the predawn darkness and wait for the first rays of sunlight, you'll be rewarded by the sight of 10–20 eagles in a single tree. (As crowds of bird-watchers and sightseers gather later in the day, the eagles start roosting farther away.) The peak viewing period is in winter, when the cottonwood trees are bare of leaves. Additionally, a flock of trumpeter swans can often be seen near the mouth of the Squamish.

The **SUNWOLF OUTDOOR CENTRE** (604/898-1537) offers naturalist-guided raft tours of the river during winter. The **BRACKENDALE ART GALLERY** (604/898-3333; *www.brackendaleartgallery.com*) pays homage to the eagles by hosting an official eagle count in January each year (dates vary). In 1994, a record 3,769 eagles were counted.

—Steven Threndyle

PEMBERTON BIKE COMPANY (1392 Portage Rd; 604/894-6625) is an integral part of the village's cycling community and the logical place to begin an off-road ramble around Pemberton and nearby Mount Currie. Pick up a detailed map of the trails that form a latticework on the east side of the Lillooet River opposite the village center. Staff will sketch in details of new trails that don't yet show up on the map, and will offer advice on travel times and ability levels on various routes.

Lillooet

As the Sea to Sky Highway winds 62 miles (100 km) east and north from Mount Currie to Lillooet, it passes through an ever-changing landscape, some of the most picturesque and notably varied terrain of its entire length. Much of the route lies in the rain shadow cast by the Coast and Cascade mountains. By the time the last moisture in the clouds has been raked off by the peaks around Cayoosh Pass (about 12 miles/19 km from Mount Currie), there's little left to water the countryside to the east. Ponderosa pine and sage take over from Douglas fir and devils club. This steep-sided section of Highway 99 is also called the Duffey Lake Road. Cayoosh Creek runs east from Duffey Lake and accompanies the highway almost to Lillooet. There's little point in trying to make time along the steep-sided, twisty route.

Instead, stop at one of the numerous pull-offs along the way. Just before Lillooet, BC Hydro's recreation area at **SETON LAKE** offers a sandy picnic beach, salmon spawning channels, and a campground with an abandoned Chinese baking oven, a relic from the Cariboo Gold Rush era. In the late 1850s, Lillooet (population 2,740) was the staging ground for an estimated 50,000 stampeders as they headed north to Clinton and beyond (see Northern British Columbia chapter).

From May to October, the **LILLOOET INFO CENTRE** (790 Main St; 250/256-4308) is located in an A-frame former church, which it shares with the town museum. While in town, be sure to check out the superb **LILLOOET BAKERY** (719 Main St; 250/256-4889). The **4 PINES MOTEL** (108 8th Ave; 250/256-4247 or 800/753-2576; *www.4pinesmotel.com*) is a good place to rest your head, particularly after an extended backcountry trip.

Lillooet, where summer temperatures are among the hottest in Canada, is the gateway to the stunning **SOUTH CHILCOTINS BACKCOUNTRY**. Jumping-off points to popular areas such as Spruce Lake and Tyaughton Creek for hikers, skiers, cyclists, as well as those traveling with pack horses or llamas, lie an hour west of town via the Bridge River Road to Gold Bridge.

RESTAURANTS

Dina's Place / ★

690 MAIN ST, LILLOOET; 250/256-4264 A whitewashed Greek restaurant suits Lillooet's often scorchy summer days. Dina's patio is the place to be in early evening, as long shadows begin to overtake the sun-drenched hillside above the Fraser River. Zesty panfried *saganaki* made with Kefalotiri goat cheese speaks to the Pulolos family's northern Greek roots. Plenty of fresh oregano in the *keftedhes scharas* (spicy meatballs) befits Lillooet's sagebrush environment. Twenty-six kinds of pizza keep one wood-fired oven going, while creamy moussaka and *paithakia* lamb chops and other entrées keep another busy. Halibut steaks and calamari are must-try recommendations. *$$; MC, V; no checks; lunch Mon–Sat, dinner every day; full bar; no reservations; on east side of Main St.* &

LODGINGS

Tyax Mountain Lake Resort / ★★☆

TYAUGHTON LAKE RD, GOLD BRIDGE; 250/238-2221 At 34,000-square feet, Tyax Mountain Lake Resort is the largest log structure on the West Coast. The lodge sits beside Tyaughton Lake with the vast South Chilcotin Provincial Park at its doorstep. Twenty-nine suites in the peeled spruce lodge have beamed ceilings, balconies, and down quilts. Five chalets each have a kitchen, a loft, and a balcony overlooking the lake. Shared amenities include a sauna, an outdoor Jacuzzi, games and workout rooms, a 100-seat restaurant, and a western lounge with a massive fireplace. Affable owner Gus Abel welcomes guests to explore the lake by canoe, rowboat, sailboat, or sailboard. The lodge's floatplanes take anglers up to the Trophy Lakes. In winter, the lodge is home base for TLH Heli-skiing (*www.tlhheliskiing.com*). *$$$; AE, MC, V; no checks; fun@tyax.com; www.tyax.com; 56 miles (90 km) west of Lillooet on Hwy 40, then 3 miles (5 km) north on Tyaughton Lake Rd.* &

Fraser Valley

The wide, fertile Fraser Valley runs 93 miles (150 km) inland from the Pacific to the small town of Hope. The Fraser River—broad, deep, and muddy—flows down the middle of the valley. River crossings are limited, forcing road travelers to choose the north (Hwy 7) or south (Hwy 1) side. Except for the cities of Maple Ridge and Mission on the north, and Abbotsford and Chilliwack south of the Fraser River, this mostly rural, fertile valley supports a blend of farming and forestry, with outdoor recreation high on everyone's list.

Fort Langley

Several historic 19th-century forts in British Columbia serve as reminders of the West's original European settlers. In Fort Langley (population 2,600), on the south side of the Fraser off Highway 1, **FORT LANGLEY NATIONAL HISTORIC SITE** (23433 Mavis St; 604/513-4777) is a preserved and restored Hudson's Bay Company post. The **LANGLEY CENTENNIAL MUSEUM** (across from fort; 604/888-3922) houses a permanent collection of memorabilia, as well as rotating displays of contemporary arts and crafts. Glover Road, Fort Langley's main street, features shops, cafés, and restaurants, many in heritage buildings. The large community hall has been lovingly preserved. Archival photographs from Fort Langley's past line the walls of **THE FORT PUB** (9273 Glover Rd; 604/888-6166; *www.fortpub.com*). The faces that stare out look remarkably similar to those of today's townsfolk.

Chilliwack

Odors born by the breeze in Chilliwack (population 62,930) are inescapably agricultural. Most travelers whizzing through the upper Fraser Valley's hub city on Hwy 1 travel too fast to get more than a pungent whiff as they pass a seemingly endless strip of box stores interspersed with the occasional barn. To get beyond the facade of fast-food franchises, building supply stores, and auto junkyards, follow historic Yale Road from Exit 116 east into the hidden heart of Chilliwack, where the town's original city hall, built in 1912, now houses the **CHILLIWACK MUSEUM** (45820 Spadina Ave; 604/795-5210; *www.chilliwack.museum.bc.ca/cm*). Designed in Classical Revival style, the museum bears an uncanny resemblance to the White House, albeit without wings. One of the best permanent collections of any BC museum is housed here and spans the history of the valley, with exhibits that range from aboriginal stone tools to quirky farm implements. Year-round information is available from the **CHILLIWACK INFO CENTRE** (44150 Luckakuck Wy; 604/858-8121 or 800/567-9535; *www.tourismchilliwack.com*).

Harrison Lake

All of 12 miles (18 km) long, the Harrison River, which drains south from Harrison Lake into the Fraser River, is among BC's shortest yet most significant waterways. Throughout fall, major runs of spawning salmon make their way upstream into numerous tributaries of the Harrison watershed. This quiet backwater is anchored by **KILBY PARK** (*wlapwww.gov.bc.ca/bcparks/*) at the crossroads community of Harrison Mills on Highway 7, on the north side of the Fraser. **KILBY HISTORIC STORE** (604/796-9576; open May–Oct and at Christmas), adjacent to Kilby Park, has a wonderful pioneer history. The restored boardinghouse, post office, and general store give a feel for life on the Fraser River at the turn of the 20th century, when stern-wheelers linked small towns with the docks downstream at Mission and New Westminster.

Bigfoot (Sasquatch, locally) is said to frequent the southern end of Harrison Lake—perhaps itching for a soak in the fabled waters of **HARRISON HOT SPRINGS**. The indoor public bathing **POOL** (224 Esplanade Ave; 604/796-2244) is one of the most inviting places in this lakefront town (population 1,345). Harrison Lake is too cold for most swimmers, but a constructed lagoon at the south end of the lake is rimmed by a wide swath of sand and a small, quiet row of low buildings. In summer, rent sailboats or bikes, or hike nearby trails. Annual events include June's long-running **HARRISON FESTIVAL OF THE ARTS**, focusing on arts and cultures of the Third World (especially Africa and Latin America), the **WORLD CHAMPIONSHIP SAND SCULPTURE** competition (second weekend in September), and the **BALD EAGLE FESTIVAL** in November. Contact the **HARRISON HOT SPRINGS VISITOR INFO CENTRE** (499 Hot Springs Rd; 604/796-3425; *harrison@uniserve.com*; *www.harrison.ca*) for details.

LODGINGS

Fenn Lodge Bed & Breakfast Retreat / ★★

15500 MORRIS VALLEY RD, HARRISON MILLS; 604/796-9798 OR 888/990-3399 Once home to a local lumber baron, this 1903 late-Victorian classic was lovingly restored in the mid-1990s. All the classic touches—parquet floors, wood-burning fireplaces, interior fixtures, mouldings, and curved banisters—were retained. Six guest rooms now occupy the expansive upper floor, two of which share a bathroom, while a family-sized converted 1950s recreation room with garden access commands the ground floor. The decor is understated and bright: creamy wallpaper, brass beds, and overstuffed duvets. Owners Diane Brady and Gary Bruce are world travelers and art collectors. It shows in exotic touches they've added to the lodge, such as the harem bed in the bridal suite and the Chinese artwork displayed throughout the rambling main floor. Two life-sized herons preside over the sitting room with its granite fireplace. In the formal dining room, Chinese bamboo instruments are arranged around a grand piano. Breakfast is served at a large kitchen table and features tasty French toast, pancakes, fresh fruit, jams, muffins, eggs—whatever suits you. The estate grounds contain a heated spring-fed swimming pool, a meditation maze based on that of San Francisco's Grace Cathedral, and a children's playground. Kayaks are available for guest use.

In autumn, the Chehalis River on the north side of the 90-acre property runs red with spawning salmon. Dinner is offered by prior arrangement. *$$–$$$; MC, V; no checks; 2-night min on long weekends and July–Aug; info@fennlodge.com; www.fennlodge.com; 2 miles (4 km) northeast of Hwy 7.*

The Harrison Hot Springs Hotel / ★★

100 ESPLANADE, HARRISON HOT SPRINGS; 604/796-2244 OR 800/663-2266
This legendary hotel on the south shore of Harrison Lake was built in 1926 to capitalize as much on its drop-dead-beautiful location as on the thermal springs that vent nearby. The current establishment has 339 rooms and suites spread among the 100-room main building and two wings built in the 1950s and 1980s. Avoid rooms in the main building, where noise seeps between the walls. A maze of hot spring pools is steps away from the newest wing, where each room has a view of the lake. If you really want to pamper yourself, request a pool walk-out room. Two indoor mineral pools are reserved for exclusive use by hotel guests. In addition, there is a full spa. Spacious grounds that surround the hotel are lovingly landscaped, with tennis courts, an exercise circuit, and 11 small rental cabins. Food and service at two hotel restaurants, the Lakeside Terrace and Copper Room, and bar are excellent. In the off-season, a roaring hearth in the large foyer takes the chill from the damp air. Children are made welcome with a water park and special menus. In 2003, the new hotel owners, Delaware North Parks Services, began an ambitious $16 million, five-year renovation. *$$–$$$; AE, DC, DIS, MC, V; checks OK; info@harrisonresort.com; www.harrisonresort.com; west end of Esplanade Ave on lake.* &

Hope

Hope (population 6,185) is a pretty little Fraser River town where the two main streets are lined with fast-food franchises. An important highway junction, the heart of town is frequently overlooked. Make a point of spending a few minutes here, if for no other reason than to breathe the incredibly fresh air that characterizes Hope. The **HOPE VISITOR INFO CENTRE** (919 Water Ave; 604/869-2021; www.hopechamber.bc.ca)—and the **HOPE MUSEUM**—at the south end of Water Street that fronts the Fraser River is a font of up-to-date news and directions to other sights within the Hope area, including popular **MANNING PARK** (16 miles/26 km east of Hope on Hwy 3; wlapwww.gov.bc.ca/bcparks/), with its family-oriented **MANNING PARK LODGE** (Hwy 3, Manning Provincial Park; 250/840-8822 or 800/330-3321; www.manningparkresort.com; 37 miles/60 km east of Hope) and **PINEWOODS DINING ROOM** (250/840-8822).

The Sunshine Coast

The Sunshine Coast lives up to its name. Bright days outnumber gloomy ones by a wide margin. The region benefits from a rain shadow cast by the Vancouver Island Mountains, which catch most of the moisture coming off the Pacific (though clouds regroup in the Coast Mountains to the east and provide sufficient winter snow to coat trails for cross-country skiing and snowshoeing, particularly in Tetrahedron Park near Sechelt). Although it may be raining when you depart from Horseshoe Bay in West Vancouver, by the time the ferry reaches Langdale, the sun may well be warming the slopes of Mount Elphinstone, inspiring the clouds to rise. As you look south across Howe Sound, Vancouver will likely still be swathed in gray.

Much of the Sunshine Coast is naturally hidden. Side roads with colorful names like Red Roof and Porpoise Bay lead to places that don't announce themselves until you all but stumble upon them, such as **SMUGGLER COVE MARINE PARK** near Sechelt and **PALM BEACH PARK** south of the town of Powell River.

The region is split into two portions, on either side of Jervis Inlet. Roughly speaking, the southern half between the ferry slips at Langdale and Earls Cove occupies the **SECHELT PENINSULA**, while the northern half between the ferry slip at Saltery Bay and the little port of Lund sits on the **MALASPINA PENINSULA**. The coastline is deeply indented by the Pacific at Howe Sound, Jervis Inlet, and Desolation Sound. Jervis and Desolation attract a steady stream of marine traffic in summer.

The world's longest highway, the **PAN-AMERICAN** (Hwys 1 and 101 in parts of the United States and Hwys 99 and 101 in Canada) stretches 9,312 miles (15,020 km) from Chile to Lund on BC's Sunshine Coast. The 87-mile (140 km) stretch of Highway 101 between Langdale and Lund leads to dozens of parks with biking, hiking, and ski trails; canoe and kayak routes; beaches; and coastal viewpoints.

ACCESS AND INFORMATION

The Sunshine Coast is only accessible from the rest of the Lower Mainland by boat or floatplane. Travelers aboard **BC FERRIES** (604/669-121; *www.bcferries.bc.ca/ferries*) leave Horseshoe Bay in West Vancouver on one of eight daily sailings for a 45-minute ride to Langdale on the Sechelt Peninsula. Highway 101 links Langdale with Earls Cove, 50 miles (80 km) north. Another ferry crosses Jervis Inlet to Saltery Bay, a 60-minute ride. **HIGHWAY 101** makes the second leg of this journey 37 miles (60 km) north to Lund. BC Ferries also connects Powell River on the Malaspina Peninsula with Comox on the east side of central Vancouver Island.

One of the best parts about enjoying the northern Sunshine Coast in the off-season (Sept–May)—particularly midweek—is catching ferries without experiencing interminable lineups. You'll still have to allow four hours to reach the Malaspina Peninsula from Horseshoe Bay, but you can do it without hurrying, enjoying the travel time just as much as the play time once you arrive. Ferry connections are scheduled to allow adequate time to make the drive from one dock to the next. Those traveling up the entire coast or returning via Vancouver Island should ask at the Horseshoe Bay terminal about special fares (saving up to 30 percent) for the circle tour (four ferry rides).

MALASPINA BUS LINE (604/885-2218 or 877/227-8287) runs daily scheduled service between Vancouver and Powell River, with stops on request anywhere in between. **PACIFIC COASTAL AIRLINES** (604/273-8666; *www.pacific-coastal.com*) flies daily between Vancouver and Powell River.

Detailed information on the Sunshine Coast, including current weather and transportation schedules, is posted at *www.suncoastcentral.com*.

Gibsons

Gibsons (population 3,900) is a colorfully low-key waterfront village 2½ miles (4 km) west of the BC Ferries dock in Langdale. Make the **GIBSONS VISITOR INFO CENTRE** (1177 Stewart Rd; 604/886-2325; *gibsonschamber@dccnet.com*; *www.gibsonschamber.com*) your first stop in the heart of town to stock up on maps and brochures. Then head to the nearby federal wharf where there's often fresh seafood for sale. Take a walk along the scenic harbor seawall that leads past a variety of character homes and boat sheds. Watch for a plaque that commemorates the arrival of George Gibson and his two sons in May 1886. The trio came ashore from the family boat, the *Swamp Angel,* and promptly took up residence. A cairn at **CHASTER REGIONAL PARK** (on Gower Point Rd; 604/886-2325) honors an even earlier arrival: British navy captain George Vancouver camped here in June 1792. He and his crew didn't enjoy themselves half as much as you will.

RESTAURANTS

Chez Philippe / ★★

1532 OCEAN BEACH ESPLANADE (BONNIEBROOK LODGE), GIBSONS; 604/886-2887 OR 877/290-9916 Parisian Philippe Lacoste trained in Normandy before coming to Vancouver, where he worked at the prestigious Le Crocodile and Le Gavroche restaurants. In the early 1990s, he and his wife, Karen, moved to Gibsons to start their own auberge. French-inspired with Northwestern influences, the menu features both à la carte selections as well as a four-course fixed-price table d'hôte offering of soup or salad, chef's appetizer special, fish or meat special of the day, and a choice of desserts. Entrées include scallops in polenta shells, seafood ragout in Nantua sauce, New York steak, chicken with wild mushrooms, rack of lamb, duck à l'orange, and a vegetarian platter. Though limited, the wine list offers reasonably priced selections. In winter, a crackling fire lights up the dining room with the old-country ambiance of a French *relais.* In summer, catch the sunset while finishing with profiteroles, filled with vanilla ice cream and topped with hot chocolate sauce. *$$$; AE, DC, MC, V; no checks; dinner every day (mid-May–mid-Sept), Fri–Sun (mid-Sept–Dec and Feb–mid-May), closed January; full bar; reservations recommended; info@bonniebrook.com; www.bonniebrook.com; follow Gower Point Rd from downtown.*

LODGINGS

Bonniebrook Lodge / ★★

1532 OCEAN BEACH ESPLANADE, GIBSONS; 604/886-2887 OR 877/290-9916 This popular, stylishly renovated 1920s-era waterfront bed-and-breakfast features four self-contained suites spread between two upper floors. Two one-bedroom ocean-view suites occupy the yellow clapboard house's second floor, with two smaller penthouse suites with private decks above. The best values are the three "romance" suites set back in the forest adjacent to the lodge. Suites come equipped with gas fireplaces, Jacuzzi tubs, overstuffed couches, wrought-iron queen bed frames, terry-cloth robes, and wooden armoires. Following the arrival of an early thermos of coffee, breakfast (perhaps a pesto omelet, fresh strawberry jam, and muffins) is delivered to each suite. Explore the lodge's stretch of private beach that leads to nearby Chaster Park. Avid outdoor adventurers, the owners also rent kayaks and operate a nearby shaded campground with RV sites. *$$; AE, MC, V; no checks; closed January; info@bonniebrook.com; www.bonniebrook.com; follow Gower Point Rd from downtown.* &

Rosewood Country House Bed and Breakfast / ★★

575 PINE ST, GIBSONS; 604/886-4714 Proprietor Frank Tonne built this Craftsman-style mansion with timber milled on his extensively gardened property and decorated it with classic fixtures rescued from Vancouver heritage homes. The result harkens back to the spacious elegance of earlier times, right down to the antique snooker table in the games room. White walls and blond wood give the house a warm, honeyed glow, a perfect setting for Oriental rugs and period furniture. Rosewood features two self-contained ground-floor suites, both with private entrances, fireplaces, stained-glass windows, and French doors that open onto the garden. The Victorian-themed Sunset Suite has its own private deck from which guests can watch as Alaska cruise ships lit up like floating palaces parade past in summer. The deluxe Garden Suite is decorated in Queen Anne style. Guests can request breakfast in bed, rolled in on a silver tea service. Co-owner Susan Tonne handles all the details. Romantic dinners (book in advance) are a specialty, served in a private dining room. Reserve several months in advance for weekends, May through October. *$$$; V; checks OK; rosewood@uniserve.com; www.rosewood countryhouse.com; 4 miles (6.4 km) west of Gibsons.* &

Roberts Creek

The free-spirited community of Roberts Creek (population 2,250) lies 4 miles (7 km) north of Gibsons on Highway 10. Stop first at **MCFARLANE'S BEACH**, a sandy crescent where the creek meets the ocean at the south end of Roberts Creek Road. Early in the 19th century, Harry Roberts operated a freight shed here. On its side he painted "Sunshine Belt"—and visitors ever since have been referring to the Sechelt Peninsula as the Sunshine Coast. From here, look north toward the sandy beaches at **ROBERTS CREEK PARK** (Hwy 101, 9 miles/14 km north of Gibsons; *wlapwww .gov.bc.ca/bcparks/*), popular for summer picnics. A reward for braving ferry traffic on **BC DAY** (first weekend in August) is taking in the annual Gumboot parade and Mr. Roberts Creek contest (604/886-2325).

RESTAURANTS

Gumboot Garden Café

1057 ROBERTS CREEK RD, ROBERTS CREEK; 604/885-4216 As you drive down what passes for Roberts Creek's main drag, look for an old maroon house with a simple sign: Café. Inside, a terracotta sun on the brightly painted yellow wall radiates warmth, as do painted linoleum table mats. The menu shines with a strong Mexican influence. Try the Huevos Gumboot, a hearty breakfast dish available all day. Popular entrées include Thai salad and homemade veggie burgers. Enjoy daily

REACHING THE PEAKS

The Coast Mountains, which begin in Vancouver and sweep north along the BC coast and through Alaska, are the tallest range in North America and among the most heavily glaciated. An imposing palisade of these peaks defines much of BC's Lower Mainland region. Some of the most rugged terrain in the province was uplifted here by a combination of glacial and volcanic activity about 12,000 years ago. Reaching the tallest peaks, such as **WEDGE MOUNTAIN** in Garibaldi Provincial Park near Whistler, requires advanced mountaineering skills. At 9,527 feet (2,904 m), Wedge is the highest peak in a park that is characterized by massive expanses of rock and ice.

If you're willing to settle for something less than the view from the loftiest pinnacles, there are less challenging approaches that still provide breathtaking panoramas. On a clear day, few skylines can compete with the six peaks—Black, Strachan, Hollyburn, Grouse, Fromme, and Seymour Mountains—on Vancouver's North Shore. Roadways climb from sea level to viewpoints in **CYPRESS PARK** and **MOUNT SEYMOUR PARK**.

If you don't have a vehicle, leave the driving to someone else and ride the Grouse Mountain Skyride gondola up **GROUSE MOUNTAIN** (604/980-9311 or 604/986-6262; www.grousemountain.com), at the north end of Capilano Road in North Vancouver. It's readily accessible by public transit via TransLink (604/521-0400; www.coastmountainbus.com). The gondola takes visitors on a thrilling ascent up the slopes

baked breads and cheesecakes, organic produce, and coffee sourced from fair-trade growers. On Friday evenings locals come to hang out and listen to music. In keeping with the community and clientele, service is relaxed. *$; MC, V; checks OK; breakfast, lunch every day, dinner Thurs–Sat; beer and wine; reservations recommended; thegumboot@yahoo.ca; www.thegumboot.com; junction of Lower Rd.* &

LODGINGS

Country Cottage B&B / ★★

1183 ROBERTS CREEK RD, ROBERTS CREEK; 604/885-7448 A perennial fave, Philip and Loragene Gaulin's 2-acre sheep farm features the vintage Rose Cottage tucked inside the front gate, and the more modern Cedar Lodge set beside the pasture. The cottage is a one-room fantasy, complete with fireplace, small kitchen, and quilt-covered bed. Farther back on the property is Cedar Cottage, a tree house for grown-ups. Wood- and stonework set its tone, as do a chandelier fashioned from deer antlers and a loft bed. Skylights brighten the interior on even the gloomiest days. A wood-burning river-rock fireplace occupies one corner. Get ready with a breakfast of fresh eggs scrambled with smoked salmon, or Belgian waffles that Loragene cooks up on her wood-burning stove. Irish wolfhound owners themselves, the Gaulins welcome well-behaved dogs to their adult-oriented retreat.

of Grouse Mountain and deposits them at 4,100 feet (1,250 m). From there, moderate hiking trails lead off from Grouse Mountain Chalet to a variety of viewpoints.

No matter which approach you choose, the views will all be dominated by the local landscape's most impressive feature: snow-covered Mount Baker (12,906 feet/3,279 m). Though this semidormant volcano is in the Cascade Mountains of nearby Washington State, its sky-raking presence rears up above the Lower Mainland like none other. Just as sensational are sweeping views of Greater Vancouver, the Strait of Georgia, and Vancouver Island.

Farther inland, gondolas and chair lifts at Whistler take visitors to lofty heights on **WHISTLER MOUNTAIN** (7,160 feet/2182 m). These are the same lifts that deposit skiers, snowboarders, snowshoers, and sightseers at the **ROUNDHOUSE LODGE** on Whistler in winter. Come summer, once the snow has melted, an extensive network of moderate-to-challenging walking and hiking trails leads off into the surrounding landscape that borders on Garibaldi Park. Here, the peaks stand out in such sharp relief that they seem to be paper cut against the backdrop of a Pacific blue sky. Chubby hoary marmots (whose distinctive whistle provided the inspiration for the mountain's name) sun themselves on warm rocks while ravens and eagles circle overhead. For more information and maps of sightseeing trails on Whistler Mountain, contact guest relations (800/766-0449 toll free, 604/932-3434 in Whistler, 604/664-5614 in Vancouver; www.whistler-blackcomb.com).

—Jack Christie

Reserve well in advance. $$–$$$; no credit cards; checks OK; 9 miles (14 km) from Langdale ferry, off Hwy 101.

Sechelt

If it weren't for a small neck of land less than a half mile wide, a large portion of the peninsula north of Sechelt would be an island. This wedge of sand backs ocean water, which flows in from the northwestern entrance to the Sechelt Inlet near Egmont. Nestled on the wedge is Sechelt (population 7,775), one of the fastest-growing towns in Canada, and home to the Sechelt First Nation, whose **HOUSE OF HEWHIWUS** (5555 Hwy 101; 604/885-8991)—House of the Chiefs—is both a cultural and an art center. Ask for a tour. The **SECHELT VISITOR INFO CENTRE** (5755 Cowrie St, Trail Bay Mall; 604/885-0662; visitorinfo@dccnet.com; www.secheltchamber.bc.ca) fills you in on the rest.

RESTAURANTS

Blue Heron Inn / ★★

🌲 **5521 DELTA RD, SECHELT; 604/885-3847 OR 800/818-8977** The Blue Heron is one of the most consistently pleasant places to dine on the Sunshine Coast—partly for the waterfront views of Sechelt Inlet (complete with blue herons, of course), partly for the food (fresh clams, veal *limonie* with prawns, grilled wild salmon with fennel, smoked black cod with hollandaise, halibut fillet with red onion and strawberry salsa, creamy Caesar salad, bouillabaisse), and partly for the romantic atmosphere (fresh flowers, candlelight, local art, live music). Gail Madeiros makes sure you're comfortable and will help with suggestions from the inn's extensive wine list. Her husband, Manuel, supervises stunning meal presentations while ensuring that the food rolls out of his kitchen like clockwork. The chef stocks his smokehouse with duck, trout, cod, chicken, and salmon. Stroll out on the nearby pier between courses to catch the sunset. In winter, a fieldstone hearth warms the solid wood-beam interior. *$$; AE, MC, V; local checks only; dinner Wed–Sun; full bar; reservations recommended; blueheron@uniserve.com; west of Hwy 101 on Wharf St, right along Porpoise Bay Rd for 1 mile (1.6 km), watch for sign on left side.* ♿

Pender Harbour

It's hard to tell where freshwater lakes end and saltwater coves begin at the north end of the Sechelt Peninsula, a confused, puzzle-shaped piece of geography. Narrow fingers of land separate the waters around Agamemnon Channel from a marvelous patchwork of small and medium-sized lakes. Three ocean-side communities—Madeira Park, Garden Bay, and Irvines Landing—lie tucked along the shoreline. Together they comprise Pender Harbour. In summer, stop by the **PENDER HARBOUR TOURIST/VISITOR INFO BOOTH** (12895 Madeira Park Rd; 604/883-2561 or 877/873-6337; *www.penderharbour.org*). As you head north of Pender Harbour towards the BC Ferries Earls Cove terminal, Highway 101 winds around Ruby Lake and climbs above it, allowing a good view of the jewel-like setting and beyond.

LODGINGS

Ruby Lake Resort / ★

👫 **RUBY LAKE, MADEIRA PARK; 604/883-2269 OR 800/717-6611** An engaging family from Milan—the Cogrossis—operate Ruby Lake Resort, with its 10 cedar cottages, each rustically appointed with pine furniture, a full kitchen, and TV. In addition, two B&B suites, with private entrances—and no TVs—are housed in the Dream Catcher cottage. This 100-acre resort is a great place to bring the kids; paddleboats are available, and you can rent canoes. The family's restaurant draws accolades for its Northern Italian cuisine and fresh seafood, such as home-smoked salmon pasta and seasonal specials such as chanterelle mushrooms in fall. Waterfowl by the hundreds flock to the resort's private lagoon. Eagles drop by for their daily feeding at 6pm. In his spare time, chef Aldo Cogrossi builds birdhouses, more than 40 of which adorn the sides of cabins, telephone poles, rooftops, and the neighboring Suncoaster Trail, a lengthy mountain bike and hiking trail. *$$; MC, V; no checks; closed Dec–Feb; talk2us@rubylakeresort.com; www.rubylakeresort .com; 6 miles (10 km) south of Earls Cove.*

Egmont

An impressive natural show occurs twice daily in **SKOOKUMCHUK NARROWS PARK** (Hwy 101; *wlapwww.gov.bc.ca/bcparks/*) in the tiny port of Egmont, about 7 miles (12 km) north of Ruby Lake. One of the largest saltwater rapids on Canada's west coast boils as tons of water force through Skookumchuk Narrows at the north end of Sechelt Inlet. A gentle 2½-mile (4 km) walking/cycling trail leads to viewing sites at North Point and nearby Roland Point. At low tide, the bays around both points display astonishingly colorful and varied forms of marine life: giant barnacles, colonies of sea stars, sea urchins, and sea anemones.

LODGINGS

West Coast Wilderness Lodge / ★★

MAPLE ROAD, EGMONT; 604/883-3667 OR 877/988-3838 Perched above island-speckled Jervis Inlet, the 20-room West Coast Wilderness Lodge's name says it all. Opened in 1998 by Paul and Patti Hansen, the sprawling lodge's most endearing feature is an expansive deck from which guests watch Pacific white-sided dolphins cavort with sea lions while swans vie with eagles for air space. Inside, high-backed rattan chairs rescued from a Trader Vic's restaurant and a bevy of comfy couches ring a fireplace that rises two floors above the inn's capacious dining area and lounge. A roster of certified guides works with guests to sharpen sea kayaking and white-water paddling skills (the renowned Skookumchuk Rapids are just 2 miles/3 km south). Try route finding on the lodge's two outdoor climbing walls or mountain biking along trails in the Coast Mountain's Caren Range. When it's all over, head for the ocean-side sauna with its view of the inlet. All-inclusive packages feature four gourmet meals, or guests can simply book a room for the night. *$$$; V, MC; checks OK; wilderness@wcwl.com; www.wcwl.com; on Maple Rd, 1 mile (1.6 km) north of Egmont harbor.* &

Powell River

Travelers looking to experience the smooth, sedate pace of ferry sailings will enjoy the journey between Earls Cove and Saltery Bay on Jervis Inlet. Get out your binoculars: the hour-long sailing is an eye-opening coastal experience. Powell River (population 12,985) is a pleasant drive 19 miles (31 km) north of the ferry terminal at Saltery Bay. This mill town on Malaspina Strait is the jumping-off point to Texada and Vancouver Islands, as well as the 12-lake Powell Forest canoe route, a full-on, 35-mile (57 km) trip that requires five to seven days to complete. This is also home to the world-renowned **INTERNATIONAL CHORAL KATHAUMIXW FESTIVAL** (*www.kathaumixw.org*) for youth and adult singers, 1,200 of whom gather to perform in early July on even-numbered years. For information on Kathaumixw (ka-thou-mew, Coast Salish for "gathering of different peoples") and the week-long black-berry festival held each August, contact the **POWELL RIVER VISITOR INFO CENTRE** (4690 Marine Ave; 604/485-4701 or 877/817-8669; *prvb@prcn.org*; *www.discover powellriver.com*) located in a storefront downtown. Nearby is the **ROCKY MOUN-TAIN PIZZA & BAKERY** (4471 Marine Ave; 604/485-9111), where you can perch on a stool and people-watch while enjoying organic coffees, chunky soups, plate-sized cinnamon buns, salads, wraps, pizza by the slice, and deli sandwiches.

RESTAURANTS

jitterbug café / ★

4643 MARINE DR, POWELL RIVER; 604/485-7797 One of Powell River's most enduring eateries, the jitterbug café shares a stylishly renovated 1920s coastal home with the Wind Spirit Gallery. Art animates the walls of the brightly lit dining room. From a window table, take in sweeping views of islands in Malaspina Strait. Better yet, enjoy a glass of sangria on the jitterbug's back deck. Wonderful homemade breads complement yummy meals laced with local ingredients. Shrimp season begins in April; blackberries appear on the menu in August. For lunch, try *torta rustica* baked with a selection of fresh veggies. Dinners offer treats such as creamy red-chili pasta with sautéed chicken and roast peanuts (also prepared vegetarian or vegan style) and meal-size salads. The steak entrée is one of the few menu concessions to red meat lovers. True to its name, the café features late-night new music on Fridays and piano stylings with dinner on Saturdays. *$$; AE, MC, V; no checks; lunch, dinner Tues–Sat; full bar; reservations recommended; allofus@wind spirit.com; www.windspirit.com; downtown.* &

Lund

Little ports don't come much better hidden than Lund, at the north end of the Sunshine Coast where the Malaspina Peninsula narrows to a thin finger of land wedged between Malaspina Strait on the west and Okeover Arm to the east. Lund retains much of the wilderness charm that drew a family of settlers from Finland here a century ago. The historic 1918 **LUND HOTEL** (1436 Hwy 101; 604/414-0474 or 877/569-3999; *www.lundhotel.com*) has recently undergone a makeover at the hands of the neighboring Sliammon First Nation. Flowers cascade from hanging baskets and carpet the hotel's garden. **NANCY'S BAKERY** (on wharf; 604/483-4180) is loaded with goodies such as blackberry sticky buns, and **FLO'S STARBOARD CAFÉ** (on Lund harbor) serves espresso in a breezy little bistro that overhangs Wolf Cove. A jolly-looking red **WATER TAXI** (604/483-9749), the *Raggedy Anne,* ferries passengers and supplies to nearby Savary Island. **OKEOVER ARM PARK** (off Hwy 101, 3 miles/5 km east of Lund; *wlapwww.gov.bc.ca/bcparks/*) is the kayakers' choice for exploring Desolation Sound.

RESTAURANTS

The Laughing Oyster Restaurant / ★★

10052 MALASPINA RD, LUND; 604/483-9775 Make a point to seek out this fine-dining restaurant with its superb waterfront location on serene Okeover Arm. The outdoor patio hums in summer, particularly during weekend brunches. On dark and stormy evenings, shelter at a cozy corner table beside the fireplace. Linen tablecloths and fresh flowers hint at the class act performed by executive chef David Bowes. Even those who aren't big oyster fans rave about the flavor of these—fresh off the restaurant dock. Laughing Seafood, a signature plate for two, includes barbecued salmon, red snapper, shrimp, oysters, prawns, scallops, mussels, and just about any fresh seafood caught that day. Like the menu says, it's big. Besides seafood, choices of lamb, chicken, and beef are extensive. Almond jambalaya and pine nut tortellini satisfy vegetarian palates. The staff is unwaveringly friendly, with the right degree of attentiveness. The reasonably priced wine list isn't deep, but is thoughtfully chosen. *$$$; AE, MC, V; no checks; lunch, dinner every day, brunch Sun (closed Mon–Tues Oct–Mar); full bar; reservations recommended; falk@prcn.org; www.laughing-oyster.bc.ca; 20 minutes north of Powell River.* &

LODGINGS

Desolation Resort / ★★

2694 DAWSON RD, LUND; 604/483-3592 Desolation Resort's forested 7-acre property clings to the steep hillside above Okeover Arm. Ten fancifully designed wooden chalets fashioned from local timber perch on log posts. Intricately inlaid fir floors flow into patterned pine walls and ceilings below steep-pitched cedar-shake roofs. Cabins are simply but tastefully furnished; duvets spread atop flannel sheets provide the warmth you'd expect of a seaside bed. Most chalets feature full kitchens. Wide verandas offer treetop views. Stairs lead to a floating dock; its pilings are adorned with carvings of herons, gulls, and even an ancient mariner. The quiet is broken only by the lapping of waves on the shore or the *awk* of ravens as they swoop among ramrod-straight firs flanking the cabins. Rental canoes and kayaks are available at the resort. Package deals include dinners at the nearby Laughing Oyster Restaurant (see review) and guided outings with Powell River Sea Kayaks. *$$; AE, MC, V; no checks; desolres@prcn.org; www.desolationresort.com; 20 minutes north of Powell River.* &

VICTORIA AND VANCOUVER ISLAND

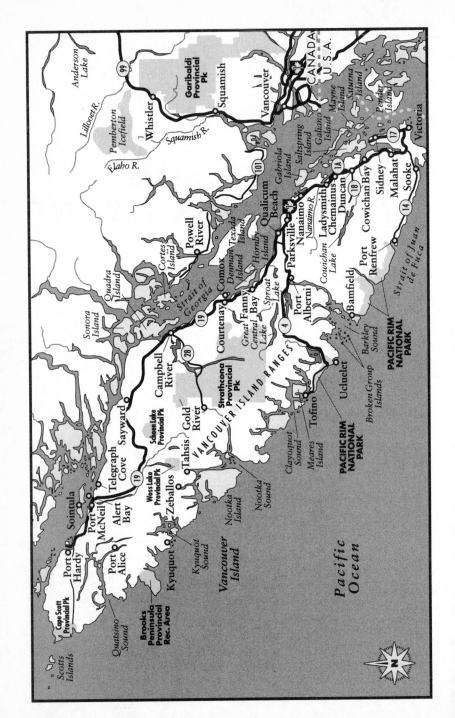

VICTORIA AND VANCOUVER ISLAND

Canadians throng to Vancouver Island because the Pacific Ocean moderates the climate to the mildest in the country: in winter, rain substitutes for snow. Wilder and less inhabited than other parts of the Pacific Northwest, this is a utopia of outdoor pursuits, from sea kayaking to mountain biking. All's not empty wilderness, of course. The island's east coast is booming with tourists and snow-weary retirees—and plenty of golf courses, marinas, restaurants, and good hotels. Victoria, a city of gardens subscribing to a whimsical "more English than the English" character, is the capital of British Columbia and most visitors' first taste of Vancouver Island.

ACCESS AND INFORMATION

It's an island, so most people get there by boat. From Seattle, the **VICTORIA CLIPPER** (206/448-5000 in Seattle, 250/382-8100 in Victoria, or 800/888-2535 elsewhere; *www.victoriaclipper.com*) zips to downtown Victoria in two or three hours via a high-speed passenger-only catamaran. You can also choose a cruise via the scenic San Juan Islands on **WASHINGTON STATE FERRIES** (206/464-6400, 888/808-7977 outside Seattle; *www.wsdot.wa.gov/ferries/*). A two- to three-hour trip runs year-round, once or twice daily, from Anacortes to Sidney, British Columbia, 17 miles (27 km) north of Victoria by highway. Reserve at least one day prior to departure. Cars should arrive at least one hour early at Anacortes; check-in times at Sidney can be longer, call ahead for details; credit cards are not accepted at the Sidney terminal. **BLACK BALL TRANSPORT** (360/457-4491 in Port Angeles, or 250/386-2202 in Victoria; *www.northolympic.com/coho*) operates the MV *Coho* car-and-passenger ferry from Port Angeles on the Olympic Peninsula to downtown Victoria, a 95-minute trip across the Strait of Juan de Fuca. There are one to four sailings daily; reservations are not accepted but call ahead for wait times. **VICTORIA SAN JUAN CRUISES** (360/738-8099 or 800/443-4552; *www.whales.com*) makes a three-hour, passenger-only cruise—including whale-watching and a salmon dinner—between Bellingham and Victoria's Inner Harbour. The service runs between mid-May and early October.

    BC FERRIES (for information: 250/386-3431, or 888/223-3779 in BC; for car reservations: 604/444-2890, or 888/724-5223 in BC; *www.bcferries.com*) runs car ferries from the British Columbia mainland (Tsawwassen terminal) into Swartz Bay, 20 miles (32 km) north of Victoria, and from Horseshoe Bay north of Vancouver to Nanaimo. Car reservations cost $15 in addition to the fare each way. Staterooms are available on some sailings for an extra $25.

    The fastest way to travel is straight to Victoria's Inner Harbour by air. **KENMORE AIR HARBOR** (425/486-1257 or 800/543-9595; *www.kenmoreair.com*) makes regular daily flights from downtown Seattle. From Sea-Tac International Airport, **HORIZON AIR** (800/547-9308; *www.horizonair.com*) flies into **VICTORIA INTERNATIONAL AIRPORT** (1640 Electra Blvd; 250/953-7500), 15 miles (25 km) north of the city. From downtown Vancouver and Vancouver International Airport, **HELIJET INTERNATIONAL** (604/273-4688 or 800/665-4354; *www.helijet.com*)

transports you to Victoria by helicopter. Seaplanes for **HARBOUR AIR** (604/274-1277 or 800/665-0212; *www.harbour-air.com*) carry passengers from Vancouver. From Vancouver International Airport, fly with **AIR CANADA** (888/247-2262; *www.aircanada.ca*).

In peak season (May–Aug), crowds are thickest, prices are highest, and tourist services are best. Gardens and greenery are freshest in May and June; days are sunniest July and August. April and September are pleasant months for quieter, reduced-rate travel (note that some hotel rates do not drop until mid-Oct). Rates are often quite low December through February, especially for U.S. travelers, who have enjoyed a favorable exchange rate in recent years. **TOURISM VANCOUVER ISLAND** (250/754-3500; *www.islands.bc.ca*) and **TOURISM VICTORIA** (250/953-2033 or 800/663-3883; *www.tourismvictoria.com*) have more information.

Victoria

Ever since Rudyard Kipling's hallowed turn-of-the-20th-century visit, Victoria has been selling itself as a wee bit of Olde England. The fancy is an appealing one, conjuring red double-decker buses and high tea as keynote themes in the Garden City. Kilted bagpipers rub shoulders with Victoria's annual 3.65 million tourists, who come from America, Europe, Asia, and Latin America to walk along the waterside causeway, sit for caricatures, marvel at jugglers, and tap their feet to the one-man blues band of Slim Chance. In the harbor, Barbra Streisand's sleek, modern yacht may rest within hailing distance of an antique three-masted sailing ship.

The great thing about Victoria—rated among the world's top 10 cities by numerous upscale travel magazines—is that in the historic downtown, everything from the elegant Parliament buildings to old Chinatown is within walking distance. In recent years Victoria has seen an explosion of whale-watching tours, and outdoor enthusiasts can sea kayak or mountain bike from the city's doorsteps. Minutes from downtown, seaside Dallas Road and Beach Drive meander through the city's finest old residential districts, offering a view of the spectacular Olympic Mountains of Washington State to the south across the Strait of Juan de Fuca.

ACCESS AND INFORMATION
A horse-drawn carriage ride is a romantic favorite: catch **VICTORIA CARRIAGE TOURS** (250/383-2207 or 877/663-2207) at the corner of Belleville and Menzies Sts; the larger **TALLY-HO** carriages (250/383-5067 or 866/383-5067) at the same corner offer rides at a family rate. The Inner Harbour is the locus of numerous popular maritime excursions. **VICTORIA HARBOUR FERRIES** (250/708-0201) offer tours of local waterways. Perched on the Inner Harbour, **TOURISM VICTORIA** (812 Wharf St; 250/953-2033; *www.tourismvictoria.com*) is brimful of brochures and helpful staff.

MAJOR ATTRACTIONS
Stroll through the main-floor hallways and shops of the venerable **FAIRMONT EMPRESS HOTEL** (721 Government St; 250/384-8111 or 800/441-1414; *www.fairmont.com/empress*), a postcard doyen since 1908. The elegant Rattenbury-

designed 1898 provincial **PARLIAMENT BUILDINGS** (501 Belleville St; 250/387-3046; *www.legis.gov.bc.ca*) have frequent historical tours. The **VICTORIA BUG ZOO** (631 Courtney St; 250/384-2847; *www.bugzoo.bc.ca*) fascinates children and adults, with features such as a surprisingly cute miniature apartment, scaled to its cockroach denizens.

   CRAIGDARROCH CASTLE (1050 Joan Crescent; 250/592-5323; *www.craig darrochcastle.com*), once visited only by 19th-century socialites, is now open to the public to take in the ballroom, grand foyer, and parlors of Victoria's richest resident, coal baron Robert Dunsmuir. Inside, fine wood banisters and paneling still glow with old money, while the quaint turret sunroom reveals the fine views the elderly Mrs. Dunsmuir enjoyed while doing needlework or plotting advantageous marriages for her 10 children. Heritage home connoisseurs enjoy **POINT ELLICE HOUSE** (2616 Pleasant St; 250/380-6506; *www.heritage.gov.bc.ca/point/ point.htm*), an early Victoria residence in tasteful Italianate style, and **EMILY CARR HOUSE** (207 Government St; 250/383-5843; *www.emilycarr.com*), the birth home of admired West Coast artist and writer Emily Carr.

MUSEUMS AND GALLERIES

Across the street from the Fairmont Empress Hotel, the **ROYAL BRITISH COLUMBIA MUSEUM** (675 Belleville St; 250/387-3014; *www.royalbcmuseum.bc.ca*) delights with its extensive collection of Canadian indigenous art—from a traditional bighouse to whaling hats and Haida masks—and the Old Town display, a reconstructed 19th-century streetscape. Kids are drawn to the Open Oceans exhibit, a simulated submarine ride, and the Imax theater. The **ART GALLERY OF GREATER VICTORIA** (1040 Moss St; 250/384-4101; *aggv.bc.ca*) is notable for its collection of Asian art; the calming courtyard garden is home to North America's only Shinto shrine.

PARKS AND GARDENS

On the southern edge of downtown, the city's beloved **BEACON HILL PARK** boasts 184 acres of manicured gardens interspersed with some natural forest and meadows. The rightfully renowned **BUTCHART GARDENS** (800 Benvenuto Ave; 250/652-5256 or 866/652-4422; *www.butchartgardens.com*) are 13 miles (21 km) north on the Saanich Peninsula. This 1904 country estate is crowded with blossoms, in the manicured precincts of the Italian Garden, Rose Garden, and the delicate Japanese Garden. For nondrivers, take city bus No. 75 Central Saanich; it stops on Douglas Street in front of Crystal Gardens.

SHOPPING

For those seeking English goods, Government Street north to Yates Street offers the best selection of tweeds and china. For men's suits and casual wear, **BRITISH IMPORTERS** (1125 Government St; 250/386-1496) will please, as will upscale **W & J WILSON** (1221 Government St; 250/383-7177), featuring fine women's wear. Irish goods are available at **IRISH LINEN STORES** (1019 Government St; 250/383-6812). **MURCHIE'S TEA & COFFEE** (1110 Government St; 250/383-3112) has the finest teas, from green Chinese Gunpowder to classic Empress blend. The **BRITISH CANDY SHOPPE** (638 Yates St; 250/382-2634) offers British treats like barley sugar and lemon acid drops. Chocolate lovers head to **ROGER'S CHOCOLATES**

VICTORIA THREE-DAY TOUR

DAY ONE: Breakfast at the **BOARDWALK CAFÉ**, at the **DELTA VICTORIA OCEAN POINTE RESORT AND SPA**, with window and patio seating overlooking the attractive **INNER HARBOUR**. Proceed on a walking and shopping tour of downtown, and lunch at **IL TERRAZZO**. Reaching the Inner Harbour (Belleville and Menzies Sts), flag down a horse-drawn carriage for a tour of **BEACON HILL PARK**. Leave the meter running at the **BEACON DRIVE-IN RESTAURANT** to grab an ice cream, and then swing by **EMILY CARR HOUSE**. After the tour, check into the view-blessed Windsor Suite at the swish **PRIOR HOUSE BED & BREAKFAST INN**. Return to the Inner Harbour to catch a pint-sized **VICTORIA HARBOUR FERRY** to the dock at Songhees Park, a five-minute meander along the waterfront to **SPINNAKERS BREWPUB**. Spend the afternoon quaffing Mount Tolmie Darks, and laze into a casual pub dinner with a view.

DAY TWO: After a lavish breakfast at **PRIOR HOUSE**, drive to **MILE ZERO** and follow Dallas Road to Clover Point. Fly your kite on the windy embankment, as the locals

(913 Government St; 250/384-7021), and **CHOCOLATES BY BERNARD CALLE-BAUT** (621 Broughton St; 250/380-1515), which sells Belgian-style chocolates. Shops such as **SASQUATCH TRADING** (1233 Government St; 250/386-9033) and **COWICHAN TRADING** (1328 Government St; 250/383-0321) offer hand-knit Cowichan sweaters, a specialty of Vancouver Island First Nations peoples. **OLD MORRIS TOBACCONISTS** (1116 Government St; 250/382-4811) sells pipes, Cuban cigars, and flasks in an authentic 19th-century shop; and stately **MUNRO'S BOOKS** (1108 Government St; 250/382-2464) offers discerning reading pleasures. In summer, buy a kite at **KABOODLES TOY STORE** (1320 Government St; 250/383-0931).

BEACON DRIVE-IN RESTAURANT (126 Douglas St; 250/385-7521) has the city's best soft ice cream. At **DEMITASSE CAFÉ** (1320 Blanshard St; 250/386-4442) breakfast is the thing. Heaping sandwiches and hearty ploughman's lunches feed hungry office workers at **SAM'S DELI** (805 Government St; 250/382-8424). Outdoor seating, along with espresso, is popular at **TORREFAZIONE ITALIA** (1234 Government St; 250/920-7203). **THE CANOE BREWPUB** (450 Swift St; 250/361-1940), near Chinatown, is a good spot for a waterfront microbrew.

Johnson Street (between Government and Wharf Sts) has quirky independent stores, highlighted by the welcoming enclosure of historic **MARKET SQUARE** (Johnson St, between Government and Store Sts). Victoria's **CHINATOWN** (Fisgard St between Government and Store Sts), is the oldest in Canada and worth visiting, especially to see narrow, shop-lined **FAN TAN ALLEY**. Outside of Old Town, **ANTIQUE ROW** (Fort St east of downtown from Blanshard to Cook Sts) beckons connoisseurs of 18th- to 20th-century goods.

do, or just stroll by the sea. Follow the **SCENIC MARINE DRIVE** signs along Beach Drive, stop at **WILLOWS BEACH**, and pass through the Uplands to gaze at million-dollar heritage homes. Head out to **BUTCHART GARDENS**, deservedly world famous for its more than one million blooms, stopping en route for lunch on the veranda at the **VICTORIA ESTATE WINERY** (1445 Benvenuto Ave; 250/652-2671). Continue your drive north to the end of the Saanich Peninsula to dine at the **DEEP COVE CHALET**, then head back to your room at **ABIGAIL'S**.

DAY THREE: After breakfast at Abigail's, visit **CRAIGDARROCH CASTLE** and see the stately signature manor of a Scottish coal baron. Back downtown, people watch at **TORREFAZIONE ITALIA** and grab a sandwich at **SAM'S DELI**. Then examine the fine First Nations arts at the **ROYAL BRITISH COLUMBIA MUSEUM**. Take in the turn-of-the-20th-century grandeur—at high tea—of the **EMPRESS HOTEL**. Relax, perhaps in the quiet orchard of **ST. ANN'S ACADEMY** (835 Humboldt St; 250/953-8828). Later, dine on fine west coast cuisine at **CAFE BRIO**. Have a change of scenery by staying the night at the **MAGNOLIA HOTEL & SPA** to conclude your Victoria tour.

PERFORMING ARTS

The **MCPHERSON PLAYHOUSE** (3 Centennial Square; 250/386-6121) is Victoria's leading live-theater venue. The **ROYAL THEATRE** (805 Broughton St; 250/386-6121) is home to a range of performances, from **PACIFIC OPERA VICTORIA** (1316B Government St; 250/385-0222) to the **VICTORIA SYMPHONY ORCHESTRA** (846 Broughton St; 250/385-6515). One of the most-anticipated public events of the year is the sunset **SYMPHONY SPLASH**, an Inner Harbour concert held the first Sunday of August. The free weekly *Monday Magazine,* available downtown in yellow boxes, has the best entertainment listings.

SPORTS AND RECREATION

The wittily named **PRINCE OF WHALES** (812 Wharf St; 250/383-4884 or 888/383-4884) outfits participants in orange survival suits for a three-hour Zodiac-boat tour of local sea life; chances of orca sightings are best May through September. Launch a self-propelled ocean adventure from the **GORGE WATERWAY**, an inlet off the Inner Harbour: you can rent a kayak at the **GORGE ROWING AND PADDLING CENTRE** (2940 Jutland Rd; 250/380-4668 or 877/380-4668); **OCEAN RIVER SPORTS** (1824 Store St; 250/381-4233 or 800/909-4233) rents kayaks and canoes and also runs guided paddles.

RESTAURANTS

Brasserie L'Ecole / ★★

1715 GOVERNMENT ST, VICTORIA; 250/475-6260 The menu changes daily at this little Chinatown brasserie, where chef Sean Brennan uses the organic bounty from local farms in his simple French country cooking. Brennan, together with sommelier Marc Morrison, has the classic brasserie look down pat,

VANCOUVER ISLAND THREE-DAY TOUR

DAY ONE: From Victoria, get a charging start with a healthful breakfast at **RE-BAR MODERN FOODS**; then head north and hop aboard one of the many Swartz Bay ferries plying the island-bejeweled waters to **SALT SPRING ISLAND**. Browse the crafts and organic produce of the popular **SATURDAY MARKET** in the heart of Ganges, the largest village in the Gulf Islands. Have a casual lunch at **MOBY'S MARINE PUB** and drive up Cranberry Road to the top of **MOUNT MAXWELL** for a panorama of the archipelago, from Salt Spring to Vancouver Island. Check into a room at the **SKY VALLEY INN** and treat yourself to a splendid dinner at **HOUSE PICCOLO**.

DAY TWO: After a delicious full breakfast at Sky Valley, zip out to **VESUVIUS BAY** on the island's western side and catch the ferry to Crofton on Vancouver Island just south of Chemainus. From there, drive north on the Trans-Canada Highway (Hwy 1). Just past Ladysmith, take a side trip to Yellow Point to lunch at the **CROW AND GATE NEIGHBOURHOOD PUB**. At Nanaimo, continue north on the inland Highway 19 to Parksville, then take Highway 4A west to visit the whimsical village of **COOMBS**; ponder

with rich pomegranate walls decked out with *fin de siecle* bistro posters, and a long bar that makes a convivial snacking spot. The menu is classic, too: mussels and frites, steak frites, and warming onion soup; most of the meat and vegetables are organic and the fish is wild. This is probably the best place in town to sample French cheeses, with a good dozen to choose from. The wine list is also predominantly French, and the imported beer selection boasts 50 mostly European varieties. Blackboards list the day's options for oysters, cheeses, and desserts, though waiters will bring the board to you at this user-friendly spot. *$$–$$$; MC, V; no checks; dinner Tues–Sat; full bar; reservations recommended; www.lecole.ca; at Herald St;* ₺

Cafe Brio / ★★★

944 FORT ST, VICTORIA; 250/383-0009 This lively Antique Row restaurant glows warmth, from the recycled fir in the weathered floor and cozy booths, to the moveable feast of lush nudes and still lifes on the warm gold walls. Owners Greg Hays and Silvia Marcolini serve contemporary regional cuisine with Italian leanings. The menu changes daily based, in part, on what's in season at local organic farms. Appetizers might include seared Alaskan scallops or confit of duck. Entrées range from red wine–braised beef short ribs to delightful and affordable dinner selections such as linguine with chanterelles, pancetta, cream, and fresh herbs. The 400-label wine list has one of the best selections of British Columbia wines available anywhere. *$$–$$$; AE, MC, V; no checks; dinner every day; full bar; reservations recommended; cafebrio@pacificcoast.net; www.cafe-brio.com; at Vancouver St.* ₺

Herald Street Caffe / ★★

546 HERALD ST, VICTORIA; 250/381-1441 This casual Old Town bistro has served fine, innovative West Coast cuisine for more than 20 years. The rich burnt-orange the goats grazing on the grass roof of the **OLD COUNTRY MARKET** and browse some shops. Continue west, joining Highway 4, and pause on the road to Port Alberni to admire the towering old-growth trees of **CATHEDRAL GROVE** in **MACMILLAN PROVINCIAL PARK**. The long drive across the island takes you over mountain passes, past lakes, and along rivers to the Pacific, where you turn north toward Tofino. Check into a waterfront room at the **MIDDLE BEACH LODGE**, just outside Tofino, and dine by the surf at **THE POINTE RESTAURANT** in the **WICKANINNISH INN**.

DAY THREE: After coffee and a muffin at Middle Beach Lodge, head out for a morning of whale-watching or kayaking—pack your suit and stop for a plunge at **HOT SPRINGS COVE** en route. Lunch at the casual **SCHOONER ON SECOND**, or at **CAFE PAMPLONA** in the **TOFINO BOTANICAL GARDENS**, driving to the inimitable Long Beach to soak in the natural splendor. If you have time, spend the night at **TAUCA LEA BY THE SEA** in Ucluelet and dine at the resort's **BOAT BASIN** restaurant. If you're heading back to the east coast, aim for a mineral pool soak, dinner, and an overnight stay at **TIGH-NA-MARA RESORT, SPA, AND CONFERENCE CENTRE** in Parksville.

interior is filled with cozy banquettes, grand floral arrangements, and eclectic local art. Appetizers such as crab cakes with cilantro-lime pesto and tomato salsa, and alder-smoked salmon on a potato latke, are delicious. Longtime favorites on the menu include a signature bouillabaisse and rack of lamb with roasted garlic, mint, and whole-grain mustard. Several fresh pasta options include the crab, scallop, prawn, and mussel-rich Seafood Splashdown. Pastas, breads, and desserts, including ice cream and sorbets, are all made in house. An excellent wine list is combined with knowledgeable, courteous service. *$$$; MC, V; no checks; dinner every day, brunch Sat–Sun; full bar; reservations recommended; heraldstcaffe@shaw.ca; members.shaw.ca/heraldstreetcaffe/; at Government St.* &

Il Terrazzo Ristorante / ★★

555 JOHNSON ST, VICTORIA; 250/361-0028 You'll find a true taste of Italy in this beautiful restaurant tucked away on Waddington Alley. Surrounded by six outdoor fireplaces and an abundance of plants and flowers, Il Terrazzo offers a haven of privacy in busy Old Town. Alfresco dining on the covered, heated terrace is possible nearly year-round. Passionate chefs create Northern Italian cuisine bursting with flavor. Classic minestrone, char-grilled baby squid, wood-oven pizzas, pastas, and entrées such as osso buco attest to the menu's diversity. An extensive wine list showcases a range of fine Italian and New World wines. *$$$; AE, DC, MC, V; no checks; lunch Mon–Sat, dinner every day (no lunch Sat–Sun in winter); full bar; reservations recommended; terrazzo@pacificcoast.net; www.ilterrazzo.com; off Waddington Alley, near Market Square.* &

J & J Wonton Noodle House / ★★

1012 FORT ST, VICTORIA; 250/383-0680 You might bypass the unassuming facade on this popular Chinese restaurant. But when the door opens and you catch the tantalizing aroma of ginger, garlic, and black beans, you won't. This busy, modest, spotlessly clean restaurant treats you to the flavors of Hong Kong, Sichuan, and northern China. A large kitchen window lets you watch chefs prepare wonton soup, imperial prawn with spicy garlic wine sauce, spicy ginger-fried chicken, or Sichuan braised beef hot pot. Noodles are made fresh daily. Service is friendly, efficient, and knowledgeable. *$–$$; AE, MC, V; no checks; lunch, dinner Tues–Sat; beer and wine; reservations for 4 or more; www.jjnoodle house.com; between Vancouver and Cook Sts.* &

Re-Bar Modern Food / ★★

50 BASTION SQUARE, VICTORIA; 250/361-9223 Victoria's original vegetarian health-food restaurant is packed at lunch and dinner. Sip one of the refreshing fresh fruit drinks, such as the Atomic Glow (apple, strawberry, and ginger juices) or the unfortunately named Cootie Bug (strawberry, pineapple, and orange) while perusing the menu. Delicious enchiladas, curries, and almond burgers are specialties, along with pastas and salads. Breads are all homemade. Honey-ginger dressing and basil vinaigrette are delicious salad-toppers. Friendly, helpful service exemplifies the Re-Bar's philosophy. *$–$$; AE, DC, MC, V; no checks; breakfast Mon–Fri, lunch every day, dinner Mon–Sat, brunch Sat–Sun; beer and wine; reservations recommended (no reservations for weekend brunch); www.rebarmodernfood.com; at Langley St.*

Spinnakers Brewpub & Guesthouse / ★

308 CATHERINE ST, VICTORIA; 250/386-2739 OR 877/838-2739 One of the first brew pubs in Canada, Spinnakers has been around since 1984. On the waterfront west of the Inner Harbour, it has one of the best views of any pub in Victoria. In the adults-only Taproom upstairs, traditional pub fare—fish-and-chips (lingcod, wild salmon, or Pacific halibut), burgers, pastas, and curries—is the order of the day. Try the Noggins chowder, fresh and consistently tasty, or one of the dinner specials, such as braised rockfish or ale-braised lamb shanks. (You'll also find pub games here.) Downstairs in the all-ages dining room, you'll find the same menu. Both levels serve beers brewed on-site, including India pale ale, Mitchell's extra special bitter, and Jameson's Scottish ale. A gift/bake shop at the entrance sells house-brewed beers, wines, spirits, house-baked goods, Spinnaker's malt vinegar, and pub memorabilia. The same owners offer rooms and suites, all delightfully decorated with art and antiques, in three nearby houses. *$$; AE, DC, MC, V; no checks; breakfast, lunch, dinner every day; full bar; reservations recommended (dining room), no reservations (Taproom); spinnakers@spinnakers.com; www .spinnakers.com; across Johnson St Bridge from downtown.*

Temple

525 FORT ST, VICTORIA; 250/383-2313 The look here is cool, blonde, and mini-malist, but there's no hiding the warmth and enthusiasm of the young team running Victoria's newest hipster hangout. The moniker derives from the name of the 1890s brick building it's housed in, but could relate to chef Sam Benedetto's devotion to fresh, organic, regional cuisine. Most of the menu, from the wild coho salmon to the raw Kusshi oysters, is Vancouver Island caught or raised; the style—light, with crisp, clean flavors and Asian touches—is also very West Coast. The menu changes weekly, but you might start with shredded duck confit, or yam-and-sage gnocchi, and follow with grilled halibut in a lemongrass miso broth, or braised lamb shank with white beans and semidried tomatoes. Local cheeses and sweets share equal billing for the third course, and the wine list is short but well rounded. Feeling decadent? Book a table in the Moroccan Room, where you lounge on low cushions as you dine; check out the antique Dutch confessional on the way out. Temple is open until 11pm on weeknights, 1am on weekends. *$$$; AE, MC, V; no checks; dinner Tues–Sun; full bar; reservations recommended; www.thetemple.ca; at Langley St.* &

The Victorian Restaurant / ★★

45 SONGHEES RD (DELTA VICTORIA OCEAN POINTE RESORT AND SPA), VICTORIA; 250/360-5800 Here's an elegant space with an unsurpassed Inner Harbour view, in one of Victoria's finest hotels, the Delta Victoria Ocean Pointe Resort and Spa (see review). Chef Craig Stoneman creates seasonal menus using a wealth of fresh regional products. A la carte starters might include lemon and avocado panna cotta, and cedar-smoked squab breast; entrées range from maple-and-ginger glazed sablefish to Cowichan Valley duck breast rubbed with orange pekoe tea. Alternately, you could splurge on the seven-course tasting menu. The extensive wine list is rich with local options and the maître d' does a remarkable job of pairing food and wine; the servers are among the most polished in town. *$$$$; AE, DC, DIS, JCB, MC, V; no checks; dinner Tues–Sat June–mid-Oct (Wed–Sat in winter); full bar; reservations recommended; vic.concierge@deltahotels.com; www.deltahotels.com; across Johnson St Bridge from downtown.* &

LODGINGS

Abigail's Hotel / ★★★

906 MCCLURE ST, VICTORIA; 250/388-5363 OR 800/561-6565 This elegant 23-room 1930 manor house overlooking Quadra Street was joined in recent years by a Coach House with additional suites. The substantial, four-story green- and rose-trimmed Tudor facade promises grandeur, and the standard rooms, thoroughly modernized and furnished with a mix of new and antique furniture, are all in good taste. Top-floor suites display more elaborate furnishings and fixtures, such as wrought-iron bedsteads, vaulted ceilings, marble bathrooms, and double Jacuzzi tubs; some feature double-sided wood-burning fireplaces, facing both bedroom and deep tub. Rooms in the Coach House have an equally luxurious feel and come at the top end of the hotel's price range. Down duvets in all rooms promise cozy nights, and mornings bring a three-course breakfast in the country-style dining room. No children under 10. *$$$–$$$$; AE, MC, V; no checks; innkeeper@abigailshotel.com; www.abigailshotel.com; at Quadra St, access from Vancouver St.*

Andersen House Bed & Breakfast / ★★★

301 KINGSTON ST, VICTORIA; 250/388-4565 OR 877/264-9988 An exceptionally ornate and well-preserved painted lady built in 1891 for a prosperous sea captain, Andersen House has four pleasing guest rooms. Inside the Queen Anne–style structure, furnishings are a mix of antiques, Persian rugs, stained glass windows, and a striking collection of contemporary art. The spacious Casablanca Room, tucked under the eaves, has a private balcony with steps to the lush garden, from where fruit harvests go into jams served at breakfast. The even roomier two-bedroom Captain's Apartment has a fridge, microwave, and room for five. Three rooms feature jetted tubs for two, and all offer private entrances, robes, coffeemakers and tea kettles, VCRs, and romantic touches such as champagne goblets and CD players. The dining room's 12-foot ceilings are rendered homey by a communal breakfast table. *$$$–$$$$; MC, V; checks OK; hosts@andersenhouse .com; www.andersenhouse.com; at Pendray St.*

Beaconsfield Inn / ★★★

998 HUMBOLDT ST, VICTORIA; 250/384-4044 This nine-room Edwardian manor, built by businessman R. P. Rithet as a wedding gift for his daughter, is tastefully furnished in Edwardian antiques. In downstairs rooms, swirling art nouveau designs glimmer in rows of stained-glass windows. The Emily Carr and Duchess suites display understated, jewel-toned elegance. Others are bright, airy retreats with flowered bedspreads. Most rooms have fireplaces and many have whirlpool tubs for two. Common rooms are the true wonders: the library, where full afternoon tea and sherry are served, harkens back to the days of smoking jackets, with wood paneling and dark leather couches. Complimentary full breakfast is served at intimate dining room tables or by the fountain in the adjacent conservatory. *$$$–$$$$; AE, JCB, MC, V; no checks; info@beaconsfieldinn.com; www.beaconsfieldinn.com; at Vancouver St.*

Delta Victoria Ocean Pointe Resort and Spa / ★★★

45 SONGHEES RD, VICTORIA; 250/360-2999 OR 800/667-4677 Dominating the Inner Harbour along with the great monuments of the Empress and the Parliament Buildings, the modern Ocean Pointe has sweeping views from the spacious lobby on up. Standard rooms, done in a rich sage and burgundy, have tall windows and great views from the water-side of the hotel. Rates in Signature Club rooms include breakfast, hors d'oeuvres, and access to a private lounge. For luxury, splurge on a suite—bedroom, two bathrooms, living and dining area, small kitchen, and miles of window views. Family parking spots, kids check-in packs, and even story time with cookies and milk in the lobby each evening make this one of Victoria's most family-friendly hotels. A full-service spa, fitness club, indoor pool, and the Victorian Restaurant (see review) round out the package. *$$$$; AE, DC, JCB, MC, V; no checks; vic.reservations@deltahotels.com; www.deltahotels.com; across Johnson St Bridge.* &

Fairmont Empress Hotel / ★★★

721 GOVERNMENT ST, VICTORIA; 250/384-8111 OR 800/441-1414 This ivy-draped complex, built in 1908 in the style of a French chateau, remains one of Victoria's key landmarks. In the public areas, tourists gather to sip afternoon tea and to admire the historic photos and antique chandeliers; a separate lobby for guests assures privacy. Standard rooms vary in size; some have great Inner Harbour views; rooms in the Fairmont Gold section have their own check-in area and private lounge. Satisfyingly luxurious rooms can be had, with stellar views to match. All the high-end facilities are here, including an indoor pool, a fitness center, and a spa, offering a range of conventional and alternative treatments, including aromatherapy, Shiatsu, and Kur treatments, which use algae, mud, and thermal water. The Empress Room is the most visually impressive dining room in Victoria. The grand space retains the original carved beams in the ceiling, tapestried walls, and spacious tables. Entrées such as garlic-rubbed rack of lamb with kalamata olive gnocchi and pistachio jus are well executed. A light, three-course spa menu is also available. *$$$$; AE, DC, DIS, JCB, MC, V; no checks; www.fairmont.com/empress; between Humboldt and Belleville Sts.* &

A Haterleigh Heritage Inn / ★★★

243 KINGSTON ST, VICTORIA; 250/384-9995 OR 866/234-2244 This turn-of-the-20th-century heritage home, which popular upper-crust architect Thomas Hooper built for himself in 1901, is decorated throughout with mint-condition antiques under soaring 12-foot ceilings. The original stained-glass windows are large and exceptional, particularly the curved set in the main lounge. The guest rooms, all phone- and TV-free, are bright, roomy, and unabashedly romantic: the main-floor Day Dreams Suite, done in airy plum, cream, and mauve, has a separate sitting area with a lush carpet, a double-jetted tub, a king bed with a satin finish scrollwork headboard, and a trio of full-length windows topped with stained-glass panels. Upstairs, the Secret Garden Room has a balcony with a view of the Olympic Mountains, the Victorian Room has its original clawfoot tub, and the Kingston is a spacious two-bedroom suite. Proprietors Paul and Elizabeth Kelly treat guests to elaborate breakfasts, with creative hot entrées and fresh home baking. Sherry is served on arrival and an Internet terminal is available for guests. *$$$–$$$$; MC, V; no checks; paulk@haterleigh.com; www.haterleigh.com; at Pendray St.*

Joan Brown's Bed & Breakfast / ★

729 PEMBERTON RD, VICTORIA; 250/592-5929 Joan Brown is a gregarious B&B proprietor, and she'll welcome you warmly into her 1883 mansion built for a former provincial lieutenant governor. Although the Rocklands neighborhood home has long lost its wood siding for stucco, all the ornate wooden fretwork and classical columns are in place as are the stained-glass windows, chandeliers, and 14-foot ceilings. The two sitting rooms are cheery with blue and yellow fabrics and contemporary art; the guest rooms favor frills, pink, and Laura Ashley prints; furnishings throughout are an eclectic (verging on eccentric) mix of antique and modern. Walk a block to the groomed gardens of the present lieutenant governor's mansion, or three blocks to the grandiose halls of Craigdarroch Castle (see the Major Attractions section in this chapter). *$$; no credit cards; checks OK; www.joanbrowns.com; off Fort St.*

Magnolia Hotel & Spa / ★★★

623 COURTNEY ST, VICTORIA; 250/381-0999 OR 877/624-6654 The 63-room Magnolia styles itself after European boutique hotels, with attentive service, tastefully luxurious rooms and suites, and a full-service spa to complete the pampering. First impressions count: the lobby is paneled in rich mahogany, and underfoot are limestone tiles. Many rooms have gas fireplaces, such as our favored seventh-floor "diamond level" corner suite, with views of the Parliament Buildings. Sumptuous bathrooms have marble counters, with deep soaker baths and separate shower stalls. Robes, minibars, coffee makers, and even umbrellas are thoughtfully provided. All rooms have floor-to-ceiling windows and side windows that open. For business travelers, rooms have desks with high-speed Internet access and multiline speaker phones; conference rooms are available. Downstairs, Hugo's Grill and Brewhouse is all dark wood and artful metal trellising. The Magnolia is just off Government Street's shopping attractions and a block from the Empress. *$$$$; AE, DC, DIS, E, JCB, MC, V; no checks; info@magnoliahotel.com; www.magnoliahotel .com; at Gordon St.* ⅗

Prior House Bed & Breakfast Inn / ★★★

620 ST. CHARLES ST, VICTORIA; 250/592-8847 OR 877/924-3300 Truly a queen among B&Bs, this large 1912 manor is sure to impress with its dramatic stonework lower levels and Tudor styling above. Gardens are splendid and visible from numerous rooms, some of which have balconies. Most luxurious is the Lieutenant Governor's Suite: the bath is glamorous with mirrored walls and ceilings, green marble air jet tub and long vanity counter, gold swan fixtures, and crystal chandeliers. The bedroom has a more traditional antique feel with a canopy bed and a garden view. The third-floor, two-bedroom Windsor Suite has French doors leading to a private balcony with a sweeping view. More private, ground-level garden suites have separate entrances, patio space, and one or two bedrooms. Every room has a TV, VCR, fridge, coffee maker, and fireplace; all but one have air jet tubs. An in-house chef creates the elaborate breakfasts and afternoon teas served daily. *$$$–$$$$; MC, V; checks OK; innkeeper@priorhouse.com; www.priorhouse.com; between Fairfield and Rockland Sts.*

Sooke to Port Renfrew

Forty minutes west of Victoria on Highway 14, Sooke is a friendly little town with little waterfront access, but the surrounding area, dotted with farmsteads, beaches, and contemplative forests and park reserves is idyllic. Beyond Sooke, the road continues past stellar beaches to Port Renfrew.

ROYAL ROADS UNIVERSITY (2005 Sooke Rd, Victoria; 250/391-2511 or 250/391-2600, ext. 4456), on the road to Sooke, is a grand former Dunsmuir family castle in medieval style; the beautiful grounds are open daily, dawn to dusk. Castle tours are available. Also on the way to Sooke is the old farmstead town of

METCHOSIN; a drive along back ways such as Rocky Point Road is a pastoral pleasure, with small farms set in rolling valleys and hills. In this area, the shallow, relatively warm waters of **WITTY'S LAGOON REGIONAL PARK** (west of Victoria via Hwy 14 and Metchosin Rd) are popular with local families. The swimming holes at **SOOKE POTHOLES PROVINCIAL PARK** (end of Sooke River Rd) are a treat on a hot day.

Locals pack the booths at the '50s-era **MOM'S CAFE** (2036 Shields Rd; 250/642-3314) for hearty diner fare; traditional pub food warms travelers at the historic **17 MILE HOUSE** (5126 Sooke Rd; 250/642-5942). For local crafts, home baking, and organic produce, stop by the **SOOKE COUNTRY MARKET** (at Otter Point and West Coast Rds; 250/642-7528; open Sat, mid-May–Sept). The entire coast between Sooke and Port Renfrew has excellent parks with trails down to ocean beaches; **CHINA BEACH** (23 miles/37 km west of Sooke) is the start of the accessible but rigorous **JUAN DE FUCA MARINE TRAIL**. **SOMBRIO BEACH** (34 miles/57 km west of Sooke) is popular with local surfers. **BOTANICAL BEACH** (follow signs at end of paved road just west of Port Renfrew) has exceptionally low tides that expose miles of sea life in sheltering pools. The **SOOKE VISITOR INFORMATION CENTRE** (in the Sooke Region Museum, 2070 Phillips Rd; 250/642-6351) has details. Hikers fuel up on mile-high cheesecakes and homemade pies at the **COUNTRY CUPBOARD CAFE**, 15 minutes west of Sooke (402 Sheringham Point Rd; 250/646-2323).

RESTAURANTS

Markus' Wharfside Restaurant

1831 MAPLE AVE S, SOOKE; 250/642-3596 Chef Markus Wieland, once a Vancouver restaurateur, has opened a Mediterranean spot in a former fisherman's cottage overlooking Sooke Harbour. Rare views of the water can be enjoyed from the two little antique-furnished dining rooms (one with a cozy fire) or from the patio. The short but interesting menu and wine list anchor a series of fresh-from-the-market specials. Risotto, Tuscan seafood soup, and baked goat cheese with roasted garlic are mainstays; the crab, when available, comes straight from the docks next door. *$$$; MC, V; no checks; lunch Mon–Sat, dinner every day, brunch Sun (check for winter closures); full bar; reservations recommended; at the foot of Maple Ave, off Hwy 14.* &

Point No Point Restaurant / ★★

1505 WEST COAST RD, SOOKE (POINT NO POINT RESORT); 250/646-2020 This little glass-enclosed restaurant, perched high on a bluff over the crashing waves, is becoming known for more than its dramatic water and mountain views. The chefs here are resolutely loyal to local organic produce and wild seafood, and use them creatively in the seasonal, made-from-scratch, lunch, dinner, and afternoon tea menus. At dinner, you can start with steamed local mussels with heirloom tomatoes, or organic squash soup with lemon crème fraîche; entrées might be wild spring salmon with sweet corn and chanterelle mushrooms, or braised halibut cheeks with tomato confit. The soup, sandwich, and pasta lunches are more casual, but a good value, and it is easier to spot passing whales in daylight (each table has binoculars for that purpose). You could also opt for a warming, post-beachcombing afternoon tea:

a set arrangement of sandwiches, tea, and homebaked goodies runs $13 per person. *$$$; AE, MC, V; no checks; lunch and afternoon tea every day, dinner Wed–Sun (no dinner in Jan); beer and wine; reservations recommended; www.pointnopointresort .com; Hwy 14, 15 miles (24 km) west of Sooke.*

Sooke Harbour House / ★★★★

1528 WHIFFEN SPIT RD, SOOKE; 250/642-3421 OR 800/889-9688 Owners Frédérique and Sinclair Philip, and their team of chefs, have garnered international attention for their rare dedication to the freshest local ingredients blended with a good deal of energy and flashes of innovation. Organically grown edible plants from the inn's own gardens complement what dedicated island farmers, fishermen, and the wilderness provide. The menu changes daily, but sample entrées range from sautéed rosethorn rockfish with a strawberry and begonia dressing, to locally raised leg of lamb marinated in fenugreek, cumin, garlic, and golden rosemary, or perhaps grilled petrale sole in a Dungeness crab-and-miso broth with grand fir-infused paprika oil. Thrill seekers can book ahead for the Gastronomic Adventure and enjoy a flight of seven to nine chef-selected courses. Sooke Harbour House's award-winning wine list, placed in the world's top 90 by *Wine Spectator* magazine, features excellent French vintages and, at 600 labels, the largest selection of British Columbia wines available anywhere; the staff here is skilled at wine pairing. The dining room, with its ocean views, roaring fire, and roomy tables, is refreshingly informal. *$$$$; DC, E, JCB, MC, V; checks OK; dinner every day; full bar; reservations recommended; info@sookeharbourhouse .com; www.sookeharbourhouse.com; end of Whiffen Spit Rd, off Hwy 14.* &

LODGINGS

Hartmann House / ★★★

5262 SOOKE RD, SOOKE; 250/642-3761 This exquisite two-room B&B exudes Northwest charm. Outside and in, the handcrafted, cedar-sided home is alive with blossoms: the bay-windowed exterior is draped with pink flowers in season; an old-fashioned porch with white wicker chairs overlooks an acre of cottage garden. Each suite has a private entrance, whirlpool tub, two-sided fireplace, kitchenette, TV and stereo, wide-plank fir floors, and loads of space (at least 600 square feet). The Honeymoon Suite is aptly named, with its romantic four-poster canopy bed and French doors leading to a private veranda. The Hydrangea Suite is also luxurious, with its wooden shower stall and secluded garden-side patio. Expect to see garden herbs, fruits, and flowers gracing the well-supplied breakfast cart delivered to your door. *$$$; V; no checks; 2-night min; info@hartmannhouse .bc.ca; www.hartmannhouse.bc.ca; 3½ miles (6 km) east of Sooke.*

Markham House / ★★★

1853 CONNIE RD, SOOKE; 250/642-7542 OR 888/256-6888 For an English country-garden setting, book into the Tudor-style Markham House. Virgil the chocolate Lab is as welcoming as innkeepers Lyall and Sally Markham, who know when to leave you alone and when to invite you to chat on the veranda. People choose Markham House for gentle pleasures: fireside sherry before turning in, tea on the patio, feather beds, and country hospitality. Immaculately groomed grounds include a hot tub in a gazebo, a small river, a trout pond, a putting green, and iris gardens with more than 100 species. All three bedrooms have private baths, though one is adjacent to its room; one has a double Jacuzzi overlooking the pond. The very private Honeysuckle Cottage, with its kitchenette, hot tub, wood stove, and cozy collection of country antiques, makes an ideal romantic hideaway. Kids and pets are welcome in the cottage. *$$–$$$; AE, DC, DIS, E, JCB, MC, V; checks OK; mail@markhamhouse.com; www.markhamhouse.com; turn south off Hwy 14 east of Sooke.*

Point No Point Resort / ★★★

1505 WEST COAST RD, SOOKE; 250/646-2020 The Soderberg family owns a mile of beach and 40 acres of undeveloped coastline facing the Strait of Juan de Fuca and the Pacific. They rent 25 cabins among the trees near the cliff, catering to those who eschew TV and phones in favor of remote beauty. Some of the older, more rustic cabins allow pets; several newer, pricier cabins have hot tubs; in-room spa services are also available. The only distractions are the crash of rolling swells and the crackle of the fire. Wood is supplied, and each cabin has a kitchen, though the restaurant (see review) serves highly rated meals. *$$$–$$$$; AE, MC, V; checks OK; 2-night min on weekends, 3-night min on long weekends; www .pointnopointresort.com; Hwy 14, 15 miles (24 km) west of Sooke.* &

Richview House / ★★★

7031 RICHVIEW DR, SOOKE; 250/642-5520 OR 866/276-2480 Views of the Strait of Juan de Fuca and the Olympic Mountains from each room's private hot tub are just part of what keeps couples returning to this adult-oriented B&B on Sooke's waterfront. Each of the three rooms in François and Joan Gething's handcrafted, modern-with-a-touch-of-Tudor-style home has a private entrance, a deck or patio (with a hot tub), and a fireplace; the lower-floor room boasts a private steam room. Much of the lovely furniture and woodwork was crafted by François himself. A three-course breakfast, with homemade bread and jam, is served at the dining table or can be delivered to your room. A kitchen is available for guests' use; for dinner, the stellar cuisine at Sooke Harbour House (see review) is a 3-minute stroll away. *$$$; MC, V; no checks; 2-night min on weekends and holidays; richview@bnbsooke.com; www.bnbsooke.com; Whiffen Spit Rd off Hwy 14, turn right onto Richview Rd.*

Sooke Harbour House / ★★★★

1528 WHIFFEN SPIT RD, SOOKE; 250/642-3421 OR 800/889-9688 This bucolic waterside establishment, owned and operated by gracious innkeepers Sinclair and Frédérique Philip, is widely considered one of British Columbia's finest inns. Sensitive additions to the original 1929 white clapboard house accommodate the inn's popularity. The Sinclairs' local art collection—among the country's most extensive and intriguing—graces the common areas, corridors, guest rooms, and grounds, even the elevator and parking lot. The gardens, too, are works of art: paths wind among meticulously tended beds of herbs, vegetables, and edible flowers destined for the dining room (see review). For the guest rooms, Frédérique works with local artists and craftspeople to create distinctive and delightful themes for each. The Mermaid Room is lavished with suitably fabled art, and the Victor Newman Longhouse Room features museum-quality First Nations art. In the Kitchen Garden room, the shower stall, of handmade, stained, and fusion glass, is a highly original thing of beauty. Most rooms have water and mountain views, fireplaces, and Japanese-style deep soaking tubs on their balconies. The lavish complimentary breakfast—hazelnut–maple syrup waffles with loganberry purée, for example—is delivered to your room. Also included is a light lunch in season (lower off-season rates include a continental breakfast). A full range of in-room spa services is also available. *$$$$; DC, E, JCB, MC, V; checks OK; info@sookeharbourhouse.com; www.sookeharbourhouse.com; end of Whiffen Spit Rd, off Hwy 14.* &

Sidney and the Saanich Peninsula

This pretty, rural area, although increasingly encroached on by development, holds some bucolic corners, particularly off W Saanich Road. En route to the floral splendor of **BUTCHART GARDENS** (800 Benvenuto Ave; 250/652-5256), stop at **VICTORIA ESTATE WINERY** (1445 Benvenuto Ave; 250/652-2671) for a tasting or for a meal on the wraparound veranda overlooking the vineyards. Bibliophiles like seaside Sidney-by-the-Sea, BC's only booktown, with 10 bookstores to browse through. While waiting in the ferry lineup to Vancouver, duck into the nearby **STONEHOUSE PUB** (2215 Canoe Cove Rd, Sidney; 250/656-3498) for a snack or a beer.

RESTAURANTS

Carden Street Café / ★★★
Wienie Wagon / ★★

164 STELLY'S CROSS RD, BRENTWOOD BAY; 250/544-1475 / 1162 STELLY'S CROSS RD, BRENTWOOD BAY; 250/544-2010 (SEASONAL) The name of this rural restaurant doesn't relate to its current address, but to its original site, the still-popular Carden Street Café in Guelph, Ontario. When the owners moved to Vancouver Island, they brought with them philosophies that made their first effort so successful: personalized service and delicious food. Area residents are frequent visitors to this charming cedar building (formerly a fruit and vegetable market). The 40-seat dining room is gardenlike and full of rich, tropical colors. The main menu is "spicy international"—inspired by the owner's many travels—and includes outstanding West African and Southeast Asian–style curries. Specials offer a range of less spicy but full-flavored tastes. The wine list is short but interesting, and a good choice of beer and fruity drinks goes well with spicier flavors. Desserts include homemade cheesecake, chocolate mousse, and light-as-air pavlovas.

Carden Street's chefs are also the talents behind the curries, falafel, veggie burgers, and all-beef kosher hot dogs sold from the little wagon outside at lunchtime during summer. The setting is basic (pull up a picnic table) but the Wienie Wagon's globe-trotting, made-from-scratch menu is inspired. Try the homemade strudel or cheesecake, strawberry or mango lassi, Mexican hot chocolate, or a low-fat gelato cone. *$$$ (café), $ (wagon); AE, MC, V; local checks only (cash only at wagon); dinner Thurs–Sun (closed Jan) (café), lunch Wed–Sun Apr–Oct (wagon); full bar (café), no alcohol (wagon); reservations recommended (café), no reservations (wagon); at W Saanich Rd.* &

Deep Cove Chalet / ★★★

11190 CHALET RD, SIDNEY; 250/656-3541 Chef-owner Pierre Koffel brings European formality to this rural seaside setting in Sidney. The large windows of this 1913 wooden lodge overlook meticulously kept lawns and a splendid view of Saanich Inlet. Guests can dine in the garden under a grape arbor on fine days. Lobster bisque, rack of lamb, coq au vin, and beef Wellington are among the Continental classics on the lengthy menu. The extensive wine list offers fine vintages from Burgundy, Bordeaux, and California. Guests can book a suite upstairs for a private dinner or an overnight stay. *$$$$; AE, MC, V; local checks only; lunch Wed–Sun, dinner Tues–Sun; full bar; reservations recommended; deepcovechalet@shaw.ca; www.deepcovechalet.com; northwest of Sidney, call for directions.* &

Dock 503 / ★★★

2320 HARBOUR RD, SIDNEY; 250/656-0828 Five hundred and two of the piers at Van Isle marina are for visiting yachts; the 503rd is for dining. Blue canvas blinds over marina-view windows create a low-key nautical air at this casual 55-seat spot, which is surrounded on three sides by water views. On fine days, you can dine at a table out on the pier. Chef-owner Simon Manvell is passionate about creating a truly Vancouver Island cuisine. He's joined forces with local farmers and fishers to stock his kitchen with wild salmon, free-range eggs and meat, and organic veggies. Although the ingredients are resolutely regional, the finished product takes its inspiration from Asia and Europe. The salad niçoise, for example, uses Salt Spring Island smoked tuna; the local free-range ostrich tenderloin comes with basil-ricotta gnocchi; and the Ahi tuna is served with soba noodles and a daikon, pine nut, and pickled ginger salad. *$$$; AE, DC, MC, V; no checks; lunch Mon–Sat, dinner every day, brunch Sun; full bar; reservations recommended; dock503@vanislemarina .com; www.dock503.vanislemarina.com; at Van Isle Marina, north of Sidney.* &

The Latch Dining Rooms / ★★

2328 HARBOUR RD (SHOAL HARBOUR INN), SIDNEY; 250/656-6622 OR 877/956-6622 This offbeat 1925 mansion was designed by noted Victoria architect Samuel Maclure as a summer home for the lieutenant governor of British Columbia. The exterior, finished with stone and slabs of Douglas fir with the bark left on is rustic BC; inside is all rich wood paneling and Old World elegance. Pacific Northwest fare, much of it locally sourced, is served in the dining room, the library, or on the patio, none of which have ocean views, despite the seaside location. The frequently changing menu might feature appetizers such as steamed mussels, or a rabbit roulade with arugula, Belgian endive, and prosciutto. Entrées range from rack of lamb to Cowichan Bay duck breast, or a vegetarian stuffed portabella mushroom. Desserts tantalize: perhaps a warm Alsatian apple tart or chocolate molten cake. Six guest suites take advantage of antique rich wood paneling hewn from local Douglas fir; one has the original 1925 10-headed shower. A modern 20-suite hotel on the property, the Shoal Harbour Inn, features water and garden vistas, fireplaces, and high-speed Internet access. *$$$; AE, DC, DIS, E, MC, V; no checks; dinner every day; full bar; reservations recommended; info@shoalharbourinn.com; www.shoal harbourinn.com; ½ mile (1 km) north of Sidney.*

Malahat

The Malahat is a talismanic word among local drivers: it signals steep roads and obscuring winter fogs. But for leisurely drives, the Malahat (Trans-Canada Hwy/Hwy 1, from Victoria to Mill Bay) is one of the prettiest drives on the island. Lush Douglas fir forests hug the narrow-laned highway, past beloved **GOLD-STREAM PROVINCIAL PARK** (3400 Trans-Canada Hwy/Hwy 1; 250/478-9414; *www.goldstreampark.com*)—where hundreds of bald eagles gather to feed on salmon between mid-December and February—and at the summit, northbound pullouts offer breathtaking views over Saanich Inlet and the surrounding undeveloped hills.

RESTAURANTS

The Dining Room at the Aerie Resort / ★★★★
Bonelli / ★★★

 600 EBEDORA LN, MALAHAT; 250/743-7115 OR 800/518-1933 Perched high on Malahat Mountain, the Aerie Resort (see review) dining room is as spectacular and inspiring as its view. Chef Christophe Letard incorporates produce from nearby organic farms, local wild mushrooms, and other forest edibles into his frequently changing multicourse tasting menus, creating such imaginative regional dishes as a local prawn and chanterelle salad, or roast of venison saddle with dark chocolate and venison sauce. Choose from a 7-course Farmers Market, Seafood, or Vegetarian menu, or an 11-course Discovery menu; diners can opt for wine pairings with any of the menus; a tea pairing is also offered with the vegetarian menu. Committed foodies should arrive by 4:30pm for Chef Letard's predinner menu discussion.

Bonelli (Italian for eagle) is the Aerie's newer, more casual dining option. Abstract paintings, wrought-iron and glass tables, and touches of leopard print make the room more dolce vita than Pacific Northwest, though views of Finlayson Arm and the Gulf Islands remind you where you really are. The back room and fireplace-heated deck have the best vistas. The Mediterranean-themed à la carte menu serves for both lunch and dinner, offering soups, salads, sandwiches, and straightforward mains such as lamb chops, beef striploin, and free-range chicken breast with morel cream sauce—all from the same high-standard, made-from-scratch kitchen as the main dining room. Local products shine here, too, with wild salmon available smoked in a salad with potatoes and greens, or in a hefty sandwich with vegetables and pesto. A plate of local artisan cheese or chocolate fondue for two are reason enough to linger for the afternoon. *$$$$ (Dining Room), $$$ (Bonelli); AE, DC, MC, V; no checks; dinner every day (Dining Room), lunch, dinner*

every day (Bonelli); full bar; reservations recommended; aerie@relaischateaux.com;
www.aerie.bc.ca; 30 minutes from downtown Victoria, take Spectacle Lake turnoff
from Trans-Canada Hwy. & (Dining Room only)

Malahat Mountain Inn / ★★

265 TRANS-CANADA HWY, MALAHAT; 250/478-1944 Funky, casual, and imaginative best describe the cuisine at this view-blessed restaurant on the Malahat drive
(Hwy 1). Wrought-iron candelabras and local art punctuate the dramatic color
scheme, booths offer cozy intimacy, and a wide deck makes the most of the eagle's-
eye view over Finlayson Arm and outlying forested hills. The menu is big on seafood
and pastas; produce is organic, and chicken is free-range. Soup specials change daily.
At dinner, vegetarians dig into the spinach primavera penne; meatier fare includes
a lamb sirloin with merlot-Stilton cream sauce, and a veal osso bucco. Finish with
a creamy lemon pie. The Malahat Mountain Inn (250/478-1979 or 800/913-1944)
operates 10 suites next door with soaker tubs, fireplaces, and, of course, views.
$$–$$$; AE, MC, V; no checks; breakfast, lunch, dinner every day; full bar; reserva-
tions recommended; info@malahatmountaininn.com; www.malahatmountaininn
.com; at top of the Malahat drive (Hwy 1).

LODGINGS

The Aerie Resort / ★★★

600 EBEDORA LN, MALAHAT; 250/743-7115 OR 800/518-1933 Celeb-
rities in search of discreet luxury seek out the Aerie Resort, which regular folk prefer for festive grandeur. The Aerie has hosted more than
600 weddings since it opened in 1991. Accolades are invariably heaped upon this
modern view resort in the lush hillsides of the Malahat region, a half-hour's drive
from downtown Victoria. Creamy white, terraced units were designed as a modern
take on Mediterranean villages. Set in 85 acres of woods and gardens, it achieves
an idyllic Isle-of-Capri mood. Most rooms feature whirlpool tubs, fireplaces, private
decks, Persian and Chinese silk carpets, and plush modern furnishings. Romantics
seeking ultimate privacy (and views) may opt for one of the six hilltop suites, several hundred feet up and away from the main building. Resort amenities such as
an indoor pool, indoor and outdoor hot tubs, a tennis court, and a spa offering
massage, aromatherapy, and other services, ensure a relaxing stay. Rates include full
breakfast in the spectacular Dining Room (see review). *$$$$; AE, DC, MC, V; no*
checks; aerie@relaischateaux.com; www.aerie.bc.ca; 30 minutes from downtown
Victoria, take Spectacle Lake turnoff from Trans-Canada Hwy.

The Gulf Islands

Stretching for 149 miles (240 km) up the broad expanse of the Strait of Georgia
are clusters of lushly forested islands, Canada's answer to the U.S. San Juans. From
the air or by boat, these islands appear positively Edenic. Well-stocked stores, bank
machines, and even restaurants are scarce to nonexistent on the more remote islands,
so plan accordingly. But natural beauty and recreational opportunities abound—all

in the rain shadow of Vancouver Island's mountains. Like Victoria, the Gulf Islands are considerably less rainy than Vancouver—but bring rain gear in winter.

The Gulf Islands fall into three groups. The best known and most populous are the southern Gulf Islands: of these, Salt Spring, Galiano, Mayne, Saturna, and Pender are accessible via the ferry terminal at Swartz Bay outside Victoria (or from Tsawwassen outside Vancouver), while Gabriola is reached from Nanaimo. Visited several times a day by ferry, the Southern Gulf Islands—particularly Salt Spring and Galiano—offer the widest selection of inns, eateries, shopping, and services. Farther north, laid-back Denman and Hornby Islands, with trails beloved by mountain bikers, are a short hop from Buckley Bay, 12 miles (20 km) south of Courtenay. Quadra, Cortes, and Sonora make up the closely linked Discovery Islands—fishing and boating meccas east of Campbell River. If you're visiting in summer, reserve accommodations before venturing onto the ferry.

ACCESS AND INFORMATION

BC FERRIES (250/386-3431 or 888/223-3779; *www.bcferries.com*) offer many trips daily, but plan ahead in summer for car traffic; popular runs fill fast. Island hopping is possible, but schedules are complex and times do not always mesh. If you are planning to island hop, ask BC Ferries about their SailPass—it may save you some money. Advance reservations are possible between the BC mainland and the Southern Gulf Islands at no extra charge. Less stressful—and less expensive—is leaving the car at home; most inns and B&Bs offer ferry pickup. Bring your own bike or rent one; the islands (with the exception of busy Salt Spring) are wonderful (if hilly) for cycling. **TOURISM VANCOUVER ISLAND** (335 Wesley St, Ste 203, Nanaimo; 250/754-3500; *www.islands.bc.ca*) has information on touring the Gulf Islands.

Salt Spring Island

Salt Spring is the largest and most populous of the Southern Gulf Islands (with 10,000 residents), and is packed densely with artisans' studios and pastoral farms. Non-native settlement here dates back to the mid-19th century, and early settlers included African Americans from San Francisco in the decades after the Civil War. The Kanakas, as the indigenous people of Hawaii were then called, also played an important role.

Today, the pioneer landscape has left an imprint of postcard farms and two sweet stone-and-wood churches on the Fulford-Ganges Road. Douglas fir forests cloak small mountains, interspersed with sparkling lakes. **MOUNT MAXWELL PROVIN-CIAL PARK** (7 miles/11 km southwest of Ganges via Fulford-Ganges Rd and Cranberry Rd), on the west side of the island 2,000 feet above sea level, has a rewarding view. For walk-in, nonreservable camping and stunning seaside walks, head for **RUCKLE PROVINCIAL PARK** (10 minutes from Fulford Harbour ferry dock, take right onto Beaver Rd; 250/539-2115 or 877/559-2115) on the island's east side. Fishing enthusiasts head to St. Mary Lake (north of Ganges on North End Rd) seeking bass and trout. St. Mary Lake and Cusheon Lake are good spots for a dip; the ocean waters are clean but chilly. **GARRY OAKS WINERY** (1880 Fulford-Ganges

Rd; 250/653-4687; *garryoakswine.com*) and **SALT SPRING VINEYARDS** (151 Lee Rd off 1700 block Fulford Ganges Rd; 250/653-9463; *www.saltspringvineyards .com*), which also has a B&B, are open for tastings between May and October.

The big draw for locals and tourists is the **SALT SPRING ISLAND SATURDAY MARKET** (Centennial Park, Ganges; 250/537-4448; *www.saltspringmarket.com*; Apr–Oct): local goat cheeses pressed with violets, organic produce, pottery, hand-smoothed wooden bowls, and more. Similarly fine wares can be found at the **ARTCRAFT** (250/537-0899) sale in Ganges's Mahon Hall, open daily June through mid-September. Dozens of arts and crafts studios throughout the island are open to the public. A Studio Tour map from the **SALT SPRING ISLAND VISITOR INFORMA-TION CENTRE** (121 Lower Ganges Rd, Ganges; 250/537-5252 or 866/216-2936; *www.saltspringtoday.com*) will show you the way. The annual (since 1896) September **SALT SPRING FALL FAIR** (Farmer's Institute, 351 Rainbow Rd) is a family favorite, with sheep shearing, crafts, animals, games for kids, baked goods, and more. Enjoy a snack and organic coffee at the vegetarian bakery and café **BARB'S BUNS** (1-121 McPhillips Ave, Ganges; 250/537-4491); views, hearty meals, and microbrews at **MOBY'S MARINE PUB** (124 Upper Ganges Rd, Ganges; 250/537-5559); live music and wholesome, made-from-scratch meals at the **TREEHOUSE CAFÉ** (106 Purvis Ln, Ganges, 250/537-5379); and wood-fired pizzas at the **RAVEN STREET MARKET CAFÉ** (321 Fernwood Rd, north end of island; 250/537-2273).

Three BC Ferries routes serve Salt Spring. From Victoria, ferries leave Swartz Bay and land 35 minutes later at Salt Spring's Fulford Harbour, a small artists' village at the island's south end. Here you can fuel up for the 20-minute drive to Ganges at **TREEHOUSE SOUTH** (2921 Fulford-Ganges Rd; 250/653-4833) or **MORNINGSIDE ORGANIC BAKERY AND CAFÉ** (107 Morningside Rd; 250/653-4414). Ferries leave less frequently from Tsawwassen on the mainland for the three-hour trip to Long Harbour on the island's northeast shore. A short hop from the Vancouver Island mill town of Crofton takes you to Salt Spring's Vesuvius Bay, on the island's northwest side, notable for the congenial waterfront **VESUVIUS NEIGHBOURHOOD PUB** (805 Vesuvius Bay Rd, northwest of Ganges; 250/537-2312).

RESTAURANTS

Calvin's Bistro / ★

133 LOWER GANGES RD, GANGES; 250/538-5551 Casual restaurants come and go in Ganges, but Calvin's, with its harbor-view patio, fresh seafood, cozy booth seating, and local popularity, should stand the test of time. The lunch menu features sandwiches, fish-and-chips, and a host of burgers: chicken, lamb, salmon, veggie, and—in a nod to the owners' European roots—schnitzel. At dinner, fresh halibut, salmon, and prawns share the menu with lamb, pasta, and, thanks to a chef who hails from Thailand, Thai specialities such as coconut prawns, pork spring rolls, and Geang Ped Kai (curried chicken with vegetables). Locals and off-season visitors mark their calendars for Calvin's Thai, French, Italian, and Swiss theme weeks. *$$–$$$; MC, V; no checks; full bar; breakfast, lunch, dinner Tues–Sat, brunch Sun; reservations for six or more; www.calvinsbistro.com; on the waterfront in Ganges.*

Hastings House / ★★★

160 UPPER GANGES RD, GANGES; 250/537-2362 OR 800/661-9255 The English country-house ambiance of this well-known inn (see review) extends to its atmospheric dining room, where an enormous Inglenook fireplace warms the foyer, and upholstered chairs, candlelight, and white linens provide understated luxury. The prix-fixe menu (choose from a three- or five-course option) changes daily, relying on fresh local ingredients (many from the inn's gardens) and offering such appetizers as celeriac and prosciutto bisque with chive cream, or seared spring salmon with pattypan squash and nasturtium jus. Entrées run from peppered pheasant breast with orchard pears to saffron-steamed halibut with rosemary ratatouille. Popular Salt Spring Island lamb is almost always available. The same menu is served on the enclosed, water-view veranda. *$$$$; AE, MC, V; no checks; dinner every day, lunch by arrangement (closed mid-Nov–mid-Mar); full bar; reservations required; info@hastingshouse.com; www.hastingshouse.com; just north of Ganges.*

The Oystercatcher Seafood Bar & Grill

104 MANSON RD, GANGES; 250/537-5041 In summer, the tables at the casual Oystercatcher Seafood Bar & Grill spill out onto the terrace, bringing a village-square buzz to sleepy Ganges evenings. Hugely popular with locals and visitors, this hip nautical spot, with its cozy booths, river-rock fireplace, and marina views, covers the ocean-going standards (oysters cooked or shucked, halibut and chips, and Dungeness crab) and does them well. Any of the five wild salmon options are a good bet. Steaks, burgers, pastas, and a kids' menu round out the offerings. Owner Barry Kazakoff has extended his franchise downstairs with Shipstones, a reasonably convincing, dark-beamed, one-room English pub, with Boddington's on tap and good value pub meals, such as steak and mushroom pie, ploughman's lunch, and fish-and-chips, listed on the chalkboard behind the bar. The same enterprising restaurateur serves Italian meals at the indoor/outdoor **LA CUCINA E TERRAZZA** (250/537-5747) just steps away along the waterfront. *$$; MC, V; no checks; lunch, dinner every day; full bar; oystercatcher@saltspring.com; at Mouat's Landing on the waterfront in Ganges.*

Restaurant House Piccolo / ★★★★

108 HEREFORD AVE, GANGES; 250/537-1844 Chef Piccolo Lyytikainen, a member of the prestigious Chaîne des Rôtisseurs, brings upscale European cuisine to this intimate Ganges restaurant, widely regarded as among the finest in the region. Set in a tiny heritage house, House Piccolo's candlelit ambiance achieves romance without formality. Starters include herb-crusted beef carpaccio and Scandinavian gravlax made with West Coast salmon. Main dishes range from charbroiled fillet of beef with Gorgonzola sauce to roasted Muscovy duck breast and local Salt Spring Island lamb. Chocolate lovers enjoy the decadent, baked-to-order warm chocolate cake. The excellent wine list includes an extensive selection of European wines and British Columbian varieties. *$$$$; AE, DC, E, MC, V; local checks only; dinner every day; full bar; reservations recommended; www.house piccolo.com; downtown Ganges.*

LODGINGS

Anne's Oceanfront Hideaway / ★★

168 SIMSON RD, SALT SPRING ISLAND; 250/537-0851 OR 888/474-2663
In this immaculate home with views of Stuart Channel and Vancouver Island, sign in to the Garry Oak Room and rest on the four-poster bed. On quiet island evenings, contemplate the sunset from the wraparound veranda and anticipate the smell of morning baking. The inn's four rooms are decorated in country floral style. Wheelchair users praise accessibility here, and others applaud the hospitality of proprietors Rick and Ruth-Anne Broad. A four-course breakfast might include eggs in phyllo pastry with lamb patties and chutney. Take advantage of the hot tub, aromatherapy massage services, canoe, and bikes. *$$$; AE, MC,V; no checks; annes@saltspring.com; www.annesoceanfront.com; north of Vesuvius ferry terminal.* &

Beddis House Bed and Breakfast / ★★

131 MILES AVE, SALT SPRING ISLAND; 250/537-1028 OR 866/537-1028
Charming Beddis House, a white-shingled farmhouse built in 1900, is on a private beach on Captain's Passage. Hidden at the end of a country road, it's far enough from town that you can see the stars at night and the seals and otters during the day. Guests make themselves at home in the modern 19th century–style coach house. It contains three very private rooms with claw-footed tubs, country-style furniture, woodstoves, and decks or balconies that look toward the water. Breakfast (including fruit from the garden) and afternoon tea are served in the old house and its guest lounge. *$$$; MC, V; no checks; closed Dec–Mar; beddis@saltspring.com; www.beddishousebandb.com; follow Beddis Rd from Ful-ford-Ganges Rd, turn left onto Miles Ave.*

Bold Bluff Retreat / ★★

1 BOLD BLUFF, SALT SPRING ISLAND; 250/653-4377 OR 866/666-4377 Families and boaters love this secluded, eco-friendly, no-smoking retreat, accessible only by boat and bordering 2,600 acres of protected land. Salty's Cabin, which sleeps up to five, sits on a rocky outcropping where the tide rushes in and out right under the deck. A 10-minute walk from the main lodge, it is utterly private; solar power, a composting toilet, and a propane stove ensure a self-sufficient holiday. Guests also enjoy the private dock, swimming cove, and hot outdoor shower. The Garden Cottage, which sleeps up to six, is nestled in an old orchard, accented by a luxuriant rose arbor. Antique furnishings, a fireplace, and a piano lend a warm glow inside the rustic shingled cottage. Amenities include a full kitchen and bath. A trampoline, swing, and beach make this an excellent family spot. Singles and couples will enjoy the single B&B room in the main house, a 1940 cedar lodge. The newest addition is a furnished tepee on the bluff's edge, with a deck, solar shower, and camp kitchen. Owner Tamar Griggs will gladly pick up guests for the 5-minute boat ride from Burgoyne Bay or the 10-minute jaunt from Maple Bay on Vancouver Island, though many guests arrive under their own paddle power. Pets are welcome in Salty's Cabin; kids are welcome throughout, but in Salty's Cabin they must be over 6 for safety reasons. *$$$ (cabins), $$–$$$ (lodge), $–$$ (tepee); AE, MC, V; checks*

OK; 1-week min in cabins Jul–Aug, Salty's Cabin closed Nov–Mar, B&B and tepee closed Oct–May; boldbluff@saltspring.com; www.boldbluff.com; accessible only by boat, from Burgoyne Bay, 10 minutes northwest of Fulford Harbour, and from Maple Bay on Vancouver Island.

Hastings House / ★★★

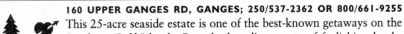

160 UPPER GANGES RD, GANGES; 250/537-2362 OR 800/661-9255 This 25-acre seaside estate is one of the best-known getaways on the Southern Gulf Islands. Past the bucolic pasture of frolicking lambs and, as the weathered barn and old farmhouse come into view, it feels as stately as England, circa 1820. Varied accommodations (18 units in all) are individually decorated with antiques and modern country plaids and florals. The Farmhouse has two two-level suites overlooking the water. In the Manor House, two upstairs suites feature the same lovely views from casement windows, warmed by stone fireplaces. The Post is a compact cabin popular with honeymooners. The current refined decor belies its history as a Hudson's Bay Company trading post. The wood-sided barn is richly weathered and divided into suites overlooking the garden and pasture. Seven Hillside Suites offer lofty ocean views in a modern, but attractively weathered, board and batten building; these, however, get some road noise and overlook the patio of the pub next door. Fireplaces or woodstoves are a given throughout, and a spa offers the full range of pampering treatments. Rates, which are roughly twice those charged at most other luxury inns in BC, include a wake-up tray delivered to your suite, a full breakfast, and an afternoon tea. The formal dining room offers refined cuisine (see review). *$$$$; AE, MC, V; no checks; 2-night min on weekends; closed mid-Nov–mid-Mar; info@hastingshouse.com; www.hastingshouse.com; just north of Ganges.*

Sky Valley Inn / ★★

421 SKY VALLEY RD, SALT SPRING ISLAND; 250/537-9800 Imagine you've been invited to stay at a friend's villa in the south of France, where you can spend your days lounging by the pool, lingering over coffee and fresh-baked goods at the breakfast table, or poking around in the garden, admiring the raspberries and sunflowers. Re-opened under new management in 2003, this adult-oriented central Salt Spring B&B replicates just that kind of Mediterranean ease, with forest trails, a friendly dog, and a nearby lake. Three rooms, in a pretty French-country style, have duvets and feather beds. Each also has a private entrance opening onto an ivy-draped courtyard, home to the inn's 20-by-40-foot heated outdoor pool. The light and airy Master Bedroom is the choicest, with a mix of French country and West Indies decor, a fireplace, and access to both the courtyard and an exterior deck with far-reaching views of the Gulf Islands and the mainland mountains. The view-blessed dining and living rooms are warm with recycled fir and a big river-rock fireplace; breakfasts are lavish homemade affairs, and wine and hors d'ouerves are served each evening. *$$$; MC, V; checks OK; 2-night min on holiday weekends; closed Dec–Jan; info@skyvalleyinn.com; www.skyvalleyinn.com; 4 miles (6 km) south of Ganges.*

North and South Pender Islands

The Penders are actually two islands, united by a small bridge. Both are green and rural, though South Pender is the less developed of the two. The population here is decidedly residential, so don't expect many restaurants, lodgings, or shops. Beaches, however, abound: **MORTIMER SPIT** (at the western tip of South Pender) and **GOWLLAND POINT BEACH** (at end of Gowlland Point Rd on South Pender) are among 30 public ocean-access points. Maps are available at the **PENDER ISLAND LIONS VISITOR INFORMATION CENTRE** (2332 Otter Bay Rd; 250/629-6541; *www.penderisland.info;* open mid-May–Labor Day) near the Otter Bay ferry terminal.

To take advantage of the fabled Gulf Island viewscape, the trails on **MOUNT NORMAN** (accessible from Ainslie Rd or Canal Rd on South Pender), part of the new **GULF ISLANDS NATIONAL PARK RESERVE**, are steep but rewarding. The gentle terrain of South Pender is particularly appealing for cyclists; rent bikes at **OTTER BAY MARINA** (2311 MacKinnon Rd; 250/629-3579) on North Pender. While waiting for the ferry at Otter Bay on North Pender, grab an excellent burger (try a venison, oyster, or ostrich variation) at the humble trailer **THE STAND** (Otter Bay Ferry Terminal; 250/629-3292).

LODGINGS

Poets Cove Seaside Resort / ★★★

9801 SPALDING RD, SOUTH PENDER ISLAND; 250/629-3212 OR 888/512-7638 This new development, known for years as Bedwell Harbour Resort, retains its idyllic location: a sheltered cove and marina, backed by a gentle, wooded hillside, with stunning sunset views. The three-story lodge, with its stone detailing and pretty rounded gables, is home to a fitness center and spa, as well as 22 ocean-view, Arts and Crafts–style rooms with fireplaces and balconies. Aurora Restaurant, also in the lodge, serves local organic produce, wild salmon, Pender Island lamb, and other regional treats in its chic dining room and on its waterfront patio; Syrens Pub has local microbrews, burgers, fish-and-chips, and other comfort fare. Farther up the hill, two- and three-bedroom Arts and Crafts–style cottages have full kitchens, rich fir cabinetry, fireplaces, and balconies; most have commanding views of the cove, and some have private hot tubs. Slightly older two- and three-bedroom villas at the top of the property also have full kitchens. A marine center for visiting yachties has an outdoor pool, a hot tub, and a café; there's another pool and hot tub on site for resort guests. A water sports center offers lessons at all levels in scuba diving, kayaking, and sailing. Fishing, whale watching, mountain biking, hiking trails, tennis courts, and overnight offsite kayaking and camping trips mean there's plenty to do, though peaceful contemplation is always an option. $$$$; AE, MC, V; no checks; reservations@poetscove.com; www.poetscove.com; from Vancouver Island, take the resort's water taxi from Sidney or BC Ferries from Swartz Bay to Otter Bay. From Otter Bay follow Canal Rd from bridge to Spalding Rd, and Spalding to Bedwell Harbour.

Saturna Island

The most remote of the Southern Gulf Islands—it takes two ferries to get here—Saturna has a scant 300 residents: no village center, no drugstore or bank machine, but two general stores, a café, and a pub overlooking the Lyall Harbour ferry stop. No camping is available on the island, but hiking abounds: climb **MOUNT WARBURTON PIKE**, the second-highest peak in the Southern Gulf Islands. **WINTER COVE PARK** (1 mile/1.6 km from ferry dock, off East Point Rd) is an inviting place to beachcomb or picnic above the Strait of Georgia, or take the scenic ocean drive to the tidal pools and sculpted sandstone of remote **EAST POINT REGIONAL PARK** at the eastern tip of the island. **SATURNA ISLAND VINEYARDS** (8 Quarry Trail; 250/539-5139 or 877/918-3388; *www.saturnavineyards.com*) is planted with merlot, semillon-chardonnay, and Gewürtztraminer. Tastings and tours are available daily in summer and by appointment in the off-season.

LODGINGS

Saturna Lodge and Restaurant / ★

130 PAYNE RD, SATURNA ISLAND; 250/539-2254 OR 888/539-8800 This lovely frame lodge sits high on a hill overlooking Boot Cove. Windows wrap around the dining room and a fire beckons in the lower-floor lounge. Seven bright and sunny rooms upstairs are individually decorated and contemporary in feel, with pleasant sitting areas and ocean or garden views. Five have private baths; the honeymoon suite has a soaker tub and private balcony. A hot tub is in the garden and bikes are on hand for touring Saturna's quiet roads. Guests are picked up from the Saturna ferry dock and boaters are welcome to use the lodge moorage. The menu at the restaurant (serving breakfast to guests, dinner to the public; reservations essential) offers Saturna-raised lamb and organic produce; the wine cellar features British Columbia vintages, including Saturna's own. $$–$$$; MC, V; *no checks; closed mid-Oct–mid-May; satlodge@gulfislands.com; www.saturna-island.bc.ca; follow signs from ferry.*

Mayne Island

During the Cariboo Gold Rush of the mid-1800s, Mayne was the Southern Gulf Islands' commercial and social hub, a way station between Victoria and Vancouver. Today, the pace of life is more serene. Rolling orchards and warm rock-strewn beaches dominate this pocket-sized island of 5 square miles (13 square km). Hike up **MOUNT PARKE** to reach Mayne's highest point, with a view of ferries plying Active Pass between the islands and mainland. A complete bicycle tour of the island takes five hours—longer if you stop for a pint at the well-worn **SPRINGWATER LODGE** (400 Fernhill Dr; 250/539-5521). At **DINNER BAY PARK**, about a half mile (1 km) south of the ferry terminal, a traditional Japanese garden commemorates the many Japanese families who settled on the island before World War II.

RESTAURANTS

Oceanwood Country Inn / ★★★

630 DINNER BAY RD, MAYNE ISLAND; 250/539-5074 Four-course dinners in the dining room overlooking Navy Channel are exquisitely prepared and feature entrée choices such as nettle and almond–stuffed sole or boneless quail stuffed with mushrooms and hazelnuts. Appetizers are strikingly unique: smoked sable fish and beet terrine with stinging nettle juice, for example. At dessert, a goat-cheese cake with walnut sabayon and rosemary caramel roasted apples might make an appearance. The careful wine list features Pacific Northwest wines. *$$$$; MC, V; Canadian checks only; dinner every day (closed Nov–Mar); full bar; reservations required; oceanwood@gulfislands.com; www.oceanwood.com; right on Dalton Dr, right on Mariners, immediate left onto Dinner Bay Rd, look for signs.*

LODGINGS

A Coachhouse on Oyster Bay / ★★

511 BAYVIEW DR, MAYNE ISLAND; 250/539-3368 OR 888/629-6322 Snuggle by the fire in one of three spacious rooms, or sit a while by your window gazing at the expansive view over the Strait of Georgia to the mainland's monumental Coast Mountains. All rooms have four-poster beds; one has an ocean-view deck with a private hot tub. Get closer to the view in the outdoor hot tub, just inches from the high tide line. The satisfying four-course breakfast often includes home-baked scones and muffins and entrées such as hot peach crepes. *$$$; AE, MC, V; Canadian checks only; coachhouse@cablelan.net; www.acoachhouse.com; just east of Georgina Point Lighthouse.*

Oceanwood Country Inn / ★★★

630 DINNER BAY RD, MAYNE ISLAND; 250/539-5074 The split-level, high-ceilinged Wisteria Room, the largest of the Oceanwood's 12 rooms, has striking views over Navy Channel from the bed and from the Japanese-style soaking tub on its private deck. Fireplaces and deep soaker tubs are features of many rooms and all but one have ocean views. Some, like the Lilac Room, are done in a floral theme with hand-stenciling; others, like the blue-hued Heron Room, come in more soothing masculine tones. Mingle with other guests in the games room or library, walk down the path to the pebbly beach after dinner, or enjoy the sea view from the hot tub. Look for fresh-squeezed fruit and vegetable juices, croissants or coffee cake, and hearty, hot country-style entrées at breakfast. After a day of kayaking, bird-watching, or cycling (the inn has bikes on hand), settle into a meal in the excellent dining room (see review). *$$$–$$$$; MC, V; Canadian checks only; closed Nov–Mar; oceanwood@gulfislands.com; www.oceanwood.com; right on Dalton Dr, right on Mariners, immediate left onto Dinner Bay Rd, look for signs.*

Galiano Island

Residents here dismiss bustling Salt Spring as "towny," as well they might on their undeveloped, secluded island. Dedicated locals work hard to protect the natural features along the island's narrow 19 miles (30 km): densely forested cliffs, towering bluffs, wildflower meadows, and sheltered harbors. Despite being the closest of the Southern Gulf Islands to the Tsawwassen ferry (one hour), Galiano has a sparse 1,000 residents and only a few services and shops, clustered at its south end.

On **BODEGA RIDGE**, a beautiful clifftop walk rewards with views across the islands in Trincomali Channel. From **BLUFFS PARK** and **MOUNT GALIANO**, you can watch eagles, ferries, and sweeping tides on Active Pass. Most Galiano roads accommodate bicycles untroubled by traffic, but there's some steep going. You can rent a bike at **GALIANO BICYCLE** (36 Burrill Rd; 250/539-9906), near the Sturdies Bay ferry terminal. **MONTAGUE HARBOUR PROVINCIAL MARINE PARK** (5 miles/8 km west of the ferry dock; 250/539-2115 or 877/559-2115 or 800/689-9025 for camping reservations) is a lovely, sheltered bay with beaches, picnic and camping areas, a boat launch, and stunning sunset views. At **MONTAGUE HARBOUR MARINA**, just east of the park, you can go kayaking with **GULF ISLANDS KAYA-KING** (250/539-2442), rent transport from **GALIANO MOPEDS & BOAT RENTALS** (250/539-3443), or stop for a beer and a barbecue on the deck of the **HARBOUR GRILL** (250/539-5733).

You'll find hearty pub food and local color at the **HUMMINGBIRD PUB** (47 Sturdies Bay Rd; 250/539-5472), vegetarian-friendly lunches at **DAYSTAR MARKET CAFÉ** (Georgeson Bay Rd at Porlier Pass Rd; 250/539-2800), and, on weekends, home-cooked, four-course dinners at **LA BÉRENGERIE** (Montague Rd; 250/539-5392), a cozy house in the woods near Montague Harbour.

While away time in the Sturdies Bay ferry lineup at **TRINCOMALI BAKERY, DELI & BISTRO** (2540 Sturdies Bay Rd; 250/539-2004) or the funky, diner-style **GRAND CENTRAL EMPORIUM** (2470 Sturdies Bay Rd; 250/539-9885). Savvy travellers grab provisions for the voyage at **MAX & MORITZ SPICY ISLAND FOOD HOUSE** (250/539-5888), a little red trailer at the ferry terminal. The **GALIANO CHAMBER OF COMMERCE** (250/539-2233; *www.galianoisland.com*) runs a small information center at Sturdies Bay in summer.

RESTAURANTS

Atrevida Restaurant at the Galiano Inn / ★★★

134 MADRONA DR, GALIANO ISLAND; 250/539-3388 OR 877/530-3939
Named for a Spanish ship that once explored these waters, Atrevida's charred-look wood floors, wrought-iron trim, and First Nations art combine Pacific Northwest and Spanish looks with grace. Chef James McNeil's light, modern fare is firmly rooted in British Columbia, however. The menu changes with the seasons, but relies on local fish, meat, and produce—organic whenever possible. The greens for a light salad with rosemary and sour cherry vinaigrette are grown on Mayne Island, the West Coast mussels come cedar-steamed with yam frites, and Salt Spring Island goat cheese is served warm on a cedar plank. Entrées range from Fraser River spring salmon with lobster butter and morels, to Gulf Island lamb with barley risotto. The wine list has a good selection of British Columbia vintages. Under a lofty open-beamed ceiling, every table in the curved atrium-style dining room has an expansive view of the seals, otters, and ferries plying Active Pass. The equally view-blessed waterfront patio, framed with cypress trees, is very Mediterranean.

$$$; MC, V; no checks; lunch, dinner every day (no lunch Oct–Apr, except for guests with packages); full bar; reservations recommended; info@galianoinn.com; www.galianoinn.com; uphill from the ferry terminal, turn left on Madrona Dr.

Woodstone Country Inn / ★★★

743 GEORGESON BAY RD, GALIANO ISLAND; 250/539-2022 OR 888/339-2022 The dining room at this inn (see review) ranks high: co-innkeeper/chef Gail Nielsen-Pich serves a fine four-course table d'hôte dinner that might include cioppino of fresh mussels, shrimp, and seafood in spicy tomato ragout; maple-baked salmon; rack of lamb; or vegetarian spinach and ricotta pie with roasted-garlic and tomato sauce. Desserts are outstanding: Galiano residents are fiercely loyal to the bread pudding with rum sauce. Enjoy the feast in a neoclassical room (think Italianate columns) overlooking serene fields. *$$$; AE, MC, V; local checks only; dinner every day (closed Dec–Jan); full bar; reservations recommended; woodstone@gulfislands.com; www.woodstoneinn.com; bear left off Sturdies Bay Rd onto Georgeson Bay Rd.* ♿

LODGINGS

The Bellhouse Inn / ★★★

29 FARMHOUSE RD, GALIANO ISLAND; 250/539-5667 OR 800/970-7464 Andrea Porter and David Birchall are consummate gentlefolk farmers, conversing with guests and feeding sheep with equal aplomb. This historic wood-shingled farmhouse, painted cream and barn red, contains three lovely upstairs guest rooms. All have balconies, duvets made with wool from the farm's own sheep, and private baths (though one is across the hall). The Kingfisher room is the largest, with picture windows allowing an expansive view of Bellhouse Bay from bed, and a Jacuzzi. Guests can play croquet or laze in a hammock. A popular wedding location, the Bellhouse is our favorite Galiano spot. Heritage touches include antique opera glasses; the comfortable guest lounge is lined with books and picture windows for spotting orcas at sea. Large breakfasts consist of fruit, granola, and hearty egg dishes such as seafood eggs Benedict. Meander the inn's 5 pleasant acres and into nearby Bellhouse Park, make your way to the sandy beach (a rare treat on Galiano), or join David for an afternoon's sailing on his 43-foot sloop. *$$–$$$; MC, V; Canadian checks only; info@bellhouse.com; www.bellhouseinn.com; uphill from ferry terminal, left on Burrill, left on Jack, right on Farmhouse.*

Galiano Inn / ★★★

134 MADRONA DR, GALIANO ISLAND; 250/539-3388 OR 877/530-3939 This new oceanfront inn, with its easy mix of Mediterranean and Northwest styles, has 10 spacious, ocean-view rooms, each with a private deck or patio, sitting area, and wood-burning fireplace. Some rooms have jetted tubs (with a separate shower), and all have luxurious touches, such as 24-carat gold-plated bathroom fixtures and velour robes. The rooms' soothing creams, yellows, and blues are just right for winding down after a soak in the hot tub or a massage at the on-site Madrona Del Mar Spa. Ten new suites and a meditation garden are planned for fall 2004. A full breakfast and afternoon tea are included, and the Atrevida

Restaurant (see review) serves Pacific Northwest fare. The inn, which is walking distance from Galiano's ferry terminal, also operates the *Chinook Key*, the island's only whale- and nature-watching boat. *$$$$; MC, V; no checks; 2-night min on weekends; info@galianoinn.com; www.galianoinn.com; uphill from the ferry terminal, left on Madrona Dr.* &

Woodstone Country Inn / ★★★

743 GEORGESON BAY RD, GALIANO ISLAND; 250/539-2022 OR 888/339-2022 This modern, executive-style manor house overlooks field and forest, and is a choice stopover for large cycling tours and business retreats. The best of the 12 rooms are on the lower level and feature private patios. The tone of the refined decor is set by classic English-print fabrics in florals and stripes; Persian and Chinese rugs warm the floors in some rooms, and antiques add country charm, as does hand-stenciling on the walls. All but two rooms have fireplaces, while one upper-end room has a double Jacuzzi. Breakfast and afternoon tea are included. Locals recommend the upscale dining room (see review). *$$–$$$; AE, MC, V; no checks; closed Dec–Jan; woodstone@gulfislands.com; www.woodstoneinn.com; bear left off Sturdies Bay Rd onto Georgeson Bay Rd.* &

Denman and Hornby Islands

Tranquil and bucolic, the sister islands of Denman and Hornby sit just off the east coast of central Vancouver Island. The larger, Denman—10 minutes by ferry from Buckley Bay, 12 miles (20 km) south of Courtenay—is known for pastoral farmlands and talented artisans. Most visitors skip right through to Hornby Island, but it is worth lingering. The sand and pebble beach at **FILLONGLEY PROVINCIAL PARK** (800/689-9025 for camping reservations) is a great place to catch the sunrise; the island's relatively flat landscape and untraveled byways make it a natural for cyclists. Work up an appetite and stop for pizza and locally roasted organic coffee at the **DENMAN BAKERY AND PIZZERIA** (3646 Denman Rd, Denman Island; 250/335-1310; closed Sun). On weekends, the **BISTRO** (at the Denman Island Guesthouse, 3806 Denman Rd; 250/335-2688) serves organic breakfasts and dinners. Rooms and dorm beds in the farmhouse are available every day of the week. Home-cooked breakfasts, lunches, and dinners are served every day at **THE DENMAN CAFÉ** (in the General Store, Northwest Rd and Denman Rd, Denman Island; 250/335-2999).

Ten minutes from Denman by ferry, Hornby is a dream for mountain bikers seeking idyllic—or hair-raising—forest trails, which fill the interior island. Downtown Hornby is centered on the **RINGSIDE MARKET**, a charming cluster of cedar-shingled craft shops and coffee bars at Central and Shields Rds. You can grab a homemade lunch at **JAN'S CAFÉ** (Ringside Market, Hornby Island; 250/335-1487). Locals also favor the burgers, Caesar salads, and ocean-view deck of the **THATCH PUB** (4305 Shingle Spit Rd, Hornby Island; 250/335-2833); kids are welcome in the restaurant section. Hornby's **HELLIWELL PROVINCIAL PARK** (far northern tip of island) impresses with dramatic seaside cliffs and lush forest, while beach lovers seek out the long stretch of sand at **TRIBUNE BAY PROVINCIAL PARK** (east shore of northern isthmus). If you're shopping for crafts, note that there are no bank machines on Denman, though there are two on Hornby (at the Hornby Island Co-op on Shields Rd and the Union Bay Credit Union near the ferry terminal).

LODGINGS

Sea Breeze Lodge / ★★

5205 FOWLER RD, HORNBY ISLAND; 250/335-2321 OR 888/516-2321 Owned for decades by the Bishop family, Sea Breeze has evolved into a comfortable family retreat with a loyal following. Most of the 16 phone- and TV-free cottages are along a bluff, with decks overlooking the sea; some have fireplaces and kitchenettes. Exteriors are simple grey cedar, but interiors are bright and cheery, with pine furniture and local art. Romantics might prefer the very rustic Nanoose Cabin, which sits alone in a seaside meadow. From the bluff, a blackberry- lined trail leads down to the rocky shoreline, past an ocean-view hot tub in a little cliffside building. Beachcombing, kayaks, a grass tennis court, beach barbecues, and a playground help occupy the kids. Cabin rates include three home-cooked meals, June through mid-September; expect comfort foods such as wholesome soups from the lodge's own cookbook, prime rib, halibut and salmon, or buffets with an Italian, Mexican, Greek, or Indian theme. The Bishops happily accommodate dietary needs, from vegetarian to vegan, and a separate kids' meal is served early. The restaurant, with its ocean-view wraparound veranda, is open to nonguests for dinner. It's open Friday and Saturday nights only in spring and fall, and is closed in winter; cabins with kitchens are available year-round. *$$$–$$$$; MC, V; checks OK; 2-night min in summer; info@seabreezelodge.com; www.seabreezelodge.com; on Tralee Point.*

Discovery Islands

The closely linked Discovery Islands—fishing and boating meccas east of Campbell River—include **QUADRA**, **CORTES**, and **SONORA**. To visit the most accessible Dis- covery Islands (Quadra and Cortes), take the 10-minute ferry ride from Campbell River to Quadra's Quathiaski Cove dock; from Heriot Bay on Quadra, another 45-minute ferry takes you to Cortes. Other islands in the chain are only accessible by private boat, water taxi from Campbell River, or float plane.

LODGINGS

April Point Lodge / ★★★

900 APRIL POINT RD, QUADRA ISLAND; 250/285-2222 OR 800/663-7090 This island getaway, centered around a cedar lodge built on pilings over the water, draws serious fisherfolk from all over the world. Though guided fishing is the major activity here, April Point also offers family-oriented activities such as bicycle, scooter, and kayak rentals; helicopter tours; and ocean-going whale- and bear-watching trips. The resort's spacious and freshly decorated accommodations range from large guest houses to lodge rooms and comfortable cabins; some have fireplaces, jetted tubs, living rooms, and kitchens, and all have sun decks with water views. At the restaurant in the main lodge, seafood (including sushi) is the focus;

wraparound windows and a sunny deck offer dramatic water views. Guests at April Point have access to the pool, hot tubs, tennis courts, and other facilities at Painter's Lodge (see review in Campbell River section), April Point's sister resort in nearby Campbell River. *$$$; AE, DC, E, MC, V; no checks; info@obmg.com; www.aprilpoint .com; 10 minutes north of ferry dock or accessible by free water taxi from Painter's Lodge.*

Tsa-Kwa-Luten Lodge and RV Park / ★★

I LIGHTHOUSE RD, QUADRA ISLAND; 250/285-2042 OR 800/665-7745 Built on an 1,100-acre forest by the Laichwiltach First Nation, this ocean-view lodge was inspired by traditional longhouse design. Native art is featured throughout the lodge and its 34 units, which include four self-contained cottages. Two beachfront and 10 forest RV sites are also available. The star attraction here, as elsewhere in the Campbell River area, is outdoor adventure: lodge staff can arrange salmon fishing, mountain biking, kayaking, river rafting, marine wildlife viewing, and sightseeing by air and sea. Alternately, stroll beaches to ponder ancient Native petroglyphs, visit the outstanding Kwagiulth Museum (a 45-minute forest walk away; 250/285-3733), walk to nearby Cape Mudge Lighthouse, or opt for a relaxing massage or reflexology treatment. The lodge hosts First Nations cultural demonstrations and traditional salmon barbecues monthly in summer. The Hamaelas dining room and lounge serves three meals every day—fresh seafood, including your own catch if you're on a fishing package, and such First Nations dishes as cedar-baked salmon, venison, and clam fritters are the star attractions; seasonal pies—try blackberry or sour cream and peach—make welcome appearances. *$$$; AE, DC, E, JCB, MC, V; no checks; open May–mid-Oct; tkllodge@connected.bc.ca; www.capemudgeresort .bc.ca; 15 minutes south of ferry dock.*

The Cowichan Valley and Southeast Shore

The Cowichan Valley is a gentle stretch of farmland and forest from the town of Shawnigan Lake north to Chemainus; the microclimate of this pleasant area lends itself to grape growing, making it the island's best known vineyard region. Try a pinot noir at **BLUE GROUSE VINEYARDS** (4365 Blue Grouse Rd, off Lakeside Rd, Duncan; 250/743-3834; *www.bluegrousevineyards.com*); also visit **CHERRY POINT VINEYARDS** (840 Cherry Point Rd, Cobble Hill; 250/743-1272 or 866/395-5252; *www.cherrypointvineyards.com*) and **GLENTERRA VINEYARDS** (3897 Cobble Hill Rd, Cobble Hill; 250/743-2330). Time your lunch for a visit to **VIGNETI ZANATTA** (5039 Marshall Rd, Duncan; 250/748-2338; *www.zanatta.com*), which has a res-taurant in a 1903 farmhouse overlooking the vineyards (lunch and dinner Wed–Sun). Or head to **MERRIDALE CIDER WORKS** (1230 Merridale Rd, Cobble Hill; 250/743-4293 or 800/998-9908; *www.merridalecider.com*), where you can enjoy a meal on the wraparound veranda. Merridale, the island's only cidery, makes cider in the English tradition; the best time to visit is mid-September to mid-October, when local apples are run through the presses. The rolling, pastoral landscape continues through the Chemainus Valley north to the hub towns of Nanaimo and Parksville. If you're traveling directly to the valley from the Sidney or Swartz Bay ferry terminal, taking the Brentwood Bay to Mill Bay ferry (BC Ferries, 250/386-3431 or 888/223-3779 in BC) saves you a drive into Victoria.

Cowichan Bay

This sweet little seaside village off Highway 1 is built on pilings over the water. Brightly painted stilt houses are home to restaurants and craft and gift shops. Houseboats, fishing boats, and yachts mingle in the busy marina. The Wooden Boat Society displays and Native artisan's studio at the **COWICHAN BAY MARITIME CENTRE AND MUSEUM** (1761 Cowichan Bay Rd; 250/746-4955; *www.classicboats.org*) are worth a visit. The **ROCK COD CAFÉ** (1759 Cowichan Bay Rd; 250/746-1550) and the **UDDER GUYS ICE CREAM PARLOUR** (1759 Cowichan Bay Rd; 250/746-4300) can fulfill seaside-induced cravings for fish, chips, and ice cream.

RESTAURANTS

The Masthead Restaurant / ★
Chowder Café

1705 COWICHAN BAY RD, COWICHAN BAY; 250/748-3714 As the Cowichan Valley nurtures its reputation as a food and wine destination, what it needs is a place to show off the local bounty. The Masthead, housed in the waterfront 1868 Columbia Hotel, may be just that place. The ingredients here are resolutely local, organic, free-range, or sustainable. The salmon is wild, vegetables come straight from local farms, and the cellar has the best selection of Vancouver Island wines available anywhere (ask if there's a winemaker's dinner scheduled soon). You might start with local oysters shucked or baked, though a favorite is the rich salmon and shrimp chowder. Depending on what's in season, mains could be crab, salmon, or halibut—all from BC waters—duck or venison from the Cowichan Valley, or Salt Spring Island lamb. All is well-executed without being overly experimental; standards like Caesar salad (prepared table-side), French onion soup, and salmon Wellington also appear. The wood-paneled, portholed, carpeted interior, dotted with model boats and fishing floats, is comfortably un-hip, though the main attraction is the sweeping bay view from the big picture windows and the wide waterfront deck. In summer (weather permitting), the Masthead's seaside deck opens as the outdoor Chowder Café, serving a casual menu of pizza, salads, sandwiches, and the same luscious chowder. *$$$ (Masthead), $ (Chowder Café); AE, MC, V; no checks; dinner every day (Masthead), lunch, dinner every day (closed Oct–Apr) (Chowder Café); full bar (Masthead), beer and wine (Chowder Café); reservations recommended (Masthead), no reservations (Chowder Café); www.themastheadrestaurant.com; at south end of the village.*

LODGINGS

Dream Weaver Bed & Breakfast / ★

1682 BOTWOOD LN, COWICHAN BAY; 250/748-7688 OR 888/748-7689 This modern wood-shake home is modeled on gabled, multistoried, Victorian-era construction. The large Magnolia Suite, nestled in the top-floor gables, is done in traditional flower prints, with a double Jacuzzi tub opposite the gas fireplace. A small balcony offers views of picturesque Cowichan Bay. Downstairs, the Rosewood Suite is Victorian and floral, with wallpaper borders and a wrought iron bedstead, while the Primrose Suite has a more masculine look, with deep plum and green hues and a Jacuzzi tub in the bedroom. Each room has a private entrance and a wealth of amenities, including a gas fireplace, jetted tub, fridge, coffee maker, TV, VCR, CD player, and robes, though only the Magnolia has a view. Hosts Cathy and Ken McAllister serve guests a full breakfast. *$$; MC, V; no checks; dreamwvr@islandnet.com; www.vancouverisland-bc.com/dreamweaver; at the south end of the village.*

Duncan

Forty-five minutes north of Victoria on the Trans-Canada Highway (Hwy 1), the City of Totems is designated by little totem poles sprinkled around the town's walkable 4-by-4-block core. Another claim to fame is the world's largest hockey stick, notably affixed to a community arena on the west side of the highway. In the old downtown, a good sandwich, wrap, or salad lunch can be had at the popular **ISLAND BAGEL COMPANY & LIVINGSTONE'S GOURMET FOODS** (48 Station St; 250/748-1988) or at **GOSSIPS** (161 Kenneth St; 250/746-6466), which also serves Asian- and Mediterranean-inspired dinners and has a pretty grapevine-draped patio. The **QUW'UTSUN' CULTURAL AND CONFERENCE CENTRE** (200 Cowichan Wy; 250/746-8119 or 877/746-8119) on Duncan's southern edge is a must-see for admirers of First Nations arts and crafts. In summer, watch as the region's renowned Cowichan sweaters—hand-knit of thick wool with indigenous designs in cream and browns or grays—are made. The center also features an open-air carving shed, where carvers craft 12- to 20-foot totem poles. The gallery and gift shop are excellent. More local crafts can be found on Saturday mornings year-round at the outdoor **SATURDAY MARKET** near the train station.

RESTAURANTS

The Quamichan Inn / ★★

1478 MAPLE BAY RD, DUNCAN; 250/746-7028 Chef Steve Mugridge turns out fresh seafood dishes and favorites such as crown of roast pork with applesauce, rack of lamb, and salmon in Creole sauce at this turn-of-the-20th-century Tudor-style country manor, owned by Pam and Clive Cunningham for the past 23 years. Red upholstered chairs, floral wallpaper, and hunting prints carry out the country-house theme in the four dining rooms. Outside, the garden is profuse with fragrant wisteria, blooming fuchsias, and colorful dahlias. The proprietors gladly pick up yachties and drop them off after dinner. Accommodations consist of four guest rooms; rates include an English hunt breakfast: fruit, eggs, bacon, sausage, and fried tomato. *$$$; AE, MC, V; local checks only; dinner Wed–Sun; full bar; reservations recommended; thequamichaninn@shaw.ca; www.thequamichaninn.com; just east of Duncan, follow the signs to Maple Bay.*

LODGINGS

Fairburn Farm / ★★

3310 JACKSON RD, DUNCAN; 250/746-4637 This lovingly restored 1894 manor house is at the heart of a 130-acre farm, where part of the charm—especially for animal-loving kids—is the chance to pitch in with chores. Always innovative, hosts Anthea and Darrel Archer operate Canada's first water buffalo dairy (and are accomplished B&B hosts). Breakfasts include farm-raised products such as freshly churned butter, homemade bread, local preserves, and frittatas of free-range eggs and organic tomatoes. The three spotlessly clean rooms are simply decorated with cozy furniture, local art, and historical photos; tall windows offer views across the gardens, fields, and surrounding forest. Some of the rooms have fireplaces and whirlpool tubs and all are phone- and TV-free; all have private baths, though one is across the hall. A two-bedroom cottage with a kitchen overlooks the fields. Trails in the woods and a canoe on the creek beckon. *$$; MC, V; checks OK; 3-night min in cottage; open Apr–mid-Oct; info@fairburnfarm.bc.ca; www.fairburnfarm.bc.ca; 7 miles (11 km) southwest of Duncan (call for directions, there are no signs to the farm).*

Chemainus

Heralded as "the little town that did," seaside Chemainus bounced back from the closure of its logging mill and turned to tourism with flair. Buildings are painted with murals depicting the town's colorful history, making Chemainus a noted tourist attraction on Highway 1A. The whole town has a theatrical feel, underlined by dinner theater productions at the popular **CHEMAINUS THEATRE** (9737 Chemainus Rd; 250/246-9820 or 800/565-7738). A new festival theater in the works for 2005 should make this little town a major theater destination.

RESTAURANTS

The Waterford Restaurant / ★★

9875 MAPLE ST, CHEMAINUS; 250/246-1046 French cookery takes a West Coast bent at the Waterford, a cozy nine-table bistro with a greenery-draped veranda ensconced in an old town heritage building. Lunch prices are surprisingly low for upscale cuisine offered by chef Dwayne Maslen: paupiette of sole, mushroom or seafood crepes, or seafood marinara. Dinner is slightly pricier: choices can include rack of lamb dijon, a traditional bouillabaisse, duck with blackberry port sauce, or local wild salmon. The wine list concentrates on local Cowichan Valley wines. *$$; AE, MC, V; no checks; lunch, dinner Tues–Sat (Oct–Apr: lunch*

Wed–Sat, dinner Thurs–Sat). Call for hours in January; full bar; reservations recommended; waterfordrestaurant@shaw.ca; a few blocks from downtown. &

LODGINGS

Bird Song Cottage / ★★

9909 MAPLE ST, CHEMAINUS; 250/246-9910 OR 866/246-9910 Bird Song Cottage is a bacchanal of imaginative Victoriana. The exterior of this lavender-and-white gingerbread cottage delights period purists. Inside, oil portraits, a baby grand piano, and a Celtic harp compete with an extensive fancy hat collection. Songs of (caged) birds are also present. Hosts Larry and Virginia Blatchford keep costumes on hand, ready to provide larger groups with a dress-up Serendipity Tea. Three guest rooms feature private baths, duvets, and fresh-cut flowers. The Bluebird and Hummingbird rooms, tucked under the gables, overflow with lace and florals, while the Nightingale is light and airy, with lace and sage green fabrics. Paintings are by Virginia's sister, a Chemainus mural artist. Friday and Saturday mornings, when the host is home, breakfast is accompanied by piano music. *$$; AE, MC, V; no checks; info@birdsongcottage.ca; www.vancouverisland accommodation.bc.ca; a few blocks from downtown.*

Castlebury Cottage / ★★

9910 CROFT ST, CHEMAINUS; 250/246-9228 OR 866/246-9910 More Medieval French castle than cottage, this two-suite hideaway is just the place to let your Lancelot and Guinevere fantasies run riot. Upstairs in the 900-square-foot Camelot Suite, you sleep beneath purple velvet bed curtains, soak in the big onyx tub, or do the Juliet thing from either of the two balconies. Though dramatically medieval right down to fireplace, vaulted ceilings, frescoed walls, and resident suit of armor, the suite also features a modern kitchenette, TV, VCR, and CD player. The smaller, less-expensive Sonnet Suite downstairs is a little more subtle, but also boasts a fireplace, rich purple fabrics, and an onyx bathtub. Hidden behind Gothic-shaped cupboards are a fridge, microwave, TV, and VCR. Privacy is assured here: each suite has its own entrance, and breakfast is delivered to the door, though for friends traveling together, there is a secret passageway between the two suites. Three-day romance packages include theater tickets, a carriage ride, and an en suite dinner with a harpist. *$$–$$$$; AE, MC, V; no checks; info@castleburycottage.com; www.castleburycottage.com; a few blocks from downtown.*

Ladysmith

RESTAURANTS

Crow and Gate Neighbourhood Pub / ★★

2313 YELLOW POINT RD, LADYSMITH; 250/722-3731 The Crow and Gate was one of the first neighborhood pubs in BC and retains pride of place as the nicest pub we have seen in this region. English fowl stroll the pastoral grounds, and quaint buildings give the feel of a gentleman's farm. Inside this popular watering hole, light from the flames of two substantial fires glints off diamond-pane windows; long plank tables invite conversation. Traditional English pub fare includes highly praised steak-and-kidney pie, ploughman's lunch, beef dip, and—in a nod to local products—panfried oysters. No kids under 19. *$; AE, MC, V; no checks; lunch, dinner every day; full bar; no reservations; 8 miles (13 km) south of Nanaimo.*

LODGINGS

Yellow Point Lodge / ★★

3700 YELLOW POINT RD, LADYSMITH; 250/245-7422 This well-loved oceanfront lodge draws guests back every year, from honeymoon to anniversary—even in winter (weekends are often booked months in advance). The log-and-timber lodge has a big ocean-view lounge with a fireplace, and simple but comfortable rooms with or without views. Cabins around the property range from very rustic, summer-only cabins to cozy one-bedroom cottages. The one-room White Beach cabins are closest to the water; each features a log-constructed bed with a view, and a wood stove nestled in a rustic, beamed interior. Water along the private 1½ miles (2.4 km) of coastline is exceptionally clear. Daily rates include most activities plus three meals and snacks served at group tables in the lodge: comfort foods such as prime rib and Yorkshire pudding, or classic BC salmon. Recreational facilities include tennis courts, kayaks, mountains bikes, walking trails, an outdoor saltwater pool, a sauna, and a hot tub. *$$$; AE, MC, V; checks OK; 2-night min on weekends, 3-night min on holidays; www.yellowpointlodge.com; 9 miles (14.5 km) east of Ladysmith, take the Cedar Rd exit off Hwy 1, south of Nanaimo.*

Nanaimo

Nanaimo is more than the strip mall it appears to be from the highway (19 and 19A join in Nanaimo). The early island settlement of Nanaimo began as a coal mining hub. The **HUDSON'S BAY COMPANY BASTION** (at Bastion and Front Sts; summer only), built in 1853, is one of the few forts of this type left standing in North America. It's part of the **NANAIMO DISTRICT MUSEUM** (100 Cameron Rd; 250/753-1821), which also has a replica of a Chinatown street.

In Nanaimo's old town, near the old train station, cafés mix with vintage shops and houseware boutiques. At **DELICADO'S** (358 Wesley St; 250/753-6524) lunch on wraps fired with chipotle sauce and black-bean-and-corn salsa, or at **GINA'S** (47 Skinner St; 250/753-5411), an ever-popular Mexican restaurant. In summer, you can hop a ferry out to the **DINGHY DOCK** (250/753-2373 for the pub; 250/753-8244 for ferry information), a nautical pub floating off shore. Nanaimo is best known as a transportation hub, with frequent sailings to Vancouver on BC Ferries (250/386-3431 or 888/223-3779 in BC only; *www.bcferries.com*), and on the new **HARBOURLYNX** (250/753-4443 or 866/206-5969; *www.harbourlynx.com*) foot-passenger service.

The island's second-largest city is also a good place to launch a scuba diving holiday. Numerous companies offer equipment rentals and guided tours. Thrill seekers head for the **BUNGY ZONE** (15 minutes south of Nanaimo; 250/753-5867 or 800/668-7771) to experience North America's only legal bungy-jumping bridge, over the Nanaimo River. Check out the **BATHTUB RACE** on the third weekend of July, a tradition since 1967. Bike trails—meandering lanes and wilderness single-tracks—snake around the city's edge.

The spit at **PIPER'S LAGOON** (northeast of downtown), extending into the Strait of Georgia, is great for bird-watching. **NEWCASTLE ISLAND PROVINCIAL MARINE PARK** is an auto-free wilderness reached by a summer foot-passenger ferry from Nanaimo's inner harbor.

Golf courses with views proliferate from Nanaimo northward. Most noteworthy is the **NANAIMO GOLF CLUB** (2800 Highland Blvd; 250/758-6332; *www.nanaimogolfclub.ca*), an 18-hole championship course 2 miles (3 km) north of the city. Others include **PRYDE VISTA GOLF COURSE** (155 Pryde Ave; 250/753-6188), 1 mile (2 km) northwest of Nanaimo, and **FAIRWINDS** (3730 Fairwinds Dr; 250/468-7666 or 888/781-2777; *www.fairwinds.bc.ca*), at Nanoose Bay. **TOURISM NANAIMO** (250/756-0106; *www.tourismnanaimo.com*) has more information.

RESTAURANTS

The Mahle House / ★★★

2104 HEMER RD, CEDAR; 250/722-3621 Find this cozy 1904 home-turned-restaurant in Cedar, just minutes southeast of Nanaimo, and sample the inventive cuisine of chef/co-owner Maureen Loucks. Begin with "porcupine" prawns, quickly deep-fried in shredded phyllo, then taste chicken stuffed with Dungeness crab and drizzled with preserved lemon sauce. Most vegetables and herbs come from the house garden; the rabbit comes from down the road, and the scallops from Qualicum Beach. Desserts are exquisite: crème brûlée Napoleon and peanut butter pie. Co-owner Delbert Horrocks takes justifiable pride in his extensive, award-winning wine list. On Wednesdays a group of four can sample 20 different dishes—all surprises selected by the chef. *$$$; AE, MC, V; no checks; dinner Wed–Sun; full bar; reservations recommended; www.mahlehouse.com; at Cedar.* &

Parksville

Parksville and the surrounding area are renowned for sandy beaches, especially in lovely **RATHTREVOR BEACH PROVINCIAL PARK** (off Hwy 19A, 1 mile/2 km south of Parksville; 800/689-9025 for camping reservations). Families love its lengthy shallows and relatively warm water temperatures, camping, and August's annual sand castle competition. **MORNINGSTAR** (525 Lowry's Rd; 250/248-2244 or 800/567-1320) offers golfing.

A little farther afield, picnic at thunderous **ENGLISHMAN RIVER FALLS PROVINCIAL PARK** (8 miles/12.8 km southwest of town; 800/689-9025 for camping reservations), and mosey along to Coombs, a tiny town on Highway 4A that hovers between cute and kitsch with its overblown pioneer theme, based on a small core of true old-time buildings. Shop for produce and gifts, or stop for a hefty sandwich lunch at the popular **OLD COUNTRY MARKET** (250/248-6272; Apr–Nov), where goats graze on the grassy roof. **MACMILLAN PROVINCIAL PARK** (20 miles/32 km west of Parksville on Hwy 4) contains Cathedral Grove, a sky-high old-growth forest of Douglas firs and cedars up to 800 years old.

LODGINGS

Tigh-Na-Mara Resort, Spa & Conference Centre / ★★★

1095 E ISLAND HWY, PARKSVILLE; 250/248-2072 OR 800/663-7373 The grotto—a swimming pool–sized thermal mineral pool complete with waterfalls and cave effects—is the centerpiece of Tigh-Na-Mara's lavish three-story spa, one of the best of the new spas springing up on Vancouver Island. The spa, combined with a wealth of supervised children's activities in summer, makes this a great spot for parents in need of a little adult time. Log cottages, spread throughout 22 acres of wooded grounds, offer privacy, kitchens, porches or patios, and barbecues, as well as fireplaces (standard in all rooms). Oceanfront condominiums are newer and spiffier, with log-beam details; some have jetted tubs and kitchens. The upscale Forest Studios and Woodland Suites surround the spa facility but are farthest from the beach. Standard hotel rooms are available in the two-story Jedediah Lodge. Guests can use the indoor pool and hot tub, steam room, tennis courts, playgrounds—and 500 feet of sandy beachfront. The log-beamed Cedar Room restaurant has Pacific Northwest fare and a spa menu. Pets are OK in some cottages during off-season. *$$–$$$; AE, DC, MC, V; local checks only; info@tigh-na-mara.com; www.tigh-na-mara.com; 1¼ miles (2 km) south of Parksville on Hwy 19A.*

Qualicum Beach

This little town 20 minutes north of Parksville on Highway 19A has a pleasant beach-front promenade and a growing downtown shopping district. For its size, it boasts a good selection of cafés—a favorite is funky coffee and lunch spot **MURPHY'S COFFEE & TEA COMPANY** (177 W 2nd Ave; 250/752-6693). For more retro character, drive 10 minutes north for a burger at the **COLA DINER** (6060 W Island Hwy; 250/757-2029), a joyful ode to a 1950s burger joint in sparkly red vinyl and chrome. Then get some exercise golfing at **EAGLECREST** (2035 W Island Hwy; 250/752-9744 or 800/567-1320). At **MILNER GARDENS AND WOODLAND** (2179 W Island Hwy; 250/752-6153) you can stroll through 10 acres of lovingly kept gardens and stop for tea in a 1930s seaside manor.

RESTAURANTS

Lefty's / ★

710 MEMORIAL AVE, QUALICUM BEACH; 250/752-7530 The bright, funky ambience and art-filled walls here rival casual café experiences of Vancouver or Victoria. Baked-on-the-premises cheesecake and chocolate fudge cake are superior. Specialties include wraps stuffed with fresh West Coast fusions like Cajun chicken; flavorful chorizo sausage pizza; or cheddar corn pie, a quichelike creation. At dinner, Lefty's transitions to pastas, stir-fries, and steak and prawns. Organic coffees are a bonus. A Parksville location (101-280 E Island Hwy, Parksville; 250/954-3886) offers the same menu. *$$; MC, V; no checks; breakfast, lunch, dinner every day; full bar; reservations recommended; leftysrestaurants@home.com; www.leftys.tv; at Fern in Qualicum Beach.*

Old Dutch Inn / ★

2690 W ISLAND HWY, QUALICUM BEACH; 250/752-6914 This place has dreamy breakfasts—and waitresses in triple-peaked, starched lace caps. The Dutch theme is taken seriously, with turned oak chairs and Delft tiles. The Dutchie is a delicious sort of French toast sandwich filled with homemade blueberry preserves. Also try classic *pannekoeken* or Eggs Benedict Old Dutch with fine smoked salmon. Join retirees and travelers at lunch for a *uitsmijter,* an open-faced sandwich with Dutch smoked ham and cheese, or Indonesian-inspired *loempia,* a 10-spice spring roll with pork and roasted peanuts. (Vegetarians are happiest here at breakfast.) Expansive windows look out on Qualicum Bay. *$; AE, DC, DIS, MC, V; no checks; breakfast, lunch, dinner every day; full bar; reservations recommended (dinner); info@olddutchinn.com; www.olddutchinn.com; on Highway 19A.*

LODGINGS

Bahari / ★

5101 W ISLAND HWY, QUALICUM BEACH; 250/752-9278 OR 877/752-9278 Enter through the modern gray-toned exterior via double carved doors dominated by a large seashell handle. Inside, the look is 1980s West Coast with Asian touches, including a Japanese kimono hung in the two-story foyer. The three enormous rooms all open onto a deck, all have fireplaces, and two have ocean views (room 3 in particular has an expansive view). Seven acres of lawn, gardens, and woods include a trail down to a pebbly beach; a private hot tub in the woods overlooks Georgia Strait and the Northern Gulf Islands. Children are welcome in the two-bedroom, 1,200-square-foot suite with a kitchen. *$$$–$$$$; AE, MC, V; no checks; 2-night min for suite; closed Dec–Feb; relax@baharibandb.com; www.baharibandb.com; 10 minutes north of town on Hwy 19A.*

Hollyford Bed & Breakfast / ★★★

106 HOYLAKE RD E, QUALICUM BEACH; 250/752-8101 OR 877/224-6511 This 1920s cottage surrounded by holly hedges and laurels has been thoughtfully renovated to add three guest rooms in a private wing. Jim Ford's collection of western and Royal Canadian Mounted Police memorabilia enhances the antique ambiance. Breakfast, served on sterling silver and Waterford crystal in the dining room, often features Marjorie Ford's gourmet takes on Irish cuisine (with recipes from her cookbook): home-baked scones, followed by tourtière with Dubliner cheese, for example. Lazy afternoons call for tea on the little patio surveying the snug garden. The hosts like to pamper guests, delivering wake-up trays of OJ and coffee to rooms before breakfast, and evening tuck-in trays of sherry, Perrier, and homemade truffles. Sodas, popcorn, coffee, and tea are available with in-room VCRs and videos. The Fords are consummate innkeepers and offer a complimentary concierge service; they will prepare itineraries to help guests tour the area. *$$$; AE, DC, JCB, MC, V; no checks; mail@hollyford.ca; www.hollyford.ca; off Hwy 4 (Memorial Ave).*

Barkley Sound and Tofino

Most visitors pass through Port Alberni on the way to Tofino via Highway 4, or wait to take the scenic boat trip on the **LADY ROSE** or **FRANCES BARKLEY** (250/723-8313 or 800/663-7192) to Bamfield, Ucluelet, or the Broken Group Islands. Boats offer passenger day trips as well as freight service.

Port Alberni

Shops, galleries, and restaurants cluster at the Harbour Quay, where boats to Barkley Sound dock in this industrial logging and fishing town. A favored nosh stop is the **CLAM BUCKET** (4479 Victoria Quay; 250/723-1315).

Bamfield

This tiny fishing village of 500, home to a marine biology research station and known for the big salmon pulled from nearby waters, is reached by boat (see Introduction to this section), or via logging road from Port Alberni or Lake Cowichan. The road extends only to the east side of the village. The west side, across Bamfield Inlet, has no vehicle access; water taxis link the two. Bamfield bustles when the **WEST COAST TRAIL** summer season hits—it's the end of the line for the world-famous, five- to seven-day, mettle-testing wilderness trail that's so popular hikers have to make reservations. For reservations and information on this spectacular, coast-hugging trek, contact **HELLO BC** (250/387-1642 or 800/435-5622; *www.hellobc.com*). The **BAMFIELD CHAMBER OF COMMERCE** (250/728-3006; *www.bamfieldchamber.com*) also has information.

LODGINGS

Wood's End Landing / ★

380 LOMBARD ST, BAMFIELD; 250/728-3383 OR 877/828-3383 These four cute cedar-shake-and-driftwood cabins are on the peaceful, car-free west side of Bamfield. Proprietor Terry Giddens built them out of materials he beachcombed and recycled from tumble-down Bamfield buildings. The cabins and two additional suites, set among 50-year-old perennial gardens, overlook Bamfield Inlet. The hilltop Woodsman cabin and Angler suite have the best views. Cabins have two loft bedrooms and cooking facilities. It's a remote area, so bring your food (town cafés offer meals in season) and toys. Canoes and rowboats are available free for guest use; Giddens also offers moorage, rents kayaks, and runs nature tours and fishing trips. *$$–$$$$; MC, V; no checks; woodsend@island.net; www.woodsend.travel .bc.ca; across inlet from government dock via water taxi (Can$3 per trip).*

Ucluelet

"Ukie" is still a little rough around the edges, as the economic staples of fishing and logging only recently began to wane, but for many visitors, that's part of its charm. This ugly duckling is making a go at becoming a tourism swan like sister town Tofino, with several new craft shops and Whiskey Landing, with a pub, restaurant, and accommodations that is set to open at the end of Main Street by Autumn 2004. A highlight is the **WILD PACIFIC TRAIL**, a two-part, 4-mile (6.5 km) path through the old growth and within sight of the pounding surf.

Budget B&B accommodations line the road into town and offer easy access to **PACIFIC RIM NATIONAL PARK RESERVE** (250/726-4212); stop by the visitor center just inside the park entrance, off Highway 4. Three separate areas of the park allow visitors to appreciate the abundant wildlife and grand vistas of the Pacific Ocean. For hikers, the West Coast Trail reigns supreme (see Bamfield section). The **BROKEN GROUP ISLANDS**, accessible only by boat, attract intrepid kayakers and scuba divers. Visitors to Ucluelet have come to enjoy the expanse of awe-inspiring Long Beach. The park's lone campground, **GREEN POINT** (at the park's midway point, well marked by signs; 800/689-9025), is often full during peak times and is closed in winter.

Six miles (10 km) north of Ucluelet, the **WICKANINNISH INTERPRETIVE CENTRE** (1 Wickaninnish Rd; 250/726-4701; open daily in summer) has oceanic exhibits and an expansive view, shared by the on-site **WICKANINNISH RESTAURANT** (not to be confused with the Wickaninnish Inn; see review in Tofino section).

During March and April, 20,000 gray whales migrate past the West Coast on their way to the Bering Sea and can often be seen from shore; orcas and humpbacks cruise the waters much of the year. For close-up views, whale-watching tours leave from both Ucluelet and Tofino; tours are easy to arrange once you arrive. The **PACIFIC RIM WHALE FESTIVAL** (250/726-7742; mid-Mar–early Apr) hosts events here and in Tofino.

RESTAURANTS

The Boat Basin / ★★

1971 HARBOUR CRES (TAUCA LEA RESORT AND SPA), UCLUELET; 250/726-4625 OR 800/979-9303 Ucluelet no longer lacks a fine-dining option, thanks to the fresh wild seafood, chic modern decor, and great harbor views laid on at Tauca Lea Resort and Spa's (see review) Boat Basin restaurant. The setting is airy, uncluttered, and very West Coast, with plenty of cedar, striking First Nations art, and a deck overlooking the local fishing fleet. Only regional seafood is served. Start with diver scallops, tuna carpaccio, or a soba noodle soup with local shrimp. Your main course could be a fishpot of local seafood, five-pepper crusted albacore tuna, or an innovative treatment of whatever was fresh at the docks that day. Meat lovers and vegetarians are well catered to, with options such as beef tenderloin with Gorgonzola sauce, or rigatoni rigatte with local goat cheese, black olives, and spinach. The wine list has a good selection of British Columbia vintages. *$$$; AE, DC, MC, V; no checks; dinner every day; full bar; reservations recommended; info@taucalearesort .com; www.taucalearesort.com; from Hwy 4 turn left onto Seaplane Base Rd.*

Matterson House / ★★

1682 PENINSULA RD, UCLUELET; 250/726-2200 Tofino residents happily make the half-hour drive to Ucluelet for a filling, satisfying breakfast or dinner (generous helpings at reasonable prices) at casual Matterson House. Breakfast standards such as eggs Benedict and huevos rancheros make way for lunch's Matterson Monster Burger, fully loaded with bacon, cheese, mushrooms, and more. Look for Caesar salads, chicken burgers, and homemade bread—and nothing deep-fried. Dinner sees hungry hikers and residents dig into prime rib, salmon filo, or veggie lasagne. Desserts feature fruit crumbles and daily cheesecakes such as Kahlúa espresso. *$$; MC, V; local checks only; breakfast, lunch, dinner every day; full bar; reservations recommended; on Hwy 4 on the way into town.*

LODGINGS

A Snug Harbour Inn / ★★

460 MARINE DR, UCLUELET; 250/726-2686 OR 888/936-5222 The million-dollar view here encompasses the rugged coast and islands where harbor seals, whales, and eagles play. Through powerful binoculars in the sitting room, guests can feel they've already taken a whale-watching tour. All rooms have private balconies and stunning views. Honeymooners favor the tiered Atlantis Room, which has a spectacular view from the bed, and the Sawadee Room, with its two-sided fireplace and sunken jetted tub. Others favor the split-level Lighthouse Room, with round brass ships' portholes and picture windows. Two rooms in a separate building feature one wheelchair-accessible unit and one pet-friendly room. *$$$–$$$$; MC, V; no checks; 2-night min; asnughbr@island.net; www.awesome view.com; through village and right on Marine Dr.*

Eagle Nook Ocean Wilderness Resort / ★★★

BARKLEY SOUND; 250/723-1000 OR 800/760-2777 No roads lead to the wilderness oasis of Eagle Nook, and that's what makes it special. It caters to the outdoors lover who revels in luxury after a day of kayaking, fishing, beachcombing, or exploring the coast by helicopter. Guests enjoy hiking the trails lacing the resort's 70 forested acres or joining nature cruises to see harbor seals, cormorants, bald eagles, and possibly whales in the Broken Group Islands, part of Pacific Rim National Park Reserve. Back at the resort, guests feast on beautifully prepared West Coast or continental meals from comfortable window seats before a roaring fire. All 23 rooms have ocean views; two one-bedroom cabins have water views and sitting areas, fireplaces, and kitchenettes. The resort's ocean-side deck features a hot tub and adjacent cedar-hut sauna. A wide range of professional massages and spa services is available. Rates include all meals and nonguided activities. Packages including airfare from Seattle or Vancouver are the most popular option. *$$$$; AE, MC, V; no checks; 2-night min; open June–Sept; www.eaglenook.com; if you're driving, arrange to meet the resort's water taxi in Ucluelet.*

Tauca Lea Resort & Spa / ★★★

1971 HARBOUR CREST, UCLUELET; 250/726-4625 OR 800/979-9303 At this resort complex set on a peninsula on the edge of Ucluelet, each of the one- and two-bedroom apartment-sized suites has a full kitchen and private balcony, gas fireplace, and Barkley Sound or marina views. Spacious, light-filled suites are decorated with leather armchairs and handcrafted furniture; a few higher-end units have hot tubs; pets are welcome in many of the units. A full-service spa offers body polishes, wraps, reflexology, thalassotherapy, and more. The resort's Boat Basin restaurant (see review) is one of the best places to eat in the area. *$$$–$$$$; AE, DC, MC, V; no checks; info@taucalearesort.com; www.taucalearesort.com; from Hwy 4 turn left onto Seaplane Base Rd.*

Tofino

At the end of Highway 4 is the wild West Coast, drawing surfers, kayakers, and nature lovers from all over the world. Tofino has been called "the next Whistler," as high-end lodges fill the forests between town and Pacific Rim National Park Preserve: we only hope careful planning keeps the spirit of this special place intact. A large number of international visitors has resulted in more excellent hotels, B&Bs, and restaurants than one would expect from a town of fewer than 2,000.

People arrive at Tofino primarily by car, via the winding mountainous route of Highway 4 (five hours from Victoria). **NORTH VANCOUVER AIR** (604/278-1608 or 800/228-6608) flies from Seattle and Vancouver—but you'll want a car here (try **BUDGET** for rentals; 250/725-2060).

You can explore the coast with one of numerous water-taxi or whale-watching companies, by floatplane, or by kayak. **TOFINO SEA KAYAKING COMPANY** (320 Main; 250/725-4222 or 800/863-4664) offers kayak rentals, or guided tours with experienced boaters and naturalists. **REMOTE PASSAGES** (71 Wharf St; 250/725-3330 or 800/666-9833) offers guided tours by kayak, Zodiac, or covered whale-watching boat. The **PACIFIC RIM WHALE FESTIVAL** (250/726-7742; mid-Mar–early Apr) hosts events here and in Ucluelet.

A number of boat and floatplane companies, including **TOFINO AIR** (50 1st St; 250/725-4454 or 866/486-3247), offer day trips to the calming pools of Hot Springs Cove; overnight at the six-room **HOT SPRINGS COVE LODGE** (250/670-1106 or 866/670-1106). The 12-acre **TOFINO BOTANICAL GARDENS** (1084 Pacific Rim Hwy; 250/725-1220) features indigenous plant life in a scenic waterfront setting.

Gift shops and galleries are sprinkled throughout town. The longhouse of the **EAGLE AERIE GALLERY** (350 Campbell St; 250/725-3235 or 800/663-0669) sells art by Coast Tsimshian artist Roy Henry Vickers. **HOUSE OF HIMWITSA** (300 Main St; 250/725-2017 or 800/899-1947) features First Nations masks, jewelry, and gifts. Get organic coffee and baked treats at the **COMMON LOAF BAKE SHOP** (180 1st St; 250/725-3915), fresh sushi at **THE INN AT TOUGH CITY** (350 Main St; 250/725-2021), or highly-rated organic global takeout from **SO-BO** (1184 Pacific Rim Hwy; 250/725-2341), a catering trailer behind the Live to Surf shop. The **TOFINO VISI-**

TORS INFO CENTRE (250/725-3414; 1426 Pacific Rim Hwy; *www.tofinobc.org*) is on Hwy 4, just south of town.

RESTAURANTS

Café Pamplona / ★★

1084 PACIFIC RIM HWY, TOFINO; 250/725-1237 With its rustic wood stove, mismatched furniture, and laid-back feel, this art-filled cedar bungalow tucked away in the Tofino Botanical Gardens brings to mind an earlier, funkier, pretourism Tofino. And, just as the gardeners focus on indigenous plant life, the chefs here concentrate on local cuisine, making the most of the bounty grown nearby, and in the gardens themselves. The menu changes frequently, but you might start with shucked oysters, organic greens, or fishcakes made with halibut, salmon, and sole; follow wild Pacific salmon with lemon risotto and saskatoonberry vinaigrette, or a pancetta-and-sage-crusted pork loin. Finish with chocolates, handmade with wild Clayoquot blackberries. *$$$; AE, MC, V; local checks only; lunch, dinner every day May–Sept (dinner Tues–Sat Oct–Apr, may close for all of Jan or Feb); full bar; reservations recommended; info@cafepamplona.com; www.cafepamplona.com; off Hwy 4, 1 mile (2 km) south of Tofino.* &

The Pointe Restaurant / ★★★

OSPREY LN AT CHESTERMAN BEACH (WICKANINNISH INN), TOFINO; 250/725-3100 OR 800/333-4604 In this truly outstanding environment, natural cedar posts and beams soar to a 20-foot ceiling, centered around a circular wood-burning stove with a hammered-copper hood and chimney. The restaurant is perched over a rocky headland; waves crash just outside the 240-degree panoramic windows, adding drama to your meal. The distinctively west coast–Canadian menu focuses on fresh, local seafood (including oysters) and produce, much of it organic. The wine list features many deserving BC vintages. An à la carte menu features Long Beach Dungeness crab, grilled wild salmon, and good vegetarian selections, but many diners opt for one of the multicourse tasting menus. All is artfully presented. *$$$$; AE, DC, MC, V; no checks; breakfast, lunch, dinner every day; full bar; reservations required for dinner, no reservations for breakfast and lunch; pointe@wickinn.com; www.wickinn.com; off Hwy 4, 3 miles (5 km) south of Tofino.* &

RainCoast Café / ★★

120 4TH ST, TOFINO; 250/725-2215 Husband-and-wife team Lisa Henderson and Larry Nicolay operate one of the best restaurants in Tofino. The decor of their intimate room (with an outdoor patio) is sleek and modern—as is the menu, which focuses on seafood, often with an Asian twist. Starters range from Thai hot and sour seafood soup, chicken satay, and samosa dragon rolls, to fresh local oysters, clams, and mussels. Popular mains include halibut in Thai red curry sauce, and trout stuffed with Dungeness crab and goat cheese. Vegetarians are well catered to: look for red lentil curry or crisp fried tofu with maple whipped yams. For dessert, try chocolate peanut butter pie. *$$$; AE, MC, V; local checks only; dinner every* *day; beer and wine; reservations recommended; www.raincoastcafe.com; near 4th St dock.* &

The Schooner on Second / ★

331 CAMPBELL ST, TOFINO; 250/725-3444 This historic central Tofino restaurant—part red clapboard building, part old schooner—has been satisfying hungry locals for almost half a century, in various incarnations. These days, the menu features fresh local seafood, island-grown produce, and plenty of hearty meat dishes. Try the Catface Bouillabaisse, a medley of finfish and shellfish in tomato-scented saffron broth. Breakfasts of huevos rancheros and eggs Benny with homemade hollandaise are popular; you can even order a whole Dungeness crab, fresh off the boat. *$$$; AE, MC, V; no checks; breakfast, lunch, dinner every day; full bar; reservations recommended; vicsdine@island.net; www.schoonerrestaurant.com; downtown, at corner of 2nd St.*

LODGINGS

Cable Cove Inn / ★

201 MAIN ST, TOFINO; 250/725-4236 OR 800/663-6449 Tucked at the edge of Tofino's town center, Cable Cove Inn's seven adult-only rooms all look out to the open sea. Rooms here exude a distinguished air, with mahogany-toned furniture and green marble whirlpool tubs or private outdoor hot tubs. All have fireplaces and private, ocean-facing decks; one corner unit has a wraparound balcony. Steps lead to the sheltered cove below the inn. A cozy wood-burning stove in the upstairs lounge is surrounded by cushy leather couches; continental breakfast is served, and a full kitchen is available for guests. Northwest Coast Native prints grace the walls. *$$$; AE, MC, V; no checks; 2-night min in summer and on long weekends; cablecin@island.net; www.cablecoveinn.com; west end of Main St.*

Clayoquot Wilderness Resorts / ★★★

QUAIT BAY; 250/726-8235 OR 888/333-5405 This resort offers among the most luxurious—and expensive—wilderness adventures on the West Coast. Choose from a room at the main lodge, which floats on a barge on the edge of Clayoquot Sound, or camp out at the inn's Wilderness Outpost on the banks of the Bedwell River. The lodge, 30 minutes by water taxi from Tofino, is moored next to a large tract of private wilderness with plenty of room to ride, hike, kayak, fish, or take a whale-watching tour. Come evening, guests dine on fine Pacific Northwest cuisine at a long table by the fire or at intimate tables for two. A full-service spa and exercise room add to the pampering. Accommodations at the Wilderness Outpost put a whole new spin on camping: guests sleep in roomy safari-style tents outfitted with Oriental rugs, propane heaters, handmade furniture, and private decks, and dine on fresh seafood and fine wine on china and crystal. By day, explore the wilderness by horse, mountain bike, canoe, or kayak; then relax in the sauna or in one of the wood-fired hot tubs and enjoy the deep silence. Rates at both locations include all meals, alcohol, activities, and airfare from Vancouver. *$$$$; AE, MC, V; no checks;*

3-night min; lodge closed Nov–Feb, outpost closed Oct–Apr; info@wildretreat.com;
www.wildretreat.com; accessible only by boat or floatplane.

InnChanter / ★★★

HOTSPRINGS COVE; 250/670-1149 Locals recommend this unique, luxuriously refitted 1920s boat moored in Hotsprings Cove. The elegant floating B&B done in velvet and chandeliers features five staterooms, a salon with a wood-burning fireplace, and a 700-square-foot sun deck. Host Shaun Shelongosky is a brilliant and quirky conversationalist, and an excellent chef who attends to all guest meals (included). He specializes in sumptuous vegetarian fare, but uses a lot of fresh seafood—look for a salmon barbecue on deck or halibut in Thai green coconut curry—and for meat eaters he prepares such dishes as lamb roast or whiskey-stuffed chicken marinated in honey and garlic. Best, when the hot springs day tours leave, you can row ashore and have them to yourself. *$$$; no credit cards; checks OK; www.innchanter.com; reach the InnChanter by floatplane, whale-watching tour, or water taxi from Tofino, call the inn for details.*

Long Beach Lodge Resort / ★★★

1441 PACIFIC RIM HWY, TOFINO; 250/725-2442 OR 877/844-7873 The newest of Tofino's string of oceanfront eco-lodges faces the crashing surf of sandy Cox Bay—the town's most popular surfing beach. A welcoming great room, home to a bar, inviting sofas, and a massive granite fireplace, takes in the view through big picture windows. Choose from beach-front rooms with gas fireplaces and surf-view balconies, lower priced forest-view rooms, or two-bedroom cottages with kitchens. All are decorated in a relaxed but luxurious West Coast style, with such natural touches as handcrafted Douglas fir furniture, slate shower tiles, wool carpets, cotton duvet covers, and microfleece robes. Lodge rooms have jetted or extra-large soaker tubs and separate showers; cottages have private hot tubs. Some pets are allowed. The restaurant, with its dramatic ocean view, is open for lunch and dinner daily and serves highly rated seafood and local organic fare. *$$$–$$$$; AE, MC, V; no checks; 2-night min in cottages, 2-night min in lodge during Jul and Aug and on weekends year-round, 3-night min during Christmas; lbl@island.net; www.longbeachlodgeresort.com; south of Tofino off Hwy 4.*

Middle Beach Lodge / ★★★

400 MACKENZIE BEACH RD, TOFINO; 250/725-2900 OR 866/725-2900 Decor is tasteful and homey at this oceanfront complex: wicker chairs, crisp natural-toned bedding and curtains, cheery colors. Each of the two main lodges has a large lobby graced with weathered antiques and a massive stone fireplace. The Lodge at the Beach is kept romantic and quiet with an adults-only policy; the rates are refreshingly low. The newer, pricier Lodge at the Headlands welcomes kids over 12 and includes some suites with full kitchens. Palatial, two-level oceanfront cabins have waterside balconies, kitchenettes, and plank flooring recovered from historic Victoria warehouses; some have private hot tubs. The lodges serve a continental breakfast of home-baked goods and jams, and high season brings fresh-fish barbecues and nightly dinners in the restaurant. *$$–$$$$; AE, MC, V; no checks;*

2-night min; restaurant open Fri and Sat, Nov–Feb; lodge@middlebeach.com; www.middlebeach.com; south of Tofino off Hwy 4.

Wickaninnish Inn / ★★★★

OSPREY LN AT CHESTERMAN BEACH, TOFINO; 250/725-3100 OR 800/333-4604 Set dramatically on the edge of the crashing surf, the Wickaninnish is known for pioneering the concept of winter storm-watching and has been touted from the time it opened in 1996. Even since adding 30 new rooms in 2003, it is still one of few places on Vancouver Island booked year-round. Service is impeccable, and the artful environment includes architectural details by master carver Henry Nolla, handmade driftwood chairs, and furniture custom-crafted from recycled old-growth fir. Rooms and suites, in both the original building and the new one, called Wickaninnish on the Beach, feature ocean views, fireplaces, private balconies, and double soaker tubs set before view windows. The soothing, full-service Ancient Cedars Spa offers aromatherapy, hydrotherapy, massages, facials, and other pamperings. The crowning glory is The Pointe Restaurant (see review). A few rooms allow pets, but these must be booked well in advance. *$$$$; AE, DC, MC, V; no checks; info@wickinn.com; www.wickinn.com; off Hwy 4, 3 miles (5 km) south of Tofino.* &

The Comox Valley

The Comox Valley, on the island's middle east coast, has skiing in winter, water sports in summer, and scenic access to Powell River on Highway 101 on the mainland Sunshine Coast via **BC FERRIES** (250/386-3431 or 888/223-3779 in BC; *www.bcferries.com*). Skiers and, in summer, hikers and mountain bikers flock to **MOUNT WASHINGTON** (250/338-1386), where five chairlifts whisk alpine skiers and boarders to the top, and cross-country skiers enjoy 33 miles (55 km) of track. The **CROWN ISLE RESORT & GOLF COMMUNITY** (399 Clubhouse Dr, 250/703-5050 or 888/338-8439) boasts the longest course on the island, an elaborate clubhouse, and chic condos.

Fanny Bay

Blink and you'll miss this tiny hamlet. For a true roadhouse experience, stop at the **FANNY BAY INN** (7480 Island Hwy; 250/335/2323)—or the FBI, as it is more familiarly known. The mostly standard pub fare menu features Fanny Bay oysters, panfried or in burgers. A few kilometers north, the tiny **HARBOUR VIEW BISTRO** (5575 Hwy 19A, Union Bay; 250/335-3277) has a loyal following; diners book months ahead for weekend dinners of duck à l'orange or poached wild salmon.

LODGINGS

Ships Point Inn / ★★

7584 SHIPS POINT RD, FANNY BAY; 250/335-1004 OR 877/742-1004 At the end of a quiet country road, this white turn-of-the-20th-century shiplap waterfront home houses six lovely rooms, individually decorated in an almost fantasy style. The Bombay room is all Raj-era elegance, in rich reds and greens, with an elephant-patterned bed canopy. The Forestview room, with its antique headboard and vintage luggage, looks set for an Edwardian traveler, while the Bayview room has a West Indies colonial style with a romantic canopy bed. Romantics also like the lower-floor Rafael room, with its cheery Mediterranean colors and enormous sunken bath. All rooms have private baths, and all are phone- and TV-free. Three large rooms in a neighboring building were planned for fall 2004. Four-course breakfasts, with Fanny Bay oysters and fresh-baked bread and muffins, are served in the view-blessed kitchen or on the wide deck with its views of water, mountains, and the occasional seal at play. Evening meals are available by prior arrangement. A sitting room and an entertainment room, each with a fireplace and an ocean view, offer plenty of hang-out space in bad weather. Outside, 2 acres of lawns and flower gardens stretch down to a seaside walkway and a pebbly shore. Enjoy the view from the hot tub in the garden gazebo. *$$–$$$; AE, MC, V; local checks only; shipspointinn@aol.com; www.shipspointinn.com; take exit 87 off Hwy 19 and follow Ships Point Rd to the end.*

Courtenay and Comox

These adjacent towns are the hub of the valley. Courtenay's in-town browsing ranges from antique, kitchenware, and retro clothing shops to the thought-of-everything **TRAVELLER'S TALE SHOP** (526 Cliffe Ave, Courtenay; 250/703-0168). Break for a delectable treat at **HOT CHOCOLATES** (238 5th St, Courtenay; 250/338-8211). Locals recommend the eclectic eats at **ATLAS CAFE** (250 6th St, Courtenay; 250/338-9838). Dinosaur fossils found in the Comox Valley are on display at the **COURTENAY AND DISTRICT MUSEUM AND PALAEONTOLOGY CENTRE** (207 4th St, Courtenay; 250/334-0686). The ferry to Denman Island leaves from Buckley Bay, about 10 minutes south of Courtenay.

RESTAURANTS

The Old House Restaurant / ★★

1760 RIVERSIDE LN, COURTENAY; 250/338-5406 This carefully restored, rambling pioneer home rests amid colorful flower gardens and verdant trees. Across the river, a working sawmill sets the tone of old Courtenay. Inside, four roaring stone fireplaces beckon on cool days, while exposed beams and garden views create a charming ambiance. Start dinner at this white-tablecloth establishment with mushrooms stuffed with shrimp, crab, spinach, and cream cheese. Next, opt for a fresh BC salmon fillet baked on a cedar plank and sparked with homemade fruit salsa, or panfried maple rye pork medallions. The chocolate kilo cake is rich white chocolate sponge and mocha mousse; also good is butter pecan bread pudding with warm caramel rum sauce. *$$–$$$; AE, DC, MC, V; no checks; lunch, dinner every day; full bar; reservations recommended; www.comoxvalleyrestaurants.ca/oldhouse .htm; just before 17th St Bridge to Comox.* &

LODGINGS

Greystone Manor / ★

4014 HAAS RD, COURTENAY; 250/338-1422 Extensive English flower gardens are the jewel of this establishment; enjoy the vibrant colors out your window and contemplate views of the Strait of Georgia and the Coast Mountains beyond. Three guest rooms with private baths (one is across the hall) give you all the basics—though ours was fairly small. Decor of this 1918 home is highlighted with antiques; the parlor has a cozy woodstove and original hardwood floors. *$$; MC, V; no checks; info@greystonemanorbb.com; www.greystonemanorbb.com; 2 miles (3 km) south of Courtenay off Hwy 19A.*

Kingfisher Oceanside Resort and Spa / ★★★

4330 S ISLAND HWY, ROYSTON; 250/338-1323 OR 800/663-7929 Kingfisher's spa features ocean-themed treatments such as seaweed body wraps and sea body polishing. Don't miss the Pacific Mist Hydropath, where you spend a decadent hour strolling through a grotto equipped with mineral pools and waterfall-like showers. Therapists offer massages in one of 20 treatment rooms or on the beach. Outdoor adventure trips and fitness and yoga classes are also available, as well as a sauna, a steam room, a hot tub, tennis courts, and an outdoor swimming pool with a mini-waterfall for massaging your neck and shoulders. The beachfront suites, with sea-themed decor, ocean views, beach-rock fireplaces, and kitchens, are the nicest accommodations. Ocean-view rooms, set back from the sea, are blander but a good value. The restaurant is worth a trip for its seafood, vegetarian choices, and spa cuisine. *$$$–$$$$; AE, DC, DIS, JCB, MC, V; no checks; 2-night min on weekends in suites; info@kingfisherspa.com; www.kingfisherspa.com; in Royston, 5 miles (8 km) south of Courtenay off Hwy 19A.*

Campbell River and
North Vancouver Island

The north end of Vancouver Island sees raw logging towns abutting unpopulated wilderness featuring plenty of outdoor pursuits, from Hemingway-worthy fishing expeditions to spectacular hiking.

If you're in Campbell River, you're probably fishing: it is known as the "salmon capital of the world." Bag your limit of Tyee, chinook, pink, or chum salmon pretty much year-round on one of many fishing charters located on the waterfront. Fly-fishing the river for pinks is gaining popularity. Seattle's **KENMORE AIR** (800/543-9595; *www.kenmoreair.com*) flies directly to local fishing lodges. From Vancouver, **AIR CANADA** (888/247-2262; *www.aircanada.ca*) and **PACIFIC COASTAL AIR** (800/663-2872; *www.pacific-coastal.com*) serve Campbell River's airport.

SURF'S UP, EH?

Ever thought to hang 10 in the Great White North? Canadian and California surfers alike get hyped on the excellent breaks and pristine beaches around Tofino. Legendary **LONG BEACH**, an 11-mile (17 km) crescent backed by Douglas fir forests, was first surfed by American draft dodgers who came to live rent-free on the then-isolated beach. In Canada, surfing is a winter sport: that's when tsunamis off Japan bring the year's best waves. As other tourists cuddle up to cozy fires to watch the storms, committed surfers hit the beach in thick hooded wet suits. With proper gear, the cold is kept at bay.

Winter waves are a little too wild for beginners, but sunny days after May 1 bring throngs of boys and girls of summer with their flowered shorts and surfboards to catch more mellow waves. A number of options exist for seasoned surfers or newbies wanting to give it a try.

SURF SISTER (250/725-4456 or 877/724-7873; *www.surfsister.com*) offers supportive women-only weekend clinics or individual lessons and surf camps for men and women. "A girl's thing is where it's at," enthuses Jenny Stewart, the school's bubbly founder. Take her word for it: she's among the best surfers, male or female, in Tofino. Taking a clinic gives newbies the pointers they need to get up on the board and stay safe in the water.

LIVE TO SURF (1180 Pacific Rim Hwy; 250/725-4464; *www.alberni.net/live_2_surf/*), run by longtime local surfer gal Liz Zed, offers lessons to men and women, and sells and rents wet suits and boards.

INNER RHYTHM SURF CAMPS (250/726-2211 or 877/393-7873; *www.inner rhythm.net*) organizes surfing safaris: let them pack the gear, and all you have to do is hop in the van and chat with the wave-loving wahine beside you.

For those not venturing as far as Tofino, good winter surfing can also be had at **JORDAN RIVER** and **SOMBRIO BEACH**, on the West Coast Highway a couple of hours from Victoria; rent gear in town (try **SPORTS RENT**, 1950 Government St, Victoria; 250/385-7368; *www.sportsrentbc.com*).

—Alisa Smith

The **MUSEUM AT CAMPBELL RIVER** (470 Island Hwy; 250/287-3103; *www.crmuseum.ca*) is one of the island's best small museums, featuring intriguing displays of First Nations art and artifacts. The museum gift shop is a good place to pick up art and jewelry.

The **CAMPBELL RIVER MARITIME HERITAGE CENTRE** (621 Island Hwy, Campbell River; 250/286-3161) opened in June 2004. The striking waterfront building is home to *BCP45*, the iconic little fishing boat that appeared on the old Canadian five-dollar bill, as well as a wealth of maritime, fishing, and cannery artifacts.

For more art, and even traditional dance performances in summer, check out the **WEI WAI KUM HOUSE OF TREASURES** (1370 Island Hwy; 250/286-1440; *www.houseoftreasures.com*). It's set in a beautiful longhouse, incongruously tucked behind a shopping mall. Locals like the fresh pastas at **FUSILLI GRILL** (220 Dogwood St; 250/830-0090).

During August's **SALMON FESTIVAL**, this mall-rich town of 30,000 is abuzz with famous and ordinary fisherfolk. The **VISITOR INFO CENTRE** (1235 Shoppers Row; 250/287-4636; *visitorinfo.incampbellriver.com*) can provide information on the festival, as well as on the region's trails and dive sites.

STRATHCONA PROVINCIAL PARK (about 25 miles/40 km west of town on Hwy 28; 800/689-9025 for camping reservations) is a place of superlatives. It contains Canada's highest waterfall as well as Vancouver Island's tallest mountain, and offers a wide range of landscapes, including a glacier, alpine meadows and lakes, and large stands of virgin cedar and Douglas fir. Mountaineers and rock climbers get their thrills here. Easily accessible by road, the park has campgrounds and boat-launching facilities at Buttle Lake. The park also has fine trout lakes and an extensive trail system for backpacking. An information kiosk is open in summer.

RESTAURANTS

Koto Japanese Restaurant / ★★

80 10TH AVE, CAMPBELL RIVER; 250/286-1422 It makes sense: a very fresh sushi bar in the middle of fishing country. Chef Takeo (Tony) Maeda has single-handedly developed the locals' taste for nigiri-sushi. Teriyaki is a big seller too—beef, chicken, or salmon—but look for more exotic food from the deep, such as freshwater eel, flying-fish roe, and octopus. *$$; AE, DC, MC, V; no checks; lunch Tues–Fri, dinner Tues–Sat; full bar; reservations recommended; behind HSBC Bank building.*

LODGINGS

Painter's Lodge / ★★

1625 MCDONALD RD, CAMPBELL RIVER; 250/286-1102 OR 800/663-7090 Fishing is the raison d'être of this lodge run by the reputable Oak Bay Marine Group of Victoria, but whale- and bear-watching tours, a pool, a hot tub, and tennis courts appeal to nonanglers, and you couldn't ask for a prettier location. Prime suites in the main lodge overlook Discovery Passage and Quadra Island. At 5am, the hotel is abustle with eager fishers, and the sounds of Boston whalers can be heard. Strive to catch the big one here, and maybe your photo will join the historic row in the plush lobby. Relax in the Fireside Lounge or Tyee Pub to hear stories of ones that got away. Fare in the Legends dining room is not especially inspired, but fresh-caught fish and seafood staples help compensate. Ask about fishing packages. A free 10-minute water taxi runs to April Point Lodge, Painter's sister resort on Quadra Island (see review in Discovery Islands section). *$$$–$$$$; AE, DC, MC, V; no checks; open Apr–late Oct; www.obmg.com; 2½ miles (4 km) north of Campbell River.*

Strathcona Park Lodge and Outdoor Education Centre / ★★

EDGE OF STRATHCONA PARK, CAMPBELL RIVER; 250/286-3122 This lakeside lodge is a mecca for those who enjoy healthful, active living. The instructors here know their stuff and gently guide even the most timid of city slickers through such outward-boundish pursuits as hiking, kayaking, rock climbing, outdoor survival skills, and orienteering. The ropes course is a hit with kids, and isn't as scary as it looks. Accommodations in the log-and-timber lodge and self-contained lakefront cabins with kitchens are modest but attractive; some of the newer suites are quite chic, and everywhere on-site are jaw-dropping views of Upper Campbell Lake and surrounding peaks. Meals are hearty, healthy, and served buffet style at long tables in the Whale Room or à la carte at the Canoe Club Café. Massage services and a waterfront sauna help soothe adventure-strained muscles. Ask about family, youth, elder, and wellness packages. *$$; MC, V; local checks only; limited facilities Dec–Feb; info@strathcona.bc.ca; www.strathcona .bc.ca; 28 miles (45 km) west of Campbell River on Hwy 28.*

Gold River

With the closure of the mill in this pretty town, many inhabitants are moving on—though retirees are moving in. From here, the utilitarian MV *Uchuck III* (on Government Dock, 7 miles/12 km past the village at the end of Hwy 28; 250/283-2325; *www.mvuchuck.com*; reservations required) embarks on one- and two-day cruises along the largely uninhabited western coast of Vancouver Island, a breathtaking stretch of rugged inlets and islands. On the way to the remote settlements of **KYUQUOT** or **ZEBALLOS**, the boat stops at **FRIENDLY COVE**, a historic site where Captain Cook first landed, which includes logging camps, fish farms, and settlers' cabins; you spend the night in a bed-and-breakfast and return the next day. **THE LODGE AT GOLD RIVER** (100 Muchalat Dr, 250/283-2900), a high-end fishing lodge, was set to open in summer 2004.

Port McNeill and Telegraph Cove

The major asset of this remote area is its proximity to all things wild and wonderful—boating, diving, whale-watching, salmon fishing, and tide pooling. The inspiring **U'MISTA CULTURAL CENTRE** (Front St; 250/974-5403; *www.umista.org*) in the nearby town of Alert Bay is only a short ferry ride from the Port McNeill waterfront (schedules are available there); learn about potlatch traditions of the local Kwakwaka'wakw people. Whale-watching (June–Oct) is superior from the town of Telegraph Cove, a village built on stilts 13 miles (21 km) south of Port McNeill. **STUBBS ISLAND WHALE WATCHING** (24 Boardwalk; 250/928-3185 or 800/665-3066) offers cruises to view orcas in Johnstone Strait. Old homes in Telegraph Cove have been gaily painted and revived as overnight lodgings. Contact **TELEGRAPH COVE RESORTS** (250/928-3131 or 800/200-4665; *www.telegraph coveresort.com*) for reservations. Kayaking and bear-watching tours are also available; check out the amazing collection of sea animal bones on display at the **BONES PROJECT** on the boardwalk.

LODGINGS

Hidden Cove Lodge / ★★

TELEGRAPH COVE; 250/956-3916 Sandra and Dan Kirby's waterfront retreat on 8½ acres is interspersed with walking trails and offers back-to-basics relaxation. Eight rooms with private baths are furnished in pine, and rates include home-cooked breakfasts such as eggs Benedict or pancakes. In summer (mid-May–mid-Oct) Sandra and the lodge staff cook dinners of Dungeness crab, baby back spareribs, salmon, halibut, or other hearty favorites. Two two-bedroom waterfront cottages with fireplaces and full kitchens allow families to cook on their own. The Kirbys can sign you up with local companies for kayaking, whale-watching, heli-fishing, or grizzly viewing; an outdoor hot tub awaits your return. A wraparound, window-lined lounge allows for quiet contemplation of herons, eagles, and whales, or a chance to mix with other guests. *$$–$$$$; MC, V; no checks; 2-night min in cottages; hidcl@island.net; www.hiddencovelodge.com; 20 minutes south of Port McNeill; take Beaver Cove/Telegraph Cove cutoff from Hwy 19.*

Port Hardy

A harborfront promenade sweetens the stay in this gritty town at the end of Highway 19. Logging, fishing, and mining have long provided most of the employment here, though these industries are fading. Travelers stop to catch the acclaimed 15-hour **BC FERRIES** (250/386-3431 or 888/223-3779; reservations required) and cruise north to Prince Rupert on the mainland or to Bella Coola and Bella Bella on the midcoast. Book summer accommodations well in advance: ferry passengers tend to fill the hotels.

The famous Edward S. Curtis silent film *In the Land of the War Canoes*—part anthropology, part fanciful potboiler—was filmed in nearby Fort Rupert (off Hwy 19, 3 miles [5 km] south of Port Hardy). **THE COPPER MAKER GALLERY** (114 Copper Way, Fort Rupert; 250/949-8491) is a good place to purchase authentic First Nations art. Some well-traveled islanders call **CAPE SCOTT PROVINCIAL PARK** (37 miles/63 km west of Port Hardy) the most beautiful place on earth. A 1½-hour drive over gravel roads west of Port Hardy, and a 45-minute walk take you to spectacular San Josef Bay; camping is permitted. A longer, more challenging hike leads to the island's northern tip; the **PORT HARDY VISITOR INFO CENTRE** (7250 Market St; 250/949-7622; www.ph-chamber.bc.ca) provides information.

SOUTHERN INTERIOR AND THE KOOTENAYS

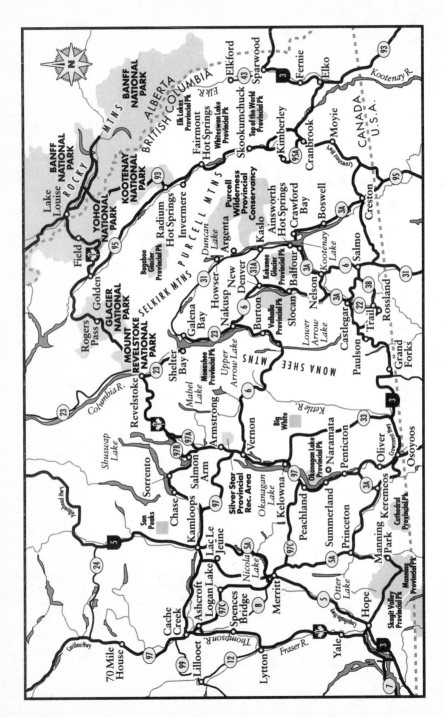

SOUTHERN INTERIOR AND THE KOOTENAYS

Welcome to the most vertically challenging landscape in British Columbia—and possibly all of Canada. Range upon range of mountains crowd up beside each other here: the Cascades, the Monashees, the Selkirks, the Purcells, the Bugaboos and the mighty Rockies. Which isn't to say there aren't open spaces among the peaks. Look no further than the Okanagan Valley in the heart of the Southern Interior. Broad, blue lakes and gently undulating benchland intensely planted with vineyards define its character. Wilder corners of the Okanagan's semidesert burn with yellow sagebrush blossoms; the flowers also dot the weather-sculpted rangelands on the adjacent Thompson Plateau.

To make sense of the West Kootenay, imagine four mountain ranges puckered together like an accordion's bellows. No wonder roads in this part of BC scatter off in more directions than windblown fireweed seeds. When the Rockies finally present themselves in the East Kootenay, they project a stateliness that makes the rest of the pack look like peaks in training. So many pinnacles vie for dominance on the skyline that some valleys in this evergreen wilderness barely receive sunlight in winter months. That's when two options start to look really good: going someplace sunny or riding deep powder from peak to glorious peak.

ACCESS AND INFORMATION

Almost every main road or highway in BC intersects the **TRANS-CANADA HIGHWAY** (Hwy 1) at some point. In this region, **HIGHWAY 1** covers 372 miles (600 km) between Hope and Field on the BC-Alberta border. Other major highways here include **HIGHWAY 5** (Yellowhead Hwy), whose 130-mile (210 km) Coquihalla Highway portion provides the most direct route between Hope and Kamloops, 45 miles (73 km) shorter than Highway 1 between those two points; **HIGHWAY 97C**, linking Highway 1 to Kelowna in the Okanagan; **HIGHWAY 97** through the Okanagan; and **HIGHWAY 3** (Crowsnest Hwy), which skirts the U.S. border for 491 miles (792 km) between Hope and the BC-Alberta border east of Fernie.

Kamloops is served by **AIR CANADA JAZZ** (888/247-2262; *www.flyjazz.ca*) and **VIA RAIL** (888/842-7245; *www.viarail.ca*). **GREYHOUND CANADA** (800/231-2222; *www.greyhound.ca*) offers daily service along the Trans-Canada Highway, through the Okanagan and the Kootenays. Kelowna is served by Air Canada Jazz, **HORIZON AIR** (800/547-9308; *www.horizonair.com*), and **WESTJET** (800/538-5696; *www.westjet.com*). Penticton is served by Air Canada Jazz. Cranbrook and Castlegar are served by Air Canada Jazz and **CENTRAL MOUNTAIN AIR** (800/663-3721).

The Thompson Plateau

As the Trans-Canada Highway (Hwy 1) and the Coquihalla Highway (Hwy 5) climb and wind their separate ways north from Hope (see Lower Mainland British Columbia chapter) before eventually crossing paths again in Kamloops, they pass through a variety of microclimates, from the semiarid canyons carved by the Fraser,

SOUTHERN INTERIOR THREE-DAY TOUR

DAY ONE: Rise early for a walk along Kelowna's lakefront promenade, stopping to enjoy breakfast al fresco at **THE GRAND OKANAGAN**. Drive over a unique floating bridge to **MISSION HILL FAMILY ESTATE** for a winery tour. Continue south along Lake Okanagan to **OSOYOOS**, stopping at one of the many roadside stalls to enjoy a picnic of your favorite variety of fruits and freshly squeezed juices. Walk off lunch along the interpretive boardwalk at the **DESERT CENTRE**, protecting Canada's only true desert. It's a three-hour drive through the wilderness of the Monashee Mountains to Rossland. Check into your room at the **RAM'S HEAD INN** before descending to town, where you'll enjoy a casual dinner at the always-popular **SUNSHINE CAFE**. Spend the rest of the evening at the inn, curled up in front of a log fire with a good book.

DAY TWO: After breakfast at the Ram's Head, drive to Nelson for a self-guided walking tour of the historic downtown precinct. Grab lunch at the **RICE BOWL RESTAURANT** (301 Baker St; 250/354-4129). After lunch, drive north on Highways 3A and 31 to **AINSWORTH HOT SPRINGS**. Trade your clothes for a bathing suit and relax in the resort's public soaking pools. Drive the short distance along Kootenay Lake

Nicola, and Thompson Rivers, to the gently rolling highlands of the Thompson Plateau.

Merritt

The waters around Merritt (population 7,200) are famous for producing fighting rainbow trout. Fly-casting is the style of choice. Close to 50 percent of BC's total **FRESHWATER SPORT FISHING** occurs in the Thompson-Nicola region: the Thompson and Nicola Rivers are historic salmon-spawning tributaries of the Fraser River, and the smaller feeder streams are also where rainbow trout, Dolly Varden char, and kokanee (freshwater salmon) spawn.

NICOLA LAKE, located about 4 miles (7 km) east of Merritt on Highway 5A, is renowned for its depth and harbors more than 26 varieties of fish, some weighing up to 20 pounds. Use the boat launch at **MONCK PARK** (off Hwy 5A, 13½ miles/22 km north of Merritt; *wlapwww.gov.bc.ca/bcparks/*). Licenses, tackle, and sound advice are available at **MCLEOD'S DEPARTMENT STORE** (2088 Quilchena Ave; 250/378-5191). The **MERRITT TOURIST/VISITOR INFO BOOTH** (2185 Voght St; 250/378-5634 or 877/330-3377; *info@merritt-chamber.bc.ca*; *www.merritt-chamber.bc.ca*), conveniently located beside Hwy 5, is a good place to take a break while stocking up on brochures. Every year in July Merritt hosts a mammoth country music–themed event, the **MOUNTAIN MUSIC FESTIVAL** (*www.mountainfest.com*).

to **KASLO**. Find a table on the patio at the **ROSEWOOD CAFE** for an early dinner, and revel in your newfound sense of well-being. Enjoy the scenic evening drive on Highway 31A between Kaslo and New Denver, and let your eyes do the work as you sightsee along Slocan and Upper Arrow Lakes. Catch the ferry across Upper Arrow Lake from Galena Bay to Shelter Bay. It's only a short drive from Shelter Bay to **MULVEHILL CREEK WILDERNESS INN** south of Revelstoke.

DAY THREE: After a leisurely breakfast, head for the inn's beach on **UPPER ARROW LAKE**. When you're ready, drive into Revelstoke and stop at **THE 112** for a weekday lunch. Point your car's nose up the Meadows in the Sky Parkway in nearby **MOUNT REVELSTOKE NATIONAL PARK**. Have plenty of film ready to record the profusion of wildflowers. Look east toward Rogers Pass and the massive **ILLECILLEWAET GLACIER**. That's where you're headed once you return to the Trans-Canada Highway (Hwy 1). Pull over at the top of the pass for a visit to the uniquely shaped information center. Primed by your crash course in a century of mountaineering tradition in **GLACIER NATIONAL PARK**, enjoy the descent past the peaks to Golden. Drive on to **EMERALD LAKE LODGE** in **YOHO NATIONAL PARK** for dinner and the night.

LODGINGS

Sundance Ranch / ★★

KIRKLAND RANCH RD, ASHCROFT; 250/453-2422 OR 800/553-3533 Set in high plateau country, the Rowe family's guest ranch offers sweeping views of the Thompson River. Sagebrush and cottonwood surround a sprawl of ranch buildings, a heated outdoor pool, and tennis courts. The real attraction here is the corral, where wranglers assemble a herd of 80 horses morning and late afternoon for daily rides, with groups split by experience. Horse temperaments run the gamut from gentle to frisky, much like the buffalo in the adjacent pasture. Immaculate guest rooms at this family-oriented ranch are divided between an adult and a kids' wing (though kids can bunk with their parents if they wish), with two separate sport lounges as well. Evening meals are often served on the sunny patio. Saturday nights there's a much-anticipated cowhand hoedown. Weekends are often booked months in advance. Visit the ranch's Web site for a detailed virtual tour. *$$$; MC, V; no checks; open Apr–Oct; sundance@wkpowerlink.com; www.sundance-ranch.com; 5 miles (8 km) south of Ashcroft.* &

Cache Creek

Nicknamed "Cash" Creek, travelers invariably pull in here for gas as they dash along the Trans-Canada Highway. Quiet, dusty Cache Creek offers few other incentives to pause. The surrounding landscape, however, is one of the most strikingly beautiful in the province—wide open views of sagebrush-covered mountainsides shaped by eons of weathering. A lonesome beauty prevails here, particularly near sundown when the earth glows. Cache Creek is the junction of Highway 97 (Cariboo Hwy; see Northern Mainland British Columbia chapter) and Highway 1. From here, Highway 1/97 leads 52 miles (84 km) east to Kamloops.

RESTAURANTS

Horstings Farm Market / ★

HWY 97, CACHE CREEK; 250/457-6546 Jars of Horstings' brand pickles, beets, and other tasty treats line the walls of Ted and Donna Horsting's rambling fruit and vegetable store. Locally produced arts and crafts jockey for space with dried fruit specialties. Best of all, nestled in the back of the store is an eight-table restaurant with a farm kitchen ambiance. Fresh daily soups, sandwiches, chili, baked goods, and ice cream comprise the modest menu. Step up and fill out an order form, then sit back and admire the pie-making team in action. Conversation flows with the same smoothness as dough under the rolling pins. Each morning Donna decides on the two soups of the day. Steaming bowls arrive with hefty dinner rolls, while sandwiches are served on thick slices of homemade bread. Take a loaf with you for munching on the road. This is *the* best place along the Trans-Canada to buy fresh fruit and vegetables. (Horstings supplies produce to many of the restaurants and guest ranches recommended in the Northern Mainland chapter.) *$; MC, V; checks OK; lunch Mon–Sun; no alcohol; no reservations; 1.2 miles (2 km) north of Cache Creek on east side of Hwy 97.* &

Kamloops

Kamloops (population 77,280), the largest city on the Trans-Canada Highway between Vancouver and Calgary, sprawls across the weathered slopes of the Thompson Plateau where the Thompson River's north and south arms converge. The town's name is taken from this important geographical intersection; it translates from the local Secwepemc language as "where the rivers meet." Summer travelers looking to take a break from the intensity of traffic on the Trans-Canada and Yellowhead Highways as they pass through Kamloops place a premium on the cottonwood tree shade in **RIVERSIDE PARK**, where a quick dip in the South Thompson is often in order as well.

Nearby **SECWEPEMC NATIVE HERITAGE PARK** (East Shuswap Road; 250/828-9801) features the largest wooden structure in Canada. Dubbed the powwow arbor, its design mimics a traditional pit house dwelling. Tall timbers thrust above the rounded arbor's square-shingled roof, which at its center opens to the sky. The **KAMLOOPA POW WOW**, held here on the third weekend in August, features more than a thousand performers, competitors, artists, and craftspeople drawn from 30 First Nations across Western Canada and the United States.

Kamloops is justly known as "the Tournament Capital," and there's always a game in town. A rough-and-tumble performance by the Western Hockey League's **KAMLOOPS BLAZERS** is assured in the sparkling **RIVERSIDE COLISEUM** (250/578-7222).

Fly-in fishing lodges are located on many of the 700 lakes in the region, where anglers cast for trophy-sized **KAMLOOPS TROUT**, a unique strain that puts on an eye-popping, acrobatic performance when hooked. The **KAMLOOPS VISITOR INFO CENTRE** (1290 W Trans-Canada Hwy; 250/374-3377 or 800/662-1994; *tourism@kamloopschamber.bc.ca*; *www.adventurekamloops.com*) offers information on all things Kamloopian.

RESTAURANTS

This Old Steak and Fish House / ★★

172 BATTLE ST, KAMLOOPS; 250/374-3227 New Mexican transplants Mickey and Betty Caldwell have been pampering guests with southern hospitality in this unique 1911 heritage home for a decade. Everything's fresh: seafood (wild salmon), local lamb (in season), ribs, and steaks, complemented by organic vegetables, authentic Southwest chili, and hot and crispy *sopaipilla*. The signature dish is an Asian sampler of seared ahi tuna, baby calamari, tiger prawns, and wonton-wrapped tiger rolls, served on a bed of shredded daikon radish. Boozy margaritas are a must-try. *$$–$$$; AE, MC, V; no checks; lunch Mon–Fri, dinner every day; full bar; stkfish@telus.net; www.steakhouse.kamloops.com.* &

Traditions Restaurant / ★★

1810 ROGERS PL, KAMLOOPS (COMFORT INN); 250/314-1174 Plain on the outside but welcoming within, Traditions draws diners who come to experience the culinary magic of French-trained chef Louis Desbiaux, once the personal cook of Prime Minister Pierre Trudeau and more recently of Umberto's in Vancouver. The chef's tour de force menu includes pepper steaks flambéed table-side, seafood crepes with fresh shrimp and crab, lobster thermidor, and chateaubriand. Caesar salads are prepared from scratch while you watch, a vanishing ritual. The cheerfully Mediterranean ambiance is augmented by tiling throughout, with tablecloths and comfy high-backed cane chairs. *$$–$$$; AE, MC, V; lunch, dinner every day, breakfast Sat–Sun, brunch Sun; full bar; comfort@kamloops.com; www.comfort.kamloops .com; Comfort Inn near Aberdeen Mall.* &

LODGINGS

Riverland Motel / ★★

1530 RIVER ST, KAMLOOPS; 250/374-1530 OR 800/663-1530 When overnighting in Kamloops, rest here on the banks of the South Thompson River. Not just because the wide river imparts a soothing quality, but also because the Riverland Motel is a traveler's dream. Centrally located, it offers quick access to major highways, and dining, shopping, and scenic attractions are within walking distance. The motel's 58 standard rooms are spotless and pleasantly furnished, all with refrigerators. Riverside rooms offer a view of the weathered palisades that rise on the Thompson's north shore. If you're traveling with a family, request a kitchen unit. If you're here to relax, there's an executive suite, complete with Jacuzzi. Soothing amenities include an indoor pool and whirlpool, laundry facilities, and complimentary continental breakfast. Turn the kids loose on the broad lawn spread between the hotel and the river. The adjacent Storms Restaurant features a full lunch and dinner menu of creative pastas, seafood, ribs, and racks, best enjoyed on the sheltered patio overlooking the river. *$–$$; AE, MC, V; no checks; riverlandmotel@kamloops.com; www.riverlandmotel.kamloops.com; from Hwy 1, take exit 374 toward Jasper, then the first left.* &

Sun Peaks Resort

Sun Peaks truly arrived as a year-round mountain resort when Canada Post officially awarded it a postal code of its own in 1998. Now that's recognition. No more living in the shadow of nearby Heffley Creek, where ranching has defined the local identity for the past century.

The finishing touches have been put on eight artfully configured slope-side hotels that anchor a village of chalets, condos, town homes, and bed-and-breakfast inns. The atmosphere feels European without (thankfully) being contrived. From November to April, Sun Peaks hosts skiers and snowboarders who come for the crisp, dry powder snow on Mounts Tod, Sundance, and Morrissey, and to ski with world champion (and Canada's woman athlete of the 20th century) Nancy Greene Raine. Her distinctive presence as the director of skiing defines the family atmosphere here. Nancy leads free daily mountain tours at 11am.

Another big draw is the wide variety of other winter activities, including cross-country and snow-cat skiing, sleigh riding, dogsledding, snowshoeing, and skating. In summer, a ski lift transports hikers and cyclists to high alpine meadows riotously strewn with wildflowers, while golfers stride the fairways of the resort's golf course below. Located 30 miles (50 km) northeast of Kamloops on Highway 5 and Tod Mountain Road, Sun Peaks takes about 45 minutes to reach, much of it a pleasant drive beside the North Thompson River. Once you arrive at the self-contained resort, you won't need your car. Contact **SUN PEAKS RESORT CORP.** (3150 Creekside Wy, Ste 50; 250/578-7842 or 800/807-3257; *info@sunpeaksresort.com; www.sunpeaksresort.com*).

LODGINGS

Father's Country Inn / ★★

TOD MOUNTAIN RD, HEFFLEY CREEK; 250/578-7306 OR 866/578-7372 A stay at Father's Country Inn, a bed-and-breakfast hideaway 4 miles (7 km) west of Sun Peaks Resort, confirms that no matter how far you roam, you'll still find surprises. Proprietor David Conover Jr. comes by his profession honestly. For decades, his parents ran a resort in BC's southern Gulf Islands. There, he learned the art of making serious coffee and killer pancakes (by prior arrangement, he also prepares dinners). Conover fills plates and cups to the brim for guests who anticipate long days outdoors. Conversation frequently turns to the photographic print business he runs from his rambling five-room inn. David markets not only his resort legacy but also the images his father took of Marilyn Monroe, whom Conover Sr. befriended while on a photo shoot for the U.S. Army in Los Angeles during World War II. Her young face brightens walls throughout the inn, the plain front of which masks the richness of its 6,000-square-foot interior, including a swimming pool (unheated). Guest rooms, each named for a season and decorated accordingly, are equipped with fireplaces and sumptuous tubs. Snow lovers will appreciate the inn's fully equipped ski room and complimentary shuttle service to Sun Peaks. *$; MC, V; checks OK; info@dconover.com; www.dconover.com; from Hwy 5, follow Tod Mountain Rd 14 miles (23 km) toward Sun Peaks Resort.*

Nancy Greene's Cahilty Lodge / ★★

220 VILLAGE WY, SUN PEAKS RESORT; 250/578-7454 OR 800/244-8424 After perfecting their hotel skills at Whistler in the 1980s, Nancy Greene Raine and her husband, Al, migrated east across the Coast Mountains in 1996 to Sun Peaks and opened the Cahilty Lodge, named for a local pioneer ranching family. This full-service condominium hotel's amenities range from rooms with modest cooking facilities to fully equipped suites that sleep eight. A hot tub and exercise room, plus a ski and mountain-bike room, share the downstairs with Macker's Bistro (250/578-7894), arguably the most consistent restaurant at Sun Peaks. Laid-back and mellow in tone, Macker's menu is imaginative, if limited, and skewed toward families and fun. Adjacent to the lodge is the resort's sports center with swimming pool and weight room, outdoor skating rink, and tennis courts. The lodge's centerpiece is Greene Raine's entranceway trophy cabinet. If the sociable hostess takes a shine to you, she might let you try on her Olympic gold medal. Service here regularly outperforms guest expectations. *$$–$$$; AE, DC, JCB, MC, V; no checks; info@cahiltylodge.com; www.cahiltylodge.com; east on Creekside Wy to Village Wy.* &

Sun Peaks Lodge / ★★★

3180 CREEKSIDE WY, SUN PEAKS RESORT; 250/578-7878 OR 800/333-9112 Some lodgings are so special that, once in your room, you simply want to drop into a comfy chair and revel in your good fortune. Such is the ambiance at Sun Peaks Lodge. The trappings are worthy of those in a quality European hotel, from harmonious decor to comfy terry robes. Wrap yourself in one and head for the sauna, steam room, and hot tub. Many of the 44 rooms feature windowed breakfast nooks. Step from the lodge to the high-speed quad chair lifts (tickets included in room rate) that ascend Mounts Tod and Sundance, winter and summer. Also here is the Val Senales fine-dining room, where a buffet breakfast (included in winter) and multi-course dinners are prepared. Tucked into the ground floor is the resort's best-kept secret: the Stube, a traditional wood-paneled European wine cellar offering lunch, après-ski, and late-evening fare. *$$–$$$; MC, V; no checks; info@sunpeakslodge .com; www.sunpeakslodge.com; in the heart of Sun Peaks Resort.* &

The Okanagan Valley

Beloved for a mild, nurturing climate and an unparalleled variety of landscape that ranges from desert to snowcapped peaks, the Okanagan has something for everyone: swimming, boating, golfing, hiking, skiing and snowboarding, orchards, and vineyards.

Highways 1 and 97 divide at Monte Creek, 19 miles (31 km) east of Kamloops. Highway 97 runs south to the head of Okanagan Lake at Vernon in the North Okanagan where it links with Hwy 97A. (Hwys 97A and 97B lead south from the Trans-Canada at Sicamous and Salmon Arm respectively. Near Enderby, Hwy 97B blends with 97A.) Orchards and vineyards testify to the presence of some of the best fruit- and vegetable-growing land in the world, while dozens of parks surround 79-mile (128 km) Okanagan Lake. As you pass through the lush South Okanagan and Similkameen regions, near the Canada-U.S. border, you'll find spectacular backcountry. Remains of old mining settlements line the highway.

Vernon and Silver Star Mountain Resort

For decades, Vernon (population 33,500) was one of the largest fruit-producing towns in the British Empire, thanks to the abundance of freshwater for irrigation. One of many farms surrounding the city, **DAVISON ORCHARDS** (Bella Vista Rd; 250/549-3266) welcomes visitors with a self-guided walk, wagon tours, a petting zoo, a café, and, of course, bountiful fresh produce for sale.

High above Vernon, **SILVER STAR MOUNTAIN RESORT** (Silver Star Rd, 11 miles/17.5 km east of Hwy 97; 250/542-0224 or 800/663-4431; *info@skisilverstar .com*; *www.silverstarmtn.com*) is the outdoor hub of the North Okanagan. Forested trails link the resort with adjacent Sovereign Lake Ski Area in **SILVER STAR PRO-VINCIAL PARK** (*wlapwww.gov.bc.ca/bcparks/*), where the Nordic lodge (250/558-3036; *www.sovereignlake.com*) sells tickets and has a café, wax room, and rental shop.

Once at Silver Star, whether you stay at a condo on Knoll Hill—where Victorian Gaslight replica homes are decorated in four or five exterior hues and trimmed with cookie-cutter moldings—or in a hotel on Main Street with its wraparound verandas and wooden walkways, everything is within walking (or skiing) distance. You can forget your car. The **BUGABOOS BAKERY CAFÉ** (and its new companion, **FRANCUCCINO'S**) (250/545-3208) is noted for robust coffee, serious strudel, and ambrosial cinnamon buns. Dutch-born baker Frank Berkers rolls a masterful cinnamon-and-sugar combo in croissant dough. Contact **VERNON TOURISM** (Hwy 97 S; 250/542-3256 or 800/665-0795; *info@vernontourism.com*; *www.vernon tourism.com*) for information on the North Okanagan.

RESTAURANTS

Eclectic Med Restaurant / ★★

3117 32ND ST, VERNON; 250/558-4646 Andrew Fradley's Eclectic Med Restaurant has been winning the hearts (and palates) of epicureans in the North Okanagan since 1996. Step inside and enter another realm: Mediterranean as much in style as in attitude. Fradley's culinary inclinations lean to Caribbean, Thai, East Indian, and other cross-pollinating influences. Tuscan tuna, Moroccan lamb, salmon Tropicana, and Calypso pork top the extensive menu. Combinations harken back to

SKIING THE SOUTHERN INTERIOR

An influx of European miners in the late 1890s introduced skiing to British Columbia. Olaus Jeldness, a legendary Norwegian who had prospected all over the West, organized a ski competition on **RED MOUNTAIN**, though he claimed it was "far too steep and the snow conditions too extreme" for a proper race. After all of the competitors—including Jeldness—hiked to the summit, Jeldness gave the starting signal, strapped on his own skis, and schussed off after the rest of the field. Despite their head start, Jeldness easily passed the other racers to become Canada's first national champion.

During the ensuing century, skiing grew in popularity with the locals as lifts were strung up over 30 mountains throughout the region. In the late 1980s and early 1990s, many of these community-owned ski hills were sold to out-of-town developers, armed with grand expansion plans that inevitably included bigger and faster lifts, accommodations, residential subdivisions, and golf courses. **SUN PEAKS**, north of Kamloops, was typical. "In the past," resident Olympic gold medalist Nancy Greene Raine recalls, "this was perceived as a place where a small group of rugged, wild, and woolly skiers went to enjoy some of the best powder skiing in the province." Mirroring other resorts throughout the interior, expansion at Sun Peaks has changed attitudes. "We see ourselves as the second step on a two-step holiday—mega and mellow," Greene Raine explains. "More visitors are coming to Canada on a two-week ski holiday. They take a week at Whistler-Blackcomb for the big hit, and then they want to come to a resort where they can get the feeling for small-town Canada. We're a small resort where you actually meet people."

Mirroring the evolution of Sun Peaks as a world-class, four-season resort are the three major Okanagan resorts, **SILVER STAR**, **BIG WHITE**, and **APEX MOUNTAIN**, as well as **PANORAMA**, in the Purcell Mountains. Transformations are continuing unabated: **FERNIE ALPINE RESORT**—legendary as a laid-back, powder-filled hideaway—doubled its size in 1999; **KICKING HORSE MOUNTAIN RESORT** replaced Golden's small local hill in 2000; while plans for **POWDER SPRINGS**—known for decades as Mount Mackenzie Ski Hill to the locals—include linking an expanded resort to the nearby town of Revelstoke by gondola.

Some things will never change, though. Whether you choose to vacation in a luxurious Sun Peaks slope-side condo or make the trek up a gravel road to lost-in-time **WHITEWATER** from Nelson, you are guaranteed a bigger bang for your buck than at better-known Whistler or Lake Louise and, more importantly, some of the world's best lift-served powder skiing.

—*Andrew Hempstead*

North African–born Fradley's dozen years in Portugal before arriving in Canada. Try the hand-mixed sangria, fresh-squeezed margaritas, or traditional martinis. The wine list features a deep selection of Okanagan estate reserve wines. *$$; AE, MC, V; no checks; lunch Mon–Fri, dinner every day; full bar; reservations recommended; www.dininginbc. info/vernon/eclecticmed/eclectic.htm; at 32nd Ave in central Vernon.* &

LODGINGS

Pinnacles Suite Hotel / ★

SILVER STAR MOUNTAIN RESORT; 250/542-4548 OR 800/551-7466 The Pinnacles Suite Hotel, poised on the open slopes above Silver Star's mountain village, has the best seat in town. Guests ski, snowboard, mountain bike, or walk from their doors onto the slopes. Come and go as you please: each suite has a private entrance, spacious living area, full bath, and kitchen, plus an outside ski locker. Relax in a rooftop hot tub after a day on the slopes. Sharing the facilities is the adjacent Kickwillie Inn, Silver Star's original day lodge renovated to hold seven self-contained suites. Suites 1 and 2 offer mountain views and, along with Suite 3, boast fireplaces. *$$; AE, MC, V; checks OK; reserve@pinnacles.com; www.pinnacles.com; 14 miles (22 km) northeast of Vernon.*

Kelowna

Sprawled on the sides of Okanagan Lake's hourglass waist, Kelowna ("grizzly bear" in the native Okanagan dialect) is the largest (population 96,290) and liveliest city in the valley. The new **CENTRE FOR THE ARTS AND KELOWNA ART GALLERY** (1315 Water St; 250/762-2226; *www.galleries.bc.ca/kelowna*) and 15,000-seat **SKYREACH PLACE** (home of the Western Hockey League's Kelowna Rockets; 1223 Water St; 250/979-0888; *www.skyreachplace.com*) herald a renaissance fueled by an influx of young professionals, many of whom work for the 200 tech firms based here. Wineries also thrive, with more than 40 open for tours and tastings. In the heart of downtown, the Okanagan's oldest winery, **CALONA WINES** (1125 Richter St; 250/762-3332 or 888/246-4472; *www.calonavineyards.ca*), is a good starting point for a wine-country tour. **MISSION HILL FAMILY ESTATE** (1730 Mission Hill Rd, Westbank; 250/768-7611 or 888/999-1713; *www.missionhillwinery.com*), perched atop a ridge on the west side of Okanagan Lake, offers one of the best views and sipping experiences in the Okanagan.

For many travelers, Kelowna is a jumping-off point for outdoor recreation, whether cycling the **MISSION CREEK GREENWAY**, kiteboarding at a lakeside beach, or exploring the **MONASHEE MOUNTAINS**. **MONASHEE ADVENTURE TOURS** (470 Cawston Ave; 250/762-9253 or 888/762-9253; *www.monasheeadventure tours.com*) rents bikes and offers guided cycle tours of nearby orchards and city greenways.

Kelowna also boasts 16 of the 39 **GOLF COURSES** (*www.golfkelowna.com*) between Vernon and Osoyoos. Most courses open in March, and some years golfers play into November. The town even has its own version of the Loch Ness monster: Ogopogo. No one has yet claimed the $2 million reward offered for providing proof of its existence, but enough sightings over the past 100 years have kept cryptologists searching and locals selling T-shirts. Contact the **KELOWNA VISITOR INFO CENTRE** (544 Harvey Ave; 250/861-1515 or 800/663-4345; *info@tourismkelowna .org*; *www.kelownachamber.org*).

RESTAURANTS

Doc Willoughby's Downtown Grill / ★

353 BERNARD AVE, KELOWNA; 250/868-8288 Darren Nicoll and Dave Willoughby (the restaurant is named for his grandfather) stripped this 1908 downtown landmark to the walls, then rebuilt with wood salvaged from a heritage site in Vancouver's Gastown neighborhood. Hardwood floors, solid maple tables, cozy booths, and a prominent floor-to-ceiling bar (featuring custom-brewed draft beers from Kelowna's Tree Brewery) provide the atmosphere; upscale pub fare and regular live music define the flavor (so too does an unfortunate reputation for spotty service). Traditional dishes such as shepherd's pie share the billing with Arizona egg rolls. Cedar-plank salmon vies with Ragin' Cajun chicken in roasted pecan-butter sauce as the priciest item on an affordable menu. Pizza, pasta, stir-fry, and hot-baked chocolate chip cookies with two scoops of vanilla ice cream and fudge sauce are other highlights. The wine bar features more than a dozen of BC's Vintners Quality Alliance (VQA) wines. Triple your fun with a flight of three samples. *$–$$; AE, MC, V; no checks; lunch Mon–Sat, dinner every day; full bar; no reservations; docwilloughby@shaw.ca; near Pandosy St.* &

Fresco / ★★★

1560 WATER ST, KELOWNA; 250/868-8805 Renowned chef Rod Butters and his entrepreneurial wife, Audrey Surrao, arrived in the Okanagan in 2001 via a string of notable BC restaurants, including the Fairmont Chateau Whistler and the Wickaninnish Inn. This welcome addition to Kelowna's fine-dining scene grew from the shell of a downtown heritage building. The dynamic duo has created a wonderfully understated atmosphere in which to enjoy some of the valley's finest culinary creations. The menu is typically West Coast with an emphasis on seafood, fusing organically grown produce with Asian flavors and a dash of European flair for presentation. The four-course, fixed-price Signature Collection showcases a short but varied range of entrées that change with the seasons. For dessert, try the chocolate mashed potato brioche with burnt almond caramel sauce and raspberry compote. *$$; AE, DC, MC, V; no checks; dinner Tues–Sun; full bar; reservations recommended; 2 blocks from Harvey Ave.* &

LODGINGS

The Grand Okanagan Lakefront Resort / ★★★

1310 WATER ST, KELOWNA; 250/763-4500 OR 800/465-4651 The Grand's modernist design harkens back to Kelowna's Mission past and complements the city's flowering cultural and entertainment center. Art galleries, restaurants, and Skyreach Place are all within steps of the resort. Rooms in the 10-story main tower have panoramic views (lake-view rooms cost a bit more). Private-access suites on the Grand Club's 9th (smoking) and 10th (nonsmoking) floors share an executive lounge, where complimentary continental breakfast is served. Other perks include robes, newspapers delivered to the door, and secured underground parking. Standard rooms have full-length windows that open onto Romeo-and-Juliet balconies. For longer stays, two-bedroom condo suites feature fireplaces, washer/dryers, and quick access to the lake (they're set just off the main lobby). Amenities include a spa, hot tubs, saunas, and an indoor/outdoor pool. Three restaurants, two lounges, a pub, and the Mind Grind Internet Café share the main floor with the adjacent Lake City Casino (*www.lakecitycasinos.com*). *$$$$; AE, DC, DIS, MC, V; business checks OK; reserve@grandokanagan.com; www.grandokanagan.com; 5 blocks north of Hwy 97.* &

Hotel Eldorado / ★★

500 COOK RD, KELOWNA; 250/763-7500 In 1990, after a fire destroyed the original Eldorado Arms, owner Jim Nixon meticulously replicated the 1920s-era hotel with hardwood floors, a stone fireplace, period furnishings, and a great collection of Okanagan memorabilia, much of it related to the water sports launched from the El's dock. Each of the reasonably priced 19 rooms (plus an upstairs boardroom that converts into a two-bedroom suite in summer) features elegant touches such as antique armoires; most have private balconies with water views; and a street-facing mountain-view room includes a Jacuzzi. The Eldorado's waterfront location and private marina cement its Kelowna landmark status. As a result, this place is extremely popular. In summer, reserve well in advance. The hotel's restaurant fare is consistently excellent, both in the dining room and casual bar. Breakfast in its sun-room or weekend brunch on the patio are pleasant ways to wake up, particularly when a soft breeze wafts in off the lake. Local wineries and a global village of beers are well represented on the beverage menus. *$$–$$$; AE, DC, MC, V; no checks; info@eldoradokelowna.com; www.eldoradokelowna.com; 4 miles (6.5 km) south of downtown on Pandosy St and Lakeshore Rd.* &

Manteo Resort / ★★★

3766 LAKESHORE RD, KELOWNA; 250/860-1031 OR 800/445-5255 Juxtaposed with its understated neighbor, the venerable Eldorado Inn, the brightly colored four-story Manteo Resort looks sunny on even the cloudiest days. Opened in 2000, the resort's 78 hotel rooms and 24 private villas are arranged in an intimate setting on the Okanagan Lake shore. Clean, quiet, and arty, the resort's Tuscan-style lobby, anchored by a soaring stone fireplace, sets the right vacation tone. Service here is superb. Thoughtful (and healthful) touches abound, such as baskets of fresh local fruit placed for guest's enjoyment. Don't forget your bathing suit and fitness gear: there's one indoor and two outdoor pools (with a water-slide), a full gym, a steam room, a sauna and spa, four outdoor hot tubs, tennis courts, and barbecues on private patios beside the beach. Kids and adults can take advantage of coaching in winter sports (including discount passes at Big White Resort) as well as an extensive summer program offered by Sunchaser Watersports (*www .sunchaserwatersports.com*). The resort's Wild Apple Grill features monthly specials inspired by fresh produce, such as May's asparagus festival. Mission Creek Greenway begins just south of the resort. *$$–$$$$; AE, DC, MC, V; no checks;*

refresh@manteo.com; www.manteo.com; 4 miles (6.5 km) south of downtown at Pandosy St. &

Big White

BIG WHITE SKI RESORT (Big White Rd, 14 miles/23 km east of Hwy 33; 250/765-3101 or 800/663-2772; cenres@bigwhite.com; *www.bigwhite.com*), second only to Whistler-Blackcomb in visitor numbers, is less than an hour's drive southeast of Kelowna on Highway 33 on the perimeter of the Monashee Mountains. Set at the highest elevation of any winter resort in BC (5,760 feet/1,755 m) Big White is the largest ski-in/ski-out resort village in Canada. The **HAPPY VALLEY ADVENTURE CENTRE** and theme park offers tubing, dogsledding, ice skating, and snowmobiling. Leave your wheels behind and hop on as the horse-drawn wagon that serves as local transportation trots by; park yourself on a hay bale and let the team of vapor-snorting Percherons do the rest. More than a dozen restaurants—**SNOWSHOE SAM'S** (250/765-5959), **COPPER KETTLE** (800/663-2772), and the **KETTLE VALLEY STEAKHOUSE** (250/491-0130) are best bets—dot the village, as do bars, boutiques, and rental shops. Check out the wood-fired bakery in the **VILLAGE CENTRE LODGE**. Its cinnamon buns are of the "big white bread" variety, with enough icing to rival the snow mounded on the slopes outside the bakery's doors.

LODGINGS

White Crystal Inn / ★★

BIG WHITE RD, KELOWNA; 800/663-2772 One of the best small resort hotels in Canada, this classic four-story chalet has grown with the mountain and now offers 49 rooms spread between two wings. So successful was the original design that it was copied for the Chateau Big White nearby. But they couldn't replicate the White Crystal's intimacy or its impeccable location adjacent to the resort's gondola and Bullet Express quad chair lift. All rooms are outfitted in cedar and slate; each comes with a fireplace, two queen-sized beds, and a small kitchen. For larger groups, some rooms feature lofts with three single beds. Downstairs you'll find a sauna, ski and snowboard lockers, plus heated parking. On the lodge's main floor are the stylish Copper Kettle Restaurant and a more casual bistro. *$$; AE, MC, V; checks OK; cenres@bigwhite.com; www.bigwhite.com; on right as you enter resort, next to the Village Centre.*

Penticton and Apex Mountain Resort

Penticton, the "Peach City" (population 30,985), might just as easily be called Festival City. There's always some serious fun going on in this town spread between Okanagan and Skaha Lakes, including the rockin'-good-time **AUGUST PEACH FESTIVAL** (250/493-4055 or 800/663-5052), now in its sixth decade; **FEST-OF-ALE** in April; weeklong **WINE FESTIVALS** in May and October (250/861-6654; *www.owfs.com*); the **MAY MEADOWLARK FESTIVAL** (250/492-5275 or 866/699-9453;

www.meadowlarkfestival.bc.ca), which celebrates the rich environmental diversity of the South Okanagan–Similkameen region; a campy **BEACH BLANKET FILM FESTIVAL** in July; and a **JAZZ FESTIVAL** in September. In addition, enough Ironmen (and Ironwomen) turn out annually for the August swim-bike-run **TRIATHLON** to throw a compass seriously out of whack. Contact the **PENTICTON VISITOR INFO CENTRE** (888 Westminster Ave W; 250/493-4055 or 800/663-5052; *visitors@penticton.org*; *www.penticton.org*) for details. Those who want to plot a wine tour itinerary (or who simply aspire to informed conversation on the 300-plus varieties of wine produced in the region) should visit the **BC WINE INFORMATION CENTRE** (250/490-2006; *www.bcwineinfo.ca*) that shares space with the visitor center.

Some of the best rock climbing in BC occurs at the Skaha Bluffs on the town's southeastern outskirts. **SKAHA ROCK ADVENTURES** (113-437 Martin St, Penticton; 250/493-1765; *www.skaharockcimbing.com*) guides climbers of all ages and abilities on many of the bluff's 120 cliffs.

APEX MOUNTAIN RESORT is 21 miles (33 km) west of town (on Green Mountain Rd; 250/292-8222 or 877/777-2739; *info@apexresort.com*; *www.apexresort.com*). Lift lines are virtually nonexistent and the powder snow is dry and sparkling. On-hill accommodations are limited to two particularly cozy lodges, **THE SADDLEBACK LODGE BED & BREAKFAST** (115 Clearview Crescent; 250/292-8118 or 800/863-1466; *info@saddlebacklodge.com*; *www.saddlebacklodge.com*) and **THE SHEEPROCK LODGE** (101 Clearview Crescent; 250/292-8558 or 877/677-1555; *info@sheeprocklodge.com*; *www.sheeprocklodge.com*). Most visitors stay in Penticton, a half-hour drive away. A shuttle bus makes the rounds of local hotels and provides handy access to the slopes. Cross-country skiing and snowshoe trails lie 4 miles (7 km) from Apex at the **NICKEL PLATE NORDIC CENTRE** (250/292-8110; *www.nickelplatenordic.org*) at the base of Beaconsfield Mountain with sweeping views across the Cascade Range into northern Washington State. Cinnamon bun baker Tjische Van Der Meer's "ooey-gooey" buns derive from an age-old Dutch recipe: a mixture of cinnamon sugar, Bavarian Cream, and most importantly, lots of raisins. You'll find them at **APEX'S HOG ON THE HILL CAFÉ**. Washed down with a potent mug of "mud for the blood," this is a great way to prepare for a day outdoors.

RESTAURANTS

Granny Bogner's Restaurant / ★★★

302 ECKHARDT AVE, PENTICTON; 250/493-2711 One of the Okanagan's oldest fine-dining restaurants is also one of the most consistent: great food, great location, and desserts that alone make the trip worthwhile. Diners relax in front of the rambling 1912 Arts and Crafts–style fireplace with an aperitif or after-dinner glass of prized Okanagan ice wine. The menu covers a broad spectrum, but what truly distinguishes Granny Bogner's is presentation. A restaurant maxim states that the eyes eat first. Nowhere more so than at Granny's, where chef Peter Hebel holds sway. Entrées arrive garnished with an eye for color and shape; vegetables are artfully arranged. Hebel loves to play with seafood. Try the baked oysters casino. His bouillabaisse is a bargain and a meal in itself. Hebel's Swiss training shines through in the beef rouladen with red cabbage and spaetzle; where he really struts his stuff is with the chateaubriand bouquetière in béarnaise sauce. Dessert specials, often using fresh local fruit, are the plum choices of the evening. The wine list admirably represents the best local estate wineries. *$$; AE, MC, V; no checks; dinner Tues–Sat; full bar; reservations recommended; 2 blocks south of Main St.* &

LODGINGS

God's Mountain Crest Chalet / ★★

4898 LAKESIDE RD, PENTICTON; 250/490-4800 Nothing prepares you for God's Mountain Crest Chalet, where interior designer Ulric Lejeune and his wife, Ghitta, have created the Club Med of B&Bs. The whitewashed Mediterranean-style mansion overlooks broad Skaha Lake and the rolling hills beyond. Inside is an eclectic blend of curios, antiques, and religious iconography. Scarves drape the length of the 60-foot-long grand salon. Quiet pervades, even at breakfast, when guests gather for sumptuous epicurean buffets. Sit in the shrouded intimacy of an opium bed or at the glass-topped table where conversation swirls around Lejeune's Teutonic presence. (On request, breakfasts are served to guest rooms on silver trays.) Nine guest rooms and suites are spread over three rambling floors with a seemingly endless labyrinth of nooks and crannies. Suite 5 features a raised tub with lake views. All suites open onto verandas or private balconies and are fitted with reflective glass for privacy and temperature control. A large swimming pool and hot tub (perfect for late-night stargazing) are surrounded by gardens and vineyards. *$$; MC, V; checks OK; godsmountain@vacationmail.com; www.godsmountain.com; 3 miles (5 km) south of Penticton.*

Naramata

North of Penticton off Hwy 97, the picturesque village of Naramata (population 1,000; 250/496-5409; *www.discovernaramata.com*) is surrounded by wineries and orchards. Rugged Naramata Road climbs through town and leads north through sage-covered slopes and bleached, vineyard-covered headlands that jut out into the broad lake. You can easily spend a day and only visit half of the 10 local wineries. Two that shouldn't be missed are **LANG VINEYARDS** (2493 Gammon Rd; 250/496-5987; *www.langvineyards.com*) and **RED ROOSTER WINERY** (910 Debeck Rd; 250/496-4041; *www.redroosterwinery.com*). Naramata lies 10 miles (16 km) from downtown Penticton; turn east from Main Street (Hwy 97) onto Jermyn Avenue and follow the signs.

LODGINGS

Sandy Beach Lodge & Resort / ★★★

4275 MILL RD, NARAMATA; 250/496-5765 Sandy Beach's log cabins are so popular that in July and August they are often completely booked two years in advance (priority is given to returning guests). That said, six B&B rooms in the restored 1940s main lodge—the real deal at this Okanagan Lake retreat—are still up for grabs. Each has its own private, covered veranda overlooking the lake. Lighted tennis courts, a swimming pool, and a hot tub bookend the lodge, which also houses a restaurant and a bright sitting room dominated by a fieldstone hearth. Thirteen two-bedroom cabins (with room for up to six each) dot the property, some on a swath of private beach. Each features a kitchen, a comfortable living area, and a deck with barbecue. Green lawns between them are perfect for croquet. Everything is immaculate and looks as if it just opened yesterday. May and September are pleasant months to visit, when competition for the resort's rowboats, canoes, and cabins is less fierce. $$–$$$$; MC, V; no checks; sandybeachresort@shaw.ca; www.sandybeachresort.com; end of Mill Rd off Robson. &

Oliver and Osoyoos

The South Okanagan is a veritable food bowl. Travelers on the 12-mile (20 km) stretch of Highway 97 between Oliver (population 4,225) and Osoyoos (population 4,295) pass the most bountiful agricultural land in the entire valley. Since the 1990s, this has become the preferred grape-growing region for classic European varietals such as pinot noir and merlot, all of which thrive in the warm climate. The **DESERT CENTRE** (west on 146th Ave off Highway 97, Osoyoos; 250/495-2420 or 877/899-0897; www.desert.org) protects a "pocket desert," where less than 12 inches of precipitation fall annually. It is desert in the truest sense, with cacti, prickly pear, sagebrush, and rattlesnakes surviving in the dry, sandy environment. Back roads on the east side of the valley lead past several award-winning wineries, including **BURROWING OWL VINEYARDS** (100 Burrowing Owl Pl, Oliver; 250/498-0620 or 877/498-0620; www.bovwine.com). From there, drivers and cyclists enjoy a unique perspective on the eroded west side of the valley. This is also the site of fledgling **SOUTH OKANAGAN NATIONAL PARK** (www.parkscanada.ca) as well as the new Okanagan Indian Band's **NK'MIP DESERT AND HERITAGE CENTRE** (1000 Ranch Creek Rd, Osoyoos; 250/495-7901 or 888/495-8555; nkmipdesert@oib.ca; www.nkmipdesert.com), a combined Native interpretive center and winery. Contact the **OLIVER VISITOR INFO CENTRE** (36205 93rd Ave; 250/498-6321; info@oliverchamber.bc.ca; www.oliverchamber.bc.ca) and the **OSOYOOS VISITOR INFO CENTRE** (Hwys 3 and 97; 250/495-3366 or 888/676-9667; obcdc@img.net; www.destinationosoyoos.com) for details.

RESTAURANTS

Campo Marina Italian Restaurant / ★

5907 MAIN ST, OSOYOOS; 250/495-7650 Friendly and courteous service is the hallmark of the Campo Marina, where variety, great food, large servings, and moderate prices add up to good value at this self-defined "funky" eatery. Don't let the name fool you. Chef-owner Mike Oran strives for a blend of continental and Mediterranean flavors. Homemade bread and salads are favorites of customers from both sides of the Canadian-U.S. border, just a stone's throw away. Campo Marina hums with activity much of the day. Even when the place is packed (which is the norm) Oran tries to personally connect with each guest. His country-style approach to cooking extends to steak with mushrooms in peppercorn sauce, veal d'Estana, chicken Albanaise with green peppers and onions in a Creole base, homemade lasagne, and salmon. Antiques and collectibles festoon the walls and tables, with an Okanagan vineyard ambiance. *$$; MC, V; checks OK; dinner Tues–Sun; full bar; no reservations; campomarina@direct.ca; across from Dairy Queen.*

Jacques' Wine Country Inn / ★★

34646 HWY 97, OLIVER; 250/498-4418 For three decades, chef Jacques Guerin and his wife (and manager of the inn), Suzi, have been championing the region's natural abundance. Guerin's classical touch betrays his Parisian roots. Seasonal vegetables grace dishes such as spiced beet cream soup with Okanagan wildflower honey; fresh salads include greens with prosciutto, wine-poached figs, local walnuts, and goat cheese croutons with aged balsamic and maple vinaigrette. Inspired entrées tempt the palate: medallions of pork slowly grilled with maple syrup and garnished with gingered pear compote and port demiglace. The house special is Guerin's pepper steak, pan seared in brandy and topped with a chardonnay-based cream sauce. A between-course rhubarb sorbet makes a superb palette cleanser. The wine-cellar atmosphere is completed by a wood-beamed ceiling, built by Okanagan pioneer Charles Cranston. Jacques' features an extensive list of local wines. For privacy, request seating in the intimate grotto. *$$; AE, MC, V; no checks; dinner Tues–Sun (closed Oct and Jan); full bar; reservations recommended; downtown at 346th St.*

LODGINGS

Vaseux Lake Lodge / ★★

9710 SUNDIAL RD, OLIVER; 250/498-0516 Perhaps the smallest resort in the Okanagan, Vaseux Lake Lodge was built by Denise and Peter Axhorn in 1995. The hidden beauty of the two-story lodge's four town homes is revealed once you step inside. Sunlight floods through skylights in the vaulted roof, as well as through floor-to-ceiling windows on the main floor that overlook the lodge's private beach. Locally made lacquered pine furniture and down duvets provide understated warmth. The one-bedroom, one-bath units are self-contained, including full kitchens and barbecues, and completely outfitted for up to four persons. Each suite has an entertainment center, including 100-channel digital TV, but no phone. Instead, each unit has its own library with books on the region's natural history; since 1922, Vaseux Lake has been a designated wildlife sanctuary. No powerboats are allowed on the shallow 2½-mile (4 km) lake. Bring your own beach toys and water craft so you can paddle with turtles and beavers, and watch as eagles and osprey practice fishing skills while bighorn sheep frolic on the slopes of nearby Eagle Bluff. Don't forget your binoculars, especially during spring and fall bird migrations. *$$; MC, V; checks OK; info@vaseuxlakelodge.com; www.vaseuxlakelodge.com; south end of Vaseux Lake, one block west of Hwy 97.*

The Kootenays

The Kootenays occupy the entire southeast portion of BC. Yahk, a small town on Highway 3 (Crowsnest Hwy) between Creston and Cranbrook, marks the great divide between the western and eastern halves. Named for the native Kootenay people's homeland, it's hard to finger what exactly characterizes the difference between the west and the east. Winter sunlight barely brushes the steep-sided valleys of the West Kootenay. Residents escape cabin fever by heading to lively towns, such as Nelson. In contrast, a brilliant winter sun splashes cheerily down on the broad slopes of the Columbia and Elk Valleys in the lightly populated East Kootenay. Open grasslands stretch out on all sides while the Rockies preside sedately above. The majestic **COLUMBIA RIVER** winds through both Kootenay regions. The river flows north from Columbia Lake for more than 186 miles (300 km) before hooking west and south to begin its 250-mile (400 km) journey to the U.S. border. For nearly half this length, it widens to form **UPPER AND LOWER ARROW LAKES**, vast reservoirs of water that moderate winter temperatures and help retain moisture in the local atmosphere, thus greatly influencing the types of vegetation found there.

Transportation in the Kootenays is primarily by road. Time zones shift between Pacific and Mountain from one town to the next, particularly in the region between Creston and Yahk in the East Kootenay, which remains on Mountain Standard Time year-round. When most parts of BC move clocks ahead in spring or back in fall, Creston, Kitchener, and Yahk don't change. East of Yahk, including Cranbrook, the Columbia Valley, and Fernie, clocks are on Mountain time. The other time zone transition point between Pacific and Mountain is on the Trans-Canada Hwy (Hwy 1) between Revelstoke and Golden in Glacier National Park. An informative Web site on all destinations in the Kootenays is *www.bcrockies.com*.

Rossland and Red Mountain Ski Area

Rossland (population 3,645) is snugly perched in the Monashee Mountains close to **RED MOUNTAIN SKI AREA** (3 miles/5 km northwest of Rossland on Hwy 3B; 250/362-7700, 250/362-7384, or 800/663-0105; *redmtn@ski-red.com*; *www.ski-red.com*). In the 1890s, when Rossland was at the peak of its gold mining boom, Red Mountain hosted the first Canadian Ski Racing Championships. The mountain has since produced two of the best women skiers to ever represent Canada, Olympic gold medal winners Nancy Greene Raine (see Sun Peaks Resort) and Kerrin Lee-Gartner (see Fernie Alpine Resort). Today the resort offers some of the country's best off-piste skiing and boarding. The **BLACK JACK CROSS-COUNTRY SKI CLUB** (Hwy 3B; 250/362-5811; *www.rossland.com/blackjack*) lies at the base of Red Mountain.

The scale of the heritage buildings that line many of Rossland's streets reflects the boom times and glory years of a century ago. Contact the **ROSSLAND VISITOR INFO CENTRE** (May–Sept; Columbia Ave and Hwy 3B; 250/362-7722 or 888/448-7444; *museum@rossland.com*; *www.rossland.com*) for details. **ROSSLAND'S WINTER CARNIVAL**, first held in 1897, is still going strong on the last weekend in January. The **RUBBERHEAD MOUNTAIN BIKE FESTIVAL** is held near Labor Day.

RESTAURANTS

Sunshine Cafe / ★

2116 COLUMBIA AVE, ROSSLAND; 250/362-5070 Everyone takes a shine to Rossland's favorite little café, which features a range of internationally inspired dishes. Sit in the front of the restaurant to do some people-watching or walk past the kitchen to the back room. The food doesn't try to be fancy, just good, and there's lots of it. Start with the Malaysian egg rolls (ground beef, coconut, and spices) dipped in a plum sauce, and then go on to one of the Mexican dishes, the Budgie Burger (boneless chicken breast with ham or Swiss), or a simple entrée such as curried chicken. Huevos rancheros is a breakfast fave. Mealtimes are crowded, and during ski season reservations are recommended. *$; MC, V; local checks only; breakfast, lunch, dinner every day; beer and wine; reservations recommended during ski season; mgypsy@direct.ca; just east of Queen St.*

LODGINGS

Angela's Bed & Breakfast and Guesthouse / ★★

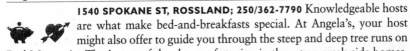

1540 SPOKANE ST, ROSSLAND; 250/362-7790 Knowledgeable hosts are what make bed-and-breakfasts special. At Angela's, your host might also offer to guide you through the steep and deep tree runs on Red Mountain. That's part of the charm of staying in these two creek-side homes. Angela Price has spent a lifetime pursuing her passion for powder skiing, the same quest that draws guests to Rossland. The comfort provided at Angela's is as attractive as the fluffy quality of Kootenay snow. Guests choose between a pair of two-bedroom suites with separate entrances. One has a fireplace in the master bedroom; a carved church window makes up one wall, with a redwood hot tub just outside the door. Another has a full kitchen. Beds are draped with comfy down duvets for those long winter nights. Across the street sits Price's newly renovated 1930s guesthouse with two more suites. Everyone feels spoiled by Price's attention to detail. Breakfasts are of the stick-to-your-ribs variety, guaranteed to fortify you for a day in the steeps: oatmeal, eggs Benedict, organic jams, and serious coffee. Time your visit to coincide with Angela's annual oyster bash in February. *$$; MC; checks OK; angela@netidea .com; www.visitangela.com; 4 blocks downhill from the Uplander Hotel.*

Ram's Head Inn / ★★★

RED MOUNTAIN RD, ROSSLAND; 250/362-9577 OR 877/267-4323 The Ram's Head Inn is *the* place to stay in the heart of the West Kootenay. What sets the inn apart is its cozy size—34 guests maximum—and little touches, such as chalet slippers at the door. The inn's location at the foot of Red Mountain Ski Area also works wonders. Conversation flows easily as guests gather for a complimentary breakfast, or, after a day exploring nearby trails, relax on an overstuffed couch beside the towering granite fireplace. Choose from 14 rooms with private baths; the larger ones have balconies; one suite has a loft and sleeps six. All are elegantly furnished with hand-hewn timber beds, maple armoires, eiderdown comforters, TVs, and telephones. The ground floor (hidden from view by snowbanks in winter) is taken up with ski lockers, a waxing room, a games room with pool table, and a sauna. A teak barrel hot tub steams outside. Dinners are offered by advance request. *$$–$$$; AE, DC, DIS, MC, V; checks OK; theinn@ramshead.bc.ca; www.ramshead.bc.ca; off Hwy 3B at Red Mountain Rd.*

Nakusp

Nakusp (population 1,700) occupies a crook in the arm of Upper Arrow Lake and is set squarely between the Monashee and Selkirk Mountains. This is hot spring country. Along Highway 23 between Nakusp and Galena Bay at the northern end of Upper Arrow Lake are two commercial and four **WILDERNESS SPRINGS**. You can't drive to the wilderness springs in winter (back roads aren't plowed), although you can reach them on snowshoes or skis. Contact the **NAKUSP VISITOR INFO CENTRE** (92 6th Ave NW; 250/265-4234 or 800/909-8819; *www.nakusphotsprings.com*) for details.

LODGINGS

Halcyon Hot Springs Resort / ★

HWY 23, NAKUSP; 250/265-3554 OR 888/689-4699 In 1999, like the proverbial phoenix, Halcyon Hot Springs Resort rose from the ashes of its predecessor, which operated here on the shores of Upper Arrow Lake between the 1890s and 1950s. One- and two-bedroom chalets sleep up to six and are equipped with en suite bathrooms, kitchenettes, TVs, phones, and sun decks. Nearby, in the sheltering forest, are four cabins that each sleep six on twin bunks and a double futon. Cabin guests share a communal bathroom. A licensed restaurant is located in the main building. *Halcyon* in Greek means "calm, serene," and that's how one feels after bathing in the two hottest pools. Mineral analysis of the water reveals a higher quantity of lithia, a natural relaxant, than any spring in this thermally active region. An outdoor swimming pool is open in summer. *$$; AE, MC, V; no checks; info@halcyon-hotsprings.com; www.halcyon-hotsprings.com; 20 miles (32 km) north of Nakusp.* &

Kaslo

Much like the beached stern-wheeler **SS MOYIE** (324 Front St; 250/353-2525; open daily, 9:30am–4:30pm mid-May–mid-Sept), this former mining hub on Kootenay Lake (almost 99 miles [160 km] long, one of BC's largest freshwater lakes) retains the flavor of its glory years. The steamer was affectionately known as "the sweetheart of the lake" in her heyday. These days, Kaslo is best known for its **JAZZ FESTIVAL** on the first weekend in August. Music lovers dig the tunes from dry land as the music flows from a stage anchored offshore. Contact **KASLO VISITOR INFO CENTRE** (May–Oct; 324 Front St; 250/353-2525; *ssmoyie@klhs.bc.ca*; *www.klhs.bc.ca*) for details.

RESTAURANTS

Rosewood Cafe / ★★

🏃 **213 5TH ST, KASLO; 250/353-7673** The Rosewood has a loyal clientele of grown-ups (and kids) from as far afield as Washington State. Reservations are a must in summer, when tourists flock to Kaslo. The fact that chef Grant Mackenzie does much of his cooking outdoors on an 8-foot barbecue helps draw a crowd. Since it opened in 1994, the capacity has expanded to 125 seats, 55 of which are on a spacious patio overlooking Kootenay Lake. You'll smell the chicken, pork, and beef ribs long before you reach the café's white picket fence. Portions are typically large; many dishes are available in both half and full size. Everything is made fresh daily and tastes like it, from mayonnaise to bread to sauces. Alberta prime rib, local venison, cedar-plank salmon with crab and shrimp, and jambalaya are specialties. Vegetarian selections, such as tortellini with curried tomato sauce, reflect chef Mackenzie's multicultural influences. The wine and cocktail menus offer a wealth of choices. *$$; MC, V; local checks only; lunch, dinner every day, brunch Sun (closed Jan); full bar; reservations recommended; rosewood@netidea.com; at east end of 5th St.* ♿

Ainsworth Hot Springs

Ainsworth Hot Springs is a sleepy spot on Highway 31, about 12 miles (19 km) south of Kaslo and 30 miles (50 km) north of Nelson. It was a boomtown during the heyday of silver, zinc, and lead mining in the Kootenays in the 1890s. Today, if it weren't for the hot springs, it's likely that few travelers would slow down through the small community perched above Kootenay Lake.

LODGINGS

Ainsworth Hot Springs Resort / ★★

🏃 🐷 **HWY 31, AINSWORTH HOT SPRINGS; 250/229-4212 OR 800/668-1171** Ainsworth Hot Springs Resort boasts a most unusual setting: a former mine shaft into which several steamy springs vent. Hot water drips from the rough-hewn granite ceiling and flows waist-deep through a narrow, horseshoe-shaped tunnel into the resort's large outdoor pool. Mist trapped in the tunnel thickens the air, further augmenting the subterranean experience. Mineral deposits have coated the walls with a smooth, ceramic-like glaze in shades of white, red, and green. The overall effect is mind bending. Hop into the glacier-fed plunge pool to restore your senses. Water inside the caves reaches 111°F (44°C) or hotter, while the plunge pool is a bracing 39°F (4°C). The Purcell Mountains float in the distance above Kootenay Lake. Upgraded in 1999, the three-story resort's accommodations range from standard hotel rooms with two twin beds to suites with kitchenettes. The Dining Room overlooks the pools. The menu features a diverse selection of entrées and desserts. Appetizers such as stuffed shiitake mushrooms and tandoori chicken tikka reflect the healthful feeling of the resort. *$$; AE, DC, MC, V; no checks;*

breakfast, lunch, dinner every day; full bar; reserve@hotnaturally.com; www.hot naturally.com; 10 miles (16 km) north of Balfour on Hwy 31. &

Crawford Bay

The tiny community of Crawford Bay (population 200) on the east side of Kootenay Lake (accessible from Balfour on Highway 3A via the world's longest free ferry ride) is home to many artisans, including Canada's only manufacturer of traditional straw brooms. Crawford Bay is popular with golfers for the picturesque and challenging **KOKANEE SPRINGS GOLF COURSE** (16082 Woolgar Rd; 250/227-9226; *info@kokaneesprings.com; www.kokaneesprings.com*).

LODGINGS

Wedgwood Manor / ★★

16002 CRAWFORD CREEK RD, CRAWFORD BAY; 250/227-9233 OR 800/862-0022 This lovely 1910 home, built on a 50-acre estate for the daughter of the renowned British china maker, is one of the finest lodgings in southeastern British Columbia. A dining room (where complimentary breakfast is served) and a parlor with a fireplace (perfect for afternoon tea) occupy the main floor, along with two suites. The four spacious upstairs rooms open onto a quiet, comfortable reading room; the lake-view Charles Darwin Room and the Commander's Room receive afternoon sun. The room off the parlor is tiny but has a garden view from the double bed. All six guest rooms have private baths. In summer, the large front porch is an idyllic spot to gaze out over the lawn and flower gardens to Kokanee Glacier across the lake. The fully equipped Wildwood Cabin, built in 2001, provides a cozy escape for up to four persons, and, unlike the inn's rooms, is available year-round. *$–$$; MC, V; checks OK; open Apr–mid-Oct; wedgwood@netidea.com; www.wedg woodcountryinn.com; east of Nelson on Hwy 3A, take Balfour ferry to Kootenay Bay.* &

Nelson

Nestled in a valley on the shore of Kootenay Lake south of Balfour, Nelson (population 9,300) thrived during the silver and gold mining boom in the late 1890s, and retains its late-Victorian character, luring filmmakers to use its downtown as a set. More than 350 heritage homes and commercial buildings are listed in this picturesque city. Pick up a map (or join a free guided tour in summer) at the **NELSON VISITOR INFO CENTRE** (225 Hall St; 250/352-3433; *www.discovernelson.com*). Built on a hillside, Nelson's steep streets are best scaled in sturdy shoes. (In winter, posties—Canadian letter carriers—occasionally resort to crampons.) The best vantage on Nelson, and the rock and ice formations that rise above Kootenay Lake, is from **GYRO PARK** (corner of Park and Morgan Sts) just east of the town center. The park has picturesque gardens and a wading pool.

A pictorial exhibit of the region's history is mounted at the **NELSON MUSEUM** (402 Anderson St; 250/352-9813). In summer, the entire town turns into an art gallery, with the work of some 100 local artists exhibited in shops, restaurants, and galleries during the **NELSON ARTWALK** (June–Aug; 250/352-2402). Art and crafts by regional artists are displayed year-round at the **CRAFT CONNECTION** (441 Baker St; 250/352-3006). Outdoor enthusiasts shop at **SNOWPACK** (333 Baker St; 250/352-6411). The **KOOTENAY BAKER** (295 Baker St; 250/352-2274) stocks the best selection of healthful foods in the region, including organic baked goods.

The Selkirk and Purcell Mountains surrounding Nelson are a magnet for hikers, backcountry skiers, and sightseers; a popular destination is **KOKANEE GLACIER PARK** (18 miles/29 km northeast of Nelson off Hwy 3A; 250/825-4421; *wlapwww .gov.bc.ca/bcparks/*). **BALDFACE SNOWCAT SKIING** (250/352-0006; *www.bald face.net*) offers cat-skiing.

WHITEWATER SKI & WINTER RESORT (12 miles/19 km south of Nelson on Hwy 6; 250/352-4944 or 800/666-9420; *info@skiwhitewater.com*; *www.skiwhitewater .com*) in the Selkirk Mountains is an old-school operation with four no-nonsense lifts. Whitewater's high base elevation of 5,400 feet (1,640 m) ensures plentiful light, dry powder. The rustic resort is also home to the **WHITEWATER NORDIC CENTRE**. The lodge's cafeteria prepares the best food at the best prices of any resort in BC—worth a visit even if you're only there to soak up a little mountain culture on the sun deck.

RESTAURANTS

All Seasons Cafe / ★★

620 HERRIDGE LN, NELSON; 250/352-0101 A storybook ambiance envelops Tracey Scanlon and Jon Langille's intimate café, situated off a narrow lane. For a quick meal, sit near the bar, sip a microbrew, and enjoy an appetizer, such as smooth-textured gravlax. Heavenly scented dishes flow from the kitchen. Halibut and prawns set your nose twitching. A steady stream of fresh sage-and-oregano bread arrives by the basket. (Ask to take a loaf home with you—they often have leftovers.) To get in the full swing of the All Seasons' professed style of "Left Coast Inland Cuisine," try the venison sausage in tomato sauce, followed by warm peach and polenta upside-down cake. Sunday brunch features creations such as an asparagus and brie flan with Italian figs and warm honey. The well-balanced wine list has won awards every year since the café opened in 1995. *$$; MC, V; local checks only; dinner every day; full bar; reservations recommended; allseas@netidea .com; www.allseasonscafe.com; between Hall and Josephine Sts.* &

Fiddler's Green / ★★

2710 LOWER SIX MILE RD, NELSON; 250/825-4466 Regardless of the season, this is Nelson's favorite spot for fine dining. Local opinion rates this estate home's three intimate rooms and one large formal area (plus summer patio) as the best atmosphere and garden dining in town. As the seasons change, chef Mark Giffin ushers in new menu offerings, such as a warm roasted winter vegetable and goat cheese tart, plus many reliable chicken, beef, pork, and lamb entrées. Fiddler's Green also caters to a growing local fondness for vegetarian and seafood dishes. Try crisp artichoke and chick-pea falafel on a bed of steamed spinach with quinoa tabbouleh and lemon parsley yogurt. The delicious house salad is a blend of locally grown mixed greens tossed with pumpkin seeds and slices of poached pear, drizzled with a Gorgonzola and cranberry vinaigrette. After savoring the salmon and prawn cakes accompanied by watercress mayo and crispy leeks, who needs dessert? As overseen by hosts Harald and Lynda Manson, service here is understated and cheerily attentive. *$$; MC, V; local checks only; dinner Wed–Sun, brunch Sun; full bar; reservations recommended; mail@fiddlersgreen.ca; www.fiddlersgreen.ca; north on Hwy 3A.*

LODGINGS

Inn the Garden B&B & Guest House / ★

408 VICTORIA ST, NELSON; 250/352-3226 OR 800/596-2337 This mostly adult B&B is where many Nelson residents book their out-of-town guests. Lynda Stevens and Jerry Van Veen decorated their Victorian home, just a block from Main Street, in a garden theme. Each room is named for a tree. Fir is the smallest and the only one with a private bath (the downside is that it adjoins the noisy bathroom shared by the other four rooms on the second floor). North-facing rooms enjoy views of Nelson's waterfront. The Tamarack Suite occupies the third floor. Complete with a small kitchen, sitting room, and bath, it's roomy enough for two couples to share. The best bargain is the adjacent three-bedroom bungalow where children are welcome. Stevens stocks the bungalow kitchen for breakfasts but leaves the rest of the meals for guests to arrange. If you run low on Stevens's home-made granola or fresh-baked muffins, hop next door to the main house to replenish the larder. *$$; AE, MC, V; checks OK; info@innthegarden.com; www.innthegarden .com; 1 block south of Baker St.*

Willow Point Lodge / ★★

2211 TAYLOR DR, NELSON; 250/825-9411 OR 800/949-2211 Mel Reasoner and Ulli Huber welcome guests at their rambling, three-story 1920 Edwardian home perched just outside Nelson amid 3½ spacious acres. Of the six guest rooms, the spacious Green Room is tops: it sports a large, private, covered balcony overlooking the Selkirk Mountains and Kootenay Lake. All rooms have en suite baths. The living room features a large stone fireplace; breakfast is served in the sumptuous dining room or on the open deck in summer. Over the past several years the already parklike setting has been further enhanced with the planting of hundreds of perennials. Enjoy the garden from the cool of a peaceful gazebo. A walking trail leads from the house to three nearby waterfalls, the farthest being a pleasant 30-minute stroll. In winter, Whitewater ski packages are available. After a day in the powder, a soak in Willow Point's large outdoor hot tub is guaranteed to soothe aches and pains. Note: The lodge fills quickly in summer; reserve well in advance. *$$; MC, V; local checks only; willowpl@uniserve.com; www .willowpointlodge.com; 2½ miles (4 km) north of Nelson.* &

Kimberley and Kimberley Alpine Resort

As with many foundering mining towns in the 1970s, Kimberley (population 6,485), on the west side of the broad Columbia Valley, looked to tourism and—like Leavenworth, Washington—chose a Bavarian theme to bolster its economy. Accordion music is played on loudspeakers at the center of the **BAVARIAN PLATZL** (the town's three-block walking street). For a quarter, a yodeling puppet pops out of the upper window of Canada's largest cuckoo clock. With so many Bavarian-themed restaurants in one place, competition among chefs is of Wagnerian proportions. If you're shopping for some goodies for your picnic lunch (or dinner at your condo), head for **KIMBERLEY SAUSAGE AND MEATS** (360 Wallinger Ave; 250/427-7766), where they also sell seafood.

At 3,650 feet (1,113 m), Kimberley is the highest city in Canada. From this height, views of the snowcapped Rockies are stunning. The **HERITAGE MUSEUM** (105 Spokane St; 250/427-7510) has an excellent display of the town's mining history and memorabilia. Gardeners shouldn't miss the teahouse, greenhouse, and immaculately kept **COMINCO GARDENS** (306 3rd Ave; 250/427-2293). A footpath leads from the Platzl to the gardens.

A frenzy of nonstop construction currently characterizes **KIMBERLEY ALPINE RESORT** (Gerry Sorenson Wy; 250/427-4881 or 800/258-7669; *info@skikimberley .com*; *www.skikimberley.com*), where a Marriott hotel anchors the resort base.

RESTAURANTS

Old Bauernhaus / ★

280 NORTON AVE, KIMBERLEY; 250/427-5133 Tony and Ingrid Schwarzenberger, who built the House Alpenglow (see review), brought a 360-year-old farmhouse to Kimberley and reassembled it. As in the Alpenglow, wood is everywhere. In a town where Bavarian flavor is as heavy as Sacher torte, this is the genuine article. You'll feel as if you've stepped through a time warp. Heidi and her grandfather might just as easily be sitting at one of the hand-carved tables. The menu reflects the Schwarzenbergers' Swiss-German roots: goulash soup, Wiener schnitzel, *raclette,* escargot-filled *maultaschen* with sautéed spinach, spicy Debrecziner sausage, home-smoked trout, an extensive selection of vegetarian entrées, apfelstrudel, homemade ice cream, and great coffee. In winter, the rough-hewn wood-plank walls ooze warmth. In summer, mountain breezes whisper among the tall sunflowers in the brightly hued garden, where patio tables are set. *$$; MC, V; local checks only; dinner every day (closed 2 weeks Nov and Apr); full bar; reservations recommended; bauernhaus@cyberlink .bc.ca; www.kimberleybc.net/bauernhaus; left off Gerry Sorenson Wy.* &

LODGINGS

House Alpenglow B&B / ★★

3 ALPENGLOW CT, KIMBERLEY; 250/427-0273 OR 877/257-3645 Merna Abel knows how to take care of guests, and it shows in her home's three spacious and lovingly furnished guest rooms, including the two-bedroom Sullivan suite with its private entrance to the outdoor hot tub and yard. The suite shares a bathroom with the upper-floor Kootenay room, designed for two to six people. The downstairs Purcell room has its own bathroom en suite. Wood paneling ensures complete quiet. Smells of fresh croissants and muffins fill the morning air, with homemade jams and jellies to sweeten the feast. After a plateful of bratwurst and cheese on homemade bread, you may not need to eat again until supper. Kimberley Alpine Resort is several minutes uphill; the Old Bauernhaus (see review), just across the road, serves dinner. *$; no credit cards; checks OK; alpenglo@rockies.net; www.kimberleybc.net/alpenglow; west side of Gerry Sorenson Wy, near Trickle Creek Golf Resort.*

Fernie

An elegant stone courthouse anchors downtown Fernie (population 4,610), a rough-and-tumble mining and logging town with a remarkably well-preserved core of historic buildings. The craggy cleft of the Lizard Range above **FERNIE ALPINE RESORT** (5339 Ski Area Rd; 250/423-4655 or 800/258-7669, 250/423-3555 snow report; *info@skifernie.com*; *www.skifernie.com*) is often likened to an open catcher's mitt. Sheer limestone faces tower above the resort, trapping snow-laden storms in massive bowls and making Fernie, along with Whitewater and Red Mountain, a must-ski on BC's powder circuit. Trails cut through dense forests on the lower slopes are visible from downtown Fernie, 3 miles (5 km) east of the resort.

In the late 1990s, Fernie began the largest expansion of any winter resort in North America, doubling its terrain with three new lifts. Seven new lodges have opened, but prime parking at the bottom of the slopes is still reserved for RVs from small towns across the prairies, the backbone of the resort's clientele. With them in mind, Fernie provides a spiffy changing room, complete with showers. The resort also offers sleigh rides (a handy way to get to the lifts from the parking lot), snowmobile tours, dogsledding, snowshoeing, as well as a twice-weekly torchlight ski run. In summer, the hills ring with the sound of horseback riders, mountain bikers, hikers, and adventure racers. Winter Olympic alpine gold medalist Kerrin Lee-Gartner settled here in 1999 to construct **SNOW CREEK LODGE** (5258 Highline Dr; 250/423-7669 or 888/558-6878; *www.fernieproperties.com*). Her medals and memorabilia are displayed in the lodge's lobby. Visitors are as likely to cross paths with the downhiller and her young family at **OUR CAPPUCCINO CORNER** (501 2nd Ave) as they are on the slopes. A good source for outdoor information and recreation equipment is **THE GUIDES HUT** (671 2nd Ave; 250/423-3650). Contact the **FERNIE INFO CENTRE** (102 Commerce Rd; 250/423-6868; *info@ferniechamber .com*; *www.ferniechamber.com*) for details. Or consult *www.fernie.com*.

LODGINGS

Griz Inn Sport Hotel / ★

5369 SKI AREA RD, FERNIE; 250/423-9221 OR 800/661-0118 When the Griz Inn opened in 1983, it signaled the beginning of a new era in tourism at Fernie Alpine Resort, which had been primarily the preserve of locals. For the next 15 years, the Griz and the lodge across the way, the Wolf Den, provided the only overnight accommodations at the base of the lifts. Since 2000, visitors can consider a sweeping list of new lodges and condos, though none outperforms the Griz's prime location. Guests enjoy second-to-none views of the mountains and trails from private balconies. Built with families in mind, the largest suites sleep 12–16 in a combination of bedrooms, lofts, and pullout couches. All suites have full kitchens and are clean and bright. The Griz features a large indoor pool, two outdoor hot tubs, and a sauna. The inn's Powderhorn Restaurant serves food from early morning breakfasts through late-night snacks. *$$; AE, MC, V; checks OK; closed briefly in late spring, early fall; reservations@grizinn.com; www.grizzinn .com; off Hwy 3 west of Fernie.* &

Fairmont Hot Springs

FAIRMONT HOT SPRINGS RESORT has graciously accommodated both soakers and skiers since the 1920s with the biggest outdoor thermal pool and the only private (guests only) ski resort in western Canada. Don't miss the view from the switchback road above the resort of the Columbia Valley to the Selkirk and Bugaboo Mountains, including the beginning of the 1,200-mile (2,000 km) Columbia River. Viewpoints in the East Kootenay don't come any better than this.

LODGINGS

Fairmont Hot Springs Resort / ★★★

FAIRMONT HOT SPRINGS; 250/345-6311 OR 800/663-4979 Fairmont Hot Springs Resort smells like a rose, and not just because—in contrast to many thermal springs—Fairmont's are odorless and sulfur-free. In summer, wild perfumes from the pine forest intermingle with those from beds of marigolds and petunias lining the walkways. Attention to detail is astonishing; all appointments have been thoughtfully chosen and blended to harmonious perfection. Archival photographs adorn the walls, reminding guests that they are partaking in a century-old tradition. Many of the 140 guest units come with kitchens partitioned from view by folding wooden doors. A dining area adjoins two queen beds. Each room has a private balcony or patio with lounge chairs. The Olympic-sized hot-springs pool lies below. Rooms 492, 494, and 496 are the most private of the ground-floor rooms. The resort has a full-service dining room, coffee shop, and lounge. *$$$; AE, DC, DIS, MC, V; no checks; info@fairmonthotsprings.com; www.fairmonthotsprings .com; turn east off Hwy 93/95.* &

Invermere and Panorama Mountain Village

Set 2 miles (3 km) west of Hwy 93/95 on Windermere Lake, **INVERMERE** (population 2,860) has a folksy main street and is the commercial hub for the nearby towns of **RADIUM HOT SPRINGS** and **FAIRMONT HOT SPRINGS**. In summer, the broad sandy beach at **JAMES CHABOT BEACH PARK** is the perfect place to swim and picnic, particularly if you've stopped at **THE QUALITY BAKERY** (1305 7th Ave; 250/342-9913). Look for an enormous pretzel poised above its roof. Espresso coffee and Swiss pastries are the feature attractions. On a slow day, locals drop by just to watch the baker at work in his open kitchen. He's as practiced and smooth as the motion of water in the nearby Columbia River. For information, contact the **COLUMBIA VALLEY VISITOR INFO CENTRE** (Hwy 93/95, Invermere; 250/342-2844; *www.mctserv.com/chamber/*).

PANORAMA MOUNTAIN VILLAGE (250/342-6941 or 800/663-2929; *paninfo @intrawest.com*; *www.panoramaresort.com*) lies at the end of a winding road 12 miles (20 km) west of Invermere. Long before you arrive, Mount Panorama appears in all its glory. Because of its remote location in the Purcell Mountains, Panorama is more of a mountain retreat. All the trappings of a destination resort are here, including outdoor hot tubs located at the base of the lifts to soak your weary bones after a day on the slopes, plus a unique outdoor heated water park at the base of its lifts. Panorama is one massive piece of work that recently expanded into the expert-only Taynton Bowl. Cross-country skiers are catered to at the village's **BECKIE SCOTT NORDIC CENTRE** (250/341-4100) named for the Olympic gold medal winner. In summer, the action switches to golfing (at the Greywolf Golf Course), playing tennis, horseback riding, hiking, and river rafting on Toby Creek.

Radium Hot Springs

Near the town of the same name, **RADIUM HOT SPRINGS** (Hwy 93, 2 miles/ 3 km from the junction of Hwy 95; 250/347-9485; *www.rhs.bc.ca*) makes an ideal soaking stop at the base of the Kootenay Range. The hot springs, open to the public year-round and wheelchair accessible, are equipped with two pools: one heated, the other cooler for swimming.

Trans-Canada Highway and the National Parks, Field

You can't go much farther east than Field, the modest commercial hub, as it were, of **YOHO NATIONAL PARK**, and still be in BC. With adjacent **BANFF, JASPER,** and **KOOTENAY NATIONAL PARKS**, Yoho is part of a vast Rocky Mountain wilderness designated by UNESCO as a World Heritage Site. The Trans-Canada Highway (Hwy 1) parallels the Kicking Horse River as it winds through a beautiful, broad valley. By the time it reaches the park's headquarters in Field, 18 miles (30 km) from its west gate, the tone of the landscape shifts to one of glaciated peaks. Extensive hiking is found along 190 miles (300 km) of trails in Yoho, a park characterized by rock walls and waterfalls. A highlight for many visitors is the strenuous hike to the **BURGESS SHALE**, a world-famous site where the mysteries of a major stage of evolution were unraveled. Access is permitted only with a registered guide from the Yoho-Burgess Shale Foundation (800/343-3006; *www.burgess-shale.bc.ca*).

Contact the **FIELD VISITOR CENTRE** (250/343-6783; *www.parkscanada.gc.ca/ yoho*). Note: A pass, available at the visitor center, is required for all visitors stopping in national parks. Permits are good in national parks throughout Canada.

LODGINGS

Emerald Lake Lodge / ★★★

🌲 **YOHO NATIONAL PARK; 250/343-6321 OR 800/663-6336** When Emerald Lake Lodge opened in 1902, it was considered the Canadian Pacific Railway's crown jewel. After falling on hard times, the lodge was restored to elegance in 1986. Set on a 13-acre peninsula that overlooks aptly named Emerald Lake, the lodge has 85 spacious rooms spread among 24 chalet-style buildings. Rooms feature twig furniture arranged around fieldstone fireplaces. Private decks open onto the lake and Presidential Range peaks. (Note: Some cabins are less than soundproof.) Built of massive hand-hewn timbers, the main lodge houses a grand salon with two towering fireplaces, the formal Mount Burgess dining room, and the Kicking Horse Bar, furnished with 1890 oak saloon fixtures brought from the Yukon. Upstairs, a majestic, green-felt billiards table anchors the game room. In summer, stop for afternoon tea on the main lodge's veranda or enjoy casual fare served at Cilantro, an airy bistro adjacent to the boathouse. *$$$$; AE, DC, MC, V; no checks; emlodge@rockies.net; www.crmr.com; 6 miles (10 km) south of Hwy 1.* &

Golden and Kicking Horse Mountain Resort

First came the railway, then logging. Now outdoor adventure draws people to Golden. In summer, white-water raft on the charging **KICKING HORSE RIVER** as it races through the Rockies to meet the Columbia River at Golden. In winter, deep powder skiing in the nearby Purcells soaks up visitors. Ice or rock climb in the Glacier and Yoho National Parks that bookend the Columbia Valley's north end near Golden. Even the town's name hints at its embarrassment of riches. Much like its neighbor, Revelstoke, on the west side of Rogers Pass, downtown Golden (population 4,020) lies hidden from those passing through on the Trans-Canada. Over the years, the Columbia River has carved a steep cutbank on the east side of town. To surmount it, traffic on Hwy 1 bypasses most of the riverfront. Not so for those exploring the Columbia Valley on Hwy 95, which conveniently leads through downtown. Contact the **GOLDEN CHAMBER OF COMMERCE** (500 10th Ave N; 250/344-7125 or 800/622-4653; *www.goldenchamber.bc.ca*) for details.

Opened in 2000, **KICKING HORSE MOUNTAIN RESORT** (866/754-5425; *www.kickinghorseresort.com*), formerly called Whitetooth Ski Area, lies 7 miles (12 km) west of Golden. The resort's Golden Eagle Express gondola deposits you at 7,710 feet (2,350 m) elevation. The superb **EAGLE'S EYE RESTAURANT** demands a visit whether you intend to schuss to the bottom or not.

LODGINGS

Hillside Lodge & Chalets / ★★

1740 SEWARD FRONTAGE RD, GOLDEN; 250/344-7281 A century ago, the Canadian Pacific Railway constructed several Alpine-style chalets in Golden to house Swiss mountain guides hired to escort climbers into nearby Glacier National Park.

More recently, Hubert and Sonja Baier built similar cabins for guests in search of a tranquil Rocky Mountain retreat. Five cabins (a two-bedroom and four one-bedrooms) and a main lodge with four en suite rooms are nestled beside the Blaeberry River on a benchland above the Columbia River Valley. Each bright cabin is furnished with a wood-burning fireplace and handcrafted Bavarian furniture. Guests share the 60-acre property with wildlife and the docile llamas that the Baiers raise. Breakfast (included) is served in the main lodge beside a cheery hearth in winter, and on the porch in summer. Fresh-baked goodies with homemade jams, muesli (Alpine granola), cold cuts, and cheese fortify guests for exploring. Dinner is available by prior arrangement. The charming Baiers can arrange white-water rafting, horseback riding, snowshoeing, tobogganing, or cross-country skiing jaunts. *$$; MC, V; no checks; info@hillsidechalets.com; www.hillsidechalets.com; 8 miles (13 km) west of Golden.*

Revelstoke

Revelstoke (population 7,500), nestled beside **MOUNT REVELSTOKE NATIONAL PARK** (250/837-7500; *www.parkscanada.gc.ca/revelstoke*), is a railway town scenically located beside the Columbia River. The town is just the right size for a stroll through well-tended neighborhood streets; pick up a self-guided heritage walking-and-driving tour brochure from the **REVELSTOKE VISITOR INFO CENTRE** (204 Campbell Ave; 250/837-5345 or 800/487-1493; *www.revelstokecc.bc.ca*). Steep-pitched metal roofs confirm the area's heavy snowfall, as does the **CANADIAN AVALANCHE CENTRE** (300 1st St W; 250/837-2435 or 800/667-1105; *canav@avalanche.ca*; *www.avalanche.ca*) located downtown, a font of information for backcountry snow trekkers. In summer, drive the 15-mile (25 km) **MEADOW IN THE SKY PARKWAY** to the highest elevation of any public road in Canada and a view of surrounding ice fields.

RESTAURANTS

The 112 / ★★

112 1ST ST E, REVELSTOKE; 250/837-2107 OR 888/245-5523 Located in downtown Revelstoke's Regent Inn (built in 1931), The 112 is a unanimous favorite among locals. The dining room's cedar-paneled interior and historic ambiance would be the pride of any town, but the great food is its biggest draw. Chef Peter Mueller specializes in veal dishes. The clams béarnaise, lasagne Florentine with Dungeness crab, seafood cioppino, and lamb provençal are also highly recommended. The wine list emphasizes BC vintners. On Sundays, when The 112 is closed, the Regent Inn's pub menu proffers a mild sampling of The 112's delights. It's solid pub fare—zesty Caesar salads, zingy wings, burgers, and a trendy selection of wraps—with a neighborhood flavor. *$$; AE, MC, V; local checks only; lunch Mon–Fri, dinner Mon–Sat; full bar; reservations recommended; regent@regentinn.com; www.regentinn.com; beside Grizzly Plaza.* &

LODGINGS

Mulvehill Creek Wilderness Inn / ★★★

4200 HWY 23S, REVELSTOKE; 250/837-8649 OR 877/837-8649 Cornelia and René Hueppi, a dynamic Swiss couple, have created a remarkable wilderness retreat south of Revelstoke. The inn, with board-and-batten construction and a small tower room, is nestled in a tranquil, brightly lit clearing. The rambling ranch house structure holds eight suites (a half suite is available for children), each furnished with original wildlife artwork and painted in soft shades. The Otter's Burrow is the largest, with private deck and Jacuzzi, perfect for honeymooners. An extensively planted yard and garden contains a heated outdoor pool and hot tub. A complimentary buffet breakfast offers homemade jams and jellies, fresh bread and muffins, fruit salad, egg dishes courtesy of the inn's chickens, and fresh cheese and produce from local suppliers. In winter, guests can snowshoe, toboggan, or cross-country ski an extensive trail network on nearby Mount McPherson. In summer, guests can canoe or make an enjoyable trek to a nearby fish-filled lake. By arrangement, Cornelia will prepare your catch. (Dinner is extra and requires a day's notice.) Reservations are a must June–August. $$; AE, MC, V; checks OK; info@mulvehillcreek.com; www.mulvehillcreek.com; 12 miles (19 km) south of Revelstoke.

NORTHERN MAINLAND BRITISH COLUMBIA

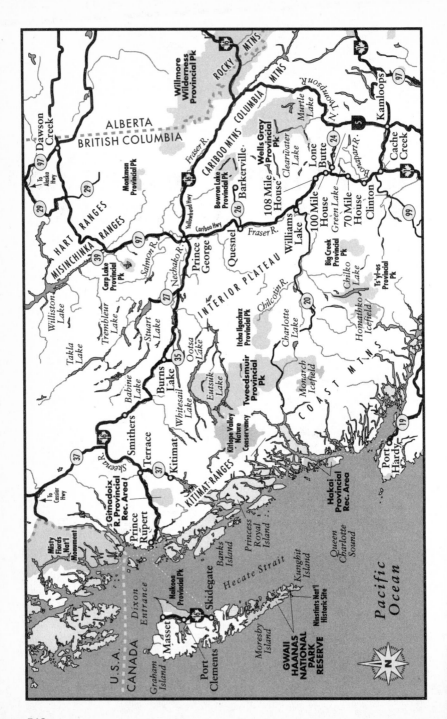

NORTHERN MAINLAND BRITISH COLUMBIA

Northern British Columbia is a vast, underpopulated wilderness—roughly the size of California and Oregon combined—that stretches from the rain-forested Central Coast to the northeastern Rockies. Legendary explorer Alexander Mackenzie walked this way in 1793, becoming the first European to cross North America by land, a full decade before the Lewis and Clark expedition duplicated that feat. Routes through the region follow centuries-old Native trading trails, or those of more recent Gold Rush and Telegraph trails.

At the heart of northern BC lies the Cariboo-Chilcotin region. This is fishing and hunting country with long, cold winters and short, hot summers. Today's travelers head into the south Cariboo via two major highway routes—the Cariboo Highway (Hwy 97) and the Yellowhead Highway (Hwy 5).

Finding the best restaurant or lodging in the most northerly parts of BC is a simple task: if they're open, they must be doing something right. This is particularly true farther north along the Alaska Highway (Hwy 97) and the Stewart-Cassiar Highway (Hwy 37).

ACCESS AND INFORMATION

HIGHWAYS 5, 16, 37, and **97** run through central and northern BC. The latter is the main access road to the Cariboo-Chilcotin region from southern BC. Many towns along Highway 97 between Clinton and Quesnel are helpfully referred to by distance from Lillooet (mile 0) north along the Gold Rush Trail that preceded construction of the Cariboo Highway. Thus 70 Mile House, for example, marks the distance between Lillooet and this point, the original site of a pioneer roadhouse. (Note: Lillooet itself lies 45 miles [75 km] west of Highway 97 on Highway 99. See Lower Mainland British Columbia chapter.) From Prince George, Highway 97 winds northeast to Dawson Creek—mile 0 on the Alaska Highway—and northwest to Watson Lake on the BC-Yukon border, via Fort St. John and Fort Nelson, 737 miles (1,228 km) in all.

PRINCE GEORGE AIRPORT (4141 Airport Rd, Prince George; 250/963-2400; *www.pgairport.ca*) is home base to **WESTJET** (800/538-5696; *www.westjet.com*), **CENTRAL MOUNTAIN AIR** (888-865-8585 or 800/663-3721; *www.cmair.com*), and **AIR CANADA JAZZ** (250/561-2905 or 888/247-2262; *www.flyjazz.ca*). Air Canada Jazz also flies from Vancouver to Sandspit on Moresby Island in Haida Gwaii (formerly known as the Queen Charlotte Islands). **CANADIAN WESTERN AIRLINES** (866-835-9292; *www.cwair.com*) links Vancouver with Williams Lake in the south Cariboo, as well as with Sandspit on Moresby Island and Masset on Graham Island in Haida Gwaii/Queen Charlotte Islands. **HARBOUR AIR SEAPLANES** (800/689-4234; *www.harbour-air.com*) flies from Prince Rupert to Sandspit, Queen Charlotte City, and Massett in Haida Gwaii/Queen Charlotte Islands. Air Canada Jazz and Central Mountain Air link southern BC with Terrace and Smithers, on Highway 16 near Kitwanga in northwestern BC.

VIA RAIL's *Skeena* (888/842-7245; *www.viarail.com*) provides east-west passenger rail service from Jasper, Alberta, to Prince George, Smithers, and Prince Rupert. The **BC FERRIES** (888-223-3779 or 250-386-3431; *www.bcferries.bc.ca*) travel west from Prince Rupert to Skidegate Landing on Graham Island in Haida Gwaii/Queen Charlotte Islands and south to Port Hardy on Vancouver Island. The **ALASKA MARINE HIGHWAY** (800/642-0066; *www.dot.state.ak.us/amhs/*) links Prince Rupert with Skagway in Alaska to the north and Bellingham, Washington, near Vancouver to the south.

TOURISM BC (800/435-5622; *www.hellobc.com/*) is a helpful source of travel information on northern British Columbia. For a virtual tour of several northern locations, follow the links at the provincial public broadcaster, the **KNOWLEDGE NETWORK** (*www.knowledgenetwork.ca/know_tool/bcmoments/index.html*).

The Cariboo Highway (Hwy 97)

Clinton

Clinton (population 740) anchors mile 47 on the historic Gold Rush Trail. This frontier trading post's history is best seen in the **SOUTH CARIBOO HISTORICAL MUSEUM** (1419 Cariboo Hwy; 250/459-24420; open June–August) housed in a former schoolhouse. Framed by wrought iron and pine, the **PIONEER MEMORIAL CEMETERY** (east side of Hwy 97) at the north end of town presents an apt gateway to northern BC. Catch the town's annual **MAY BALL RODEO** (250/459-2261) that kicks off with the Ball and Tea, the longest continually held event in British Columbia (more than 130 years). For more information on Clinton, contact the mayor's office (306 Lebourdais Ave; 250/459-2261) or the **CLINTON AND DISTRICT CHAMBER OF COMMERCE** (1522 Cariboo Hwy; 250/459-2224; open daily June–Sept).

LODGINGS

Big Bar Guest Ranch / ★

BOX 27, JESMOND; 250/459-2333 Cowboy pride doesn't get any thicker than at Big Bar Ranch. Generations of greenhorns have cut their teeth here and return season after season for more riding and roping, skiing and skating, fishing and gold panning, hiking and swimming, snowshoeing and dogsledding. Big Bar offers plain but functional guest rooms in the Sagebrush Lodge, one-bedroom log cabins, the six-bedroom Coyote Lodge (for groups), plus tepees (summer only) dotted among the ponderosa pines. As they say at Big Bar, "You arrive a city slicker, and go home a cowboy." *$$$$; MC, V; checks OK; two-night min; info@bigbarranch.com; www.bigbarranch.com; 25 miles (40 km) west of Hwy 97 on Big Bar Road.*

Echo Valley Ranch Resort / ★★★★

BOX 16, JESMOND; 250/459-2386 OR 800/253-8831 Echo Valley is the Cariboo's premier adult-oriented working guest ranch and spa. After vacationing at nearby Big Bar Ranch, owners Norm and Nan Dove

NORTHERN MAINLAND BC THREE-DAY TOUR

DAY ONE: Start your day in Prince Rupert with a walk through downtown. Begin at the **MUSEUM OF NORTHERN BRITISH COLUMBIA**, where you'll learn about interpretations of carving styles throughout the Northwest Coast. Tour the harbor and nearby Dodge Cove with the **PRINCE RUPERT WATER TAXI**, or rent a kayak at **ECO-TREKS ADVENTURES** and go for a paddle. Lunch at the **COW BAY CAFÉ** before heading to the **NORTH PACIFIC CANNERY VILLAGE NATIONAL HIS-TORIC SITE** in nearby Port Edward. Afterward, check into **EAGLE BLUFF BED & BREAKFAST** and relax to the sound of the ocean lapping against the wharf. Then it's off to dinner at nearby **SMILE'S SEAFOOD CAFÉ**.

DAY TWO: After breakfast at Eagle Bluff, head for the nearby BC Ferries terminal for the 6-hour crossing to Haida Gwaii/Queen Charlotte Islands. Lunch on the ferry, then on arrival at Skidegate Landing visit the **HAIDA GWAII MUSEUM** before heading to either the **COPPER BEECH HOUSE** (where dinner may be available by prior arrangement) or the **ALASKA VIEW LODGE** in Masset.

DAY THREE: Breakfast with your hosts, then head 16 miles (26 km) north to explore Rose Spit. Lunch at **MARJ'S CAFE** (1645 Man St, Masset, 250/626-9344) before following Hwy 16 south to Tlell, where a sip of spring water from St. Mary's Well will guarantee you'll return one day to these islands at the boundary of the world. Dinner in Queen Charlotte City at **OCEANIA CHINESE & CONTINENTAL RESTAURANT** (3119 3rd Ave; 250/559-8683). Afterward, stroll the town's waterfront before heading to Skidegate Landing to catch the overnight ferry sailing back to the mainland at Prince Rupert.

bought the adjacent property and built six imposing peeled-log cabins and lodges, plus an east-meets-west Baan Thai wellness center, that sit artfully positioned on an open shoulder of land above Cripple Creek, with the Marble Range mountains spread off to the north as a backdrop. It's all here: welcoming ambiance, pampering amenities, as well as sumptuous gourmet meals. Guest accommodations range from the central six-bedroom Dove Lodge; the nine-bedroom Lookout Lodge; two private cabins (with private bedrooms, bathrooms, sitting areas, fireplaces, lofts, and private decks); or one special cabin set aside in a refuge of its own with a four-poster bed, fireplace, romantically furnished sitting area, and private deck with outdoor Jacuzzi. (A video preview of the resort is posted at the ranch's Web site.) *$$$$; MC, V; no checks; 3-night min, Wed or Sat arrival dates May–Sept, or 2-night min Oct and Dec–Apr; evranch@uniserve.com; www.evranch.com; on unpaved Big Bar Rd 30 miles (50 km) west of Clinton on Hwy 97.* ⅃

Interlakes District

Head east off Highway 97 at either 70 Mile or 93 Mile House and you'll be in the Interlakes microregion. **GREEN LAKE** is the first of hundreds of lakes, large and larger, strung between here and Hwy 5 on the North Thompson River. For a quick sample, drive the Green Lake scenic loop north from Green Lake to Lone Butte on Highway 24. Each lake boasts at least one guest ranch or fishing camp.

LODGINGS

Crystal Waters Guest Ranch / ★★

BOX 100 NORTH BONAPARTE RD, BRIDGE LAKE; 250/593-4252 OR 888/593-2252 At Crystal Waters, rodeo man Gary Cleveland and his wife, Marisa Peters, have distilled the appealing essence of a small guest ranch experience: intimacy and spontaneity. Their secret: empower the guest. Spend a day exploring the 640-acre spread on one of the ranch's herd of paints and palominos. Soak off your saddle sores in the wood-fired, lake-shore hot tub before chowing down on hearty ranch-raised organic repasts. Fish for rainbow trout or simply paddle on pristine Crystal Lake. Seven honey-hued log cabins (two at lakeside) equipped with hot plates, small refrigerators, and cowboy outhouses, accommodate 2 to 12 guests each. Request the Loon's Nest, a BPNW fave. (Note: Guests must supply their own sleeping bags or duvets.) A firelit guest lodge rebuilt from the old homestead and relocated near lakeside provides a quiet retreat. Non-riding rates are also available. *$$$$; MC, V; checks OK; open Dec–Oct; holiday@crystal watersranch.com; www.crystalwatersranch.com; 3 miles (5 km) southwest of Hwy 24 at Bridge Lake on North Bonaparte Rd.* &

Flying U Guest Ranch / ★

70 MILE HOUSE, BC; 250/456-7717 Founded by rodeo star Jack Boyd in 1924, the Flying U is as original as guest ranches come. All you need to know about the Flying U—Canada's oldest working guest ranch—is embodied in the soft, smoky smell that emanates from the main lodge's stone fireplace. For nearly 100 years, countless blazes have imbued the main house's interior with the peaty ambiance of single-malt whisky. The Longhorn Saloon, swinging doors and all, is just up the street in this miniature ranch town. A horseshoe of 25 rustic cabins lines the long approach road that climbs the gently sloping hillside above Green Lake. Choose your horse when you check in and ride off—unsupervised, if you wish—into the sunset to explore the ranch's 25,000-acre property. Vintage western movies, bonfires, hayrides, or square dancing often follow dinner. As is traditional in the Cariboo, everything the ranch offers is included in one price. *$$$$; MC, V; checks OK; open Apr–Oct; 2-night min mid-Apr–Jun and Sept–Oct; 3-night min Jul–Aug; flyingu@bcinternet.net; www.flyingu.com; 12 miles (20 km) east of 70 Mile House on N Green Lake Rd.*

100 Mile House

100 Mile House (population 1,740) is home to the annual 50-kilometer "classic technique" Cariboo Cross-Country Ski Marathon. Just to show how seriously locals take their sticks, the world's largest pair of skinny skis, accompanied by a 30-foot (9 m) pair of poles, point skyward in front of the modern peeled-log cabin that houses the **SOUTH CARIBOO VISITOR INFO CENTRE** (422 Cariboo Hwy 97S; 877/511-5353). Arguably the best track-set, cross-country skiing in BC is found on the 120 miles (200 km) of community trails that loop between here and nearby 108 Mile Ranch. For information on cross-country skiing and mountain biking in the Cariboo, contact **GUNNER'S CYCLE AND X-COUNTRY SKI SHOP** (800/664-5414) in 108 Mile Ranch.

RESTAURANTS

Trails End Restaurant/1871 Lodge / ★★

HWY 97 (THE HILLS HEALTH AND GUEST RANCH), 108 MILE HOUSE; 250/791-5225 OR 800/668-2233 Trails End Restaurant sits in the main lodge of the Hills Health and Guest Ranch (see review). On weekends, adjacent 1871 Lodge favors a more informal approach. Both dining rooms are characterized by cozy fireside tables amid *fin de siècle* frontier decor. The Trails End menu includes generously portioned Cariboo Country selections and, in keeping with the ranch's healthful theme, lighter spa fare. The emphasis is on grain-fed meat, fresh seafood, and vegetarian dishes, prepared by Swiss chef Stephan Witner, whose inspired touch can also be seen in the 1871 Lodge's dinner menu, which includes all-you-can-eat fondue, hot-rock steaks that guests cook themselves, plus a nightly chef's special. *$$–$$$; AE, MC, V; checks OK; breakfast, lunch, dinner every day, brunch Sun; full bar; reservations required (dinner); info@thehillsbc.com; www.spabc.com; east side of Hwy 97 just north of main intersection.* ♿

LODGINGS

The Hills Health and Guest Ranch / ★★★

HWY 97, 108 MILE HOUSE; 250/791-5225 OR 800/668-2233 In 1983, Pat and Juanita Corbett began pioneering a combined spa-and-ranch experience. The Corbetts wanted their spread to stand apart, while epitomizing the essence of the Cariboo region: hard-working, free-spirited, family-centered, and health-oriented. Three "International Specialty Spa of the Year" awards later, their guest roster includes well-known Canadian entertainers as well as former prime minister Jean Chrétien. Some visitors stay for months. Choose from hotel-style rooms in either the Ranch House or Manor House Lodge (breakfast included), or private self-contained chalets that sleep as many as six. Lodge rooms are outfitted with twin beds, rocking chairs, and festive touches, such as floral wreathes. Best views are from the Manor House rooms (request odd-numbered rooms, 31–47) that overlook the ranch's private ski and snowboard hill. Chalets 1–4 also adjoin the hill with ski-in/ski-out potential. The faux-log chalets are more simply furnished than lodge rooms and come equipped with complete kitchens and large decks with gas barbeques, and are pet friendly. Main ranch attractions

TOUR OF THE TOTEMS

One of the most unique scenic drives in BC leads around a well-marked circuit in the Hazelton Valley called the **TRAIL OF THE TOTEMS**. The **HAZELTON INFO CENTRE** (on Hwy 16, halfway between Prince George and Prince Rupert; 250/842-6071) has information on the self-guided Tour of the Totems as well as the Hands of History Tour.

First stop is just north of Highway 16 on Highway 37 in the village of **KITWANGA**. A dozen poles face the Skeena River beside a century-old wooden bell tower and church. The weathered poles are carved with an array of animal and human images.

The more than 20 intricately carved and thought-provoking poles in the small village of **KITWANCOOL**, about 12 miles (20 km) north along Highway 37, are reputed to be the oldest and finest such examples. Little people crowd together on some poles like townsfolk on the exterior of a medieval European cathedral. Some of the tallest poles are surmounted by figures of raven, bear, eagle, wolf, or humans. Nearby, a shed houses some of the oldest poles, weathered almost beyond recognition, with just an eye or a beak to suggest the original design. A freshly cut log often lies beside the shed, awaiting the carver's adze. (Note: The Gitanyow have banned photographing or video

include a large spa and fitness center, with a heated swimming pool, saunas, and hydrotherapy pools. Hundreds of kilometers of cross-country ski trails network the woods. In summer, mountain bikes, guided hikes, and a corral of patient horses are at guests' disposal. *$$$; AE, MC, V; checks OK; info@thehillsbc.com; www.spabc .com; east side of Hwy 97 just north of main intersection.* ⅙

The Wolf Den Country Inn / ★★

CANIM LAKE RD, FOREST GROVE; 250/397-2108 OR 877/397-2108
The spirits of Sgt. Preston of the Yukon and his lead dog, King, live on in the sheltering folds of the Cariboo Mountains, most noticeably at this country inn and outdoor adventure center that Chantelle and Jamie Ross established in 1992. Their rambling log rancher has four guest rooms, each with its own floor-to-ceiling window overlooking Bridge Creek. Snuggle on the Pendleton blanket–draped couches beside the fieldstone fireplace that blazes in the private guest living room. An outdoor hot tub on the broad deck completes the scene. Purebred Siberian huskies sit kenneled in the 20-acre pasture below the inn. Exceptionally quiet, these dogs are both clean and great with children. Book an intimate (six-person max) dogsledding adventure in winter, or guided horseback and canoe outings in summer. Stay for the night just to wake up to one of Chantelle's farm-fresh breakfasts. She also takes requests for much-lauded gourmet lunches or dinners. *$–$$; MC, V; checks OK; info@wolfden-adventures.com; www.wolfden-adventures.com; 19 miles (30 km) east of Hwy 97 at 100 Mile House.*

recording their poles. Please respect their wishes.)

Return to Highway 16 and travel east to **KITSEGUECLA**, a small Skeena River settlement near Hazelton. Two wonderfully unique poles are here, and large sculptures grace the front yards of several homes in the community.

Just north of Hazelton on a paved side road, pull into the **'KSAN HISTORICAL VILLAGE** (Box 326, Hazelton; 250/842-5544) to see its rich display of totems, jewelry, and clothing. A museum in one of the longhouses honors the Gitksan ancestors who beautified the items they carved for everyday use. Seven lovingly decorated longhouses are grouped at the confluence of the Skeena and Bulkley Rivers, and several are open to visitors at no charge. Guided tours are offered of the Fireweed, Wolf, and Frog Clan houses for a small fee.

Continuing north, the **KISPIOX** ceremonial poles are the most animated, with carved tears dripping from eyes of inlaid abalone. The 18 poles here have the appearance of being held in the palm of the Creator. Kispiox is built on high ground, about 18 miles (30 km) north of Hazelton on a side road, from where the view of the Skeena River is stunning.

—Jack Christie

Williams Lake

One of the most exciting times to visit Williams Lake (population 11,150) is on the last weekend in June, when this lumber and cattle town hosts its annual **WILLIAMS LAKE STAMPEDE** (*www.williamslakestampede.com*)—second only to Calgary's in stature. From here, Hwy 20 leads 274 miles (456 km) west across the Chilcotin Plateau and the Coast Mountains to Bella Coola on BC's central coast. For more information, contact the **WILLIAMS LAKE VISITOR INFO CENTRE** (1148 Broadway S; 250/392-5025; *www.bcadventure.com/wlcc/*).

Prince George

Although Prince George, the largest city in the BC interior (population 72,400), sits near the geographical center of BC (that honor belongs to Vanderhoof, 60 miles [100 km] northwest on Hwy 16), it's still thought of as deep in the northern half of the province. "P. G." or the "City of Bridges" sits at a crossroads of rivers, railroads, and highways. The mighty Fraser and Nechako Rivers blend near old **FORT GEORGE** (south end of 20th Ave), now a municipal park; get information from the **FRASER-FORT GEORGE REGIONAL MUSEUM** (333 Becott Pl; 250/562-1612; *www.theexploration place.com*). Walk or bike the park's riverside pathways to sense the site's importance in the destiny of the region. Highway 16 leads east to the Rockies and west to Prince Rupert; Highway 97 leads northeast to Dawson Creek and the Alaska Highway.

A municipal pool, art gallery, and park are downtown close to the **COAST INN OF THE NORTH** (770 Brunswick St, Prince George, 250/563-0121 or 800/663-1144; *www.coasthotels.com*) the best bet if you're overnighting. For more information, contact the **PRINCE GEORGE VISITOR INFO CENTRE** (1198 Victoria St; 250/562-3700 or 800/668-7646; *www.tourismpg.bc.ca*).

The Northwest Coast

Prince Rupert

Wet days outnumber dry ones by a 2–1 margin in Prince Rupert (population 14,640), BC's northernmost port. Fortunately, the rain is often light and the region offers plenty of interesting things to do *indoors*. Don't miss the **MUSEUM OF NORTHERN BRITISH COLUMBIA** (1st Ave E and McBride; 250/624-3207; *www.museumof northernbc.com*). Under its cedar-shaked, copper-flashed roof sits one of the finest collections of Native art in BC. While you visit, a local artist may be creating a piece, such as a ceremonial apron woven from mountain-goat hair. From the museum, an elevated walkway leads to the waterfront and the **KWINITSA STATION RAILWAY MUSEUM** (north end of Bill Murray Dr in Waterfront Park; 250/624-3207).

Prince Rupert is home to one of the best totem pole displays on the west coast. In summer, the Museum of Northern British Columbia offers guided walking tours, or you can take a self-guided tour beginning at the **PRINCE RUPERT VISITOR INFO CENTRE** (215 Cow Bay Rd; 250/624-5637 or 800/667-1994; *prtravel@citytel.net*; *www.tourismprincerupert.com*).

Tour the harbor with the **PRINCE RUPERT WATER TAXI** (Cow Bay; 250/624-3337) or **WEST COAST LAUNCH** (718 Smithers St; 800/201-8377; *www.westcoast launch.com*), or rent a kayak at **ECO-TREKS ADVENTURES** (203 Cow Bay Rd; 250/624-8311; *www.citytel.net/ecotreks*), in a boathouse on the wharf. A good spot to warm up afterward is the **COW BAY CAFÉ** (205 Cow Bay Rd; 250/624-1212).

Just south of town in Port Edward is the **NORTH PACIFIC CANNERY VILLAGE NATIONAL HISTORIC SITE** (1889 Skeena Dr, 7 miles/11 km southwest of Hwy 16; 250/628-3538; open May 15–Sept 15). Until the 1970s, it employed as many as 1,500 workers. Boardwalks link offices, stores, cafés, and homes with the west coast's oldest standing cannery, perched at the mouth of the Skeena River.

RESTAURANTS

Smile's Seafood Café / ★

131 COW BAY RD, PRINCE RUPERT; 250/624-3072 The spirit of Prince Rupert's fish plant heyday lives on at Smile's. Tucked demurely on the waterfront, Smile's and its neighbor, Love Electric, set the mood here on the wharves of Cow Bay, and fresh seafood sets the pace. If your little Bart Simpson has a cow about that, he'll more than thank you for bringing him here when he tastes the home-cut French fries still in their jackets. *$$; MC, V; no checks; breakfast, lunch, dinner every day (open Feb–Dec); full bar; no reservations; 2 blocks east of McBride on 3rd Ave to Cow Bay Rd.*

LODGINGS

Eagle Bluff Bed & Breakfast / ★

201 COW BAY RD, PRINCE RUPERT; 250/627-4955 OR 800/833-1550
Eagle Bluff is like a storybook come alive. The ocean laps beneath the pilings on Cow Bay, where owners Mary Allen and Brian Cox have restored five rustically elegant rooms in a former marine chandlery. Fireplaces in two of the rooms (Captain's Quarters and the Heron Room) impart warmth and a feeling of well-being, especially if stormy weather's brewing outdoors. A two-bedroom suite sits atop Allen and Cox's adjacent home and is ideal for families. Breakfast specialties include smoked salmon, eggs Benedict, fresh fruit salad, and Mary's muffins—or just about anything else you request. *$–$$; MC, V; no checks; eaglebed@citytel.net; www.citytel.net/eaglebluff; 1 block west of Hwy 16 on the harbor.* &

Haida Gwaii/Queen Charlotte Islands

These islands present one of the most beautiful and diverse landscapes in the world. Sometimes called Canada's Galapagos, they are home to a distinctive ecosystem and people, the Haida First Nation. Dubbed the Queen Charlotte Islands by an 18th-century British sea captain, the older Haida name for this place is Xhaaidlagha Gwaayyaai, or Haida Gwaii, "Islands at the Boundary of the World."

Haida Gwaii lies 60 miles (100 km) west of the BC mainland. Moresby and Graham are the largest of the 150 islands. Moresby, home to **GWAII HAANAS NATIONAL PARK RESERVE** (250/559-8818), lies to the south. Most of Moresby is inaccessible except by chartered boat, sea kayak, floatplane, or logging roads. The island's main airport is on Moresby at Sandspit, where a small ferry links with Queen Charlotte City (population 1,045) on nearby Graham Island.

Ferry traffic between Prince Rupert and Haida Gwaii docks at the BC Ferries' terminal at Skidegate Landing on Graham Island. Just north of the terminal is the **HAIDA GWAII MUSEUM** (at Qay'llnagaay, east of Hwy 16 at Second Beach; 250/559-4643), where whale spotting is almost guaranteed. Queen Charlotte City, with a serene waterfront, lies 2½ miles (4 km) west of Skidegate on Hwy 16. For those exploring by car or bike, Graham Island holds both cultural and recreational appeal. From Skidegate Landing, Hwy 16 leads 68 miles (109 km) north to Masset, home of the Haida First Nation, and the long, hard-packed beach at Rose Spit in **NAIKOON PROVINCIAL PARK** (250/557-4390; wlapwww.gov.bc.ca/bcparks/), from where the shoreline of southeastern Alaska can be glimpsed through the ocean mist. The Haida plan to construct three longhouses in Masset, where the offices of the First Nation are headquartered, to complement the surge of cultural activity at Skidegate Landing.

When choosing where to rest your head, our picks are the **ALASKA VIEW LODGE** (12291 Tow Hill Rd, Box 116, Masset, BC V0T 1M0; 800/661-0019; info@alaskaviewlodge.com; www.alaskaviewlodge.com) on South Beach, and

COPPER BEECH HOUSE (1590 Delkatlah St, Box 97, Masset, BC V0T 1S0; 250/626-5441; *www.copperbeechhouse.com/*) on the Masset harbor.

For information on all aspects of a visit to the Queen Charlottes, contact the **VISITOR INFORMATION CENTRE** (3220 Wharf St, Queen Charlotte City; 250/559-8316; *www.qcinfo.com*); the interpretive center is well worth a visit. For tourism information on Graham Island, contact the **MASSET INFO CENTRE** (1455 Old Beach Rd, Box 116, Masset, BC V0T 1M0; 888/352-9292; *www.massetbc.com/*).

Few roads link communities on the islands, and distances are not great. Car rentals are available at the Sandspit Airport, in Queen Charlotte City, and in Massett. **EAGLE CABS** (250/559-4461) runs a regular bus system with stops throughout Graham Island.

Index

A

Abacela Vineyards & Winery, 130
Abendblume Pension, 323
Aberdeen, 342–44
Abigail's Hotel, 477, 481
Abruzzo, 37–38
Ace Hotel, 199
Adam's Place, 53, 72
Adventure Kayak, 118
Aerie Resort, The, 491
Afrikando, 183
Agua Verde Cafe & Paddle Club,
    184
Ainsworth Hot Springs, 549–50
Ainsworth Hot Springs Restaurant,
    549–50
Air Canada, 474, 522
Air Canada Jazz, 529, 563
Airial Hot Air Balloon Company,
    217
Airports
    Eugene Airport, 51
    Portland International
        Airport, 3
    Prince George Airport, 563
    Seattle-Tacoma International
        Airport, 178, 210, 213
    Spokane International Airport,
        395
    Vancouver International
        Airport, 413, 443
    Victoria International Airport,
        473
Ajax Cafe, 279
Alaska Marine Highway System,
    234
Alaska View Lodge, 571–72
Albany, 67–68
Albany Convention and Visitors
    Center, 67
Alderbrook Resort and Spa, 277
Alec's by the Sea, 345
Alessandro's 120, 53, 65
Alexander's Country Inn &
    Restaurant, 335
Alexis Hotel, 199
Alice's Restaurant, 266
Ali's Thai Kitchen, 136
All Seasons Cafe, 551
All Seasons River Inn, 324
Alligator Soul, 215
Aloha Beachside Bed and Breakfast,
    261
Alpenglow Cafe, 132, 150
Alta Crystal Resort, 334

Altezzo, 255
Alton Baker Park, 71–72
Ambrosia, 72
American Hop Museum, 370
American Museum of Radio, 233
Amici's Bistro, 216–17
Amtrak, 3
Amuse Restaurant, 141–42
Amy's Manor Inn, 312
Anacortes, 239–40
Anacortes Museum, 214, 240
Ancestral Spirits Gallery, 280
Anchorage Inn, 224
Andersen House Bed & Breakfast,
    482
Anderson House on Oro Bay, 262
Anderson Island, 261–62
Andina, 8–9
Angela's Bed & Breakfast and
    Guesthouse, 547
Anjou Bakery, 321, 327
Ann Starrett Mansion, 283
Anna Lena's Pantry, 354
Anne's Oceanfront Hideaway, 495
Annie's at the Airport, 66
Annzpanz, 37
Anthony Lakes Ski Area, 169
Anthony's Homeport, 259
Anthony's Pier 66, 184
Apex Mountain Resort, 542–43
April Point Lodge, 503–4
April's, 83, 103
Aqua Riva, 420
Araxi Restaurant & Bar, 447–48
Arbor Café, The, 65
Arch Cape, 90–91
Archer Ale House, 234
Argosy, 207
Argyle House, The, 249
Ark Restaurant, The, 356
Arlene Schnitzer Concert Hall, 7
Arnold's Country Inn, 266
Art Gallery of Greater Victoria, 475
Art museums, 5–6, 115, 178,
    180–81, 253
Artattack Theater Ensemble, 137
Artists Repertory Theatre, 7
Arts Alive, 226
Ashford, 335–36
Ashland, 140–45
Ashland Community Food Store,
    140
Ashland Racquet Club, 132
Ashland Vineyards, 140

Astoria, 82, 84–86
Atlas Cafe, 521
Atomic Ale Brewpub & Eatery,
    374, 380
Atrevida Restaurant at the Galiano
    Inn, 500–501
Aurora, 61–62
Autovue Drive-In, 405
Avalon Hotel & Spa, 24
Azalea Park, 124

B

Bacchus, 359
Bacchus Ristorante, 419–20
Bacco, 178
Back Bay Inn, 252
Bagel Haven Bakery & Cafe,
    278–79
Bahari, 512
Bahn Thai, 273
Bair Restaurant at the Bair Drug and
    Hardware Store, The, 262
Baker City, 169–70
Bakery at the Store, The, 240
Bald eagles, 456
Baldface Snowcat Skiing, 551
Baldwin Hotel Museum, 146
Baldwin Saloon, 37, 42
Ballet, 7, 181
Baltic Room, 182
Bamfield, 513
Bandon, 117–20
Bandon Dunes Golf Resort, 119
Bandon Fisheries, 117
Bandon Gourmet, 117
Bar 98, 439
Barb's Buns, 493
Barkley Sound, 513
Barley Brown's Brewpub, 170
Barnacle Bill's Seafood Market, 97
Barnard Griffin Winery, 389
Barnes & Noble, 205
Barrel House, 373
Bavarian Clothing Company, The,
    322
Bay Cafe, The, 242
Bay City, 93–94
Bay Cottage, 283–84
Bay House, 98
Bayleaf, 223
Bayview State Park, 230
BC Ferries, 413, 461, 473, 492,
    564

BC Lions, 419
Beach Cottages on Marrowstone, 279
Beach Store Café, 237
Beach Street Bed and Breakfast, 119
Beacon Drive-In Restaurant, 476
Beacon Rock State Park, 385
Beaconsfield Inn, 482
Beanery, The, 68
Beddis House Bed and Breakfast, 495
Bella, 169
Bella Isola at Nantucket Inn, 240
Bella Italia, 289
Bella Union, 138
Bellevue (OR), 59–60,
Bellevue (WA), 205–6
Bellevue Club Hotel, 206
Bellevue Square, 205
Bellhouse Inn, The, 501
Bellingham, 232–37
Bellingham Music Festival, 233
Belltown Billiards, 182
Ben Franklin Transit, 370
Ben Moore's, 264
Bend, 149–54
Bend Phoenix Inn, The, 152
Benjamin Young Inn, 85
Benson Farmstead Bed & Breakfast, 232
Benson Hotel, The, 24
Benson's Restaurant, 274
Bento Sushi, 188
Benton County Courthouse, 68
Beppe and Gianni's Trattoria, 73
Bert's Restaurant, 422
Best Western Heritage Inn, 235–36
Best Western Lakeside Lodge, 314
Best Western Wesley Inn, 260
BeWon Korean Restaurant, 9
Bicycling, 183
Big Bar Guest Ranch, 564
Big Lava Bed, 364
Big River, 69
Big Rock Garden Park, 233
Big White, 541
Bijou Café, 5, 9
Bilbo's Festivo, 243–44
Bill's Tavern & Brewhouse, 83, 88
Billy Ray's, 241
Billy's Bar and Grill, 342
Bin 941 Tapas Parlour, 417, 420–21
Bin 942 Tapas Parlour, 420–21
Birchfield Manor, 373–74
Bird Song Cottage, 508
Bishop's, 421

Bistro, The, 89
Bistro Maison, 53, 57–58
Bistro Pastis, 421
Black Ball Transport, 473
Black Butte Ranch, 157
Black Diamond, 333
Black Diamond Winery, 289
Black Forest Steak & Schnitzel House, 301
Black Jack Cross-Country Ski Club, 546
Blackcomb Helicopters, 447
Blackcomb Mountain, 446
Blackfish Cafe, 83, 98–99
Blaine, 238–39
Blau Oyster Company, 230–31
Blue C Sushi, 188
Blue Fox Drive-In Theater and Brattland Go-Karts, 225
Blue Grouse Vineyards, 504
Blue Heron Art Center, 251
Blue Heron Bistro, 116
Blue Heron Inn, 358, 466
Blue Sky Cafe, 83, 92
Blue Water Cafe, 417, 421–22
Bluehour, 9–10
Bluewood Ski Resort, 387
Boardwalk Café, 476
Boat Basin, The, 514
Boat Shed, 272
Boatyard Inn, 220
Boccherini's Coffee and Tea House, 67
Boehm's Chocolates, 274
Bold Bluff Retreat, 495–96
Bombs Away Cafe, 69
Bonelli, 490–91
Bonneville Dam, 35–36
Bonneville Fish Hatchery, 35–36
Bonneville Hot Springs Resort, 362
Bonniebrook Lodge, 462–63
Bon's Off Broadway, 422
Bookmark, 416
Boreas Bed & Breakfast, 355
Bosch Garden, 324
Boundary Bay Brewery, 233
Brackendale Art Gallery and Theatre Restaurant, 446
Brady's Oysters, 348
Braeburn, 219
Brandy Peak Distillery, 124–25
Brandywine Falls Park, 446
Brasa, 184–85
Brasserie L'Ecole, 477–78
Bread and Ink Café, 5, 10
Bread and Ocean, 92
Bread and Roses Bakery, 280

Breadboard Restaurant & Bakery, 142
Bremerton, 272
Brew Creek Lodge, 452–53
Brew Pub at Mount Hood Brewing Co., 44
Brewers on the Bay, 102
Brian Scott Gallery & The Snug Ocean View Coffee House, 124
Brian's Pourhouse, 36, 38
Brian's Windsurfing, 36
Brick, The, 331
Bridge of the Gods, 36
Bridges, 342–43, 422
Bridgeview Vineyards & Winery, 135
British Candy Shoppe, 475
British Columbia
Lower Mainland, 442–69
Northern Mainland, 562–72
British Importers, 475
Britt Festival, 138
Broadway Center for the Performing Arts, 253–54
Broken Top Restaurant, 151
Bronco Billy's Ranch Grill and Saloon, 156–57
Bronze Antler B&B, 162, 168
Brookings, 124–26
Budd Bay Cafe, 264
Buena Vista Ferry, 66
Buena Vista House Café and Lodging, 66–67
Bugaboos Bakery Café, 536
Bullards Beach State Park, 117
Bungy Zone, 509–10
Burke Museum of Natural History and Culture, 180
Burns, 172–73
Burrowing Owl Vineyards, 544
Bush House, 53, 64
Butchart Gardens, 475

C

C, 422–23
C & M Stables, 112
Cable Cove Inn, 518
Cachalot, 348
Cache Creek, 531–32
Cafe Brio, 477, 478
Cafe Francais, 112–13
Cafe Italiano, 406
Cafe Juanita, 207
Cafe Langley, 214, 219
Café Luna, 252
Cafe Mango, 89
Cafe Mozart, 323

Café Nicholas, 371, 374
Cafe Olga, 244
Café Pamplona, 479, 517
Café Soriah, 73
Café Toulouse, 233
Caffe Bisbo, 57
Caffe Mingo, 5, 10
Calico Cupboard, 214, 227–28, 240
Calona Wines, 538
Calumet Restaurant, The, 234
Calvin's Bistro, 493
Camano Island, 218
Camano Island Inn, 214, 218
Camaraderie Cellars, 289
Camp Sherman, 157
Campagne, 178, 185
Campbell House, 76
Campbell House Cafe, 314
Campbell River, 522–25
Campbell River Maritime Heritage Center, 523
Campbell's Resort on Lake Chelan, 300, 314–15
Campiche Studios, 354
Campo Marina Italian Restaurant, 544–45
Canadian Snowmobile Adventures, 447
Canadian Western Airlines, 563
Canlis, 185–86
Cannery Cafe, 83–84
Cannery Seafood House, The, 423–24
Cannon Beach, 88–90
Cannon Beach Hotel, 89–90
Cannon Street Grill, 397–98
Canoe Brewpub, The, 476
Canoe Ridge Vineyard, 389
Canoe Room Cafe, The, 350
Canyon Way Restaurant and Bookstore, 103–4
Cap Sante Marina, 240
Cape Arago State Park, 116
Cape Blanco Lighthouse, 120
Cape Blanco State Park, 120
Cape Disappointment State Park, 343, 350
Cape Lookout State Park, 94
Cape Meares Lighthouse, 94
Cape Meares State Park, 94
Cape Perpetua Interpretive Center, 97, 107
Cape Scott Provincial Park, 526
Cape Sebastian, 121
Capilano Suspension Bridge, 439
Capitol Theater, 263

Caprial's Bistro, 10–11
Captain George Flavel House, 82
Captain Jacks, 281
Captain Whidbey Inn, 214, 224
Car rentals, 3, 51, 413
Carambal, 449
Carden Street Café, 488–89
Carlton, 56–57
Carmelita, 186
Carnation, 329
Caroline Inn, 343, 346
Carson, 362–63
Casa Chapala, 381
Cascade Dining Room, 44
Cascade Harbor Inn, 245
Cascade Lakes Area, 148
Cascade Locks, 35–36
Cascades, The
    access to, 129
    map of, 128
    three-day tour of, 132
Cascadia Restaurant, 186
Cashmere, 327
Castagna, 5, 11
Castle Rock, 358
Castlebury Cottage, 508
Caswell's on the Bay Bed & Breakfast, 357
Catacombs Pub, 398–99
Caterina Winery, 403
Caterina's Trattoria, 138–39
Cayuse Vineyards, 389
Cedar Grill, 116
Cedarbrook Herb Farm, 285
Cedars Pier 1, 381
Celilo Falls, 45
Cellar Jazz Club, 419
Central Cascades, 318–37
Central Coast Watersports, 112
Central Library, 6
Central Mountain Air, 529, 563
Central Washington Agricultural Museum, 371
Central Washington University, 371
Central Whidbey Chamber of Commerce, 223
Centre for the Arts and Kelowna Art Gallery, 538
Century Ballroom, 182
C'est Si Bon, 270, 289–90
Chamber Music Northwest, 7
Champagne Creek, 130
Champoeg State Park, 62
Channel House, 102
Chanterelle, 73–74, 213
Chanticleer Inn, 143 .
Charburger, 36
Charles at Smugglers Cove, 217

Charleston, 114–17
Charleston Station, 114, 115
Chartwell, 424
Chateau Ste. Michelle, 208
Chateau Westport, 348
Chateaulin, 142
Chauntecleer House, Dove House, and Potting Shed Cottages, 220–21
Cheesemonger's Shop, The, 321
Chef Bernard's Café, 449
Chelan, 96, 313–15
Chemainus, 507–8
Cherry Point Vineyards, 504
Chestnut Cottage, 290
Chetco River Inn Bed and Breakfast Retreat, 125–26
Chetzemoka Park, 280
Chewelah, 405
Chez Chaz Bistro, 381–82
Chez Philippe, 462
Chicken-n-More, 399
Chicochai Antiques, 417
Chief Timothy State Park, 384
Children's Museum, 180
Children's Museum 2nd Generation (CM2), 4
Chilliwack, 458
Chilliwack Museum, 458
Chimacum Cafe, 278
China Beach Retreat, 343, 351
China Bend Winery, 405
Chinaberry Hill, 257
Chinatown, 417
Chinese Classical Garden, 415
Chinoise Café, 179, 186
Chinook, 349
Chinook's at Salmon Bay, 187
Chiso, 188
Chives, 122
Chocolates by Bernad Callebaut, 476
Christina's, 244
Chrysalis Inn & Spa, The, 236
Chuckanut Drive, 230–32
Chuck's Seafood, 115
Churchyard Inn B&B, The, 391
CinCin Restaurant & Bar, 424
Cinedome Theater, The, 358
Cinnamon Twisp, 300, 311
Cioppino's Enoteca, 424–25
Cioppino's Mediterranean Grill, 424–25
Circolo, 425
Clallam Bay, 292–93
Clark County Historical Museum, 359

clarklewis, 11
Clayoquot Wilderness Resorts, 518–19
Cle Elum, 331–32
Clementine's Bed and Breakfast, 85
Cliff House (Freeland), 222
Cliff House (Tacoma), 255
Cliff House at Arbor Crest Wine Cellars, 402
Cliff House Bed and Breakfast, 106
Clinton, 564–65
Clyde, The, 219
Clymer Museum and Gallery, 371
Coachhouse on Oyster Bay, A, 499
Coast Cabins, 93
Coast Inn of the North, 570
Coast Wenatchee Center Hotel, 329
Coeur D'Alene Resort, 395
Coho Charters, 350
Cola Diner, 511
Collector's Choice, 217
Colophon Café, The, 234
Columbia Gorge, 352
Columbia Gorge Discovery Center, 45
Columbia Gorge Hotel, 36, 39
Columbia Gorge Interpretive Center, 361
Columbia River Exhibition of History, Science & Technology, 379–80
Columbia River Gorge, 32–48, 361
Columbia River Gorge National Scenic Area, 34
Columbia River Gorge Visitors Association, 34
Columbia River Maritime Museum, 82
Columbia Winery, 208
Columbian Cafe, 83–84
Colville, 405–6
Commodore Ballroom, 419
Common Load Bake Shop, 516
Comox, 521–22
Comox Valley, The, 520
Condon, 164
Condos at Wapato Point, 313
Connie Hansen Garden, 97
Contemporary Crafts Museum & Gallery, 6
Contemporary Theatre, 181
Cooley's Iris Display Gardens, 63
Coombs, 478
Cooper Beech House, 572
Cooper Spur, 43
Coos Art Museum, 115

Coos Bay, 114–17
Coos Bay Manor Bed & Breakfast, 116–17
Copalis, 346–47
Coppa Mediterranean Bistro, 234–35
Copper Kettle, 541
Copper Maker Gallery, The, 526
Coquille River Lighthouse, 117
Corpeny's, 86–87
Corvallis, 67–71
Corvallis Art Center, 68
Cottage Coffee Shop, The, 423
Cottons, 226
Cougar Mountain Wilderness Adventures, 447
Coulee Dam Casino, 407
Country Cottage B&B, 464–65
Country Cupboard Cafe, 485
Country Village Nutrition Shoppe and Cafe, 357
Country Willows Inn, 143–44
Coupeville, 223–24
Courtenay, 521–22
Covered Bridge Society of Oregon, 67–68
Cow Bay Café, 565, 570
Cowboy Cafe, 163
Cowichan Bay, 505–6
Cowichan Trading, 476
Cowichan Valley, 504–5
Cowslip's Belle, 132, 144
Cozy Rose Private Country Suites, 378
Craigdarroch Castle, 475, 477
Cranberry Museum and Gift Shop, 354
Crater Lake Lodge, 148
Crater Lake National Park, 132, 147–48
Craterian Ginger Rogers Theater, 136
Crawford Bay, 550
Creek at Qualchan, 407
Creek Town Café, 374, 383
Crocodile Cafe, 182
Crooked River Dinner Train, 155
Crosby Library, 397
Cross-country skiing, 305
Crossroads Shopping Center, 205
Crow and Gate Neighbourhood Pub, 478, 508–9
Crown Isle Resort & Golf Community, 520
Cru, 425
Crystal Crane Hot Springs, 172
Crystal Mountain, 334

Crystal Springs Rhododendron Garden, 6
Crystal Waters Guest Ranch, 566
Cucina Biazzi, 142–43
Cuneo Cellars, 56
Cup of Magic, A, 132
Cypress Park, 464

D

Dahlia Lounge, 187
Dalles, The, 41–42
Dalles Convention & Visitors Bureau, The, 45
Dalles Dam, The, 42
Dams
   Bonneville Dam, 35
   Dalles Dam, The, 42
   Grand Coulee Dam, 397, 406–7
Dancing Coyote Gallery, 100
Daniel's Broiler Prime Steak & Chops, 187–88
Darlingtonia Botanical Wayside, 112
Davenport Hotel, 397, 401–2
Daystar Market Café, 500
Dayton (OR), 55–56
Dayton (WA), 387–89
Deception Pass State Park, 214, 225
Deep Cove Chalet, 489
Deer Harbor Inn and Restaurant, 245
Delicado's, 509
Delta Victoria Ocean Pointe Resort and Spa, 476, 482
Delta Whistler Resort, 453
Deming, 301
Demitasse Café, 476
Denino Umpqua River Vineyards, 130
Denman Bakery and Pizzeria, 502
Denman Café, The, 502
Denman Island, 502–3
Den's Wood Den, 276
Depoe Bay, 100–102
Depot Restaurant, The, 351–52
Deschutes River Area, 155
Deschutes State Park, 42
Desolation Resort, 469
Diablo, 304
Diamond, 173
Diamond Lake, 148
Die Musik Box, 322
Dimitriou's Jazz Alley, 182
Dina's Place, 447, 457
Dinghy Dock, 509

Dining Room at the Aerie Resort, The, 490–91
Dinner at Dykstra House Restaurant, 374
Discovery Islands, 503–4
Discovery Park, 181
Diva at the Met, 425–26
D&M Coffee, 371
Doc Willoughby's Downtown Grill, 539
Dock 503, 489
Dock of the Bay Marina, 105
Dog House, 219
Dolce Skamania Lodge, 362
Dolphin Bay Bicycles, 243
Domaine Madeleine, 290–91
Donut House, The, 240
Dorris Ranch Living History Farm, 78
Douglas County Museum of History and Natural History, 130
Dr. Sun Yat-Sen Classical Chinese Garden, 416
Dragon Fire Gallery, 88
Dream Weaver Bed & Breakfast, 506
Drift Inn, The, 107
Duck Brand Hotel & Cantina, 300, 308
Duck Soup Inn, 248
Duncan, 506–7
Dundee, 54–55
Dundee Bistro, 54–55
Dungeness Crab & Seafood Festival, 289
Dungeness Spit, 285–86
Dungeness Valley, 285–87
Durlacher Hof Alpine Country Inn, 453
Dusty Strings, 181
Dutch Bakery, 238
Dykstra House Restaurant, 377

E

Eagle Aerie Gallery, 516
Eagle Bluff Bed & Breakfast, 565, 571
Eagle Cabs, 572
Eagle Cap Wilderness Pack Station, 162, 166
Eagle Creek Winery, 322
Eagle Nook Ocean Wilderness Resort, 515
Eagle Point Inn, 294
Eaglecrest, 511
Eagle's View Bed & Breakfast, 95–96
Earshot Jazz Festival, 182

Earthen Works, 280
Earthworks Gallery, 106
East & West Cafe, 255
East King County Convention & Visitors Bureau, 205
Eastern Oregon, 160–74
Eastside, 205
Eatonville, 335
Echo Valley Ranch Resort, 564–65
Eclectic Med Restaurant, 536, 538
Ecola Seafood Market, 88
Ecola State Park, 83, 88, 97
Eco-Treks Adventure, 570
Edel Haus, 323
Eden Hall, 99
Edenwild Inn, 242
Edgefield, 16
Edgewater, The, 200
Edgewater Cottages, 106
Edgewater Lodge, 447, 453–54
Edmonds, 213
Edmonds Harbor Inn, 213
Edwin K Bed & Breakfast, 113–14
Egmont, 467
El Gaucho (Portland), 5, 11–12
El Gaucho (Seattle), 188
El Gaucho (Tacoma), 255
Elevated Ice Cream, 280
Elixir, 426
Elk Cove Vineyards, 29
Elk Lake, 155
Elk Lake Resort, 155
Elk Public House, The, 399
Ellensburg Valley, 370–72
Elliott Bay Book Co., 178, 182
Elliott's Oyster House, 178, 189
Elusive Trout Pub, The, 48
Embassy Suites Portland Downtown, 24
Emerald Lake Lodge, 557
Emily Carr House, 475
Emily Carr Institute of Art and Design, 415
Emory's Lake House, 215
Enchanted Forest, 64
Encore! Theater, 260
End of the Oregon Trail Interpretive Center, 30
Engine House No 9, 254
Englishman River Falls Provincial Park, 510
Enterprise, 166
ER Rogers Mansion, 262
Ernest Bloch Music Festival, 101
Esmeralda Golf Course, 407
Esparza's Tex-Mex Café, 12
Eugene, 71–76

Eugene Airport, 51
Euphoria, 71
Eva Restaurant and Wine Bar, 189
Everett, 214–16
Everett Events Center, 215
Everett Performing Arts Center, 215
Evergreen Aviation Museum, 53, 57
Evergreen State College, The, 263
Everson, 301
Excelsior Inn, 76
Excelsior Inn Ristorante Italiano, 74
Express Cuisine, 252
Ezogiku Noodle Cafe, 426
Ezra Meeker Mansion, 258

F

Fairburn Farm, 507
Fairhaven Village Inn, 236
Fairmont Chateau Whistler Resort, 454
Fairmont Empress Hotel, 474–75, 483
Fairmont Hot Springs, 555
Fairmont Hot Springs Resort, 555
Fairmont Hotel Vancouver, 434
Fairmont Olympic Hotel, 200
Fairmont Vancouver Airport Place, 438–39
Fairwinds, 510
Falcon's Crest Inn, 44
Fall Kite Festival, 101
Fanny Bay, 520–21
Father's Country Inn, 534–35
Favell Museum of Western Art and Indian Artifacts, 145
Feenie's, 426–27
Fenn Lodge Bed & Breakfast Retreat, 459–60
Fenton & Lee, 71
Fernando's Hideaway, 12
Fernie, 554–55
Ferry
    BC Ferries, 413, 461, 473, 492, 564
    Washington State Ferry, 179, 213, 239, 251, 269, 473
Festivals, 101, 115, 233, 304, 418
Fiddlehead Bistro, 300, 311
Fiddler's Green, 551–52
Fidel's, 352, 363
Fifth Avenue Public Market, 72
5th Avenue Suites Hotel, 5, 24–25
5th Avenue Theatre, 181
Fillongley Provincial Park, 502
Fiorella's, 146
Firehouse, The, 114

Firehouse Restaurant, 113
Fire's Eye, 60
First Presbyterian Church, 254
Fish Bowl, The, 219–20
Fish House at Stanley Park, The, 427
Fishing, 45
Five SeaSuns, 291
Fiery Manor, 134
Fleuri, 417
Florence, 112–13
Flo's Starboard Café, 468
Flounder Bay Cafe, 241
Fly Fisher's Place, The, 156
Flying Dutchman Winery, 100
Flying Fish, 189–90
Flying L Ranch, 364–65
Flying M Ranch, 56
Flying U Guest Ranch, 566
Foley Station, 164–65
Forest Grove, 29
Forest Park, 6, 8
Foris Vineyards, 132, 135
Forks, 293–95
Fort Casey Inn, 224
Fort Casey State Park, 223
Fort Clatsop National Memorial, 82–83, 385
Fort Columbia State Park, 349
Fort Dalles Museum, 42
Fort Ebey State Park, 214, 223
Fort Flagler State Park, 279
Fort Langley, 458
Fort Rock State Monument, 147
Fort Simcoe State Park, 376
Fort Stevens State Park, 82–83
Fort Vancouver, 359
Fort Walla Walla Museum, 374, 383
Fort Worden, 284
Fort Worden State Park, 281
49 Degrees North, 405
42nd Street Café, The, 352–53
Fotheringham House, 402–3
Fountain Cafe, 281
4 Pines Motel, 447, 457
Four Seasons, The, 434
Franz Hardware, 37
Fraser Valley, 458
Fraser-Fort George Regional Museum, 569
Freed Gallery, 98
Freeland, 222
Freeland Café and Lounge, 222
Freestone Inn, 305–6
Freestone Inn and Early Winters Cabin, 306
Frenglen, 173–74

Frenglen Hotel, 174
Fresco, 539
Fresh Palate Café, 60
Friday Harbor House, 249
Friday's Historic Inn, 249–50
From the Bayou, 258–59
Frye Art Museum, 180
Fugazzi, 397
Fujiya, 256
Fulio's Pastaria, 84
Full Sail Brewery and Pub, 37

G

Gaches Mansion, 226
Galiano Inn, 501–2
Galiano Island, 499–502
Galleries
    in Portland, 6
    in Vancouver, 414–15
    in Victoria, 475
    See also specific gallery
Gallery at Salishan, 99
Galway Bay Restaurant & Pub, 343, 345
Gameworks, 179
Garden(s)
    in Portland, 6–7
    in Seattle, 181
    in Vancouver, 415
    in Victoria, 475
    See also specific garden
Garden of the Awakening Orchid, 6
Garden Path Suites, The, 221
Gardner's Seafood and Pasta, 264
Garibaldi, 93–94
Garibaldi Park, 446
Garry Oaks Winery, 492–93
Gas Works Park, 181
Gaskill–Olson Gallery, 219
Gasperetti's Restaurant, 375
Gateway Mall, 77
Gearhart, 86–88
Geiser Grand Hotel, 170
Genoa, 12–13
George, 370
Geppetto's, 240
Gere-A-Deli, 240
Gibsons, 462
Gig Harbor, 259–61
Gig Harbor Kayak Center, 259
Gilbert House Children's Museum, 64
Gilbert Inn, 88
Gilman Village, 210
Gina's, 509
Gina's Bakery, 289
Giorgio's, 13

Girardet, 130
Glacier, 302
Glacier National Park, 531
Gleneden Beach, 99–100
Glenterra Vineyards, 504
Glenwood, 364–65
Go Outside, 226
God's Mountain Crest Chalet, 543
Gold Beach, 121–24
Gold Beach Books and Biscuit Coffeehouse & Art Gallery, 121
Gold River, 525
Golden, 557–58
Golden Valley Brewery & Pub, 53, 58
Goldendale, 365
Goldstream Provincial Park, 490
Golf courses, 407, 538
Gonzaga University, 396
Gorge Rowing and Paddling Centre, 477
Gotham Steakhouse & Cocktail Bar, 427
Governor Hotel, The, 25
Grand Central Emporium, 500
Grand Coulee Dam, 397, 406–7
Grand Lodge, 16
Grand Okanagan Lakefront Resort, The, 539–40
Grande Ronde, 60
Grandview, 377–78
Granny Bogner's Restaurant, 542–43
Grant's Brewery Pub, 375
Grants Pass, 133–35
Granville Island, 417
Granville Island Museums, 415
Granville Island Tea Co., 416
Grapefields, 383–84
Grateful Bread Bakery, 95
Gray Line Airport Express, 178
Grayline of Portland Airport Express, 3
Grays Harbor, 342
Great American Smokehouse & Seafood Company, The, 125
Great Columbia Crossing and Silver Salmon Festival, 101
Great Times, 223
Greater Newport Chamber of Commerce, 82
Green Gables Inn, 386
Green Turtle, The, 260
Greenbank, 222–23
Greenhouse, 233
Greenwater, 334
Greyhound, 4

Greystone Manor, 522
Grimm's Gourmet & Deli, 447, 455
Griz Inn Sport Hotel, 554–55
Grouse Mountain, 464
Grove Cantina, The, 132
Groveland Cottage, 287
Guest House Log Cottages, 222–23
Guides Hut, The, 554
Gulf Islands, The, 491–92
Gulf Islands Kayaking, 500
Gumboot Garden Café, 463–64
Gunner's Cycle and X-Country Ski Shop, 567
Gusto di Quattro, 439
Gwaii Haanas National Park Reserve, 571

H
Habibi's, 427–28
Hacienda del Mar, 290
Haida Gwaii, 571–72
Haida Gwaii Museum, 565, 571
Haines, 169–70
Haines Steak House, 170
Halcyon Hot Springs Resort, 548
Halfway, 168–69
Haller Fountain, 280
Hallie Ford Museum of Art, 64
Hamilton River House, 133
Hampton Inn, 374, 380
Hangman Valley, 407
Hans, 151
Hanson Country Inn, 53, 70–71
Hansville, 275
Harbinger Inn, 265
Harbor Lights, 256
Harbour Air, 474
Harbour Air Seaplanes, 563
Harbour Grill, 500
Harbour View Bistro, 520
Harbourlynx, 509
Harp's on the Bay Restaurant, 118
Harris Beach State Park, 124
Harrison Hot Springs Hotel, The, 460
Harrison House Bed and Breakfast, 71
Harrison House Suites, 250
Harrison Lake, 459–60
Harry and David's Country Village, 132, 136
Hart Mountain National Antelope Refuge, 174
Hartmann House, 486
Harvest Vine, 190

Hastings House, 494, 496
Hastings House/Old Consulate Inn, 284
Haterleigh Heritage Inn, A, 483
Hatfield Marine Science Center, 103
Haus Rohrbach Pension, 324
Hawk Creek Cafe, 96
Hawthorne District, 5
Hawthorne Street Alehouse, 5
Haystack Rock, 88
Heathman Hotel, The, 5, 25
Heathman Lodge, 352, 361
Heathman Restaurant and Bar, The, 13
Heceta Head Lighthouse, 112
Hedges Cellars, 388
Heirloom Old Garden Roses, 62
Helijet International, 473–74
Hellebore Glass Gallery, 219
Hellgate Jetboat Excursions, 133
Hells Canyon, 163–64, 169
Henderson Books, 233
Hendricks Park, 72
Henry Art Gallery, 180
Henry Estate Winery, 130
Herald Street Caffe, 478–79
Herbfarm, The, 209
Heritage Museum, 82
Heron and Beaver Pub, The, 353
Heron Haus Bed and Breakfast, 25–26
Heron Inn & Watergrass Day Spa, 229
Heron's Nest, 251
Hi Strung Music & Pickin' Parlor, 322
Hidden Cove Lodge, 526
Hidden Valley Guest Ranch, 331–32
Higgins, 5, 13–14
High Desert Museum, 132, 150
Highland Inn, 250
Highway 99, 444
Hillcrest, 130
Hills Health and Guest Ranch, The, 567–68
Hill's Someplace Else, 399–400
Hillsdale Brewery and Pub, 16
Hillside Lodge & Chalets, 557–58
Hilltop Restaurant, 390
Hilton Eugene and Conference Center, 76–77
Hilton Seattle Airport Hotel, 210
Historic Columbia River Highway, 36–37
Historic Mission Mill Village, 64

Hogue Cellars, 388
Hoh River Valley, 293
Holly B's Bakery, 241
Hollyford Bed & Breakfast, 512
Holt Renfrew, 416
Home by the Sea Bed and Breakfast, 121
Homegrown Cafe, The, 252–53
Homestead Farms Golf Resort, 238
Hon's Wun Tun House, 428
Hood Canal, 276–85
Hood River, 36–40
Hood River County Chamber of Commerce, 37
Hood River Hotel, 39
Hoodsport Winery, 276
Hope, 460
Hoquiam, 342–44
Hoquiam's Castle Bed & Breakfast, 344
Horizon Air, 111
Hornby Island, 502–3
Horseback riding, 112
Horstings Farm Market, 532
Hot Chocolates, 521
Hot Springs Cove Lodge, 516
Hotel Bellwether, 236
Hotel Condon, 164
Hotel Diamond, 173
Hotel Eldorado, 540
Hotel Elliott, 83, 85–86
Hotel Le Soleil, 435
Hotel Lucia, 26
Hotel Lusso, 397, 403–4
Hotel Monaco, 200–201
Hotel Oregon, 58–59
Hotel Packwood, 337
Hotel Pension Anna, 324
Hotel Planter, 229
Hotel Rio Vista, 309
Hotel Vintage Park, 201
Hotel Vintage Plaza, 26
House Alpenglow B&B, 553–54
House of Hewhiwus, 465
House of Himwitsa, 516
House of Myrtlewood, The, 114–15
House Piccolo, 478
Houseboats, 406
Howard Prairie Lake Resort, 140–41
Howe Sound Inn & Brewing Company, 445–46
Hoyt Arboretum, 5–6
Hoz's Pub & El Tipo's Mexican Grill, 446, 449–50
Huckleberry Lodge, 294

Hudson's Bar & Grill, 352, 360
Hudson's Bay Company Bastion, 509
Hula Grill Cafe, 274
Humbug Mountain State Park, 120
Hummingbird Pub, 500
Hungry Belly, 314
Hunter's Hot Springs, 146
Hurricane Creek Llama Treks, 166

I

Icefire Glassworks, 88
Icicle Creek Music Center, 321
Icicle Ridge Winery, 321
Il Terrazzo Carmine, 190–91
Il Terrazzo Ristorante, 476, 479
Illecillewaet Glacier, 531
Ilwaco, 350–51
Imperial Chinese Seafood
 Restaurant, 428
In Good Taste, 7
Independence, 66–67
India Bistro, 191
India Grill, 233
Indian Salmon Bake, 101
Inn @ Northup Station, 26
Inn at Abeja, 386
Inn at Blackberry Creek, 386
Inn at Eagle Crest, 155–56
Inn at Goose Creek, The, 372
Inn at Harbor Steps, 201–2
Inn at Langley, 214, 221
Inn at Manzanita, The, 83, 93
Inn at Mount Baker, 302
Inn at Nesika Beach, 123
Inn at Port Gardner, The, 216
Inn at Ship Bay, 244
Inn at Spanish Head, 97
Inn at Swifts Bay, 242
Inn at the Market, 202
Inn at Tough City, The, 516
Inn of the Seventh Mountain, 132,
 152
Inn of the White Salmon, 352,
 363–64
Inn on Orcas Island, The, 245
Inn the Garden B&B & Guest
 House, 552
InnChanter, 519
Inner Rhythm Surf Camps, 523
Interlakes District, 566
International Museum of Carousel
 Art, 37
International Pinot Noir
 Celebration, 57
International Rose Test Garden, 5–6
Invermere, 555–56
Iovino's, 53, 69–70

Irish Linen Stores, 475
Iron Horse Inn B&B, 332
Iron Springs Ocean Beach Resort,
 346–47
Island Bagel Company &
 Livingstone's Gourmet Foods,
 506
Island County Historical Museum,
 214, 223
Island Dive & Water Sports, 248
Island Tyme, 221
Issaquah, 210
Italian Kitchen, The, 400

J

J & J Wonton Noodle House, 480
j. james restaurant, 53, 65
Jacksonville, 137–39
Jacksonville Inn, 139
Jacksonville Museum, 132, 138
Jacques' Wine Country Inn, 545
Jake's Famous Crawfish, 14
James House, The, 284–85
Jan's Café, 502
Japanese Garden, 5–6
Jayde, 450
Jazz, 182, 344, 418, 542
Jeffrey Hull Gallery, 88
Jerry's Rogue River Jet Boat Trips,
 121
Jessie M. Honeyman State Park,
 114
jitterbug café, 468
Joan Brown's Bed & Breakfast,
 483–84
Job Carr's Cabin, 253
Joel Palmer House, 53, 55–56
John Day, 170–71
John Horan House, 328
Johnson Heritage House, 435
Jolly Roger Seafoods, 355
Jonsrud Viewpoint, 48
Joseph, 166–68
Juan de Fuca Cottages, 287

K

Kaboodles Toy Store, 476
Kahler Glen Golf and Ski Resort,
 320
Kah-Nee-Ta High Desert Resort,
 158
Kalypso, 87
Kam Wah Chung Museum, 170–71
Kamiak Butte County Park, 389
Kamloops, 532–34
Karpeles Manuscript Museum, 253

Kaslo, 548–49
Kasteel Franssen, 225
Kayaking, 227, 500
K-Diamond-K Guest Ranch, 405
Kelly's Resort, 315
Kelowna, 538–41
Kenmore Air, 239, 522
Kenmore Air Harbor, 473
Kennedy School, The, 16, 27
Kennewick, 381–82
Kerstin's, 214, 228
Kettle Falls, 405–6
Kettle Valley Steakhouse, 541
Keystone Ferry, 223
Khu Larb Thai II, 286
Khun Pic's Bahn Thai, 14
Kicking Horse Mountain Resort,
 557–58
Kilby Historic Store, 459
Kilby Park, 459
Kimberley, 553–54
Kimberley Alpine Resort, 553–54
Kimberley Sausage and Meats, 553
Kingfish Café, 191
Kingfisher Oceanside Resort and
 Spa, 522
Kirkland, 207–8
Kirkland Performance Center, 207
Kisaku, 188
Kitsap Peninsula, 271
Kitseguecla, 569
Kitsilano, 416
Kitwancool, 568
Kitwanga, 568
Klamath County Museum, 145–46
Klamath Falls, 145–46
Kla-Mo-Ya Casino, 145
Knead & Feed, 214, 223
Knipprath Cellars, 403
Koin Cinemas, 5
Kokanee Cafe, 157
Kokanee Glacier Park, 551
Kootenay Baker, 551
Kootenays, The, 529, 545–48
Kopachuck State Park, 260
Koto Japanese Restaurant, 524
K-R Drive-In, 130
Kramer Vineyards, 29
Kris Kringl, 322
Kruse Farms, 130
'Ksan Historical Village, 569
Kuraya's, 78
Kwinitsa Station Railway Museum,
 570

L

La Calaca Comelona, 14

La Conner, 226–30
La Conner Country Inn, 229
La Garza Cellars & Gourmet
    Kitchen, 130
La Grande, 164–65
La Morenita Tortilleria, 61
La Presa, 408
La Push, 295
La Régalade, 428
La Rua Restaurante, 450
La Serre, 107–8
La Toscana Winery, 321
Ladysmith, 508–9
Lake Chelan, 312–13
Lake County, 146
Lake Crescent, 291–92
Lake Crescent Lodge, 291–92
Lake Oswego, 30
Lake Quinault, 295–96
Lake Quinault Lodge, 295–96
Lake Wenatchee, 320
Lakedale Resort, 247
Lakeview, 146
Lakewold Gardens, 254
Lampreia, 191–92
Lang Vineyards, 543
Langley, 219–22
Langley Village Bakery, 219
Lark, 192
Larrabee State Park, 231
Laslow's Northwest, 15
Latah Creek Wine Cellars, 402
Latch Dining Rooms, The, 489–90
Laughing Oyster Restaurant, The,
    469
Laurel Ridge Winery, 29
Lava Lands Visitor Center, 149
Lawrence Gallery, 59–60
Le Bistro, 70
Le Bouchon, 15
Le Crocodile, 428–29
Le Gourmand, 192–93
Le Pichet, 193
Leavenworth, 322–27
L'Ecole No. 41, 389
Left Coast Siesta, 91
Lefty's, 511–12
Legends Casino, 376
Lemon Grass Café, 233
Lemongrass Thai, 15
Les Schwab Amphitheater, 150
Lewis and Clark College, 30
Lewis and Clark Trail State Park,
    384
Liberty Bay Bakery and Cafe, 274
Liberty Lake, 407
Liberty Orchards, 327

Lighthouse(s), 83, 88, 94, 102,
    112, 114, 117, 120
Lighthouse Bed and Breakfast,
    115, 120
Lighthouse Brewpub, 97
Lighthouse Park, 417
Lil' Bayou, 87
Lillooet, 447, 456–57
Lillooet Bakery, 457
Lincoln City, 96–99
Lindaman's Gourmet To Go, 397,
    400
Lion and the Rose, The, 27
Live to Surf, 523
Lively Park Swim Center, 77–78
Lloyd Center Mall, 7
Local Myth Pizza, 314
LocoMotive Restaurant, The, 74
Lodgings
    in Portland, 24–29
    in Seattle, 199–205
    in Vancouver, 434–38
    in Victoria, 481–84
    in Whistler, 452–55
    See also specific lodging
Loeb Park, 124
Lonesome Cove Resort, 250
Long Beach, 354–55
Long Beach Lodge Resort, 519
Long Beach Peninsula, 348–49
Longhorn Saloon & Grill, 231
Longmire, 337
Longview, 357
Lonny's, 282
Lonsdale Quay, 439
Lopez Island, 241–43
Lord Bennett's, 118
Lost Lake Park, 447
Lost Mountain Lodge, 287
Lost Mountain Winery, 289
Love Dog Café, 241
Lucère, 15–16
Lucy's Table, 16–17
Lumière, 417, 429
Lummi Island, 237–38
Luna, 397, 400
Lund, 468–69
Lund Hotel, 468
Lupita's Restaurant, 61
Lyle, 365
Lyle Hotel, 352, 365
Lynden, 238
Lyons Ferry State Park, 390

M

MacKaye Harbor Inn, 243
MacMaster House, 27

MacMillan Provincial Park, 510–11
Macrina Bakery and Cafe, 179, 193
Made in Oregon, 7
Magenta, 70
Magnolia Hotel & Spa, 477, 484
Mahle House, The, 510
Mail Boat Hydro-Jets, 121
Malahat, 490–91
Malahat Mountain Inn, 491
Malaspina Bus Line, 461
Malay Satay Hut, 193–94
Malheur National Wildlife Refuge,
    172
Mallard's Bistro & Grill, 343
Mallory Hotel, 27
Mama Vallone's Steak House, 331
Manning Park, 460
Manor Farm Inn, 275
Manresa Castle, 282
Manteo Resort, 540–41
Manuel Museum and Studio, 166
Manzanita, 91–93
Manzanita News and Espresso, 91
Marblemount, 303
Marché, 74–75
Marco's Ristorante Italiano, 260
Marcus Whitman, 386–87
Marianna Stoltz House, 404
Marina Village Inn, 216
Marine Discovery Tours, 97
Marine Science Center, 281
Marinepolis Sushi Land, 188
Maritime Inn, The, 261
Marjorie, 194
Marj's Cafe, 565
Mark, The, 264–65
Mark Spencer Hotel, The, 28
Markham House, 486–87
Markus' Wharfside Restaurant, 485
Marrowstone Island, 279
Marsh's Free Museum, 343, 354
Maryhill Museum of Art, 365, 385
Maryhill State Park, 385
Maryhill Winery, 365
Marymoor Park, 207
Marymoor Velodrome, 207
Mary's Peak, 68
Marz Planetary Bistro, 151
Marzano's, 91, 259
Mashiko, 188
Masset Info Centre, 572
Masthead Restaurant, The/
    Chowder Café, 505
Matterson House, 515
Matt's in the Market, 194
Matuskaze, 133

Max & Moritz Spicy Island Food House, 500
May Ball Rodeo, 564
May Meadowlark Festival, 541
Mayflower Park Hotel, 202
Mayne Island, 498–99
Mazama, 304–5
Mazama Country Inn, 306–7
Mazama Ranch House, 307
Mazama Village Motor Inn, 148
McCormick & Schmick's Seafood Restaurant, 17
McCully House Inn, 139
McDonald State Forest, 68
McFarlane's Beach, 463
McKenzie River, 71–72
McKenzie View Bed & Breakfast, 78
McKenzie's, 280
McLeod's Department Store, 530
McMenamin's, 16
McMenamin's Edgefield, 35–36
McMenamin's on the Columbia, 352, 360
McMinnville, 57–59
McMinnville Chamber of Commerce, 57
McPherson Playhouse, 477
Meadowlark Guest House, 372–73
Meadowwood, 407
Medford, 136
Melange, 375
Melrose Vineyards, 130
Memorial Coliseum, 8
Memphis Blues Barbeque house, 429–30
Merchants Ltd., 384
Merenda Restaurant and Wine Bar, 132, 151–52
Merino Seafoods, 348
Merridale Cider Works, 504
Merritt, 530–31
Methow Music Festival, 304
Methow Valley, The, 304
Metolius River Resort, 157
Metro Transit, 178
Mexico Lindo, 61
Meydenbauer Center, 205
Middle Beach Lodge, 519–20
Mike's Seafood, 346
Milagros Mexican Folk Art, 181
Milano's Restaurant and Deli, 302
Mill Creek Inn, 66
Mill Resort & Casino, 114
Milner Gardens and Woodland, 511
Mint, 17
Mission Hill Family Estate, 530, 538

Mizuna, 401
Moby Dick Hotel and Oyster Farm, 356
Moby's Marine Pub, 478, 493
Moclips, 347
Molly's Cafe, 423
Mombasa Coffee Company, 289
Momokawa Sake, 29
Mom's Cafe, 485
Monashee Mountains, 538
Monck Park, 530
Monet, 143
Monsoon, 194–95
Montague Harbour Provincial Marine Park, 500
Monte Clark Gallery, 415
Monteith Riverpark, 67
Montinore Vineyards, 29
Montri's Thai Restaurant, 430
Mookie's Place, 78
Moondance, 227
Moran State Park, 243
Morning Star Cafe, 86
Morningside Organic Bakery and Cafe, 493
Morningstar, 510
Morrison's Rogue River Lodge, 134
Morton's Bistro Northwest, 66
Morton's of Chicago, 17
Mosier, 40–41
Mosier House Bed & Breakfast, 41
Mother's, 132
Mother's Bistro & Bar, 5, 17–18
Moulton Falls, 359
Mount Adams, 361–62
Mount Angel, 62
Mount Angel Abbey, 62
Mount Angel Brewing Company, 62
Mount Ashland Inn, 144
Mount Bachelor, 149, 154
Mount Bachelor Village, 153
Mount Bailey, 148
Mount Baker, 299–301
Mount Baker Ski Area, 299–300
Mount Baker Theatre, 233
Mount Baker Vineyards, 233
Mount Currie, 455–56
Mount Hood, 32–34, 43
Mount Hood Hamlet Bed & Breakfast, 37, 44–45
Mount Hood Information Center, 34
Mount Hood Meadows, 43
Mount Hood Railroad, 36–37
Mount Hood Skibowl, 43
Mount Maxwell, 478
Mount Maxwell Provincial Park, 492

Mount Rainier National Park, 332–33
Mount Revelstoke National Park, 531, 558
Mount Seymour Park, 464
Mount St. Helens National Volcanic Monument, 352, 358
Mount Vernon, 226
Mountain Dome Winery, 402
Mountain Home Lodge, 325
Mountain Loop Highway, 310–11
Mountain Meadows Inn and B&B, 336
Mountain Springs Lodge, 320
Mukilteo, 216–17
Mukilteo Ferry, 214
Multnomah Falls Lodge, 34–36
Mulvehill Creek Wilderness Inn, 559
Munro's Books, 476
Munson Creek Falls, 94
Murchie's Tea & Coffee, 475
Murphy's Coffee & Tea Company, 511
Musashi's, 188
Museo, 219
Museum(s)
    in Portland, 6
    in Seattle, 180
    in Vancouver, 414–15
    in Victoria, 475
    See also specific museum
Museum at Campbell River, 523
Museum at Warm Springs, 158
Museum of Anthropology, The, 415
Museum of Flight, 180
Museum of Glass International Center for Contemporary Art, 253
Museum of Northern British Columbia, 570
Museum of Northwest Art, 226
Music festivals, 101, 115, 233, 304, 418
MV Coho, 270
Myrtlewood, 124

N

Naches, 376
Nahcotta, 355–57
Naikoon Provincial Park, 571
Nakusp, 548
Nanaimo, 509–10
Nanaimo Golf Club, 510
Nancy Greene's Cahilty Lodge, 535
Nancy's Bakery, 468
Naramata, 543–44

Nasty Jack's Antiques, 226
Natapoc Lodging, 320–21
National Historic Oregon Trail
　Interpretive Center, 169
Nat's New York Pizzeria, 430
Nature Store, 8
Navarre, 18
Neah Bay, 293
Neahkahnie Mountain, 83, 91
Necanicum River, 86
Nehalem Bay State Park, 91
Nehalem River Inn, 92–93
Neighbors, 182
Nell Thorn Restaurant & Pub,
　214, 228
Nelson, 550–52
Neskowin, 96
New Morning Bakery, 68
New Sammy's Cowboy Bistro,
　132, 139–40
Newberg, 54
Newberry National Volcanic
　Monument, 141, 149
Newport, 102–5
Nichols Brothers Boat Builders, 222
Nickel Plate Nordic Centre, 542
Nick's Italian Café, 58
Nicola Lake, 530
Nightlife
　in Portland, 8
　in Seattle, 182
　in Vancouver, 419
Niko's II Greek and Middle Eastern
　Restaurant, 397, 401
Nishino, 188
Nisqually Lodge, 336
Nisqually National Wildlife Refuge,
　263
Nk'Mip Desert and Heritage
　Centre, 544
Noodles on the Move, 335
Nordland General Store, 279
Nordstrom, 179, 181
North Bend, 114–17
North Cascades, 298–316
North Cascades National Park,
　303–4
North Cascades Scenic Highway,
　302–3
North Fork, The, 301
North Oak Brasserie, 38
North Olympic Peninsula Visitor &
　Convention Bureau, 271
North Pacific Cannery Village
　National Historic Site, 570
North Pender Island, 497
North Vancouver, 439–40
North Vancouver Island, 522–25

Northeast Corner, The, 276–85
Northeastern Washington, 404–9
Northern Lights Expeditions, 227
Northern Oregon Coast, 80–108
　access to, 81–82
　map of, 80
　three-day tour of, 83
Northwest Asian American Theater,
　179
Northwest Folklife Festival, 182
Northwest Outdoor Center, 183
Notaras Lodge, 397, 408–9
NW 23rd Avenue, 5, 7
Nye Beach Hotel & Café, 104–5

O

"O Canada" House, 435
Oak Harbor, 225
Oak Table Cafe, 286
¡Oba!, 18
Ocean, 348
Ocean Crest Resort, 347
Ocean Inn, 93
Ocean Lodge, The, 90
Ocean Palace, 344
Ocean Park, 355–57
Ocean Shores, 342, 344–46
Oceanaire Seafood Room, The,
　195
Oceania Chinese & Continental
　Restaurant, 565
Oceanic Arts Center, 102
Oceanside, 94–95
Oceanwood Country Inn, 499
Odell Lake, 149
Odell Lake Lodge and Resort, 149
O'dysius Hotel, 99
Odyssey, The Maritime Discovery
　Center, 180
Okanagan Valley, The, 535–36
Okeover Arm Park, 468
Oktoberfest, 62
Old Aurora Colony Museum, 62
Old Bauernhaus, 553
Old City Hall, 254
Old Dutch Inn, 512
Old House Restaurant, The,
　521–22
Old Morris Tobacconists, 476
Old Parkdale Inn, 46
Old Tower House, The, 117
Old Town Cafe, 162, 167
Old Welches Inn, 47
Olive Shoppe, 226
Oliver, 544–45
Olympia, 262–65
Olympic Cellars Winery, 289

Olympic Game Farm, 285
Olympic National Park, 288
Olympic Peninsula, 267–96
Olympic Raft and Kayak Service,
　289
Omak, 409
112, The, 531, 558
100 Mile House, 567–68
Opera, 181–82, 418
Opus Hotel, 416, 435–36
Orange Torpedo Trips, 133
Orcas Hotel, 243
Orcas Island, 243–47
Orchard In B&B, 375
Oregon
　Eastern, 160–74
　Southern, 128–58
　See also specific city
Oregon Ballet Theater, 7
Oregon Cabaret Theater, 137
Oregon Candy Farm, 48
Oregon Caves Lodge, 135
Oregon Caves National
　Monument, 135–36
Oregon City, 30
Oregon Coast
　Northern, 80–108
　Southern, 110–26
Oregon Coast Aquarium, 83, 103
Oregon Coast Music Festival, 115
Oregon Coast Trail, 82, 121
Oregon Department of
　Transportation, 33, 52, 161
Oregon Dunes National Recreation
　Area, 113, 123
Oregon History Center, 4–5
Oregon Islands National Wildlife
　Refuge, 116
Oregon Museum of Science and
　Industry, 4
Oregon Shakespeare Festival, 132
Oregon State Fair, 64
Oregon State University, 68
Oregon Symphony Orchestra, 7
Oregon Tea Garden, 63
Oregon Wine Advisory Board,
　52–53
Oregon Wine Tasting Room, 60
Oregon Zoo, 4, 5
Osoyoos, 530, 544–45
Oswald West State Park, 91
Otto's, 48
Our Cappuccino Corner, 554
Out 'n' About Treesort, 135–36
Outlook, 377–78
Outlook Guest House, 378
Outlook Inn, 245–46
Ouzeri, 430

Over the Moon Café, 256
Owen's Meats, 321
Oyster Bar on Chuckanut Drive, 231
Oystercatcher, The, 223–24
Oystercatcher Seafood Bar & Grill, The, 494
Oysterville, 355–57

P

Pacific Beach, 347
Pacific Bento, 86
Pacific Cafe, 235
Pacific Centre, 416
Pacific City, 95–96
Pacific Coastal Airlines, 461, 522
Pacific Dunes Golf Course, 114–15
Pacific Northwest Ballet, 181
Pacific Ocean, 295
Pacific Ocean Victoria, 477
Pacific Oyster Company, 93
Pacific Rim National Park Reserve, 514
Pacific Science Center, 180
Pacific Way Bakery & Cafe, 87
Padilla Bay National Estuarine Research Reserve and Breazeale Interpretive Center, 230
Painter's Lodge, 524
Palace Kitchen, 195–96
Paley's Place, 18–19
Palisade, 196
Palmers at the Lighthouse, 228
Palotai Vineyards, 130
Palouse Falls State Park, 390
Pan Pacific Hotel, 436
Pan Pacific Lodge, 454
Panama Hotel, 202–3
Panini Bakery, 102
Panorama Mountain Village, 556
Pantages Theater, 254
Panzanella Artisan Bakery and Italian Deli, 36, 38–39
Papa Haydn, 19
Paprika, 401
Paradise, 337
Paradise Cabaret Theatre, 260
Paramount Hotel, The, 28
Paramount Theatre, 181
Park(s)
    in Portland, 6–7
    in Seattle, 181
    in Vancouver, 415
    in Victoria, 475
    See also specific park
Park Bench, The, 396

Parker House Bed and Breakfast, 163
Parkland, 258–59
Parkside, 430–31
Parksville, 510–11
Pasco, 382
Pateros, 312
Patit Creek Restaurant, 387
Paulina Peak, 132
Pauly's Bistro, 343, 350
Pavé, 215
Pavz, 321–23
Pearl District, 5–7
Pearl's on Pearl Wine Bar & Bistro, 371–72
Peavy Arboretum, 68
Peco's Pit BBQ, 179
Peerless Hotel, 144–45
Pelican Pub & Brewery, 83
Pemberton, 455–56
Pend Oreille, 404–5
Pender Harbour, 466–67
Pendleton, 161–63
Pendleton Underground Tours, 161–62
Pendleton Woolen Mills, 161
Peninsula Gardens Nursery, 260
Pensione Nichols, 203
Penticton, 541–43
Pepper Sisters, 235
Performing arts
    in Portland, 7–8
    in Seattle, 181–82
    in Vancouver, 418
    in Victoria, 477
Petals Garden Cafe, 286
Peter Kirk Park, 207
PGE Park, 8
Pheasant Valley Orchards Bed and Breakfast, 40
Pho Van, 19
PICA, 8
Piccadilly Circus, 217
Pike Place Market, 179
Pilot Butte State Park, 132, 150
Pine Ridge Inn, 153
Pine Room Cafe, 172–73
Pine Tavern Restaurant, 152
Pinewoods Dining Room, 460
Pinnacles Suite Hotel, 538
Pioneer Courthouse Square, 4
Pioneer Museum, 238
Pioneer Place, 7
Pioneer Square, 179–80
Pizza 'A Fetta, 83, 88
Place Bar & Grill, The, 248
Plain, 320–21
Plainfield's Mayur, 19–20

Poets Cove Seaside Resort, 497
Point Atkinson, 417
Point Defiance Park, 254
Point Ellice House, 475
Point No Point Resort, 487
Point No Point Restaurant, 485–86
Pointe Restaurant, The, 479, 517
Ponderosa Guest Ranch, The, 171
Pony Espresso, 455
Port Alberni, 513
Port Angeles, 288–91
Port Book and News, 289
Port Gamble, 275
Port Gamble General Store, 270
Port Hadlock, 278–79
Port Hardy, 526
Port Ludlow, 278
Port McNeill, 525–26
Port Orchard, 271–72
Port Orford, 120–21
Port Orford Breadworks, 120
Port Townsend, 280–85
Port Townsend Antique Mall, 280
Port Townsend Chamber of Commerce Visitor Information Center, 271
Porteau Cove Park, 446
Portland
    access to, 3–4
    attractions in, 4–6
    galleries in, 6
    gardens in, 6–7
    lodgings in, 24–29
    map of, 2
    museums in, 6
    nightlife in, 8
    parks in, 6–7
    performing arts in, 7–8
    recreation in, 8
    restaurants in, 8–23
    shopping in, 7
    sports in, 8
    three-day tour of, 5
    transportation to, 3–4
Portland Art Museum, 5–6
Portland Beavers, 8
Portland Center for the Performing Arts, 7
Portland Center Stage, 7
Portland Guest House, 28
Portland Institute for Contemporary Art, 8
Portland International Airport, 3
Portland Spirit, 5
Portland Streetcar, 4
Portland Timbers, 8
Portland Trail Blazers, 8
Portland Winter Hawks, 8

Portland's White House, 28
Portofino, 265
Portteus, 388
Poulsbo, 274–75
Powell River, 467–68
Powell's City of Books, 5–7
Prairie City, 171
Primo Grill, The, 256–57
Prince George, 569–70
Prince George Airport, 563
Prince of Whales, 477
Prince Rupert, 570–71
Prince Rupert Water Taxi, 565
Prior House, 476
Prior House Bed & Breakfast Inn, 476, 484
Prosser, 379
Public House, The, 282
Puget Sound, 212–66
Puget Sound Express, 281
Pullman, 389–91
Punjabi Market, 417–18
Purple House B&B Inn, 388
Puyallup, 258
Pyrde Vista Golf Course, 510
Pyromania Glass Studio, 102
Pythian Lodge, 254

Q
Qualicum Beach, 511–12
Quality Bakery, The, 555–56
Qualman Oyster Farms, 115
Quamichan Inn, The, 506–7
Quatat Marine Park, 86
Quattro at Whistler, 450–51
Quattro on Fourth, 431
Queen Charlotte Islands, 571–72
Quilcene, 278
Quilt Museum, 226
Quimper Inn, 270
Quimper Inn Bed and Breakfast, 285
Quinault Beach Resort and Casino, 344
Quw'utsun' Cultural and Conference Centre, 506

R
Radium Hot Springs, 556
Raincity Grill, 431
RainCoast Café, 517–18
Raindrop Café, 270
Ram's Head, The, 5
Ram's Head Inn, 530, 547–48
Raphael's, 162

Rathtrevor Beach Provincial Park, 510
Raven Street Market Café, 493
Ray Klebba's White Salmon Boat Works, 363
Ray's Boathouse, 196
RD Steeves Imports, 56
Re-Bar Modern Foods, 478, 480
Recreation
   in Portland, 8
   in Seattle, 182–83
   in Vancouver, 419
   in Victoria, 477
Red Agave, 53, 75
Red Heather Grill & Brew Pub, 445
Red Hills Provincial Dining, 55
Red Lion Hotel Pasco, 382
Red Lion Silverdale Hotel, 274
Red Mountain Ski Area, 546
Red Rooster Winery, 543
Red Star Tavern & Restaurant, 20
Redhook Ale Brewery, 208–9
Redmond (OR), 155–56
Redmond (WA), 206–7
Redmond Town Center and Cinemas, 207
Reedsport, 113–14
Reflections Bed and Breakfast Inn, 272
Regional Arts and Culture Council, 6
Reiersgaard Theatre, 7
Rendezvous Grill and Tap Room, The, 47
Resort at Port Ludlow, The, 278
Resort at the Mountain, The, 47–48
Resort Semiahmoo, 238–39
Restaurant(s)
   in Portland, 8–23
   in Seattle, 183–99
   in Vancouver, 420–34
   in Victoria, 477–81
   in Whistler, 448–52
   See also specific restaurant
Restaurant House Piccolo, 494
Restaurant Murata, 20
Revelstoke, 558–59
Rhododendron Cafe, The, 231
Rhododendron Festival, 281
Rice Bowl Restaurant, 530
Ricenroll, 188
Richland, 379–80
Richmond, 438–39
Richview House, 487
Ridgefield National Wildlife Refuge, 359

Rim Rock Cafe and Oyster Bar, 451
Ring of Fire, 75
Rising Sun Farm, 132
River Gallery, 66
Riverfront Park, 53, 68
Riverland Motel, 533–34
RiverPlace Hotel, 29
Riverrun Coffee, 270
Rivers Restaurant, 20
Riverside Coliseum, 532–33
Riverside Inn, 133
Roberts Creek, 463–65
Robin Hood, 277–78
Roche Harbor Resort, 250–51
Rock Cod Café, 505
Rock Springs Guest Ranch, 153
Rockwood Bakery, 396
Rocky Mountain Pizza & Bakery, 468
Rodeway Inn, The, 409
Rodney's Oyster House, 417, 432
Roger's Chocolates, 475–76
Rogue Ales Public House, 102
Rogue Outdoor Store, 121
Rogue River Valley, The, 133
Rogue Valley Creamery, 132
Romeo Inn, 145
Romul's, 42
Roots Restaurant, 360
Roozengarde, 214
Rosario Resort & Spa, 246
Rose French Bakery and Pastry Shop, 240
Rose Garden Arena, 8
Roseanna's Oceanside Café, 94–95
Rosebriar Hotel, 86
Roseburg, 129–31
Roseburg Station Pub & Brewery, 130–31
Rosewood Cafe, 531, 549
Rosewood Country House Bed and Breakfast, 463
Roslyn, 331
Ross Lake, 304
Ross Ragland Theater, 146
Rossland, 546–48
Rover's, 196–97
Royal British Columbia Museum, 475
Royal Roads University, 484–85
Royal Victoria Tours, 270
Ruby Lake Resort, 466–67
Ruckle Provincial Park, 492
Run of the River, 325
Running Y Ranch Resort, 145
Ryan Gallery, 97

S

Sacajawea State Park, 379, 384–85
Saddleback Lodge Bed & Breakfast, The, 542
Safeco Field, 182–83
Saffron Salmon, 104
Sage Country Inn, 173
Saito's Japanese Cafe & Bar, 197
Salem, 61, 64–66
Salem Chamber of Commerce, 64
Salem Visitor Information Center, 64
Salish Lodge & Spa, 321, 330
Salishan Lodge & Golf Resort, 100
Salt Spring Island, 492–96
Salt Spring Vineyards, 493
Salumi, 197
Salvador's Bakery, 61
Samish Point by the Bay, 232
Samovar, 136
Sam's Deli, 476–77
Samuel H. Boardman Park, 124
San Juan Island, 247–51
San Juan Island Bed and Breakfast Association, 247
San Juan Island Commuter, 234
San Juan Safaris, 227
Sanctuary Restaurant, The, 349
Sandpiper, 347
Sandy, 48
Sandy Beach Lodge & Resort, 543–44
Sanmi Sushi, 188
Sans Souci, 205–6
Santosh, 264
Sarah Spurgeon Gallery, 371
Saratoga Inn, 221–22
Sasquatch Trading, 476
Saturna Island, 498
Saturna Island Vineyards, 498
Saturna Lodge and Restaurant, 498
Saucebox, 21
Savary Island Pie Company, 417
Savoure, 71
Scandinavian Midsummer Festival, 101
Schnauzer Crossing, 237
Schneider Museum of Art, 140
Schooner on Second, 479, 518
Science Fiction Museum and Hall of Fame, 180
Sea Breeze Charters, 350
Sea Breeze Lodge, 503
Sea Lion Caves, 112, 114
Sea Quest Bed & Breakfast, 108
Sea to Sky Highway, 444, 446–47
Seabeck, 273

Seafood & Wine Festival, 101
Seafood City, 416
Seaside, 86–88
Seaside Visitors Bureau, 82
Seastar Restaurant and Raw Bar, 206
Seattle
    access to, 177–78
    attractions in, 179–80
    gardens in, 181
    information regarding, 177–78
    lodgings in, 199–205
    map of, 176
    museums in, 180
    nightlife in, 182
    parks in, 181
    performing arts, 181–82
    recreation in, 182–83
    restaurants in, 183–99
    shopping in, 181
    sports in, 182–83
    three-day tour of, 178–79
Seattle Aquarium, 180
Seattle Art Museum, 178, 180
Seattle Asian Art Museum, 181
Seattle Center, 180
Seattle Children's Theatre, 181
Seattle City Light, 304
Seattle International Film Festival, 182
Seattle Mariners, 182–83
Seattle Opera, 181–82
Seattle Repertory Theatre, 181
Seattle Seahawks, 183
Seattle Sounders, 183
Seattle Storm, 183
Seattle Supersonics, 183
Seattle Symphony, 178, 181
Seattle-King County Convention and Visitors Bureau, 179
Seattle's Best Coffee, 252
Seattle-Tacoma International Airport, 178, 210, 213
Seaview, 351–54
Sechelt, 465–66
Second Street Gallery, 117
Secret Garden, 77
Secwepemc Native Heritage Park, 532
Sehome Hill Arboretum, 233
Sekiu, 292–93
Sentosa, 270
Sentosa Sushi, 282–83
Sequim, 285–87
Serenity's Village, 364
Seven Feathers Hotel and Casino Resort, 131

Seven Hills Winery, 389
750 ml, 21
17 Mile House, 485
7th Street Theatre, 342
Shady Nook Cottage, 270, 294–95
Shafer Museum, 300, 307
Shafer Vineyards, 29
Shaka Rock Adventures, 542
Shakespeare festivals, 132, 137
Shakti Cove Cottages, 357
Shakti's, 328
Shark's Seafood Bar & Steamer Co., 102
Shearwater Kayak Tours, 227
Sheeprock Lodge, The, 542
Shelburne Country Inn, 353–54
Shelburne Inn, 343
Shell Creek Grill & Wine Bar, 213
Shelton, 277
Shilo Inn, The, 346
Ship Harbor Inn, 240
Ships Point Inn, 521
Shoalwater Cove Gallery, 350
Shoalwater Restaurant, The, 353
Shopping
    in Portland, 7
    in Seattle, 181
    in Vancouver, 415–16
    in Victoria, 475–76
Shore Acres State Park, 116
Side Door Cafe, 99
Sidney, 488–90
Silver Bay Inn, 316
Silver Cloud Inn, 217, 257
Silver Falls State Park, 63
Silver Grille Café & Wines, 63
Silver Lake Winery, 321
Silver Skis Chalet, 334
Silver Star Mountain Resort, 536–38
Silverdale, 273–74
Silvertips, 215
Silverton, 63
Silverwater Café, 270, 283
Silverwood Gallery, 251–52
Sinclair Centre, 416
Sirens, 280
Sisters (town), 155–57
Sisters, The (restaurant), 216
Sisters Coffee Company, 156
Siuslaw River Coffee Roasters, 112
Skagit Bay Hideaway, 229
Skagit Valley, 225–26
Skiing, 305, 537, 551
Skookumchuck Narrows Park, 467
Sky Valley Inn, 478, 496
Skydive Snohomish, 217
Sleeping Lady, 325–27

Sluy's Bakery, 274
Smelt Sands State Recreation Area, 107
Smile's Seafood Café, 565, 570–71
Smith Family Bookstore, 71
Smith Rock State Park, 155
Snipes Mountain Microbrewery & Restaurant, 378
Snohomish, 217
Snohomish Pie Company, 217
Snoqualmie, 330
Snoqualmie Pass, 330–31
Snowpack, 551
Snowshoe Sam's, 541
Snug Harbour Inn, A, 515
Soap Lake, 408–9
So-Bo, 516
Sol Duc Hot Springs, 292
Sol Duc Hot Springs Resort, 292
Sooke Harbour House, 486–88
Sooke to Port Renfrew, 484–88
Sophie's Cosmic Cafe, 416, 432
Sorrento Hotel, 203
South Beach State Park, 103
South Cariboo Visitor Info Centre, 567
South Coast Inn, 126
South Pender Island, 497
South Slough National Estuarine Research Center Reserve, 115
Southeast High Desert, 172
Southeast Shore, 504–5
Southeast Washington, 368–91
Southern Interior, 528–59
Southern Oregon, 128–58
Southern Oregon Coast, 110–26
Southwest Washington, 340–65
Spar Cafe and Bar, The, 254, 265
Spencer Spit State Park, 241
Spencer's Butte, 53, 72
Spinnakers Brewpub & Guesthouse, 476, 480
Spinner's Seafood, Steak & Chop House, 122
Spirit Mountain Casino, 60
Spirit Mountain Lodge, 60
Splitz Grill, 451
Spokane
    access to, 395–96
    information regarding, 395–96
    lodgings in, 401–3
    map of, 394
    restaurants in, 398–401
Spokane International Airport, 395
Spokane Symphony, 397–98
Sporthaven Marina, 125

Sports
    in Portland, 8
    in Seattle, 182–83
    in Vancouver, 419
    in Victoria, 477
Spring Bay Inn, 246
Springbrook Hazelnut Farm, 54
Springfield, 77–78
Squamish, 444–45
SS Moyie, 548
St. Ann's Academy, 477
St. Bernards, 91
St. Peter's Landmark, 42
Stange Manor Inn, 165
Stanley and Seaforts Steak, Chop, and Fish House, 257
Stanley Park, 415
Stanwood, 218
Stanwood Grill, 218
Star Bistro Café and Bar, 214, 220
Star Center Mall, 217
Starbucks, 178
State Capitol Museum, 263
Steamboat Inn, 131
Steelhead, 71
Stehekin, 315–16
Steiger Haus Inn, 59
Steilacoom, 261–62
Steilacoom Tribal Museum, 261
Stephanie Inn, 90
Sternwheeler Columbia Gorge, 35–36
Stevens Pass, 319–20
Stevenson, 362
Stonehedge Gardens, 39
Stork's, 240
Stormking Spa and Cabins, 336
Stormy Weather Arts Festival, 101
Strait of Juan de Fuca, 288–91
Strathcona Park Lodge and Outdoor Education Centre, 525
Strathcona Provincial Park, 524
Strawberry Mountain Inn, 171
Stray Dog Cafe, 253
Stubbs Island Whale Watching, 525
Su Casa Imports, 61
Summer Jo's, 133–34
Summer Lake, 147
Summer Lake Hot Springs, 146
Summer Lake Inn, 147
Summit Meadow Cabins, 46
Sun Mountain Lodge, 308–9
Sun Peaks Lodge, 535
Sun Peaks Resort, 534–35
Sun Sui Wah Seafood Restaurant, 432
Sundance Grill, 374, 380
Sundance Ranch, 531

Sunflower Books, 162
Sungari Pearl, 21
Sungari Restaurant, 21
Sunny Farms Country Store, 270
Sunnyside, 377–78
Sunrise, 334
Sunriver Lodge, 154
Sunset Bay State Park, 115
Sunshine Cafe, 530, 547
Sunshine Coast, The, 460–61
SunWolf Outdoor Centre, 445
Suquamish, 275
Surf Sister, 523
Surfing, 523
Sushi, 188
Sushi Village, 451–52
Sutton Place Hotel, The, 436–37
Swain's General Store, 289
Sweet Oasis, 264
Sweet Williams, 355
Swilly's Cafe & Catering, 390–91
Swiss Pub, 254
Sybaris, 68
Sylvia Beach Hotel, 83, 105
Sylvia Hotel, 437
Symphony, 7, 178, 181, 397–98, 418, 477
Syun Izakaya, 22

T

Tables of Content, 83
Tacoma, 253–58
Tacoma Art Museum, 253
Tacoma Dome, 254
Tad's Chicken 'n' Dumplins, 35
Talent, 139–40
Talk and Coffee, 397, 405
Támastslikt, 162
Taqueria El Rey, 61
Taqueria La Fogata, 374, 378, 388
Taqueria Nueve, 22
Tasting Room, The, 56
Tauca Lea by the Sea, 479
Tauca Lea Resort & Spa, 516
Taylor Shellfish Farms, 231
Taylor's Fountain and Gift, 66
Tea & Tomes Ltd, 102
Tea Room Café, The, 124
Tefft Cellars, 388
Telegraph Cove, 525–26
Temple, 480–81
Ten Depot Street, 165
Tenino, 266
Terminal Gravity Brewery, 166
Terra Blanca, 388
Terra Breads, 416
Thai Orchid, 360–61

Thaiku, 198
Thatch Pub, 502
This Old Steak and Fish House, 533
Thistledown House, 440
Thompson Plateau, The, 529–30
Thornewood Caste B&B Inn, 257–58
Three Capes Scenic Drive, 83
Three Girls Bakery, 178
Ticketmaster, 182
Tidal Raves, 100–101
Tides Tavern, 260–61
Tidewind Charters, 125
Tigh-Na-Mara Resort, Spa & Conference Centre, 511
Tillamook, 93–94
Tillamook Air Museum, 94
Tillamook Bay, 93
Tillamook Cheese Plant, 83
Tillamook County Creamery Association, 94
Tillamook County Fair, 101
Tillamook Rock Lighthouse, 88
Timber Museum, 294
Timberline Lodge, 43, 46
Tina's, 55
Toby's 1890 Tavern, 214, 223
Tofino, 513, 516–20
Tofino Botanical Gardens, 479
Tojo's, 432–33
Tole Tree, 106
Tolovana Park, 88–89
Tolt Macdonald Memorial Park, 329
Tom McCall Waterfront Park, 5
Tomahawk, The, 439–40
Tony's Coffees, 234
Topo Café, 300, 308
Toppenish, 376
Torrefazione Italia, 476
Tost, 182
Totems, 568–69
Touch of Europe B&B, A, 376
Touchstone Gallery, 106
Tours
    of Columbia River Gorge, 36–37
    of Eastern Oregon, 162–63
    of Northeastern Washington, 397
    of Northern Mainland British Columbia, 565
    of Northern Oregon Coast, 83
    of Portland, 5
    of Seattle, 178–79
    of Spokane, 397
    of Victoria, 476–77
    of Willamette Valley, 53

Townshend Cellar, 403
Tractor Tavern, 182
Traditions Restaurant, 533
Trails End Restaurant/1871 Lodge, 567
Trains, 3–4
Trans-Canada Highway, 556–57
Trattoria di Umberto, 452
Trattoria Giuseppe, 220
Traveller's Tale Shop, 521
Treehouse Café, 493
Treehouse South, 493
Tri-Cities, 379
Tri-Met, 4
Trincomali Bakery, Deli & Bistro, 500
Trout Lake, 364
Troutdale, 34–35
Troutdale Chamber of Commerce, 34
Tryon Creek State Park, 30
Tsa-Kwa-Luten Lodge and RV Park, 504
Tu Tu'Tun Lodge, 115, 124
Tualatin Estate Vineyards, 29
Tudor Inn, 270, 291
Tula's, 182
Turtleback Farm Inn, 246–47
Twisp, 310–12
Twisp River Pub, 312
Twist, 7
Tyax Mountain Lake Resort, 457
Tygres Heart, 7
Typhoon!, 22

U
Ucluelet, 514–16
Udder Guys Ice Cream Parlour, 505
U'Mista Cultural Centre, 525
Umpqua Discovery Center Museum, 113–14
Umpqua Lighthouse, 114
Under the Greenwood Tree, 136
Union, 165, 198, 277–78
Union Hotel, 165
Union Station, 3–4
University of British Columbia, The, 415
University of Oregon, 71
University of Washington, 183, 254
US Highway 2, 319–20
Utsalady Grocery, 218

V
Vagabond Lodge, 36, 40

Val d'Isère, 452
Valley Cafe, The, 372
Valley River Inn, 77
Valley View Winery, 132, 138
Vancouver (BC), 412–38
    food and wine in, 418–19
    galleries in, 414–15
    gardens in, 415
    lodgings in, 434–38
    museums in, 414–15
    music in, 418
    nightlife in, 419
    parks in, 415
    performing arts in, 418
    restaurants in, 420–34
    shopping in, 415–16
    sports and recreation in, 419
    theater in, 418
    three-day tour of, 416–17
Vancouver (WA), 359–61
Vancouver Art Gallery, 414–15
Vancouver Canucks, 419
Vancouver Centre, 416
Vancouver Folk Music Festival, 418
Vancouver International Airport, 413, 443
Vancouver Island
    map of, 472
    three–day tour of, 478–79
Vancouver Opera, 418
Vancouver Playhouse Theatre Company, 418
Vancouver Symphony Orchestra, 418
Vancouver Whitecaps, 419
Vandusen Botanical Garden, 415
Vantage, 370
Varsity Grill, 423
Vaseux Lake Lodge, 545
Vashon Island, 251–53
Vashon Island Kayak Company, 252
Vera Project, 182
Veritable Quandary, 22–23
Vernon, 536–38
Vesuvius Bay, 478
Vesuvius Neighbourhood Pub, 493
Victoria
    access to, 473–74
    attractions in, 474–75
    galleries in, 475
    gardens in, 475
    lodgings in, 481–84
    map of, 472
    museums in, 475
    parks in, 475
    performing arts in, 477
    restaurants in, 477–81
    shopping in, 475–76

sports and recreation in, 477
three-day tour of, 476–77
Victoria Bug Zoo, 475
Victoria Clipper, 473
Victoria Estate Winery, 477
Victoria Express, 270
Victoria International Airport, 473
Victoria San Juan Cruises, 234, 473
Victoria Symphony Orchestra, 477
Victorian Restaurant, The, 481
Vietnam Veterans' Living Memorial, 6
Vigneti Zanatta, 504
Vij's, 433
Villa del Lupo, 433
Village Baker, 278
Village Books, 234
Village Theatre, 210
Vineyards. See specific vineyard
Vinny's, 248–49
Vintner's Inn at Hinzerling Winery, 379
Visconti's, 323
Vista House, The, 34
Volunteer Park, 181

W

W & J Wilson, 475
W Seattle Hotel, 203–4
Waldport, 105–6
Waldport Ranger District, 68–69
Walla Walla, 382–87
Wallowa Lake Lodge, 168
Wallowa Llamas, 168
Wallowa Mountains Visitor Center, 166
Wallowa Valley Stage Lines, 161
Wallowas, 164
Wanda's Cafe, 83
Warm Springs, 157–58
Warm Springs Inn, The, 329
Warner Canyon Ski Area, 146
Warren House Pub, 89
Wasco County Historical Museum, 37, 41–42
Washington
   Northeastern, 404–9
   Southeast, 368–91
   Southwest, 340–65
   See also specific city
Washington Park, 6
Washington Park Arboretum, 181
Washington Park International Rose Test Garden, 5
Washington State Ferry, 179, 213, 239, 251, 269, 473

Washington State History Museum, 253
Washington State Library, 263
Washington State University, 390
Water Street Inn Bed and Breakfast, 63
Waterbrook Winery, 389
Waterford Restaurant, The, 507–8
Watertown, 204
Waucoma Books, 37
Waverly Place Bed & Breakfast, 404
Weasku Inn, 135
Wedge Mountain, 464
Wedge Mountain Winery, 321
Wedgewood Hotel, The, 437
Wedgwood Manor, 550
Wei Wai Kum House of Treasures, 524
Weinhard Hotel, The, 389
Weinhard Inn, The, 388–89
Weisinger's of Ashland Winery, 140
Welches, 47–48
Wellspring, 336
Wenatchee, 327–29
West, 417, 433–34
West Coast Game Park Safari, 118
West Coast Launch, 570
West Coast Wilderness Lodge, 467
West End Guest House, 437–38
West Hills, 5
West Linn, 30
Westcott Bay Sea Farms, 248
Western Washington University, 232
Westin Seattle, The, 204–5
Westjet, 529
Westport, 347–48
Westport Maritime Museum, 348
Westport Seafood, 348
Westward Ho!, 112, 114
Wet Planet, 363
Whale's Tale, 104
Whale-watching, 97, 525
Wharfside Bed & Breakfast on the Slowseason, 251
Whatcom Museum of History and Art, 233
Wheeler on the Bay Lodge, 91
Whidbey Island, 218–19
Whidbey Island Winery, 219
Whidbey's Greenbank Farm, 222
Whiskers Cafe, 226
Whistler
   description of, 446–47
   lodgings in, 452–55
   restaurants in, 448–52
Whistler Air, 444
Whistler Golf Club, 448

Whistler Heli-Skiing, 447
Whistler Mountain, 465
Whistler Village Inn & Suites, 454–55
Whistlin' Jack Lodge, 376
White Bird, 7, 88
White Crystal Inn, 541
White Pass, 337
White Salmon, 363–64
White Swan Guest House, 229–30
Whitehouse-Crawford, 385
Whitewater Ski & Winter Resort, 551
Whitman College, 383
Whittaker's Bunkhouse, 335
Wickaninnish Inn, 520
Wickaninnish Interpretive Center, 514
Wicked Wheel Pizza, 455
Wiegardt Studio Gallery, 355
Wienie Wagon, 488–89
Wild Duck, 71
Wild Ginger Asian Restaurant and Satay Bar, 198–99
Wild Iris Inn, The, 230
Wild River Brewing & Pizza Company, 124
Wild Rose Bistro, 118
Wildflour Bakery, 162, 167–68
Wildflower Café, 41
Wildlife Safari, 130
Wildwood, 23
Willamette Gables Riverside Estate, 62
Willamette River, 71–72
Willamette University, 64
Willamette Valley, 50–78
   access to, 51–52
   description of, 51
   map of, 50
   three-day tour of, 53
Wine Country, 52–54
Willamette Valley Visitor's Association, 52
Willapa Bay, 348–49
Willapa Bay Interpretive Center, 355
Willcox House, 273
William James Bookseller, 280
Williamette Valley Vineyards, 53, 64
Williams Lake, 569
Willow Point Lodge, 552
Willow Springs Guest Ranch, 146
Willows Inn, The, 237–38
Willows Lodge, 209–10
Winchester Bay, 113–14
Windmill, The, 328
Wine Country, 52–54

Wine Country Farm, 56
Wine Seller, 280
Wineglass Cellars, 388
Wineries, 388–89, 402–3
　　See also specific winery
Wing Luke Asian Museum, 178–79, 180
Winterborne, 23
Winthrop, 307–10
Winthrop Brewing Company, 307
Wolf Creek Inn, 131
Wolf Den Country Inn, 568
WolfRidge Resort, 309–10
Wood Gallery, 102
Woodinville, 208–10
Woodmark Hotel on Lake Washington, The, 208
Wood's End Landing, 513
Woodstone Country Inn, 501–2
Woodward Canyon Winery, 389

Working Girl's Hotel, The, 163
Working Waterfront Museum, 253
World Kite Museum and Hall of Fame, 354
Wyatt's Eatery & Brewhouse, 67
Wyvern Cellars, 403

X

Xinh's Clam & Oyster House, 277

Y

Yachats, 106–8
Yacht Club Broiler, 273–74
Yakima Valley, 373–76
Yaletown, 415–16
Yamhill, 56–57
Yamhill County Wineries Association, 52

Yaquina Bay Lighthouse, 102
Yaquina Head Lighthouse, 83
Yarrow Bay Grill, 208
Yellow Point Lodge, 509
Yelm, 266
Youngberg Hill Vineyards & Inn, 53, 59
YWCA Hotel/Residence, 416, 438

Z

Zell's: An American Café, 5, 23
Zenon Cafe, 75–76
Ziggurat Bed & Breakfast, 108
Zigzag Ranger District, 43
Zillah, 377
Zoller's Outdoor Odyssey, 363
Zoo, Oregon, 4

We Stand By Our Reviews

Sasquatch Books is proud of *Best Places Northwest*. Our editors and contributors go to great lengths and expense to see that all of the restaurant and lodging reviews are as accurate, up-to-date, and honest as possible. If we have disappointed you, please accept our apologies; however, if a recommendation in this 15th edition of *Best Places Northwest* has seriously misled you, Sasquatch Books would like to refund your purchase price. To receive your refund:

1. Tell us where and when you purchased your book and return the book and the book-purchase receipt to the address below.
2. Enclose the original restaurant or lodging receipt from the establishment in question, including date of visit.
3. Write a full explanation of your stay or meal and how *Best Places Northwest* misled you.
4. Include your name, address, and phone number.

Refund is valid only while this 15th edition of *Best Places Northwest* is in print. If the ownership, management, or chef has changed since publication, Sasquatch Books cannot be held responsible. Tax and postage on the returned book is your responsibility. Please allow six to eight weeks for processing.

Please address to Satisfaction Guaranteed, *Best Places Northwest*, and send to:
Sasquatch Books
119 South Main Street, Suite 400
Seattle, WA 98104

Best Places Northwest Report Form

Based on my personal experience, I wish to nominate the following restaurant, place of lodging, shop, nightclub, sight, or other as a "Best Place"; or confirm/correct/disagree with the current review.

_____

_____

_____

_____

(Please include address and telephone number of establishment, if convenient.)

REPORT

Please describe food, service, style, comfort, value, date of visit, and other aspects of your experience; continue on another piece of paper if necessary.

_____

_____

_____

_____

_____

_____

I am not associated, directly or indirectly, with the management or ownership of this establishment.

_____

SIGNED

_____

ADDRESS

_____

_____

PHONE   **DATE**

Please address to _Best Places Northwest_ and send to:
SASQUATCH BOOKS
119 SOUTH MAIN STREET, SUITE 400
SEATTLE, WA 98104
Feel free to email feedback as well: **CUSTSERV@SASQUATCHBOOKS.COM**